American
Working-Class
Literature

American Working-Class Literature

An Anthology

EDITED BY

Nicholas Coles
University of Pittsburgh

Janet Zandy
Rochester Institute of Technology

New York   Oxford
OXFORD UNIVERSITY PRESS
2007

Oxford University Press, Inc., publishes works that further Oxford University's objective of excellence in research, scholarship, and education.

Oxford New York
Auckland Cape Town Dar es Salaam Hong Kong Karachi
Kuala Lumpur Madrid Melbourne Mexico City Nairobi
New Delhi Shanghai Taipei Toronto

With offices in
Argentina Austria Brazil Chile Czech Republic France Greece
Guatemala Hungary Italy Japan Poland Portugal Singapore
South Korea Switzerland Thailand Turkey Ukraine Vietnam

Published by Oxford University Press, Inc.
198 Madison Avenue, New York, New York 10016
http://www.oup.com

Oxford is a registered trademark of Oxford University Press

Library of Congress Cataloging-in-Publication Data

American working-class literature : an anthology / edited by Nicholas Coles, Janet Zandy.
    p.   cm.
  Includes bibliographical references and index.
  ISBN 978-0-19-514456-7
    1. Working class writings, American.   2. Working class–Literary collections.
I. Coles, Nicholas. II. Zandy, Janet, 1945–

PS508.W73A835 2006
810.8′09220623–dc22

2005053945

Frontispiece: Elizabeth Olds, *Harlem Dancers*, 1939 (wood cut).
The University of Michigan Museum of Art, gift of the U.S. Government,
W.P.A. Federal Art Project.

Printing number: 9 8 7 6 5 4

Printed in the United States of America
on acid-free paper

To first generation college students

And to Tillie Olsen and her vision of creativity "as an enormous and *universal* human capacity"

J. Z.

To John and Carmel Coles
for their love and their sense of justice

N. C.

Contents

---

* Items in brackets are titles assigned by the editors.

Preface

American Working-Class Literature introduces readers to the long, and sometimes concealed, tradition of writing by and about America's working people. Gathering three hundred texts that span the centuries from colonial times to the early 2000s, this anthology presents a range of working-class literature that includes not only the industrial proletariat, but also enslaved and peonage labor, unpaid domestic work, immigrant and migrant labor, and low-paid service work. The writers are as diverse in race, gender, culture, and region as America's working class itself. Their writing represents the full range of genres: fiction, poetry, drama, memoir, reportage, oratory, manifestos, letters, oral history, song lyrics, and other mixed or hybrid forms of expression. Because the working-class cultural tradition has at times been submerged or suppressed, the anthology includes work by little-known, even anonymous, authors, alongside such writers as Frederick Douglass, Upton Sinclair, Tillie Olsen, Philip Levine, Maxine Hong Kingston, and Leslie Marmon Silko.

Designed for general readers, as well as students of American literature and history, *American Working-Class Literature* is arranged historically in seven parts, each with an introduction to the period and its literature. Individual headnotes provide biographical and historical context for reading. An introduction by the editors traces the tradition of working-class writing in the United States and discusses the uses of such literature in American culture. Additional resources include a bibliography, a timeline of working-class history, and a rich array of illustrations and documentary photographs.

This anthology of labor and literature, class and culture, emerges at a critical juncture in American history. It invites teachers and students to view literary expression through the lens of class at a time when work itself—because of deindustrialization, downsizing, globalization, and technology—is rapidly changing. While organized historically, this collection of working-class writings does not suggest in any way that the class system in America is "history." Instead, it places class differences in a long historical continuum showing how people created culture out of their economic circumstances and social relationships.

The editors have organized this material so that students can begin to explore not only a rich and often hidden literary world, but also the historical contexts for the writing. This anthology also offers an opportunity for students to see the interrelationships and inseparability of class with race, ethnicity, and gender, as well as other cultural differences and layered identities. It invites a deeper appreciation of the ideals and struggles of ordinary American people in all their diversity through their literature.

What about literature? The editors understand "literature" not as an isolated aesthetic object, but as what Raymond Williams called "writing in society," an ongoing process of writing that is practiced widely across social spaces inside and outside the academy.[1] As such, this collection of working-class literature not only expands the canonical understandings of students who are English majors, but offers all students a living connection to a legacy of American culture that may have been hidden from them.

In working with these texts, we as teachers have raised with our students such questions and topics as the following:

- How might traditional conceptions of "literature"—how it is made, where it comes from, how it is received and used—be revised and expanded to account for this alternative tradition? How do working-class experience, identity, history, and struggle shape literary expression? What cultural work does this literature perform, in terms of what it allows us, as readers and writers, to see, understand, and produce?
- Work as a subject is at the center of much of this literature, as it is or will be at the center of much of our lives. These text allow us to ask: What is work, and what has it been in America? What are the conditions of work and the relationships of the workplace for those who do the hardest and often most physically demanding work in the society?
- Class also shapes all our lives, and consciousness of class informs all the literature that follows. If we understand class as a set of lived relationships shaped by historical forces and expressed in shared culture, we can ask: What are the connections between the work that people do and their experience of class? What does it mean to be a part of America's "working-class majority"?[2] What are the human consequences of the class system?

Responses to the questions just posed can be as multiple and varied as the 150 voices gathered here. Our aim is not to define these fluid and contested terms once and for all, but rather, to stimulate a process of dialogue and interpretation, grounded in the literature and its contexts, that will be continued by readers individually, in groups, and in classrooms. As Constance Coiner wrote, "We want readers to decipher the cultural work done by working-class texts and the ways in which readers are invited to participate in that cultural work."[3]

To initiate and frame this process, the Introduction looks further into the implications of the key terms that name the project of this book—*American*, *working class*, and *literature*—explaining as we go what has motivated us, as teachers and participants in this tradition, to gather these texts into an anthology. We then examine particular processes of "cultural formation" through which working-class literature is produced, received, and used. Finally, we describe the way in which the book itself was constructed and how it is organized so as to make this literature accessible and its contexts clear. Just as we argue that working-class literature enacts collective traditions of reading and writing, we also suggest that studying it can open a much fuller understanding of how culture is formed, sustained, and carried from one generation to another.

In this way, *American Working-Class Literature* is designed to engage readers in working-class literature as an ongoing tradition of cultural expression. The work collected here invites students, teachers, scholars, and writers not only to discover and study this tradition, but also to contribute to it.

ACKNOWLEDGMENTS

As with any project of this scope, *American Working-Class Literature* is the product not only of the labor of its editors, but also of the published and unpublished writings, oral and cultural traditions, scholarship, critical perceptions, and progressive commitments of too many people to name here. This collection does, in Walt Whitman's phrase, contain multitudes. The final outcome, honed and refined, emerges out of a process of difficult choices and necessary consultation. For detailed suggestions on the contents and design of the book, for their advice and scholarship, we especially thank our editorial advisers John Crawford, Florence Howe, Barbara Smith, Cary Nelson, and Laura Hapke. We are grateful for their knowledge and their support. Oxford University Press would also like to acknowledge the expertise of the scholars who served as outside reviewers on this project and whose counsel informed it final shape: Michael Elliott, Emory University; Gavin

Jones, Stanford University; Barry Maxwell, Cornell University; Cary Nelson, the University of Illinois; Xiomara A Santamarina, the University of Michigan; and Gustvus Stadler, Haverford College.

Although the majority of headnotes were written by the editors, our thanks are also due to a number scholars who contributed notes on particular authors: Ken Boas, Eric Lief Davin, and Lois Williams at the University of Pittsburgh, John Crawford at West End Press, David Demarest at Carnegie Mellon University, Babak Elahi at the Rochester Institute of Technology, Richard Ellis at University of Birmingham, UK, Ted Genoways at the University of Virginia, John Marsh at the University of Illinois, Florence Howe of The Feminist Press and Larry Smith at Firelands College and Bottom Dog Press.

In addition to those named above, Nicholas Coles has benefited from collegial discussion with Jim Daniels, John Gilgun, Michael Helfand, Donald Petesch, Richard Oestereicher, Marcus Rediker, and Scott Smith. He particularly wishes to acknowledge Eric Lief Davin for his astute editorial advice on the book's historical sections and to Jennifer Matesa for her diligent work on securing permissions to reprint copyrighted material. Timely research help was provided by Sara Grozanick, Laura Hoover, Kirstin Collins, and Will Seung-Hwan, students at the University of Pittsburgh. Coles wishes to thank administrators of Pitt's English Department and School of Arts and Sciences for the grant of release time and other resources toward the completion of this project. He is deeply grateful to Jennifer Matesa for her fine editing and constant support through the years of work represented here.

Janet Zandy wishes to recognize John Crawford's "installments" of literary history, theory, and scholarship, especially in the area of radical and multicultural writers. She thanks the many conference audiences and panel participants who have contributed to the recognition of American working-class literature, particularly comments and advice from Paul Lauter and Barbara Foley. She also thanks the Rochester Institute of Technology for a Faculty Development Grant and professional leave for providing time to complete this and other projects. At a critical juncture, RIT's Provost Stanley McKenzie and Dean Andrew Moore generously provided financial support to defray permission costs. Her family and friends have sustained her through this long book, as well as many other professional commitments. Many thanks.

The editors also wish to recognize these individuals at Oxford University Press for their editorial advice and professional commitment to this project: Anthony English, Jan Beatty, Talia Krohn, Jackie Ardam, and Marta Peimer. We appreciate the careful work of Lisa Grzan, production editor, Wendy Almeleh, copyeditor, and Annika Sarin, designer, who saw this book through the process of final production. We thank the many people who granted permissions to reprint copyrighted material, librarians who offered advice, and contemporary visual artists who allowed the reproduction of their images.

Finally, anyone who has completed an anthology of any size is aware of the hard choices that must be made in the face of necessary restrictions that are imposed by a book's length and by the cost of permission to reprint copyrighted material. We regret that we have not been able to include many fine contemporary writers whose work belongs in the tradition of American working-class literature. We invite readers to consider the work of these and other writers, who are listed in the extended bibliography.

We hope this book will contribute to the restoration of a nearly lost literary legacy. We thank the writers, alive and dead, for their work.

Nicholas Coles
Pittsburgh, Pennsylvania 2005

Janet Zandy
Rochester, New York 2005

Notes

1. "Writing," in *Writing in Society* (London: Verso, 1985), 1–7.

2. See Michael Zweig, *The Working-Class Majority: America's Best Kept Secret* (Ithaca, NY: ILR/Cornell University Press, 2000).

3. Constance Coiner, "U.S. Working-Class Women's Fiction: Notes Toward an Overview," in Janet Zandy, ed., *What We Hold in Common: An Introduction to Working-Class Studies* (New York: Feminist Press, 2001), 230.

Introduction

Class . . . [and] its relationship to works of literature: the great unexamined.
—Tillie Olsen, Silences

American Working-Class Literature invites readers to explore a world of writing that until recently has largely been left out of the mainstream literary canon. Workers have been singing, reciting, performing, telling stories, writing, and publishing since the beginning of the settlements that became the United States—and they are still doing so. This collection aims to represent this tradition of more than 250 years of literary witness to the ways in which working-class people have lived, labored, and given meaning to their experiences inside and outside the workplace.

Often during its history, this alternative literary tradition has been hidden or forgotten, marginalized as folklore, or actively suppressed as political propaganda. From time to time, such as during the rise of proletarian struggles in the 1930s, working-class writers found wider audiences and greater opportunities for publication, only to have their work muted or submerged when political backlash suppressed populist expression. Still, culture produced out of the experience and creativity of workers continued, albeit sometimes in fragmentary and unrecognized forms. In the context of the social changes that gathered force through the 1960s, writers, small-press publishers, editors, students, teachers, and activists challenged narrowly constructed views of literature. This anthology of working-class writings owes much to previous work of reclamation and recovery of the cultures of working people, especially those of women and writers of color.[1] But it goes further in that it foregrounds what worker-writer Tillie Olsen calls "the great unexamined": class.

As a continuing tradition of cultural expression, responsive to historical and economic pressures and changes, working-class literature is rooted for the most part outside the academy. This anthology bridges the space between the circumstances of the writing—the site of its original production and reception—and the academic location of reading and engaging with the text in its present form. To connect these worlds, to see how they intersect, and increasingly overlap in contemporary writing, it is important to understand the concepts of "literature" and "working class" in elastic, expansive ways. This anthology represents the full range of genres that writers of and about the working class have drawn upon. These genres include, but are not limited to, fiction, poetry, memoir, reportage, manifestos, letters, oral history, speeches, songs, and plays, as well as mixed forms, such as illustrated poem-cards, oral history "lifelets," and collective "autobiography." Within this range, readers will find selections by well-known American writers of the working class, such as Tillie Olsen, Jack London, and Langston Hughes, alongside work that has been more obscure, local, or ephemeral. Texts have been chosen for both their historical and literary value. This is writing that illuminates key moments, locations, and conditions in working-class life and that does so in language and in forms that are vivid, compelling, and artful. And it meets the standard that Lillian Robinson proposed for literature that is "honest": "[It] should help us learn about the way things are, in as much depth and fullness as possible and by any means necessary."[2]

Like the term *"literature,"* *"working class"* is also defined inclusively here. This is much more than a "blue-collar" collection. Collars—blue, white, pink, brown, or missing entirely—can be misleading signifiers. To categorize this writing as "labor literature," that is, work associated mainly with organized labor movements, is too narrow as well. Although the industrial workplace is well represented, along with the literature of labor struggles, the writers collected here also represent preindustrial workers and those whose labor was appropriated through enslavement, peonage, or indentured servitude.[3] Also included is writing by those who perform unpaid work at home and those who work in the burgeoning service economy with little control over the compensation, conditions, or products of their labor. Defined broadly, in terms of the relative lack of economic and political power, "the great majority of Americans form the working-class," according to economist Michael Zweig. "They are skilled and unskilled, in manufacturing and services, men and women of all races, nationalities, and religions."[4]

Working-class identity is, of course, much more than a matter of one's economic position; it is also a lived experience, a set of relationships, expectations, legacies, and entitlements (or the lack of them). Literature illuminates those experiences and relationships, revealing how class as a shaping force is inseparable from other markers of identity: gender, sexuality, race, region, and ethnicity. The writing included here is therefore as multiethnic and multiracial as the working class itself, and it fully demonstrates how women's work is also "classed" labor.[5] "Working-class" is—of necessity and circumstance—not a single discreet identity, but an uneasy and unstable amalgam of multiple identities. These identities may be hybrid and fluid, but class of birth, the lives and economic circumstances of one's parents, cannot be separated out.[6]

Working-class literature opens to readers the intricate interior world of class experience and sets it in the context of U.S. history as it is lived by the majority of ordinary Americans. As a framework for reading, consider the implications of the key terms:

AMERICAN / WORKING-CLASS / LITERATURE

American

Let America be the dream the dreamers dreamed.
                              —*Langston Hughes*

First, a word about the meanings of *American*. Although some of the literature collected here predates 1776, it was all produced or published in the territory that now comprises the United States. However, the concept of national identity is complicated by the fact that many of these early writers did not have access to the rights of citizenship, since some were slaves, indentured servants, illegal immigrants, disenfranchised women, and propertyless men. Cohesive assumptions about national identity are rightly troubled by careful readings of the historical and biographical contexts of these writers. That said, however, this book belongs in the category of "American literature," rather than North American (although its themes of work and class can be read as international, even global). Canadian writing has reluctantly been excluded, as has writing from south of the border, although the thriving Mexican American tradition is well represented.

The working-class literature collected here can be read as constituting an alternative and evolving national narrative, one that consciously begins with the perspective and circumstances of the least powerful and confronts the many paradoxes and contradictions between professed American beliefs and revealed actions. Indeed, many of the writers who were champions of the poor and working class also saw themselves as patriots, drawing on Enlightenment ideals of liberty and justice to urge America to be true to itself. Seen as a body of work, working-class literature documents the rift between America's inclusive promise and its exclusionary (for some) historical reality without losing sight of repair and redemption.

One of the foundations of dominant American ideology is that the United States is an essentially classless society. *Class* and *rank* are terms commonly associated with European histories of monarchy and feudalism, and the rigid social stratification that went with them. America, in contrast, is often viewed in "exceptionalist" terms as a land of possibility and mobility for all. Work hard and you will succeed. While it is true that America has produced some rags-to-riches success stories, and that it remains to this day a country where immigrants seek refuge and economic opportunity, the larger historical picture is more complicated and less sanguine. The workers (slave, free, indentured, sojourners, immigrants, male, female, black, brown, and white) who labored to build the country rarely owned or controlled the products of their labor. Those who were not of the elite propertied class had to struggle for their rights within a capitalistic system that offered opportunity for some, but also exploited, suppressed, and limited the freedom of many others. This literature represents and documents the conflict within this system, and, as such, it can be considered a literature of resistance, endurance, and struggle. "All men are created equal" in theory, but not in fact if you were enslaved or propertyless, female or nonwhite. In the words of Langston Hughes's poem "Let America Be America Again":

> O, let my land be a land where Liberty
> Is crowned with no false patriotic wreath,
> But opportunity is real, and life is free,
> Equality is in the air we breathe.
> (There's never been equality for me,
> Nor freedom in this homeland of the free.) (See page 372)

Hughes is referring, of course, to the historical fact that the United States was founded not only on a set of inspiring ideals and principles, but also on a set of economic and political imperatives. These entailed the violent expropriation of land from the native inhabitants and the forced importation of masses of Africans who were wrenched from their homeland to provide both the resources and the labor power for what would become the most powerful capitalist nation on earth. American history has been shaped by class conflict all along, even in those rare periods that were not marked by slave revolts, labor strikes, race riots, mass demonstrations, or overt political repression.

Working-Class

There is not a person in this crowd in whom I do not find a part of myself.
—*Clifford Odets*[7]

If we accept that American society is, in fact, stratified and divided by class, what does it mean to be working-class in the United States? Michael Zweig makes the distinction this way:

> For all their differences, working-class people share a common place in production, where they have relatively little control over the pace and content of their work, and aren't anybody's boss. They produce the wealth of nations, but receive from that wealth only what they can buy with the wages their employers pay them.[8]

There is an argument and a history embedded in the term "working class" that provides an essential framework for the literature presented here. It argues, first of all, that this is a class of people that works, producing the goods and services that build the economy and meet social needs. It is also the class that, because of its relative lack of economic and political power, is frequently out of work, as when decisions made in boardrooms result in the closing of a factory or the offshoring of a work center. Working-class life is marked by this insecurity as much as by the often-injurious effects of the job itself.

These effects, and workers' responses to them, reveal themselves in palpable ways in this literature. The writing employs a common language of the body at work, showing how workers face occupational hazards and physical risks that mark the body and the text. The physicality of the job—hard muscles, swollen legs, enlarged hands, or missing fingers—is inscribed on a worker's body, recognizable to other workers. Through its focus on physical labor, this writing presents worlds of work that are usually hidden or not deemed appropriate subjects for literary expression.[9] We see the fatigue of working in kitchens, the dangers of steel production, or the labor of birthing, but we also become more fully aware of an interior consciousness that is rarely attributed to working-class characters, as well as their deep sense of pride in the dignity of work and craft. Through often-lyrical and feisty language, these workers witness the conditions of working-class lives, the power of resistance, and the necessity of struggle—not only in a political or labor context, but also in the dailiness of providing and "making do." These voices emerge despite efforts to silence them through strikebreaking, militias, red-baiting, corporate dominance, and political unwillingness to name the class that, as Zweig makes clear, encompasses the majority of Americans.[10]

The second word in the compound term "*working class*" also carries an argument; it proposes that we live and work not only as individuals, but as members of groups and in relation to the history of our "classed" society. British historian. E. P. Thompson defines class as "an historical phenomenon . . . something which in fact happens (and can be shown to have happened) in human relationships":

> And class happens when some [people], as a result of common experiences (inherited or shared), feel and articulate the identity of their interests as between themselves, and as against other [people] whose interest are different from (and usually opposed to) theirs. The class experience is largely determined by the productive relations into which [people] are born— or enter involuntarily. Class-consciousness is the way in which these experiences are handled in cultural terms: embodied in traditions, value-systems, ideas, and institutional forms.[11]

And, of course, embodied in literature. Two lasting and linked common ideas in the history of working-class people, ideas that animate this writing, have been the value of solidarity and the tradition of struggle. At the level of lived history, improvement in material conditions has come largely through processes of mutual aid and shared action, celebrated in songs like Ralph Chaplin's "Solidarity Forever" and Florence Reese's "Which Side Are You On?" (presented in this volume). At the level of the writing, much of this literature necessarily moves away from the stereotyped view of the author as isolated genius. Most of these authors are also workers, and many of them are activists. Their writing challenges reverence for disconnected artistic individualism by providing another kind of model—of reciprocal understanding—and another kind of movement—a collective mobility that improves working and living conditions for many, not just the lucky few.

This, then, is literature by, about, and in the interests of the working class. Many of the more contemporary texts gathered here are by writers who come from working-class families. Some of the authors are self-identified as worker-writers (Jack Conroy, Sue Doro, and Joseph Kalar). Some are second-generation immigrants, educated in America (Pietro DiDonato, Hisaye Yamamoto, and Tomas Rivera). Some are middle-class authors writing in allegiance with workers (Upton Sinclair, Meridel LeSueur, and William Attaway). As poet Thomas McGrath puts it: "All of us live twice at the same time—once uniquely and once representatively. I am interested in those moments when my unique personal life intersects with something bigger."[12] Whether narrating their own stories or witnessing for others, all are telling a larger story about work and class in the United States.

Literature

> I do not write mere words. I write of human flesh and blood . . . with roots in experience and conviction.
>
> —*Agnes Smedley*[13]

An important claim of this book is that the working class is not only a class that works—that produces goods and services; it is also a class that produces culture, including literature. "Literature" is, like "working class," an unstable and contested concept. Literary culture as anthologized in texts that are intended for classroom use is frequently presented as either a timeless artifact of the past or as emerging out of the sensibilities of individual writers. As Raymond Williams explains the development of the term *literature* over the past two centuries, its meanings have gradually narrowed from a reference to the broad social practices of reading and writing to the point at which it now marks a set of works of "high imagination," which, because they were particularly well written ("literary"), were taken to be of lasting value.[14] These texts became the centerpieces of the English profession's "canon," repeatedly taught in schools and universities and regularly republished.

In light of this mainstream tradition of what counts as "literary," some readers will find linking the words "working class" and "literature" puzzling. Perhaps more than any other identity-related field of writing—gay, women's, Latino, or African American literature—working-class writing has been subject to questions about literary quality and to assumptions about the limitations of writers' abilities. This anthology challenges these assumptions as signs of class prejudice. Working-class literature—both within the historical contexts in which it was produced and as we read it today—is as lively, engaging, and "well written" as one would find in standard literature textbooks. But it is also unfamiliar and, to some, unsettling.

Readers are challenged, for example, to imagine these texts as not necessarily written in the quiet of "a room of one's own," but rather fitted in around the demands of job, family, and home life. Some of the writing here was composed in jail, on the road, or in a work camp. As Paul Lauter explains the distinctiveness of this literary culture:

> Much working-class art is created and experienced in group situations—not in the privacy of the study, but in the church . . . the work site, the meeting hall, the quilting bee, or the picket line. It is thus rooted in the experiences of a particular group of people facing particular problems at a particular time. It is not conceived as timeless and transcedent.[15]

Consequently, some of this literature stretches the boundaries of what is commonly understood as a "text." It calls on readers to imagine themselves as part of a participatory audience, as witnesses, or as fellow workers by singing along with the ballad, "hearing" the speech being delivered, or "witnessing" factory girls jumping from ninth-floor windows of a blazing factory. It calls on readers to reenter the urgency of the moment, to venture inside the circumstances out of which the text was created.

Although this is a textbook designed for use in academic settings, it is important to recognize that many of the writings, songs, and speeches come from these other labor contexts and were not originally designed for the interpretative and defining frameworks of the academy. Unlike a strictly formalist approach to literature that views a text as an isolated artifact to be admired and analyzed, working-class literature is marked by its roots in ordinary people's experiences of particular places and historical moments. And this affects how the literature is received by its audiences, now and at the time of creation. It is more important that the writing have agency and usefulness than that it celebrate solo achieve-ment. Proletarian writer and magazine editor Jack Conroy puts it this way, referring to his 1933 novel *The Disinherited*: "I wanted to be a witness to the times, to show how it feels to be without work and with no prospect of any, and with the imminent fear of starvation, to move people to think about these things, and, what was more important, to do some-thing about it."[16] Working-class literature has use-value as protest, mourning, celebration, affirmation, testimony, call to action, and transformation. At its best, it becomes a form of cultural "commons."

Among the many genres encompassed by working-class literature—poetry, short story, novels, autobiography, memoir, drama, reportage, oratory, manifestos, letters, oral history, documentary, and speeches—songs are a powerful example of this process of collective sensibility and shared use. As John Steinbeck explained in his foreword to the collection *Hard Hitting Songs for Hard Hit People*:

> The songs of the working people have always been their sharpest statement and the one state-ment which cannot be destroyed. You can burn books, buy newspapers, you can guard against handbills and pamphlets, but you cannot prevent singing. . . . You can learn more about people by listening to their songs than in any other way, for into the songs go all the hopes and hurts, the angers, fears, the wants and aspirations.[17]

Woody Guthrie, one of the songwriters who compiled *Hard Hitting Songs*, puts a similar point with characteristic humor: "This song is Copyrighted in U.S., under Seal of Copyright # 154085, for a period of 28 years, and anybody caught singin it without our permission, will be mighty good friends of ours, cause we don't give a dern. Publish it. Write it. Sing it. Swing to it. Yodel it. We wrote it, that's all we wanted to do."[18]

It is important to note, too, that just as there is no single working-class identity, there is no single working-class literary aesthetic. Because the American working class is large and particularly diverse, its literature is multivocal, embracing the richness of language differences and styles of utterance. Cary Nelson makes it clear in his work on modern American poetry that the working-class and radical traditions are no less innovative in their forms and genres than are works in the "high modernist" tradition.[19] As writers on the margins gave shape to the new content and new awareness engendered by the struggles of working-class people, they rewrote conventions, crossed genre boundaries, and created new experimental forms, such as blues poetry, the proletarian portrait, and the revolution-ary sonnet. Let us look more closely at the processes of cultural formation through which this literature is forged.

CULTURAL FORMATIONS

> I feel any writer serves many aspects of culture, including language,
> but you also serve history, you serve the mythic structure that you're a
> part of, the people, the earth, and so on—and none of these are separate.
> —*Joy Harjo*[20]

As consumers we are accustomed to seeing a finished product. What is visible is the sleek new computer, but not the interior wiring or the human process of design and assembly. In calling attention to cultural formations, we evoke an older craft tradition involving an exposure of the various steps of production—in making a carpet, for example, the carding, cleaning, dyeing of the wool, the design, the work of loom and hand. Culture is, in Raymond Williams's words, "a noun of process," and working-class literature particularly calls for attention to the process of cultural formation.[21] So, then, in noting the differences in language and content between, for example, the writing of Frederick Douglass and Richard Wright or Tillie Olsen and Gloria Anzaldúa, we can also trace their shared process of cultural formation—of the carding and weaving necessary between solo voice and communal sensibility.

How working-class writers respond to historical events is one example of cultural formation. Literary antecedents are often not so much dominant canonical "fathers" as events, legacies, histories, and actions that affect working-class people. To illustrate this process, the book includes "clusters" of writing that juxtapose a historical event and the writing produced at that time with later writings by contemporary authors who express particular affinities with this past. For example, in addition to the poetry written shortly after the Triangle Shirtwaist factory fire in 1911, the Contents includes recent "fire poetry" that reclaims the event in labor history and imaginatively restores the subjectivities of the workers at the time. Other instances of this version of cultural formation—in which historical events and their literary traces serve as provocations for working-class writers who come after—occur in the clusters of writing on the Dust Bowl migration in the 1930s and on the legacy in song and memoir of IWW (Industrial Workers of the World) song-writer and organizer Joe Hill.

Another version of the process of cultural formation can be seen in the ways in which working-class artist have adopted and rewritten traditional forms, especially those that are validated in mainstream culture, and have articulated them to new purposes. Joe Hill was a master at this, especially in the form of parody, as when he rewrote the gospel ballad "In the Sweet Bye and Bye" as a scathing attack on sanctimonious providers of charity in "The Preacher and the Slave":

> You will eat, bye and bye
> In that glorious land in the sky
> Work and pray, live on hay
> You'll get pie in the sky when you die (that's a lie). (See p. 296)

In a more serious vein, Hill's fellow-Wobbly Ralph Chaplin set his 1915 song "Solidarity Forever"—which has since become an unofficial anthem of the American labor movement —to the tune of the Civil War marching song "John Brown's Body," bringing forward the fighting spirit of the struggle for emancipation into a celebration of the strength of union solidarity. Often, the same song will "travel" across historical and geographic contexts, with new verses being patched in to address the new occasion. For example, "Which Side Are You On?" written in the 1930s by Florence Reece, a Kentucky union activist and coal miner's wife (and itself set to the tune of a Baptist hymn), was adapted and sung by Pete Seeger in reference to a longshoremen's strike and again by British socialist folksinger Billy Bragg during a 1980s printers' strike in London.

The conscious use of intertextuality is another form of cultural formation—especially for twentieth-century writers who have had the benefit of higher education and/or wide reading. A writer may quote or cite, explicitly or implicitly, other writers in order to create an internal dialogue with other texts or statements. In John Gligun's poem "Counting Tips," for example, a well-known poem of W. B. Yeats is cited to emphasize the distance between the mother's work world and the son's college education:

> My mother came home from work,
> sat down at the kitchen table
> and counted her tips, nickel by nickel,
> quarter by quarter, dime by dime.
> I sat across from her reading Yeats.
> No moonlight graced our window
> and it wasn't Pre-Raphaelite pallor

> that bleached my mother's cheeks.
> I've never been able to forget
> the moment she said—
> interrupting *The Lake Isle of Innisfree*—
> "I told him to go to hell."
> A Back Bay businessman
> had held back the tip, asking,
> "How much do you think you're worth?"
> And she'd said, "You can go to hell."
> All evening at the Winthrop Room she'd fed
> stockbrokers, politicians, mafioso capos.
> I was eighteen, a commuter student at BU,
> riding the MTA to classes every day
> and she was forty-one in her frilly cap,
> pink uniform, and white dress shoes.
> "He just laughed but his wife was there
> and she complained and the boss fired me." (See p. 690)

In addition to the explicit ironic reference to Yeats and his romantic lyric celebrating escape from the grayness of the city, there is a piece of "silent" quoting in the line "No moonlight graced our window," which Gilgun explains as a response to line in Philip Levine's poem "You Can Have It" (see page 670). In Levine's poem, the speaker's brother comes home from work in the middle of the night and collapses into bed:

> The moonlight streams in the window
> and his unshaven face is whitened
> like the face of the moon. He will sleep
> long after noon and waken to find me gone.

Gilgun explains his process of intertextuality this way:

> I honor Philip Levine as one of the few poets in my time who's written on working-class themes. I consider his work essential and I always taught "You Can Have It" each semester because Missouri Western College is an Open Door, working-class, community college. My students needed to know that poems on work and working-class people were being written and that these poems applied to their lives as working-class people. "*This is your life and here it is in poetry.*" "*Can we write like that?*" "*Why not? Levine does.*"
>
>   However, there are a few things I disagree with in Levine's "You Can Have It" and my poem "Counting Tips" is my way of "getting it right," that is, specifically, it is my way of writing a working-class poem in which no moonlight shines through a window to put a poetic gloss on the gritty, dirt-under-fingernails "reality" of what work really means to a working-class person.[22]

Gilgun explains further that, although his mother did work as a waitress, the specific incident narrated in the poem—and the line "How much do you think you are worth?"—is adapted from an interview with the waitress Dolores Dante in Studs Terkel's oral history collection *Working* (see page 652). The poem is then constructed partly, in Gilgun's words, as "text on text on text," but it is also, he insists, "working-class autobiography," true to his life and his mother's and the world of work and money that both unites and separates them.

   Attending to the complexity of processes of cultural formation, the call and response of workers and writers within a larger literary or historical continuum, reminds us that a national narrative of labor—told from the perspective of workers—is often underrepresented or completely missing from the classroom and curriculum. This collection, then, is simultaneously old and new, looking back to a forgotten history and culture and providing a new framing for contemporary readers. It offers a critical dialogue between early and recent cultural forms, and it invites readers to continue that conversation through further research and study. And, as Gilgun suggests, it invites us to participate in this living cultural tradition as writers as well as readers.

FORMING THE BOOK

There has also been a process of cultural formation in the construction of this book, and although it has been a relatively deliberate and academic process, it has been a collective one, drawing on the ideas and texts and energies of many people. The two editors, with different class backgrounds but a common commitment to teaching and publishing working-class literature, have collaborated across the distance between their homes and universities for many years. They have been supported in this work by a group of editorial advisers, scholars, and publishers who have made suggestions for inclusion and responded to drafts of the designs for the book. Beyond them is the wider circle of colleagues—writers, teachers, artists, and scholars in many disciplines—who contribute to the growing field of working-class studies. And, of course, there would be no book without an interested press that is willing to commit the resources to publish a body of work that has never before been collected and made available to readers in the form of an anthology.

As a result of this collective process of formation, here is a body of work called "American working-class literature," but the fact that it is collected between the covers of a book does not make it definitive or complete. Any anthology has finite limits of size and costs, and a large number of appropriate texts have regrettably had to be left out. For each one of the more than 300 pieces included here, the editors have considered dozens of other possible selections for the book. To give readers a sense of the scope of the field and as a guide to further reading and study, a detailed bibliography lists longer works of literature for recommended reading, as well as critical commentary on this literature and on the history of work and class in America.

The editors recognize the complexity of audience for a book that does not quite fit conventional expectations of literature textbooks—a book that will be of interest to teachers and students of history and sociology as well as of literature and writing. Our readers are invited to engage in a process of "reading backward"—that is, understanding the material in its own historical time and for its own historical audience—and reading in the present and for the future, discovering writing that is of relevance to our own (classed) times. The book is designed to facilitate this reading process—a dialogue involving history as read through literature and literature as read through history.

The organization is broadly historical, rather than strictly chronological. To illuminate a continuum of literary expression, the texts are grouped around key historical and cultural developments in working-class life. They are arranged in seven parts, each containing works from a particular span of years in which life changed in major ways for working-class people, including colonial times and slavery days, the first industrial revolution, mass immigration and urbanization, the Great Depression, and the rise of the service economy. Each part is introduced by a short essay that places the literature of the period in the context of these historical developments. Additional historical framing is provided in the timeline of significant events in working-class history (See p. 903). Each selection in the book (with the exception of some early texts in Part I, many of which are anonymous) is introduced by a brief headnote, providing information about the author's life and writing, and an account of the context—historical, artistic, political—in which that text was produced.

Part VII, writing from 1980 to 2005—the most recent being Martín Espada's poem "Alabanza: In Praise of Local 100" about the September 11 attack on the World Trade Center—is arranged chronologically by the author's date of birth. Our aim in Part VII, the book's largest, is to gather work by writers from the full range of identities that make up the contemporary American working class. These writings express not only the diverse voices of America's working people, but also their commonality across the many differences of identity and location. The literature reveals filaments of connection across differences of race, gender, ethnicity, geography, and generations, among people who share common and subordinate relationships to the owning classes.

Two of the primary commonalities in working-class experience, threaded throughout the book, are the value of solidarity and the necessity of struggle. This literature underscores how improvement in material conditions—whether in the neighborhoods, barrios, villages, or borders of American life or in the global structure of economic trade—has come and can come through a process of connection and shared work. This book is, in one sense, an effort to recall and recuperate the language and the vision of solidarity, expressed in the IWW slogan "an injury to one is an injury to all." This is a continuing historical struggle whose uncertainties and promises are embedded within the literature itself. Consequently, this is a collection not only of critique and exposé, but of possibility and hope. We invite readers to become better acquainted with this distinctive American literature and the compelling history it illuminates.

Notes

1. The list of the writers, scholars, and teachers who were involved in this work is as long as the process of recovery itself. It includes works listed in our bibliography by Paula Gunn Allen, Pamela Annas, Gloria Anzaldua, Constance Coiner, John Crawford, Jim Daniels, Michael Denning, Barbara Foley, Gloria T. Hall, Laura Hapke, Florence Howe, Paul Lauter, Sherry Linkon, Cherríe Moraga, Bill Mullen, Cary Nelson, Tillie Olsen, Patricia Bell Scott, Barbara Smith, Larry Smith, Ronald Takaki, Alan Wald, Mary Helen Washington, Tom Wayman, and Janet Zandy.

2. Lillian Robinson, "Working/Women/Writing" in *Sex, Class, and Culture* (Bloomington: Indiana University Press, 1978), 230.

3. Some readers may be surprised by the inclusion of slave writing in this collection, especially if their definition of *working class* follows Marx's classic account of the (industrial) proletariat. David Roediger has addressed this issue in an afterword to his classic study *The Wages of Whiteness* (New York: Verso, 1991, 1999) which was (mis-) taken by many to argue that the American working-class was an essentially white formation: "I had long argued that slavery in the US was part of a capitalist system of social relations, that slaves were workers and that slavery must be central to any rethinking of labor's past . . . [T]he Civil War would demonstrate that slaves were not just a part of the working class but its most politicized and combative sector" (188–189).

4. Michael Zweig, *The Working Class Majority: America's Best Kept Secret* (Ithaca, NY: ILR/Cornell University Press, 2000), 3.

5. In discussing "the obfuscation of class as a category of literary analysis," Constance Coiner describes its displacement in classrooms by the more identifiable markers of race, gender, and ethnicity, noting, for example, that Rita Mae Brown's *Rubyfruit Jungle* (1973) is identified "as a lesbian but not also a working-class novel . . . [and] Ann Petry's *The Street* (1946) as both African American and women's writing but not a working-class novel as well" ("US Working-Class Women's Fiction," in Janet Zandy, ed., *What We Hold in Common*, [New York: Feminist Press, 2001], 233).

6. As Dorothy Allison, best known as a lesbian-feminist author, has expressed it: "But what may be the central fact of my life is that I was born in 1949 in Greenville, South Carolina, the bastard daughter of a white woman from a desperately poor family, a girl who had left the seventh grade the year before, worked as a waitress, and was just a month past fifteen when she had me. That fact, the inescapable impact of being born in a condition of poverty that this society finds shameful, contemptible, and somehow deserved, has had dominion over me." (*Skin: Talking about Sex, Class, and Literature*, Ann Arbor, MI: Firebrand Books, 1994).

7. Quoted in Harold Clurman's Introduction to Cifford Odets, *Waiting for Lefty and Other Plays* (New York: Grove Press, 1975), x.

8. Zweig, *The Working-Class Majority*, 3.

9. See Janet Zandy, *Hands: Physical Labor, Class, and Cultural Work* (New Brunswick, NJ: Rutgers University Press, 2004).

10. Zweig, *The Working-Class Majority.*

11. E. P. Thompson, *The Making of the English Working Class* (New York: Vintage, 1963), 9–10. We altered Thompson's generic male "men" to "people."

12. From McGrath's Foreword to the first collected edition of the poetry of Edwin Rolfe, *Permit Me Refuge* (1955), quoted in Frederick Stern, ed., *The Revolutionary Poet in the United States: The Poetry of Thomas McGrath* (Columbia: University of Missouri Press, 1988).

13. *Daughter of Earth*, (1929; New York: Feminist Press, 1987), 246.

14. Raymond Williams, *Keywords: A Vocabulary of Culture and Society* (New York: Oxford University Press, 1976), 183–188.

15. "Working-Class Women's Literature: An Introduction to Study," *Radical Teacher* 15 (December 1979), 16–26; reprinted in *Women in Print I*, ed. Joan E. Hartman and Ellen Messer-Davidow (New York: Modern Language Association, 1982), 109–125.

16. "Introduction to the 1982 Edition" of *The Disinherited* (1933; Columbia: University of Missouri Press, 1982), 28.

17. *Hard Hitting Songs for Hard-Hit People*, compiled by Alan Lomax, introduction by Woody Guthrie, edited by Pete Seeger (1967; Lincoln: University of Nebraska Press), 8.

18. Quoted on the web site http://eff.org/deeplinks/archives/001765.php. Ironically, the holder of copyright to many of Guthrie's best known songs, including "This Land is Your Land," refused permission to reprint his work in this anthology. However, lyrics to most of his songs are available at the website of the Woody Guthrie Foundation, which granted permission to print the songs included in Part V.

19. Cary Nelson, *Repression and Recovery: Modern American Poetry and the Politics of Cultural Memory* (Madison: University of Wisconsin Press, 1989).

20. From an interview with Marilyn Kallett, *Kenyon Review* 15, 3 (Summer 1993), 57–66.

21. *Marxism and Literature* (New York, Oxford University Press, 1977), 13.

22. From Email correspondence, January 30, 2004, quoted with permission.

I

Early American Labor: Hard, Bound, and Free

Now the pleasant time approaches;
Gentlemen do ride in coaches,
But poor men they don't regard,
That to maintain them labour hard.[1]

To look at the beginning of American literature from the perspective of the people who "labour[ed] hard" to *maintain* the early colonial society is to see indentured servants, enslaved Africans, transported felons, disenfranchised mechanics, and any number of nameless seamstresses, shoemakers, sailors, ship builders, and housemaids. This perspective allows us to tilt the history of the early American colonies away from merchants and founders and toward those whose labor was essential to the making of a nation. The epigraph at the beginning of this section emerged out of political agitation and resentment caused by restrictive laws that allowed only those who owned property access to the ballot box "as the pleasant time approaches" (election day?). But as the literature demonstrates, this is a larger story than suffrage or even nation building. It is a story of how human labor (by some) equals accumulated wealth (for others). It is also a story of speaking back, of how individuals, through a variety of forms—ballads, poems, songs, letters, petitions, and speeches—expressed their subjective, interior experiences, especially the physicality of labor, even as they were conscious of exterior, structural forces that regulated and controlled their labor and their freedom. This compelling tension between the imposition of power and the formation and re-formation of culture shapes not only the colonial and revolutionary period, but also the tradition of working-class literature to the present day.[2]

From its beginning, colonial and postcolonial American society was controlled and organized to serve the interests of the wealthy and powerful; that is, it was a *classed* economic and political system. An oligarchic policy of divide and conquer, of subverting possible alliances among blacks, poor whites, and Indians, and of fostering an ideology of white racial supremacy sticks like resin to the very fiber and root of the United States. This early American writing exposes the relational and hierarchical structure of labor, the commonalities and differences among indentured servants, transported felons, enslaved workers, child laborers, wage earners, and immigrants in a transatlantic context, a continuum of labor that is harsh, relentlessly physical, and without closure for some. Whether through ballads or broadsides, letters or petitions, readers confront a tactile world of labor—the flesh, bone, and human endurance beneath the historical facts. "The only labor system foreordained," writes historian Jacqueline Jones about the seventeenth- and early eighteenth-century colonies in Virginia, Maryland, and Georgia, "was the 'hard usage' of men, women, and children, whether red, white or black. Indeed, almost all workers . . .

found themselves bound to some form of exploitative relationship—children governed by their elders, servants by their masters, sharecroppers and tenants by their landlords, hirelings by their employers, women by their fathers and husbands, Indians and Africans by white men, criminals and sexual renegades by the state and church."[3] Jones adds that "each of these groups devised means of resistance to the people who sought to work them hard" (p. 25). As readers, we are asked to hear and really listen to the voices that document that hard usage and attempt to resist it. We also have the advantage of seeing these texts in relation to each other, a mutuality of vision that was often denied to these historical participants.

We begin not with literary certainty of authorship and date, but with the uncertain fluidity of early ballads and poems. Set to well-known tunes, ballads or broadsides were ephemeral, pasted on the walls of ale houses and cottages, and not collected until the early seventeenth century. It is likely that "The Trappan'd Maiden" is a mid-1600s ballad. It also appears in Samuel Pepys's late seventeenth-century ballad collection.[4]

The ballad's tale of a single maiden's possible entrapment and subsequent indenture would likely have been familiar to audiences on either side of the Atlantic, since indentured or "indented" labor was fundamental to the founding of the colonies. Historians estimate that at the time of the American Revolution, roughly 60 percent to 77 percent of all European immigrants arrived as indentured servants.[5]

The "Trappan'd Maiden" is a ballad of complaint against harsh treatment, although deception may be involved as well, as the first line, "Give ear unto a Maid, that lately was betray'd," suggests. It is likely that she was indentured—although "cunningly so"—and not kidnapped and then sold, as was the fate of some unfortunate children in London of 1645 who would be "spirited away" by kidnappers known as "spirits" (Firth xxx). Perhaps, beneath the litany of spoken woes, the listeners to the ballad might have also heard or imagined a warning to women of the sexual dangers they might face as servants in the colonies. In a 1756 letter written by Elizabeth Sprigs from Maryland to her father John in London, we hear a plea from a "Destress[ed] Daughter" in language more blunt and direct than the ballad form might allow:

> What we unfortunat English People suffer here is beyond the probability of you in England to Conceive, let it suffice that I one of the unhappy Number, am toiling almost Day and Night, and very often in the Horses druggery, . . . and then tied up and whipp'd to that Degree that you'd not serve an Animal . . . and the comfort after slaving dureing Masters pleasure, what rest we can get is to rap ourselves up in a Blanket and ly upon the Ground, this is the deplorable Condition your poor Betty endures.[6]

Both "The Trappan'd Maiden" and James Revel's "The Poor, Unhappy Transported Felon" begin with an appeal to the reader to hear ("give ear," "lend an Ear") the story that follows of lament, regret, complaint, woe, and, in Revel's case, of lessons learned and not to be repeated. Scholars tend to agree that Revel's tale is likely to have come out of the seventeenth century because of the significant number—an estimated 30,000—of trans-ported felons to the colonies during the mid-1600s and because of his use of place names. Revel's poem is an interesting starting point for a study of working-class literature because of its specificity about the physical conditions of prison labor. Essentially, it is a tale of a young man, born to humble but good parents, who fell in with the wrong crowd, got arrested more than once for thievery, and, as punishment, was transported to the Virginia colony to work for fourteen years. Revel presents a detailed picture of how he and others were, upon landing, offered to potential buyers, inspected and purchased, chained, and then shipped up river to work hoeing tobacco on a plantation. The narrator worked along-side five other transports and "eighteen Negroes," while four transported women were house servants. Revel is overcome by illness and harsh labor and contrasts the treatment of his "inhuman brutal master" to the "pity the poor Negroe slaves bestowed" on him and each other. Finally, Revel is sold to a more kindly master (a craftsman, rather than a plan-tation owner), sees his conditions improve as a servant, rather than a slave, and eventually returns to the embrace of his long-suffering parents.

For contemporary readers of Gottlieb Mittelberger's account of the most wretched conditions faced by ship passengers, particularly women and children, it may be difficult to imagine how Europeans, no matter how hopeless and poor their lot, would accept an indentured labor contract and agree to sail to the colonies. Yet, between 1749 and 1754, more than 30,000 Germans came to Philadelphia, driven out of Europe by starvation or false claims of a better existence in the American colonies. Gottlieb Mittleberger, an organist and schoolteacher who eventually returned to Germany after three years in America, witnessed and described the prolonged weeks at sea, the disease and filth, lice, scurvy, packed quarters, and frequent deaths. These emigrants were called "redemp-tioners" because if they survived the journey (and half of Mittelberger's fellow passengers did not), their debts were "redeemed" by unscrupulous "entrepreneurs" who later sold them into indentured bondage.[7] Children who survived the passage seem to have fared the worst, often having to absorb the debts of their parents if they were orphaned at sea, and some were sold by their parents. Mittelberger wrote and published *Journey to Pennsylvania* (1756) as a warning to Germans not to be lured by the promises of eventual freedom in America. Judging by the number of "redemptioners" who arrived in Philadelphia each year, many either did not hear his advice or, if they did, thought that the American gamble was worth the risks.[8]

Early America was a world in which slavery and bondage were normative—and profitable. What distinguished white slaves, indentured servants, or transported felons from enslaved blacks was the possibility of freedom for whites and the certitude of bondage for blacks and their descendents. The "Petition of a Grate Number of Blackes" to General Thomas Gage, commander-in-chief of British forces in North America and governor of Massachusetts, is a reasoned, if unheeded, appeal for a legislative act to remedy the injustice of slavery on the basis of the natural rights of human beings to freedom. We can access a biography of General Gage, but what do we know about the identities of the enslaved black writers of the petition, how they organized themselves, acquired literacy, and how many were men, how many women and children? This petition is framed to illuminate the contradiction of slavery in a "Christian land," a contradiction that Maria Stewart, Frederick Douglass, and others would address during the nineteenth century. It also suggests a more complex, even insurrectionist, interpretation of religion and the Christian Bible, a revivalism of spiritual egalitarianism spread by itinerant preachers in the 1730s and 1740s.[9]

Like the black petitioners, Olaudah Equiano claims to have been kidnapped (at the age of eleven) and sold into slavery. In the excerpt from his life story, *The Interesting Narrative of Olaudah Equiano or Gustavus Vassa, the African, Written by Himself* (1790), readers learn the accumulating horrors of the African slave trade and the unimaginable brutality of the slave ships, every "new refinement in cruelty," as told by Equiano in a literary style of grace, clarity, and true refinement. While Equiano's birthplace has been questioned by recent scholarship,[10] the power of his narrative to *represent* the middle passage for the thousands (millions?) who did not survive to tell their stories cannot be denied. Historians Linebaugh and Rediker also highlight Equiano's internal passage "from personal redemp-tion to liberation theology" (p. 246). In contrast to the physical dynamism of Equiano's lived experiences as a sailor and activist, Phillis Wheatley's relatively stationary life and writing are more opaque. Also kidnapped and enslaved as a child, frail house-servant to the Wheatley family, she was able to demonstrate her intellectual prowess and hone her observations about liberty and slavery within a conventional, constrained verse form. Her poem/petition to the British Earl of Dartmouth, in its studied, embroidered neoclassical style, illuminates the profound contradictions in the air and at the base of the emerging American nation.

But what about the lives of white, "free," wage earners? In his rich compilation of American labor songs, Philip S. Foner writes, "While the shortage of labor made the lot of the free [male?] workers of the colonial period a better one than that of their European counterparts, they were often reduced to poverty by long periods of unemployment, high prices, and competition from indentured servants and black slaves" (p. 1). These songs are feisty complaints, calls for recognition, and critiques of the social order. The "Sea Song" contrasts the cushy and safe existence of the gentlemen "who stay at home at ease" with the dangers of storms and enemies encountered (pirates?) on rough seas. It is also a reminder of the transatlantic cultural fluidity of this period, in which the same song might be sung about similar laboring experience in pubs in London and Boston. "The Raising: A New Song for Federal Mechanics" was sung at a procession that included eighty-eight tradesmen in Philadelphia on July 4, 1788, to celebrate Pennsylvania's adoption of the Constitution.[11] This song, with its emphasis on workers' tools and skills, links the erection of a building with the formation of a new nation. These earlier songs offer some insight into the political sensibilities of artisans as they insisted on recognition of their importance (as skilled workers but also as builders of a democracy) in opposition to elite governing bodies and property rights. "Address to the Journeymen Cordwainers L. B. of Philadelphia" by John McIlvaine signifies a historical shift in the artisans' societies to move beyond mutual aid and toward more defined labor organizations that were willing to strike to protect their jobs and wages. The Federal Society of Journeymen Cordwainers (shoemakers) of Philadelphia existed as a fledgling union from 1791 to 1806 (Foner 11). The loss of their ten-week strike against a reduction in wages and subsequent legal appeals presages the difficulties that laboring people would face in organizing themselves into unions from the beginnings of the nation to the present. This is not so much a matter of false or missing consciousness, but a realization of how the institutions of power—judicial, governmental, media, and military—were arrayed against the economic interests of working people.

What if poor free whites united with servants and enslaved blacks in a common struggle against merchants and landowners? "Only one fear was greater than the fear of black rebellion in the new American colonies," Howard Zinn writes. "That was the fear that discontented whites would join black slaves to overthrow the existing order."[12] And some did: "Servants and debt-ridden farmers, along with runaway slaves, joined together in conflicts against masters or creditors in almost every colony" reports historian Philip Yale Nicholson.[13] Given the imbalance of institutional power, most uprisings were unsuccessful, often resulting in brutal reprisals.

A consciousness of collective action as a strategy of resistance infuses Tecumseh's speech to the Osages during the winter of 1811 and 1812. We conclude this section with Tecumseh's presence as a reminder that the expansion of the new nation by whites before and after the revolution to secure independence from England meant the usurpation of Indian territories and the removal and murder of Native people.

What do we see in this early period that prepares us for the more class-specific literature that follows? First, the literature pries beneath the rhetoric of liberty, progress, and freedom and focuses on the often-unfree human labor that built a new country. Second, it demonstrates the interpenetration of race and class. An ideology of racial supremacy supported a technological system that was designed to amass wealth for the few, divide poor whites from enslaved blacks, and justify the expulsion of Native Americans. Three, the literature demonstrates foundational impulses in working-class literature. These specific ballads, narratives, and poems engage a collective sensibility and are not merely focused on individual trajectories. Individual narratives of enslavement or commonly sung ballads about navy tars or trapped maidens are acts of kinship that give voice and visibility to thousands of others. This writing asks the reader not only to see the human costs of nation building, but also to listen to the beat of struggle.

Notes

1. Issac N. P. Stokes, *The Iconography of Manhattan Island 1498 to 1909* (New York, 1915–1928), vol. 4, p. 536. Reprinted in Philip S. Foner, *American Labor Songs of the Nineteenth Century* (Urbana: University of Illinois Press, 1975), 2.

2. See Herbert G. Gutman, *Essays on the American Working Class*, edited with an introduction by Ira Berlin (New York: Pantheon Books, 1987), 45.

3. Jacqueline Jones, *American Work: Four Centuries of Black and White Labor* (New York: Norton), 25.

4. C. H. Firth, ed., *An American Garland, Being a Collection of Ballads Relating to America 1563–1759* (Oxford, England: B. H. Blackwell, 1915, reprinted Detroit: Singing Tree Press, 1969).

5. Priscilla Murolo and A. B. Chitty, with illustrations by Joe Sacco, *From the Folks Who Brought You the Weekend: A Short, Illustrated History of Labor in the United States* (New York: New Press, 2001), 7.

6. In Nancy Cott, ed., *Root of Bitterness: Documents of the Social History of American Women* (New York: E. P. Dutton, 1972), p. 89.

7. Murolo and Chitty, *From the Folks Who Brought You the Weekend*, 9.

8. Ibid.

9. See Peter Linebaugh and Marcus Rediker, *The Many-Headed Hydra: Sailors, Slaves, Commoners, and the Hidden History of the Revolutionary Atlantic*, (Boston: Beacon Press, 2000), 190–193.

10. For an account of the debate about Equiano's birthplace and the facts unearthed by literary scholar Vincent Carretta, see Jennifer Howard, "Unraveling the Narrative," *Chronicle of Higher Education*, September 9, 2005: A11–A15.

11. Pennsylvania was one of the few states at that time without property qualifications for voting. See Foner, *American Labor Songs of the Nineteenth Century* (Urbana: University of Illinois Press, 1975), 5.

12. Howard Zinn, *A People's History of the United States* (New York: Harper Perennial, 1980), 37.

13. Philip Yale Nicholson, *Labor's Story in the United States* (Philadelphia: Temple University Press, 2004), 21.

The Women

"Sweep the house, dress up the dishboard and set all things in good order. Milk the kine, suckle the calves, strain the milk, take up and dress the children, provide breakfast, dinner and supper. . . . Send corn and malt to the mill for baking and brewing . . . make butter and cheese . . . feed the swine morning and evening and the poultry in the morning. Look after the hen and goose eggs. Take care of the chickens.

"Get the garden in order, keep it weeded. Sew flax and hemp for sheets, board cloths, towels, shirts, smocks, other necessities . . . Other duties are winnowing corn, washing, haymaking, harvesting, spreading manure, plow driving, loading hay or corn, going to market to sell produce and to buy all household requisites."

—A woman's journal, late 1700s

Source: Pete Serger and Bob Reiser, *Carry It on! A History in Song and Picture of the Working-men and Women of America.* New York: Fireside Editions, Simon and Schustern, 1986, 6.

THE TRAPPAN'D MAIDEN: OR, THE DISTRESSED DAMSEL

This Girl was cunningly Trappan'd, sent to Virginny from England,
Where she doth Hardship undergo, there is no Cure it must be so:
  But if she lives to cross the Main, she vows she'll ne'r go there again.

    Tune of *Virginny*, OR, *When that I was weary, weary, O.*

    Give ear unto a Maid, that lately was betray'd,
      And sent into Virginny, O:
    In brief I shall declare, what I have suffer'd there,
      When that I was weary, weary, weary, weary, O.

5   [Since] that first I came to this Land of Fame,
      Which is called Virginny, O,
    The Axe and the Hoe have wrought my overthrow,
      When that I was weary, weary, weary, weary, O.

    Five years served I, under Master Guy,
10   In the land of Virginny, O,
    Which made me for to know sorrow, grief and woe,
      When that I was weary, weary, weary, weary, O.

    When my Dame says "Go" then I must do so,
      In the land of Virginny, O;
15   When she sits at Meat, then I have none to eat,
      When that I am weary, weary, weary, weary, O.

    The Cloath[e]s that I brought in, they are worn very thin,
      In the land of Virginny, O,
    Which makes me for to say, "Alas, and Well-a-day!"
20   *When that I am weary, weary, weary, weary, O.*

    Instead of Beds of Ease, to lye down when I please,
      In the Land of Virginny, O;
    Upon a bed of straw, I lye down full of woe,
      When that I am weary, weary, weary, weary, O.

25   Then the Spider, she, daily waits on me,
      In the Land of Virginny, O;
    Round about my bed, she spins her web [of thread],
      When that I am weary, weary, weary, weary, O.

    So soon as it is day, to work I must away,
30   In the Land of Virginny, O;
    Then my Dame she knocks, with her tinder-box,
      When that I am weary, weary, weary, weary, O.

    I have play'd my part both at Plow and Cart,
      In the Land of Virginny, O;
35   Billets from the Wood upon my back they load,
      When that I am weary, weary, weary, weary, O.

    Instead of drinking Beer, I drink the water clear,
      In the Land of Virginny, O;
    Which makes me pale and wan, do all that e'er I can,
40   *When that I am weary, weary, weary, weary, O.*

If my Dame says "Go!" I dare not say no,
  In the Land of Virginny, O;
The Water from the Spring, upon my head I bring,
  When that I am weary, weary, weary, weary, O.

45 When the Mill doth stand, I'm ready at command,
  In the Land of Virginny, O;
The Morter for to make, which makes my heart to ake,
  When that I am weary, weary, weary, weary, O.

When the Child doth cry, I must sing "By-a-by!"
50   In the Land of Virginny, O;
No rest that I can have, whilst I am here a Slave,
  When that I am weary, weary, weary, weary, O.

A thousand woes beside, that I do here abide,
  In the Land of Virginny, O;
55 In misery I spend my time that hath no end,
  When that I am weary, weary, weary, weary, O.

Then let Maids beware, all by my ill-fare,
  In the Land of Virginny, O;
Be sure to stay at home, for if you do here come,
60   *You all will be weary, weary, weary, weary, O.*

But if it be my chance, Homewards to advance,
  From the Land of Virginny, O;
If that I, once more, land on English Shore,
  I'll no more be weary, weary, weary, weary, O.

———

James Revel

THE POOR, UNHAPPY TRANSPORTED FELON

Tune of Death and the Lady

My loving Countrymen pray lend an Ear,
  To this Relation which I bring you here,
My sufferings at large I will unfold,
  Which tho' 'tis strange, 'tis true as e'er was told,
5   Of honest parents I did come (tho' poor,)
Who besides me had never Children more;
  Near Temple Bar was born their darling son,
And for some years in virtue's path did run.
  My parents in me took great delight,
10 And brought me up at School to read and write,
  And cast accompts likewise, as it appears,
Until that I was aged thirteen years.
  Then to a Tin-man I was Prentice bound,

My master and mistress good I found,
15   They lik'd me well, my business I did mind,
From me my parents comfort hop'd to find.
    My master near unto Moorfields did dwell,
Where into wicked company I fell;
To wickedness I quickly was inclin'd,
20   Thus soon is tainted any youthful mind.
    I from my master then did run away,
And rov'd about the streets both night and day:
Did with a gang of rogues a thieving go,
Which filled my parents heart with grief and woe.
25   At length my master got me home again,
And used me well, in hopes I might reclaim,
My father tenderly to me did say,
My dearest child, what made you run away?
    If you had any cause at all for grief,
30   Why came you not to me to seek relief?
I well do know you did for nothing lack,
Food for your belly and cloaths to your back.
    My mother cry'd, dear son I do implore,
That you will from your master go no more,
35   Your business mind, your master ne'er forsake,
Lest you again to wicked courses take.
    I promis'd fair, but yet could not refrain,
But to my vile companions went again:
For vice when once, alas! it taints the mind,
40   Is not soon rooted out again we find.
    With them again I did a thieving go,
But little did my tender parents know,
I follow'd courses that could be so vile,
My absence griev'd them, being their only child[,]
45   A wretched life I liv'd, I must confess,
In fear and dread and great uneasiness;
Which does attend such actions that's unjust,
For thieves can never one another trust.
    Strong liquor banish'd all the thoughts of fear,
50   But Justice stops us in our full career:
One night was taken up one of our gang,
Who five impeach'd & three of these were hang'd.
    I was one of the five was try'd and cast,
Yet transportation I did get at last;
55   A just reward for my vile actions past,
Thus justice overtook me at the last.
    My Father griev'd, my mother she took on,
And cry'd, Alas! alas! my only Son:
My Father cry'd, It cuts me to the heart,
60   To think on such a cause as this we part.
    To see them grieve thus pierc'd my very soul,
My wretched case I sadly did condole;
With grief and shame my eyes did overflow,
And had much rather chuse to die than go.

65   In vain I griev'd, in vain my parents weep,
For I was quickly sent on board the Ship:
With melting kisses and a heavy heart,
I from my dearest parents then did part.

Part II

In a few Days we left the river quite,
And in short time of land we lost the sight,
The Captain and the sailors us'd us well,
But kept us under lest we should rebel.
5   We were in number much about threescore,
A wicked lowsey crew as e'er went o'er;
Oaths and Tobacco with us plenty were,
For most did smoak, and all did curse and swear.
Five of our number in our passage died,
10   Which were thrown into the Ocean wide:
And after sailing seven Weeks and more,
We at Virginia all were put on shore.
Where, to refresh us, we were wash'd and cleaned
That to our buyers we might the better seem;
15   Our things were gave to each they did belong,
And they that had clean linnen put it on.
Our faces shav'd, comb'd out our wigs and hair,
That we in decent order might appear,
Against the planters did come down to view,
20   How well they lik'd this fresh transported crew.
The Women s[e]parated from us stand,
As well as we, by them for to be view'd;
And in short time some men up to us came,
Some ask'd our trades, and others ask'd our names.
25   Some view'd our limbs, and other's turn'd us round
Examening like Horses, if we're sound,
What trade are you, my Lad, says one to me,
A Tin-man, Sir, that will not do, says he[.]
Some felt our hands and view'd our legs and feet,
30   And made us walk, to see we were compleat;
Some view'd our teeth, to see if they were good,
Or fit to chew our hard and homely Food.
If any like our look, our limbs, our trade,
The Captain then a good advantage made:
35   For they a difference made it did appear,
'Twixt those for seven and for fourteen year.
Another difference there is alow'd,
They who have money have most favour show'd;
For if no cloaths nor money they have got,
40   Hard is their fate, and hard will be their lot.
At length a grim old Man unto me came,
He ask'd my trade, and likewise ask'd my Name:
I told him I a Tin-man was by trade,
And not quite eighteen years of age I said.
45   Likewise the cause I told that brought me there,

That I for fourteen years transported were,
And when he this from me did understand,
He bought me of the Captain out of hand.

Part III

Down to the harbour I was took again,
    On board of a sloop, and loaded with a chain;
Which I was forc'd to wear both night and day,
For fear I from the Sloop should get away.
5   My master was a man but of ill fame,
Who first of all a Transport thither came;
In Reppahannock county we did dwell,
Up Reppahannock river known full well,
    And when the Sloop with loading home was sent
10   An hundred mile we up the river went
The weather cold and very hard my fare,
My lodging on the deck both hard and bare.
    At last to my new master's house I came,
At the town of Wicocc[o]moco call'd by name,
15   Where my Europian clothes were took from me,
Which never after I again could see.
    A canvas shirt and trowsers then they gave,
With a hop-sack frock in which I was to slave:
No shoes nor stockings had I for to wear,
20   Nor hat, nor cap, both head and feet were bare.
    Thus dress'd into the Field I nex[t] must go,
Amongst tobacco plants all day to hoe,
At day break in the morn our work begun,
And so held to the setting of the Sun.
25   My fellow slaves were just five Transports more,
With eighteen Negroes, which is twenty four:
Besides four transport women in the house,
To wait upon his daughter and his Spouse.
    We and the Negroes both alike did fare,
30   Of work and food we had an equal share;
But in a piece of ground we call our own,
The food we eat first by ourselves were sown,
    No other time to us they would allow,
But on a Sunday we the same must do:
35   Six days we slave for our master's good,
The seventh day is to produce our food.
    Sometimes when that a hard days work we've done,
Away unto the mill we must be gone;
Till twelve or one o'clock a grinding corn,
40   And must be up by daylight in the morn.
    And if you run in debt with any one,
It must be paid before from thence you come;
For in publick places they'll put up your name,
That every one their just demands may claim.
45   And if we offer for to run away,
For every hour we must serve a day;

For every day a Week, They're so severe,
For every week a month, for every month a year
But if they murder, rob or steal when there,
50   Then straightway hang'd, the Laws are so severe;
For by the Rigour of that very law
They're much kept under and to stand in awe.

Part IV

At length, it pleased God I sick did fall
But I no favour could receive at all,
For I was Forced to work while I could stand,
Or hold the hoe within my feeble hands.
5   Much hardships then in deed I did endure,
No dog was ever nursed so I'm sure,
More pity the poor Negroe slaves bestowed
Than my inhuman brutal master showed.
       Oft on my knees the Lord I did implore,
10   To let me see my native land once more;
For through God's grace my life I would amend
And be a comfort to my dearest friends.
       Helpless and sick and being left alone,
I by myself did use to make my moan;
15   And think upon my former wicked ways,
How they had brought me to this wretched case.
       The Lord above who saw my Grief and smart,
Heard my complaint and knew my contrite heart,
His gracious Mercy did to me afford,
20   My health again was unto me restor'd.
       It pleas'd the Lord to grant me so much Grace,
That tho' I was in such a barbarous place,
I serv'd the Lord with fervency and zeal,
By which I did much inward comfort feel.
25   Thus twelve long tedious years did pass away,
And but two more by law I had to stay:
When Death did for my cruel Master call,
But that was no relief to us at all.
       The Widow would not the Plantation hold,
30   So we and that were both for to be sold,
A lawyer rich who at James-Town did dwell,
Came down to view it and lik'd it very well.
       He bought the Negroes who for life were slaves,
But no transported Fellons would he have,
35   So we were put like Sheep into a fold,
There unto the best bidder to be sold.

Part V

A Gentleman who seemed something grave,
Unto me said, how long are you to slave;
Not two years quite, I unto him reply'd,
That is but very short indeed he cry'd.
5   He ask'd my Name, my trade, and whence I came

And what vile Fate had brought me to that shame?
I told him all at which he shook his head,
I hope you have seen your folly now, he said,
   I told him yes and truly did repent,
10   But that which made me most of all relent
That I should to my parents prove so vile,
I being their darling and their only child.
   He said no more but from me short did turn,
While from my Eyes the tears did trinkling run,
15   To see him to my overseer go,
But what he said to him I do not know.
   He straightway came to me again,
And said no longer here you must remain,
For I have bought you of that Man said he,
20   Therefore prepare yourself to come with me.
   I with him went with heart oppressed with woe,
Not knowing him, or where I was to go;
But was surprised very much to find,
He used me so tenderly and kind.
25   He said he would not use me as a slave,
But as a servant if I well behav'd;
And if I pleased him when my time expir'd,
He'd send me home again if I required.
   My kind new master did at James Town dwell;
30   By trade a Cooper, and liv'd very well:
I was his servant on him to attend,
Thus God, unlook'd for raised me up a friend.

Part VI

Thus did I live in plenty and at ease,
   Having none but my master for to please,
And if at any time he did ride out,
I with him rode the country round about.
5   And in my heart I often cry'd to see,
So many transport fellons there to be;
Some who in England had lived fine and brave,
Were like old Horses forced to drudge and slave.
   At length my fourteen years expired quite,
10   Which fill'd my very soul with fond delight;
To think I shoud no longer there remain,
But to old England once return again.
   My master for me did express much love,
And as good as his promise to me prov'd:
15   He got me ship'd and I came home again
With joy and comfort tho' I went asham'd,
   My Father and my Mother wel[l] I found,
Who to see me, with Joy did much abound:
My Mother over me did weep for Joy,
20   My Father cry'd once more to see my Boy;
   Whom I thought dead, but does alive remain,
And is resumed to me once again;
I hope God has so wrought upon your mind,

No more wickedness you'll be inclined,
25 I told them all the dangers I went thro'
Likewise my sickness and my hardships too;
   Which fill'd their tender hearts with sad surprise,
While tears ran trinkling from their aged eyes.
   I begg'd them from all grief to refrain,
30 Since God had brought me to them home again,
The Lord unto me so much grace will give,
For to work for you both while I live,
   My country men take warning e'er too late,
Lest you should share my hard unhappy fate;
35 Altho' but little crimes you here have done,
Consider seven or fourteen years to come,
   Forc'd from your friends and country for to go,
Among the Negroes to work at the hoe;
   In distant countries void of all relief,
40 Sold for a slave because you prov'd a thief.
   Now young men with speed your lives amend,
Take my advice as one that is your friend:
For tho' so slight you make of it while here,
Hard is your lot when once the[y] get you there.

Gottlieb Mittelberger

GOTTLIEB MITTELBERGER'S JOURNEY TO PENNSYLVANIA IN THE YEAR 1750 AND RETURN TO GERMANY IN THE YEAR 1754 (1754)

Both in Rotterdam and in Amsterdam the people are packed densely, like herrings so to say, in the large sea-vessels. One person receives a place of scarcely 2 feet width and 6 feet length in the bedstead, while many a ship carries four to six hundred souls; not to mention the innumerable implements, tools, provisions, waterbarrels and other things which likewise occupy much space.

On account of contrary winds it takes the ships sometimes 2, 3 and 4 weeks to make the trip from Holland to . . . England. But when the wind is good, they get there in 8 days or even sooner. Everything is examined there and the custom-duties paid, whence it comes that the ships ride there 8, 10 to 14 days and even longer at anchor, till they have taken in their full cargoes. During that time every one is compelled to spend his last remaining money and to consume his little stock of provisions which had been reserved for the sea; so that most passengers, finding themselves on the ocean where they would be in greater need of them, must greatly suffer from hunger and want. Many suffer want already on the water between Holland and Old England.

When the ships have for the last time weighed their anchors near the city of Kaupp [Cowes] in Old England, the real misery begins with the long voyage. For from there the ships, unless they have good wind, must often sail 8, 9, 10 to 12 weeks before they reach Philadelphia. But even with the best wind the voyage lasts 7 weeks.

But during the voyage there is on board these ships terrible misery, stench, fumes, horror, vomiting, many kinds of sea-sickness, fever, dysentery, headache, heat, consti- pation, boils, scurvy, cancer, mouth-rot, and the like, all of which come from old and sharply salted food and meat, also from very bad and foul water, so that many die miserably.

Add to this want of provisions, hunger, thirst, frost, heat, dampness, anxiety, want, afflictions and lamentations, together with other trouble, . . . [and] the lice abound so frightfully, especially on sick people, that they can be scraped off the body. The misery reaches the climax when a gale rages for 2 or 3 nights and days, so that every one believes that the ship will go to the bottom with all human beings on board. In such a visitation the people cry and pray most piteously.

When in such a gale the sea rages and surges, so that the waves rise often like high mountains one above the other, and often tumble over the ship, so that one fears to go down with the ship; when the ship is constantly tossed from side to side by the storm and waves, so that no one can either walk, or sit, or lie, and the closely packed people in the berths are thereby tumbled over each other, both the sick and the well—it will be readily understood that many of these people, none of whom had been prepared for hardships, suffer so terribly from them that they do not survive it.

I myself had to pass through a severe illness at sea, and I best know how I felt at the time. These poor people often long for consolation, and I often entertained and comforted them with singing, praying and exhorting; and whenever it was possible and the winds and waves permitted it, I kept daily prayer-meetings with them on deck. Besides, I baptized five children in distress, because we had no ordained minister on board. I also held divine service every Sunday by reading sermons to the people; and when the dead were sunk in the water, I commended them and our souls to the mercy of God.

Among the healthy, impatience sometimes grows so great and cruel that one curses the other, or himself and the day of his birth, and sometimes come near killing each other. Misery and malice join each other, so that they cheat and rob one another. One always reproaches the other with having persuaded him to undertake the journey. Frequently children cry out against their parents, husbands against their wives and wives against their husbands, brothers and sisters, friends and acquaintances against each other. But most against the soul-traffickers.

Many sigh and cry: "Oh, that I were at home again, and if I had to lie in my pig-sty!" Or they say: "O God, if I only had a piece of good bread, or a good fresh drop of water." Many people whimper, sigh and cry piteously for their homes; most of them get home-sick. Many hundred people necessarily die and perish in such misery, and must be cast into the sea, which drives their relatives, or those who persuaded them to undertake the journey, to such despair that it is almost impossible to pacify and console them.

No one can have an idea of the sufferings which women in confinement have to bear with their innocent children on board these ships. Few of this class escape with their lives; many a mother is cast into the water with her child as soon as she is dead. One day, just as we had a heavy gale, a woman in our ship, who was to give birth and could not give birth under the circumstances, was pushed through a loop-hole [port-hole] in the ship and dropped into the sea, because she was far in the rear of the ship and could not be brought forward.

Children from 1 to 7 years rarely survive the voyage. I witnessed misery in no less than 32 children in our ship, all of whom were thrown into the sea. The parents grieve all the more since their children find no resting-place in the earth, but are devoured by the monsters of the sea.

That most of the people get sick is not surprising, because, in addition to all other trials and hardships, warm food is served only three times a week, the rations being very poor and very little. Such meals can hardly be eaten, on account of being so unclean. The water which is served out on the ships is often very black, thick and full of worms, so that one cannot drink it without loathing, even with the greatest thirst. Toward the end we were compelled to eat the ship's biscuit which had been spoiled long ago; though in a whole biscuit there was scarcely a piece the size of a dollar that had not been full of red worms and spiders nests.

At length, when, after a long and tedious voyage, the ships come in sight of land, so that the promontories can be seen, which the people were so eager and anxious to see, all creep from below on deck to see the land from afar, and they weep for joy, and pray and sing, thanking and praising God. The sight of the land makes the people on board the ship, especially the sick and the half dead, alive again, so that their hearts leap within them; they shout and rejoice, and are content to bear their misery in patience, in the hope that they may soon reach the land in safety. But alas!

When the ships have landed at Philadelphia after their long voyage, no one is permitted to leave them except those who pay for their passage or can give good security; the others, who cannot pay, must remain on board the ships till they are purchased, and are released from the ships by their purchasers. The sick always fare the worst, for the healthy are naturally preferred and purchased first; and so the sick and wretched must often remain on board in front of the city for 2 or 3 weeks, and frequently die, whereas many a one, if he could pay his debt and were permitted to leave the ship immediately, might recover and remain alive.

The sale of human beings in the market on board the ship is carried on thus: Every day Englishmen, Dutchmen and High-German people come from the city of Philadelphia and other places, in part from a great distance, say 20, 30, or 40 hours away, and go on board the newly arrived ship that has brought and offers for sale passengers from Europe, and select among the healthy persons such as they deem suitable for their business, and bargain with them how long they will serve for their passage money, which most of them are still in debt for. When they have come to an agreement, it happens that adult persons bind themselves in writing to serve 3, 4, 5 or 6 years for the amount due by them, according to their age and strength. But very young people, from 10 to 15 years, must serve till they are 21 years old.

Many parents must sell and trade away their children like so many head of cattle; for if their children take the debt upon themselves, the parents can leave the ship free and unrestrained; but as the parents often do not know where and to what people their children are going, it often happens that such parents and children, after leaving the ship, do not see each other again for many years, perhaps no more in all their lives.

It often happens that whole families, husband, wife, and children, are separated by being sold to different purchasers, especially when they have not paid any part of their passage money.

When a husband or wife has died at sea, when the ship has made more than half of her trip, the survivor must pay or serve not only for himself or herself, but also for the deceased.

When both parents have died over half-way at sea, their children, especially when they are young and have nothing to pawn or to pay, must stand for their own and their parents' passage, and serve till they are 21 years old. When one has served his or her term, he or she is entitled to a new suit of clothes at parting; and if it has been so stipulated, a man gets in addition a horse, a woman, a cow.

When a serf has an opportunity to marry in this country, he or she must pay for each year which he or she would have yet to serve, 5 to 6 pounds. But many a one who has thus purchased and paid for his bride, has subsequently repented his bargain, so that he would gladly have returned his exorbitantly dear ware, and lost the money besides.

If some one in this country runs away from his master, who has treated him harshly, he cannot get far. Good provision has been made for such cases, so that a runaway is soon recovered. He who detains or returns a deserter receives a good reward.

If such a runaway has been away from his master one day, he must serve for it as a punishment a week, for a week a month, and for a month half a year.

"Petition of a Grate Number of Blackes" to Thomas Gage (May 25, 1774)

The Petition of a Grate Number of Blackes of this Province who by divine permission are held in a state of Slavery within the bowels of a free and christian Country

Humbly Shewing

That your Petitioners apprehind we have in common with all other men a naturel right to our freedoms without Being depriv'd of them by our fellow men as we are a free-born Pepel and have never forfeited this Blessing by aney compact or agreement whatever. But we were unjustly dragged by the cruel hand of power from our dearest frinds and sum of us stolen from the bosoms of our tender Parents and from a Populous Pleasant and plentiful country and Brought hither to be made slaves for Life in a Christian land. Thus are we deprived of every thing that hath a tendency to make life even tolerable, the endearing ties of husband and wife we are strangers to for we are no longer man and wife then our masters or mestreses thinkes proper marred or onmarred. Our children are also taken from us by force and sent maney miles from us wear we seldom or ever see them again there to be made slaves of for Life which sumtimes is vere short by Reson of Being dragged from their mothers Breest[.] Thus our Lives are imbittered to us on these accounts[.] By our deplorable situation we are rendered incapable of shewing our obedience to Almighty God[.] [H]ow can a slave perform the duties of a husband to a wife or parent to his child[?] How can a husband leave master and work and cleave to his wife[?] How can the wife submit themselves to there husbands in all things[?] How can the child obey thear parents in all things[?] . . .

How can the master be said to Beare my Borden when he Beares me down whith the Have chanes of slavery and operson [oppression] against my will and how can we fulfill our parte of duty to him whilst in this condition[?] [A]nd as we cannot searve our God as we ought whilst in this situation Nither can we reap an equal benefet from the laws of the Land which doth not justifi but condemns Slavery or if there had bin aney Law to hold us in Bondege we are Humbely of the Opinon ther never was aney to inslave our children for life when Born in a free Countrey. We therfor Bage your Excellency and Honours will give this its deu weight and consideration and that you will accordingly cause an act of the legislative to be pessed that we may obtain our Natural right our freedoms and our children be set at lebety [liberty].

Olaudah Equiano (1745–1797)

According to his account in *The Interesting Narrative of the Life of Olaudah Equiano, or Gustavus Vassa, the African*, Equiano was kidnapped as a child from his family home in what is today Nigeria, to be sold as a chattel slave in the New World. Recent research by Vincent Carretta, however, has called into question Equiano's claim of African birth and with it the authenticity of his being transported across the Atlantic aboard a slave ship. Whether it is based on his own experience or on the stories of other Igbo slaves, Equiano's account of the encounter with this horrifying new reality—part trading vessel, part instrument of terror—forms the powerful centerpiece of the chapter that follows. In setting up this encounter, Equiano takes care to inform his potentially abolitionist readers that the land from which he and his kin were stolen was not the dark continent of racist stereotype, but had admirable "customs and manners" and a functioning village economy.

Negroes for Sale.

A Cargo of very fine stout Men and Women, in good order and fit for immediate service, just imported from the Windward Coast of Africa, in the Ship Two Brothers.—— Conditions are one half Cash or Produce, the other half payable the first of January next, giving Bond and Security if required.

The Sale to be opened at 10 o'Clock each Day, in Mr. Bourdeaux's Yard, at No. 48, on the Bay.

May 19, 1784.   JOHN MITCHELL.

Thirty Seasoned Negroes

To be Sold for Credit, at Private Sale.

AMONGST which is a Carpenter, none of whom are known to be dishonest.

Also, to be sold for Cash, a regular bred young Negroe Man-Cook, born in this Country, who served several Years under an exceeding good French Cook abroad, and his Wife a middle aged Washer-Woman, (both very honest) and their two Children. Likewise, a young Man a Carpenter.

For Terms apply to the Printer.

"Negroes for Sale" and "Thirty Seasoned Negroes," 1784. *Courtesy of Library of Congress, LC-USZ62-10474.*

After surviving the Middle Passage, according to the *Interesting Narrative*, Equiano (or Gustavus Vassa, as his owner was to name him) was sold in Virginia to a British sea captain. He worked as a sailor on merchant vessels and fighting ships for much of his life, recrossing the Atlantic many times both as a slave, and after he saved enough to purchase his freedom in 1766. His narrative is therefore "interesting" as a remarkable early piece of travel writing, as well as an eloquent account of the horrors of slavery. As one of the most traveled men in his time, as well as an ex-slave, Equiano understood slavery both intimately and as part of a global economic system. His critique of its evils is inspired by biblical prophecy and by the writing of Milton and Blake, which he came to know in the course of an education that he picked up from shipmates and during his sojourns in England. *The Narrative* was first published in London in 1789, during fierce Parliamentary debates over abolition of the slave trade. The title's insistence that his autobiography was "Written by Himself"—a phrase also employed by Frederick Douglass—was made necessary by the common suspicion that black slaves lacked the literacy to author their own stories. It sold through nine editions in England and Ireland before it was reissued in the United States in 1791. It has been called "the most important single literary contribution to the campaign for abolition," and doubts of the authenticity of its early chapters are unlikely to change that assessment.

"I Was in Another World: The Slave Ship"

*The author's birth and parentage—His being kidnapped with his sister—Their separation—
Surprise at meeting again—Are finally separated—Account of the different places and incidents
the author met with till his arrival on the coast—The effect the sight of a slave ship had on
him—He sails for the West Indies—Horrors of a slave ship—Arrives at Barbadoes, where the
cargo is sold and dispersed.*

I hope the reader will not think I have trespassed on his patience in introducing myself
to him with some account of the manners and customs of my country. They had been
implanted in me with great care, and made an impression on my mind, which time could
not erase, and which all the adversity and variety of fortune I have since experienced served
only to rivet and record; for, whether the love of one's country be real or imaginary, or a
lesson of reason, or an instinct of nature, I still look back with pleasure on the first scenes
of my life, though that pleasure has been for the most part mingled with sorrow.

I have already acquainted the reader with the time and place of my birth. My father,
besides many slaves, had a numerous family, of which seven lived to grow up, including
myself and a sister, who was the only daughter. As I was the youngest of the sons, I became,
of course, the greatest favourite with my mother, and was always with her; and she used
to take particular pains to form my mind. I was trained up from my earliest years in the art
of war; my daily exercise was shooting and throwing javelins; and my mother adorned
me with emblems, after the manner of our greatest warriors. In this way I grew up till
I was turned the age of eleven, when an end was put to my happiness in the following
manner:—Generally when the grown people in the neighborhood were gone far in the
fields to labour, the children assembled together in some of the neighbours' premises to
play; and commonly some of us used to get up a tree to look out for any assailant, or
kidnapper, that might come upon us; for they sometimes took those opportunities of our
parents' absence to attack and carry off as many as they could seize. One day, as I was
watching at the top of a tree in our yard, I saw one of those people come into the yard
of our next neighbour but one, to kidnap, there being many stout young people in it.
Immediately on this I gave the alarm of the rogue, and he was surrounded by the stoutest
of them, who entangled him with cords, so that he could not escape till some of the grown
people came and secured him. But alas! ere long it was my fate to be thus attacked, and to
be carried off, when none of the grown people were nigh. One day, when all our people
were gone out to their works as usual, and only I and my dear sister were left to mind
the house, two men and a woman got over our walls, and in a moment seized us both, and,
without giving us time to cry out, or make resistance, they stopped our mouths, and ran
off with us into the nearest wood. Here they tied our hands, and continued to carry us as
far as they could, till night came on, when we reached a small house, where the robbers
halted for refreshment, and spent the night. We were then unbound, but were unable to
take any food; and, being quite overpowered by fatigue and grief, our only relief was some
sleep, which allayed our misfortune for a short time. The next morning we left the house,
and continued travelling all the day. For a long time we had kept the woods, but at last we
came into a road which I believed I knew. I had now some hopes of being delivered; for
we had advanced but a little way before I discovered some people at a distance, on which
I began to cry out for their assistance: but my cries had no other effect than to make them
tie me faster and stop my mouth, and then they put me into a large sack. They also stopped
my sister's mouth, and tied her hands; and in this manner we proceeded till we were
out of the sight of these people. When we went to rest the following night they offered
us some victuals; but we refused it; and the only comfort we had was in being in one
another's arms all that night, and bathing each other with our tears. But alas! we were soon

deprived of even the small comfort of weeping together. The next day proved a day of greater sorrow than I had yet experienced; for my sister and I were then separated, while we lay clasped in each other's arms. It was in vain that we besought them not to part us; she was torn from me, and immediately carried away, while I was left in a state of distraction not to be described. I cried and grieved continually; and for several days I did not eat any thing but what they forced into my mouth. . . .

The wretchedness of the situation was redoubled by my anxiety after her fate, and my apprehensions lest her sufferings should be greater than mine, when I could not be with her to alleviate them. Yes, thou dear partner of all my childish sports! thou sharer of my joys and sorrows! happy should I have ever esteemed myself to encounter every misery for you, and to procure your freedom by the sacrifice of my own. Though you were early forced from my arms, your image has been always rivetted in my heart, from which neither *time nor fortune* have been able to remove it; so that, while the thoughts of your sufferings have damped my prosperity, they have mingled ,with adversity and increased its bitterness. To that Heaven which protects the weak from the strong, I commit the care of your innocence and virtues, if they have not already received their full reward, and if your youth and delicacy have not long since fallen victims to the violence of the African trader, the pestilential stench of a Guinea ship, the seasoning in the European colonies, or the lash and lust of a brutal and unrelenting overseer. . . .

Thus I continued to travel, sometimes by land, sometimes by water, through different countries and various nations, till, at the end of six or seven months after I had been kidnapped, I arrived at the sea coast. It would be tedious and uninteresting to relate all the incidents which befell me during this journey, and which I have not yet forgotten; of the various hands I passed through, and the manners and customs of all the different people among whom I lived: I shall therefore only observe, that in all the places where I was the soil was exceedingly rich; the pomkins, eadas, plantains, yams, &c. &c. were in great abundance, and of incredible size. There were also vast quantities of different gums, though not used for any purpose; and every where a great deal of tobacco. The cotton even grew quite wild; and there was plenty of red-wood. I saw no mechanics whatever in all the way, except such as I have mentioned. The chief employment in all these countries was agriculture, and both the males and females, as with us, were brought up to it, and trained in the arts of war.

The first object which saluted my eyes when I arrived on the coast was the sea, and a slave ship, which was then riding at anchor, and waiting for its cargo. These filled me with astonishment, which was soon converted into terror when I was carried on board. I was immediately handled and tossed up to see if I were sound by some of the crew; and I was now persuaded that I had gotten into a world of bad spirits, and that they were going to kill me. Their complexions too differing so much from ours, their long hair, and the language they spoke, (which was very different from any I had ever heard) united to confirm me in this belief. Indeed such were the horrors of my views and fears at the moment, that, if ten thousand worlds had been my own, I would have freely parted with them all to have exchanged my condition with that of the meanest slave in my own country. When I looked round the ship too and saw a large furnace or copper boiling, and a multitude of black people of every description chained together, every one of their countenances expressing dejection and sorrow, I no longer doubted of my fate; and, quite overpowered with horror and anguish, I fell motionless on the deck and fainted. When I recovered a little I found some black people about me, who I believed were some of those who brought me on board, and had been receiving their pay; they talked to me in order to cheer me, but all in vain. I asked them if we were not to be eaten by those white men with horrible looks, red faces, and loose hair. They told me I was not; and one of the crew brought me a small portion of spirituous liquor in a wine glass; but, being afraid of him, I would not take it out of his hand. One of the blacks therefore took it from him and gave it to me, and I took a little down my palate, which, instead of reviving me, as they thought it would, threw me into the greatest consternation at the strange feeling it produced, having never tasted any such liquor before. Soon after this the blacks who brought me on board went off, and left me abandoned to despair. I now saw myself deprived of all chance of returning to my native country, or even the least glimpse of hope of gaining the shore, which I now considered as friendly; and I even wished for my former slavery in preference to my present situation, which was filled with horrors of every kind, still heightened by my ignorance of what I was to undergo. I was not long suffered to indulge my grief; I was soon put down under the decks, and there I received such a salutation in my nostrils as I had never experienced in my life: so that, with the loathsomeness of the stench, and crying together, I became so sick and low that I was not able to eat, nor had I the least desire to taste any thing. I now wished for the last friend, death, to relieve me; but soon, to my grief, two of the white men offered me eatables; and, on my refusing to eat, one of them held me fast by the hands, and laid me across I think the windlass, and tied my feet, while the other flogged me severely. I had never experienced any thing of this kind before; and although, not being used to the water, I naturally feared that element the first time I saw it, yet nevertheless, could I have got over the nettings, I would have jumped over the side, but I could not; and, besides, the crew used to watch us very closely who were not chained down to the decks, lest we should leap into the water: and I have seen some of these poor African prisoners most severely cut for attempting to do so, and hourly whipped for not eating. This indeed was often the case with myself. In a little time after, amongst the poor chained men, I found some of my own nation, which in a small degree gave ease to my mind. I inquired of these what was to be done with us; they gave me to understand we were to be carried to these white people's country to work for them. I then was a little revived, and thought, if it were no worse than working, my situation was not so desperate: but still I feared I should be put to death, the white people looked and acted, as I thought, in so savage a manner; for I had never seen among any people such instances of brutal cruelty; and this not only shewn towards us blacks, but also to some of the whites themselves. One white man in particular I saw, when we were permitted to be on deck, flogged so unmercifully with a large rope near the foremast, that he died in consequence of it; and they tossed him over the side as they would have done a brute. This made me fear these people the more; and I expected nothing less than to be treated in the same manner. I could not help expressing my fears and apprehensions to some of my countrymen: I asked them if these people had no country, but lived in this hollow place (the ship): they told me they did not, but came from a distant one. "Then," said I, "how comes it in all our country we never heard of them?" They told me because they lived so very far off. I then asked where were their women? had they any like themselves? I was told they had: "and why," said I, "do we not see them?" they answered, because they were left behind. I asked how the vessel could go? they told me they could not tell; but that there were cloths put upon the masts by the help of the ropes I saw, and then the vessel went on; and the white men had some spell or magic they put in the water when they liked in order to stop the vessel. I was exceedingly amazed at this account, and really thought they were spirits. I therefore wished much to be from amongst them, for I expected they would sacrifice me: but my wishes were vain; for we were so quartered that it was impossible for any of us to make our escape. While we stayed on the coast I was mostly on deck; and one day, to my great astonishment, I saw one of these vessels coming in with the sails up. As soon as the whites saw it, they gave a great shout, at which we were amazed; and the more so as the vessel appeared larger by approaching nearer. At last she came to an anchor in my sight, and when the anchor was let go I and my countrymen who saw it were lost in astonishment to observe the vessel stop; and were now convinced it was done by magic. Soon after this the other ship got her boats out, and they came on board of us, and the people of both ships seemed very glad to see each other. Several of the strangers also shook hands with us black people, and made motions with their hands, signifying I suppose we were to go to their country; but we did not understand them. At last, when the ship we were in had got in all her cargo, they made ready with many fearful noises, and we were all put under deck, so that we could not see how they managed the vessel. But this disappointment was the least of my sorrow. The stench of the hold while we were on the coast was so intolerably loathsome, that it was dangerous to remain there for any time, and some of us had been permitted to stay on the deck for the fresh air; but now that the whole ship's cargo were confined together, it became absolutely pestilential. The closeness of the place, and the heat of the climate, added to the number in the ship, which was so crowded that each had scarcely room to turn himself, almost suffocated us. This produced copious perspirations, so that the air soon became unfit for respiration, from a variety of loathsome smells, and brought on a sickness among the slaves, of which many died, thus falling victims to the improvident avarice, as I may call it, of their purchasers. This wretched situation was again aggravated by the galling of the chains, now become insupportable; and the filth of the necessary tubs, into which the children often fell, and were almost suffocated. The shrieks of the women, and the groans of the dying, rendered the whole a scene of horror almost inconceivable. Happily perhaps for myself I was soon reduced so low here that it was thought necessary to keep me almost always on deck; and from my extreme youth I was not put in fetters. In this situation I expected every hour to share the fate of my companions, some of whom were almost daily brought upon deck at the point of death, which I began to hope would soon put an end to my miseries. Often did I think many of the inhabitants of the deep much more happy than myself. I envied them the freedom they enjoyed, and as often wished I could change my condition for theirs. Every circumstance I met with served only to render my state more painful, and heighten my apprehensions, and my opinion of the cruelty of the whites. One day they had taken a number of fishes; and when they had killed and satisfied themselves with as many as they thought fit, to our astonishment who were on the deck, rather than give any of them to us to eat as we expected, they tossed the remaining fish into the sea again, although we begged and prayed for some as well as we could, but in vain; and some of my countrymen, being pressed by hunger, took an opportunity, when they thought no one saw them, of trying to get a little privately; but they were discovered, and the attempt procured them some very severe floggings. One day, when we had a smooth sea and moderate wind, two of my wearied countrymen who were chained together (I was near them at the time), preferring death to such a life of misery, somehow made through the nettings and jumped into the sea: immediately another quite dejected fellow, who, on one account of his illness, was suffered to be out of irons, also followed their example; and I believe many more would very soon have done the same if they had not been prevented by the ship's crew, who were instantly alarmed. Those of us that were the most active were in a moment put down under the deck, and here was such a noise and confusion amongst the people of the ship as I never heard before, to stop her, and get the boat out to go after the slaves. However two of the wretches were drowned, but they got the other, and afterwards flogged him unmercifully for thus attempting to prefer death to slavery. In this manner we continued to undergo more hardships than I can now relate, hardships which are inseparable from this accursed trade. Many a time we were near suffocation from the want of fresh air, which we were often without for whole days together. This, and the stench of the necessary tubs, carried off many. During our passage I first saw flying fishes, which surprised me very much: they used frequently to fly across the ship, and many of them fell on the deck. I also now first saw the use of the quadrant; I had often with astonishment seen the mariners make observations with it, and I could not think what it meant. They at last took notice of my surprise; and one of them, willing to increase it, as well as to gratify my curiosity, made me one day look through it. The clouds appeared to me to be land, which disappeared as they passed along. This heightened my wonder; and I was now more persuaded than ever that I was in another world, and that every thing about me was magic. At last we came in sight of the island of Barbadoes, at which the whites on board gave a great shout, and made many signs of joy to us. We did not know what to think of this; but as the vessel drew nearer we plainly saw the harbour, and other ships of different kinds and sizes; and we soon anchored amongst them off Bridge Town. Many merchants and planters now came on board, though it was in the evening. They put us in separate parcels, and examined us attentively. They also made us jump, and pointed to the land, signifying we were to go there. We thought by this we should be eaten by these ugly men, as they appeared to us; and, when soon after we were all put down under the deck again, there was much dread and trembling among us, and nothing but bitter cries to be heard all the night from these apprehensions, insomuch that at last the white people got some old slaves from the land to pacify us. They told us we were not to be eaten, but to work, and were soon to go on land, where we should see many of our country people. This report eased us much; and sure enough, soon after we were landed, there came to us Africans of all languages. We were conducted immediately to the merchant's yard, where we were all pent up together like so many sheep in a fold, without regard to sex or age. As every object was new to me every thing I saw filled me with surprise. What struck me first was that the houses were built with stories, and in every other respect different from those in Africa: but I was still more astonished on seeing people on horseback. I did not know what this could mean; and indeed I thought these people were full of nothing but magical arts. While I was in this astonishment one of my fellow prisoners spoke to a countryman of his about the horses, who said they were the same kind they had in their country. I understood them, though they were from a distant part of Africa, and I thought it odd I had not seen any horses there; but afterwards, when I came to converse with different Africans, I found they had many horses amongst them, and much larger than those I then saw. We were not many days in the merchant's custody before we were sold after their usual manner, which is this:—On a signal given, (as the beat of a drum) the buyers rush at once into the yard where the slaves are confined, and make choice of that parcel they like best. The noise and clamour with which this is attended, and the eagerness visible in the countenances of the buyers, serve not a little to increase the apprehensions of the terrified Africans, who may well be supposed to consider them as the ministers of that destruction to which they think themselves devoted. In this manner, without scruple, are relations and friends separated, most of them never to see each other again. I remember in the vessel in which I was brought over, in the men's apartment, there were several brothers, who, in the sale, were sold in different lots; and it was very moving on this occasion to see and hear their cries at parting. O, ye nominal Christians! might not an African ask you, learned you this from your God, who says unto you, Do unto all men as you would men should do unto you? Is it not enough that we are torn from our country and friends to toil for your luxury and lust of gain? Must every tender feeling be likewise sacrificed to your avarice? Are the dearest friends and relations, now rendered more dear by their separation from their kindred, still to be parted from each other, and thus prevented from cheering the gloom of slavery with the small comfort of being together and mingling their sufferings and sorrows? Why are parents to lose their children, brothers their sisters, or husbands their wives? Surely this is a new refinement in cruelty, which, while it has no advantage to atone for it, thus aggravates distress, and adds fresh horrors even to the wretchedness of slavery.

Phillis Wheatley (1753?–1784)

She was a frail child of about eight years when she was kidnapped from her West African home, shipped as human cargo, and arrived in Boston in 1761. Purchased as a house servant by John Wheatley, a prosperous merchant and tailor, for his wife Susanna who named her after the slave ship, the *Phillis*, her life, like her given name, was circumscribed by the institution and economics of slavery. The Wheatley family responded to her intellectual prowess by educating her in English, Latin, and the Bible and decreasing her duties to allow her to write. Her first poem appeared in 1767, and Phillis acquired wide fame as a poet with an elegy on the death of a prominent evangelist. In addition to elegies, her literary genius found expression in a series of poems addressed to prominent worthies, including George Washington. John Wheatley succeeded in convincing influential leaders of the Massachusetts Colony that she was, indeed, the author of poetry, a fact that challenged even enlightened assumptions about the innate inferiority of enslaved blacks. *Poems on Various Subjects, Religious and Moral by Phillis Wheatley, Negro Servant to Mr. John Wheatley, of Boston, in New England* was published in London in September 1773. At the age of twenty-one, Phillis was emancipated by John Wheatley, but stayed with the family until his death when she married John Peters, a free black man. It was at this pivotal point that the intertwined constraints of caste and class limited her development as a poet. Her three children did not survive infancy, and Peters was unable to support his family, which became increasingly impoverished. Phillis Wheatley Peters published no poetry during the first five years of her marriage and was unsuccessful in acquiring sufficient promised subscriptions to persuade a publisher to issue a new volume of her verse. She died at the age of thirty. In the poem presented here, she insightfully links the "iron chain[s]" restraining America's freedom to her own kidnapping and enslavement, persuasively arguing the legitimacy of her own subjectivity as having experienced "wanton Tyranny" and, knowing it intimately, links her own ordeal to an enlarged vision, the necessity of freedom, so that "Others may never feel tyrannic sway."

Job Advertisement

Wanted at a Seat about half a day's journey from Philadelphia, on which are good improvements and domestics, A Single Woman of unsullied Reputation, an affable, cheerful, active and amiable Disposition; cleanly, industrious, perfectly qualified to direct and manage the female Concerns of country business, as raising small stock, dairying, marketing, combing, carding, spinning, knitting, sewing, pickling, preserving, etc., and occasionally to instruct two young Ladies in those Branches of Oeconomy, who, with their father, compose the Family. Such a person will be treated with respect and esteem, and meet with every encouragement due to such a character.

Pennsylvania Packet, September 23, 1780

America's Working Women: A Documentary History-1600 to the Present, eds. Rosalyn Baxandall, Linda Gordon, and Susan Reverby (New York: Random House, 1976).

To the Right Honourable William, Earl of Dartmouth, His Majesty's Principal Secretary of State for North-America, &c

Hail, happy day, when, smiling like the morn,
Fair *Freedom* rose *New-England* to adorn:
The northern clime beneath her genial ray,
Dartmouth, congratulates thy blissful sway:
5 Elate with hope her race no longer mourns,
Each soul expands, each grateful bosom burns,
While in thine hand with pleasure we behold
The silken reins, and *Freedom's* charms unfold.
Long lost to realms beneath the northern skies
10 She shines supreme, while hated *faction* dies:
Soon as appear'd the *Goddess* long desir'd,
Sick at the view, she lanquish'd and expir'd;
Thus from the splendors of the morning light
The owl in sadness seeks the caves of night.

15 No more, *America*, in mournful strain
Of wrongs, and grievance unredress'd complain,
No longer shalt thou dread the iron chain,
Which wanton *Tyranny* with lawless hand
Had made, and with it meant t' enslave the land.

20 Should you, my lord, while you peruse my song,
Wonder from whence my love of *Freedom* sprung,
Whence flow these wishes for the common good,
By feeling hearts alone best understood,
I, young in life, by seeming cruel fate
25 Was snatch'd from *Afric's* fancy'd happy seat:
What pangs excruciating must molest,
What sorrows labour in my parent's breast?
Steel'd was that soul and by no misery mov'd
That from a father seiz'd his babe belov'd:
30 Such, such my case. And can I then but pray
Others may never feel tyrannic sway?

For favours past, great Sir, our thanks are due,
And thee we ask thy favours to renew,
Since in thy pow'r, as in thy will before,
35 To sooth the griefs, which thou did'st once deplore.
May heav'nly grace the sacred sanction give
To all thy works, and thou for ever live
Not only on the wings of fleeting *Fame*,
Though praise immortal crowns the patriot's name,
40 But to conduct to heav'ns refulgent fane,
May fiery coursers sweep th' ethereal plain,
And bear thee upwards to that blest abode,
Where, like the prophet, thou shalt find thy God.

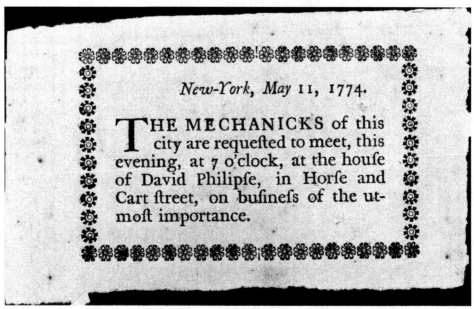

New-York, May 11, 1774.

THE MECHANICKS of this city are requested to meet, this evening, at 7 o'clock, at the house of David Philipse, in Horse and Cart street, on business of the utmost importance.

"The Mechanics," May 11, 1774. *Courtesy of Library of Congress, LC-USZ62-59808.*

A Sea Song

You gentlemen of England who stay at home at ease
How little do you think of the Dangers of the Seas
Give ear unto any bold Mariners and they will plainly Sho
The fears and the cares we poor Seamen undergo.

If you intend to be Seamen you must have a valliant heart
And when your on the raging Seas you must think to start
Neither be faint hearted at hail, rain, frost or snow
Or to think for to sink whilst the stormy winds do blow.

When we meet our Enemies as often times we do
We'll either drive them off our Coast or else we'll bring them too
Our roaring guns shall teach them our vallor for to show
For we'll real on her keale while the stormy winds do blow

Sometimes in absent Bosom our ship she is toss'd with waves
Expecting every moment the Seas would prove our graves
It's up aloft she mounts Boys then down again so low
For we'll real on her keale whilst the stormy winds do blow.

When to Boston we return our wages for our pains
The tapster and the miller shall share in all our gains
We'll call for Licker round boys we'll pay before we go
For we'll rore on the shore while the stormy winds do blow.

The Raising: A New Song for
Federal Mechanics, by A. B. (Francis Hopkinson)

Come muster my Lads, your mechanical Tools,
Your Saws and Your Axes, your Hammers and Rules;
Bring your Mallets and Planes, your Level and Line,
And Plenty of Pins of American Pine;
5   *For our Roof we will raise, and our Song still shall be—*
    A Government firm, and our Citizens free.

Come, up with the *Plates*, lay them firm on the Wall,
Like the People at Large, they're the Ground-work of all,
Examine them well, and see that they're Sound,
10   Let no rotten Parts in our Building be found;
    For our Roof we will raise, and our Song still shall be—
    Our Government firm, and our Citizens free.

Now hand up the *Girders*, lay each in his Place,
Between them the *Joists* must divide all the Space,
15   Like Assembly-men, *these* should lye level along,
Like *Girders*, our Senate prove level and Strong;
    For our Roof we will raise, and our Song still shall be—
    A Government firm, over citizens free.

The *Rafters* now frame . . . your *King-Posts* and *Braces*,
20   And drive your Pins home, to keep all in their Places;
Let Wisdom and Strength in the Fabric Combine,
And your Pins be all made of American Pine.
    For our Roof we will raise, and our Song still shall be—
    A Government firm, and our Citizens free.

25   Our *King-Posts* are Judges—how upright they stand,
Supporting the *Braces*, the Laws of the Land—
The Laws of the Land, which divide Right from Wrong,
And Strengthen the Weak, by weak'ning the Strong;
    For our Roof we will raise, and our Song still shall be—
30   *Laws equal and just, for a People that's free.*

Up! Up with the Rafters—each Frame is a State!
How nobly they rise! their Span, too, how great!
From the North to the South, o'er the Whole they extend,
And rest on the Walls, while the Walls they defend!
35 *For our Roof we will raise, and our Song still shall be—*
    Combine in Strength, yet as Citizens free.

Now enter the *Purlins*, and your Pins through,
And see that your Joints are drawn home, and all true;
The *Purlins* will bind all the Rafters together,
40   The Strength of the Whole shall defy Wind and Weather;
    For our Roof we will raise, and our Song still shall be—
    United as States, but as Citizens free.

Come, raise up the Turret, our Glory and Pride—
In the Centre it stands, o'er the Whole to preside;

45   The Sons of Columbia shall view with Delight
      Its Pillars, and Arches, and towering Height;
          Our Roof is now rais'd, and our Song still shall be—
          A Federal Head, o'er people still free.

      Huzza! my brave Boys, our Work is complete,
50   The World shall admire *Columbia's* fair Seat;
      Its Strength against Tempests and Time shall be Proof.
      And Thousands shall come to dwell under our ROOF.
          Whilst we drain the deep Bowl, our Toast still shall be—
          A Government firm, and our Citizens free.

John McIlvaine

Address to the Journeymen Cordwainers L. B. of Philadelphia

      Cordwainers! Arouse! The time has now come!
          When our rights should be fully protected;
      And every attempt to reduce any one
          By all should be nobly rejected.

5   Fellow-Craft-men! Arouse! We united should be
          And each man should be hailed as a brother,
      Organized we should be in this hallowed cause,
          To love and relieve one another.

      Speak not of failure, in our attempt to maintain,
10   For our labor a fair compensation;
      All that we want is assistance from you,
          To have a permanent organization.

      A commencement we've made, associations we have.
          From one to thirteen inclusive,
15   Come join them my friends, and be not afraid,
          Of them being in the least delusive.

      Go join No. 1, and in it you'll find,
          Men of courage and firmness, devoting
      Their time and their money, in fact all they have
20   Your interest and mine they're promoting.

      And join No. 2, if you wish to maintain,
          For your labor a fair compensation,
      You will find them at work for you and for me
          Their success has far beat expectation.

25   If you join No. 3, you will find them aroused,
          For much do they dread the oppression

They have been subject to in years gone by,
    Go give them a friendly expression.

Join No. 4, defer not a day,
30   But go and with them unite,
Ah! give them assistance, for you they're at work,
    And they'll ten times your trouble requite.

If you join No. 5, you'll find them awake,
    Awake to the pledge they have taken:
35   Their hearts are all true, add yours to them too,
    And by them you ne'er shall be forsaken.

Or join No. 6, if you wish to be
    Raised from your present condition,
To rank with mechanics in wages and name,
40   And be able to keep that position.

Nos. 7, 8, and 9, if you with them join,
    Your interest they have justly at heart,
Their motives you'll love, and with them you'll move.
    And from them you ne'er will depart.

45   Come join No. 10, if you wish to find,
    Men, whose hearts beat with love and devotion,
For the organization, to which they belong,
    Come assist them to keep it in motion.

Or cross o'er to Jersey, if you be not afraid,
50   Of its native disease called the chills,
You will find men united their wages to raise,
    On pump springs, welts, turns and heels.

Then join us my friends, and be not afraid,
    That we will extort from our employers
55   Prices that will injure our fair city's trade,
    Or frighten away from us buyers.

TECUMSEH'S SPEECH TO THE OSAGES
(WINTER 1811–12)

Brothers,—We all belong to one family; we are all children of the Great Spirit; we walk in the same path; slake our thirst at the same spring; and now affairs of the greatest concern lead us to smoke the pipe around the same council fire!

Brothers,—We are friends; we must assist each other to bear our burdens. The blood of many of our fathers and brothers has run like water on the ground, to satisfy the avarice of the white men. We, ourselves, are threatened with a great evil; nothing will pacify them but the destruction of all the red men.

Brothers,—When the white men first set foot on our grounds, they were hungry; they had no place on which to spread their blankets, or to kindle their fires. They were feeble; they could do nothing for themselves. Our father commiserated their distress, and shared freely with them whatever the Great Spirit had given his red children. They gave them food when hungry, medicine when sick, spread skins for them to sleep on, and gave them grounds, that they might hunt and raise corn.

Brothers,—The white people are like poisonous serpents: when chilled, they are feeble and harmless; but invigorate them with warmth, and they sting their benefactors to death.

The white people came among us feeble; and now we have made them strong, they wish to kill us, or drive us back, as they would wolves and panthers.

Brothers,—The white men are not friends to the Indians: at first, they only asked for land sufficient for a wigwam; now, nothing will satisfy them but the whole of our hunting grounds, from the rising to the setting sun.

Brothers,—The white men want more than our hunting grounds; they wish to kill our warriors; they would even kill our old men, women and little ones.

Brothers,—Many winters ago, there was no land; the sun did not rise and set: all was darkness. The Great Spirit made all things. He gave the white people a home beyond the great waters. He supplied these grounds with game, and gave them to his red children; and he gave them strength and courage to defend them.

Brothers—My people wish for peace; the red men all wish for peace; but where the white people are, there is no peace for them, except it be on the bosom of our mother.

Brothers,—The white men despise and cheat the Indians; they abuse and insult them; they do not think the red men sufficiently good to live.

The red men have borne many and great injuries; they ought to suffer them no longer. My people will not; they are determined on vengeance; they have taken up the tomahawk; they will make it fat with blood; they will drink the blood of the white people.

Brothers,—My people are brave and numerous; but the white people are too strong for them alone. I wish you to take up the tomahawk with them. If we all unite, we will cause the rivers to stain the great waters with their blood.

Brothers,—If you do not unite with us, they will first destroy us, and then you will fall an easy prey to them. They have destroyed many nations of red men because they were not united, because they were not friends to each other.

Brothers,—The white people send runners amongst us; they wish to make us enemies that they may sweep over and desolate our hunting grounds, like devastating winds, or rushing waters.

Brothers,—Our Great Father, over the great waters, is angry with the white people, our enemies. He will send his brave warriors against them; he will send us rifles, and whatever else we want—he is our friend, and we are his children.

Brothers,—Who are the white people that we should fear them? They cannot run fast, and are good marks to shoot at: they are only men; our fathers have killed many of them; we are not squaws, and we will stain the earth red with blood.

Brothers,—The Great Spirit is angry with our enemies; he speaks in thunder, and the earth swallows up villages, and drinks up the Mississippi. The great waters will cover their lowlands; their corn cannot grow; and the Great Spirit will sweep those who escape to the hills from the earth with his terrible breath.

Brothers,—We must be united; we must smoke the same pipe; we must fight each other's battles; and more than all, we must love the Great Spirit: he is for us; he will destroy our enemies, and make all his red children happy.

II

New Kinds of Work, Old Practices: 1820s–1850s

> What I come through in life,
> if I go down in meself for it, I could
> make a book.
>
> *J. W. White, former slave*[1]

In his 1832 "Address to the Working-Men of New-England," Massachusetts carpenter and labor reformer Seth Luther describes two tours through a cotton mill in Waltham, Massachusetts. In the first, a United States senator observes "with increased delight" the efficiency of a large cotton manufactory and the "happy countenances" of the women workers. In the second, Luther presents the mills from the perspective of the "lower orders," likening the conditions in the cotton mills to New England prisons. "We do not believe there can be a single person found east of the mountains who ever thanked God for permission to work in a cotton mill." Luther's speech encapsulates critical tensions in postrevolutionary, early industrial America. Will the "American system" be one "where education and intelligence are generally diffused, and the enjoyment of life and liberty secured to all?" Or will America be controlled by men of property, "those who produce nothing and who enjoy all"? Luther asks.[2]

Consider Luther's questions in the context of the technological and industrial changes in the decades leading up to the Civil War. Power generated by steam and water, faster transportation systems of canals and rails, machines with interchangeable parts, and power textile looms were tools and systems that dramatically altered the rhythms of labor. However, they did not necessarily translate into improved living conditions for workers. Structured hierarchies of labor—white, immigrant, women, children, slave and free— served the interests of industrialists and inhibited solidarity among workers.

With historical hindsight, we can trace some of the political shifts and undercurrents that mark this period as well. In 1848, some three hundred women and a few men (including Frederick Douglass) met in Seneca Falls, New York, to forge a declaration on the rights of women that borrowed the language and rhythm of the Declaration of Independence. In 1848, Karl Marx and Frederick Engels published *The Communist Manifesto*, in which they critiqiued the impact of capitalism on the human condition. In the same year, the war in Mexico ended with the expansion of the United States, heightening the debate over slave-owning states and territories. The passage of the Fugitive Slave Act in 1850 requiring citizens to assist in the recovery of fugitive slaves implicated free citizens and free states in upholding the legal status of slavery. Although the act spurred abolitionists to greater resistance, it also escalated the dangers that escaped slaves faced along the Underground Railroad stations.

We see in this section the development of an American working-class literature that was responsive to these economic and political shifts and the fissures in what Luther calls the American system. This section begins and ends with one of the oldest and most

Facing Page: "Am I Not a Man and a Brother?" (woodcut). *Courtesy of Library of Congress, LC-USZ62-44265.*

accessible forms of cultural expression—songs. The haunting sorrow songs and spirituals of enslaved blacks testify to the brutality of slave systems and yet buoy the human spirit with hope of liberation and freedom. The work songs narrate with humor as well as pain the gritty particulars of laboring lives—at home, on the farm, in the small shops, and on the railroad.

The stories, narratives, orations, and poems that follow offer contemporary readers a way of understanding the relational nature of class identity. In his paired stories, Herman Melville narrates key moments—a dinner party and a factory tour—that mirror two systems, interdependent but unequal: lawyers in their "Temple" and girls in a paper mill, capital and labor. He does so from a writer's distance, as Whittier does in his poem about the process of shipbuilding, in which he takes the reader from the raw forest to the finished ship. For a closer look, we turn to Frederick Douglass, who as a worker takes us into the heat, noise, and physicality of the shipyard. Caulking was a critical trade, crucial to the sea-worthiness of ships. Who did the work? In these excerpts from his autobiographies, Douglass goes beyond telling his singular story and analyzes the violence that is inherent in a system that sets wage-earning white workers against enslaved black laborers. Douglass's "Address" is a call for mutuality among blacks, but also a plea for them to work with abolitionist whites and to seek the means for economic self-sufficiency.

This period is by no means just a story about the laboring practices of men. While middle-class and upper-class women were encouraged to stay in their separate domestic spheres, other women were trading their laboring lives on farms for the regimentation of the mills. By 1850, 181,000 women worked in factories, half of them in textile mills.[3] The literature on the "operatives" of the "model" mill town of Lowell, Massachusetts, documents the historical shift from farm to factory and offers insights into the subjectivities of these early industrial workers. To be sure, they were feistier and more vocal than Melville's blank paper-mill girls. In response to a reduction in wages, "factory girls" in Dover, New Hampshire, "turned out" by the hundreds in 1834, declaring, "However freely the epithet of 'factory slaves' may be bestowed upon us, we will never deserve it by a base and cringing submission to proud wealth or haughty insolence."[4]

These strikes and others that were often crushed by mill owners and militias demonstrate workers' consciousness about their working conditions and their resistance to dehumanization and regimentation as factory hands. The cluster of texts by and about the Lowell mill girls suggests some of the ambivalence about the new factory system by the women workers themselves. On the one hand, as Thomas Dublin noted, most of the Lowell girls did not come from destitute backgrounds, nor were they forced by circumstances to work in the mills.[5] Mary Paul asked her father's permission to work at Lowell at the age of 15 or 16, expressing the need for income to buy new clothes (Dublin 36). Others sought urban amenities and educational and other opportunities for a measure of economic and social independence (Dublin 40). On the other hand, women worked thirteen-hour days, about seventy-three hours a week; some were proponents of the Ten-Hour Day movement, and many complained about the poor ventilation in the boarding houses and factory floors. As working conditions deteriorated in the 1840s and 1850s, the Yankee mill girls left and were replaced by immigrants, about half of whom were Irish.[6] These immigrant workers had fewer choices about work and could not so easily return to their family farms.

It was also during this period that class distinctions sharpened between "the lady" and "the mill girl." Newspapers and magazines elevated "true womanhood" as a separate domestic sphere apart from the world of work.[7] Fanny Fern offers another, more realistic, view in her reports of housemaids and working girls. Frances Ellen Watkins Harper's poem exposes the racial hypocrisy that was inherent in the idealization of motherhood. Maria Stewart, as early as 1832, addressed the double oppressions of race and gender, obstacles to self-sufficiency that Stewart understood deeply as a black woman.

The literature of this period also embraces the ideal and the utopian. How the promise of America, a country where "all men are created equal," might be realized in the lives of laboring people is a theme that working-class writers turn to repeatedly. In 1829, the Quaker poet John Greenleaf Whittier linked the cause of the workingman with the cause of the country: "The people—the 'bone and sinew' of the nation are calling forth their giant energies and who shall arrest this progress?"[8] Walt Whitman gives flesh to that bone and sinew in his poetic and inclusive embrace of all work. In "The Wound Dresser," he is most literal—an old man making his way with "bandages, water and sponge" to dress the wounds of Union soldiers. In "Song for Occupations," Whitman offers an idealized paean for a democracy of labor, a literary response to the fissures and shifts of the times.

Notes

1. Quoted in James Mellon, ed. *Bullwhip Days: The Slaves Remember: An Oral History* (New York: Grove Press, 1988).
2. Quoted in Philip S. Foner, *History of the Labor Movement in the United States: From the Colonial Times to the Founding of the American Federation of Labor* (New York: International Publishers, 1947), 106–107.
3. Howard Zinn, *A People's History of the United States* (New York: Harper Perennial, 1980), 253.
4. Quoted in Foner, *History of the Labor Movement,* 109.
5. See Thomas Dublin, *Women at Work: The Transformation of Work and Community in Lowell, Massachusetts, 1826–1860* (New York: Columbia University Press, 1979), 35–57.
6. Benita Eisler, "Introduction," *The Lowell Offering: Writings by New England Mill Women (1840–1845)* (New York: Harper & Row, 1977), 29.
7. Gerda Lerner, "The Lady and the Mill Girl," in Nancy F. Cott and Elizabeth H. Pleck, *A Heritage of Her Own* (New York: Simon and Schuster, 1979), 182–196.
8. Quoted in Foner, *History of the Labor Movement,* 127.

Sorrow Songs and Spirituals

Frederick Douglass called them "wild" and "rude" and "apparently incoherent," yet possessing such deep meaning that "the mere hearing of those songs would do more to impress some minds with the horrible character of slavery, than the reading of whole volumes of philosophy on the subject could do." Douglass's reflection on the slave songs he heard as a youth stresses the songs' compressed depth and power to enlarge consciousness. Sorrow songs, work songs, field songs, secular songs, and spirituals defy clear distinctions and systems of classification. To "hear" them involves setting aside academic concerns of originality, authenticity, and exact dates and entering a space where music and sound are inseparable from experience; where individual voices are linked to community; and where oppression is met with agency, endurance, and hope. These small songs tell large stories. Their crucial legacy is that the most subjugated of enslaved people are doing the telling.

In *The Souls of Black Folk,* W. E. B. Du Bois identifies ten master songs, including "Nobody knows the trouble I've seen," "Swing low, sweet chariot," and "Steal away" that are presented in this section. Folklorist Alan Lomax comments on their functionality— to lighten the burden of labor; to offer consolation and hope; and, through equivocal language, to speak back to their white masters. "Many thousands gone" or "No more auction block for me" is a sweeping historical narrative of loss and liberation. Lomax describes it as a "spiritual of resistance" tracing its antebellum origins to escaped slaves in Nova Scotia in the 1830s and later written down by abolitionists as they encountered Negro Union soldiers during the Civil War. Historian Lawrence Levine notes the versatility of "Breddren, don't git weary," as a sacred song and work song, reportedly heard sung by slave boatmen in the late 1850s. Dynamic and interchangeable, these songs emerged from what Levine calls an "improvisational communal consciousness." Where did they come from? A freedman during the Civil War offered a simple but full answer: "Dey make em, sah."

NOBODY KNOWS DE TROUBLE I'VE SEEN

Nobody knows de trouble I've seen
Nobody knows but Jesus
Nobody knows de trouble I've seen
Glory Hallelujah!

Sometimes I'm up, sometimes I'm down
Oh, yes, Lord
Sometimes I'm almost to de groun'
Oh, yes, Lord

Although you see me goin' 'long so
Oh, yes, Lord
I have my trials here below
Oh, yes, Lord

Advertisement for purchasing slaves. *Courtesy of Library of Congress, LC-USZ62-62799.*

If you get there before I do
Oh, yes, Lord
Tell all-a my friends I'm coming too
Oh, yes, Lord

STEAL AWAY TO JESUS

Steal away, steal away, steal away to Jesus
Steal away, steal away home
I ain't got long to stay here

My Lord, He calls me
He calls me by the thunder
The trumpet sounds within-a my soul
I ain't got long to stay here

Green trees are bending
Po' sinner stand a-trembling
The trumpet sounds within-a my soul
I ain't got long to stay here

SWING LOW, SWEET CHARIOT

Swing low, sweet chariot,
Coming for to carry me home
Swing low, sweet chariot,
Coming for to carry me home

I looked over Jordan, and what did I see
Coming for to carry me home?
A band of angels coming after me
Coming for to carry me home

If you get there before I do
Coming for to carry me home
Tell all my friends I coming too
Coming for to carry me home

I'm sometimes up, I'm sometimes down
Coming for to carry me home
But still my soul feels heavenly bound
Coming for to carry me home

MANY THOUSAND GONE

No more auction block for me,
No more, no more,
No more auction block for me,
Many thousand gone.

No more peck o'corn for me,
No more, no more,
No more peck o 'corn for me,
Many thousand gone.

No more driver's lash for me,
No more, no more,
No more driver's lash for me,
Many thousand gone.

No more pint o' salt for me,
No more, no more.
No more pint o' salt for me
Many thousand gone.

No more hundred lash for me
No more, no more.
No more hundred lash for me,
Many thousand gone.

No more mistress' call for me,
No more, no more
No more mistress' call for me.
Many thousand gone.

BREDDREN, DON' GIT WEARY

Breddren, don' git weary,
Breddren, don' git weary,
Breddren, don' git weary,
Fo' de work is most done.

De ship is in de harbor, harbor, harbor,
De ship is in de harbor,
To wait upon de Lord. . . .

'E got 'e ca'go raidy, raidy, raidy,
'E got 'e ca'go raidy,
Fo' to wait upon de Lord.

W. E. B. Du Bois (1868–1963)

One of the great public intellectuals and civil rights activists of twentieth-century America, William Edward Burghart Du Bois was born in Great Barrington, Massachusetts, into one of the town's few African American families. His encounters with racism in the public schools prompted both an introspective turn and what became a life-long commitment to understanding the roots of discrimination and to combating its effects on his own prospects and on the development of his race. By age fifteen, Du Bois was writing political editorials as a local correspondent for the *New York Globe*. After high school, supported by funds raised among kinfolk and friends, he attended Fisk University in Nashville, Tennessee, a school founded in 1866 to provide a Harvard-style education to freed southern blacks. After three years in the segregated South, Du Bois was admitted to Harvard itself on a full scholarship and later became the first African American to receive a Harvard Ph.D. His dissertation, *The Suppression of the African Slave Trade to the United States of America*, was published in 1896. Du Bois went on to teach at Wilberforce College in Ohio and held positions at the University of Pennsylvania and Atlanta University, where he produced his renowned studies of African American social and cultural life: *Phildelphia Negro* (1899) and *The Souls of Black Folk* (1903), of which "The Sorrow Songs" is an excerpt. In this chapter, Du Bois rehearses his consistent argument for the centrality of black experience to American culture, presenting the songs as not only "the articulate message of the slave to the world," but also "the most beautiful expression of human experience born this side the seas."

Always an activist as well as a teacher and writer, Du Bois's political engagements over a career of sixty years included leading roles in the NAACP (he edited its journal *Crisis*), in the Socialist Party, in the Pan-Africanist movement, in the American Labor Party (he ran as its senatorial candidate for New York in 1950), and in the antinuclear Peace Information Center (for which he was tried as a "subversive"). He ended his days as a member of the Communist Party, living in Accra, Ghana, where he had relocated at the invitation of President Nkrumah to direct *Encyclopedia Africana*, an extensive project on the history and conditions of people of African descent. *The Autobiography of W. E. B. Du Bois* was published in 1968, on the centenary of his birth.

THE SORROW SONGS

I walk through the churchyard
To lay this body down;
I know moon-rise, I know star-rise;
I walk in the moonlight, I walk in the starlight;
I'll lie in the grave and stretch out my arms,
I'll go to judgment in the evening of the day,
And my soul and thy soul shall meet that day,
When I lay this body down.

Negro Song

They that walked in darkness sang songs in the olden days—Sorrow Songs—for they were weary at heart. And so before each thought that I have written in this book I have set a phrase, a haunting echo of these weird old songs in which the soul of the black slave spoke to men. Ever since I was a child these songs have stirred me strangely. They came out of the South unknown to me, one by one, and yet at once I knew them as of me and of mine. Then in after years when I came to Nashville I saw the great temple builded of these songs towering over the pale city. To me Jubilee Hall seemed ever made of the songs themselves, and its bricks were red with the blood and dust of toil. Out of them rose for me morning, noon, and night, bursts of wonderful melody, full of the voices of my brothers and sisters, full of the voices of the past.

Little of beauty has America given the world save the rude grandeur God himself stamped on her bosom; the human spirit in this new world has expressed itself in vigor and ingenuity rather than in beauty. And so by fateful chance the Negro folk-song—the rhythmic cry of the slave—stands to-day not simply as the sole American music, but as the most beautiful expression of human experience born this side the seas. It has been neglected, it has been, and is, half despised, and above all it has been persistently mistaken and misunderstood; but notwithstanding, it still remains as the singular spiritual heritage of the nation and the greatest gift of the Negro people.

Away back in the thirties the melody of these slave songs stirred the nation, but the songs were soon half forgotten. Some, like "Near the lake where drooped the willow," passed into current airs and their source was forgotten; others were caricatured on the "minstrel" stage and their memory died away. Then in war-time came the singular Port Royal experiment after the capture of Hilton Head, and perhaps for the first time the North met the Southern slave face to face and heart to heart with no third witness. The Sea Islands of the Carolinas, where they met, were filled with a black folk of primitive type, touched and moulded less by the world about them than any others outside the Black Belt. Their appearance was uncouth, their language funny, but their hearts were human and their singing stirred men with a mighty power. Thomas Wentworth Higginson hastened to tell of these songs, and Miss McKim and others urged upon the world their rare beauty. But the world listened only half credulously until the Fisk Jubilee Singers sang the slave songs so deeply into the world's heart that it can never wholly forget them again.

There was once a blacksmith's son born at Cadiz, New York, who in the changes of time taught school in Ohio and helped defend Cincinnati from Kirby Smith. Then he fought at Chancellorsville and Gettysburg and finally served in the Freedman's Bureau at Nashville. Here he formed a Sunday school class of black children in 1866, and sang with them and taught them to sing. And then they taught him to sing, and when once the glory of the Jubilee songs passed into the soul of George L. White, he knew his life-work was to let those Negroes sing to the world as they had sung to him. So in 1871 the pilgrimage of the Fisk Jubilee Singers began. North to Cincinnati they rode,—four half-clothed black boys and five girl-women,—led by a man with a cause and a purpose. They stopped at Wilberforce, the oldest of Negro schools, where a black bishop blessed them. Then they went, fighting cold and starvation, shut out of hotels, and cheerfully sneered at, ever northward; and ever the magic of their song kept thrilling hearts, until a burst of applause in the Congregational Council at Oberlin revealed them to the world. They came to New York and Henry Ward Beecher dared to welcome them, even though the metropolitan dailies sneered at his "Nigger Minstrels." So their songs conquered till they sang across the land and across the sea, before Queen and Kaiser, in Scotland and Ireland, Holland and Switzerland. Seven years they sang, and brought back a hundred and fifty thousand dollars to found Fisk University.

Since their day they have been imitated—sometimes well, by the singers of Hampton and Atlanta, sometimes ill, by straggling quartettes. Caricature has sought again to spoil the quaint beauty of the music, and has filled the air with many debased melodies which vulgar ears scarce know from the real. But the true Negro folk-song still lives in the hearts of those who have heard them truly sung and in the hearts of the Negro people.

What are these songs, and what do they mean? I know little of music and can say nothing in technical phrase, but I know something of men, and knowing them, I know that these songs are the articulate message of the slave to the world. They tell us in these eager days that life was joyous to the black slave, careless and happy. I can easily believe this of some, of many. But not all the past South, though it rose from the dead, can gainsay the heart-touching witness of these songs. They are the music of an unhappy people, of the children of disappointment; they tell of death and suffering and unvoiced longing toward a truer world, of misty wanderings and hidden ways.

The songs are indeed the siftings of centuries; the music is far more ancient than the words, and in it we can trace here and there signs of development. My grandfather's grandmother was seized by an evil Dutch trader two centuries ago; and coming to the valleys of the Hudson and Housatonic, black, little, and lithe, she shivered and shrank in the harsh north winds, looking longingly at the hills, and often crooned a heathen melody to the child between her knees, thus:

The child sang it to his children and they to their children's children, and so two hundred years it has travelled down to us and we sing it to our children, knowing as little as our fathers what its words may mean, but knowing well the meaning of its music.

This was primitive African music; it may be seen in larger form in the strange chant which heralds "The Coming of John":

> "You may bury me in the East,
> You may bury me in the West,
> But I'll hear the trumpet sound in that morning,"

—the voice of exile.

Ten master songs, more or less, one may pluck from this forest of melody—songs of undoubted Negro origin and wide popular currency, and songs peculiarly characteristic of the slave. One of these I have just mentioned. Another whose strains begin this book is "Nobody knows the trouble I've seen." When, struck with a sudden poverty, the United States refused to fulfill its promises of land to the freedmen, a brigadier-general went down to the Sea Islands to carry the news. An old woman on the outskirts of the throng began singing this song; all the mass joined with her, swaying. And the soldier wept.

The third song is the cradle-song of death which all men know,—"Swing low, sweet chariot,"—whose bars begin the life story of "Alexander Crummell." Then there is the song of many waters, "Roll, Jordan, roll," a mighty chorus with minor cadences. There were many songs of the fugitive like that which opens "The Wings of Atalanta," and the more familiar "Been a-listening." The seventh is the song of the End and the Beginning— "My Lord, what a mourning! when the stars begin to fall"; a strain of this is placed before "The Dawn of Freedom." The song of groping—"My way's cloudy"—begins "The Meaning of Progress"; the ninth is the song of this chapter—"Wrestlin' Jacob, the day is a-breaking,"—a pæan of hopeful strife. The last master song is the song of songs—"Steal away,"—sprung from "The Faith of the Fathers."

There are many others of the Negro folk-songs as striking and characteristic as these, as, for instance, the three strains in the third, eighth, and ninth chapters; and others I am sure could easily make a selection on more scientific principles. There are, too, songs that seem to me a step removed from the more primitive types: there is the mazelike medley, "Bright sparkles," one phrase of which heads "The Black Belt"; the Easter carol, "Dust, dust and ashes"; the dirge, "My mother's took her flight and gone home"; and that burst of melody hovering over "The Passing of the First-Born"—"I hope my mother will be there in that beautiful world on high."

These represent a third step in the development of the slave song, of which "You may bury me in the East" is the first, and songs like "March on" (chapter six) and "Steal away" are the second. The first is African music, the second Afro-American, while the third is a blending of Negro music with the music heard in the foster land. The result is still distinctively Negro and the method of blending original, but the elements are both Negro and Caucasian. One might go further and find a fourth step in this development, where the songs of white America have been distinctively influenced by the slave songs or have incorporated whole phrases of Negro melody, as "Swanee River" and "Old Black Joe." Side by side, too, with the growth has gone the debasements and imitations—the Negro "minstrel" songs, many of the "gospel" hymns, and some of the contemporary "coon" songs,—a mass of music in which the novice may easily lose himself and never find the real Negro melodies.

In these songs, I have said, the slave spoke to the world. Such a message is naturally veiled and half articulate. Words and music have lost each other and new and cant phrases of a dimly understood theology have displaced the older sentiment. Once in a while we catch a strange world of an unknown tongue, as the "Mighty Myo," which figures as a river of death; more often slight words or mere doggerel are joined to music of singular sweetness. Purely secular songs are few in number, partly because many of them were turned into hymns by a change of words, partly because the frolics were seldom heard by the stranger, and the music less often caught. Of nearly all the songs, however, the music is distinctly sorrowful. The ten master songs I have mentioned tell in word and music of trouble and exile, of strife and hiding; they grope toward some unseen power and sigh for rest in the End.

The words that are left to us are not without interest, and, cleared of evident dross, they conceal much of real poetry and meaning beneath conventional theology and unmeaning rhapsody. Like all primitive folk, the slave stood near to Nature's heart. Life was a "rough and rolling sea" like the brown Atlantic of the Sea Islands; the "Wilderness" was the home of God, and the "lonesome valley" led to the way of life. "Winter'll soon be over," was the picture of life and death to a tropical imagination. The sudden wild thunderstorms of the South awed and impressed the Negroes,—at times the rumbling seemed to them "mournful," at times imperious:

> "My Lord calls me,
> He calls me by the thunder,
> The trumpet sounds it in my soul."

The monotonous toil and exposure is painted in many words. One sees the ploughmen in the hot, moist furrow, singing:

> "Dere's no rain to wet you,
> Dere's no sun to burn you,
> Oh, push along, believer,
> I want to go home."

The bowed and bent old man cries, with thrice-repeated wail:

> "O Lord, keep me from sinking down,"

and he rebukes the devil of doubt who can whisper:

> "Jesus is dead and God's gone away."

Yet the soul-hunger is there, the restlessness of the savage, the wail of the wanderer, and the plaint is put in one little phrase:

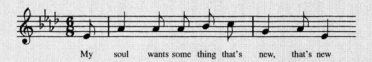

My   soul   wants some thing that's   new,   that's new

Over the inner thoughts of the slaves and their relations one with another the shadow of fear ever hung, so that we get but glimpses here and there, and also with them, eloquent omissions and silences. Mother and child are sung, but seldom father; fugitive and weary wanderer call for pity and affection, but there is little of wooing and wedding; the rocks and the mountains are well known, but home is unknown. Strange blending of love and helplessness sings through the refrain:

> "Yonder's my ole mudder,
> Been waggin' at de hill so long;
> 'Bout time she cross over,
> Git home bime-by."

Elsewhere comes the cry of the "motherless" and the "Farewell, farewell, my only child."

Love-songs are scarce and fall into two categories—the frivolous and light, and the sad. Of deep successful love there is ominous silence, and in one of the oldest of these songs there is a depth of history and meaning:

Poor   Ro - sy,   poor   gal;   Poor   Ro - sy,

poor   gal;   Ro - sy   break   my   poor   heart.

Heav'n   shall - a - be   my   home.

A black woman said of the song, "It can't be sung without a full heart and a troubled sperrit." The same voice sings here that sings in the German folk-song:

> "Jetz Geh i' an's brunele, trink' aber net."

Of death the Negro showed little fear, but talked of it familiarly and even fondly as simply a crossing of the waters, perhaps—who knows?—back to his ancient forests again. Later days transfigured his fatalism, and amid the dust and dirt the toiler sang:

> "Dust, dust and ashes, fly over my grave,
> But the Lord shall bear my spirit home."

The things evidently borrowed from the surrounding world undergo characteristic change when they enter the mouth of the slave. Especially is this true of Bible phrases. "Weep, O captive daughter of Zion," is quaintly turned into "Zion, weep-a-low," and the wheels of Ezekiel are turned every way in the mystic dreaming of the slave, till he says:

> "There's a little wheel a-turnin' in-a-my heart."

As in olden time, the words of these hymns were improvised by some leading minstrel of the religious band. The circumstances of the gathering, however, the rhythm of the songs, and the limitations of allowable thought, confined the poetry for the most part to single or double lines, and they seldom were expanded to quatrains or longer tales, although there are some few examples of sustained efforts, chiefly paraphrases of the Bible. Three short series of verses have always attracted me,—the one that heads this chapter, of one line of which Thomas Wentworth Higginson has fittingly said, "Never, it seems to me, since man first lived and suffered was his infinite longing for peace uttered more plaintively." The second and third are descriptions of the Last Judgment,—the one a late improvisation, with some traces of outside influence:

> "Oh, the stars in the elements are falling,
> And the moon drips away into blood,
> And the ransomed of the Lord are returning unto God,
> Blessed be the name of the Lord."

And the other earlier and homelier picture from the low coast lands:

> "Michael, haul the boat ashore,
> Then you'll hear the horn they blow,
> Then you'll hear the trumpet sound,
> Trumpet sound the world around,
> Trumpet sound for rich and poor,
> Trumpet sound the Jubilee,
> Trumpet sound for you and me."

Through all the sorrow of the Sorrow Songs there breathes a hope—a faith in the ultimate justice of things. The minor cadences of despair change often to triumph and calm confidence. Sometimes it is faith in life, sometimes a faith in death, sometimes assurance of boundless justice in some fair world beyond. But whichever it is, the meaning is always clear: that sometime, somewhere, men will judge men by their souls and not by their skins. Is such a hope justified? Do the Sorrow Songs sing true?

The silently growing assumption of this age is that the probation of races is past, and that the backward races of today are of proven inefficiency and not worth the saving. Such an assumption is the arrogance of peoples irreverent toward Time and ignorant of the deeds of men. A thousand years ago such an assumption, easily possible, would have made it difficult for the Teuton to prove his right to life. Two thousand years ago such dogmatism, readily welcome, would have scouted the idea of blond races ever leading civilization. So wofully unorganized is sociological knowledge that the meaning of progress, the meaning of "swift" and "slow" in human doing, and the limits of human perfectability, are veiled, unanswered sphinxes on the shores of science. Why should Æschylus have sung two thousand years before Shakespeare was born? Why has civilization flourished in Europe, and flickered, flamed, and died in Africa? So long as the world stands meekly dumb before such questions, shall this nation proclaim its ignorance and unhallowed prejudices by denying freedom of opportunity to those who brought the Sorrow Songs to the Seats of the Mighty?

Your country? How came it yours? Before the Pilgrims landed we were here. Here we have brought our three gifts and mingled them with yours: a gift of story and song—soft, stirring melody in an ill-harmonized and unmelodious land; the gift of sweat and brawn to beat back the wilderness, conquer the soil, and lay the foundations of this vast economic empire two hundred years earlier than your weak hands could have done it; the third, a gift of the Spirit. Around us the history of the land has centered for thrice a hundred years; out of the nation's heart we have called all that was best to throttle and subdue all that was worst; fire and blood, prayer and sacrifice, have billowed over this people, and they have found peace only in the altars of the God of Right. Nor has our gift of the Spirit been merely passive. Actively we have woven ourselves with the very warp and woof of this nation,—we fought their battles, shared their sorrow, mingled our blood with theirs, and generation after generation have pleaded with a headstrong, careless people to despise not Justice, Mercy, and Truth, lest the nation be smitten with a curse. Our song, our toil, our cheer, and warning have been given to this nation in blood-brotherhood. Are not these gifts worth the giving? Is not this work and striving? Would America have been America without her Negro people?

Even so is the hope that sang in the songs of my father well sung. If somewhere in this whirl and chaos of things there dwells Eternal Good, pitiful yet masterful, then anon in His good time America shall rend the Veil and the prisoned shall go free. Free, free as the sunshine trickling down the morning into these high windows of mine, free as yonder fresh young voices welling up to me from the caverns of brick and mortar below—swelling with song, instinct with life, tremulous treble and darkening bass. My children, my little children, are singing to the sunshine, and thus they sing:

And the traveller girds himself, and sets his face toward the Morning, and goes his way.

THE AFTERTHOUGHT

Hear my cry, O God the Reader; vouchsafe that this my book fall not still-born into the world-wilderness. Let there spring, Gentle One, from out its leaves vigor of thought and thoughtful deed to reap the harvest wonderful. (Let the ears of a guilty people tingle with truth, and seventy millions sigh for the righteousness which exalteth nations, in this drear day when human brotherhood is mockery and a snare.) Thus in Thy good time may infinite reason turn the tangle straight, and these crooked marks on a fragile leaf be not indeed

THE END

Maria W. Stewart (1803–1879)

"How long shall the fair daughters of Africa be compelled to bury their minds and talents beneath a load of iron pots and kettles?" asks Maria Stewart in the speech delivered in Boston in 1832, the first such public lecture by an American-born woman of any race. In a set of "Meditations" published in the year of her death, Stewart summarized her early life with poignant brevity:

> I was born in Hartford, Connecticut, 1803; was left an orphan at five years of age; was bound out [as a servant] in a clergyman's family; had the seeds of virtue and piety early sewn in my mind; but was deprived of the advantages of education, though my soul thirsted for knowledge. Left them at fifteen years of age; attended Sabbath schools until I was twenty; in 1826 was married to James W. Stewart; was left a widow in 1829.

Cheated out of her husband's military pension but determined to avoid further domestic service, Stewart turned to teaching school as a livelihood. Now a convinced Christian—"a strong advocate for the cause of God and the cause of freedom," causes she regarded as closely aligned—Stewart began writing the "devotional essays" that were brought to the attention of William Lloyd Garrison, a leading Boston abolitionist and editor of *The Liberator*. It was with his encouragement that she began her brief but effective career as a public political activist, giving stirring speeches to the Afric-America Female Intelligence Society and broader audiences. A former house servant speaking largely to other domestics and day laborers, Stewart critiqued not only slavery, but also the degraded labor to which "free" blacks in the North were confined. Like Phillis Wheatley before her, Stewart held no attachment to "fallen Africa." She looked to Christian principle, ideals of female respectability, and the American promise of equal citizenship as the grounds for advancement of her race and class. Stewart soon came to find the "notoriety" of public speaking distasteful, and she devoted the rest of her working life to teaching, eventually, after many costly failures, starting successful Christian schools in New York, Baltimore, and Washington, DC.

LECTURE DELIVERED AT THE FRANKLIN HALL
BOSTON, SEPTEMBER 21, 1832

Why sit ye here and die? If we say we will go to a foreign land, the famine and the pestilence are there, and there we shall die. If we sit here, we shall die. Come let us plead our cause before the whites: if they save us alive, we shall live—and if they kill us, we shall but die.

Methinks I heard a spiritual interrogation—"Who shall go forward, and take off the reproach that is cast upon the people of color? Shall it be a woman?" And my heart made this reply—"If it is thy will, be it even so, Lord Jesus!"

I have heard much respecting the horrors of slavery; but may Heaven forbid that the generality of my color throughout these United States should experience any more of its horrors than to be a servant of servants, or hewers of wood and drawers of water! Tell us no more of southern slavery; for with few exceptions, although I may be very erroneous in my opinion, yet I consider our condition but little better than that. Yet, after all, methinks there are no chains so galling as the chains of ignorance—no fetters so binding as those that bind the soul, and exclude it from the vast field of useful and scientific knowledge. O, had I received the advantages of early education, my ideas would, ere now, have expanded far and wide; but, alas! I possess nothing but moral capability—no teachings but the teachings of the Holy spirit.

I have asked several individuals of my sex, who transact business for themselves, if providing our girls were to give them the most satisfactory references, they would not be willing to grant them an equal opportunity with others? Their reply has been—for their own part, they had no objection; but as it was not the custom, were they to take them into their employ, they would be in danger of losing the public patronage.

And such is the powerful force of prejudice. Let our girls possess what amiable qualities of soul they may; let their characters be fair and spotless as innocence itself; let their natural taste and ingenuity be what they may; it is impossible for scarce an individual of them to rise above the condition of servants. Ah! why is this cruel and unfeeling distinction? Is it merely because God has made our complexion to vary? If it be, O shame to soft, relenting humanity! "Tell it not in Gath! publish it not in the streets of Askelon!" Yet, after all, methinks were the American free people of color to turn their attention more assiduously to moral worth and intellectual improvement, this would be the result:

prejudice would gradually diminish, and the whites would be compelled to say, unloose those fetters!

> Though black their skins as shades of night,
> Their hearts are pure, their souls are white.

Few white persons of either sex, who are calculated for any thing else, are willing to spend their lives and bury their talents in performing mean, servile labor. And such is the horrible idea that I entertain respecting a life of servitude, that if I conceived of there being no possibility of my rising above the condition of a servant, I would gladly hail death as a welcome messenger. O, horrible idea, indeed! to possess noble souls aspiring after high and honorable acquirements, yet confined by the chains of ignorance and poverty to lives of continual drudgery and toil. Neither do I know of any who have enriched themselves by spending their lives as house-domestics, washing windows, shaking carpets, brushing boots, or tending upon gentlemen's tables. I can but die for expressing my sentiments; and I am as willing to die by the sword as the pestilence; for I am a true born American; your blood flows in my veins, and your spirit fires my breast.

I observed a piece in the *Liberator* a few months since, stating that the colonizationists had published a work respecting us, asserting that we were lazy and idle. I confute them on that point. Take us generally as a people, we are neither lazy nor idle; and considering how little we have to excite or stimulate us, I am almost astonished that there are so many industrious and ambitious ones to be found; although I acknowledge, with extreme sorrow, that there are some who never were and never will be serviceable to society. And have you not a similar class among yourselves?

Again. It was asserted that we were "a ragged set, crying for liberty." I reply to it, the whites have so long and so loudly proclaimed the theme of equal rights and privileges, that our souls have caught the flame also, ragged as we are. As far as our merit deserves, we feel a common desire to rise above the condition of servants and drudges. I have learnt, by bitter experience, that continual hard labor deadens the energies of the soul, and benumbs the faculties of the mind; the ideas become confined, the mind barren, and, like the scorching sands of Arabia, produces nothing; or, like the uncultivated soil, brings forth thorns and thistles.

Again, continual hard labor irritates our tempers and sours our dispositions; the whole system becomes worn out with toil and failure; nature herself becomes almost exhausted, and we care but little whether we live or die. It is true, that the free people of color throughout these United States are neither bought nor sold, nor under the lash of the cruel driver; many obtain a comfortable support; but few, if any, have an opportunity of becoming rich and independent; and the employments we most pursue are as unprofitable to us as the spider's web or the floating bubbles that vanish into air. As servants, we are respected; but let us presume to aspire any higher, our employer regards us no longer. And were it not that the King eternal has declared that Ethiopia shall stretch forth her hands unto God, I should indeed despair.

I do not consider it derogatory, my friends, for persons to live out to service. There are many whose inclination leads them to aspire no higher; and I would highly commend the performance of almost any thing for an honest livelihood; but where constitutional strength is wanting, labor of this kind, in its mildest form, is painful. And doubtless many are the prayers that have ascended to Heaven from Africa's daughters for strength to perform their work. Oh, many are the tears that have been shed for the want of that strength! Most of our color have dragged out a miserable existence of servitude from the cradle to the grave. And what literary acquirements can be made, or useful knowledge derived, from either maps, books or charm, by those who continually drudge from Monday morning until Sunday noon? O, ye fairer sisters, whose hands are never soiled, whose nerves and muscles are never strained, go learn by experience! Had we had the opportunity that you have had, to improve our moral and mental faculties, what would have hindered our intellects from being as bright, and our manners from being as dignified as yours? Had it been our lot to have been nursed in the lap of affluence and ease, and to have basked beneath the smiles and sunshine of fortune, should we not have naturally supposed that we were never made to toil? And why are not our forms as delicate, and our constitutions as slender, as yours? Is not the workmanship as curious and complete? Have pity upon us, have pity upon us, O ye who have hearts to feel for other's woes; for the hand of God has touched us. Owing to the disadvantages under which we labor, there are many flowers among us that are

> "—born to bloom unseen,
> And waste their fragrance on the desert air."

My beloved brethren, as Christ has died in vain for those who will not accept of offered mercy, so will it be vain for the advocates of freedom to spend their breath in our behalf, unless with united hearts and souls you make some mighty efforts to raise your sons and daughters from the horrible state of servitude and degradation in which they are placed. It is upon you that woman depends; she can do but little besides using her influence; and it is for her sake and yours that I have come forward and made myself a hissing and a reproach among the people; for I am also one of the wretched and miserable daughters of the descendants of fallen Africa. Do you ask, why are you wretched and miserable? I reply, look at many of the most worthy and interesting of us doomed to spend our lives in gentlemen's kitchens. Look at our young men, smart, active and energetic, with souls filled with ambitious fire; if they look forward, alas! what are their prospects? They can be nothing but the humblest laborers, on account of their dark complexions; hence many of them lose their ambition, and become worthless. Look at our middle-aged men, clad in their rusty plaids and coats; in winter, every cent they earn goes to buy their wood and pay their rents; their poor wives also toil beyond their strength, to help support their families. Look at our aged sires, whose heads are whitened with the front of seventy winters, with their old wood-saws on their backs. Alas, what keeps us so? Prejudice, ignorance and poverty. But ah! methinks our oppression is soon to come to an end; yes, before the Majesty of heaven, our groans and cries have reached the ears of the Lord of Sabaoth. As the prayers and tears of Christians will avail the finally impenitent nothing; neither will the prayers and tears of the friends of humanity avail us any thing, unless we possess a spirit of virtuous emulation within our breasts. Did the pilgrims, when they first landed on these shores, quietly compose themselves, and say, "the Britons have all the money and all the power, and we must continue their servants forever?" Did they sluggishly sigh and say, "our lot is hard, the Indians own the soil, and we cannot cultivate it?" No; they first made powerful efforts to raise themselves and then God raised up those illustrious patriots Washington and Lafayette to assist and defend them. And, my brethren, have you made a powerful effort? Have you prayed the Legislature for mercy's sake to grant you all the rights and privileges of free citizens, that your daughters may raise to that degree of respectability which true merit deserves, and your sons above the servile situations which most of them fill?

The Lowell Factory Girls

The poet John Greenleaf Whittier described Lowell, Massachusetts, as "a city springing up, like the enchanted palaces of the Arabian Tales." As one of the first designed and built industrial cities in the United States, Lowell emerged more by dint of Yankee technological know-how, industrial espionage, corporate alliances, the harnessing of natural energy resources, and a workforce of able young women than by any literary enchantment. Lowell marks the growth in manufacturing in the Northeast between 1825 and 1860 that transformed the landscape of labor in America. A model corporate city, Lowell integrated boarding houses, mills, churches, libraries, and shops into a functioning, highly controlled, and organized manufacturing center that was fueled by the water power generated by the Pawtucket Falls, the confluence of the Merrimack and Concord Rivers, and miles of canals dug by Irish laborers. Now a historic site, visitors can don earplugs and walk among the clattering looms, see a replica of a boarding house, and learn about the historic and technical forces that brought New England farm girls into the mills and about the changing working conditions that drove them away to be replaced by generations of immigrants. The visitor does not experience the speed of the machines, the dirt and lack of ventilation in the boarding houses, or the dust and lint in the air that the "factory girls" of Lowell knew too well. Less visible, as well, is the relationship between the wage-earning workers who produced cloth in the North and the enslaved workers who picked raw cotton in the South.

The selections that follow take us inside the world of Lowell. Industrial or factory tours are familiar literary devices for guiding middle-class readers into subterranean worlds of harsh physical labor, a device used by Herman Melville, Rebecca Harding Davis, and Upton Sinclair in their fiction that is included in this collection. The Lowell tour, however, is from the inside out. In "A Second Peep at Factory Life," the writer, Josephine L. Baker, takes her reader into the mill and through the various cloth-processing departments. She uses strategies of imagined or actual "overheard" conversations to present grievances about pay and working conditions in the mills. A necessary indirection, perhaps, since the story was published in *The Lowell Offering* (1840–1845), which claimed to emphasize literary expression, not working issues. However, beneath the self-conscious literary language, many writers in the *Offering* managed to illuminate actual conditions within the paternalistic corporate "utopia." Baker and the other *Lowell Offering* writers offer a complex, mixed picture of factory work: tedious, long hours and frequently cut wages, on the one hand, but access to books, lectures, the companionship of other young women, and a degree of financial independence, on the other hand. In Mary Paul's letters to her father, we have a more subjective view of the promise of Lowell and the realities of work injuries and reduced pay. The anonymous ballad "The Lowell Factory Girl," despite the jaunty rhythm, is a long complaint about deteriorating conditions in the mills. In "Characteristics of the Early Factory Girls," Harriet Hanson Robinson, author of *Loom and Spindle: Or Life Among the Early Mill Girls* (1898) appraises the early days in the mills with a sympathetic description of the feisty "turn outs" (strikes) in the early 1830s over reduced wages and increased costs. Like the poet Whittier, Robinson takes issue with condescending stereotypes about factory workers and their cultural expressions. Workers, like Samuel Johnson's "dancing dog," were not expected to produce genuine culture any more than dogs could dance. Robinson puts that prejudice to rest by insisting on the intellectuality and creativity of workers. The last selection in this cluster, "From the Same Cloth," by the contemporary poet Helena Minton, is a tribute to the labor legacy of the Lowell girls, as well as a poetic answer to the regulating bells, incessant machinery, and physical costs of factory work.

JOSEPHINE L. BAKER, A SECOND PEEP AT FACTORY LIFE

There is an old saying, that "When we are with the Romans, we must do as the Romans do." And now, kind friend, as we are about to renew our walk, I beg that you will give heed to it, and do as factory girls do. After this preliminary, we will proceed to the factory.

There is the "counting-room," a long, low, brick building, and opposite is the "store-house," built of the same material, after the same model. Between them, swings the ponderous gate that shuts the mills in from the world without. But, stop; we must get "a pass," ere we go through, or "the watchman will be after us." Having obtained this, we will stop on the slight elevation by the gate, and view the mills. The one to the left rears high its huge sides of brick and mortar, and the belfry, towering far above the rest, stands out in bold relief against the rosy sky. The almost innumerable windows glitter, like gems, in the morning sunlight. It is six and a half stories high, and, like the fabled monster of old, who guarded the sacred waters of Mars, it seems to guard its less aspiring sister to the right; that is five and a half stories high, and to it is attached the repair-shop. If you please, we will pass to the larger factory,—but be careful, or you will get lost in the mud, for this yard is not laid out in such beautiful order, as some of the factory yards are, nor can it be.

We will just look into the first room. It is used for cleaning cloth. You see the scrubbing and scouring machines are in full operation, and gigging and fulling are going on in full perfection. As it is very damp, and the labor is performed by the other half of creation, we will pass on, for fear of incurring their jealousy. But the very appearance might indicate that there are, occasionally, *fogs* and *clouds*; and not only fogs and clouds, but sometimes plentiful showers. In the second room the cloth is "*finished*," going through the various operations of burling, shearing, brushing, inking, fine-drawing, pressing, and packing for market. This is the pleasantest room on the corporation, and consequently they are never in want of help. The shearing, brushing, pressing and packing is done by males, while the burling, inking, marking and fine-drawing is performed by females. We will pass to the third room, called the "cassimere weaving-room," where all kinds of cloths are woven, from plain to the most exquisite fancy. There are between eighty and ninety looms, and part of the dressing is also done here. The fourth is the "broad weaving-room," and contains between thirty and forty looms; and broad sure enough they are. Just see how lazily the lathe drags backward and forward, and the shuttle—how spitefully it hops from one end of it to the other. But we must not stop longer, or perchance it will hop at us. You look weary; but, never mind! there was an end to Jacob's ladder, and *so* there is a termination to these stairs. Now if you please we will go up to the next room, where the spinning is done. Here we have spinning jacks or jennies that dance merrily along whizzing and singing, as they spin out their "long yarns," and it seems but pleasure to watch their movements; but it is hard work, and requires good health and much strength. Do not go too near, as we shall find that they do not understand the established rules of *etiquette*, and might unceremoniously knock us over. We must not stop here longer, for it is twelve o'clock, and we have the "carding-room" to visit before dinner. There are between twenty and thirty set of cards located closely together, and I beg of you to be careful as we go amongst them, or you will get caught in the machinery. You walk as though you were afraid of getting blue. Please excuse me, if I ask you not to be afraid. 'Tis a wholesome color, and soap and water will wash it off. The girls, you see, are partially guarded against it, by over-skirts and sleeves; but as it is not *fashionable* to wear masks, they cannot keep it from their faces. You appear surprised at the hurry and bustle now going on in the room, but your attention has been so engaged that you have forgotten the hour. Just look at the clock, and you will find that it wants but five minutes to "bell time." We will go to the door, and be ready to start when the others do; and now, while we are waiting, just cast your eyes to the stair-way, and you will see another flight of stairs, leading to another spinning-room; a picker is located somewhere in that region, but I cannot give you a description of it, as I have never had the courage to ascend more than five flight of stairs at a time. And—but the bell rings.

Now look out—not for the engine—but for the rush to the stair-way. O mercy! what a crowd. I do not wonder you gasp for breath; but, keep up courage; we shall soon be on terra firma again. Now, safely landed, I hope to be excused for taking you into such a crowd. Really, it would not be fair to let you see the factory girls and machinery for nothing. I shall be obliged to hurry you, as it is some way to the boarding-house, and we have but thirty minutes from the time the bell begins to ring till it is done ringing again; and then all are required to be at their work. There is a group of girls yonder, going our way; let us overtake them, and hear what they are talking about. Something unpleasant I dare say, from their earnest gestures and clouded brows.

"Well, I do think it is too bad," exclaims one.

"So do I," says another. "This cutting down wages *is not* what they cry it up to be. I wonder how they'd like to work as hard as we do, digging and drudging day after day, from morning till night, and then, every two or three years, have their wages reduced. I rather guess it wouldn't set very well."

"And, besides this, who ever heard, of such a thing as their being raised again," says the first speaker. "I confess that I never did, so long as I've worked in the mill, and that's been these ten years."

"Well, it is real provoking any how," returned the other, "for my part I should think they had made a clean sweep this time. I wonder what they'll do next."

"Listeners never hear any good of themselves" is a trite saying, and, for fear it may prove true in our case, we will leave this busy group, and get some dinner. There is an open door inviting us to enter. We will do so. You can hang your bonnet and shawl on one of those hooks, that extend the length of the entry for that purpose, or you can lay them on the banisters, as some do. Please to walk into the diningroom. Here are two large square tables, covered with checked clothes and loaded down with smoking viands, the odor of which is very inviting. But we will not stop here; there is the long table in the front room, at which ten or fifteen can be comfortably seated. You may place yourself at the head. Now do not be bashful or wait to be helped, but comply with the oft-made request, "help your-self" to whatever you like best; for you have but a few minutes allotted you to spend at the table. The reason why, is because you are a rational, intelligent, thinking being, and ought to know enough to swallow your food whole; whereas a horse or an ox, or any other dumb beast knows no better than to spend an hour in the *useless* process of mastication. The bell rings again, and the girls are hurrying to the mills; you, I suppose, have seen enough of them for one day, so we will walk up stairs and have a *tete-a-tete*.

You ask, if there are so many things objectionable, why we work in the mill. Well, simply for this reason,—every situation in life, has its trials which must be borne, and factory life has no more than any other. There are many things we do not like; many occurrences that send the warm blood mantling to the cheek when they must be borne in silence, and many harsh words and acts that are not called for. There are objections also to the number of hours we work, to the length of time allotted to our meals, and to the low wages allowed for labor; objections that must and will be answered; for the time has come when something, besides the clothing and feeding of the body is to be thought of; when the mind is to be clothed and fed; and this cannot be as it should be, with the present system of labor. Who, let me ask, can find that pleasure in life which they should, when it is spent in this way. Without time for the laborer's own work, and the improvement of the mind, save the few evening hours; and even then if the mind is enriched and stored with useful knowledge, it must be at the expense of health. And the feeling too, that comes over us (there is no use in denying it) when we hear the bell calling us away from repose that tired nature loudly claims—the feeling, that we are *obliged to go*. And these few hours, of which we have spoken, are far too short, three at the most at the close of day. Surely, methinks, every heart that lays claim to humanity will feel 'tis not enough. But this, we hope will, ere long, be done away with, and labor made what it should be; pleasant and inviting to every son and daughter of the human family.

There is a brighter side to this picture, over which we would not willingly pass without notice, and an answer to the question, why we work here? The time we *do* have is our own. The money we earn comes promptly; more so than in any other situation; and our work, though laborious is the same from day to day; we know what it is, and when finished we feel perfectly free, till it is time to commence it again.

Besides this, there are many pleasant associations connected with factory life, that are not to be found elsewhere.

There are lectures, evening schools and libraries, to which all may have access. The one thing needful here, is the time to improve them as we ought.

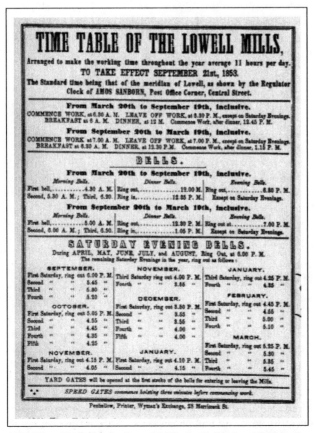

1853 Time Table for the Lowell Mills (probably Lowell Manufacturing Company, makers of worsted yarns and carpets). *Source*: Merrimack Valley Textile Museum.

There is a class, of whom I would speak, that work in the mills, and will while they continue in operation. Namely, the many who have no home, and who come here to seek, in this busy, bustling "City of Spindles," a competency that shall enable them in after life, to live without being a burden to society,—the many who toil on, without a murmur, for the support of an aged mother or orphaned brother and sister. For the sake of them, we earnestly hope labor may be reformed; that the miserable, selfish spirit of competition, now in our midst, may be thrust from us and consigned to eternal oblivion.

There is one other thing that must be mentioned ere we part, that is the practice of sending agents through the country to decoy girls away from their homes with the promise of high wages, when the market is already stocked to overflowing. This is certainly wrong, for it lessens the value of labor, which should be ever held in high estimation, as the path marked out by the right hand of God, in which man should walk with dignity.

And now, kind friend, we must part. I beg pardon for intruding so long upon your time and patience, and also for not introducing you to Dorcas Hardscrabble. I feared I should weary you, and besides, many hardscrabbling Dorcases may be found among the factory girls.

One word for what has been said. It has been uttered for *truth's* sake, and because called for. If it does not answer your expectations, a companion must be sought, that will please the fancy better.

MARY PAUL, "LETTERS TO HER FATHER"

[Woodstock, Vt.] Saturday Sept. 13th 1845[1]

Dear Father

I received your letter this afternoon by Wm Griffith. You wished me to write if I had seen Mr. Angell. I have neither written to him nor seen him nor has he written to me. I began to write but I could not write what I wanted to. I think if I could see him I could convince him of his error if he would let me talk. I am very glad you sent my shoes. They fit very well indeed they [are] large enough.

I want you to consent to let me go to Lowell if you can. I think it would be much better for me than to stay about here. I could earn more to begin with than I can any where about here. I am in need of clothes which I cannot get if I stay about here and for that reason I want to go to Lowell or some other place. We all think if I could go with some steady girl that I might do well. I want you to think of it and make up your mind. Mercy Jane Griffith is going to start in four or five weeks. Aunt Miller and Aunt Sarah think it would be a good chance for me to go if you would consent—which I want you to do if possible. I want to see you and talk with you about it.

Aunt Sarah gains slowly.

Mary

Bela Paul

---

[1] The postmark of this letter and its contents indicate that Mary has left the Angells and come to Woodstock, about eight miles from Barnard, where she is staying with the Millers. (The footnotes to Mary Paul's letters are from Thomas Dublin ed., *Farm to Factory: Women's Letters, 1830–1860* [New York: Columbia University, Press, 1981, 1993]. Reprinted with permission.)

Woodstock Nov 8 1845

Dear Father

As you wanted me to let you know when I am going to start for Lowell, I improve this opportunity to write you. Next Thursday the 13th of this month is the day set or the Thursday afternoon. I should like to have you come down. If you come bring Henry if you can for I should like to see him before I go. Julius has got the money for me.[2]

Yours Mary

Lowell Nov 20th 1845

Dear Father

An opportunity now presents itself which I improve in writing to you. I started for this place at the time I talked of which was Thursday. I left Whitneys at nine o'clock stopped at Windsor at 12 and staid till 3 and started again. Did not stop again for any length of time till we arrived at Lowell. Went to a boarding house and staid until Monday night. On Saturday after I got here Luthera Griffith went round with me to find a place but we were unsuccessful. On Monday we started again and were more successful. We found a place in a spinning room and the next morning I went to work. I like very well have 50 cts first payment increasing every payment as I get along in work have a first rate overseer and a very good boarding place. I work on the Lawrence Corporation. Mill is No 2 spinning room.[3] I was very sorry that you did not come to see me start. I wanted to see you and Henry but I suppose that you were otherways engaged. I hoped to see Julius but did not much expect to for I s[up]posed he was engaged in other matters. He got six dollars for me which I was very glad of. It cost me $3.25 to come. Stage fare was $3.00 and lodging at Windsor, 25 cts. Had to pay only 25 cts for board for 9 days after I got here before I went into the mill. Had 2.50 left with which I got a bonnet and some other small articles. Tell Harriet Burbank to send me paper. Tell her I shall send her one as soon as possible. You must write as soon as you receive this. Tell Henry I should like to hear from him. If you hear anything from William write for I want to know what he is doing.[4] I shall write to Uncle Millers folks the first opportunity. Aunt Nancy presented me with a new alpacca dress before I came away from there which I was very glad of. I think of staying here a year certain, if not more. I wish that you and Henry would come down here. I think that you might do well. I guess that Henry could get into the mill and I think that Julius might get in too. Tell all friends that I should like to hear from them.

excuse bad writing and mistakes
This from your own daughter
Mary

P.S. Be sure and direct to No. 15 Lawrence Corporation.
Bela Paul   Mary S Paul

---

[2] The references here are to two of Mary's brothers, Henry and Julius, both apparently living with their father at this time. Henry was thirteen and Julius twenty-seven. Paul Family Genealogy, VHS.

[3] Surviving payrolls reveal that Mary Paul earned $0.30 per day in her first month in the mill, making $1.80 per week, or $0.55 above the cost of room and board. Lawrence Manufacturing Company Records, Vol. GB-8, Spinning Room No. 2, Nov. 20, 1845.

[4] There are repeated references to William, a third brother who lived and married in Tennessee during these years. Paul Family Genealogy; Letters of William Paul, VHS.

Lowell Dec 21st 1845

Dear Father

I received your letter on Thursday the 14th with much pleasure. I am well which is one comfort. My life and health are spared while others are cut off. Last Thursday one girl fell down and broke her neck which caused instant death. She was going in or coming out of the mill and slipped down it being very icy. The same day a man was killed by the cars.[5] Another had nearly all of his ribs broken. Another was nearly killed by falling down and having a bale of cotton fall on him. Last Tuesday we were paid. In all I had six dollars and sixty cents paid $4.68 for board. With the rest I got me a pair of rubbers and a pair of 50.cts shoes. Next payment I am to have a dollar a week beside my board.[6] We have not had much snow the deepest being not more than 4 inches. It has been very warm for winter. Perhaps you would like something about our regulations about going in and coming out of the mill. At 5 o'clock in the morning the bell rings for the folks to get up and get breakfast. At half past six it rings for the girls to get up and at seven they are called into the mill. At half past 12 we have dinner are called back again at one and stay till half past seven.[7] I get along very well with my work. I can doff as fast as any girl in our room. I think I shall have frames before long. The usual time allowed for learning is six months but I think I shall have frames before I have been in three as I get along so fast. I think that the factory is the best place for me and if any girl wants employment I advise them to come to Lowell. Tell Harriet that though she does not hear from me she is not forgotten. I have little time to devote to writing that I cannot write all I want to. There are half a dozen letters which I ought to write to day but I have not time. Tell Harriet I send my love to her and all of the girls. Give my love to Mrs. Clement. Tell Henry this will answer for him and you too for this time.

This from
Mary S Paul

Bela Paul
Henry S Paul

Lowell April 12th 1846

Dear Father

I received your letter with much pleasure but was sorry to hear that you had been lame. I had waited for a long time to hear from you but no letter came so last Sunday I thought I would write again which I did and was going to send it to the [post] office Monday but at noon I received a letter from William and so I did not send it at all. Last Friday I received a letter from you. You wanted to know what I am doing. I am at work in a spinning room and tending four sides of warp which is one girls work. The overseer

---

[5] These were probably the cars of the Boston and Lowell Railroad. Each firm had railroad siding running right up to the mills to facilitate transport of raw cotton and finished cloth.

[6] In fact, Mary earned only $2.04 per week during the payroll period which ended January 10, 1846, making $0.79 above the cost of room and board. She worked as a doffer removing full bobbins of yarn from the spinning frames and replacing them with empty ones. The work called for speed and dexterity, but it was intermittent, requiring only about fifteen minutes of activity out of each hour. Doffers were almost always children, usually sons or daughters of boardinghouse keepers or skilled workers.

[7] Mary is outlining the winter schedule, when operatives took breakfast before beginning work. In the summer months, as the next letter indicates, work began at 5:00 A.M. and operatives had short breaks for breakfast and dinner during the working day.

tells me that he never had a girl get along better than I do and that he will do the best he can by me. I stand it well, though they tell me that I am growing very poor. I was paid nine shillings a week last payment and am to have more this one though we have been out considerable for backwater which will take off a good deal.[8] The Agent promises to pay us nearly as much as we should have made but I do not think that he will. The payment was up last night and we are to be paid this week.[9] I have a very good boarding place have enough to eat and that which is good enough. The girls are all kind and obliging. The girls that I room with are all from Vermont and good girls too. Now I will tell you about our rules at the boarding house. We have none in particular except that we have to go to bed about 10. o'clock. At half past 4 in the morning the bell rings for us to get up and at five for us to go into the mill. At seven we are called out to breakfast are allowed half an hour between bells and the same at noon till the first of May when we have three quarters [of an hour] till the first of September. We have dinner at half past 12 and supper at seven. If Julius should go to Boston tell him to come this way and see me. He must come to the Lawrence Counting room and call for me. He can ask some one to show him where the Lawrence is. I hope he will not fail to go. I forgot to tell you that I have not seen a particle of snow for six weeks and it is settled going we have had a very mild winter and but little snow. I saw Ann Hersey last Sunday. I did not know her till she told me who she was. I see the Griffith girls often. I received a letter from a girl in Bridgewater in which she told me that Mrs Angell had heard some way that I could not get work and that she was much pleased and said that I was so bad that no one would have me. I believe I have written all so I will close for I have a letter to write to William this afternoon.

Yours affectionately
Mary S Paul

Mr. Bela Paul
P.S. Give my love to all that enquire for me and tell them to write me a long long letter. Tell Harriet I shall send her a paper.

Lowell Nov 5th 1848[10]

Dear Father

Doubtless you have been looking for a letter from me all the week past. I would have written but wished to find whether I should be able to stand it—to do the work that

---

[8] Mary tended four sides of warp spinning frames, each with 128 spindles, the normal complement for spinners in these years. She quoted her wages in English currency, though she was undoubtedly paid American money, nine shillings being equal to $1.50. As in the earlier cases, Mary is referring to her wages exclusive of room and board charges. "Backwater," mentioned here, was a common problem in the spring, when heavy run-off due to rains and melting snow led to high water levels, causing water to back up and block the waterwheel. Mills often had to cease operations for several days at a time. The April payroll at the Lawrence Company indicates that Mary worked only fifteen of the normal twenty-four days in the payroll period.

[9] It was standard practice to post on a blackboard in each room of the mills the production and the earning of each worker several days before the monthly payday, to enable operatives to see what they would be paid and to complain if the posted production figures did not agree with their own records of the work.

[10] Mary Paul has left and returned to Lowell since her previous letter. She remained at the Lawrence Company until the end of October 1846. Lawrence Company payrolls, Vol. GB-8. This letter is addressed to Claremont, N.H., where her father has recently moved.

I am now doing. I was unable to get my old place in the cloth room on the Suffolk or on any other corporation. I next tried the dressrooms on the Lawrence Cor[poration], but did not succe[e]d in getting a place. I almost concluded to give up and go back to Claremont, but thought I would try once more. So I went to my old overseer on the Tremont Cor. I had no idea that he would want one, but he *did*, and I went to work last Tuesday—warping—the same work I used to do.[11]

It is *very* hard indeed and sometimes I think I shall not be able to endure it. I never worked so hard in my life but perhaps I shall get used to it. I shall try hard to do so for there is no other work that I can do unless I spin and that I shall not undertake on any account. I presume you have heard before this that the wages are to be reduced on the 20th of this month. It is *true* and there seems to be a good deal of excitement on the subject but I can not tell what will be the consequence.[12] The companies pretend they are losing immense sums every *day* and therefore they are obliged to lessen the wages, but this seems perfectly absurd to me for they are constantly making *repairs* and it seems to me that this would not be if there were really any danger of their being obliged to *stop* the mills.

It is very difficult for any one to get into the mill on any corporation. All seem to be very full of help. I expect to be paid about two dollars a week but it will be dearly earned.[13] I cannot tell how it is but never since I have worked in the mill have I been so very tired as I have for the last week but it may be owing to the long rest I have had for the last six months. I have not told you that I do not board on the Lawrence. The reason of this is because I wish to be nearer the mill and I do not wish to pay the extra $.12-1/2 per week (I should not be obliged to do it if I boarded at 15) and I know that they are not able to give it me. Beside this I am so near I can go and see them as often as I wish. So considering all things I think I have done the best I could. I do not like here very well and am very sure I never shall as well as at Mother Guilds.[14] I can now realize how very kind the whole family have ever been to me. It seems like going *home* when I go there which is every day. But now I see I have not told you yet where I do board. It is at No. 5 Tremont Corporation. Please enlighten all who wish for information. There is one thing which I forgot to bring with me and which I want very

---

[11] The "dressroom" mentioned here would be a dressing room in the mill where warp yarn was prepared for the weaving process. Generally speaking, more experienced women worked in the dressing room, wages and conditions of work being considerably better there than in the carding and spinning rooms.

[12] Wages were reduced in all of the Lowell mills in November 1848. See Henry Hall to John Aiken, September 4, 1848, Lawrence Company Records; Henry Hall to John Wright, September[4], 1848, Vol. FB-3, Tremont-Suffolk Mills Records, Baker Library, Harvard Business School.

[13] This wage figure, $2.00 per week, again refers to earnings exclusive of charges for room and board. The overall figure of $3.25 weekly was extremely low for warpers, usually among the best-paid women workers in the mills. Thomas Dublin, *Women at Work: The Transformation of Work and Community in Lowell, Massachusetts, 1826–1860* (New York: Columbia University Press, 1979), pp. 66, 159.

[14] "Mother Guild" refers to Mrs. Betsey Guild who, with her husband, kept a boardinghouse at 15 Lawrence Company at least between 1847 and 1853. Mary Paul did get to know and like the "whole family," as she indicates, for in 1857 she married a son, Isaac, and settled in Lynn. Lowell *Directory*, 1847–1853; Massachusetts Bureau of Vital Records, vol. 109, p. 147.

much. That is my *rubbers*. They hang in the back room at uncle Jerrys.[15] If Olive comes down here I presume you can send them by her, but if you should not have the opportunity to send them do not trouble yourself about them. There is another thing I wish to mention—about my fare down here. If you paid it all the way as I understand you did there is something wrong about it. When we stopped at Concord to take the cars, I went to the ticket office to get a ticket which I knew I should be obliged to have. When I called for it I told the man that my fare to Lowell was paid all the way and I wanted a ticket to Lowell. He told me if this was the case the Stagedriver would get the ticket for me and I supposed of course he would. But he did *not*, and when the ticket master called for my ticket in the *cars*, I was obliged to give him a dollar. Sometimes I have thought that the fare might *not* have been paid beside farther than Concord. If this is the case all is right. But if it is not, then I have paid a dollar too much and gained the character of trying to cheat the company out of my fare, for the man thought I was lying to him. I suppose I want to know how it is and wish it could be settled for I do not like that *any* one should think *me* capable of such a thing, even though that person be an utter stranger. But enough of this. The Whigs of Lowell had a great time on the night of the 3rd. They had an immense procession of men on foot bearing *torches* and *banners* got up for the occasion. The houses were illuminated (Whigs houses) and by the way I should think the whole of *Lowell* were Whigs. I went out to see the illuminations and they did truly look splendid. The Merrimack house was illuminated from attic to cellar.[16] Every pane of glass in the house had a half candle to it and there were many others lighted in the same way. One entire block on the Merrimack Cor[poration] with the exception of one tenement which doubtless was occupied by a free soiler who would not illuminate on any account whatever.[17]

(Monday Eve) I have been to work today and think I shall manage to get along with the work. I am not so tired as I was last week. I have not yet found out what wages I shall get but presume they will be about $2.00 per week exclusive of board. I think of nothing further to write excepting I wish you to prevail on *Henry* to write to me, also tell *Olive* to write and *Eveline* when she comes.[18]

Give my love to uncle Jerry and aunt Betsey and tell little Lois that "Cousin Carra" thanks her very much for the *apple* she sent her. Her health is about the same that it was when she was at Claremont. No one has much hope of her ever being any better.

Write soon. Yours affectionately
Mary S Paul

Mr. Bela Paul
P.S. Do not forget to direct to No. 5 Tremont Cor and tell all others to do the same.

---

[15] Jerry refers to Jeremiah Paul who lived with his wife, Betsey, and two young children in Claremont, N.H. "Little Lois," mentioned at the end of this letter, was their two-year-old daughter. 1850 Census of Claremont, dwelling 407.

[16] The Merrimack House was the leading hotel in Lowell and usually housed distinguished visitors and millowners when they came to town. The date of the illumination, November 3, suggests it was part of election day festivities.

[17] The Free Soil Party was a third party opposed to the extension of slavery into the territories acquired in the recent Mexican War. Former President Martin Van Buren ran on its ticket in 1848.

[18] Eveline here is Eveline Sperry Paul, the wife of Seth Paul, another younger brother of Bela. Subsequent letters also refer to their oldest son, Seth Jr. Paul Family Genealogy, VHS; 1850 Census for Claremont, dwelling 135.

THE LOWELL FACTORY GIRL

When I set out for Lowell,
Some factory for to find,
I left my native country,
And all my friends behind.

5   Refrain:

Then sing hit–re–i–re–a–re–o
Then sing hit–re–i–re–a

But now I am in Lowell,
And summon'd by the bell,
10   I think less of the factory
Than of my native dell.

The factory bell begins to ring,
And we must all obey,
And to our old employment go,
15   Or else be turned away.

Come all ye weary factory girls,
I'll have you understand,
I'm going to leave the factory
And return to my native land.

20   No more I'll put my bonnet on
And hasten to the mill,
While all the girls are working hard,
Here I'll be lying still.

No more I'll lay my bobbins up,
25   No more I'll take them down;
No more I'll clean my dirty work,
For I'm going out of town.

No more I'll take my piece of soap,
No more I'll go to wash,
30   No more my overseer shall say,
"Your frames are stopped to doff."

Come all you little doffers
That work in the Spinning room;
Go wash your face and comb your hair,
35   Prepare to leave the room.

No more I'll oil my picker rods,
No more I'll brush my loom,
No more I'll scour my dirty floor
All in the Weaving room.

40   No more I'll draw these threads
All through the harness eye;
No more I'll say to my overseer,
Oh! dear me, I shall die.

No more I'll get my overseer
45   To come and fix my loom,

No more I'll say to my overseer
Can't I stay out 'till noon?

Then since they've cut my wages down
To nine shillings per week,
50　If I cannot better wages make,
Some other place I'll seek.

No more he'll find me reading,
No more he'll see me sew,
No more he'll come to me and say
55　"Such works I can't allow."

I do not like my overseer,
I do not mean to stay,
I mean to hire a Depot-boy
To carry me away.

60　The Dress-room girls they needn't think
Because they higher go,
That they are better than the girls
That work in the rooms below.

The overseers they need not think
65　Because they higher stand,
That they are better than the girls
That work at their command.

'Tis wonder how the men
Can such machinery make,
70　A thousand wheels together roll
Without the least mistake.

Now soon you'll see me married
To a handsome little man,
'Tis then I'll say to you factory girls,
75　Come and see me when you can.

HARRIET HANSON ROBINSON, "CHARACTERISTICS OF THE EARLY FACTORY GIRLS" (1898)

When I look back into the factory life of fifty or sixty years ago, I do not see what is called "a class" of young men and women going to and from their daily work, like so many ants that cannot be distinguished one from another; I see them as individuals, with personalities of their own. This one has about her the atmosphere of her early home. That one is impelled by a strong and noble purpose. The other,—what she is, has been an influence for good to me and to all womankind.

Yet they were a class of factory operatives, and were spoken of (as the same class is spoken of now) as a set of persons who earned their daily bread, whose condition was fixed, and who must continue to spin and to weave to the end of their natural existence. Nothing but this was expected of them, and they were not supposed to be capable of social or mental improvement. That they could be educated and developed into something more than workpeople, was an idea that had not yet entered the public mind. So little does one class of persons really know about the thoughts and aspirations of another! It was the good fortune of these early mill-girls to teach the people of that time that this sort of labor is not degrading; that the operative is not only "capable of virtue," but also capable of self-cultivation.

At the time the Lowell cotton-mills were started, the factory girl was the lowest among women. In England, and in France particularly, great injustice had been done to her real character; she was represented as subjected to influences that could not fail to destroy her purity and self-respect. In the eyes of her overseer she was but a brute, slave, to be beaten, pinched, and pushed about.

It was to overcome this prejudice that such high wages had been offered to women that they might be induced to become mill-girls, in spite of the opprobrium that still clung to this "degrading occupation." At first only a few came; for, though tempted by the high wages to be regularly paid in "cash," there were many who still preferred to go on working at some more genteel employment at seventy-five cents a week and their board.

But in a short time the prejudice against the factory labor wore away, and the Lowell mills became filled with blooming and energetic New England women. They were naturally intelligent, had mother-wit, and fell easily into the ways of their new life. They soon began to associate with those who formed the community in which they had come to live, and were invited to their houses. They went to the same church, and sometimes married into some of the best families. Or if they returned to their secluded homes again, instead of being looked down upon as "factory girls" by the squire's or lawyer's family, they were more often welcomed as coming from the metropolis, bringing new fashions, new books, and new ideas with them.

In 1831 Lowell was little more than a factory village. Several corporations were started, and the cotton-mills belonging to them were building. Help was in great demand; and the stories were told all over the country of the new factory town, and the high wages that were offered to all classes of work-people,—stories that reached the ears of mechanics' and farmers' sons, and gave new life to lonely and dependent women in distant towns and farmhouses. Into this Yankee El Dorado, these needy people began to pour by the various modes of travel known to those slow old days. The stage-coach and the canal-boat came every day, always filled with the new recruits for this army of useful people. The mechanic and machinist came, each with his home-made chest of tools, and oftentimes his wife and little ones. The widow came with her little flock of scanty housekeeping goods to open a boarding-house or variety store, and so provided a home for her fatherless children. Many farmers' daughters came to earn money to complete their wedding outfit, or buy the bride's share of housekeeping articles.

Women with past histories came, to hide their griefs and their identity, and to earn an honest living in the "sweat of their brow." Single young men came, full of hope and life, to get money for an education, or to lift the mortgage from the home-farm. Troops of young girls came by stages and baggage-wagons, men often being employed to go to other States and to Canada, to collect them at so much a head, and deliver them to the factories. . . .

These country girls had queer names, which added to the singularity of their appearance. Samantha, Triphena, Plumy, Kezia, Aseneth, Elgardy, Leafy, Ruhamah, Lovey, Almaretta, Sarepta, and Florilla were among them.

Their dialect was also very peculiar. On the broken English and Scotch of their ancestors was ingrafted the nasal Yankee twang; so that many of them, when they had just come down, spoke a language almost unintelligible. But the severe discipline and ridicule which met them was as good as a school education, and they were soon taught the "city way of speaking." . . .

One of the first strikes of the cotton-factory operatives that ever took place in this country was that in Lowell, in October, 1836. When it was announced that wages were to be cut down, great indignation was felt, and it was decided to strike, en masse. This was done. The mills were shut down, and the girls went in procession from their several corporations to the "grove" on Chapel Hill, and listened to "incendiary" speeches from early labor reformers.

One of the girls stood on a pump, and gave vent to the feelings of her companions in a neat speech, declaring that it was their duty to resist all attempts at cutting down the wages. This was the first time a woman had spoken in public in Lowell, and the event caused surprise and consternation among her audience.

Cutting down the wages was not their only grievance, nor the only cause of this strike. Hitherto the corporations had paid twenty-five cents a week towards the board of each operative, and now it was their purpose to have the girls pay the sum; and this, in addition to the cut in wages, would make a difference of at least one dollar a week. It was estimated that as many as twelve or fifteen hundred girls turned out, and walked in procession through the streets. . . .

My own recollection of this first strike (or "turn out" as it was called) is very vivid. I worked in a lower room, where I had heard the proposed strike fully, if not vehemently, discussed; I had been an ardent listener to what was said against this attempt at "oppression" on the part of the corporation, and naturally I took sides with the strikers. When the day came on which the girls were to turn out, those in the upper rooms started first, and so many of them left that our mill was at once shut down. Then, when the girls in my room stood irresolute, uncertain what to do, asking each other, "Would you?" or "Shall we turn out?" and not one of them having the courage to lead off, I, who began to think they would not go out, after all their talk, became impatient, and started on ahead, saying, with childish bravado, "I don't care what you do, *I* am going to turn out, whether any one else does or not;" and I marched out, and was followed by the others.

As I looked back at the long line that followed me, I was more proud than I have ever been at any success I may have achieved.

Massachusetts House of Representatives hearings on industrial conditions, 1845

The first petitioner who testified was Eliza R. Hemingway. She had worked 2 years and 9 months in the Lowell factories; 2 years in the Middlesex, and 9 months in the Hamilton Corporations. Her employment is weaving—works by the piece. . . . She complained of the hours for labor being too many, and the time for meals too limited. In the summer season, the work is commenced at 5 o'clock, a.m., and continued til 7 o'clock, p.m., with half an hour for breakfast and three quarters of an hour for dinner. During eight months of the year but half an hour is allowed for dinner. The air in the room she considered not to be wholesome. There were 293 small lamps and 61 large lamps lighted in the room in which she worked, when evening work is required. These lamps are also lighted sometimes in the morning. About 130 females, 11 men, and 12 children (between the ages of 11 and 14) work in the room with her. She thought the children enjoyed about as good health as children generally do. The children work but 9 months out of 12. The other 3 months they must attend school. Thinks that there is no day when there are less than six of the females out of the mill from sickness. Has known as many as thirty. She herself is out quite often on account of sickness. . . . She thought there was a general desire among the females to work but ten hours, regardless of pay. . . . She knew of one girl who last winter went into the mill at half past four o'clock, a.m., and worked till half past 7 o'clock, p.m. She did so to make more money. She earned from $25 to $30 per month.

Norman Ware. *The Industrial Worker, 1840–1860.* New York: Quadrangle, 1964. John R. Commons et al. *Documentary History of American Industrial Society.* Cleveland: A. H. Clark Co., 1911.

HELENA MINTON, "FROM THE SAME CLOTH: FOR THE MILL GIRLS, LOWELL, MASSACHUSETTS, CIRCA 1840"

The city fathers dreamed these girls
the way they dreamed the town:
to scale, pale colors on a map, dolls
bending at looms by day, reading
5　the classics by night. Now I imagine them
as they rise to bells, break ice
in washing bowls, file at dawn
to the mills, their breath pouring before them.
All day they stand, each girl
10　at a different task: to guide raw
cotton through the spindle, blend dye
for yellow calico, count each bolt
for dish towels, sheets, their future husbands'
shirts, their own petticoats.
15　They hear machines roar the way the river
roars, breast wheels turning.
Do they whisper sonnets to themselves
or think of Cleopatra on the Nile,
clay banks where men lie sleeping?
20　Do they dream of being loved like that?
Each time a girl writes home, part of her
follows the letter across the border
to New Hampshire, growing damp
as it passes the sea, then safe,
25　unfolded by her mother's hands.
When she places her cheek on cold cotton
she sees the years ahead
like yards of undyed linen,
and yearns to watch a warehouse full
30　of dimity catch fire.
She wants to walk past the row
of beds, down to the river's most
seductive bend, to lie on the grass,
wet blades staining her nightgown,
35　feeling the hush, the sound
of nothing being made.

Frederick Douglass (1818–1895)

Born into slavery, Frederick Douglass would transform himself into one of slavery's fiercest critics and one of the nation's most accomplished literary and political writers. Prior to the Civil War, Douglass's autobiographies and speeches exposed the horrors of slavery and challenged the country to make good on its commitment to liberty and justice for all. After the Civil War, Douglass used his authority as speaker, writer, and publisher to address the injustices of a failed Reconstruction in the South, particularly institutionalized segregation that limited jobs for blacks and widespread lynching and acts of violence and intimidation against blacks.

Always troubled by not knowing the exact year of his birth, Frederick Augustus Washington Bailey was born, according to plantation records, in February 1818 and was part of the fifth generation of the Bailey family in America. He lived his early years as a slave on a plantation in eastern Maryland before being sent when he was eight years old to Baltimore, where he worked as a house servant and taught himself how to read and write with some help from his mistress and neighborhood white boys. In 1833, Douglass was sent back to rural Maryland to work as a field hand. Unsuited physically and mentally for farm labor after years as a "city" slave, he soon turned "rebellious" and was sent to a "slave breaker," Edward Covey. Degraded and brutalized, Douglass fought Covey and won, declaring later, "You have seen how a man was made a slave; you shall see how a slave was made a man." After a failed escape attempt, Douglass was returned to Baltimore, where he learned a trade as a caulker in the shipyards. Deprived of the marginal dignity of wage-earning labor, Douglass planned his escape disguised as a free black sailor and made his way north to New Bedford, Massachusetts. Now married and a father, he supported his family as a "common laborer" on the New Bedford wharves and began speaking publicly about the abolition of slavery. In 1845, he published his first autobiography, *Narrative of the Life of Frederick Douglass, an American Slave, Written by Himself*. After traveling in Ireland, England, and Scotland, and having his freedom purchased by British antislavery friends, Douglass founded his abolitionist newspaper, *The North Star*, and published an expanded version of his autobiography, *My Bondage and My Freedom* (1855). Under the heading, "In the Shipyards," the following excerpts from both the 1845 and 1855 narratives tell and retell an incident in which Douglass was brutally attacked by wage-earning whites. In the second telling, Douglass shows how an ideology of white supremacy channels fears about lost jobs into anger at blacks, rather than at those who own the means of production. Douglass's concern for black economic independence and brotherhood are voiced in his "Address to the National Negro Convention," published in the *North Star* in September 1848.

John Marsh

"In the Shipyards" (1845)

In a few weeks after I went to Baltimore, Master Hugh hired me to Mr. William Gardner, an extensive ship-builder, on Fell's Point. I was put there to learn how to calk. It, however, proved a very unfavorable place for the accomplishment of this object. Mr. Gardner was engaged that spring in building two large man-of-war brigs, professedly for the Mexican government. The vessels were to be launched in the July of that year, and in failure thereof, Mr. Gardner was to lose a considerable sum; so that when I entered, all was hurry. There was no time to learn any thing. Every man had to do that which he knew how to do. In entering the ship-yard, my orders from Mr. Gardner were, to do whatever the carpenters commanded me to do. This was placing me at the beck and call of about seventy-five men. I was to regard all these as masters. Their word was to be my law. My situation was a most trying one. At times I needed a dozen pair of hands. I was called a dozen ways in the space of a single minute. Three or four voices would strike my ear at the same moment. It was— "Fred., come help me to cant this timber here."—"Fred., come carry this timber yonder." —"Fred., bring that roller here."—"Fred., go get a fresh can of water."—"Fred., come help saw off the end of this timber."—"Fred., go quick, and get the crowbar."—"Fred.,

hold on the end of this fall."—"Fred., go to the blacksmith's shop, and get a new punch."—
"Hurra, Fred.! run and bring me a cold chisel."—"I say, Fred., bear a hand, and get up
a fire as quick as lightning under that steam-box."—"Halloo, nigger! come, turn this
grindstone."—"Come, come! move, move! and *bowse* this timber forward."—"I say,
darky, blast your eyes, why don't you heat up some pitch?"—"Halloo! halloo! halloo!"
(Three voices at the same time.) "Come here!—Go there!—Hold on where you are!
Damn you, if you move, I'll knock your brains out!"

    This was my school for eight months; and I might have remained there longer, but
for a most horrid fight I had with four of the white apprentices, in which my left eye
was nearly knocked out, and I was horribly mangled in other respects. The facts in the case
were these: Until a very little while after I went there, white and black ship-carpenters
worked side by side, and no one seemed to see any impropriety in it. All hands seemed to
be very well satisfied. Many of the black carpenters were freemen. Things seemed to be
going on very well. All at once, the white carpenters knocked off, and said they would not
work with free colored workmen. Their reason for this, as alleged, was, that if free colored
carpenters were encouraged, they would soon take the trade into their own hands, and
poor white men would be thrown out of employment. They therefore felt called upon at
once to put a stop to it. And, taking advantage of Mr. Gardner's necessities, they broke off,
swearing they would work no longer, unless he would discharge his black carpenters. Now,
though this did not extend to me in form, it did reach me in fact. My fellow-apprentices
very soon began to feel it degrading to them to work with me. They began to put on airs,
and talk about the "niggers" taking the country, saying we all ought to be killed; and, being
encouraged by the journeymen, they commenced making my condition as hard as they
could, by hectoring me around, and sometimes striking me. I, of course, kept the vow
I made after the fight with Mr. Covey, and struck back again, regardless of consequences;
and while I kept them from combining, I succeeded very well; for I could whip the whole
of them, taking them separately. They, however, at length combined, and came upon me,
armed with sticks, stones, and heavy handspikes. One came in front with a half brick.
There was one at each side of me, and one behind me. While I was attending to those in
front, and on either side, the one behind ran up with the handspike, and struck me a heavy
blow upon the head. It stunned me. I fell, and with this they all ran upon me, and fell to
beating me with their fists. I let them lay on for a while, gathering strength. In an instant,
I gave a sudden surge, and rose to my hands and knees. Just as I did that, one of their
number gave me, with his heavy boot, a powerful kick in the left eye. My eyeball seemed
to have burst. When they saw my eye closed, and badly swollen, they left me. With this
I seized the handspike, and for a time pursued them. But here the carpenters interfered,
and I thought I might as well give it up. It was impossible to stand my hand against so many.
All this took place in sight of not less than fifty white ship-carpenters, and not one inter-
posed a friendly word; but some cried, "Kill the damned nigger! Kill him! kill him!
He struck a white person." I found my only chance for life was in flight. I succeeded in
getting away without an additional blow, and barely so; for to strike a white man is death
by Lynch law,—and that was the law in Mr. Gardner's ship-yard; nor is there much of any
other out of Mr. Gardner's ship-yard.

    I went directly home, and told the story of my wrongs to Master Hugh; and I am
happy to say of him, irreligious as he was, his conduct was heavenly, compared with that
of his brother Thomas under similar circumstances. He listened attentively to my narration
of the circumstances leading to the savage outrage, and gave many proofs of his strong
indignation at it. The heart of my once overkind mistress was again melted into pity. My
puffed-out eye and blood-covered face moved her to tears. She took a chair by me, washed
the blood from my face, and, with a mother's tenderness, bound up my head, covering the
wounded eye with a lean piece of fresh beef. It was almost compensation for my suffering

to witness, once more, a manifestation of kindness from this, my once affectionate old mistress. Master Hugh was very much enraged. He gave expression to his feelings by pouring out curses upon the heads of those who did the deed. As soon as I got a little the better of my bruises, he took me with him to Esquire Watson's, on Bond Street, to see what could be done about the matter. Mr. Watson inquired who saw the assault committed. Master Hugh told him it was done in Mr. Gardner's ship-yard, at mid-day, where there were a large company of men at work. "As to that," he said, "the deed was done, and there was no question as to who did it." His answer was, he could do nothing in the case, unless some white man would come forward and testify. He could issue no warrant on my word. If I had been killed in the presence of a thousand colored people, their testimony combined would have been insufficient to have arrested one of the murderers. Master Hugh, for once, was compelled to say this state of things was too bad. Of course, it was impossible to get any white man to volunteer his testimony in my behalf, and against the white young men. Even those who may have sympathized with me were not prepared to do this. It required a degree of courage unknown to them to do so; for just at that time, the slightest manifestation of humanity toward a colored person was denounced as abolitionism, and that name subjected its bearer to frightful liabilities. The watchwords of the bloody-minded in that region, and in those days, were, "Damn the abolitionists!" and "Damn the niggers!" There was nothing done, and probably nothing would have been done if I had been killed. Such was, and such remains, the state of things in the Christian city of Baltimore.

Master Hugh, finding he could get no redress, refused to let me go back again to Mr. Gardner. He kept me himself, and his wife dressed my wound till I was again restored to health. He then took me into the shipyard of which he was foreman, in the employment of Mr. Walter Price. There I was immediately set to calking, and very soon learned the art of using my mallet and irons. In the course of one year from the time I left Mr. Gardner's, I was able to command the highest wages given to the most experienced calkers. I was now of some importance to my master. I was bringing him from six to seven dollars per week. I sometimes brought him nine dollars per week: my wages were a dollar and a half a day. After learning how to calk, I sought my own employment, made my own contracts, and collected the money which I earned. My pathway became much more smooth than before; my condition was now much more comfortable. When I could get no calking to do, I did nothing. During these leisure times, those old notions about freedom would steal over me again. When in Mr. Gardner's employment, I was kept in such a perpetual whirl of excitement, I could think of nothing, scarcely, but my life; and in thinking of my life, I almost forgot my liberty. I have observed this in my experience of slavery,—that whenever my condition was improved, instead of its increasing my contentment, it only increased my desire to be free, and set me to thinking of plans to gain my freedom. I have found that, to make a contented slave, it is necessary to make a thoughtless one. It is necessary to darken his moral and mental vision, and, as far as possible, to annihilate the power of reason. He must be able to detect no inconsistencies in slavery; he must be made to feel that slavery is right; and he can be brought to that only when he ceases to be a man.

I was now getting, as I have said, one dollar and fifty cents per day. I contracted for it; I earned it; it was paid to me; it was rightfully my own; yet, upon each returning Saturday night, I was compelled to deliver every cent of that money to Master Hugh. And why? Not because he earned it,—not because he had any hand in earning it,—not because I owed it to him,—nor because he possessed the slightest shadow of a right to it; but solely because he had the power to compel me to give it up. The right of the grim-visaged pirate upon the high seas is exactly the same. . . .

I had somehow imbibed the opinion that, in the absence of slaves, there could be no wealth, and very little refinement. And upon coming to the north, I expected to meet with a rough, hard-handed, and uncultivated population, living in the most Spartan-like simplicity, knowing nothing of the ease, luxury, pomp, and grandeur of southern slave-holders. Such being my conjectures, any one acquainted with the appearance of New Bedford may very readily infer how palpably I must have seen my mistake.

In the afternoon of the day when I reached New Bedford, I visited the wharves, to take a view of the shipping. Here I found myself surrounded with the strongest proofs of wealth. Lying at the wharves, and riding in the stream, I saw many ships of the finest model, in the best order, and of the largest size. Upon the right and left, I was walled in by granite warehouses of the widest dimensions, stowed to their utmost capacity with the necessaries and comforts of life. Added to this, almost every body seemed to be at work, but noiselessly so, compared with what I had been accustomed to in Baltimore. There were no loud songs heard from those engaged in loading and unloading ships. I heard no deep oaths or horrid curses on the laborer. I saw no whipping of men; but all seemed to go smoothly on. Every man appeared to understand his work, and went at it with a sober, yet cheerful earnestness, which betokened the deep interest which he felt in what he was doing, as well as a sense of his own dignity as a man. To me this looked exceedingly strange. From the wharves I strolled around and over the town, gazing with wonder and admiration at the splendid churches, beautiful dwellings, and finely-cultivated gardens; evincing an amount of wealth, comfort, taste, and refinement, such as I had never seen in any part of slaveholding Maryland.

Every thing looked clean, new, and beautiful. I saw few or no dilapidated houses, with poverty-stricken inmates; no half-naked children and barefooted women, such as I had been accustomed to see in Hillsborough, Easton, St. Michael's, and Baltimore. The people looked more able, stronger, healthier, and happier, than those of Maryland. I was for once made glad by a view of extreme wealth, without being saddened by seeing extreme poverty. But the most astonishing as well as the most interesting thing to me was the condition of the colored people, a great many of whom, like myself, had escaped thither as a refuge from the hunters of men. I found many, who had not been seven years out of their chains, living in finer houses, and evidently enjoying more of the comforts of life, than the average of slaveholders in Maryland. I will venture to assert that my friend Mr. Nathan Johnson (of whom I can say with a grateful heart, "I was hungry, and he gave me meat; I was thirsty, and he gave me drink; I was a stranger, and he took me in") lived in a neater house; dined at a better table; took, paid for, and read, more newspapers; better understood the moral, religious, and political character of the nation,—than nine tenths of the slaveholders in Talbot county, Maryland. Yet Mr. Johnson was a working man. His hands were hardened by toil, and not his alone, but those also of Mrs. Johnson. I found the colored people much more spirited than I had supposed they would be. I found among them a determination to protect each other from the blood-thirsty kidnapper, at all hazards. Soon after my arrival, I was told of a circumstance which illustrated their spirit. A colored man and a fugitive slave were on unfriendly terms. The former was heard to threaten the latter with informing his master of his whereabouts. Straightway a meeting was called among the colored people, under the stereotyped notice, "Business of import-ance!" The betrayer was invited to attend. The people came at the appointed hour, and organized the meeting by appointing a very religious old gentleman as president, who, I believe, made a prayer, after which he addressed the meeting as follows: *Friends, we have got him here, and I would recommend that you young men just take him outside the door, and kill him!* With this, a number of them bolted at him; but they were intercepted by some more timid than themselves, and the betrayer escaped their vengeance, and has not been seen in New Bedford since. I believe there have been no more such threats, and should there be hereafter, I doubt not that death would be the consequence.

I found employment, the third day after my arrival, in stowing a sloop with a load of oil. It was new, dirty, and hard work for me; but I went at it with a glad heart and a willing hand. I was now my own master. It was a happy moment, the rapture of which can be understood only by those who have been slaves. It was the first work, the reward of which was to be entirely my own. There was no Master Hugh standing ready, the moment I earned the money, to rob me of it. I worked that day with a pleasure I had never before experienced. I was at work for myself and newly-married wife. It was to me the starting-point of a new existence. When I got through with that job, I went in pursuit of a job of calking; but such was the strength of prejudice against color, among the white calkers, that they refused to work with me, and of course I could get no employment.[1] Finding my trade of no immediate benefit, I threw off my calking habiliments, and prepared myself to do any kind of work I could get to do. Mr. Johnson kindly let me have his wood-horse and saw, and I very soon found myself a plenty of work. There was no work too hard—none too dirty. I was ready to saw wood, shovel coal, carry the hod, sweep the chimney, or roll oil casks,—all of which I did for nearly three years in New Bedford, before I became known to the anti-slavery world.

In about four months after I went to New Bedford, there came a young man to me, and inquired if I did not wish to take the "Liberator." I told him I did; but, just having made my escape from slavery, I remarked that I was unable to pay for it then. I, however, finally became a subscriber to it. The paper came, and I read it from week to week with such feelings as it would be quite idle for me to attempt to describe. The paper became my meat and my drink. My soul was set all on fire. Its sympathy for my brethren in bonds—its scathing denunciations of slaveholders—its faithful exposures of slavery—and its powerful attacks upon the upholders of the institution—sent a thrill of joy through my soul, such as I had never felt before!

I had not long been a reader of the "Liberator," before I got a pretty correct idea of the principles, measures and spirit of the anti-slavery reform. I took right hold of the cause. I could do but little; but what I could, I did with a joyful heart, and never felt happier than when in an anti-slavery meeting. I seldom had much to say at the meetings, because what I wanted to say was said so much better by others. But, while attending an anti-slavery convention at Nantucket, on the 11th of August, 1841, I felt strongly moved to speak, and was at the same time much urged to do so by Mr. William C. Coffin, a gentleman who had heard me speak in the colored people's meeting at New Bedford. It was a severe cross, and I took it up reluctantly. The truth was, I felt myself a slave, and the idea of speaking to white people weighed me down. I spoke but a few moments, when I felt a degree of freedom, and said what I desired with considerable ease. From that time until now, I have been engaged in pleading the cause of my brethren—with what success, and with what devotion, I leave those acquainted with my labors to decide.

"In the Shipyards" (1855)

Such, dear reader, is a glance at the school which was mine, during the first eight months of my stay at Baltimore. At the end of eight months, Master Hugh refused longer to allow me to remain with Mr. Gardiner. The circumstance which led to his taking me away, was a brutal outrage, committed upon me by the white apprentices of the ship-yard. The fight was a desperate one, and I came out of it most shockingly mangled. I was cut and bruised in sundry places, and my left eye was nearly knocked out of its socket. The facts, leading

---

[1] I am told that colored persons can now get employment at calking in New Bedford—a result of anti-slavery effort.

to this barbarous outrage upon me, illustrate a phase of slavery destined to become an important element in the overthrow of the slave system, and I may, therefore state them with some minuteness. That phase is this: *the conflict of slavery with the interests of the white mechanics and laborers of the south.* In the country, this conflict is not so apparent; but, in cities, such as Baltimore, Richmond, New Orleans, Mobile, &c., it is seen pretty clearly. The slaveholders, with a craftiness peculiar to themselves, by encouraging the enmity of the poor, laboring white man against the blacks, succeeds in making the said white man almost as much a slave as the black slave himself. The difference between the white slave, and the black slave, is this: the latter belongs to one slaveholder, and the former belongs to all the slaveholders, collectively. The white slave has taken from him, by indirection, what the black slave has taken from him, directly, and without ceremony. Both are plundered, and by the same plunderers. The slave is robbed, by his master, of all his earnings, above what is required for his bare physical necessities; and the white man is robbed by the slave system, of the just results of his labor, because he is flung into competition with a class of laborers who work without wages. The competition, and its injurious consequences, will, one day, array the nonslaveholding white people of the slave states, against the slave system, and make them the most effective workers against the great evil. At present, the slaveholders blind them to this competition, by keeping alive their prejudice against the slaves, as men—not against them as slaves. They appeal to their pride, often denouncing emancipation, as tending to place the white working man, on an equality with negroes, and, by this means, they succeed in drawing off the minds of the poor whites from the real fact, that, by the rich slave-master, they are already regarded as but a single remove from equality with the slave. The impression is cunningly made, that slavery is the only power that can prevent the laboring white man from falling to the level of the slave's poverty and degradation. To make this enmity deep and broad, between the slave and the poor white man, the latter is allowed to abuse and whip the former, without hinderance. But—as I have suggested—this state of facts prevails mostly in the country. In the city of Baltimore, there are not unfrequent murmurs, that educating the slaves to be mechanics may, in the end, give slavemasters power to dispense with the services of the poor white man altogether. But, with characteristic dread of offending the slaveholders, these poor, white mechanics in Mr. Gardiner's ship-yard—instead of applying the natural, honest remedy for the apprehended evil, and objecting at once to work there by the side of slaves—made a cowardly attack upon the free colored mechanics, saying they were eating the bread which should be eaten by American freemen, and swearing that they would not work with them. The feeling was, really, against having their labor brought into competition with that of the colored people at all; but it was too much to strike directly at the interest of the slaveholders; and, therefore—proving their servility and cowardice—they dealt their blows on the poor, colored freeman, and aimed to prevent him from serving himself, in the evening of life, with the trade with which he had served his master, during the more vigorous portion of his days. Had they succeeded in driving the black freemen out of the ship yard, they would have determined also upon the removal of the black slaves. The feeling was very bitter toward all colored people in Baltimore, about this time (1836), and they—free and slave—suffered all manner of insult and wrong.

AN ADDRESS TO THE COLORED PEOPLE OF THE UNITED STATES

Fellow Countrymen:

Under a solemn sense of duty, inspired by our relation to you as fellow sufferers under the multiplied and grievous wrongs to which we as a people are universally subjected,—we, a portion of your brethren, assembled in National Convention, at Cleveland, Ohio, take the liberty to address you on the subject of our mutual improvement and social elevation.

The condition of our variety of the human family, has long been cheerless, if not hopeless, in this country. The doctrine perseveringly proclaimed in high places in church and state, that it is impossible for colored men to rise from ignorance and debasement, to intelligence and respectability in this country, has made a deep impression upon the public mind generally, and is not without its effect upon us. Under this gloomy doctrine, many of us have sunk under the pall of despondency, and are making no effort to relieve ourselves, and have no heart to assist others. It is from this despond that we would deliver you. It is from this slumber we would rouse you. The present, is a period of activity and hope. The heavens above us are bright, and much of the darkness that overshadowed us has passed away. We can deal in the language of brilliant encouragement, and speak of success with certainty. That our condition has been gradually improving, is evident to all, and that we shall yet stand on a common platform with our fellow countrymen, in respect to political and social rights, is certain. The spirit of the age—the voice of inspiration—the deep longings of the human soul—the conflict of right with wrong—the upward tendency of the oppressed throughout the world, abound with evidence complete and ample, of the final triumph of right over wrong, of freedom over slavery, and equality over caste. To doubt this, is to forget the past, and blind our eyes to the present, as well as to deny and oppose the great law of progress, written out by the hand of God on the human soul.

Great changes for the better have taken place and are still taking place. The last ten years have witnessed a mighty change in the estimate in which we as a people are regarded, both in this and other lands. England has given liberty to nearly one million, and France has emancipated three hundred thousand of our brethren, and our own country shakes with the agitation of our rights. Ten or twelve years ago, an educated colored man was regarded as a curiosity, and the thought of a colored man as an author, editor, lawyer or doctor, had scarce been conceived. Such, thank Heaven, is no longer the case. There are now those among us, whom we are not ashamed to regard as gentlemen and scholars, and who are acknowledged to be such, by many of the most learned and respectable in our land. Mountains of prejudice have been removed, and truth and light are dispelling the error and darkness of ages. The time was, when we trembled in the presence of a white man, and dared not assert, or even ask for our rights, but would be guided, directed, and governed, in any way we were demanded, without ever stopping to enquire whether we were right or wrong. We were not only slaves, but our ignorance made us willing slaves. Many of us uttered complaints against the faithful abolitionists, for the broad assertion of our rights; thought they went too far, and were only making our condition worse. This sentiment has nearly ceased to reign in the dark abodes of our hearts; we begin to see our wrongs as clearly, and comprehend our rights as fully, and as well as our white countrymen. This is a sign of progress; and evidence which cannot be gainsayed. It would be easy to present in this connection, a glowing comparison of our past with our present condition, showing that while the former was dark and dreary, the present is full of light and hope. It would be easy to draw a picture of our present achievements, and erect upon it a glorious future.

But, fellow countrymen, it is not so much our purpose to cheer you by the progress we have already made, as it is to stimulate you to still higher attainments. We have done much, but there is much more to be done.—While we have undoubtedly great cause to thank God, and take courage for the hopeful changes which have taken place in our condition, we are not without cause to mourn over the sad condition which we yet occupy. We are yet the most oppressed people in the world. In the Southern states of this Union, we are held as slaves. All over that wide region our paths are marked with blood. Our backs are yet scarred by the lash, and our souls are yet dark under the pall of slavery.—Our sisters are sold for purposes of pollution, and our brethren are sold in the market, with beasts of burden. Shut up in the prison-house of bondage—denied all rights, and deprived of all privileges, we are blotted from the page of human existence, and placed beyond the limits of human regard. Death, moral death, has palsied our souls in that quarter, and we are a murdered people.

In the Northern states, we are not slaves to individuals, not personal slaves, yet in many respects we are the slaves of the community. We are, however, far enough removed from the actual condition of the slave, to make us largely responsible for their continued enslavement, or their speedy deliverance from chains. For in the proportion which we shall rise in the scale of human improvement, in that proportion do we augment the probabilities of a speedy emancipation of our enslaved fellow-countrymen. It is more than a mere figure of speech to say, that we are as a people, chained together. We are one people—one in general complexion, one in a common degradation, one in popular estimation. As one rises, all must rise, and as one falls all must fall. Having now, our feet on the rock of freedom, we must drag our brethren from the slimy depths of slavery, ignorance, and ruin. Every one of us should be ashamed to consider himself free, while his brother is a slave.— The wrongs of our brethren, should be our constant theme. There should be no time too precious, no calling too holy, no place too sacred, to make room for this cause. We should not only feel it to be the cause of humanity, but the cause of christianity, and fit work for men and angels. We ask you to devote yourselves to this cause, as one of the first, and most successful means of self improvement. In the careful study of it, you will learn your own rights, and comprehend your own responsibilities, and, scan through the vista of coming time, your high, and God-appointed destiny. Many of the brightest and best of our number, have become such by their devotion to this cause, and the society of white abolitionists. The latter have been willing to make themselves of no reputation for our sake, and in return, let us show ourselves worthy of their zeal and devotion. Attend anti-slavery meetings, show that you are interested in the subject, that you hate slavery, and love those who are laboring for its overthrow.—Act with white Abolition societies wherever you can, and where you cannot, get up societies among yourselves, but without exclusiveness. It will be a long time before we gain all our rights; and although it may seem to conflict with our views of human brotherhood, we shall undoubtedly for many years be compelled to have institutions of a complexional character, in order to attain this very idea of human brotherhood. We would, however, advise our brethren to occupy memberships and stations among white persons, and in white institutions, just so fast as our rights are secured to us.

Never refuse to act with a white society or institution because it is white, or a black one, because it is black. But act with all men without distinction of color. By so acting, we shall find many opportunities for removing prejudices and establishing the rights of all men. We say avail yourselves of *white* institutions, not because they are white, but because they afford a more convenient means of improvement. But we pass from these suggestions, to others which may be deemed more important. In the Convention that now addresses you, there has been much said on the subject of labor, and especially those departments of it, with which we as a class have been long identified. You will see by the resolutions there adopted on that subject, that the Convention regarded those employments though right in themselves, as being nevertheless, degrading to us as a class, and therefore, counsel you to abandon them as speedily as possible, and to seek what are called the more respectable employments. While the Convention do not inculcate the doctrine that any kind of needful toil is in itself dishonorable, or that colored persons are to be exempt from what are called menial employments, they do mean to say that such employments have been so long and universally filled by colored men, as to become a badge of degradation, in that it has established the conviction that colored men are only fit for such employments. We therefore, advise you by all means, to cease from such employments, as far as practicable, by pressing into others. Try to get your sons into mechanical trades; press them into the black-smith's shop, the machine shop, the joiner's shop, the wheelwright's shop, the cooper's shop, and the tailor's shop.

Every blow of the sledge hammer, wielded by a sable arm, is a powerful blow in support of our cause. Every colored mechanic, is by virtue of circumstances, an elevator of his race. Every house built by black men, is a strong tower against the allied hosts of prejudice. It is impossible for us to attach too much importance to this aspect of the subject. Trades are important. Wherever a man may be thrown by misfortune, if he has in his hands a useful trade, he is useful to his fellow man, and will be esteemed accordingly; and of all men in the world who need trades we are the most needy.

Understand this, that independence is an essential condition of respectability. To be dependent, is to be degraded. Men may indeed pity us, but they cannot respect us. We do not mean that we can become entirely independent of all men; that would be absurd and impossible, in the social state. But we mean that we must become equally independent with other members of the community. That other members of the community shall be as dependent upon us, as we upon them.—That such is not now the case, is too plain to need an argument. The houses we live in are built by white men—the clothes we wear are made by white tailors—the hats on our heads are made by white hatters, and the shoes on our feet are made by white shoe-makers, and the food that we eat, is raised and cultivated by white men. Now it is impossible that we should ever be respected as a people, while we are so universally and completely dependent upon white men for the necessaries of life. We must make white persons as dependent upon us, as we are upon them. This cannot be done while we are found only in two or three kinds of employments, and those employ-ments have their foundation chiefly, if not entirely, in the pride and indolence of the white people. Sterner necessities, will bring higher respect.

The fact is, we must not merely make the white man dependent upon us to shave him but to feed him; not merely dependent upon us to black his boots, but to make them. A man is only in a small degree dependent on us when he only needs his boots blacked, or his carpet bag carried; as a little less pride, and a little more industry on his part, may enable him to dispense with our services entirely. As wise men it becomes us to look forward to a state of things, which appears inevitable. The time will come, when those menial employments will afford less means of living than they now do. What shall a large class of our fellow countrymen do, when white men find it economical to black their own boots, and shave themselves. What will they do when white men learn to wait on them-selves? We warn you brethren, to seek other and more enduring vocations.

Let us entreat you to turn your attention to agriculture. Go to farming. Be tillers of the soil. On this point we could say much, but the time and space will not permit. Our cities are overrun with menial laborers, while the country is eloquently pleading for the hand of industry to till her soil, and reap the reward of honest labor. We beg and intreat you, to save your money—live economically—dispense with finery, and the gaities which have rendered us proverbial, and save your money. Not for the senseless purpose of being better off than your neighbor, but that you may be able to educate your children, and render your share to the common stock of prosperity and happiness around you. It is plain that the equality which we aim to accomplish, can only be achieved by us, when we can do for others, just what others can do for us. We should therefore, press into all the trades, professions and callings, into which honorable white men press.

We would in this connection, direct your attention to the means by which we have been oppressed and degraded. Chief among those means, we may mention the press. This engine has brought to the aid of prejudice, a thousand stings. Wit, ridicule, false philosophy, and an impure theology, with a flood of low blackguardism, come through this channel into the public mind; constantly feeding and keeping alive against us, the bitterest hate.

The pulpit too, has been arrayed against us. Men with sanctimonious face, have talked of our being descendants of Ham—that we are under a curse, and to try to improve our condition, is virtually to counteract the purposes of God!

It is easy to see that the means which have been used to destroy us, must be used to save us. The press must be used in our behalf: aye! we must use it ourselves; we must take and read newspapers; we must read books, improve our minds, and put to silence and to shame, our opposers.

Dear Brethren, we have extended these remarks beyond the length which we had allotted to ourselves, and must now close, though we have but hinted at the subject. Trusting that our words may fall like good seed upon good ground; and hoping that we may all be found in the path of improvement and progress,

We are your friends and servants,
(Signed by the Committee, in behalf of the Convention)
Frederick Douglass,
H. Bibb,
W. L. Day,
D. H. Jenkins,
A. H. Francis.

The North Star, September 29, 1848

Herman Melville (1819–1891)

Born in New York City, Herman Melville was one of eight children of Allan and Maria Gansevoort Melville, descendents of English and Dutch colonial families. When he was twelve years old, Melville's life altered sharply after the bankruptcy of the family's merchant business and the death of his father. Melville left Albany Classical School at the age of fifteen and worked as a clerk, farmhand, and teacher in upstate New York. He loved the sea and shipped out as a cabin boy on a vessel that was bound for Liverpool in 1839, an adventure later described in his novel *Redburn* (1849). He returned to New York, taught school for a short while, and then embarked on a series of adventures that began as a sailor on a whaling ship bound for the South Seas and included a sojourn in the Marquesas, living as a captive in Typee, and working as a field laborer in Tahiti.

As a sailor, Melville observed the technology of whale oil production firsthand and combined that knowledge, his sense of adventure, his erudition, and his metaphysical inclinations in the great epic novel, *Moby Dick* (1851). His reading public, however, was more interested in his early stories of harrowing adventure on the high seas—*Typee* (1846), *Omoo* (1847), and *Mardi* (1849)—than in the Shakespearean cadences of *Moby Dick*. "What I feel most moved to write, that is banned—it will not pay," he famously complained to his Massachusetts neighbor, Nathaniel Hawthorne, in 1851. "Yet altogether, write the *other* way I cannot. So the product is a final hash, and all my books are botches." Tensions between economic necessity and intellectual and aesthetic desire haunted Melville all his life as he struggled to sustain a family on his earnings as a writer, then as a lecturer, and finally as a customs inspector on the New York docks. In a 1877 letter he wrote, "They talk of the *dignity of work*. Bosh. True work is the *necessity* of poor humanity's earthly condition. The dignity is in leisure." The class relationship between some people's dignified leisure and others' necessity of labor is illustrated in these combined tales of overfed British bachelor lawyers and desexualized American paper mill maidens. "The Paradise of Bachelors and The Tartarus of Maids," was originally published in *Harper's New Monthly Magazine*, April 1855.

THE PARADISE OF BACHELORS AND THE TARTARUS OF MAIDS

I. THE PARADISE OF BACHELORS

It lies not far from Temple-Bar.
 Going to it, by the usual way, is like stealing from a heated
plain into some cool, deep glen, shady among harboring hills.

Sick with the din and soiled with the mud of Fleet Street—where the Benedick tradesmen are hurrying by, with ledger-lines ruled along their brows, thinking upon rise of bread and fall of babies—you adroitly turn a mystic corner—not a street—glide down a dim, monastic way, flanked by dark, sedate, and solemn piles, and still wending on, give the whole care-worn world the slip, and, disentangled, stand beneath the quiet cloisters of the Paradise of Bachelors.

Sweet are the oases in Sahara; charming the isle-groves of August prairies; delectable pure faith amidst a thousand perfidies: but sweeter, still more charming, most delectable, the dreamy Paradise of Bachelors, found in the stony heart of stunning London.

In mild meditation pace the cloisters; take your pleasure, sip your leisure, in the garden waterward; go linger in the ancient library; go worship in the sculptured chapel: but little have you seen, just nothing do you know, not the sweet kernel have you tasted, till you dine among the banded Bachelors, and see their convivial eyes and glasses sparkle. Not dine in bustling commons, during term-time, in the hall; but tranquilly, by private hint, at a private table; some fine Templar's hospitably invited guest.

Templar? That's a romantic name. Let me see. Brian de Bois Guilbert was a Templar, I believe. Do we understand you to insinuate that those famous Templars still survive in modern London? May the ring of their armed heels be heard, and the rattle of their shields, as in mailed prayer the monk-knights kneel before the consecrated Host? Surely a monk-knight were a curious sight picking his way along the Strand, his gleaming corselet and snowy surcoat spattered by an omnibus. Long-bearded, too, according to his order's rule; his face fuzzy as a pard's; how would the grim ghost look among the crop-haired, close-shaven citizens? We know indeed—sad history recounts it—that a moral blight tainted at last this sacred Brotherhood. Though no sworded foe might outskill them in the fence, yet the worm of luxury crawled beneath their guard, gnawing the core of knightly troth, nibbling the monastic vow, till at last the monk's austerity relaxed to wassailing, and the sworn knights-bachelors grew to be but hypocrites and rakes.

But for all this, quite unprepared were we to learn that Knights-Templars (if at all in being) were so entirely secularized as to be reduced from carving out immortal fame in glorious battling for the Holy Land, to the carving of roast-mutton at a dinner-board. Like Anacreon, do these degenerate Templars now think it sweeter far to fall in banquet than in war? Or, indeed, how can there be any survival of that famous order? Templars in modern London! Templars in their red-cross mantles smoking cigars at the Divan! Templars crowded in a railway train, till, stacked with steel helmet, spear, and shield, the whole train looks like one elongated locomotive!

No. The genuine Templar is long since departed. Go view the wondrous tombs in the Temple Church; see there the rigidly-haughty forms stretched out, with crossed arms upon their stilly hearts, in everlasting and undreaming rest. Like the years before the flood, the bold Knights-Templars are no more. Nevertheless, the name remains, and the nominal society, and the ancient grounds, and some of the ancient edifices. But the iron heel is changed to a boot of patent-leather; the long two-handed sword to a one-handed quill; the monk-giver of gratuitous ghostly counsel now counsels for a fee; the defender of the sarcophagus (if in good practice with his weapon) now has more than one case to defend; the vowed opener and clearer of all highways leading to the Holy Sepulchre, now has it in particular charge to check, to clog, to hinder, and embarrass all the courts and avenues of Law; the knight-combatant of the Saracen, breasting spear-points at Acre, now fights law-points in Westminster Hall. The helmet is a wig. Struck by Time's enchanter's wand, the Templar is today a Lawyer.

But, like many others tumbled from proud glory's height—like the apple, hard on the bough but mellow on the ground—the Templar's fall has but made him all the finer fellow.

I dare say those old warrior-priests were but gruff and grouty at the best; cased in Birmingham hardware, how could their crimped arms give yours or mine a hearty shake? Their proud, ambitious, monkish souls clasped shut, like horn-book missals; their very faces clapped in bomb-shells; what sort of genial men were these? But best of comrades, most affable of hosts, capital diner is the modern Templar. His wit and wine are both of sparkling brands.

The church and cloisters, courts and vaults, lanes and passages, banquet-halls, refectories, libraries, terraces, gardens, broad walks, domicils, and dessert-rooms, covering a very large space of ground, and all grouped in central neighborhood, and quite sequestered from the old city's surrounding din; and every thing about the place being kept in most bachelor-like particularity, no part of London offers to a quiet wight so agreeable a refuge.

The Temple is, indeed, a city by itself. A city with all the best appurtenances, as the above enumeration shows. A city with a park to it, and flower-beds, and a river-side—the Thames flowing by as openly, in one part, as by Eden's primal garden flowed the mild Euphrates. In what is now the Temple Garden the old Crusaders used to exercise their steeds and lances; the modern Templars now lounge on the benches beneath the trees, and, switching their patent-leather boots, in gay discourse exercise at repartee.

Long lines of stately portraits in the banquet-halls, show what great men of mark—famous nobles, judges, and Lord Chancellors—have in their time been Templars. But all Templars are not known to universal fame; though, if the having warm hearts and warmer welcomes, full minds and fuller cellars, and giving good advice and glorious dinners, spiced with rare divertisements of fun and fancy, merit immortal mention, set down, ye muses, the names of R.F.C. and his imperial brother.

Though to be a Templar, in the one true sense, you must needs be a lawyer, or a student at the law, and be ceremoniously enrolled as member of the order, yet as many such, though Templars, do not reside within the Temple's precincts, though they may have their offices there, just so, on the other hand, there are many residents of the hoary old domicils who are not admitted Templars. If being, say, a lounging gentleman and bachelor, or a quiet, unmarried, literary man, charmed with the soft seclusion of the spot, you much desire to pitch your shady tent among the rest in this serene encampment, then you must make some special friend among the order, and procure him to rent, in his name but at your charge, whatever vacant chamber you may find to suit.

Thus, I suppose, did Dr. Johnson, that nominal Benedick and widower but virtual bachelor, when for a space he resided here. So, too, did that undoubted bachelor and rare good soul, Charles Lamb. And hundreds more, of sterling spirits, Brethren of the Order of Celibacy, from time to time have dined, and slept, and tabernacled here. Indeed, the place is all a honeycomb of offices and domicils. Like any cheese, it is quite perforated through and through in all directions with the snug cells of bachelors. Dear, delightful spot! Ah!

when I bethink me of the sweet hours there passed, enjoying such genial hospitalities beneath those time-honored roofs, my heart only finds due utterance through poetry; and, with a sigh, I softly sing, "Carry me back to old Virginny!"

Such then, at large, is the Paradise of Bachelors. And such I found it one pleasant afternoon in the smiling month of May, when, sallying from my hotel in Trafalgar Square, I went to keep my dinner-appointment with that fine Barrister, Bachelor, and Bencher, R.F.C. (he *is* the first and second, and *should be* the third; I hereby nominate him), whose card I kept fast pinched between my gloved forefinger and thumb, and every now and then snatched still another look at the pleasant address inscribed beneath the name, "No.—, Elm Court, Temple."

At the core he was a right bluff, care-free, right comfortable, and most companionable Englishman. If on a first acquaintance he seemed reserved, quite icy in his air— patience; this Champagne will thaw. And if it never do, better frozen Champagne than liquid vinegar.

There were nine gentlemen, all bachelors, at the dinner. One was from "No.—, King's Bench Walk, Temple;" a second, third, and fourth, and fifth, from various courts or passages christened with some similarly rich resounding syllables. It was indeed a sort of Senate of the Bachelors, sent to this dinner from widely-scattered districts, to represent the general celibacy of the Temple. Nay it was, by representation, a Grand Parliament of the best Bachelors in universal London; several of those present being from distant quarters of the town, noted immemorial seats of lawyers and unmarried men—Lincoln's Inn, Furnival's Inn; and one gentleman, upon whom I looked with a sort of collateral awe, hailed from the spot where Lord Verulam once abode a bachelor—Gray's Inn.

The apartment was well up toward heaven. I know not how many strange old stairs I climbed to get to it. But a good dinner, with famous company, should be well earned. No doubt our host had his dining-room so high with a view to secure the prior exercise necessary to the due relishing and digesting of it.

The furniture was wonderfully unpretending, old, and snug. No new shining mahogany, sticky with undried varnish; no uncomfortably luxurious ottomans, and sofas too fine to use, vexed you in this sedate apartment. It is a thing which every sensible American should learn from every sensible Englishman, that glare and glitter, gimcracks and gewgaws, are not indispensable to domestic solacement. The American Benedick snatches, down-town, a tough chop in a gilded show-box; the English bachelor leisurely dines at home on that incomparable South Down of his, off a plain deal board.

The ceiling of the room was low. Who wants to dine under the dome of St. Peter's? High ceilings! If that is your demand, and the higher the better, and you be so very tall, then go dine out with the topping giraffe in the open air.

In good time the nine gentlemen sat down to nine covers, and soon were fairly under way.

If I remember right, ox-tail soup inaugurated the affair. Of a rich russet hue, its agreeable flavor dissipated my first confounding of its main ingredient with teamster's gads and the raw-hides of ushers. (By way of interlude, we here drank a little claret.) Neptune's was the next tribute rendered—turbot coming second; snow-white, flaky, and just gelatinous enough, not too turtleish in its unctuousness.

(At this point we refreshed ourselves with a glass of sherry.) After these light skirmishers had vanished, the heavy artillery of the feast marched in, led by that well-known English generalissimo, roast beef. For aids-de-camp we had a saddle of mutton, a fat turkey, a chicken-pie, and endless other savory things; while for avantcouriers came nine silver flagons of humming ale. This heavy ordnance having departed on the track of the light skirmishers, a picked brigade of game-fowl encamped upon the board, their camp-fires lit by the ruddiest of decanters.

Tarts and puddings followed, with innumerable niceties; then cheese and crackers. (By way of ceremony, simply, only to keep up good old fashions, we here each drank a glass of good old port.)

The cloth was now removed; and like Blucher's army coming in at the death on the field of Waterloo, in marched a fresh detachment of bottles, dusty with their hurried march.

All these manœuvrings of the forces were superintended by a surprising old field-marshal (I can not school myself to call him by the inglorious name of waiter), with snowy hair and napkin, and a head like Socrates. Amidst all the hilarity of the feast, intent on important business, he disdained to smile. Venerable man!

I have above endeavored to give some slight schedule of the general plan of operations. But any one knows that a good, genial dinner is a sort of pell-mell, indiscriminate affair, quite baffling to detail in all particulars. Thus, I spoke of taking a glass of claret, and a glass of sherry, and a glass of port, and a mug of ale—all at certain specific periods and times. But those were merely the state bumpers, so to speak. Innumerable impromptu glasses were drained between the periods of those grand imposing ones.

The nine bachelors seemed to have the most tender concern for each other's health. All the time, in flowing wine, they most earnestly expressed their sincerest wishes for the entire well-being and lasting hygiene of the gentlemen on the right and on the left. I noticed that when one of these kind bachelors desired a little more wine (just for his stomach's sake, like Timothy), he would not help himself to it unless some other bachelor would join him. It seemed held something indelicate, selfish, and unfraternal, to be seen taking a lonely, unparticipated glass. Meantime, as the wine ran apace, the spirits of the company grew more and more to perfect genialness and unconstraint. They related all sorts of pleasant stories. Choice experiences in their private lives were now brought out, like choice brands of Moselle or Rhenish, only kept for particular company. One told us how mellowly he lived when a student at Oxford; with various spicy anecdotes of most frank-hearted noble lords, his liberal companions. Another bachelor, a gray-headed man, with a sunny face, who, by his own account, embraced every opportunity of leisure to cross over into the Low Countries, on sudden tours of inspection of the fine old Flemish architecture there—this learned, white-haired, sunny-faced old bachelor, excelled in his descriptions of the elaborate splendors of those old guild-halls, town-halls, and stadthold-houses, to be seen in the land of the ancient Flemings. A third was a great frequenter of the British Museum, and knew all about scores of wonderful antiquities, of Oriental manuscripts, and costly books without a duplicate. A fourth had lately returned from a trip to Old Granada, and, of course, was full of Saracenic scenery. A fifth had a funny case in law to tell. A sixth was erudite in wines. A seventh had a strange characteristic anecdote of the private life of the Iron Duke, never printed, and never before announced in any public or private company. An eighth had lately been amusing his evenings, now and then, with translating a comic poem of Pulci's. He quoted for us the more amusing passages.

And so the evening slipped along, the hours told, not by a water-clock, like King Alfred's, but a wine-chronometer. Meantime the table seemed a sort of Epsom Heath, a regular ring, where the decanters galloped round. For fear one decanter should not with sufficient speed reach his destination, another was sent express after him to hurry him; and then a third to hurry the second; and so on with a fourth and fifth. And throughout all this nothing loud, nothing unmannerly, nothing turbulent. I am quite sure, from the scrupulous gravity and austerity of his air, that had Socrates, the field-marshal, perceived aught of indecorum in the company he served, he would have forthwith departed without giving warning. I afterward learned that, during the repast, an invalid bachelor in an adjoining chamber enjoyed his first sound refreshing slumber in three long, weary weeks.

It was the very perfection of quiet absorption of good living, good drinking, good feeling, and good talk. We were a band of brothers. Comfort—fraternal, household comfort, was the grand trait of the affair. Also, you could plainly see that these easy-hearted men had no wives or children to give an anxious thought. Almost all of them were travelers, too; for bachelors alone can travel freely, and without any twinges of their consciences touching desertion of the fire-side.

The thing called pain, the bugbear styled trouble—those two legends seemed preposterous to their bachelor imaginations. How could men of liberal sense, ripe scholarship in the world, and capacious philosophical and convivial understandings—how could they suffer themselves to be imposed upon by such monkish fables? Pain! Trouble! As well talk of Catholic miracles. No such thing.—Pass the sherry, Sir.—Pooh, pooh! Can't be!—The port, Sir, if you please. Nonsense; don't tell me so.—The decanter stops with you, Sir, I believe.

And so it went.

Not long after the cloth was drawn our host glanced significantly upon Socrates, who, solemnly stepping to a stand, returned with an immense convolved horn, a regular Jericho horn, mounted with polished silver, and otherwise chased and curiously enriched; not omitting two life-like goat's heads, with four more horns of solid silver, projecting from opposite sides of the mouth of the noble main horn.

Not having heard that our host was a performer on the bugle, I was surprised to see him lift this horn from the table, as if he were about to blow an inspiring blast. But I was relieved from this, and set quite right as touching the purposes of the horn, by his now inserting his thumb and forefinger into its mouth; whereupon a slight aroma was stirred up, and my nostrils were greeted with the smell of some choice Rappee. It was a mull of snuff. It went the rounds. Capital idea this, thought I, of taking snuff about this juncture. This goodly fashion must be introduced among my countrymen at home, further ruminated I.

The remarkable decorum of the nine bachelors—a decorum not to be affected by any quantity of wine—a decorum unassailable by any degree of mirthfulness—this was again set in a forcible light to me, by now observing that, though they took snuff very freely, yet not a man so far violated the proprieties, or so far molested the invalid bachelor in the adjoining room as to indulge himself in a sneeze. The snuff was snuffed silently, as if it had been some fine innoxious powder brushed off the wings of butterflies.

But fine though they be, bachelors' dinners, like bachelors' lives, can not endure forever. The time came for breaking up. One by one the bachelors took their hats, and two by two, and arm-in-arm they descended, still conversing, to the flagging of the court; some going to their neighboring chambers to turn over the Decameron ere retiring for the night; some to smoke a cigar, promenading in the garden on the cool river-side; some to make for the street, call a hack, and be driven snugly to their distant lodgings.

I was the last lingerer.

"Well," said my smiling host, "what do you think of the Temple here, and the sort of life we bachelors make out to live in it?"

"Sir," said I, with a burst of admiring candor—"Sir, this is the very Paradise of Bachelors!"

II.   THE TARTARUS OF MAIDS

It lies not far from Woedolor Mountain in New England. Turning to the east, right out from among bright farms and sunny meadows, nodding in early June with odorous grasses, you enter ascendingly among bleak hills. These gradually close in upon a dusky pass, which, from the violent Gulf Stream of air unceasingly driving between its cloven walls of haggard rock, as well as from the tradition of a crazy spinster's hut having long ago stood somewhere hereabouts, is called the Mad Maid's Bellows'-pipe.

Winding along at the bottom of the gorge is a dangerously narrow wheel-road, occupying the bed of a former torrent. Following this road to its highest point, you stand as within a Dantean gateway. From the steepness of the walls here, their strangely ebon hue, and the sudden contraction of the gorge, this particular point is called the Black Notch. The ravine now expandingly descends into a great, purple, hopper-shaped hollow, far sunk among many Plutonian, shaggy-wooded mountains. By the country people this hollow is called the Devil's Dungeon. Sounds of torrents fall on all sides upon the ear. These rapid waters unite at last in one turbid brick-colored stream, boiling through a flume among enormous boulders. They call this strange-colored torrent Blood River. Gaining a dark precipice it wheels suddenly to the west, and makes one maniac spring of sixty feet into the arms of a stunted wood of gray-haired pines, between which it thence eddies on its further way down to the invisible lowlands.

Conspicuously crowning a rocky bluff high to one side, at the cataract's verge, is the ruin of an old saw-mill, built in those primitive times when vast pines and hemlocks superabounded throughout the neighboring region. The black-mossed bulk of those immense, rough-hewn, and spike-knotted logs, here and there tumbled all together, in long abandonment and decay, or left in solitary, perilous projection over the cataract's gloomy brink, impart to this rude wooden ruin not only much of the aspect of one of rough-quarried stone, but also a sort of feudal, Rhineland, and Thurmberg look, derived from the pinnacled wildness of the neighboring scenery

Not far from the bottom of the Dungeon stands a large white-washed building, relieved, like some great whited sepulchre, against the sullen background of mountain-side firs, and other hardy evergreens, inaccessibly rising in grim terraces for some two thousand feet.

The building is a paper-mill.

Having embarked on a large scale in the seedsman's business (so extensively and broadcast, indeed, that at length my seeds were distributed through all the Eastern and Northern States, and even fell into the far soil of Missouri and the Carolinas), the demand for paper at my place became so great, that the expenditure soon amounted to a most important item in the general account. It need hardly be hinted how paper comes into use with seedsmen, as envelopes. These are mostly made of yellowish paper, folded square; and when filled, are all but flat, and being stamped, and superscribed with the nature of the seeds contained, assume not a little the appearance of business-letters ready for the mail. Of these small envelopes I used an incredible quantity—several hundreds of thousands in a year. For a time I had purchased my paper from the wholesale dealers in a neighboring town. For economy's sake, and partly for the adventure of the trip, I now resolved to cross the mountains, some sixty miles, and order my future paper at the Devil's Dungeon paper-mill.

The sleighing being uncommonly fine toward the end of January, and promising to hold so for no small period, in spite of the bitter cold I started one gray Friday noon in my pung, well fitted with buffalo and wolf robes; and, spending one night on the road, next noon came in sight of Woedolor Mountain.

The far summit fairly smoked with frost; white vapors curled up from its white-wooded top, as from a chimney. The intense congelation made the whole country look like one petrifaction. The steel shoes of my pung craunched and gritted over the vitreous, chippy snow, as if it had been broken glass. The forests here and there skirting the route, feeling the same all-stiffening influence, their inmost fibres penetrated with the cold, strangely groaned—not in the swaying branches merely, but likewise in the vertical trunk—as the fitful gusts remorselessly swept through them. Brittle with excessive frost, many colossal tough-grained maples, snapped in twain like pipe-stems, cumbered the unfeeling earth.

Flaked all over with frozen sweat, white as a milky ram, his nostrils at each breath sending forth two horn-shaped shoots of heated respiration, Black, my good horse, but six years old, started at a sudden turn, where, right across the track—not ten minutes fallen—an old distorted hemlock lay, darkly undulatory as an anaconda.

Gaining the Bellows'-pipe, the violent blast, dead from behind, all but shoved my high-backed pung up-hill. The gust shrieked through the shivered pass, as if laden with lost spirits bound to the unhappy world. Ere gaining the summit, Black, my horse, as if exasperated by the cutting wind, slung out with his strong hind legs, tore the light pung straight up-hill, and sweeping grazingly through the narrow notch, sped downward madly past the ruined saw-mill. Into the Devil's Dungeon horse and cataract rushed together.

With might and main, quitting my seat and robes, and standing backward, with one foot braced against the dash-board, I rasped and churned the bit, and stopped him just in time to avoid collision, at a turn, with the bleak nozzle of a rock, couchant like a lion in the way—a road-side rock.

At first I could not discover the paper-mill.

The whole hollow gleamed with the white, except, here and there, where a pinnacle of granite showed one wind-swept angle bare. The mountains stood pinned in shrouds— a pass of Alpine corpses. Where stands the mill? Suddenly a whirling, humming sound broke upon my ear. I looked, and there, like an arrested avalanche, lay the large white-washed factory. It was subordinately surrounded by a cluster of other and smaller buildings, some of which, from their cheap, blank air, great length, gregarious windows, and comfortless expression, no doubt were boarding-houses of the operatives. A snow-white hamlet amidst the snows. Various rude, irregular squares and courts resulted from the somewhat picturesque clusterings of these buildings, owing to the broken, rocky nature of the ground, which forbade all method in their relative arrangement. Several narrow lanes and alleys, too, partly blocked with snow fallen from the roof, cut up the hamlet in all directions.

When, turning from the traveled highway, jingling with bells of numerous farmers— who, availing themselves of the fine sleighing, were dragging their wood to market—and frequently diversified with swift cutters dashing from inn to inn of the scattered villages— when, I say, turning from that bustling main-road, I by degrees wound into the Mad Maid's Bellows'-pipe, and saw the grim Black Notch beyond, then something latent, as well as something obvious in the time and scene, strangely brought back to my mind my first sight of dark and grimy Temple-Bar. And when Black, my horse, went darting through the Notch, perilously grazing its rocky wall, I remembered being in a runaway London omnibus, which in much the same sort of style, though by no means at an equal rate, dashed through the ancient arch of Wren. Though the two objects did by no means com-pletely correspond, yet this partial inadequacy but served to tinge the similitude not less with the vividness than the disorder of a dream. So that, when upon reining up at the protruding rock I at last caught sight of the quaint groupings of the factory-buildings, and with the traveled highway and the Notch behind, found myself all alone, silently and privily stealing through deep-cloven passages into this sequestered spot, and saw the long, high-gabled main factory edifice, with a rude tower—for hoisting heavy boxes—at one end, standing among its crowded outbuildings and boarding-houses, as the Temple Church amidst the surrounding offices and dormitories, and when the marvelous retirement of this mysterious mountain nook fastened its whole spell upon me, then, what memory lacked, all tributary imagination furnished, and I said to myself, "This is the very counterpart of the Paradise of Bachelors, but snowed upon, and frost-painted to a sepulchre."

Dismounting, and warily picking my way down the dangerous declivity—horse and man both sliding now and then upon the icy ledges—at length I drove, or the blast drove me, into the largest square, before one side of the main edifice. Piercingly and shrilly the shotted blast blew by the corner; and redly and demoniacally boiled Blood River at one side. A long wood-pile, of many scores of cords, all glittering in mail of crusted ice, stood crosswise in the square. A row of horse-posts, their north sides plastered with adhesive snow, flanked the factory wall. The bleak frost packed and paved the square as with some ringing metal.

The inverted similitude recurred—"The sweet, tranquil Temple garden, with the Thames bordering its green beds," strangely meditated I.

But where are the gay bachelors?

Then, as I and my horse stood shivering in the wind-spray, a girl ran from a neighboring dormitory door, and throwing her thin apron over her bare head, made for the opposite building.

"One moment, my girl; is there no shed hereabouts which I may drive into?"

Pausing, she turned upon me a face pale with work, and blue with cold; an eye supernatural with unrelated misery.

"Nay," faltered I, "I mistook you. Go on; I want nothing."

Leading my horse close to the door from which she had come, I knocked. Another pale, blue girl appeared, shivering in the doorway as, to prevent the blast, she jealously held the door ajar.

"Nay, I mistake again. In God's name shut the door. But hold, is there no man about?"

That moment a dark-complexioned well-wrapped personage passed, making for the factory door, and spying him coming, the girl rapidly closed the other one.

"Is there no horse-shed here, Sir?"

"Yonder, to the wood-shed," he replied, and disappeared inside the factory.

With much ado I managed to wedge in horse and pung between the scattered piles of wood all sawn and split. Then, blanketing my horse, and piling my buffalo on the blanket's top, and tucking in its edges well around the breast-band and breeching, so that the wind might not strip him bare, I tied him fast, and ran lamely for the factory door, stiff with frost, and cumbered with my driver's dread-naught.

Immediately I found myself standing in a spacious place, intolerably lighted by long rows of windows, focusing inward the snowy scene without.

At rows of blank-looking counters sat rows of blank-looking girls, with blank, white folders in their blank hands, all blankly folding blank paper.

In one corner stood some huge frame of ponderous iron, with a vertical thing like a piston periodically rising and falling upon a heavy wooden block. Before it—its tame minister—stood a tall girl, feeding the iron animal with half-quires of rose-hued note paper, which, at every downward dab of the piston-like machine, received in the corner the impress of a wreath of roses. I looked from the rosy paper to the pallid cheek, but said nothing.

Seated before a long apparatus, strung with long, slender strings like any harp, another girl was feeding it with foolscap sheets, which, so soon as they curiously traveled from her on the cords, were withdrawn at the opposite end of the machine by a second girl. They came to the first girl blank; they went to the second girl ruled.

I looked upon the first girl's brow, and saw it was young and fair; I looked upon the second girl's brow, and saw it was ruled and wrinkled. Then, as I still looked, the two— for some small variety to the monotony—changed places; and where had stood the young, fair brow, now stood the ruled and wrinkled one.

Perched high upon a narrow platform, and still higher upon a high stool crowning it, sat another figure serving some other iron animal; while below the platform sat her mate in some sort of reciprocal attendance.

Not a syllable was breathed. Nothing was heard but the low, steady, overruling hum of the iron animals. The human voice was banished from the spot. Machinery— that vaunted slave of humanity—here stood menially served by human beings, who served mutely and cringingly as the slave serves the Sultan. The girls did not so much seem accessory wheels to the general machinery as mere cogs to the wheels.

All this scene around me was instantaneously taken in at one sweeping glance—even before I had proceeded to unwind the heavy fur tippet from around my neck. But as soon as this fell from me the dark-complexioned man, standing close by, raised a sudden cry, and seizing my arm, dragged me out into the open air, and without pausing for a word instantly caught up some congealed snow and began rubbing both my cheeks.

"Two white spots like the whites of your eyes," he said; "man, your cheeks are frozen."

"That may well be," muttered I; "'tis some wonder the frost of the Devil's Dungeon strikes in no deeper. Rub away."

Soon a horrible, tearing pain caught at my reviving cheeks. Two gaunt bloodhounds, one on each side, seemed mumbling them. I seemed Actæon.

Presently, when all was over, I re-entered the factory, made known my business, concluded it satisfactorily, and then begged to be conducted throughout the place to view it.

"Cupid is the boy for that," said the dark-complexioned man. "Cupid!" and by this odd fancy-name calling a dimpled, red-cheeked, spirited-looking, forward little fellow, who was rather impudently, I thought, gliding about among the passive-looking girls—like a gold fish through hueless waves—yet doing nothing in particular that I could see, the man bade him lead the stranger through the edifice.

"Come first and see the water-wheel," said this lively lad, with the air of boyishly-brisk importance.

Quitting the folding-room, we crossed some damp, cold boards, and stood beneath a great wet shed, incessantly showering with foam, like the green barnacled bow of some East Indiaman in a gale. Round and round here went the enormous revolutions of the dark colossal water-wheel, grim with its one immutable purpose.

"This sets our whole machinery a-going, Sir; in every part of all these buildings; where the girls work and all."

I looked, and saw that the turbid waters of Blood River had not changed their hue by coming under the use of man.

"You make only blank paper; no printing of any sort, I suppose? All blank paper, don't you?"

"Certainly; what else should a paper-factory make?"

The lad here looked at me as if suspicious of my common-sense.

"Oh, to be sure!" said I, confused and stammering; "it only struck me as so strange that red waters should turn out pale chee—paper, I mean."

He took me up a wet and rickety stair to a great light room, furnished with no visible thing but rude, manger-like receptacles running all round its sides; and up to these mangers, like so many mares haltered to the rack, stood rows of girls. Before each was vertically thrust up a long, glittering scythe, immovably fixed at bottom to the manger-edge. The curve of the scythe, and its having no snath to it, made it look exactly like a sword. To and fro, across the sharp edge, the girls forever dragged long strips of rags, washed white, picked from baskets at one side; thus ripping asunder every seam, and converting the tatters almost into lint. The air swam with the fine, poisonous particles, which from all sides darted, subtilely, as motes in sun-beams, into the lungs.

"This is the rag-room," coughed the boy.

"You find it rather stifling here," coughed I, in answer; "but the girls don't cough."

"Oh, they are used to it."

"Where do you get such hosts of rags?" picking up a handful from a basket.

"Some from the country round about; some from far over sea—Leghorn and London."

"'Tis not unlikely, then," murmured I, "that among these heaps of rags there may be some old shirts, gathered from the dormitories of the Paradise of Bachelors. But the buttons are all dropped off. Pray, my lad, do you ever find any bachelor's buttons hereabouts?"

"None grow in this part of the country. The Devil's Dungeon is no place for flowers."

"Oh! you mean the *flowers* so called—the Bachelor's Buttons?"

"And was not that what you asked about? Or did you mean the gold bosom-buttons of our boss, Old Bach, as our whispering girls all call him?"

"The man, then, I saw below is a bachelor, is he?"

"Oh, yes, he's a Bach."

"The edges of those swords, they are turned outward from the girls, if I see right; but their rags and fingers fly so, I can not distinctly see."

"Turned outward."

Yes, murmured I to myself; I see it now; turned outward; and each erected sword is so borne, edge-outward, before each girl. If my reading fails me not, just so, of old, condemned state-prisoners went from the hall of judgment to their doom: an officer before, bearing a sword, its edge turned outward, in significance of their fatal sentence. So, through consumptive pallors of this blank, raggy life, go these white girls to death.

"Those scythes look very sharp," again turning toward the boy.

"Yes; they have to keep them so. Look!"

That moment two of the girls, dropping their rags, plied each a whet-stone up and down the sword-blade. My unaccustomed blood curdled at the sharp shriek of the tormented steel.

Their own executioners; themselves whetting the very swords that slay them; meditated I.

"What makes those girls so sheet-white, my lad?"

"Why"—with a roguish twinkle, pure ignorant drollery, not knowing heartlessness— "I suppose the handling of such white bits of sheets all the time makes them so sheety."

"Let us leave the rag-room now, my lad."

More tragical and more inscrutably mysterious than any mystic sight, human or machine, throughout the factory, was the strange innocence of cruel-heartedness in this usage-hardened boy.

"And now," said he, cheerily, "I suppose you want to see our great machine, which cost us twelve thousand dollars only last autumn. That's the machine that makes the paper, too. This way, Sir."

Following him, I crossed a large, bespattered place, with two great round vats in it, full of a white, wet, woolly-looking stuff, not unlike the albuminous part of an egg, soft-boiled.

"There," said Cupid, tapping the vats carelessly, "these are the first beginnings of the paper; this white pulp you see. Look how it swims bubbling round and round, moved by the paddle here. From hence it pours from both vats into that one common channel yonder; and so goes, mixed up and leisurely, to the great machine. And now for that."

He led me into a room, stifling with a strange, blood-like, abdominal heat, as if here, true enough, were being finally developed the germinous particles lately seen.

Before me, rolled out like some long Eastern manuscript, lay stretched one continuous length of iron frame-work—multitudinous and mystical, with all sorts of rollers, wheels, and cylinders, in slowly-measured and unceasing motion.

"Here first comes the pulp now," said Cupid, pointing to the nighest end of the machine. "See; first it pours out and spreads itself upon this wide, sloping board; and then—look—slides, thin and quivering, beneath the first roller there. Follow on now, and see it as it slides from under that to the next cylinder. There; see how it has become just a very little less pulpy now. One step more, and it grows still more to some slight con-sistence. Still another cylinder, and it is so knitted—though as yet mere dragon-fly wing—that it forms an air-bridge here, like a suspended cobweb, between two more separated rollers; and flowing over the last one, and under again, and doubling about there out of sight for a minute among all those mixed cylinders you indistinctly see, it reappears here, looking now at last a little less like pulp and more like paper, but still quite delicate and defective yet awhile. But—a little further onward, Sir, if you please—here now, at this further point, it puts on something of a real look, as if it might turn out to be something you might possibly handle in the end. But it's not yet done, Sir. Good way to travel yet, and plenty more of cylinders must roll it."

"Bless my soul!" said I, amazed at the elongation, interminable convolutions, and deliberate slowness of the machine; "it must take a long time for the pulp to pass from end to end, and come out paper."

"Oh! not so long," smiled the precocious lad, with a superior and patronizing air; "only nine minutes. But look; you may try it for yourself. Have you a bit of paper? Ah! here's a bit on the floor. Now mark that with any word you please, and let me dab it on here, and we'll see how long before it comes out at the other end."

"Well, let me see," said I, taking out my pencil; "come, I'll mark it with your name."

Bidding me take out my watch, Cupid adroitly dropped the inscribed slip on an exposed part of the incipient mass.

Instantly my eye marked the second-hand on my dial-plate.

Slowly I followed the slip, inch by inch; sometimes pausing for full half a minute as it disappeared beneath inscrutable groups of the lower cylinders, but only gradually to emerge again; and so, on, and on, and on—inch by inch; now in open sight, sliding along like a freckle on the quivering sheet; and then again wholly vanished; and so, on, and on, and on—inch by inch; all the time the main sheet growing more and more to final firmness—when, suddenly, I saw a sort of paper-fall, not wholly unlike a water-fall; a scissory sound smote my ear, as of some cord being snapped; and down dropped an unfolded sheet of perfect foolscap, with my "Cupid" half faded out of it, and still moist and warm.

My travels were at an end, for here was the end of the machine.

"Well, how long was it?" said Cupid.

"Nine minutes to a second," replied I, watch in hand.

"I told you so."

For a moment a curious emotion filled me, not wholly unlike that which one might experience at the fulfillment of some mysterious prophecy. But how absurd, thought I again; the thing is a mere machine, the essence of which is unvarying punctuality and precision.

Previously absorbed by the wheels and cylinders, my attention was now directed to a sad-looking woman standing by.

"That is rather an elderly person so silently tending the machine-end here. She would not seem wholly used to it either."

"Oh," knowingly whispered Cupid, through the din, "she only came last week. She was a nurse formerly. But the business is poor in these parts, and she's left it. But look at the paper she is piling there."

"Ay, foolscap," handling the piles of moist, warm sheets, which continually were being delivered into the woman's waiting hands. "Don't you turn out any thing but foolscap at this machine?"

"Oh, sometimes, but not often, we turn out finer work—cream-laid and royal sheets, we call them. But foolscap being in chief demand, we turn out foolscap most."

It was very curious. Looking at that blank paper continually dropping, dropping, dropping, my mind ran on in wonderings of those strange uses to which those thousand sheets eventually would be put. All sorts of writings would be writ on those now vacant things—sermons, lawyers' briefs, physicians' prescriptions, love-letters, marriage certificates, bills of divorce, registers of births, death-warrants, and so on, without end. Then, recurring back to them as they here lay all blank, I could not but bethink me of that celebrated comparison of John Locke, who, in demonstration of his theory that man had no innate ideas, compared the human mind at birth to a sheet of blank paper; something destined to be scribbled on, but what sort of characters no soul might tell.

Pacing slowing to and fro along the involved machine, still humming with its play, I was struck as well by the inevitability as the evolvement-power in all its motions.

"Does that thin cobweb there," said I, pointing to the sheet in its more imperfect stage, "does that never tear or break? It is marvelous fragile, and yet this machine it passes through is so mighty."

"It never is known to tear a hair's point."

"Does it never stop—get clogged?"

"No. It *must* go. The machinery makes it go just *so*; just that very way, and at that very pace you there plainly *see* it go. The pulp can't help going."

Something of awe now stole over me, as I gazed upon this inflexible iron animal. Always, more or less, machinery of this ponderous, elaborate sort strikes, in some moods, strange dread into the human heart, as some living, panting Behemoth might. But what made the thing I saw so specially terrible to me was the metallic necessity, the unbudging fatality which governed it. Though, here and there, I could not follow the thin, gauzy vail of pulp in the course of its more mysterious or entirely invisible advance, yet it was indubitable that, at those points where it eluded me, it still marched on in unvarying docility to the autocratic cunning of the machine. A fascination fastened on me. I stood spell-bound and wandering in my soul. Before my eyes—there, passing in slow procession along the wheeling cylinders, I seemed to see, glued to the pallid incipience of the pulp, the yet more pallid faces of all the pallid girls I had eyed that heavy day. Slowly, mournfully, beseechingly, yet unresistingly, they gleamed along, their agony dimly outlined on the imperfect paper, like the print of the tormented face on the handkerchief of Saint Veronica.

"Halloa! the heat of the room is too much for you," cried Cupid, staring at me.

"No—I am rather chill, if any thing."

"Come out, Sir—out—out," and, with the protecting air of a careful father, the precocious lad hurried me outside.

In a few moments, feeling revived a little, I went into the folding-room—the first room I had entered, and where the desk for transacting business stood, surrounded by the blank counters and blank girls engaged at them.

"Cupid here has led me a strange tour," said I to the dark-complexioned man before mentioned, whom I had ere this discovered not only to be an old bachelor, but also the principal proprietor. "Yours is a most wonderful factory. Your great machine is a miracle of inscrutable intricacy."

"Yes, all our visitors think it so. But we don't have many. We are in a very out-of-the-way corner here. Few inhabitants, too. Most of our girls come from far-off villages."

"The girls," echoed I, glancing round at their silent forms. "Why is it, Sir, that in most factories, female operatives, of whatever age, are indiscriminately called girls, never women?"

"Oh! as to that—why, I suppose, the fact of their being generally unmarried—that's the reason, I should think. But it never struck me before. For our factory here, we will not have married women; they are apt to be off-and-on too much. We want none but steady workers: twelve hours to the day, day after day, through the three hundred and sixty-five days, excepting Sundays, Thanksgiving, and Fast-days. That's our rule. And so, having no married women, what females we have are rightly enough called girls."

"Then these are all maids," said I, while some pained homage to their pale virginity made me involuntarily bow.

"All maids."

Again the strange emotion filled me.

"Your cheeks look whitish yet, Sir," said the man, gazing at me narrowly. "You must be careful going home. Do they pain you at all now? It's a bad sign, if they do."

"No doubt, Sir," answered I, "when once I have got out of the Devil's Dungeon, I shall feel them mending."

"Ah, yes; the winter air in valleys, or gorges, or any sunken place, is far colder and more bitter than elsewhere. You would hardly believe it now, but it is colder here than at the top of Woedolor Mountain."

"I dare say it is, Sir. But time presses me; I must depart."

With that, remuffling myself in dread-naught and tippet, thrusting my hands into my huge seal-skin mittens, I sallied out into the nipping air, and found poor Black, my horse, all cringing and doubled up with the cold.

Soon, wrapped in furs and meditations, I ascended from the Devil's Dungeon.

At the Black Notch I paused, and once more bethought me of Temple-Bar. Then, shooting through the pass, all alone with inscrutable nature, I exclaimed—Oh! Paradise of Bachelors! and oh! Tartarus of Maids!

John Greenleaf Whittier (1807–1892)

Born into a Massachusetts farm family of modest circumstances, John Greenleaf Whittier described the family house as "built by my first American ancestor, two hundred years ago." His parents were Quakers; the farm was secluded, and the young Whittier lived what he described as a "dual life"—"a world of fancy" and a "world of plain matter-of-fact." Influenced by the poetry of Robert Burns as well as antislavery newspapers, Whittier became a staunch abolitionist and prolific poet. His first poems were published in the Newburyport *Free Press*, edited by William Lloyd Garrison (1826). "As a member of the Society of Friends [Quakers], I had been educated to regard Slavery as a great and dangerous evil," he wrote in an 1882 autobiographical letter. Whittier served as a delegate to the first National Anti-Slavery Convention in Philadelphia in 1833 and published "Pennsylvania Freeman," a paper associated with the Anti-Slavery Society, where his office was sacked and burned by a pro-slavery mob. He published at his own expense, a pamphlet *Justice and Expediency* (1833), but was unable to make a living as a journalist, and he later observed: "Indeed, my pronounced views on Slavery made my name too unpopular for a publisher's uses."

Whittier was one of the founders of the Liberty Party, which later became the Republican Party of Abraham Lincoln. After the Civil War, he devoted himself to poetry. In 1837, Ticknor and Fields published his first volume of poetry. Other volumes include *Songs of Labor* (1850), from which the poem presented here is taken; *In War Time* (1864); and his most famous poem, *Snow-bound* (1863). "The Ship-Builders" is a miniature portrait of the process of building a mid-nineteenth-century ship that looks beneath the finished project and recognizes the dignity and skill of labor, yet cautions that the ship carry "No groaning cargo of despair." Whittier's poetic sentiments may be usefully juxtaposed with Frederick Douglass's enslaved labor as a caulker in a Baltimore shipyard in the 1830s.

The Ship-Builders

The sky is ruddy in the East,
    The earth is gray below,
And, spectral in the river-mist,
    The ship's white timbers show.
5   Then let the sounds of measured stroke
    And grating saw begin;
The broad-axe to the gnarléd oak,
    The mallet to the pin!

Hark!—roars the bellows, blast on blast,
10   The sooty smithy jars,
And fire-sparks, rising far and fast,
    Are fading with the stars.
All day for us the smith shall stand
    Beside that flashing forge;
15   All day for us his heavy hand
    The groaning anvil scourge.

From far-off hills, the panting team
    For us is toiling near;
For us the raftsmen down the stream
20   Their island barges steer.
Rings out for us the axe-man's stroke
    In forests old and still,—
For us the century-circled oak
    Falls crashing down his hill.

25   Up!—up!—in nobler toil than ours
    No craftsmen bear a part:
We make of Nature's giant powers
    The slaves of human Art.
Lay rib to rib and beam to beam,
30   And drive the treenails free;
Nor faithless joint nor yawning seam
    Shall tempt the searching sea!

Where'er the keel of our good ship
    The sea's rough field shall plough—
35   Where'er her tossing spars shall drip
    With salt-spray caught below—
That ship must heed her master's beck,
    Her helm obey his hand,
And seamen tread her reeling deck
40   As if they trod the land.

Her oaken ribs the vulture-beak
    Of Northern ice may peel;
The sunken rock and coral peak
    May grate along her keel;
45   And know we well the painted shell
    We give to wind and wave,

Must float, the sailor's citadel,
    Or sink, the sailor's grave!

Ho!—strike away the bars and blocks,
50   And set the good ship free!
Why lingers on these dusty rocks
    The young bride of the sea?
Look! how she moves adown the grooves,
    In graceful beauty now!
55 How lowly on the breast she loves
    Sinks down her virgin prow!

God bless her! wheresoe'er the breeze
    Her snowy wing shall fan,
Aside the frozen Hebrides,
60   Or sultry Hindostan!
Where'er, in mart or on the main,
    With peaceful flag unfurled,
She helps to wind the silken chain
    Of commerce round the world!

65 Speed on the ship!—But let her bear
    No merchandise of sin,
No groaning cargo of despair
    Her roomy hold within.
No Lethean drug for Eastern lands,
70   Nor poison-draught for ours;
But honest fruits of toiling hands
    And Nature's sun and showers.

Be hers the Prairie's golden grain,
    The Desert's golden sand,
75 The clustered fruits of sunny Spain,
    The spice of Morning-land!
Her pathway on the open main
    May blessings follow free,
And glad hearts welcome back again
80   Her white sails from the sea!

Fanny Fern (Sara Payson Willis Parton) (1811–1872)

In large part because of the expanding number of common schools, a generation of white middle-class Americans became readers in the 1850s and 1860s and, consequently, a prime audience for newspaper columnists and journalists. Sara Payson Willis, whose father Nathaniel Willis established a religious newspaper, later credited her more broadminded mother as the source of her talent. As a young widow, then divorcée escaping a bad second marriage, she turned to writing as a means of supporting herself and her children. Choosing the pseudonym Fanny Fern, she began writing weekly columns to a receptive audience of mostly women readers. She was enormously successful, as astute at the business of journalism as she was lively as a writer, earning $100 a week for her column in the *New York Ledger* in 1855. Fern became a popular commentator on white middle-class women's domestic lives, but also turned her sympathetic eye to conditions of women's labor, imagining the life of a housemaid in "Soliloquy" (presented here) and reporting on the contrasting lives of women workers in "The Working Girls of New York" (an urban companion piece to Herman Melville's "Tartarus of Maids"). She republished her columns in six collections and wrote two novels, including the well-received *Ruth Hall* (1855), and several books for children. *Fern Leaves from Fanny's Port-Folio* (1853) sold nearly 100,000 copies in England and America. Fern used satire, wit, and vernacular language to comment on women's rights and suffrage, particularly economic independence for women. As her writing matured, she addressed issues of poverty, prostitution, prisons, and labor exploitation. She was one of the first writers to praise publicly Walt Whitman's *Leaves of Grass*.

Soliloquy of a Housemaid

Oh, dear, dear! Wonder if my mistress *ever* thinks I am made of flesh and blood? Five times, within half an hour, I have trotted up stairs, to hand her things, that were only four feet from her rocking-chair. Then, there's her son, Mr. George,—it does seem to me, that a great able-bodied man like him, need n't call a poor tired woman up four pair of stairs to ask "what's the time of day?" Heigho!—its "*Sally* do this," and "*Sally* do that," till I wish I never had been baptized at all; and I might as well go farther back, while I am about it, and wish I had never been born.

Now, instead of ordering me round so like a dray horse, if they would only look up smiling-like, now and then; or ask me how my "rheumatiz" did; or say good morning, Sally; or show some sort of interest in a fellow-cretur, I could pluck up a bit of heart to work for them. A kind word would ease the wheels of my treadmill amazingly, and wouldn't cost *them* anything, either.

Look at my clothes, all at sixes and sevens. I can't get a minute to sew on a string or button, except at night; and then I'm so sleepy it is as much as ever I can find the way to bed; and what a bed it is, to be sure! Why, even the pigs are now and then allowed clean straw to sleep on; and as to bed-clothes, the less said about them the better; my old cloak serves for a blanket, and the sheets are as thin as a charity school soup. Well, well; one wouldn't think it, to see all the fine glittering things down in the drawing-room. Master's span of horses, and Miss Clara's diamond ear-rings, and mistresses rich dresses. I *try* to think it is all right, but it is no use.

To-morrow is Sunday—"day of *rest*," I believe they *call* it. H-u-m-p-h!—more cooking to be done—more company—more confusion than on any other day in the week. If I own a soul I have not heard how to take care of it for many a long day. Wonder if my master and mistress calculate to pay me for *that*, if I lose it? It is a *question* in my mind. Land of Goshen! I aint sure I've got a mind—there's the bell again!

The Working-Girls of New York

Nowhere more than in New York does the contest between squalor and splendor so sharply present itself. This is the first reflection of the observing stranger who walks its streets. Particularly is this noticeable with regard to its women. Jostling on the same pavement with the dainty fashionist is the care-worn working-girl. Looking at both these women, the question arises, which lives the more miserable life—she whom the world styles "fortunate," whose husband belongs to three clubs, and whose only meal with his family is an occasional breakfast, from year's end to year's end; who is as much a stranger to his own children as to the reader; whose young son of seventeen has already a detective on his track employed by his father to ascertain where and how he spends his nights and his father's money; swift retribution for that father who finds food, raiment, shelter, equipages for his household; but love, sympathy, companionship—never? Or she—this other woman—with a heart quite as hungry and unappeased, who also faces day by day the same appalling question: *Is this all life has for me?*

A great book is yet unwritten about women. Michelet has aired his wax-doll theories regarding them. The defender of "woman's rights" has given us her views. Authors and authoresses of little, and big repute, have expressed themselves on this subject, and none of them as yet have begun to grasp it: men—because they lack spirituality, rightly and justly to interpret women; women—because they dare not, or will not tell us that which most interests us to know. Who shall write this bold, frank, truthful book remains to be seen. Meanwhile woman's millennium is yet a great way off; and while it slowly progresses, conservatism and indifference gaze through their spectacles at the seething elements of to-day, and wonder "what ails all our women?"

Let me tell you what ails the working-girls. While yet your breakfast is progressing, and your toilet unmade, comes forth through Chatham Street and the Bowery, a long procession of them by twos and threes to their daily labor. Their breakfast, so called, has been hastily swallowed in a tenement house, where two of them share, in a small room, the same miserable bed. Of its quality you may better judge, when you know that each of these girls pays but three dollars a week for board, to the working man and his wife where they lodge.

The room they occupy is close and unventilated, with no accommodations for personal cleanliness, and so near to the little Flinegans that their Celtic night-cries are distinctly heard. They have risen unrefreshed, as a matter of course, and their ill-cooked breakfast does not mend the matter. They emerge from the doorway where their passage is obstructed by "nanny goats" and ragged children rooting together in the dirt, and pass out into the street. They shiver as the sharp wind of early morning strikes their temples. There is no look of youth on their faces; hard lines appear there. Their brows are knit; their eyes are sunken; their dress is flimsy, and foolish, and tawdry; always a hat, and feather or soiled artificial flower upon it; the hair dressed with an abortive attempt at style; a soiled petticoat; a greasy dress, a well-worn sacque or shawl, and a gilt breast-pin and earrings.

Now follow them to the large, black-looking building, where several hundred of them are manufacturing hoop-skirts. If you are a woman you have worn plenty; but you little thought what passed in the heads of these girls as their busy fingers glazed the wire, or prepared the spools for covering them, or secured the tapes which held them in their places. *You* could not stay five minutes in that room, where the noise of the machinery used is so deafening, that only by the motion of the lips could you comprehend a person speaking.

Five minutes! Why, these young creatures bear it, from seven in the morning till six in the evening; week after week, month after month, with only half an hour at midday to eat their dinner of a slice of bread and butter or an apple, which they usually eat in the building, some of them having come a long distance. As I said, the roar of machinery in that room is like the roar of Niagara. Observe them as you enter. Not one lifts her head. They might as well be machines, for any interest or curiosity they show, save always to know *what o'clock it is*. Pitiful! pitiful, you almost sob to yourself, as you look at these young girls. *Young?* Alas! it is only in years that they are young.

Frances Ellen Watkins Harper (1825–1911)

In her long, extraordinary, and heroic life, Frances Ellen Watkins Harper embodied the role of a public and creative intellectual. As an author, lecturer, activist, feminist, and educator, she addressed the most pressing issues of her day and linked them to a vision of a future America where African Americans were essential to the building of a democratic nation. Born to free black parents in Baltimore, Maryland, Frances Watkins was orphaned at age three and raised by her uncle William Watkins, an educator and preacher. She started her young working life as a domestic and then became a teacher. She became the first woman to teach at Union Seminary in Wilberforce, Ohio, where John M. Brown (later leader of the Harper's Ferry revolt) was principal at the time. Her poetry appeared in abolitionist newspapers, and her first poetry collection, *Forest Leaves*, was published in 1845. Watkins witnessed the crux of fear and relief in the lives of escaped slaves when, as a teacher in Pennsylvania, she lived in a home that served as a station on the Underground Railroad. In 1854, she experienced exile firsthand when new slave laws made it unsafe to return to Maryland. These events sharpened her political consciousness as she began giving antislavery speeches in the Northeast and Canada while continuing to write poetry, essays, and sketches, and more than fifteen books over a long lifetime, including *Iola Leroy* (1892), one of the first novels published by a black woman. Slipping poems into her speeches, infusing her writing with the urgency of struggle, Watkins never separated her literary imagination from her political consciousness. As a feminist, she lectured on equal rights and, ahead of her time, perceived the tangled relationships of class, race, and gender. She recognized the importance of suffrage, but also insisted on the necessity of ensuring the survival and safety of blacks first. She married Fenton Harper in 1860, gave birth to their daughter Mary in 1862, and temporarily retired from public life until Harper's death in 1863. In the 1870s, she lived in Philadelphia while traveling and lecturing widely and continuing to write and publish. She envisioned a future for women as not only sustainers of the home, but also as catalysts for transforming society. "The Slave Mother" speaks to that impulse as she coaxes her reader to hear the anguish of a mother who has been separated from her child.

The Slave Mother

Heard you that shriek? It rose
  So wildly on the air,
It seemed as if a burden'd heart
  Was breaking in despair.

5   Saw you those hands so sadly clasped—
  The bowed and feeble head—
The shuddering of that fragile form—
  That look of grief and dread?

Saw you the sad, imploring eye?
10   Its every glance was pain,
As if a storm of agony
  Were sweeping through the brain.

She is a mother, pale with fear,
   Her boy clings to her side,
15 And in her kirtle vainly tries
   His trembling form to hide.

He is not hers, although she bore
   For him a mother's pains;
He is not hers, although her blood
20   Is coursing through his veins!

He is not hers, for cruel hands
   May rudely tear apart
The only wreath of household love
   That binds her breaking heart.

25 His love has been a joyous light
   That o'er her pathway smiled,
A fountain gushing ever new,
   Amid life's desert wild.

His lightest word has been a tone
30   Of music round her heart,
Their lives a streamlet blent in one—
   Oh, Father! must they part?

They tear him from her circling arms,
   Her last and fond embrace.
35 Oh! never more may her sad eyes
   Gaze on his mournful face.

No marvel, then, these bitter shrieks
   Disturb the listening air:
She is a mother, and her heart
40   Is breaking in despair.

Harriet E. Wilson (1828?–1900?)

Harriet E. Wilson's *Our Nig* (1859) depicts the cruel mistreatment of Frado, a young mulatto woman living in New England shortly before the Civil War. Despite being a Northern "free black," Frado is treated as badly as many a Southern slave. Having been deserted as a child of six by her white mother, she is taken in by a family of white farmers, the Bellmonts, and put to work as an indentured servant. Mrs. Bellmont and her daughter, Mary, treat Frado with such cruelty that her health breaks down never fully to recover, even after coming of age and leaving the Bellmonts. The book then depicts how Frado meets a young man, Samuel, posing as a runaway slave, marries him, and has his child. She experiences further acute poverty when he deserts her, which finally forces her to separate from her child.

This story seems largely autobiographical. Wilson (née Adams) was born in 1828 or 1829, probably in Milford, New Hampshire. By 1840, she was living with the Haywards, moderately affluent Milford farmers. The history of the Haywards closely matches that of the Bellmonts, just as Frado's story closely matches Wilson's life, even down to her marriage to an African American (Thomas Wilson) and the birth of a son, George Mason Wilson, who, after a long period of penury both in and out of his mother's care, died in Milford in 1860. Probably Wilson herself moved to Boston, became a spirit medium, and died in 1900.

Our Nig also emphasizes how the rural poor generally may be ground down by free enterprise. Frado leads the life of a farm servant: domestic farmhouse duties are matched by field and dairy work. The word *work* becomes a constant chorus, occurring thirty-seven times, as Frado's life is circumscribed by debilitating profit extraction. *Our Nig* thus stands as an early portrait of American farm life by a working-class writer and, indeed, one of the first prose accounts written from the point of view of the rural *female* laboring class. To establish this innovative antipastoral trajectory, Wilson's story, effectively modelless, almost necessarily draws upon the slave narrative's inevitable stress upon heavy labor's human cost.

It also reveals how the "inalienable rights . . . of liberty and the pursuit of happiness" extend to neither slaves nor "free" blacks, particularly since African American indenturing was so common in the antebellum North. But it does more than this. It shows how "slavery's shadow" fell on Northern labor more widely. Wilson's tale closely engages with power, economics, and their deployment in New England's countryside. In this excerpt, Frado's worth is judged and economically weighed by the Bellmont family.

Richard Ellis

"Keep her. . . . She's real handsome and bright, and not very black, either."

"Keep her," said Jack. "She's real handsome and bright, and not very black, either."

"Yes," rejoined Mary; "that's just like you, Jack. She'll be of no use at all these three years, right under foot all the time."

"Poh! Miss Mary; if she should stay, it wouldn't be two days before you would be telling the girls about *our* nig, *our* nig!" retorted Jack.

"I don't want a nigger 'round me, do you, mother?" asked Mary.

"I don't mind the nigger in the child. I should like a dozen better than one," replied her mother. "If I could make her do my work in a few years, I would keep her. I have so much trouble with girls I hire, I am almost persuaded if I have one to train up in my way from a child, I shall be able to keep them awhile. I am tired of changing every few months."

"Where could she sleep?" asked Mary. "I don't want her near me."

"In the L chamber," answered the mother.

"How'll she get there?" asked Jack. "She'll be afraid to go through that dark passage, and she can't climb the ladder safely."

"She'll have to go there; it's good enough for a nigger," was the reply.

Jack was sent on horseback to ascertain if Mag was at her home. He returned with the testimony of Pete Greene that they were fairly departed, and that the child was intentionally thrust upon their family.

The imposition was not at all relished by Mrs. B., or the pert, haughty Mary, who had just glided into her teens.

"Show the child to bed, Jack," said his mother. "You seem most pleased with the little nigger, so you may introduce her to her room."

He went to the kitchen, and, taking Frado gently by the hand, told her he would put her in bed now; perhaps her mother would come the next night after her.

It was not yet quite dark, so they ascended the stairs without any light, passing through nicely furnished rooms, which were a source of great amazement to the child. He opened the door which connected with her room by a dark, unfinished passageway. "Don't bump your head," said Jack, and stepped before to open the door leading into her apartment,— an unfinished chamber over the kitchen, the roof slanting nearly to the floor, so that the bed could stand only in the middle of the room. A small half window furnished light and air. Jack returned to the sitting room with the remark that the child would soon outgrow those quarters.

"When she *does*, she'll outgrow the house," remarked the mother.

"What can she do to help you?" asked Mary. "She came just in the right time, didn't she? Just the very day after Bridget left," continued she.

"I'll see what she can do in the morning," was the answer. While this conversation was passing below, Frado lay, revolving in her little mind whether she would remain or not until her mother's return. She was of wilful, determined nature, a stranger to fear, and would not hesitate to wander away should she decide to. She remembered the conversation of her mother with Seth, the words "given away" which she heard used in reference to herself; and though she did not know their full import, she thought she should, by remaining, be in some relation to white people she was never favored with before. So she resolved to tarry, with the hope that mother would come and get her some time. The hot sun had penetrated her room, and it was long before a cooling breeze reduced the temperature so that she could sleep.

Frado was called early in the morning by her new mistress. Her first work was to feed the hens. She was shown how it was *always* to be done, and in no other way; any departure from this rule to be punished by a whipping. She was then accompanied by Jack to drive the cows to pasture, so she might learn the way. Upon her return she was allowed to eat her breakfast, consisting of a bowl of skimmed milk, with brown bread crusts, which she was told to eat, standing, by the kitchen table, and must not be over ten minutes about it. Meanwhile the family were taking their morning meal in the dining-room. This over, she was placed on a cricket to wash the common dishes; she was to be in waiting always to bring wood and chips, to run hither and thither from room to room.

A large amount of dish-washing for small hands followed dinner. Then the same after tea and going after the cows finished her first day's work. It was a new discipline to the child. She found some attractions about the place, and she retired to rest at night more willing to remain. The same routine followed day after day, with slight variation; adding a little more work, and spicing the toil with "words that burn," and frequent blows on her head. These were great annoyances to Frado, and had she known where her mother was, she would have gone at once to her. She was often greatly wearied, and silently wept over her sad fate. At first she wept aloud, which Mrs. Bellmont noticed by applying a raw hide, always at hand in the kitchen. It was a symptom of discontent and complaining which must be "nipped in the bud," she said.

Thus passed a year. No intelligence of Mag. It was now certain Frado was to become a permanent member of the family. Her labors were multiplied; she was quite indispensable, although but seven years old. She had never learned to read, never heard of a school until her residence in the family.

Mrs. Bellmont was in doubt about the utility of attempting to educate people of color, who were incapable of elevation. This subject occasioned a lengthy discussion in the family. Mr. Bellmont, Jane and Jack arguing for Frado's education; Mary and her mother objecting. At last Mr. Bellmont declared decisively that she should go to school. He was a man who seldom decided controversies at home. The word once spoken admitted of no appeal; so, notwithstanding Mary's objection that she would have to attend the same school she did, the word became law. . . .

The interim of [school] terms was filled up with a variety of duties new and peculiar. At home, no matter how powerful the heat when sent to rake hay or guard the grazing herd, she was never permitted to shield her skin from the sun. She was not many shades darker than Mary now; what a calamity it would be ever to hear the contrast spoken of. Mrs. Bellmont was determined the sun should have full power to darken the shade which nature had first bestowed upon her as best befitting. . . .

Spring was now retiring. James, one of the absent sons, was expected home on a visit. He had never seen the last acquisition to the family. Jack had written faithfully of all the merits of his colored *protégé*, and hinted plainly that mother did not always treat her just right. Many were the preparations to make the visit pleasant, and as the day approached when he was to arrive, great exertions were made to cook the favorite viands, to prepare the choicest table-fare.

The morning of the arrival day was a busy one. Frado knew not who would be of so much importance; her feet were speeding hither and thither so unsparingly. Mrs. Bellmont seemed a trifle fatigued, and her shoes which had, early in the morning, a methodic squeak, altered to an irregular, peevish snap.

"Get some little wood to make the fire burn," said Mrs. Bellmont, in a sharp tone. Frado obeyed, bringing the smallest she could find.

Mrs. Bellmont approached her, and, giving her a box on her ear, reiterated the command.

The first the child brought was the smallest to be found; of course, the second must be a trifle larger. She well knew it was, as she threw it into a box on the hearth. To Mrs. Bellmont it was a greater affront, as well as larger wood, so she "taught her" with the raw-hide, and sent her the third time for "little wood."

Nig, weeping, knew not what to do. She had carried the smallest; none left would suit her mistress; of course further punishment awaited her; so she gathered up whatever came first, and threw it down on the hearth. As she expected, Mrs. Bellmont, enraged, approached her, and kicked her so forcibly as to throw her upon the floor. Before she could rise, another foiled the attempt, and then followed kick after kick in quick succession and power, till she reached the door. Mr. Bellmont and Aunt Abby, hearing the noise, rushed in, just in time to see the last of the performance. Nig jumped up, and rushed from the house, out of sight.

Aunt Abby returned to her apartment, followed by John, who was muttering to himself.

"What were you saying?" asked Aunt Abby.

"I said I hoped the child never would come into the house again."

"What would become of her? You cannot mean that," continued his sister.

"I do mean it. The child does as much work as a woman ought to; and just see how she is kicked about!"

"Why do you have it so, John?" asked his sister.

"How am I to help it? Women rule the earth, and all in it."

"I think I should rule my own house, John,"__

"And live in hell meantime," added Mr. Bellmont. . . .

James' visit concluded. Frado had become greatly attached to him, and with sorrow she listened and joined in the farewells which preceded his exit. The remembrance of his kindness cheered her through many a weary month, and an occasional word to her in letters to Jack, were like "cold waters to a thirsty soul." Intelligence came that James would soon marry; Frado hoped he would, and remove her from such severe treatment as she was subject to. There had been additional burdens laid on her since his return. She must now *milk* the cows, she had then only to drive. Flocks of sheep had been added to the farm, which daily claimed a portion of her time. In the absence of the men, she must harness the horse for Mary and her mother to ride, go to mill, in short, do the work of a boy, could one be procured to endure the tirades of Mrs. Bellmont. She was first up in the morning, doing what she could towards breakfast. Occasionally, she would utter some funny thing for Jack's benefit, while she was waiting on the table, provoking a sharp look from his mother, or expulsion from the room.

On one such occasion, they found her on the roof of the barn. Some repairs having been necessary, a staging had been erected, and was not wholly removed. Availing herself of ladders, she was mounted in high glee on the topmost board. Mr. Bellmont called sternly for her to come down; poor Jane nearly fainted from fear. Mrs. B. and Mary did not care if she "broke her neck," while Jack and the men laughed at her fearlessness. Strange, one spark of playfulness could remain amid such constant toil; but her natural temperament was in a high degree mirthful, and the encouragement she received from Jack and the hired men, constantly nurtured the inclination. When she had none of the family around to be merry with, she would amuse herself with the animals. Among the sheep was a willful leader, who always persisted in being first served, and many times in his fury he had thrown down Nig, till, provoked, she resolved to punish him. The pasture in which the sheep grazed was bounded on three sides by a wide stream, which flowed on one side at the base of precipitous banks. The first spare moments at her command, she ran to the pasture with a dish in her hand, and mounting the highest point of land nearest the stream, called the flock to their mock repast. Mr. Bellmont, with his laborers, were in sight, though unseen by Frado. They paused to see what she was about to do. Should she by any mishap lose her footing, she must roll into the stream, and, without aid, must drown. They thought of shouting; but they feared an unexpected salute might startle her, and thus ensure what they were anxious to prevent. They watched in breathless silence. The willful sheep came furiously leaping and bounding far in advance of the flock. Just as he leaped for the dish, she suddenly jumped one side, when down he rolled into the river, and swimming across, remained alone till night. The men lay down, convulsed with laughter at the trick, and guessed at once its object. Mr. Bellmont talked seriously to the child for exposing herself to such danger; but she hopped about on her toes, and with laughable grimaces replied, she knew she was quick enough to "give him a slide." . . .

She was now able to do all the washing, ironing, baking, and the common et cetera of household duties, though but fourteen. Mary left all for her to do, though she affected great responsibility. She would show herself in the kitchen long enough to relieve herself of some command, better withheld; or insist upon some compliance to her wishes in some department which she was very imperfectly acquainted with, very much less than the person she was addressing; and so impetuous till her orders were obeyed, that to escape the turmoil, Nig would often go contrary to her own knowledge to gain a respite.

Nig was taken sick! What could be done? The *work*, certainly, but not by Miss Mary. So Nig would work while she could remain erect, then sink down upon the floor, or a chair, till she could rally for a fresh effort. Mary would look in upon her, chide her for her laziness, threaten to tell mother when she came home, and so forth.

"Nig!" screamed Mary, one of her sickest days, "come here, and sweep these threads from the carpet." She attempted to drag her weary limbs along, using the broom as support. Impatient of delay, she called again, but with a different request. "Bring me some wood, you lazy jade, quick." Nig rested the broom against the wall, and started on the fresh behest.

Too long gone. Flushed with anger, she rose and greeted her with, "What are you gone so long, for? Bring it in quick, I say."

"I am coming as quick as I can," she replied, entering the door.

"Saucy, impudent nigger, you! is this the way you answer me?" and taking a large carving knife from the table, she hurled it, in her rage, at the defenceless girl.

Dodging quickly, it fastened in the ceiling a few inches from where she stood. There rushed on Mary's mental vision a picture of bloodshed, in which she was the perpetrator, and the sad consequences of what was so nearly an actual occurrence.

"Tell anybody of this, if you dare. If you tell Aunt Abby, I'll certainly kill you," said she, terrified. She returned to her room, brushed her threads herself; was for a day or two more guarded, and so escaped deserved and merited penalty.

Walt Whitman (1819–1892)

The second son of Walter Whitman, Sr., a carpenter and farmer of English heritage, and Lousia (Van Velsor) Whitman of Dutch and Welsh heritage, Walt Whitman was born on Long Island, but his childhood was largely spent in Brooklyn, New York, where the family moved in search of work. After six years in school, he began work at age eleven as an office boy and, by age twelve, was an apprentice printer for the radical Democratic *Long Island Patriot* newspaper. In 1836, Whitman began five years of teaching school around Long Island, during which he also tried starting his own newspaper and began to publish short fiction and journalism. In 1846, he became editor-in-chief of the *Brooklyn Eagle*, where he wrote both literary reviews and political commentary on issues of the day, including slavery and working-class conditions in the cities. Fired by the paper's pro-slavery editor, Whitman moved to New Orleans, where, still earning his living as a journalist, he began to experiment seriously with poetry. The first edition of *Leaves of Grass* appeared in 1855, self-published, and was revised and expanded through eleven editions until 1891, the year before his death.

Although the poem's radical politics and homoerotic undertones later cost him his post–Civil War government job, Whitman's reputation as a founder of modern American poetry and as bard and critic of the United States's democratic experiment rests on this masterpiece, with its rolling free-verse lines and its generous embrace. "Song of Occupations," which began as a section of *Leaves of Grass*, celebrates the broad array of ways of making a living in his time and argues for the fundamental equality of workers with those who boss and govern them. The poem also makes a strong claim for the socially necessary power of the poet: "I own publicly who you are, if nobody else owns. . . . You workmen and workwomen of these States having your own divine and strong life."

The mature Whitman's closest, and life-changing, contact with workers came when he volunteered as a nurse tending the wounded, both in hospital and on the battlefield, during the Civil War. The poems collected in *Drum-taps* (1865) are among his most tender, reflecting the pain of a loving witness as both the bodies of young men and the American "Union" he cherished were being torn apart. After the war, Whitman turned again to prose, publishing *Democratic Vistas* (1871) and *Specimen Days* (1882). In 1873, he suffered the first of a series of strokes and moved to be with his family in Camden, New Jersey, where he worked on further editions of *Leaves*, the sixth of which was banned in Boston because of its inclusion of poems about prostitution. The resulting scandal boosted sales and earned Whitman the first significant poetic royalties of his life.

A Song for Occupations

1

A song for occupations!
In the labor of engines and trades and the labor of fields I find the developments,
And find the eternal meanings.

Workmen and Workwomen!
5   Were all educations practical and ornamental well display'd out of me, what would
    it amount to?

Were I as the head teacher, charitable proprietor, wise statesman, what would it
    amount to?
Were I to you as the boss employing and paying you, would that satisfy you?

10   The learn'd, virtuous, benevolent, and the usual terms,
A man like me and never the usual terms.

Neither a servant nor a master I,
I take no sooner a large price than a small price, I will have my own whoever
    enjoys me,
15   I will be even with you and you shall be even with me.

If you stand at work in a shop I stand as nigh as the nighest in the same shop,
If you bestow gifts on your brother or dearest friend I demand as good as your
    brother or dearest friend,
If your lover, husband, wife, is welcome by day or night, I must be personally as
20   welcome,
If you become degraded, criminal, ill, than I become so for your sake,
If you remember your foolish and outlaw'd deeds, do you think I cannot
    remember my own foolish and outlaw'd deeds?
If you carouse at the table I carouse at the opposite side of the table,
25   If you meet some stranger in the streets and love him or her, why I often meet
    strangers in the street and love them.

Why what have you thought of yourself?
Is it you then that thought yourself less?
Is it you that thought the President greater than you?
30   Or the rich better off than you? or the educated wiser than you?

(Because you are greasy or pimpled, or were once drunk, or a thief,
Or that you are diseas'd, or rheumatic, or a prostitute,
Or from frivolity or impotence, or that you are no scholar and never saw your
    name in print,
35   Do you give in that you are any less immortal?)

2

Souls of men and women! it is not you I call unseen, unheard, untouchable and
    untouching,
It is not you I go argue pro and con about, and to settle whether you are alive or no,
I own publicly who you are, if nobody else owns.

40   Grown, half-grown and babe, of this country and every country, in-doors and
    out-doors, one just as much as the other, I see,
And all else behind or through them.

The wife, and she is not one jot less than the husband,
The daughter, and she is just as good as the son,
45   The mother, and she is every bit as much as the father.
Offspring of ignorant and poor, boys apprenticed to trades,
Young fellows working on farms and old fellows working on farms,
Sailor-men, merchant-men, coasters, immigrants,
All these I see, but nigher and farther the same I see,
50   None shall escape me and none shall wish to escape me.

I bring what you much need yet always have,
Not money, amours, dress, eating, erudition, but as good,
I send no agent or medium, offer no representative of value, but offer the value
  itself.

55   There is something that comes to one now and perpetually,
It is not what is printed, preach'd, discussed, it eludes discussion and print,
It is not to be put in a book, it is not in this book,
It is for you whoever you are, it is no farther from you than your hearing and sight
  are from you,
60   It is hinted by nearest, commonest, readiest, it is ever provoked by them.

You may read in many languages, yet read nothing about it,
You may read the President's message and read nothing about it there,
Nothing in the reports from the State department or Treasury department, or in
  the daily papers or weekly papers,
65   Or in the census or revenue returns, prices current, or any accounts of stock.

3

The sun and stars that float in the open air,
The apple-shaped earth and we upon it, surely the drift of them is something
  grand,
I do not know what it is except that it is grand, and that it is happiness,
70   And that the enclosing purport of us here is not a speculation or bonmot or
  reconnoissance,
And that it is not something which by luck may turn out well for us, and without
  luck must be a failure for us,
And not something which may yet be retracted in a certain contingency.

75   The light and shade, the curious sense of body and identity, the greed that with
  perfect complaisance devours all things,
The endless pride and outstretching of man, unspeakable joys and sorrows,
The wonder every one sees in every one else he sees, and the wonders that fill
  each minute of time forever,
80   What have you reckon'd them for, camerado?
Have you reckon'd them for your trade or farm-work? or for the profits of your
  store?
Or to achieve yourself a position? or to fill a gentleman's leisure, or a lady's leisure?

Have you reckon'd that the landscape took substance and form that it might be
85   painted in a picture?
Or men and women that they might be written of, and songs sung?
Or the attraction of gravity, and the great laws of harmonious combinations and
  the fluids of the air, as subjects for the savans?
Or the brown land and the blue sea for maps and charts?
90   Or the stars to be put in constellations and named fancy names?
Or that the growth of seeds is for agricultural tables, or agriculture itself?

Old institutions, these arts, libraries, legends, collections, and the practice handed
  along in manufactures, will we rate them so high?
Will we rate our cash and business high? I have no objection,
95   I rate them as high as the highest—then a child born of a woman and man I rate
  beyond all rate.

We thought our Union grand, and our Constitution grand,
I do not say they are not grand and good, for they are,
I am this day just as much in love with them as you,
100   Then I am in love with You, and with all my fellows upon the earth.

We consider bibles and religions divine—I do not say they are not divine,
I say they have all grown out of you, and may grow out of you still,
It is not they who give the life, it is you who give the life,
Leaves are not more shed from the trees, or trees from the earth, than they are
105   shed out of you.

4

The sun of all known reverence I add up in you whoever you are,
The President is there in the White House for you, it is not you who are here
    for him,
The Secretaries act in their bureaus for you, not you here for them,
110   The Congress convenes every Twelfth-month for you,
Laws, courts, the forming of States, the charters of cities, the going and coming
    of commerce and mails, are all for you.

List close my scholars dear,
Doctrines, politics and civilization exurge from you,
115   Sculpture and monuments and any thing inscribed anywhere are tallied in you,
The gist of histories and statistics as far back as the records reach is in you this
    hour, and myths and tales the same,
If you were not breathing and walking here, where would they all be?
The most renown'd poems would be ashes, orations and plays would be
120   vacuums.

All architecture is what you do to it when you look upon it,
(Did you think it was in the white or gray stone? or the lines of the arches and
    cornices?)

All music is what awakes from you when you are reminded by the instruments,
125   It is not the violins and the cornets, it is not the oboe nor the beating drums, nor
    the score of the baritone singer singing his sweet romanza, nor that of the men's
    chorus, nor that of the women's chorus,
It is nearer and farther than they.

5

Will the whole come back then?
130   Can each see signs of the best by a look in the looking-glass? is there nothing
    greater or more?
Does all sit there with you, with the mystic unseen soul?
Strange and hard that paradox true I give,
Objects gross and the unseen soul are one.

135   House-building, measuring, sawing the boards,
Blacksmithing, glass-blowing, nail-making, coopering, tin-roofing,
    shingle-dressing,
Ship-joining, dock-building, fish-curing, flagging of sidewalks by flaggers,
The pump, the pile-driver, the great derrick, the coal-kiln and brick-kiln,

140   Coal-mines and all that is down there, the lamps in the darkness, echoes, songs,
           what meditations, what vast native thoughts looking through smutch'd faces,
       Iron-works, forge-fires in the mountains or by river-banks, men around feeling
           the melt with huge crowbars, lumps of ore, the due combining of ore,
           limestone, coal,
145   The blast-furnace and the puddling-furnace, the loup-lump at the bottom of the
           melt at last, the rolling-mill, the stumpy bars of pig-iron, the strong clean-shaped
           T-rail for railroads,
       Oil-works, silk-works, white-lead-works, the sugar-house, steam-saws, the great
           mills and factories,
150   Stone-cutting, shapely trimmings for façades or window or door-lintels, the mallet,
           the tooth-chisel, the jib to protect the thumb,
       The calking-iron, the kettle of boiling vault-cement, and the fire under the kettle,
       The cotton-bale, the stevedore's hook, the saw and buck of the sawyer, the mould
           of the moulder, the working-knife of the butcher, the ice-saw, and all the work
155   with ice,
       The work and tools of the rigger, grappler, sail-maker, block-maker,
       Goods of gutta-percha, papier-maché, colors, brushes, brush making, glazier's
           implements,
       The veneer and glue-pot, the confectioner's ornaments, the decanter and glasses,
160   the shears and flat-iron,
       The awl and knee-strap, the pint measure and quart measure, the counter and
           stool, the writing-pen of quill or metal, the making of all sorts of edged tools,
       The brewery, brewing, the malt, the vats, every thing that is done by brewers,
           wine-makers, vinegar-makers,
165   Leather-dressing, coach-making, boiler-making, rope-twisting, distilling,
           sign-painting, lime-burning, cotton-picking, electroplating, electrotyping,
           stereotyping,
       Stave-machines, planing-machines, reaping-machines, ploughing-machines,
           thrashing-machines, steam-wagons,
170   The cart of the carman, the omnibus, the ponderous dray,
       Pyrotechny letting off color'd fireworks at night, fancy figures and jets;
       Beef on the butcher's stall, the slaughter-house of the butcher, the butcher in his
           killing-clothes,
       The pens of live pork, the killing-hammer, the hog-hook, the scalder's tub,
175   gutting, the cutter's cleaver, the packer's maul, and the plenteous winterwork
           of pork-packing,
       Flour-works, grinding of wheat, rye, maize, rice, the barrels and the half and
           quarter barrels, the loaded barges, the high piles on wharves and levees,
       The men and the work of the men on ferries, railroads, coasters, fishboats,
180   canals;
       The hourly routine of your own or any man's life, the shop, yard, store,
           or factory,
       These shows all near you by day and night—workman! whoever you are, your
           daily life!
185   In that and them the heft of the heaviest—in that and them far more than you
           estimated, (and far less also,)
       In them realities for you and me, in them poems for you and me,
       In them, not yourself—you and your soul enclose all things, regardless of
           estimation,
190   In them the development good—in them all themes, hints, possibilities.

I do not affirm that what you see beyond is futile, I do not advise you to stop,
I do not say leadings you thought great are not great,
But I say that none lead to greater than these lead to.

6

Will you seek afar off? you surely come back at last,
195   In things best known to you finding the best, or as good as the best,
In folks nearest to you finding the sweetest, strongest, lovingest,
Happiness, knowledge, not in another place but this place, not for another hour
       but this hour,
Man in the first you see or touch, always in friend, brother, nighest neighbor—
200   woman in mother, sister, wife,
The popular tastes and employments taking precedence in poems or anywhere,
You workwomen and workmen of these States having your own divine and
       strong life,
And all else giving place to men and women like you.

205   When the psalm sings instead of the singer,
When the script preaches instead of the preacher,
When the pulpit descends and goes instead of the carver that carved the
       supporting desk,
When I can touch the body of books by night or by day, and when they touch by
210   body back again,
When a university course convinces like a slumbering woman and child convince,
When the minted gold in the vault smiles like the night-watchman's daughter,
When warrantee deeds loafe in chairs opposite and are my friendly companions,
I intend to reach them my hand, and make as much of them as I do of men and
215   women like you.

THE WOUND-DRESSER

1

An old man bending I come among new faces,
Years looking backward resuming in answer to children,
Come tell us old man, as from young men and maidens that love me,
(Arous'd and angry, I'd thought to beat the alarum, and urge relentless war,
5   But soon my fingers fail'd me, my face droop'd and I resign'd myself,
To sit by the wounded and soothe them, or silently watch the dead;)
Years hence of these scenes, of these furious passions, these chances,
Of unsurpass'd heroes (was one side so brave? the other was equally brave;)
Now be witness again, paint the mightiest armies of earth,
10   Of those armies so rapid so wondrous what saw you to tell us?
What stays with you latest and deepest? of curious panics,
Of hard-fought engagements or sieges tremendous what deepest remains?

2

O maidens and young men I love and that love me,
What you ask of my days those the strangest and sudden your talking recalls,
15   Soldier alert I arrive after a long march cover'd with sweat and dust,
  In the nick of time I come, plunge in the fight, loudly shout in the rush of
      successful charge,
Enter the captur'd works—yet lo, like a swift-running river they fade,
Pass and are gone they fade—I dwell not on soldiers' perils or soldiers' joys
20   (Both I remember well—many the hardships, few the joys, yet I was content).
But in silence, in dreams' projections,
While the world of gain and appearance and mirth goes on,
So soon what is over forgotten, and waves wash the imprints off the sand,
With hinged knees returning I enter the doors (while for you up there,
25   Whoever you are, follow without noise and be of strong heart).

Bearing the bandages, water and sponge,
Straight and swift to my wounded I go,
Where they lie on the ground after the battle brought in,
Where their priceless blood reddens the grass, the ground,
30   Or to the rows of the hospital tent, or under the roof'd hospital,
To the long rows of cots up and down each side I return,
To each and all one after another I draw near, not one do I miss,
An attendant follows holding a tray, he carries a refuse pail,
Soon to be fill'd with clotted rags and blood, emptied, and fill'd again.

35   I onward go, I stop,
With hinged knees and steady hand to dress wounds,
I am firm with each, the pangs are sharp yet unavoidable,
One turns to me his appealing eyes—poor boy! I never knew you,
Yet I think I could not refuse this moment to die for you, if that would save you.

3

40   On, on I go, (open doors of time! open hospital doors!)
The crush'd head I dress (poor crazed hand tear not the bandage away),
The neck of the cavalry-man with the bullet through and through I examine,
Hard the breathing rattles, quite glazed already the eye, yet life struggles hard
(Come sweet death! be persuaded O beautiful death!
45   In mercy come quickly).

From the stump of the arm, the amputated hand,
I undo the clotted lint, remove the slough, wash off the matter and blood,
Back on his pillow the soldier bends with curv'd neck and side-falling head,
His eyes are closed, his face is pale, he dares not look on the bloody stump,
50   And has not yet look'd on it.

I dress a wound in the side, deep, deep,
But a day or two more, for see the frame all wasted and sinking,
And the yellow-blue countenance see.
I dress the perforated shoulder, the foot with the bullet-wound,
55   Cleanse the one with a gnawing and putrid gangrene, so sickening, so offensive,
While the attendant stands behind aside me holding the tray and pail.

I am faithful, I do not give out,
The fractur'd thigh, the knee, the wound in the abdomen,
These and more I dress with impassive hand (yet deep in my breast a fire, a
60   burning flame).
Thus in silence in dreams' projections,
Returning, resuming, I thread my way through the hospitals,
The hurt and wounded I pacify with soothing hand,
I sit by the restless all the dark night, some are so young,
65   Some suffer so much, I recall the experience sweet and sad,
(Many a soldier's loving arms about this neck have cross'd and rested,
Many a soldier's kiss dwells on these bearded lips).

Nineteenth-Century Work Songs

Songs and singing have always been part of working-class popular cultures, a vital way to express and share common experiences. The focus of the songs that follow is work itself, in particular, the work of a shoemaker, a housekeeper, a farmer, and two railroad workers, Irish and African American. Although we can hear in each of these songs the distinctive voices of particular workers, all are "anonymous," in that it is not possible to establish exactly when or by whom they were first composed and sung. The songs functioned as collective cultural property, circulating and performed as a living tradition of witness and response to the working life. "Peg and Awl" is likely the earliest of them. Shoemaking was, along with spinning and weaving cloth (see "The Lowell Factory Girl" presented earlier), one of the first industries to be mechanized at the start of the nineteenth century. As competition from factory-produced goods depressed the prices of handmade shoes, and with them the wages of once-proud craftsmen, it is no coincidence that the country's first labor unions were organized by shoemakers (see "Address to Journeymen Cordwainers" in Part I). The song, of course, does not make clear whether the protagonist, having thrown away his pegs, will submit to factory discipline and learn to operate the new machines or leave the trade altogether.

"Paddy Works on the Railway" is a traditional English industrial ballad given new content as the story of an Irish immigrant railroad worker. Although the dates that structure the song's sequence of verses (in a manner similar to "Peg and Awl") are earlier than those of the Irish Potato Famine (1846–1850), which forced the mass emigration of workers, mostly to the United States, the song's popularity likely owes a lot to the experience of displacement and disappointment that were common to tens of thousands of mid-century immigrants. "The Housekeeper's Lament," also known by its refrain "Life Is a Toil," has remained a popular song of protest on the theme that "women's work is never done," targeting, with tragicomic exaggeration, the perennial and repetitive futility of much domestic work. Folklorists trace the song to the mid-nineteenth century, when the majority of households were still rural (and dirt was a serious challenge).

Like most popular folksongs, these "work songs" exist in multiple versions, since they were sung on particular occasions in different parts of the country. The lyrics were passed from singer to singer, picking up new verses and dropping older ones as they responded to new events, experiences, and group feelings. "John Henry" is a prime example of this creative mutability. In part because it so powerfully communicates deeply rooted themes in the lives of working people, the many versions of this story of the African American steel driver as tragic superhero carry differing emphases: on the victory of man over machine as a form of resistance to job loss through mechanization; on the physical strength and endurance of the black worker under the racial subordination of his white "captain"; on the continuity of that tradition of strength and endurance in labor within the family, uniting John's father, John, Polly Ann, and their son; other versions stress John Henry's sexual prowess and numerous women friends. "John Henry" has been sung in prisons, on work gangs, in union halls, and by bluesmen, bluegrass performers, and folksingers, from Woody Guthrie to Johnny Cash. The version that follows is drawn from the popular contemporary songbook *Rise Up Singing*.

"The Farmer Is the Man" is probably contemporary with John Henry in its origins, although it deals with a very different set of labor conditions. It arose among western farmers after the Civil War and came to serve as an informal anthem for the agrarian political movements of the century's last decades (the Greenback Party in the 1880s and the People's Party in the 1890s). The song deftly critiques the economic system of high-interest merchants' credit and bankers' mortgages that was driving farmers into permanent debt (see Hamlin Garland's "Under the Lion's Paw" in Part III). At the same time, the song asserts the indispensable value of what farmers' work produces, feeding us all. At a time when a majority of the population was moving to the cities and into various forms of industrial work, the song insists that the farmer—like the steel-driving John Henry in another context—is still "the man."

PEG AN' AWL

> In the days of eighteen and one,
>   Peg an' awl,
> In the days of eighteen and one,
>   Peg an' awl,
> 5 In the days of eighteen and one,
> Peggin' shoes is all I done,
>   Hand me down my pegs, my pegs, my pegs, my awl.
>
> In the days of eighteen and two,   (x3)
> Peggin' shoes was all I'd do,
> 10   Hand me down my pegs, my pegs, my pegs, my awl.
>
> In the days of eighteen and three,   (x3)
> Peggin' shoes is all you'd see,
>   Hand me down my pegs, my pegs, my pegs, my awl.
>
> In the days of eighteen and four,   (x3)
> 15 I said I'd peg them shoes no more,
>   Throw away my pegs, my pegs, my pegs, my awl.
>
> They've invented a new machine,   (x3)
> The prettiest little thing you ever seen,
>   I'll throw away my pegs, my pegs, my pegs, my awl.
>
> 20 Make a hundred pair to my one,   (x3)
> Peggin' shoes, it ain't no fun.
>   Throw away my pegs, my pegs, my pegs, my awl.

Paddy Works on the Railway

In eighteen hundred and forty-one
I put my corduroy breeches on.
I put my corduroy breeches on
To work upon the railway.

Chorus
5   Fill-i-me-oo-ree-i-ree-ay (three times)
To work upon the railway.

In eighteen hundred and forty-two
I left the Old World for the New.
Bad cess to the luck that brought me through
10   To work upon the railway.

When Pat left Ireland to come here
And spend his latter days in cheer,
His bosses they did drink strong beer
While Pat worked on the railway.

15   In eighteen hundred and forty-three
'Twas then that I met sweet Biddy McGee.
An elegant wife she's been to me
While working on the railway.

In eighteen hundred and forty-four
20   I traveled the land from shore to shore,
I traveled the land from shore to shore
To work upon the railway.

In eighteen hundred and forty-five
I found myself more dead than alive.
25   I found myself more dead than alive
From working on the railway.

It's "Pat do this" and "Pat do that,"
Without a stocking or cravat,
Nothing but an old straw hat
30   While I worked on the railway.

In eighteen hundred and forty-seven
Sweet Biddy McGee she went to heaven;
If she left one kid she left eleven,
To work upon the railway.

35   In eighteen hundred and forty-eight
I learned to take me whiskey straight.
'Tis an elegant drink and can't be bate
For working on the railway.

THE HOUSEKEEPER'S LAMENT

One day as I wandered, I heard a complaining,
and saw an old woman, the picture of gloom.
She gazed at the mud on her doorstep ('twas raining)
and this was her song as she wielded her broom:

5   "Oh life is a toil and love is a trouble,
And beauty will fade and riches will flee,
Oh, pleasures they dwindle and prices they double,
And nothing is as I would wish it to be.

"It's sweeping at six and it's dusting at seven;
10   It's victuals at eight and it's dishes at nine.
It's potting and panning from ten to eleven;
We scarce break our fast till we plan how to dine.

"There's too much of worriment goes in a bonnet;
There's too much of ironing goes in a shirt.
15   There's nothing that pays for the time you waste on it;
There's nothing that lasts us but trouble and dirt.

"In March it is mud, it is snow in December;
The mid-summer breezes are loaded with dust.
In fall the leaves litter; in rainy September
20   The wallpaper rots and the candlesticks rust.

"Last night in my dreams I was stationed forever
On a far little isle in the midst of the sea.
My one chance for life was a ceaseless endeavor
To sweep off the waves ere they swept over me.

25   "Alas, 'twas no dream, for ahead I behold it;
I know I am helpless my fate to avert."
She put down her broom and her apron she folded,
Then lay down and died, and was buried in dirt.

Jackson, Mississippi, June 20, 1866

Mayor Barrows
Dear Sir:

At a meeting of the colored Washerwomen of this city, on the evening of the 18th of June, the subject of raising the wages was considered, and the following preamble and resolution were unanimously adopted:

Whereas, under the influence of the present high prices of all the necessaries of life, and the attendant high rates of rent, we, the washerwomen of the city of Jackson, State of Mississippi, thinking it impossible to live uprightly and honestly in laboring for the present daily and monthly recompense, and hoping to meet with the support of all good citizens, join in adopting unanimously the following resolution:

Be it resolved by the washerwomen of this city and county, That on and after the foregoing date, we join in charging a uniform rate for our labor, and any one belonging to the class of washerwomen, violating this, shall be liable to a fine regulated by the class. We do not wish in the least to charge exorbitant prices, but desire to be able to live comfortably if possible from the fruits of our labor. We present the matter to your Honor, and hope you will not reject it. The prices charged are:

$1.50 per day for washing

$15.00 per month for family washing

$10.00 per month for single individuals

We ask you to consider the matter in our behalf, and should you deem it just and right, your sanction of the movement will be gratefully received.

Yours, very truly,
The washerwomen of Jackson

Source: Dorothy Sterling, ed. *We Are Your Sisters: Black Women in the Nineteenth Century.* New York: W.W. Norton, 1984, 355–56.

THE FARMER IS THE MAN

Oh, the farmer comes to town
With his wagon broken down,
But the farmer is the man who feeds them all.
If you'll only look and see,
5   I think you will agree
That the farmer is the man who feeds them all.

Chorus
The farmer is the man,
The farmer is the man,
Lives on credit till the fall,
10   Then they take him by the hand
And they lead him from the land,
And the merchant is the man who gets it all.

When the lawyer hangs around
While the butcher cuts a pound,
15   Oh, the farmer is the man who feeds them all.
When the preacher and the cook
Go a-strolling by the brook,
Oh, the farmer is the man who feeds them all.

When the banker says he's broke
20   And the merchant's up in smoke,
They forget that it's the farmer feeds them all.
It would put them to the test
If the farmer took a rest;
Then they'd know that it's the farmer feeds them all.

Last chorus
25   The farmer is the man,
The farmer is the man,
Lives on credit till the fall.
With the interest rate so high
It's a wonder he don't die,
30   For the mortgage man's the one who gets it all.

JOHN HENRY

John Henry was a little baby
Sittin' on his papa's knee
He picked up a hammer & a little piece of steel
Said "Hammer's gonna be the death of me, Lord, Lord!
5   Hammer's gonna be the death of me."

The captain said to John Henry
"Gonna bring that steam drill 'round
Gonna bring that steam drill out on the job
Gonna whop that steel on down, down, down!
10   Whop that steel on down."

John Henry told his captain
"A man ain't nothin' but a man
But before I let your steam drill beat me down
I'll die with a hammer in my hand, Lord, Lord!
15   I'll die with a hammer in my hand."

John Henry said to his Shaker
"Shaker, why don't you sing?
I'm throwin' 30 lbs. from my hips on down
Just listen to that cold steel ring, Lord, Lord!
20   Listen to that cold steel ring."

John Henry said to his Shaker
"Shaker, you'd better pray
'Cause if I miss that little piece of steel

Tomorrow be your buryin' day! Lord, Lord!
25 Tomorrow be your buryin' day."

The Shaker said to John Henry
"I think this mountain's cavin' in!"
John Henry said to his Shaker, "Man
That ain't nothin' but my hammer suckin' wind! Lord, Lord!
30 Nothin' but my hammer suckin' wind."

The man that invented the steam drill
Thought he was mighty fine
But John Henry made 15 ft.
The steam drill only made nine, Lord, Lord!
35 The steam drill only made nine.

John Henry hammered in the mountain
His hammer was striking fire
But he worked so hard, he broke his poor heart
He laid down his hammer and he died, Lord, Lord,
40 Laid down his hammer and he died.

John Henry had a little woman
Her name was Polly Ann
John Henry took sick & went to his bed
Polly Ann drove steel like a man, Lord, Lord!
45 Polly Ann drove steel like a man.

John Henry had a little baby
You could hold him in the palm of your hand
The last words I heard that poor boy say
"My daddy was a steel-driving man, Lord, Lord!
50 My daddy was a steel-driving man."

They took John Henry to the graveyard
And they buried him in the sand
And every locomotive comes a-roaring by
Says "There lies a steel-driving man, Lord, Lord!
55 There lies a steel-driving man."

Well every Monday morning
When the bluebirds begin to sing
You can hear John Henry a mile or more
You can hear John Henry's hammer ring, Lord, Lord!
60 You can hear John Henry's hammer ring.

III

Beneath the Gilded Surface: Working-Class Fictions and Realities, 1860s–1890s

> Remember that your future position
> depends mainly upon yourself, and that it
> will be high or low as you choose to make it.
> *Horatio Alger,* Ragged Dick *(1868)*

The name Horatio Alger has come to signify an ideology and literary motif of individual progress: strive and with some "luck and pluck," you will succeed.[1] The writer Horatio Alger, author of *Ragged Dick* (1868) and about a hundred other formulaic "stories for boys," offered a bourgeois model of thrift, honesty, and the postponement of pleasure for the gain of a respectable middle-class life.[2] Genuinely sympathetic to the plight of neglected and abandoned children in New York's streets and alleys, he presents a sanitized version of these "street arabs," later depicted more naturalistically in the words and photographs of Jacob Riis in *How the Other Half Lives* (1890). Implicit in Alger's model is the possibility, even promise, of class mobility within a dynamic and fluid capitalistic economy. Not revealed in his postbellum stories of ragged Dick's "making it" are the forces inhibiting mobility and the huge disparities of wealth and power in what Mark Twain called "The Gilded Age."

The literature in this section offers a view of the Gilded Age from the perspective of workers whose actual lives belie the easy possibility of Alger's ascension narrative. Realistic accounts of unemployed men, indebted farmers, and dehumanized industrial workers can be read in relation to significant labor movements to improve conditions for workers and to salvage an ethos of liberty and societal well-being. These movements were forged—not through luck and pluck, but through alliances with other workers as they struggled to understand and attempted to resist the full weight of the powers that were aligned against them.

This section spans four transformative decades in American history. It was a time of enormous shifts, migrations, upheavals, and problematic advances in technology. Between 1860 and 1890, 10 million immigrants, primarily from the British Isles, Germany, and Scandinavia, arrived in the United States.[3] Many of these immigrants settled in already overcrowded tenements in rapidly expanding northern cities. No longer primarily an agrarian nation, the United States was transformed by the forces of urbanization and industrialization and the power of capital and corporations. Manufacturing doubled from 1860 to 1890.[4] By 1880, America had become the world's number one industrial nation. The expansion of railroads had a wide-ranging catalytic effect. Material goods could be moved more swiftly and widely. Coal mining and iron and steel production accelerated.

Facing Page: Grand demonstration of workingmen, Sept. 5, 1882—NYC—procession passing the reviewing stand at Union Square, *Frank Leslie's Illustrated Newspaper. Courtesy of Library of Congress, LC-USZ62-83164.*

Native Americans fought and lost their battles to retain their own land. The West was settled, and the western frontier officially ceased to exist in 1890. And increasingly, the disparities of wealth between the owning "robber barons" and the laborers who produced the goods, mined the coal, farmed the fields, and poured the molten steel belied the Jeffersonian ideal of American democracy.

Organized labor challenged the new industrial order. Nearly 300,000 workers were represented by unions in 1872 and more than 700,000 in 1886.[5] According to historian Leon Fink, "the American working class—in terms of organization, militancy, and collective self-consciousness—appeared more advanced than its European counterparts."[6] The songs and documentary materials that are included here—on the Knights of Labor, the eight-hour-day movement, the militant words of Lucy Parsons to the jobless men who were forced to leave home and "tramp" for work, and the iconic Battle of Homestead— dramatize some of labor's collective efforts during the Gilded Age to turn "the plowshares of a consensual political past into a sword of class conflict" (Fink 4). It is not an exaggeration to use the language of war and battle to describe the upheaval and struggle of labor against capital during this period of ruthless exploitation.

In the South, the immediate postwar period of Reconstruction extended political and civil rights for emancipated blacks, but also improved conditions for the white working class. That period ended in 1876 with the withdrawal of federal troops, opening the door for the Ku Klux Klan to increase its terrorism and for the expanded use of convict labor, the rolling back of public education, and the restoration of the power of the southern owning class. Legal intimidation through the passage of Jim Crow segregation laws in the 1880s and 1890s and illegal vigilantism of mob violence and lynching propagated a structural racism that thwarted any Horatio Alger ascendancy for blacks.

Memoir and autobiography enrich the historical record and give contemporary readers insight into the daily lives of people who lived during this period. The life stories of the anonymous "Georgia Negro Peon" and "Negro Nurse," although published after the turn of the twentieth century, give flesh and blood to the abstractions of facts and dates in the aftermath of Reconstruction. James Williams's account of his life as a coastal seaman and union organizer offers an alternative story of possible class solidarity despite institutional and structural racism.

Literary realism intersects with industrial change in Rebecca Harding Davis's prescient novella, *Life in the Iron Mills*. Harding Davis's narrative—written for a middle-class audience —sets the stage for the industrial novels of social realism that would follow decades later. Harding Davis asks her readers to smell, hear, and see, not just the industrial landscape, but the human workers who are more than cogs, who have their own needs for beauty, love, and creative expression. It is a story of critical exposure by a sympathetic outsider. In a similar vein, Stephen Crane's impressionistic "The Men in the Storm" and Hamlin Garland's rural "Under the Lion's Paw" take readers to the underside of the Horatio Alger ascension narratives. Edwin Markham's famous poem "The Man with the Hoe" offers a sympathetic but objectified portrait of a rural laborer, a "thing" beaten down and without subjectivity.

Reading working-class literature involves a consciousness of the peripheral in relation to the status quo. Many of the works that are included in this collection challenge assumptions about what is at the center of American culture. The excerpt from Maxine Hong Kingston's genre-bending *China Men* is an imaginatively autobiographical and historical reconstruction of the lives of the Chinese men who performed the most dangerous work in building the Western railroads during the 1860s and 1870s. Hong Kingston centers Chinese men as essential builders of America. Chinese immigrant laborers were perceived as efficient laborers by railroad managers and as alien threats to their livelihoods by most workers and unions; they were driven out and officially excluded after the railroads were completed. Yet, the Chinese continued to claim America in the decades that followed. The selections from the many poems that were etched on the walls of the West Coast immigration station "Angel Island" document not just the obstacles and racism that Chinese immigrants faced, but also the immigrants' personal longings, desires, and insistence that they were more than just numerical categories. They and the diverse voices in this section insist that the promise of America can and should be claimed by all others as well.

Notes

1. Laura Hapke, *Labor's Text: The Worker in American Fiction* (New Brunswick, NJ: Rutgers University Press), 5, 48.

2. Alan Trachtenberg, "Introduction," Horatio Alger, Jr., *Ragged Dick Or, Street Life in New York with the Boot-blacks* (1868; New York: Signet Classic/Penguin, 1990), v–xx.

3. David M. Katzman and William M. Tuttle, Jr., "Introduction," *Plain Folk: The Life Stories of Undistinguished Americans* (Urbana: University of Illinois Press, 1982), xiii.

4. Bruce Levin et al., *Who Built America, Vol. 1* (New York: Pantheon Books, 1989), 523.

5. Philip Yale Nicholson, *Labor's Story in the United States* (Philadelphia: Temple University Press, 2004), 103.

6. Leon Fink, *Workingmen's Democracy: The Knights of Labor and American Politics* (Urbana: University of Illinois Press, 1983), 5.

Civil War, Reconstruction, Gilded Age

Rebecca Harding Davis (1831–1910)   *1861*

Strength, solidarity, and survival

A pivotal figure in the history of working-class literature, Rebecca Harding Davis observed the smoky industrial landscape of ironworks and the procession of workers in and out of the mill from her parents' home in Wheeling, Virginia (later West Virginia). She was thirty years old, unmarried, and a dutiful daughter to her successful, conservative father when her novella, *Life in the Iron Mills* was published in the prestigious *Atlantic Monthly* in 1861. It was "an instant sensation" and a "literary landmark," according to Tillie Olsen, whose recovery of the text led to its republication in 1972 by the Feminist Press. Rebecca Harding wrote directly to her middle-class readers, challenging them to "hide [their] disgust" and descend with her into an industrial reality, the "thickest of the fog and mud and foul effluvia." For her imaginative leap into the world of "furnace-hands," she won not only her first earnings as a professional writer, but the attention and respect of the most prominent New England authors of her day, especially Nathaniel Hawthorne. In her long career, she wrote hundreds of journalistic articles, short stories, children's stories, editorials, several novels, and an autobiography, often compromising her artistic aspirations because of the exigencies of sustaining a middle-class life for her husband L. Clarke Davis, a lawyer and journalist, and their three children. Her life was circumscribed by the societal restrictions on women, the necessary caring for young children, and by the constraints that were imposed by her middle-class audience. She advised her son Richard, who would later become a famous journalist: "I've had 30 years experience and I know how much depends on the articles suiting the present needs of the magazine, and also on the mood of the editor. . . . Develop . . . your keen sympathy with all kinds of people" (quoted by Tillie Olsen).

strength
solidarity
survival

LIFE IN THE IRON-MILLS

"Is this the end?
O Life, as futile, then, as frail!
What hope of answer or redress?"[1]

A cloudy day: do you know what that is in a town of iron-works? The sky sank down before dawn, muddy, flat, immovable. The air is thick, clammy with the breath of crowded human beings. I open the window, and, looking out, can scarcely see through the rain the grocer's shop opposite, where a crowd of drunken Irishmen are puffing Lynchburg[2] tobacco in their pipes. I can detect the scent through all the foul smells ranging loose in the air.

characteristic

The idiosyncrasy of this town is smoke. It rolls sullenly in slow folds from the great chimneys of the iron-foundries, and settles down in black, slimy pools on the muddy streets. Smoke on the wharves, smoke on the dingy boats, on the yellow river,—clinging in a coating of greasy soot to the house-front, the two faded poplars, the faces of the passers-by. The long train of mules, dragging masses of pig-iron through the narrow street, have a foul vapor hanging to their reeking sides. Here, inside, is a little broken figure of an' angel pointing upward from the mantel-shelf; but even its wings are covered with smoke, clotted and black. Smoke everywhere! A dirty canary chirps desolately in a cage beside me. Its dream of green fields and sunshine is a very old dream—almost worn, out, I think.

From the back-window I can see a narrow brick-yard sloping down to the river-side, strewed with rain-butts and tubs. The river, dull and tawny-colored, (*la bella rivière!*) drags itself sluggishly along, tired of the heavy weight of boats and coal-barges. What wonder? When I was a child, I used to fancy a look of weary, dumb appeal upon the face of the negro-like river slavishly bearing its burden day after day. Something of the same idle notion comes to me to-day, when from the street-window I look on the slow stream of human life creeping past, night and morning, to the great mills. Masses of men, with dull, besotted faces bent to the ground, sharpened here and there by pain or cunning; skin and muscle and flesh begrimed with smoke and ashes; stooping all night over boiling cauldrons of metal, laired by day in dens of drunkenness and infamy; breathing from infancy to death an air saturated with fog and grease and soot, vileness for soul and body. What do you make of a case like that, amateur psychologist? You call it an altogether serious thing to be alive: to these men it is a drunken jest, a joke,—horrible to angels perhaps, to them common-place enough. My fancy about the river was an idle one: it is no type of such a life. What if it be stagnant and slimy here? It knows that beyond there waits for it odorous sunlight,— quaint old gardens, dusky with soft, green foliage of apple-trees, and flushing crimson with roses,—air, and fields, and mountains. The future of the Welsh puddler[3] passing just now is not so pleasant. To be stowed away, after his grimy work is done, in a hole in the muddy graveyard, and after that,—*not* air, nor green fields, nor curious roses.

---

[1] "*Is this . . . redress?*": The second and third lines of Davis's epigraph are from Alfred, Lord Tennyson's *In Memoriam* 56.25–27. The first line is Davis's own. [Unless identified otherwise, all footnotes were written by Cecelia Tichi, editor of The Bedford Cultural Edition of *Life in the Iron Mills* (Boston: Bedford/St. Martins, 1998). Reprinted with permission.]

[2] *Lynchburg*: City in Virginia known for its production of tobacco.

[3] *puddler*: A worker who converts pig iron into wrought iron or steel by *puddling*—that is, by subjecting the metal to heat and stirring it in a furnace.

Can you see how foggy the day is? As I stand here, idly tapping the window-pane, and looking out through the rain at the dirty back-yard and the coal-boats below, fragments of an old story float up before me,—a story of this old house into which I happened to come to-day. You may think it a tiresome story enough, as foggy as the day, sharpened by no sudden flashes of pain or pleasure.—I know: only the outline of a dull life, that long since, with thousands of dull lives like its own, was vainly lived and lost: thousands of them,—massed, vile, slimy lives, like those of the torpid lizards in yonder stagnant water-butt.—Lost? There is a curious point for you to settle, my friend, who study psychology in a lazy, *dilettante*[4] way. Stop a moment. I am going to be honest. This is what I want you to do. I want you to hide your disgust, take no heed to your clean clothes, and come right down with me,—here, into the thickest of the fog and mud and foul effluvia. I want you to hear this story. There is a secret down here, in this nightmare fog, that has lain dumb for centuries: I want to make it a real thing to you. You, Egoist, or Pantheist, or Arminian,[5] busy in making straight paths for your feet on the hills, do not see it clearly,—this terrible question which men here have gone mad and died trying to answer. I dare not put this secret into words. I told you it was dumb. These men, going by with drunken faces and brains full of unawakened power, do not ask it of Society or of God. Their lives ask it; their deaths ask it. There is no reply. I will tell you plainly that I have a great hope; and I bring it to you to be tested. It is this: that this terrible dumb question is its own reply; that it is not the sentence of death we think it, but, from the very extremity of its darkness, the most solemn prophecy which the world has known of the Hope to come. I dare make my meaning no clearer, but will only tell my story. It will, perhaps, seem to you as foul and dark as this thick vapor about us, and as pregnant with death; but if your eyes are free as mine are to look deeper, no perfume-tinted dawn will be so fair with promise of the day that shall surely come.

My story is very simple,—only what I remember of the life of one of these men,—a furnace-tender in one of Kirby & John's rolling-mills,[6]—Hugh Wolfe. You know the mills? They took the great order for the Lower Virginia railroads there last winter; run usually with about a thousand men. I cannot tell why I choose the half-forgotten story of this Wolfe more than that of myriads of these furnace-hands. Perhaps because there is a secret underlying sympathy between that story and this day with its impure fog and thwarted sunshine,—or perhaps simply for the reason that this house is the one where the Wolfes lived. There were the father and son,—both hands, as I said, in one of Kirby & John's mills for making railroad-iron,—and Deborah, their cousin, a picker in some of the cotton-mills. The house was rented then to half a dozen families. The Wolfes had two of the cellar-rooms. The old man, like many of the puddlers and feeders of the mills, was Welsh,—had

---

[4] *dilettante*: From the Italian verb *dilettare*, which means "to take delight in," a dilettante is a person who appreciates or loves the fine arts; the term, however, is often used disparagingly, since a dilettante tends to dabble in art, usually viewing it as one pastime among many rather than as a subject for serious or rigorous analysis.

[5] *Egoist . . . Arminian*: Not to be confused with egotists, who focus on themselves and their own worth, *egoists* assert that good can be found by pursuing self-interest; that is, for an egoist, the improvement of a person's welfare will lead to an ultimate sense of perfection and happiness. An adherent of *pantheism*, a doctrine popular with the English romantics, believes that God is everything and, conversely, that everything is God. *Arminians* belonged to a religious sect that began in Holland in the seventeenth century and then made its way to England and the American colonies. Unlike Calvinism, which it broke away from, Arminianism rejected the doctrine of absolute predestination as well as beliefs about the elect and the human will.

[6] *rolling-mills*: Mills producing iron rolled into sheets.

spent half of his life in the Cornish tin-mines.[7] You may pick the Welsh emigrants, Cornish miners, out of the throng passing the windows, any day. They are a trifle more filthy; their muscles are not so brawny; they stoop more. When they are drunk, they neither yell, nor shout, nor stagger, but skulk along like beaten hounds. A pure, unmixed blood, I fancy: shows itself in the slight angular bodies and sharply-cut facial lines. It is nearly thirty years since the Wolfes lived here. Their lives were like those of their class: incessant labor, sleeping in kennel-like rooms, eating rank pork and molasses, drinking—God and the distillers only know what; with an occasional night in jail, to atone for some drunken excess. Is that all of their lives?—of the portion given to them and these their duplicates swarming the streets to-day?—nothing beneath?—all? So many a political reformer will tell you,—and many a private reformer too, who has gone among them with a heart tender with Christ's charity, and come out outraged, hardened.

One rainy night, about eleven o'clock, a crowd of half-clothed women stopped outside of the cellar-door. They were going home from the cotton-mill.

"Good-night, Deb," said one, a mulatto, steadying herself against the gas-post. She needed the post to steady her. So did more than one of them.

"Dah's a ball to Miss Potts' to-night. Ye'd best come."

"Inteet, Deb, if hur'll[8] come, hur'll hef fun," said a shrill Welsh voice in the crowd.

Two or three dirty hands were thrust out to catch the gown of the woman, who was groping for the latch of the door.

"No."

"No? Where's Kit Small, then?"

"Begorra![9] on the spools. Alleys behint, though we helped her, we dud. An wid ye! Let Deb alone! It's ondacent frettin' a quite body. Be the powers, an' we'll have a night of it! there'll be lashin's o' drink,—the Vargent[10] be blessed and praised for't!"

They went on, the mulatto inclining for a moment to show fight, and drag the woman Wolfe off with them; but, being pacified, she staggered away.

Deborah groped her way into the cellar, and, after considerable stumbling, kindled a match, and lighted a tallow dip, that sent a yellow glimmer over the room. It was low, damp,—the earthen floor covered with a green, slimy moss,—a fetid air smothering the breath. Old Wolfe lay asleep on a heap of straw, wrapped in a torn horse-blanket. He was a pale, meek little man, with a white face and red rabbit-eyes. The woman Deborah was like him; only her face was even more ghastly, her lips bluer, her eyes more watery. She wore a faded cotton gown and a slouching bonnet. When she walked, one could see that she was deformed, almost a hunchback. She trod softly, so as not to waken him, and went through into the room beyond. There she found by the half-extinguished fire an iron saucepan filled with cold boiled potatoes, which she put upon a broken chair with a pint-cup of ale. Placing the old candlestick beside this dainty repast, she untied her bonnet, which hung limp and wet over her face, and prepared to eat her supper. It was the first food that had touched her lips since morning. There was enough of it, however: there is not always. She was hungry,—one could see that easily enough,—and not drunk, as most of her companions would have been found at this hour. She did not drink, this woman,— her face told that, too,—nothing stronger than ale. Perhaps the weak, flaccid wretch had

---

[7] *Cornish tin-mines*: That is, in Cornwall, a county in southwest England where much mining was done.

[8] *hur'll*: Dialectal pronoun used instead of *she, he, her,* and *him.*

[9] *Begorra*: Irish-English euphemism for "by God."

[10] *Vargent*: The Virgin Mary, mother of Jesus.

some stimulant in her pale life to keep her up,—some love or hope, it might be, or urgent need. When that stimulant was gone, she would take to whiskey. Man cannot live by work alone. While she was skinning the potatoes, and munching them, a noise behind her made her stop.

"Janey!" she called, lifting the candle and peering into the darkness. "Janey, are you there?"

A heap of ragged coats was heaved up, and the face of a young girl emerged, staring sleepily at the woman.

"Deborah," she said, at last, "I'm here the night."

"Yes, child. Hur's welcome," she said, quietly eating on.

The girl's face was haggard and sickly; her eyes were heavy with sleep and hunger: real Milesian[11] eyes they were, dark, delicate blue, glooming out from black shadows with a pitiful fright.

"I was alone," she said, timidly.

"Where's the father?" asked Deborah, holding out a potato, which the girl greedily seized.

"He's beyant,[12]—wid Haley,—in the stone house." (Did you ever hear the word *jail* from an Irish mouth?) "I came here. Hugh told me never to stay me-lone."[13]

"Hugh?"

"Yes."

A vexed frown crossed her face. The girl saw it, and added quickly,—

"I have not seen Hugh the day, Deb. The old man says his watch lasts till the mornin'."

The woman sprang up, and hastily began to arrange some bread and flitch[14] in a tin pail, and to pour her own measure of ale into a bottle. Tying on her bonnet, she blew out the candle.

"Lay ye down, Janey dear," she said, gently, covering her with the old rags. "Hur can eat the potatoes, if hur's hungry."

"Where are ye goin', Deb? The rain's sharp."

"To the mill, with Hugh's supper."

"Let him bide till-th' morn. Sit ye down."

"No, no,"—sharply pushing her off. "The boy'll starve."

She hurried from the cellar, while the child wearily coiled herself up for sleep. The rain was falling heavily, as the woman, pail in hand, emerged from the mouth of the alley, and turned down the narrow street, that stretched out, long and black, miles before her. Here and there a flicker of gas lighted an uncertain space of muddy footwalk and gutter; the long rows of houses, except an occasional lager-bier shop, were closed; now and then she met a band of mill-hands skulking to or from their work.

Not many even of the inhabitants of a manufacturing town know the vast machinery of system by which the bodies of workmen are governed, that goes un-ceasingly from year to year. The hands of each mill are divided into watches that relieve each other as regularly as the sentinels of an army. By night and day the work goes on, the unsleeping engines groan and shriek, the fiery pools of metal boil and surge. Only for a day in the week, a half-courtesy to public censure, the fires are partially veiled; but as soon as the clock strikes

---

11 *Milesian*: A synonym for *Irish*, *Milesian* refers to the followers and descendants of Miledh, who, according to the mythical history of Ireland, came from the East through Spain and into Ireland around 1,000 B.C.

12 *beyant*: Beyond.

13 *me-lone*: Alone.

14 *flitch*: Salted, cured pork; commonly, it refers to a side of bacon.

midnight, the great furnaces break forth with renewed fury, the clamor begins with fresh, breathless vigor, the engines sob and shriek like "gods in pain."

As Deborah hurried down through the heavy rain, the noise of these thousand engines sounded through the sleep and shadow of the city like far-off thunder. The mill to which she was going lay on the river, a mile below the city-limits. It was far, and she was weak, aching from standing twelve hours at the spools. Yet it was her almost nightly walk to take this man his supper, though at every square she sat down to rest, and she knew she should receive small word of thanks.

Perhaps, if she had possessed an artist's eye, the picturesque oddity of the scene might have made her step stagger less, and the path seem shorter; but to her the mills were only "summat deilish to look at by night."

The road leading to the mills had been quarried from the solid rock, which rose abrupt and bare on one side of the cinder-covered road, while the river, sluggish and black, crept past on the other. The mills for rolling iron are simply immense tent-like roofs, covering acres of ground, open on every side. Beneath these roofs Deborah looked in on a city of fires, that burned hot and fiercely in the night. Fire in every horrible form: pits of flame waving in the wind; liquid metal-flames writhing in tortuous streams through the sand; wide caldrons filled with boiling fire, over which bent ghastly wretches stirring the strange brewing; and through all, crowds of half-clad men, looking like revengeful ghosts in the red light, hurried, throwing masses of glittering fire. It was like a street in Hell. Even Deborah muttered, as she crept through, " 'T looks like t' Devil's place!" It did,—in more ways than one.

She found the man she was looking for, at last, heaping coal on a furnace. He had not time to eat his supper; so she went behind the furnace, and waited. Only a few men were with him, and they noticed her only by a "Hyur comes t' hunchback, Wolfe."

Deborah was stupid with sleep; her back pained her sharply; and her teeth chattered with cold, with the rain that soaked her clothes and dripped from her at every step. She stood, however, patiently holding the pail, and waiting.

"Hout,[15] woman! ye look like a drowned cat. Come near to the fire,"—said one of the men, approaching to scrape away the ashes.

She shook her head. Wolfe had forgotten her. He turned, hearing the man, and came closer.

"I did no' think; gi' me my supper, woman."

She watched him eat with a painful eagerness. With a woman's quick instinct, she saw that he was not hungry,—was eating to please her. Her pale, watery eyes began to gather a strange light.

"Is't good, Hugh? T'ale was a bit sour, I feared."

"No, good enough." He hesitated a moment. "Ye're tired, poor lass! Bide here till I go. Lay down there on that heap of ash, and go to sleep."

He threw her an old coat for a pillow, and turned to his work. The heap was the refuse of the burnt iron, and was not a hard bed; the half-smothered warmth, too, penetrated her limbs, dulling their pain and cold shiver.

Miserable enough she looked, lying there on the ashes like a limp, dirty rag,—yet not an unfitting figure to crown the scene of hopeless discomfort and veiled crime: more fitting, if one looked deeper into the heart of things,—at her thwarted woman's form, her colorless life, her waking stupor that smothered pain and hunger,—even more fit to be a type of her class. Deeper yet if one could look, was there nothing worth reading in this wet, faded thing, half-covered with ashes? no story of a soul filled with groping passionate

---

[15] *Hout*: Exclamatory greeting.

love, heroic unselfishness, fierce jealousy? of years of weary trying to please the one human being whom she loved, to gain one look of real heart-kindness from him? If anything like this were hidden beneath the pale, bleared eyes, and dull, washed-out-looking face, no one had ever taken the trouble to read its faint signs: not the half-clothed furnace-tender, Wolfe, certainly. Yet he was kind to her: it was his nature to be kind, even to the very rats that swarmed in the cellar: kind to her in just that same way. She knew that. And it might be that very knowledge had given to her face its apathy and vacancy more than her low, torpid life. One sees that dead, vacant look steal sometimes over the rarest, finest of women's faces,—in the very midst, it may be, of their warmest summer's day; and then one can guess at the secret of intolerable solitude that lies hid beneath the delicate laces and brilliant smile. There was no warmth, no brilliancy, no summer for this woman; so the stupor and vacancy had time to gnaw into her face perpetually. She was young, too, though no one guessed it; so the gnawing was the fiercer. *young but tired*

She lay quiet in the dark corner, listening, through the monotonous din and uncertain glare of the works, to the dull plash of the rain in the far distance,—shrinking back whenever the man Wolfe happened to look towards her. She knew, in spite of all his kindness, that there was that in her face and form which made him loathe the sight of her. She felt by instinct, although she could not comprehend it, the finer nature of the man, which made him among his fellow-workmen something unique, set apart. She knew, that, down under all the vileness and coarseness of his life, there was a groping passion for whatever was beautiful and pure,—that his soul sickened with disgust at her deformity, even when his words were kindest. Through this dull consciousness, which never left her, came, like a sting, the recollection of the little Irish girl she had left in the cellar. The recollection struck through even her stupid intellect with a vivid glow of beauty and grace. Little Janey, timid, helpless, clinging to Hugh as her only friend: that was the sharp thought, the bitter thought, that drove into the glazed eyes a fierce light of pain. You laugh at it? Are pain and jealousy less savage realities down here in this place I am taking you to than in your own house or your own heart,—your heart, which they clutch at sometimes? The note is the same, I fancy, be the octave high or low.

If you could go into this mill where Deborah lay, and drag out from the hearts of these men the terrible tragedy of their lives, taking it as a symptom of the disease of their class, no ghost Horror would terrify you more. A reality of soul-starvation, of living death, that meets you every day under the besotted faces on the street,—I can paint nothing of this, only give you the outside outlines of a night, a crisis in the life of one man: whatever muddy depth of soul-history lies beneath you can read according to the eyes God has given you.

Wolfe, while Deborah watched him as a spaniel its master, bent over the furnace with his iron pole, unconscious of her scrutiny, only stopping to receive orders. Physically, Nature had promised the man but little. He had already lost the strength and instinct vigor of a man, his muscles were thin, his nerves weak, his face (a meek, woman's face) haggard, yellow with consumption. In the mill he was known as one of the girl men: "Molly Wolfe" was his *sobriquet*.[16] He was never seen in the cockpit,[17] did not own a terrier, drank but seldom; when he did, desperately. He fought sometimes, but was always thrashed, pommelled to a jelly. The man was game enough, when his blood was up: but he was no favorite in the mill; he had the taint of school-learning on him,—not to a dangerous extent, only a quarter or so in the free-school[18] in fact, but enough to ruin him as a good hand in a fight. *description of Wolfe*

---

[16] *sobriquet*: "Nickname" (French).

[17] *cockpit*: Area where gamecocks fought and spectators wagered on the outcome.

[18] *free-school*: Public school.

For other reasons, too, he was not popular. Not one of themselves, they felt that, though outwardly as filthy and ash-covered; silent, with foreign thoughts and longings breaking out through his quietness in innumerable curious ways: this one, for instance. In the neighboring furnace-buildings lay great heaps of the refuse from the ore after the pig-metal is run. *Korl* we call it here: a light, porous substance, of a delicate, waxen, flesh-colored tinge. Out of the blocks of this korl, Wolfe, in his off-hours from the furnace, had a habit of chipping and moulding figures,—hideous, fantastic enough, but sometimes strangely beautiful: even the mill-men saw that, while they jeered at him. It was a curious fancy in the man, almost a passion. The few hours for rest he spent hewing and hacking with his blunt knife, never speaking, until his watch came again,—working at one figure for months, and, when it was finished, breaking it to pieces perhaps, in a fit of disappointment. A morbid, gloomy man, untaught, unled, left to feed his soul in grossness and crime, and hard, grinding labor.

I want you to come down and look at this Wolfe, standing there among the lowest of his kind, and see him just as he is, that you may judge him justly when you hear the story of this night. I want you to look back, as he does every day, at his birth in vice, his starved infancy; to remember the heavy years he has groped through as boy and man,—the slow, heavy years of constant, hot work. So long ago he began, that he thinks sometimes he has worked there for ages. There is no hope that it will ever end. Think that God put into this man's soul a fierce thirst for beauty,—to know it, to create it; to *be*—something, he knows not what,—other than he is. There are moments when a passing cloud, the sun glinting on the purple thistles, a kindly smile, a child's face, will rouse him to a passion of pain,—when his nature starts up with a mad cry of rage against God, man, whoever it is that has forced this vile, slimy life upon him. With all this groping, this mad desire, a great blind intellect stumbling through wrong, a loving poet's heart, the man was by habit only a coarse, vulgar laborer, familiar with sights and words you would blush to name. Be just: when I tell you about this night, see him as he is. Be just,—not like man's law, which seizes on one isolated fact, but like God's judging angel, whose clear, sad eye saw all the countless cankering days of this man's life, all the countless nights, when, sick with starving, his soul fainted in him, before it judged him for this night, the saddest of all.

I called this night the crisis of his life. If it was, it stole on him unawares. These great turning-days of life cast no shadow before, slip by unconsciously. Only a trifle, a little turn of the rudder, and the ship goes to heaven or hell.

Wolfe, while Deborah watched him, dug into the furnace of melting iron with his pole, dully thinking only how many rails the lump would yield. It was late,—nearly Sunday morning; another hour, and the heavy work would be done,—only the furnaces to replenish and cover for the next day. The workmen were growing more noisy, shouting, as they had to do, to be heard over the deep clamor of the mills. Suddenly they grew less boisterous,—at the far end, entirely silent. Something unusual had happened. After a moment, the silence came nearer; the men stopped their jeers and drunken choruses. Deborah, stupidly lifting up her head, saw the cause of the quiet. A group of five or six men were slowly approaching, stopping to examine each furnace as they came. Visitors often came to see the mills after night: except by growing less noisy, the men took no notice of them. The furnace where Wolfe worked was near the bounds of the works; they halted there hot and tired: a walk over one of these great foundries is no trifling task. The woman, drawing out of sight, turned over to sleep. Wolfe, seeing them stop, suddenly roused from his indifferent stupor, and watched them keenly. He knew some of them: the overseer, Clarke,—a son of Kirby, one of the mill-owners,—and a Doctor May, one of the town-physicians. The other two were strangers. Wolfe came closer. He seized eagerly every chance that brought him into contact with this mysterious class that shone down on him perpetually with the glamour of another order of being. What made the difference between them? That was the mystery of his life. He had a vague notion that perhaps to-night he could find it out. One of the strangers sat down on a pile of bricks, and beckoned young Kirby to his side.

"This *is* hot, with a vengeance. A match, please?"—lighting his cigar. "But the walk is worth the trouble. If it were not that you must have heard it so often, Kirby, I would tell you that your works look like Dante's Inferno."[19]

Kirby laughed.

"Yes. Yonder is Farinata[20] himself in the burning tomb,"—pointing to some figure in the shimmering shadows.

"Judging from some of the faces of your men," said the other, "they bid fair to try the reality of Dante's vision, some day."

Young Kirby looked curiously around, as if seeing the faces of his hands[21] for the first time.

"They're bad enough, that's true. A desperate set, I fancy. Eh, Clarke?"

The overseer did not hear him. He was talking of net profits just then,—giving, in fact, a schedule of the annual business of the firm to a sharp peering little Yankee, who jotted down notes on a paper laid on the crown of his hat: a reporter for one of the city-papers, getting up a series of reviews of the leading manufactories. The other gentlemen had accompanied them merely for amusement. They were silent until the notes were finished, drying their feet at the furnaces, and sheltering their faces from the intolerable heat. At last the overseer concluded with—

"I believe that is a pretty fair estimate, Captain."

"Here, some of you men!" said Kirby, "bring up those boards. We may as well sit down, gentlemen, until the rain is over. It cannot last much longer at this rate."

"Pig-metal,"—mumbled the reporter,—"um!—coal facilities,—um!—hands employed, twelve hundred,—bitumen,—um!—all right, I believe, Mr. Clarke;—sinking-fund,[22] —what did you say was your sinking-fund?"

"Twelve hundred hands?" said the stranger, the young man who had first spoken. "Do you control their votes,[23] Kirby?"

"Control? No." The young man smiled complacently. "But my father brought seven hundred votes to the polls for his candidate last November. No force-work, you understand,—only a speech or two, a hint to form themselves into a society, and a bit of red and blue bunting to make them a flag. The Invincible Roughs,—I believe that is their name. I forget the motto: 'Our country's hope,' I think."

---

19 *Dante's Inferno*: The Italian poet Dante Alighieri (1265–1321) is best known as the author of *The Divine Comedy*, an epic poem completed in 1321 and divided into three sections: *Inferno* ("hell"), *Purgatorio* ("purgatory"), and *Paradiso* ("paradise"). In the *Inferno*, the poet and his guide, the spirit of the classical poet Virgil, visit the nine levels of hell, which descend conically into the earth.

20 *Farinata*: In the sixth circle of hell (canto 10), Dante meets Farinata degli Uberti, a famous Florentine patriot whose family was an enemy of Dante's people, the Guelfs. After Farinata discusses his role in Florentine politics and explains how people in hell can see the future without understanding the present, Dante leaves with a new respect for his enemy.

21 *hands*: Common term for workers in the nineteenth century.

22 *coal facilities . . . sinking-fund*: Mill visitors' language of capitalist control of finance and production. *Bitumen* refers to coal, *sinking-fund* to sums set aside and invested, at interest, to pay debt and meet depreciation expenses.

23 *control their votes*: Vote control refers to efforts of business capitalists to designate political candidates favorable to their interests and, through bribes and threats, to control the outcome of elections.

There was a laugh. The young man talking to Kirby sat with an amused light in his cool gray eye, surveying critically the half-clothed figures of the puddlers, and the slow swing of their brawny muscles. He was a stranger in the city,—spending a couple of months in the borders of a Slave State,[24] to study the institutions of the South,—a brother-in-law of Kirby's,—Mitchell. He was an amateur gymnast,—hence his anatomical eye; a patron, in a *blasé* way, of the prize-ring; a man who sucked the essence out of a science or philosophy in an indifferent, gentlemanly way; who took Kant, Novalis, Humboldt,[25] for what they were worth in his own scales; accepting all, despising nothing, in heaven, earth, or hell, but one-idead men; with a temper yielding and brilliant as summer water, until his Self was touched, when it was ice, though brilliant still. Such men are not rare in the States.

As he knocked the ashes from his cigar, Wolfe caught with a quick pleasure the contour of the white hand, the blood-glow of a red ring he wore. His voice, too, and that of Kirby's, touched him like music,—low, even, with chording cadences. About this man Mitchell hung the impalpable atmosphere belonging to the thorough-bred gentleman. Wolfe, scraping away the ashes beside him, was conscious of it, did obeisance to it with his artist sense, unconscious that he did so.

The rain did not cease. Clarke and the reporter left the mills; the others, comfortably seated near the furnace, lingered, smoking and talking in a desultory way. Greek would not have been more unintelligible to the furnace-tenders, whose presence they soon forgot entirely. Kirby drew out a newspaper from his pocket and read aloud some article, which they discussed eagerly. At every sentence, Wolfe listened more and more like a dumb, hopeless animal, with a duller, more stolid look creeping over his face, glancing now and then at Mitchell, marking acutely every smallest sign of refinement, then back to himself, seeing as in a mirror his filthy body, his more stained soul.

Never! He had no words for such a thought, but he knew now, in all the sharpness of the bitter certainty, that between them there was a great gulf never to be passed. Never!

The bell of the mills rang for midnight. Sunday morning had dawned. Whatever hidden message lay in the tolling bells floated past these men unknown. Yet it was there. Veiled in the solemn music ushering the risen Saviour was a key-note to solve the darkest secrets of a world gone wrong,—even this social riddle which the brain of the grimy puddler grappled with madly to-night.

The men began to withdraw the metal from the caldrons. The mills were deserted on Sundays, except by the hands who fed the fires, and those who had no lodgings and slept usually on the ash-heaps. The three strangers sat still during the next hour, watching the men cover the furnaces, laughing now and then at some jest of Kirby's.

"Do you know," said Mitchell, "I like this view of the works better than when the glare was fiercest? These heavy shadows and the amphitheatre of smothered fires are ghostly, unreal. One could fancy these red smouldering lights to be the half-shut eyes of wild beasts, and the spectral figures their victims in the den."

---

[24] *borders of a Slave State*: Wheeling, once part of Virginia, a slave state, bordered the free states of Ohio and Pennsylvania.

[25] *Kant, Novalis, Humboldt*: The German philosopher Immanuel Kant (1724–1804) explored rational understanding in his *Critique of Pure Reason*, *Critique of Practical Reason*, and *Critique of Judgment*. Novalis, the pen name of Friedrich von Hardenberg (1762–1801), was a novelist and leading poet of early German romanticism who believed in the mystical oneness of all things. Baron Alexander von Humboldt (1769–1859), a German naturalist and explorer, traveled throughout Latin America and studied its geography and meteorology; in *Kosmos*, his principal work, he described the physical universe.

Kirby laughed. "You are fanciful. Come, let us get out of the den. The spectral figures, as you call them, are a little too real for me to fancy a close proximity in the darkness,—unarmed, too."

The others rose, buttoning their overcoats, and lighting cigars.

"Raining, still," said Doctor May, "and hard. Where did we leave the coach, Mitchell?"

"At the other side of the works.—Kirby, what's that?"

Mitchell started back, half-frightened, as, suddenly turning a corner, the white figure of a woman faced him in the darkness,—a woman, white, of giant proportions, crouching on the ground, her arms flung out in some wild gesture of warning.

"Stop! Make that fire burn there!" cried Kirby, stopping short.

The flame burst out, flashing the gaunt figure into bold relief.

Mitchell drew a long breath.

"I thought it was alive," he said, going up curiously.

The others followed.

"Not marble, eh?" asked Kirby, touching it.

One of the lower overseers stopped.

"Korl, Sir."

"Who did it?"

"Can't say. Some of the hands; chipped it out in off-hours."

"Chipped to some purpose, I should say. What a flesh-tint the stuff has! Do you see, Mitchell?"

"I see."

He had stepped aside where the light fell boldest on the figure, looking at it in silence. There was not one line of beauty or grace in it: a nude woman's form, muscular, grown coarse with labor, the powerful limbs instinct with some one poignant longing. One idea: there it was in the tense, rigid muscles, the clutching hands, the wild, eager face, like that of a starving wolf's. Kirby and Doctor May walked around it, critical, curious. Mitchell stood aloof, silent. The figure touched him strangely.

"Not badly done," said Doctor May. "Where did the fellow learn that sweep of the muscles in the arm and hand? Look at them! They are groping,—do you see?—clutching: the peculiar action of a man dying of thirst."

"They have ample facilities for studying anatomy," sneered Kirby, glancing at the half-naked figures.

"Look," continued the Doctor, "at this bony wrist, and the strained sinews of the instep! A working-woman,—the very type of her class."

"God forbid!" muttered Mitchell.

"Why?" demanded May. "What does the fellow intend by the figure? I cannot catch the meaning."

"Ask him," said the other, dryly. "There he stands,"—pointing to Wolfe, who stood with a group of men, leaning on his ash-rake.

The Doctor beckoned him with the affable smile which kindhearted men put on, when talking to these people.

"Mr. Mitchell has picked you out as the man who did this,—I'm sure I don't know why. But what did you mean by it?"

"She be hungry."

Wolfe's eyes answered Mitchell, not the Doctor.

"Oh-h! But what a mistake you have made, my fine fellow! You have given no sign of starvation to the body. It is strong,—terribly strong. It has the mad, half-despairing gesture of drowning."

Wolfe stammered, glanced appealingly at Mitchell, who saw the soul of the thing, he knew. But the cool, probing eyes were turned on himself now,—mocking, cruel, relentless.

"Not hungry for meat," the furnace-tender said at last.

"What then? Whiskey?" jeered Kirby, with a coarse laugh.

Wolfe was silent a moment, thinking.

"I dunno," he said, with a bewildered look. "It mebbe. Summat to make her live, I think,—like you. Whiskey ull do it, in a way."

The young man laughed again. Mitchell flashed a look of disgust somewhere,—not at Wolfe.

"May," he broke out impatiently, "are you blind? Look at that woman's face! It asks questions of God, and says 'I have a right to know.' Good God, how hungry it is!"

They looked a moment; then May turned to the mill-owner:—

"Have you many such hands as this? What are you going to do with them? Keep them at puddling iron?"

Kirby shrugged his shoulders. Mitchell's look had irritated him.

"*Ce n'est pas mon affaire.*[26] I have no fancy for nursing infant geniuses. I suppose there are some stray gleams of mind and soul among these wretches. The Lord will take care of his own; or else they can work out their own salvation. I have heard you call our American system a ladder which any man can scale. Do you doubt it? Or perhaps you want to banish all social ladders, and put us all on a flat table-land,—eh, May?"

The Doctor looked vexed, puzzled. Some terrible problem lay hid in this woman's face, and troubled these men. Kirby waited for an answer, and, receiving none, went on, warming with his subject.

"I tell you, there's something wrong that no talk of '*Liberté*' or '*Egalité*'[27] will do away. If I had the making of men, these men who do the lowest part of the world's work should be machines,—nothing more,—hands. It would be kindness. God help them! What are taste, reason, to creatures who must live such lives as that?" He pointed to Deborah, sleeping on the ash-heap. "So many nerves to sting them to pain. What if God had put your brain, with all its agony of touch, into your fingers, and bid you work and strike with that?"

"You think you could govern the world better?" laughed the Doctor.

"I do not think at all."

"That is true philosophy. Drift with the stream, because you cannot dive deep enough to find bottom, eh?"

"Exactly," rejoined Kirby. "I do not think. I wash my hands of all social problems,— slavery, caste, white or black. My duty to my operatives has a narrow limit,—the pay-hour on Saturday night. Outside of that, if they cut korl, or cut each other's throats, (the more popular amusement of the two,) I am not responsible."

The Doctor sighed,—a good honest sigh, from the depths of his stomach.

"God help us! Who is responsible?"

"Not I, I tell you," said Kirby, testily. "What has the man who pays them money to do with their souls' concerns, more than the grocer or butcher who takes it?"

"And yet," said Mitchell's cynical voice, "look at her! How hungry she is!"

Kirby tapped his boot with his cane. No one spoke. Only the dumb face of the rough image looking into their faces with the awful question, "What shall we do to be saved?" Only Wolfe's face, with its heavy weight of brain, its weak, uncertain mouth, its desperate eyes, out of which looked the soul of his class,—only Wolfe's face turned towards Kirby's. Mitchell laughed,—a cool, musical laugh.

---

[26] *Ce n'est pas mon affaire*: "It's not my concern" or "it's none of my business" (French).

[27] "*Liberté*" or "*Egalité*": "Liberté, égalité, fraternité" ("liberty, equality, fraternity") was the motto of the French Revolution.

"Money has spoken!" he said, seating himself lightly on a stone with the air of an amused spectator at a play. "Are you answered?"—turning to Wolfe his clear, magnetic face.

Bright and deep and cold as Arctic air, the soul of the man lay tranquil beneath. He looked at the furnace-tender as he had looked at a rare mosaic in the morning; only the man was the more amusing study of the two.

"Are you answered? Why, May, look at him! '*De profundis clamavi.*'[28] Or, to quote in English, 'Hungry and thirsty, his soul faints in him.' And so Money sends back its answer into the depths through you, Kirby! Very clear the answer, too!—I think I remember reading the same words somewhere:—washing your hands in Eau de Cologne, and saying, 'I am innocent of the blood of this man. See ye to it!'"[29]

Kirby flushed angrily.

"You quote Scripture freely."

"Do I not quote correctly? I think I remember another line, which may amend my meaning: 'Inasmuch as ye did it unto one of the least of these, ye did it unto me.' Deist?[30] Bless you, man, I was raised on the milk of the Word. Now, Doctor, the pocket of the world having uttered its voice, what has the heart to say? You are a philanthropist, in a small way,—*n'est ce pas?*[31] Here, boy, this gentleman can show you how to cut korl better,—or your destiny. Go on, May!"

"I think a mocking devil possesses you to-night," rejoined the Doctor, seriously.

He went to Wolfe and put his hand kindly on his arm. Something of a vague idea possessed the Doctor's brain that much good was to be done here by a friendly word or two: a latent genius to be warmed into life by a waited-for sunbeam. Here it was: he had brought it. So he went on complacently:—

"Do you know, boy, you have it in you to be a great sculptor, a great man?—do you understand?" (talking down to the capacity of his hearer: it is a way people have with children, and men like Wolfe,)—"to live a better, stronger life than I, or Mr. Kirby here? A man may make himself anything he chooses. God has given you stronger powers than many men,—me, for instance."

May stopped, heated, glowing with his own magnanimity. And it was magnanimous. The puddler had drunk in every word, looking through the Doctor's flurry, and generous heat, and self-approval, into his will, with those slow, absorbing eyes of his.

"Make yourself what you will. It is your right."

"I know," quietly. "Will you help me?"

Mitchell laughed again. The Doctor turned now, in a passion,—

"You know, Mitchell, I have not the means. You know, if I had, it is in my heart to take this boy and educate him for"——

"The glory of God, and the glory of John May."

May did not speak for a moment; then, controlled, he said,—

"Why should one be raised, when myriads are left?—I have not the money, boy," to Wolfe, shortly.

---

28 "*De profundis clamavi*": "We shout out of the deep" (Latin version of Psalm 130:1). Thus, a bitter, wretched cry for help.

29 "*I am innocent. . . . See ye to it!*": A reference to the words of Pontius Pilate, the Roman procurator of Judea (ca. 26–36 A.D.) who allowed Christ to be crucified but would not accept responsibility for his actions. See Matthew 27:24.

30 *Deist*: Deists believe in a personal God and base their religion on reason, not revelation; Deism emerged as a result of the burgeoning interest in science that started in the Renaissance and lasted into the eighteenth century.

31 *n'est ce pas?*: "Isn't it so?" (French).

"Money?" He said it over slowly, as one repeats the guessed answer to a riddle, doubt-fully. "That is it? Money?"

"Yes, money,—that is it," said Mitchell, rising, and drawing his furred coat about him. "You've found the cure for all the world's diseases.—Come, May, find your good-humor, and come home. This damp wind chills my very bones. Come and preach your Saint-Simonian[32] doctrines to-morrow to Kirby's hands. Let them have a clear idea of the rights of the soul, and I'll venture next week they'll strike for higher wages. That will be the end of it."

"Will you send the coach-driver to this side of the mills?" asked Kirby, turning to Wolfe.

He spoke kindly: it was his habit to do so. Deborah, seeing the puddler go, crept after him. The three men waited outside. Doctor May walked up and down, chafed. Suddenly he stopped.

"Go back, Mitchell! You say the pocket and the heart of the world speak without meaning to these people. What has its head to say? Taste, culture, refinement? Go!"

Mitchell was leaning against a brick wall. He turned his head indolently, and looked into the mills. There hung about the place a thick, unclean odor. The slightest motion of his hand marked that he perceived it, and his insufferable disgust. That was all. May said nothing, only quickened his angry tramp.

"Besides," added Mitchell, giving a corollary to his answer, "it would be of no use. I am not one of them."

"You do not mean"—said May, facing him.

"Yes, I mean just that. Reform is born of need, not pity. No vital movement of the people's has worked down, for good or evil; fermented, instead, carried up the heaving, cloggy mass. Think back through history, and you will know it. What will this lowest deep—thieves, Magdalens,[33] negroes—do with the light filtered through ponderous Church creeds, Baconian theories, Goethe schemes?[34] Some day, out of their bitter need will be thrown up their own light-bringer,—their Jean Paul, their Cromwell,[35] their Messiah."

"Bah!" was the Doctor's inward criticism. However, in practice, he adopted the theory; for, when, night and morning, afterwards, he prayed that power might be given these degraded souls to rise, he glowed at heart, recognizing an accomplished duty.

Wolfe and the woman had stood in the shadow of the works as the coach drove off. The Doctor had held out his hand in a frank, generous way, telling him to "take care of

---

[32] *Saint-Simonian*: The Saint-Simonians based their protosocialist movement on the writings of the French social philosopher Claude Henry de Rouvroy, comte de Saint-Simon (1760–1825). In a series of lectures published from 1828 to 1830, the Saint-Simonians called for public control of the means of production and an end to individual inheritance.

[33] *Magdalens*: Prostitutes or reformed prostitutes; the name refers to Mary Magdalene, a follower of Christ who may have been a prostitute.

[34] *Baconian theories, Goethe schemes*: Sir Francis Bacon (1561–1626), English philosopher, statesman, and essayist who stressed the importance of developing a systemic way of amassing empirical knowl-edge about the natural world; Johann Wolf-gang von Goethe (1749–1832), German poet, playwright, and novelist who was perhaps the greatest figure of the German romantic period.

[35] *their Jean Paul, their Cromwell*: Jean Paul Marat (1743–1793), Swiss-born French politician and physician who participated in the French Revolution, first by publishing the paper *L'Ami du peuple* (*The Friend of the People*) and later by helping Danton and Robespierre overthrow the Girondists, a middle-class political party; Oliver Cromwell (1599–1658), English Puritan leader who dissolved Parliament in 1653 and became lord protector of England (1653–1658).

himself, and to remember it was his right to rise." Mitchell had simply touched his hat, as to an equal, with a quiet look of thorough recognition. Kirby had thrown Deborah some money, which she found, and clutched eagerly enough. They were gone now, all of them. The man sat down on the cinder-road, looking up into the murky sky.

"'T be late, Hugh. Wunnot hur come?"

He shook his head doggedly, and the woman crouched out of his sight against the wall. Do you remember rare moments when a sudden light flashed over yourself, your world, God? when you stood on a mountain-peak, seeing your life as it might have been, as it is? one quick instant, when custom lost its force and every-day usage? when your friend, wife, brother, stood in a new light? your soul was bared, and the grave,—a fore-taste of the nakedness of the Judgment-Day? So it came before him, his life, that night. The slow tides of pain he had borne gathered themselves up and surged against his soul. His squalid daily life, the brutal coarseness eating into his brain, as the ashes into his skin: before, these things had been a dull aching into his consciousness; to-night, they were reality. He griped[36] the filthy red shirt that clung, stiff with soot, about him, and tore it savagely from his arm. The flesh beneath was muddy with grease and ashes,—and the heart beneath that! And the soul? God knows.

Then flashed before his vivid poetic sense the man who had left him,—the pure face, the delicate, sinewy limbs, in harmony with all he knew of beauty or truth. In his cloudy fancy he had pictured a Something like this. He had found it in this Mitchell, even when he idly scoffed at his pain: a Man all-knowing, all-seeing, crowned by Nature, reigning,— the keen glance of his eye falling like a sceptre on other men. And yet his instinct taught him that he too—He! He looked at himself with sudden loathing, sick, wrung his hands with a cry, and then was silent. With all the phantoms of his heated, ignorant fancy, Wolfe had not been vague in his ambitions. They were practical, slowly built up before him out of his knowledge of what he could do. Through years he had day by day made this hope a real thing to himself,—a clear, projected figure of himself, as he might become.

Able to speak, to know what was best, to raise these men and women working at his side up with him: sometimes he forgot this defined hope in the frantic anguish to escape,— only to escape,—out of the wet, the pain, the ashes, somewhere, anywhere,—only for one moment of free air on a hill-side, to lie down and let his sick soul throb itself out in the sunshine. But to-night he panted for life. The savage strength of his nature was roused; his cry was fierce to God for justice.

"Look at me!" he said to Deborah, with a low, bitter laugh, striking his puny chest savagely. "What am I worth, Deb? Is it my fault that I am no better? My fault? My fault?"

He stopped, stung with a sudden remorse, seeing her hunchback shape writhing with sobs. For Deborah was crying thankless tears, according to the fashion of women.

"God forgi' me, woman! Things go harder wi' you nor me. It's a worse share."

He got up and helped her to rise; and they went doggedly down the muddy street, side by side.

"It's all wrong," he muttered, slowly,—"all wrong! I dunnot understan'. But it'll end some day."

"Come home, Hugh!" she said, coaxingly; for he had stopped, looking around bewildered.

"Home,—and back to the mill!" He went on saying this over to himself, as if he would mutter down every pain in this dull despair.

She followed him through the fog, her blue lips chattering with cold. They reached the cellar at last. Old Wolfe had been drinking since she went out, and had crept nearer

---

[36] *griped*: Gripped.

the door. The girl Janey slept heavily in the corner. He went up to her, touching softly the worn white arm with his fingers. Some bitterer thought stung him, as he stood there. He wiped the drops from his forehead, and went into the room beyond, livid, trembling. A hope, trifling, perhaps, but very dear, had died just then out of the poor peddler's life, as he looked at the sleeping, innocent girl,—some plan for the future, in which she had borne a part. He gave it up that moment, then and forever. Only a trifle, perhaps, to us: his face grew a shade paler,—that was all. But, somehow, the man's soul, as God and the angels looked down on it, never was the same afterwards.

Deborah followed him into the inner room. She carried a candle, which she placed on the floor, closing the door after her. She had seen the look on his face, as he turned away: her own grew deadly. Yet, as she came up to him, her eyes glowed. He was seated on an old chest, quiet, holding his face in his hands.

"Hugh!" she said, softly.

He did not speak.

"Hugh, did hur hear what the man said,—him with the clear voice? Did hur hear? Money, money,—that it wud do all?"

He pushed her away,—gently, but he was worn out; her rasping tone fretted him.

"Hugh!"

The candle flared a pale yellow light over the cobwebbed brick walls, and the woman standing there. He looked at her. She was young, in deadly earnest; her faded eyes, and wet, ragged figure caught from their frantic eagerness a power akin to beauty.

"Hugh, it is true! Money ull do it! Oh, Hugh, boy, listen till me! He said it true! It is money!"

"I know. Go back! I do not want you here."

"Hugh, it is t' last time. I'll never worrit[37] hur again."

There were tears in her voice now, but she choked them back.

"Hear till me only to-night! If one of t' witch people wud come, them we heard of t' home, and gif hur all hur wants, what then? Say, Hugh!"

"What do you mean?"

"I mean money."

Her whisper shrilled through his brain.

"If one of t' witch dwarfs wud come from t' lane moors to-night, and gif hur money, to go out,—out, I say,—out, lad, where t' sun shines, and t' heath grows, and t' ladies walk in silken gownds, and God stays all t' time,—where t' man lives that talked to us to-night, —Hugh knows,—Hugh could walk there like a king!"

He thought the woman mad, tried to check her, but she went on, fierce in her eager haste.

"If I were t' witch dwarf, if I had t' money, wud hur thank me? Wud hur take me out o' this place wid hur and Janey? I wud not come into the gran' house hur wud build, to vex hur wid t' hunch,—only at night, when t' shadows were dark, stand far off to see hur."

Mad? Yes! Are many of us mad in this way?

"Poor Deb! poor Deb!" he said, soothingly.

"It is here," she said, suddenly jerking into his hand a small roll. "I took it! I did it! Me, me!—not hur! I shall be hanged, I shall be burnt in hell, if anybody knows I took it! Out of his pocket, as he leaned against t' bricks. Hur knows?"

She thrust it into his hand, and then, her errand done, began to gather chips together to make a fire, choking down hysteric sobs.

"Has it come to this?"

---

[37] *worrit*: Worry.

That was all he said. The Welsh Wolfe blood was honest. The roll was a small green pocket-book containing one or two gold pieces, and a check for an incredible amount, as it seemed to the poor puddler. He laid it down, hiding his face again in his hands.

"Hugh, don't be angry wud me! It's only poor Deb,—hur knows?"

He took the long skinny fingers kindly in his.

"Angry? God help me, no! Let me sleep. I am tired."

He threw himself heavily down on the wooden bench, stunned with pain and weariness. She brought some old rags to cover him.

It was late on Sunday evening before he awoke. I tell God's truth, when I say he had then no thought of keeping this money. Deborah had hid it in his pocket. He found it there. She watched him eagerly, as he took it out.

"I must gif it to him," he said, reading her face.

"Hur knows," she said with a bitter sigh of disappointment. "But it is hur right to keep it."

His right! The word struck him. Doctor May had used the same. He washed himself, and went out to find this man Mitchell. His right! Why did this chance word cling to him so obstinately? Do you hear the fierce devils whisper in his ear, as he went slowly down the darkening street?

The evening came on, slow and calm. He seated himself at the end of an alley leading into one of the larger streets. His brain was clear to-night, keen, intent, mastering. It would not start back, cowardly, from any hellish temptation, but meet it face to face. Therefore the great temptation of his life came to him veiled by no sophistry, but bold, defiant, owning its own vile name, trusting to one bold blow for victory.

He did not deceive himself. Theft! That was it. At first the word sickened him; then he grappled with it. Sitting there on a broken cartwheel, the fading day, the noisy groups, the church-bells' tolling passed before him like a panorama,[38] while the sharp struggle went on within. This money! He took it out, and looked at it. If he gave it back, what then? He was going to be cool about it.

People going by to church saw only a sickly mill-boy watching them quietly at the alley's mouth. They did not know that he was mad, or they would not have gone by so quietly: mad with hunger; stretching out his hands to the world, that had given so much to them, for leave to live the life God meant him to live. His soul within him was smothering to death; he wanted so much, thought so much, and knew—nothing. There was nothing of which he was certain, except the mill and things there. Of God and heaven he had heard so little, that they were to him what fairy-land is to a child: something real, but not here; very far off. His brain, greedy, dwarfed, full of thwarted energy and unused powers, questioned these men and women going by, coldly, bitterly, that night. Was it not his right to live as they,—a pure life, a good, true-hearted life, full of beauty and kind words? He only wanted to know how to use the strength within him. His heart warmed, as he thought of it. He suffered himself[39] to think of it longer. If he took the money?

Then he saw himself as he might be, strong, helpful, kindly. The night crept on, as this one image slowly evolved itself from the crowd of other thoughts and stood triumphant. He looked at it. As he might be! What wonder, if it blinded him to delirium,—the madness that underlies all revolution, all progress, and all fall?

You laugh at the shallow temptation? You see the error underlying its argument so clearly,—that to him a true life was one of full development rather than self-restraint?

---

[38] *panorama*: The extended paintings, of a landscape or other scene, that were often displayed a section at a time before nineteenth-century audiences as a form of entertainment.

[39] *suffered himself*: Allowed himself.

that he was deaf to the higher tone in a cry of voluntary suffering for truth's sake than in the fullest flow of spontaneous harmony? I do not plead his cause. I only want to show you the mote in my brother's eye: then you can see clearly to take it out.[40]

The money,—there it lay on his knee, a little blotted slip of paper, nothing in itself; used to raise him out of the pit; something straight from God's hand. A thief! Well, what was it to be a thief? He met the question at last, face to face, wiping the clammy drops of sweat from his forehead. God made this money—the fresh air, too—for his children's use. He never made the difference between poor and rich. The Something who looked down on him that moment through the cool gray sky had a kindly face, he knew,—loved his children alike. Oh, he knew that!

There were times when the soft floods of color in the crimson and purple flames, or the clear depth of amber in the water below the bridge, had somehow given him a glimpse of another world than this,—of an infinite depth of beauty and of quiet somewhere,—somewhere,—a depth of quiet and rest and love. Looking up now, it became strangely real. The sun had sunk quite below the hills, but his last rays struck upward, touching the zenith. The fog had risen, and the town and river were steeped in its thick, gray, damp; but overhead, the sun-touched smoke-clouds opened like a cleft ocean,—shifting, rolling seas of crimson mist, waves of billowy silver veined with blood-scarlet, inner depths unfathomable of glancing light. Wolfe's artist-eye grew drunk with color. The gates of that other world! Fading, flashing before him now! What, in that world of Beauty, Content, and Right, were the petty laws, the mine and thine, of mill-owners and mill-hands?

A consciousness of power stirred within him. He stood up. A man,—he thought, stretching out his hands,—free to work, to live, to love! Free! His right! He folded the scrap of paper in his hand. As his nervous fingers took it in, limp and blotted, so his soul took in the mean temptation, lapped it in fancied rights, in dreams of improved existences, drifting and endless as the cloud-seas of color. Clutching it, as if the tightness of his hold would strengthen his sense of possession, he went aimlessly down the street. It was his watch at the mill. He need not go, need never go again, thank God!—shaking off the thought with unspeakable loathing.

Shall I go over the history of the hours of that night? how the man wandered from one to another of his old haunts, with a half-consciousness of bidding them farewell,—lanes and alleys and back-yards where the mill-hands lodged,—noting, with a new eagerness, the filth and drunkenness, the pig-pens, the ash-heaps covered with potato-skins, the bloated, pimpled women at the doors,—with a new disgust, a new sense of sudden triumph, and, under all, a new, vague dread, unknown before, smothered down, kept under, but still there? It left him but once during the night, when, for the second time in his life, he entered a church. It was a sombre Gothic pile,[41] where the stained light lost itself in far-retreating arches; built to meet the requirements and sympathies of a far other class than Wolfe's. Yet it touched, moved him uncontrollably. The distances, the shadows, the still, marble figures, the mass of silent kneeling worshippers, the mysterious music, thrilled, lifted his soul with a wonderful pain. Wolfe forgot himself, forgot the new life he was going to live, the mean terror gnawing underneath. The voice of the speaker strengthened the charm; it was clear, feeling, full, strong. An old man, who had lived much, suffered much; whose brain was keenly alive, dominant; whose heart was summer-warm with

---

[40] *I only want to show you . . . take it out*: A reference to Christ's words in the Sermon on the Mount: "And why beholdest thou the mote that is in thy brother's eye, but considerest not the beam that is in thine own eye? Or how wilt thou say to thy brother, let me pull out the mote out of thine eye, and, behold, a beam is in thine own eye?" See Matthew 7:3–4.

[41] *pile*: Large building.

charity. He taught it to-night. He held up Humanity in its grand total; showed the great world-cancer to his people. Who could show it better? He was a Christian reformer; he had studied the age thoroughly; his outlook at man had been free, world-wide, over all time. His faith stood sublime upon the Rock of Ages; his fiery zeal guided vast schemes by which the gospel was to be preached to all nations. How did he preach it to-night? In burning, light-laden words he painted the incarnate Life, Love, the universal Man: words that became reality in the lives of these people,—that lived again in beautiful words and actions, trifling, but heroic. Sin, as he defined it, was a real foe to them; their trials, temptations, were his. His words passed far over the furnace-tender's grasp, toned to suit another class of culture; they sounded in his ears a very pleasant song in an unknown tongue. He meant to cure this world-cancer with a steady eye that had never glared with hunger, and a hand that neither poverty nor strychnine-whiskey[42] had taught to shake. In this morbid, distorted heart of the Welsh puddler he had failed.

Wolfe rose at last, and turned from the church down the street. He looked up; the night had come on foggy, damp; the golden mists had vanished, and the sky lay dull and ash-colored. He wandered again aimlessly down the street, idly wondering what had become of the cloud-sea of crimson and scarlet. The trial-day of this man's life was over, and he had lost the victory. What followed was mere drifting circumstance,—a quicker walking over the path,—that was all. Do you want to hear the end of it? You wish me to make a tragic story out of it? Why, in the police-reports of the morning paper you can find a dozen such tragedies: hints of shipwrecks unlike any that ever befell on the high seas; hints that here a power was lost to heaven,—that there a soul went down where no tide can ebb or flow. Commonplace enough the hints are,—jocose sometimes, done up in rhyme.

Doctor May, a month after the night I have told you of, was reading to his wife at breakfast from this fourth column of the morning-paper: an unusual thing,—these police-reports not being, in general, choice reading for ladies; but it was only one item he read.

"Oh, my dear! You remember that man I told you of, that we saw at Kirby's mill?—that was arrested for robbing Mitchell? Here he is; just listen:—'Circuit Court. Judge Day. Hugh Wolfe, operative in Kirby & John's Loudon Mills. Charge, grand larceny. Sentence, nineteen years hard labor in penitentiary.'—Scoundrel! Serves him right! After all our kindness that night! Picking Mitchell's pocket at the very time!"

His wife said something about the ingratitude of that kind of people, and then they began to talk of something else.

Nineteen years! How easy that was to read! What a simple word for Judge Day to utter! Nineteen years! Half a lifetime!

Hugh Wolfe sat on the window-ledge of his cell, looking out. His ankles were ironed. Not usual in such cases; but he had made two desperate efforts to escape. "Well," as Haley, the jailer, said, "small blame to him! Nineteen years' imprisonment was not a pleasant thing to look forward to." Haley was very good-natured about it, though Wolfe had fought him savagely.

"When he was first caught," the jailer said afterwards, in telling the story, "before the trial, the fellow was cut down at once,—laid there on that pallet like a dead man, with his hands over his eyes. Never saw a man so cut down in my life. Time of the trial, too, came the queerest dodge of any customer I ever had. Would choose no lawyer. Judge gave him one, of course. Gibson it was. He tried to prove the fellow crazy; but it wouldn't go. Thing was plain as daylight: money found on him. 'Twas a hard sentence,—all the law allows; but it was for 'xample's sake. These mill-hands are gettin' on-bearable. When the sentence was read, he just looked up, and said the money was his by rights, and that all the world had

---

[42] *strychnine-whiskey*: Sickening alcoholic spirits.

gone wrong. That night, after the trial, a gentleman came to see him here, name of Mitchell,—him as he stole from. Talked to him for an hour. Thought he came for curiosity, like. After he was gone, thought Wolfe was remarkable quiet, and went into his cell. Found him very low; bed all bloody. Doctor said he had been bleeding at the lungs. He was as weak as a cat; yet, if ye'll b'lieve me, he tried to get a-past me and get out. I just carried him like a baby, and threw him on the pallet. Three days after, he tried it again: that time reached the wall. Lord help you! he fought like a tiger,—giv' some terrible blows. Fightin' for life, you see; for he can't live long, shut up in the stone crib down yonder. Got a death-cough now. 'T took two of us to bring him down that day; so I just put the irons on his feet. There he sits, in there. Goin' to-morrow, with a batch more of 'em. That woman, hunchback, tried with him,—you remember?—she's only got three years. 'Complice. But *she's* a woman, you know. He's been quiet ever since I put on irons: giv' up, I suppose. Looks white, sick-lookin'. It acts different on 'em, bein' sentenced. Most of 'em gets reckless, devilish-like. Some prays awful, and sings them vile songs of the mills, all in a breath. That woman, now, she's desper't'. Been beggin' to see Hugh, as she calls him, for three days. I'm a-goin' to let her in. She don't go with him. Here she is in this next cell. I'm a-goin' now to let her in."

He let her in. Wolfe did not see her. She crept into a corner of the cell, and stood watching him. He was scratching the iron bars of the window with a piece of tin which he had picked up, with an idle, uncertain, vacant stare, just as a child or idiot would do.

"Tryin' to get out, old boy?" laughed Haley. "Them irons will need a crowbar beside your tin, before you can open 'em."

Wolfe laughed, too, in a senseless way.

"I think I'll get out," he said.

"I believe his brain's touched," said Haley, when he came out.

The puddler scraped away with the tin for half an hour. Still Deborah did not speak. At last she ventured nearer, and touched his arm.

"Blood?" she said, looking at some spots on his coat with a shudder.

He looked up at her. "Why, Deb!" he said, smiling,—such a bright, boyish smile, that it went to poor Deborah's heart directly, and she sobbed and cried out loud.

"Oh, Hugh, lad! Hugh! dunnot look at me, when it wur my fault! To think I brought hur to it! And I loved hur so! Oh, lad, I dud!"

The confession, even in this wretch, came with the woman's blush through the sharp cry.

He did not seem to hear her,—scraping away diligently at the bars with the bit of tin.

Was he going mad? She peered closely into his face. Something she saw there made her draw suddenly back,—something which Haley had not seen, that lay beneath the pinched, vacant look it had caught since the trial, or the curious gray shadow that rested on it. That gray shadow,—yes, she knew what that meant. She had often seen it creeping over women's faces for months, who died at last of slow hunger or consumption. That meant death, distant, lingering: but this——Whatever it was the woman saw, or thought she saw, used as she was to crime and misery, seemed to make her sick with a new horror. Forgetting her fear of him, she caught his shoulders, and looked keenly, steadily, into his eyes.

"Hugh!" she cried, in a desperate whisper,—"oh, boy, not that! for God's sake, not *that!*"

The vacant laugh went off his face, and he answered her in a muttered word or two that drove her away. Yet the words were kindly enough. Sitting there on his pallet, she cried silently a hopeless sort of tears, but did not speak again. The man looked up furtively at her now and then. Whatever his own trouble was, her distress vexed him with a momentary sting.

It was market-day. The narrow window of the jail looked down directly on the carts and wagons drawn up in a long line, where they had unloaded. He could see, too, and hear distinctly the clink of money as it changed hands, the busy crowd of whites and blacks shoving, pushing one another, and the chaffering[43] and swearing at the stalls. Somehow, the sound, more than anything else had done, wakened him up,—made the whole real to him. He was done with the world and the business of it. He let the tin fall, and looked out, pressing his face close to the rusty bars. How they crowded and pushed! And he,—he should never walk that pavement again! There came Neff Sanders, one of the feeders at the mill, with a basket on his arm. Sure enough, Neff was married the other week. He whistled, hoping he would look up; but he did not. He wondered if Neff remembered he was there,—if any of the boys thought of him up there, and thought that he never was to go down that old cinder-road again. Never again! He had not quite understood it before; but now he did. Not for days or years, but never!—that was it.

How clear the light fell on that stall in front of the market! and how like a picture it was, the dark-green heaps of corn, and the crimson beets, and golden melons! There was another with game: how the light flickered on that pheasant's breast, with the purplish blood dripping over the brown feathers! He could see the red shining of the drops, it was so near. In one minute he could be down there. It was just a step. So easy, as it seemed, so natural to go! Yet it could never be—not in all the thousands of years to come—that he should put his foot on that street again! He thought of himself with a sorrowful pity, as of some one else. There was a dog down in the market, walking after his master with such a stately, grave look!—only a dog, yet he could go backwards and forwards just as he pleased: he had good luck! Why, the very vilest cur, yelping there in the gutter, had not lived his life, had been free to act out whatever thought God had put into his brain; while he—No, he would not think of that! He tried to put the thought away, and to listen to a dispute between a countryman and a woman about some meat; but it would come back. He, what had he done to hear this?

Then came the sudden picture of what might have been, and now. He knew what it was to be in the penitentiary,—how it went with men there. He knew how in these long years he should slowly die, but not until soul and body had become corrupt and rotten,—how, when he came out, if he lived to come, even the lowest of the mill-hands would jeer him,—how his hands would be weak, and his brain senseless and stupid. He believed he was almost that now. He put his hand to his head, with a puzzled, weary look. It ached, his head, with thinking. He tried to quiet himself. It was only right, perhaps; he had done wrong. But was there right or wrong for such as he? What was right? And who had ever taught him? He thrust the whole matter away. A dark, cold quiet crept through his brain. It was all wrong; but let it be! It was nothing to him more than the others. Let it be!

The door grated, as Haley opened it.

"Come, my woman! Must lock up for t' night. Come, stir yerself!"

"Good-night, Deb," he said, carelessly.

She had not hoped he would say more; but the tired pain on her mouth just then was bitterer than death. She took his passive hand and kissed it.

"Hur'll never see Deb again!" she ventured, her lips growing colder and more bloodless.

What did she say that for? Did he not know it? Yet he would not be impatient with poor old Deb. She had trouble of her own, as well as he.

"No, never again," he said, trying to be cheerful.

She stood just a moment, looking at him. Do you laugh at her, standing there, with her hunchback, her rags, her bleared, withered face, and the great despised love tugging at her heart?

"Come, you!" called Haley, impatiently.

---

[43] *chaffering*: Teasing.

She did not move.

"Hugh!" she whispered.

It was to be her last word. What was it?

"Hugh, boy, not THAT!"

He did not answer. She wrung her hands, trying to be silent, looking in his face in an agony of entreaty. He smiled again, kindly.

"It is best, Deb. I cannot bear to be hurted any more."

"Hur knows," she said, humbly.

"Tell my father good-bye; and—and kiss little Janey."

She nodded, saying nothing, looked in his face again, and went out of the door. As she went, she staggered.

"Drinkin' to-day?" broke out Haley, pushing her before him. "Where the Devil did you get it? Here, in with ye!" and he shoved her into her cell, next to Wolfe's, and shut the door.

Along the wall of her cell there was a crack low down by the floor, through which she could see the light from Wolfe's. She had discovered it days before. She hurried in now, and, kneeling down by it, listened, hoping to bear some sound. Nothing but the rasping of the tin on the bars. He was at his old amusement again. Something in the noise jarred on her ear, for she shivered as she heard it. Hugh rasped away at the bars. A dull old bit of tin, not fit to cut korl with.

He looked out of the window again. People were leaving the market now. A tall mulatto girl, following her mistress, her basket on her head, crossed the street just below, and looked up. She was laughing; but, when she caught sight of the haggard face peering out through the bars, suddenly grew grave, and hurried by. A free, firm step, a clear-cut olive face, with a scarlet turban tied on one side, dark, shining eyes, and on the head the basket poised, filled with fruit and flowers, under which the scarlet turban and bright eyes looked out half-shadowed. The picture caught his eye. It was good to see a face like that. He would try to-morrow, and cut one like it. *To-morrow!* He threw down the tin, trembling, and covered his face with his hands. When he looked up again, the daylight was gone.

Deborah, crouching near by on the other side of the wall, heard no noise. He sat on the side of the low pallet, thinking. Whatever was the mystery which the woman had seen on his face, it came out now slowly, in the dark there, and became fixed,—a something never seen on his face before. The evening was darkening fast. The market had been over for an hour; the rumbling of the carts over the pavement grew more infrequent: he listened to each, as it passed, because he thought it was to be for the last time. For the same reason, it was, I suppose, that he strained his eyes to catch a glimpse of each passer-by, wondering who they were, what kind of homes they were going to, if they had children, —listening eagerly to every chance word in the street, as if—(God be merciful to the man! what strange fancy was this?)—as if he never should hear human voices again.

It was quite dark at last. The street was a lonely one. The last passenger, he thought, was gone. No,—there was a quick step: Joe Hill, lighting the lamps. Joe was a good old chap; never passed a fellow without some joke or other. He remembered once seeing the place where he lived with his wife. "Granny Hill" the boys called her. Bedridden she was; but so kind as Joe was to her! kept the room so clean!—and the old woman, when he was there, was laughing at "some of t' lad's foolishness." The step was far down the street; but he could see him place the ladder, run up, and light the gas. A longing seized him to be spoken to once more.

"Joe!" he called, out of the grating. "Good-bye, Joe!"

The old man stopped a moment, listening uncertainly; then hurried on. The prisoner thrust his hand out of the window, and called again, louder; but Joe was too far down the street. It was a little thing; but it hurt him,—this disappointment.

"Good-bye, Joe!" he called, sorrowfully enough.

"Be quiet!" said one of the jailers, passing the door, striking on it with his club.

Oh, that was the last, was it?

There was an inexpressible bitterness on his face, as he lay down on the bed, taking the bit of tin, which he had rasped to a tolerable degree of sharpness, in his hand,—to play with, it may be. He bared his arms, looking intently at their corded veins and sinews. Deborah, listening in the next cell, heard a slight clicking sound, often repeated. She shut her lips tightly, that she might not scream; the cold drops of sweat broke over her, in her dumb agony.

"Hur knows best," she muttered at last, fiercely clutching the boards where she lay.

If she could have seen Wolfe, there was nothing about him to frighten her. He lay quite still, his arms outstretched, looking at the pearly stream of moonlight coming into the window. I think in that one hour that came then he lived back over all the years that had gone before. I think that all the low, vile life, all his wrongs, all his starved hopes, came then, and stung him with a farewell poison that made him sick unto death. He made neither moan nor cry, only turned his worn face now and then to the pure light, that seemed so far off, as one that said, "How long, O Lord? how long?"

The hour was over at last. The moon, passing over her nightly path, slowly came nearer, and threw the light across his bed on his feet. He watched it steadily, as it crept up, inch by inch, slowly. It seemed to him to carry with it a great silence. He had been so hot and tired there always in the mills! The years had been so fierce and cruel! There was coming now quiet and coolness and sleep. His tense limbs relaxed, and settled in a calm languor. The blood ran fainter and slow from his heart. He did not think now with a savage anger of what might be and was not; he was conscious only of deep stillness creeping over him. At first he saw a sea of faces: the mill-men,—women he had known, drunken and bloated,—Janeys timid and pitiful,—poor old Debs: then they floated together like a mist, and faded away, leaving only the clear, pearly moonlight.

Whether, as the pure light crept up the stretched-out figure, it brought with it calm and peace, who shall say? His dumb soul was alone with God in judgment. A Voice may have spoken for it from far-off Calvary, "Father, forgive them, for they know not what they do!"[44] Who dare say? Fainter and fainter the heart rose and fell, slower and slower the moon floated from behind a cloud, until, when at last its full tide of white splendor swept over the cell, it seemed to wrap and fold into a deeper stillness the dead figure that never should move again. Silence deeper than the Night! Nothing that moved, save the black, nauseous stream of blood dripping slowly from the pallet to the floor!

There was outcry and crowd enough in the cell the next day. The coroner and his jury, the local editors, Kirby himself, and boys with their hands thrust knowingly into their pockets and heads on one side, jammed into the corners. Coming and going all day. Only one woman. She came late, and outstayed them all. A Quaker, or Friend,[45] as they call themselves. I think this woman was known by that name in heaven. A homely body, coarsely dressed in gray and white. Deborah (for Haley had let her in) took notice of her. She watched them all—sitting on the end of the pallet, holding his head in her arms—with the ferocity of a watch-dog, if any of them touched the body. There was no meekness, no sorrow, in her face; the stuff out of which murderers are made, instead. All the time Haley and the woman were laying straight the limbs and cleaning the cell, Deborah sat still,

---

44 "*Father, forgive them, . . . what they do!*": Christ's words on the cross in reference to his persecutors.

45 *A Quaker, or Friend*: The Society of Friends is a Christian religious sect formed in England by George Fox around 1650. Although Quakers have no precisely articulated doctrine, they believe in pacifism, the refusal to take oaths, and the guidance of an inner light.

keenly watching the Quaker's face. Of all the crowd there that day, this woman alone had not spoken to her,—only once or twice had put some cordial to her lips. After they all were gone, the woman, in the same still, gentle way, brought a vase of wood-leaves and berries, and placed it by the pallet, then opened the narrow window. The fresh air blew in, and swept the woody fragrance over the dead face. Deborah looked up with a quick wonder.

"Did hur know my boy wud like it? Did hur know Hugh?"

"I know Hugh now."

The white fingers passed in a slow, pitiful way over the dead, worn face. There was a heavy shadow in the quiet eyes.

"Did hur know where they'll bury Hugh?" said Deborah in a shrill tone, catching her arm.

This had been the question hanging on her lips all day.

"In t' town-yard? Under t' mud and ash? T' lad'll smother, woman! He wur born on t' lane moor, where t' air is frick[46] and strong. Take hur out, for God's sake, take hur out where t' air blows!"

The Quaker hesitated, but only for a moment. She put her strong arm around Deborah and led her to the window.

"Thee sees the hills, friend, over the river? Thee sees how the light lies warm there, and the winds of God blow all the day? I live there,—where the blue smoke is, by the trees. Look at me." She turned Deborah's face to her own, clear and earnest. "Thee will believe me? I will take Hugh and bury him there to-morrow."

Deborah did not doubt her. As the evening wore on, she leaned against the iron bars, looking at the hills that rose far off, through the thick sodden clouds, like a bright, unattainable calm. As she looked, a shadow of their solemn repose fell on her face: its fierce discontent faded into a pitiful, humble quiet. Slow, solemn tears gathered in her eyes: the poor weak eyes turned so hopelessly to the place where Hugh was to rest, the grave heights looking higher and brighter and more solemn than ever before. The Quaker watched her keenly. She came to her at last, and touched her arm.

"When thee comes back," she said, in a low, sorrowful tone, like one who speaks from a strong heart deeply moved with remorse or pity, "thee shall begin thy life again,—there on the hills. I came too late; but not for thee,—by God's help, it may be."

Not too late. Three years after, the Quaker began her work. I end my story here. At evening-time it was light. There is no need to tire you with the long years of sunshine, and fresh air, and slow, patient Christ-love, needed to make healthy and hopeful this impure body and soul. There is a homely pine house, on one of these hills, whose windows over-look broad, wooded slopes and clover-crimsoned meadows,—niched into the very place where the light is warmest, the air freest. It is the Friends' meeting-house. Once a week they sit there, in their grave, earnest way, waiting for the Spirit of Love to speak, opening their simple hearts to receive His words. There is a woman, old, deformed, who takes a humble place among them: waiting like them: in her gray dress, her worn face, pure and meek, turned now and then to the sky. A woman much loved by these silent, restful people; more silent than they, more humble, more loving. Waiting: with her eyes turned to hills higher and purer than these on which she lives,—dim and far off now, but to be reached some day. There may be in her heart some latent hope to meet there the love denied her here,—that she shall find him whom she lost, and that then she will not be all-unworthy. Who blames her? Something is lost in the passage of every soul from one eternity to the other,—something pure and beautiful, which might have been and was not: a hope, a talent, a love, over which the soul mourns, like Esau deprived of his

---

[46] *frick*: Fresh.

birthright.[47] What blame to the meek Quaker, if she took her lost hope to make the hills of heaven more fair?

Nothing remains to tell that the poor Welsh puddler once lived, but this figure of the mill-woman cut in korl. I have it here in a corner of my library. I keep it hid behind a curtain,—it is such a rough, ungainly thing. Yet there are about it touches, grand sweeps of outline, that show a master's hand. Sometimes,—to-night, for instance,—the curtain is accidentally drawn back, and I see a bare arm stretched out imploringly in the darkness, and an eager, wolfish face watching mine: a wan, woful face, through which the spirit of the dead korl-cutter looks out, with its thwarted life, its mighty hunger, its unfinished work. Its pale, vague lips seem to tremble with a terrible question. "Is this the End?" they say,—"nothing beyond?—no more?" Why, you tell me you have seen that look in the eyes of dumb brutes,—horses dying under the lash. I know.

The deep of the night is passing while I write. The gas-light wakens from the shadows here and there the objects which lie scattered through the room: only faintly, though; for they belong to the open sunlight. As I glance at them, they each recall some task or pleasure of the coming day. A half-moulded child's head; Aphrodite;[48] a bough of forest-leaves; music; work; homely fragments, in which lie the secrets of all eternal truth and beauty. Prophetic all! Only this dumb, woful face seems to belong to and end with the night. I turn to look at it. Has the power of its desperate need commanded the darkness away? While the room is yet steeped in heavy shadow, a cool, gray light suddenly touches its head like a blessing, and its groping arm points through the broken cloud to the far East, where, in the flickering, nebulous crimson, God has set the promise of the Dawn.

Isaac G. Blanchard

Blanchard's "Eight Hours," with its clear, radical claim—"We mean to make things over / We are tired of toil for naught"—became the unofficial anthem of the movement for a shorter workday in the late nineteenth century. According to historian Philip Foner, it may have been the most popular labor song before the appearance of "Solidarity Forever" by Ralph Chaplin (presented in Part IV). In 1850, the typical workweek averaged about seventy hours. The earliest factory workers had campaigned for a ten-hour day, but it was not until after the Civil War that eight hours became a key unifying aim of labor organizations. Isaac G. Blanchard, a Boston printer and newspaper editor, first published "Eight Hours" as a poem in his paper, *Boston Daily Voice*, in August 1866. The poem was republished as a song, with music written by the Rev. Jesse H. Jones, in the July 1878 issue of *Labor Standard*, at a time when the Knights of Labor were gathering strength and members.

The focused nationwide push for the eight-hour day began in 1884 with a declaration by the Federation of Organized Trades and Labor Unions that "eight hours shall constitute a legal day's work from and after May 1, 1886," the first (unofficial) May Day. Blanchard's poem, now a song, served as a rallying cry during the widespread agitation that

---

[47] *Esau deprived of his birthright*: In the Old Testament, Esau was the eldest son of Isaac and Rebekah. Upon returning from an unsuccessful hunting expedition, a hungry Esau sold his birthright to his twin brother, Jacob, for some red pottage (soup). See Genesis 25:33–34.

[48] *Aphrodite*: Greek goddess of erotic love and marriage.

preceded that day and the general strikes by hundreds of thousands of workers in multiple cities on May 1 itself. "Eight Hours" stated the goal, made the case for it, and spurred those who embraced the cause to join "forces," wave the "banner," and raise the "shout": "Eight hours for work, eight hours for rest, eight hours for what we will." As events unfolded, the movement was stymied by the repression that followed the Haymarket affair of May 1886. The eight-hour day was not guaranteed by federal legislation until 1938.

EIGHT HOURS

We mean to make things over,
We are tired of toil for naught
With but bare enough to live upon
And ne'er an hour for thought.
5   We want to feel the sunshine
And we want to smell the flow'rs
We are sure that God has willed it
And we mean to have eight hours;
We're summoning our forces
10 From the shipyard, shop and mill.

Eight hours for work, eight hours for rest
Eight hours for what we will;
Eight hours for work, eight hours for rest
Eight hours for what we will.

15 The beasts that graze the hillside,
And the birds that wander free,
In the life that God has meted,
Have a better life than we.
Oh, hands and hearts are weary,
20 And homes are heavy with dole;
If our life's to be filled with drudg'ry,
What need of a human soul.
Shout, shout the lusty rally,
From shipyard, shop, and mill.

25 Eight hours for work, eight hours for rest
Eight hours for what we will;
Eight hours for work, eight hours for rest
Eight hours for what we will.

The voice of God within us
30 Is calling us to stand
Erect as is becoming
To the work of His right hand.
Should he, to whom the Maker
His glorious image gave,
35 The meanest of His creatures crouch,
A bread-and-butter slave?
Let the shout ring down the valleys
And echo from every hill.

Eight hours for work, eight hours for rest
40   Eight hours for what we will;
Eight hours for work, eight hours for rest
Eight hours for what we will.

Ye deem they're feeble voices
That are raised in labor's cause,
45   But bethink ye of the torrent,
And the wild tornado's laws.
We say not toil's uprising
In terror's shape will come,
Yet the world were wise to listen
50   To the monetary hum.
Soon, soon the deep toned rally
Shall all the nations thrill.

Eight hours for work, eight hours for rest
Eight hours for what we will;
55   Eight hours for work, eight hours for rest
Eight hours for what we will.

From factories and workshops
In long and weary lines,
From all the sweltering forges,
60   And from out the sunless mines,
Wherever toil is wasting
The force of life to live
There the bent and battered armies
Come to claim what God doth give
65   And the blazon on the banner
Doth with hope the nation fill:

Eight hours for work, eight hours for rest
Eight hours for what we will;
Eight hours for work, eight hours for rest
70   Eight hours for what we will.

Hurrah, hurrah for labor,
For it shall arise in might
It has filled the world with plenty,
It shall fill the world with light.
75   Hurrah, hurrah for labor,
It is mustering all its powers
And shall march along to victory
With the banner of Eight Hours.
Shout, shout the echoing rally
80   Till all the welkin thrill.

Eight hours for work, eight hours for rest
Eight hours for what we will;
Eight hours for work, eight hours for rest
Eight hours for what we will.

Lucy Parsons (1853–1942)

If Lucy Parsons is remembered at all, it is as the widow of Haymarket martyr Albert Parsons, who in 1886 was falsely accused and subsequently hanged for inciting violence at a protest meeting he never actually attended. A fiery and compelling orator in her day, her correspondence, writings, and library were confiscated and probably destroyed by the Chicago police and the FBI after her death in a house fire in 1942. Born in Texas in 1853 of black, Mexican, and Native American ancestry, she witnessed firsthand the brutality of Klan violence in the post-Civil War South. After "marrying" (miscegenation laws may have made an official marriage impossible) Albert Parsons, she left Waco, Texas, for Chicago, where they lived among the poorest of Chicago's recent immigrants and became involved in militant proletarian struggles in the 1870s and 1880s. When Albert was blackballed as a printer because of his political activism, Lucy supported their family of two children as a self-employed dressmaker.

For fifty years, Lucy Parsons was a movement activist and social revolutionary, who gravitated to political organizations that were committed to the end of "wage slavery" and the overthrow of the exploitative capitalist system. One of the first women to join the Knights of Labor, she was a founding member of the International Working People's Association, as well as the Industrial Workers of the World. She fought in defense of those who were falsely accused—the Scottsboro Eight, Sacco and Vanzetti, and Tom Mooney. In 1884, Parsons' "To Tramps" appeared on the front page of the first issue of *Alarm*, an English-language paper published by the International Working People's Association. "To Tramps" was a message of hope and of "revolution by [sometimes violent] deed" to those homeless and unemployed men who "tramped" the roads looking for work and who considered suicide as an alternative to dying of hunger. Her militancy answered the rhetoric of violence of Chicago's ruling class and its leading newspapers, typified by this quote from the *Chicago Tribune*: "When a tramp asks you for bread, put strychnine or arsenic on it and he will not trouble you any more, and others will keep out of the neighborhood." By the 1890s, Parsons reassessed a political strategy of "propaganda by deed," advocating instead trade union activism. She was buried, as she wished, at the Haymarket monument in Waldheim Cemetery.

To Tramps,
The Unemployed, the Disinherited, and Miserable

A word to the 35,000 now tramping the streets of this great city, with hands in pockets, gazing listlessly about you at the evidence of wealth and pleasure of which you own no part, not sufficient even to purchase yourself a bit of food with which to appease the pangs of hunger now knawing at your vitals. It is with you and the hundreds of thousands of others similarly situated in this great land of plenty, that I wish to have a word.

Have you not worked hard all your life, since you were old enough for your labor to be of use in the production of wealth? Have you not toiled long, hard and laboriously in producing wealth? And in all those years of drudgery do you not know you have produced thousand upon thousands of dollars' worth of wealth, which you did not then, do not now, and unless you ACT, never will, own any part in? Do you not know that when you were harnessed to a machine and that machine harnessed to steam, and thus you toiled your 10, 12 and 16 hours in the 24, that during this time in all these years you received only enough of your labor product to furnish yourself the bare, coarse necessaries of life, and that when you wished to purchase anything for yourself and family it always had to be of the cheapest quality? If you wanted to go anywhere you had to wait until Sunday, so little did you receive for your unremitting toil that you dare not stop for a moment, as it were? And do you not know that with all your squeezing, pinching and economizing you never were enabled to keep but a few days ahead of the wolves of want? And that at last when the caprice of your employer saw fit to create an artificial famine by limiting production, that the fires in the furnace were extinguished, the iron horse to which you had been harnessed was stilled; the factory door locked up, you turned upon the highway a tramp, with hunger in your stomach and rags upon your back?

Yet your employer told you that it was overproduction which made him close up. Who cared for the bitter tears and heart-pangs of your loving wife and helpless children, when you bid them a loving "God bless you" and turned upon the tramper's road to seek employment elsewhere? I say, who cared for those heartaches and pains? You were only a tramp now, to be execrated and denounced as a "worthless tramp and a vagrant" by that very class who had been engaged all those years in robbing you and yours. Then can you not see that the "good boss" or the "bad boss" cuts no figure whatever? that you are the common prey of both, and that their mission is simply robbery? Can you not see that it is the INDUSTRIAL SYSTEM and not the "boss" which must be changed?

Now, when all these bright summer and autumn days are going by and you have no employment, and consequently can save up nothing, and when the winter's blast sweeps down from the north and all the earth is wrapped in a shroud of ice, hearken not to the voice of the hyprocrite who will tell you that it was ordained of God that "the poor ye have always"; or to the arrogant robber who will say to you that you "drank up all your wages last summer when you had work, and that is the reason why you have nothing now, and the workhouse or the workyard is too good for you; that you ought to be shot." And shoot you they will if you present your petitions in too emphatic a manner. So hearken not to them, but list! Next winter when the cold blasts are creeping through the rents in your seedy garments, when the frost is biting your feet through the holes in your worn-out shoes, and when all wretchedness seems to have centered in and upon you, when misery has marked you for her own and life has become a burden and existence a mockery, when you have walked the streets by day and slept upon hard boards by night, and at last determine by your own hand to take your life,—for you would rather go out into utter nothingness than to longer endure an existence which has become such a burden—so, perchance, you determine to dash yourself into the cold embrace of the lake rather than longer suffer thus. But halt, before you commit this last tragic act in the drama of your simple existence. Stop! Is there nothing you can do to insure those whom you are about to orphan, against a like fate? The waves will only dash over you in mockery of your rash act; but stroll you down the avenues of the rich and look through the magnificent plate windows into their voluptuous homes, and here you will discover the *very identical robbers* who have despoiled you and yours. Then let your tragedy be enacted *here!* Awaken them from their wanton sport at your expense! Send forth your petition and let them read it by the red glare of destruction. Thus when you cast "one long lingering look behind" you can be assured that you have spoken to these robbers in the only language which they have ever been able to understand, for they have never yet deigned to notice any petition from their slaves that they were not *compelled* to read by the red glare bursting from the cannon's mouths, or that was not handed to them upon the point of the sword. You need no organization when you make up your mind to present this kind of petition. In fact, an organization would be a detriment to you; but each of you hungry tramps who read these lines, avail yourselves of those little methods of warfare which Science has placed in the hands of the poor man, and you will become a power in this or any other land.

Learn the use of explosives!

Dedicated to the tramps by Lucy E. Parsons.

Songs of the Knights of Labor

"An Injury to One is an Injury to All" was the slogan of the Noble and Holy Order of the Knights of Labor, expressing its commitment to the ethic of solidarity among the "universal brotherhood" of workers. What became the first truly national labor organization of the 19th century began in 1869 as a secret society of Philadelphia garment workers. Knights "assemblies" multiplied gradually in other cities and trades until 1881 when, under the leadership of railroad machinist Terence Powderly, the Knights went public. Membership started to grow rapidly, from about 30,000 in 1881 to more than 700,000 by 1886, when the Knights led more than 1,400 strikes, many of them for the eight-hour day, which became a key goal and rallying cry. The Order was more than a labor union, however; assemblies sponsored lectures, dances, and picnics, set up consumer and producer cooperatives, and ran candidates for office. Despite their masculine title, the Knights were uniquely inclusive, welcoming unskilled as well as craft workers, foreign-born immigrants, women, and African American workers (albeit in segregated locals in the South). The glaring exception was Chinese workers whom the Knights, along with much of the white working class of the time, targeted for sometimes violent exclusion. The Order declined rapidly after 1886 and the Haymarket Affair, collapsing under a combination of internal political divisions and brutal suppression by the newly centralized industrial corporations, aided in several strikes by state militia and federal troops.

Like the more famously musical Wobblies (Industrial Workers of the World, founded in 1905), the Knights of Labor was a movement that understood the power of songs to instruct and inspire its members. Its songs differ from the earlier work songs, many of which arose anonymously out of folk traditions, in that they were authored by individual members and published as broadsheets or in journals, such *Labor Enquirer* and the *Journal of United Labor*. Set to popular tunes and anthems, many—including the rousing "Knights of Labor" and "Storm the Fort, Ye Knights"—were designed to be sung during assembly meetings or strike rallies. Others aimed to educate the public ("Thirty Cents a Day"), to pillory monopolists and corporate crooks ("America," "Father Gander's Melodies"), or to envision the future workers' commonwealth ("One More Battle to Fight"). In the words of the Order's *Labor Reform Songster* (1892): "All movements which have for their object the uplifting of humanity have been greatly helped by their poets. . . . Armed with such songs, we can sing the new gospel of human brotherhood into the hearts of the people."

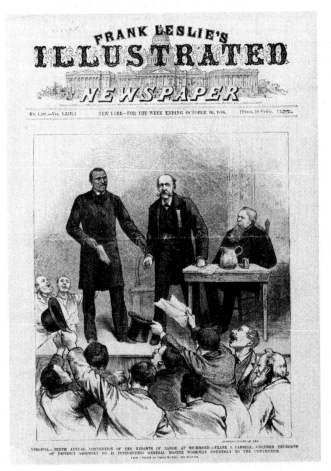

Tenth annual convention of the Knights of Labor at Richmond, Virginia. Frank J. Farrell, delegate of District Assembly No. 49, introducing General Master Workman Powderly to the convention. From a sketch by Joseph Becker. *Frank Leslie's Illustrated Newspaper*, October 16, 1886. *Courtesy of the Library of Congress, LC-USZ62-120765.*

Knights of Labor

Composed and Sung by Budd Harris

I'll sing of an order that lately has done
　　Some wonderful things in our land,
Together they pull, great battles have won,
　　A popular hard working band.
5　Their numbers are legion great strength they possess,
　　They strike good and strong for their rights,
From the North to the South from the East to the West,
　　God speed each Assembly of Knights.

　　Then conquer we must,
10　Our cause it is just,
　　　What power the uplifted hand,
　　Let each Labor Knight
　　Be brave in the fight,
　　　Remember united we stand.

15　They ask nothing wrong you can plainly see,
　　　All that they demand is but fair,
　　A lesson they'll teach with me you'll agree,
　　　To every purse-proud millionaire.
　　Fair wages they want, fair wages they'll get,
20　　Good tempered they wage all their fights,
　　Success to the cause may the sun never set,
　　　On each brave Assembly of Knights.

　　Then conquer we must, &c.

　　Then fight on undaunted, you brave working men,
25　　Down the vampires who oppress the poor,
　　You use noble weapons, the tongue and the pen,
　　　Successful you'll be I'm sure.
　　With hope for your watchword and truth for your shield,
　　　Prosperity for your pathway lights,
30　Then let labor make proud capital yield,
　　　God speed each Assembly of Knights.

　　Then conquer we must, &c.

Storm the Fort, Ye Knights

Tune—"Hold the Fort"

Toiling millions now are waking,
　　See them marching on;
All the tyrants now are shaking,
　　Ere their power is gone.

5　　　Storm the fort, ye Knights of Labor,
　　　　Battle for your cause;
　　　Equal rights for every neighbor,
　　　　Down with tyrant laws!

Lazy drones steal all the honey
10　From hard labor's hives;
Banks control the nation's money
　　And destroy your lives.

　　　Chorus

Do not load the workman's shoulder
　　With an unjust debt;
15　Do not let the rich bondholder
　　Live by blood and sweat.

　　　Chorus

Why should those who fought for freedom
　　Wear old slavery's chains?
Workingmen will quickly break them
20　When they use their brains.

　　　Chorus

THIRTY CENTS A DAY!

Air—"The Faded Coat of Blue"

In a dim-lighted chamber a dying maiden lay,
The tide of her pulses was ebbing fast away;
In the flush of her youth she was worn with toil and care,
And starvation showed its traces on the features once so fair.

5   No more the work-bell calls the weary one.
Rest, tired wage-slave, in your grave unknown;
Your feet will no more tread life's thorny, rugged way,
They have murdered you by inches upon thirty cents a day!

From earliest childhood she'd toiled to win her bread;
10   In hunger and rags, oft she wished that she were dead;
She knew naught of life's joys or the pleasures wealth can bring,
Or the glory of the woodland in the merry days of spring.

No more the work-bell, etc.

By the rich she was tempted to eat the bread of shame,
15   But her mother dear had taught her to value her good name;
Mid want and starvation she waved temptation by,
As she would not sell her honor she in poverty must die.

No more the work-bell, etc.

She cried in her fever: "I pray you let me go,
20   For my work is yet to finish, I cannot leave it so;
The foreman will curse me and dock my scanty pay,
I am starving amid plenty upon thirty cents a day!"

No more the work-bell, etc.

Too late, Christian ladies! You cannot save her now,
25   She breathes out her life—see the death-damp on her brow;
Full soon she'll be sleeping beneath the churchyard clay,
While you smile on those who killed her with thirty cents a day.

No more the work-bell, etc.

AMERICA

New Version by Ralph E. Hoyt, Los Angeles, Cal.

Our Country, 'tis of thee,
Sweet land of knavery,
   Of thee we sing!
Sweet land of Jobs and Rings,
5   And various crooked things—
Our social system brings
   Full many a sting.

Our boodlers sometimes flee,
Far off to Cana-da,

10   To save their bacon.
        But thousands more, we fear,
        Will still continue here,
        Each other's hearts to cheer—
          With hopes unshaken.

15   Land of the great defaulter,
        Of knaves who need the halter,
          Where gold is king.
        Land where fond hopes have died,
        Where demagogues reside,
20   Monopolies preside,
          And misery bring.

        We love thy rocks and rills,
        But not thy bitter ills—
          And griefs that follow.
25   Thy boasts of "equal rights,"
        Made through thy leading lights,
        In rhetoric proud flights—
          Are somewhat hollow.

        Sweet Land, sweet Liberty,
30   Let Truth and Justice be
          Allowed full sway.
        When none shall toil in vain,
        Monopoly cease to reign,
        No heart be pierced with pain
35   By cruel wrong.

        Land of true liberty,
        We'll sound loud praise to thee,
          In cheerful song.
        Then will the oppressed arise,
40   The dawn salute all eyes,
        Souls swell with glad surprise—
          God speed the day!

FATHER GANDER'S MELODIES

        "Sing a song o' swindle
          Safe full of stocks;
        The man who tends the spindle
          Going without socks!

5   "The loafer in his parlor
          Counting up his gold;
        The worker in his garret
          Perishing from cold!

        "See him in his mansion!
10   Man of might and means,

Who never knew the earning
Of one poor pot of beans!

"Yonder man is toiling
From dawn till dewy eve,
15   Two-thirds of his earnings
Go to fatten thieves!"

One More Battle to Fight

Air—"One More River to Cross"

The car of progress rolls along,
    One more battle to fight;
The voice of the people is growing strong,
    One more battle to fight.

5   One more battle,
        One more battle for freedom;
    One more battle,
        One more battle to fight.

Too long have the poor been bought and sold,
10   One more battle to fight;
And men bowed down to the shrine of gold,
        One more battle to fight.

One more battle, etc.

Too long have the many like me and you,
15   One more battle to fight;
Enriched with our labor the wealthy few,
        One more battle to fight.

One more battle, etc.

The signal sounds from shore to shore,
20   One more battle to fight;
To manhood rise! Be slaves no more!
        One more battle to fight.

One more battle, etc.

We'll teach the world a wiser plan,
25   One more battle to fight;
When the little rag-baby becomes a man,
        One more battle to fight.

One more battle, etc.

No more shall loafers own the soil,
30   One more battle to fight;
Nor bond-thieves fatten on poor men's toil,
        One more battle to fight.

One more battle, etc.

Oppression shall perish and freedom reign,
35   One more battle to fight;
The people shall come to their own again,
One more battle to fight.

One more battle, etc.

The Battle of Homestead, 1892

The Homestead strike of 1892 was one of the pivotal confrontations between labor and capital in the Gilded Age. In this western Pennsylvania steel town, one of the country's most powerful industrial corporations faced off against one of its strongest craft unions in a struggle whose centerpiece became a bloody riverfront battle that left ten dead. These dramatic events immediately generated a flourishing literature of songs and poems that gave voice to the experience of steelworkers and their families, communicating their side of the story.

In Homestead, Andrew Carnegie had built the world's largest and most technologically advanced steel-making plant, employing more than one third of the town's population. Of these workers, only the most skilled belonged to the Amalgamated Association of Iron and Steel Workers (AAISW); however, the union had negotiated a wage scale in 1889 whose benefits extended to the company's huge unskilled workforce. Homestead was a union town as much as a company town—its mayor and most civic leaders were AAISW members—and when Carnegie Steel announced in May 1892 that it would reduce wages and no longer recognize the union if it did not agree to the cuts, the townspeople united across ethnic lines in opposition to this attack on their livelihoods. Carnegie's new partner Henry Clay Frick, fresh from breaking the unions in the coke regions of southwestern Pennsylvania, had been deputized to lead the attack, while the steel baron himself was on vacation at his castle in Scotland. When the deadline for compliance passed on June 30, Frick shut down the plant and locked out the workers. He built a tall security fence around the mill and hired the Pinkerton Detective Agency to import and protect "scab" workers. The Homestead workers, meanwhile, had organized patrols and lookouts to deter strikebreaking and keep order in the town. On July 6, 1892, they spotted barges carrying three hundred Pinkertons up the Monogahela River to the plant under cover of darkness. When this "invading force" tried to come ashore, a fierce battle ensued, in which the barges were set on fire. By day's end, seven workers and three Pinkertons were killed. The mercenaries surrendered and were marched through Homestead to the roundhouse from where they were later shipped out of town by rail. However, the victory that was celebrated in the songs that follow was short-lived. Pennsylvania's governor ordered the state militia to wrest control of Homestead away from the workers' committees. Soldiers rounded up union leaders and imported strikebreakers to operate the mill. By November, the strike had collapsed, and the union was effectively broken.

The songs that are presented here dramatize and interpret the battle of Homestead, both for those who were directly affected and for a larger public that was hungry for images and information. In telling the story of the battle and events surrounding it, the songs share common themes and persuasive strategies; they vilify the wealthy "tyrants" Carnegie and Frick, who dominate in the manner of feudal lords; they celebrate the heroism of those who defended their jobs and homes against this domination; and they argue, through

Labor Troubles at Homestead, Pennsylvania. Attack of the strikers and their sympathizers on the surrendered Pinkerton men, drawn by Miss G.A. Davis, from a sketch by C. Upham, *Frank Leslie's Illustrated Weekly*, July 14, 1892. *Courtesy of Library of Congress, LC-USZ62-75205.*

references to slavery and the Civil War, that the workers' campaign was a defense of the basic American "liberties" that were fought for and won in the First and Second American Revolutions. Homestead songs were composed by both professional songwriters and worker-poets around the country, and they were published with the rapidity of news stories. "A Man Named Carnegie" first appeared anonymously in Stockton, California, on July 7, the day after the battle. "A Fight for Home and Honor" by John W. Kelly, a former Chicago steelworker who had taken to the minstrel stage as the Rolling Mill Man, was copyrighted with the Library of Congress by July 16. "Tyrant Frick" was published in the National Labor Tribune on August 27, while the date of the bitter elegy "Father Was Killed by the Pinkerton Men" is unknown.

The defeat at Homestead was a disaster for labor both locally and nationally. Although Carnegie presented the town with one of his signature free public libraries, his workers had little time to use it, since they were working twelve-hour shifts, seven days a week, and at wages that were reduced by one third from those negotiated in the 1889 contract. Their union was marginalized, its leaders blacklisted and put on trial. More broadly, the events of 1892 demonstrated that even a well-organized "craft" union, whose members' skills

were being replaced by machines operated by unskilled labor, was no match for an aggress-
ive corporation with deep pockets, especially when backed up by the press, the courts,
and the state. When concerned sociologists began to study living conditions in working-
class towns and neighborhoods in the early 1900s, Homestead was found to be one of the
worst, with high levels of hunger, prostitution, and alcoholism (*The Pittsburgh Survey*,
1906). However, when Big Steel was finally organized in the 1930s under the grassroots
industrial unionism of the CIO (Congress of Industrial Organizations), Homestead was
again a center of the struggle.

AAISW PREAMBLE

Year after year the capital of the country becomes more and more concentrated in the
hands of the few; and, in proportion, as the wealth of the country becomes centralized,
its power increases and the laboring classes are more or less impoverished. It therefore
becomes us as men who have to *battle* with the stern realities of life, to look this matter fair
in the face. There is no *dodging* the question. Let every man give it a fair, full and candid
consideration, and then act according to his honest convictions. What position are we,
the Iron and Steel Workers of America, to hold in our society? Are we to receive an
equivalent for our labor sufficient to maintain us in comparative independence and
respectability, to procure the means with which to educate our children and qualify them
to play their part in the world drama?

"In union there is strength," and in the formation of a National Amalgamated
Association, embracing every Iron and Steel Worker in the country, a union founded
upon a basis broad as the land in which we live lies our only hope. Single-handed we can
accomplish nothing, but united there is no power of wrong we may not openly defy.

Let the Iron and Steel Workers of such places as have not already moved in this
matter, organize as quickly as possible and connect themselves with the National Association.
Do not be humbugged with the idea that this thing cannot succeed. We are not theorists;
this is no visionary plan, but one eminently practicable. Nor can injustice be done to
anyone; no undue advantage should be taken of any of our employers. There is not, there
can not be any good reason why they should not pay us a fair price for our labor, and there
is no good reason why we should not receive a fair equivalent therefor.

To rescue our trades from the condition into which they have fallen, and raise ourselves to that condition in society to which we, as mechanics, are justly entitled; to place
ourselves on a foundation sufficiently strong to secure us from encroachments: to elevate
the moral, social and intellectual condition of every Iron and Steel Worker in the country,
is the object of our National Association.

TYRANT FRICK

> In days gone by before the war
>   All freemen did agree
> The best of plans to handle slaves
>   Was to let them all go free;
> 5 But the slave-drivers then, like now,
>   Contrived to make a kick
> And keep the slaves in bondage tight,
>   Just like our Tyrant Frick.

Chorus
   Of all slave-drivers, for spite and kick,
10   No one so cruel as Tyrant Frick.

The brave Hungarians, sons of toil,
   When seeking which was right,
Were killed like dogs by tyrants' hands
   In the coke districts' fight.
15   Let labor heroes all be true—
   Avenge the *bloody trick*!
Be firm like steel, true to the cause,
   And conquer Tyrant Frick.

   Of all slave-drivers, for spite and kick,
20   No one so cruel as Tyrant Frick.

The traitorous Pinkerton low tribe,
   In murdering attack,
Tried hard to take our lives and homes,
   But heroes drove them back.
25   O! sons of toil, o'er all the land,
   Now hasten, and be quick
To aid us, in our efforts grand,
   To down this Tyrant Frick.

   Of all slave-drivers, for spite and kick,
30   No one so cruel as Tyrant Frick.

The battle of "Fort Frick" is stamped
   On page of history,
And marked with blood of freemen true,
   Against this tyranny!
35   The sons of toil, for ages to come,
   His curse will always bring;
The name of *Frick* will be well known—
   The Nigger driver King!

   Of all slave-drivers, for spite and kick,
40   No one so cruel as Tyrant Frick.

A MAN NAMED CARNEGIE

Sing ho, for a man named Carnegie,
   Who owns us, controls us, his cattle, at will.
Doff hats to himself and his lady;
   Let the sigh of the weary be stiller and still.
5   Drink, boys, to the health of Carnegie,
   Who gives his slaves freedom to live—if they can.
Bend knees, and cheer, chattels, cheer. He
   May still be a chattel who can't be a man.

But, oh, there was weeping last night at the Homestead!
10   The river ran red on its way to the sea,
And curses were muttered and bullets whistling,
   And Riot was King of the land of the free.

Sing ho, for we know you, Carnegie;
   God help us and save us, we know you too well;
15 You're crushing our wives and you're starving our babies;
   In our homes you have driven the shadow of hell.
Then bow, bow down to Carnegie,
   Ye men who are slaves to his veriest whim;
If he lowers your wages cheer, vassals, then cheer. Ye
20   Are nothing but chattels and slaves under him.

But, oh, did you hear it, that mad cry for vengeance,
   Which drowned with its pulses the cannon's loud roar?
For women were weeping last night at the Homestead,
   And the river ran red from shore unto shore.

25 Then woe to the man named Carnegie!
   His vassals are rising, his bondsmen awake,
And there's woe for the lord and there's grief for his lady
   If his slaves their manacles finally break.
Let him call his assassins; we've murder for murder.
30   Let him arm them with rifles; we've cannon to greet.
We are guarding our wives and protecting our babies,
   And vengeance for bloodshed we sternly will mete.

And, oh, did you hear it, that wild cry for mercy
   The Pinkertons raised as they fell 'neath our fire?
35 They came armed with guns for shooting and killing,
   But they cowered like curs 'neath our death-dealing ire.

Sing ho, if the man named Carnegie
   Were under our guns, where the Pinkertons stood,
He would shrink like a dog and would cry like a baby;
40   But his country he's left for his country's best good.
He rides in a carriage; his workmen "protected"
   Pray God for a chance that their dear ones may live;
For he's crushing our wives and he's starving our babies,
   And we would be hounds to forget or forgive.

45 But, oh, it was awful, that day at Homestead,
   When the river ran red on its way to the sea.
When brave men were falling and women were weeping.
   And Riot was King of the land of the free!

FATHER WAS KILLED BY THE PINKERTON MEN

'Twas in a Pennsylvania town not very long ago
Men struck against reduction of their pay
Their millionaire employer with philanthropic show
Had closed the work till starved they would obey
5 They fought for home and right to live where they had toiled so long
But ere the sun had set some were laid low
There're hearts now sadly grieving by that sad and bitter wrong,
   God help them for it was a cruel blow.

Chorus:
God help them tonight in their hour of affliction
Praying for him whom they'll ne'er see again
10 Hear the poor orphans tell their sad story
"Father was killed by the Pinkerton men."

Ye prating politicians, who boast protection creed,
Go to Homestead and stop the orphans' cry,
Protection for the rich man ye pander to his greed,
15 His workmen they are cattle and may die.
The freedom of the city in Scotland far away
'Tis presented to the millionaire suave,
But here in Free America with protection in full sway
His workmen get the freedom of the grave.

20 God help them tonight in their hour of affliction
Praying for him whom they'll ne'er see again
Hear the poor orphans tell their sad story
"Father was killed by the Pinkerton men."

A FIGHT FOR HOME AND HONOR
(SOMETIMES CALLED "THE HOMESTEAD STRIKE")

We are asking one another as we pass the time of day,
Why men must have recourse to arms to get their proper pay;
And why the labor unions now must not be recognized.
While the actions of a syndicate must not be criticised.
5 The trouble down at Homestead was brought about this way,
When a grasping corporation had the audacity to say;
You must all renounce your unions and forswear your liberty,
And we'll promise you a chance to live and die in slavery.

Chorus:
For the man that fights for honor, none can blame him;
10 May luck attend wherever he may roam;
And no song of his will ever live to shame him
While liberty and honor rule his home.

When a crowd of well armed ruffians came without authority,
Like thieves at night, while decent men were sleeping peacefully,
15 Can you wonder why all honest men with indignation burn,
Why the slimy worm that crawls the earth when trod upon will turn?
When the locked out men at Homestead saw they were face to face
With a lot of paid detectives then they knew it was their place
To protect their homes and families and that was nobly done,
20 And the angels will applaud them for the victory they won.

See that sturdy band of working men start at the break of day,
Determination in their eyes that surely meant to say;
No men can drive us from our homes for which we've toiled so long,
No men shall take our places now for here's where we belong.

25   A woman with a rifle saw her husband in a crowd;
        She handed him the weapon and they cheered her long and loud.
        He kissed her and said, "Mary, you go home 'til we are through."
        She answered, "No, if you must fight, my place is here with you."

━━━━━━

Stephen Crane (1871–1900)

Stephen Crane was born in Newark, New Jersey, the fourteenth child of a Methodist minister and elder. Both his parents wrote temperance articles and decried social excesses of gambling, smoking, and drinking, which their youngest child later embraced. A precocious writer, Crane began publishing articles in the *New York Tribune* at the age of 16. He attended Pennington Seminary and Hudson River Institute (a military academy) and completed a term each at Lafayette College and Syracuse University, although he was at best an indifferent student. Freelance writer, journalist, war correspondent, novelist, poet, and short story writer, Crane is best known to contemporary readers as the author of the Civil War novel, *The Red Badge of Courage* (1895)—a remarkable achievement for a twenty-four year old who had never, to that point, seen a battlefield—and of memorable short stories, such as "The Open Boat." In 1890 he moved to New York and into an apartment in the Bowery slums. There he led a bohemian life and gathered research for his first novella, *Maggie: A Girl of the Streets* (1893), which was originally self-published on borrowed money under the pseudonym Johnston Smith. Although its account of an Irish working girl's descent into prostitution initially had few readers, *Maggie* received critical praise from Hamlin Garland and William Dean Howells and is now considered a milestone in literary naturalism, particularly in depicting how environmental conditions affect character. A collection of impressionistic poems, *The Black Rider* (1895), led to better reporting assignments, and Crane traveled to Greece, Cuba, Texas, and Mexico as a war correspondent. His health was affected by his shipwreck experience (the factual base of "The Open Boat") and malarial fever contracted in Cuba. He moved to Sussex, England, in 1898, where he became friends with Joseph Conrad, H. G. Wells, and Henry James. Crane returned to Cuba in 1899 to cover the Spanish-American war, but illness forced his return to England. He died from tuberculosis on June 5, 1900, at Badenweiler, Germany, and is buried in Hillside, New Jersey. "The Men in the Storm," a sketch from Crane's time on the Bowery during the nineteenth century's worst economic depression, was originally published in *The Arena* in 1894.

THE MEN IN THE STORM

The blizzard began to swirl great clouds of snow along the streets, sweeping it down from the roofs, and up from the pavements, until the faces of pedestrians tingled and burned as from a thousand needle-prickings. Those on the walks huddled their necks closely in the collars of their coats, and went along stooping like a race of aged people. The drivers of vehicles hurried their horses furiously on their way. They were made more cruel by the exposure of their position, aloft on high seats. The street cars, bound up-town, went slowly, the horses slipping and straining in the spongy brown mass that lay between the rails. The drivers, muffled to the eyes, stood erect, facing the wind, models of grim philosophy. Overhead, trains rumbled and roared, and the dark structure of the elevated railroad, stretching over the avenue, dripped little streams and drops of water upon the mud and snow beneath.

All the clatter of the street was softened by the masses that lay upon the cobbles, until, even to one who looked from a window, it became important music, a melody of life made necessary to the ear by the dreariness of the pitiless beat and sweep of the storm. Occasionally one could see black figures of men busily shovelling the white drifts from the walks. The sounds from their labour created new recollections of rural experiences which every man manages to have in a measure. Later, the immense windows of the shops became aglow with light, throwing great beams of orange and yellow upon the pavement. They were infinitely cheerful, yet in a way they accentuated the force and discomfort of the storm, and gave a meaning to the pace of the people and the vehicles, scores of pedestrians and drivers, wretched with cold faces, necks, and feet, speeding for scores of unknown doors and entrances, scattering to an infinite variety of shelters, to places which the imagination made warm with the familiar colours of home.

There was an absolute expression of hot dinners in the pace of the people. If one dared to speculate upon the destination of those who came trooping, he lost himself in a maze of social calculation; he might fling a handful of sand and attempt to follow the flight of each particular grain. But as to the suggestion of hot dinners, he was in firm lines of thought, for it was upon every hurrying face. It is a matter of tradition; it is from the tales of childhood. It comes forth with every storm.

However, in a certain part of a dark west-side street, there was a collection of men to whom these things were as if they were not. In this street was located a charitable house where for five cents the homeless of the city could get a bed at night, and in the morning coffee and bread.

During the afternoon of the storm, the whirling snows acted as drivers, as men with whips, and at half-past three the walk before the closed doors of the house was covered with wanderers of the street, waiting. For some distance on either side of the place they could be seen lurking in the doorways and behind projecting parts of buildings, gathering in close bunches in an effort to get warm. A covered wagon drawn up near the curb sheltered a dozen of them. Under the stairs that led to the elevated railway station, there were six or eight, their hands stuffed deep in their pockets, their shoulders stooped, jiggling their feet. Others always could be seen coming, a strange procession, some slouching along with the characteristic hopeless gait of professional strays, some coming with hesitating steps, wearing the air of men to whom this sort of thing was new.

It was an afternoon of incredible length. The snow, blowing in twisting clouds, sought out the men in their meagre hiding-places, and skilfully beat in among them, drenching their persons with showers of fine stinging flakes. They crowded together, muttering, and fumbling in their pockets to get their red inflamed wrists covered by the cloth.

New-comers usually halted at one end of the groups and addressed a question, perhaps much as a matter of form, "Is it open yet?"

Those who had been waiting inclined to take the questioner seriously and became contemptuous. "No; do yeh think we'd be standin' here?"

The gathering swelled in numbers steadily and persistently. One could always see them coming, trudging slowly through the storm.

Finally, the little snow plains in the street began to assume a leaden hue from the shadows of evening. The buildings upreared gloomily save where various windows became brilliant figures of light, that made shimmers and splashes of yellow on the snow. A street lamp on the curb struggled to illuminate, but it was reduced to impotent blindness by the swift gusts of sleet crusting its panes.

In this half-darkness, the men began to come from their shelter-places and mass in front of the doors of charity. They were of all types, but the nationalities were mostly American, German, and Irish. Many were strong, healthy, clear-skinned fellows, with that stamp of countenance which is not frequently seen upon seekers after charity. There were men of undoubted patience, industry, and temperance, who, in time of ill-fortune, do not habitually turn to rail at the state of society, snarling at the arrogance of the rich, and bemoaning the cowardice of the poor, but who at these times are apt to wear a sudden and singular meekness, as if they saw the world's progress marching from them, and were trying to perceive where they had failed, what they had lacked, to be thus vanquished in the race. Then there were others, of the shifting Bowery element, who were used to paying ten cents for a place to sleep, but who now came here because it was cheaper.

But they were all mixed in one mass so thoroughly that one could not have discerned the different elements, but for the fact that the labouring men, for the most part, remained silent and impassive in the blizzard, their eyes fixed on the windows of the house, statues of patience.

The sidewalk soon became completely blocked by the bodies of the men. They pressed close to one another like sheep in a winter's gale, keeping one another warm by the heat of their bodies. The snow came upon this compressed group of men until, directly from above, it might have appeared like a heap of snow-covered merchandise, if it were not for the fact that the crowd swayed gently with a unanimous rhythmical motion. It was wonderful to see how the snow lay upon the heads and shoulders of these men, in little ridges an inch thick perhaps in places, the flakes steadily adding drop and drop, precisely as they fall upon the unresisting grass of the fields. The feet of the men were all wet and cold, and the wish to warm them accounted for the slow, gentle rhythmical motion. Occasionally some man whose ear or nose tingled acutely from the cold winds would wriggle down until his head was protected by the shoulders of his companions.

There was a continuous murmuring discussion as to the probability of the doors being speedily opened. They persistently lifted their eyes toward the windows. One could hear little combats of opinion.

"There's a light in th' winder!"

"Naw; it's a reflection f'm across th' way."

"Well, didn't I see 'em light it?"

"You did?"

"I did!"

"Well, then, that settles it!"

As the time approached when they expected to be allowed to enter, the men crowded to the doors in an unspeakable crush, jamming and wedging in a way that, it seemed, would crack bones. They surged heavily against the building in a powerful wave of push-ing shoulders. Once a rumour flitted among all the tossing heads.

"They can't open th' door! Th' fellers er smack up agin 'em."

Then a dull roar of rage came from the men on the outskirts; but all the time they strained and pushed until it appeared to be impossible for those that they cried out against to do anything but be crushed into pulp.

"Ah, git away f'm th' door!"

"Git outa that!"

"Throw 'em out!"

"Kill 'em!"

"Say, fellers, now, what th' 'ell? G've 'em a chance t' open th' door!"

"Yeh damn pigs, give 'em a chance t' open th' door!"

Men in the outskirts of the crowd occasionally yelled when a boot-heel of one of trampling feet crushed on their freezing extremities.

"Git off me feet, yeh clumsy tarrier!"

"Say, don't stand on me feet! Walk on th' ground!"

A man near the doors suddenly shouted: "O-o-oh! Le' me out—le' me out!" And another, a man of infinite valour, once twisted his head so as to half face those who were pushing behind him. "Quit yer shovin', yeh"—and he delivered a volley of the most powerful and singular invective, straight into the faces of the men behind him. It was as if he was hammering the noses of them with curses of triple brass. His face, red with rage, could be seen, upon it an expression of sublime disregard of consequences. But nobody cared to reply to his imprecations; it was too cold. Many of them snickered, and all continued to push.

In occasional pauses of the crowd's movement the men had opportunities to make jokes; usually grim things, and no doubt very uncouth. Nevertheless, they were notable— one does not expect to find the quality of humour in a heap of old clothes under a snowdrift.

The winds seemed to grow fiercer as time wore on. Some of the gusts of snow that came down on the close collection of heads cut like knives and needles, and the men huddled, and swore, not like dark assassins, but in a sort of American fashion, grimly and desperately, it is true, but yet with a wondrous under-effect, indefinable and mystic, as if there was some kind of humour in this catastrophe, in this situation in a night of snow-laden winds.

Once the window of the huge dry-goods shop across the street furnished material for a few moments of forgetfulness. In the brilliantly lighted space appeared the figure of a man. He was rather stout and very well clothed. His beard was fashioned charmingly after that of the Prince of Wales. He stood in an attitude of magnificent reflection. He slowly stroked his moustache with a certain grandeur of manner, and looked down at the snow-encrusted mob. From below, there was denoted a supreme complacence in him. It seemed that the sight operated inversely, and enabled him to more clearly regard his own delightful environment.

One of the mob chanced to turn his head, and perceived the figure in the window. "Hello, look-it 'is whiskers," he said genially.

Many of the men turned then, and a shout went up. They called to him in all strange keys. They addressed him in every manner, from familiar and cordial greetings to carefully worded advice concerning changes in his personal appearance. The man presently fled, and the mob chuckled ferociously, like ogres who had just devoured something.

They turned then to serious business. Often they addressed the stolid front of the house.

"Oh, let us in fer Gawd's sake!"

"Let us in, or we'll all drop dead!"

"Say, what's th' use o' keepin' us poor Indians out in th' cold?"

And always some one was saying, "Keep off my feet."

The crushing of the crowd grew terrific toward the last. The men, in keen pain from the blasts, began almost to fight. With the pitiless whirl of snow upon them, the battle for shelter was going to the strong. It became known that the basement door of the foot of a little steep flight of stairs was the one to be opened, and they jostled and heaved in this direction like labouring fiends. One could hear them panting and groaning in their fierce exertion.

Usually some one in the front ranks was protesting to those in the rear—"O-o-ow! Oh, say now, fellers, let up, will yeh? Do yeh wanta kill somebody?"

A policeman arrived and went into the midst of them, scolding and berating, occasionally threatening, but using no force but that of his hands and shoulders against these men who were only struggling to get in out of the storm. His decisive tones rang out sharply—"Stop that pushin' back there! Come, boys, don't push! Stop that! Here you, quit yer shovin'! Cheese that!"

When the door below was opened, a thick stream of men forced a way down the stairs, which were of an extraordinary narrowness, and seemed only wide enough for one at a time. Yet they somehow went down almost three abreast. It was a difficult and painful operation. The crowd was like a turbulent water forcing itself through one tiny outlet. The men in the rear, excited by the success of the others, made frantic exertions, for it seemed that this large band would more than fill the quarters, and that many would be left upon the pavements. It would be disastrous to be of the last, and accordingly men with the snow biting their faces writhed and twisted with their might. One expected that, from the tremendous pressure, the narrow passage to the basement door would be so choked and clogged with human limbs and bodies that movement would be impossible. Once indeed the crowd was forced to stop, and a cry went along that a man had been injured at the foot of the stairs. But presently the slow movement began again, and the policeman fought at the top of the flight to ease the pressure of those that were going down.

A reddish light from a window fell upon the faces of the men when they, in turn, arrived at the last three steps and were about to enter. One could then note a change of expression that had come over their features. As they stood thus upon the threshold of their hopes, they looked suddenly contented and complacent. The fire had passed from their eyes and the snarl had vanished from their lips. The very force of the crowd in the rear, which had previously vexed them, was regarded from another point of view, for it now made it inevitable that they should go through the little doors into the place that was cheery and warm with light.

The tossing crowd on the sidewalk grew smaller and smaller. The snow beat with merciless persistence upon the bowed heads of those who waited. The wind drove it up from the pavements in frantic forms of winding white, and it seethed in circles about the huddled forms passing in one by one, three by three, out of the storm.

Hamlin Garland (1860–1940)

Although less well known today than his contemporaries Jack London or Upton Sinclair, Hamlin Garland was, at the turn of the century, the leading writer of America's farming frontier. In his short stories and memoirs, he celebrated the hard work, plain language, and mutual caring of his midwestern people, as well as the beauty and harshness of the land they worked. He also exposed the cruel realities underneath the pioneer dream, which, with the help of railroad advertising and unscrupulous banks, fueled the westward migration of working people who were seeking economic independence.

Born on a farm in the La Crosse valley of Wisconsin, Garland moved with his family to several homesteads in Iowa and South Dakota, doing his full share of the farmwork and attending school during the winters. He left home at age twenty-one to take up teaching and found his way to Boston, where, in 1894, unable to afford university admission, he devoted himself to a thorough literary education in the public library. He became a teacher at Moses True Brown's Boston School of Oratory and began contributing articles and stories to journals like *Harper's Weekly*.

A trip back to South Dakota in 1887, where he found his family living in deep poverty, led to the writing of the stories collected in *Main-Travelled Roads* (1891), from which "Under the Lion's Paw" is taken. The book was dedicated to the "silent heroism" of his parents, "whose half-century pilgrimage on the main traveled road of life has brought them only toil and deprivation." Garland's socialism dates from this period, when he lectured and campaigned for the People's Party of Iowa. Through the books that followed—short story collections *Prairie Folks* (1892) and *Other Main-Traveled Roads* (1910), a series of political novels, and the later memoirs, such as *A Son of the Middle Border* (1917), which brought him his greatest success—Garland developed a literary aesthetic he called "veritism," which anticipated the social realism of the 1930s. Stephen Crane described it this way: "The realist or veritist is really an optimist, a dreamer. He sees life in terms of what it might be, as well as in terms of what it is; but he writes of what is, and, at his best, suggests what is to be."

Under the Lion's Paw

"Along this main-travelled road trailed an endless line of prairie schooners, coming into sight at the east, and passing out of sight over the swell to the west. We children used to wonder where they were going and why they went."

It was the last of autumn and first day of winter coming together. All day long the plowmen on their prairie farms had moved to and fro on their wide level field through the falling snow, which melted as it fell, wetting them to the skin—all day, notwithstanding the frequent squalls of snow, the dripping, desolate clouds, and the muck of the furrows, black and tenacious as tar.

Under their dripping harness the horses swung to and fro silently, with that marvelous uncomplaining patience which marks the horse. All day the wild geese, honking wildly as they sprawled sidewise down the wind, seemed to be fleeing from an enemy behind, and with neck out-thrust and wings extended, sailed down the wind, soon lost to sight.

Yet the plowman behind his plow, though the snow lay on his ragged greatcoat and the cold clinging mud rose on his heavy boots, fettering him like gyves, whistled in the very beard of the gale. As day passed, the snow, ceasing to melt, lay along the plowed land and lodged in the depth of the stubble, till on each slow round the last furrow stood out black and shining as jet between the plowed land and the gray stubble.

When night began to fall, and the geese, flying low, began to alight invisibly in the near cornfield, Stephen Council was still at work "finishing a land." He rode on his sulky-plow when going with the wind, but walked when facing it. Sitting bent and cold but cheery under his slouch hat, he talked encouragingly to his four-in-hand.

"Come round there, boys!—round agin! We got t' finish this land. Come in there, Dan! *Stiddy*, Kate!—stiddy! None o' y'r tantrums, Kittie. It's purty tuff, but gotta be did. *Tchk! tchk!* Step along, Pete! Don't let Kate git y'r single tree on the wheel. *Once* more!"

They seemed to know what he meant, and that this was the last round, for they worked with greater vigor than before.

"Once more, boys, an' sez I oats, an' a nice warm stall, an' sleep f'r all."

By the time the last furrow was turned on the land it was too dark to see the house, and the snow changing to rain again. The tired and hungry man could see the light from the kitchen shining through the leafless hedge, and lifting a great shout, he yelled, "Sup*per* f'r a half a dozen!"

It was nearly eight o'clock by the time he had finished his chores and started for supper. He was picking his way carefully through the mud when the tall form of a man loomed up before him with a premonitory cough.

"Waddy ye want?" was the rather startled question of the farmer.

"Well, ye see," began the stranger in a deprecating tone, "we'd like t' git in f'r the night. We've tried every house f'r the last two miles, but they hadn't any room f'r us. My wife's jest about sick, 'n' the children are cold and hungry—"

"Oh, y' want a stay all night, eh?"

"Yes, sir; it 'ud be a great accom—"

"Waal, I don't make it a practice t' turn anybuddy away hungry, not on sech nights as this. Drive right in. We ain't got much, but sech as it is—"

But the stranger had disappeared. And soon his steaming, weary team, with drooping heads and swinging single trees, moved past the well to the block beside the path. Council stood at the side of the "schooner" and helped the children out—two little half-sleeping children—and then a small woman with a babe in her arms.

"There ye go!" he shouted jovially to the children. "*Now* we're all right. Run right along to the house there, an' tell M'am Council you wants sumpthin' t' eat. Right this way, Mis'—keep right off t' the right there. I'll go an' git a lantern. Come," he said to the dazed and silent group at his side.

"Mother," he shouted as he neared the fragrant and warmly lighted kitchen "here are some wayfarers an' folks who need sumpthin t' eat an' a place t'snooze." He ended by pushing them all in.

Mrs. Council, a large, jolly, rather coarse-looking woman, took the children in her arms. "Come right in, you little rabbits. 'Most asleep, hay? Now here's a drink o' milk f'r each o' ye. I'll have s'm tea in a minute. Take off y'r things and set up t' the fire."

While she set the children to drinking milk, Council got out his lantern and went out to the barn to help the stranger about his team, where his loud, hearty voice could be heard as it came and went between the haymow and the stalls.

The woman came to light as a small, timid, and discouraged-looking woman, but still pretty, in a thin and sorrowful way.

"Land sakes! An' you've travelled all the way from Clear Lake t'day in this mud! Waal! waal! No wonder you're all tired out. Don't wait f'r the men, Mis'—" She hesitated, waiting for the name.

"Haskins."

"Mis' Haskins, set right up to the table an' take a good swig o' tea, whilst I make y' s'm toast. It's green tea, an' it's good. I tell Council as I git older I don't seem t' enjoy Young Hyson n'r Gunpowder. I want the reel green tea, jest as it comes off'n the vines. Seems t' have more heart in it some way. Don't s'pose it has. Council says it's all in m' eye."

Going on in this easy way, she soon had the children filled with bread and milk and the woman thoroughly at home, eating some toast and sweet-melon pickles and sipping the tea.

"See the little rats!" she laughed at the children. "They're full as they can stick now, and they want to go to bed. Now don't git up, Mis' Haskins; set right where you are an' let me look after 'em. I know all about young ones, though I am all alone now. Jane went an' married last fall. But, as I tell Council, it's lucky we keep our health. Set right there, Mis' Haskins; I won't have you stir a finger."

It was an unmeasured pleasure to sit there in the warm, homely kitchen, the jovial chatter of the housewife driving out and holding at bay the growl of the impotent, cheated wind.

The little woman's eyes filled with tears which fell down upon the sleeping baby in her arms. The world was not so desolate and cold and hopeless, after all.

"Now I hope Council won't stop out there and talk politics all night. He's the greatest man to talk politics an' read the *Tribune*. How old is it?"

She broke off and peered down at the face of the babe.

"Two months 'n' five days," said the mother, with a mother's exactness.

"Ye don't say! I want t' know! The dear little pudzy-wudzy!" she went on, stirring it up in the neighborhood of the ribs with her fat forefinger.

"Pooty tough on 'oo to go gallivant'n' 'cross lots this way."

"Yes, that's so; a man can't lift a mountain," said Council, entering the door. "Sarah, this is Mr. Haskins from Kansas. He's been eat up 'n' drove out by grasshoppers."

"Glad t' see yeh! Pa, empty that washbasin 'n' give him a chance t' wash."

Haskins was a tall man with a thin, gloomy face. His hair was a reddish brown, like his coat, and seemed equally faded by the wind and sun. And his sallow face, though hard and set, was pathetic somehow. You would have felt that he had suffered much by the line of his mouth showing under his thin, yellow mustache.

"Hain't Ike got home yet, Sairy?"

"Hain't seen 'im."

"W-a-a-l, set right up, Mr. Haskins; wade right into what we've got; 'tain't much, but we manage to live on it—she gits fat on it," laughed Council, pointing his thumb at his wife.

After supper, while the women put the children to bed, Haskins and Council talked on, seated near the huge cooking stove, the steam rising from their wet clothing. In the Western fashion, Council told as much of his own life as he drew from his guest. He asked but few questions; but by and by the story of Haskins's struggles and defeat came out. The story was a terrible one, but he told it quietly, seated with his elbows on his knees, gazing most of the time at the hearth.

"I didn't like the looks of the country, anyhow," Haskins said, partly rising and glancing at his wife. "I was ust t' northern Ingyannie, where we have lots a timber 'n' lots o' rain, 'n' I didn't like the looks o' that dry prairie. What galled me the worst was goin' s' far away acrosst so much fine land layin' all through here vacant."

"And the 'hoppers eat ye four years hand running, did they?"

"Eat! They wiped us out. They chawed everything that was green. They jest set around waitin' f'r us to die t' eat us, too. My God! I ust t' dream of 'em sitt'n' 'round on the bedpost, six feet long, workin' their jaws. They eet the fork handles. They got worse 'n' worse till they jest rolled on one another, piled up like snow in winter. Well, it ain't no use; if I was t' talk all winter I couldn't tell nawthin'. But all the while I couldn't help thinkin' of all that land back here that nobuddy was usin', that I ought a had 'stead o' bein' out there in that cussed country."

"Waal, why didn't ye stop an' settle here?" asked Ike, who had come in and was eating his supper.

"Fer the simple reason that you fellers wantid ten 'r fifteen dollars an acre fer the bare land, and I hadn't no money fer that kind o' thing."

"Yes, I do my own work," Mrs. Council was heard to say in the pause which followed. "I'm a-gettin' purty heavy t' be on m' laigs all day, but we can't afford t' hire, so I rackin' around somehow, like a foundered horse. S' lame—I tell Council he can't tell how lame I am f'r I'm jest as lame in one laig as t'other." And the good soul laughed at the joke on herself as she took a handful of flour and dusted the biscuit board to keep the dough from sticking.

"Well, I hain't *never* been very strong," said Mrs. Haskins. "Our folks was Canadians an' small-boned, and then since my last child I hain't got up again fairly. I don't like t' complain—Tim has about all he can bear now—but they was days this week when I jest wanted to lay right down an' die."

"Waal, now, I'll tell ye," said Council from his side of the stove, silencing everybody with his good-natured roar, "I'd go down and *see* Butler, *anyway*, if I was you. I guess he'd let you have his place purty cheap; the farm's all run down. He's ben anxious t' let t' some-buddy next year. It 'ud be a good chance fer you. Anyhow, you go to bed and sleep like a babe. I've got some plowin' t' do anyhow, an' we'll see if somethin' can't be done about your case. Ike, you go out an' see if the horses is all right, an' I'll show the folks t' bed."

When the tired husband and wife were lying under the generous quilts of the spare bed, Haskins listened a moment to the wind in the eaves, and then said with a slow and solemn tone:

"There are people in this world who are good enough t' be angels, an' only haff t' die to *be* angels."

II

Jim Butler was one of those men called in the West "land poor." Early in the history of Rock River he had come into the town and started in the grocery business in a small way, occupying a small building in a mean part of the town. At this period of his life he earned all he got, and was up early and late, sorting beans, working over butter, and carting his goods to and from the station. But a change came over him at the end of the second year, when he sold a lot of land for four times what he paid for it. From that time forward he believed in land speculation as the surest way of getting rich. Every cent he could save or spare from his trade he put into land at forced sale, or mortgages on land, which were "just as good as the wheat," he was accustomed to say.

Farm after farm fell into his hands, until he was recognized as one of the leading landowners of the county. His mortgages were scattered all over Cedar County, and as they slowly but surely fell in he sought usually to retain the former owner as tenant.

He was not ready to foreclose; indeed, he had the name of being one of the "easiest" men in the town. He let the debtor off again and again, extending the time whenever possible.

"I don't want y'r land," he said. "All I'm after is the int'rest on my money—that's all. Now if y' want 'o stay on the farm, why, I'll give y' a good chance. I can't have the land layin' vacant." And in many cases the owner remained as tenant.

In the meantime he had sold his store; he couldn't spend time in it; he was mainly occupied now with sitting around town on rainy days, smoking and "gassin' with the boys," or in riding to and from his farms. In fishing time he fished a good deal. Doc Grimes, Ben Ashley, and Cal Cheatham were his cronies on these fishing excursions or hunting trips in the time of chickens or partridges. In winter they went to northern Wisconsin to shoot deer.

In spite of all these signs of easy life, Butler persisted in saying he "hadn't money enough to pay taxes on his land," and was careful to convey the impression that he was poor in spite of his twenty farms. At one time he was said to be worth fifty thousand dollars, but land had been a little slow of sale of late, so that he was not worth so much. A fine farm, known as the Higley place, had fallen into his hands in the usual way the previous year, and he had not been able to find a tenant for it. Poor Higley, after working himself nearly to death on it, in the attempt to lift the mortgage, had gone off to Dakota, leaving the farm and his curse to Butler.

This was the farm which Council advised Haskins to apply for; and the next day Council hitched up his team and drove down town to see Butler.

"You jest le' *me* do the talkin'," he said. "We'll find him wearin' out his pants on some salt barrel somew'er's; and if he thought you *wanted* a place, he'd sock it to you hot and heavy. You jest keep quiet; I'll fix 'im."

Butler was seated in Ben Ashley's store, telling "fish yarns," when Council sauntered in casually.

"Hello, But, lyin' agin, hay?"

"Hello, Steve! how goes it?"

"Oh, so-so. Too dang much rain these days. I thought it was goin' t' freeze f'r good last night. Tight squeak if I git m' plowin' done. How's farmin' with *you* these days?"

"Bad. Plowin' ain't half done."

"It 'ud be a religious idee f'r you t' go out an' take a hand y'rself."

"I don't haff to," said Butler with a wink.

"Got anybody on the Higley place?"

"No. Know of anybody?"

"Waal, no; not eggsackly. I've got a relation back t' Michigan who's b'en hot an' cold on the idee o' comin' West f'r some time. *Might* come if he could get a good layout. What do you talk on the farm?"

"Well, I d' know. I'll rent it on shares, or I'll rent it money rent."

"Waal how much money, say?"

"Well, say ten percent on the price—two-fifty."

"Waal, that ain't bad. Wait on 'im till 'e thrashes?"

Haskins listened eagerly to his important question, but Council was coolly eating a dried apple which he had speared out of a barrel with his knife. Butler studied him carefully.

"Well, knocks me out of twenty-five dollars interest."

"My relation 'll need all he's got t' git his crops in," said Council in the same indifferent way.

"Well, all right; *say* wait," concluded Butler.

"All right; this is the man. Haskins, this is Mr. Butler—no relation to Ben—the hardest working man in Cedar county."

On the way home Haskins said: "I ain't much better off. I'd like that farm; it's a good farm, but it's all run down, an' so'm I. I could make a good farm of it if I had half a show. But I can't stock it n'r seed it."

"Waal, now, don't you worry," roared Council in his ear. "We'll pull y' through somehow till next harvest. He's agreed t' hire it plowed, an' you can earn a hundred dollars ploughin', an' y' c'n git the seed o' me, an' pay me back when y' can."

Haskins was silent with emotion, but at last he said, "I ain't got nothin' t' live on."

"Now don't you worry 'bout that. You jest make your headquarters at ol' Steve Council's. Mother 'll take a pile o' comfort in havin' y'r wife an children 'round. Y' see Jane's married off lately, an' Ike's away a good 'eal, so we'll be darn glad t' have ye stop with us this winter. Nex' spring we'll see if y' can't git a start agin," and he chirruped to the team, which sprang forward with the rumbling, clattering wagon.

"Say, looky here, Council, you can't do this. I never saw—" shouted Haskins in his neighbor's ear.

Council moved about uneasily in his seat and stopped his stammering gratitude by saying: "Hold on, now; don't make such a fuss over a little thing. When I see a man down, an' things all on top of 'm, I jest like t' kick em off an' help 'm up. That's the kind of religion I got, an' it's about the *only* kind."

They rode the rest of the way home in silence. And when the red light of the lamp shone out into the darkness of the cold and windy night, and he thought of this refuge for his children and wife, Haskins could have put his arm around the neck of his burly companion and squeezed him like a lover; but he contented himself with saying: "Steve Council, you'll git y'r pay f'r this some day."

"Don't want any pay. My religion ain't run on such business principles."

The wind was growing colder, and the ground was covered with a white frost, as they turned into the gate of the Council farm, and the children came rushing out, shouting "Papa's come!" They hardly looked like the same children who had sat at the table the night before. Their torpidity under the influence of sunshine and Mother Council had given way to a sort of spasmodic cheerfulness, as insects in winter revive when laid on the earth.

III

Haskins worked like a fiend, and his wife, like the heroic woman that she was, bore also uncomplainingly the most terrible burdens. They rose early and toiled without inter-mission till the darkness fell on the plain, then tumbled into bed, every bone and muscle aching with fatigue, to rise with the sun next morning to the same round of the same ferocity of labor.

The eldest boy, now nine years old, drove a team all through the spring, plowing and seeding, milked the cows, and did chores innumerable, in most ways taking the place of a man; an infinitely pathetic but common figure—this boy—on the American farm, where there is no law against child labor. To see him in his coarse clothing, his huge boots, and his ragged cap, as he staggered with a pail of water from the well, or trudged in the cold and cheerless dawn out into the frosty field behind his team, gave the city-bred visitor a sharp pang of sympathetic pain. Yet Haskins loved his boy, and would have saved him from this if he could, but he could not.

By June the first year the result of such Herculean toil began to show on the farm. The yard was cleaned up and sown to grass, the garden plowed and planted, and the house mended. Council had given them four of his cows.

"Take 'em an' run 'em on shares. I don't want a milk s' many. Ike's away s' much now, Sat'd'ys an' Sund'ys, I can't stand the bother anyhow."

Other men, seeing the confidence of Council in the newcomer, had sold him tools on time; and as he was really an able farmer, he soon had round him many evidences of his care and thrift. At the advice of Council he had taken the farm for three years, with the privilege of rerenting or buying at the end of the term.

"It's a good bargain, an' y' want 'o nail it," said Council. "If you have any kind ov a crop, you can pay y'r debts an' keep seed an' bread."

The new hope which now sprang up in the heart of Haskins and his wife grew great almost as a pain by the time the wide field of wheat began to wave and rustle and swirl in the winds of July. Day after day he would snatch a few moments after supper to go and look at it.

"Have ye seen the wheat t'day, Nettie?" he asked one night as he rose from supper.

"No, Tim, I ain't had time."

"Well, take time now. Le's go look at it."

She threw an old hat on her head—Tommy's hat—and looking almost pretty in her thin sad way, went out with her husband to the hedge.

"Ain't it grand, Nettie? Just look at it."

It was grand. Level, russet here and there, heavy-headed, wide as a lake, and full of multitudinous whispers and gleams of wealth, it stretched away before the gazers like the fabled field of the cloth of gold.

"Oh, I think—I *hope* we'll have a good crop, Tim; and oh, how good the people have been to us!"

"Yes; I don't know where we'd be t'day if it hadn't ben f'r Council and his wife."

"They're the best people in the world," said the little woman with a great sob of gratitude.

"We'll be in the field on Monday, sure," said Haskins, griping the rail on the fence as if already at the work of the harvest.

The harvest came, bounteous, glorious, but the winds came and blew it into tangles, and the rain matted it here and there close to the ground, increasing the work of gathering it threefold.

Oh, how they toiled in those glorious days! Clothing dripping with sweat, arms aching, filled with briers, fingers raw and bleeding, backs broken with the weight of heavy bundles, Haskins and his man toiled on. Tommy drove the harvester while his father and a hired man bound on the machine. In this way they cut ten acres every day, and almost every night after supper, when the hand went to bed, Haskins returned to the field, shocking the bound grain in the light of the moon. Many a night he worked till his anxious wife came out to call him in to rest and lunch.

At the same time she cooked for the men, took care of the children, washed and ironed, milked the cows at night, made the butter, and sometimes fed the horses and watered them while her husband kept at the shocking. No slave in the Roman galleys could have toiled so frightfully and lived, for this man thought himself a free man, and that he was working for his wife and babes.

When he sank into his bed with a deep groan of relief, too tired to change his grimy, dripping clothing, he felt that he was getting nearer and nearer to a home of his own, and pushing the wolf of want a little farther from his door.

There is no despair so deep as the despair of a homeless man or woman. To roam the roads of the country or the streets of the city, to feel there is no rood of ground on which the feet can rest, to halt weary and hungry outside lighted windows and hear laughter and song within—these are the hungers and rebellions that drive men to crime and women to shame.

It was the memory of this homelessness, and the fear of its coming again, that spurred Timothy Haskins and Nettie, his wife, to such ferocious labor during that first year.

IV

"'M, yes; 'm, yes; first-rate," said Butler as his eye took in the great garden, the pigpen, and the well-filled barnyard. "You're git'n' quite a stock around yer. Done well, eh?"

Haskins was showing Butler around the place. He had not seen it for a year, having spent the year in Washington and Boston with Ashley, his brother-in-law, who had been elected to Congress.

"Yes, I've laid out a good deal of money during the last three years. I've paid out three hundred dollars f'r fencin'."

"Um—h'm! I see, I see," said Butler while Haskins went on.

"The kitchen there cost two hundred; the barn ain't cost much in money, but I've put o lot o' time on it. I've dug a new well, and I—"

"Yes, yes. I see! You've done well. Stalk worth a thousand dollars," said Butler, picking his teeth with a straw.

"About that," said Haskins modestly. "We begin to feel 's if we wuz git'n' a home f'r ourselves; but we've worked hard. I tell ye we begin to feel it, Mr. Butler, and we're goin' t' begin t' ease up purty soon. We've been kind o' plannin' a trip back t' *her* folks after the fall plowin's done."

"*Eggs*-actly!" said Butler, who was evidently thinking of something else. "I suppose you've kine o' kalklated on stayin' here three years more?"

"Well, yes. Fact is, I think I c'n buy the farm this fall, if you'll give me a reasonable show."

"Um—m! What do you call a reasonable show?"

"Waal; say a quarter down and three years' time."

Butler looked at the huge stacks of wheat which filled the yard, over which the chickens were fluttering and crawling, catching grasshoppers, and out of which the crickets were singing innumerably. He smiled in a peculiar way as he said, "Oh, I won't be hard on yer. But what did you expect to pay f'r the place?"

"Why, about what you offered it for before, two thousand five hundred, or *possibly* the three thousand dollars," he added quickly as he saw the owner shake his head.

"This farm is worth five thousand and five hundred dollars," said Butler in a careless but decided voice.

"*What!*" almost shrieked the astounded Haskins. "What's that? Five thousand? Why, that's double what you offered it for three years ago."

"Of course; and it's worth it. It was all run down then; now it's in good shape. You've laid out fifteen hundred dollars in improvements, according to your own story."

"But *you* had nothin' t' do about that. It's my work an' my money."

"You bet it was; but it's my land."

"But what's to pay me for all my—?"

"Ain't you had the use of 'em?" replied Butler, smiling calmly into his face.

Haskins was like a man struck on the head with a sandbag; he couldn't think; he stammered as he tried to say: "But—I never 'd git the use—You'd rob me. More'n that: you agreed—you promised that I could buy or rent at the end of three years at—"

"That's all right. But I didn't say I'd let you carry off the improvements, nor that I'd go on renting the farm at two-fifty. The land is doubled in value, it don't matter how; it don't enter into the question; an' now you can pay me five hundred dollars a year rent, or take it on your own terms at fifty-five hundred, or—git out."

He was turning away when Haskins, the sweat pouring from his face, fronted him, saying again:

"But *you've* done nothing to make it so. You hain't added a cent. I put it all there myself, expectin' to buy. I worked an' sweat to improve it. I was workin' f'r myself an' babes—"

"Well, why didn't you buy when I offered to sell? What y' kickin' about?"

"I'm kickin' about payin' you twice f'r my own things—my own fences, my own kitchen, my own garden."

Butler laughed. "You're too green t' eat, young feller. *Your* improvements! The law will sing another tune."

"But I trusted your word."

"Never trust anybody, my friend. Besides, I didn't promise not to do this thing. Why, man, don't look at me like that. Don't take me for a thief. It's the law. The reg'lar thing. Everybody does it."

"I don't care if they do. It's stealin' jest the same. You take three thousand dollars of my money. The work o' my hands and my wife's." He broke down at this point. He was not a strong man mentally. He could face hardship, ceaseless toil, but he could not face the cold and sneering face of Butler.

"But I don't take it," said Butler coolly. "All you've got to do is to go on jest as you've been a-doin', or give me a thousand dollars down and a mortgage at ten percent on the rest."

Haskins sat down blindly on a bundle of oats nearby and, with staring eyes and drooping head, went over the situation. He was under the lion's paw. He felt a horrible numbness in his heart and limbs. He was hid in a mist, and there was no path out.

Butler walked about, looking at the huge stacks of grain and pulling now and again a few handfuls out, shelling the heads in his hands and blowing the chaff away. He hummed a little tune as he did so. He had an accommodating air of waiting.

Haskins was in the midst of the terrible toil of the last year. He was walking again in the rain and the mud behind his plow, he felt the dust and dirt of the threshing. The ferocious husking time, with its cutting wind and biting, clinging snows, lay hard upon him. Then he thought of his wife, how she had cheerfully cooked and baked, without holiday and without rest.

"Well, what do you think of it?" inquired the cool, mocking, insinuating voice of Butler.

"I think you're a thief and a liar!" shouted Haskins, leaping up. "A black-hearted houn'!" Butler's smile maddened him; with a sudden leap he caught a fork in his hands and whirled it in the air. "You'll never rob another man, damn ye!" he grated through his teeth, a look of pitiless ferocity in his accusing eyes.

Butler shrank and quivered, expecting the blow; stood, held hypnotized by the eyes of the man he had a moment before despised—a man transformed into an avenging demon. But in the deadly hush between the lift of the weapon and its fall there came a gush of faint, childish laughter, and then across the range of his vision, far away and dim, he saw the sun-bright head of his baby girl as, with the pretty tottering run of a two-year-old, she moved across the grass of the dooryard. His hands relaxed; the fork fell to the ground; his head lowered.

"Make out y'r deed an' morgige, an' git off'n my land, an' don't ye never cross my line agin; if y' do, I'll kill ye."

Butler backed away from the man in wild haste and, climbing into his buggy with trembling limbs, drove off down the road, leaving Haskins seated dumbly on the sunny pile of sheaves, his head sunk into his hands.

Edwin Markham (1852–1940)

Charles Edwin Anson Markham was born in the Oregon Territory but soon moved with his divorced mother and five older siblings to her family ranch near Suisun, California, where as a child he learned firsthand the rigors of manual labor and farm life. Against his mother's practical wishes, he studied literature at three different colleges, eventually earning his teacher's certification at California College at Vacaville. Markham was a popular teacher in several California school districts. He was elected El Dorado County superintendent of schools in 1879 and in 1890 became principal of a school in Oakland, all the while sending poems out for magazine publication and developing an acquaintance with influential writers, such as Ambrose Bierce, Hamlin Garland, and Jack London.

In 1898, Markham wrote the poem for which he is best known. "The Man with the Hoe" was first published in the *San Francisco Examiner* on January 15, 1899. Inspired by François Millet's 1862 painting of the same name (now available for viewing on the Getty Museum's web site), the poem describes the oppression of the agricultural day laborer as a crime against divine purpose. It issues a direct moral challenge to "masters, lords and rulers in all lands," who should fear the "whirlwinds of rebellion" that their crimes against the poor will stir up. A contemporary reviewer commented on the immediate and widespread appeal of the poem, which "appears everywhere to have stimulated thought upon social problems. . . . Clergy made the poem their text; platform orators dilated upon it; college professors lectured upon it; debating societies discussed it; schools took it up for study in their literary courses; and it was the subject of conversation in social circles and on the street" (Edward B. Payne, 1899). Ultimately reprinted in 10,000 newspapers in more than 40 languages, "The Man with the Hoe" made Markham's reputation and became the title poem of his first book. Markham moved with his family to New York City, where he made his living as a poet, editor, and lecturer on labor and radical topics. His other books of poetry include *Lincoln and Other Poems* (1901), *Shoes of Happiness* (1915), and *Eighty Songs at Eighty* (1932). His 1914 nonfiction work *Children in Bondage* was a key text in the campaign to abolish child labor in the United States.

THE MAN WITH THE HOE

(Written after seeing Millet's world-famous painting)

Bowed by the weight of centuries he leans
Upon his hoe and gazes on the ground,
The emptiness of ages in his face,
And on his back the burden of the world.
5   Who made him dead to rapture and despair,
A thing that grieves not and that never hopes,
Stolid and stunned, a brother to the ox?
Who loosened and let down this brutal jaw?
Whose was the hand that slanted back this brow?
10   Whose breath blew out the light within this brain?

Is this the Thing the Lord God made and gave
To have dominion over sea and land;
To trace the stars and search the heavens for power;
To feel the passion of Eternity?
15   Is this the dream He dreamed who shaped the suns
And marked their ways upon the ancient deep?
Down all the caverns of Hell to their last gulf
There is no shape more terrible than this—
More tongued with censure of the world's blind greed—
20   More filled with signs and portents for the soul—
More packt with danger to the universe.

What gulfs between him and the seraphim!
Slave of the wheel of labor, what to him
Are Plato and the swing of Pleiades?
25   What the long reaches of the peaks of song,
The rift of dawn, the reddening of the rose?
Through this dread shape the suffering ages look;
Time's tragedy is in that aching stoop;
Through this dread shape humanity betrayed,
30   Plundered, profaned, and disinherited,
Cries protest to the Judges of the World,
A protest that is also prophecy.

O masters, lords and rulers in all lands,
Is this the handiwork you give to God,
35   This monstrous thing distorted and soul-quenched?
How will you ever straighten up this shape;
Touch it again with immortality;
Give back the upward looking and the light;
Rebuild in it the music and the dream;
40   Make right the immemorial infamies,
Perfidious wrongs, immedicable woes?

O masters, lords and rulers in all lands,
How will the Future reckon with this man?
How answer his brute question in that hour
45   When whirlwinds of rebellion shake all shores?

How will it be with kingdoms and with kings—
With those who shaped him to the thing he is—
When this dumb terror shall rise to judge the world,
After the silence of the centuries?

Lifelets: "Life Stories of Undistinguished Americans" from the *Independent*

Between 1902 and 1912, the *Independent*, a progressive, national journal, published a series of short life stories, or "lifelets," by "ordinary" Americans. These were stories of individual "types"—a bootblack, a miner, a sweatshop girl, a priest, a college professor, a summer hotel waitress, a street car conductor, a chorus girl, and the four personal narratives that are included in this collection—the anonymous, "Georgia Negro Peon" and "A Negro Nurse" and the identified stories of two labor leaders, the African American seamen, James Williams, and the Jewish garment worker, Rose Schneiderman (See "A Cap Maker's Story" and the Triangle fire in Part IV). Hamilton Holt, an editor of the *Independent*, collected and published sixteen of these seventy-five autobiographies as *The Life Stories of Undistinguished Americans* (1906). Published at a time of nativist anxiety over foreign immigration in relation to American identity, these "lifelets" offered ordinary people, mostly workers, an opportunity to present themselves directly to readers through their own written words or through interviews that were later written down and then read to and approved by the storyteller. Akin to a direct style of photographic portraiture, the stories are reminiscent of early occupational tintypes and similar to Lewis Hine's photos of Ellis Island immigrants and child laborers. Indeed, photographs occasionally accompanied the stories that were published in the *Independent*. While it is impossible to measure the degree of mediation and editing involved in the original texts (they have a uniformity of middle-class grammar), the stories included here are valuable historical accounts of the deliberate failure of Reconstruction in the South and the instances of interracial labor resistance among coastal seamen, as well as interclass affiliations of garment workers in the North. They also move beyond the representation of types and into the detailed daily lives of women and men whose stories of endurance illuminate the inseparability of race and gender to class struggle. These selections are from *Plain Folk* (1982), a second edition of stories culled from the *Independent*, edited by David M. Katzman and William M. Tuttle.

A GEORGIA NEGRO PEON

I am a negro and was born some time during the war in Elbert Country, Georgia, and I reckon by this time I must be a little over forty years old. My mother was not married when I was born and I never knew who my father was or anything about him. Shortly after the war my mother died, and I was left to the care of my uncle. All this happened before I was eight years old, and so I can't remember very much about it. When I was about ten years old my uncle hired me out to Captain—. I had already learned how to plow, and was also a good hand at picking cotton. I was told that the Captain wanted me for his house-boy, and that later on he was going to train me to be his coachman. To be a coachman in those days was considered a post of honor, and, young as I was, I was glad of the chance. But I had not been at the Captain's a month before I was put to work on the farm, with some twenty or thirty other negroes—men, women and children. From the beginning the boys had the same tasks as the men and women. There was no difference. We all worked hard during the week, and would frolic on Saturday nights and often on Sundays. And everybody was happy. The men got $3 a week and the women $2. I don't know what the children got. Every week my uncle collected my money for me, but it was very little of it that I ever saw. My uncle fed and clothed me, gave me a place to sleep, and allowed me ten or fifteen cents a week for "spending change," as he called it. I must have been seventeen or eighteen years old before I got tired of that arrangement; and felt that I was man enough to be working for myself and handling my own things. The other boys about my age and size were "drawing" their own pay, and they used to laugh at me and call me "Baby" because my old uncle was always on hand to "draw" my pay. Worked up by these things, I made a break for liberty. Unknown to my uncle or the Captain I went off to a neighboring plantation and hired myself out to another man. The new landlord agreed to give me forty cents a day and furnish me one meal. I thought that was doing fine. Bright and early one Monday morning I started to work, still not letting the others know anything about it. But they found out before sundown. The Captain came over to the new place and brought some kind of officer of the law. The officer pulled out a long piece of paper from his pocket and read it to my new employer. When this was done I heard my new boss say:

"I beg your pardon, Captain. I didn't know this nigger was bound out to you, or I wouldn't have hired him."

"He certainly is bound out to me," said the Captain. "He belongs to me until he is twenty-one, and I'm going to make him know his place."

So I was carried back to the Captain's. That night he made me strip off my clothing down to my waist, had me tied to a tree in his backyard, ordered his foreman to give me thirty lashes with a buggy whip across my bare back, and stood by until it was done. After that experience the Captain made me stay on his place night and day, —but my uncle still continued to "draw" my money.

I was a man nearly grown before I knew how to count from one to one hundred. I was a man nearly grown before I ever saw a colored school teacher. I never went to school a day in my life. To-day I can't write my own name, tho I can read a little. I was a man nearly grown before I ever rode on a railroad train, and then I went on an excursion from Elberton to Athens. What was true of me was true of hundreds of other negroes around me—'way off there in the country, fifteen or twenty miles from the nearest town.

When I reached twenty-one the Captain told me I was a free man, but he urged me to stay with him. He said he would treat me right, and pay me as much as anybody else would. The Captain's son and I were about the same age, and the Captain said that, as he had owned my mother and uncle during slavery, and as his son didn't want me to leave them (since I had been with them so long), he wanted me to stay with the old family. And I stayed. I signed a contract—that is, I made my mark—for one year. The Captain was to give me $3.50 a week, and furnish me a little house on the plantation—a one-room log cabin similar to those used by his other laborers.

During that year I married Mandy. For several years Mandy had been the house-servant for the Captain, his wife, his son and his three daughters, and they all seemed to think a good deal of her. As an evidence of their regard they gave us a suit of furniture, which cost about $25, and we set up housekeeping in one of the Captain's two-room shanties. I thought I was the biggest man in Georgia. Mandy still kept her place in the "Big House" after our marriage. We did so well for the first year that I renewed my contract for the second year, and for the third, fourth and fifth year I did the same thing. Before the end of the fifth year the Captain had died, and his son, who had married some two or three years before, took charge of the plantation. Also, for two or three years, this son had been serving at Atlanta in some big office to which he had been elected. I think it was in the Legislature or something of that sort—anyhow, all the people called him Senator. At the end of the fifth year the Senator suggested that I sign up a contract for ten years; then, he said, we wouldn't have to fix up papers every year. I asked my wife about it; she consented; and so I made a ten-year contract.

Not long afterward the Senator had a long, low shanty built on his place. A great big chimney, with a wide, open fireplace, was built at one end of it, and on each side of the house, running lengthwise, there was a row of frames of stalls just large enough to hold a single mattress. The places for these mattresses were fixed one above the other; so that there was a double row of these stalls or pens on each side. They looked for all the world like stalls for horses. Since then I have seen cabooses similarly arranged as sleeping quarters for railroad laborers. Nobody seemed to know what the Senator was fixing for. All doubts were put aside one bright day in April when about forty able-bodied negroes bound in iron chains, and some of them handcuffed, were brought out to the Senator's farm in three big wagons. They were quartered in the long, low shanty, and it was afterward called the stockade. This was the beginning of the Senator's convict camp. These men were prisoners who had been leased to the Senator from the State of Georgia at about $200 each per year, the State agreeing to pay for guards and physicians, for necessary inspection, for inquests, all rewards for escaped convicts, the costs of litigation and all other incidental camp expenses. When I saw these men in shackles, and the guards with their guns, I was scared nearly to death. I felt like running away, but I didn't know where to go. And if there had been any place to go to, I would have had to leave my wife and child behind. We free laborers held a meeting. We all wanted to quit. We sent a man to tell the Senator about it. Word came back that we were all under contract for ten years and that the Senator would hold us to the letter of the contract, or put us in chains and lock us up—the same as the other prisoners. It was made plain to us by some white people we talked to that in the contracts we had signed we had all agreed to be locked up in a stockade at night or at any other time that our employer saw fit; further, we learned that we could not lawfully break our contract for any reason and go and hire ourselves to somebody else without the consent of our employer; and, more than that, if we got mad and ran away, we could be run down by bloodhounds, arrested without process of law, and be returned to our employer, who according to the contract, might beat us brutally or administer any other kind of punishment that he thought proper. In other words, we had sold ourselves into slavery—and what could we do about it? The white folks had all the courts, all the guns, all the hounds, all the railroads, all the telegraph wires, all the newspapers, all the money, and nearly all the land—and we had only our ignorance, our poverty and our empty hands. We decided that the best thing to do was to shut our mouths, say nothing, and go back to work. And most of us worked side by side with those convicts during the remainder of the ten years.

But this first batch of convicts was only the beginning. Within six months another stockade was built, and twenty or thirty other convicts were brought to the plantation, among them six or eight women! The Senator had bought an additional thousand acres of land, and to his already large cotton plantation he added two great big saw-mills and went into the lumber business. Within two years the Senator had in all nearly 200 negroes working on his plantation—about half of them free laborers, so-called, and about half of them convicts. The only difference between the free laborers and the others was that the free laborers could come and go as they pleased, at night—that is, they were not locked up at night, and were not, as a general thing, whipped for slight offenses. The troubles of the free laborers began at the close of the ten-year period. To a man, they all wanted to quit when the time was up. To a man, they all refused to sign new contracts—even for one year, not to say anything of ten years. And just when we thought that our bondage was at an end we found that it had really just begun. Two or three years before, or about a year and a half after the Senator had started his camp, he had established a large store, which was called the commissary. All of us free laborers were compelled to buy our supplies—food, clothing, etc.—from that store. We never used any money in our dealings with the commissary, only tickets or orders, and we had a general settlement once each year, in October. In this store we were charged all sorts of high prices for goods, because every year we would come out in debt to our employer. If not that, we seldom had more than $5 or $10 coming to us—and that for a whole year's work. Well, at the close of the tenth year, when we kicked and meant to leave the Senator, he said to some of us with a smile (and I never will forget that smile—I can see it now):

"Boys, I'm sorry you're going to leave me. I hope you will do well in your new places—so well that you will be able to pay me the little balances which most of you owe me."

Word was sent out for all of us to meet him at the commissary at 2 o'clock. There he told us that, after we had signed what he called a written acknowledgment of our debts, we might go and look for new places. The storekeeper took us one by one and read to us statements of our accounts. According to the books there was no man of us who owed the Senator less than $100; some of us were put down for as much as $200. I owed $165, according to the bookkeeper. These debts were not accumulated during one year, but ran back for three and four years, so we were told—in spite of the fact that we understood that we had had a full settlement at the end of each year. But no one of us would have dared to dispute a white man's word—oh, no; not in those days. Besides, we fellows didn't care anything about the amounts—we were after getting away; and we had been told that we might go, if we signed the acknowledgments. We would have signed anything, just to get away. So we stepped up, we did, and made our marks. That same night we were rounded up by a constable and ten or twelve white men, who aided him, and we were locked up, every one of us, in one of the Senator's stockades. The next morning it was explained to us by the two guards appointed to watch us that, in the papers we had signed the day before, we had not only made acknowledgment of our indebtedness, but that we had also agreed to work for the Senator until the debts were paid by hard labor. And from that day forward we were treated just like convicts. Really we had made ourselves lifetime slaves, or peons, as the laws called us. But, call it slavery, peonage, or what not, the truth is we lived in a hell on earth what time we spent in the Senator's peon camp.

I lived in that camp, as a peon, for nearly three years. My wife fared better than I did, as did the wives of some of the other negroes, because the white men about the camp used these unfortunate creatures as their mistresses. When I was first put in the stockade my wife was still kept for a while in the "Big House," but my little boy, who was only nine years old, was given away to a negro family across the river in South Carolina, and I never saw or heard of him after that. When I left the camp my wife had had two children for some one of the white bosses, and she was living in fairly good shape in a little house off to herself. But the poor negro women who were not in the class with my wife fared about as bad as the helpless negro men. Most of the time the women who were peons or convicts were compelled to wear men's clothes. Sometimes, when I have seen them dressed like men, and plowing or hoeing or hauling logs or working at the blacksmith's trade, just the same as men, my heart would bleed and my blood would boil, but I was powerless to raise a hand. It would have meant death on the spot to have said a word. Of the first six women brought to the camp, two of them gave birth to children after they had been there more than twelve months—and the babies had white men for their fathers!

The stockades in which we slept were, I believe, the filthiest places in the world. They were cesspools of nastiness. During the thirteen years that I was there I am willing to swear that a mattress was never moved after it had been brought there, except to turn it over once or twice a month. No sheets were used, only dark-colored blankets. Most of the men slept every night in the clothing that they had worked in all day. Some of the worst characters were made to sleep in chains. The doors were locked and barred each night, and tallow candles were the only lights allowed. Really the stockades were but little more than cow lots, horse stables or hog pens. Strange to say, not a great number of these people died while I was there, tho a great many came away maimed and bruised and, in some cases, disabled for life. As far as I remember only about ten died during the last ten years that I was there, two of these being killed outright by the guards for trivial offenses.

It was a hard school that peon camp was, but I learned more there in a few short months by contact with those poor fellows from the outside world than ever I had known before. Most of what I learned was evil, and I now know that I should have been better off without the knowledge, but much of what I learned was helpful to me. Barring two or three severe and brutal whippings which I received, I got along very well, all things considered; but the system is damnable. A favorite way of whipping a man was to strap him down to a log, flat on his back, and spank him fifty or sixty times on his bare feet with a shingle or a huge piece of plank. When the man would get up with sore and blistered feet and an aching body, if he could not then keep up with the other men at work he would be strapped to the log again, this time face downward, and would be lashed with a buggy trace on his bare back. When a woman had to be whipped it was usually done in private, tho they would be compelled to fall down across a barrel or something of the kind and receive the licks on their backsides. . . .

One of the usual ways of securing laborers for a large peonage camp is for the proprietor to send out an agent to the little courts in the towns and villages, and where a man charged with some petty offenses has no friends or money the agent will urge him to plead guilty, with the understanding that the agent will pay his fine, and in that way save him from the disgrace of being sent to jail or the chain-gang! For this high favor the man must sign beforehand a paper signifying his willingness to go to the farm and work out the amount of the fine imposed. When he reaches the farm he has to be fed and clothed, to be sure, and these things are charged up to his account. . . . [E]very year many convicts were brought to the Senator's camp from a certain county in South Georgia, 'way down in the turpentine district. The majority of these men were charged with adultery, which is an offense against the law of the great and sovereign State of Georgia! Upon inquiry I learned that down in that county a number of negro lewd women were employed by certain white men to entice negro men into their houses; and then on certain nights, at a given signal, when all was in readiness, raids would be made by the officers upon these houses, and the men would be arrested and charged with living in adultery. Nine out of ten of these men, so arrested and so charged, would find their way ultimately to some convict camp, and, as I said, many of them found their way every year to the Senator's camp while I was there. The low-down women were never punished in any way. On the contrary, I was told that they always seemed to stand in high favor with the sheriffs, constables and other officers. There can be no room to doubt that they assisted very materially in furnishing laborers for the prison pens of Georgia, and the belief was general among the men that they were regularly paid for their work. I could tell more, but I've said enough to make anybody's heart sick. . . .

But I didn't tell you how I got out. I didn't get out—they put me out. When I had served as a peon for nearly three years—and you remember that they claimed that I owed them only $165—when I had served for nearly three years one of the bosses came to me and said that my time was up. He happened to be the one who was said to be living with my wife. He gave me a new suit of overalls, which cost about seventy-five cents, took me in a buggy and carried me across the Broad River into South Carolina, set me down and told me to "git." I didn't have a cent of money, and I wasn't feeling well, but somehow I managed to get a move on me. I begged my way to Columbia. In two or three days I ran across a man looking for laborers to carry to Birmingham, and I joined his gang. I have been here in the Birmingham district since they released me, and I reckon I'll die either in a coal mine or an iron furnace. It don't make much difference which. Either is better than a Georgia peon camp. And a Georgia peon camp is hell itself!

The Autobiography of a Labor Leader: James Williams

I drifted into the labor movement as naturally as a ship goes with the tide or before a leading wind. I was originally endowed with a fair share of common sense, strong democratic tendencies and a sympathetic nature. I knew the tricks of the trade and sympathized with my associates in misfortune, whose sufferings I shared. I first became identified with the labor movement at Calcutta, India. All I knew of trade union tactics at that time was what I had gleaned from time to time from newspaper reports of strikes, lockouts, boycotts, labor riots, etc., and I must confess right here that I was not prejudiced in their favor.

I had not yet had an opportunity to investigate the causes which lead to such unpleasant effects. I was only a sailor, and like most others of my class had a sublime and abiding reverence for law and order, and always bowed supinely to the rules promulgated by my masters.

But there is always a point at which "patience ceases to be a virtue," and where oppression becomes the parent of rebellion. So it was in my case. I had already endured the onerous exactions and cruel conditions of the unjust American shipping system more than half my life and always noticed that the more I yielded the more I had to yield and the less thanks I got. I wanted to make a stand for what I considered my rights somehow, but did not know exactly how to proceed.

I could hand, reef and steer, box the compass or send down a royal yard, but I knew nothing of trade union principles. The conditions existing at Calcutta at that time were certainly not calculated to redound to the sailor's best interests.

As individuals we were powerless against the crimps who infested the port and who, owing to the indifference of the officials, continued to deprive us of our rights and our earnings from voyage to voyage with monotonous regularity.

I had often observed in hoisting a topsail we all pulled, not only in the same direction, but in unison and with the same purpose—to raise the yard. This idea set me thinking. If by concentrated effort we could raise a topsail yard, why could we not raise our wages by the same method?

I consulted with some of my shipmates and we decided to write to England for permission to establish a branch of the Amalgamated Sailors' and Firemen's Union in Calcutta.

We also asked the president of the Board of Trade in London to have the rules of the board enforced in Calcutta. Both requests were granted.

After a short but rather exciting period of agitation we succeeded in inducing a majority of the seamen in port to enroll in the union.

The sailor's chaplain at Calcutta then was the Reverend Father Hopkins, a Church of England minister, and since none of our members could or would accept the position we elected him secretary.

Father Hopkins had manifested much interest in our cause and entered heartily into all our plans. He always counseled us to confine our arguments among the "black legs" to moral suasion, and we always did, tho sometimes with the assistance of a hardwood club.

Father Hopkins had two assistant missionaries to assist him in his work among the seamen and he permitted them to act as walking delegates for the union.

Sailors, as a rule, are prejudiced against "sky pilots" and "devil dodgers." So it was that shortly after the leading spirits of the movement had left the port the organization began to decline, and when I returned to Calcutta two years afterward it had degenerated into a guild.

A sky pilot is all right in a Pulpit, but it takes a laborer to run a trade union. Altho, indirectly, I have devoted some of my attention to all seamen's unions, my direct labors among seafaring men have been confined to the men sailing on this coast. "The Atlantic Coast Seamen's Union" was organized in 1889. At that time I was homeward bound from a deep water voyage, and first heard of the movement at Demerara, B. G. On reaching the coast I made inquiries concerning the condition, purposes and policy of the union, and after consideration I decided to become a member.

I first came into prominence in 1893. In the early part of that year the sailors had succeeded, through the power of organization, in raising their wages from $16 to $30 per month, but they had made the mistake of utilizing the crimps as their principal organizers.

In December I reached Boston and found that there was a strike on. The shipowners and crimps had decided that $18 per month was enough for a man before the mast and that $2 for the chance was about the right figure. Later on the wages were further reduced to $16 per month, and the shipping fee accordingly raised to $3.

I shall never forget that terrible winter siege. At the beginning our finances were low, but as the shipowners were obliging enough to lay up about 50 percent of their tonnage so that union men would not have to work, and managed to sail the remainder with scabs, we were soon in sore straits. Then it was we perceived the folly of temporizing with our enemies.

We had a large meeting room at 152 Commercial Street. Besides the meeting room and office we had two large upper floors. From the middle of December, 1893, until the 10th of March, 1894, there were from 200 to 300 sailors sleeping on the hard, bare floors and benches every night. So many hungry men were hard to control, and somehow, altho our secretary was a good man, I gradually and unconsciously assumed actual charge of the situation.

The winter was an unusually severe one even for New England, and many others beside sailors were suffering from want. Soup kitchens and bean foundries were opened at various points in the poorer quarters of the city, and I often walked for miles through banks of snow in the piercing wind to find the place where I could get the largest plate of beans or the largest bowl of soup for a nickel.

I took a leading part in all the many meetings we held that winter, and, as a rule, my advice was adopted. Mass meetings were held almost daily to keep up the enthusiasm of the men. The crowd was divided into squads of four. Every morning each squad would separate, each man going in a different direction to see what he could bum. In the evening when the squads assembled each man was to share with the other members of his squad whatever he had found, borrowed or stolen. Persuasion committees were organized to watch and report, and intimidate scabs. A "hall" committee was appointed to preserve order in the hall at night and no one could gain admission after 10 p.m. Each member was required to assist in keeping the hall clean.

Thus we struggled along, until long before spring we had succeeded in practically tying up the shipping of the port. The crimps tried in every way to continue their business and we tried in every way to circumvent them.

There was one crimp who was particularly obnoxious to us. He was the most persistent and unprincipled scoundrel of them all. He kept a boarding house and was also a shipping agent—a double headed jackal. He owned a horse and wagon and was in the habit of putting crews on board vessels at night. I decided to put a stop to his night work and I did.

I induced a chum of mine to go to this man's house and board a few days, get the bearings of the house and report to me from time to time what was going on. One bitter cold evening my chum reported that a crew of scabs was to be sent away after midnight to join a vessel lying at South Boston. I told him to get the key to the barn. While he was gone I went to the office and took a sling shot from the desk and putting it in my pocket returned to my chum, who had in the meantime got the key. Then I went after a hammer and cold chisel. We unlocked the stable door and went in. After some difficulty we got the horse's shoes off. These we took, with the harness and threw over the dock. Next I took a wrench and slacked up the nuts on the wagon wheels, leaving them just on a thread. Then we locked the door. My chum returned the key to its place and went to bed. The cold was intense, but I waited patiently outside the stable until about half past one before Mr. B. came out to harness his horse. When he missed his harness his rage was really pathetic and his profanity was so extreme that I almost fancied I could smell brimstone. While he was invoking all the blessings of perdition on the sailors' union I was nearly exploding with merriment.

He did not notice his horse's hoofs nor his wagon wheels until he left the stable, when his wagon got shipwrecked and he found himself and six scabs and two big policemen sitting on an ice patch at the spot where I had accidentally thrown several buckets of water the night before.

This was only one of the many tricks we played on the crimps that winter, but it is illustrative of our methods.

Mr. C. A. Walker was secretary of our union at that time, and he often urged me to accept an official position in the organization, but I declined. On March 1st, 1894, the sailors of Boston made a demand for an increase of $10 per month in wages and the abolition of shipping fees. The struggle was short but bitter, and there were many broken heads before we were through. In ten days, however, we won.

In April, 1894, I went to Providence, R. I., where we had a branch in charge of Mr. Horace Atkinson. On the day of my arrival Mr. Atkinson showed me a telegram from our New York agent advising him that a crew had been sent to his port from New York, at $7 per month below the regular wages. Next morning a committee was sent to the depot to intercept them, but failed. The men and their baggage were taken on board and the vessel, being light, hauled out into the stream. About midnight that night Mr. Atkinson and I went out in a small boat to "pull" the scabs. It was an ideal night for such a venture. There was not a breath of wind, the water was smooth and drizzling rain was falling. There was no moon.

We pulled quietly alongside the schooner, and after much difficulty I climbed over her rail at the port fore rigging and dropped on deck right abreast the forecastle door. Mr. Atkinson remained in the boat.

It was a very hazardous undertaking, as I knew the captain and mate were keeping watch on the poop and would not hesitate to shoot me if I was discovered. Besides I knew that when I gained the forecastle I would have six men to deal with single-handed.

Darkness favored me and I gained the forecastle unobserved. When I got inside the six seamen were all asleep in their bunks. I awoke them and at once began to stow their clothing in their canvas bags. They wanted to know what I was doing. I told them that there was a fleet of boats alongside loaded with union men and that I had been sent on board as a committee to notify them that unless they went quietly with me a committee of twenty would be sent on board to drag them out.

They took the bluff and proceeded to pack up with my assistance. As fast as their bags were ready I lowered them over the side one by one into the boat, where Mr. Atkinson received them. The men followed, and as we had a gun in the rowboat they made no disturbance while we rowed toward the shore. The next day the vessel shipped a crew of union men.

On July 2d, 1894, I was elected delegate to Philadelphia, Pa., while Mr. Atkinson was elected business agent at the same port. We had a strike while I was there and won it in a week.

During the strike I organized a persuasion committee, consisting of six of the best fighting men I could find—the worst cards in the pack. Whenever we learned that a non-union crew was to be signed we would go round the other way and waylay them. They were seldom eager to ship when our committee was through arguing with them.

Shortly after the strike was over I was sent to New York with instructions to close up the branch. New York had been a drain on our resources for a long time and had never paid running expenses.

On my way to New York I determined not to close the branch, as directed by headquarters, but to organize the sailors instead. I could not bear to haul down the union's colors and become the leader of an unconditional surrender.

I have always been proud of that decision, for the years that have passed by now witness the splendid condition of our union at this port. The shipping of the port is now practically in the hands of the union and at least 95 percent of the coasting sailors are members of it. Besides this we have formed a Marine Firemen's Union and have already enrolled more than 2,000 marine firemen. It now requires a large staff of officers to conduct the business of the union and no one is allowed to ship except through our offices, of which there are now four. And still the good work goes on. In 1894 there were but four branches on the Atlantic Coast. Now there are eleven, while our International Union embraces some 35 locals controlled from three headquarters. And still the good work goes on and will continue to go on until we have a union as wide as the world is round, so that the sailor can be assured of good treatment, good wages and equitable conditions at any place where fortune sends him.

In January, 1899, I went to Baltimore, and arriving there with 19 cents in my pocket, succeeded, after a hard struggle, in organizing the sailors of that port, and we have a good, substantial branch there now.

I have been instrumental in breaking up the gangs of organized crimps at New York, Baltimore and Norfolk, and have done a large share of the work which preceded the enactment of the new shipping law by Congress in 1898. I was greatly assisted in this work by the Social Reform Club of New York, and my connection with the club was a liberal education to me, and I shall always remember my association with it as the pleasantest and most useful period of my life.

In May, 1895, I was sent to Albany and appeared before a Senate Committee having charge of a bill to protect seamen in New York Harbor, and in April, 1902, I was sent to Washington with a delegation to protest against the re-enactment by Congress of the Seamen's Imprisonment Bill, introduced by Mr. Allen, of Maine, last January.

At present I am an ex-officer of the union, but expect eventually to return to harness. It seems to be my life's work.

Dear reader, before you proceed to criticise these confessions, pause to investigate and do not condemn until you know.

If the shipowners and crimps would be as frank with you as I have been you might be disposed to alter your opinions in our favor. A conflict between labor and capital is an industrial war and I have never resorted to any unfair methods unless I thought the ends justified the means.

If it were not for oppression there would be no unions, and if it were not for Satan there would be no churches.

On Christmas Day when you sit before your cheerful fire at your loaded board, surrounded by your smiling wife and smiling children, with a prospect of a comfortable bed and sweet repose, please give a thought to the brave and generous men who must forego their own comfort that you may enjoy these blessings.

Think of the noble, hardy men who at that moment are rushing down through the Roaring Forties, facing the rigors and desolation of Cape Horn, running their "Easting" down or pounding their bleeding hands on frozen canvas off stormy Labrador.

The sailor is the half-brother of the world and that nation is wisest which best protects him. He has no wife to plead nor children to cry for him, therefore little is known about him.

Our merchant marine is our first line of defense. Protect your sailors and you need have no fear of a foreign invader reaching your shores. You may rest secure in the thought that all your possessions are safe and that all your wants will be supplied, for the sailor is the errand boy of the world.

The rule of the sea is the survival of the fittest, and no man will long continue to follow the sea unless he is able to fight.

New York City

A Negro Nurse

I am a negro woman, and I was born and reared in the South. I am now past forty years of age and am the mother of three children. My husband died nearly fifteen years ago, after we had been married about five years. For more than thirty years—or since I was ten years old—I have been a servant in one capacity or another in white familes in a thriving Southern city, which has at present a population of more than 50,000. In my early years I was at first what might be called a "house-girl," or, better, a "house-boy." I used to answer the doorbell, sweep the yard, go on errands and do odd jobs. Later on I became a chambermaid and performed the usual duties of such a servant in a home. Still later I was graduated into a cook, in which position I served at different times for nearly eight years in all. During the last ten years I have been a nurse. I have worked for only four different families during all these thirty years. But, belonging to the servant class, which is the majority class among my race at the South, and associating only with servants, I have been able to become intimately acquainted not only with the lives of hundreds of household servants, but also with the lives of their employers. I can, therefore, speak with authority on the so-called servant question; and what I say is said out of an experience which covers many years.

To begin with, then, I should say that more than two-thirds of the negroes of the town where I live are menial servants of one kind or another, and besides that more than two-thirds of the negro women here, whether married or single, are compelled to work for a living,—as nurses, cooks, washerwomen, chambermaids, seamstresses, hucksters, janitresses, and the like. I will say, also, that the condition of this vast host of poor colored people is just as bad as, if not worse than, it was during the days of slavery. Tho today we are enjoying nominal freedom, we are literally slaves. And, not to generalize, I will give you a sketch of the work I have to do—and I'm only one of many.

I frequently work from fourteen to sixteen hours a day. I am compelled by my contract, which is oral only, to sleep in the house. I am allowed to go home to my own children, the oldest of whom is a girl of 18 years, only once in two weeks, every other Sunday afternoon—even then I'm not permitted to stay all night. I not only have to nurse a little white child, now eleven months old, but I have to act as playmate or "handy-andy," not to say governess, to three other children in the home, the oldest of whom is only nine years of age. I wash and dress the baby two or three times each day; I give it its meals, mainly from a bottle; I have to put it to bed each night; and, in addition, I have to get up and attend to its every call between midnight and morning. If the baby falls to sleep during the day, as it has been trained to do every day about eleven o'clock, I am not permitted to rest. It's "Mammy, do this," or "Mammy, do that," or "Mammy, do the other," from my mistress, all the time. So it is not strange to see "Mammy" watering the lawn in front with the garden hose, sweeping the sidewalk, mopping the porch and halls, dusting around the house, helping the cook, or darning stockings. Not only so, but I have to put the other three children to bed each night as well as the baby, and I have to wash them and dress them each morning. I don't know what it is to go to church; I don't know what it is to go to a lecture or entertainment or anything of the kind. I live a treadmill life; and I see my own children only when they happen to see me on the streets when I am out with the children, or when my children come to the "yard" to see me, which isn't often, because my white folks don't like to see their servants' children hanging around their premises. You might as well say that I'm on duty all the time—from sunrise to sunrise, every day in the week. I am the slave, body and soul, of this family. And what do I get for this work—this lifetime bondage? The pitiful sum of ten dollars a month! And what am I expected to do with these ten dollars? With this money I'm expected to pay my house rent, which is four dollars per month, for a little house of two rooms, just big enough to turn round in; and I'm expected, also, to feed and clothe myself and three children. For two years my oldest child, it is true, has helped a little toward our support by taking in a little washing at home. She does the washing and ironing of two white families, with a total of five persons; one of these families pays her $1.00 per week, and the other 75 cents per week, and my daughter has to furnish her own soap and starch and wood. For six months my youngest child, a girl about thirteen years old, has been nursing, and she receives $1.50 per week but has no night work. When I think of the low rate of wages we poor colored people receive, and when I hear so much said about our unreliability, our untrustworthiness, and even our vices, I recall the story of the private soldier in a certain army who, once upon a time, being upbraided by the commanding officer because the heels of his shoes were not polished, is said to have replied: "Captain, do you expect all the virtues for $13 per month?"

Of course, nothing is being done to increase our wages, and the way things are going at present it would seem that nothing could be done to cause an increase of wages. We have no labor unions or organizations of any kind that could demand for us a uniform scale of wages for cooks, washerwomen, nurses, and the like; and, for another thing, if some negroes did here and there refuse to work for seven and eight and ten dollars a month, there would be hundreds of other negroes right on the spot ready to take their places and do the same work, or more, for the low wages that had been refused. So that, the truth is, we have to work for little or nothing or become vagrants! And that, of course, in this State would mean that we would be arrested, tried, and despatched to the "State Farm," where we would surely have to work for nothing or be beaten with many stripes!

Nor does this low rate of pay tend to make us efficient servants. The most that can be said of us negro household servants in the South—and I speak as one of them—is that we are to the extent of our ability willing and faithful slaves. We do not cook according to scientific principles because we do not know anything about scientific principles. Most of our cooking is done by guesswork or by memory. We cook well when our "hand" is in, as we say, and when anything about the dinner goes wrong, we simply say, "I lost my hand today!" We don't know anything about scientific food for babies, nor anything about what science says must be done for infants at certain periods of their growth or when certain symptoms of disease appear; but somehow we "raise" more of the children than we kill, and, for the most part, they are lusty chaps—all of them. But the point is, we do not go to cooking-schools nor to nurse-training schools and so it cannot be expected that we should make as efficient servants without such training as we should make were such training provided. And yet with our cooking and nursing, such as it is, the white folks seem to be satisfied—perfectly satisfied. I sometimes wonder if this satisfaction is the outgrowth of the knowledge that more highly trained servants would be able to demand better pay!

Perhaps some might say, if the poor pay is the only thing about which we have to complain, then the slavery in which we daily toil and struggle is not so bad after all. But the poor pay isn't all—not by any means! I remember very well the first and last place from which I was dismissed. I lost my place because I refused to let the madam's husband kiss me. He must have been accustomed to undue familiarity with his servants, or else he took it as a matter of course, because without any love-making at all, soon after I was installed as cook, he walked up to me, threw his arms around me, and was in the act of kissing me, when I demanded to know what he meant, and shoved him away. I was young then, and newly married, and didn't know then what has been a burden to my mind and heart ever since: that a colored woman's virtue in this part of the country has no protection. I at once went home, and told my husband about it. When my husband went to the man who had insulted me, the man cursed him, and slapped him, and—had him arrested! The police judge fined my husband $25. I was present at the hearing, and testified on oath to the insult offered me. The white man, of course, denied the charge. The old judge looked up and said: "This court will never take the word of a nigger against the word of a white man." Many and many a time since I have heard similar stories repeated again and again by my friends. I believe nearly all white men take, and expect to take, undue liberties with their colored female servants—not only the fathers, but in many cases the sons also. Those servants who rebel against such familiarity must either leave or expect a mighty hard time, if they stay. By comparison, those who tamely submit to these improper relations live in clover. They always have a little "spending change," wear better clothes, and are able to get off from work at least once a week—and sometimes oftener. This moral debasement is not at all times unknown to the white women in these homes. I know of more than one colored woman who was openly importuned by white women to become the mistresses of their white husbands, on the ground that they, the white wives, were afraid that, if their husbands did not associate with colored women, they would certainly do so with outside white women, and the white wives, for reasons which ought to be perfectly obvious, preferred to have their husbands do wrong with colored women in order to keep their husbands *straight*! And again, I know at least fifty places in my small town where white men are positively raising two families—a white family in the "Big House" in front, and a colored family in a "Little House" in the backyard. In most cases, to be sure, the colored women involved are the cooks or chambermaids or seamstresses, but it cannot be true that their real connection with the white men of the families is unknown to the white women of the families. The results of this concubinage can be seen in all of our colored churches and in all of our colored public schools in the South, for in most of our churches and schools the majority of the young men and women and boys and girls are light-skinned mulattoes. The real, Simon-pure, blue-gum, thick-lip, coal-black negro is passing away— certainly in the cities; and the fathers of the new generation of negroes are white men, while their mothers are unmarried colored women.

Another thing—it's a small indignity, it may be, but an indignity just the same. No white person, not even the little chidren just learning to talk, no white person at the South ever thinks of addressing any negro man or woman as *Mr.*, or *Mrs.*, or *Miss*. The women are called, "Cook," or "Nurse," or "Mammy," or "Mary Jane," or "Lou," or "Dilcey," as the case might be, and the men are called "Bob," or "Boy," or "Old Man," or "Uncle Bill," or "Pate." In many cases our white employers refer to us, and in our presence, too, as their "niggers." No matter what they call us—no matter what they teach their children to call us—we must tamely submit, and answer when we are called; we must enter no protest; if we did object, we should be driven out without the least ceremony, and, in applying for work at other places, we should find it very hard to procure another situation. In almost every case, when our intending employers would be looking up our record, the information would be give by telephone or otherwise that we were "impudent," "saucy," "dishonest," and "generally unreliable." In our town we have no such thing as an employment agency or intelligence bureau, and, therefore, when we want work, we have to get out on the street and go from place to place, always with hat in hand, hunting for it.

Another thing. Sometimes I have gone on the street cars or the railroad trains with the white children, and, so long as I was in charge of the children, I could sit anywhere I desired, front or back. If a white man happened to ask some other white man, "What is that nigger doing in here?" and was told, "Oh, she's the nurse of those white children in front of her!" immediately there was the hush of peace. Everything was all right, so long as I was in the white man's part of the street car or in the white man's coach as a servant— a slave—but as soon as I did not present myself as a menial, and the relationship of master and servant was abolished by my not having the white children with me, I would be forthwith assigned to the "nigger" seats or the "colored people's coach." Then, too, any day in my city, and I understand that it is so in every town in the South, you can see some "great big black burly" negro coachman or carriage driver huddled up beside some aristocratic Southern white woman, and nothing is said about it, nothing is done about it, nobody resents the familiar contact. But let that same colored man take off his brass buttons and his high hat, and put on the plain livery of an average American citizen, and drive one block down any thoroughfare in any town in the South with that same white woman, as her equal or companion or friend, and he'd be shot on the spot!

You hear a good deal nowadays about the "service pan." The "service pan" is the general term applied to "left-over" food, which in many a Southern home is freely placed at the disposal of the cook or, whether so placed or not, it is usually disposed of by the cook. In my town, I know, and I guess in many other towns also, every night when the cook starts for her home she takes with her a pan or a plate of cold victuals. The same thing is true on Sunday afernoons after dinner—and most cooks have nearly every Sunday afternoon off. Well, I'll be frank with you, if it were not for the service pan, I don't know what the majority of our Southern colored families would do. The service pan is the mainstay in many a home. Good cooks in the South receive on an average $8 per month. Porters, butlers, coachmen, janitors, "office boys" and the like receive on an average $16 per month. Few and far between are the colored men in the South who receive $1 or more per day. Some mechanics do; as for example, carpenters, brick masons, wheelwrights, blacksmiths, and the like. The vast majority of negroes in my town are serving in menial capacities in homes, stores and offices. Now taking it for granted, for the sake of illustration, that the husband receives $16 per month and the wife $8. That would be $24 between the two. The chances are that they will have anywhere from five to thirteen children between them. Now, how far will $24 go toward housing and feeding and clothing ten or twelve persons for thirty days? And, I tell you, with all of us poor people the service pan is a great institution; it is a great help to us, as we wag along the weary way of life. And then most of the white folks expect their cooks to avail themselves of these perquisites; they allow it; they expect it. I do not deny that the cooks find opportunity to hide away at times, along with the cold "grub," a little sugar, a little flour, a little meal, or a little piece of soap; but I indignantly deny that we are thieves. We don't steal; we just "take" things—they are a part of the oral contract, exprest or implied. We understand it, and most of the white folks understand it. Others may denounce the service pan, and say that it is used only to support idle negroes, but many a time, when I was a cook, and had the responsibility of rearing my three children upon my lone shoulders, many a time I have had occasion to bless the Lord for the service pan!

I have already told you that my youngest girl was a nurse. With scores of other colored girls who are nurses, she can be seen almost any afternoon, when the weather is fair, rolling the baby carriage or lolling about on some one of the chief boulevards of our town. The very first week that she started out on her work she was insulted by a white man, and many times since has been improperly approached by other white men. It is a favorite practice of young white sports about town—and they are not always young, either—to stop some colored nurse, inquire the name of the "sweet little baby," talk baby talk to the child, fondle it, kiss it, make love to it, etc., etc., and in nine of ten cases every such white man will wind up by making love to the colored nurse and seeking an appointment with her.

I confess that I believe it to be true that many of our colored girls are as eager as the white men are to encourage and maintain these improper relations; but where the girl is not willing, she has only herself to depend upon for protection. If their fathers, brothers or husbands seek to redress their wrongs, under our peculiar conditions, the guiltless negroes will be severely punished, if not killed, and the white blackleg will go scot-free!

Ah, we poor colored women wage earners in the South are fighting a terrible battle, and because of our weakness, our ignorance, our poverty, and our temptations we deserve the sympathies of mankind. Perhaps a million of us are introduced daily to the privacy of a million chambers thruout the South, and hold in our arms a million white children, thousands of whom, as infants, are suckled at our breasts—during my lifetime I myself have served as "wet nurse" to more than a dozen white children. On the one hand, we are assailed by white men, and, on the other hand, we are assailed by black men, who should be our natural protectors; and, whether in the cook kitchen, at the washtub, over the sewing machine, behind the baby carriage, or at the ironing board, we are but little more than pack horses, beasts of burden, slaves! In the distant future, it may be, centuries and centuries hence, a monument of brass or stone will be erected to the Old Black Mammies of the South, but what we need is present help, present sympathy, better wages, better hours, more protection, and a chance to breathe for once while alive as free women. If none others will help us, it would seem that the Southern white women themselves might do so in their own defense, because we are rearing their children—we feed them, we bathe them, we teach them to speak the English language, and in numberless instances we sleep with them—and it is inevitable that the lives of their children will in some measure be pure or impure according as they are affected by contact with their colored nurses.

Georgia

Maxine Hong Kingston (1940)

Maxine Hong Kingston was born in Stockton, California, the first American child of Chinese immigrants, Tom Hong and Chew Ying Lan. She claims that the mixture of imagination and reality in her books was a form that she created to protect her parents from deportation. Her double identity, Chinese and American, fuels her imaginative use of history, memoir, myths, and facts. "My hands are writing English," she says, "but my mouth is speaking Chinese." Her father, who named himself after Thomas Edison, was educated as a scholar and poet in China and managed laundries and gambling houses in New York and California. Her mother, whose first two children died in China, trained as a midwife and doctor, and worked in America as a maid, laundress, cannery worker, and produce picker. Maxine, named after a lucky gambler, and her three American siblings grew up absorbing her mother's "talk stories" and her father's silences. She says, "I began writing when I was nine . . . all of a sudden this poem started coming out of me. On and on I went, oblivious to everything, and when it was over I had written 30 verses." Maxine Hong won scholarships to Berkeley where she began her studies in engineering, switched to English, and there met her husband, Earll Kingston, an actor. They protested the American war in Vietnam and lived in Hawaii before returning to California. In 1991 Maxine Hong Kingston lost her home and her book manuscript, *The Fourth Book of Peace*, in a devastating fire in the Oakland Hills that killed an estimated twenty-five people and took thousands of homes. Out of that loss emerged a new book, *The Fifth Book of Peace* (2003). Her other published works include *To Be The Poet* (2002), *Tripmaster Monkey: His Fake Book* (1989), *Hawaii One Summer* (1978, 1987), *China Men* (1980), and the book that established her reputation as a great American writer, *The Woman Warrior: Memoirs of a Girlhood Among Ghosts* (1976).

Woman Warrior and *China Men* are companion volumes, the first tracing her mother's story, the second recalling her father's history. In *China Men* she constructs a multi-generational, class-conscious history of Chinese men as builders of America. At the book's center are "The Laws," her historical summation of national laws aimed at the exclusion of one ethnic group—the Chinese. Countering the official record of racial exclusion, Hong Kingston offers another narrative—a history of the Chinese as "binding and building ancestors." In writing a story of four generations of "China Men" (not chinamen), Hong Kingston begins around 1850 where William Carlos Williams's epic *In the American Grain* (1925) ends. In this excerpt, she tells a blended story of imagination and fact about a grandfather, "Ah Goong," who "built the railroad."

The Grandfather of the Sierra Nevada Mountains

The trains used to cross the sky. The house jumped and dust shook down from the attic. Sometimes two trains ran parallel going in opposite directions; the railroad men walked on top of the leaning cars, stepped off one train onto the back of the other, and traveled the opposite way. They headed for the caboose while the train moved against their walk, or they walked toward the engine while the train moved out from under their feet. Hoboes ran alongside, caught the ladders, and swung aboard. I would have to learn to ride like that, choose my boxcar, grab a ladder at a run, and fling myself up and sideways into an open door. Elsewhere I would step smoothly off. Bad runaway boys lost their legs trying for such rides. The train craunched past—pistons stroking like elbows and knees, the coal cars dropping coal, cows looking out between the slats of the cattlecars, the boxcars almost stringing together sentences—Hydro-Cushion, Georgia Flyer, Route of the Eagle—and suddenly sunlight filled the windows again, the slough wide again and waving with tules, for which the city was once named; red-winged blackbirds and squirrels settled. We children ran to the tracks and found the nails we'd placed on them; the wheels had flattened them into knives that sparked.

Once in a while an adult said, "Your grandfather built the railroad." (Or "Your grandfathers built the railroad." Plural and singular are by context.) We children believed that it was that very railroad, those trains, those tracks running past our house; our own giant grandfather had set those very logs into the ground, poured the iron for those very spikes with the big heads and pounded them until the heads spread like that, mere nails to him. He had built the railroad so that trains would thunder over us, on a street that inclined toward us. We lived on a special spot of the earth, Stockton, the only city on the Pacific coast with three railroads—the Santa Fe, Southern Pacific, and Western Pacific. The three railroads intersecting accounted for the flocks of hoboes. The few times that the train stopped, the cows moaned all night, their hooves stumbling crowdedly and banging against the wood.

Grandfather left a railroad for his message: We had to go somewhere difficult. Ride a train. Go somewhere important. In case of danger, the train was to be ready for us.

The railroad men disconnected the rails and took the steel away. They did not come back. Our family dug up the square logs and rolled them downhill home. We collected the spikes too. We used the logs for benches, edged the yard with them, made bases for fences, embedded them in the ground for walkways. The spikes came in handy too, good for paperweights, levers, wedges, chisels. I am glad to know exactly the weight of ties and the size of nails.

Grandfather's picture hangs in the dining room next to an equally large one of Grandmother, and another one of Guan Goong, God of War and Literature. My grandparents' similarity is in the set of their mouths; they seem to have hauled with their mouths. My mouth also feels the tug and strain of weights in its corners. In the family album, Grandfather wears a greatcoat and Western shoes, but his ankles show. He hasn't shaved either. Maybe he became sloppy after the Japanese soldier bayoneted his head for not giving directions. Or he was born slow and without a sense of direction.

The photographer came to the village regularly and set up a spinet, potted trees, an ornate table stacked with hardbound books of matching size, and a backdrop with a picture of paths curving through gardens into panoramas; he lent his subjects dressy ancient mandarin clothes, Western suits, and hats. An aunt tied the fingers of the lame cousin to a book, the string leading down his sleeve; he looks like he's carrying it. The family hurried from clothes chests to mirrors without explaining to Grandfather, hiding Grandfather. In the family album are group pictures with Grandmother in the middle, the family arranged on either side of her and behind her, second wives at the ends, no Grandfather. Grandmother's earrings, bracelets, and rings are tinted jade green, everything and everybody else black and white, her little feet together neatly, two knobs at the bottom of her gown. My mother, indignant that nobody had readied Grandfather, threw his greatcoat over his nightclothes, shouted, "Wait! Wait!" and encouraged him into the sunlight. "Hurry," she said, and he ran, coat flapping, to be in the picture. She would have slipped him into the group and had the camera catch him like a peeping ghost, but Grandmother chased him away. "What a waste of film," she said. Grandfather always appears alone with white stubble on his chin. He was a thin man with big eyes that looked straight ahead. When we children talked about overcoat men, exhibitionists, we meant Grandfather, Ah Goong, who must have yanked open that greatcoat—no pants.

MaMa was the only person to listen to him, and so he followed her everywhere, and talked and talked. What he liked telling was his journeys to the Gold Mountain. He wasn't smart, yet he traveled there three times. Left to himself, he would have stayed in China to play with babies or stayed in the United States once he got there, but Grandmother forced him to leave both places. "Make money," she said. "Don't stay here eating." "Come home," she said.

Ah Goong sat outside her open door when MaMa worked. (In those days a man did not visit a good woman alone unless married to her.) He saw her at her loom and came running with his chair. He told her that he had found a wondrous country, really gold, and he himself had gotten two bags of it, one of which he had had made into a ring. His wife had given that ring to their son for his wedding ring. "That ring on your finger," he told Mother, "proves that the Gold Mountain exists and that I went there."

Another of his peculiarities was that he heard the crackles, bangs, gunshots that go off when the world lurches; the gears on its axis snap. Listening to a faraway New Year, he had followed the noise and come upon the blasting in the Sierras. (There is a Buddhist instruction that that which is most elusive must, of course, be the very thing to be pursued; listen to the farthest sound.) The Central Pacific hired him on sight; chinamen had a natural talent for explosions. Also there were not enough workingmen to do all the labor of building a new country. Some of the banging came from the war to decide whether or not black people would continue to work for nothing.

Slow as usual, Ah Goong arrived in the spring; the work had begun in January 1863. The demon that hired him pointed up and up, east above the hills of poppies. His first job was to fell a redwood, which was thick enough to divide into three or four beams. His tree's many branches spread out, each limb like a little tree. He circled the tree. How to attack it? No side looked like the side made to be cut, nor did any ground seem the place for it to fall. He axed for almost a day the side he'd decided would hit the ground. Halfway through, imitating the other lumberjacks, he struck the other side of the tree, above the cut, until he had to run away. The tree swayed and slowly dived to earth, creaking and screeching like a green animal. He was so awed, he forgot what he was supposed to yell. Hardly any branches broke; the tree sprang, bounced, pushed at the ground with its arms. The limbs did not wilt and fold; they were a small forest, which he chopped. The trunk lay like a long red torso; sap ran from its cuts like crying blind eyes. At last it stopped fighting. He set the log across sawhorses to be cured over smoke and in the sun.

He joined a team of men who did not ax one another as they took alternate hits. They blew up the stumps with gunpowder. "It was like uprooting a tooth," Ah Goong said. They also packed gunpowder at the roots of a whole tree. Not at the same time as the bang but before that, the tree rose from the ground. It stood, then plunged with a tearing of veins and muscles. It was big enough to carve a house into. The men measured themselves against the upturned white roots, which looked like claws, a sun with claws. A hundred men stood or sat on the trunk. They lifted a wagon on it and took a photograph. The demons also had their photograph taken.

Because these mountains were made out of gold, Ah Goong rushed over to the root hole to look for gold veins and ore. He selected the shiniest rocks to be assayed later in San Francisco. When he drank from the streams and saw a flash, he dived in like a duck; only sometimes did it turn out to be the sun or the water. The very dirt winked with specks.

He made a dollar a day salary. The lucky men gambled, but he was not good at remembering game rules. The work so far was endurable. "I could take it," he said.

The days were sunny and blue, the wind exhilarating, the heights godlike. At night the stars were diamonds, crystals, silver, snow, ice. He had never seen diamonds. He had never seen snow and ice. As spring turned into summer, and he lay under that sky, he saw the order in the stars. He recognized constellations from China. There—not a cloud but the Silver River, and there, on either side of it—Altair and Vega, the Spinning Girl and the Cowboy, Car, far apart. He felt his heart breaking of loneliness at so much blue-black space between star and star. The railroad he was building would not lead him to his family. He jumped out of his bedroll. "Look! Look!" Other China Men jumped awake. An accident? An avalanche? Injun demons? "The stars," he said. "The stars are here." "Another China Man gone out of his mind," men grumbled. "A sleepwalker." "Go to sleep, sleepwalker." "There. And there," said Ah Goong, two hands pointing. "The Spinning Girl and the Cowboy. Don't you see them?" "Homesick China Man," said the China Men and pulled their blankets over their heads. "Didn't you know they were here? I could have told you they were here. Same as in China. Same moon. Why not same stars?" "Nah. Those are American stars."

Pretending that a little girl was listening, he told himself the story about the Spinning Girl and the Cowboy: A long time ago they had visited earth, where they met, fell in love, and married. Instead of growing used to each other, they remained enchanted their entire lifetimes and beyond. They were too happy. They wanted to be doves or two branches of the same tree. When they returned to live in the sky, they were so engrossed in each other that they neglected their work. The Queen of the Sky scratched a river between them with one stroke of her silver hairpin—the river a galaxy in width. The lovers suffered, but she did devote her time to spinning now, and he herded his cow. The King of the Sky took pity on them and ordered that once each year, they be allowed to meet. On the seventh day of the seventh month (which is not the same as July 7), magpies form a bridge for them to cross to each other. The lovers are together for one night of the year. On their parting, the Spinner cries the heavy summer rains.

Ah Goong's discovery of the two stars gave him something to look forward to besides meals and tea breaks. Every night he located Altair and Vega and gauged how much closer they had come since the night before. During the day he watched the magpies, big black and white birds with round bodies like balls with wings; they were a welcome sight, a promise of meetings. He had found two familiars in the wilderness: magpies and stars. On the meeting day, he did not see any magpies nor hear their chattering jaybird cries. Some black and white birds flew overhead, but they may have been American crows or late magpies on their way. Some men laughed at him, but he was not the only China Man to collect water in pots, bottles, and canteens that day. The water would stay fresh forever and cure anything. In ancient days the tutelary gods of the mountains sprinkled corpses with this water and brought them to life. That night, no women to light candles, burn incense, cook special food, Grandfather watched for the convergence and bowed. He saw the two little stars next to Vega—the couple's children. And bridging the Silver River, surely those were black flapping wings of magpies and translucent-winged angels and faeries. Toward morning, he was awakened by rain, and pulled his blankets into his tent.

The next day, the fantailed orange-beaked magpies returned. Altair and Vega were beginning their journeys apart, another year of spinning and herding. Ah Goong had to find something else to look forward to. The Spinning Girl and the Cowboy met and parted six times before the railroad was finished.

When cliffs, sheer drops under impossible overhangs, ended the road, the workers filled the ravines or built bridges over them. They climbed above the site for tunnel or bridge and lowered one another down in wicker baskets made stronger by the lucky words they had painted on four sides. Ah Goong got to be a basketman because he was thin and light. Some basketmen were fifteen-year-old boys. He rode the basket barefoot, so his boots, the kind to stomp snakes with, would not break through the bottom. The basket swung and twirled, and he saw the world sweep underneath him; it was fun in a way, a cold new feeling of doing what had never been done before. Suspended in the quiet sky, he thought all kinds of crazy thoughts, that if a man didn't want to live any more, he could just cut the ropes or, easier, tilt the basket, dip, and never have to worry again. He could spread his arms, and the air would momentarily hold him before he fell past the buzzards, hawks, and eagles, and landed impaled on the tip of a sequoia. This high and he didn't see any gods, no Cowboy, no Spinner. He knelt in the basket though he was not bumping his head against the sky. Through the wickerwork, slivers of depths darted like needles, nothing between him and air but thin rattan. Gusts of wind spun the light basket. "Aiya," said Ah Goong. Winds came up under the basket, bouncing it. Neighboring baskets swung together and parted. He and the man next to him looked at each other's faces. They laughed. They might as well have gone to Malaysia to collect bird nests. Those who had done high work there said it had been worse; the birds screamed and scratched at them. Swinging near the cliff, Ah Goong stood up and grabbed it by a twig. He dug holes, then inserted gunpowder and fuses. He worked neither too fast nor too slow, keeping even with the others. The basketmen signaled one another to light the fuses. He struck match after match and dropped the burnt matches over the sides. At last his fuse caught; he waved, and the men above pulled hand over hand hauling him up, pulleys creaking. The scaffolds stood like a row of gibbets. Gallows trees along a ridge. "Hurry, hurry," he said. Some impatient men clambered up their ropes. Ah Goong ran up the ledge road they'd cleared and watched the explosions, which banged almost synchronously, echoes booming like war. He moved his scaffold to the next section of cliff and went down in the basket again, with bags of dirt, and set the next charge.

This time two men were blown up. One knocked out or killed by the explosion fell silently, the other screaming, his arms and legs struggling. A desire shot out of Ah Goong for an arm long enough to reach down and catch them. Much time passed as they fell like plummets. The shreds of baskets and a cowboy hat skimmed and tacked. The winds that pushed birds off course and against mountains did not carry men. Ah Goong also wished that the conscious man would fall faster and get it over with. His hands gripped the ropes, and it was difficult to let go and get on with the work. "It can't happen twice in a row," the basketmen said the next trip down. "Our chances are very good. The trip after an accident is probably the safest one." They raced to their favorite basket, checked and double-checked the four ropes, yanked the strands, tested the pulleys, oiled them, reminded the pulleymen about the signals, and entered the sky again.

Another time, Ah Goong had been lowered to the bottom of a ravine, which had to be cleared for the base of a trestle, when a man fell, and he saw his face. He had not died of shock before hitting bottom. His hands were grabbing at air. His stomach and groin must have felt the fall all the way down. At night Ah Goong woke up falling, though he slept on the ground, and heard other men call out in their sleep. No warm women tweaked their ears and hugged them. "It was only a falling dream," he reassured himself.

Across a valley, a chain of men working on the next mountain, men like ants changing the face of the world, fell, but it was very far away. Godlike, he watched men whose faces he could not see and whose screams he did not hear roll and bounce and slide like a handful of sprinkled gravel.

After a fall, the buzzards circled the spot and reminded the workers for days that a man was dead down there. The men threw piles of rocks and branches to cover bodies from sight.

The mountainface reshaped, they drove supports for a bridge. Since hammering was less dangerous than the blowing up, the men played a little; they rode the baskets swooping in wide arcs; they twisted the ropes and let them unwind like tops. "Look at me," said Ah Goong, pulled open his pants, and pissed overboard, the wind scattering the drops. "I'm a waterfall," he said. He had sent a part of himself hurtling. On rare windless days he watched his piss fall in a continuous stream from himself almost to the bottom of the valley.

One beautiful day, dangling in the sun above a new valley, not the desire to urinate but sexual desire clutched him so hard he bent over in the basket. He curled up, overcome by beauty and fear, which shot to his penis. He tried to rub himself calm. Suddenly he stood up tall and squirted out into space. "I am fucking the world," he said. The world's vagina was big, big as the sky, big as a valley. He grew a habit: whenever he was lowered in the basket, his blood rushed to his penis, and he fucked the world.

Then it was autumn, and the wind blew so fiercely, the men had to postpone the basketwork. Clouds moved in several directions at once. Men pointed at dust devils, which turned their mouths crooked. There was ceaseless motion; clothes kept moving; hair moved; sleeves puffed out. Nothing stayed still long enough for Ah Goong to figure it out. The wind sucked the breath out of his mouth and blew thoughts from his brains. The food convoys from San Francisco brought tents to replace the ones that whipped away. The baskets from China, which the men saved for high work, carried cowboy jackets, long underwear, Levi pants, boots, earmuffs, leather gloves, flannel shirts, coats. They sewed rabbit fur and deerskin into the linings. They tied the wide brims of their cowboy hats over their ears with mufflers. And still the wind made confusing howls into ears, and it was hard to think.

The days became nights when the crews tunneled inside the mountain, which sheltered them from the wind, but also hid the light and sky. Ah Goong pickaxed the mountain, the dirt filling his nostrils through a cowboy bandanna. He shoveled the dirt into a cart and pushed it to a place that was tall enough for the mule, which hauled it the rest of the way out. He looked forward to cart duty to edge closer to the entrance. Eyes darkened, nose plugged, his windy cough worse, he was to mole a thousand feet and meet others digging from the other side. How much he'd pay now to go swinging in a basket. He might as well have gone to work in a tin mine. Coming out of the tunnel at the end of a shift, he forgot whether it was supposed to be day or night. He blew his nose fifteen times before the mucus cleared again.

The dirt was the easiest part of tunneling. Beneath the soil, they hit granite. Ah Goong struck it with his pickax, and it jarred his bones, chattered his teeth. He swung his sledgehammer against it, and the impact rang in the dome of his skull. The mountain that was millions of years old was locked against them and was not to be broken into. The men teased him, "Let's see you fuck the world now." "Let's see you fuck the Gold Mountain now." But he no longer felt like it. "A man ought to be made of tougher material than flesh," he said. "Skin is too soft. Our bones ought to be filled with iron." He lifted the hammer high, careful that it not pull him backward, and let it fall forward of its own weight against the rock. Nothing happened to that gray wall; he had to slam with strength and will. He hit at the same spot over and over again, the same rock. Some chips and flakes broke off. The granite looked everywhere the same. It had no softer or weaker spots anywhere, the same hard gray. He learned to slide his hand up the handle, lift, slide and swing, a circular motion, hammering, hammering, hammering. He would bite like a rat through that mountain. His eyes couldn't see; his nose couldn't smell; and now his ears were filled with the noise of hammering. This rock is what is real, he thought. This rock is what real is, not clouds or mist, which make mysterious promises, and when you go through them are nothing. When the foreman measured at the end of twenty-four hours of pounding, the rock had given a foot. The hammering went on day and night. The men worked eight hours on and eight hours off. They worked on all eighteen tunnels at once. While Ah Goong slept, he could hear the sledgehammers of other men working in the earth. The steady banging reminded him of holidays and harvests; falling asleep, he heard the women chopping mincemeat and the millstones striking.

The demons in boss suits came into the tunnel occasionally, measured with a yardstick, and shook their heads. "Faster," they said. "Faster. Chinamen too slow. Too slow." "Tell us we're slow," the China Men grumbled. The ones in top tiers of scaffolding let rocks drop, a hammer drop. Ropes tangled around the demons' heads and feet. The cave China Men muttered and flexed, glared out of the corners of their eyes. But usually there was no diversion—one day the same as the next, one hour no different from another—the beating against the same granite.

After tunneling into granite for about three years, Ah Goong understood the immovability of the earth. Men change, men die, weather changes, but a mountain is the same as permanence and time. This mountain would have taken no new shape for centuries, ten thousand centuries, the world a still, still place, time unmoving. He worked in the tunnel so long, he learned to see many colors in black. When he stumbled out, he tried to talk about time. "I felt time," he said. "I saw time. I saw world." He tried again, "I saw what's real. I saw time, and it doesn't move. If we break through the mountain, hollow it, time won't have moved anyway. You translators ought to tell the foreigners that."

Summer came again, but after the first summer, he felt less nostalgia at the meeting of the Spinning Girl and the Cowboy. He now knew men who had been in this country for twenty years and thirty years, and the Cowboy's one year away from his lady was no time at all. His own patience was longer. The stars were meeting and would meet again next year, but he would not have seen his family. He joined the others celebrating Souls' Day, the holiday a week later, the fourteenth day of the seventh month. The supply wagons from San Francisco and Sacramento brought watermelon, meat, fish, crab, pressed duck. "There, ghosts, there you are. Come and get it." They displayed the feast complete for a moment before falling to, eating on the dead's behalf.

In the third year of pounding granite by hand, a demon invented dynamite. The railroad workers were to test it. They had stopped using gunpowder in the tunnels after avalanches, but the demons said that dynamite was more precise. They watched a scientist demon mix nitrate, sulphate, and glycerine, then flick the yellow oil, which exploded off his fingertips. Sitting in a meadow to watch the dynamite detonated in the open, Ah Goong saw the men in front of him leap impossibly high into the air; then he felt a shove as if from a giant's unseen hand—and he fell backward. The boom broke the mountain silence like fear breaking inside stomach and chest and groin. No one had gotten hurt; they stood up laughing and amazed, looking around at how they had fallen, the pattern of the explosion. Dynamite was much more powerful than gunpowder. Ah Goong had felt a nudge, as if something kind were moving him out of harm's way. "All of a sudden I was sitting next to you." "Aiya. If we had been nearer, it would have killed us." "If we were stiff, it would have gone through us." "A fist." "A hand." "We leapt like acrobats." Next time Ah Goong flattened himself on the ground, and the explosion rolled over him.

He never got used to the blasting; a blast always surprised him. Even when he himself set the fuse and watched it burn, anticipated the explosion, the bang—*bahng* in Chinese—when it came, always startled. It cleaned the crazy words, the crackling, and bingbangs out of his brain. It was like New Year's, when every problem and thought was knocked clean out of him by firecrackers, and he could begin fresh. He couldn't worry during an explosion, which jerked every head to attention. Hills flew up in rocks and dirt. Boulders turned over and over. Sparks, fires, debris, rocks, smoke burst up, not at the same time as the boom (*bum*) but before that—the sound a separate occurrence, not useful as a signal.

The terrain changed immediately. Streams were diverted, rockscapes exposed. Ah Goong found it difficult to remember what land had looked like before an explosion. It was a good thing the dynamite was invented after the Civil War to the east was over.

The dynamite added more accidents and ways of dying, but if it were not used, the railroad would take fifty more years to finish. Nitroglycerine exploded when it was jounced on a horse or dropped. A man who fell with it in his pocket blew himself up into red pieces. Sometimes it combusted merely standing. Human bodies skipped through the air like puppets and made Ah Goong laugh crazily as if the arms and legs would come together again. The smell of burned flesh remained in rocks.

In the tunnels, the men bored holes fifteen to eighteen inches deep with a power drill, stuffed them with hay and dynamite, and imbedded the fuse in sand. Once, for extra pay, Ah Goong ran back in to see why some dynamite had not gone off and hurried back out again; it was just a slow fuse. When the explosion settled, he helped carry two-hundred-, three-hundred-, five-hundred-pound boulders out of the tunnel.

As a boy he had visited a Taoist monastery where there were nine rooms, each a replica of one of the nine hells. Lifesize sculptures of men and women were spitted on turning wheels. Eerie candles under the suffering faces emphasized eyes poked out, tongues pulled, red mouths and eyes, and real hair, eyelashes, and eyebrows. Women were split apart and men dismembered. He could have reached out and touched the sufferers

and the implements. He had dug and dynamited his way into one of these hells. "Only
here there are eighteen tunnels, not nine, plus all the tracks between them," he said.

One day he came out of the tunnel to find the mountains white, the evergreens and
bare trees decorated, white tree sculptures and lace bushes everywhere. The men from
snow country called the icicles "ice chopsticks." He sat in his basket and slid down the
slopes. The snow covered the gouged land, the broken trees, the tracks, the mud, the
campfire ashes, the unburied dead. Streams were stilled in mid-run, the water petrified.
That winter he thought it was the task of the human race to quicken the world, blast the
freeze, fire it, redden it with blood. He had to change the stupid slowness of one sunrise
and one sunset per day. He had to enliven the silent world with sound. "The rock," he
tried to tell the others. "The ice." "Time."

The dynamiting loosed blizzards on the men. Ears and toes fell off. Fingers stuck to
the cold silver rails. Snowblind men stumbled about with bandannas over their eyes. Ah
Goong helped build wood tunnels roofing the track route. Falling ice scrabbled on the
roofs. The men stayed under the snow for weeks at a time. Snowslides covered the
entrances to the tunnels, which they had to dig out to enter and exit, white tunnels and
black tunnels. Ah Goong looked at his gang and thought, If there is an avalanche, these are
the people I'll be trapped with, and wondered which ones would share food. A party of
snowbound barbarians had eaten the dead. Cannibals, thought Ah Goong, and looked
around. Food was not scarce; the tea man brought whiskey barrels of hot tea, and he
warmed his hands and feet, held the teacup to his nose and ears. Someday, he planned, he
would buy a chair with metal doors for putting hot coal inside it. The magpies did not
abandon him but stayed all winter and searched the snow for food.

The men who died slowly enough to say last words said, "Don't leave me frozen under
the snow. Send my body home. Burn it and put the ashes in a tin can. Take the bone jar
when you come down the mountain." "When you ride the fire car back to China, tell my
descendants to come for me." "Shut up," scolded the hearty men. "We don't want to hear
about bone jars and dying." "You're lucky to have a body to bury, not blown to
smithereens." "Stupid man to hurt yourself," they bawled out the sick and wounded. How
their wives would scold if they brought back deadmen's bones. "Aiya. To be buried here,
nowhere." "But this is somewhere," Ah Goong promised. "This is the Gold Mountain.
We're marking the land now. The track sections are numbered, and your family will know
where we leave you." But he was a crazy man, and they didn't listen to him.

Spring did come, and when the snow melted, it revealed the past year, what had happened, what they had done, where they had worked, the lost tools, the thawing bodies,
some standing with tools in hand, the bright rails. "Remember Uncle Long Winded
Leong?" "Remember Strong Back Wong?" "Remember Lee Brother?" "And Fong Uncle?"
They lost count of the number dead; there is no record of how many died building
the railroad. Or maybe it was demons doing the counting and chinamen not worth
counting. Whether it was good luck or bad luck, the dead were buried or cairned next to
the last section of track they had worked on. "May his ghost not have to toil," they said
over graves. (In China a woodcutter ghost chops eternally; people have heard chopping in
the snow and in the heat.) "Maybe his ghost will ride the train home." The scientific
demons said the transcontinental railroad would connect the West to Cathay. "What if he
rides back and forth from Sacramento to New York forever?" "That wouldn't be so bad.
I hear the cars will be like houses on wheels." The funerals were short. "No time. No
time," said both China Men and demons. The railroad was as straight as they could build
it, but no ghosts sat on the tracks; no strange presences haunted the tunnels. The blasts
scared ghosts away.

When the Big Dipper pointed east and the China Men detonated nitroglycerine and
shot off guns for the New Year, which comes with the spring, these special bangs were not

as loud as the daily bangs, not as numerous as the bangs all year. Shouldn't the New Year be the loudest day of all to obliterate the noises of the old year? But to make a bang of that magnitude, they would have to blow up at least a year's supply of dynamite in one blast. They arranged strings of chain reactions in circles and long lines, banging faster and louder to culminate in a big bang. And most importantly, there were random explosions—surprise. Surprise. SURPRISE. They had no dragon, the railroad their dragon.

The demons invented games for working faster, gold coins for miles of track laid, for the heaviest rock, a grand prize for the first team to break through a tunnel. Day shifts raced against night shifts, China Men against Welshmen, China Men against Irishmen, China Men against Injuns and black demons. The fastest races were China Men against China Men, who bet on their own teams. China Men always won because of good teamwork, smart thinking, and the need for the money. Also, they had the most workers to choose teams from. Whenever his team won anything, Ah Goong added to his gold stash. The Central Pacific or Union Pacific won the land on either side of the tracks it built.

One summer day, demon officials and China Man translators went from group to group and announced, "We're raising the pay—thirty-five dollars a month. Because of your excellent work, the Central Pacific Railroad is giving you a four-dollar raise per month." The workers who didn't know better cheered. "What's the catch?" said the smarter men. "You'll have the opportunity to put in more time," said the railroad demons. "Two more hours per shift." Ten-hour shifts inside the tunnels. "It's not ten hours straight," said the demons. "You have time off for tea and meals. Now that you have dynamite, the work isn't so hard." They had been working for three and a half years already, and the track through the Donner Summit was still not done.

The workers discussed the ten-hour shift, swearing their China Man obscenities. "Two extra hours a day—sixty hours a month for four dollars." "Pig catcher demons." "Snakes." "Turtles." "Dead demons." "A human body can't work like that." "The demons don't believe this is a human body. This is a chinaman's body." To bargain, they sent a delegation of English speakers, who were summarily noted as troublemakers, turned away, docked.

The China Men, then, decided to go on strike and demand forty-five dollars a month and the eight-hour shift. They risked going to jail and the Central Pacific keeping the pay it was banking for them. Ah Goong memorized the English, "Forty-five dollars a month—eight-hour shift." He practiced the strike slogan: "Eight hours a day good for white man, all the same good for China Man."

The men wrapped barley and beans in ti leaves, which came from Hawai'i via San Francisco, for celebrating the fifth day of the fifth month (not May but mid-June, the summer solstice). Usually the way the red string is wound and knotted tells what flavors are inside—the salty barley with pickled egg, or beans and pork, or the gelatin pudding. Ah Goong folded ti leaves into a cup and packed it with food. One of the literate men slipped in a piece of paper with the strike plan, and Ah Goong tied the bundle with a special pattern of red string. The time and place for the revolution against Kublai Khan had been hidden inside autumn mooncakes. Ah Goong looked from one face to another in admiration. Of course, of course. No China Men, no railroad. They were indispensable labor. Throughout these mountains were brothers and uncles with a common idea, free men, not coolies, calling for fair working conditions. The demons were not suspicious as the China Men went gandying up and down the tracks delivering the bundles tied together like lines of fish. They had exchanged these gifts every year. When the summer solstice cakes came from other camps, the recipients cut them into neat slices by drawing the string through them. The orange jellies, which had a red dye stick inside soaked in lye, fell into a series of sunrises and sunsets. The aged yolks and the barley also looked like suns. The notes gave a Yes strike vote. The yellow flags to ward off the five evils—centipedes, scorpions, snakes, poisonous lizards, and toads—now flew as banners.

The strike began on Tuesday morning, June 25, 1867. The men who were working at that hour walked out of the tunnels and away from the tracks. The ones who were sleeping slept on and rose as late as they pleased. They bathed in streams and shaved their moustaches and wild beards. Some went fishing and hunting. The violinists tuned and played their instruments. The drummers beat theirs at the punchlines of jokes. The gamblers shuffled and played their cards and tiles. The smokers passed their pipes, and the drinkers bet for drinks by making figures with their hands. The cooks made party food. The opera singers' falsettos almost perforated the mountains. The men sang new songs about the railroad. They made up verses and shouted Ho at the good ones, and laughed at the rhymes. Oh, they were madly singing in the mountains. The storytellers told about the rise of new kings. The opium smokers when they roused themselves told their florid images. Ah Goong sifted for gold. All the while the English-speaking China Men, who were being advised by the shrewdest bargainers, were at the demons' headquarters repeating the demand: "Eight hours a day good for white man, all the same good for China Man." They had probably negotiated the demons down to nine-hour shifts by now.

The sounds of hammering continued along the tracks and occasionally there were blasts from the tunnels. The scabby white demons had refused to join the strike. "Eight hours a day good for white man, all the same good for China Man," the China Men explained to them. "Cheap John Chinaman," said the demons, many of whom had red hair. The China Men scowled out of the corners of their eyes.

On the second day, artist demons climbed the mountains to draw the China Men for the newspapers. The men posed bare-chested, their fists clenched, showing off their arms and backs. The artists sketched them as perfect young gods reclining against rocks, wise expressions on their handsome noble-nosed faces, long torsos with lean stomachs, a strong arm extended over a bent knee, long fingers holding a pipe, a rope of hair over a wide shoulder. Other artists drew faeries with antennae for eyebrows and brownies with elvish pigtails; they danced in white socks and black slippers among mushroom rings by moonlight.

Ah Goong acquired another idea that added to his reputation for craziness: The pale, thin Chinese scholars and the rich men fat like Buddhas were less beautiful, less manly than these brown muscular railroad men, of whom he was one. One of ten thousand heroes.

On the third day, in a woods—he would be looking at a deer or a rabbit or an Injun watching him before he knew what he was seeing—a demon dressed in a white suit and tall hat beckoned him. They talked privately in the wilderness. The demon said, "I Citizenship Judge invite you to he U.S. citizen. Only one bag gold." Ah Goong was thrilled. What an honor. He would accept this invitation. Also what advantages, he calculated shrewdly; if he were going to be jailed for this strike, an American would have a trial. The Citizenship Judge unfurled a parchment sealed with gold and ribbon. Ah Goong bought it with one bag of gold. "You vote," said the Citizenship Judge. "You talk in court, buy land, no more chinaman tax." Ah Goong hid the paper on his person so that it would protect him from arrest and lynching. He was already a part of this new country, but now he had it in writing.

The fourth day, the strikers heard that the U. S. Cavalry was riding single file up the tracks to shoot them. They argued whether to engage the Army with dynamite. But the troops did not come. Instead the cowardly demons blockaded the food wagons. No food. Ah Goong listened to the optimistic China Men, who said, "Don't panic. We'll hold out forever. We can hunt. We can last fifty days on water." The complainers said, "Aiya. Only saints can do that. Only magic men and monks who've practiced." The China Men refused to declare a last day for the strike.

The foresighted China Men had cured jerky, fermented wine, dried and strung orange and grapefruit peels, pickled and preserved leftovers. Ah Goong, one of the best hoarders, had set aside extra helpings from each meal. This same quandary, whether to give away food or to appear selfish, had occurred during each of the six famines he had lived through. The foodless men identified themselves. Sure enough, they were the shiftless, piggy, arrogant type who didn't worry enough. The donors scolded them and shamed them the whole while they were handing them food: "So you lived like a grasshopper at our expense." "Fleaman." "You'll be the cause of our not holding out long enough." "Rich man's kid. Too good to hoard." Ah Goong contributed some rice crusts from the bottoms of pans. He kept how much more food he owned a secret, as he kept the secret of his gold. In apology for not contributing richer food, he repeated a Mohist saying that had guided him in China: " 'The superior man does not push humaneness to the point of stupidity.' " He could hear his wife scolding him for feeding strangers. The opium men offered shit and said that it calmed the appetite.

On the fifth and sixth days, Ah Goong organized his possessions and patched his clothes and tent. He forebore repairing carts, picks, ropes, baskets. His work-habituated hands arranged rocks and twigs in designs. He asked a reader to read again his family's letters. His wife sounded like herself except for the polite phrases added professionally at the beginnings and the ends. "Idiot," she said, "why are you taking so long? Are you wasting the money? Are you spending it on girls and gambling and whiskey? Here's my advice to you: Be a little more frugal. Remember how it felt to go hungry. Work hard." He had been an idle man for almost a week. "I need a new dress to wear to weddings. I refuse to go to another banquet in the same old dress. If you weren't such a spendthrift, we could be building the new courtyard where we'll drink wine among the flowers and sit about in silk gowns all day. We'll hire peasants to till the fields. Or lease them to tenants, and buy all our food at market. We'll have clean fingernails and toenails." Other relatives said, "I need a gold watch. Send me the money. Your wife gambles it away and throws parties and doesn't disburse it fairly among us. You might as well come home." It was after one of these letters that he had made a bonus investigating some dud dynamite.

Ah Goong did not spend his money on women. The strikers passed the word that a woman was traveling up the railroad and would be at his camp on the seventh and eighth day of the strike. Some said she was a demoness and some that she was a Chinese and her master a China Man. He pictured a nurse coming to bandage wounds and touch foreheads or a princess surveying her subjects; or perhaps she was a merciful Jesus demoness. But she was a pitiful woman, led on a leash around her waist, not entirely alive. Her owner sold lottery tickets for the use of her. Ah Goong did not buy one. He took out his penis under his blanket or bared it in the woods and thought about nurses and princesses. He also just looked at it, wondering what it was that it was for, what a man was for, what he had to have a penis for.

There was rumor also of an Injun woman called Woman Chief, who led a nomadic fighting tribe from the eastern plains as far as these mountains. She was so powerful that she had four wives and many horses. He never saw her though.

The strike ended on the ninth day. The Central Pacific announced that in its benevolence it was giving the workers a four-dollar raise, not the fourteen dollars they had asked for. And that the shifts in the tunnels would remain eight hours long. "We were planning to give you the four-dollar raise all along," the demons said to diminish the victory. So they got thirty-five dollars a month and the eight-hour shift. They would have won forty-five dollars if the thousand demon workers had joined the strike. Demons would have listened to demons. The China Men went back to work quietly. No use singing and shouting over a compromise and losing nine days' work.

There were two days that Ah Goong did cheer and throw his hat in the air, jumping up and down and screaming Yippee like a cowboy. One: the day his team broke through the tunnel at last. Toward the end they did not dynamite but again used picks and sledge-hammers. Through the granite, they heard answering poundings, and answers to their shouts. It was not a mountain before them any more but only a wall with people breaking through from the other side. They worked faster. Forward. Into day. They stuck their arms through the holes and shook hands with men on the other side. Ah Goong saw dirty faces as wondrous as if he were seeing Nu Wo, the creator goddess who repairs cracks in the sky with stone slabs; sometimes she peeks through and human beings see her face. The wall broke. Each team gave the other a gift of half a tunnel, dug. They stepped back and forth where the wall had been. Ah Goong ran and ran, his boots thudding to the very end of the tunnel, looked at the other side of the mountain, and ran back, clear through the entire tunnel. All the way through.

He spent the rest of his time on the railroad laying and bending and hammering the ties and rails. The second day the China Men cheered was when the engine from the West and the one from the East rolled toward one another and touched. The transcontinental railroad was finished. They Yippee'd like madmen. The white demon officials gave speeches. "The Greatest Feat of the Nineteenth Century," they said. "The Greatest Feat in the History of Mankind," they said. "Only Americans could have done it," they said, which is true. Even if Ah Goong had not spent half his gold on Citizenship Papers, he was an American for having built the railroad. A white demon in top hat tap-tapped on the gold spike, and pulled it back out. Then one China Man held the real spike, the steel one, and another hammered it in.

While the demons posed for photographs, the China Men dispersed. It was danger-ous to stay. The Driving Out had begun. Ah Goong does not appear in railroad photo-graphs. Scattering, some China Men followed the north star in the constellation Tortoise the Black Warrior to Canada, or they kept the constellation Phoenix ahead of them to South America or the White Tiger west or the Wolf east. Seventy lucky men rode the Union Pacific to Massachusetts for jobs at a shoe factory. Fifteen hundred went to Fou Loy Company in New Orleans and San Francisco, several hundred to plantations in Mississippi, Georgia, and Arkansas, and sugarcane plantations in Louisiana and Cuba. (From the South, they sent word that it was a custom to step off the sidewalk along with the black demons when a white demon walked by.) Seventy went to New Orleans to grade a route for a railroad, then to Pennsylvania to work in a knife factory. The Colorado State Legislature passed a resolution welcoming the railroad China Men to come build the new state. They built railroads in every part of the country—the Alabama and Chattanooga Railroad, the Houston and Texas Railroad, the Southern Pacific, the railroads in Louisiana and Boston, the Pacific Northwest, and Alaska. After the Civil War, China Men banded the nation North and South, East and West, with crisscrossing steel. They were the binding and building ancestors of this place.

Ah Goong would have liked a leisurely walk along the tracks to review his finished handiwork, or to walk east to see the rest of his new country. But instead, Driven Out, he slid down mountains, leapt across valleys and streams, crossed plains, hid sometimes with companions and often alone, and eluded bandits who would hold him up for his railroad pay and shoot him for practice as they shot Injuns and jackrabbits. Detouring and backtracking, his path wound back and forth to his railroad, a familiar silver road in the wilderness. When a train came, he hid against the shaking ground in case a demon with a shotgun was hunting from it. He picked over camps where he had once lived. He was careful to find hidden places to sleep. In China bandits did not normally kill people, the booty the main thing, but here the demons killed for fun and hate. They tied pigtails to horses and dragged chinamen. He decided that he had better head for San Francisco, where he would catch a ship to China.

Perched on hillsides, he watched many sunsets, the place it was setting, the direction he was going. There were fields of grass that he tunneled through, hid in, rolled in, dived and swam in, suddenly jumped up laughing, suddenly stopped. He needed to find a town and human company. The spooky tumbleweeds caught in barbed wire were peering at him, waiting for him; he had to find a town. Towns grew along the tracks as they did along rivers. He sat looking at a town all day, then ducked into it by night.

At the familiar sight of a garden laid out in a Chinese scheme—vegetables in beds, white cabbages, red plants, chives, and coriander for immortality, herbs boxed with boards—he knocked on the back door. The China Man who answered gave him food, the appropriate food for the nearest holiday, talked story, exclaimed at how close their ancestral villages were to each other. They exchanged information on how many others lived how near, which towns had Chinatowns, what size, two or three stores or a block, which towns to avoid. "Do you have a wife?" they asked one another. "Yes. She lives in China. I have been sending money for twenty years now." They exchanged vegetable seeds, slips, and cuttings, and Ah Goong carried letters to another town or China.

Some demons who had never seen the likes of him gave him things and touched him. He also came across lone China Men who were alarmed to have him appear, and, unwelcome, he left quickly; they must have wanted to be the only China Man of that area, the special China Man.

He met miraculous China Men who had produced families out of nowhere—a wife and children, both boys and girls. "Uncle," the children called him, and he wanted to stay to be the uncle of the family. The wife washed his clothes, and he went on his way when they were dry.

On a farm road, he came across an imp child playing in the dirt. It looked at him, and he looked at it. He held out a piece of sugar; he cupped a grassblade between his thumbs and whistled. He sat on the ground with his legs crossed, and the child climbed into the hollow of his arms and legs. "I wish you were my baby," he told it. "My baby." He was very satisfied sitting there under the humming sun with the baby, who was satisfied too, no squirming. "My daughter," he said. "My son." He couldn't tell whether it was a boy or a girl. He touched the baby's fat arm and cheeks, its gold hair, and looked into its blue eyes. He made a wish that it not have to carry a sledgehammer and crawl into the dark. But he would not feel sorry for it; other people must not suffer any more than he did, and he could endure anything. Its mother came walking out into the road. She had her hands above her like a salute. She walked tentatively toward them, held out her hand, smiled, spoke. He did not understand what she said except "Bye-bye." The child waved and said, "Bye-bye," crawled over his legs, and toddled to her. Ah Goong continued on his way in a direction she could not point out to a posse looking for a kidnapper chinaman.

Explosions followed him. He heard screams and went on, saw flames outlining black windows and doors, and went on. He ran in the opposite direction from gunshots and the yell—*eeha awha*—the cowboys made when they herded cattle and sang their savage songs.

Good at hiding, disappearing—decades unaccounted for—he was not working in a mine when forty thousand chinamen were Driven Out of mining. He was not killed or kidnapped in the Los Angeles Massacre, though he gave money toward ransoming those whose toes and fingers, a digit per week, and ears grotesquely rotting or pickled, and scalped queues, were displayed in Chinatowns. Demons believed that the poorer a chinaman looked, the more gold he had buried somewhere, that chinamen stuck together and would always ransom one another. If he got kidnapped, Ah Goong planned, he would whip out his Citizenship Paper and show that he was an American. He was lucky not to be in Colorado when the Denver demons burned all chinamen homes and businesses, nor in Rock Springs, Wyoming, when the miner demons killed twenty-eight or fifty china-men. The Rock Springs Massacre began in a large coal mine owned by the Union Pacific; the outnumbered chinamen were shot in the back as they ran to Chinatown, which the demons burned. They forced chinamen out into the open and shot them; demon women and children threw the wounded back in the flames. (There was a rumor of a good white lady in Green Springs who hid China Men in the Pacific Hotel and shamed the demons away.) The hunt went on for a month before federal troops came. The count of the dead was inexact because bodies were mutilated and pieces scattered all over the Wyoming Territory. No white miners were indicted, but the government paid $150,000 in repara-tions to victims' families. There were many family men, then. There were settlers—abiding China Men. And China Women. Ah Goong was running elsewhere during the Drivings Out of Tacoma, Seattle, Oregon City, Albania, and Marysville. The demons of Tacoma packed all its chinamen into boxcars and sent them to Portland, where they were run out of town. China Men returned to Seattle, though, and refused to sell their land and stores but fought until the army came; the demon rioters were tried and acquitted. And when the Boston police imprisoned and beat 234 chinamen, it was 1902, and Ah Goong had already reached San Francisco or China, and perhaps San Francisco again.

In Second City (Sacramento), he spent some of his railroad money at the theater. The main actor's face was painted red with thick black eyebrows and long black beard, and when he strode onto the stage, Ah Goong recognized the hero, Guan Goong; his puppet horse had red nostrils and rolling eyes. Ah Goong's heart leapt to recognize hero and horse in the wilds of America. Guan Goong murdered his enemy—crash! bang! of cymbals and drum—and left his home village—sad, sad flute music. But to the glad clamor of cymbals entered his friends—Liu Pei (pronounced the same as Running Nose) and Chang Fei. In a joyful burst of pink flowers, the three men swore the Peach Garden Oath. Each friend sang an aria to friendship; together they would fight side by side and live and die one for all and all for one. Ah Goong felt as warm as if he were with friends at a party. Then Guan Goong's archenemy, the sly Ts'ao Ts'ao, captured him and two of Liu Pei's wives, the Lady Kan and the Lady Mi. Though Ah Goong knew they were boy actors, he basked in the presence of Chinese ladies. The prisoners traveled to the capital, the soldiers waving horse-hair whisks, signifying horses, the ladies walking between horizontal banners, signifying palanquins. All the prisoners were put in one bedroom, but Guan Goong stood all night outside the door with a lighted candle in his hand, singing an aria about faithfulness. When the capital was attacked by a common enemy, Guan Goong fought the biggest man in one-to-one combat, a twirling, jumping sword dance that strengthened the China Men who watched it. From afar Guan Goong's two partners heard about the feats of the man with the red face and intelligent horse. The three friends were reunited and fought until they secured their rightful kingdom.

Ah Goong felt refreshed and inspired. He called out Bravo like the demons in the audience, who had not seen theater before, Guan Goong, the God of War, also God of War and Literature, had come to America—Guan Goong, Grandfather Guan, our own ancestor of writers and fighters, of actors and gamblers, and avenging executioners who mete out justice. Our own kin. Not a distant ancestor but Grandfather.

In the Big City (San Francisco), a goldsmith convinced Ah Goong to have his gold made into jewelry, which would organize it into one piece and also delight his wife. So he handed over a second bag of gold. He got it back as a small ring in a design he thought up himself, two hands clasping in a handshake. "So small?" he said, but the goldsmith said that only some of the ore had been true gold.

He got a ship out of San Francisco without being captured near the docks, where there was a stockade full of jailed chinamen; the demonesses came down from Nob Hill and took them home to be servants, cooks, and baby-sitters.

Grandmother liked the gold ring very much. The gold was so pure, it squished to fit her finger. She never washed dishes, so the gold did not wear away. She quickly spent the railroad money, and Ah Goong said he would go to America again. He had a Certificate of Return and his Citizenship Paper.

But this time, there was no railroad to sell his strength to. He lived in a basement that was rumored to connect with tunnels beneath Chinatown. In an underground arsenal, he held a pistol and said, "I feel the death in it." "The holes for the bullets were like chambers in a beehive or wasp nest," he said. He was inside the earth when the San Francisco Earthquake and Fire began. Thunder rumbled from the ground. Some say he died falling into the cracking earth. It was a miraculous earthquake and fire. The Hall of Records burned completely. Citizenship Papers burned, Certificates of Return, Birth Certificates, Residency Certificates, passenger lists, Marriage Certificates—every paper a China Man wanted for citizenship and legality burned in that fire. An authentic citizen, then, had no more papers than an alien. Any paper a China Man could not produce had been "burned up in the Fire of 1906." Every China Man was reborn out of that fire a citizen.

Some say the family went into debt to send for Ah Goong, who was not making money; he was a homeless wanderer, a shiftless, dirty, jobless man with matted hair, ragged clothes, and fleas all over his body. He ate out of garbage cans. He was a louse eaten by lice. A fleaman. It cost two thousand dollars to bring him back to China, his oldest sons signing promissory notes for one thousand, his youngest to repay four hundred to one neighbor and six hundred to another. Maybe he hadn't died in San Francisco, it was just his papers that burned; it was just that his existence was outlawed by Chinese Exclusion Acts. The family called him Fleaman. They did not understand his accomplishments as an American ancestor, a holding, homing ancestor of this place. He'd gotten the legal or illegal papers burned in the San Francisco Earthquake and Fire; he appeared in America in time to be a citizen and to father citizens. He had also been seen carrying a child out of the fire, a child of his own in spite of the laws against marrying. He had built a railroad out of sweat, why not have an American child out of longing?

Angel Island Poems

Chinese sojourners and settlers came to "*Gum Sahn*," or Gold Mountain, to pan for gold in the 1850s and to work on the construction of the Central Pacific Railroad in the 1860s. Underpaid and overworked, they had little choice but to take the most dangerous and labor-intensive jobs. After the completion of the railroad, they faced the "great driving out," waves of violence from whites and virulent racism in the press and among business owners that melded into national racist policies and laws. In 1882, Congress passed the Chinese Exclusion Act, barring, for the first time, a single ethnic group from immigrating to the United States. The act was targeted at laborers, but did allow a small number of Chinese merchants and teachers into the country. Some immigrants came through this loophole in the law, claiming to be the "paper sons" of Chinese merchants who held American citizenship. Those whose papers did not pass initial inspection in San Francisco were sent to Angel Island in San Francisco Bay, a detention center where men were held separately from women and young children. New arrivals were not allowed to talk with other detainees before their questioning by immigration officials. They waited sometimes for months. The conditions were crowded and prisonlike; detainees protested meager and poor-quality food. While they waited, the Chinese formed small self-help communities within Angel Island, and some expressed their subjective feelings about their confinement in poems they etched on the wooden barracks walls. As one wrote: "This island is not angelic." After an earthquake and fire that destroyed the administration building, the Immigration Station on Angel Island was closed in 1943. Chinese Exclusion Laws were partially repealed in 1943 and fully repealed in 1965. The detention barracks, scheduled for demolition, were saved because an alert park ranger brought the carved markings on the walls to the public's attention; the barracks are now a historic landmark at Angel Island State Park. These poems are from the versions that were recorded by two former detainees, Smiley Jann and Tet Yee, and are included in the book *Island: Poetry and History of Chinese Immigrants on Angel Island 1910–1940*, edited by Him Mark Lai, Genny Lim, and Judy Yung (1991).

ANGEL ISLAND POEMS (1910–1940)

[1]

POEM BY ONE NAMED XU, FROM XIANGSHAN, CONSOLING HIMSELF

Over a hundred poems are on the walls.
Looking at them, they are all pining at the delayed progress.
What can one sad person say to another?
Unfortunate travellers everywhere wish to commiserate.
5   Gain or lose, how is one to know what is predestined?
Rich or poor, who is to say it is not the will of heaven?
Why should one complain if he is detained and imprisoned here?
From ancient times, heroes often were the first ones to face adversity.

[2]

This place is called an island of immortals,
When, in fact, this mountain wilderness is a prison.
Once you see the open net, why throw yourself in?
It is only because of empty pockets I can do nothing else.

[3]

I raise my brush to write a poem to tell my dear wife,
Last night at the third watch I sighed at being apart
The message you gave with tender thoughts is still with me;
I do not know what day I can return home.

[4]

Leaving behind my writing brush and removing my sword, I came to America.
Who was to know two streams of tears would flow upon arriving here?
If there comes a day when I will have attained my ambition and become successful,
I will certainly behead the barbarians and spare not a single blade of grass.

[5]

I have lingered here three days moving again and again.
It is difficult to compare this to the peacefulness at home.
Life need not be so demeaning.
Rushing about so much, smoke came out of my mouth.

IV

Revolt, Repression, and Cultural Formations: 1900–1929

The working class and the employing class have nothing
in common. There can be no peace as long as hunger
and want are found among millions of working people,
and the few who make up the employing class have all
the good things of life.
—from the manifesto of the Industrial Workers
of the World (IWW), 1905

These fighting words of the IWW, written one hundred years ago, may seem like so much exaggerated rhetoric from a contemporary perspective. History, as told and retold in textbooks, tends to filter out emotion and flatten into discernible periods: the Progressive Era, a period around 1900–1917 of modest reform; then the Jazz Age or Roaring Twenties, a time of flappers, illegal booze, and excess; and bridging these two decades, World War I (1914–1918), which the United States entered in 1917. The language of class warfare is rarely part of the historical discursive mix. But for the working poor, it was a time of intense class struggle with more defeats than victories, many casualties and deaths, and the undermining of civil liberties and constitutional rights.

Political, social, and labor movements forged various strategies, from incremental reform to radical change, to resist the flagrant wealth and power of the robber barons. The IWW emerged in 1905 partly in response to the conservatism and exclusionary policies of the AFL (American Federation of Labor). In 1912, the Socialist Party, with Eugene Debs as its presidential candidate, polled 6 percent of the total vote and elected 1,200 candidates in municipal elections throughout the country. Newspapers and periodicals with socialist and working-class perspectives proliferated in English and foreign-language editions.[1] Novels, such as Upton Sinclair's *The Jungle*, exposed horrendous working conditions in industry, and investigations by "muckracking" journalists were serialized in magazines that reached a wider middle-class audience.

With resistance came repression and the arrests of numerous "agitators" perceived by business owners as threats to the natural order of capitalism. The wartime Espionage Act of 1917 restricted free speech and was the catalyst for the imprisonment of hundreds of Americans (including Eugene V. Debs). The Russian Revolution of 1917, championed by the American Left as a working-class revolution, was viewed by business and government leaders as an intolerable threat. In 1918, over one hundred IWW members were arrested and put on trial for their opposition to war; all were found guilty.[2] The Palmer Raids

Facing Page: Lewis Hine, Child Laborers. Clockwise: spinner in a New England cotton mill, North Pownal, Vermont, 1910; young West Virginia coal miner; glass factory worker, Alexandria, Virginia, 1911; seven-year-old Rosie, an experienced oyster shucker, Bluffton, South Carolina, 1913.

(1918–1921) that followed the end of the war intensified political repression against dissenters and were aimed particularly at communists, anarchists, and "alien" immigrants. During this period of the "Red Scare," Emma Goldman was deported, and in 1920 Italian immigrants and anarchists Nicola Sacco and Bartolomeo Vanzetti were arrested on charges of robbery and murder. Despite the international efforts of writers and activists who argued for their innocence, they were executed in 1927. For those who were on the side of free speech, labor rights, and economic justice, the first three decades of the twentieth century were, in the words of Mother Jones, a time of "martyrs and saints."

It was also a time for important intersections among public space (including mass meetings, processions, and marches), private consciousness, and shared labor experience. Miners' work poetry, union songs of censure or parody, stirring speeches, court statements, and engaged journalism were some of the cultural forms that linked public spaces, physical labor, and struggle. These expressions of working-class culture were highly instrumental, intended to advance a cause, rouse the masses, or instruct the middle and upper classes about the actual existence of the working class. Edwin Markham's generic lonely "Man with a Hoe" was replaced by the clamor of women, men, and children claiming public spaces as participants and as an engaged audience.

Speech making was central to the spirit of the time. From 1908 to 1916, the IWW headed free-speech campaigns in key cities across the West. Elizabeth Gurley Flynn began addressing crowds at the age of fifteen, asserting in a speech in Missoula, Montana, that "full freedom for women was impossible under capitalism."[3] Labor organizers, agitators, and strike leaders were peripatetic, crisscrossing the country inspiring workers to strike or sustain their strikes. Imagine a speaker, perhaps a diminutive young woman or a wiry older man, standing on a soap box or a shaky platform addressing the crowd with the familiar salutation, "Fellow workers and friends." The speech might focus on opposition to war, the cruelty of child labor, the injustice of an industrial fire, or the necessity of a strike. The speaker might be fervently ideological or resistant to any political categorization. It is likely that she or he would appeal to the audience's feelings about foundational American values of liberty, justice, and equality. To the police, local jurists, and politicians, the speaker might be viewed as a dangerous radical who should be thrown in jail. To workers, she might be viewed as a mother, sister, or comrade. Hated or beloved, one thing is clear—the speaker would have a moral authority, a sense of urgency and outrage at economic injustice, and call not only for "bread," but for "roses," too. If the speech was effective, the crowd would come away with a sense of connection, knowing that they were not isolated workers, but part of a larger movement and vision. Elizabeth Gurley Flynn called it a revolutionary spirit: "For workers to go back with a class-conscious spirit, with an organized and determined attitude toward society means that even if they have made no economic gain they have the possibility of gaining in the future."[4]

This literature also illustrates an important aspect of working-class cultural formation. Not only were such events as the Triangle shirtwaist factory fire of 1911 catastrophic to the many immigrant families who were affected by the deaths of 146 workers, but also the memory of that event is carried in time and inspires contemporary cultural expressions. Labor history is more than static fact; it has resonance for writers with working-class consciousness in the present. Furthermore, this is a reciprocal cultural process—the contemporary poets imaginatively witness the lives and deaths of the workers—and the event itself gives subject matter and voice to the poets. This process of reclamation is also evident in the iconic memory of Joe Hill and the songs and memoirs related to his life and death that followed. These are instances of cultural reciprocity, of how writers of the working class recognize and answer each other across time.

In the 1920s and early 1930s, the emigration of blacks out of the Jim Crow South to northern cities generated a confluence of culture and geography. Race and place converged during this period in Harlem, New York, sparking a rich outpouring of writing, painting, music, and photography known as the New Negro Movement or the Harlem Renaissance. Claude McKay, James Weldon Johnson, Jean Toomer, Sterling Brown, Langston Hughes (included in Part V), and others produced writing that drew on the legacy of black oppression and spoke back to it in traditional and experimental literary forms. Although he had some quarrels with individual writers, W. E. B. Du Bois remarked in 1934: "It is the class-conscious workingmen uniting together who will eventually emancipate labor throughout the world. It is the race-conscious Black cooperating together in his own institutions and movements who will eventually emancipate the colored race."[5]

When women finally won the right to vote in 1920, what did it mean for working-class women? Mother Jones—who never had too much faith in the electoral process for laboring men—would likely answer, "not much." Issues of safe and sanitary working conditions, dignity as women workers, a living family wage sufficient to sustain a family, that is, concerns about the immediacy of daily existence, took precedence over suffrage. In addition to the public speeches of labor organizers and Socialists, this section includes writings by and about working-class women that reveal the private realm as well. Anzia Yezierska brings the subjectivity of an immigrant Jewish woman to Progressive Era attitudes toward American assimilation. Edith Summers Kelley's censored chapter, "Billy's Birth," is a powerful rendering of childbirth. Agnes Smedley's yearning for beauty and knowledge, her frankness (and ambivalence) about sex, her commitment to movements for social justice, especially in China, and her kinship and quarrel with the deterministic fate of working-class women inaugurates a proletarian feminism that will resonate for generations of women writers.

The 1920s roared back against organized labor. Strikes were defeated one by one, and total union memberships declined to about 3.6 million. By 1926, Debs was dead, and IWW leader Bill Haywood died in the Soviet Union in 1928.[6] In 1929, the stock market crashed, but the blame could not be placed on workers, their unions, or radical organizations.[7] Workers could not purchase what they produced with insufficient pay. "We have been naught, we shall be all" sang the founding members of the IWW in 1905.[8] The song's intent did not come to fruition, but within this era of resistance and repression lay the seeds for an momentous awakening of worker consciousness and cultural expression in the decade that followed.

Notes

1. Paul Le Blanc, *A Short History of the U.S. Working Class* (Amherst, NY: Humanity Books, 1999), 64.

2. Howard Zinn, *A People's History of the United States* (New York: Harper Perennial, 1980), 364.

3. Philip S. Foner, ed., *Fellow Workers and Friends: I. W. W. Free-Speech Fights as Told by Participants* (Westport, CT: Greenwood Press, 1981), 23.

4. Quoted in Le Blanc, 65.

5. Quoted in Manning Marable, *W. E. B. Du Bois: Black Radical Democrat* (Boston: Twayne Publishers, 1986), 121.

6. Priscilla Murolo and A. B. Chitty, *From the Folks Who Brought You the Weekend* (New York: The New Press, 2001), 172–173.

7. Philip Yale Nicholson, *Labor's Story in the United States* (Philadelphia: Temple University Press, 2004), 200.

8. Quoted in Joyce L. Kornbluh, ed., *Rebel Voices: An I. W. W. Anthology* (Ann Arbor: The University of Michigan Press, 1964), v.

Eugene V. Debs (1855–1926)

Eugene V. Debs began working on the railroads at age fourteen and eventually became a charismatic leader beloved by millions, as well as America's principal Socialist spokesman between 1897 and his death in 1926. His evolution into socialism began in 1894 when he organized the American Railway Union (ARU). Unlike craft unions, which organized workers by particular jobs—such as conductors, engineers, brakemen, or firemen—the ARU embraced everyone who worked on the railroads. However, the ARU was crushed by the federal government in the famous Pullman Strike of 1894, and Debs was sentenced to six months in prison. While in prison, he began reading socialist literature and emerged committed to the goal of total social transformation (see "How I Became a Socialist" in this section).

In 1900, Debs ran for president as leader of the Social Democratic Party, and the next year, he helped organize the Socialist Party of America. In 1905, he helped found the Industrial Workers of the World, which aimed to unite laborers in all industries and of all nationalities into "one big union." Debs opposed the exclusion of Chinese immigrants, even when California Socialists supported it. In an age of entrenched sexism, he also argued that, "If the revolutionary movement . . . stands for anything it stands for the absolute equality of the sexes." For Debs, the "movement" was for all the oppressed, regardless of job, race, gender, or any other obstacle that divided working people. Debs was also a committed pacifist, declaring, "I am opposed to every war but one, and that is the world wide war of the social revolution."

When America entered World War I in 1917, Debs remained opposed. In June 1918, he delivered an antiwar speech, for which he was tried under the 1917 Espionage Act. Upon being sentenced to ten years in prison, Debs restated his ideals: "While there is a lower class, I am in it. While there is a criminal element, I am of it. While there is a soul in prison, I am not free" ("Statement to the Court," presented in this section).

In 1920, with Debs in prison, his party ran him for president for the fifth and last time. His campaign buttons carried the slogan, "Vote for Prisoner 9653," and he received 912,000 votes, his highest total. In 1921, President Warren G. Harding pardoned Debs. True to his belief in solidarity with the oppressed, Debs sent his five dollars in release money to the defense committee for Sacco and Vanzetti, the Italian anarchists who were imprisoned in Massachusetts.

Eric Leif Davin

How I Became a Socialist

As I have some doubt about the readers of *The Comrade* having any curiosity as to "how I became a socialist" it may be in order to say that the subject is the editor's, not my own; and that what is here offered is at his bidding—my only concern being that he shall not have cause to wish that I had remained what I was instead of becoming a socialist.

On the evening of February 27, 1875, the local lodge of the Brotherhood of Locomotive Firemen was organized at Terre Haute, Indiana, by Joshua A. Leach, then grand master, and I was admitted as a charter member and at once chosen secretary. "Old Josh Leach," as he was affectionately called, a typical locomotive fireman of his day, was the founder of the brotherhood, and I was instantly attracted by his rugged honesty, simple manner and homely speech. How well I remember feeling his large, rough hand on my shoulder, the kindly eye of an elder brother searching my own as he gently said: "My boy, you're a little young, but I believe you're in earnest and will make your mark in the brotherhood." Of course, I assured him that I would do my best. What he really thought at the time flattered my boyish vanity not a little when I heard of it. He was attending a meeting at St. Louis some months later, and in the course of his remarks said: "I put a towheaded boy in the brotherhood at Terre Haute not long ago, and some day he will be at the head of it."

Twenty-seven years, to a day, have played their pranks with "Old Josh" and the rest of us. When last we met, not long ago, and I pressed his good right hand, I observed that he was crowned with the frost that never melts; and as I think of him now:

> Remembrance wakes, with all her busy train,
> Swells at my breast and turns the past to pain.

My first step was thus taken in organized labor and a new influence fired my ambition and changed the whole current of my career. I was filled with enthusiasm and my blood fairly leaped in my veins. Day and night I worked for the brotherhood. To see its watchfires glow and observe the increase of its sturdy members were the sunshine and shower of my life. To attend the "meeting" was my supreme joy, and for ten years I was not once absent when the faithful assembled.

At the convention held in Buffalo in 1878 I was chosen associate editor of the magazine, and in 1880 I became grand secretary and treasurer. With all the fire of youth I entered upon the crusade which seemed to fairly glitter with possibilities. For eighteen hours at a stretch I was glued to my desk reeling off the answers to my many correspondents. Day and night were one. Sleep was time wasted and often, when all oblivious of her presence in the still small hours my mother's hand turned off the light, I went to bed under protest. Oh, what days! And what quenchless zeal and consuming vanity! All the firemen everywhere—and they were all the world—were straining:

> To catch the beat
> On my tramping feet

My grip was always packed; and I was darting in all directions. To tramp through a railroad yard in the rain, snow or sleet half the night, or till daybreak, to be ordered out of the roundhouse for being an "agitator," or put off a train, sometimes passenger, more often freight, while attempting to dead-head over the division, were all in the program, and served to whet the appetite to conquer. One night in midwinter at Elmira, New York, a conductor on the Erie kindly dropped me off in a snowbank, and as I clambered to the top I ran into the arms of a policeman, who heard my story and on the spot became my friend.

I rode on the engines over mountain and plain, slept in the cabooses and bunks, and was fed from their pails by the swarthy stokers who still nestle close to my heart, and will until it is cold and still.

Through all these years I was nourished at Fountain Proletaire. I drank deeply of its waters and every particle of my tissue became saturated with the spirit of the working class. I had fired an engine and been stung by the exposure and hardship of the rail. I was with the boys in their weary watches, at the broken engine's side and often helped to bear their bruised and bleeding bodies back to wife and child again. How could I but feel the burden of their wrongs? How could the seed of agitation fail to take deep root in my heart?

And so I was spurred on in the work of organizing, not the firemen merely, but the brakemen, switchmen, telegraphers, shopmen, trackhands, all of them in fact, and as I had now become known as an organizer, the calls came from all sides and there are but few trades I have not helped to organize and less still in whose strikes I have not at some time had a hand.

In 1894 the American Railway Union was organized and a braver body of men never fought the battle of the working class.

Up to this time I had heard but little of socialism, knew practically nothing about the movement, and what little I did know was not calculated to impress me in its favor. I was bent on thorough and complete organization of the railroad men and ultimately the whole working class, and all my time and energy were given to that end. My supreme conviction was that if they were only organized in every branch of the service and all acted together in concert they could redress their wrongs and regulate the conditions of their employment. The stockholders of the corporation acted as one, why not the men? It was such a plain proposition—simply to follow the example set before their eyes by their masters— surely they could not fail to see it, act as one, and solve the problem.

It is useless to say that I had yet to learn the workings of the capitalist system, the resources of its masters and the weakness of its slaves. Indeed, no shadow of a "system" fell athwart my pathway; no thought of ending wage misery marred my plans. I was too deeply absorbed in perfecting wage servitude and making it a "thing of beauty and a joy forever."

It all seems very strange to me now, taking a backward look, that my vision was so focalized on a single objective point that I utterly failed to see what now appears as clear as the noonday sun—so clear that I marvel that any workingman, however dull, uncomprehending, can resist it.

But perhaps it was better so. I was to be baptized in socialism in the roar of conflict and I thank the gods for reserving to this fitful occasion the fiat, "Let there be light!"— the light that streams in steady radiance upon the broad way to the socialist republic.

The skirmish lines of the A.R.U. were well advanced. A series of small battles was fought and won without the loss of a man. A number of concessions was made by the corporations rather than risk an encounter. Then came the fight on the Great Northern, short, sharp, and decisive. The victory was complete—the only railroad strike of magnitude ever won by an organization in America.

Next followed the final shock—the Pullman strike—and the American Railway Union again won, clear and complete. The combined corporations were paralyzed and helpless. At this juncture there was delivered, from wholly unexpected quarters, a swift succession of blows that blinded me for an instant and then opened wide my eyes—and in the gleam of every bayonet and the flash of every rifle *the class struggle was revealed*. This was my first practical lesson in socialism, though wholly unaware that it was called by that name.

An army of detectives, thugs and murderers was equipped with badge and beer and bludgeon and turned loose; old hulks of cars were fired; the alarm bells tolled; the people were terrified; the most startling rumors were set afloat; the press volleyed and thundered, and over all the wires sped the news that Chicago's white throat was in the clutch of a red mob; injunctions flew thick and fast, arrests followed, and our office and headquarters, the heart of the strike, was sacked, torn out and nailed up by the "lawful" authorities of the federal government; and when in company with my loyal comrades I found myself in Cook County Jail at Chicago, with the whole press screaming conspiracy, treason and murder, and by some fateful coincidence I was given the cell occupied just previous to his execution by the assassin of Mayor Carter Harrison, Sr., overlooking the spot, a few feet distant, where the anarchists were hanged a few years before, I had another exceedingly practical and impressive lesson in socialism.

Acting upon the advice of friends we sought to employ John Harlan, son of the Supreme Justice, to assist in our defense—a defense memorable to me chiefly because of the skill and fidelity of our lawyers, among whom were the brilliant Clarence Darrow and the venerable Judge Lyman Trumbull, author of the thirteenth amendment to the Constitution, abolishing slavery in the United States.

Mr. Harlan wanted to think of the matter overnight; and the next morning gravely informed us that he could not afford to be identified with the case, "for," said he, "you will be tried upon the same theory as were the anarchists, with probably the same result." That day, I remember, the jailer, by way of consolation, I suppose, showed us the blood-stained rope used at the last execution and explained in minutest detail, as he exhibited the gruesome relic, just how the monstrous crime of lawful murder is committed.

But the tempest gradually subsided and with it the bloodthirstiness of the press and "public sentiment." We were not sentenced to the gallows, nor even to the penitentiary—though put on trial for conspiracy—for reasons that will make another story.

The Chicago jail sentences were followed by six months at Woodstock and it was here that socialism gradually laid hold of me in its own irresistible fashion. Books and pamphlets and letters from socialists came by every mail and I began to read and think and dissect the anatomy of the system in which workingmen, however organized, could be shattered and battered and splintered at a single stroke. The writings of Bellamy and Blatchford early appealed to me. The *Cooperative Commonwealth* of Gronlund also impressed me, but the writings of Kautsky were so clear and conclusive that I readily grasped not merely his argument, but also caught the spirit of his socialist utterance—and I thank him and all who helped me out of darkness into light.

It was at this time, when the first glimmerings of socialism were beginning to penetrate, that Victor L. Berger—and I have loved him ever since—came to Woodstock, as if a providential instrument, and delivered the first impassioned message of socialism I had ever heard—the very first to set the "wires humming in my system." As a souvenir of that visit there is in my library a volume of *Capital*, by Karl Marx, inscribed with the compliments of Victor L. Berger, which I cherish as a token of priceless value.

The American Railway Union was defeated but not conquered—overwhelmed but not destroyed. It lives and pulsates in the socialist movement, and its defeat but blazed the way to economic freedom and hastened the dawn of human brotherhood.

STATEMENT TO THE COURT

SEPTEMBER 18, 1918

Your Honor, years ago I recognized my kinship with all living beings, and I made up my mind that I was not one bit better than the meanest on earth. I said then, and I say now, that while there is a lower class, I am in it, and while there is a criminal element I am of it, and while there is a soul in prison, I am not free.

I listened to all that was said in this court in support and justification of this prosecution, but my mind remains unchanged. I look upon the Espionage Law as a despotic enactment in flagrant conflict with democratic principles and with the spirit of free institutions. . . .

Your Honor, I have stated in this court that I am opposed to the social system in which we live; that I believe in a fundamental change—but if possible by peaceable and orderly means. . . .

Standing here this morning, I recall my boyhood. At fourteen I went to work in a railroad shop; at sixteen I was firing a freight engine on a railroad. I remember all the hardships and privations of that earlier day, and from that time until now my heart has been with the working class. I could have been in Congress long ago. I have preferred to go to prison. . . .

I am thinking this morning of the men in the mills and the factories; of the men in the mines and on the railroads. I am thinking of the women who for a paltry wage are compelled to work out their barren lives; of the little children who in this system are robbed of their childhood and in their tender years are seized in the remorseless grasp of Mammon and forced into the industrial dungeons, there to feed the monster machines while they themselves are being starved and stunted, body and soul. I see them dwarfed and diseased and their little lives broken and blasted because in this high noon of Christian civilization money is still so much more important than the flesh and blood of childhood. In very truth gold is god today and rules with pitiless sway in the affairs of men.

In this country—the most favored beneath the bending skies—we have vast areas of the richest and most fertile soil, material resources in inexhaustible abundance, the most marvelous productive machinery on earth, and millions of eager workers ready to apply their labor to that machinery to produce in abundance for every man, woman, and child— and if there are still vast numbers of our people who are the victims of poverty and whose lives are an unceasing struggle all the way from youth to old age, until at last death comes to their rescue and lulls these hapless victims to dreamless sleep, it is not the fault of the Almighty: it cannot be charged to nature, but it is due entirely to the outgrown social system in which we live that ought to be abolished not only in the interest of the toiling masses but in the higher interest of all humanity. . . .

I believe, Your Honor, in common with all Socialists, that this nation ought to own and control its own industries. I believe, as all Socialists do, that all things that are jointly needed and used ought to be jointly owned—that industry, the basis of our social life, instead of being the private property of a few and operated for their enrichment, ought to be the common property of all, democratically administered in the interest of all. . . .

I am opposing a social order in which it is possible for one man who does absolutely nothing that is useful to amass a fortune of hundreds of millions of dollars, while millions of men and women who work all the days of their lives secure barely enough for a wretched existence.

This order of things cannot always endure. I have registered my protest against it. I recognize the feebleness of my effort, but, fortunately, I am not alone. There are multiplied thousands of others who, like myself, have come to realize that before we may truly enjoy the blessings of civilized life, we must reorganize society upon a mutual and cooperative basis; and to this end we have organized a great economic and political movement that spreads over the face of all the earth.

There are today upwards of sixty millions of Socialists, loyal, devoted adherents to this cause, regardless of nationality, race, creed, color, or sex. They are all making common cause. They are spreading with tireless energy the propaganda of the new social order. They are waiting, watching, and working hopefully through all the hours of the day and the night. They are still in a minority. But they have learned how to be patient and to bide their time. They feel—they know, indeed—that the time is coming, in spite of all opposition, all persecution, when this emancipating gospel will spread among all the peoples, and when this minority will become the triumphant majority and, sweeping into power, inaugurate the greatest social and economic change in history.

In that day we shall have the universal commonwealth—the harmonious cooperation of every nation with every other nation on earth. . . .

Your Honor, I ask no mercy and I plead for no immunity. I realize that finally the right must prevail. I never so clearly comprehended as now the great struggle between the powers of greed and exploitation on the one hand and upon the other the rising hosts of industrial freedom and social justice.

I can see the dawn of the better day for humanity. The people are awakening. In due time they will and must come to their own.

When the mariner, sailing over tropic seas, looks for relief from his weary watch, he turns his eyes toward the southern cross, burning luridly above the tempest-vexed ocean. As the midnight approaches, the southern cross begins to bend, the whirling worlds change their places, and with starry finger-points the Almighty marks the passage of time upon the dial of the universe, and though no bell may beat the glad tidings, the lookout knows that the midnight is passing and that relief and rest are close at hand. Let the people everywhere take heart of hope, for the cross is bending, the midnight is passing, and joy cometh with the morning.

Miners' and Other Labor Poems

As the Knights of Labor and the Homestead strike made clear, working people, especially those who were active in struggles for democratic and labor rights, have often turned to poetry and songs to communicate their vision. The following selection brings together two particular instances of poetry designed to address conditions of labor and the possibilities of organized resistance in the early twentieth century: the poems of Colorado miners, published in the weekly magazine of the Western Federation of Miners (WFM), and the "poem cards" that were used in organizing by the Industrial Workers of the World (IWW) and other unions of the day.

Dan Tannacito, the scholar who first republished these pieces from *Miners Magazine*, notes their origins in the aftermath of the bitter Cripple Creek strike of 1903–1904.[1] During a time of violent change when both the WFM and mining corporations were growing rapidly, workers' poetry, writes Tannacito, "contributed to the mining community's definition of its common life, work, and goals." Tannacito distinguishes several subgenres among these poems, according to the function they performed for the community. *Poems of praise* celebrate heroes of the workplace or of the struggle for labor rights; in the case of "The Man Behind the Pick," the hero is the anonymous common laborer who gets his work done without complaint. "Scab, Scab, Scab" is an example of *poems of censure and condemnation*, which, like "St. Peter and the Scab" twenty years later, treats the object of scorn with cleverly dramatized comic irony. "The Eight Hour Day" is one of many *poems of struggle*, published in the *Miners Magazine*, calling workers to united action for a particular cause, in this case the shorter workday that had been a longstanding goal of the labor movement. The lovingly detailed narrative poem "A Colorado Miner's Fourth" and Berton Braley's intensely realized challenge to exploiters in "The Worker" belong to the genre of *work poems*. "The *work poem*," according to Tannacito, "arises from acute observation and intense feeling while participating in labor; it communicates the social experience shared by all members of the group."

The poem-cards that follow are from the collection of scholar Cary Nelson and were reproduced by him under the heading, "Modern Poems We Have Wanted to Forget".[2] The earliest of these poem-cards, Thompson's four-line "Union Poem" and "Labor Speaks" (technically anonymous, but presented as the voice of a universal "unknown worker" who can speak for all), were published together by the IWW on a folded poem-card, around 1909. Such cards, circulated by organizers and offered for sale in bulk, were a common union recruiting device, along with the song-making for which the Wobblies were famous. Joe Foley's rousing "Whadda Ya Want to Break Your Back For the Boss For," a poem-card from around 1917, was set to the familiar tune "What Do You Want to Make Those Eyes at Me For?" Other poem-cards were produced in response to a particular moment of need or crisis. Eugene Barnett's "Political Prisoners" (1921) dates from the Red Scare after the World War I, when scores of IWW leaders and members were rounded up and imprisoned. Barnett was arrested when an IWW meeting in Centralia, Washington, was attacked by armed vigilantes (who castrated and lynched one of the

---

[1] "Poetry of the Colorado Miners, 1903–1906" *Radical Teacher* 15 (March 1980), 1–13.

[2] *Revolutionary Memory: Recovering the Poetry of the American Left* (New York: Routledge, 2001), 28–36.

United Mine Workers of America. *Courtesy of Library of Congress, LC-USZ62-2082.*

Wobblies). Framed and sentenced to twenty-five to forty years, Barnett composed his illustrated poem in prison. It was distributed in the form of a card as part of the amnesty campaign for the release of those suffering persecution for exercising what Barnett symbolizes as the freedoms of the "American Eagle." The final poem presented here, "St. Peter and the Scab," was printed on one side of a card inviting Chicago railroad workers to an "amalgamation meeting" of the city's sixteen railroad unions. "The poem is published without an author's name," Nelson writes, "because it voices collective rather than uniquely held or subjective values. Its authorship is, in effect, transferable" to its readers. If its readers find that the poem speaks for them, they may be drawn to attend the meeting announced on the card's reverse side.

What these labor poets have in common is a conviction that their writing will be useful to the people they belong to and represent, as well as an awareness that they are writing within an honorable tradition that is different from the literary mainstream. As Nelson expresses this tradition: "Over several decades, the labor movement used poetry not only to build or unify membership but also to educate workers and to restate core beliefs and values. Poetry was the ongoing discourse of pride in the labor movement's universal common sense. It elevated that common sense to a principle of identity and solidarity."

J. A. EDGERTON, THE MAN BEHIND THE PICK

There has been all kinds of gush about the man who is "behind"—
And the man behind the cannon has been toasted, wined and dined.
There's the man behind the musket and the man behind the fence;
And the man behind his whiskers, and the man behind his rents,
5   And the man behind his plow beam, and the man behind the hoe;
And the man behind the ballot and the man behind the dough;
And the man behind the jimmy, and the man behind the bars;
And the Johnny that goes snooping on the stage behind the "stars";
And the man behind the kisser, and the man behind the fist;
10 And the girl behind the man behind the gun is on the list;
But they've missed one honest fellow, and I'm raising of a kick,
That they didn't make a mention of the man behind the pick.

Up the rugged mountain side, a thousand feet he takes his way,
Or as far into darkness from the cheerful light of day;
15 He is shut out from the sunlight in the glimmer of the lamps;
He is cut off from the sweet air in the sickly fumes and damps;
He must toil in cramped positions; he must take his life in his hand;
For he works in deadly peril, that but few can understand;
But he does it all in silence and he seldom makes a kick.
20 Which is why I sing the praises of the man behind the pick.

He unlocks the belted portals of the mountains to the stores
Hid in nature's vast exchequer in her treasure house of ores;
He applies a key of dynamic, and the gates are backward rolled.
And the ancient rocks are riven to their secret heart of gold.
25 Things of comfort and of beauty, and of usefulness are mined,
By the brave, heroic fellow, who toils on all begrimmed,
Trampled down and underpaid, works on without a kick;
So I lift my hat in honor to the man behind the pick.

ANONYMOUS, SCAB, SCAB, SCAB

Altho' it's not my color, I'm feeling mighty blue,
I have a lot of trouble, I'll tell it all to you.
I'm certainly clean disgusted with life and that's a fact,
Because my job is scabby and because my character is black.
5 My girl she took a notion against the scabby race.
She said if I would win her I'd have to change my place.
She said if she would wed me that she'd regret it bad,
Because I am an unfair man and working as a scab.

Chorus:
Scab, scab, scab, I wish my color would fade,
10 Scab, scab, scab, I wish my job was played,
Scab, scab, scab, I give my life for the maid.
I wish I was a union man instead of scab, scab, scab.

I had my white shirt laundered and gave my hair a cut,
I put my bran' new suit on—I certainly did loom up.
15   I started out to see her just twenty minutes of nine.
I had in mind the question to ask her to be mine.
And when I popped the question she said, "You made me sad.
Do you know I can marry a union man? Do you think I'd look at a scab?
My father is a W.F.M., my brother is the same,
20   My mother *joined* the auxiliary—I guess I'll not take your name."

Tune: "Coon, Coon, Coon"

Shorty P., The Eight Hour Day

In Telluride the strike is still on
    And on there it will stay
Until we get just what we want—
    It is an eight-hour day.

5   Eight months we have been out on strike
    Up to the first of May.
And eight months more we'll stay on strike
    Just for an eight-hour day.

Though gatling guns and cannonade
10   Surround the town, oh, say,
I wonder what they'll do with them
    After the eight-hour day!

They may deport us from our homes,
    And tell us to stay away;
15   But then we'll not call off the strike
    Until the eight-hour day.

We have labored hard for many a year,
    We have labored night and day,
But when the people cast the votes,
20   It was for an eight-hour day.

They may confine some men in jail,
    But they can't win out that way,
For our cause is just and we won't quit
    Until the eight-hour day.

25   Now working men from Telluride,
    I say just stay away;
The fight is yours as well as ours,
    To get an eight-hour day.

Joe R. Lazure, A Colorado Miner's Fourth

Oh stranger, this is a great day on this part of the earth—
it's "Independence Day" of ours, which gave our nation birth,

When our patriots assembled and declared, "It shall not be,
We'll stand no more oppression; our country shall be free."
5   While from the call of duty these miners will not shirk,
This is the one day in the year on which they will not work.

I never worked on but one fourth, and that one was the last
Fourth of July I'll ever mine, where'er my lot be cast.
'Twas at a place called Goldfield in the county of Pinal,
10   Way down in Arizona, I was working with a "pal,"
There were nothing doing on this fourth, there was no place to go,
So we decided we would work and try to save some "dough."

The day it passed off quickly, we were young then, full of life,
We've since had many ups and downs in this hard world of strife.
15   So when the shades of evening fell we thought it was our right,
With other kindred spirits there, to celebrate that night.
The boys had scarcely settled down to have a quiet time,
With refreshments by the bottle, and several different kinds.

When in rushed old Riel Morse, his face as pale as death,
20   And says: "Come boys, get out of here!" when he could catch his breath.
"For that old stope has caved in, clear down to the 2;
Come get your digging clothes on, boys, for there'll be need of you."
If Stevens was back in his drift, we knew there was some hope.
His orders were, that very day, "not to go through that stope."

25   We jumped into our harness, for the mine we made a dash,
And there we found Bolitho, for he had heard the crash.
Our foreman in the mine was he, and right here let me say,
He was a good one, stranger, he sleeps beneath the clay.
Near the new shaft he was standing, and with steady voice and slow,
30   Says he: "Now I want one of you to go with me below.

"We'll go down to the 7; I think the shaft's all right,
To see if Jimmy Lee is safe—he's working there to-night."
On the bucket there with Billy stepped the Kid without a word.
They found Lee on the 7, he knew not what occurred.
35   To the surface on the bucket, and back down to the 3,
They went, to find the quickest way to set poor Stevens free.

But that old stope was working—you could hear the timbers pop—
So Billy thought it safer to sink down from the top.
He picked out four of us at once to work on that night shift.
40   We started through the old cave there to tap poor Jimmy's drift.
Then Billy called up all the boys, and these words to them said:
"I'll want you in the morning, boys, now you can go to bed.

"I want you all to stay in camp, we will need all of you,
For I'll work every man I can to carry that shaft through."
45   But every man was anxious, each one in the crew,
With strong hands and willing hearts to help on this rescue.

While Stevens, he was working too, we heard him digging in
To reach a little air-shaft which was not far from him.
But the ground was dry as powder, like sand it ran in fast,
50   And, with no light or timbers, he gave it up at last.

The time they made on this first shaft was pretty hard to beat;
It had taken just three days to sink it fifty feet.
But there we struck some timbers which came from that old stope.
We could not drive our spike in, and with them could not cope.
55 The morning of the 8th, then, Billy says: "We'll have to quit
And start a shaft thro' solid land; I know we can sink it."

The place where they then started in was right above Jim's drift,
And a small stope, some eighteen feet there, gave them quite a lift.
Two rows of stulls they threw in there and lagged up good and tight,
60 And how those miners made the "muck" fly was a pretty sight.
For they all worked like demons; there were many feet to drive,
We never thought to find poor Jimmy Stevens there alive.

Not one man in ten thousand could stand it, do you think?
Entombed alive for thirteen days, and without food or drink.
65 But Jimmy bore up bravely, and when the boys would drill,
They'd rap upon the foot-wall and he'd rap back with a will.
And this would cheer the boys up, and they'd dig in like a Turk.
They never needed any boss to make them do their work.

One hundred six and twenty feet that new shaft had to go.
70 Before they made connection with Jimmy's drift below.
The morning of the 17th the sun rose bright and fair,
You'd see by groups of miners who were scattered here and there.
By subdued voices, anxious faces, each one felt the strain,
And hoped that all their gallant efforts had not been in vain.

75 The "graveyard" shift had just come up, they knew the end was near,
They knew that Stevens was alive, but would his mind be clear?
The morning shift had been on thirty minutes, or about,
When up the shaft came ringing a glad and joyful shout:

"We've reached him, boys, he is all right, we have just now broke thro'!"
80 Then down the shaft a doctor went, to tell them what to do.
And when the doctor looked at Jim, he says: "Why he's all right,
But we will keep him here a while, the sunlight is too bright."
In Colorado, all this time, their loving hearts did yearn,
His wife and little children, praying for his safe return.

85 For Jimmy, he had told me: "On the 15th I'll go home,
To see my wife and family, for I'm too old to roam."
There, with aching heart, she waited; she knew about the cave,
How hard at work his comrades were, her husband's life to save.
How proud those happy miners were when they sent the news that night
90 To his wife in Central City: "Your Jimmy's safe, all right!"

The miners won't forget them if they live till Judgment Day;
For when they heard the story of these miners' brave rescue
That Stevens was all right once more, they knew just what to do.
They commenced to cooking chickens, cakes and pies, and brought the band
95 And with their wives and daughters came to shake them by the hand.

The way those hard-worked miners the whole bakery did take,
They say it was no "cake-walk," but walking into cake.

And how they stowed those "gumys" away, it surely was a fright.
They danced and ate, and ate and danced, till early morning light
100 While Jimmy Stevens, so they say, gained seven pounds that night
"'Twas time for one to pick up some, who's forty-eight pounds light."

The good people from that valley, to them it was a treat
To see those chickens disappear and watch those miners eat.
They showed a Christian spirit, true, and when they bade adieu,
105 Invited every miner there to come and see them, too.
And when with hearts and baskets light they journeyed home again
They left kind memories of them which always will remain.

Up home in Central City, when Jimmy stepped down off the train
With a band his friends had gathered there to welcome him again,
110 The meeting with his loving wife who found him safe from harm,
His joy to see his little ones, and clasp them in his arms,
This picture is too sacred, pard; I'll draw the curtain here,
For scenes like this are apt to start from me a pensive tear.

And there I fain would leave him now, alive and doing well.
115 But alas! poor Jimmy's story, the sad truth I must tell:
Far up in Colorado's hills he sleeps beneath the sod.
Caught in a cave in a mine there, he went to meet his God.
So, stranger, when each glorious Fourth of July rolls around,
I think of Jimmy Stevens, and stay from under ground.

J. P. Thompson, Union Poem

You cannot be a Union Man,
   No matter how you try,
Unless you think in terms of "We,"
   Instead of terms of "I."

Unknown Worker, Labor Speaks

I built your ships and your railroads,
   And worked in your factories and mines;
I built the good roads that you ride on,
   And crushed your ripe grapes into wine.

I built the fine house that you live in,
   And gathered the grain for your bread;
I worked late at nights on your garments,
   And printed the fine books that your read.

I linked two great oceans together,
   And spanned your rivers with steel,
I built your towering skyscrapers,
   And also your automobile.

Wherever there is progress you will find me,
  For the world without me could not live,
And yet you seek to destroy me
  With the meagre pittance you give.

I am master of field and of factories,
  I am mighty and you are but few,
So, no longer will I bow into submission,
  I am Labor and I ask for my due.

JOE FOLEY, WADDA YA WANT TO BREAK YOUR BACK FOR THE BOSS FOR

Tune: What Do You Want to Make Those Eyes at Me For?

Toiling along in life from morn' til night,
Wearin' away your all for the Parasite;
Workin' like a mule with a number two,
Puffin' like a bellows when the day is through;
5 Stearing a load of gravel through the muck and slop,
Packing a hod of mustard til you damn near flop;
Trying to bust a gut for two twenty-five,
Pluggin' like a sucker til five.

Chorus
So whadda ya want to break your back for the boss for,
10 When it don't mean life to you;
Do you think it right to struggle day and night,
And plow like Hell for the Parasite;
So whadda ya want to break your back for the boss for,
When there's more in life for you.
15 Slow up Bill! that's the way to beat the System;
Join the Wobbly gang, they've got the bosses guessing;
So whadda ya want to break your back for the boss for,
When it don't mean life to you.

Do it all today and you'll soon find out,
20 Tomorrow there'll be nothing but to hang about,
Looking at the "job sign," wondering why you rave,
With a wrinkle on your belly like an ocean wave;
Doughnuts then begin to hang a little high,
You're pinched by the Bull for a "German spy";
25 You're nothing but a bum, says the Judge with a smile,
Thirty days on the Rock Pile.

Chorus

BERTON BRALEY, THE WORKER

I have broken my hands on your granite,
I have broken my strength on your steel;

I have sweated through years for your pleasure,
I have worked like a slave for your weal;
5   And what is the wage you have paid me?
You masters and drivers of men—
Enough so I come in my hunger
    To beg for more labor again!

I have given my manhood to serve you,
10   I have given my gladness and youth,
    You have used me, and spent me, and crushed me
And thrown me aside without ruth;
You have shut my eyes off from the sunlight—
My lungs from the untainted air,
15   You have housed me in horrible places
    Surrounded by squalor and care.

I have built you the world in its beauty,
I have brought you the glory and spoil;
You have blighted my sons and my daughters,
20   You have scourged me again to my toil,
Yet I suffer it all in my patience,
For, somehow, I dimly have known
That someday the worker will conquer
    In a world that was meant for his own.

Eugene Barnett, Political Prisoners

Hail! the American eagle,
Emblem of men once free;
Languishing now in prison,
In its own loved country.
Though its heart is broken,
Its spirit is defiant still;
Though prisons break its body,
They cannot break its will.

Anonymous, St. Peter and the Scab

St. Peter stood guard at the golden gate
With solemn mien and air sedate,
When up at the top of the golden stair
A shrouded figure ascended there,
5   Applied for admission. He came and stood
Before St. Peter, so great and good,
In hope the City of Peace to win,
And asked St. Peter to let him in.

St. Peter said with a gleam in his eye,
10   "Who is tending this gate, sir, you or I?
I've heard of you and your gift of gab;

Poem Cards from the collection of Cary Nelson, as published in *Revolutionary Memory: Recovering the Poetry of the American Left* (New York: Routledge, 2003).

St. Peter and the Scab

St. Peter stood guard at the golden gate
With solemn mien and air sedate,
When up at the top of the golden stair
A shrouded figure ascended there,
Applied for admission. He came and stood
Before St. Peter, so great and good,
In hope the City of Peace to win,
And asked St. Peter to let him in.

St. Peter said with a gleam in his eye,
"Who is tending this gate, sir, you or I?
I've heard of you and your gift of gab;
You are what is known on earth as a scab."
Thereupon he arose in his stature tall
And pressed a button upon the wall,
And said to the imp who answered the bell:
"Escort this fellow around to Hell."

"Tell Satan to give him a seat alone
On a red-hot griddle up near the throne;
But stay, e'en the Devil can't stand the smell
Of a cooking scab on a griddle in Hell.
It would cause a revolt, a strike, I know,
If I sent you down to the imps below.
Go back to your masters on earth and tell
That they don't even want a scab in Hell."

[Over]

UNION PRESS 483 ◆ 2066 N. California Ave.

RAILROADERS ⟨logo⟩ **UNIONISTS**
Amalgamation Mass Meeting
SUNDAY, FEBRUARY 25TH, 3 P. M.
at
WEST SIDE AUDITORIUM
SO. RACINE AVE. AND TAYLOR ST.

SPEAKERS:

O. H. WANGERIN, Secretary, and
G. H. KENNEDY, Chairman, National Committee for Amalgamation, of St. Paul, Minn.
WILLIAM Z. FOSTER, Editor The Labor Herald and other prominent speakers
Latest news, developments and plans. Come and hear why Railroaders must Amalgamate

P. JENSEN, Chairman   ADMISSION FREE

Auspices Chicago Committee for Amalgamation of the Sixteen Standard Railroad Unions   [Over]

You are what is known on earth as a scab."
Thereupon he arose in his stature tall
And pressed a button upon the wall,
15   And said to the imp who answered the bell:
"Escort this fellow around to Hell."

"Tell Satan to give him a seat alone
On a red-hot griddle up near the throne;

But stay, e'en the Devil can't stand the smell
20   Of a cooking scab on a griddle in Hell.
It would cause a revolt, a strike, I know,
If I sent you down to the imps below.
Go back to your masters on earth and tell
That they don't even want a scab in Hell."

———

Upton Sinclair (1878–1968)

Born in Baltimore into a family with connections to southern aristocracy, Sinclair's childhood was marked by wide fluctuations between poverty and affluence, especially after the family's move to New York City when Upton was ten years old. "One night I would be sleeping on a vermin-ridden sofa in a lodging-house, and the next night under silken coverlets in a fashionable home. It all depended on whether my father had the money for that week's board." His father's alcoholism and early death required Sinclair to fend for himself and, by age 15, he began writing jokes for magazines, short stories for boys' weeklies, and dime novels to pay his way through City College and later graduate school at Columbia University. Always a writer, as well as an organizer and political candidate, Sinclair produced almost one hundred books in his long career, including *Springtime and Harvest* (1901), *The Jungle* (1906), *King Coal* (1917), *Oil!* (1927), *Boston* (1928, on the Sacco and Vanzetti case), *Dragon's Teeth* (1942), and his *Autobiography* (1962).

Written on assignment for *The Appeal to Reason*—the socialist journal paid Sinclair a $500 advance and underwrote a seven-week visit to Chicago's "packingtown"—*The Jungle* is Sinclair's best-known novel, a leading example of the "muckraking" tradition in American writing. It was one of the few such works of fiction before the 1930s to mobilize a working-class protagonist, the Lithuanian immigrant Jurgis Rudkis whose struggles in Chicago's brutal workplaces, bars, unions, and political parties lead him by the novel's end to (an albeit inarticulate) socialism. In the excerpt that follows, Jurgis and two family members are taken on a tour of a meatpacking plant, much as Sinclair was during his visit. The tone of an official tour guide's statistics-laced account of the wonders of industrial food production is undercut by ironic reflections on the fate of the "innocent" hogs and cattle that provide the raw material—a fate that, as Jurgis will later learn, mirrors that of the workers. *The Jungle*, dedicated to "the workingmen of America," quickly became a best-seller on the strength of its lurid exposure of the underworld of urban industrial work life. But despite Jack London's prediction that "What *Uncle Tom's Cabin* did for the black slaves *The Jungle* has a large chance to do for the white slaves of today," the novel's greatest impact came in the form of legislation for food hygiene, not, as Sinclair had hoped, in better pay and working conditions for the industry's apparently expendable workers.

"The Hog-Squeal of the Universe"

In his capacity as delicatessen vender, Jokubas Szedvilas had many acquaintances. Among these was one of the special policemen employed by Durham, whose duty it frequently was to pick out men for employment. Jokubas had never tried it, but he expressed a certainty that he could get some of his friends a job through this man. It was agreed, after consultation, that he should make the effort with old Antanas and with Jonas. Jurgis was confident of his ability to get work for himself, unassisted by any one.

As we have said before, he was not mistaken in this. He had gone to Brown's and stood there not more than half an hour before one of the bosses noticed his form towering above the rest, and signalled to him. The colloquy which followed was brief and to the point:

"Speak English?"

"No; Lít-uanian." (Jurgis had studied this word carefully.)

"Job?"

"Je." (A nod.)

"Worked here before?"

"No 'stand."

(Signals and gesticulations on the part of the boss. Vigorous shakes of the head by Jurgis.)

"Shovel guts?"

"No 'stand." (More shakes of the head.)

"Zarnos. Pagaiksztis. Szluota!" (Imitative motions.)

"Je."

"See door. Durys?" (Pointing.)

"Je."

"To-morrow, seven o'clock. Understand? Rytoj! Priesz-pietys! Septyni!"

"Dekui, tamistai!" (Thank you, sir.) And that was all. Jurgis turned away, and then in a sudden rush the full realization of his triumph swept over him, and he gave a yell and a jump, and started off on a run. He had a job! He had a job! And he went all the way home as if upon wings, and burst into the house like a cyclone, to the rage of the numerous lodgers who had just turned in for their daily sleep.

Meantime Jokubas had been to see his friend the policeman, and received encouragement, so it was a happy party. There being no more to be done that day, the shop was left under the care of Lucija, and her husband sallied forth to show his friends the sights of Packingtown. Jokubas did this with the air of a country gentleman escorting a party of visitors over his estate; he was an old-time resident, and all these wonders had grown up under his eyes, and he had a personal pride in them. The packers might own the land, but he claimed the landscape, and there was no one to say nay to this.

They passed down the busy street that led to the yards. It was still early morning, and everything was at its high tide of activity. A steady stream of employees was pouring through the gate—employees of the higher sort, at this hour, clerks and stenographers and such. For the women there were waiting big two-horse wagons, which set off at a gallop as fast as they were filled. In the distance there was heard again the lowing of the cattle, a sound as of a far-off ocean calling. They followed it this time, as eager as children in sight of a circus menagerie—which, indeed, the scene a good deal resembled. They crossed the railroad tracks, and then on each side of the street were the pens full of cattle; they would have stopped to look, but Jokubas hurried them on, to where there was a stairway and a raised gallery, from which everything could be seen. Here they stood, staring, breathless with wonder.

There is over a square mile of space in the yards, and more than half of it is occupied by cattle pens; north and south as far as the eye can reach there stretches a sea of pens. And they were all filled—so many cattle no one had ever dreamed existed in the world. Red cattle, black, white, and yellow cattle; old cattle and young cattle; great bellowing bulls and little calves not an hour born; meek-eyed milch cows and fierce, long-horned Texas steers. The sound of them here was as of all the barnyards of the universe; and as for counting them—it would have taken all day simply to count the pens. Here and there ran long alleys, blocked at intervals by gates; and Jokubas told them that the number of these gates was twenty-five thousand. Jokubas had recently been reading a newspaper article which was full of statistics such as that, and he was very proud as he repeated them and made his guests cry out with wonder. Jurgis too had a little of this sense of pride. Had he not just gotten a job, and become a sharer in all this activity, a cog in this marvelous machine?

Here and there about the alleys galloped men upon horseback, booted, and carrying long whips; they were very busy, calling to each other, and to those who were driving the cattle. They were drovers and stock-raisers, who had come from far states, and brokers and commission-merchants, and buyers for all the big packing houses. Here and there they would stop to inspect a bunch of cattle, and there would be a parley, brief and businesslike. The buyer would nod or drop his whip, and that would mean a bargain; and he would note it in his little book, along with hundreds of others he had made that morning. Then Jokubas pointed out the place where the cattle were driven to be weighed upon a great scale that would weigh a hundred thousand pounds at once and record it automatically. It was near to the east entrance that they stood, and all along this east side of the yards ran the railroad tracks, into which the cars were run, loaded with cattle. All night long this had been going on, and now the pens were full; by tonight they would all be empty, and the same thing would be done again.

"And what will become of all these creatures?" cried Teta Elzbieta.

"By tonight," Jokubas answered, "they will all be killed and cut up; and over there on the other side of the packing houses are more railroad tracks, where the cars come to take them away."

There were two hundred and fifty miles of track within the yards, their guide went on to tell them. They brought about ten thousand head of cattle every day, and as many hogs, and half as many sheep—which meant some eight or ten million live creatures turned into food every year. One stood and watched, and little by little caught the drift of the tide, as it set in the direction of the packing houses. There were groups of cattle being driven to the chutes, which were roadways about fifteen feet wide, raised high above the pens. In these chutes the stream of animals was continuous; it was quite uncanny to watch them, pressing on to their fate, all unsuspicious—a very river of death. Our friends were not poetical, and the sight suggested to them no metaphors of human destiny; they thought only of the wonderful efficiency of it all. The chutes into which the hogs went climbed high up—to the very top of the distant buildings, and Jokubas explained that the hogs went up by the power of their own legs, and then their weight carried them back through all the processes necessary to make them into pork.

"They don't waste anything here," said the guide, and then he laughed and added a witticism, which he was pleased that his unsophisticated friends should take to be his own: "They use everything about the hog except the squeal." In front of Brown's General Office building there grows a tiny plot of grass, and this, you may learn, is the only bit of green thing in Packingtown; likewise this jest about the hog and his squeal, the stock in trade of all the guides, is the one gleam of humor that you will find there.

After they had seen enough of the pens, the party went up the street, to the mass of buildings which occupy the centre of the yards. These buildings, made of brick and stained with innumerable layers of Packingtown smoke, were painted all over with advertising signs, from which the visitor realized suddenly that he had come to the home of many of the torments of his life. It was here that they made those products with the wonders of which they pestered him so—by placards that defaced the landscape when he traveled, and by staring advertisements in the newspapers and magazines—by silly little jingles that he could not get out of his mind, and gaudy pictures that lurked for him around every street corner. Here was where they made Brown's Imperial Hams and Bacon, Brown's Dressed Beef, Brown's Excelsior Sausages! Here was the headquarters of Durham's Pure Leaf Lard, of Durham's Breakfast Bacon, Durham's Canned Beef, Potted Ham, Deviled Chicken, Peerless Fertilizer!

Entering one of the Durham buildings, they found a number of other visitors waiting, and before long there came a guide, to escort them through the place. They make a great feature of showing strangers through the packing plants, for it is a good advertisement. But Ponas Jokubas whispered maliciously that the visitors did not see any more than the packers wanted them to.

They climbed a long series of stairways outside of the building, to the top of its five or six stories. Here were the chute, with its river of hogs, all patiently toiling upward; there was a place for them to rest to cool off, and then through another passageway they went into a room from which there is no returning for hogs.

It was a long, narrow room, with a gallery along it for visitors. At the head there was a great iron wheel, about twenty feet in circumference, with rings here and there along its edge. Upon both sides of this wheel there was a narrow space, into which came the hogs at the end of their journey; in the midst of them stood a great burly Negro, bare-armed and bare-chested. He was resting for the moment, for the wheel had stopped while men were cleaning up. In a minute or two, however, it began slowly to revolve, and then the men upon each side of it sprang to work. They had chains which they fastened about the leg of the nearest hog, and the other end of the chain they hooked into one of the rings upon the wheel. So, as the wheel turned, a hog was suddenly jerked off his feet and borne aloft.

At the same instant the ear was assailed by a most terrifying shriek; the visitors started in alarm, the women turned pale and shrank back. The shriek was followed by another, louder and yet more agonizing—for once started upon that journey, the hog never came back; at the top of the wheel he was shunted off upon a trolley, and went sailing down the room. And meantime another was swung up, and then another, and another, until there was a double line of them, each dangling by a foot and kicking in frenzy—and squealing. The uproar was appalling, perilous to the eardrums; one feared there was too much sound for the room to hold—that the walls must give way or the ceiling crack. There were high squeals and low squeals, grunts, and wails of agony; there would come a momentary lull, and then a fresh outburst, louder than ever, surging up to a deafening climax. It was too much for some of the visitors—the men would look at each other, laughing nervously, and the women would stand with hands clenched, and the blood rushing to their faces, and the tears starting in their eyes.

Meantime, heedless of all these things, the men upon the floor were going about their work. Neither squeals of hogs nor tears of visitors made any difference to them; one by one they hooked up the hogs, and one by one with a swift stroke they slit their throats. There was a long line of hogs, with squeals and life-blood ebbing away together, until at last each started again, and vanished with a splash into a huge vat of boiling water.

It was all so very businesslike that one watched it fascinated. It was pork-making by machinery, pork-making by applied mathematics. And yet somehow the most matter-of-fact person could not help thinking of the hogs; they were so innocent, they came so very trustingly; and they were so very human in their protests—and so perfectly within their rights! They had done nothing to deserve it, and it was adding insult to injury, as the thing was done here, swinging them up in this cold-blooded, impersonal way, without a pretence at apology, without the homage of a tear. Now and then a visitor wept, to be sure; but this slaughtering machine ran on, visitors or no visitors. It was like some horrible crime committed in a dungeon, all unseen and unheeded, buried out of sight and of memory.

One could not stand and watch very long without becoming philosophical, without beginning to deal in symbols and similes, and to hear the hog-squeal of the universe. Was it permitted to believe that there was nowhere upon the earth, or above the earth, a heaven for hogs, where they were requited for all this suffering? Each one of these hogs was a separate creature. Some were white hogs, some were black; some were brown, some were spotted; some were old, some were young; some were long and lean, some were monstrous. And each of them had an individuality of his own, a will of his own, a hope and a heart's desire; each was full of self-confidence, of self-importance, and a sense of dignity. And trusting and strong in faith he had gone about his business, the while a black shadow hung over him and a horrid Fate waited in his pathway. Now suddenly it had swooped upon him, and had seized him by the leg. Relentless, remorseless, it was; all his protests, his screams, were nothing to it—it did its cruel will with him, as if his wishes, his feelings, had simply no existence at all; it cut his throat and watched him gasp out his life. And now was one to believe that there was nowhere a god of hogs, to whom this hog-personality was precious, to whom these hog-squeals and agonies had a meaning? Who would take this hog into his arms and comfort him, reward him for his work well done, and show him the meaning of his sacrifice? Perhaps some glimpse of all this was in the thoughts of our humble-minded Jurgis, as he turned to go on with the rest of the party, and muttered: "*Dieve*—but I'm glad I'm not a hog!"

The carcass hog was scooped out of the vat by machinery, and then it fell to the second floor, passing on the way through a wonderful machine with numerous scrapers, which adjusted themselves to the size and shape of the animal, and sent it out at the other end with nearly all of its bristles removed. It was then again strung up by machinery, and sent upon another trolley ride; this time passing between two lines of men, who sat upon a raised platform, each doing a certain single thing to the carcass as it came to him. One scraped the outside of a leg; another scraped the inside of the same leg. One with a swift stroke cut the throat; another with two swift strokes severed the head, which fell to the floor and vanished through a hole. Another made a slit down the body; a second opened the body wider; a third with a saw cut the breastbone; a fourth loosened the entrails; a fifth pulled them out—and they also slid through a hole in the floor. There were men to scrape each side and men to scrape the back; there were men to clean the carcass inside, to trim it and wash it. Looking down this room, one saw, creeping slowly, a line of dangling hogs a hundred yards in length; and for every yard there was a man, working as if a demon were after him. At the end of this hog's progress every inch of the carcass had been gone over several times, and then it was rolled into the chilling room, where it stayed for twenty-four hours, and where a stranger might lose himself in a forest of freezing hogs.

Before the carcass was admitted here, however, it had to pass a government inspector, who sat in the doorway and felt of the glands in the neck for tuberculosis. This government inspector did not have the manner of a man who was worked to death; he was apparently not haunted by a fear that the hog might get by him before he had finished his testing. If you were a sociable person, he was quite willing to enter into conversation with you, and to explain to you the deadly nature of the ptomaines which are found in tubercular pork; and while he was talking with you you could hardly be so ungrateful as to notice that a dozen carcasses were passing him untouched. This inspector wore an imposing silver badge, and he gave an atmosphere of authority to the scene, and, as it were, put the stamp of official approval upon the things which were done in Durham's.

Jurgis went down the line with the rest of the visitors, staring open-mouthed, lost in wonder. He had dressed hogs himself in the forest of Lithuania; but he had never expected to live to see one hog dressed by several hundred men. It was like a wonderful poem to him, and he took it all in guilelessly—even to the conspicuous signs demanding immaculate cleanliness of the employees. Jurgis was vexed when the cynical Jokubas translated these signs with sarcastic comments, offering to take them to the secret rooms where the spoiled meats went to be doctored.

The party descended to the next floor, where the various waste materials were treated. Here came the entrails, to be scraped and washed clean for sausage casings; men and women worked here in the midst of a sickening stench, which caused the visitors to hasten by, gasping. To another room came all the scraps to be "tanked," which meant boiling and pumping off the grease to make soap and lard; below they took out the refuse, and this, too, was a region in which the visitors did not linger. In still other places men were engaged in cutting up the carcasses that had been through the chilling rooms. First there were the "splitters," the most expert workmen in the plant, who earned as high as fifty cents an hour, and did not a thing all day except chop hogs down the middle. Then there were "cleaver men," great giants with muscles of iron; each had two men to attend him— to slide the half carcass in front of him on the table, and hold it while he chopped it, and then turn each piece so that he might chop it once more. His cleaver had a blade about two feet long, and he never made but one cut; he made it so neatly, too, that his implement did not smite through and dull itself—there was just enough force for a perfect cut, and no more. So through various yawning holes there slipped to the floor below—to one room hams, to another forequarters, to another sides of pork. One might go down to this floor and see the pickling rooms, where the hams were put into vats, and the great smoke rooms, with their airtight iron doors. In other rooms they prepared salt pork—there were whole cellars full of it, built up in great towers to the ceiling. In yet other rooms they were putting up meat in boxes and barrels, and wrapping hams and bacon in oiled paper, sealing and labeling and sewing them. From the doors of these rooms went men with loaded trucks, to the platform where freight cars were waiting to be filled; and one went out there and realized with a start that he had come at last to the ground floor of this enormous building.

Then the party went across the street to where they did the killing of beef—where every hour they turned four or five hundred cattle into meat. Unlike the place they had left, all this work was done on one floor, and instead of there being one line of carcasses which moved to the workmen, there were fifteen or twenty lines, and the men moved from one to another of these. This made a scene of intense activity, a picture of human power wonderful to watch. It was all in one great room, like a circus amphitheater, with a gallery for visitors running over the center.

Along one side of the room ran a narrow gallery, a few feet from the floor, into which gallery the cattle were driven by men with goads which gave them electric shocks. Once crowded in here, the creatures were prisoned, each in a separate pen, by gates that shut, leaving them no room to turn around, and while they stood bellowing and plunging, over the top of the pen there leaned one of the "knockers," armed with a sledge hammer, and watching for a chance to deal a blow. The room echoed with the thuds in quick succession, and the stamping and kicking of the steers. The instant the animal had fallen, the "knocker" passed on to another, while a second man raised a lever, and the side of the pen was raised, and the animal, still kicking and struggling, slid out to the "killing bed." Here a man put shackles about one leg, and pressed another lever, and the body was jerked up into the air. There were fifteen or twenty such pens, and it was a matter of only a couple of minutes to knock fifteen or twenty cattle and roll them out. Then once more the gates were opened, and another lot rushed in; and so out of each pen there rolled a steady stream of carcasses, which the men upon the killing beds had to get out of the way.

The manner in which they did this was something to be seen and never forgotten. They worked with furious intensity, literally upon the run—at a pace with which there is nothing to be compared except a football game. It was all highly specialized labor, each man having his task to do; generally this would consist of only two or three specific cuts, and he would pass down the line of fifteen or twenty carcasses, making these cuts upon each. First there came the "butcher," to bleed them; this meant one swift stroke, so swift that you could not see it—only the flash of the knife; and before you could realize it, the man had darted on to the next line, and a stream of bright red was pouring out upon the floor. This floor was half an inch deep with blood, in spite of the best efforts of men who kept shoveling it through holes; it must have made the floor slippery, but no one could have guessed this by watching the men at work.

The carcass hung for a few minutes to bleed; there was no time lost, however, for there were several hanging in each line, and one was always ready. It was let down to the ground, and there came the "headsman," whose task it was to sever the head, with two or three swift strokes. Then came the "floorsman," to make the first cut in the skin; and then another to finish ripping the skin down the center; and then half a dozen more in swift succession, to finish the skinning. After they were through, the carcass was again swung up, and while a man with a stick examined the skin, to make sure that it had not been cut, and another rolled it up and tumbled it through one of the inevitable holes in the floor, the beef proceeded on its journey. There were men to cut it, and men to split it, and men to gut it and scrape it clean inside. There were some with hoses which threw jets of boiling water upon it, and others who removed the feet and added the final touches. In the end, as with the hogs, the finished beef was run into the chilling room, to hang its appointed time.

The visitors were taken there and shown them, all neatly hung in rows, labelled conspicuously with the tags of the government inspectors—and some, which had been killed by a special process, marked with the sign of the "kosher" rabbi, certifying that it was fit for sale to the orthodox. And then the visitors were taken to the other parts of the building, to see what became of each particle of the waste material that had vanished through the floor; and to the pickling rooms, and the salting rooms, the canning rooms, and the packing rooms, where choice meat was prepared for shipping in refrigerator cars, destined to be eaten in all the four corners of civilization. Afterward they went outside, wandering about among the mazes of buildings in which was done the work auxiliary to this great industry. There was scarcely a thing needed in the business that Durham and Company did not make for themselves. There was a great steam power plant and an electricity plant. There was a barrel factory, and a boiler repair shop. There was a building to which the grease was piped, and made into soap and lard, and then there was a factory for making lard cans, and another for making soap boxes. There was a building in which the bristles were cleaned and dried, for the making of hair cushions and such things; there was a building where the skins were dried and tanned, there was another where heads and feet were made into glue, and another where bones were made into fertilizer. No tiniest particle of organic matter was wasted in Durham's. Out of the horns of the cattle they made combs, buttons, hairpins, and imitation ivory; out of the shin bones and other big bones they cut knife and tooth brush handles, and mouthpieces for pipes; out of the hoofs they cut hairpins and buttons, before they made the rest into glue. From such things as feet, knuckles, hide clippings, and sinews came such strange and unlikely products as gelatin, isinglass, and phosphorus, bone black, shoe blacking, and bone oil. They had curled-hair works for the cattle tails, and a "wool pullery" for the sheep skins; they made pepsin from the stomachs of the pigs, and albumen from the blood, and violin strings from the ill-smelling entrails. When there was nothing else to be done with a thing, they first put it into a tank and got out of it all the tallow and grease, and then they made it into fertilizer. All these industries were gathered into buildings near by, connected by galleries and railroads with the main establishment, and it was estimated that they had handled nearly a quarter of a billion of animals since the founding of the plant by the elder Durham a generation and more ago. If you counted with it the other big plants—and they were now really all one—it was, so Jokubas informed them, the greatest aggregation of labor and capital ever gathered in one place. It employed thirty thousand men; it supported directly two hundred and fifty thousand people in its neighborhood, and indirectly it supported half a million. It sent its products to every country in the civilized world, and it furnished the food for no less than thirty million people!

To all of these things our friends would listen openmouthed—it seemed to them impossible of belief that anything so stupendous could have been devised by mortal man.

That was why to Jurgis it seemed almost profanity to speak about the place as did Jokubas, sceptically; it was a thing as tremendous as the universe—the laws and ways of its working no more than the universe to be questioned or understood. All that a mere man could do, it seemed to Jurgis, was to take a thing like this as he found it, and do as he was told; to be given a place in it and a share in its wonderful activities was a blessing to be grateful for, as one was grateful for the sunshine and the rain. Jurgis was even glad that he had not seen the place before meeting with his triumph, for he felt that the size of it would have overwhelmed him. But now he had been admitted—he was a part of it all! He had the feeling that this whole huge establishment had taken him under its protection, and had become responsible for his welfare. So guileless was he, and ignorant of the nature of business, that he did not even realize that he had become an employee of Brown's, and that Brown and Durham were supposed by all the world to be deadly rivals—were even required to be deadly rivals by the law of the land, and ordered to try to ruin each other under penalty of fine and imprisonment!

Jack London (1876–1916)

One of America's most popular (and, in his time, financially successful) writers of adventure fiction, Jack London was also one of the nation's most trenchant social critics. Described by E. L. Doctrow as a "great gobbler-up of the world," London produced more than fifty books and a thousand stories and articles between the time he began publishing in the *Overland Monthly* in 1899 and his early death in 1916. As an adolescent in San Francisco, he dropped out of school and turned to hard labor to earn money to support his unmarried mother, working twelve- to eighteen-hour days in a cannery, pirating for oysters in the Bay, then (switching sides of the law) serving on the California Fish Patrol, and shipping out on a Pacific sealing voyage. He brought this work-ethic to writing, eventually coming to see a life of letters as a way out of an impoverished existence as a worker always threatened with falling into "the Social Pit." He got firsthand knowledge of life in the Pit while traveling the country with other jobless hoboes during the depression of 1893–1894. The prison narrative presented here is drawn from London's life-changing experience during this time, of arrest and imprisonment for the crime of being out of work.

London joined the Socialist Labor Party in 1896 and gained a reputation as the "Boy Socialist" of Oakland for his speech making in the City Park. At age twenty-one, he spent the winter as a prospector in the Yukon Territory and soon after began to produce the stories, including *The Call of the Wild* (1903), that made his name and allowed him to devote himself to writing as a livelihood. An extended visit to the East End of London led to his exposé, in *The People of the Abyss* (1903), of the extreme poverty at the heart of what was then the world's greatest capitalist empire. In the quasi-autobiographical novel *Martin Eden* (1909), London recounts his own experiences as a "work-beast" and his painstaking emergence as a writer and socialist, who ironically finds himself isolated between the labor class to which he no longer belongs and the bourgeoisie to whom he is equally alien. The 1906 story "The Apostate" presents a different image of what happens to the work-beast when he abandons all allegiance to wage work. London's literary success permitted him in 1910 to settle on what would become his beloved ranch in Sonoma County, California, where he devoted himself to animal husbandry and environmental conservation while producing a series of less distinguished novels. Of this later period, he would confess, "I write a book for no other reason than to add three or four hundred acres to my magnificent estate." The example of his searing early work, nevertheless, inspired later generations of worker-writers.

THE APOSTATE

Now I wake me up to work;
I pray the Lord I may not shirk.
If I should die before the night,
I pray the Lord my work's all right.
                    AMEN

"If you don't git up, Johnny, I won't give you a bite to eat!"

The threat had no effect on the boy. He clung stubbornly to sleep, fighting for its oblivion as the dreamer fights for his dream. The boy's hands loosely clenched themselves, and he made feeble, spasmodic blows at the air. These blows were intended for his mother, but she betrayed practised familiarity in avoiding them as she shook him roughly by the shoulder.

"Lemme 'lone!"

It was a cry that began, muffled, in the deeps of sleep, that swiftly rushed upward, like a wail, into passionate belligerence, and that died away and sank down into an inarticulate whine. It was a bestial cry, as of a soul in torment, filled with infinite protest and pain.

But she did not mind. She was a sad-eyed, tired-faced woman, and she had grown used to this task, which she repeated every day of her life. She got a grip on the bedclothes and tried to strip them down; but the boy, ceasing his punching, clung to them desperately. In a huddle, at the foot of the bed, he still remained covered. Then she tried dragging the bedding to the floor. The boy opposed her. She braced herself. Hers was the superior weight, and the boy and bedding gave, the former instinctively following the latter in order to shelter against the chill of the room that bit into his body.

As he toppled on the edge of the bed it seemed that he must fall head-first to the floor. But consciousness fluttered up in him. He righted himself and for a moment perilously balanced. Then he struck the floor on his feet. On the instant his mother seized him by the shoulders and shook him. Again his fists struck out, this time with more force and directness. At the same time his eyes opened. She released him. He was awake.

"All right," he mumbled.

She caught up the lamp and hurried out, leaving him in darkness.

"You'll be docked," she warned back at him.

He did not mind the darkness. When he had got into his clothes, he went out into the kitchen. His tread was very heavy for so thin and light a boy. His legs dragged with their own weight, which seemed unreasonable because they were such skinny legs. He drew a broken-bottomed chair to the table.

"Johnny!" his mother called sharply.

He arose as sharply from the chair, and, without a word went to the sink. It was a greasy, filthy sink. A smell came up from the outlet. He took no notice of it. That a sink should smell was to him part of the natural order, just as it was a part of the natural order that the soap should be grimy with dishwater and hard to lather. Nor did he try very hard to make it lather. Several splashes of the cold water from the running faucet completed the function. He did not wash his teeth. For that matter he had never seen a tooth-brush, nor did he know that there existed human beings in the world who were guilty of so great a foolishness as tooth washing.

"You might wash yourself wunst a day without bein' told," his mother complained.

She was holding a broken lid on the pot as she poured two cups of coffee. He made no remark, for this was a standing quarrel between them, and the one thing upon which his mother was hard as adamant. "Wunst" a day it was compulsory that he should wash his face. He dried himself on a greasy towel, damp and dirty and ragged, that left his face covered with shreds of lint.

"I wish we didn't live so far away," she said, as he sat down. "I try to do the best I can. You know that. But a dollar on the rent is such a savin', an we've more room here. You know that."

He scarcely followed her. He had heard it all before, many times, the range of her thought was limited, and she was ever harking back to the hardship worked upon them by living so far from the mills.

"A dollar means more grub," he remarked sententiously. "I'd sooner do the walkin' and git the grub."

He ate hurriedly, half chewing the bread and washing the unmasticated chunks down with coffee. The hot and muddy liquid went by the name of coffee. Johnny thought it was coffee—and excellent coffee. That was one of the few of life's illusions that remained to him. He had never drunk real coffee in his life.

In addition to the bread, there was a small piece of cold pork. His mother refilled his cup with coffee. As he was finishing the bread, he began to watch if more was forthcoming. She intercepted his questioning glance.

"Now, don't be hoggish, Johnny," was her comment. "You've had your share. Your brothers an' sisters are smaller 'n you."

He did not answer the rebuke. He was not much of a talker. Also, he ceased his hungry glancing for more. He was uncomplaining, with a patience that was as terrible as the school in which it had been learned. He finished his coffee, wiped his mouth on the back of his hand, and started to rise.

"Wait a second," she said hastily. "I guess the loaf can stand another slice—a thin un."

There was legerdemain in her actions. With all the seeming of cutting a slice from the loaf for him, she put loaf and slice back in the bread box and conveyed to him one of her own two slices. She believed she had deceived him, but he had noted her sleight-of-hand. Nevertheless, he took the bread shamelessly. He had a philosophy that his mother, what of her chronic sickliness, was not much of an eater anyway.

She saw that he was chewing the bread dry, and reached over and emptied her coffee cup into his.

"Don't set good somehow on my stomach this morning," she explained.

A distant whistle, prolonged and shrieking, brought both of them to their feet. She glanced at the tin alarm-clock on the shelf. The hands stood at half-past five. The rest of the factory world was just arousing from sleep. She drew a shawl about her shoulders, and on her head put a dingy hat, shapeless and ancient.

"We've got to run," she said, turning the wick of the lamp and blowing down the chimney.

They groped their way out and down the stairs. It was clear and cold, and Johnny shivered at the first contact with the outside air. The stars had not yet begun to pale in the sky, and the city lay in blackness. Both Johnny and his mother shuffled their feet as they walked. There was no ambition in the leg muscles to swing the feet clear of the ground.

After fifteen silent minutes, his mother turned off to the right.

"Don't be late," was her final warning from out of the dark that was swallowing her up.

He made no response, steadily keeping on his way. In the factory quarter, doors were opening everywhere, and he was soon one of a multitude that pressed onward through the dark. As he entered the factory gate the whistle blew again. He glanced at the east. Across a ragged sky-line of housetops a pale light was beginning to creep. This much he saw of the day as he turned his back upon it and joined his work-gang.

He took his place in one of many long rows of machines. Before him, above a bin filled with small bobbins, were large bobbins revolving rapidly. Upon these he wound the jute-twine of the small bobbins. The work was simple. All that was required was celerity. The small bobbins were emptied so rapidly, and there were so many large bobbins that did the emptying, that there were no idle moments.

He worked mechanically. When a small bobbin ran out, he used his left hand for a brake, stopping the large bobbin and at the same time, with thumb and forefinger, catching the flying end of twine. Also, at the same time, with his right hand, he caught up the loose twine-end of a small bobbin. These various acts with both hands were performed simultaneously and swiftly. Then there would come a flash of his hands as he looped the weaver's knot and released the bobbin. There was nothing difficult about the weaver's knots. He once boasted he could tie them in his sleep. And for that matter, he sometimes did, toiling centuries long in a single night at tying an endless succession of weaver's knots.

Some of the boys shirked, wasting time and machinery by not replacing the small bobbins when they ran out. And there was an overseer to prevent this. He caught Johnny's neighbor at the trick, and boxed his ears.

"Look at Johnny there—why ain't you like him?" the overseer wrathfully demanded.

Johnny's bobbins were running full blast, but he did not thrill at the indirect praise. There had been a time . . . but that was long ago, very long ago. His apathetic face was expressionless as he listened to himself being held up as a shining example. He was the perfect worker. He knew that. He had been told so, often. It was a commonplace, and besides it didn't seem to mean anything to him any more. From the perfect worker he had evolved into the perfect machine. When his work went wrong, it was with him as with the machine, due to faulty material. It would have been as possible for a perfect nail-die to cut imperfect nails as for him to make a mistake.

And small wonder. There had never been a time when he had not been in intimate relationship with machines. Machinery had almost been bred into him, and at any rate he had been brought up on it. Twelve years before, there had been a small flutter of excitement in the loom room of this very mill. Johnny's mother had fainted. They stretched her out on the floor in the midst of the shrieking machines. A couple of elderly women were called from their looms. The foreman assisted. And in a few minutes there was one more soul in the loom room than had entered by the doors. It was Johnny, born with the pounding, crashing roar of the looms in his ears, drawing with his first breath the warm, moist air that was thick with flying lint. He had coughed that first day in order to rid his lungs of the lint; and for the same reason he had coughed ever since.

The boy alongside of Johnny whimpered and sniffed. The boy's face was convulsed with hatred for the overseer who kept a threatening eye on him from a distance; but every bobbin was running full. The boy yelled terrible oaths into the whirling bobbins before him; but the sound did not carry half a dozen feet, the roaring of the room holding it in and containing it like a wall.

Of all this Johnny took no notice. He had a way of accepting things. Besides, things grow monotonous by repetition, and this particular happening he had witnessed many times. It seemed to him as useless to oppose the overseer as to defy the will of a machine. Machines were made to go in certain ways and to perform certain tasks. It was the same with the overseer.

But at eleven o'clock there was excitement in the room. In an apparently occult way the excitement instantly permeated everywhere. The one-legged boy who worked on the other side of Johnny bobbed swiftly across the floor to a bin truck that stood empty. Into this he dived out of sight, crutch and all. The superintendent of the mill was coming along, accompanied by a young man. He was well dressed and wore a starched shirt—a gentleman, in Johnny's classification of men, and also, "the Inspector."

He looked sharp at the boys as he passed along. When he did so, he was compelled to shout at the top of his lungs, at which moments his face was ludicrously contorted with the strain of making himself heard. His quick eye noted the empty machine alongside of Johnny's, but he said nothing. Johnny also caught his eye, and he stopped abruptly. He caught Johnny by the arm to draw him back a step from the machine; but with an exclamation of surprise he released the arm.

"Pretty skinny," the superintendent laughed anxiously.

"Pipe stems," was the answer. "Look at those legs. The boy's got the rickets—incipient, but he's got them. If epilepsy doesn't get him in the end, it will be because tuberculosis gets him first."

Johnny listened, but did not understand. Furthermore he was not interested in future ills. There was an immediate and more serious ill that threatened him in the form of the inspector.

"Now, my boy, I want you to tell me the truth," the inspector said, or shouted, bending close to the boy's ear to make him hear. "How old are you?"

"Fourteen," Johnny lied, and he lied with the full force of his lungs. So loudly did he lie that it started him off in a dry, hacking cough that lifted the lint which had been settling in his lungs all morning.

"Looks sixteen at least," said the superintendent.

"Or sixty," snapped the inspector.

"He's always looked that way."

"How long?" asked the inspector quickly.

"For years. Never gets a bit older."

"Or younger, I dare say. I suppose he's worked here all those years?"

"Off and on—but that was before the new law was passed," the superintendent hastened to add.

"Machine idle?" the inspector asked, pointing at the unoccupied machine beside Johnny's, in which the part-filled bobbins were flying like mad.

"Looks that way." The superintendent motioned the overseer to him and shouted in his ear and pointed at the machine. "Machine's idle," he reported back to the inspector.

They passed on, and Johnny returned to his work, relieved in that the ill had been averted. But the one-legged boy was not so fortunate. The sharp-eyed inspector hauled him out at arm's length from the bin truck. His lips were quivering, and his face had all the expression of one upon whom was fallen profound and irremediable disaster. The overseer looked astounded, as though for the first time he had laid eyes on the boy, while the superintendent's face expressed shock and displeasure.

"I know him," the inspector said. "He's twelve years old. I've had him discharged from three factories inside the year. This makes the fourth."

He turned to the one-legged boy. "You promised me, word and honor, that you'd go to school."

The one-legged boy burst into tears. "Please, Mr. Inspector, two babies died on us, and we're awful poor."

"What makes you cough that way?" the inspector demanded, as though charging him with crime.

And as in denial of guilt, the one-legged boy replied: "It ain't nothin'. I jes' caught a cold last week, Mr. Inspector, that's all."

In the end the one-legged boy went out of the room with the inspector, the latter accompanied by the anxious and protesting superintendent. After that monotony settled down again. The long morning and the longer afternoon wore away and the whistle blew for quitting time. Darkness had already fallen when Johnny passed out through the factory gate. In the interval the sun had made a golden ladder of the sky, flooded the world with its gracious warmth, and dropped down and disappeared in the west behind a ragged sky-line of housetops.

Supper was the family meal of the day—the one meal at which Johnny encountered his younger brothers and sisters. It partook of the nature of an encounter, to him, for he was very old, while they were distressingly young. He had no patience with their excess-ive amazing juvenility. He did not understand it. His own childhood was too far behind him. He was like an old and irritable man, annoyed by the turbulence of their young spirits that was to him arrant silliness. He glowered silently over his food, finding compensation in the thought that they would soon have to go to work. That would take the edge off of them and make them sedate and dignified—like him. Thus it was, after the fashion of the human, that Johnny made of himself a yardstick with which to measure the universe.

During the meal, his mother explained in various ways and with infinite repetition that she was trying to do the best she could; so that it was with relief, the scant meal ended, that Johnny shoved back his chair and arose. He debated for a moment between bed and the front door, and finally went out the latter. He did not go far. He sat down on the stoop, his knees drawn up and his narrow shoulders drooping forward, his elbows on his knees and the palms of his hand supporting his chin.

As he sat there, he did no thinking. He was just resting. So far as his mind was concerned, it was asleep. His brothers and sisters came out, and with other children played noisily about him. An electric globe on the corner lighted their frolics. He was peevish and irritable, that they knew; but the spirit of adventure lured them into teasing him. They joined hands before him, and, keeping time with their bodies, chanted in his face weird and uncomplimentary doggerel. At first he snarled curses at them—curses he had learned from the lips of various foremen. Finding this futile, and remembering his dignity, he relapsed into dogged silence.

His brother Will, next to him in age, having just passed his tenth birthday, was the ringleader. Johnny did not possess particularly kindly feelings toward him. His life had early been imbittered by continual giving over and giving way to Will. He had a definite feeling that Will was greatly in his debt and was ungrateful about it. In his own playtime, far back in the dim past, he had been robbed of a large part of that playtime by being compelled to take care of Will. Will was a baby then, and then, as now, their mother had spent her days in the mills. To Johnny had fallen the part of little father and little mother as well.

Will seemed to show the benefit of the giving over and the giving way. He was well-built, fairly rugged, as tall as his elder brother and even heavier. It was as though the lifeblood of the one had been diverted into the other's veins. And in spirits it was the same. Johnny was jaded, worn out, without resilience, while his younger brother seemed bursting and spilling over with exuberance.

The mocking chant rose louder and louder. Will leaned closer as he danced, thrusting out his tongue. Johnny's left arm shot out and caught the other around the neck. At the same time he rapped his bony fist to the other's nose. It was a pathetically bony fist, but that it was sharp to hurt was evidenced by the squeal of pain it produced. The other children were uttering frightened cries, while Johnny's sister, Jenny, had dashed into the house.

He thrust Will from him, kicked him savagely on the shins, then reached for him and slammed him face downward in the dirt. Nor did he release him till the face had been rubbed into the dirt several times. Then the mother arrived, an anaemic whirlwind of solicitude and maternal wrath.

"Why can't he leave me alone?" was Johnny's reply to her upbraiding. "Can't he see I'm tired?"

"I'm as big as you," Will raged in her arms, his face a mess of tears, dirt, and blood. "I'm as big as you now, an' I'm goin' to git bigger. Then I'll lick you—see if I don't."

"You ought to be to work, seein' how big you are," Johnny snarled. "That's what's the matter with you. You ought to be to work. An' it's up to your ma to put you to work."

"But he's too young," she protested. "He's only a little boy."

"I was younger'n him when I started to work."

Johnny's mouth was open, further to express the sense of unfairness that he felt, but the mouth closed with a snap. He turned gloomily on his heel and stalked into the house and to bed. The door of his room was open to let in warmth from the kitchen. As he undressed in the semi-darkness he could hear his mother talking with a neighbor woman who had dropped in. His mother was crying, and her speech was punctuated with spiritless sniffles.

"I can't make out what's gittin' into Johnny," he could hear her say. "He didn't used to be this way. He was a patient little angel."

"An' he is a good boy," she hastened to defend. "He's worked faithful, an' he did go to work too young. But it wasn't my fault. I do the best I can, I'm sure."

Prolonged sniffling from the kitchen, and Johnny murmured to himself as his eyelids closed down, "You betcher life I've worked faithful."

The next morning he was torn bodily by his mother from the grip of sleep. Then came the meagre breakfast, the tramp through the dark, and the pale glimpse of day across the housetops as he turned his back on it and went in through the factory gate. It was another day, of all the days, and all the days were alike.

And yet there had been variety in his life—at the times he changed from one job to another, or was taken sick. When he was six, he was little mother and father to Will and the other children still younger. At seven he went into the mills—winding bobbins. When he was eight, he got work in another mill. His new job was marvellously easy. All he had to do was to sit down with a little stick in his hand and guide a stream of cloth that flowed past him. This stream of cloth came out of the maw of a machine, passed over a hot roller, and went on its way elsewhere. But he sat always in the one place, beyond the reach of daylight, a gas-jet flaring over him, himself part of the mechanism.

He was very happy at that job, in spite of the moist heat, for he was still young and in possession of dreams and illusions. And wonderful dreams he dreamed as he watched the steaming cloth streaming endlessly by. But there was no exercise about the work, no call upon his mind, and he dreamed less and less, while his mind grew torpid and drowsy. Nevertheless, he earned two dollars a week, and two dollars represented the difference between acute starvation and chronic underfeeding.

But when he was nine, he lost his job. Measles was the cause of it. After he recovered, he got work in a glass factory. The pay was better, and the work demanded skill. It was piece-work, and the more skillful he was, the bigger wages he earned. Here was incentive. And under this incentive he developed into a remarkable worker.

It was simple work, the tying of glass stoppers into small bottles. At his waist he carried a bundle of twine. He held the bottles between his knees so that he might work with both hands. Thus, in a sitting position and bending over his own knees, his narrow shoulders grew humped and his chest was contracted for ten hours each day. This was not good for the lungs, but he tied three hundred dozen bottles a day.

The superintendent was very proud of him, and brought visitors to look at him. In ten hours three hundred dozen bottles passed through his hands. This meant that he had attained machine-like perfection. All waste movements were eliminated. Every motion of his thin arms, every movement of a muscle in the thin fingers, was swift and accurate. He worked at high tension, and the result was that he grew nervous. At night his muscles twitched in his sleep, and in the daytime he could not relax and rest. He remained keyed up and his muscles continued to twitch. Also he grew sallow and his lint-cough grew worse. Then pneumonia laid hold of the feeble lungs within the contracted chest, and he lost his job in the glassworks.

Now he had returned to the jute mills where he had first begun with winding bobbins. But promotion was waiting for him. He was a good worker. He would next go on the starcher, and later he would go into the loom room. There was nothing after that except increased efficiency.

The machinery ran faster than when he had first gone to work, and his mind ran slower. He no longer dreamed at all, though his earlier years had been full of dreaming. Once he had been in love. It was when he first began guiding the cloth over the hot roller, and it was with the daughter of the superintendent. She was much older than he, a young woman, and he had seen her at a distance only a paltry half-dozen times. But that made no difference. On the surface of the cloth stream that poured past him, he pictured radiant futures wherein he performed prodigies of toil, invented miraculous machines, won to the mastership of the mills, and in the end took her in his arms and kissed her soberly on the brow.

But that was all in the long ago, before he had grown too old and tired to love. Also, she had married and gone away, and his mind had gone to sleep. Yet it had been a wonderful experience, and he used often to look back upon it as other men and women look back upon the time they believed in fairies. He had never believed in fairies nor Santa Claus; but he had believed implicitly in the smiling future his imagination had wrought into the steaming cloth stream.

He had become a man very early in life. At seven, when he drew his first wages, began his adolescence. A certain feeling of independence crept up in him, and the relationship between him and his mother changed. Somehow, as an earner and breadwinner, doing his own work in the world, he was more like an equal with her. Manhood, full-blown manhood, had come when he was eleven, at which time he had gone to work on the night shift for six months. No child works on the night shift and remains a child.

There had been several great events in his life. One of these had been when his mother bought some California prunes. Two others had been the two times when she cooked custard. Those had been events. He remembered them kindly. And at that time his mother had told him of a blissful dish she would sometime make—"floating island," she had called it, "better than custard." For years he had looked forward to the day when he would sit down to the table with floating island before him, until at last he had relegated the idea of it to the limbo of unattainable ideals.

Once he found a silver quarter lying on the sidewalk. That, also, was a great event in his life, withal a tragic one. He knew his duty on the instant the silver flashed on his eyes, before even he had picked it up. At home, as usual, there was not enough to eat, and home he should have taken it as he did his wages every Saturday night. Right conduct in this case was obvious; but he never had any spending of his money, and he was suffering from candy hunger. He was ravenous for the sweets that only on red-letter days he had ever tasted in his life.

He did not attempt to deceive himself. He knew it was sin, and deliberately he sinned when he went on a fifteen-cent candy debauch. Ten cents he saved for a future orgy; but not being accustomed to the carrying of money, he lost the ten cents. This occurred at the time when he was suffering all the torments of conscience, and it was to him an act of divine retribution. He had a frightened sense of the closeness of an awful and wrathful God. God had seen, and God had been swift to punish, denying him even the full wages of sin.

In memory he always looked back upon that event as the one great criminal deed of his life, and at the recollection his conscience always awoke and gave him another twinge. It was the one skeleton in his closet. Also, being so made and circumstanced, he looked back upon the deed with regret. He was dissatisfied with the manner in which he had spent the quarter. He could have invested it better, and, out of his later knowledge of the quickness of God, he would have beaten God out by spending the whole quarter at one fell swoop. In retrospect he spent the quarter a thousand times, and each time to better advantage.

There was one other memory of the past, dim and faded, but stamped into his soul everlastingly by the savage feet of his father. It was more like a nightmare than a remembered vision of a concrete thing—more like the race-memory of man that makes him fall in his sleep and that goes back to his arboreal ancestry.

This particular memory never came to Johnny in broad daylight when he was wide awake. It came at night, in bed, at the moment that his consciousness was sinking down and losing itself in sleep. It always aroused him to frightened wakefulness, and for the moment, in the first sickening start, it seemed to him that he lay cross-wise on the foot of the bed. In the bed were the vague forms of his father and mother. He never saw what his father looked like. He had but one impression of his father, and that was that he had savage and pitiless feet.

His earlier memories lingered with him, but he had no late memories. All days were alike. Yesterday or last year were the same as a thousand years—or a minute. Nothing ever happened. There were no events to mark the march of time. Time did not march. It stood always still. It was only the whirling machines that moved, and they moved nowhere—in spite of the fact that they moved faster.

When he was fourteen, he went to work on the starcher. It was a colossal event. Something had at least happened that could be remembered beyond a night's sleep or a week's pay-day. It marked an era. It was a machine Olympiad, a thing to date from. "When I went to work on the starcher," or, "after," or "before I went to work on the starcher," were sentences often on his lips.

He celebrated his sixteenth birthday by going into the loom room and taking a loom. Here was an incentive again, for it was piece-work. And he excelled, because the clay of him had been moulded by the mills into the perfect machine. At the end of three months he was running two looms, and, later, three and four.

At the end of his second year at the looms he was turning out more yards than any other weaver, and more than twice as much as some of the less skillful ones. And at home things began to prosper as he approached the full stature of his earning power. Not, however, that his increased earnings were in excess of need. The children were growing up. They ate more. And they were going to school, and schoolbooks cost money. And somehow, the faster he worked, the faster climbed the prices of things. Even the rent went up, though the house had fallen from bad to worse disrepair.

He had grown taller; but with his increased height he seemed leaner than ever. Also, he was more nervous. With the nervousness increased peevishness and irritability. The children had learned by many bitter lessons to fight shy of him. His mother respected him for his earning power, but somehow her respect was tinctured with fear.

There was no joyousness in life for him. The procession of the days he never saw. The nights he slept away in twitching unconsciousness. The rest of the time he worked, and his consciousness was machine consciousness. Outside this his mind was a blank. He had no ideals, and but one illusion; namely, that he drank excellent coffee. He was a work-beast. He had no mental life whatever; yet deep down in the crypts of his mind, unknown to him, were being weighed and sifted every hour in his toil, every movement of his hands, every twitch of his muscles, and preparations were making for a future course of action that would amaze him and all his little world.

It was in the late spring that he came home from work one night aware of unusual tiredness. There was a keen expectancy in the air as he sat down to the table, but he did not notice. He went through the meal in moody silence, mechanically eating what was before him. The children um'd and ah'd and made smacking noises with their mouths. But he was deaf to them.

"D'ye know what you're eatin'?" his mother demanded at last, desperately.

He looked vacantly at the dish before him, and vacantly at her.

"Floatin' island," she announced triumphantly.

"Oh," he said.

"Floating island!" the children chorused loudly.

"Oh," he said. And after two or three mouthfuls, he added, "I guess I ain't hungry to-night."

He dropped the spoon, shoved back his chair, and arose wearily from the table.

"An' I guess I'll go to bed."

His feet dragged more heavily than usual as he crossed the kitchen floor. Undressing was a Titan's task, a monstrous futility, and he wept weakly as he crawled into bed, one shoe still on. He was aware of a rising, swelling something inside his head that made his brain thick and fuzzy. His lean fingers felt as big as his wrist, while in the ends of them was a remoteness of sensation vague and fuzzy like his brain. The small of his back ached intolerably. All his bones ached. He ached everywhere. And in his head began the shrieking, pounding, crashing, roaring of a million looms. All space was filled with flying shuttles. They darted in and out, intricately, amongst the stars. He worked a thousand looms himself, and ever they speeded up, faster and faster, and his brain unwound, faster and faster, and became the thread that fed the thousand flying shuttles.

He did not go to work next morning. He was too busy weaving colossally on the thousand looms that ran inside his head. His mother went to work, but first she sent for the doctor. It was a severe attack of la grippe, he said. Jennie served as nurse and carried out his instructions.

It was a very severe attack, and it was a week before Johnny dressed and tottered feebly across the floor. Another week, the doctor said, and he would be fit to return to work. The foreman of the loom room visited him on Sunday afternoon, the first day of his convalescence. The best weaver in the room, the foreman told his mother. His job would be held for him. He could come back to work a week from Monday.

"Why don't you thank 'im, Johnny?" his mother asked anxiously.

"He's ben that sick he ain't himself yet," she explained apologetically to the visitor.

Johnny sat hunched up and gazing steadfastly at the floor. He sat in the same position long after the foreman had gone. It was warm outdoors, and he sat on the stoop in the afternoon. Sometimes his lips moved. He seemed lost in endless calculations.

Next morning, after the day grew warm, he took his seat on the stoop. He had pencil and paper this time with which to continue his calculations, and he calculated painfully and amazingly.

"What comes after millions?" he asked at noon, when Will came home from school. "An' how d'ye work 'em?"

That afternoon finished his task. Each day, but without paper and pencil, he returned to the stoop. He was greatly absorbed in the one tree that grew across the street. He studied it for hours at a time, and was unusually interested when the wind swayed its branches and fluttered its leaves. Throughout the week he seemed lost in a great communion with himself. On Sunday, sitting on the stoop, he laughed aloud, several times, to the perturbation of his mother, who had not heard him laugh in years.

Next morning, in the early darkness, she came to his bed to rouse him. He had had his fill of sleep all week, and awoke easily. He made no struggle, nor did he attempt to hold on to the bedding when she stripped it from him. He lay quietly, and spoke quietly.

"It ain't no use, ma."

"You'll be late," she said, under the impression that he was still stupid with sleep.

"I'm awake, ma, an' I tell you it ain't no use. You might as well lemme alone. I ain't goin' to git up."

"But you'll lose your job!" she cried.

"I ain't goin' to git up," he repeated in a strange, passionless voice.

She did not go to work herself that morning. This was sickness beyond any sickness she had ever known. Fever and delirium she could understand; but this was insanity. She pulled the bedding up over him and sent Jennie for the doctor.

When that person arrived Johnny was sleeping gently, and gently he awoke and allowed his pulse to be taken.

"Nothing the matter with him," the doctor reported. "Badly debilitated, that's all. Not much meat on his bones."

"He's always been that way," his mother volunteered.

"Now go 'way, ma, an' let me finish my snooze."

Johnny spoke sweetly and placidly, and sweetly and placidly he rolled over on his side and went to sleep.

At ten o'clock he awoke and dressed himself. He walked out into the kitchen, where he found his mother with a frightened expression on her face.

"I'm goin' away, ma," he announced, "an' I jes' want to say good-by."

She threw her apron over her head and sat down suddenly and wept. He waited patiently.

"I might a-known it," she was sobbing.

"Where?" she finally asked, removing the apron from her head and gazing up at him with a stricken face in which there was little curiosity.

"I don't know—anywhere."

As he spoke, the tree across the street appeared with dazzling brightness on his inner vision. It seemed to lurk just under his eyelids, and he could see it whenever he wished.

"An' your job?" she quavered.

"I ain't never goin' to work again."

"My God, Johnny!" she wailed, "don't say that!"

What he had said was blasphemy to her. As a mother who hears her child deny God, was Johnny's mother shocked by his words.

"What's got into you, anyway?" she demanded, with a lame attempt at imperativeness.

"Figures," he answered. "Jes' figures. I've ben doin' a lot of figurin' this week, an' it's most surprisin'."

"I don't see what that's got to do with it," she sniffled.

Johnny smiled patiently, and his mother was aware of a distinct shock at the persistent absence of his peevishness and irritability.

"I'll show you," he said. "I'm plum' tired out. What makes me tired? Moves. I've ben movin' ever since I was born. I'm tired of movin', an' I ain't goin' to move any more. Remember when I worked in the glass-house? I used to do three hundred dozen a day. Now I reckon I made about ten different moves to each bottle. That's thirty-six thousan' moves a day. Ten days, three hundred an' sixty thousan' moves a day. One month, one million an' eighty thousan' moves. Chuck out the eighty thousan'—" he spoke with the complacent beneficence of a philanthropist—"chuck out the eighty thousan', that leaves a million moves a month—twelve million moves a year.

"At the looms I'm movin' twic'st as much. That makes twenty-five million moves a year, an' it seems to me I've ben a-movin' that way 'most a million years.

"Now this week I ain't moved at all. I ain't made one move in hours an' hours. I tell you it was swell, jes' settin' there, hours an' hours, an' doin' nothin'. I ain't never ben happy before. I never had any time. I've ben movin' all the time. That ain't no way to be happy. An' I ain't goin' to do it any more. I'm jes' goin' to set, an' set, an' rest, an' rest, and then rest some more."

"But what's goin' to come of Will an' the children?" she asked despairingly.

"That's it, 'Will an' the children,'" he repeated.

But there was no bitterness in his voice. He had long known his mother's ambition for the younger boy, but the thought of it no longer rankled. Nothing mattered any more. Not even that.

"I know, ma, what you've ben plannin' for Will—keepin' him in school to make a bookkeeper out of him. But it ain't no use, I've quit. He's got to go to work."

"An' after I have brung you up the way I have," she wept, starting to cover her head with the apron and changing her mind.

"You never brung me up," he answered with sad kindliness. "I brung myself up, ma, an' I brung up Will. He's bigger'n me, an' heavier an' taller. When I was a kid, I reckon I didn't git enough to eat. When he come along an' was a kid, I was workin' an' earnin' grub for him too. But that's done with. Will can go to work, same as me, or he can go to hell, I don't care which. I'm tired. I'm goin' now. Ain't you goin' to say good-by?"

She made no reply. The apron had gone over her head again, and she was crying. He paused a moment in the doorway.

"I'm sure I done the best I knew how," she was sobbing.

He passed out of the house and down the street. A wan delight came into his face at the sight of the lone tree. "Jes' ain't goin' to do nothin'," he said to himself, half aloud, in a crooning tone. He glanced wistfully up at the sky, but the bright sun dazzled and blinded him.

It was a long walk he took, and he did not walk fast. It took him past the jute-mill. The muffled roar of the looms came to his ears, and he smiled. It was a gentle, placid smile. He hated no one, not even the pounding, shrieking machines. There was no bitterness in him, nothing but an inordinate hunger for rest.

The houses and factories thinned out and the open spaces increased as he approached the country. At last the city was behind him, and he was walking down a leafy lane beside the railroad track. He did not walk like a man. He did not look like a man. He was a travesty of the human. It was a twisted and stunted and nameless piece of life that shambled like a sickly ape, arms loose-hanging, stoop-shouldered, narrow-chested, grotesque and terrible.

He passed by a small railroad station and lay down in the grass under a tree. All afternoon he lay there. Sometimes he dozed, with muscles that twitched in his sleep. When awake, he lay without movement, watching the birds or looking up at the sky through the branches of the tree above him. Once or twice he laughed aloud, but without relevance to anything he had seen or felt.

After twilight had gone, in the first darkness of the night, a freight train rumbled into the station. When the engine was switching cars on to the sidetrack, Johnny crept along the side of the train. He pulled open the side-door of an empty box-car and awkwardly and laboriously climbed in. He closed the door. The engine whistled. Johnny was lying down, and in the darkness he smiled.

"Pinched": A Prison Experience

I rode into Niagara Falls in a "side-door Pullman," or, in common parlance, a boxcar. A flat car, by the way, is known among the fraternity as a "gondola," with the second syllable emphasized and pronounced long. But to return. I arrived in the afternoon and headed straight from the freight-train to the falls. Once my eyes were filled with that wonderful vision of downrushing water, I was lost. I could not tear myself away long enough to "batter" the "privates" (domiciles) for my supper. Even a set-down could not have lured me away. Night came on, a beautiful night of moonlight, and I lingered by the falls until after eleven. Then it was up to me to hunt for a place to "kip."

"Kip," "doss," "flop," "pound your ear," all mean the same thing, namely, to sleep. Somehow I had a "hunch" that Niagara Falls was a "bad" town for hoboes, and I headed out into the country. I climbed a fence and "flopped" in a field. John Law would never find me there, I flattered myself. I lay on my back in the grass and slept like a babe. It was so balmy warm that I woke up not once all night. But with the first gray daylight my eyes opened, and I remembered the wonderful falls. I climbed the fence and started down the road to have another look at them. It was early—not more than five o'clock—and not until eight o'clock could I begin to batter for my breakfast. I could spend at least three hours by the river. Alas! I was fated never to see the river nor the falls again.

The town was asleep when I entered it. As I came along the quiet street, I saw three men coming towards me along the sidewalk. They were walking abreast. Hoboes, I decided, who, like myself, had got up early. In this surmise I was not quite correct. I was only sixty-six and two-thirds percent correct. The men on each side were hoboes all right, but the man in the middle wasn't. I directed my steps to the edge of the sidewalk in order to let the trio go by. But it didn't go by. At some word from the man in the center, all three halted, and he of the center addressed me.

I piped the lay on the instant. He was a "fly-cop," and the two hoboes were his prisoners. John Law was up and out after the early worm. I was a worm. Had I been richer by the experiences that were to befall me in the next several months, I should have turned and run like the very devil. He might have shot at me, but he'd have had to hit me to get me. He'd never run after me, for two hoboes in the hand are worth more than one on the get-away. But like a dummy I stood still when he halted me. Our conversation was brief.

"What hotel are you stopping at?" he queried.

He had me. I wasn't stopping at any hotel, and, since I did not know the name of a hotel in the place, I could not claim residence in any of them. Also, I was up too early in the morning. Everything was against me.

"I just arrived," I said.

"Well, you just turn around and walk in front of me, and not too far in front. There's somebody wants to see you."

I was "pinched." I knew who wanted to see me. With that "fly-cop" and the two hoboes at my heels, and under the direction of the former, I led the way to the city jail. There we were searched and our names registered. I have forgotten now under which name I was registered. I gave the name of Jack Drake, but when they searched me they found letters addressed to Jack London. This caused trouble and required explanation, all of which has passed from my mind, and to this day I do not know whether I was pinched as Jack Drake or Jack London. But one or the other, it should be there to-day in the prison register of Niagara Falls. Reference can bring it to light. The time was somewhere in the latter part of June, 1894. It was only a few days after my arrest that the great railroad strike began.

From the office we were led to the "Hobo" and locked in. The "Hobo" is that part of a prison where the minor offenders are confined together in a large iron cage. Since hoboes constitute the principal division of the minor offenders, the aforesaid iron cage is called the "Hobo." Here we met several hoboes who had been pinched already that morning, and every little while the door was unlocked and two or three more were thrust in with us. At last, when we totaled sixteen, we were lead upstairs into the court-room. And now I shall faithfully describe what took place in that court-room, for know that my patriotic American citizenship there received a shock from which it has never fully recovered.

In the court-room were the sixteen prisoners, the judge, and two bailiffs. The judged seemed to act as his own clerk. There were no witnesses. There were no citizens of Niagara Falls present to look on and see how justice was administered in their community. The judge glanced at the list of cases before him and called out a name. A hobo stood up. The judge glanced at a bailiff. "Vagrancy, your honor," said the bailiff. "Thirty days," said his honor. The hobo sat down, and the judge was calling another name and another hobo was rising to his feet.

The trial of that hobo had taken just about fifteen seconds. The trial of the next hobo came off with equal celerity. The bailiff said, "Vagrancy, your honor," and his honor said, "Thirty days." This it went like clockwork, fifteen seconds to a hobo—and thirty days.

They are poor dumb cattle, I thought to myself. But wait till my turn comes; I'll give his honor a "spiel." Part way along in the performance his honor, moved by some whim, gave one of us an opportunity to speak. As chance would have it, this man was not a genuine hobo. He bore none of the earmarks of the professional "stiff." Had he approached the rest of us, while waiting at a water-tank for a freight, we should have unhesitatingly classified him as a gay-cat. "Gay-cat" is the synonym for tenderfoot in Hoboland. This gay-cat was well along in years—somewhere around forty-five, I should judge. His shoulders were humped a trifle, and his face was seamed and weather-beaten.

For many years, according to his story, he had driven team for some firm in (if I remember rightly) Lockport, New York. The firm had ceased to prosper, and finally, in the hard times of 1893, had gone out of business. He had been kept on to the last, though toward the last his work had been very irregular. He went on and explained at length his difficulties in getting work (when so many were out of work) during the succeeding months. In the end, deciding that he would find better opportunities for work on the lakes, he had started for Buffalo. Of course he was "broke," and there he was. That was all.

"Thirty days," said his honor, and called another hobo's name.

Said hobo got up. "Vagrancy, your honor," said the bailiff, and his honor said, "Thirty days."

And so it went, fifteen seconds and thirty days to each hobo. The machine of justice was grinding smoothly. Most likely, considering how early it was in the morning, his honor had not yet had his breakfast and was in a hurry.

But my American blood was up. Behind me there were the many generations of my American ancestry. One of the kinds of liberty those ancestors of mine had fought and died for was the right of trial by jury. This was my heritage, stained sacred by their blood, and it devolved upon me to stand up for it. All right, I threatened to myself; just wait till he gets to me.

He got to me. My name, whatever it was, was called, and I stood up. The bailiff said, "Vagrancy, your honor," and I began to talk. But the judge began talking at the same time, and he said, "Thirty days." I started to protest, but at that moment his honor was calling the name of the next hobo on the list. His honor paused long enough to say to me, "Shut up!" The bailiff forced me to sit down. And the next moment that next hobo received thirty days, and the succeeding hobo was just in the process of getting his.

When we had all been disposed of, thirty days to each stiff, his honor, just as he was about to dismiss us, suddenly turned to the teamster from Lockport, the one man he had allowed to talk.

"Why did you quit your job?" his honor asked.

Now the teamster had already explained how his job had quit him, and the question took him aback. "Your honor," he began confusedly, "isn't that a funny question to ask?"

"Thirty days more for quitting your job," said his honor, and the court was closed. That was the outcome. The teamster got sixty days altogether, while the rest of us got thirty days.

We were taken down below, locked up, and given breakfast. It was a pretty good breakfast, as prison breakfasts go, and it was the best I was to get for a month to come.

As for me, I was dazed. Here was I, under sentence, after a farce of a trial wherein I was denied not only my right of trial by jury, but my right to plead guilty or not guilty. Another thing my fathers had fought for flushed through my brain—habeas corpus. I'd show them. But when I asked for a lawyer, I was laughed at. Habeas corpus was all right, but of what good was it to me when I could communicate with no one outside the jail? But I'd show them. They couldn't keep me in jail forever. Just wait till I got out, that was all. I'd make them sit up. I knew something about the law and my own rights, and I'd expose their maladministration of justice. Visions of damage suits and sensational newspaper head-lines were dancing before my eyes, when the jailers came in and began hustling us out into the main office.

A policeman snapped a handcuff on my right wrist. (Aha! thought I, a new indignity. Just wail till I get out.) On the left wrist of a negro he snapped the other handcuff of that pair. He was a very tall negro, well past six feet—so tall was he that when we stood side by side his hand lifted mine up a trifle in the manacles. Also, he was the happiest and the raggedest negro I have ever seen.

We were all handcuffed similarly, in pairs. This accomplished, a bright, nickel-steel chain was brought forth, run down through the links of all the handcuffs, and locked at front and rear of the double line. We were now a chain-gang. The command to march was given, and out we went upon the street, guarded by two officers. The tall negro and I had the place of honor. We led the procession.

After the tomb-like gloom of the jail, the outside sunshine was dazzling. I had never known it to be so sweet as now when, a prisoner with clanking chains, I knew that I was soon to see the last of it for thirty days. Down through the streets of Niagara Falls we marched to the railroad station, stared at by curious passers-by and, especially, by a group of tourists on the veranda of a hotel that we marched passed.

There was plenty of slack in the chain, and with much rattling and clanking we sat down, two and two, in the seats of the smoking car. Afire with indignation as I was at the outrage that had been perpetrated on me and my forefathers, I was nevertheless too prosaically practical to lose my head over it. This was all new to me. Thirty days of mystery were before me, and I looked about me to find somebody who knew the ropes. For I had already learned that I was not bound for a petty jail with a hundred or so prisoners in it, but for a full-grown penitentiary with a couple of thousand prisoners in it doing anywhere from ten days to ten years.

In the seat behind me, attached to the chain by his wrist, was a squat, heavily built, powerfully muscled man. He was somewhere between thirty-five and forty years of age. I sized him up. In the corners of his eyes I saw humor and laughter and kindliness. As for the rest of him, he was a brute-beast, wholly unmoral, and with all the passion and turgid violence of the brute-beast. What saved him, what made him possible for me, were those corners of his eyes—the humor and laughter and kindliness of the beast when unaroused.

He was my "meat." I cottoned to him. While my cuff-mate, the tall negro, mourned with chucklings and laughter over some laundry he was sure to lose through his arrest, and while the train rolled on toward Buffalo, I talked with the man in the seat behind me.

He had an empty pipe. I filled it for him with my precious cigarette tobacco—enough in a single filling to make a dozen cigarettes. Nay, the more we talked the surer I was that he was my meat, and I divided all my tobacco with him.

Now it happens that I am a fluid sort of organism, with sufficient kinship with life to fit myself in 'most anywhere. I laid myself out to fit in with that man, though little did I dream to what extraordinary good purpose I was succeeding. He had never been in the particular penitentiary to which we were going, but he had done "one," "two," and "five spots" in various other penitentiaries (a "spot" is a year), and he was filled with wisdom. We became pretty chummy, and my heart bounded when he cautioned me to follow his lead. He called me "Jack," and I called him "Jack."

The train stopped at a station about five miles from Buffalo, and we, the chain-gang, got off. I do not remember the station, but I am confident that it is some one of the following; Rocklyn, Rockwood, Black Rock, Rockcastle, or Newcastle. But whatever the name of the place, we were walked a short distance and then put on a street-car. It was an old-fashioned car, with a seat, running the full length, on each side. All the passengers who sat on one side were asked to move over to the other side, and we, with a great clanking of chain, took their places. We sat facing them, I remember, and I remember, too, the awed expression on the faces of the women, who took us, undoubtedly, for convicted murderers and bank-robbers. I tried to look my fiercest, but that cuff-mate of mine, the too happy negro, insisted on rolling his eyes, laughing, and reiterating, "Oh, Lawdy! Lawdy!"

We left the car, walked some more, and were led into the office of the Erie County penitentiary. Here we were to register, and on that register one or the other of my names will be found. Also, we were informed that we must leave in the office all our valuables, money, tobacco, matches, pocket-knives, and so forth.

My new pal shook his head at me.

"If you do not leave your things here, they will be confiscated inside," warned the official.

Still my pal shook his head. He was busy with his hands, hiding his movements behind the other fellows. (Our handcuffs had been removed.) I watched him and followed suit, wrapping up in a bundle in my handkerchief all the things I wanted to take in. These bundles the two of us thrust into our shirts. I noticed that our fellow-prisoners, with the exception of one or two who had watches, did not turn over their belongings to the man in the office. They were determined to smuggle them in somehow, trusting to luck; but they were not so wise as my pal, for they did not wrap their things in bundles.

Our erstwhile guardians gathered up the handcuffs and chain and departed for Niagara Falls, while we, under new guardians, were led away into the prison. While we were in the office our number had been added to by other squads of newly arrived prisoners, so that we were now a procession of forty or fifty strong.

Know, ye unimprisoned, that traffic is as restricted inside a large prison as commerce was in the Middle Ages. Once inside a penitentiary, one cannot move about at will. Every few steps are encountered great steel doors or gates which are always kept locked. We were bound for the barber-shop, but we encountered delays in the unlocking of doors for us. We were thus delayed in the first hall we entered. A "hall" is not a corridor. Imagine an oblong structure, built of bricks and rising six stories high, each story a row of cells, say fifty cells in a row—in short, imagine an oblong of colossal honey-comb. Place this on the ground and enclose it in a building with a roof overhead and walls all around. Such an oblong and encompassing building constitute a "hall" in the Erie County penitentiary. Also, to complete the picture, see a narrow gallery, with a steel railing, running the full length of each tier of cells, and at the ends of the oblong see all these galleries, from both sides, connected by a fire-escape system of narrow steel stairways.

We were halted in the first hall, waiting for some guard to unlock a door. Here and there, moving about, were convicts, with close-cropped heads and shaven faces, and garbed in prison stripes. One such convict I noticed above us on the gallery of the third tier of cells. He was standing on the gallery and leaning forward, his arms resting on the railing, apparently oblivious of our presence. He seemed staring into vacancy. My pal made a slight hissing noise. The convict glanced down. Motioned signals passed between them. Then through the air soared the handkerchief bundle of my pal. The convict caught it, and like a flash it was out of sight in his shirt. And he was staring into vacancy. My pal had told me to follow his lead. I watched my chance when the guard's back was turned, and my bundle followed the other one into the shirt of the convict.

A minute later the door was unlocked, and we filed into the barbershop. Here were more men in convict stripes. They were prison barbers. Also, there were bath-tubs, hot water, soap, and scrubbing-brushes. We were ordered to strip and bathe, each man to scrub his neighbors back—a needless precaution, this compulsory bath, for the prison swarmed with vermin. After the bath, we were each given a prison clothes-bag.

"Put all your clothes in the bags," said the guard. "It's no good trying to smuggle anything in. You've got to line up naked for inspection. Men for thirty days or less keep their shoes and suspenders. Men for more than thirty days keep nothing."

This announcement was received with consternation. How could naked men smuggle anything past an inspection? Only my pal and I were safe. But it was right here that the convict barbers got in their work. They passed among the poor newcomers, kindly volunteering to take charge of their precious little belongings, and promised to return them later in the day. Those barbers were philanthropists—to hear them talk. As in the case of Fra Lippo Lippi, there was prompt disemburdening. Matches, tobacco, rice-paper, pipes, knives, money, everything, flowed into the capacious shirts of the barbers. They fairly bulged with the spoil, and the guards made believe not to see. To cut the story short, nothing was ever returned. The barbers never had any intention of returning what they had taken. They considered it legitimately theirs. It was the barber-shop graft. There were many grafts in that prison, as I was to learn, and I, too, was destined to become a grafter— thanks to my new pal.

There were several chairs, and the barbers worked rapidly. The quickest shaves and hair-cuts I have ever seen were given in that shop. The men lathered themselves, and the barbers shaved them at the rate of a man a minute. A hair-cut took a trifle longer. In three minutes the down of eighteen was scraped from my face and my head was a smooth as a billiard-ball just sprouting a crop of bristles. Beards, mustaches, like our clothes and everything, came off. Take my word for it, we were a villainous-looking gang when they got through with us. I had not realized before how really altogether bad we were.

Then came the line-up, forty or fifty of us, naked as Kipling's heroes who stormed Lungtungpen. To search us was easy. There were only our shoes and ourselves. Two or three rash spirits, who had doubted the barbers, had the goods found on them—which goods, namely, tobacco, pipes, matches, and small change, were quickly confiscated.

This over, our new clothes were brought to us—stout prison shirts, and coats and trousers conspicuously striped. I had always lingered under the impression that the convict stripes were put on a man only after he had been convicted of a felony. I lingered no longer, but put on the insignia of shame and got my first taste of marching the lock-step.

In single file, close together, each man's hands on the shoulders of the man in front, we marched on into another large hall. Here we were ranged up against the wall in a long line and ordered to strip our left arms. A youth, a medical student who was getting in his practice on cattle such as we, came down the line. He vaccinated just about four times as rapidly as the barbers shaved. With a final caution to avoid rubbing our arms against anything, we were led away to our cells.

In my cell was another man who was to be my cell-mate. He was a young, manly fellow, not talkative, but very capable, indeed as splendid a fellow as one could meet with in a day's ride, and this in spite of the fact that he had just recently finished a two-year term in some Ohio penitentiary.

Hardly had we been in our cell half an hour when a convict sauntered down the gallery and looked in. It was my pal. He had the freedom of the hall, he explained. He was to be unlocked at six in the morning and not locked up again till nine at night. He was in with the "push" in that hall, and had been promptly appointed a trusty of the kind technically known as "hall-man." The man who had appointed him was also a prisoner and a trusty, and was known as "first hall-man." There were thirteen hall-men in that hall. Ten of them had charge each of a gallery of cells, and over them were the first, second, and third hall-men.

We newcomers were to stay in our cells for the rest of the day, my pal informed me, so that the vaccine would have a chance to take. Then next morning we would be put to hard labor in the prison-yard.

"But I'll get you out of the work as soon as I can," he promised. "I'll get one of the hall-men fired and have you put in his place."

He put his hand into his shirt, drew out the handkerchief containing my precious belongings, passed it in to me through the bars, and went on down the gallery.

I opened the bundle. Everything was there. Not even a match was missing. I shared the makings of a cigarette with my cell-mate. When I started to strike a match for a light, he stopped me. A flimsy, dirty comforter lay in each of our bunks for bedding. He tore off a narrow strip of the thin cloth and rolled it tightly and telescopically into a long and slender cylinder. This he lighted with a precious match. The cylinder of tight-rolled cotton cloth did not flame. On the end a coal of fire slowly smoldered. It would last for hours, and my cell-mate called it a "punk." When it burned short, all that was necessary was to make a new punk, put the end of it against the old, blow on them, and so transfer the glowing coal. Why, we could have given Prometheus pointers on the conserving of fire.

At twelve o'clock dinner was served. At the bottom of our cage-door was a small opening like the entrance of a runway in a chicken-yard. Through this were thrust two hunks of dry bread and two pannikins of "soup." A portion of soup consisted of about a quart of hot water with a lonely drop of grease floating on its surface. Also, there was some salt in the water.

We drank the soup, but we did not eat the bread. Not that we were not hungry, and not that the bread was uneatable. It was fairly good bread. But we had reasons. My cell-mate had discovered that our cell was alive with bedbugs. In all the cracks and interstices between the bricks where the mortar had fallen out great colonies flourished. The natives even ventured out in the broad daylight and swarmed over the walls and ceilings by hundreds. My cell-mate was wise in the ways of the beasts. Like Childe Roland, dauntless the slug-horn to his lips he bore. Never was there such a battle. It lasted for hours. It was a shambles. And when the last survivors fled to their brick-and-mortar fastnesses, our work was only half done. We chewed mouthfuls of our bread until it was reduced to the consistency of putty, and when a fleeing belligerent escaped into a crevice between the bricks, we promptly walled him in with a daub of the chewed bread. We toiled on until the light grew dim and until every hole, nook, and cranny was closed. I shudder to think of the tragedies of starvation and cannibalism that must have ensued behind those bread-plastered ramparts.

We threw ourselves on our bunks, tired out and hungry, to wait for supper. It was a good day's work well done. In the weeks to come we at least should not suffer from the hosts of vermin. We had foregone our dinner, saved our hides at the expense of our stomachs; but we were content. Alas for the futility of human effort! Scarcely was our long task completed when a guard unlocked our door. A redistribution of prisoners was being made, and we were taken to another cell and locked in two galleries higher up.

Early next morning our cells were unlocked, and down in the hall the several hundred prisoners of us formed the lock-step and marched out into the prison-yard to go to work. The Erie Canal runs right by the back yard of the Erie County penitentiary. Our task was to unload canal-boats, carrying huge stay-bolts on our shoulders, like railroad ties, into the prison. As I worked I sized up the situation and studied the chances for a get-away. There wasn't the ghost of a show. Along the tops of the walls marched guards armed with repeating rifles, and I was told, furthermore, that there were machine-guns in the sentry-towers.

I did not worry. Thirty days were not so long. I'd stay those thirty days, and add to the store of material I intended to use, when I got out, against the harpies of justice. I'd show what an American boy could do when his rights and privileges had been trampled on the way mine had. I had been denied my right of trial by jury. I had been denied my right to plead guilty or not guilty; I had been denied a trial even (for I couldn't consider that what I had received at Niagara Falls was a trial); I had not been allowed to communicate with a lawyer or anyone, and hence had been denied my right for suing for a writ of habeas corpus; my face had been shaved, my hair cropped close, convict stripes has been put upon my body; I was forced to toil hard on a diet of bread and water and to march the shameful lock-step with armed guards over me—and all for what? What had I done? What crime had I committed against the good citizens of Niagara Falls that all this vengeance should be wreaked upon me? I had not even violated their "sleeping-out" ordinance. I had slept in the country, outside their jurisdiction, that night. I had not even begged for a meal, or battered for a "light-piece" on the streets. All that I had done was to walk along their sidewalk and gaze at their picayune waterfall. And what crime was there in that? Technically I was guilty of no misdemeanor. All right, I'd show them when I got out.

The next day I talked with a guard. I wanted to send for a lawyer. The guard laughed at me. So did the other guards. I really was *incommunicado* so far as the outside world was concerned. I tried to write a letter out, but I learned that all letters were read and censored or confiscated by the prison authorities, and that "short-timers" were not allowed to write letters, anyway. A little later I tried smuggling letters out by men who were released, but I learned that they were searched and the letters found and destroyed. Never mind. It all helped to make it a blacker case when I did get out.

But as the prison days went by (which I shall describe in the next chapter), I "learned a few." I heard tales of the police, and police courts, and lawyers, that were unbelievable and monstrous. Men, prisoners, told me of personal experiences with the police of great cities that were awful. And more awful were the hearsay tales they told me concerning men who had died at the hands of the police and therefore could not testify for themselves. Years afterward, in the report of the Lexow Committee, I was to read tales true and more awful than those told to me. But in the meantime, during the first days of my imprisonment, I scoffed at what I heard.

As the days went by, however, I began to be convinced. I saw with my own eyes, there in that prison, things unbelievable and monstrous. And the more convinced I became, the profounder grew the respect in me for the sleuth-hounds of the law and for the whole institution of criminal justice. My indignation ebbed away, and into my being rushed the tides of fear. I saw at last, clear-eyed, what I was up against. I grew meek and lowly. Each day I resolved more emphatically to make no rumpus when I got out. All I asked, when I got out, was a chance to fade away from the landscape. And that was just what I did do when I was released. I kept my tongue between my teeth, walked softly, and sneaked for Pennsylvania, a wiser and humbler man.

Rose Schneiderman (1882 [?]–1972)

Born in Russian Poland, Rose Schneiderman emigrated to the United States with her Orthodox Jewish family in 1890. Her father earned a living as a tailor in New York. After his unexpected death, Rose, a bright student, had to leave school for a time to help sustain the family. Her first job was as a low-paid department store clerk, but she soon found relatively better-paying work in the garment industry. She and her friend Bessie Braut organized a local chapter of the Cap Maker's Union that included women workers and actively participated in their 1903 strike. An invitation to speak at a meeting of the New York Women's Trade Union League (WTUL) enabled Schneiderman to see the advantages of cross-class affiliations between the progressive leaders of the National Women's Trade Union League and working-class women. Schneiderman became vice president of the New York chapter while she worked full time as an organizer. After the Triangle fire of 1911, she helped establish the International Ladies' Garment Workers Union and became president of the National Women's Trade Union League, where she lobbied for legislation for the eight-hour day and the minimum wage. She was active in the founding of the Bryn Mawr Summer School for Women Workers and began in 1921 a long friendship with Eleanor Roosevelt, who joined the WTUL and supported it financially. In 1933, Franklin Delano Roosevelt named Schneiderman to the National Recovery Administration (NRA). After the Supreme Court declared the NRA unconstitutional, Schneiderman returned to New York, where she was the president of the New York WTUL until it ceased operations in 1955. She also served as secretary to the New York State Department of Labor. "A Cap Maker's Story" originally appeared as a short autobiography, or "lifelet," in the *Independent* in 1905 (edited by Hamilton Holt) and was later included in her aptly titled autobiography, *All for One* (1967).

A CAP MAKER'S STORY

My name is Rose Schneiderman, and I was born in some small city of Russian Poland. I don't know the name of the city, and have no memory of that part of my childhood. When I was about five years of age my parents brought me to this country and we settled in New York.

So my earliest recollections are of living in a crowded street among the East Side Jews, for we also are Jews.

My father got work as a tailor, and we lived in two rooms on Eldridge Street, and did very well, though not so well as in Russia, because mother and father both earned money, and here father alone earned the money, while mother attended to the house. There were then two other children besides me, a boy of three and one of five.

I went to school until I was nine years old, enjoying it thoroughly and making great progress, but then my father died of brain fever and mother was left with three children and another one coming. So I had to stay at home to help her and she went out to look for work.

A month later the baby was born, and mother got work in a fur house, earning about $6 a week and afterward $8 a week, for she was clever and steady.

I was the house worker, preparing the meals and looking after the other children—the baby, a little girl of six years, and a boy of nine. I managed very well, tho the meals were not very elaborate. I could cook simple things like porridge, coffee and eggs, and mother used to prepare the meat before she went away in the morning, so that all I had to do was to put it in the pan at night.

The children were not more troublesome than others, but this was a hard part of my life with few bright spots in it. I was a serious child, and cared little for children's play, and I knew nothing about the country, so it was not so bad for me as it might have been for another. Yet it was bad, tho I did get some pleasure from reading, of which I was very fond: and now and then, as a change from the home, I took a walk in the crowded street.

Mother was absent from half-past seven o'clock in the morning till half-past six o'clock in the evening.

I was finally released by my little sister being taken by an aunt, and the two boys going to the Hebrew Orphan Asylum, which is a splendid institution, and turns out good men. One of these brothers is now a student in the City College, and the other is a page in the Stock Exchange.

When the other children were sent away mother was able to send me back to school and I stayed in this school (Houston Street Grammar) till I had reached the Sixth Grammar Grade.

Then I had to leave in order to help support the family. I got a place in Hearn's as cash girl, and after working there three weeks changed to Ridley's, where I remained for two and a half years. I finally left because the pay was so very poor and there did not seem to be any chance of advancement, and a friend told me that I could do better making caps.

So I got a place in the factory of Hein & Fox. The hours were from 8 a.m. to 6 p.m., and we made all sorts of linings—or, rather, we stitched in the linings—golf caps, yachting caps, etc. It was piece work, and we received from $3^1/2$ cents to 10 cents a dozen, according to the different grades. By working hard we could make an average of about $5 a week. We would have made more but had to provide our own machines, which cost us $45, we paying for them on the installment plan. We paid $5 down and $1 a month after that.

I learned the business in about two months, and then made as much as the others, and was consequently doing quite well when the factory burned down, destroying all our machines—150 of them. This was very hard on the girls who had paid for their machines. It was not so bad for me, as I had only paid a little of what I owed.

The bosses got $500,000 insurance, so I heard, but they never gave the girls a cent to help them bear their losses. I think they might have given them $10, anyway,

Soon work went on again in four lofts, and a little later I became assistant sample maker. This is a position which, tho coveted by many, pays better in glory than in cash. It was still piece work, and tho the pay per dozen was better the work demanded was of a higher quality, and one could not rush through samples as through the other caps. So I still could average only about $5 per week.

After I had been working as a cap maker for three years it began to dawn on me that we girls needed an organization. The men had organized already, and had gained some advantages, but the bosses had lost nothing, as they took it out of us.

We were helpless; no one girl dare stand up for anything alone. Matters kept getting worse. The bosses kept making reductions in our pay, half a cent a dozen at a time. It did not sound important, but at the end of the week we found a difference.

We didn't complain to the bosses; we didn't say anything except to each other. There was no use. The bosses would not pay any attention unless we were like the men and could make them attend.

One girl would say that she didn't think she could make caps for the new price, but another would say that she thought she could make up for the reduction by working a little harder, and then the first would tell herself:

"If she can do it, why can't I?"

They didn't think how they were wasting their strength.

A new girl from another shop got in among us. She was Miss Bessie Brout, and she talked organization as a remedy for our ills. She was radical and progressive, and she stimulated thoughts which were already in our minds before she came.

Finally Miss Brout and I and another girl went to the National Board of United Cloth Hat and Cap Makers when it was in session, and asked them to organize the girls.

They asked us:

"How many of you are there willing to be organized?"

"In the first place about twelve," we said. We argued that the union label would force the bosses to organize their girls, and if there was a girls' union in existence the bosses could not use the union label unless their girls belonged to the union.

We were told to come to the next meeting of the National Board, which we did, and then received a favorable answer, and were asked to bring all the girls who were willing to be organized to the next meeting, and at the next meeting, accordingly, we were there twelve strong and were organized.

When Fox found out what had happened he discharged Miss Brout, and probably would have discharged me but that I was a sample maker and not so easy to replace. In a few weeks we had all the girls in the organization, because the men told the girls that they must enter the union or they would not be allowed to work in the shop.

Then came a big strike. Price lists for the coming season were given in to the bosses, to which they did not agree. After some wrangling a strike was declared in five of the biggest factories. There are 30 factories in the city. About 100 girls went out.

The result was a victory, which netted us—I mean the girls—$2 increase in our wages on the average.

All the time our union was progressing very nicely. There were lectures to make us understand what trades unionism is and our real position in the labor movement. I read upon the subject and grew more and more interested, and after a time I became a member of the National Board, and had duties and responsibilities that kept me busy after my day's work was done.

But all was not lovely by any means, for the bosses were not at all pleased with their beating and had determined to fight us again.

They agreed among themselves that after the 26th of December, 1904, they would run their shops on the "open" system.

This agreement was reached last fall, and soon notices, reading as follows, were hung in the various shops:

Notice

After the 26th of December, 1904, this shop will be run on the open shop system, the bosses having the right to engage and discharge employees as they see fit, whether the latter are union or nonunion.

Of course, we knew that this meant an attack on the union. The bosses intended gradually to get rid of us, employing in our place child labor and raw immigrant girls who would work for next to nothing.

On December 22nd the above notice appeared, and the National Board, which had known about it all along, went into session prepared for action.

Our people were very restive, saying that they could not sit under that notice, and that if the National Board did not call them out soon they would go out of themselves.

At last word was sent out, and at 2.30 o'clock all the workers stopped, and, laying down their scissors and other tools, marched out, some of them singing the "Marseillaise."

We were out for thirteen weeks, and the girls established their reputation. They were on picket duty from seven o'clock in the morning till six o'clock in the evening, and gained over many of the nonunion workers by appeals to them to quit working against us.

Our theory was that if properly approached and talked to few would be found who would resist our offer to take them into our organization. No right thinking person desires to injure another. We did not believe in violence and never employed it.

During this strike period we girls each received $3 a week; single men $3 a week, and married men $5 a week. This was paid us by the National Board.

We were greatly helped by the other unions, because the open shop issue was a tremendous one, and this was the second fight which the bosses had conducted for it.

Their first was with the tailors, whom they beat. If they now could beat us the outlook for unionism would be bad.

Some were aided and we stuck out, and won a glorious victory all along the line. That was only last week. The shops are open now for all union hands and for them only.

While the strike lasted I tried to get work in a factory that was not affected, but found that the boss was against me.

Last spring I had gone as a member of a committee to appeal to this boss on behalf of a girl who had been four years in his employ and was only getting $7 a week. She wanted $1 raise and all legal holidays. Previously she had had to work on holidays. After argument we secured for her the $1 raise and half a day on every legal holiday.

When the strike broke out, looking for work, I went to this boss, and he stared at me, and said:

"What do you want?"

"You asked for a girl."

"You—you—I don't want you," said he. "Can't I have my choice?"

"Certainly," said I, "I could never work where I'm not wanted."

I suppose he expected me to revenge myself by keeping other girls away, but I sent him others till he filled the place.

He resented my having served on the committee, and so he did not want me, but I felt honored by the manner in which I was treated. It showed that I had done my duty.

The bosses try to represent this open shop issue as tho they were fighting a battle for the public, but really it is nothing of the sort. The open shop is a weapon to break the unions and set men once more cutting each other's throats by individual competition.

Why, there was a time in the cap trade when men worked fourteen hours a day, and then took the heads of their machines home in bags and setting them up on stands, put mattresses underneath to deaden the sound and worked away till far into the morning.

We don't want such slavery as that to come back.

The shops are open now for all union people, and all nonunion people can join the union. In order to take in newcome foreigners we have for them cut the initiation fees down to one-half what we Americans have to pay, and we trust them till they get work and their wages.

In order to give the newcomers a chance we have stopped night work, which doesn't suit the bosses, because it causes them to pay more rent when they can't use their buildings night and day. It costs them the price of another loft instead of costing the workers their health and lives as in the old days.

Our trade is well organized, we have won two victories and are not going backward.

But there is much to be done in other directions. The shop girls certainly need organization, and I think that they ought to be easy to organize, as their duties are simple and regular and they have a regular scale of wages.

Many saleswomen on Grand and Division streets, and, in fact, all over the East Side, work from 8 a.m. till 9 p.m. week days, and one-half a day on Sundays for $5 and $6 a week; so they certainly need organization.

The waitresses also could easily be organized, and perhaps the domestic servants. I don't know about stenographers. I have not come in contact with them.

Women have proved in the late strike that they can be faithful to an organization and to each other. The men give us the credit of winning the strike.

Certainly our organization constantly grows stronger, and the Woman's Trade Union League makes progress.

The girls and women by their meetings and discussions come to understand and sympathize with each other, and more and more easily they act together.

It is the only way in which they can hope to hold what they now have or better present conditions.

Certainly there is no hope from the mercy of the bosses.

Each boss does the best he can for himself with no thought of the other bosses, and that compels each to gouge and squeeze his hands to the last penny in order to make a profit.

So we must stand together to resist, for we will get what we can take—just that and no more.

New York, March 20, 1905

The Triangle Shirtwaist Fire, March 25, 1911

The workday had nearly ended that late Saturday afternoon when a fire started on the eighth, ninth, and tenth floors of the Triangle Shirtwaist Company. Located in a loft building adjacent to New York University and a block from Washington Square Park, Triangle was the largest manufacturer of the popular shirtwaist blouse, and a nonunion shop. On the street below, witnesses heard glass explode and thought they saw bales of fabric fall from the windows. One caught the wind. It was not expensive fabric; it was a young woman. The Triangle Shirtwaist Company fire took the lives of 146 workers, 123 women and 23 men. Many of the women were young Italian and Jewish immigrants whose earnings were crucial to their families' survival. Some were active in the Uprising of the 20,000, a major strike of women garment workers in 1909–1910, but most were nonunion garment workers who lost the right to a shorter Saturday workday. The fire was sudden and rapidly fed by flammable cloth and tissue-thin blouse patterns. So many workers died because their means of escape were blocked by doors that were locked from the outside and hindered by one narrow and inadequate fire escape that reached only to the second floor and collapsed under the weight of fleeing workers. More than sixty victims were forced by the flames to jump to their deaths. State-of-the-art fire equipment brought the fire under control within twenty minutes, but the fire hoses barely reached the seventh floor. New York newspapers published front-page illustrations, photos of the dead, and columns "encased in unashamed emotion," according to Leon Stein who wrote the first and perhaps most compelling account of the fire at a time when survivors were still alive

Mourning the Triangle Shirt-waist Fire victims in the rain, 1911. *(UNITE HERE Archives, Kheel Center, Cornell University)*

(*The Triangle Fire*, 1962). Triangle owners Isaac Harris and Max Blanck, who escaped onto the roof, were indicted and charged with manslaughter, primarily because of the illegally locked exit doors, and acquitted by a jury of businessmen. Public outrage at the accumulated injustices to workers resulted in the establishment of a Factory Investigating Commission and, eventually, more than thirty regulatory laws.

The 1911 Triangle shirtwaist factory fire has a particular resonance for working-class people. In her stirring memorial speech at the Metropolitan Opera House two months after the fire, Women's Trade Union League organizer Rose Schneiderman indicted her audience of well-to-do New Yorkers for turning a blind eye to an exploitative and unsafe factory system and acquiescing to police brutality against striking union workers. She called for the working class to save—and lead—themselves. Four days after the March 25 fire, Morris Rosenfeld published his mournful poem in Yiddish on the front page of the *Jewish Daily Forward*. This solemn dirge speaks to and for an angry and grieving immigrant community. In subsequent labor journals of the period, other writers recall the Triangle fire in commentary and poetry.

More than a single tragic event, isolated in the past, the Triangle fire has also inspired contemporary poets, writing independently of each other, to return to the 1911 newspaper accounts, photographs, court testimonies, artifacts, survivors' stories, and even the still-standing building to re-create the event for a new generation of readers. Unlike other poetry about work that is often site- and job-specific to the authors, these writers are from various regions of the country and different races and ethnicities and do not necessarily come from families of garment workers. These "fire poems" illustrate an important vein of working-class literature and a process of historical and cultural reciprocity—the dead give voice to the poetry, and the poets give meaning to their lost lives through language. Among these contemporary poets are Mary Fell, Chris Llewellyn, Safiya Henderson-Holmes, and Carol Tarlen. Mary Fell's sequenced series of poems, *The Triangle Fire* (1983), was first published in a limited edition chap book and later included in her collection *The Persistence of Memory* (1984). Chris Llewellyn's book-length *Fragments from the Fire* (1987) won the Walt Whitman Award of the Academy of American Poets, Safiya Henderson-Holmes's poem "rituals of spring (for the 78th anniversary of the shirtwaist factory fire)" was included in her collection, *Madness and a Bit of Hope* (1990), and Carol Tarlen's "Sisters in the Flames" appeared in the anthology *What We Hold in Common: An Introduction to Working-Class Studies* (2001), edited by Janet Zandy. In commenting on this process, Mary Fell said, "At the time I wrote 'Triangle Fire' I didn't know anyone else had written about it. I felt I'd re-created it." The linkage of the personal and the historical is evident in Carol Tarlen's remarks as well: "Despite the tragedy [the fire] represents solidarity and resistance. . . . I have always been moved that the women embraced each other and jumped together."

Rose Schneiderman, "Triangle Memorial Speech"

I would be a traitor to these poor burned bodies if I came here to talk good fellowship. We have tried you good people of the public and we have found you wanting: The old Inquisition had its rack and its thumbscrews and its instruments of torture with iron teeth. We know what these things are today: the iron teeth are our necessities, the thumbscrews the high-powered and swift machinery close to which we must work, and the rack is here in the "fire-proof" structures that will destroy us the minute they catch on fire.

This is not the first time girls have been burned alive in the city. Each week I must learn of the untimely death of one of my sister workers. Every year thousands of us are maimed. The life of men and women is so cheap and property is so sacred. There are so many of us for one job it matters little if 143 of us are burned to death.

We tried you, citizens; we are trying you now, and you have a couple of dollars for the sorrowing mothers and daughters and sisters by way of a charity gift. But every time the workers come out in the only way they know to protest against conditions which are unbearable, the strong hand of the law is allowed to press down heavily upon us.

Public officials have only words of warning to us—warning that we must be intensely orderly and must be intensely peaceable, and they have the workhouse just back of all their warnings. The strong hand of the law beats us back when we rise into the conditions that make life bearable.

I can't talk fellowship to you who are gathered here. Too much blood has been spilled. I know from my experience it is up to the working people to save themselves. The only way they can save themselves is by a strong working-class movement.

Morris Rosenfeld, "Requiem on the Triangle Fire" [from the Jewish Daily Forward]

Neither battle nor fiendish pogrom
Fills this great city with sorrow;
Nor does the earth shudder or lightning rend the heavens,
No clouds darken, no cannon's roar shatters the air.
5   Only hell's fire engulfs these slave stalls
And Mammon devours our sons and daughters.

Fellow Workers!

Join in rendering a last sad tribute of sympathy and affection for the victims of the Triangle Fire. THE FUNERAL PROCESSION will take place Wednesday, April 5th, at 1 P. M. Watch the newspapers for the line of march.

צו דער לויה שוועסטער און ברידער !

די לויה פֿון די היילינע קרבנות פֿון דעם טריִיִענגעל פֿיַיר וועם זיַין סימוואך, דעם לטטן אפריל, 1 אודר נאכטיטטמאג.

קיינער פֿון אייך מער ניט פֿערלייבען אין די שעפער ! שליסם זיך אַן אין די רייהען פֿון די טרוייערענדע ! דריקם אייס אייער סימפאטיע און מיטעגפן בּעדוייערין אין אייך דעם גרוייסען אַבּרילום וואס די ערבייטערוועלט האָט געהטאט.

געבּיינען די קעפ — סיס ציסעווּתעע העירצער וועלען מיר פֿיהרען סיר אונזערע פֿהייעע שפּעֿרטע צו וייער לעצטער רוה.

העֿמם די ציַימוּנגען דורך וועלכע סיר וועלעע לאֿוען וויסעע וואו איהר קעער זיך צוזעמענגוסעע.

צו דער לויה פֿון די היילינע קרבנות,
קוּם שוועסטער און ברידער !

Operai Italiani!

Unitevi compatti a rendere l'ultimo tributo d'affetto alle vittime dell'imane sciagura della Triangle Waist Co. IL CORTEO FUNEBRE avra luogo mercoledi, 5 Aprile, alle ore 1 P. M. Traverete nei giornali l'ordine della marcia.

Source: William Cahn, *A Pictorial History of American Labor.* New York: Crown Publishers, 1972, 189.

Wrapt in scarlet flames, they drop to death from his maw
And death receives them all.

Sisters mine, oh my sisters; brethren
10 Hear my sorrow:
See where the dead are hidden in dark corners,
Where life is choked from those who labor.
Oh, woe is me, and woe is to the world
On this Sabbath
15 When an avalanche of red blood and fire
Pours forth from the god of gold on high
As now my tears stream forth unceasingly.
Damned be the rich!

Damned be the system!
20   Damned be the world!

Over whom shall we weep first?
Over the burned ones?
Over those beyond recognition?
Over those who have been crippled?
25   Or driven senseless?
Or smashed?
I weep for them all.

Now let us light the holy candles
And mark the sorrow
30   Of Jewish masses in darkness and poverty.
This is our funeral,
These our graves,
Our children,
The beautiful, beautiful flowers destroyed,
35   Our lovely ones burned,
Their ashes buried under a mountain of caskets.

There will come a time
When your time will end, you golden princes.
Meanwhile,
40   Let this haunt your consciences:
Let the burning building, our daughters in flame
Be the nightmare that destroys your sleep,
The poison that embitters your lives,
The horror that kills your joy.
45   And in the midst of celebrations for your children,
May you be struck blind with fear over the
Memory of this red avalanche
Until time erases you.

Contemporary Poems on the Triangle Shirtwaist Factory Fire

Mary Fell, The Triangle Fire

1. Havdallah

This is the great divide
by which God split
the world:
on the Sabbath side
5   he granted rest,
eternal toiling
on the workday side.

But even one
revolution of the world
10   is an empty promise
where bosses
where bills to pay
respect no heavenly bargains.
Until each day is ours

15   let us pour
darkness in a dish
and set it on fire,
bless those who labor
as we pray, praise God
20   his holy name,
strike for the rest.

2. Among the Dead

First a lace of smoke
decorated the air of the workroom,
the far wall unfolded
into fire. The elevator shaft
5   spun out flames like a bobbin,
the last car sank.
I leaped for the cable,
my only chance. Woven steel
burned my hands as I wound
10   to the bottom.

I opened my eyes. I was lying
in the street. Water and blood
washed the cobbles, the sky
rained ash. A pair of shoes
15   lay beside me, in them
two blistered feet.
I saw the weave in the fabric
of a girl's good coat,
the wilted nosegay pinned to her collar.
20   Not flowers, what I breathed then,
awake among the dead.

3. Asch Building

In a window,
lovers embrace
haloed by light.
He kisses her, holds her
5   gently, lets her go
nine stories to the street.

Even the small ones
put on weight

as they fall:
10 eleven thousand pounds split
the fireman's net,
implode the deadlights

on the Greene Street side,
until the basement catches them
15 and holds. Here
two faceless ones are found
folded neatly over the steam pipes
like dropped rags.

I like the one
20 on that smoky ledge, taking stock
in the sky's deliberate mirror
She gives her hat
to wind, noting its style,
spills her week's pay

25 from its envelope, a joke
on those who pretend
heaven provides, and chooses
where there is no choice
to marry air, to make
30 a disposition of her life.

4. Personal Effects

One lady's
handbag, containing
rosary beads, elevated
railroad ticket, small pin
5 with picture, pocket knife,
one small purse containing
$1.68 in cash,
handkerchiefs,
a small mirror, a pair of gloves,
10 two thimbles, a Spanish
comb, one yellow metal ring,
five keys, one
fancy glove button,
one lady's handbag containing
15 one gent's watch case
number of movement 6418593
and a $1 bill,
one half dozen postal cards,
a buttonhook, a man's photo,
20 a man's garter,
a razor strap,
one portion of limb and hair
of human being.

5. Industrialist's Dream

This one's
dependable won't
fall apart
under pressure doesn't
5   lie down on the job
doesn't leave early
come late
won't join unions
strike
10   ask for a raise
unlike one hundred
forty six
others I could name
who couldn't
15   take the heat this one's
still at her machine
and doubtless
of spotless moral
character you
20   can tell by the bones
pure white
this one
does what she's told
and you don't hear
25   her complaining.

6. The Witness

Woman, I might have watched you
sashay down Washington Street
some warm spring evening
when work let out,
5   your one thin dress
finally right for the weather,
an ankle pretty
as any flower's stem, full
breasts the moon's envy, eyes bold
10   or modest as you passed me by.

I might have thought, as heat
climbed from the pavement,
what soft work you'd make
for a man like me:
15   even the time clock, thief of hours,
kinder, and the long day
passing in a dream.
Cradled in that dream
I might have slept
20   forever, but today's nightmare

vision woke me:
your arms aflame, wings
of fire, and you a falling star,
a terrible lump of coal
25 in the burning street.
No dream, your hair of smoke,
your blackened face.
No dream the fist I make,
taking your hand
30 of ashes in my own.

7. Cortege

A cold rain comforts the sky.
Everything ash-colored under clouds.
I take my place in the crowd,

move without will as the procession moves,
5   a gray wave breaking against the street.
Up ahead, one hundred and forty seven

coffins float, wreckage of lives. I follow
the box without a name. In it
whose hand encloses whose heart? Whose mouth

10 presses the air toward a scream?
She is no one, the one I claim
as sister. When the familiar is tagged

and taken away, she remains.
I do not mourn her. I mourn no one.
15 I do not praise her. No one

is left to praise. Seventy years after
her death, I walk in March rain behind her.
She travels before me into the dark.

CHRIS LLEWELLYN, FOUR FROM SONYA

Is the room swept, blankets
pressed and folded chairs
lined in readiness straight
oh hang the heavenly picture.

5   Writing poems with a cardboard
bookcase my only company
the poplar tree shifting shades
and whispering: remember me.

Boarding houses yes
10 lived in four or five or more.

Don't think I'll ever get
the smell of urine, frying
potatas and Evening in Paris
outa my head.

15 Going outside sunny sunny
rubbing leaves try to
out eclipse each other.

CHRIS LLEWELLYN, "I AM APPALLED"

New York Governor Dix

The Police Commissioner
points to the Mayor who gripes at
the Governor, "I am appalled,"
who sets on the State Labor Commissioner
5   who blames the National Fire Underwriters
who turn on the Fire Commissioner
who cites the "City Beautiful"
(for finding fire escapes ugly)
who then faults the Architects
10 who place it on Tenement Housing
who says failure of the Health Department
who then proclaim conspiracy
between the Utility Companies and
the Police Commissioner.

CHRIS LLEWELLYN, SURVIVOR'S CENTO[1]

All through the day rain ever and again.
The quartet from the Elks Lodge sang "Abide with Me."
They lost both daughters, Sara and Sarafine.
Last year I was one of the pickets arrested and fined.
5   We were striking for open doors, better fire escapes.
Freda Velakowski, Ignatzia Bellota, Celia Eisenberg.
You knew the families from the flowers nailed to the doors.
That's my mama. Her name's Julia Rosen.
I know by her hair. I braid it every morning.
10 Now the same police who clubbed the strikers
keep the crowd from trampling on our bodies.
Sadie Nausbaum, Gussie Bierman, Anna Cohen, Israel Rosen.

---

[1] *Cento* is a Latin word for a garment made of patches.

I know that's my daughter, Sophie Salemi.
See that darn in her knee? Mended her stockings, yesterday.
15 Box one-twelve: female, black stockings, black shoes,
part of a skirt, a white petticoat, hair ribbons.
I would be a traitor to these poor burned bodies
if I came to talk good fellowship: Jennie Franco,
Julia Aberstein, Joseph Wilson, Nicolina Nicolese.
20 I found a mouse on the ninth floor, took it home,
kept it for a pet. At least it was still alive.
Our children go to work in firetraps, come home and sleep
in firetraps. Day and night they are condemned.
Ninth floor looked like a kindergarten. We were eight,
25 nine, ten. If the Inspector came, they hid us in bins.
Rose Feibush, Clotild Terdanova, Mary Leventhal.
That one's Catherine Maltese, and those, her daughters.
Lucia, she's twenty. Rosalie—she'd be fourteen.
Those two are sisters. Bettina and Frances Miale. M-I-A-L-E.
30 We asked the Red Cross worker how to help
and she said bring books—Tolstoy, Shakespeare in Yiddish.
Benny Costello said he knew his sister Della by her new shoes.
Anna Ardito, Gussie Rosenfield, Sara Kupla, Essie Bernstein,
reminders to spend my life fighting these conditions. Antonia
35 Colleti, Daisy Lopez Fitze, Surka Brenman, Margaret Schwartz.
One coffin read: Becky Kessler, call for tomorrow.
The eighth casket had neither name nor number. It contained
fragments from the Fire, picked up but never claimed.

CHRIS LLEWELLYN, SEAR

July 1982

Always adding. Revising this manuscript.
I plant *direct quotations* on the page,
arranging line-breaks, versification.

Newspaper files: Frances Perkins speaks
5 from the street, *I felt I must sear it
not only on my mind but on my heart
forever.* One mother, *When will it be
safe to earn our bread?* Their words.
Yet some call that schmaltz, soap-opera-

10 *Sentiment, Victorian melodrama.* Riding
the subway, smoke fizzes in my ears and
in my room, electric heater coils glow
Cs and Os in the box. To write about *them*
yet not interfere, although I'm told
15 a poet's task is to create a little world.

A testimony: Two tried to stay together
on the ledge, but one suddenly twisted
and plunged, a burning bundle. The other
looked ahead, arms straight out, speaking
20   and shouting *as if addressing an invisible*
audience. She gestured an embrace then

Jumped. Her name was Celia
Weintraub. She lived
on Henry Street.

Carol Tarlen, Sisters in the Flames

for Leah

Spectators saw again and again pitiable companionships formed in the instant
of death—girls who placed their arms around each other as they leaped.
In many cases their clothing was flaming or their hair flaring as they fell.
— *"The Triangle Fire,"* New York World, *26 March 1911*

Greenhorn
bent over the machine
your hair a mess of red curls
like flames I said
5   my words extinguished
by the wailing motors
we never spoke
together we sewed
fine linen shirtwaists
10   for fine ladies we worked
in our coarse gowns
and muslin aprons twelve hours
in the dank rooms
nine floors above the street
15   our fingers worked
the soft cloth
our coarse hands
fed the machines

Stranger
20   I saw you once in the elevator
going down going home
your eyes laughed
when I whispered too loud
strands of red hair falling
25   over your cheek and neck I
touched your red rough hand
my shoulders ached

my pay envelope tucked
in my coat pocket
30   for Papa for Mama
for the rent I need
a new skirt I need
a day in the sun
I need to unlock the doors
35   of this factory
I'm still young
I whispered and you laughed
because of course
we all were young

40   Sister
of the flames
take my hand
I will hold you in the cradle
of my billowing skirt
45   in the ache of my shoulders
the center of my palm
our sisters already dance
on the sidewalk nine
floors below the fire
50   is leaping through my hair
Sister I will hold you
the air will lick our thighs
grab my hand
together now fly
55   the sky is an unlocked door
and the machines are burning

SAFIYA HENDERSON-HOLMES, RITUALS OF SPRING

(FOR THE 78TH ANNIVERSARY OF THE SHIRTWAIST FACTORY FIRE)

from bareness to fullness flowers do bloom
whenever, however spring enters a room
oh, whenever, however spring enters a room

march 25th, 1911
5   at the triangle shirtwaist factory
a fire claimed the lives of 146 people, mostly women,
mostly children in the plume of their lives,
in the room of their lives
begging for spring, toiling and begging for spring

10   *and in my head*
      as i read the history, afraid to touch the pictures
      i imagine the room, i imagine the women
      dressed in pale blues and pinks,
      some without heads or arms—sitting
15   some without legs or waist—hovering
      hundreds of flowering girls tucking spring into sleeves,
      tucking and tugging at spring to stay alive

      and so a shirtwaist for spring
      a dress with a mannish collar, blousing over breast,
20   blousing over sweat, tapering to fit a female waist,
      tapering to fit a female breath
      sheer silk, cotton, linen
      hand-done pleats, hands done in by pleats
      hands done in by darts and lace

25   *colors of spring*
      pale blues, pale pinks, yellows, magentas, lavender, peach

      secret thoughts of spring
      falling in love under a full moon, forever young
      with money enough to buy a flower or two,
30   time enough to smell it
      yes, from bareness to fullness a flower will bloom
      anytime, everytime spring enters a room
      and here, near these machines, hundreds of flowering girls

      shirtwaist factory room 1911
35   crowded, hard, fast, too fast, closed windows,
      locked doors, smell of piss, of sweat,
      of wishes being cut to bits,
      needle stabs, electric shocks, miscarriages over silk,
      fading paisley, fading magenta,
40   falling in love will get you fired, forever old,
      never fast enough, buying flowers is wasteful
      so hurry, hurry, grind your teeth and soul
      six dollars a week send to grandfather,
      four dollars a week send to aunt ruth, sleep over the
45   machine and you're done for, way before you open your
      eyes ma'm, madam, miss, mrs., mother, girlie
      hundreds of flowering green spring girls in rows
      waiting with needles in hands for spring to show

      women workers
50   from ireland, poland, germany, france,
      england, grenada, mississippi
      thin clothes, thinner hopes, months full of why,
      of how, of when
      answers always less than their pay
55   but the sewing machines grew like weeds,
      thick snake roots strangling the flowers everyday
      strangling the roses, daises, lilies everyday

hundreds of blooming girls
hundreds of blooming, spring girls

60   *the shirtwaist building 1911*
135-feet-high, wooden, cold, three floors,
not enough stairs,
one fire escape ending in midair,
ending in the spring midair
65   a tender room of hundreds of blooming bright girls
hundreds of daisy bud girls who pray for spring
to enter their world,
who pray and sweat for spring to enter their world

  the strike the year before
70   and they shouted; open the doors,
unwire the windows, more air,
more stairs, more quiet time, more fire escapes
and to the ground damn you,
and more toilets, more time to be sick,
75   more time to be well,
and remove the fear and slow it down,
for god's sake, slow it all time, it's spring

  they shouted
hundreds of flowering girls,
80   hundreds of flowering girls shouted
for spring to hurry, hurry and enter their world

  and
triangle won a half-day
but the doors remained locked,
85   windows remained wired, no extra air,
no extra quiet time, or sick time, the fear stayed,
nothing slowed
and god watched hundreds of flowering girls twirl
hundreds of flowering girls willow and twirl

90   *march 25th 1911 at triangle*
a worker is expendable
a sewing needle is not
a worker is bendable
a sewing needle is not
95   a worker can be sent straight to hell
a sewing needle is heaven sent
and must be protected well
a sewing needle is the finger of god
and must be protected well
100   over hundreds of flowering girls,
hundreds of flowering sweet dandelion girls

  march 25th, smoke
smoke, stopping the machines
run to wired windows, run to locked doors,
105   run to the one and only fire escape,

everyone run to the air
hundreds of flowering girls

smoke
stopping eyes, stopping hearts, stopping worlds
110   elevator move faster, elevator you are a machine
managed by a human being move faster, c'mon faster
carry all the flowering girls, carry all the sweet,
sweet orchid girls

fire
115   catching bouquets of girls in a corner, tall, long
stemmed lilies on fire in a corner,
from bloom to ashes in a corner, smell
them in the rain hundreds of tulip girls

on a window ledge
120   pliés for life, on a window ledge lovely, ribboned young
ladies on their tiptoes twirling, twirling
an arabesque for life
hundreds of flowering girls
smell them in the rain
125   hundreds of jasmine girls

the ladders were too short
the hoses were too short
the men holding the nets were not gods, only men
who were never trained to catch falling bodies, or
130   falling stars, or hundreds of flowering girls, hundreds
of carnation bud girls

and the girls
were girls not angels jumping,
not goddesses flying or hovering
135   they smashed, they broke into
large pieces, smell them in the rain

and the sidewalks
opened in shame to meet the flowering girls
the sidewalks opened in such horrible shame to cradle
140   the remains of violets
and the gutters
bled for hours, choking on bones, shoes, buttons,
ribbons, holy sewing needles
the gutters bled for hours all the colors of spring
145   the cool magenta of delicate spring

and the fire ate
the locked doors and the wired windows,
ate the fast machines
in their narrow rooms, ate the lace and hand-done pleats,
150   the silk, the cotton, the linen,
the crisp six dollars a week, the

eternal buzz of someone else's dreams
nightmares and screams of quiet girls,
loud skull-cracking noises from shy girls
155   smell them in the rain, the lilacs, daffodils
in the rain

spring, 78 years later
triangle is now part of a university, with offices
and polished intellect, arched unwired windows,
160   hydraulically controlled and unlocked doors,
air conditioning, swivel chairs, marble walls and fire
alarms

but oh, hundreds of flowering girls still roam
hundreds of blushing spring girls still roam
165   78 years later in the paint, in the chrome
in the swivel of the chairs
hundreds of blossoms twirling in the air
daring to descend if ever, oh ever the fire comes again

yes, like lead they will drop
170   if ever, oh ever the fire comes again
to hundreds of flowering girls
smell them in the rain, iris, peonies, magnolias,
bending for the rain

James Oppenheim (1882–1932)

"**B**read and Roses," as a poem, a song, and a slogan for working women's rights, has traditionally been associated with the 1912 Textile Strike in Lawrence, Massachusetts, one of the most successful labor actions organized by the Industrial Workers of the World. The story goes that Oppenheim was inspired by a banner reading "We want Bread, and Roses too" carried by a contingent of young women strikers. In fact, the poem was written before the strike and published in the December 1911 edition of the *American Magazine*, with the attribution "Bread for all, and Roses, too—a slogan of the women of the West," a reference, Oppenheim later explained, to "Chicago Women Trade Unionists" whose garment workers' strike he had observed in 1911. Whatever the source of its most famous phrase, the poem struck a chord and was reprinted in several magazines and in Upton Sinclair's influential *The Cry for Justice: An Anthology of the Literature of Social Protest* (1915). Set to music by Caroline Kohlsaat, "Bread and Roses" has become an enduring worldwide anthem of both the labor and feminist movements.

Born in St. Paul, Minnesota, Oppenheim spent most of his life in New York City, working as a social worker at the Hudson Settlement house on the Lower East Side and as a teacher at the Hebrew Technical Institute for Girls before he devoted himself full time to writing. While producing sentimental fiction to support his family, he developed his craft as a poet and a keen social observer. *Monday Morning and Other Poems* (1909) was followed by *Pay Envelopes: Tales of the Mill, the Mine, and the City Street* (1911), a collection of stories about workers in New York and throughout the Midwest. From 1916 to 1917, Oppenheim published the journal *The Seven Arts*, which provided a haven for socialist and pacifist writers during the repressive years after the U.S. entry into World War I. Several volumes of poetry followed before his death in 1932 after years of poverty and illness.

BREAD AND ROSES

As we come marching, marching, in the beauty of the day,
. A million darkened kitchens, a thousand mill-lofts gray
Are touched with all the radiance that a sudden sun discloses,
For the people hear us singing, "Bread and Roses, Bread and Roses."

5   As we come marching, marching, we battle, too, for men—
For they are women's children and we mother them again.
Our lives shall not be sweated from birth until life closes—
Hearts starve as well as bodies: Give us Bread, but give us Roses!

As we come marching, marching, unnumbered women dead
10 Go crying through our singing their ancient song of Bread;
Small art and love and beauty their drudging spirits knew—
Yes, bread we fight for—but we fight for Roses, too.

As we come marching, marching, we bring the Greater Days—
The rising of the women means the rising of the race—
15 No more the drudge and idler—ten that toil where one reposes—
But sharing of life's glories: Bread and Roses, Bread and Roses!

Arturo Giovannitti (1884–1959)

Arturo Giovannitti first gained national fame from his role in the 1912 Lawrence, Massachusetts, textile strike, one of the few significant labor victories in this period, won by a multiethnic workforce led by the Industrial Workers of the World (IWW). His poem "The Walker" comes from the time of his imprisonment during that signal event in his life. Giovannitti continued to organize and write—poems, essays, speeches, and plays—for decades after the Lawrence strike, and in many ways his life and writings mirror the larger fortunes both of Italian immigrants in the United States and of political radicals who sought to improve workers' lives in the first half of the twentieth century.

Born in a small town in southern Italy in 1884, Giovannitti joined the wave of roughly 3 million Italian immigrants who made their way to North America between 1890 and the start of World War I. He settled in Montreal, studying theology with the hope of joining the church, but in 1904 left for New York City, where he became involved in left-wing politics, eventually (by 1911) assuming editorship of *Il Proletario*, the Italian-language journal of the Industrial Workers of the World. In 1912, Giovannitti traveled to Lawrence to help organize Italian workers in the strike against the American Woolen Company, during which the state militia killed a young woman, sixteen-year-old Anna LoPizzo.

Giovannitti and another IWW organizer, Joe Ettor, were arrested and charged as accessories to murder, even though neither of them had been present when the shooting occurred. They served a year in prison before a jury found them innocent of the fabricated charges. Once out of prison, Giovannitti contributed poetry and essays to mainstream journals, such as the *Atlantic Monthly*, as well as to left-wing journals like *Masses*, the *Liberator*, *New Masses*, and several Italian-language political journals. In the 1920s and 1930s, he helped establish the Italian Dress Makers Union, an affiliate of the International Ladies Garment Workers Union, and contributed poems to the ILGWU newspaper, *Justice*. Giovannitti's family and friends assembled and published *The Collected Poems of Arturo Giovannitti* in 1962.

"The Walker" emerged from Giovannitti's imprisonment following the Lawrence textile strike and reflects on the experience of prison itself: its confinement, its inhumanity, and the desperation for freedom it inspires in those who are subjected to it. The poem underscores the unusual solidarity and even equality between prisoners that results from their confinement—thus posing the question of whether, as Giovannitti believed, we should view prisoners not as criminal deviants, but as in some way part of the working class, subject to (and perhaps even the products of) the same economic laws as other workers.

John Marsh

THE WALKER

I hear footsteps over my head all night.
They come and they go. Again they come and they go all night.
They come one eternity in four paces and they go one eternity in
four paces, and between the coming and the going there is
5   silence and the Night and the Infinite.
For infinite are the nine feet of a prison cell, endless is the march
of him who walks between the yellow brick wall and the red
iron gate, thinking things that cannot be chained and cannot
be locked, but that wander far away in the sunlit world, each
10   in a wild pilgrimage after a destined goal.

Throughout the restless night I hear the footsteps over my head.
Who walks? I know not. It is the phantom of the jail, the sleepless
brain, a man, the man, the Walker.
One-two-three-four: four paces and the wall.
15   One-two-three-four: four paces and the iron gate.
He has measured his pace, he has measured it accurately, scrupulously,
minutely, as the hangman measures the rope and the
gravedigger the coffin—so many feet, so many inches so
many fractions of an inch for each of the four paces.
20   One-two-three-four. Each step sounds heavy and hollow over my
head, and the echo of each step sounds hollow within my head
as I count them in suspense and in dread that once, perhaps, in
the endless walk, there may be five steps instead of four
between the yellow brick wall and the red iron gate.
25   But he has measured the space so accurately, so scrupulously, so
minutely that nothing breaks the grave rhythm of the slow,
fantastic march.

When All are asleep, (and who knows but I when all sleep?) three
things are still awake in the night. The Walker, my heart

30   and the old clock which has the soul of a fiend—for never,
      since a coarse hand with red hair on its fingers swung for
      the first time the pendulum in the jail, has the old clock tick—
      tocked a full hour of joy.

      Yet the old clock which marks everything and records everything,
35   and to everything tolls the death knell, the wise old
      clock that knows everything, does not know the number of
      the footsteps of the Walker nor the throbs of my heart.

      For not for the Walker, nor for my heart is there a second, a
      minute, an hour or anything that is in the old clock—there
40   is nothing but the night, the sleepless night, the watchful
      night, and footsteps that go, and footsteps that come and the
      wild, tumultuous beatings that trail after them forever.

      All the sounds of the living beings and inanimate things, and all
      the voices and all the noises of the night I have heard in my
45   wistful vigil.
      I have heard the moans of him who bewails a thing that is dead
      and the sighs of him who tries to smother a thing that will
      not die;
      I have heard the stifled sobs of the one who weeps with his head
50   under the coarse blankets, and the whisperings of the one
      who prays with his forehead on the hard, cold stone of the
      floor;
      I have heard him who laughs the shrill sinister laugh of folly at
      the horror rampant on the yellow wall and at the red eyes
55   of the nightmare glaring through the iron bars;
      I have heard in the sudden icy silence him who coughs a dry
      ringing cough and wished madly that his throat would not
      rattle so and that he would not spit on the floor, for no sound
      was more atrocious than that of his sputum upon the floor;
60   I have heard him who swears fearsome oaths which I listen to in
      reverence and awe, for they are holier than the virgin's
      prayer;
      And I have heard, most terrible of all, the silence of two hundred
      brains all possessed by one single, relentless, unforgiving
65   desperate thought.
      All this have I heard in the watchful night,
      And the murmur of the wind beyond the walls,
      And the tolls of a distant bell,
      And the woeful dirge of the rain
70   And the remotest echoes of the sorrowful city
      And the terrible beatings, wild beatings, mad beatings of the One
      Heart which is nearest to my heart.

      All this have I heard in the still night;
      But nothing is louder, harder, drearier, mightier or more awful than
75   the footsteps I hear over my head all night.

      Yet fearsome and terrible are all the footsteps of men upon this
      earth, for they either descend or climb.

They descend from little mounds and high peaks and lofty altitudes
    through wide roads and narrow paths, down noble marble
80   stairs and creaky stairs of wood—and some go down to the
    cellar, and some to the grave, and some down to the pits of
    shame and infamy, and still come to the glory of an unfathomable
    abyss where there is nothing but the staring white, stony
    eyeballs of Destiny.
85   And again other footsteps climb. They climb to life and to love,
    to fame, to power, to vanity, to truth, to glory and to the
    scaffold—to everything but Freedom and the Ideal.
And they all climb the same roads and the same stairs others go
    down; for never, since man began to think how to overcome
90   and overpass man, have other roads and other stairs been
    found.
They descend and they climb, the fearful footsteps of men, and
    some limp, some drag, some speed, some trot, some run—
    they are quiet, slow, noisy, brisk, quick, feverish, mad, and
95   most awful is their cadence to the ears of the one who stands
    still.
But of all the footsteps of men that either descend or climb, no
    footsteps are so fearsome and terrible as those that go straight
    on the dead level of a prison floor, from a yellow stone wall
100   to a red iron gate.

All through the night he walks and he thinks. Is it more frightful
    because he walks and his footsteps sound hollow over my
    head, or because he thinks and speaks not his thoughts?
But does he think? Why should he think? Do I think? I only hear
105   the footsteps and count them. Four steps and the wall. Four
    steps and the gate. But beyond? Beyond? Where goes he
    beyond the gate and the wall?

He goes not beyond. His thought breaks there on the iron gate
    Perhaps it breaks like a wave of rage, perhaps like a sudden
110   flood of hope, but it always returns to beat the wall like a
    billow of helplessness and despair.
He walks to and fro within the narrow whirlpit of this ever storming
    and furious thought. Only one thought—constant, fixed
    immovable, sinister without power and without voice.
115   A thought of madness, frenzy, agony and despair, a hellbrewed
    thought, for it is a natural thought. All things natural are
    things impossible while there are jails in the world—bread,
    work, happiness, peace, love.
But he thinks not of this. As he walks he thinks of the most superhuman,
120   the most unattainable, the most impossible thing in
    the world:
He thinks of a small brass key that turns just half around and
    throws open the red iron gate.

That is all the Walker thinks, as he walks throughout the night.
125   And that is what two hundred minds drowned in the darkness and
    the silence of the night think, and that is also what I think.

Wonderful is the supreme wisdom of the jail that makes all think
　　the same thought. Marvelous is the providence of the law
　　that equalizes all, even, in mind and sentiment. Fallen is the
130　last barrier of privilege, the aristocracy of the intellect.
The democracy of reason has leveled all the two hundred minds
　　to the common surface of the same thought.
I, who have never killed, think like the murderer;
I, who have never stolen, reason like the thief;
135　I think, reason, wish, hope, doubt, wait like the hired assassin
　　the embezzler, the forger, the counterfeiter, the incestuous,
　　the raper, the drunkard, the prostitute, the pimp, I, I who
　　used to think of love and life and flowers and song and
　　beauty and the ideal.
140　A little key, a little key as little as my little finger, a little key of
　　shining brass.
All my ideas, my thoughts, my dreams are congealed in a little
　　key of shiny brass.
All my brain, all my soul, all that suddenly surging latent power
145　of my deepest life are in the pocket of a white-haired man
　　dressed in blue.

He is great, powerful, formidable, the man with the white hair,
　　for he has in his pocket the mighty talisman which makes
　　one man cry, and one man pray, and one laugh, and one
150　cough, and one walk, and all keep awake and listen and think
　　the same maddening thought.
Greater than all men is the man with the white hair and the small
　　brass key, for no other man in the world could compel two
　　hundred men to think for so long the same thought. Surely
155　when the light breaks I will write a hymn unto him which
　　shall hail him greater than Mohammed and Arbues and
　　Torquemada and Mesmer, and all the other masters of other
　　men's thoughts. I shall call him Almighty, for he holds
　　everything of all and of me in a little brass key in his pocket.

160　Everything of me he holds but the branding iron of contempt and
　　the claymore of hatred for the monstrous cabala that can
　　make the apostle and the murderer, the poet and the procurer,
　　think of the same gate, the same key and the same
　　exit on the different sunlit highways of life.

165　My brother, do not walk any more.
　　It is wrong to walk on a grave. It is a sacrilege to walk four
　　steps from the headstone to the foot and four steps from the
　　foot to the headstone.
If you stop walking, my brother, no longer will this be a grave,
170　—for you will give me back my mind that is chained to your
　　feet and the right to think my own thoughts.
I implore you, my brother, for I am weary of the long vigil, weary
　　of counting your steps, and heavy with sleep.
Stop, rest, sleep, my brother, for the dawn is well nigh and it is
175　not the key alone that can throw open the gate.

John Reed (1887–1920)

Journalist, poet, novelist, and political activist, John Reed witnessed and reported on the most dramatic historical changes of his time. He covered the Mexican Revolution in the early 1910s (*Insurgent Mexico*, 1914), the horrific fighting in Germany and Eastern Europe during World War I (*The War in Eastern Europe*, 1916), and the October 1917 revolution in Russia (*Ten Days That Shook the World*, 1920). His life as a bohemian intellectual and revolutionary adventurer is depicted in the 1981 film *Reds*.

Born in "Cedar Hill," his grandfather's estate in Portland, Oregon, the son of a businessman father and socially prominent mother, Reed chafed against the social restrictions of his class, but delighted in the natural beauty of the Northwest. After graduating from Harvard in 1910 and traveling to Europe, he began his career as a journalist for leftist magazines, writing for the *New Review*, *The Masses*, and *Metropolitan Magazine*, and became an active participant in the politically radical and intellectually charged world of Greenwich Village in the 1910s.

Although not a political theorist, Reed had a sustained awareness of the structural relationship of class differences: "All I know is that my happiness is built on the misery of others, so that I eat because others go hungry, that I am clothed when other people go almost naked through the frozen cities in winter; and that fact poisons me, disturbs my serenity, makes me write propaganda when I would rather play." Propaganda here should be understood as journalism that takes political sides. As one example, his reporting on the 1913 silk workers' strike in Paterson, New Jersey, resulted in Reed's arrest and brief imprisonment in the Paterson County Jail. Workers in hundreds of mills went on strike to protest the use of high-speed looms and the firing of fellow workers. Reed helped organize a Paterson Strike Pageant in Madison Square Garden to raise funds for the strikers. Despite the cross-class support, the strike was lost, and the workers were forced back to work. Reed died of typhus in Moscow on October 19, 1920, but his revolutionary spirit continued in the many John Reed Clubs for radical writers and artists that were established throughout the United States.

WAR IN PATERSON

JUNE 1913

There's war in Paterson. But it's a curious kind of war. All the violence is the work of one side—the Mill Owners. Their servants, the Police, club unresisting men and women and ride down law-abiding crowds on horse-back. Their paid mercenaries, the armed Detectives, shoot and kill innocent people. Their newspapers, the Paterson *Press* and the Paterson *Call*, publish incendiary and crime-inciting appeals to mob-violence against the strike leaders. Their tool, Recorder Carroll, deals out heavy sentences to peaceful pickets that the police-net gathers up. They control absolutely the Police, the Press, the Courts.

Opposing them are about twenty-five thousand striking silk-workers, of whom perhaps ten thousand are active, and their weapon is the picket-line. Let me tell you what I saw in Paterson and then you will say which side of this struggle is "anarchistic" and "contrary to American ideals."

At six o'clock in the morning a light rain was falling. Slate-grey and cold, the streets of Paterson were deserted. But soon came the Cops—twenty of them—strolling along with their night-sticks under their arms. We went ahead of them toward the mill district. Now we began to see workmen going in the same direction, coat collars turned up, hands in their pockets. We came into a long street, one side of which was lined with silk mills, the other side with the wooden tenement houses. In every doorway, at every window of the houses clustered foreign-faced men and women, laughing and chatting as if after breakfast on a holiday. There seemed no sense of expectancy, no strain or feeling of fear. The sidewalks were almost empty, only over in front of the mills a few couples—there couldn't have been more than fifty—marched slowly up and down, dripping with the rain. Some were men, with here and there a man and woman together, or two young boys. As the warmer light of full day came the people drifted out of their houses and began to pace back and forth, gathering in little knots on the corners. They were quick with gesticulating hands, and low-voiced conversation. They looked often toward the corners of side streets.

Suddenly appeared a policeman, swinging his club. "Ah-h-h!" said the crowd softly.

Six men had taken shelter from the rain under the canopy of a saloon. "Come on! Get out of that!" yelled the policeman, advancing. The men quietly obeyed. "Get off this street! Go on home, now! Don't be standing here!" They gave way before him in silence, drifting back again when he turned away. Other policemen materialized, hustling, cursing, brutal, ineffectual. No one answered back. Nervous, bleary-eyed, unshaven, these officers were worn out with nine weeks incessant strike duty.

On the mill side of the street the picket-line had grown to about four hundred. Several policemen shouldered roughly among them, looking for trouble. A workman appeared, with a tin pail, escorted by two detectives. "Boo! Boo!" shouted a few scattered voices. Two Italian boys leaned against the mill fence and shouted a merry Irish threat, "Scab! Come outa here I knocka you' head off!" A policeman grabbed the boys roughly by the shoulder. "Get to hell out of here!" he cried, jerking and pushing them violently to the corner, where he kicked them. Not a voice, not a movement from the crowd.

A little further along the street we saw a young woman with an umbrella, who had been picketing, suddenly confronted by a big policeman.

"What the hell are *you* doing here?" he roared. "God damn you, you go home!" and he jammed his club against her mouth. "I *no* go home!" she shrilled passionately, with blazing eyes. "You bigga stiff!"

Silently, steadfastly, solidly the picket-line grew. In groups or in couples the strikers patrolled the sidewalk. There was no more laughing. They looked on with eyes full of hate. These were fiery-blooded Italians, and the police were the same brutal thugs that had beaten them and insulted them for nine weeks. I wondered how long they could stand it.

It began to rain heavily. I asked a man's permission to stand on the porch of his house. There was a policeman standing in front of it. His name, I afterwards discovered, was McCormack. I had to walk around him to mount the steps.

Suddenly he turned round, and shot at the owner: "Do all them fellows live in that house?" The man indicated the three other strikers and himself, and shook his head at me.

"Then you get to hell off of there!" said the cop, pointing his club at me.

"I have the permission of this gentleman to stand here," I said. "He owns this house."

"Never mind! Do what I tell you! Come off of there, and come off damn quick!"

"I'll do nothing of the sort."

With that he leaped up the steps, seized my arm, and violently jerked me to the sidewalk. Another cop took my arm and they gave me a shove.

"Now you get to hell off this street!" said Officer McCormack.

"I won't get off this street or any other street. If I'm breaking any law, you arrest me!"

Officer McCormack, who is doubtless a good, stupid Irishman in time of peace, is almost helpless in a situation that requires thinking. He was dreadfully troubled by my request. He didn't want to arrest me, and said so with a great deal of profanity.

"I've *got* your number," said I sweetly. "Now will you tell me your name?"

"Yes," he bellowed, "an' I got *your* number! I'll arrest you." He took me by the arm and marched me up the street.

He was sorry he *had* arrested me. There was no charge he could lodge against me. I hadn't been doing anything. He felt he must make me say something that could be construed as a violation of the Law. To which end he God damned me harshly, loading me with abuse and obscenity, and threatened me with his night-stick, saying, "You big — — lug, I'd like to beat the hell out of you with this club."

I returned airy persiflage to his threats.

Other officers came to the rescue, two of them, and supplied fresh epithets. I soon found them repeating themselves, however, and told them so. "I had to come all the way to Paterson to put one over on a cop!" I said. Eureka! They had at last found a crime! When I was arraigned in the Recorder's Court that remark of mine was the charge against me!

Ushered into the patrol-wagon, I was driven with much clanging of gongs along the picket-line. Our passage was greeted with "Boos" and ironical cheers, and enthusiastic waving. At Headquarters I was interrogated and lodged in the lockup. My cell was about four feet wide by seven feet long, at least a foot higher than a standing man's head, and it contained an iron bunk hung from the side-wall with chains, and an open toilet of disgusting dirtiness in the corner. A crowd of pickets had been jammed into the same lockup only three days before, *eight or nine in a cell*, and kept there without food or water for *twenty-two hours!* Among them a young girl of seventeen, who had led a procession right up to the Police Sergeant's nose and defied him to arrest them. In spite of the horrible discomfort, fatigue and thirst, these prisoners had *never let up cheering and singing* for a day and a night!

In about an hour the outside door clanged open, and in came about forty pickets in charge of the police, joking and laughing among themselves. They were hustled into the cells, two in each. Then pandemonium broke loose! With one accord the heavy iron beds were lifted and slammed thunderingly against the metal walls. It was like a cannon battery in action.

"Hooray for I. W. W.!" screamed a voice. And unanimously answered all the voices as one, "Hooray!"

"Hooray for Chief Bums!" (Chief of Police Bimson).

"Boo-o-o-o!" roared forty pairs of lungs—a great boom of echoing sound that had more of hate in it than anything I ever heard.

"To hell wit' Mayor McBride!"

"Boo-o-o-o!" It was an awful voice in that reverberant iron room, full of menace.

"Hooray for Haywood! One bigga da Union! Hooray for da Strike! To hell wit' da police! Boo-o-o-o! Boo-o-o-o! Hooray! Killa da A. F. of L.! A. F. of *Hell*, you mean! Boo-o-o-o!"

"Musica! Musica!" cried the Italians, like children. Whereupon one voice went "Plunk-plunk! Plunk-plunk!" like a guitar, and another, a rich tenor, burst into the first verse of the Italian-English song, written and composed by one of the strikers to be sung at the strike meetings. He came to the chorus:

> "Do you lika Miss Flynn?"
> (Chorus) "Yes! Yes! Yes! Yes!"
> "Do you like Carlo Tresca?"
> (Chorus) "Yes! Yes! Yes! Yes!"
> "Do you like Major McBride?"
> (Chorus) "No! *No!* NO! *NO!!!*"
> "Hooray for I. W. W.!"
> "Hooray! Hooray!! Hooray!!!"

"*Bis! Bis!*" shouted everybody, clapping hands, banging the beds up and down. An officer came in and attempted to quell the noise. He was met with "Boos" and jeers. Some one called for water. The policeman filled a tin cup and brought it to the cell door. A hand reached out swiftly and slapped it out of his fingers on the floor. "Scab! Thug!" they yelled. The policeman retreated. The noise continued.

The time approached for the opening of the Recorder's Court, but word had evidently been brought that there was no more room in the County Jail, for suddenly the police appeared and began to open the cell doors. And so the strikers passed out, cheering wildly. I could hear them outside, marching back to the picket-line with the mob who had waited for them at the jail gates.

And then I was taken before the Court of Recorder Carroll. Mr. Carroll has the intelligent, cruel, merciless face of the ordinary police court magistrate. But he is worse than most police court magistrates. He sentences beggars to *six months' imprisonment* in the County Jail without a chance to answer back. He also sends little children there, where they mingle with dope-fiends, and tramps, and men with running sores upon their bodies—to the County Jail, where the air is foul and insufficient to breathe, and the food is full of dead vermin, and grown men become insane.

Mr. Carroll read the charge against me. I was permitted to tell my story. Officer McCormack recited a clever *mélange* of lies that I am sure he himself could never have concocted. "John Reed," said the Recorder. "Twenty days." That was all.

And so it was that I went up to the County Jail. In the outer office I was questioned again, searched for concealed weapons, and my money and valuables taken away. Then the great barred door swung open and I went down some steps into a vast room lined with three tiers of cells. About eighty prisoners strolled around, talked, smoked, and ate the food sent in to them by those outside. Of this eighty almost half were strikers. They were in their street clothes, held in prison under $500 bail to await the action of the Grand Jury. Surrounded by a dense crowd of short, dark-faced men, Big Bill Haywood towered in the center of the room. His big hand made simple gestures as he explained something to them. His massive, rugged face, seamed and scarred like a mountain, and as calm, radiated strength. These slight, foreign-faced strikers, one of many desperate little armies in the vanguard of the battle-line of Labor, quickened and strengthened by Bill Haywood's face and voice, looked up at him lovingly, eloquently. Faces deadened and dulled with grinding routine in the sunless mills glowed with hope and understanding. Faces scarred and bruised from policemen's clubs grinned eagerly at the thought of going back on the picket-line. And there were other faces, too—lined and sunken with the slow starvation of a nine weeks' poverty—shadowed with the sight of so much suffering, or the hopeless brutality of the police—and there were those who had seen Modestino Valentino shot to death by a private detective. But not one showed discouragement; not one a sign of faltering or of fear. As one little Italian said to me, with blazing eyes: "We all one bigga da Union. I. W. W.—dat word is pierced de heart of de people!"

"Yes! Yes! Dass righ'! I. W. W.! One bigga da Union"—they murmured with soft, eager voices, crowding around.

I shook hands with Haywood, who introduced me to Pat Quinlan, the thin-faced, fiery Irishman now under indictment for speeches inciting to riot.

"Boys," said Haywood, indicating me, "this man wants to *know* things. You tell him everything"—

They crowded around me, shaking my hand, smiling, welcoming me. "Too bad you get in jail," they said, sympathetically. "We tell you ever't'ing. You ask. We tell you. Yes. Yes. You good feller."

And they did. Most of them were still weak and exhausted from their terrible night before in the lockup. Some had been lined up against a wall, as they marched to and fro in front of the mills, and herded to jail on the charge of "unlawful assemblage!" Others had been clubbed into the patrolwagon on the charge of "rioting," as they stood at the track, on their way home from picketing, waiting for a train to pass! They were being held for the Grand Jury that indicted Haywood and Gurley Flynn. *Four of these jurymen were silk manufacturers, another the head of the local Edison company—which Haywood tried to organize for a strike—and not one a workingman!*

"We not take bail," said another, shaking his head. "We stay here. Fill up de damn jail. Pretty soon no more room. Pretty soon can't arrest no more picket!"

It was visitors' day. I went to the door to speak with a friend. Outside the reception room was full of women and children, carrying packages, and pasteboard boxes, and pails full of dainties and little comforts lovingly prepared, which meant hungry and ragged wives and babies, so that the men might be comfortable in jail. The place was full of the sound of moaning; tears ran down their work-roughened faces; the children looked up at their fathers' unshaven faces through the bars and tried to reach them with their hands.

"What nationalities are all the people?" I asked. There were Dutchmen, Italians, Belgians, Jews, Slovaks, Germans, Poles—

"What nationalities stick together on the picket-line?"

A young Jew, pallid and sick-looking from insufficient food, spoke up proudly. "T'ree great nations stick togedder like dis." He made a fist. "T'ree great nations—Italians, Hebrews an' Germans"—

"But how about the Americans?"

They all shrugged their shoulders and grinned with humorous scorn. "English peoples not go on picket-line," said one, softly. "'Mericans no lika fight!" An Italian boy thought my feelings might be hurt, and broke in quickly: "Not all lika dat. Beeg Beell, *he* 'Merican. *You* 'Merican. Quinl', Miss Flynn, 'Merican. *Good! Good!* 'Merican workman, he lika talk too much."

This sad fact appears to be true. It was the English-speaking group that held back during the Lawrence strike. It is the English-speaking contingent that remains passive at Paterson, while the "wops," the "kikes," the "hunkies"—the "degraded and ignorant races from Southern Europe"—go out and get clubbed on the picket-line and gaily take their medicine in Paterson jail.

But just as they were telling me these things the keeper ordered me to the "convicted room," where I was pushed into a bath and compelled to put on regulation prison clothes. I shan't attempt to describe the horrors I saw in that room. Suffice it to say that forty-odd men lounged about a long corridor lined on one side with cells; that the only ventilation and light came from one small skylight up a funnel-shaped air-shaft; that one man had syphilitic sores on his legs and was treated by the prison doctor with sugar-pills for "nervousness"; that a seventeen-year-old boy *who had never been sentenced* had remained in that corridor without ever seeing the sun for over *nine months*; that a cocaine-fiend was getting his "dope" regularly from the inside, and that the background of this and much more was the monotonous and terrible shouting of a man who had lost his mind in that hell-hole and who walked among us.

There were about fourteen strikers in the "convicted" room—Italians, Lithuanians, Poles, Jews, one Frenchman and one "free-born" Englishman! That Englishman was a peach. He was the only Anglo-Saxon striker in prison except the leaders—and perhaps the only one who *had been* there for picketing. He had been sentenced for insulting a mill-owner who came out of his mill and ordered him off the sidewalk. "Wait till I get out!" he said to me. "If them damned English-speaking workers don't go on picket *I'll* put the curse o'Cromwell on 'em!"

Then there was a Pole—an aristocratic, sensitive chap, a member of the local Strike Committee, a born fighter. He was reading Bob Ingersoll's lectures, translating them to the others. Patting the book, he said with a slow smile: "Now I don' care if I stay in here one year." One thing I noticed was the utter and reasonable irreligion of the strikers—the Italians, the Frenchman—the strong Catholic races, in short—and the Jews, too.

"Priests, it is a profesh'. De priest, he gotta work same as any workin' man. If we ain't gotta no damn Church we been strikin' t'ree hund'd years ago. Priest, he iss all a time keeping working-man down!"

And then, with laughter, they told me how the combined clergy of the city of Paterson had attempted from their pulpits to persuade them back to work—back to wage-slavery and the tender mercies of the mill-owners on grounds of religion! They told me of that disgraceful and ridiculous conference between the Clergy and the Strike Committee, with the Clergy in the part of Judas. It was hard to believe that until I saw in the paper the sermon delivered the previous day at the Presbyterian Church by the Reverend William A. Littell. He had the impudence to flay the strike leaders and advise workmen to be respectful and obedient to their employers—to tell them that the saloons were the cause of their unhappiness—to proclaim the horrible depravity of Sabbath-breaking workmen, and more rot of the same sort. And this while living men were fighting for their very existence and singing gloriously of the Brotherhood of Man!

The lone Frenchman was a lineal descendant of the Republican doctrinaires of the French Revolution. He had been a Democrat for thirteen years, then suddenly had become converted to Socialism. Blazing with excitement, he went round bubbling with arguments. He had the same blind faith in Institutions that characterized his ancestors, the same intense fanaticism, the same willingness to die for an idea. Most of the strikers were Socialists already—but the Frenchman was bound to convert every man in that prison. All day long his voice could be heard, words rushing forth in a torrent, tones rising to a shout, until the Keeper would shut him up with a curse. When the fat Deputy-Sheriff from the outer office came into the room the Frenchman made a dive for him, too.

"You're not producing anything," he'd say, eyes snapping, finger waving violently up and down, long nose and dark, excited face within an inch of the Deputy's. "You're an unproductive worker—under Socialism we'll get what we're working for—we'll get all we make. Capital's not necessary. Of course it ain't! Look at the Post Office—is there any private capital in that? Look at the Panama Canal. That's Socialism. The American Revolution was a smuggler's war. Do you know what is the Economic Determinism?" This getting swifter and swifter, louder and louder, more and more fragmentary, while a close little circle of strikers massed round the Deputy, watching his face like hounds on a trail, waiting till he opened his mouth to riddle his bewildered arguments with a dozen swift retorts. Trained debaters, all these, in their Locals. For a few minutes the Deputy would try to answer them, and then, driven into a corner, he'd suddenly sweep his arm furiously around, and bellow:

"Shut up, you damned dagos, or I'll clap you in the dungeon!" And the discussion would be closed.

Then there was the strike-breaker. He was a fat man, with sunken, flabby cheeks, jailed by some mistake of the Recorder. So completely did the strikers ostracize him— rising and moving away when he sat by them, refusing to speak to him, absolutely ignoring his presence—that he was in a pitiable condition of loneliness.

"I've learned my lesson," he moaned. "I ain't never goin' to scab on working-men no more!"

One young Italian came up to me with a newspaper and pointed to three items in turn. One was "American Federation of Labor hopes to break the Strike next week"; another, "Victor Berger says 'I am a member of the A. F. of L., and I have no love for the I. W. W. in Paterson'"; and the third, "Newark Socialists refuse to help the Paterson Strikers."

"I no un'erstand," he told me, looking up at me appealingly. "You tell me. I Socialis'—I belong Union—I strike wit' I. W. W. Socialis', he say, 'Worke'men of de worl'. Unite!' A. F. of L., he say, 'All workmen join togedder.' Bot' dese or-gan-i-zashe, he say, 'I am for de Working Class.' Awri', I say, I am de Working Class. I unite, I strike. Den he say, 'No! You *cannot* strike!' Why dat? I no un'erstan'. You explain me."

But I could not explain. All I could say was that a good share of the Socialist Party and the American Federation of Labor have forgotten all about the Class Struggle, and seem to be playing a little game with Capitalistic rules, called "Button, button, who's got the Vote!"

When it came time for me to go out I said good-bye to all those gentle, alert, brave men, ennobled by something greater than themselves. *They* were the strike—not Bill Haywood, not Gurley Flynn, not any other individual. And if they should lose all their leaders other leaders would arise from the ranks, even as *they* rose, and the strike would go on! Think of it! Twelve years they have been losing strikes—twelve solid years of disappointments and incalculable suffering. They must not lose again! They can not lose!

And as I passed out through the front room they crowded around me again, patting my sleeve and my hand, friendly, warm-hearted, trusting, eloquent. Haywood and Quinlan had gone out on bail.

"You go out," they said softly. "Thass nice. Glad you go out. Pretty soon we go out. Then we go back on picket-line"—

Fellow Workers: IWW Oral Histories

When some two hundred men and women met in Chicago on June 27, 1905, to found the IWW (Industrial Workers of the World), Big Bill Hayywood brought the convention to order with the salutation, "Fellow workers." The collection *Solidarity Forever: An Oral History of the IWW* (1985) by Steward Bird, Dan Georgakas, and Deborah Shaffer, a book based on the documentary film *The Wobblies* (1979), includes oral histories from elderly Wobblies who recall that spirit of solidarity, signified by "fellow workers." Sophie Cohen, who grew up around the Paterson, New Jersey, textile mills, offers an insider perspective of the heyday of the IWW and the failed Paterson strike of 1913. James Fair, a black dockworker and Wobbly, describes the hazardous working conditions in the shipyards and the hopes and losses of the IWW.

SOPHIE COHEN, "PATERSON HAD A PRISON-LIKE FEELING"

Paterson had a prison-like feeling when you walked through the narrow streets where the mills were. They were red brick buildings with small, dirty windows set very high. The mills were next to the Passaic River. We lived about two blocks from the river, so when I had to bring lunch to my father, I had to go uphill. Whenever you walked from the center of town, you walked up.

My father collapsed at one of the mills when I was young, and he was told never to go back again. That was a terrible time for us. My mother had a child that died during birth and my little brother died from diptheria. Somehow, though, my mother and father got together with another family, and they managed to put a deposit on a farm outside of town. I remember the fields and how hard they worked, but they couldn't keep up the payments. That's when we came back to Paterson.

My father couldn't go back to the mills, but he was able to set up a laundry. We'd get shirts and things from our family doctor and other people who were a bit wealthier and could afford to send lace curtains and things like that to a laundry. Childhood was not unhappy for us. For Christmas or Hanukkah, my father would take us to Broadway where there was an Italian fruit shop and he'd buy big California oranges. That was a big treat. There was one group that said it would give toys to all the children of the workers. I think it was the Salvation Army, but I'm not sure. My sister and I went. We stood in line and went into a house where they gave us a little package. They said not to open it up until we got home. But we couldn't wait. We opened it up and found a broken toy. That was the closest to toys we ever got. We used to play with mud pies. We dug holes and things like that. Sometimes, my father would take us to the woods. One thing that was very different from now is when we had a meeting, everyone went. Adults and children attended as long as they were part of the shop. We didn't divide ourselves by age.

There were a lot of nationalities in Paterson. A lot of the textile workers were Italian, and there were Jewish people, Poles, and some Germans. When we went to a picnic or mass meeting, we didn't care if someone was a different nationality. The children played together and the people talked together, as well as they could. The children would be sent over to get beer for the adults. It made no difference whether you were Italian or Jewish or Polish. The barrels of beer were for everyone. There was a lot of singing too, at the picnics and at the meetings.

During the strike, Carlo Tresca was one of our leaders. You didn't have to understand Italian to feel what he was saying. Everyone spoke with accents but that didn't get in the way. There was a refrain everyone knew:

> Do you like Mr. Boss? No, no, no!
> Do you like Miss Flynn? Yes, yes, yes!
> The IWW! Hurray! Hurray!

A lot of speakers would use that in their talks. They'd yell out, "Do you like Mr. Boss?" and people would laugh and shout back as loud as they could, "No, no, no!" Those were tremendous events for us when we were children.

We children didn't have many entertainments. Only three stand out in my mind. One was the Italian organ grinder. He had a little monkey who tried to get money into his cup. There was little money, but after a lot of giggling, screaming, and singing, he would sometimes get a penny. The minute he would get a coin, the organ grinder would leave. That was all he was waiting for, but in the meantime, we had a lot of fun with him and his monkey. On Fridays a violinist came. He would play and tell the story of the fire that happened in the Triangle Shirt Waist Company in New York. He would try to get some pennies too, but he wanted to make us aware of political issues. The other thing we did was walk to the Passaic Falls. Other than that, there was school and the mills.

When I was graduating from the eighth grade, the principal came around to tell us that there was a new shirt company opening that was perfect for young people because it was not noisy and dirty like the textile mills. The factory was offering five dollars a week, which seemed a tremendous amount then. I was only fourteen at the time, and girls my age were not allowed to come to work at the usual starting time of seven. We waited until eight and then stayed until five; on Saturdays, we worked until one. At the end of the week, we got either $3.75 or $3.95, because they had deducted the hour we didn't come in. Our job was to box shirts. The conditions were dreadful. If you went to the bathroom more than twice a day and were more than a few minutes, you were reported to the office by the floorwalker.

Most of the girls were taught how to weave by their parents. Since my father was not in the mills at that time, I went to an office where the bolts of cloth were shipped. In return for helping them, I was taught how to weave. They never paid me, and as soon as I thought I knew enough, I left. Soon afterwards, I went with one of the girls I had met at a Wobbly picnic to look for a job. I told them I was a weaver. It was all right for a while, then a filling got stuck. I didn't know what to do. I got so frightened I never went back after lunch. I didn't even go to ask for the money I had already earned.

I finally did learn to weave and got my first job as a weaver. One of the big issues for us was the loom system. They used to get people to work four and even six looms at a time. That's the reason men brought their wives with them. It was too much for one person. If a thread broke or a piece fell down, the fine threads would be flawed. You couldn't let this happen, so you had to stop the loom to fix it. When you did that, you weren't making cloth. You had to keep going from the front. You had to inject the filling and then go around the back to see how the threads there were. To keep four or six looms going was just impossible. Even if you somehow managed, you still didn't earn enough for the fundamentals of living.

I remember the clanging of those looms, the sound of steel against steel. You couldn't speak with one another unless you shouted. Many of the weavers brought a piece of wood to stand on to get relief from the cement floor. It didn't relieve anything for me. The first time I walked out of the mill, I couldn't hear normally and although I knew my feet were touching the ground, it felt strange. After a time, I got used to the noise. There seemed to be a certain rhythm to the loom. It encouraged me to sing. The only way I could endure that work was to sing along to the rhythm of the loom. Most of the discomfort could be forgotten that way. Maybe that's why we used to sing so many Wobbly songs.

About this time, the AFL tried to organize the school teachers. A number of the teachers were quite sympathetic. They felt sorry for young girls who could only go to the eighth grade and then were sent to the mills. They started to teach us in small groups on Sunday. We'd read Shakespeare and Dreiser, and they tried to help as much as they could. When the school system found out, the teachers were fired. There was never a union for them.

Everyone worked long days then. My mother would go to the farmers' market at four in the morning pushing a baby carriage. The farmers had come from the night before, and anything they didn't sell, they would let you have cheap or for nothing. Sometimes she'd get potatoes or big sacks of vegetables. The neighbors would come in and they'd divide up whatever they got. Before I started working in the mills, my mother used to send me to the butcher to buy meat. If you bought meat, he'd always give you a lot of bones, and some days you would get liver. I would ask for liver "for my cat." Of course, it wasn't for the cat. My mother always had a big pot of soup on the stove. People would often come to ask my father to help him find a job or to discuss a problem. My mother always managed to have a bowl of soup to offer. It was always from the bones, but to get the bones and liver free, you had to buy some meat.

My parents could read, write, and speak German, Russian, and Hebrew. Our home became a nucleus for people who wanted to write home but were illiterate. They would come to our house to have my mother write their letters. But people from Warsaw and Lodz tended to be well-educated; and they were the ones who became leaders in our strike. People used to meet in our house to talk about conditions. You weren't allowed to belong to a union or organize one. If you were heard talking about that at work, you would be blacklisted immediately. Many of the Polish people worked in the dye factories. The smell was so bad that when we'd pass by, we had to hold our breath and run. Even from the outside, we could hardly breathe. They worked in water up to their knees. The clothes most of us wore were hand-me-downs. People would crowd in about three rooms and then take a boarder to make ends meet. You couldn't get credit from the butcher, but the grocer used to sell a few odd pieces of meat which helped. Many of the men couldn't take it. Instead of going home with their pay, many headed straight for the saloon. There was one on our corner, and I would see children running to find their fathers, or wives coming to see if they could rescue some money before the husbands drank it all. I couldn't blame the men that much. There was nothing to look forward to after pay day. They had to start the same thing all over again. Conditions became worse and worse until either you had to just stop living or become a rebel. That's when the IWW came in.

Everyone would go out to the IWW picnics and meetings. Haywood came to speak. Gurley Flynn came. There was Tresca, Scott Nearing, Norman Thomas, Roger Baldwin. I remember once I didn't want to go. I said, "Pop, all they do is talk." He said, "Listen." One time they refused to let the IWW meet in the Turn Hall. We had to walk all the way to Haledon, a small town outside Paterson where they had a socialist mayor who allowed us to have picnics in the woods and to hold meetings.

Gurley Flynn looked just like the pictures we see of her now. She was young, vibrant, enthusiastic. She wasn't really a good speaker, but she gave so much of herself in her talks. She would come at night to the soup kitchens. There were big caldrons of soup set up in a lot next to the church and she would get up on a platform. There were red flares around her, and she'd get them singing and then she'd talk with them. It was just the thing people needed to keep them together and give them courage.

Although my father was very sympathetic to the IWW, he couldn't be a member; he had a store. But he always went to the meetings and picnics. When he spoke of Scott Nearing, he would lower his voice as if he was talking about a person so great he was almost holy. We liked Haywood, too. He seemed a tower of strength. He was a big fellow and had one eye closed. He didn't wear a patch. The eye was just closed.

It's important to realize that we were very proud to be Americans. Even though we were radical, strikers always carried the flag. In those days, during the elections, newspapers would flash images on sheets attached to the side of the buildings. Candidates would soapbox in front of them and sometimes they'd have arguments. My father always took me, and he would say, "This is America. They say whatever they want during the election; but afterwards, they shake hands. It isn't like other countries where they shoot one another and kill one another. This is America."

During the actual strike, most of the children were sent away to people in New York. They wore red sashes and were put into trucks, yelling and screaming like it was a lot of fun. They were in front of our laundry and I wanted to go too, but my father said, "Shhh, you have something to eat. They have nothing." It wasn't easy for the families to give up their children, but my father was right. There was no income and the strike fund was low. The grocer fed most of the workers on credit, and there were soup kitchens. The strike lasted until the summer, then groups began to fall away.

The police would be violent when there was picketing, but the Paterson workers were never violent. That was the last thing on our minds. We had no guns. I don't believe anyone I knew could operate a gun. There was one Italian man shot on the picket line. There was a collection to raise money for his widow, who, I think, opened an Italian grocery afterwards. The police also raided homes. There was a Wobbly who had important files in his room. One night after an IWW dance, someone suggested we go to New York. I had never been to New York, to Greenwich Village, and a whole group of us decided to do it. We went to Long John Silver's, the Pirates' Den, where the waiters wore patches for atmosphere. We missed the last train home and didn't get back until dawn, on the milk run. There was someone waiting to tell us that the Wobbly's room had been raided. I saw it. The room was in a private house, but they had pulled open all the drawers and taken things away. The police weren't gentle, and of course they arrested many people.

We had a big pageant for the strike. That was much more our way of doing things. John Reed was involved in that. It was to show exactly what had happened in Paterson. It showed how the looms had stopped, how a striker was shot, how the picket lines were. Although the pageant seemed to siphon off some of the energy we had, there really wasn't much more that could have been done. The employers were stronger. The workers had nothing but their enthusiasm and courage.

I wasn't an official organizer, but when I became a weaver, a girlfriend and I would take jobs in unorganized factories and try to organize them. We would refuse the four looms, saying it was too much for us. Because we were young girls, we were permitted to work only two. After a few weeks, we would hand out leaflets and call for an organizing meeting. We looked so innocent that the managers never thought we were capable of even believing in a union. In one place, they locked us out. They called the police, and we had to get our pay at a little booth. When the police handed us the pay and our tools, I refused the tools because I considered the factory to be on strike. The cop got angry and said if I didn't take them there, I could come for them at the station. Rather than be organized, that particular factory closed and left town to start again somewhere in Pennsylvania.

The companies never stopped putting the pressure on. If you said you were an IWW, it was like saying you were a criminal. For years there were people who would not let you know they had been IWWs. They would deny it out of simple fear. If you were an IWW in Paterson, you were blacklisted. I got a lesson on how much they feared the IWW when I was just starting to work. I used to teach children on the block some IWW songs. I'd always come home for lunch, and one day while I was eating, there was a bang on the door. My mother, who was very short, opened the door, and there was a gigantic police-men standing there. He said he wanted to see me. She led him to the table where I was eating. He looked down at me, and he must have realized how ridiculous the situation was. He had been sent to find a dangerous rebel, and there was a fifteen year old girl eating lunch. He left. But imagine! A little girl sang a song in school and the teacher reported it and the principal called the police and the police came to my door. For a song.

I guess I had no choice about becoming a rebel. The first dress I ever bought that was mine was after I had earned my first pay as a weaver. I wanted to go to a Wobbly dance, but I had to bring that money home, because we never had any extra spending money. On the way home, I saw a pretty dress. I opened my paycheck and took some money out and bought the dress. When I got home I told my mother someone saw me looking at the dress, bought it, and gave it to me. It was a ridiculous story. It was having to make excuses like that that kept you fighting.

The IWW left people with a taste for organization. Every time workers win a strike, it helps straighten out their backs a little bit more and lifts their heads a bit higher. Even though the big strike was lost in Paterson, there was a feeling of togetherness among the workers. We had a medium of expression. From then on, there were a series of strikes and every shop had to be reorganized. Every shop refought the eight hour day all the way down the line—and the four loom system. We used to carry placards: "Eight hours work— eight hours play—eight hours sleep." Well, there was always some shop going on strike for one reason or another. The thing in 1913 that we really acted on and won was the two loom system.

I'm still with the IWW. The AFL-CIO was organized along the lines of a big corporation with the president receiving a fabulous amount and the workers just like commodities. The IWW was more than a union. It wanted to bring forth a new form of society. The IWW taught that the worker has nothing in common with the employer. The average worker still doesn't understand that. The eight hour day and pensions are taken for granted. They can't understand there was a time when the word *vacation* was foreign. The IWW tried to educate people to be more than horses, more than cogs in a wheel. The IWW never had high paid officials. How can a president who earns so much understand the plight of a working mother who has to deposit her child in a day care center and run off to her job still worrying about a fever the child might have? The president worries about the best college to send his kids to. They can't understand each other. There is a big division. The leaders have political jobs. They need the workers so they can exist, but they do not function in the interest of the worker, of the working class.

The IWW fought for new values, for a society where every person can be a full human being. We saw that men were bored from doing the same ritual work, day after day, week after week. Of course, they drank too much. We had a slogan: "You can't fight booze and the boss at the same time." We were against drink and in favor of education. What the worker needs most is not more pennies per hour but education. We thought that when workers got to understand their situation, they could have a general strike and through the general work stoppage, workers would get their various goals.

If you are not a rebel, it is easy to be pessimistic. How can people live with themselves? I fought whenever I could. During the Sacco and Vanzetti struggle, I soapboxed on South Street. I told the audience that we should cut the powerlines so they couldn't electrocute them. Another time, I was there and got swept into the safety of a restaurant when the police came through swinging clubs from their horses. When I moved to New York, it was different than Paterson. There were no mills. But I would work for and organize dances for the General Recruiting Union. I never charged any expenses. When my husband was working—he was a carpenter—I thought, how can you take money for doing things for the organization? We couldn't. We struggled as best we could and we always sang those wonderful songs.

James Fair, "Working the Docks"

Conditions on our farm in the South were just bad. My parents heard that in Pennsylvania, well, so to speak, you could rake up money from the street. We decided to move North. Soon as I arrived, I went out and got a job where I got twenty-five cents an hour. I had to do sweeping and cleaning, because that's all I knew how to do other than plowing. Later, I heard about a job on the waterfront. I heard about people belonging to a union called the Industrial Workers of the World. I went down and got some information and joined. That was 1917, the beginning of my union life. At that time, there was no such thing as the AF of L on the riverfront of this port. Didn't know what it was. We became affiliated with them much later, and then the CIO came in.

Those days two men would work a hand truck with two iron wheels. Our freight was things like flour, corn meal, grits. We'd take it over rough floors to the side of the ship to be loaded. We worked ten hours with an hour for lunch. The wage was about eighty-five cents an hour. Our problem was that people were getting hurt. We had no medical or safety rules or anything like that. The first accident I incurred was on Christmas Eve, 1919. I had worked up from the docks and was aboard a ship. We had what they call a turn hole. You're on the deck and have to work with a machine. I got caught in the turn. Its head caught my trousers and pulled me around. When they stopped the machine, my head was down and my legs were up in the air. I sustained a strained left knee. They carried me to the hospital, and I laid there in the hospital practically all afternoon before they even examined me. Since I didn't have anything broken, they sent me home. When I recovered enough to go back to work, I found I had no job.

The IWW tried to change those conditions, but it wasn't favored by most workers and companies didn't like it at all. I learned that the companies considered it a subversive organization, but we kept fighting and fighting. Striking was unlawful then; when we were on strike, people were transported from different parts of the country to break it. Every time we had a strike, they'd transport those men in vans with police escorts right from the starting points to the job. Strikers would have as much chance before a strikebreaker as a rabbit would have before a gunner. In nineteen and twenty-two, the IWW was out on strike all the month of September. We tried to do something at lunchtime, but the companies would feed the strikebreakers right on the docks. They won out. We had one stevedoring company come here and work right on Pier 78 which is in operation now. They helped to break the strike. This was something that I experienced.

The IWW was for the laboring man, not just black or white. That's why it was so opposed by the capitalists. I'm not a radical, not by any means. I do believe in moderation. I also believe in getting the most for my labor. I don't believe in getting something for nothing. I think labor is entitled to a fair turn, and that's what the IWW, in my eyes, stood for. But without a certain amount of radicalism, we wouldn't have had decent homes to live in. Now, this thing of working ten or fifteen minutes past the hour and not getting paid for it—they didn't stand for that. We finally got that in a contract years later, but there was a time when the companies cheated us on that.

Everyone got along fairly good working on the docks of Philadelphia. Now, when we left the job, that was different. But when we worked, we worked on the decks together, we worked on the wharves together, and we worked in the hole together. Yes, we were given the roughest jobs, of course. Because more than one time, if a white came along, I didn't have no job. My experience involved whites beginning from my advance from the truck to working on the deck. Maybe they took a liking to how I worked. If they told me something, I did it and I did it with speed. I wanted to advance. That was the way I got away from this hard labor, this worrisome work on the docks. It was rough. Nowadays a lot of automation has cut down the number of jobs, but I can appreciate the changes. Despite the things being as bad as they are, what longshoremen do today is not as back breaking as it was.

In those days, we didn't have a checkoff system. We wore buttons with a different color for each month, and it was marked with the name of the month. Men could be working who were far behind in their dues and the IWW might have to call a job action because the boss would not knock those men off. It was similar to a strike. The only time I remember a formal strike would be later, after we had contracts. There was no such thing as a picket line, because unions didn't have that right. We didn't have news media like today. Word just got around: we weren't working. I don't know much about what it was like before the IWW, because when I first came to the docks, the IWW was already there. They were the only thing on the riverfront to represent the worker.

We had some good leaders. Ben Fletcher was a Negro—we say "black" now—and we had another guy whose first name I don't remember, but his last name was Nef, and he was white. I don't remember his nationality, but he was a very dedicated union man. Both of them were. For as long as the IWW existed, our meetings were at 121 Catherine Street. They would call the meeting to order and read the minutes. Then we'd talk about whatever was on the agenda: working conditions and what-not were discussed. I think it was very democratic.

As far as blacks were concerned, things were rough. To my knowing, the IWW was the only union, at that time, accepting black workers freely. They advocated just one thing—solidarity. Ben Fletcher would tell us we had to live together and work together. His pet words were: "All for one and one for all." Solidarity was the main thing. That sank in with a lot of us. It paid off, and it's paying off today. You see, the IWW was something for the working man. It didn't make any difference who you was, what kind of work you did. They wanted to organize *all* the working people.

Fletcher was not only just in Philadelphia. He was a national organizer. Some of us were very hurt when he was arrested. We knew what he was doing was something for us to earn a livelihood, to support ourselves and our families. It was just like, well, I would say it was something like Martin Luther King, but turned to organized labor and improving our standards of life. I don't think how the IWW felt about the war had anything to do with what happened. As far as I know of, the union, the IWW, supported the war. We longshoremen, a good many of us, would extend our hours without any hesitation. I was on ships myself in the Philadelphia navy yard at that time. We would be working, and they would ask us to work through, working at nights, for instance. They'd say the ship has got to go. Some would agree to work until seven. If we weren't finished, the order would come down to work until the job was done. Naturally, we would have some who would rebel. Some wanted to get something to eat and would get food off the ship. The companies began to station guards and marines so that no one could leave the ship. We'd have to stay until the ship was finished. That was because a war was going on. There were men overseas fighting for you, giving their lives. You couldn't refuse to supply them with food and arms and what-not. What I'm saying is not a fairy tale. I experienced it myself. In all walks of life, we find some people going to the extreme; but on the whole, I think the IWW promoted fairness. They said if you were hired, you should work. They didn't say break your neck, but they advocated work.

The charges against Fletcher and Nef were trumped up just to get rid of them. Since it wasn't local, they didn't go to a city or state jail, but to a federal prison. With them gone, activities gradually ceased here in Philadelphia. The IWW wasn't effective, anymore. We had several other organizers come along to do what they could do, but the odds were against us. I remember seeing Fletcher and Nef going off to prison. Being locked up affected their natural health a lot. I saw them after they came out, and they were very thin. How long they lasted after that, I just don't know.

Mother Jones (Mary Harris Jones) (1837–1930)

In his introduction to the *Autobiography of Mother Jones* (1925), the famed lawyer Clarence Darrow described Mary Harris Jones as an "individualist" and "crusader." That she was strong-willed and devoted to the cause of improving the lives of the working poor there is little historical doubt. She was an individualist in a larger-than-life sense, someone who defied the societal constraints of age and gender by using her wit, energy, sympathy, and oratory to confront authority and shame the powerful into seeing the unjust disparities of wealth and poverty. She told a reporter in 1912: "I am simply a social revolutionist. I believe in collective ownership of the means of wealth. . . . My life work has been to try to educate the worker to a sense of the wrongs he has had to suffer and does suffer—and to stir up the oppressed to a point of getting off their knees and demanding that which I believe to be rightfully theirs."

Although Mother Jones liked to claim that she was born on May 1, 1830, historians agree that her birth was on August 1, 1837, in County Cork, Ireland. Her family immigrated to Toronto, Canada, and later settled in Michigan. As a young woman, she faced extraordinary tragedy when her husband George Jones and their four children died in a yellow fever epidemic in 1867 in Memphis, Tennessee. Mother Jones moved to Chicago and supported herself as a dressmaker, but soon lost her shop and home to the great

Chicago fire in 1871. Her life as a radical labor organizer and champion of workers and their families parallels significant events in American labor history: the general railroad strike of 1877, the early years of the Knights of Labor, union organizing in the coal fields of Pennsylvania and West Virginia in 1897, the founding convention of the Industrial Workers of the World in 1905, and the Pennsylvania steel strike of 1919. Always ready to travel to support labor struggles, Mother Jones lived in no fixed place: "My address is like my shoes: it travels with me." She was called the "Angel of the Miners" because of her deep sympathy with miners, their wives and children. "Mining is cruel work," she wrote simply. "The March of the Mill Children," shows Mother Jones as a strategist and publicist, using imaginative street theater, processions, music, and the physically damaged bodies of young workers themselves to battle the evils of child labor.

THE MARCH OF THE MILL CHILDREN

In the spring of 1903 I went to Kensington, Pennsylvania, where seventy-five thousand textile workers were on strike. Of this number at least ten thousand were little children. The workers were striking for more pay and shorter hours. Every day little children came into Union Headquarters, some with their hands off, some with the thumb missing, some with their fingers off at the knuckle. They were stooped things, round shouldered and skinny. Many of them were not over ten years of age, the state law prohibited their working before they were twelve years of age.

The law was poorly enforced and the mothers of these children often swore falsely as to their children's age. In a single block in Kensington, fourteen women, mothers of twenty-two children all under twelve, explained it was a question of starvation or perjury. That the fathers had been killed or maimed at the mines.

I asked the newspaper men why they didn't publish the facts about child labor in Pennsylvania. They said they couldn't because the mill owners had stock in the papers.

"Well, I've got stock in these little children," said I, "and I'll arrange a little publicity."

We assembled a number of boys and girls one morning in Independence Park and from there we arranged to parade with banners to the court house where we would hold a meeting. A great crowd gathered in the public square in front of the city hall. I put the little boys with their fingers off and hands crushed and maimed on a platform. I held up their mutilated hands and showed them to the crowd and made the statement that Philadelphia's mansions were built on the broken bones, the quivering hearts and drooping heads of these children. That their little lives went out to make wealth for others. That neither state or city officials paid any attention to these wrongs. That they did not care that these children were to be the future citizens of the nation.

The officials of the city hall were standing the open windows. I held the little ones of the mills high up above the heads of the crowd and pointed to their puny arms and legs and hollow chests. They were light to lift.

I called upon the millionaire manufactures to cease their moral murders, and I cried to the officials in the open windows opposite, "Some day the workers will take possession of your city hall, and when we do, no child will be sacrificed on the altar of profit."

The officials quickly closed the windows, as they had closed their eyes and hearts.

The reporters quoted my statement that Philadelphia mansions were built on the broken bones and quivering hearts of children. The Philadelphia papers and the New York papers got into a squabble with each other over the question. The universities discussed it. Preachers began talking. That was what I wanted. Public attention on the subject of child labor.

The matter quieted down for a while and I concluded the people needed stirring up again. The Liberty Bell that a century ago rang out for freedom against tyranny was touring the country and crowds were coming to see it everywhere. That gave me an idea. These little children were striking for some of the freedom that childhood ought to have, and I decided that the children and I would go on a tour.

I asked some of the parents if they would let me have their little boys and girls for a week or ten days, promising to bring them back safe and sound. They consented. A man named Sweeny was marshal for our "army." A few men and women went with me to help with the children. They were on strike and I thought, they might as well have a little recreation.

The children carried knapsacks on their backs which was a knife and fork, a tin cup and plate. We took along a wash boiler in which to cook the food on the road. One little fellow had a drum and another had a fife. That was our band. We carried banners that said, "We want more schools and less hospitals." "We want time to play." "Prosperity is here. Where is ours?"

We started from Philadelphia where we held a great mass meeting. I decided to go with the children to see President Roosevelt to ask him to have Congress pass a law prohibiting the exploitation of childhood. I thought that President Roosevelt might see these mill children and compare them with his own little ones who were spending the summer on the seashore at Oyster Bay. I thought too, out of politeness, we might call on Morgan in Wall Street who owned the mines where many of these children's fathers worked.

The children were very happy, having plenty to eat, taking baths in the brooks and rivers every day. I thought when the strike is over and they go back to the mills, they will never have another holiday like this. All along the line of march the farmers drove out to meet us with wagon loads of fruit and vegetables. Their wives brought the children clothes and money. The interurban trainmen would stop their trains and give us free rides.

Marshal Sweeny and I would go ahead to the towns and arrange sleeping quarters for the children, and secure meeting halls. As we marched on, it grew terribly hot. There was no rain and the roads were heavy with dust. From time to time we had to send some of the children back to their homes. They were too weak to stand the march.

We were on the outskirts of New Trenton, New Jersey, cooking our lunch in the wash boiler, when the conductor on the interurban car stopped and told us the police were coming down to notify us that we could not enter the town. There were mills in the town and the mill owners didn't like our coming.

I said, "All right, the police will be just in time for lunch." Sure enough, the police came and we invited them to dine with us. They looked at the little gathering of children with their tin plates and cups around the wash boiler. They just smiled and spoke kindly to the children, and said nothing at all about not going into the city.

We went in, held our meeting, and it was the wives of the police who took the little children and cared for them that night, sending them back in the morning with a nice lunch rolled up in paper napkins.

Everywhere we had meetings, showing up with living children, the horrors of child labor. At one town the mayor said we could not hold a meeting because he did not have sufficient police protection. "These little children have never known any sort of protection, your honor" I said, "and they are used to going without it." He let us have our meeting. One night in Princeton, New Jersey, we slept in the big cool barn on Grover Cleveland's great estate. The heat became intense. There was much suffering in our ranks, for our little ones were not robust. The proprietor of the leading hotel sent for me. "Mother," he said, "order what you want and all you want for your army, and there's nothing to pay."

I called on the mayor of Princeton and asked for permission to speak opposite the campus of the University. I said I wanted to speak on higher education. The mayor gave me permission. A great crowd gathered, professors and students and the people; and I told them that the rich robbed these little children of any education of the lowest order that they might send their sons and daughters to places of higher education. That they used the hands and feet of little children that they might buy automobiles for their wives and police dogs for their daughters to talk French to. I said the mill owners take babies almost from the cradle. And I showed those professors children in our army who could scarcely read or write because they were working ten hours a day in the silk mills of Pennsylvania.

"Here's a text book on economics," I said pointing to a little chap, James Ashworth, who was ten years old and who was stooped over like an old man from carrying bundles of yarn that weighed seventy-five pounds. "He gets three dollars a week and his sister who is fourteen gets six dollars. They work in a carpet factory ten hours a day while the children of the rich are getting their higher education."

That night we camped on the banks of Stony Brook where years and years before the ragged Revolutionary Army camped, Washington's brave soldiers that made their fight for freedom.

From Jersey City we marched to Hoboken. I sent a committee over to the New York Chief of Police, Ebstein, asking for permission to march up Fourth Avenue to Madison Square where I wanted to hold a meeting. The chief refused and forbade our entrance to the city.

I went over myself to New York and saw Mayor Seth Low. The mayor was most courteous but he said he would have to support the police commissioner. I asked him what the reason was for refusing us entrance to the city and he said that we were not citizens of New York.

"Oh, I think we will clear that up, Mr. Mayor," I said. "Permit me to call your attention to an incident which took place in this nation just a year ago. A piece of rotten royalty came over here from Germany, called Price Henry. The Congress of the United States voted $45,000 to fill that fellow's stomach for three weeks and to entertain him. His highness was getting $4,000,000 dividends out of the blood of the workers in this country. Was he a citizen of this land?"

"And it was reported, Mr. Mayor, that you and all the officials of New York and the University Club entertained that chap." And repeated, "Was he a citizen of New York!"

"No, Mother," said the mayor, "he was not."

"And a Chinaman called Lee Woo was also entertained by the officials of New York. Was he a citizen of New York?"

"No, Mother, he was not."

"Did they ever create any wealth for our nation!"

"No, Mother, they did not," said he.

"Well, Mr. Mayor, these are the little citizens of the nation and they also produce its wealth. Aren't we entitled to enter your city!"

"Just wait," says he, and he called the commissioner of police over to his office. Well, finally they decided to let the army come in. We marched up Fourth Avenue to Madison Square and police officers, captains, sergeants, roundsmen and reserves from three precincts accompanied us. But the police would not let us hold a meeting in Madison Square. They insisted that the meeting be held in Twentieth Street.

I pointed out to the captain that the single taxers were allowed to hold meetings in the square. "Yes," he said, "but they won't have twenty people and you might have twenty thousand." We marched to Twentieth Street. I told an immense crowd of the horrors of child labor in the mills around the anthracite region and I showed them some of the children. I showed them Eddie Dunphy, a little fellow of twelve, whose job it was to sit all day on a high stool, handing in the right thread to another worker. Eleven hours a day he sat on the high stool with dangerous machinery all about him. All day long, winter and summer, spring and fall, for three dollars a week.

And then I showed them Gussie Rangnew, a little girl from whom all the childhood had gone. Her face was like an old woman's. Gussie packed stockings in a factory, eleven hours a day for a few cents a day.

We raised a lot of money for the strikers and hundreds of friends offered their homes to the little ones while we were in the city. The next day we went to Coney Island at the invitation of Mr. Bostick who owned the wild animal show The children had a wonderful day such as they never had in all their lives. After the exhibition of the trained animals, Mr. Bostick let me speak to the audience. There was a back drop to the tiny stage of the Roman Coliseum with the audience painted in and two Roman emperors down in front with their thumbs down. Right in front of the emperors were the empty iron cages of the animals. I put my little children in the cages and they clung to the iron bars while I talked.

I told the crowd that the scene was typical of the aristocracy of employers with their thumbs down to the little ones of the mills and factories, and people sitting dumbly by.

"We want President Roosevelt to hear the wail of the children who never have a chance to go to school but work eleven and twelve hours a day in the textile mills of Pennsylvania; who weave the carpets that he and you walk upon and the lace curtains in your windows, and the clothes of the people. Fifty years ago there was a cry against slavery and men gave up their lives to stop the selling of black children on the block. Today the white child is sold for two dollars a week to the manufacturers. Fifty years ago the black babies were sold C.O.D. Today the white baby is sold on the installment plan.

"In Georgia where children work day and night in the cotton mills they have just passed a bill to protect song birds. What about little children from whom all song is gone?

"I shall ask the president in the name of the aching hearts of these little ones that he emancipate them from slavery. I will tell the president that the prosperity he boasts of is the prosperity of the rich wrung from the poor and the helpless.

"The trouble is that no one in Washington cares. I saw our legislators in one hour pass three bills for the relief of the railways but when labor cries for aid for the children they will not listen.

"I asked a man in prison once how he happened to be there and he said he had stolen a pair of shoes. I told him if he had stolen a railroad he would be a United States Senator.

"We are told that every American boy has the chance of being president. I tell you that these little boys in the iron cages would sell their chance any day for good square meals and a chance to play. These little toilers whom I have taken from the mills—deformed, dwarfed in body and soul, with nothing but toil before them—have never heard that they have a chance, the chance of every American male citizen, to become the president.

"You see those monkeys in those cages over there." I pointed to a side cage. "The professors are trying to teach them to talk. The monkeys are too wise for they fear that the manufacturers would buy them for slaves in their factories."

I saw a stylishly dressed young man down in the front of the audience. Several times he grinned. I stopped speaking and pointing to him I said, "Stop your smiling, young man! Leave this place! Go home and beg the mother who bore you in pain, as the mothers of these little children bore them, go home and beg her to give you brains and a heart."

He rose and slunk out, followed by the eyes of the children in the cage. The people sat stone still and out in the rear a lion roared.

The next day we left Coney Island for Manhattan Beach to visit Senator Platt, who had made an appointment to see me at nine o'clock in the morning. The children got stuck in the sand banks and I had a time cleaning the sand off the littlest ones. So we started to walk on the railroad track. I was told it was private property and we had to get off. Finally a saloon keeper showed us a short cut into the sacred grounds of the hotel and suddenly the army appeared in the lobby. The little fellows played "Hail, hail, the gang's all here" [on] their fifes and drums, and Senator Platt when he saw the little army ran away through the back door to New York.

I asked the manager if he would give children breakfast and charge it up to the Senator as we had an invitation to breakfast that morning with him. He gave us a private room and he gave those children such a breakfast as they had never had in all their lives. I had breakfast too, and a reporter from one of the Hearst papers and I charged it all to Senator Platt.

We marched down to Oyster Bay but the president refused to see us and he would not answer my letters. But our march had done its work. We had drawn the attention of the nation to the crime of child labor. And while the strike of the textile workers in Kensington was lost and the children driven back to work, not long afterward the Pennsylvania legislature passed a child labor law that sent thousands of children home from the mills, and kept thousands of others from entering the factory until they were fourteen years of age.

The Wobblies, the "Little Red Song Book," and The Legacy of Joe Hill (1879–1915)

The name Joe Hill is inseparable from the history of the Industrial Workers of the World (the IWW, or Wobblies), labor songs, and an esprit de corps among those on the side of workers' rights. Founded in 1905, the IWW had a vision of "one big union" that would not only improve conditions in the here and now for all workers, but would revolutionize the whole society. The Preamble to the IWW constitution declares: "The working class and the employing class have nothing in common. There can be no peace so long as hunger and want are found among millions of working people, and the few, who make up the employing class, have all the good things of life." The IWW faced brutal hostility and vigilante violence in its campaigns for free speech and for a radical unionism that would unify all workers in an international solidarity. Songs—witty, sarcastic parodies and stirring anthems—were highly portable and enjoyable organizing tools, sung to familiar tunes and intended "to fan the flames of discontent." The IWW published its first edition of the *Little Red Song Book* in 1909, and there have been over thirty editions since, including more than 180 songs. With its red paper cover and pocket size, the *Little Red Song Book* is a genuine example of culture for and by workers, intended to instruct, build morale, and poke fun at the owning class. Included in this section are Ralph H. Chaplin's enduring anthem "Solidarity Forever," T-Bone Slim's witty "The Popular Wobbly," and selected songs by Joe Hill.

Perhaps the most gifted and prolific songwriter of them all, Joe Hill gave collective voice and cultural meaning to forgotten workers and itinerant laborers. His songs and life personified the idealism and fighting spirit of the Wobblies. His death—seemingly larger than his life—became a powerful symbol of labor struggle and generated memorable cultural responses, such as Alfred Hayes's poem, "I Dreamed I Saw Joe Hill Last Night" (1925), set to music by Earl Robinson and sung internationally by Paul Robeson and later by

Joan Baez. Self-described "wharf-rat" and artist, Joe Hill was a working-class poet who happened to be in Salt Lake City, Utah, the night of a double murder in 1914. Accused, convicted, and condemned to death on circumstantial evidence and within a highly hostile judicial system, his definite innocence or guilt has never been clearly determined. But many saw him then and see him now as a labor martyr and hero. In one of his farewell letters, he wrote, "Don't waste any time mourning, organize!" a line—part secular prayer, part urgent message—that has become iconic in American labor history.

Joe Hill or Joseph Hillstrom (his first Americanized name) was born Joel Emmanuel Hagglund on October 7, 1879, in Gavle, Sweden, one of six surviving children in a religious and musical family. His father was injured and subsequently died when Joel was eight years old, and Joel was treated for tuberculosis as a young boy, enduring several operations. After the death of his mother around 1900, the family home was sold and the family was split up. Joel and his brother Paul emigrated to the United States in 1902, having the advantage over other immigrants of speaking English. He worked in New York and Chicago at various laboring jobs and changed his name to Joe Hill supposedly to avoid blacklisting for organizing workers. He joined the IWW in 1910 in San Pedro, California, and became a secretary of the local and apparently was involved in several strikes, including the dockworkers' strike in San Pedro in 1912. Hill worked intermittently, traveled, and wrote songs and poems as life circumstances transformed him from hopeful immigrant to, in his own words, "a rebel true-blue" by the time he arrived in Utah and was accused of murder in January 1914.

Losing his petition for a new trial, and despite the letters and petitions of the Swedish ambassador to the United States, of Helen Keller, and even of President Woodrow Wilson to the governor of Utah, Hill was executed by firing squad on November 9, 1915. One of his staunchest defenders was Elizabeth Gurley Flynn, a strike leader for the IWW and a great orator and activist for labor and free speech. Hill's song, "The Rebel Girl," was written while he was in prison and is dedicated to "Gurley" Flynn. Included here are the song's lyrics, Hill's letter to Flynn written the night before his death, and Flynn's reflections on his life and death as told from her own Wobbly perspective.

Hill's legacy has not died. Kenneth Patchen's poem, "Joe Hill Listens to the Praying" (in Part V) evokes Hill's memory in the context of the 1930s, and Cheri Register, in her memoir of growing up as a "packinghouse daughter" (2000), inscribes her own Minnesota memories of labor and community onto the life of Joe Hill.

Elizabeth Gurley Flynn, Joe Hill—Martyred Troubador of Labor

After the gruesome year of 1914, relieved only by a trip to Tampa, I was glad to go on a cross-country speaking trip in 1915, my first to California. I visited many cities I had never seen—Denver, a mile high in the Rockies, Salt Lake City, with its windswept wide streets and long blocks, Los Angeles, and last but not least in my memory—the fairest of them all—San Francisco.

The outstanding event on this trip was my visit to Joe Hill in the County Jail in Salt Lake City. He was a troubador of the IWW, who wrote songs "to fan the flames of discontent." Some were written to popular tunes, some to religious airs and some to his own musical composition. They were very catchy and were heard at IWW street and hall meetings, on picket lines and in jails from coast to coast. Sometimes he played the piano in meetings to accompany his songs. Among his most famous songs are "Casey Jones," "Mr. Block," "Long Haired Preachers" or "Pie in the Sky," "Workers of the World Awaken," "Hallelujah, I'm a Bum," and two anti-war songs, "Don't Take My Papa Away from Me" and "Should I Ever Be a Soldier." While in prison he sent me a copy of "The Rebel Girl" which he wrote there and dedicated to me.

Joe Hill's full name was Joseph Hillstrom. He was an immigrant from Sweden who had drifted to the West and become a migratory worker. What caused him to stand out and to become a target for employers' special attacks were his songs. He had been active in the San Diego free speech fight. The IWW had been trying in 1914 to organize the copper mines owned by the Guggenheim interests. Joe went there and was active in an IWW strike at Tucker, Utah, involving 1,500 miners. In January 1914 a holdup and murder of a grocery man occurred in Salt Lake City. The police looked for IWWs to fasten the crime upon, and a crude frame-up was created against Joe Hill. It was built around his refusal to give an alibi and the fact that he had been shot that night. The story was that he had had a love affair with a married woman and to the day of his execution he refused to name her or her husband who presumably had shot him. The legal case was the flimsiest imaginable, but so great was the fear and prejudice against the IWW that it was made to stick.

I had never met Joe Hill before I went to see him in jail. He was tall, slender, very blond, with deep blue eyes. He was 31 years old—"the age when Jesus was crucified," he said to me. We sat in the sheriff's office, looking out the open barred door at the wide expanse of a beautiful lawn. It was spring in the garden city of Salt Lake, encircled by great mountains, crowned with eternal snows. In springtime its green shimmer, high altitude, and clear pure air were like wine. But the familiar fetid jail odor assailed the nostrils, the clang of the keys, the surly permission to enter, the damp air loaded with the sickening smell of disinfectants, all marked the prison abode. It was the first time Joe had been allowed to receive a visitor in the office and to shake hands with a visitor. The head jailer was one of the detectives who made up the case and they hoped that Joe would "talk." He was expected to prove himself innocent.

He had little to say to me about his case. I knew his appeal—taken over at the eleventh hour by Judge O. N. Hilton, long the chief counsel of the Western Federation of Miners—was pending. The case was a legal mess because his first lawyer, a local Socialist, was timid and inept and had made no real defense, had registered no proper objections and exceptions to "protest the record," as the lawyers put it. Joe finally stood up in court and fired him, telling the judge he did not need two prosecutors. The judge reappointed the same lawyer forthwith and Joe refused to participate further in the case. Joe had questioned at one time the advisability of an appeal because of the expense involved but we had persuaded him otherwise. In spite of all the legal difficulties, we were optimistic as to the outcome, with the victories of Moyer, Haywood and Pettibone, and Ettor and Giovannitti behind us.

Joe Hill did not share our optimism but he did not oppose our efforts. He said to me: "*I am not afraid of death, but I'd like to be in the fight a little longer.*" He saw I was downcast as I left. A feeling of foreboding clutched my heart as I said good-bye to him. He joked about a bearded old man mowing the lawn outside. "He's lucky, Gurley. He's a Mormon and he's had two wives and I haven't even had one yet!" I can see him standing behind the barred door, "smiling with his eyes" as the modern song describes. Many young people of today may think Joe Hill is a mythical figure, like Paul Bunyan. They know him only through the song with its haunting refrain, "I never died, said he." The real story of this martyred troubador of the IWW is a tragic chapter of the infamous frame-up system against workers.

Judge Hilton came East and laid all the information before the Swedish Minister, W. A. F. Ekengren, who had heard from Sweden of tremendous protests there. He interceded with President Wilson, who had no power in a state case. However, he sent a request to Governor Spry of Utah, and the execution which was set for October 1 was postponed to allow the Swedish Minister to present his views to the governor. While Judge Hilton was in New York City, I introduced him to Mr. and Mrs. J. Sargent Cram. Mrs. Cram was a liberal, an avowed pacifist. Prior to World War I she rented stores in various parts of the city for neighborhood exhibitions of Robert Minor's magnificent antiwar cartoons. She made all her appointments at the swanky Colony Club in New York and occasionally took me to her summer home in Old Westbury, Long Island. She introduced me to Judge Lovett, president of the Union Pacific Railroad, who lived in a palatial home nearby and who was "amazed" that I thought he had "influence" with the governor of Utah. She also introduced me to one of the Guggenheims, owners of the mines in Utah. For me it was like talking to creatures from another planet!

Judge Hilton and I went to Long Island to see Mr. Cram. He was a portly, bald-headed, shrewd Democratic politician who thought we were all slightly goofy. But he was impressed with Judge Hilton's presentation of the case and he liked me as "a sensible woman," particularly because I enjoyed the rare wines from his cellar. So he agreed to arrange an interview with President Woodrow Wilson for Mrs. Cram and me. We had gone once before on September 28, 1915, to try to see him, but had been referred then to Acting Secretary of State Polk. Mr. Cram had led the New York delegation to vote for Wilson at the nominating convention and had easy access to the White House.

We went down on November 11, 1915. We had breakfast with Gifford Pinchot, Mrs. Cram's Republican brother-in-law, who escorted us to the White House. Mr. Tumulty, the President's Secretary, was friendly. He knew of me from the Paterson strike of 1913. When the President came in he greeted us cordially, in fact he held Mrs. Cram's hand. He listened attentively while we presented our appeal. He said he had once intervened at the request of the Swedish Minister. He wondered if further insistence might do more harm than good. Not knowing the etiquette of talking to the President, I interrupted: "But he's sentenced to death. You can't make it worse, Mr. President." He smiled and said: "Well, that's true!" and promised to consider the matter.

As the days passed we felt that our mission had failed. But fortunately the American Federation of Labor, meeting in San Francisco, wired a plea on November 17 to the President, signed by Samuel Gompers. President Wilson, under pressure, sent a second message to Governor Spry as follows: "With unaffected hesitation but with a very earnest consideration of the importance of the case, I again venture to urge upon Your Excellency the justice and advisability of a thorough reconsideration of the case of Joseph Hillstrom." Governor Spry curtly rejected this message from the President of the United States as "unwarranted interference."

In Utah a condemned man had the right to choice—to be hanged or to be shot by a firing squad. It was a remnant of the old West. Joe chose to be shot. On November 19, 1915, five masked men, one with a blank in his gun, were brought to the prison in a carriage with all the curtains drawn so the identities of those who fired the fatal shots would be unknown. Joe's last words were: "*Don't mourn, organize.*" His wish "not to be found dead in the state of Utah," was respected and the IWW took his body to Chicago for cremation. I was unable to attend because of my pending trial in Paterson. Judge Hilton was the principal speaker at the services in Ashland Auditorium and because of his speech he was disbarred in the state of Utah from further practice there. This is the first labor case I know of where a lawyer was penalized for defending his client. It was a forerunner of such a procedure against similar attorneys over three decades later in Smith Act cases.

JOE HILL, THE REBEL GIRL

There are women of many descriptions
In this queer world, as everyone knows.
Some are living in beautiful mansions,
And are wearing the finest of clothes.
5   There are blue blooded queens and princesses,

Cover art from the *Joe Hill Songbook*, "The Rebel Girl." *IWW Collection, Walter P. Reuther Library, Wayne State University.*

Who have charms made of diamonds and pearl;
But the only and thoroughbred lady
Is the Rebel Girl.

Chorus
That's the Rebel Girl, that's the Rebel Girl!
10   To the working class she's a precious pearl.
She brings courage, pride and joy
To the fighting Rebel Boy.
We've had girls before, but we need some more
In the Industrial Workers of the World.
15   For it's great to fight for freedom
With a Rebel Girl.

Yes, her hands may be hardened from labor,
And her dress may not be very fine;
But a heart in her bosom is beating
20   That is true to her class and her kind.
And the grafters in terror are trembling
When her spite and defiance she'll hurl;
For the only and thoroughbred lady
Is the Rebel Girl.

Joe Hill, Letter to Elizabeth Gurley Flynn

Salt Lake City Nov. 18. 1915
10-P.M.
Elizabeth Gurley Flynn 511–134th
N.Y. City

Dear Friend Gurley:

I have been saying Good Bye, so much now that it is becoming monotonous but I just cannot help to send you a few more lines because you have been more to me than a Fellow Worker. You have been an inspiration and when I composed The Rebel Girl you was right there and helped me all the time. As you furnished the idea I will, now that I am gone, give you all the credit for that song, and be sure to locate a few more Rebel Girls like yourself because they are needed and needed badly—I gave Busters picture Hilda and she will watch so his pony doesn't run away. With a warm handshake across the continent and a last fond Good-Bye to all. I remain Yours as Ever.

Joe Hill

From *The Little Red Song Book*

PREAMBLE OF THE INDUSTRIAL WORKERS OF THE WORLD

The working class and the employing class have nothing in common. The can be no peace so long as hunger and want are found among millions of the working people and the few, who make up the employing class, have all the good things of life.

Between these two classes a struggle must go on until the workers of the world organize as a class, take possession of the earth and the machinery of production, and abolish the wage system.

We find that the centering of the management of industries into fewer and fewer hands makes the trade unions unable to cope with the ever growing power of the employing class. The trade unions foster a state of affairs which allows one set of workers to be pitted against another set of workers in the same industry, thereby helping to defeat one another in wage wars. Moreover, the trade unions aid the employing class to mislead the workers into the belief that the working class have interests in common with their employers.

These conditions can be changed and the interest of the working class upheld only by an organization formed in such a way that all its members in any one industry, or in all industries if necessary, cease work whenever a strike or lockout is on in any department thereof, thus making an injury to one an injury to all.

Instead of the conservative motto, "A fair day's wage for a fair day's work," we must inscribe on our banner the revolutionary watchword, "Abolition of the wage system."

It is the historic mission of the working class to do away with capitalism. The army of production must be organized, not only for the everyday struggle with capitalists, but also to carry on production when capitalism shall have been overthrown. By organizing industrially we are forming the structure of the new society within the shell of the old.

JOE HILL, THE TRAMP

If you all will shut your trap,
I will tell you 'bout a chap,
That was broke and up against it, too, for fair
He was not the kind that shirk,
5   He was looking hard for work,
But he heard the same old story everywhere:

Chorus:
Tramp, tramp, tramp, keep on a-tramping,
Nothing doing here for you;
If I catch you 'round again,
10   You will wear the ball and chain,
Keep on tramping, that's the best thing you can do.

He walked up and down the street,
'Till the shoes fell off his feet,
In a house he spied a lady cooking stew,
15   And he said, "How do you do,
May I chop some wood for you?"
What the lady told him made him feel so blue:

Chorus

'Cross the street a sign he read,
"Work for Jesus," so it said,
20   And he said, "Here is my chance, I'll surely try."
And he kneeled upon the floor,
'Till his knees got rather sore,
But at eating-time he heard the preacher cry:

Chorus

Down the street he met a cop,
25   And the Copper made him stop,
And he asked him, "When did you blow into town?
Come with me up to the judge."
But the judge he said, "Oh, fudge,
Bums that have no money needn't come around."

Chorus

30   Finally came that happy day
When his life did pass away,
He was sure he'd go to heaven when he died.
When he reached the pearly gate,
Santa Peter, mean old skate,
35   Slammed the gate right in his face and loudly cried:

Chorus

In despair he went to Hell,
With the Devil for to dwell,
For the reason he'd no other place to go.
And he said, "I'm full of sin,
40   So for Christ's sake, let me in!"
But the Devil said, "Oh, beat it! You're a 'bo!"

Chorus

RALPH CHAPLIN, SOLIDARITY FOREVER!

(Tune: "John Brown's Body")

When the Union's inspiration through the worker's blood shall run,
There can be no power greater anywhere beneath the sun.
Yet what force on earth is weaker than the feeble strength of one?
    But the Union makes us strong.

Chorus
5   Solidarity forever!
    Solidarity forever!
    Solidarity forever!
    But the Union makes us strong.

    Is there aught we hold in common with the greedy parasite
10 Who would lash us into serfdom and would crush us with his might?
    Is there anything left for us but to organize and fight?
        For the Union makes us strong.

    It is we who plowed the prairies; built the cities where they trade.
    Dug the mines and built the workshops; endless miles of railroad laid.
15 Now we stand, outcast and starving, 'mid the wonders we have made;
        But the Union makes us strong.

    All the world that's owned by idle drones, is ours and ours alone.
    We have laid the wide foundations; built it skywards, stone by stone.
    It is ours, not to slave in, but to master and to own,
20   While the Union makes us strong.

    They have taken untold millions that they never toiled to earn.
    But without our brain and muscle not a single wheel can turn.
    We can break their haughty power; gain our freedom when we learn
        That the Union makes us strong.

25 In our hands is placed a power greater than their hoarded gold;
    Greater than the might of armies, magnified a thousand fold.
    We can bring to birth the new world from the ashes of the old,
        For the Union makes us strong.

JOE HILL, THE PREACHER AND THE SLAVE

(Tune: "Sweet Bye and Bye")

Long-haired preachers come out every night,
Try to tell you what's wrong and what's right;
But when asked how 'bout something to eat
They will answer with voices so sweet:

Chorus
5   You will eat, bye and bye,
    In that glorious land above the sky;
    Work and pray, live on hay,
    You'll get pie in the sky when you die.

And the starvation army they play,
10   And they sing and they clap and they pray,
Till they get all your coin on the drum,
Then they tell you when you're on the bum:

Holy Rollers and Jumpers come out,
And they holler, they jump and they shout
15   "Give your money to Jesus," they say,
"He will cure all diseases today."

If you fight hard for children and wife—
Try to get something good in this life—
You're a sinner and bad man, they tell,
20   When you die you will sure go to hell.

Workingmen of all countries, unite,
Side by side we for freedom will fight:
When the world and its wealth we have gained
To the grafters we'll sing this refrain:

Last Chorus
25   **You will eat, bye and bye,**
When you've learned how to cook and to fry;
Chop some wood, 'twill do you good,
And you'll eat in the sweet bye and bye.

T-BONE SLIM, THE POPULAR WOBBLY

(*Air: "They Go Wild, Simply Wild Over Me"*)

I'm as mild manner'd man as can be
And I've never done them harm that I can see,
Still on me they put a ban and they threw me in the can,
They go wild, simply wild over me.

5   They accuse me of ras—cal—i—ty
But I can't see why they always pick on me,
I'm as gentle as a lamb, but they take me for a ram,
They go wild, simply wild over me.

Oh the "bull" he went wild over me
10   And he held his gun where everyone could see,
He was breathing rather hard when he saw my union card—
He went wild, simply wild over me.

Then the judge he went wild over me
And I plainly saw we never would agree,
15   So I let the man obey what his conscience had to say,
He went wild, simply wild over me.

Oh the jailer went wild over me
And he locked me up and threw away the key—
It seems to be the rage so they keep me in a cage,
20   They go wild, simply wild over me.

They go wild, simply wild over me,
I'm referring to the bed-bug and the flea,
They disturb my slumber deep and I murmur in my sleep,
They go wild, simply wild over me.

25   Even God, he went wild over me,
This I found out when I knelt upon my knee,
Did he hear my humble yell? No, he told me "Go to hell,"
He went wild, simply wild over me.

Will the roses grow wild over me
30   When I'm gone to the land that is to be?
When my soul and body part in the stillness of my heart—
Will the roses grow wild over me?

JOE HILL'S LAST WILL

(Written in his cell, November 18, 1915, on the eve of his execution.)

My will is easy to decide,
For there is nothing to divide.
My kin don't need to fuss and moan—
"Moss does not cling to a rolling stone."
5   My body? Ah, if I could choose,
I would to ashes it reduce,
And let the merry breezes blow
My dust to where some flowers grow.
Perhaps some fading flower then
10   Would come to life and bloom again.
This is my last and final will.
Good luck to all of you,

JOE HILL.

RALPH CHAPLIN, MOURN NOT THE DEAD

Mourn not the dead that in the cool earth lie—
    Dust unto dust—
The calm sweet earth that mothers all who die
    As all men must;

5   Mourn not your captive comrades who must dwell—
    Too strong to strive—
Within each steel bound coffin of a cell,
    Buried alive;

But rather mourn the apathetic throng—
10   The cowed and the meek—
Who see the world's great anguish and its wrong
    And dare not speak!

ALFRED HAYES, JOE HILL

I dreamed I saw Joe Hill last night
Alive as you or me
Says I, But Joe, you're ten years dead
I never died, says he
5 I never died, says he

In Salt Lake, Joe, says I to him
Him standing by my bed
They framed you on a murder charge
Says Joe, But I ain't dead
10 Says Joe, But I ain't dead

The copper bosses killed you, Joe
They shot you, Joe, says I
Takes more than guns to kill a man
Says Joe, I didn't die
15 Says Joe, I didn't die

And standing there as big as life
And smiling with his eyes
Joe says, What they forgot to kill
Went on to organize
20 Went on to organize

Joe Hill ain't dead, he says to me
Joe Hill ain't never died
Where working men are out on strike
Joe Hill is at their side
25 Joe Hill is at their side

From San Diego up to Maine
In every mine and mill
Where workers strike and organize
Says he, You'll find Joe Hill
30 Says he, You'll find Joe Hill

I dreamed I saw Joe Hill last night
Alive as you or me
Says I, But Joe, you're ten years dead
I never died, says he
35 I never died, says he

CHERI REGISTER, A DREAM OF JOE HILL

"I dreamed I saw Joe Hill last night alive as you or me," a popular labor song begins. I don't literally dream about Joe Hill, but the IWW troubadour has haunted my waking hours since I first read about him in novelist John Dos Passos's *U.S.A.* My discovery of Dos Passos while still in high school endures as a literary and political epiphany. Joe Hill, a Swedish

immigrant allegedly framed on a murder charge by antilabor schemers and executed in 1915, seemed a perfect hero for a Scandinavian-American girl from a working-class family, especially one with literary aspirations and a passion for history. As a martyred songwriter, he stirred my imagination, and as an itinerant laborer born Joel Hägglund in a country next door to my ancestral Denmark, he could help push my roots a little deeper.

That's what I reminded myself when Swedish director Bo Widerberg's film *Joe Hill* arrived at the Varsity Theater in Minneapolis's Dinkytown neighborhood in 1971. I had recently moved away from the campus of the University of Chicago, where I often felt displaced among fellow intellectuals unfamiliar with factory whistles and the tense uncertainty of a long-lasting strike. Yet I felt no more at home in my new life. My husband, fresh out of law school, had been hired by a prestigious Minneapolis law firm that paid its new associates nearly twice as much as my dad was earning after twenty-eight years of skilled labor. We were flush enough to be homeowners already, which had taken my parents fourteen years of married life, carpentry skills, and a mail-order catalog of house blueprints. A dose of Joe Hill promised both a familiar anchor and the excitement of the new: a rare chance to listen to Swedish dialogue. I had made one last attachment to home by pursuing a Ph.D. in Scandinavian languages and literatures.

Walking from the car to the theater alongside my wary husband, who preferred James Bond to Joe Hill, I replayed Grandma Petersen's boastful stories about hiding in the fruit trees at age twelve when she heard the *tap-tap* of the cane her employer, the orchard owner, used on his inspection and disciplinary rounds. I wondered what stories Grandpa might have told about the cigar factory, had I taken time to ask him. Joe Hill had left Sweden just five years before my grandpa arrived in America, perhaps with similar dreams of "scraping gold off the streets."

The movie was a disappointment, and I soon chimed in with my husband's whispered cynical commentary. Actor Thommy Berggren was too sleek and fine-featured to be a convincing laborer. I had expected a body type I recognized, one that showed the effects of hefting sheaves of wheat and prying copper loose from walls of rock. I wanted him to be an average Joe, a man-on-*my*-street. (Now, having seen photographs of Joe Hill, I realize that casting Thommy Berggren was not farfetched. Joe Hill was just a bit lankier and more craggy-faced, a familiar type of Swedish physiognomy.)

The film's story of capitalist cruelty versus worker idealism was too simplistic to engage my intellect or to further my budding understanding of the factional disputes in labor organizing. Despite their plea for "one big union" and their creativity and vitality, the Industrial Workers of the World—the "Wobblies"—captured only the fringe of the labor movement. They were certainly not the whole of it, as the movie would have us believe. Worst of the disappointments, the movie's dialogue wasn't even in Swedish. Of course, the setting was America and Joe Hill had presumably left the oppressive narrowness of Swedish culture behind. Never mind the historical record, which, though meager, shows that he frequently sought shelter with other Swedish immigrants as he roamed the country.

Hard as I tried to keep pace with my husband's cynicism, however, I was soon blinded by the hazy wash of light that bathed Joe/Thommy's lovely face in glory. I sniffed. I dabbed at my eyes. I mocked myself for being undone, once again, by the manipulative sentimentality of a dumb tearjerker. Finally, at the end of the movie, nostalgia for his homeland overtakes poor doomed Joe Hill and he utters a bit of Swedish. As he stands blindfolded before the firing squad, a bird chirps and sings beyond the prison wall. Joe cocks his head to listen. "*Fågel*"—"bird"—he whispers just before the guns go off. I left the theater red-eyed, clutching my saturated Kleenex, with my disgruntled husband clucking at my side.

I wasn't at all prepared for what happened next. As we headed toward Bridgeman's Ice Cream, where we would likely rehash and pan the movie, three young men, dressed like the student radicals at the nearby University of Minnesota, came striding by, singing Joe Hill songs at full voice in a triumphant camaraderie. Their joy should have been contagious. What better high could there be than to leave a movie singing? A surge of emotion nearly lifted me from the sidewalk, but instead of joining in the chorus, I burst into sobs. This was not the sentimental sorrow the movie had evoked, but the righteous anger of the deprived, the disinherited.

The realization struck hard: I had never sung a Joe Hill song, had never even heard one sung until college introduced me to Folkways records. We didn't sing Joe Hill at Christmas parties in Albert Lea's Union Center. I don't remember hearing a single labor song during the Wilson strike of 1959, when silence was prudence. There was no Joe Hill sheet music on our battered, out-of-tune basement piano, no renditions of Joe Hill songs in our collection of 78-RPM records. I wondered if Grandma and Grandpa Petersen even knew of him, if his execution had been reported in the Danish-American newspapers, assuming they even subscribed. The year of his death was the year they lost their first little girl to brain fever. Private sorrows always overwhelm public tragedy. That seemed to be the case even now, for me.

I cried out of grief for my lost heritage, but the hurt ran deeper than that. I was jealous and angry over these boys' gleeful appropriation of what was rightfully mine, over their acceptance of moviedom's mythologized Joe Hill as a symbol for the grueling work, the curtailed aspirations, the arbitrary decisions, the physical dangers that shaped the lives of blue-collar families. And now they were carrying him back to campus, where his songs would nourish their self-styled, unthreatened radicalism on the University's grassy mall. I had a sudden inclination to throw the man out with the myth. Joe Hill may be worth dreaming about, but neither his song lyrics nor his martyrdom told the truth as I knew it. He was a hero for those privileged to rally around the glorious margins of labor-movement history without ever wading into its turbid mainstream. And yet I wanted him so badly to be an icon for me, torn as I was between pragmatism and poetry.

"*Fågel, fågel*," whispered in my brain the following week. Where was that bird? How did it manage to fly away? Where were the songs that ought to have fed my dad's spirit as he packed up his dinner pail and drove off to the packinghouse before dawn, just as the birds began tuning up for the day? Where was the songbird that could have parried the accusations cast at the strikers, turned them into satire, let us laugh and sing and feel radical as we drowned out the opposition with Joe Hill's own "pie in the sky"? When I pronounced the word "bird" in Danish—*fugl*—I thought I had hit on an answer. *Fugl* to an English speaker sounds like "fool." "Fool," I guessed, is how Dad would characterize the young, naive Joe Hill, so carried away by idealism that he'd forget to watch his back, so convinced of his righteousness that he'd put others in jeopardy for the sake of an unattainable vision. Dad wouldn't say all this. "Foolish" would be enough—as foolish as the Wilson strikers who threw rocks at scabs' cars, thinking this could stop the company's efforts at union-busting. As foolish as the nightriders who broke windows and burned down corncribs in unrestrained surges of bitterness. They risked losing their jobs forever and forgot to think twice about jeopardizing their fellow workers with families to support and dwindling possibilities at forty, forty-five, fifty. Our family's hero was not the songbird with the wild fantasies but the plodding drafthorse, organizing, negotiating, attention riveted on the point-by-point compromise. I hadn't known Joe Hill, but the face of CIO President John L. Lewis, bushy eyebrows drawn inward for his signature scowl, had been etched in my memory since early childhood.

The labor songs I never learned to sing still stir me to tears and incite me to an anger that has no clear object. Sometimes I want to bite the singer, but that's no consolation. Pete Seeger, for example, is so benign, so gentle. How can I begrudge him his genuine sympathy for the miner's plight, just because his musical talent and cultured Manhattan upbringing spared him from descending into the dark stagnation of the mine day after day? Often, I glare at the stomping, cheering audience, whooping in scornful glee at the singer's lampoon of the boss's greed. "What do *you* know?" I want to demand. Sometimes I just look away in shame, silenced by a gnawing suspicion that if these songs truly represent working-class culture, then what I have lived is not the real thing.

Why not just accept the Joe Hill legend as romanticized history, as innocently distorted as Johnny Appleseed or as Davy Crockett killing a b'ar when he was only three? Why not just enjoy the sing-along, as though it were "Oh, Susanna" or "Yankee Doodle," melodic ditties whose original meaning has been left behind in a past irrelevant to present needs? Why not refuse to listen altogether, ignore the rowdy chorus and hide away in the tiny niche I've earned among the intelligentsia? I am welcome to drown my sorrows in Vivaldi and Mahler on public-radio broadcasts. As I consider these obvious, reasonable questions, each song I add to the repertoire becomes another provocation.

"That's the Rebel Girl, that's the Rebel Girl, to the working class she's a precious pearl." I'd like to pretend we sang this song around the kitchen table, that my parents taught me Elizabeth Gurley Flynn's defiant courage. But it was not the Rebel Girl I longed to be. It was the Clearasil Personality of the Month, her smooth, blemish-free face spread across the shiny pages of *Teen* magazine, which also listed her supergirl accomplishments: straight As, first chair violin, hospital candystriper, homecoming queen. Joe Hill, even as Thommy Berggren, was no match for Frankie Avalon and Fabian, true working-class troubadours— urban ethnic greasers—who crooned about teenage romance, the most pressing problem in my little world. Would Joe Hill, reimagined as an outlaw hero-of-the-people for a TV western, have torn me away from *Gunsmoke*? We working-class kids were subject to the same empty but persuasive commercial culture that seduced most American children of the 1950s and 1960s. Without a television set, it might have been different. Or maybe not. My sisters, who listened to swing bands and the strange harmonies of the Four Lads and the Four Freshmen on the radio, were even less acquainted with Joe Hill. We did learn to sing one labor song, I remember now: *"Look for the union label."* It was performed as a radio and television jingle promoting the International Ladies' Garment Workers Union. We took the message to heart, too. Turning clothes inside out at Penney's to find the union "bug" sewn into the seam became my family's ritual of solidarity. No, that's badly overstated. We just did because it was right.

Dream of Joe Hill alive as you or me? I was more likely to dream that I walked the picket line in my Maidenform bra. Maybe that silly magazine advertisement holds the key to my tangled maze of emotions. Why would a fantasy of being exposed in public in my underwear induce me to buy Maidenform? Why would a self-conscious teenager, obsessed with the competitive pace of anatomic development, give in to such perversion? I wouldn't be caught dead in my Maidenform bra, with or without a union label. To be caught in public stumbling over the lyrics to "The Preacher and the Slave" is equally humiliating. Better to avoid the risk altogether, or to impute dishonest motives to the people who sing along easily. Consider this actual dream:

I am teaching a class, sitting at a table before rows of college students at desks with writing arms. The music of "The Internationale" begins playing outside the classroom windows. A few students immediately stand up, reverently, at attention. Gradually, others join them, though these students look either confused or apprehensive. I rise up partway, unsure whether this song is indeed "The Internationale." I'm afraid I might have it mixed up with "La Marseillaise," and I don't need to stand for that, since I'm not French. Uncertainty keeps me in an awkward crouch until the very last verse, when I decide it has to be "The Internationale" and lurch upright, unnaturally stiff. I'm greatly embarrassed, having exposed my ignorance to my students.

The day after I awoke from that dream, snatches of the melody kept playing in my mind. I wanted to sing along, but of course I didn't know the words. The dream, I concluded, smug in my reading of its symbolism, was about "taking a stand," which is not as easy as it might seem.

"Which side are you on? Which side are you on?" Never has this song struck my ears so discordantly as it did in 1985, in the turmoil of the Hormel strike in Austin, Minnesota. The lyrics presuppose a clear choice, and told to check a box for labor or management, I would not hesitate. My loyalties are firm. I do not cross picket lines. But when the complexities of survival in a declining economy degenerate into a simplistic either/or choice, a "with us or against us" ultimatum, I balk. Witnessing the support of Twin Cities intellectuals for Austin's Local P-9, which was conducting a strike of its own despite negotiations underway by the United Food and Commercial Workers international union, I felt shamefully ambivalent, as if I were being asked to choose between bread and roses, between slow, persistent, behind-the-scenes argument and a showy gamble for total justice. Friends and acquaintances spoke with enthusiasm about the rallies and fund-raisers they were attending on behalf of the Hormel workers. They expected I'd be there, or at least be impressed by their allegiance to my people. They thought they were speaking my native tongue. Some even thought I was from Austin, a common but annoying error. I seldom felt that I could explain my dampened enthusiasm intelligibly, or as succinctly as the occasion required. Nor could I talk about the awful vulnerability I felt when my ambivalence was exposed. Which side *was* I on?

Nothing about Austin is simple for an Albert Lea girl. Like a favored sister, Austin, in my teenage years, had everything we wanted: a strip-mall shopping center, a junior college, specialist doctors, a Frank Lloyd Wright house, the Terp ballroom with live rock and roll, well-equipped athletic teams that consistently beat ours, Scholastic Aptitude Tests (college-bound Albert Lea kids had to drive to Austin to take the SAT), easy girls who stole away our boyfriends, smooth-talking boys who seduced our best friends. Our parents, too, had much to envy: a benevolent hometown meatpacking company that paid well, offered bonuses when profits were up, treated its employees respectfully, and never threatened to pull out of town at contract time. Hormel's hadn't had a strike since the organizing days of the 1930s, thanks to the company's "me too" policy: after the workers at Armour, Cudahy, Swift, and Wilson had battled out a master agreement, Hormel's went with the terms, and then some.

Even after the tide turned at Hormel's and the reward system was trimmed back, the Austin workers had the best pay scale in the meatpacking industry. The company's withdrawal of profit-sharing incentives still left them better off, in plain wages, than their counterparts in Albert Lea. Wilson workers, remember, cut back from a base wage of $10.69 to $6.50 by the company's bankruptcy, had gone on strike and renegotiated pay at $8.50. Though this was a drastic cut in income most people realized that no more could be pumped from a drying well. With fears of the plant closing altogether, it was not easy to work up sympathy for dissatisfied but better-off neighbors. Bucking the national union and refusing the concessions called for in the industry-wide contract might put the long-term job security of packinghouse workers across the country at risk. The Hormel strike was, on its face, a courageous stand, a simple insistence on what's right, but, considering the trend toward bankruptcies, downsizing, and plant closings, it looked self-destructive.

I was eager to know where Dad stood, but he, normally garrulous and opinionated, seemed to be avoiding conversation. It hurts a great deal to admit that your strongest loyalties are suffering strain. At the mention of Ray Rogers, the charismatic showman brought in to lead a "corporate campaign" directed at Hormel's stockholders and business investments, Dad's hackles rose a bit. He shook his head and muttered, "Leading them down the primrose path." A songbird, a *fugl*, I suspected, who might even fly low enough to eat the bread crumbs that could show the lost souls their way back home. Years later, someone offered, as a semi-apology for Rogers, that his most valuable contribution was the creation of a "strike culture" that the local leadership could never have inspired. It was fun to hang around the union hall. There was real spirit there. A rousing chorus of Joe Hill songs, I imagined, to ease the bitterness of lost jobs and long-lasting animosities.

This time a movie affirmed rather than provoked my sensitivities. Barbara Kopple's Academy Award–winning *American Dream*, a documentary about the Hormel strike, debuted in Austin on a weekend when I was visiting my parents in Albert Lea. I mentioned it to Dad but got no response. When it turned up at my neighborhood theater several weeks later, I determined to go, but not alone and certainly not with a cynic. I called my old Albert Lea friend Linda. Our junior high friendship had survived the Wilson strike, even though her dad, a salesman, had to report for work across the picket line. Linda's husband Dick, a therapist who works with teenage lawbreakers, had made regular weekly visits to a group home in Austin all through the strike. He could see beyond the rebellious fervor to the toll it took on families. Tears dribbled down our faces as we watched the strike come to life on-screen and relived the ache of ambivalence. Kopple had left the complexities unresolved and had let the players speak for themselves, though of course she kept the privilege of editing their words. There were no romantic heroes, no happy tunes to hum. Some members of the audience clearly wanted it otherwise. They laughed knowingly with Ray Rogers whenever he said something clever. They booed at Lewie Anderson, the dogged negotiator for the UFCW. Afterward, Linda, Dick, and I took refuge in a restaurant down the street, where we spent an hour in intense but sober conversation. Had someone dared to burst into labor songs in that charged atmosphere, I might have burst into bits.

I really do long to sing. I'd love to send my quaking, middle-aged voice soaring in a chorus of "*Oh, you can't scare me, I'm stickin' to the union. I'm stickin' to the union till the day I die.*" Most labor songs are feel-good songs, meant to charge up the crowd and pare away any hint of pessimism, any factional differences, any subtleties that dim belief in the common vision: society will reward work fairly. They are meant to be sung heartily the way Welsh church congregations sing, not like the old joke about Unitarians, who can't sing with gusto because they are too busy reading ahead to see if they agree with what comes next. But these are difficult times for singing. Can music stem the disappearance of blue-collar jobs from the U.S. economy? I still look for the union label whenever I shop for clothes, but I rarely see one. "Made in El Salvador," "Made in Macao," the labels say. What songs do the garment workers sing while they work for pennies an hour in the maquiladoras, turning out clothing that produces megadollars for big-name fashion designers? Perhaps because the labor situation has deteriorated so badly, casting greed and poverty in such stark, unambiguous relief, I am feeling the necessity for song, for a swooping flock of noisy birds to keep the chorus going. I have even begun to sing along.

One Saturday night I had arranged to go out with my friend Sara for a rare evening without our kids. Dinner and a movie was the original plan, but thumbing through the newspaper, I had come upon a feature article about Joe Glaser, a seventy-five-year-old man billed as "labor's troubadour" who was performing that evening as the finale of a conference on "Arts in Solidarity." I was curious, intrigued, and wary. Sara is one friend I can trust with my mistrust of romanticism about the working class. A history professor who teaches and writes about American women's history, she is exceedingly sane and fair on the subject of labor history, which overlaps her own field in ways other scholars often ignore. My dad has bestowed his highest mark of approval on Sara. "Real common and ordinary," he called her once, and she and I laughed at how those words would sound to her proper, Carolina-bred mother, to whom they mean crass and unmannered.

"There's a concert of labor songs," I began. "Oh, let's go!" Sara urged. She needed to learn a few new ones, she said, for her undergraduate survey course in U.S. history. In sessions billed as "history karaoke," she flashes lyrics on the overhead projector and invites the class to sing songs commemorating the events they are studying. "I don't know," I balked. "If it's a bunch of intellectuals playing at working-class radicalism, I may wish I hadn't come." When I checked to see where it was being held, my fears eased a little. The Machinists' Union local on the industrial edge of Sara's middle-class neighborhood certainly wouldn't tolerate sham labor-symps.

Sara had been taking a course on stress relief that required her to spend forty-five minutes a day listening to a taped "body scan" exercise. She had saved it for my arrival, so we spent the start of the evening stretched out on our backs in a near-hypnotic state, though the monotone voice on the tape kept assuring us that we were "fully aware." When I finally peeled myself off the carpet and stood on rubber legs, I felt resilient enough for any provocation, like one of those weighted children's toys that refuses to be knocked over.

Still, I lingered over our dinner at a neighborhood café, not wanting to be among the first to arrive for the concert. Like a secular Jew or a lapsed Catholic at holy day services, I wanted to slip in unnoticed and not risk betraying myself by responding shyly to a hearty greeting or bumbling a new ritual I hadn't learned. There were just a few parking spaces left when we pulled into the lot alongside the Machinists' Hall. Inside, folding chairs were arranged in rows, already three-quarters filled with elderly couples, families with children, and a few political activists. We recognized at least one other history professor.

I don't know if it was the residue of the relaxation tape or the comfort of home that settled over me as Sara and I draped our jackets over two chairs at the end of the second row. The setting was so familiar, the union hall just as utilitarian and unadorned— all Sheetrock and linoleum, just as permeated with cigarette smoke as the meeting room in Albert Lea's Union Center where I had recently spent hours looking through strike memorabilia. A labor-history exhibit brought in for the occasion lined one long wall of the room. Just to my right stood a panel headed "Minnesota National Guard vs. Packinghouse Workers" with a subheading "Albert Lea, 1959." I stepped over, took off my glasses, and leaned in close to check out the three newspaper pages displayed, then smiled to myself when I spotted Chuck Lee, the retired president of Local 6, whom I had recently interviewed. He had told me that the iww was the first union to try to organize the packinghouse. The "Independent" Workers of the World, he called them. Wobblies in Albert Lea? Humming on the hog kill? Why hadn't I known? (Actually, it was the Independent Union of All Workers, no direct relation to the iww, though its chief organizer, Frank Ellis of Austin, had been a Wobbly.)

The emcee for the evening, a man about forty years old named Mike, stepped up onto the low platform that functioned as a stage and called us all to attention. He had the muscular, foreshortened arms, the barrel chest, and squat neck of a man whose job demands body strength. "My kind of guy," I whispered to Sara, recalling the adult men of my family and my old neighborhood, a different species from Cary Grant and Gregory Peck. Mike introduced Joe Glaser, an elderly man I had noticed wandering around the room, in and out of conversations with the crowd, seemingly unconcerned about turning his personality "on" for a performance. He ambled up to the stage, chatted a bit with Mike, opened the conversation to us, his audience, then sang a couple of rousing songs. This was no star from the Coast flown in first-class for the show. The lights never dimmed, no spot-light set him apart from the rest of us. "Labor's troubadour" was hardly a death-defying, righteousness-exuding romantic hero; he was just an old guy with a clear voice and a good heart, whose vocation is to make songs of a truck driver's weekly routine and the grievances of hospital employees out on strike. Pragmatic poetry, you might call it.

With a generosity most audiences would neither expect nor tolerate, he quickly invited up some of the locals who were leaning around the edges of the room with guitars slung over their shoulders or resting on their laps. Larry Long, an institution on the Twin Cities folk-and-protest-music scene, sang a song he wrote not just about but *with* seven women who walked out of the American Linen Company in Hibbing, an Iron Range city with a vigorous history of labor conflict. There was not a "union maid" or a "rebel girl" among them—just Ruth and Bev and their coworkers. A UPS driver from the Teamsters' Union put in a pitch for part-time workers like herself, a mom who wanted time to pass on her union legacy to her children. Her contribution was a Marvin Gaye song done a cappella because no one in the group could provide the instrumentation to match. Except for the guitars, the instruments were make-do. An ensemble of AFSCME members—clerical employees from the university—and their children played bongos, homemade drums, and plastic ice-cream pails, to accompany a rap they had written on newsprint and taped to the wall.

I was glad it was Sara sitting next to me. I could be sure that she would find this event fun and even a bit silly. She'd make no effort to exalt it as the prelude to a proletarian revolution. On the other hand, there would be no eye-rolling to contend with, no belittling chuckles, not even the puzzled silence and polite applause of the respectful outsider. I could think of other friends who might have relished the amateur performances as kitsch. My limbs still humming with stress-free pleasure, I was content to set my misgivings aside and let the event be what it was. We, the audience, had been invited to witness a proud display of shared values and renewed hopes, and we were welcome to sing along. I sang in full voice.

As I reviewed the evening, later, its historical meaning became clear. This was not a celebration of burly stevedores tossing cargo into the bay, nor a lament for miners trapped in the shaft while their wives weep at the gate. The New American Worker is a mom in her thirties risking carpal tunnel syndrome, eyestrain, and the unexamined dangers of electromagnetism in order to boost her kids a little higher on the social scale.

Joe Hill did make his requisite appearance. A local folksinger, Barb Tilsen, interwove the lyrics of "Joe Hill" with a poem by Meridel Le Sueur which makes reference to Joe Hill's death and the legendary distribution of his ashes to IWW locals around the country. She didn't tell us, but surely many of us knew that Barb Tilsen is Meridel Le Sueur's granddaughter, one of a family of politically engaged Tilsens noted for their support of labor and human-rights issues. I felt a twinge of envy—oh, to be the heir of this inspired family line—and then came sorrow about all that isn't said and isn't passed from one generation to the next in "common and ordinary" families. Had I been born a Tilsen, I would surely be teaching labor songs to my children. Of course the Tilsens are not laborers. The family matriarch was a poet with labor sympathies and radical politics that got her blacklisted and kept her literary career muffled for decades. Her son-in-law is a lawyer who represents the underdog—sometimes a political activist prosecuted on a possibly concocted felony charge, the modern-day Joe Hill. The Tilsens are troubadours, songbirds. Let them sing.

As I drove home from the concert, with two of Joe Glaser's tapes tucked in my purse, I finally came to terms with my attraction and resistance to Joe Hill. I am not a songbird, neither *fågel* nor *fugl*. Nor am I the all-suffering drafthorse. A troubadour in prose is the best I can be. I will learn to sing out in my own dry, critical voice, lightened by a touch of whimsy, my saving grace in this divisive world:

I Dreamed I Saw Joe Hill Last Night . . . in My Maidenform Bra

I dreamed I saw Joe Hill last night, alive as you or me. Well, not quite that alive. He was looking thin and ashen-faced. The smell of his musty black coat nearly bowled me over.

"*Hej* Joe," I said. "*Det är 80 långa år sen du gick bort.*" You're eighty years dead!

"*Jag har aldrig dött,*" *sade han.* "I never died," said he.

As I shook his bony hand, the skin of his palm flaked onto mine. He saw me wipe my hand against my skirt, and he gave me a wistful look.

"It takes more than guns to kill a man," he sighed.

"You're a martyr to the cause you loved," I said. "It's a great honor."

"Don't you know it!" he said. "I fell hard for this martyr business. I just didn't expect to end up as a *gengångare*."

"What's that, Joe?" I interrupted.

"*Gengångare*, a ghost, one of those restless souls doomed to wander until their mission is accomplished."

"Or vengeance is done," I caught on. "Like Elsalill in Selma Lagerlöf's story."

"Right. It's just wander and wander endlessly," he complained. "*From San Diego up to Maine, in every mine and mill, where workers strike and organize, it's there you'll find Joe Hill.* That's a whole lot more traveling than I bargained for."

"Sounds like you need some rest," I said, as I gave him a comforting pat on the shoulder. A puff of dust and mold rose up out of his coat and I turned away to stifle a cough.

"*Ja,*" he nodded. "The working class needs a new troubadour, one with a little more energy than I've got left."

"There's Joe Glaser," I suggested, "though he's getting a bit old. We have Larry Long right here in Minnesota, and of course Pete Seeger's been trying for years. Would Bruce Springsteen do?"

"Naw," he protested. "Gotta pay your dues. It's gotta be somebody who can still feel the work in his muscles."

"You're not looking at me then," I said with some relief.

"No, no. You're too prosy . . . and you think too much."

But he *was* looking at me, and it was getting very disconcerting. I found it harder and harder to make contact with his glazed eyes. He kept looking at my chest. I should have known; another hero unmasked. Elizabeth Gurley Flynn's good friend was just an everyday male with a boob fixation.

I dropped my eyes, dejected, and immediately felt the blood course up my neck and into my cheeks. I was talking to Joe Hill in my Maidenform bra!

"What is that thing?" he asked, after a long silence. "*Vad är det för något?*"

"A bra . . ." I began.

"*Bra, ja,*" he laughed. "You can say that again." Of course. *Bra* means "good" in Swedish.

"The bra—the brassiere—took over for corsets and camisoles about a decade after you died, or didn't die as the case may be. I'm not sure it's an improvement."

He stepped closer, hunched his pointed shoulders, and jutted his long Swedish jaw toward my chest. "Look at that workmanship," he mused. "How do they shape that fabric and keep those tiny seams flat? Must be some skilled sewers in that Garment Union."

"I hate to tell you this, Joe, but the union label is deader than you are. There's hardly even a garment factory left in the United States."

"So who made this, uh, bra then?"

"I don't know," I said as I spun around. "If you flip that band in the back over, you'll find a label right near the hooks. Tell me what it says."

He kept a tight grip on the elastic as he leaned back to focus his vision on the tiny printing. "Made in Hon-du-ras," he sounded out. "Where's that?"

"It's a country in Central America." I said, "where union organizers disappear mysteriously and people work for next to nothing. I wouldn't be surprised if this bra was cut and stitched by a line of fifteen-year-old girls."

"Central America?" he moaned. "Way down south of Mexico? I thought my territory was San Diego to Maine."

"It's called the globalization of the economy," I scoffed, "just a fancy term for drawing higher profits out of low-wage workers in impoverished parts of the world."

"Well, I'm off to Honduras then," he sighed. "No rest for the *gengångare.*"

"Not unless we find you a replacement," I suggested.

"Or an avenger," he added. He was staring off into the horizon with a forlorn expression. Suddenly his head cocked to one side and he held up his hand to shush me.

"*Fågel*," he whispered.

I listened, and I began to hear it too: a sweet melody far off in the distance. I strained to tune it in. The song was in Spanish. I could pick up only scattered words: *Trabajadoras. Libertad.*

I wound my arm gently around his fragile waist. "*Kom, Julle Hägglund*," I said, addressing him by his childhood name. "We'll find her. She's going to give Joe Hill a long-deserved rest."

Sarah N. Cleghorn (1876–1959)

On January 23, 1915, the *New York Tribune* published Sarah Cleghorn's potent four-line poem linking men golfers and children mill workers. This observant poem, crafted after a visit to a South Carolina cotton factory, is indicative of Cleghorn's socially committed writing and life. Cleghorn was born in Virginia, the daughter of a Scottish immigrant and an investment banker, and moved to Vermont after the death of her mother. She was raised in Manchester by two aunts, and there she befriended writer Dorothy Canfield Fisher, with whom she would collaborate on two books of essays. She wrote poems, essays, an autobiography, letters to newspapers, and novels. A Quaker, Cleghorn was educated at Radcliffe College and became keenly interested in educational reform and education for workers. She taught at Brookwood School in Katonah, New York, which was connected with the worker education movement. Cleghorn was also a proponent of Montessori schools for children and later taught at Vassar College. She was active in major reform movements of her day—peace, women's suffrage, antilynching, prison reform, and, as the poem would suggest, opposition to child labor. She joined the Socialist Party in 1911. Her books include *A Turnpike Lady* (1907), *The Spinster* (1916), *Portraits and Protests* (1917), *Ballad of Eugene Debs* (1928), *Threescore: The Autobiography of Sarah N. Cleghorn* (1936), *Poems of Peace and Freedom* (1945), and *The Seamless Robe* (1945).

Through the needle's eye

1. Comrade Jesus

Thanks to Saint Matthew, who had been
At mass meetings in Palestine,
We know whose side was spoken for
When Comrade Jesus had the floor.

5   "Where sore they toil and hard they lie,
Among the great unwashed, dwell I.
The tramp, the convict, I am he;
Cold-shoulder him, cold-shoulder me."

By Dives' door, with thoughtful eye,
10   He did tomorrow prophesy.
"The kingdom's gate is low and small;
The rich can scarce wedge through at all."

"A dangerous man," said Caiaphas,
"An ignorant demagogue, alas,
15   Friend of low women, it is he
Slanders the upright Pharisee."

For law and order, it was plain
For holy church, he must be slain.
The troops were there to awe the crowd
20   And "violence" was not allowed.

The clumsy force with force to foil
His strong, clean hands he would not soil.
He saw their childishness quite plain
Between the lightnings of his pain.

25   Between the twilights of his end
He made his fellow-felon friend;
With swollen tongue and blinding eyes
Invited him to paradise.

2. Quatrain

The golf links lie so near the mill
   That almost every day
The laboring children can look out
   And see the men at play.

Carl Sandburg (1878–1967)

One of the most popular and prolific American writers, Carl Sandburg wrote poetry, biography, history, fiction, and journalism. He was a broadcaster, a writer of children's stories, and a singer and collector of folk songs. He was also a committed socialist, who saw his work with words—whether written, spoken, or sung—as a celebration of the energy and diversity of his "people" and a critique of the injustices that marked the rapid industrialization of the first half of the twentieth century. As a poet, Sandburg shared both the democratic vision and some of the formal experimentation of Walt Whitman, about whom he lectured under the title "An American Vagabond." As he wrote in the preface to *The American Songbag* (1927), a collection of folksongs gathered during his travels throughout the United States, "A wide human procession marches through these pages. . . . Pioneers, pick and shovel men, teamsters, mountaineers, and people often called ignorant have their hands and voices in this book." This claim applies equally to his own poetry.

Sandburg was born in Galesburg, Illinois, the son of Swedish immigrants; his father worked on the railroad, his mother as a hotel maid. Quitting school after the eighth grade, Sandburg worked as a delivery boy and a housepainter and spent time hoboing out west in search of work before enlisting in 1898 for service in the Spanish-American War. He attended Lombard College in his hometown, leaving without a degree but with a passion for reading and writing poetry. After several years of traveling as a salesman and lecturer, Sandburg settled in Milwaukee, where he worked as an organizer for the Social-Democratic Party and as secretary to Milwaukee's socialist mayor. He moved in 1912 to Chicago, the city with which his writing is most associated, where he wrote for the *Chicago Evening World* and other newspapers. His first recognition as a poet came in 1914, when "Chicago" appeared in the journal *Poetry*, to be followed by the collection, *Chicago Poems*, published in 1916.

Sandburg's other major works include *Smoke and Steel* (poems, 1920), *Abraham Lincoln: The Prairie Years* (1927), *The People, Yes* (1936, excerpted here), *Abraham Lincoln: The War Years* (1939, Pulitzer Prize in history), *Rememberance Rock* (1948, his only novel), and *Complete Poems* (1950, Pulitzer Prize in poetry). His *Rootabaga Stories* and *Poetry for Young People* also remain in print today.

CHICAGO

Hog Butcher for the World,
Tool Maker, Stacker of Wheat,
Player with Railroads and the Nation's Freight Handler;
Stormy, husky, brawling,
5   City of the Big Shoulders:

They tell me you are wicked and I believe them, for I have seen your painted
    women under the gas lamps luring the farm boys.
And they tell me you are crooked and I answer: Yes, it is true I have seen the
    gunman kill and go free to kill again.
And they tell me you are brutal and my reply is: On the faces of women and
    children I have seen the marks of wanton hunger.

And having answered so I turn once more to those who sneer at this my city, and
    I give them back the sneer and say to them:
10   Come and show me another city with lifted head singing so proud to be alive and
    coarse and strong and cunning.
Flinging magnetic curses amid the toil of piling job on job, here is a tall bold
    slugger set vivid against the little soft cities;
Fierce as a dog with tongue lapping for action, cunning as a savage pitted against
    the wilderness,
Bareheaded,
Shoveling,
15   Wrecking,
Planning,
Building, breaking, rebuilding,
Under the smoke, dust all over his mouth, laughing with white teeth,
Under the terrible burden of destiny laughing as a young man laughs,
20   Laughing even as an ignorant fighter laughs who has never lost a battle,
Bragging and laughing that under his wrist is the pulse, and under his ribs the heart
    of the people,
Laughing!
Laughing the stormy, husky, brawling laughter of Youth, half-naked, sweating,
    proud to be Hog Butcher, Tool Maker, Stacker of Wheat, Player with Railroads
    and Freight Handler to the Nation.

MUCKERS

Twenty men stand watching the muckers.
    Stabbing the sides of the ditch
    Where clay gleams yellow,
    Driving the blades of their shovels
5   Deeper and deeper for the new gas mains,
    Wiping sweat off their faces
      With red bandanas.

The muckers work on . . . pausing . . . to pull
Their boots out of suckholes where they slosh.

10   Of the twenty looking on
Ten murmur, "O, it's a hell of a job,"
Ten others, "Jesus, I wish I had the job."

CHILD OF THE ROMANS

The dago shovelman sits by the railroad track
Eating a noon meal of bread and bologna.
    A train whirls by, and men and women at tables
    Alive with red roses and yellow jonquils,
5   Eat steaks running with brown gravy,
    Strawberries and cream, eclairs and coffee.

The dago shovelman finishes the dry bread and bologna,
Washes it down with a dipper from the water-boy,
And goes back to the second half of a ten-hour day's work
10   Keeping the road-bed so the roses and jonquils
Shake hardly at all in the cut glass vases
Standing slender on the tables in the dining cars.

FROM *THE PEOPLE, YES*

     The people will live on.
The learning and blundering people will live on.
     They will be tricked and sold and again sold
And go back to the nourishing earth for rootholds,
5   The people so peculiar in renewal and comeback,
     You can't laugh off their capacity to take it.
The mammoth rests between his cyclonic dramas.

The people so often sleepy, weary, enigmatic,
is a vast huddle with many units saying:
10   "I earn my living.
I make enough to get by
and it takes all my time.
If I had more time
I could do more for myself
15   and maybe for others.
I could read and study
and talk things over
and find out about things.
It takes time.
20   I wish I had the time."
The people is a tragic and comic two-face:
hero and hoodlum: phantom and gorilla
twisting to moan with a gargoyle mouth:
"They buy me and sell me . . . it's a game . . .
25   sometime I'll break loose . . ."

     Once having marched
Over the margins of animal necessity,
Over the grim line of sheer subsistence
     Then man came
30   To the deeper rituals of his bones,
To the lights lighter than any bones,
To the time for thinking things over,
To the dance, the song, the story;
Or the hours given over to dreaming,
35   Once having so marched.

Between the finite limitations of the five senses
and the endless yearnings of man for the beyond
the people hold to the humdrum bidding of work and food

while reaching out when it comes their way
40   for lights beyond the prisms of the five senses,
for keepsakes lasting beyond any hunger or death.
    This reaching is alive.
The panderers and liars have violated and smutted it.
    Yet this reaching is alive yet
45   for lights and keepsakes.

The people know the salt of the sea
and the strength of the winds
lashing the corners of the earth.
The people take the earth
50   as a tomb of rest and a cradle of hope.
Who else speaks for the Family of Man?
They are in tune and step
with constellations of universal law.

The people is a polychrome,
55   a spectrum and a prism
held in a moving monolith,
a console organ of changing themes,
a clavilux of color poems
wherein the sea offers fog
60   and the fog moves off in rain
and the labrador sunset shortens
to a nocturne of clear stars
serene over the shot spray
of northern lights.

65   The steel mill sky is alive.
The fire breaks white and zigzag
Shot on a gun-metal gloaming.
Man is a long time coming.
Man will yet win.
70   Brother may yet line up with brother:

This old anvil laughs at many broken hammers.
    There are men who can't be bought.
    The fireborn are at home in fire.
    The stars make no noise.
75   You can't hinder the wind from blowing.
    Time is a great teacher.
    Who can live without hope?

In the darkness with a great bundle of grief
    the people march.
80   In the night, and overhead a shovel of stars for
    keeps, the people march:
                           "Where to? what next?"

Lola Ridge (1873–1941)

The author of "The Ghetto," a remarkable poem of Jewish life in and around New York's Hester Street, came to the city as an adult immigrant by way of Ireland, Australia, and New Zealand. Born Rose Emily Ridge in Dublin, she experienced poverty both before and after moving with her mother to New Zealand, where her stepfather, a miner of Scots descent, was apparently given to violent rages. Ridge attended Trinity College in Sydney, Australia, and studied painting at an arts academy before returning to New Zealand at age twenty-two as the wife of the manager of a gold mine. The marriage dissolved sometime before Ridge moved to the United States in 1907, eventually settling in New York's Greenwich Village and adopting the preferred name Lola, under which she would later begin her career as a poet and literary editor. In the meantime, she supported herself as a factory worker, model, illustrator, and writer of advertising copy.

The poem that established Ridge's reputation first appeared in *The New Republic* in 1918 and was published in *The Ghetto and Other Poems* the same year. Reviewers quickly noted the power and freshness of her vision of what Louis Untermeyer called the city's beauties and brutalities: "'The Ghetto' is at once personal in its piercing sympathy and epical in its sweep. . . . It glows with a color that is barbaric, exotic, and as local as Grand Street." Epithets like "barbaric" and "exotic" were common in reference to immigrant communities of America's large cities, but what is striking about Ridge's achievement in "The Ghetto" is the way in which its nine chapters, arranged in a distinctly modernist montage of fluid scenes and images, evoke the sharp complexities of Jewish American identities, male and female, without reducing them to stereotype.

Ridge published regularly in small radical journals, such as Emma Goldman's *Mother Earth*, as well as mainstream literary journals. She became a contributing editor at *New Masses* in 1926. Four volumes of poetry followed *The Ghetto*: *Sun-Up and Other Poems* (1920), *Red Flag* (1927), *Firehead* (1929), and *Dance of Fire* (1935).

THE GHETTO

I

Cool, inaccessible air
Is floating in velvety blackness shot with steel-blue lights,
But no breath stirs the heat
Leaning its ponderous bulk upon the Ghetto
5   And most on Hester street . . .

The heat . . .
Nosing in the body's overflow,
Like a beast pressing its great steaming belly close,
Covering all avenues of air . . .

10 The heat in Hester street,
Heaped like a dray
With the garbage of the world.

Bodies dangle from the fire escapes
Or sprawl over the stoops . . .
15   Upturned faces glimmer pallidly—
Herring-yellow faces, spotted as with a mold,
And moist faces of girls
Like dank white lilies,
And infants' faces with open parched mouths that suck at the air
20   as at empty teats.

Young women pass in groups,
Converging to the forums and meeting halls,
Surging indomitable, slow
Through the gross underbrush of heat.
25   Their heads are uncovered to the stars,
And they call to the young men and to one another
With a free camaraderie.
Only their eyes are ancient and alone . . .

The street crawls undulant,
30   Like a river addled
With its hot tide of flesh
That ever thickens.
Heavy surges of flesh
Break over the pavements,
35   Clavering like a surf—

Flesh of this abiding
Brood of those ancient mothers who saw the dawn break over Egypt . . .
And turned their cakes upon the dry hot stones
And went on
40   Till the gold of the Egyptians fell down off their arms . . .
Fasting and athirst . . .
And yet on . . .

Did they vision—with those eyes darkly clear,
That looked the sun in the face and were not blinded—
45   Across the centuries
The march of their enduring flesh?
Did they hear—
Under the molten silence
Of the desert like a stopped wheel—
50   (And the scorpions tick-ticking on the sand . . .)
The infinite procession of those feet?

II

I room at Sodos'—in the little green room that was Bennie's—
With Sadie
And her old father and her mother,
55   Who is not so old and wears her own hair.

Old Sodos no longer makes saddles.
He has forgotten how.
He has forgotten most things—even Bennie who stays away
   and sends wine on holidays—
60 And he does not like Sadie's mother
Who hides God's candles,
Nor Sadie
Whose young pagan breath puts out the light—
That should burn always,
65 Like Aaron's before the Lord.

Time spins like a crazy dial in his brain,
And night by night
I see the love-gesture of his arm
In its green-greasy coat-sleeve
70 Circling the Book,
And the candles gleaming starkly
On the blotched-paper whiteness of his face,
Like a miswritten psalm . . .
Night by night
75 I hear his lifted praise,
Like a broken whinnying
Before the Lord's shut gate.

Sadie dresses in black.
She has black-wet hair full of cold lights
80 And a fine-drawn face, too white.
All day the power machines
Drone in her ears . . .
All day the fine dust flies
Till throats are parched and itch
85 And the heat—like a kept corpse—
Fouls to the last corner.

Then—when needles move more slowly on the cloth
And sweaty fingers slacken
And hair falls in damp wisps over the eyes—
90 Sped by some power within,
Sadie quivers like a rod . . .
A thin black piston flying,
One with her machine.

She—who stabs the piece-work with her bitter eye
95 And bids the girls: "Slow down—
You'll have him cutting us again!"
She—fiery static atom,
Held in place by the fierce pressure all about—
Speeds up the driven wheels
100 And biting steel—that twice
Has nipped her to the bone.

Nights, she reads
Those books that have most unset thought,

New-poured and malleable,
105   To which her thought
Leaps fusing at white heat,
Or spits her fire out in some dim manger of a hall,
Or at a protest meeting on the Square,
Her lit eyes kindling the mob . . .
110   Or dances madly at a festival.
Each dawn finds her a little whiter,
Though up and keyed to the long day,
Alert, yet weary . . . like a bird
That all night long has beat about a light.

115   The Gentile lover, that she charms and shrews,
Is one more pebble in the pack
For Sadie's mother,
Who greets him with her narrowed eyes
That hold some welcome back.
120   "What's to be done?" she'll say,
"When Sadie wants she takes . . .
Better than Bennie with his Christian woman . . .
A man is not so like,
If they should fight,
125   To call her Jew . . ."

Yet when she lies in bed
And the soft babble of their talk comes to her
And the silences . . .
I know she never sleeps
130   Till the keen draught blowing up the empty hall
Edges through her transom
And she hears his foot on the first stairs.

Sarah and Anna live on the floor above.
Sarah is swarthy and ill-dressed.
135   Life for her has no ritual.
She would break an ideal like an egg for the winged thing at the core.
Her mind is hard and brilliant and cutting like an acetylene torch.
If any impurities drift there, they must be burnt up as in a clear flame.
It is droll that she should work in a pants factory.
140   —Yet where else . . . tousled and collar awry at her olive throat.
Besides her hands are unkempt.
With English . . . and everything . . . there is so little time.
She reads without bias—
Doubting clamorously—
145   Psychology, plays, science, philosophies—
Those giant flowers that have bloomed and withered, scattering their seed . . .
—And out of this young forcing soil what growth may come—
      what amazing blossomings.

Anna is different.
150   One is always aware of Anna, and the young men turn their heads
      to look at her.

She has the appeal of a folk-song
And her cheap clothes are always in rhythm.
When the strike was on she gave half her pay.
155   She would give anything—save the praise that is hers
And the love of her lyric body.

But Sarah's desire covets nothing apart.
She would share all things . . .
Even her lover.

III

160   The sturdy Ghetto children
March by the parade,
Waving their toy flags,
Prancing to the bugles—
Lusty, unafraid . . .
165   Shaking little fire sticks
At the night—
The old blinking night—
Swerving out of the way,
Wrapped in her darkness like a shawl.

170   But a small girl
Cowers apart.
Her braided head,
Shiny as a black-bird's
In the gleam of the torch-light,
175   Is poised as for flight.
Her eyes have the glow
Of darkened lights.

She stammers in Yiddish,
But I do not understand,
180   And there flits across her face
A shadow
As of a drawn blind.
I give her an orange,
Large and golden,
185   And she looks at it blankly.
I take her little cold hand and try to draw her to me,
But she is stiff . . .
Like a doll . . .

Suddenly she darts through the crowd
190   Like a little white panic
Blown along the night—
Away from the terror of oncoming feet . . .
And drums rattling like curses in red roaring mouths . . .
And torches spluttering silver fire
195   And lights that nose out hiding-places . . .
To the night—

Squatting like a hunchback
Under the curved stoop—
The old mammy-night
200 That has outlived beauty and knows the ways of fear—
The night—wide-opening crooked and comforting arms,
Hiding her as in a voluminous skirt.

The sturdy Ghetto children
March by the parade,
205 Waving their toy flags,
Prancing to the bugles,
Lusty, unafraid.
But I see a white frock
And eyes like hooded lights
210 Out of the shadow of pogroms
Watching . . . watching . . .

IV

Calicoes and furs,
Pocket-books and scarfs,
Razor strops and knives
215 (Patterns in check . . .)

Olive hands and russet head,
Pickles red and coppery,
Green pickles, brown pickles,
(Patterns in tapestry . . .)

220 Coral beads, blue beads,
Beads of pearl and amber,
Gew gaws, beauty pins—
Bijoutry for chits—
Darting rays of violet,
225 Amethyst and jade . . .
All the colors out to play,
Jumbled iridescently . . .
(Patterns in stained glass
Shivered into bits!)

230 Nooses of gay ribbon
Tugging at one's sleeve,
Dainty little garters
Hanging out their sign . . .
Here a pout of frilly things—
235 There a sonsy feather . . .
(White beards, black beards
Like knots in the weave . . .)
And ah, the little babies—
Shiny black-eyed babies—
240 (Half a million pink toes
Wriggling altogether.)

Baskets full of babies
Like grapes on a vine.

Mothers waddling in and out,
245 Making all things right—
Picking up the slipped threads
In Grand street at night—
Grand street like a great bazaar,
Crowded like a float,
250 Bulging like a crazy quilt
Stretched on a line.

But nearer seen
This litter of the East
Takes on a garbled majesty.

255 The herded stalls
In dissolute array . . .
The glitter and the jumbled finery
And strangely juxtaposed
Cans, paper, rags
260 And colors decomposing,
Faded like old hair,
With flashes of barbaric hues
And eyes of mystery . . .
Flung
265 Like an ancient tapestry of motley weave
Upon the open will of this new land.

Here, a tawny-headed girl . . .
Lemons in a greenish broth
And a huge earthen bowl
270 By a bronzed merchant
With a tall black lamb's wool cap upon his head . . .
He has no glance for her.
His thrifty eyes
Bend—glittering, intent
275 Their hoarded looks
Upon his merchandise,
As though it were some splendid cloth
Or sumptuous raiment
Stitched in gold and red . . .

280 He seldom talks
Save of the goods he spreads—
The meager cotton with its dismal flower—
But with his skinny hands
That hover like two hawks
285 Above some luscious meat,
He fingers lovingly each calico,
As though it were a gorgeous shawl,
Or costly vesture
Wrought in silken thread,

290   Or strange bright carpet
        Made for sandaled feet . . .

        Here an old grey scholar stands.
        His brooding eyes—
        That hold long vistas without end
295   Of caravans and trees and roads,
        And cities dwindling in remembrance—
        Bend mostly on his tapes and thread.

        What if they tweak his beard—
        These raw young seed of Israel
300   Who have no backward vision in their eyes—
        And mock him as he sways
        Above the sunken arches of his feet—
        They find no peg to hang their taunts upon.
        His soul is like a rock
305   That bears a front worn smooth
        By the coarse friction of the sea,
        And, unperturbed, he keeps his bitter peace.

        What if a rigid arm and stuffed blue shape,
        Backed by a nickel star
310   Does prod him on,
        Taking his proud patience for humility . . .
        All gutters are as one
        To that old race that has been thrust
        From off the curbstones of the world . . .
315   And he smiles with the pale irony
        Of one who holds
        The wisdom of the Talmud stored away
        In his mind's lavender.

        But this young trader,
320   Born to trade as to a caul,
        Peddles the notions of the hour.
        The gestures of the craft are his
        And all the lore
        As when to hold, withdraw, persuade, advance . . .
325   And be it gum or flags,
        Or clean-all or the newest thing in tags,
        Demand goes to him as the bee to flower.
        And he—appraising
        All who come and go
330   With his amazing
        Slight-of-mind and glance
        And nimble thought
        And nature balanced like the scales at nought—
        Looks Westward where the trade-lights glow,
335   And sees his vision rise—
        A tape-ruled vision,
        Circumscribed in stone—
        Some fifty stories to the skies.

V

As I sit in my little fifth-floor room—
340   Bare,
Save for bed and chair,
And coppery stains
Left by seeping rains
On the low ceiling
345   And green plaster walls,
Where when night falls
Golden lady-bugs
Come out of their holes,
And roaches, sepia-brown, consort . . .
350   I hear bells pealing
Out of the gray church at Rutgers street,
Holding its high-flung cross above the Ghetto,
And, one floor down across the court,
The parrot screaming:
355   *Vorwärts . . . Vorwärts . . .*

The parrot frowsy-white,
Everlastingly swinging
On its iron bar.

A little old woman,
360   With a wig of smooth black hair
Gummed about her shrunken brows,
Comes sometimes on the fire escape.
An old stooped mother,
The left shoulder low
365   With that uneven droopiness that women know
Who have suckled many young . . .
Yet I have seen no other than the parrot there.

I watch her mornings as she shakes her rugs
Feebly, with futile reach
370   And fingers without clutch.
Her thews are slack
And curved the ruined back
And flesh empurpled like old meat,
Yet each conspires
375   To feed those guttering fires
With which her eyes are quick.

On Friday nights
Her candles signal
Infinite fine rays
380   To other windows,
Coupling other lights,
Linking the tenements
Like an endless prayer.

She seems less lonely than the bird
385   That day by day about the dismal house

Screams out his frenzied word . . .
That night by night—
If a dog yelps
Or a cat yawls
390 Or a sick child whines,
Or a door screaks on its hinges,
Or a man and woman fight—
Sends his cry above the huddled roofs:
Vorwärts . . . Vorwärts . . .

VI

395 In this dingy cafe
The old men sit muffled in woollens.
Everything is faded, shabby, colorless, old . . .
The chairs, loose-jointed,
Creaking like old bones—
400 The tables, the waiters, the walls,
Whose mottled plaster
Blends in one tone with the old flesh.

Young life and young thought are alike barred,
And no unheralded noises jolt old nerves,
405 And old wheezy breaths
Pass around old thoughts, dry as snuff,
And there is no divergence and no friction
Because life is flattened and ground as by many mills.

And it is here the Committee—
410 Sweet-breathed and smooth of skin
And supple of spine and knee,
With shining unpouched eyes
And the blood, high-powered,
Leaping in flexible arteries—
415 The insolent, young, enthusiastic, undiscriminating Committee,
Who would placard tombstones
And scatter leaflets even in graves,
Comes trampling with sacrilegious feet!

The old men turn stiffly,
420 Mumbling to each other.
They are gentle and torpid and busy with eating.
But one lifts a face of clayish pallor,
There is a dull fury in his eyes, like little rusty grates.
He rises slowly,
425 Trembling in his many swathings like an awakened mummy,
Ridiculous yet terrible.
—And the Committee flings him a waste glance,
Dropping a leaflet by his plate.

A lone fire flickers in the dusty eyes.
430 The lips chant inaudibly.
The warped shrunken body straightens like a tree.

And he curses . . .
With uplifted arms and perished fingers,
Claw-like, clutching . . .
435   So centuries ago
The old men cursed Acosta,
When they, prophetic, heard upon their sepulchres
Those feet that may not halt nor turn aside for ancient things.

VII

Here in this room, bare like a barn,
440   Egos gesture one to the other—
Naked, unformed, unwinged
Egos out of the shell,
Examining, searching, devouring—
Avid alike for the flower or the dung . . .
445   (Having no dainty antennae for the touch and withdrawal—
Only the open maw . . .)

Egos cawing,
Expanding in the mean egg . . .
Little squat tailors with unkempt faces,
450   Pale as lard,
Fur-makers, factory-hands, shop-workers,
News-boys with battling eyes
And bodies yet vibrant with the momentum of long runs,
Here and there a woman . . .

455   Words, words, words,
Pattering like hail,
Like hail falling without aim . . .
Egos rampant,
Screaming each other down.
460   One motions perpetually,
Waving arms like overgrowths.
He has burning eyes and a cough
And a thin voice piping
Like a flute among trombones.

465   One, red-bearded, rearing
A welter of maimed face bashed in from some old wound,
Garbles Max Stirner.
His words knock each other like little wooden blocks.
No one heeds him,
470   And a lank boy with hair over his eyes
Pounds upon the table.
—He is chairman.

Egos yet in the prime,
Hearing world-voices
475   Chanting grand arias . . .
Majors resonant,
Stunning with sound . . .

Baffling minors
Half-heard like rain on pools . . .
480   Majestic discordances
Greater than harmonies . . .
—Gleaning out of it all
Passion, bewilderment, pain . . .

Egos yearning with the world-old want in their eyes—
485   Hurt hot eyes that do not sleep enough . . .
Striving with infinite effort,
Frustrate yet ever pursuing
The great white Liberty,
Trailing her dissolving glory over each hard-won barricade—
490   Only to fade anew . . .

Egos crying out of unkempt deeps
And waving their dreams like flags—
Multi-colored dreams,
Winged and glorious . . .

495   A gas jet throws a stunted flame,
Vaguely illumining the groping faces.
And through the uncurtained window
Falls the waste light of stars,
As cold as wise men's eyes . . .
500   Indifferent great stars,
Fortuitously glancing
At the secret meeting in this shut-in room,
Bare as a manger.

VIII

Lights go out
505   And the stark trunks of the factories
Melt into the drawn darkness,
Sheathing like a seamless garment.

And mothers take home their babies,
Waxen and delicately curled,
510   Like little potted flowers closed under the stars.

Lights go out
And the young men shut their eyes,
But life turns in them . . .

Life in the cramped ova
515   Tearing and rending asunder its living cells . . .
Wars, arts, discoveries, rebellions, travails, immolations,
        cataclysms, hates . . .
Pent in the shut flesh.
And the young men twist on their beds in languor and dizziness
520   unsupportable . . .
Their eyes—heavy and dimmed

With dust of long oblivions in the gray pulp behind—
Staring as through a choked glass.
And they gaze at the moon—throwing off a faint heat—
525   The moon, blond and burning, creeping to their cots
Softly, as on naked feet . . .
Lolling on the coverlet . . . like a woman offering her white body.

Nude glory of the moon!
That leaps like an athlete on the bosoms of the young girls stripped
530   of their linens;
Stroking their breasts that are smooth and cool as mother-of-pearl
Till the nipples tingle and burn as though little lips plucked at them.
They shudder and grow faint.
And their ears are filled as with a delirious rhapsody,
535   That Life, like a drunken player,
Strikes out of their clear white bodies
As out of ivory keys.

Lights go out . . .
And the great lovers linger in little groups, still passionately debating,
540   Or one may walk in silence, listening only to the still summons of Life—
Life making the great Demand . . .
Calling its new Christs . . .
Till tears come, blurring the stars
That grow tender and comforting like the eyes of comrades;
545   And the moon rolls behind the Battery
Like a word molten out of the mouth of God.

Lights go out . . .
And colors rush together,
Fusing and floating away . . .
550   Pale worn gold like the settings of old jewels . . .
Mauves, exquisite, tremulous, and luminous purples
And burning spires in aureoles of light
Like shimmering auras.

They are covering up the pushcarts . . .
555   Now all have gone save an old man with mirrors—
Little oval mirrors like tiny pools.
He shuffles up a darkened street
And the moon burnishes his mirrors till they shine like phosphorus . . .
The moon like a skull,
560   Staring out of eyeless sockets at the old men trundling home the pushcarts.

IX

A sallow dawn is in the sky
As I enter my little green room.
Sadie's light is still burning . . .
Without, the frail moon
565   Worn to a silvery tissue,
Throws a faint glamour on the roofs,
And down the shadowy spires

Lights tip-toe out . . .
Softly as when lovers close street doors.

570 Out of the Battery
A little wind
Stirs idly—as an arm
Trails over a boat's side in dalliance—
Rippling the smooth dead surface of the heat,
575 And Hester street,
Like a forlorn woman over-born
By many babies at her teats,
Turns on her trampled bed to meet the day.

LIFE!
Startling, vigorous life,
580 *That squirms under my touch,*
And baffles me when I try to examine it,
Or hurls me back without apology.
Leaving my ego ruffled and preening itself.

Life,
585 *Articulate, shrill,*
Screaming in provocative assertion,
Or out of the black and clotted gutters,
Piping in silvery thin
Sweet staccato
590 *Of children's laughter,*

Or clinging over the pushcarts
Like a litter of tiny bells
Or the jingle of silver coins,
Perpetually changing hands,
595 *Or like the Jordan somberly*
Swirling in tumultuous uncharted tides,
Surface-calm.

Electric currents of life,
Throwing off thoughts like sparks,
600 *Glittering, disappearing,*
Making unknown circuits,
Or out of spent particles stirring
Feeble contortions in old faiths
Passing before the new.

605 *Long nights argued away*
In meeting halls
Back of interminable stairways—
In Roumanian wine-shops
And little Russian tea-rooms . . .

610 *Feet echoing through deserted streets*
In the soft darkness before dawn . . .
Brows aching, throbbing, burning—
Life leaping in the shaken flesh
Like flame at an asbestos curtain.

615   *Life—*
      Pent, overflowing
      Stoops and façades,
      Jostling, pushing, contriving,
      Seething as in a great vat . . .

620   *Bartering, changing, extorting,*
      Dreaming, debating, aspiring,
      Astounding, indestructible
      Life of the Ghetto . . .

      Strong flux of life,
625   *Like a bitter wine*
      Out of the bloody stills of the world . . .
      Out of the Passion eternal.

Anzia Yezierska (1881–1970)

In 1890, Anzia Yezierska emigrated with her family from Plotzk in Russian Poland to New York's Lower East Side. After working in laundries and sweatshops, she attended college aided by the Clara de Hirsch Home for Working Girls, which insisted that she study domestic science. Yezierska graduated from Columbia University Teachers College in 1904 and, after teaching for several years, began to write fiction of intensity and pathos about Jewish immigrant life on the Lower East Side. She divorced twice and gave birth to a daughter, Louise. In 1917, Yezierska audited John Dewey's seminar on Ethics and Educational Problems, and sought his help in securing a better teaching position. Much like a scene from one of her novels, in which an immigrant working girl meets a scholarly American male, Yezierska and Dewey had a three-year romantic relationship. Dewey wrote love poems to Yezierska, and their (unconsummated?) affair became the subject of her last novel, *All I Could Never Be* (1932). In 1918, she was one of the researchers for Dewey's study of Polish immigrants in Philadelphia.

Meanwhile, her story collection *Hungry Hearts* (1920) and the novel *Salome of the Tenements* (1923) were adapted into films by Goldwyn studios. Her Hollywood persona as the "sweatshop Cinderella" helped promote her books *Children of Loneliness* (1923), *Arrogant Beggar* (1927), and her best-known novel *Bread Givers* (1925), which depicted her sense of being caught between an Orthodox rabbi father and a cold materialistic American society. By the 1930s, however, the emotional intensity of her style fell out of favor, leaving her in relative obscurity for two decades. Working in the WPA Writers' Project in the 1930s, Yezierska met other writers, including Richard Wright. Her autobiography, *Red Ribbon on a White Horse* (1950), documented these experiences and brought her back into public life. By the 1960s, she became a public and passionate advocate for the poor and elderly. "The Free Vacation House," her first short story, captures the rhythms of ghetto dialect and humorously satirizes upper-middle-class charity workers whose patronizing "good intentions" ignored working-class immigrants' familial structures and a mother's sense of dignity.

Babak Elahi

THE FREE VACATION HOUSE

How came it that I went to the free vacation house was like this:

One day the visiting teacher from the school comes to find out for why don't I get the children ready for school in time; for why are they so often late.

I let out on her my whole bitter heart. I told her my head was on wheels from worrying. When I get up in the morning, I don't know on what to turn first: should I nurse the baby, or make Sam's breakfast, or attend on the older children. I only got two hands.

"My dear woman," she says, "you are about to have a nervous breakdown. You need to get away to the country for a rest and vacation."

"Gott im Himmel!" says I. "Don't I know I need a rest? But how? On what money can I go to the country?"

"I know of a nice country place for mothers and children that will not cost you anything. It is free."

"Free! I never heard from it."

"Some kind people have made arrangements so no one need pay," she explains.

Later, in a few days, I just finished up with Masha and Mendel and Frieda and Sonya to send them to school, and I was getting Aby ready for kindergarten, when I hear a knock on the door, and a lady comes in. She had a white starched dress like a nurse and carried a black satchel in her hand.

"I am from the Social Betterment Society," she tells me. "You want to go to the country?"

Before I could say something, she goes over to the baby and pulls out the rubber nipple from her mouth, and to me, she says, "You must not get the child used to sucking this; it is very unsanitary."

"Gott im Himmel!" I beg the lady. "Please don't begin with that child, or she'll holler my head off. She must have the nipple. I'm too nervous to hear her scream like that."

When I put the nipple back again in the baby's mouth, the lady takes herself a seat, and then takes out a big black book from her satchel. Then she begins to question me. What is my first name? How old I am? From where come I? How long I'm already in this country? Do I keep any boarders? What is my husband's first name? How old he is? How long he is in this country? By what trade he works? How much wages he gets for a week? How much money do I spend out for rent? How old are the children, and everything about them.

"My goodness!" I cry out. "For why is it necessary all this to know? For why must I tell you all my business? What difference does it make already if I keep boarders, or I don't keep boarders? If Masha had the whooping-cough or Sonya had the measles? Or whether I spend out for my rent ten dollars or twenty? Or whether I come from Schnipishock or Kovner Gubernie?"

"We must make a record of all the applicants, and investigate each case," she tells me. "There are so many who apply to the charities, we can help only those who are most worthy."

"Charities!" I scream out. "Ain't the charities those who help the beggars out? I ain't no beggar. I'm not asking for no charity. My husband, he works."

"Miss Holcomb, the visiting teacher, said that you wanted to go to the country, and I had to make out this report before investigating your case."

"Oh! Oh!" I choke and bit my lips. "Is the free country from which Miss Holcomb told me, is it from the charities? She was telling me some kind people made arrangements for any mother what needs to go there."

"If your application is approved, you will be notified," she says to me, and out she goes.

When she is gone I think to myself, I'd better knock out from my head this idea about the country. For so long I lived, I didn't know nothing about the charities. For why should I come down among the beggars now?

Then I looked around me in the kitchen. On one side was the big wash-tub with clothes, waiting for me to wash. On the table was a pile of breakfast dishes yet. In the sink was the potatoes, waiting to be peeled. The baby was beginning to cry for the bottle. Aby was hollering and pulling me to take him to kindergarten. I felt if I didn't get away from here for a little while, I would land in a crazy house, or from the window jump down. Which was worser, to land in a crazy house, jump from the window down, or go to the country from the charities?

In about two weeks later around comes the same lady with the satchel again in my house.

"You can go to the country to-morrow," she tells me. "And you must come to the charity building to-morrow at nine o'clock sharp. Here is a card with the address. Don't lose it, because you must hand it to the lady in the office."

I look on the card, and there I see my name wrote; and by it, in big printed letters, that word "CHARITY."

"Must I go to the charity office?" I ask, feeling my heart to sink. "For why must I come there?"

"It is the rule that everybody comes to the office first, and from there they are taken to the country."

I shivered to think how I would feel, suppose somebody from my friends should see me walking into the charity office with my children. They wouldn't know that it is only for the country I go there. They might think I go to beg. Have I come down so low as to be seen by the charities? But what's the use? Should I knock my head on the walls? I had to go.

When I come to the office, I already found a crowd of women and children sitting on long benches and waiting. I took myself a seat with them, and we were sitting and sitting and looking on one another, sideways and crosswise, and with lowered eyes, like guilty criminals. Each one felt like hiding herself from all the rest. Each one felt black with shame in the face.

We may have been sitting and waiting for an hour or more. But every second was seeming years to me. The children began to get restless. Mendel wanted water. The baby on my arms was falling asleep. Aby was crying for something to eat.

"For why are we sittin' here like fat cats?" says the woman next to me. "Ain't we going to the country to-day yet?"

At last a lady comes to the desk and begins calling us our names, one by one. I nearly dropped to the floor when over she begins to ask: Do you keep boarders? How much do you spend out for rent? How much wages does your man get for a week?

Didn't the nurse tell them all about us already? It was bitter enough to have to tell the nurse everything, but in my own house nobody was hearing my troubles, only the nurse. But in the office there was so many strangers all around me. For why should everybody have to know my business? At every question I wanted to holler out: "Stop! Stop! I don't want no vacations! I'll better run home with my children." At every question I felt like she was stabbing a knife into my heart. And she kept on stabbing me more and more, but I could not help it, and they were all looking at me. I couldn't move from her. I had to answer everything.

When she got through with me, my face was red like fire. I was burning with hurts and wounds. I felt like everything was bleeding in me.

When all the names was already called, a man doctor with a nurse comes in, and tells us to form a line, to be examined. I wish I could ease out my heart a little, and tell in words how that doctor looked on us, just because we were poor and had no money to pay. He only used the ends from his finger-tips to examine us with. From the way he was afraid to touch us or come near us, he made us feel like we had some catching sickness that he was trying not to get on him.

The doctor got finished with us in about five minutes, so quick he worked. Then we was told to walk after the nurse, who was leading the way for us through the street to the car. Everybody what passed us in the street turned around to look on us. I kept down my eyes and held down my head and I felt like sinking into the sidewalk. All the time I was trembling for fear somebody what knows me might yet pass and see me. For why did they make us walk through the street, after the nurse, like stupid cows? Weren't all of us smart enough to find our way without the nurse? Why should the whole world have to see that we are from the charities?

When we got into the train, I opened my eyes, and lifted up my head, and straightened out my chest, and again began to breathe. It was a beautiful, sunshiny day. I knocked open the window from the train, and the fresh-smelling country air rushed upon my face and made me feel so fine! I looked out from the window and instead of seeing the iron fire-escapes with garbage-cans and bedclothes, that I always seen when from my flat I looked—instead of seeing only walls and wash-lines between walls, I saw the blue sky, and green grass and trees and flowers.

Ah, how grand I felt, just on the sky to look! Ah, how grand I felt just to see the green grass—and the free space—and no houses!

"Get away from me, my troubles!" I said. "Leave me rest a minute. Leave me breathe and straighten out my bones. Forget the unpaid butcher's bill. Forget the rent. Forget the wash-tub and the cook-stove and the pots and pans. Forget the charities!"

"Tickets, please," calls the train conductor.

I felt knocked out from heaven all at once. I had to point to the nurse what held our tickets, and I was feeling the conductor looking on me as if to say, "Oh, you are only from the charities."

By the time we came to the vacation house I already forgot all about my knock-down. I was again filled with the beauty of the country. I never in all my life yet seen such a swell house like that vacation house. Like the grandest palace it looked. All round the front, flowers from all colors was smelling out the sweetest perfume. Here and there was shady trees with comfortable chairs under them to sit down on.

When I only came inside, my mouth opened wide and my breathing stopped still from wonder. I never yet seen such an order and such a cleanliness. From all the corners from the room, the cleanliness was shining like a looking-glass. The floor was so white scrubbed you could eat on it. You couldn't find a speck of dust on nothing, if you was looking for it with eyeglasses on.

I was beginning to feel happy and glad that I come, when, Gott im Himmel! again a lady begins to ask us out the same questions what the nurse already asked me in my home and what was asked over again in the charity office. How much wages my husband makes out for a week? How much money I spend out for rent? Do I keep boarders?

We were hungry enough to faint. So worn out was I from excitement, and from the long ride, that my knees were bending under me ready to break from tiredness. The children were pulling me to pieces, nagging me for a drink, for something to eat and such like. But still we had to stand out the whole list of questionings. When she already got through asking us out everything, she gave to each of us a tag with our name written on it. She told us to tie the tag on our hand. Then like tagged horses at a horse sale in the street, they marched us into the dining-room.

There was rows of long tables, covered with pure-white oilcloth. A vase with bought flowers was standing on the middle from each table. Each person got a clean napkin for himself. Laid out by the side from each person's plate was a silver knife and fork and spoon and teaspoon. When we only sat ourselves down, girls with white starched aprons was passing around the eatings.

I soon forgot again all my troubles. For the first time in ten years I sat down to a meal what I did not have to cook or worry about. For the first time in ten years I sat down to the table like a somebody. Ah, how grand it feels, to have handed you over the eatings and everything you need. Just as I was beginning to like it and let myself feel good, in comes a fat lady all in white, with a teacher's look on her face. I could tell already, right away by the way she looked on us, that she was the boss from this place.

"I want to read you the rules from this house, before you leave this room," says she to us.

Then she began like this: We dassen't stand on the front grass where the flowers are. We dassen't stay on the front porch. We dassen't sit on the chairs under the shady trees. We must stay always in the back and sit on those long wooden benches there. We dassen't come in the front sitting-room or walk on the front steps what have carpet on it—we must walk on the back iron steps. Everything on the front from the house must be kept perfect for the show for visitors. We dassen't lay down on the beds in the daytime, the beds must always be made up perfect for the show for visitors.

"Gott im Himmel!" thinks I to myself; "ain't there going to be no end to the things we dassen't do in this place?"

But still she went on. The children over two years dassen't stay around by the mothers. They must stay by the nurse in the play-room. By the meal-times, they can see their mothers. The children dassen't run around the house or tear up flowers or do anything. They dassen't holler or play rough in the play-room. They must always behave and obey the nurse.

We must always listen to the bells. Bell one was for getting up. Bell two, for getting babies' bottles. Bell three, for coming to breakfast. Bell four, for bathing the babies. If we come later, after the ring from the bell, then we'll not get what we need. If the bottle bell rings and we don't come right away for the bottle, then the baby don't get no bottle. If the breakfast bell rings, and we don't come right away down to the breakfast, then there won't be no breakfast for us.

When she got through with reading the rules, I was wondering which side of the house I was to walk on. At every step was some rule what said don't move here, and don't go there, don't stand there, and don't sit there. If I tried to remember the endless rules, it would only make me dizzy in the head. I was thinking for why, with so many rules, didn't they also have already another rule, about how much air in our lungs to breathe.

On every few days there came to the house swell ladies in automobiles. It was for them that the front from the house had to be always perfect. For them was all the beautiful smelling flowers. For them the front porch, the front sitting-room, and the easy stairs with the carpet on it.

Always when the rich ladies came the fat lady, what was the boss from the vacation house, showed off to them the front. Then she took them over to the back to look on us, where we was sitting together, on long wooden benches, like prisoners. I was always feeling cheap like dirt, and mad that I had to be there, when they smiled down on us.

"How nice for these poor creatures to have a restful place like this," I heard one lady say.

The next day I already felt like going back. The children what had to stay by the nurse in the play-room didn't like it neither.

"Mamma," says Mendel to me, "I wisht I was home and out in the street. They don't let us do nothing here. It's worser than school."

"Ain't it a play-room?" asks I. "Don't they let you play?"

"Gee wiss! play-room, they call it! The nurse hollers on us all the time. She don't let us do nothing."

The reason why I stayed out the whole two weeks is this: I think to myself, so much shame in the face I suffered to come here, let me at least make the best from it already. Let me at least save up for two weeks what I got to spend out for grocery and butcher for my back bills to pay out. And then also think I to myself, if I go back on Monday, I got to do the big washing; on Tuesday waits for me the ironing; on Wednesday, the scrubbing and cleaning, and so goes it on. How bad it is already in this place, it's a change from the very same sameness of what I'm having day in and day out at home. And so I stayed out this vacation to the bitter end.

But at last the day for going out from this prison came. On the way riding back, I kept thinking to myself: "This is such a beautiful vacation house. For why do they make it so hard for us? When a mother needs a vacation, why must they tear the insides out from her first, by making her come down to the charity office? Why drag us from the charity office through the streets? And when we live through the shame of the charities and when we come already to the vacation house, for why do they boss the life out of us with so many rules and bells? For why don't they let us lay down our heads on the bed when we are tired? For why must we always stick in the back, like dogs what have got to be chained in one spot? If they would let us walk around free, would we bite off something from the front part of the house?

"If the best part of the house what is comfortable is made up for a show for visitors, why ain't they keeping the whole business for a show for visitors? For why do they have to fool in worn-out mothers, to make them think they'll give them a rest? Do they need the worn-out mothers as part of the show? I guess that is it, already."

When I got back in my home, so happy and thankful I was I could cry from thankfulness. How good it was feeling for me to be able to move around my own house, like I pleased. I was always kicking that my rooms was small and narrow, but now my small rooms seemed to grow so big like the park. I looked out from my window on the fire-escapes, full with bedding and garbage-cans, and on the wash-lines full with the clothes. All these ugly things was grand in my eyes. Even the high brick walls all around made me feel like a bird what just jumped out from a cage. And I cried out, "Gott sei dank! Gott sei dank!"

Edith Summers Kelley (1884–1956)

E dith Summers Kelley's novel *Weeds* is the story of Judith Pippinger Blackford, whose artistic potential is thwarted by the circumstances of her life as the wife of a tenant tobacco farmer. Set in the hollows of rural Kentucky, the novel relates the production of tobacco, a crop that exhausts the land, with the lives of the earnest, hardworking tenant farmers whose work is subject to the vagaries of weather and the tobacco companies' set prices. Summers Kelley also shows the intertwined relationship between the labor of farming and the labor of birth and mothering. Shortly before the novel's publication in 1923, Summers Kelley's editors at Harcourt, Brace recommended that the chapter "Billy's Birth" be condensed or removed completely because they argued that childbirth is "common to the lot of all women and not to Kentucky alone. It has been done over and over again in modern realistic novels." That chapter, reproduced here, was cut and not restored until 1982, when the novel was republished by the Feminist Press. Contrary to her first editors' judgment, Summers Kelley's description of protracted labor, "like the ever-recurring drive of some great piston," was and still is one of the most detailed, graphic, and original stage-by-stage accounts of a first birth in American literature.

Edith Summers was born in Toronto, Canada, in 1884, graduated from the University of Toronto in 1903, and, wanting to be a writer, moved to New York City, where she became a part of the intellectual and creative circles of Greenwich Village. From 1906 to 1907, she was secretary to novelist Upton Sinclair and lived at Helicon Hall, an experimental community of intellectuals and writers. There she met Sinclair Lewis, to whom she was briefly engaged, and her first husband, Allan Updegraff, with whom she had two children. She returned to Greenwich Village after a fire destroyed Helicon Hall in 1907. After her divorce from Updegraff, she lived with the sculptor C. Fred Kelley and left New York with Kelley to manage a tobacco ranch in Kentucky. They faced a series of financial losses as they moved from Kentucky to New Jersey and then to California, where they struggled to make a living at farming and chicken raising. *Weeds* was written amid farmwork and bringing up three children, including her son with Fred Kelley. Her only other work, a second novel *The Devil's Hand*, was published posthumously in 1974.

BILLY'S BIRTH

Judith disliked, too, Aunt Mary's extreme femininity, her niceness and decency and care for the minutiae of the small properties of her little world. Her attention to detail in every tiny matter bored and wearied Judith and her fastidiousness annoyed her. She could not help thinking of Aunt Mary as a cat, a cleanly cat that attends to its toilet with great care and purrs by the domestic hearth and nurses its kittens tenderly and considers that the world revolves about itself and its offspring, and spits and scratches at anyone who approaches the kittens. She could not refrain from the pleasure of occasionally teasing the cat. She found that if she said anything disparaging about Jerry or any of his habits, the cat would bridle and raise its fur and stretch its sharp claws out of its soft, velvet paws. This amused Judith, and she often made such criticisms in order to get the inevitable reaction from her mother-in-law.

When Jerry returned with his mother, Judith had washed the dishes and put the house in order and made such preparations as she could for her confinement. Her pains were occurring only infrequently; and between the pains she felt no particular discomfort. But she was obsessed with a desire to be doing something, and kept finding more things to attend to so that she might not be left unoccupied. After the arrival of Jerry's mother she was all the more determined to keep busy; for she did not want to have to sit down and talk to Aunt Mary.

"Tain't a bit of use your goin' for the doctor now, Jerry," advised Aunt Mary, who was experienced in such situations. "This is Judy's first, an' it won't come in a hurry. Her pains ain't a-comin' near fast enough. The two of you had best go to bed an' try to git some sleep. You won't need the doctor afore mornin' anyway."

"But can't he give her sumpin to stop the pain?" inquired Jerry anxiously. A smile of amused condescension, in which Judith thought she detected a trace of malice, passed over Aunt Mary's face.

"I reckon she'll have to go through a deal more pain nor what she's doin' afore the baby's born. Fu'st babies don't come so easy. An' I kin tell you for sure the doctor won't be able to do a single thing for her. He'd jes' take a look at her an' go away agin."

Aunt Mary spoke with such conviction that the young couple were convinced. They went to bed in the kitchen, giving up their bedroom to their visitor. At first neither of them could sleep, Judith on account of the ever-recurring pains, which grew steadily worse, and Jerry because of his excitement and anxiety. At last, however, Jerry began to doze and soon fell from the doze into a deep, healthy sleep.

He was startled out of this sleep by Judith shaking him violently.

"Jerry, Jerry," she cried, "git up an' fetch the doctor quick. I've waited as long as I kin. I can't stand this no longer. It's a-comin'. I know it's a-comin'. An' there must be sumpin wrong. I'm jes' a-bein' tore up alive."

Her voice was vibrant with anguish and terror. It was different from any voice that Jerry had ever heard before in his life.

He leapt from the bed and struggled into his clothes, scarcely awake, yet keenly conscious of the one urgent thing that was required of him. They had left a lamp burning dimly in a far corner of the kitchen and it threw a faint light over the objects in the room. Judith was sitting on the foot of the bed clutching one of the posts, her hair hanging wildly about her face. He found the lantern and fumbled with the chimney, finding it in his excitement hard to open. At last he managed to open it and struck a match, which flared and went out. He cursed the match, struck another and at last had the lantern lighted and closed. Grabbing it by the handle he flung out of the door, and a few minutes later galloped past the house on Nip's back. There was no moon, but the sky was clear and the stars gave enough light for him to vaguely see the path. As he guided the horse up the steep hill that led to the ridge road, he heard, suddenly shattering the peace of the night, a terrible sound, a shriek of agony vibrating on two notes, shrill, piercing, utterly unearthly and seeming as though it would never stop. If it ever did stop, the end would surely be the silence of death. Nobody could scream like that who was not about to die. The prickly feeling of sudden sweat broke out all over Jerry, and he kicked the horse in the side to urge him on. The doctor! The doctor! He must fetch the doctor! He pounded along the top of the ridge with all the speed into which Nip could be urged. But he was sick with a dreadful certainty that however quickly he fetched the doctor, he would come too late.

In the meantime Aunt Mary had risen and lighted her lamp and came out into the kitchen with a shawl thrown over her nightgown. Judith was still clinging to the post at the foot of the bed, her cheeks flushed a bright scarlet. Drops of sweat stood out on her forehead and upper lip, and she constantly clenched and unclenched her hands. As Aunt Mary entered the kitchen, she was seized with the worst paroxysm of pain that she had yet had; and, gripping the bedpost, she uttered the scream that had struck terror into Jerry's heart as he was riding up the hill.

But the scream caused no such perturbation of spirit in Aunt Mary. She who went into spasms of anxious excitement over a mislaid male collar button, was here calm as the matron of a foundling asylum. She waited till the cry of agony and terror was over. Then she said,

"Try not to take on so, Judy. It on'y makes it seem worse when you screech."

Judith made no answer, but began to pace up and down the room, still clenching and unclenching her hands.

Aunt Mary went into the bedroom and put on her clothes. Then she came back and lighted the fire, filled the kettle and put it on, swept up the floor about the stove, and made everything neat in her fussy, meticulous way. Having done this, she went into the bedroom again and prepared the bed for Judith's confinement.

All the time Judith paced up and down the kitchen floor like a wild tigress newly caged. When the terrific spasm of pain would grind through her body, she would grasp the nearest object and utter, again and again, the strangely unhuman shriek, a savage, elemental, appalling sound that seemed as though it could have its origin nowhere upon the earth.

It did not, however, seem to greatly disturb the equanimity of Aunt Mary. She bustled about feeding the fire and putting on more water to heat and doing a hundred and one small things about the kitchen.

Having made every preparation that she could think of, she turned to Judith, speaking soothingly with an undertone of irritation, as one addresses a fretful child who has been causing annoyance.

"Naow then, Judy, you'd best come in the bedroom an' lay daown. I've fixed up the bed all nice, an' you'll be better off there. If you prance up an' down an' screech yer lungs out, you won't have no strength left when you'll be a-needin' it by an' by."

Judith only glared at her and made no answer. She continued to pace up and down.

The swift-coming summer dawn reached pale arms into the room, and with it came Jerry galloping back. He burst into the kitchen and could hardly believe his eyes to see Judith still alive and standing on her feet. With a great rush of joy and tenderness he took her in his arms and covered her face and neck with kisses.

"Judy, Judy, I was sure you was gone," he cried and broke into great, gulping sobs.

She gripped him by the shoulders and herself burst into hysterical weeping; then began to laugh foolishly. Jerry laughed too between his sobs; and they clung together, crying and laughing in one breath. Aunt Mary, forgotten and unnoticed, sat coldly by the stove.

All at once he felt her stiffening in his arms. As she stiffened, she trembled violently with terror of what was to befall her; and her hands clenched hard. He closed his arms about her as if he could ward off what was coming. But there was no saving her. In the iron grip of the demon, she grew first rigid as a statue, then bent, twisted, writhed in a hopeless, yet desperate, attempt to wrench herself away from his hold. Again and again came the dreadful shriek. When at last the fiend loosened his grip, she was left trembling, panting, breathless, and wet all over with the sweat of agony.

Jerry, almost as flushed and perspiring as she, stood aghast and speechless before this dreadful thing.

"My God, Judy, this is awful!" he managed to gasp out at last.

The spasm had left Judith exhausted. She sank back into a chair and her eyes closed for a moment. But it was only for a moment. She had gone past the stage when she was able to relax between the paroxysms. The fiend was now constantly at her side and would not leave her in peace a moment, but kept jabbing at her with sharp, vicious stabs which, although they were nothing like the great onslaught, kept her nerves taut and strained. At every moment she stirred uneasily, her knees trembled, and her hands alternately fluttered and clenched.

The doctor had not been at home when Jerry arrived at his house. He was away attending a critical pneumonia case, his wife said; but she would phone him to go directly from there to Jerry's. Jerry kept looking out of the window and imagining he heard the chugging of a car, although he felt sure the doctor would not arrive so soon.

In the meantime Aunt Mary had prepared breakfast and placed the steaming cakes and coffee on the table. Judith, between her spasms of pain, managed to drink a little coffee; and Jerry gulped down several cupfuls boiling hot, but could not swallow a mouthful of the cakes. Aunt Mary made her usual meal, eating as she always did in a dainty, pecking, birdlike manner. When crumbs fell on the table she brushed them away with her small, fidgety hands.

After breakfast Jerry went to attend to the horses and feed the hogs and chickens. The barnyard seemed to him an unreal place and the farm animals mere painted creatures. He fed them mechanically, scarcely knowing what he was doing. Snap, the shepherd pup, now grown into a playful and intelligent young dog, barked joyfully at his heels, asking for attention.

"Down, Snap," he said absently, and kicked him gently aside. Even the dog seemed a phantom creature. The only real thing that penetrated to his senses was the shattering scream that came from the house. As he went about his chores, he found himself waiting for it, stiffening and gasping when he heard it, then waiting for it again.

When he went back into the house, he found that by some miracle the demon had left Judith's side for a few moments and she had fallen asleep of exhaustion. She lay back in the old rocking chair in which Uncle Nat Carberry had died, breathing heavily, her black hair dropping in a long, tousled wisp over the side of the chair, her features pale and drawn, her arms hanging limply, the long hands dangling from the ends like dead things. He moved about noiselessly so as not to disturb her.

"Ain't it dreadful that she has to suffer like this," he said more to himself than to his mother.

"It's God's will," answered Aunt Mary piously.

"Looks to me a damn sight more like the devil's will."

Judith was not allowed to rest for long. The first premonitory twinges of the great throe which was about to rack her roused her out of her sleep; and opening her eyes very wide she looked at Jerry with such horror and dismay, such abject fear, such beseeching, pitiful appeal that his knees went weak under him. She was asking him to help her, and he could give her no help. He held her and gritted his teeth till she had struggled once more with the demon and sank back limply in his arms.

About ten o'clock they heard the throb of an engine; and rushing out of the door, Jerry saw Doctor McTaggert's battered Ford on the ridge above. The doctor got out and came down the hill on foot, carrying a small leather satchel. Jerry was so glad to see him that he ran to meet him as a dog runs to meet his master.

Doctor McTaggert looked exactly as he had looked seven years before when he had attended Judith's mother in her last illness. He was still shabby, dust-colored, of unguessable age, and he still wore the same air of resignation to his lot. He was a very commonplace-looking little man; but the Angel Gabriel in all his heavenly finery could not have shone more gloriously in Jerry's eyes.

Eagerly ushered into the house by Jerry, he went up to Judith and held her hand with a firm, soothing pressure while he felt her pulse.

"You're getting along fine, Judy, my girl," he said, in the quiet, hopeful tone that experience had taught him to use toward expectant mothers. "You have a good, firm, steady pulse. Nothing wrong with *your* heart. Come now and lie down, and we'll see how far along you are."

In the bedroom the doctor made his examination.

"Haow is she?" demanded Jerry, anxiously drawing the doctor outside the kitchen door, when the examination was over.

"She's all right," answered the doctor in a low tone, "But it's a slow case. She's in absolutely no danger at present. Her symptoms are quite normal and natural so far. But the baby won't be born for a long time. Don't tell her that. She's always been a very active girl, and there's a good deal of muscular rigidity which must be overcome. We must leave nature to do it; and nature takes her own time. That's what makes the false pains so bad and makes them last so long."

"Good God, Doc, if these is *false* pains, what's the real ones like?" demanded Jerry.

The doctor smiled. "It's just a name that's been given them," he explained wearily. "I guess they're all real enough. Try to keep her courage up, and don't let her know how long it's going to last. I'm going home now to turn in. I had two hours' sleep last night and three the night before. I'll be here first thing tomorrow morning. If anything unusual happens, you can get me on the phone from Uncle Ezra's."

Tomorrow morning! Jerry was dumbfounded. Desperately he gripped the doctor by the front of his coat, as though to hold him against his will.

"But Doc, how's she a-goin' to *live* till tomorrow mornin' through such pain?"

The doctor smiled again. "She'll live all right," was all he said.

He was gone, and Jerry was left with his terrible task before him. Tomorrow morning seemed to stretch centuries away into the distant future. He gritted his teeth and went back into the chamber of torture where once more she was struggling desperately with the fiend.

"Where's the doctor? Why don't he come back?" she demanded eagerly, when the spasm was over.

"He's a-comin' back right soon, Judy."

All through the rest of the long day and all through the dreadful, crawling hours of the night, he was by her side. When the pains tore at her vitals and she shrieked and flung her arms wildly and aimlessly in the air protesting that she couldn't bear it, she couldn't bear it, she wanted to die and have it over with, he could do nothing but stand by the bedside feeling bitterly his own worthlessness. When she clung to him, as she sometimes did and dug her nails into his flesh, he supported her as best he could, glad to seem to be of some help to her, and waited, tense as she, through minutes that seemed like hours, till she fell back again into the pillows. During the short intervals when she was not suffering so keenly, he bathed her hot face, arranged her pillows, lied to her heroically, and tried to say a few soothing words of hope and comfort.

From time to time Aunt Mary offered to take his place, but Judith would have none of her. Her manner of offering suggested that she considered it a rather indecent thing for Jerry to be there at all. She had a way, which Judith hated, of suggesting things quite definitely without the use of words.

During the night it began to rain. The patter of the drops falling on the roof and beating against the window pane seemed to shut Jerry in with the tortured girl in a great loneliness, as though all the rest of the world had withdrawn itself far away and forgotten them.

As the night wore on and her exhaustion became greater, she slept in the intervals of the pains, short as these intervals had now become. The instant the demon relaxed his grip upon her, she would fall asleep, breathe heavily for a few seconds, then wake moaning with pain and terror of what was to come, as the inexorable iron grip tightened once more upon her. Outside the rain fell steadily and peacefully.

Toward morning she was granted a short respite. When Jerry saw that her body was no longer rent by pain, that she was not even moaning, and had actually fallen into a deep, quiet sleep, his nerves, strained tight for so many hours, all at once relaxed; and he dropped his head into the quilts at the foot of the bed and sobbed for a long time.

When he had emptied his reservoir of tears he felt much better and went out into the kitchen and awkwardly made himself a cup of coffee and devoured four large corn cakes that he found in the cupboard. Aunt Mary, who had lain down in her clothes and was sleeping fitfully, woke up as he was drinking the coffee and asked him why he had not called her to make it for him. When he went back into the bedroom Judith was still sleeping. He sat down in a low rocking chair and instantly fell asleep.

He awoke the moment that he heard her stirring and was on his feet and listening terrified to a sound that he had never heard before, a deep-toned, gutteral, growling sound that ended in a snarl. It was not like that of an ordinary dog; but more as Jerry imagined some wild, doglike creature, inhabitant of lonely waste country, might growl and snarl over its prey. Could it be Judith who was making this savage sound?

He was at the bedside looking at her. The veins in her forehead were purple and swollen. The muscles of her cheeks stood out tense and hard. Her eyes, wide open, stared at the ceiling with the look of eyes that see nothing; and her gums were fleshed in the snarl like the gums of an angry wolf. Her hands were clenched into iron balls, her whole body rigid and straining heavily downward. As she gave vent to this prolonged, wolfish noise, she held her breath. He watched in helpless, horrified suspense.

When at last the strange spasm passed, she took breath again with a gasp and looked up at Jerry as one who has returned from another world.

"That's better," said Aunt Mary, who, had come into the room. "That means the baby'll be born afore long."

This news changed Jerry's terror into joy and helped to cheer him through the trials that were yet before him.

There were hours upon hours of this, dragging endlessly into eternity. Like the ever-recurring drive of some great piston which went on its way relentless and indomitable, the irresistible force drove through her quivering body, drew back and drove again. At first there was a moment or two of breathing space between the drives when she could look up at Jerry declaring that she could not bear it a moment longer, begging him frantically to save her, bring the doctor, do *something*. But as time passed the great drives became as regular and as incessant as clockwork, with no stop, no slightest pause, no abating of the terrific, invincible energy.

She no longer saw Jerry nor heard his voice nor cared anything about him. For her there was no longer any return from the ghastly No Man's Desert of pain into which she had been snatched by a strong, pitiless hand again and again for so many long hours. She was there now quite alone and cut off from all humankind. Out of it there led but one sinister canyon through which she must pass to come back to the world of men. All other ways were closed but this. Nature that from her childhood had led kindly and blandly through pleasant paths and had at last betrayed her, treacherously beguiling her into this desolate region, now sternly pointed her the one way out: the dread and cruel pass of herculean struggle through tortures unspeakable. Through no volition of her own, but following only the grimly pointing finger, because follow she must, as a leaf is drawn upon a downward current, the girl entered between the towering entrance boulders of that silent canyon and passed far away from the life of the world. There was no time any more, nor space, nor measure of anything. It was her fate only to struggle on desperately, blindly, knowing only one thing: that each struggle meant the suffering of anguish that is unbearable and that yet must and will be borne; and to do this endlessly, endlessly, endlessly, without rest, without respite.

Her eyes were closed now, her face a dark purple with dreadfully swollen veins and salient muscles; her body driving, driving, driving, with the force and regularity of some great steel and iron monster. It seemed to Jerry impossible that a creature made of mere flesh and blood could struggle and suffer like this through so many hours and continue to hold the spark of life.

"If she'd been a caow, she'd a been dead long ago," he muttered; then started violently, shocked at his own comparison.

The rain stopped as the dawn began to grow in the room. With the approach of the sun, roosters crew and hens cackled in a chatty, gossiping way, as though nothing unusual were happening. Snap, the dog, full of morning vivacity, rushed among them and scattered them, barking joyously. They half ran half flew from his approach and cackled in loud tones, at first with fright, then with indignation, and went back to their scratching. Robins and orioles greeted the rain-washed morning with song; and a meadow lark, perched on a rail fence a few rods from the house, uttered at regular intervals its trill of melody. After the rain everything beamed, sparkled, and gave forth all it had of color and fragrance.

These things in which Judith was wont to take delight were all as nothing to her now. Stretched out on the bed as on some grisly rack of torture, she still gasped, strained, ground her teeth and uttered again and again the growl of struggle ending in the fierce snarl of agony. To Jerry's sleep-dulled mind she took on gigantic proportions. She was no longer Judith; she was something superhuman, immense and overpowering.

The sun rose over the brow of the ridge and made the pattern of the half open window on the floor. Through the open door shaded by the grape vine came the pungent smell of flowering grapes exhaling their intense wet fragrance into the warm sunshine. Aunt Mary flitted about, doing such things as she deemed necessary; and Jerry, having done his morning chores, sat by the bed in a sort of dazed stupor. He was too tired now to care very much what happened.

The sun rose higher and higher, whitening with its glare the deep morning blue of the sky. And still the never-ending struggle went on, and still the doctor did not come.

It was nearly eleven o'clock when at last Jerry heard, as if dimly through a dream, the chug of his engine. He came in and having felt her pulse nodded in a reassuring way.

"She's got a good strong heart all right," he said, as he washed his hands at the washstand. Having made his examination, he smiled with a sort of weary satisfaction to find that he would not have long to wait. He washed his hands again, and this time the water in the basin was red with blood.

"Is it all right?" asked Jerry anxiously.

"Perfectly all right. Everything normal. No complications."

"Now then, Judy," he said, bending over the struggling girl. "Try to bear down just as long and hard as you can each time, and you'll be out of pain before you know it."

He asked for a handkerchief; and having taken a little bottle of chloroform from his bag, poured a few drops on the handkerchief and handed it to Jerry.

"Hold that over her nose," he said.

She breathed deep of the sweet, suffocating, merciful fumes; and as she drew them into her lungs the intense, tearing agony changed to a strong but dull straining pressure, as though she were still being pulled apart but lost most of the power of sensation. She still felt the great drives going through her, she still strained with all the power of her muscles, and she still felt pain, but in a dull-edged, far off way. Her mind, released from the present, wandered aimlessly into the past, picking up a shred here and a scrap there.

"Ain't he a handsome mule, Elmer? An' don't he smile for all the world like Uncle Sam Whitmarsh?"

"I'm a-goin' to have a pink dress an' a pink sunbonnet, like Hat's, on'y nicer made, an' slippers with two straps an' white stockings."

"Oh land, I wisht she'd go. I hate all these old wimmin. She smells bad too."

"You gotta let me have all them terbaccer sticks, Jerry, 'cause I wanta build a cage with 'em to break up my settin' hens. No, them old rotten pickets won't do. I want the terbaccer sticks, an' I'm a-goin' to have 'em. Hiram Stone's a rich man; he won't miss a few terbaccer sticks."

"All right, dad. I'm a-comin'. I'm a-fetchin' 'em. Git along, Blackie. He there, Spot. Land, ain't a caow a o'nery beast!"

The doctor stood over her with patient watchfulness, encouraging, exhorting. (Aunt Mary flitted about in the background.)

"Hold fast, Judy. A little longer. A little longer. It'll soon be all over. There. Once more. Just once more."

She heard him and instinctively responded with her body, although his voice seemed to be far, far away, and his words of but vague import.

There came at last one great drive that did not recoil upon her as the others had done from the impact against something hard, solid, and immovable. This time something gave way. Encouraged by the far away voice of the doctor and the more clearly heard accents of nature, she kept on straining, straining, straining, as though she would never stop. She vaguely sensed the doctor working rapidly above her, tense, sweating, straining with all his might even as she was straining. And miraculously something started to come and kept on coming, coming, coming, as though it would never have an end.

But there was an end at last; and with a great sigh she fell back into the bosom of an immense peace.

It was over, and the doctor triumphantly held up nature's reward for all the anguish: a little, bloody, groping, monkey-like object, that moved its arms and legs with a spasmodic, froglike motion and uttered a sound that was not a cry nor a groan nor a grunt nor anything of the human or even the animal world, but more like a harsh grating of metal upon metal. It was a reward about the worthwhileness of which not a few women have had serious doubts, especially when first confronted with what seems to the inexperienced eye a deformed abortion. Judith was too far sunk into semi-unconsciousness to care anything about it one way or the other.

Aunt Mary, however, entertained no doubts. It was her first grandchild.

"Ah, but ain't he the fine boy!" she cried, taking the creature from the hands of the doctor and wrapping it carefully in a woolen shawl, "Der naow, he was des the best boy his granny every had, yes he was."

She approached her face to that of the weird mannikin, waggling it up and down, and actually began to chirp and twitter ecstatically to the bloody little squirming object. The sight gave Jerry a shiver of revulsion. It did not occur to him that he himself had once looked just like this; and if it had his feelings would probably not have been different.

"Ain't he a splendid boy, Jerry?" she cried, carrying him over toward her son.

"Aw, take the durn thing away," growled Jerry impatiently, and bent over his wife.

It was astonishing how quickly the color came back into Judith's cheeks, and how soon her muscles, strained and aching from the two days of incessant struggle, became relaxed and rested. The baby, too, was greatly improved in appearance by being washed and dressed. Judith's first impulse was to dislike the child because, before she even saw it, she heard its grandmother in the other room making such a silly fuss over it. But when the little stranger, who seemed to have miraculously appeared from nowhere, was brought to her dressed in white muslin garments, she was completely captivated by the appeal of the soft, yet-strong, little body, the perfect hands and feet, the eyes, bright yet vague, like those of a young kitten, and the foolish, groping little mouth. His finger nails, exquisitely pure and clean, were pink like the inside of a sea shell, and they had already grown too long. So she must have Jerry get the scissors and cut them at once, although Aunt Mary said that to cut his nails before he was a month old would surely bring bad luck to the baby. Jerry, too, who had been assured by Doctor McTaggert that the baby would "come out all right," began to take an interest in the child and to watch him curiously as he unfolded day by day into more human likeness.

"You know, Judy, he turns a diff'rent color every day," he said to Judith, when the baby was about a week old. "The fu'st day he was purple, the next day red, the next day a kind of Chinaman yaller; an' naow he's a-gittin' to be jes' nice an' pink an' white like a kid otta be."

The little house was beset with visitors. Everybody in the neighborhood dropped in to see the new baby; and the relatives came from miles around. An air of festivity clung about the house and the visitors, as though even in Scott County it was a good thing to be born. Aunt Abigail, whose hard, shiny black hair still showed no streak of gray, presented Judith with a cream colored baby cape which her son Noey had worn when he was a baby. Luella brought two white muslin dresses elaborately tucked and trimmed with lace. Lizzie May came proudly carrying her own child, a round-eyed, puffy-cheeked, rather stodgy-looking boy, now several months old, to whom she had attached the name of Granville. Lizzie May looked better and younger than before the birth of the child, and seemed to take Dan's shortcomings less seriously. Hat came and old Aunt Selina Cobb and Aunt Sally Whitmarsh and Cissy and Aunt Eppie Pettit and a dozen others.

Most of these women brought their men with them and left them in the kitchen to chew and spit and talk about the dry spell while they themselves went into the bedroom and admired the baby and asked Judith how she felt.

Of the men only her father and Jabez Moorhouse came in to see her. Bill looked his grandson over and decided that he would pass.

"Purty good size an' strong fer bein' on'y a heifer's calf, Judy," he said, showing the twinkle in his gray eyes.

Judith laughed gaily. She was glad her father was pleased with the baby. These few words of praise from him meant more to her than the cooings and gurglings of all the women. Between Bill and his youngest girl there had always been a strong bond of silent sympathy.

Jabez was the only one of the visitors who did not say something "nice." He had not had a drink that day, and was in one of his melancholy moods. He cast an unseeing glance of indifference at the baby and then looked at Judith with eyes at once vague and intense that seemed to look through and beyond her into some gloomy and unfathomable distance.

"I s'pose it's a fine brat," he drawled. "They all are when they fu'st git borned. But somehaow I don't like to see you a-gittin' yerse'f all cluttered up with babies, Judy. There's plenty enough wimmin likes to mess about over babies in the kitchen. You'd otta a left it to the like o' them. It hain't fit work for a gal like you. But that's haow young folks is. You can't tell 'em nothing for their good. You can't tell 'em nothing. They gotta find it out for their selves—when it's too late. Ah well, it's nater. It's nater, that must have her fun with all of us, like a cat that likes to have a nice long play with every mouse she ketches."

He sat with his chin propped on one great, heavy-veined hand and looked gloomily out of the little window. He had dropped in on his way from setting tobacco and his hands were caked with dried earth. The buttons were gone from his faded blue shirt, and the lean cords of his neck vibrated above his hairy chest.

"This here stuffy bedroom hain't no place for you to be this fine day, Judy," he went on, sniffing the air, which was faintly suggestive of wet diapers. "You'd otta be out over the hills a-stalkin' turkeys or a-fetchin' up the caows, or a-ridin' hoss back over the roads up hill an' down dale, or else jes' a-runnin' wild with the res' o' the wild things: grass an' wind an' rabbits an' ants an' brier roses an' woodchucks an' sech. That's where you'd otta be, Judy. But I expect you won't never git back there no more. Waal, I s'pose the world has gotta be kep' a-goin'."

Poetry of the Harlem Renaissance

The Harlem Renaissance, named for the city-within-a-city that was its cultural center, flourished during the 1920s and early 1930s, producing a body of writing, theater, art, and music that inscribed its legacy deeply on twentieth-century American literature. The New Negro Renaissance, as it was better known at the time, represented the artistic and intellectual expression of a broad social and political movement. Although many of its best-known writers circulated in the fashionable literary salons and published with mainstream presses, the movement had its roots in the collective historical experience of poor and working-class African Americans. The promise of political rights and economic independence, encoded in the post–Civil War Reconstruction period, had been betrayed by decades of disenfranchisement, Jim Crow segregation, and debt peonage for the majority of southern blacks. Escaping not only poverty but what had become, with the rise of the Ku Klux Klan, a campaign of terror against their communities, tens of thousands joined the Great Migration to northern cities in search of industrial jobs that were generated by military spending for World War I. Black soldiers returning home in 1918, the year with a record number of lynchings, found families dispersed and the "Red Scare" repression of labor in full swing.

It was in this context of violence, dislocation, and new possibility that African American writers framed their individual and communal literary responses. They were inspired by the example of leading, although ideologically disparate, black intellectuals

Booker T. Washington and W. E. B. Du Bois to deploy their talents in the service of "racial uplift." The poetry of protest and celebration produced by the Harlem Renaissance is remarkably diverse in its formal conventions and innovations, from the European sonnets of Countee Cullen and Claude McKay, through the multigenre experiment of Jean Toomer (1894–1967) in *Cane*, to the urban speech idioms and musical inflections of Sterling Brown and Langston Hughes (whose poems follow in Part V).

We begin this cluster with James Weldon Johnson (1871–1938), whose early poem "O Black and Unknown Bards" looks back, through the lens provided by Du Bois, to celebrate the "black slave singers, gone, forgot, and unfamed" whose "songs of sorrow, love and faith, and hope" inspired the current generation. Johnson, whose novel *The Autobiography of an Ex-Colored Man* (published anonymously in 1912) is considered a foundational text for the New Negro movement, collected these songs for his contemporaries in two books of *American Negro Spirituals* (1925, 1926). His 1922 collection, *The Book of American Negro Poetry* brought many of the writers presented here to a larger public for the first time.

Claude McKay (1889–1948) was born into a farming family in Jamaica. He left for the United States in 1912, having published his first book of poems *Songs of Jamaica* while working as a policeman in Spanish Town, and settled in New York in 1914. Published anonymously in 1917, "The Harlem Dancer" adapts the traditional form of the sonnet to the new material of urban nightlife, with the sonnet's closing couplet turning the gaze to the dancer's own experience of her work. "If We Must Die," written at a time when McKay and his work mates were hounded by the threat of racial violence, caught the attention of the white editors of radical journals such as *The Liberator*, of which McKay later became an editor. Unlike the working-class socialist McKay, Countee Cullen (1903–1946), adopted and raised by a prominent black minister, was academically trained (NYU and Harvard), socially distinguished (married for a time to Du Bois's daughter), and won more recognition and prizes for his poetry than any of his peers. Like McKay, however, he filled the sonnet's concise music and elevated diction (Keats and Shelley were his models) with a new energy of political protest and promise in poems such as "From the Dark Tower." The literary politics of Sterling Brown's poetry were less explicit, being expressed through his embrace of southern black culture, in particular its spoken dialect, work rhythms, and music—blues and jazz. Raised in a middle-class family in segregated Washington, DC, and educated, like Cullen, at Harvard, Brown (1901–1989) headed for the South after graduation in 1923 to teach college and to learn about his people's cultural roots. The resulting poetry, collected in *Southern Road* (1932), deploys the wit and energy of dialect to critique the power relations of race and class and to affirm the alternative knowledge and values of African-American communities.

The two poets who conclude this selection, Alice Dunbar-Nelson (1875–1935) and Angelina Weld Grimke (1880–1958) are less celebrated than their male contemporaries (the major female figures of the Harlem Renaissance were novelists Nella Larson and Zora Neal Hurston). Born in New Orleans of creole (mixed white, black, and Native American) parentage, Dunbar-Nelson wrote short fiction, as well as popular newspaper columns for the Washington, DC-based *Eagle*, but she had difficulty finding publishers for poems that addressed race and class oppression. Grimke's ancestry was differently mixed. Her father was a white slave owner and her grandmother his slave; Grimke herself never knew her mother. Primarily a dramatist—*Rachel* (1916) was her major success—she also published a small number of poems in the journals of the day. The undated "Fragment" was found among her papers after her death. In bringing forward the work lives of their poetic subjects—women who "sit and sew" while their menfolk are dying in the trenches or the black women who "toil just to eat / in the cold and in the heat"—and speaking through these women in the first-person singular, Grimke and Dunbar-Nelson offer a link between Harlem's literary renaissance and the "worker-writers" of the proletarian renaissance that was to follow.

James Weldon Johnson, O Black and Unknown Bards

O black and unknown bards of long ago,
How came your lips to touch the sacred fire?
How, in your darkness, did you come to know
The power and beauty of the minstrel's lyre?
5 Who first from midst his bonds lifted his eyes?
Who first from out the still watch, lone and long,
Feeling the ancient faith of prophets rise
Within his dark-kept soul, burst into song?

Heart of what slave poured out such melody
10 As "Steal away to Jesus"? On its strains
His spirit must have nightly floated free,
Though still about his hands he felt his chains.
Who heard great "Jordan roll"? Whose starward eye
Saw chariot "swing low"? And who was he
15 That breathed that comforting, melodic sigh,
"Nobody knows de trouble I see"?

What merely living clod, what captive thing,
Could up toward God through all its darkness grope,
And find within its deadened heart to sing
20 These songs of sorrow, love and faith, and hope?
How did it catch that subtle undertone,
That note in music heard not with the ears?
How sound the elusive reed so seldom blown,
Which stirs the soul or melts the heart to tears.

25 Not that great German master in his dream
Of harmonies that thundered amongst the stars
At the creation, ever heard a theme
Nobler than "Go down, Moses." Mark its bars
How like a mighty trumpet-call they stir
30 The blood. Such are the notes that men have sung
Going to valorous deeds; such tones there were
That helped make history when Time was young.

There is a wide, wide wonder in it all,
That from degraded rest and servile toil
35 The fiery spirit of the seer should call
These simple children of the sun and soil.
O black slave singers, gone, forgot, unfamed,
You—you alone, of all the long, long line
Of those who've sung untaught, unknown, unnamed,
40 Have stretched out upward, seeking the divine.

You sang not deeds of heroes or of kings;
No chant of bloody war, no exulting paean
Of arms-won triumphs; but your humble strings
You touched in chord with music empyrean.
45 You sang far better than you knew; the songs
That for your listeners' hungry hearts sufficed

Still live,—but more than this to you belongs:
You sang a race from wood and stone to Christ.

JEAN TOOMER, REAPERS

Black reapers with the sound of steel on stones
Are sharpening scythes. I see them place the hones
In their hip-pockets as a thing that's done,
And start their silent swinging, one by one.
5 Black horses drive a mower through the weeds,
And there, a field rat, startled, squealing bleeds.
His belly close to ground. I see the blade,
Blood-stained, continue cutting weeds and shade.

CLAUDE McKAY, THE HARLEM DANCER

Applauding youths laughed with young prostitutes
And watched her perfect, half-clothed body sway;
Her voice was like the sound of blended flutes
Blown by black players upon a picnic day.
5 She sang and danced on gracefully and calm,
The light gauze hanging loose about her form;
To me she seemed a proudly-swaying palm
Grown lovelier for passing through a storm.
Upon her swarthy neck black shiny curls
10 Luxuriant fell; and tossing coins in praise,
The wine-flushed, bold-eyed boys, and even the girls,
Devoured her shape with eager, passionate gaze;
But looking at her falsely-smiling face,
I knew her self was not in that strange place.

CLAUDE McKAY, IF WE MUST DIE

If we must die, let it not be like hogs
Hunted and penned in an inglorious spot,
While round us bark the mad and hungry dogs,
Making their mock at our accursed lot.
5 If we must die, O let us nobly die,
So that our precious blood may not be shed
In vain; then even the monsters we defy
Shall be constrained to honor us though dead!
O kinsmen! we must meet the common foe!
10 Though far outnumbered let us show us brave,
And for their thousand blows deal one deathblow!
What though before us lies the open grave?
Like men we'll face the murderous, cowardly pack,
Pressed to the wall, dying, but fighting back!

CLAUDE McKAY, THE LYNCHING

His Spirit in smoke ascended to high heaven.
His father, by the cruelest way of pain,
Had bidden him to his bosom once again;
The awful sin remained still unforgiven.
5   All night a bright and solitary star
(Perchance the one that ever guided him,
Yet gave him up at last to Fate's wild whim)
Hung pitifully o'er the swinging char.
Day dawned, and soon the mixed crowds came to view
10 The ghastly body swaying in the sun.
The women thronged to look, but never a one
Showed sorrow in her eyes of steely blue.

And little lads, lynchers that were to be,
Danced round the dreadful thing in fiendish glee.

COUNTEE CULLEN, FOR A LADY I KNOW

She even thinks that up in heaven
    Her class lies late and snores,
While poor black cherubs rise at seven
    To do celestial chores.

COUNTEE CULLEN, FROM THE DARK TOWER

(To Charles S. Johnson)

We shall not always plant while others reap
The golden increment of bursting fruit,
Not always countenance, abject and mute,
That lesser men should hold their brothers cheap;
5   Not everlastingly while others sleep
Shall we beguile their limbs with mellow flute,
Not always bend to some more subtle brute;
We were not made eternally to weep.

The night whose sable breast relieves the stark,
10 White stars is no less lovely being dark,
And there are buds that cannot bloom at all
In light, but crumple, piteous, and fall;
So in the dark we hide the heart that bleeds,
And wait, and tend our agonizing seeds.

STERLING A. BROWN, MA RAINEY

I

When Ma Rainey
Comes to town,
Folks from anyplace
Miles aroun',
5   From Cape Girardeau,
Poplar Bluff,
Flocks in to hear
Ma do her stuff;
Comes flivverin' in,
10 Or ridin' mules,
Or packed in trains,
Picknickin' fools. . . .
That's what it's like,
Fo' miles on down,
15 To New Orleans delta
An' Mobile town,
When Ma hits
Anywheres aroun'.

II

Dey comes to hear Ma Rainey from de little river settlements,
20 From blackbottom cornrows and from lumber camps;
Dey stumble in de hall, jes a-laughin' an' a-cacklin',
Cheerin' lak roarin' water, lak wind in river swamps.

An' some jokers keeps deir laughs a-goin' in de crowded aisles,
An' some folks sits dere waitin' wid deir aches an' miseries,
25 Till Ma comes out before dem, a-smilin' gold-toofed smiles,
An' Long Boy ripples minors on de black an' yellow keys.

III

O Ma Rainey,
Sing yo' song;
Now you's back
30 Whah you belong,
Git way inside us,
Keep us strong. . . .
O Ma Rainey,
Li'l an' low;
35 Sing us 'bout de hard luck
Roun' our do';
Sing us 'bout de lonesome road
We mus' go. . . .

IV

I talked to a fellow, an' the fellow say,
40   "She jes' catch hold of us, somekindaway.
She sang Backwater Blues one day:

> 'It rained fo' days an' de skies was dark as night,
> Trouble taken place in de lowlands at night.

> 'Thundered an' lightened an' the storm begin to roll
45   Thousan's of people ain't got no place to go.

> 'Den I went an' stood upon some high ol' lonesome hill,
> An' looked down on the place where I used to live.'

An' den de folks, dey natchally bowed dey heads an' cried,
Bowed dey heavy heads, shet dey moufs up tight an' cried,
50   An' Ma lef' de stage, an' followed some de folks outside."

Dere wasn't much more de fellow say:
She jes' gits hold of us dataway.

STERLING A. BROWN, SCOTTY HAS HIS SAY

Whuh folks, whuh folks; don' wuk muh brown too hahd!

> 'Cause Ise crazy 'bout muh woman,
> An' ef yuh treats huh mean,
> I gonna sprinkle goofy dus'
5   In yo' soup tureen.

Whuh folks, whuh folks; don' wuk muh brown too hahd!
Muh brown what's tendin' chillen in yo' big backyahd.

> Oh, dat gal is young an' tender,
> So jes' don' mistreat huh please,
10   Or I'll put a sprig of pisen ivy
> In yo' B.V.D.'s.

> I got me a Blackcat's wishbone,
> Got some Blackcat's ankle dus',
> An' yuh crackers better watch out
15   Ef I sees yo' carcass fus'—

Whuh folks, whuh folks; don' wuk muh brown too hahd!
Muh brown what's wringin' chicken necks in yo' backyahd.

> 'Cause muh brown an' me, we'se champeens
> At de St. Luke's Hall;
20   An' yo' cookin' an' yo' washin'
> Jes' ain't in it, not at all,

> Wid de way we does de Chahlston,
> De Black Bottom an' cake walkin',
> Steppin' on de puppies' tail;

25   Whuh folks, ain' no need in talkin',—

You is got muh purty brownskin
In yo' kitchen an' yo' yahd,
Lemme tell yuh rebs one sho thing
Doncha wuk muh brown too hahd—

30   Whuh folks, whuh folks; don' wuk muh brown too hahd!
Who's practisin' de Chahlston in yo' big backyahd.

STERLING A. BROWN, CALL BOY

Git out o' bed, you rascals,
Take it up from de covers,
Bring it to de strawboss
Fast as you can;
5   Down to de railroads
De day is beginnin',
An' day never waited
Fo' no kinda man.

Sun's jes a-peekin'
10 Over top o' de mountains,
An' de fogclouds a-liftin'
Fo' de break of day;
Number Forty-four's pantin',
Takin' on coal an' water,
15 An' she's strainin' ready
Fo' to git away.

Leave yo' wives an' yo' sweethearts,
Yo' pink and yo' yaller,
Yo' blue black and stovepipe,
20 Yo' chocolate brown;
All you backbitin' rascals,
Leave de other men's women,
De night crew from de roundhouse
Is a-roundin' roun'.

25 O you shifters and humpers,
You boiler washers,
You oilers and you greasers
Of de drivin' rods,
You switchers and flagmen,
30 Tile layers and tampers,
Youse wanted at de Norfolk
And Western yards.

You cooks got to cook it
From here to Norfolk,
35 You waiters got to dish it
From here to Tennessee,

You porters got to run
From here to Memphis,
Gotta bring de man's time,
40   Dontcha see, dontcha see?

De air may be cold, an'
Yo' bed may be easy,
Yo' babe may be comfy
An' warm by yo' side;
45   But don't snore so loud
Dat you can't hear me callin',
Don't ride no nightmare,
Dere's engines to ride.

Git up off o' yo shirt-tails,
50   You dumb lazy rounders,
Think I'm gonna let you
Sleep all day?
Bed has done ruint
Dem as can't leave it,
55   You knows you can't make it
Actin' datway. . . .

ALICE DUNBAR-NELSON, I SIT AND SEW

I sit and sew—a useless task it seems,
My hands grown tired, my head weighed down with dreams—
The panoply of war, the martial tread of men,
Grim-faced, stern-eyed, gazing beyond the ken
5   Of lesser souls, whose eyes have not seen Death
Nor learned to hold their lives but as a breath—
But—I must sit and sew.

I sit and sew—my heart aches with desire—
That pageant terrible, that fiercely pouring fire
10   On wasted fields, and writhing grotesque things
Once men. My soul in pity flings
Appealing cries, yearning only to go
There in that holocaust of hell, those fields of woe—
But—I must sit and sew.—

15   The little useless seam, the idle patch;
Why dream I here beneath my homely thatch,
When there they lie in sodden mud and rain,
Pitifully calling me, the quick ones and the slain?
You need, me, Christ! It is no roseate seam
20   That beckons me—this pretty futile seam,
It stifles me—God, must I sit and sew?

ANGELINA WELD GRIMKÉ, FRAGMENT

I am the woman with the black black skin
I am the laughing woman with the black black face
I am living in the cellars and in every crowded place
    I am toiling just to eat
5   In the cold and in the heat
      And I laugh
I am the laughing woman who's forgotten how to weep
I am the laughing woman who's afraid to go to sleep

John Beecher (1904–1980)

In his principled and peripatetic life, John Beecher was a steelworker and an English professor, a New Deal administrator and a journalist, a small farmer and a small-press publisher, and a proletarian poet. A great-great-nephew of abolitionist and novelist Harriet Beecher Stowe, John (Henry Newman) Beecher was born in New York City and moved as a child to Birmingham, Alabama, where his father was an executive of the Tennessee Coal, Iron and Railroad Company (TCI), later acquired by U.S. Steel. He attended Birmingham public schools, as well as various military camps, studied engineering at Cornell and writing and literature at the University of Alabama, Harvard, the Sorbonne, the University of Wisconsin, and the University of North Carolina. As a young man he worked at TCI as a steelworker and metallurgist pulling long shifts (eleven-hour days and thirteen-hour nights) in the open-hearth furnace. He was seriously injured on the job in 1925. A year later he married, returned to graduate school, and became an instructor of English.

During the Great Depression, Beecher worked in various New Deal agencies and carried out the first study of migrant farm labor in Florida. In 1940, the same year he published his first long poem, *And I Will Be Heard*, he testified on migrant labor conditions to Congress and worked as a journalist and editor for a Birmingham newspaper. A second volume of poetry, which included the long narrative poem, "Here I Stand," was published the following year. In 1943, Beecher joined the Liberty Ship *S.S. Booker T. Washington*, the first integrated warship, an experience that he wrote about in *All Brave Sailors* (1945). After the war, Beecher directed displaced persons' camps around Stuttgart, Germany. In 1948, he became a professor of sociology at San Francisco State College but was discharged in 1950 when he refused to sign a loyalty oath. Beecher became a small farmer in Sonoma County, north of San Francisco, where he and his wife founded the Morning Star Press in 1956. He moved the press to Arizona and renamed it Rampart Press, where his *Report to the Stockholders & Other Poems, 1932–1962* was published to critical success. In 1966, Beecher served as visiting professor at Miles College, a traditionally black institution, and reported on the civil rights movement for the *San Francisco Chronicle* and *Ramparts*. His other published works include *To Live and Die in Dixie and Other Poems* (1966) and *Collected Poems 1924–1974* (1974). He died in San Francisco in 1980.

REPORT TO THE STOCKHOLDERS

I

he fell off his crane
and his head hit the steel floor and broke like an egg
he lived a couple of hours with his brains bubbling out
and then he died
5 and the safety clerk made out a report saying
it was carelessness
and the craneman should have known better
from twenty years experience
than not to watch his step
10 and slip in some grease on top of his crane
and then the safety clerk told the superintendent
he'd ought to fix that guardrail

II

out at the open hearth
they all went to see the picture
15 called *Men of Steel*
about a third-helper who
worked up to the top
and married the president's daughter
and they liked the picture
20 because it was different

III

a ladle burned through
and he got a shoeful of steel
so they took up a collection through the mill
and some gave two bits
25 and some gave four
because there's no telling when

IV

the stopper-maker
puts a sleeve brick on an iron rod
and then a dab of mortar
30 and then another sleeve brick
and another dab of mortar
and when he has put fourteen sleeve bricks on
and fourteen dabs of mortar
and fitted on the head
35 he picks up another rod
and makes another stopper

V

a hot metal car ran over the Negro switchman's leg
and nobody expected to see him around here again
except maybe on the street with a tin cup
40   but the superintendent saw what an ad
the Negro would make with his peg leg
so he hung a sandwich on him
with safety slogans
and he told the Negro just to keep walking
45   all day up and down the plant
and be an example

VI

he didn't understand why he was laid off
when he'd been doing his work
on the pouring tables OK
50   and when men with less age than he had
weren't laid off
and he wanted to know why
but the superintendent told him to get the hell out
so he swung on the superintendent's jaw
55   and the cops came and took him away

VII

he's been working around here ever since there was a plant
he started off carrying tests when he was fourteen
and then he third-helped
and then he second-helped
60   and then he first-helped
and when he got to be sixty years old
and was almost blind from looking into furnaces
the bosses let him
carry tests again

VIII

65   he shouldn't have loaded and wheeled
a thousand pounds of manganese
before the cut in his belly was healed
but he had to pay his hospital bill
and he had to eat
70   he thought he had to eat
but he found out
he was wrong

IX

in the company quarters
you've got a steelplant in your backyard
75   very convenient

gongs bells whistles mudguns steamhammers and slag-pots blowing up
you get so you sleep through it
but when the plant shuts down
you can't sleep for the quiet

BEAUFORT TIDES

Low tide.
The scavenging gulls
scour the reaches of mud.
No slavers ride
5   at anchor in the roads. Rotting hulls
are drawn up on the shore.

Full stood
the tide here
when through this colonnaded door
10   into the raw land passed bond and free,
the one in hope leading the other in fear,
chained each to each by destiny.

Not only tide
but time and blood
15   can turn, can ebb and flow.
Time ebbs, blood flows, the fear
shows in the master's eye while jubilee
bursts from the bondsman's throat.

Now
20   no shout
rings out.
Neither hopes. Both fear.
What future tide will free
these captives of their history?

Bartolomeo Vanzetti (1888–1927)

Vanzetti's "Last Speech to the Court" was originally neither a poem nor a speech actually made in court. Vanzetti's words, remarks passed along to friends and a final statement to a reporter, were reprinted as verse by Selden Rodman in his 1938 collection, *A New Anthology of Modern Poetry*. Rodman describes Vanzetti's language as "eloquent with compassion and anguish, fall[ing] into lines as easily as the frost into crystals." Shoe trimmer Nicola Sacco and fish peddler Bartolomeo Vanzetti, Italian immigrants and pro-

Ben Shahn, *Passion of Sacco and Vanzetti*, 1958. Art © Estate of Ben Shahn / Licensed by VAGA, New York, NY.

letarian anarchists, were tried and convicted for murder and robbery, and after seven years in prison, were executed on August 23, 1927. Their real crime, their supporters believe, was their Italian immigrant status and their radical politics. Leading writers, scientists, and artists lobbied on their behalf during a period of repressive political hysteria known as the Red Scare (1919–1920). Long after their execution, their case inspired poetry, novels, documentaries, music, and visual art, notably Ben Shahn's Sacco and Vanzetti series.

Bartolomeo Vanzetti was born in Villafelletto, Italy, to a loving mother and fairly prosperous father. A serious and spiritual boy, he left school at age thirteen at his father's insistence that he apprentice himself to the owner of a pastry shop, where he worked fifteen-hour days. When he became ill with pleurisy, he convalesced by reading deeply in philosophy and religion. After his mother's death, Vanzetti emigrated to America in 1908. He preferred outdoor labor to the confinement of restaurant kitchens and labored in construction gangs, stone pits, brickyards, and ice works before supporting himself as a carpenter and fish peddler. His reading turned from religion to theories of radical social change. In his actual speech to the court before being sentenced to death, Vanzetti declared his innocence, saying: "Everybody that knows these two arms knows very well that I did not need to go into the streets and kill a man or try to take money. . . . I never committed a crime in my life. . . . I would not wish to a dog or to a snake, to the most low

and misfortunate creature of the earth—I would not wish to any of them what I have had
to suffer for things that I am not guilty of. I am suffering because I am a radical and indeed
I am a radical; I have suffered because I was an Italian, and indeed I am an Italian. . . . you
can only kill me once but if you could execute me two times, and I could be reborn two
other times, I would live again to do what I have done already."

Last Speech to the Court

    I have talk a great deal of myself
    but I even forgot to name Sacco.
    Sacco too is a worker,
    from his boyhood a skilled worker, lover of work,
5   with a good job and pay,
    a bank account, a good and lovely wife,
    two beautiful children and a neat little home
    at the verge of a wood, near a brook.

    Sacco is a heart, a faith, a character, a man;
10 a man, lover of nature, and mankind;
    a man who gave all, who sacrifice all
    to the cause of liberty and to his love for mankind:
    money, rest, mundane ambition,
    his own wife, his children, himself
15 and his own life.

    Sacco has never dreamt to steal, never to assassinate.
    He and I have never brought a morsel
    of bread to our mouths, from our childhood to today
    which has not been gained by the sweat of our brows.
20 Never . . .

    Oh, yes, I may be more witful, as some have put it;
    I am a better babbler than he is, but many, many times
    in hearing his heartful voice ringing a faith sublime,
    in considering his supreme sacrifice, remembering his
25   heroism,
    I felt small at the presence of his greatness
    and found myself compelled to fight back
    from my eyes the tears,
    and quanch my heart
30 trobling to my throat to not weep before him:
    this man called thief and assassin and doomed.

    But Sacco's name will live in the hearts of the people
    and in their gratitude when Katzmann's bones
    and yours will be dispersed by time;
35 when your name, his name, your laws, institutions,
    and your false god are but a dim rememoring
    of a cursed past in which man was wolf
    to the man. . . .

If it had not been for these thing
40   I might have live out my life
talking at street corners to scorning men.
I might have die, unmarked, unknown, a failure.
Now we are not a failure.
This is our career and our triumph. Never
45   in our full life could we hope to do such work
for tolerance, for justice, for man's understanding
of man, as now we do by accident.
Our words, our lives, our pains—nothing!
The taking of our lives—lives of a good shoemaker and
50   a poor fishpeddler—
all! That last moment belongs to us—
that agony is our triumph.

Agnes Smedley (1892–1950)

Born on a tenant farm in Missouri and raised in company-owned coal mining camps and towns in southern Colorado, Agnes Smedley was haunted by the memory of her mother's hands blackened by constant labor and her song-loving father's desertions and crushed hopes for economic success. After briefly attending Tempe, Arizona, Normal School, she became a country schoolteacher, and then varying circumstances, including her own writing, political acumen, vision, and pluck, led her from California to New York to Berlin to Moscow and then to China. She lived and wrote in the most radical and intellectual circles of her day. Smedley participated in the campaign for (Asian) Indian independence, was involved with the Berlin Freudians in the mid-1920s, campaigned for birth control rights (for which she was imprisoned), and throughout the 1930s was an active participant in and reporter of the Chinese revolutionary movement. She wrote hundreds of articles for socialist and progressive newspapers and journals, a classic working-class autobiographical novel, *Daughter of Earth* (1929), and six books on China, including *Battle Hymn of China* (1943).

In her peripatetic and protean life, Smedley found the soil for revolutionary change in China. Her style and language reflect both the bitterness of her impoverished youth and the lyrical beauty of her native Southwest. She believed that writing could be an agent for social change. She returned to the United States in 1942 deservedly expecting to establish herself as an expert on China, but her political commitments and allegiance to the perspectives of peasants collided with publishers' ideological conservatism. Falsely accused of being a Soviet spy and hounded by the FBI, Smedley left for England, where she died unexpectedly at the age of fifty-eight. After nearly being lost to the anticommunism of the 1950s, her books and interest in her life were revived with the republication by the Feminist Press of *Daughter of Earth* (1973, 1986) and *Portraits of Chinese Women in Revolution* (1976), both excerpted in this section. Her words in the first chapter of *Daughter of Earth* speak not just to her individual life, but to the struggles of the poor expressed in working-class literature: "I belong to those who do not die for the sake of beauty. I belong to those who die from other causes—exhausted by poverty, victims of wealth and power, fighters in a great cause." Her ashes are buried in China.

"The Wanderlust in My Blood"

Had it not been for the wanderlust in my blood—my father's gift to me—and had I not inherited his refusal to accept my lot as ordained by a God, I might have remained in the mining towns all my life, married some working man, borne him a dozen children to wander the face of the earth, and died in my early thirties. Such was the fate of all women about me. But settled things were enemies to me and soon lost their newness and color. The unknown called.

Within a year after we moved to Tercio, I found myself a school teacher—I, who had not finished the grammar school, who could not add one figure to another without mistakes, who could not remember one rule in grammar. And I was teaching children of six and boys of my own age: far out in New Mexico, on top of one of the purple-green-red mesas that suddenly rear themselves from the great plains and plateaus, a broad, flat mesa above the timber-line, surrounded by perpendicular rim-rocks that caught the lightning in the fierce storms sweeping over the mountain ranges.

There, out near the edge of the rim-rock, I lived in isolation in a two-room school house, the front room serving as my class-room, the back room as my livingroom where I slept, cooked my food and corrected my school papers. It was May when I arrived, but at night the snow still flew before the wind and beat the rope hanging from the school bell against the side of the house: a dull, ghostly sound mingling with the hoarse wailing of the wind and the creaking of the bell above.

From the broad sweeping mesa, little boys and girls came to school; from the deep canyons below, Mexicans and half-breed Indians came; from the plains that stretched as far as eye could reach to the south, a few boys and girls from the ranches came riding on cow-ponies. I was ignorant, yes, but I was learned compared with those about me. And I possessed a native cunning. When a smaller child could not do a problem in arithmetic, and I saw that I also could not do it, I called upon one of the older boys to demonstrate his knowledge before the classroom. He did it proudly, and all of us learned something.

I was "teacher," and it was considered an honor to have me in a ranch house. Children brought me food as presents, a horse was always at my disposal, and I rode through a rough but kindly land—and I rode safely, as all women rode safely, for it was a land not only where strong men lived, but it was a land where women were strong also; or, if not, where the gun slung at their sides could answer their needs. But neither physical force nor guns were necessary. I recall now the years of my girlhood and youth amongst the men of the far West—unlettered, rough working-men who had tasted the worst of life: and with but one exception—that of a barber in a small town—I had never suffered insult and not one man had tried to lay a hand on me in violence. Perhaps I was too young or too ignorant. I had many suitors for marriage, for there were few women in that land. But I was wiser than most girls about me. My intellect, rough and unshod as it was, was wiser than my emotions. All girls married, and I did not know how I would escape, but escape I determined to. I remember that almost without words, my mother supported me in this.

There in New Mexico I rode with men far and wide, singly and in groups, at midday, or to and from dances at night. I danced with them in ranch houses down in the dark canyons or on the plains. They were honorable men, and I was safer with them than are girls within convent walls—far safer. Of sex I thought not at all, for not only was I little more than a child, but I was too busy. There were so many other things to think about; and then, I had no intention of marrying.

I now recall with joy those hearty, rough, hairy-chested, unshaven men. I recall the rougher, unhappy men in the mining camps, and their silent, unhappy wives. It is with a feeling of sadness and of affection that I think of them now. But there were years when, in search of what I thought were better, nobler things, I denied these, my people, and my family. I forgot the songs they sung—and most of those songs are now dead; I erased their dialect from my tongue; I was ashamed of them and their ways of life. But now—yes, I love them; they are a part of my blood; they, with all their virtues and their faults, played a great part in forming my way of looking at life.

Back in Tercio I had, by the purest chance, met the camp school teacher, a woman from a normal school. At first I was resentful and suspicious of her because she was an educated woman. At last we became friends. We borrowed horses from the camp and rode and hunted together in the hills. She had urged me to study with her, take the county teachers' examination, and become a teacher. Before the year was finished she had loaned me one of her blouses and skirts, and I rode across the Divide to a New Mexico town where the teachers' examination was held.

"Say you are eighteen," she warned. "Lie—it won't hurt anybody."

"I'm not afraid of lyin'," I replied.

"Lie!" Big Buck later exclaimed when I told him of it. "Why, you can lie quicker'n a jackrabbit can jump!"

In fear and trembling I sat among older, better-educated women and took the examination. Two days passed and the County Superintendent of Schools sent for me. He was a tall, lean, black-eyed Mexican, intelligent and kindly.

"You have low grades in arithmetic, and grammar, and school law, and a few more things," he announced, "but if you can speak a little Mexican, here is a school. It is lonely. It is so cold that school is held only in the summer. It is rough and far from town. You will have to cook your own food and wash your own clothes. The life is rough . . . cattle men, you know!"

I didn't understand, but wisdom taught me to listen and look intelligent; it was news to me that there were people who did not cook their own food; and I thought that everybody except rich people washed their own clothing. Then "rough people" . . . what could he mean, I wondered . . . he must mean people who hang around saloons . . . yet that was not possible, for he said it was a lonely place. I would just wait and see; it never occurred to me that I myself belonged to just such rough people as he referred to.

So it was that I became a teacher. I had no fear of loneliness or the cold or wild animals . . . and as for roughness . . . well, I waited to see what it would be like. I never saw any of it. Everybody acted just like I did. Even when, up there on the mesa, I was stunned by lightning that struck the rim-rock a short distance from my house, and I was left lying stretched unconscious across my doorway for hours, it really never occurred to me to be either afraid or give up the school. I merely dragged myself into my room, crept to bed, and waited to get better. The school was the best thing I had ever known. I was making forty dollars a month and sending part of it to my mother. And she, delicate and gentle, proudly made shirts and skirts and sent them to her school-teacher daughter! She had always known I would become "edjicated." Now, when she met the wife of the Superintendent of the camp at Tercio, she did not try to hide her big-veined hands and pass by without being seen; she raised her head proudly and said:

"Howdye do, Mis' Richards . . . it's a nice day t'day, ain't it?"

Up there on the mesa I found a cheap, monthly, housewife's magazine that contained continued love stories, patterns for dresses, recipes for cooking, beauty hints, and odds and ends of a thousand kinds. There was also a list of names and addresses of men and women who wished to exchange picture post cards. From this list I chose the name of a man—the most beautiful name there—a Robert Hampton, whose address was Columbus, Ohio. That was a city far back East, and I had great ideas of the beauty and learning and culture of cities. I sent him a post card. He replied, and as the summer wore on one card gave way to two, then to four in an envelope. He wrote that he was finishing high school—a learned man, in my eyes! He began sending me his old books to read—history, literature, botany—and I studied them, even the things that were dry and uninteresting. Then I sent them on to my mother; for I wanted her to study also. When the school closed and I went home in the autumn, I found my mother sitting by the kitchen window patiently studying one of the books. It had taken her weeks and she was not yet half finished. It was so very new and difficult for her, yet she, as I, felt that it was necessary to know these things.

That was a great home-coming for me . . . I, the triumphant, conquering daughter of sixteen! I was now one of the chief supports of our family. My father was working on a far-away ranch. He came to Tercio, where my mother now lived, while I was there. I still remember how he came. My mother was sitting by the window, her face enthusiastic as I told of my teaching and of the new school I was to have during the winter. I told her of Robert Hampton, who had sent me a picture of himself—how he was handsome and learned like the men in books. She replied nothing; perhaps she thought it best that I fell in love with a distant hero rather than a near-by reality. As we talked, her eyes wandered to the hillside beyond and I saw her face become suddenly miserable. I noticed how gray her hair had become, although she was but in her late thirties. My eyes followed her, and there from beyond the Company store came my father, walking heavily, his big shoulders stooped, his head down, his hands moving as if talking to some imaginary person.

I went almost immediately to my other school. It lay in a canyon far back of Primero, another of the C. F. & I. Company camps. There, for four months, I heard no English except that spoken in my school; even my students talked to me in Mexican. At night I went to my room in a Mexican adobe house. The man of the house was a Mexican on the school board and he felt it his right, as a man and as an official, to talk at length with the most intellectual woman in the countryside. And that woman was I! His wife was a broad, good-natured Mexican with no ambitions and no ideas. He always ate his supper with me and she waited table, moving back and forth from the kitchen to the room which was the dining-room, the living-room, and my bedroom, all in one. Later, she and her child ate their supper in the kitchen. Her husband spoke a remarkable jargon that was half Mexican and half English, although he led her to believe that he spoke perfect and fluent English. His contempt for her was great and he was always trying to let me see how humiliating it was for a man of his position and intelligence to be married to such a woman. I dared show no sympathy with the woman . . . such would have been a deadly insult to the man and perhaps I would have lost my position.

I wearied of his talk. But he thought a woman should always listen to a man and improve her intellect . . . a woman always knew less than a man; it mattered not who or what she was. I longed for the comfort of silence in which I could read the new book and the letter that had come from Robert Hampton in the East. Those letters were the most important things in my life; they were written in a handwriting that was perfect. While I was in my school the Mexican read them, without my permission, then questioned me about their contents. He understood little, but he knew the handwriting was incomparable and he respected me more for having learned friends. At night I sat for hours with them propped before me, trying to learn to write like that, and to this day my handwriting bears a similarity to them. I knew that if I could ever learn to write so beautifully my education would be complete.

My distant correspondent became the ideal who guided my life. He must have felt like a god, he, sitting back there reading the humble, groping, scrawling letters from a lonely canyon in the Rocky Mountains. Over my little table stood his picture and on the table his old books; if my emotions ever wandered to some dark, handsome Mexican-Indian boy in the neighborhood—as they often did, for I was a wanderer in all things—I fought them, and felt ashamed of myself at night when I went home. But it was not easy. There was an

Indian boy just my age in school; he watched me with worshipful eyes, not daring to approach so learned a person as I. His homage to me was the discipline he exercised over all the other pupils—a blink of an eyelash against me from one of them and he escorted them to the edge of the forest at recess time!

One day as I was standing before my classroom and trying to induce my school to talk to me in English—my chief occupation—the door opened and my Mexican host appeared. A telephone call had come from beyond the hills, from Tercio; my mother was sick and I must go home. I stood staring at him, as if he were a messenger of death. He repeated the message. I turned without a word, took my hat and coat hanging in the corner and left the school building. It never occurred to me to dismiss the school. I only knew that my mother was dying . . . had I not dreamed it the night before?

The man caught up with me at his house. He would drive me over the hills tomorrow, he said, for now his team was up in the timber hauling props for the mines. Only one train a day came up the canyons from Trinidad and stopped at all the coal camps. It would reach Primero at two in the afternoon and Tercio in another hour. It was now eleven. I said I would walk to Primero. No, he protested, the snow was deep in the canyons and it was freezing cold. . . . It was dangerous. I hardly heard him. I went into my room, strapped my gun tightly about my waist beneath my coat, and started. He and his wife stood in the door watching in amazement as I started up the canyon road and turned to take the short-cut across the Divide. The snow was heavy, but a herd of sheep had been driven that way and had beaten it down. I climbed the slippery slope, pulling myself up here and there with the tough scrub oak that fastened itself in the frozen ground. If I could only reach the top of the Divide, the rest would be easy, for there I would reach the road. The cold, the possibility of meeting wild animals, the danger of slipping and falling and lying with a broken leg—nothing came to my mind except the top of the hills. Thinking nothing, feeling nothing, seeing nothing, I climbed.

At last I reached it. It had been swept clear of snow by a fierce wind, and was rutty and frozen. I hid my head in my coat collar for a second to warm my lungs. Then I began a slow, easy, steady trot that makes it possible to cover long distances and still not be too exhausted. My mind watched my body as if the two were separate units. My body was tough and strong —as tough as the mountain oak. My mind knew that when the body was so exhausted that it seemed unable to go further, a new energy would flow through it—the "second wind" would come. My mind was I, down that long hard road with the wind lashing my back—my body was a foreign thing. I—my mind—as clear as the winter air, was concentrated on one point—to reach the mining camp by two o'clock; my body was a foreign thing that must be coaxed and humored into doing it. The chief thing, I assured myself over and over again, was to keep the legs steady until the second wind came. There was a time when my legs trembled, weak and faltering. I turned a bend and there, far beyond and below, I saw the smoke of Primero. I lifted my chin—a new warm energy was coursing through my blood, and down the slope, my mouth buried in the neck of my coat to warm the air entering my lungs, my hands free to catch myself in case I should fall, I swung along, running in that slow, steady trot.

I reached the outskirts of Primero, turned to run past the Company store and take the road, black with coal dust, leading to the station. But I was not the only one running— other people, with horror-stricken faces, were rushing through the streets, and I saw that the windows in the Company store were shattered into bits . . . across the street the windows of other houses were also broken. A woman with a plaid shawl over her head stumbled by, weeping in wild terror and crying out in some foreign tongue.

Without faltering in my trot, I turned the corner of the store to pass the mouth of a mine on the hillside that lay before the station. The road was filled with people. Two working men met and ran toward the mine, one shouting at the other:

"They're shuttin' the air-shafts, the God damned . . ."

The mine was belching black smoke, like some primeval Fafnir. Men were drawing ropes around the base of the slag dump and were trying to beat back the struggling women, who fought with the savageness of wild beasts. Their men were penned in the mines, I heard . . . the air-shafts were being closed to save the coal . . . but the fumes would smother the men to death. Such was the burden of their cries. Coal was dear . . . life was cheap.

I ran on. I stumbled onto the station platform and up the steps of the train without even thinking of a ticket. I threw myself face downward on a seat. My lungs were tight and cold. Beyond . . . miles beyond the other side of the humming . . . humming . . . came the scream of a woman.

For three days and nights I watched by her bedside. A movement would awaken me as I dozed. Her blue-black eyes were tender as they followed me back and forth. The doctor who made his weekly rounds from mining town to mining town was out of patience . . . there seemed nothing wrong with her as he could see. Yes—pains in the stomach, of course . . . that was from bad food and from too little . . . what else could you expect, he said, if she insisted on living on potatoes and flour-and-water gravy! She must have better food . . . she was under-nourished. I wondered what "under-nourished" could mean. No, he answered my question, even if she wanted it, she could have no more bicarbonate of soda to ease the pain.

During the first two days she talked with me. Annie had died two weeks before . . . that she had written me. She had gone to her, away down on the desolate plain of western Oklahoma where Annie and Sam worked like animals on their homestead. Annie had left the baby . . . a tiny thing, lying in the next room. I warmed milk and fed it, and it watched me with wistful blue eyes; strange it was that its coming should have caused my sister's death.

My mother was very happy as I sat by her. But I think she knew that death was near, for she said strange things to me—things touching the emotions that she would never have dared say otherwise, for affection between parents and children was never shown among my people. She called me "my daughter"—a thing she had never said before in her life.

"I don't know how I could of lived till now if it hadn't been fer you," she said once, as if the words were wrung from her.

Once in the middle of the night she woke me to say: "Promise me you'll go on an' git a better edjication." Her hand closed upon mine, steady and strong, as if asking for a pledge. A wave of unfamiliar emotion swept over me. I clasped her hand.

When the doctor came the next day I said, "Please give her somethin' . . . she's goin' to die." He was disgusted . . . he had a lot to do and was sick of my telephoning down for him to come all the way up there when there was nothing wrong with my mother except that she needed decent food for a while, he said.

I watched him go. Then, standing by my mother's bedside, I realized that we faced death alone . . . and that I was helpless. She pleaded for the forbidden bicarbonate of soda. I would not give it. But she pleaded again and again and the look in her eyes appalled me. Then, in my ignorance, I gave it. But when I did it, I turned and ran up the alley to the school building, burst into the schoolroom and, without thinking, called aloud to Beatrice, George and Dan.

When we reached her bedside, my father, who had come home that morning, was there. He had fallen on his knees and had buried his face in the covers. My mother's eyes were large and glistening, and she turned them on me in an appeal beyond all speech. I bent over the bed and, for the first time in my life, took her in my arms and held her close to my trembling body. "Marie!" My name was the last word she ever uttered.

The lids closed down over the glistening eyes. The body grew limp. I tore back the covering and listened to her breast, so flat, so thin, so poor. The heart throbbed twice, stopped . . . throbbed once more. I listened an eternity . . . intensely yearning . . . but no sound came. My father pulled me to my feet. With difficulty I could stand on my feet. But there were no tears in me. I only knew that I stood by the body of the woman who had given me life. I understood nothing except that this thing I could not understand. In my mind a brilliant light ran in circles, then contracted until it was a tiny I black spot, then became lost in nothingness, and nothingness throbbed in beats, like the waves of a sea against a cliff.

Helen came. She and my father touched hands in the room where my mother's body lay in a white pine-board coffin. Her hair was still a burnished bronze with flashes of dull gold. Her cheeks and lips were painted. She wore a fur coat of great beauty. Her eyes traveled about the room—to the cold, bare floor, the rickety old bureau in the corner, the little rusty stove, the cheap white curtain at the window. Then she turned back the sheet from my mother's body and gazed at the worn, wrinkled face, wistful in death as in life; at the rough, big-veined hands almost black from work, clasped across the thin breast; at the hair, almost gray, although my mother was still young. Turning away to hide her face from us, she stepped into the sleeping room at the side, removed her cloak and stood watching the tiny bit of kicking baby on the bed—the baby that belonged to Sam, the first and perhaps the only love in her life.

We were to take my mother's body to Oklahoma to bury it beside Annie. We had waited only for Helen's coming. In the afternoon the pine coffin was put into the baggage car of the train, and we began our journey.

We left the train at a station on the plains of western Oklahoma where Sam met us in a big rough wagon. When he caught sight of Helen he walked away, but turned back to grasp her hand and look at his baby lying in her arms.

It was January and the earth was hard and cold, swept almost clean by a bitter wind that rushed across the plains. A lonely clump of trees stood here and there, but apart from these the plains stretched endlessly, freezing and bare, the road a rutty, winding trail across the waste. After a long time we reached a gaunt, frame house where Sam and Annie had lived, and where Sam now lived alone. The coffin was placed in the bare front room.

By the next morning crude board benches and a few chairs stood in rows before the coffin. A number of men and women had gathered from farmhouses, together with the ignorant minister who was to preach the sermon. This minister now stood on the other side of my mother's coffin and talked to us. He was illiterate, crude and vulgar, even more than we. He said things that had nothing to do with my mother's body lying there, or with the poverty and unhappiness that had killed her. He looked squarely at Helen, sitting there in her fur coat . . . he looked at my father sitting with his head bent, chewing a cud of tobacco, his shoulders round and stooped. He looked accusingly at us all, one by one, and spoke to us without calling our individual names. We were not Christians, he said,—and dared touch the coffin of my mother! He warned us that we were going the way of sin . . . some of us the way of scarlet sin . . . his eyes swooped upon Helen as a vulture swoops upon its prey; God had punished us by taking my mother from us, but He would punish us still more!

My father arose and went up to the preacher and knelt down, the imprint of a bottle in his hip pocket showing through his coat as he bent. The preacher reached down and laid his hand piously on his head—one soul saved! He turned to Helen and his lips parted for speech. But with a gasp of disgust and anger, Helen arose and walked out of the room, deliberately and with quiet dignity. I followed her, and the mourners and the preacher stared in scandalized silence.

The funeral ceremony came to an end, lamely and unimpressively, and amidst a shocked silence Helen and I joined the small group to proceed to the cemetery. We drove a long distance and entered a graveyard by a fence made of one single barbed wire stretched on crazy posts leaning in every direction. Perhaps twelve mounds were in the lot, all with one straight piece of board at the head and one smaller one at the foot. On these had once been written the names of the dead, but the wind and rain and snow had long since eradicated them. The name of my sister was still readable, and near her grave lay the mound of fresh earth that had been thrown up for the grave of my mother. We stood among the graves and listened once more to the preacher calling down the blessing of God upon my mother and a warning upon those who failed to heed him.

Then we were told to look at my mother's face for the last time. I did not weep. Helen did not weep . . . her face was filled with a hard white misery as she gazed down on the sister she had so dearly loved . . . for "greater love hath no woman than she who will sell her body for the sister she loves."

For months I followed the road that I had marked out for myself. With resolve I determined to care for my brothers and sister and my dead sister's baby. So I gave up my school and came back to Tercio, to cooking, washing, ironing and sewing. My father returned home. I tried to make things homelike—it seemed to me that if my mother had perhaps done that, my father would not have drunk himself into stupidity all the time. I bought a carpet and new window curtains, a round brown table, a few pictures for the wall— pictures of children with angel's wings—and I bought white spreads for the beds.

But the daily housework and worry of our little house bore heavily upon me and I thought ceaselessly of my mother. I was succeeding no better with my father than she had. To think of years and years of living like this, as she had done! My conflicts with him became frequent and my desire to go away grew stronger and tormented me. The transient atmosphere that had always been a part of our life had become a part of me, and I was restless, unhappy, resentful.

One day my father returned home drunk. Dan had done something to displease him, and the boy watched him in terror, for my father had a long horsewhip in his hand. He reached for Dan, who rushed behind me and threw his arms about my waist, keeping me between him and my father. I held the little hands tightly about me . . . my father cursed and ordered him into the center of the room where he would "teach him a lesson." Then my father lunged toward him, but I kept my body between them. He made a dive around me, but with all my might I pushed him back. Not a word was spoken between us . . . I felt him grasp my shoulder to throw me out of the way, and without thinking I hurled myself upon him, striking with my clenched fists, blow upon blow.

Then he was standing motionless. He and I stood looking at each other. He turned and picked up the whip from the floor. I watched like an animal, ready to spring, for he should never use it! He looked at the whip, then turned and slowly passed out of the door, the whip dragging along the floor behind him.

MINING FAMILIES

Today I visited the miner Partisans again. I talked with three miners who helped the Eighth Route Army fight the Japanese at Kwangyangchen. One of them told me his story. He was once a soldier in General Feng Yu-hsiang's army, and later became a miner in the Kailin mines at Tangshan, Hopei Province. The Japanese invasion left him unemployed and he found a job in the terrible coal mines at Tatung, North Shansi, where he worked for twenty to thirty cents a day and lived like a dog. When the Communist Party began organizing the men he was arrested and sentenced to twelve years in the Taiyuan prison.

With the Japanese invasion and the building of the national front, he was released and was sent to Yangchüan, on the Chentai railway, to organize the miners there into Partisans. The mines were closed and but two hundred miners remained. He organized them into an armed Partisan group, along with the railway workers there. They blew up the railway as the Japanese advanced; they helped the Eighth Route Army blow up the railroad line at various other places, and finally they fought from November 2nd to 4th at Kwangyangchen (south-west of Yangchüan) and helped the Eighth Route Army score its victory in the afternoon and night of November 4th.

The Partisans have their families with them. Li-po talked with the old mother of one of the men. She is sixty-one years old, grey-haired, strong, militant. She told him that she had two sons, one of whom is a Partisan here and the other a Volunteer. "Do not think of taking care of me," she told them. "Go and fight the enemy. I order you!" She is now with the elder son and is sewing and knitting socks for all the Partisans. She is the mother of the whole group.

As they came down from Yangchüan the miners saw the dead bodies of many slaughtered Chinese youths. In many places the Japanese had taken one, two or three men from each family and killed them; they had sometimes killed all the young men of a village. They roped them together and then split their heads open with swords, on the general theory that living Chinese—particularly youths—are "dangerous." Many people, the miners said, merely watched the Japanese come. But now they have learned a bloody lesson. They know now what the Japanese occupation means—and they are fighting it.

It was difficult to realize, except for the language, that I was talking to Chinese miners, and their wives, sisters and daughters. Some way or other, the miners of all countries look alike, move alike, have the same kind of hands into which coal dust is beaten or rubbed. There is a decision about them, a kind of grim attitude that is still friendly, and an intelligence that arouses respect. Their problems are almost the same, though the problems of the Chinese miners are greater and more difficult than those of Americans. They told of their miserable conditions of life, of their struggle to organize, and of imprisonment and torture. And yet, when the Japanese invasion began, they took up arms to defend their country. They have a great advantage, however, over the oppressed of other countries: they have the Eighth Route Army, an army of workers and peasants, to help them, to train them, to take them into its ranks.

We met groups of armed miners escorting more of their women to the rear. The women might have been the wives or daughters of American or European miners. Like their men, they were grim—perhaps a bit more grim than the men. Their hair was a bit stringy about their faces, they stood firmly on their feet, and they sometimes propped their hands on their hips or folded them across their waists in front of them.

I left the miners feeling once more that I am nothing but a writer, a mere onlooker. I look at their big, black-veined hands, at their cloth shoes worn down to their socks or bare feet, at their soiled shirts. I know there is no chance for me ever to know them and share their lives. I remain a teller of tales, a writer of things through which I have not lived. The real story of China can be told only by the Chinese workers and peasants themselves. To-day that is impossible. I do not believe that my companions, Chinese though they are, can write the real story of the struggle of the Chinese people. They are true Chinese intellectuals, as removed from the life of the masses as I am. And one of them, Hsu Chuen, is first of all interested in "style."

If you ask him about a book, he will tell you first of its style. Later on you can pry out of him something of the content. Li-po is more interested in content, it is true. But the life he lives is so hard now that he is often too weary to make use of his experiences. Later on he will become hardened to this way of life, I think. What I write is not the essence of the Chinese struggle for liberation. It is the record of an observer.

V

Economic Depression and Cultural Resurgence: 1930s

[A] poet's mind
Is as useful as a carpenter's hammer,
As real for plain people as the color red.
–*Genevieve Taggard, "Words Property of the People" (1934)*

The 1930s—from the stock market crash of 1929 through U.S. entry into World War II in 1941—were years of economic disaster, bringing widespread suffering and dislocation to America's working people. The Great Depression also brought with it a resurgence in the country's labor movement, as well as a "New Deal" from the federal government designed to ensure a measure of social well-being to the broad mass of the population. During the 1930s, new forms of "proletarian" writing came to the cultural forefront to dramatize the turbulence of these years and give literary shape to new possibilities arising from it. "For the first time in American literature," writes Laura Hapke, "a truly wide landscape emerged, peopled by sharecropping blacks, Mexican farmworkers, Dust Bowl migrants, Detroit autoworkers, men in lumber, men in sweatshops, and women in canneries, peafields, homes, and commercialized sex venues."[1] In the 1930s, most of the authors of this wider literary landscape were worker-writers—the poet and the carpenter in one person—giving voice to their stories and social visions in their own language.

At the lowest point of the Great Depression, with industrial production cut by half and thousands of businesses failing, an estimated one-third of Americans were unemployed, and as many as another third worked only occasionally. Hunger was endemic, families were torn apart, and homeless workers roamed the country in search of jobs, food, and shelter. A severe drought across the nation's agricultural belt, combined with terrifying dust storms in the lower Plains, compounded the disaster of homelessness, forcing tens of thousands of farm families to join the flood of refugees (as we see in the work of Sanora Babb, John Steinbeck, Wilma Elizabeth McDaniel, and Woody Guthrie). In the cities, where soup kitchens and Salvation Army shelters could not accommodate the need for relief, police rounded up and jailed panhandlers for the crime of "vagrancy." Yip Harburg's song "Brother, Can You Spare a Dime" (1932) became an anthem of the early depression years: "Once I built a railroad, made it run, made it race against time. Once I built a railroad. Now it's done. Brother, can you spare a dime." In an age before unemployment benefits or social security—both of which were created as a part of the New Deal response to the depression—the scale and extremity of human suffering shattered any faith left over from the "Roaring Twenties" that capitalism could deliver a better life for the majority of Americans.

The 1930s were, though, not only a time of need and disillusionment; they were also a time of anger at the government and at corporate monopolies, which were blamed for

Facing Page: Rockwell Kent, "The Workers of the World Unite," 1938. *Courtesy of Library of Congress, LC-USZ62-63874.*

the economic collapse, and a time of vigorous political and cultural activism on behalf of, and on the part of, the working class. The constant low-level class war between the homeless and the police erupted into full-scale conflict when the "Bonus Army"—World War I veterans demanding immediate payment of their military bonuses—marched on Washington, DC, in 1932. President Herbert Hoover ordered the U.S. Army to keep the veterans away from the capitol; General Douglas MacArthur took it upon himself to attack and burn down their "Hooverville" colony of tents and shacks, at the cost of several lives. The sight of thousands of former soldiers and their families being driven out with teargas, bayonets, and tanks did irreparable damage to Hoover's credibility. Hoover lost the election of 1932 to a little-known Democrat, Franklin Delano Roosevelt, who, by the mid-1930s, would put in place the New Deal legislation—including the WPA (Works Progress Administration) job-creation program and the Wagner Act's recognition of the rights of unions to organize and bargain—which provided some relief from unemployment and gave legitimacy to the mass organizing drives of the 1930s.

After decades of defeats, from the 1890s through the 1920s, labor was again on the move. Unemployed Councils staged mass protests and organized mutual aid at the local level: patrols rehoused evicted tenants, while unemployed electricians reconnected homes whose power had been shut off. The political Left rebounded from the repression of the 1920s, with many socialists now joining with the Communist Party in providing leadership and vision to the new mass movements. With capitalism apparently collapsing and fascism on the rise in Europe, the communists' revolutionary ideal of full democracy and shared resources had wide appeal. The 1934 general strikes in San Francisco and Minneapolis, which writers Tillie Olsen (San Francisco) and Meridel LeSueur (Minneapolis) participated in and recorded, shut down entire cities and demonstrated the power of mass action. Within the ranks of labor, a new coalition arose—the CIO (Congress of Industrial Organizations)—to organize, in the words of the miners' leader John L. Lewis, the "great reservoir of workers here numbering millions and millions of men and women [willing] to join with us in this great fight for the maintenance of the rights of workers and for the upholding of the standards of modern democracy."[2] Labor rights were also civil rights—as Thurgood Marshall put it, "The program of the CIO has become a Bill of Rights for Negro labor in America"—and many organizers were active against Jim Crow laws and racial violence across the South (as seen in Richard Wright's "Fire and Cloud"). The Flint sit-down strike against General Motors, among others in 1936, demonstrated the success of the new industry-wide approach. In the same year, even antiunion giant U.S. Steel signed a contract with the Steel Workers Organizing Committee (a victory that is celebrated at the conclusion of Thomas Bell's novel of immigrant labor in the Pittsburgh steel towns, *Out of This Furnace*). A Fair Labor Standards Act became law in 1938, and by 1941 33 percent of American workers (and close to 100 percent in the mass production industries) belonged to unions.

On the cultural front, writers were fully engaged in the struggles of the 1930s. They produced a body of work which, along with the burgeoning art, music, theater, and photography of the time, made visible the human cost of the Great Depression, critiqued the systems that produced it, and implicitly or overtly argued for radical social change. Some writers, inspired by Mike Gold's proletarian manifestos (see "Go Left, Young Writers"), sought to create literature "as useful as a carpenter's hammer / As real to plain folk as the color red," as poet Genevieve Taggard expressed this mission. The journal *New Masses*, which Gold edited from 1929 to 1934, published a number of the writers whose works are gathered in this section: little-known worker-writers like Tillie Olsen, Joseph Kalar, and Richard Wright; established authors like John Dos Passos and Mary Heaton Vorse, who embraced and recorded working-class life and struggle; as well as the radical Harlem Renaissance poet Langston Hughes. Joseph North described the journal's impact on a young worker-writer: "The monthly *New Masses* arrived at my mailbox in a Pennsylvania city and I could not wait until I tore the wrapper off. . . . My father was a blacksmith who had never mastered the reading or writing of English; my mother a seamstress who taught herself to read and write; I, myself, a rivet-passer in the shipyard when I wasn't in the books."[3] A major goal of the proletarian literary movement was to produce not only new readers for new forms of writing, but new writers as well.

Many emerging writers like North were nurtured in the John Reed Clubs, venues for discussion of art and politics, which formed in most major cities, supported (as was the New York-based *New Masses*) by the Communist Party. Many found outlets for their work in the numerous independent "mushroom mags" that were cropping up across the country with names like *Blast, Dynamo, Hub, Outlander, The New Tide*, and *Challenge* (a Boston-based journal of African American writing). From 1933 to 1936, the leading proletarian magazine was the *Anvil: Stories for Workers*, edited by Jack Conroy in Moberly, Illinois, initially as a publication of the Rebel Poets. Still other writers produced their work relatively removed from this thriving literary left wing: Tom Kromer's narratives of being "on the bum," Zora Neale Hurston's folk sociology, Don West's southern mountain poetry, Pietro Di Donato's Italian American work-fiction, Wilma Elizabeth McDaniel's Dust Bowl vignettes, "Boxcar Bertha"'s stories of hobo women, and the Appalachian songs of Aunt Molly Jackson and Florence Reese. Together, their contributions produced a broad shift in American culture: a democratization of writing and publishing that has never since been fully reversed. "Proletarian literature," writes Michael Denning, "enfranchised a generation of writers of ethnic, working-class origins; it allowed them to represent—to speak for and to depict—their families, their neighborhoods, their aspirations, and their nightmares" (Denning 229). Their combined cultural production transformed American literature for decades to come, opening the territory on which the multicultural writers, men and women, of the postwar and contemporary periods would build their work.

Notes

1. Laura Hapke, *Labor's Text: The Worker in American Fiction* (New Brunswick, NJ: Rutgers University Press, 2001), 221.

2. Quoted in Paul Le Blanc, *A Short History of the U.S. Working Class* (Amherst, NY: Humanity Books, 1999), 85–86.

3. Quoted in Michael Denning, *The Cultural Front: The Laboring of American Culture in the Twentieth Century* (London: Verso, 1997), 205.

Langston Hughes (1902–1967)

From the publication of *The Weary Blues* in 1926 through the 1950s, Langston Hughes was the best-known African American poet. He was a major figure in both the Harlem Renaissance and in left-wing resistance to fascism and economic injustice. A prolific writer, he produced twelve volumes of poetry, several plays, a novel, an autobiography, and a long-running series of newspaper sketches that presented dialogues in a Harlem café with a character named Simple. Hughes was also a reporter with the Abraham Lincoln Brigade in the Spanish Civil War; a translator of Frederico Garcia Lorca; and an editor, with Arna Bontemps, of *The Poetry of the Negro, 1746–1949*. Born in Joplin, Missouri, Hughes grew up in Lawrence, Kansas, moving to Cleveland, Ohio, and other cities in his mother's search for work after his father left the family. He eventually settled in New York City, working a series of low-wage jobs and shipping out as a merchant seaman. As a sailor, he traveled to Africa and Europe; later, as a writer and cultural ambassador, he visited the Soviet Union, Japan, and China. Harlem was Hughes's home base; its street life and its music, jazz and blues, were deep influences on his art.

Hughes was a "popular" writer in a double sense: he wrote for and about the people he knew and lived among, recording their day-to-day struggles and joys; and he was widely read and appreciated, both in the United States and internationally. He was also a political writer, exposing the contradictions of racial and class subordination with deceptive simplicity and sharp irony. He was admired and criticized for both his popularity and his politics. Academic critics and some fellow writers discounted his apparently simple style and common subjects. For his radicalism, and especially his association with American and international communists, Hughes was persecuted both officially by J. Edgar Hoover's FBI, and unofficially through a racist hate campaign. Under this pressure, Hughes's self-edited *Selected Poems* (1959) left out many of his most radical pieces—including "Christ in Alabama"—which were not fully restored to his canon until the 1990s.

THE WEARY BLUES

Droning a drowsy syncopated tune,
Rocking back and forth to a mellow croon,
    I heard a Negro play.
Down on Lenox Avenue the other night
5   By the pale dull pallor of an old gas light
       He did a lazy sway. . . .
       He did a lazy sway. . . .
To the tune o' those Weary Blues.
With his ebony hands on each ivory key
10   He made that poor piano moan with melody.
       O Blues!
Swaying to and fro on his rickety stool
He played that sad raggy tune like a musical fool.
       Sweet Blues!
15   Coming from a black man's soul.
       O Blues!
In a deep song voice with a melancholy tone
I heard that Negro sing, that old piano moan—
      "Ain't got nobody in all this world,
20   Ain't got nobody but ma self.
      I's gwine to quit ma frownin'
      And put ma troubles on the shelf."

Thump, thump, thump, went his foot on the floor.
He played a few chords then he sang some more—
25   "I got the Weary Blues
      And I can't be satisfied.
      Got the Weary Blues
      And can't be satisfied—
      I ain't happy no mo'
30   And I wish that I had died."

And far into the night he crooned that tune.
The stars went out and so did the moon.
The singer stopped playing and went to bed
While the Weary Blues echoed through his head.
35 He slept like a rock or a man that's dead.

JOHANNESBURG MINES

In the Johannesburg mines
There are 240,000
Native Africans working.
What kind of poem
Would you
5   Make out of that?
240,000 natives
Working in the
Johannesburg mines.

CHRIST IN ALABAMA

Christ is a nigger,
Beaten and black:
Oh, bare your back!

Mary is His mother:
5   Mammy of the South,
Silence your mouth.

God is His father:
White Master above
Grant Him your love.

10 Most holy bastard
Of the bleeding mouth,
    Nigger Christ
    On the cross
    Of the South.

PARK BENCH

I live on a park bench.
You, Park Avenue.
Hell of a distance
Between us two.

5   I beg a dime for dinner—
You got a butler and maid.
But I'm wakin' up!
Say, ain't you afraid

That I might, just maybe,
10   In a year or two,
Move on over
To Park Avenue?

Let America Be America Again

Let America be America again.
Let it be the dream it used to be.
Let it be the pioneer on the plain
Seeking a home where he himself is free.

5   (America never was America to me.)

Let America be the dream the dreamers dreamed—
Let it be that great strong land of love
Where never kings connive nor tyrants scheme
That any man be crushed by one above.

10   (It never was America to me.)

O, let my land be a land where Liberty
Is crowned with no false patriotic wreath,
But opportunity is real, and life is free,
Equality is in the air we breathe.

15   (There's never been equality for me,
Nor freedom in this "homeland of the free.")

Say, who are you that mumbles in the dark?
And who are you that draws your veil across the stars?

I am the poor white, fooled and pushed apart,
20   I am the Negro bearing slavery's scars.
I am the red man driven from the land,
I am the immigrant clutching the hope I seek—
And finding only the same old stupid plan
Of dog eat dog, of mighty crush the weak.

25   I am the young man, full of strength and hope,
Tangled in that ancient endless chain
Of profit, power, gain, of grab the land!
Of grab the gold! Of grab the ways of satisfying need!
Of work the men! Of take the pay!
30   Of owning everything for one's own greed!

I am the farmer, bondsman to the soil.
I am the worker sold to the machine.
I am the Negro, servant to you all.
I am the people, humble, hungry, mean—
35   Hungry yet today despite the dream.
Beaten yet today—O, Pioneers!
I am the man who never got ahead,
The poorest worker bartered through the years.

Yet I'm the one who dreamt our basic dream
40   In that Old World while still a serf of kings,
Who dreamt a dream so strong, so brave, so true,
That even yet its mighty daring sings
In every brick and stone, in every furrow turned
That's made America the land it has become.
45   O, I'm the man who sailed those early seas
In search of what I meant to be my home—
For I'm the one who left dark Ireland's shore,
And Poland's plain, and England's grassy lea,
And torn from Black Africa's strand I came
50   To build a "homeland of the free."

The free?

Who said the free? Not me?
Surely not me? The millions on relief today?
The millions shot down when we strike?
55   The millions who have nothing for our pay?
For all the dreams we've dreamed
And all the songs we've sung
And all the hopes we've held
And all the flags we've hung,
60   The millions who have nothing for our pay—
Except the dream that's almost dead today.

O, let America be America again—
The land that never has been yet—
And yet must be—the land where *every* man is free.
65   The land that's mine—the poor man's, Indian's, Negro's, ME—
Who made America,
Whose sweat and blood, whose faith and pain,
Whose hand at the foundry, whose plow in the rain,
Must bring back our mighty dream again.

70   Sure, call me any ugly name you choose—
The steel of freedom does not stain.
From those who live like leeches on the people's lives,
We must take back our land again,
America!

75   O, yes,
I say it plain,
America never was America to me,
And yet I swear this oath—
America will be!

80   Out of the rack and ruin of our gangster death,
The rape and rot of graft, and stealth, and lies,
We, the people, must redeem
The land, the mines, the plants, the rivers.
The mountains and the endless plain—
85   All, all the stretch of these great green states—
And make America again!

OFFICE BUILDING: EVENING

When the white folks get through
Here come you:

Got to clean awhile.

When daytime folks
5   Have made their dough,
Away they go:

You clean awhile.

When white collars get done,
You have your "fun"
10   Cleaning awhile.

"But just wait, chile . . ."

Genevieve Taggard (1894–1948)

Celebrated by the literary establishment as one of the foremost "New Woman" lyric poets of the 1920s, Genevieve Taggard was also the editor in 1925 of *May Days*, a collection of poetry from the radical journals *The Liberator* and *The Masses*. She went on to become a leading radical poet of the 1930s, with her poems heard on records and the radio and sung at Carnegie Hall accompanied by the music of Aaron Copland.

Born in Waitsburg, Washington, Taggard spent her childhood in Hawaii, where her parents, missionaries of the Disciples of Christ, founded and ran a school. She attended the University of California at Berkeley, where she edited a small literary magazine. On graduating in 1919, Taggard moved to New York's Greenwich Village. There she became a familiar face among a Bohemian feminist circle of avant-garde poets, artists, and scholars. Her first book of poetry in 1923, *For Eager Lovers*, catapulted her into the front rank of American poets. In 1927, *The Nation* published her autobiographical memoir as a representative of the "modern woman's rebellion." The recipient of a Guggenheim Fellowship and a college teacher, Taggard was routinely grouped with such poets of the day as Edna St. Vincent Millay, Amy Lowell, and Louise Bogan. In 1930, she published *The Life and Mind of Emily Dickinson*.

When the Jazz Age gave way to the Great Depression of the 1930s, Taggard immersed herself in the new political struggles. Her poetry remained feminist, but also became increasingly class conscious and concerned with poverty and hunger, protest and resistance. Her poetry of these years, gathered in *Calling Western Union* (1936) and *Long View* (1942), also demonstrates her internationalist concern with the rise of fascism and her support for the partisans in the Spanish Civil War. As her poetry became more politically conscious, Taggard's literary reputation went into decline. Critics who had praised her in the 1920s denigrated her in the late 1930s. The FBI began monitoring her activities, and congressional committees attacked the Guggenheim Foundation for supporting her. Taggard began to be ignored in the anthologies and critical histories of modern poetry. By the time of her death, she had been relegated to almost complete obscurity. The arc of her career reveals much about how the literary canon is constructed. With Taggard, the evaluation of political poetry became the political evaluation of poetry.

Eric Leif Davin

Words Property of the People

By me used hopefully to stammer
What cannot except by miracle be said;
Anxious to show that a poet's mind
Is as useful as a carpenter's hammer,
As real for plain people as the color red.

Life of the Mind, 1935

The words in the books are not true
If they do not act in you.

Fret fools the days away,
Best-sellers for their food,
5   And bad philosophy,
Fret fools.

   But we,

We dare not read for long.
We snatch our thought, our song,
10   As soldiers do their meat.
Necessity to eat,
Necessity to act,
And act aright, renews
The mind's link with the arm.
15   Imperative to choose,
Imperative to do,
Our time's dynamic form.
Once we were students—then
Grave faces hours poured
20   Over the activity stored—
The energy of great men.

That time must come again.
If not for us, for those
We will to endow once more
25   With the tested word-in-deed.
Poetry and the great prose
Born in a like uproar
Where someone had to bleed.

The battle of the mind,
30   Tranquillity, too, the kind
Quick teacher's face, the jest,

Keen argument with a friend,
That sport and the sweet zest,—
All fall, must fall, behind.
35   That time is at an end.

Now action like a sword.
Now to redeem the word.
Now blood for stubborn proof
No one may cut apart
40   Word from the living deed,
Or live this life aloof.
Fear is a flimsy creed.
"I believe with all my heart."
In the one way to believe:
45   *"This thing is good—I give*
My living to see it live."

Bleak thought and a bastard art,
How easy to relinquish both!
So to be wise, so learned
50   If never more returned
To temporary peace.
So not to die of sloth
Or live best-sellers' ease.
But to stand upon our oath.

At Last the Women Are Moving

Last, walking with stiff legs as if they carried bundles
Came mothers, housewives, old women who knew why they abhorred war.
Their clothes bunched about them, they hobbled with anxious steps
To keep with the stride of the marchers, erect, bearing wide banners.

5   Such women looked odd, marching on American asphalt.
Kitchens they knew, sinks, suds, stew-pots and pennies . . .
Dull hurry and worry, clatter, wet hands and backache.
Here they were out in the glare on the militant march.

How did these timid, the slaves of breakfast and supper
10   Get out in the line, drop for once dish-rag and broom?
Here they are as work-worn as stitchers and fitters.
Mama have you got some grub, now none of their business.

Oh, but these who know in their growing sons and their husbands
How the exhausted body needs sleep, how often needs food,
15   These, whose business is keeping the body alive,
These are ready, if you talk their language, to strike.

Kitchen is small, the family story is sad.
Out of the musty flats the women come thinking:
Not for me and mine only. For my class I have come
20   *To walk city miles with many, my will in our work.*

Mary Heaton Vorse (1874–1966)

Mary Heaton Vorse was one of America's foremost labor journalists in the first half of the twentieth century, covering (and sometimes participating in) major strikes, from Lawrence, Massachusetts, in 1912, through the steel strike of 1919, the 1920s uprisings in textiles, and the 1937 sit-down strike at Chevrolet in Flint, Michigan. The topics of her more than four hundred articles included infant mortality, child labor, working-class housing, and women's suffrage. A pacifist and a feminist, Vorse was also a war correspondent and a popular writer of women's fiction.

Born in New York City into a wealthy New England family, Mary Heaton traveled widely as a child and became fluent in several languages. After sojourns in art school and in Paris, she began her journey into progressive politics with a move to Greenwich Village around the time of her husband Albert Vorse's death in 1910. In 1912, she married Joseph O'Brien, a radical journalist, and in the same year formed what would be a long-lasting friendship with Elizabeth Gurley Flynn. In 1915, she joined other left-wing writers, including John Reed and Edna St. Vincent Millay, in forming the Provincetown Theatre Group. Widowed again in the same year, Vorse became a single mother and supported herself through her writing, which appeared in the *New Yorker*, *Harper's*, *Atlantic Monthly* and *Ladies Home Journal*, as well as in the radical magazines of the time, *Masses* and *New Masses*. She was the author of *The Breaking-In of a Yatchsman's Wife* (1908), *Autobiography of an Elderly Woman* (1910), *Men and Steel* (1921), and *Labor's New Millions* (1938). Her novel *Strike!* (1930) about the bloody 1929 conflict around the textile mills of Gastonia, North Carolina, was republished by the University of Illinois Press in 1991. The best of her shorter works are collected in *Rebel Pen* (1985), edited by Dee Garrison. Vorse was also the author of the classic maxim: "The art of writing is the art of applying the seat of the pants to the seat of the chair." "The Emergency Brigade at Flint" appeared in *The New Republic* in 1937.

THE EMERGENCY BRIGADE AT FLINT

About the time that the pressure of the crowd waiting to get into the injunction hearing was tearing off the hinges of the courtroom door, word came to union headquarters that there was fighting in the Chevrolet plant.

Anyone experienced in strike atmosphere could have told at the mass meeting on Sunday night that there was something in the air. The meeting, which was addressed by Father J. W. R. Maguire and Mrs. Cornelia Bryce Pinchot, was no ordinary mass meeting. It was an assembly of men and women who are on the march. It was almost impossible to get through the good-natured crowd. Every seat was taken. Workers were packed close against the wall. They thronged the stairway while Father Maguire was talking to the overflow.

One felt that this special meeting was the molten core of this historic automobile strike. Here was a strike whose outcome might influence the labor movement for many years. Its success or its failure did not concern automobiles alone. It took in its sweep steel, coal, rubber, electrical workers. The fate of the whole labor movement was bound up in it. It had emerged from the frame of unionism and had become a contest now between industrial leaders, like the duPonts, Morgans, Sloans, and a president and administration favorable to organized labor. Here in this hall was the burning center of this momentous strike. Failing immediate settlement, action of some sort was inevitable.

The action came. All that week the Chevrolet workers had been holding meetings about the discharge of workers for union activities. Now there was a sit-down in the Chevrolet plant. Plant Manager Lenz would not meet the union to iron out the trouble. First he agreed to do this, then he withdrew. This is one striker's story of what happened:

"A hundred of us started walking through the plant calling a sit-down. The company police and thugs sprang up from nowhere. They kept them shut up in the employment office and sprung them loose on us. In a moment there was fighting everywhere. Fighters were rolling on the floor. They had clubs and we were unarmed. They started shooting off tear gas. I saw one fellow hit on the head and when he swung backwards he cut his head on the machinery. He started to stagger out. Two of the thugs knocked him down again. I let go on a couple of thugs. You kind of go crazy when you see thugs beating up men you know."

There were about eighteen casualties in all. Two of them had to be taken to the hospital. Most of them came up to the room in the Pengelly Building, where there is a nurse, a striker's wife, in attendance all the time. The room was soon full of bleeding men, the table heaped high with crimson gauze. None of the casualties happened outside the plant. All the injuries occurred inside, showing who made the trouble. Union headquarters say they have definite proof that there are 500 thugs from a strike-breaking detective agency in St. Louis scattered in the plant. At the present moment the majority have barricaded themselves in Plant No. 8 of Chevrolet.

The Women's Emergency Brigade had come back from their first march past the plant. One of the women I knew was wiping her eyes, which were smarting with tear gas. Around her clung the acrid smell of gas. "They were fighting inside and outside the factory," she said. "The fighting would have been much worse if it hadn't been for us. We walked right along with our flag at our head. The gas floated right out toward us. But we have been gassed and we went right on."

Someone speaking admiringly of the Women's Brigade said, "Gee, those women can sure break windows fast!" But they didn't want to break them. "We had to break windows, I tell you, to get air to the boys who were being gassed inside. We don't want violence. We just want to protect our husbands and we are going to." These women were veterans of the battle for Fisher No. 2, known in Flint as "Bulls Run" because the police ran away. I have seen women do yeoman service in strikes. I have seen some pretty good women's auxiliaries in my time, but I have never before seen such splendid organization or such determination as there is in the women's auxiliary of Flint.

Who are these women? They are strikers' wives and mothers, normally homebodies. Ma and the girls in fact. They are most of them mature women, the majority married, ranging in age from young mothers to grandmothers. In the auxiliary room there are always some children playing around. A big crowd comes after school to find out what Ma's doing, more come in after movies, and there's always a baby or two.

I should judge the majority of the brigade have been to high school, and all are neatly and carefully dressed. There isn't a flaming-eyed Joan of Arc among them. One and all are normal, sensible women who are doing this because they have come to the mature conclusion it must be done if they and their children are to have a decent life. So they are behind their husbands as long as there is need, with the same matter-of-fact capability— and inevitablity—with which they get the children off to school.

Today their job was "protecting their men." I went down to the Chevrolet plant with two of them. The workers had now captured Plant No. 4. The street was full of people; there were about twenty police behind the bridge and the high plant gate. The police were quiet and unprovocative so the crowd of pickers was good-natured. The sound truck was directing operations as usual.

The use of the sound truck is new to me in strike procedure and it is hard to know how a strike was ever conducted without it. As we came down past the policemen a great voice, calm and benignant, proclaimed that everything was in hand, the plant was under control. Next the great disembodied voice, really the voice of auburn-haired young Roy Reuther, urged the men in the plant to barricade themselves from tear gas. Every now and then the voice came, "Protection squad. Attention! Guard your sound car. Protection squad, attention!"

Then the voice addressed the workers who crowded the windows of the lower levels. At the top of the steep flight of steps were other workers, lunch buckets under their arms, waving at the pickets in the street, and still more workers fringed the roof. The sound truck inquired if they were union men. They shouted, "Yes." The crowd cheered.

The measured, soothing voice of the sound truck boomed: "Word has come to us that there are men in the crowd anxious to join the union. Go to the last car, you will find the cards ready to sign. If you have no money for dues with you you can come to Pengelly Hall later." The sound car strikes up "Solidarity," the men at the top of the steps, on top of the plant, in the street, all sing. A woman's voice next. She tells the crowd that the women have gone to the auxiliary hall to wipe their eyes clear of the tear gas and will soon be back. "We don't want any violence, we don't want any trouble. We are going to do everything we can to keep from trouble, but we are going to protect our husbands."

The Chevrolet plant covers eighty acres and has twelve departments. Plant No. 4 is the key plant, because it makes the motors. Without Plant No. 4 Chevrolet cannot make cars. This plant is set in a hollow, below a little hill about five hundred feet long. Down this hill presently came a procession, preceded by an American flag. The women's bright red caps showed dramatically in the dark crowd. They were singing "Hold the Fort."

There was something moving to all the crowd to see the women return after having been gassed. A cheer went up; the crowd joined in the song. The line of bright-capped women spread themselves out in front of the high barbed-wire-protected gate. Some of the men who had jumped over the gate went back, amid the cheers of the crowd.

I went to the top of the little hill where a string of men were coming out of the back of the building.

"Are you going home?" I asked.

"Home? Hell, no! Half of us are sitting down inside, and half of us are coming out to picket from the street."

"How many of you are for the sit-down?"

"Ninety percent," a group of them chorused.

It is getting dark, the crowd has grown denser. A black fringe of pickets and spectators is silhouetted against the brilliant green lights of the plant windows. "Protection squad! Guard your sound car!" the voice warns solemnly. I go with members of the women's auxiliary to Flint No. 2 to get salamanders and material for a shack for the night picket line. The women are going to stay all night.

There is plenty of excitement in union headquarters a mile and a half away, a meeting is being held. You can hear the cheers as you push up the crowded stairway. Presently some of the Women's Emergency Brigade come in to warm up; the night is bitter. "The Guard has been called out," they report. "We met the soldiers going down as we came back." Why has the National Guard been brought out? I have been in scores of crowds where trouble hung on the edge of a knife. This crowd in front of Chevrolet No. 4 was not so terrifying as a Christmas crowd. After the first fighting was over there was not even the semblance of trouble.

I was at a union meeting at the Cadillac-Fleetwood Hall in Detroit, where a pale organizer started his speech with emotion, saying, "Your hardsweated wages are being used to pay hired thugs and gunmen!" This was Organizer Mayo, who, with three other organizers, had been surrounded by a mob in a hotel in Bay City. They appealed for police protection, which must have been meager, since the organizers were kidnapped in Saginaw. Mayo escaped and made his way to Detroit. The other organizers were sideswiped by the thugs' car on the outskirts of Flint and are still in the hospital, one in critical condition.

It is not only in Flint that one gets the impression of a vital movement. In all the union meetings I have attended there is this sense of direction of workers knowing what they are doing and where they are going. Here at this meeting in Detroit were reports from the picket captains; the welfare committee, which had been in Lansing and had succeeded in cutting red tape for strikers under relief; the "chiselers'" committee, which goes to various merchants to get donations of food; the recreation committee; and the strategy board, which is always in contact with the central strategy board of the union in Detroit. There is also a women's auxiliary, which cooks the food, goes on picket duty, and so forth.

The vitality of this movement shows itself by the many spontaneous cultural movements that are springing up on all sides. Inside Fisher Body Nos. 1 and 2 the sitters are going to classes run by the union.

Since last Monday the plants have been turned into workers' educational institutions. Classes conducted by Merlin D. Bishop include parliamentary procedure, public speaking, and collective bargaining. The workers are writing their own plays. There are two groups of strikers who want to put on incidents of the strike in a living newspaper. Classes in journalism and workers' writing classes have been started with a graduate student from the University of Michigan journalism school as an instructor. This is a strike, Model 1937.

Mike Gold (1893–1967)

As a writer and a literary organizer, Mike Gold profoundly influenced the American proletarian renaissance of the 1930s, many of whose authors he published as editor of the *New Masses*. Born Yitzhak Granich, the eldest son of Jewish immigrants to New York, he grew up in the ghetto tenements and streets of the ethnically mixed Lower East Side. Here, in his family and among their neighbors, he witnessed grinding poverty and ill health, the constant struggle to make ends meet, and rich examples of poor people's caring for one another. He started work at twelve years of age, after the failure of his father's business, and quickly developed a hatred for the pushing and gauging of bosses and landlords. This anger developed into a thoroughgoing critique of capitalism during the years of the World War I, which, like many radicals of the time Gold opposed as a "rich man's war, poor man's fight."

Gold moved to Mexico in 1917 to avoid being conscripted and, in 1919, changed his name to Michael Gold (after a Jewish freedom fighter) in hopes of protecting himself from persecution during the Palmer Raids. Gold had meanwhile discovered *The Masses* (publisher of Jack London, Upton Sinclair, John Reed, and others) and in 1914 had the first of many poems and stories published in that radical journal. After *The Masses* (1911–1917) was succeeded by the *Liberator*, Gold became an editor in 1921, announcing its new cultural direction in the essay "Towards Proletarian Art." In 1926, Gold helped found *New Masses*, and as its editor-in-chief from 1928 on, he dedicated the journal to a literature whose politics are grounded in "a knowledge of working-class life in America gained from first hand contacts . . . a flesh and blood reality, however crude" ("Go Left, Young Writers!" 1929). In one sense, Gold's now-classic novel *Jews Without Money* (1930) meets this criterion, based as it is on his own childhood and family struggles. But it is far from crude, having been artfully assembled from sketches that Gold was writing throughout the 1920s. Although it looked back to the urban tenement writing of the early twentieth century, *Jews Without Money* provided the example of a fictional autobiography of marginalized people that would soon be transformed by such midwestern worker-writers as Jack Conroy and Tom Kromer, who lived through the labor struggles, unemployment, and homelessness of the Depression years. Gold, who remained a member of the Communist Party until his death, also published *The Damned Agitator and Other Stories* (1926), *Hoboken Blues* (1927), and *Change the World* (1937).

GO LEFT, YOUNG WRITERS!

LITERATURE is one of the products of a civilization like steel or textiles. It is not a child of eternity, but of time. It is always the mirror of its age. It is not any more mystic in its origin than a ham sandwich.

It is easy to understand the lacquer of cynicism, smartness and ritzy sophistication with which popular American writing is now coated. This is a product of "our" sudden prosperity, the gesture of our immense group of *nouveau riches*.

The epic melancholy of Dreiser, the romantic democracy of Carl Sandburg, the social experimentation of Frank Norris, Stephen Crane, Mark Twain, Edgar Lee Masters and other men of the earlier decades, is as dead as the Indian's Manitou.

We are living in another day. It is dominated by a hard, successful, ignorant jazzy bourgeois of about thirty-five, and his leech-like young wife.

Just as European tours, night clubs, Florida beaches and streamline cars have been invented for this class, just so literature is being produced for them. They have begun to have time, and now read books occasionally to fill in the idle moments between cocktail parties.

They need novels that will take the place of the old fashioned etiquette books to teach them how to spend their money smartly.

Ernest Hemingway is one of the caterers to this demand.

The liberals have become disheartened and demoralized under the strain of American prosperity. Are there any liberals left in America? I doubt it. The *Nation* was the last organ of the liberals in this country. It has been swinging right in the last few years. When it surrendered itself body and soul to Tammany Hall in the last campaign, I think it performed a logical suicide.

Its editorials now read like the New York *World*. Its book reviews and dramatic criticisms are no different in viewpoint from those in New York *Times* or *Tribune*. In fact the same group of writers fill the columns of both liberal and conservative press, and no one can detect the difference.

There isn't any difference.

There isn't a centrist liberal party in our politics any more, or in our literature. There is an immense overwhelming, right wing which accepts the American religion of "prosperity." The conservatives accept it joyfully, the liberals "soulfully." But both accept it.

There is also a left wing, led in politics by the Communists, and in literature by the *New Masses*. Will someone inform us if there is something vital between these two extremes of right and left?

This is in some ways a depressing situation. Can there be a battle between such unequal forces? Will it not rather be a massacre of a lion carelessly crushing the rabbit that has crossed his path?

No. The great mass of America is not "prosperous" and it is not being represented in the current politics of literature. There are at least forty million people who are the real America.

They are Negroes, immigrants, poor farmers and city proletarians and they live in the same holes they did ten years ago. Upon their shoulders the whole gaudy show palace rests. When they stir it will and must fall.

It was the same in Rome, in France, in Russia; it is the same here.

Let us never be dazzled by appearances. The American orgy has been pitched on the crater of the historic social volcano.

This volcano is as certain to erupt eventually as is Mount Etna.

By default, the liberals have presented us writers and revolutionists of the left wing with a monopoly on the basic American mass. We have a wonderful virgin field to explore; titanic opportunities for creative work.

Let us be large, heroic and self-confident at our task.

The best and newest thing a young writer can now do in America, if he has the vigor and the guts, is to go leftward. If he gets tangled up in the other thing he will make some money, maybe, but he will lose everything else. Neither the *Saturday Evening Post* or the *Nation* can any longer nourish the free heroic soul. Try it and see.

When I say "go leftward," I don't mean the temperamental bohemian left, the stale old Paris posing, the professional poetizing, etc. No, the real thing; a knowledge of working-class life in America gained from first-hand contacts, and a hard precise philosophy of 1929 based on economics, not verbalisms.

The old *Masses* was a more brilliant but a more upper class affair. The *New Masses* is working in a different field. It goes after a kind of flesh and blood reality, however crude, instead of the smooth perfect thing that is found in books.

The America of the working class is practically undiscovered. It is like a lost continent. Bits of it come above the surface in our literature occasionally and everyone is amazed. But there is no need yet of going to Africa or the Orient for strange new pioneering. The young writer can find all the primitive material he needs working as a wage slave around the cities and prairies of America.

In the past eight months the *New Masses* has been slowly finding its path toward the goal of a proletarian literature in America. A new writer has been appearing; a wild youth of about twenty-two, the son of working-class parents, who himself works in the lumber camps, coal mines, and steel mills, harvest fields and mountain camps of America. He is sensitive and impatient. He writes in jets of exasperated feeling and has no time to polish his work. He is violent and sentimental by turns. He lacks self confidence but writes because he must—and because he has a real talent.

He is a Red but has few theories. It is all instinct with him. His writing is no con-scious straining after proletarian art, but the natural flower of his environment. He writes that way because it is the only way for him. His "spiritual" attitudes are all mixed up with tenements, factories, lumber camps and steel mills, because that is his life. He knows it in the same way that one of Professor Baker's students know the six different ways of ending a first act.

A Jack London or a Walt Whitman will come out of this new crop of young workers who write in the *New Masses*. Let us not be too timid or too modest in our judgments. This is a fact. Keene Wallis, for instance, an ex-harvest worker and I.W.W., will take Carl Sandburg's place in five years. Why ought one to hesitate about stating such a conviction?

The *New Masses*, by some miracle, has gotten out eight issues under the present management, after the magazine had been declared bankrupt, and was about to suspend. We have received no subsidies; we have earned our way.

We can announce now that another year is certain. We feel that year will be fruitful, and may see further clarification of our groping experiment.

Once more we appeal to our readers:

Do not be passive. Write. Your life in mine, mill and farm is of deathless significance in the history of the world. Tell us about it in the same language you use in writing a letter. It may be literature—it often is. Write. Persist. Struggle.

"JEWS AND CHRISTIANS," FROM *JEWS WITHOUT MONEY*

1

My mother never learned to like shoes. In Hungary, in her native village, she had rarely worn them, and she could see no reason for wearing them here.

"Does one wear shoes on one's hands?" she would ask. "How can one work in shoes? Shoes are only for people to show off in."

So she paddled about in bare feet whenever she could. This annoyed my father at those times when he was ambitious. To him not wearing shoes was like confessing to the world that one was poor. But my mother had no such false pride, and would even walk barefooted in the street.

Once my father bought her a diamond ring on the installment plan. It was during one of his periods of greatness, when he had earned a big week's pay, and the Boss had hinted at a foreman's job for him.

It was on a Saturday night, and he had been drinking beer with his fellow-workmen. He came home flushed and dramatic. With many flourishes and the hocus-pocus of a magician he extracted the ring from his vest pocket and placed it on my mother's finger.

"At last, Katie!" he said, kissing her with great ceremony, "at last you have a diamond ring! At last you can write home to Hungary that you too are wearing diamonds in America!"

"Pouf!" said my mother angrily, pushing him away. She snatched the ring from her finger as if it burned her. "What foolishness!"

"Foolishness!" my father exclaimed, indignantly. "What! it is foolish to wear diamonds?"

"Yes," said my stubborn mother.

"Every one wears diamonds!" said my father, "every one with a little pride."

"Let others be proud! I am a work horse," said my mother.

My father spat in disgust, and stalked off to find some intelligent males.

The ring remained in the family. It was our only negotiable capital. It was hidden among some towels and sheets in the bureau. In time of need it traveled to the pawnshop, to buy us food and rent. Many East Side families aspired to jewelry for this reason. Money vanished. Jewelry remained. This was the crude credit system of the East Side.

2

My mother was fond of calling herself a work horse. She was proud of the fact that she could work hard. She wanted no diamond rings, no fancy dresses, no decorations. She had a strong sense of reality, and felt that when one was poor, only strength could help one. But my father was a romantic, and dreamed of a bright easy future.

My humble funny little East Side mother! How can I ever forget this dark little woman with bright eyes, who hobbled about all day in bare feet, cursing in Elizabethan Yiddish, using the forbidden words "ladies" do not use, smacking us, beating us, fighting with her neighbors, helping her neighbors, busy from morn to midnight in the tenement struggle for life.

She would have stolen or killed for us. She would have let a railroad train run over her body if it could have helped us. She loved us all with the fierce painful love of a mother-wolf, and scolded us continually like a magpie.

Mother! Momma! I am still bound to you by the cords of birth. I cannot forget you. I must remain faithful to the poor because I cannot be faithless to you! I believe in the poor because I have known you. The world must be made gracious for the poor! Momma, you taught me that!

3

What a hard life she had led. She had known nothing but work since her tenth year. Her father had died then, and she was the oldest child of a large family. She went to work in a bakery, then did a man's labor on a farm.

When she was eighteen, relatives gathered seventy-five gulden, and sent her to America as the last hope for her family. She was to work here and send for her brothers and sisters.

The crossing made a deep mark on her mind. She spent seventeen agonized days in the filthy steerage, eating nothing but herrings and potatoes, because there was no *kosher* food.

Her first night in America was spent amid groans and confusion on the floor of a crowded cellar for immigrants. It was called the Nigger House.

A relative found her the next morning. He took her to a job. It was in an East Side restaurant where she was paid five dollars a month, with meals. She slept on a mattress in the evil, greasy kitchen. The working hours were from five to midnight.

In a year she saved enough money to send a ship ticket to her oldest brother.

"Yes, I have had all kinds of good times in America," she would chuckle grimly, when she told us of this time. "Yes, that first year in the restaurant I had lots of fun with the pots and pans.

"It's lucky I'm alive yet. It is a good land, but not for the poor. When the Messiah comes to America, he had better come in a fine automobile, with a dozen servants. If he comes here on a white horse, people will think he is just another poor immigrant. They may set him to work washing dishes in a restaurant."

4

She and my father had married in the old Jewish style; that is, they were brought together by a professional matrimonial broker. He charged them a commission for the service. It is as good a method as any. My parents came to love each other with an emotion deeper than romance; I am sure my father would have died for my mother. But she also made his head ache, and he told her so often.

She was a buttinsky. She tried to "reform" everybody, and fought people because they were "bad." She spoke her mind freely, and told every one exactly where the path of duty lay. She was always engaged in some complicated ethical brawl, and my father had to listen to all the details.

Or she was always finding people in trouble who needed her help. She helped them for days, weeks and months, with money, food, advice and the work of her hands.

She was a midwife in many hasty births, a nurse in sickness, a peacemaker in family battles.

She knew how to make a poultice for boils by chewing bread and mixing it with yellow soap; and how to cure colds with kerosene, and the uses of herbs and other peasant remedies. She was a splendid cook and breadmaker, and shared all these secrets with the neighbors.

When a woman fell sick, the distracted husband appealed to my mother; and for weeks she'd drop in there twice a day, to cook the meals, and scrub the floors, and bathe the children, to joke, gossip, scold, love, to scatter her strength and goodness in the dark home.

It would have shocked her if any one had offered to pay for these services. It was simply something that had to be done for a neighbor.

Once there was a woman on our street who was going crazy. Her cigarmaker husband had deserted her and two children. The woman had spells, and could not sleep at night. She begged my mother to sleep with her. She was afraid she would kill her children during one of her spells.

So my mother slept there every night for more than a month.

How often have I seen my mother help families who were evicted because they could not pay rent. She wrapped herself in her old shawl, and went begging through the tenements for pennies. Puffing with bronchitis, she dragged herself up and down the steep landings of a hundred tenements, telling the sad tale with new emotion each time and begging for pennies.

But this is an old custom on the East Side; whenever a family is to be evicted, the neighboring mothers put on their shawls and beg from door to door.

5

My poor father, worrying over his own load of American troubles, had to listen to the tremendous details of all these tragedies. My mother could discover so many sick people! And so many bad people who needed to be fought! No wonder my father drank beer! No wonder he grabbed his head between his hands, and groaned:

"Stop! you give me a headache! I can't listen any more!"

"It is not your head, but your selfishness!" scoffed my mother.

"One has to be selfish in America," said my father. "It is dog eat dog over here. But you, you neglect your own family to help every passing stranger."

"*Pfui*, what a lie!" my mother spat. "When have my children been neglected?"

"But for God's sake," said my father, "haven't we enough troubles of our own? You're like a man with consumption. It is not enough for him to have this, he has to go skating so that he can break his leg, too."

"*Nu*, I can stand a broken leg," said my mother. "What is a leg when there is so much misery in the world?"

6

My mother was opposed to the Italians, Irish, Germans and every other variety of Christian with whom we were surrounded.

"May eight and eighty black years fall on these *goys!*" she said, her black eyes flashing. "They live like pigs; they have ruined the world. And they hate and kill Jews. They may seem friendly to us to our faces, but behind our backs they laugh at us. I know them well. I have seen them in Hungary."

My father sat one evening at the supper table, drinking beer and reading a Yiddish newspaper. In the hot kitchen my mother was washing the dishes, and humming a Hungarian folk song.

"*Nu, nu!*" my father exclaimed, striking the table with his fist, "another railroad accident! Katie, I have always said it is dangerous to travel on these American railroads!"

"What has happened?" my mother gasped, appearing from the kitchen with steaming hands and face.

"What has happened, you ask?" my father repeated in the important tone of a pedant. "What has happened is that seventeen innocent people were killed in a railroad accident in New Jersey! And whose fault was it? The fault of the rich American railroads!"

My mother was horrified. She wiped her boiling face with her apron and muttered: "God help us and shield us! Were there any Jews among the dead?"

My father glanced rapidly through the list of names. "No," he said, "only Christians were killed."

My mother sighed with relief. She went back into her kitchen. She was no longer interested; Christians did not seem like people to her. They were abstractions. They were the great enemy, to be hated, feared and cursed. In Hungary three Christian peasant girls had once taunted her. Then they had gone in swimming, and had been drowned. This was God's punishment on them for persecuting a Jew. Another peasant had once plucked the beard of an old reverend Jew, and God struck him with lightning a week later. My mother was full of such anecdotes.

The East Side never forgot Europe. We children heard endless tales of the pogroms. Joey Cohen, who was born in Russia, could himself remember one. The Christians had hammered a nail into his uncle's head, and killed him. When we passed a Christian church we were careful to spit three times; otherwise bad luck was sure to befall us. We were obsessed by wild stories of how the Christians loved to kidnap Jewish children, to burn a cross on each cheek with a redhot poker. They also cut off children's ears, and made a kind of soup. Nigger had once seen Jewish ears for sale in the window of a Christian butcher shop.

"In the old days," my mother said, "the Christians hunted the Jews like rabbits. They would gather thousands in a big marketplace, and stuff pork down their throats with swords, and ask the Jews to be baptized. The Jews refused, of course. So they were burnt in great fires, and the Christians laughed, danced and made merry when they saw the poor Jews burning up like candles. Such are the Christians. May they burn some day, too."

These impressions sank into my heart, and in my bad dreams during the hot summer nights, dark Christian ogres the size of tenements moved all around me. They sat on my chest, and clutched my throat with slimy remorseless fingers, shrieking, "Jew, Jew! Jew!"

And I would spend long daylight hours wondering why the Christians hated us so, and form noble plans of how I would lead valiant Jewish armies when I grew up, in defense of the Jews.

7

But my mother was incapable of real hatred. Paradoxically she had many warm friends among the Italian and Irish neighbors. She was always apologetic about this. "These are not like other Christians," she would say, "these are good people." How could she resist another human being in trouble? How could she be indifferent when another was in pain?

Her nature was made for universal sympathy, without thought of prejudice. Her hatred of Christians was really the outcry of a motherly soul against the boundless cruelty in life.

Betsy was an Italian woman who lived in the next tenement. She had a long, emaciated face covered with moles, engraved with suffering like an old yellow wood carving. Her coffee-colored eyes always seemed to have a veil over them, as if she were hiding a terrible secret. She avoided people; swathed in her long black scarf she stole down the street furtively, as if conscious of the eyes of the world.

Her husband was in jail for murder. One summer night (I shall never forget it), he burst from the tenement into the street, screaming like a madman. A revolver was in his hand. We were sitting on the stoop, calmly eating ice-cream cones. The spectacle of this wild swarthy Italian in his undershirt, shrieking, and waving a pistol, appalled us like a hallucination. He rushed by us, and dived into a cellar. A crowd gathered. A policeman ran up. He hadn't the nerve to follow the Italian into the cellar, but stood uncertainly on the sidewalk, growling: "Get up out of there, before I shoot yuh." At last the Italian stumbled out, sobbing like a child. His bronzed, rocky face was grotesquely twisted with grief. He wrung his hands, beat his chest, and clawed at his cheeks until the blood spurted. I have never heard such dreadful animal howls, the ferocious and dangerous agony of a dying wolf. He had just killed his brother in a quarrel over a card game.

This passion-blinded assassin was Betsy's husband. She was left with three children, and no friends. She could speak only Italian. My mother visited her, and through sheer sympathy, learned, in the course of several visits, a kind of pigeon-Italian. It was marvelous to hear my mother hold hour-long conversations with this woman, in a polyglot jargon that was a mixture of Italian, Yiddish, Hungarian and English. But the women understood each other.

My mother helped Betsy find a clothing shop that would give her basting work to do at home. My mother helped the Christian in many ways. And Betsy worshipped her. In the midst of her miseries she found time to knit a large wool shawl as a surprise for my mother. She brought it in one night, and cried and jabbered excitedly in Italian, and kissed my mother's hands. And my mother cried, and kissed her, too. We could not understand a word of what they were saying, but my mother kept repeating in Yiddish: "Ach, what a good woman this is! What a dear woman!" My mother treasured this shawl more than anything she owned. She liked to show it to every one, and tell the story of how Betsy had made it.

A shawl like that was worth over ten dollars, more than Betsy earned in a week. It must have taken weeks to knit, many overtime nights under the gaslight after a weary sixteen-hour day at basting clothing. Such gifts are worthy to be treasured; they are knitted in love.

8

There was an Irish family living on the top floor of our tenement. Mr. O'Brien was a truck-driver, a tall gloomy giant with a red face hard as shark-leather. He came home from work at nine and ten o'clock each night. Powerful and hairy in his blue overalls, he stamped ponderously up the stairs. If we children were playing in the halls, he brushed through our games, scowling at us as if he hated children.

"Get the hell out of my way; you're thick as bedbugs," he muttered, and we scattered from under the feet of the ferocious great Christian.

His wife was also large and red-faced, a soft, sad mountain of flesh waddling around under perpetual baskets of laundry. All Christian ladies did washing, all except the Italians. Mrs. O'Brien was kinder to children than her husband, but we feared her almost as much.

This couple was one of the scandals of the tenement. Night after night, in the restless sleep of our little commune, we heard as in a coöperative nightmare the anguished screams of the Irish mother down the airshaft. Her husband was drunk and was beating her.

"No, no, Jack, don't!" she screamed. "You'll frighten the boy."

This couple had a mysterious child whom nobody had ever seen, and the mother always mentioned him in these brutal midnight scenes.

"Tuh hell with the boy!" roared the man's voice, formidable and deep as a mad bull's. "Tuh hell with everything!"

Crash! he had knocked her down over a table. Windows flew open; heads popped into the airshaft from every side like a shower of curious balloons; the tenement was awake and fascinated. We could hear a child's frightened whimpering, then crash! another powerful blow struck at a soft woman's body.

"Jack, don't! The neighbors will hear!"

"Tuh hell with the kikes! I'll set fire to the damn house and make the sheenies run like rats?"

Bang, crash, scream! The tenement listened with horror. These were the Christians again. No Jew was ever as violent as that. No Jew struck a woman. My mother, ever an agitator, led a campaign against the Irish couple, to force the landlord to put them out. "It is worse than the whores," said my mother, "having Christians in a tenement is worse."

<h2 style="text-align:center">9</h2>

But one quiet afternoon, who should burst into my mother's kitchen, pale and stammering with fright, but the Irish washerlady.

"Quick, my boy is choking to death! Help me! Get a doctor, for God's sake!"

My mother, without a superfluous word, sped like a fireman up the stairs, to help the child. It had swallowed a fishbone. My mother, expert and brave in such emergencies, put her finger down his throat and dislodged the bone. Then she had a long intimate talk with the Irish mother.

That night at the supper table, while my workweary father was trying to eat hamburger steak, and read the Yiddish newspaper, and drink beer, and think about his troubles, and smoke and talk all at the same time, my mother irritated him by sighing profoundly.

"Ach, Herman," she said, "that Irish washerlady has so many misfortunes."

"*Pfui!*" my father spat impatiently, "so have I!"

"She is a good woman," said my mother, "even if she is a Christian. Her husband beats her, but she is sorry for him. He is not a bad man. He is only sad."

"*Gottenu!*" my father groaned in disgust with female logic. "I hope he beats you, too!"

"He was a farmer in Ireland," my mother went on dreamily. "He hates the city life here, but they are too poor to move to the country. And their boy has been sick for years. All their money goes for doctors. That's why he drinks and beats her, but her heart bleeds for him."

"Enough!" said my father, clutching his hair. "Enough, or I will go mad!"

My mother saw that he was really angry, so she took the empty soup plates into the kitchen. There she stirred something in a pot, and opened the stove to take out the noodle pudding. She brought this to the table.

"And, Herman," she said pensively, with the steaming pudding in her hands, "that woman used to gather mushrooms in the forest in Ireland. Just the way I gathered them in Hungary."

<h2 style="text-align:center">10</h2>

I was playing with the boys. We had been seized with the impulse to draw horses in chalk on the pavement. Then there was a fight, because Joey Cohen had written under his horse,

"NIGGER LOVES LEAH." He also wrote this on an express wagon, on the stoop steps, and on the bock beer sign standing in front of the saloon. Nigger was about ready to punch Joey on the nose, when Mrs. O'Brien shambled up to us, slow, sad and huge, looming above us with the perpetual basket of laundry on her arm.

"Don't fight, boys," she said kindly in her clear Christian speech. "Will one of you do something for me? I will give any boy a nickel who will go up and play with my little boy. He is sick."

We were dumfounded with fear. We stared at her and our mouths fell open. Even Nigger was scared.

Mrs. O'Brien looked right at me. "Will you do it?" she pleaded. I blushed, and suddenly ran off as if I had seen a devil. The other boys scattered. Mrs. O'Brien sighed, picked up her heavy basket, and hobbled on her way.

I told my mother that night. What did it mean? Was the Christian washerlady trying to snare me into her home, where she would burn a cross on my face with a hot poker?

"No," said my mother thoughtfully. "Go up there; it will be a good deed. The Christian child is lonely. Nothing can happen to you."

She took me there herself the next morning. And I found nothing to fear. It was a gray humid morning. In the yellow gloom of a bedroom narrow and damp like a coffin, a child with shrunken face lay in bed. His forehead was pale as marble. It was streaked with blue veins, and altogether too round and large for his head. His head was too large for his body. It dangled clumsily, though supported by a steel brace at the neck.

He looked at me with great mournful eyes. His nose wrinkled like a baby's, and he cried.

"Don't be frightened, Johnnie," said his mother, "this boy is a friend who has come to play with you."

I wound my top and spun it on the floor. He craned his stiff neck to watch. Then I put the top in his hand and tried to teach him to spin it, too. But he was too feeble for this sport. So he wept once more, and I was grieved for him. Was this one of the dreaded Christians?

Appalachian Voices

Derived from a Native American word meaning "endless mountain range," Appalachia is a geographic region, a complex and diverse culture, and a historical crossroad for working-class oppression and struggle. Marked by rugged hills and hollows, southern Appalachia encompasses the intersecting boundaries of Ohio, West Virginia, Kentucky, Virginia, Tennessee, North and South Carolina, and Georgia. At once enclosed by their mountain boundaries and exposed to the scrutiny of outsiders, the Appalachian working classes are descendents of revolutionary war-era settlers. *Hillbilly* is a term of pride in their sense of kinship and culture when used by these mountain people and a slur in the mouths of outsiders. By the turn of the twentieth century, cash-poor farmers, who sold their timber and mineral rights of their land to industrialists, left their farms to mine deep coal under murderous safety conditions, and for low wages that were paid in scrip. They lived in squalid company housing, were forced to pay high prices at the company store, and saw their families suffer from disease and malnutrition. As conditions deteriorated further in the early 1930s, miners and their wives sought relief by organizing themselves and seeking the support of unions. Their efforts were met by entrenched resistance, including the hiring of "company thugs," with shootings, beatings, intimidation, and deaths on both sides. The songs, narratives, reports, and poems that follow illuminate one period in the colonized history of the Appalachian working class.

Born in 1880, Aunt Molly Jackson was a mountaineer midwife and union organizer whose father, husband, and son suffered death and injury in the coal mines. She saw children starve to death and once robbed the company store at gunpoint when she was refused credit for some food to take to starving families. She was the half-sister of another famous Kentucky singer, Sarah Ogan Gunning, also a coal miner's wife and daughter, and the mother of a baby who died from starvation. About her life, Ogan Gunning said, "I never was ashamed of myself or my parents in my life. I know I was poor, and I've been hungry many a time. . . . I'm not ashamed of being a hillbilly—I'm proud of it."

Florence Reece's famous song "Which Side Are You On?" gives contemporary readers a sense of the intensity of the class wars in Kentucky's mining towns and backroads in the 1930s and some insight into the process of cultural formation. The song was written on a page torn from a wall calendar and sung to the tune of an old Baptist hymn, "Lay the Lily Low." "My songs," Reece said, "always goes to the underdog—to the worker. I'm one of them and I feel like I've got to be with them. . . . Some people say, 'I don't take sides— I'm neutral.' There's no such thing as neutral. You *have* to be on one side or the other. In Harlan Country there wasn't no neutral. If you wasn't a gun thug, you was a union man. You *had* to be."

There was often a price in human lives for taking sides, as the story of Harry Simms, told by Kentucky coal-mine union organizers Jim Garland and Tilman Cadle, shows. While miners sought the help of established unions and tried to organize themselves, they also received material support and publicity from northerners, including many writers and

Marion Post Wolcott, coal miners, the "lady's man" and the "smart guy," Bertha Hill, West Virginia, 1938. *Courtesy of Library of Congress, LC-USF33-30209.*

labor sympathizers. During the Harlan County mine strike of 1931–1931, the National Committee for the Defense of Political Prisoners sent a group of writers, headed by Theodore Dresier, to Evart, in Harlan County, Kentucky, to investigate and report on the conditions surrounding the strike. John Dos Passos (1896–1970), author of *USA Trilogy*— *The 43nd Parallel* (1930), *1919* (1932), and *The Big Money* (1936)—was a member of that commission. Using an intertextual technique of interpolating songs and testimony with his own commentary, Dos Passos presents what it means to "Work Under the Gun" in Harlan County, Kentucky. His report was originally published separately from the Dresier Committee's pamphlet in *The New Republic* (December 1931).

This cluster concludes with poems by contemporary poet Maggie Anderson. Anderson's parents were generational exceptions—although born and raised in West Virginia into working-class families, they left the mountains, earned college educations, and became educators. Anderson was born in New York City but returned frequently to West Virginia, especially after the death of her mother when she was nine years old. These poems are journeys back to Appalachia. The first two are through the West Virginia photographs of Walker Evans as the poet seeks out the subjectivities of the people who are framed in Walker's still photographs. In "Long Story," she shows the inseparability of external history from family stories and memories and, in the telling, reveals the necessary work of poems and poets to mine that past.

Aunt Molly Jackson, Kentucky Miners' Wives Ragged Hungry Blues

I'm sad and weary; I've got the hungry ragged blues;
I'm sad and weary; I've got the hungry ragged blues;
Not a penny in my pocket to buy the thing I need to use.

5 I woke up this morning with the worst blues I ever had in my life;
I woke up this morning with the worst blues I ever had in my life;
Not a bite to cook for breakfast, a poor coal miner's wife.

When my husband works in the coal mines, he loads a car on every trip,
When my husband works in the coal mines, he loads a car on every trip,
Then he goes to the office that evening and gits denied of scrip.

10 Just because it took all he had made that day to pay his mine expense,
Just because it took all he had made that day to pay his mine expense,
A man that'll work for coal-light and carbide, he ain't got a speck of sense.

All the women in the coal camps are a-sitting with bowed-down heads,
All the women in the coal camps are a-sitting with bowed-down heads,
15 Ragged and barefooted, the children a-crying for bread.

No food, no clothes for our children, I'm sure this ain't no lie,
No food, no clothes for our children, I'm sure this ain't no lie,
If we can't git more for our labor, we will starve to death and die.

Listen, friends and comrades, please take a friend's advice,
20   Listen, friends and comrades, please take a friend's advice,
Don't load no more that dirty coal till you git a living price.

Don't go under the mountains with the slate a-hanging over your heads,
Don't go under the mountains with the slate a-hanging over your heads,
And work for just coal-light and carbide and your children a-crying for bread.

25   This mining town I live in is a sad and lonely place,
This mining town I live in is a sad and lonely place,
Where pity and starvation is pictured on every face.

Ragged and hungry, no slippers on our feet,
Ragged and hungry, no slippers on our feet,
30   We're bumming around from place to place to get a little bite to eat.

All a-going round from place to place bumming for a little food to eat.
Listen, my friends and comrades, please take a friend's advice,
Don't put out no more of your labor, till you get a living price.

Some coal operators might tell you the hungry blues are not bad;
35   Some coal operators might tell you the hungry blues are not bad;
They are the worst blues this poor woman ever had.

SARAH OGAN GUNNING,
I AM A GIRL OF CONSTANT SORROW

I am a girl of constant sorrow,
I've seen trouble all my days.
I bid farewell to old Kentucky,
The state where I was born and raised.

5   My mother, how I hated to leave her,
Mother dear who now is dead,
But I had to go and leave her
So my children could have bread.

Perhaps, dear friends, you are wondering
10   What the miners eat and wear.

This question I will try to answer,
For I'm sure that it is fair.

For breakfast we had bulldog gravy,
For supper we had beans and bread.
15 The miners don't have any dinner,
And a tick of straw they call a bed.

Well, we call this Hell on earth, friends,
I must tell you all good-bye.
Oh, I know you all are hungry,
20 Oh, my darling friends, don't cry.

KATHY KAHN, THEY SAY THEM CHILD BRIDES DON'T LAST

FLORENCE REECE, ELLISTOWN, TENNESSEE

Wake up, wake up, you working folks, what makes you sleep so sound?
The company thugs are coming to burn your homeplace down.
They're slipping around that mountain town with guns and dynamite
To try to murder the sleeping folks that led the Harlan strike.

During the union organizing of the twenties and thirties in the Southern coal fields, several songs were written about the struggle by women who were going through it. Sarah Ogan Gunning was a miner's wife in Harlan, Kentucky, and she wrote the famous song, "I Am a Girl of Constant Sorrow." Aunt Molly Jackson, a midwife in Bell and Harlan counties, wrote many songs, including one called, "I Am a Union Woman." One of the verses to that song goes like this:

The bosses ride big fine horses,
While we walk in the mud.
Their banner is the dollar sign,
While ours is striped with blood.

The women used their songs to organize coal mining families into the union. They were one of the most effective organizing tools because they captured the spiritual, emotional, and physical feelings of people who were dying of starvation while they fought some of the bloodiest battles union organizing has ever known.

Perhaps the most famous song coming out of that time is "Which Side Are You On?" which Florence Reece wrote while she and her husband, Sam, were organizing miners in Eastern Kentucky.

The songs of Florence Reece, Aunt Molly Jackson, and Sarah Ogan Gunning brought spirit to coal mining families during their time of hardship and struggle. Today, they recall vividly just how brutal those times were for the people in the coal fields of the Southern mountains.

Sam went in the mines when he was eleven years old. Sixty cents a day. And there wasn't no such thing as hours. He'd come out of there way in the dark of the night. And him just a little boy.

As soon as a boy'd get up to be ten or eleven years old, he'd have to go in the mines to help feed the others in his family. As soon as he got sixteen years old, he'd marry and it'd start revolving over.

I was fourteen when we got married and Sam was nineteen. Child bride. They say them child brides don't last, but they do. When the gun thugs was coming around we had eight children. We had ten altogether. And every one of them was born at home.

My father was killed in the coal mines. He was loading a ton and a half of coal for thirty cents, and pushing it. And that's what he got killed for, for nothing. That was Fork Ridge, Tennessee; they call it Mingo Holler now.

In the morning when they'd go to work before daylight, you could see the kerosene lamps they wore on their hats. It was just like fireflies all around the mountain. They'd go under that mountain every day, never knowing whether they'd come out alive. Most every day they'd bring out a dead man. Sometimes, two or three.

I never knew whether Sam would come out of the mines alive or not. I've seen him come home and his clothes would be froze into ice. He'd have to lay down in the water and dig the coal, and then carry a sack of coal home to keep us warm and to cook. But he had to go, had to go somewhere cause the children had to eat. Sam joined the union in nineteen and seventeen.

Well, it was in Harlan County, Kentucky, and they was on strike. John Henry Blair, see, he was the High Sheriff, and he'd hire these men to go and get the miners. He'd hire these men that was real tough, and they'd give them good automobiles to drive and good guns to carry and they'd give them whiskey to drink, to beat the miners down, keep them down so they couldn't went in the union. They called these men "deputy sheriffs" but they was gun thugs. That was the coal operators with John Henry Blair.

We was living in Molus in Harlan County, Kentucky, then. In 1930 the coal miners went out on strike against the coal operators. Well, Sam had a garage down below where we lived. The miners would come there and hang out and talk about how they wasn't going back to work. So some of the bosses and officials come and asked Sam if he'd go back to work and Sam said did that mean that they got the union contract. And they said no. So Sam said, well, he wouldn't go back to work. From that beginning they started on him.

First, they arrested him, they took him to jail, said he was selling whiskey, anything they could put on him. And he wasn't fooling with whiskey at all, no, not at all. That was in nineteen and thirty.

It seems like a bad dream when you think about it, that it happened to your own children. They didn't have no clothes, nor enough to eat, they was always sick and you could see they was hungry. We was all just starving, and so the miners would go out and kill cows or goats or just anything. They belonged to the coal companies, you know.

I've seen little children, their little legs would be so tiny and their stomachs would be so big from eating green apples, anything they could get. And I've seen grown men staggering they was so hungry. One of the company bosses said he hoped the children'd have to gnaw the bark off the trees.

In Molus they didn't have nothing to eat. The miners and their families was starving and a lot of people had that pellagra. One woman come to my house to get something to eat and she had that. All scaly all over, you know. Someone said, "Aren't you afraid you'll catch that from her?" I said, "No. She got that at the table cause she didn't have no food."

While we lived in Molus and Sam was away, he wasn't just hiding from the gun thugs. He was organizing with the union. One time he was gone a week and I didn't know where he was dead or alive. Well, one night he slipped in way long about one o'clock in the morning. We had a garden, it had corn and he slipped in through the back way, up through the corn. And I stayed up all that night watching for them to come after Sam.

The thugs made my mind up for me right off, which side I was on. They would come to our house in four and five carloads and they all had guns and belts around them filled with cartridges, and they had high powers. They'd come here looking for Sam cause he was organizing and on strike.

One night they killed eleven. That was "Evart's Fight." That was in May of 1931. It was at the Greenville crossing. A little boy heard the thugs a-talkin', saying they was going to meet the miners there at the railroad crossing and kill them. This little boy run and told his daddy and his daddy run and told the miners. The miners was there to meet the gun thugs and killed seven of them. Four miners got killed in the fight and the rest of them got sent to the penitentiary. One of them was a Negro man. But the thugs, they didn't get nothing.

Do you remember Harry Simms? He was from New York, he was a organizer. Sam was in the holler with Harry Simms, and Sam had just come out when the thugs backed Simms up on a flatcar and shot him. Well, the miners took him to Pineville after he was shot and he bled to death on the steps of the hospital. They wouldn't let him in cause he was a union man. They killed Harry Simms on Brush Creek. He was nineteen year old.

The gun thugs would take the union men out and kill them. The miners would go out in the woods and the cemeteries and hide. So then they had the state militia out after them. We'd find men's bones up there on Pine Mountain where they'd take them out and shoot them.

There was one man, a organizer, he come to our house. His back was beat to a bloody gore, he was beat all to pieces. He took off his shirt, went out back and laid in the sun for a long time. He stayed here all day. We pleaded with him not to go back. But he says, "Somebody's got to do it. I'm going back." When one gets killed, somebody's got to go back and take his place a-organizin'. And he went back and we never heard from him again.

One old man come to our house. Dan Brooks. They had a thousand or two thousand dollars on his head. I kept him in our house. He come in here from Pennsylvania to organize. He stayed two nights then left for a day. Then he came sneaking back to the house and that night he held a meeting on our porch. He told the miners, "Somebody's got to lose their lives in this, but won't it be better for them that's left?" And that's right. If we lose our lives a-doin' something like this, struggling, trying to get higher wages and better conditions for the workers, better homes, schools, hospitals, well then, if they kill us but yet if the people get those things, then it'd be better that we'd lose our lives for what'd help the workers.

Well, the thugs kept coming and coming. One day Sam went down to the garage and I saw them coming. I knowed from what had happened to other people that they was going to search the house.

Sam had a shotgun and he had a high power. Well, I was setting on the porch with my baby. They come on in and I got up and went in after them. My eleven-year-old daughter got that shotgun and that rifle and jumped out the window and ran, went up in the cornfields and hid.

We had shells hid inside the record player and I didn't want them to get them cause Sam would go hunting, you know. Well, one of them started to play the record player . . . it was one of them old ones you got to crank . . . he started a-crankin' it. I said, "You can't play that. It's broke." "Oh." And he stopped cranking it. I knowed if they'd started a-playin' it they'd've killed every one of us cause there was shells in there.

They looked in the beds, under the beds, through the dirty clothes, through folded clean clothes. Said they was a-lookin' for guns and literature. I'd never studied papers, I'd never heared tell of the International Workers of the World till they come, I didn't know what it meant. So that worried me. I told them, I said, "I'm not used to such stuff as this. All I do is just stay at home and take care of my children and go to church." One of them said, "As long as these communists is in here, you'll have trouble." I didn't even know what a communist was, I never heared tell of a communist before. But every time a body starts to do one good thing, he's branded a communist.

So they kept harder and harder a-pushin' us. One day when Sam was gone, they come with high powers and a machine gun. They come down the back road they was a-guardin'. They was intending to get Sam. So I sent my son and my sister's son down the front road to Bell County to tell the miners not to come, the gun thugs was a-waitin' on them. The thugs didn't get nothing that time.

But then they was back again. Says, "Here we are back." I said. "There's nothing here but a bunch of hungry children." But they come in anyway. They hunted, they looked in suitcases, opened up the stove door, they raised up the mattresses. It was just like Hitler Germany.

Down at that little garage we had, there was a man that worked there, his name was Tuttle. The gun thugs thought he was so dumb he wouldn't listen at nothing, he was all dirty and greasy. Well, Tuttle heared something and come up and told me. Said, "They're going to get you or Harvey"—Harvey was my fourteen-year-old son—"and hold one of you till Sam comes." Well, I couldn't wait for nothing. Harvey was up at Wallens Creek tending to Sam's chickens and Tuttle went up there, told Harvey they was coming to get him. So Harvey come back down to the house. I told him, "Harvey, the thugs is going to get you or me and hold until your Daddy comes. Now," I says, "you go to Mrs. Brock's and tell her if she'll keep you all night till you can get out of here, I'll give her anything in my house, anything. And," I said, "tell her not to let them know you're there."

Well, he went. But he didn't stop at Mrs. Brock's at all. He went right on through the woods. The stooges was always a-watchin' the house and they saw him a-goin'. So Harvey walked eighteen miles through the woods, him fourteen year old. And they followed him along, these stooges did.

The next morning we was a-movin' out of our house, getting out fast. Tuttle was a-helpin' us and he was scared to death. So we come on down to Mrs. Brock's and we couldn't see Harvey nowhere. She said she hadn't seen him at all, he hadn't been there. We figured they got him between our place and Mrs. Brock's.

Well, we went down to Pineville. We called at the hospitals and the jails a-lookin' for Harvey. But we couldn't find him. So we went down to our friends, the Dilbecks. I said, "Has Harvey been here?" He says, "Yes, he come here last night and we put him in the bed. And," he said, "he'd got up and left it was peeping daylight." We went on then, with all our things, and made it to the Tennessee-Kentucky line. There, on the Tennessee side, a-settin' on the fence was Harvey a-waitin' on us.

I was thirty when I wrote "Which Side Are You On?" We couldn't get word out any way. So I just had to do something. It was the night Sam had sneaked in through the cornfields and I was up a-watchin' for the thugs to come after him. That's when I wrote the song. We didn't have any stationery cause we didn't get nothing, we was doing good to live. So I just took the calendar off the wall and wrote that song, "Which Side Are You On?":

Which Side Are You On?
by Florence Reece

Come all you poor workers,
Good news to you I'll tell,
How the good old union
Has come in here to dwell.

(Chorus:)
5   Which side are you on?
Which side are you on?

We're starting our good battle,
We know we're sure to win,
Because we've got the gun thugs
10   A-lookin' very thin.

Which Side Are You On?

WORDS: FLORENCE REECE
MUSIC: "LAY THE LILY LOW"

Come all of you good work-ers, Good news to you I'll tell___ Of how the good old un-ion Has come in here to dwell. Which side are you on? Which side are you on?

Come all of you good workers,
Good news to you I'll tell
Of how the good old union
Has come in here to dwell.
   Which side are you on?
   Which side are you on?
   Which side are you on?
   Which side are you on?

My daddy was a miner
And I'm a miner's son,
And I'll stick with the union
Till ev'ry battle's won.
   Which side are you on? etc.

They say in Harlan County
There are no neutrals there;
You'll either be a union man
Or a thug for J. H. Blair.
   Which side are you on? etc.

Oh, workers, can you stand it?
Oh, tell me how you can.
Will you be a lousy scab
Or will you be a man?
   Which side are you on? etc.

Don't scab for the bosses,
Don't listen to their lies.
Us poor folks haven't got a chance
Unless we organize.
   Which side are you on? etc.

(Chorus:)
Which side are you on?
Which side are you on?

If you go to Harlan County,
There is no neutral there,
15　You'll either be a union man
Or a thug for J. H. Blair.

(Chorus:)
Which side are you on?
Which side are you on?

They say they have to guard us
20　To educate their child,
Their children live in luxury,
Our children almost wild.

(Chorus:)
Which side are you on?
Which side are you on?

25　With pistols and with rifles
They take away our bread,
And if you miners hinted it
They'll sock you on the head.

(Chorus:)
Which side are you on?
30　Which side are you on?

Gentlemen, can you stand it?
Oh, tell me how you can?
Will you be a gun thug
Or will you be a man?

(Chorus:)
35　Which side are you on?
Which side are you on?

My daddy was a miner,
He's now in the air and sun,[1]
He'll be with you fellow workers
40　Till every battle's won.

(Chorus:)
Which side are you on?
Which side are you on?

The music to the song is an old hymn. I can't remember what was that hymn, but I've got to look in the songbooks and find out what that was a tune to.

Now, I got a song, I like it, a lot of people like it:

We're tearing up an old recipe
Of poverty and war
We don't know why we're hungry
Nor what we're fighting for.

---

[1] Blacklisted and without a job.

5   This old recipe is yellow with age
It's been used far too long
People are shuffling to and fro
They know there's something wrong.

If the sun would stand still
10   Till the people are fed, all wars cease to be
Houses, hospitals, schools, a-built . . .
We must have a new recipe.

Sam says it's better I don't have music with my songs cause then they can understand every word you're saying. When you're past going out and organizing, well, then maybe you can sing a song or write a song to help.

Sometimes I can cry, and sometimes I get hurt too bad, tears won't come. I cry inside. It hurts worse. The ones that don't want the poor to win, that wants to keep us down in slavery, they'll hire these gun thugs, like they did over in Harlan County, to beat the workers down. And all in the world we people wanted was enough to feed and clothe and house our children. We didn't want what the coal operators had at all, just a decent living.

The workers offered all they had. They offered their hands, most of them offered their prayers, they'd pray . . . well, they'd also drink moonshine. But they was good, them coal miners.

Jim Garland, The Murder of Harry Simms

Come and listen to my story, come and listen to my song,
I'll tell you of a hero who now is dead and gone,
I'll tell you of a young lad, his age was just nineteen,
He was the bravest union man that I have ever seen.

5   Harry Simms was a pal of mine, we labored side by side,
Expecting to be shot on sight or taken for a ride
By the dirty coal-operator gun thugs that roamed from town to town
Shooting down the union men where'er they could be found.

Harry Simms and I were parted at 12 o'clock that day
10   Be careful, my dear comrade, to Harry I did say.
But I must do my duty, was his reply to me,
If I get killed by gun thugs, don't grieve after me.

Harry Simms was walking down the track that bright sunshiny day.
He was a youth of courage, his step was light and gay.
15   He did not know the gun thugs were hiding on the way
To kill our dear young comrade that bright sunshiny day.

Harry Simms was killed on Brush Creek in 1932,
He organized the miners into the NMU,
He gave his life in struggle, it was all that he could do,
20   He died for the union, he died for me and you.

Tillman Cadle, Commentary on Harry Simms

Harry Simms was a young organizer who came into Kentucky when the miners were on strike. He was murdered on Brush Creek in 1932. He was a real good organizer—he was having a lot of influence, mainly among the young people.

A lot of people had been going up to New York to speak about the miners' plight. Aunt Molly Jackson had gone and was speaking and singing around at mass meetings. And these people didn't believe what was going on in Kentucky. A committee (the Dreiser Committee) came to investigate. They said, "We'll just go and see for ourselves what's going on there." They brought a truckload of food, milk, and clothes for the children.

We was going to form a demonstration to go and meet these people to welcome them to Kentucky. We had organizers to go into different sections—Straight Creek, parts of Harlan County. I was to lead them out of Clear Fork. There was a junction there where they could all come together. Harry Simms and Green Lawson was delegated to go and lead the miners out of Brush Creek.

There was two of these company gun men came along on one of these little cars that travel on the railroad tracks. When they saw Harry Simms and Green Lawson walking up the tracks, they stopped and got off and shot Harry Simms. They weren't interested in killing Green Lawson—they knew he was just a local boy. But Harry Simms was an outsider—as they're so fond of calling them.

I was on the committee to go and claim his body from the chief of police.

John Dos Passos, Harlan: Working Under the Gun

Everybody knows that the coal industry is sick and that the men working at our most dangerous occupation (every sixth man is injured in the course of a year) are badly off, but few Americans outside of the miners themselves understand how badly off, or how completely the "American standard of living" attained in some sections during boom years, with strong unions working under the Jacksonville agreement, has collapsed. The coal operators, who have been unable to organize their industry commercially or financially along modern lines, have taken effective common action in only one direction: in an attack against the unions, the wage scales and the living conditions of the men who dig the coal out for them. Harlan County in eastern Kentucky, which has been brought out into the spotlight this summer by the violence with which the local Coal Operators' Association has carried on this attack, is, as far as I can find out, a pretty good medium exhibit of the entire industry: living conditions are better than in Alabama and perhaps a little worse than in the Pittsburgh district. The fact that the exploited class in Harlan County is of old American pre-Revolutionary stock, that the miners still speak the language of Patrick Henry and Daniel Boone and Andrew Jackson and conserve the pioneer traditions of the Revolutionary War and of the conquest of the West, will perhaps win them more sympathy from the average American than he would waste on the wops and bohunks he is accustomed to see get the dirty end of the stick in labor troubles.

I: WAR ZONE

> I am sad and weary, I've got the
> 　　hongry ragged blues,
> Not a penny in my pocket
> 　　to buy one thing I need to use

I was up this mornin
  with the worst blues ever had in my life
Not a bit to cook for breakfast
  or for a coalminer's wife.

The mines in Harlan County are in the forks and creeks of the upper part of the Cumberland River. A comparatively new coal field, first developed on a large scale during the boom in production that went along with the European War, its output is said to be a very high grade of bituminous. The miners were organized 90 percent by the United Mine Workers of America around 1917. In the 1920 boom a union miner was sometimes able, hiring several "chalkeyes" (inexperienced helpers) at $8 a day, to clear two or three hundred dollars a month. Railways pushed into the leafy valleys of the Cumberland range, fairly prosperous towns grew up. The population of Harlan County increased three or fourfold. Local business men who had managed to get hold of coal lands prospered on leases and royalties. Mountaineers who had lived poor and free on their hillside farms came down into the valleys to work in the mines and live in "patches" of temporary houses, put up by the companies. The race for riches went to the heads of the operators. The fact of having a little cash every two weeks went to the heads of the miners. The union turned into a racket and lapsed. Financiers skimmed the cream off the coal companies and left them overcapitalized and bankrupt. In the fat years no one thought of taking any measures of civic organization to help tide them over the lean years that were to follow—a typical American situation. Headlong deflation left the coal operators broke and the miners starving.

Last winter was pretty bad. When spring came along, the miners around Evarts began to think something ought to be done to revive the old locals of the U. M. W. of A. Wages had been steadily slipping. Conditions of safety were getting worse. A few old Wobblies and radicals began to talk class war; some of the youngsters began to wonder about socialism. A meeting was held in Pineville to talk about union organization. Two hundred men lost their jobs and were blacklisted. The coal operators, scared by the flood of anti-Red propaganda fed them through detective agencies and professional labor-baiting organizations, began to hire extra guards. Their position depended on their underselling the coal regions where traces of unionism still remained. Trusting to the terrible unemployment to break any strike that might be pulled, they took the offensive. In April they started evicting active union men from their houses. In the eastern counties of Kentucky every man considers himself entitled to carry a gun and to protect himself with it against insult and aggression. It was not long before a skirmish took place between miners and guards sworn in as deputies. This was followed, on May 5, by an out-and-out battle on the road outside of Evarts.

The townspeople of Evarts explain it this way: The town was full of evicted miners who seem to have had the pretty complete sympathy of the townspeople (the small merchants and storekeepers are against the mine operators because they force the miners to trade at the company commissaries). Feeling was running high. The mine guards made a practice of riding slowly through the town with their cars in second, machine guns and sawed-off shotguns sticking out of the windows, "tantalizing us," as one man put it. The morning of the fight, a rumor went around that the sheriff was going to bring in some carloads of scabs. Miners congregated on the road across the bridge from Evarts. The Coal Operators' Association claims that the miners were lying in ambush, an assertion which the miners deny. A carload of deputies came in from Harlan town. Shooting began, and lasted for thirty minutes. In the course of it three deputies were killed and several wounded; one miner was also killed and others wounded. Deputies then took Evarts by storm and arrested everybody they could lay their hands on. For some time the town had been under the cross-fire of their machine guns. The next morning Judge D. C. Jones—his wife is a member of the Hall family, which has mining interests in the vicinity—called a grand jury which the miners assert was illegally picked, made them a fiery speech denouncing I. W. W.'s and Reds. This grand jury returned thirty triple-murder indictments and thirty indictments for banding and confederating. Among those indicted were the town clerk and chief of police of Evarts. From then on through the summer the elected town officers of Evarts were superseded by the high sheriff's men, whose salaries are paid by the coal operators. No indictments were returned against mine guards or deputy sheriffs who had taken part in the battle, or against a mine guard who later killed Chasteen, a restaurant owner in Evarts who was on the miners' side.

About that time, so far as I can make out, the communist-affiliated National Miners' Union, which was conducting a strike against the Pittsburgh Terminal Company, sent organizers into eastern Kentucky, and N. M. U. locals began to be formed out of the wreckage of the old U. M. W. of A. In Evarts itself the I. W. W. seems to have had more influence than the Communists. The thing is that the miners felt that they were fighting for their lives and were ready to join any organization that would give them back solidarity and support them in their struggle against intolerable conditions. I talked to men who had joined all three unions.

Meanwhile the Coal Operators' Association was out to crush radicalism in Harlan County. The automobile of the I. L. D. relief worker was mysteriously dynamited. The soup kitchen in Evarts, which was feeding four hundred men, women and children a day, was blown up. In an attack on another soup kitchen at the swimming hole near Wallins Creek, two union men were killed and several wounded. Union organizers were beaten and run out of the county. Bruce Crawford of Crawford's Weekly, who greatly annoyed Sheriff Blair by publishing the miners' side of the story, was mysteriously shot from ambush. Boris Israel, Federated Press correspondent, was seized on the steps of the courthouse at Harlan, taken for a ride in perfect Chicago style, thrown out of the car on a lonely road and shot. Houses were raided, and many union sympathizers (among them Arnold Johnson, a theological student, who was an investigator for the American Civil Liberties Union) were arrested and jailed on the charge of criminal syndicalism. The Knoxville News Sentinel, a Scripps-Howard paper which printed stories about the frightful plight of the miners, was taken out of the newsstands in Harlan and its reporters were so intimidated the editor never dared send the same man up to Harlan twice.

All this time in the adjacent Bell County, where living conditions among the miners are worse if possible than in Harlan, the high sheriff has told the coal operators that if they make any trouble, he will cancel the deputy commissions of the mine guards, with the result that there has been no bloodshed, although there have been successful strikes in several small mines along Straight Creek.

II: ENTER THE WRITERS' COMMITTEE

When my husband works in the coalmines,
    he loads a car on every trip,
Then he goes to the office that evenin
    an gits denied of scrip—
Jus because it took all he had made that day
    to pay his mine expenses—
Jus because it took all he had made that day
    to pay his mine expenses.
A man that'll jus work for coal light an carbide
    he ain't got a speck of sense.

Breakfast in the station at Cincinnati. After that the train crosses the Ohio River and starts winding through the shallow valleys of the rolling section of central Kentucky. At lunch time to get to the dining car we have to walk through a federal prison car on its way to Atlanta. Change at Corbin onto a local train for Pineville. The Louisville papers say Governor Sampson is sending a detachment of militia into Harlan County. As we get near Pineville the valleys deepen. Steep hills burnished with autumn cut out the sky on either side. There's the feeling of a train getting near the war zone in the old days.

At the station is a group of miners and their wives come to welcome the writers' committee: they stand around a little shyly, dressed in clean ragged clothes. A little coaldust left in men's eyebrows and lashes adds to the pallor of scrubbed faces, makes you think at once what a miserable job it must be keeping clean if you work in coal. At the Hotel Continental Mr. Dreiser is met by newspaper men, by the mayor and town clerk of Pineville, who offer their services "without taking sides." Everybody is very polite. A reporter says that Judge D. C. Jones is in the building. A tall man in his thirties, built like a halfback, strides into the lobby. There's something stiff and set about the eyes and the upper part of his face; a tough customer. When he comes up to you you realize he must stand six-feet-six in his stocking feet. He and Mr. Dreiser meet and talk rather guardedly. Judge Jones says he's willing to answer any questions put to him about the situation in Harlan County. Mr. Dreiser and Judge Jones are photographed together on the steps of the hotel. Mrs. Grace of Wallins Creek, the wife of Jim Grace, a union organizer who was beaten up and run out of the county, comes up and asks Judge Jones why the sheriff's deputies raided her house and ransacked her things and her boarders' rooms. The interview comes abruptly to an end.

When the members of the committee settle down at a long table in a room off the lobby to decide on a plan of procedure, stories start pouring in.

Mr. Dreiser, after questioning Mrs. Grace about her husband's former employment— a former miner now working in a store, he was prominent in organizing the N. M. U.— asks her how he was arrested:

A. I was not with him, but he was arrested in Letcher County. Neon. Him and Tom Myerscough were together.

Q. What were they doing?

A. They were trying to get the union organized. They were organizing against starvation. They were establishing a union for better conditions.

Q. What happened to him?

A. After they came to the house looking for him, he went away and stayed at a friend's house and then he and Tom went to Neon, Letcher County. There he was arrested and took to jail in Neon. Then he was turned over to the Jenkins' bunch of gunmen.

Q. Well, what happened then?

A. Him and Myerscough were turned over to the Harlan County bunch and they takes them over to the Big Black Mountains of Virginia. They bust him in the face and broke his cheek bone. They kicked him in the back. He ran into the woods and they fired at him.

Q. How many shots did they fire?

A. About fifty I guess.

Q. Did they hit him?

A. Well he was grazed at the elbow.

Q. What did he do?

A. He went on to Middlesboro and stayed at a friend's house. But I didn't know. When I first got word that Mr. Grace and Tom was held in jail, I didn't know whether he was in Harlan, Jenkins, or Neon. I goes out and went to get somebody to find out. We thought they were killed. I started to get hold of the I. L. D. and I just happened in where

Mr. Grace was and I asked the lady whether her husband was there and I found out that Jim was there. His face and eyes was swollen black and blue. He was crazy as a loon.

Then she testified to raids on her house and her boarders' rooms being searched for I. W. W. and Com-MU-nist literature. Then an organizer for the union testified about having his house broken into and his guns seized (the possession of firearms is legal in Kentucky), a vice president of the Kentucky State Federation of Labor turned over some documents to the effect that when the state militia came in after the Evarts battle last spring the operators had promised the U. M. W. of A. that they wouldn't take that opportunity of importing scabs, and in spite of that had imported scabs. A young man brought a mysterious message warning the writers' committee not to attend the meeting called by the National Miners' Union at Wallins Creek on Sunday, as there'd surely be trouble there. Bruce Crawford told the story of his quarrel with Sheriff John Henry Blair: how Blair had gone to see him in Norton and complained of the attitude of his paper, had taken a subscription and left, and how the next time Crawford went to Harlan several shots had been fired at him as he crossed the swinging footbridge over the river, one of them nicking him in the ankle. The most moving testimony was that of Jeff Baldwin, whose brother Julius had been killed by deputies at the swimming-hole soup kitchen. His story was that two or more deputies had driven up the dirt road that leads up the hill from the main road to the shack where the soup kitchen was located, had stopped the sedan so that the headlights shone full in the door dazzling the group of miners standing around it, that one deputy, Lee Fleener by name, had first yelled "Put up your hands" and then immediately opened fire. Baldwin's brother and another man had been killed and he himself wounded in the shoulder as he ducked for shelter inside the shack. In spite of the fact that the coroner's jury had named Lee Fleener and other persons unknown as the murderers, no action had been taken by the county prosecutor.

Next day the committee went up to Harlan, a fine ride up the magnificent valley of the Cumberland River. Harlan is a lively little town; stores and bank buildings attest to the slightly flimsy prosperity of the boom period; the handsome courthouse takes away a little from the gimcrack air of a Southern industrial town.

Meanwhile, in a crowded room in the Llewellyn Hotel, miners and their wives were telling their stories:

Q. For how many years have you been a miner?

A. From twenty to twenty-five years.

Q. Have you done most of your mining here in Harlan County?

A. Since 1917. . . .

Q. When you were in good standing with this union [the United Mine Workers] how much did you make a day?

A. When we had a union here I could make from four dollars to five dollars to six dollars a day.

Q. How much did you make a month?

A. Anywhere maybe along from eighty dollars to one hundred.

Q. How much did you work for after the union broke up?

A. They kept cutting wages down till you hardly couldn't make anything at all. . . .

Q. This thirty dollars that you would get, was it in scrip or in cash?

A. No, sir, you hardly ever drew any money on that. You traded your scrip in at the store, the company store, and part of the time they had you in debt.

Q. Did you buy clothing at the company store or food?

A. Food. I couldn't get enough to buy clothes.

Q. How did you get clothing?

A. I generally sent out to beg and did the best I could.

This miner testified that since he'd been fired he had lived "on the mercy of the people." Being asked what criminal syndicalism, the charge on which he had been arrested and bonded over to keep the peace, meant to him, he said: "The best I can give it is going against your country, but that is something I never did do. I never thought about such a thing. . . . My family always fought for the country and I've always been for it."

Then Mr. Dreiser questioned a woman who refused to give her name, saying she was afraid her husband would lose his job if the boss found out she'd testified. They were living in a company house, where they'd been living for three weeks. In that time the husband had received only scrip.

Q. How do you manage to live?

A. We have just managed to exist. I will tell you that I've had just one dollar in the last three days to live on, my husband and myself and two children.

Q. I wonder how you distribute that money around.

A. We live on beans and bread. We don't get no dinner. . . . There don't none of you know how hard a man works that works in the mines and I'll tell you what I had to put in his bucket this morning for him to eat and work hard all day. There was a little cooked punkin and what you folks call white meat, just fat white bacon, and that's what he took to the mines to eat and work on and he had water gravy for breakfast and black coffee.

Q. And what's water gravy?

A. Water and grease and a little flour in it.

Q. What do you give the children?

A. They had the same breakfast and they don't get no dinner. . . . They're not in a situation to go to school because they have no shoes on their feet and no underwear on them and the few clothes they have, they are through them.

In the afternoon Mr. Dreiser visited Sheriff Blair in his office and asked him some questions. The sheriff said that the National Mine Workers was a Communist organization and that the U. M. W. of A. had not been, that he considered The Daily Worker and all other Communist, I. W. W. or Red publications illegal, and explained that most of the deputies he had sworn in were mine guards paid by the coal operators. He didn't know how many deputies he had sworn in. The only money they got from his office were fees for arrests and summonses. He brought the interview to a lively close by serving Bruce Crawford with a $50,000 civil suit for slander.

Next morning County Prosecutor Will Brock was interviewed. He said he approved of unionism, if it was a legal unionism like that of the U. M. W. of A., but that he considered all this I. W. W.–Communist agitation illegal and seditious. As an example of a fellow that he'd thought at first was decent and that had then turned out to be a Communist, he mentioned Arnold Johnson, investigator for the American Civil Liberties Union. The interview was made fairly tense by the interruptions of an attorney named Jones, who shares his office with him, who said he was just waiting to tell the whole damned bunch what he thought of them; on being asked about a deputy named Heywood who was reputed to be a Chicago gunman, he said grimly through his teeth: "All right, if you want to see him so bad, you'll see him." We learned afterward that his brother had been killed in the Evarts fight, and that he himself had taken part in raids on miners' houses.

III: THE MEETING IN STRAIGHT CREEK

All the women in this coalcamp
        are sittin with bowed down heads
All the women in this coalcamp
        are sittin with bowed down heads
Ragged an barefooted an their
        children acryin for bread
No food no clothes for our children
        I'm sure this ain't no lie
No food no clothes for our children
        I'm sure this ain't no lie
If we can't get no more for our labor
        we will starve to death and die.

Straight Creek is the section of Bell County that has been organized fairly solid under the National Miners' Union. Owing, the miners say, to the fair-minded attitude of the sheriff, who has not allowed the mine guards to molest them, there has been no bloodshed, and a three weeks' strike ended the week before we got there with several small independent operators signing agreements with the union at thirty-eight cents a ton and allowing a union checkweighman. They say thirty-eight cents is not a living wage but that it's something to begin on. The committee had been invited to attend a meeting of the N. M. U. local at the Glendon Baptist Church and walked around the miners' houses first. The militia officers who accompanied us were impressed with the utter lack of sanitation and the miserable condition of the houses, tumble-down shacks set up on stilts with the keen mountain wind blowing through the cracks in the floor.

The midwife at Straight Creek, Aunt Molly Jackson, who later spoke at the meeting and sang these blues of her own composing that I've been quoting at the heads of the sections, was questioned by Mr. Dreiser:

Q. Can you tell us something about the conditions of the people in this hollow?

A. The people in this country are destitute of anything that is really nourishing to the body. That is the truth. Even the babies have lost their lives and we have buried from four to seven a week during the warm weather . . . on account of cholera, flux, famine, stomach trouble brought on by undernourishment. Their food is very bad, such as beans and harsh foods fried in this lard that is so hard to digest . . . Families have had to depend on the Red Cross. The Red Cross put out some beans and corn.

Q. Do they give it to everyone that asks?

A. No, they stop it when they know a man belongs to the union.

Q. What did they say about it?

A. The Red Cross is against a man who is trying to better conditions. They are for the operators and they want the mines to be going, so they won't give anything to a man unless he does what the operators want him to. . . . I talked to the Red Cross lady over in Pineville. I said there's a lot of little children in destitution. Their feet are on the ground. They have come so far. They are going to get pneumonia and flu this winter that will kill them children off.

Q. Did she offer to give you any relief?

A. No, because they was members of the National Miners' Union. They said, "We are not responsible for those men out on strike. They should go back to work and work for any price that they will take them on for."

The meeting in the Baptist Church was conducted by a young fellow who'd been a preacher. Men and women spoke. Two representatives of the I. L. D. made speeches. One of the miners said in his speech that the reason they called them Reds was because the miners were so thin an' poor that if you stood one of 'em up against the sun you'd see red through him. All through the meeting a stout angry woman, who we were told was the bookkeeper at the Carey mine and the Red Cross distributor, stood in the aisle with her arms akimbo glaring at the speakers as if she was going to start trouble of some kind. All she did was occasionally to taunt the chairman with the fact that he owed her ten dollars. The high point of the meeting was Aunt Molly Jackson's singing of her blues:

> Please don't go under those mountains
>   with the slate ahangin over your head,
> Please don't go under those mountains
>   with the slate ahangin over your head
> An work for jus coal light and carbide
>   an your children acryin for bread;
> I pray you take my council
>   please take a friend's advice:
> Don't load no more, don't put out no more
>   till you get a livin price.

IV: LAST VESTIGE OF DEMOCRACY

> This minin town I live in
>   is a sad an a lonely place,
> This minin town I live in
>   is a sad an a lonely place,
> For pity and starvation
>   is pictured on every face,
> Everybody hongry and ragged,
>   no slippers on their feet,
> Everybody hongry and ragged,
>   no slippers on their feet,
> All goin round from place to place
>   bummin for a little food to eat.
> Listen my friends and comrades
>   please take a friend's advice,
> Don't put out no more of your labor
>   till you get a livin price.

Evarts is probably one of the few towns in the United States that still has democratic government. In spite of the fact that it's hemmed in on every side by coal-company property, that the chief of police and town clerk were arrested and charged with murder after the battle in May and that the town policing was done all summer by company guards, at the November election they put in a pro-miner town council by something like 200 to 80 votes. Most of the men at present on trial for their lives come from Evarts, and as far as I could find out from talking around, they have the complete sympathy of the local population. It is in Evarts that the union movement started, and there the miners were first accused of being Reds when it was discovered by the Coal Operators' Association that one of the U. M. W. of A. locals had taken out an I. W. W. charter. The miners on trial for murder are being defended by the General Defense Committee, the old Wobbly defense, that is unwilling to coöperate with the Communist-affiliated I. L. D. defending the criminal syndicalism and banding and confederating cases that have grown out of attempts to suppress the National Miners' Union. So far as I could make out, the county authorities

consider members of either organization equally without human rights. Possibly the
I. W. W. occupies a slightly better position, owing to its connection with U. M. W. of A.
officials who have contacts with state (Democratic) politics, and to its soft pedaling of class-
war talk. But the real point is that the situation of the miners is so desperate that they'll
join anything that promises them even temporary help. I asked one man if he'd go to work
again under the present scale, supposing he could get past the blacklist. He said, "You starve
if you work an' you starve if you don't work. A man 'ud rather starve out in the woods
than starve workin' under the gun."

The meeting at Wallins Creek took place in the high-school building and passed off
without disorder, though you got the impression that the people who attended it were pretty
nervous. The local small merchants seemed strong for the N. M. U. and somebody had put
up a banner across the main street that read, "Welcome I. L. D., National Miners' Union,
Writers' Committee." The next morning the committee packed up its testimony and left for
New York, to be followed by the "toothpick indictment" of Mr. Dreiser and a general indictment of all concerned, including the speakers at the miners' meeting, for criminal syndicalism.

Maggie Anderson, Among Elms and Maples, Morgantown, West Virginia, August, 1935

Houses are wedged between the tall stacks
of Seneca Glass beside the Monongahela
and waffle up steep hills. Here, the terrain
allows photographers to appear acrobatic.
5   Walker Evans liked standing on a hill, focusing
down so it seemed he was poised on a branch.
He liked the single telephone pole against
the flat sky, crossed off-center like a crucifix.
Beneath it, among elms and maples, is the house
10   my mother lived in with her sister and their mother
nearly fifty years ago. In this shot, Evans
only wanted the rough surfaces of clapboard
houses, their meshed roofs and slanted gables.
He didn't want my mother peeling the thin skin
15   from tomatoes with a sharp knife, my clumsy
Aunt Grace chasing the ones she'd dropped
around the linoleum floor. That would be another
picture, not this one. I look back from the future,
past the undulating, unremitting line of hills
20   Evans framed my family in, through the shaggy fronds
of summer ferns he used as foreground and as border.

Mining Camp Residents, West Virginia, July, 1935

They had to seize something in the face of the camera.
The woman's hand touches her throat as if feeling
for a necklace that isn't there. The man buries one hand

in his overall pocket, loops the other through a strap,
5   and the child twirls a strand of her hair as she hunkers
in the dirt at their feet. Maybe Evans asked them to stand
in that little group in the doorway, a perfect triangle
of people in the morning sun. Perhaps he asked them
to hold their arms that way, or bend their heads. It was
10   his composition after all. And they did what he said.

LONG STORY

To speak in a flat voice
Is all that I can do.
                    —*James Wright*

I need to tell you that I live in a small town
in West Virginia you would not know about.
It is one of the places I think of as home.

When I go for a walk, I take my basset hound
5   whose sad eyes and ungainliness always draw
a crowd of children. She tolerates anything
that seems to be affection, so she lets the kids
put scarves and ski caps on her head
until she starts to resemble the women who have to dress
10   from rummage sales in poverty's mismatched polyester.

The dog and I trail the creek bank with the kids,
past clapboard row houses with Christmas seals
pasted to the windows as a decoration.
Inside, television glows around the vinyl chairs
15   and curled linoleum, and we watch someone old
perambulating to the kitchen on a shiny walker.
Up the hill in town, two stores have been
boarded up beside the youth center, and miners
with amputated limbs are loitering outside
20   the Heart and Hand. They wear Cat diesel caps
and spit into the street. The wind
carries on, whining through the alleys,
rustling down the sidewalks, agitating
leaves, and circling the courthouse steps
25   past the toothless Field sisters who lean
against the flagpole holding paper bags
of chestnuts they bring to town to sell.

History is one long story of what happened to us,
and its rhythms are local dialect and anecdote.
30   In West Virginia a good story takes awhile,
and if it has people in it, you have to swear

that it is true. I tell the kids the one about
my Uncle Craig who saw the mountain move
so quickly and so certainly it made the sun
35   stand in a different aspect to his little town
until it rearranged itself and settled down again.
This was his favorite story. When he got old,
he mixed it up with baseball games, his shift boss
pushing scabs through a picket line, the Masons
40   in white aprons at a funeral, but he remembered
everything that ever happened, and he knew how far
he lived from anywhere you would have heard of.

Anything that happens here has a lot of versions,
how to get from here to Logan twenty different ways.
45   The kids tell me convoluted country stories
full of snuff and bracken, about how long
they sat quiet in the deer blind with their fathers
waiting for the ten-point buck that got away.
They like to talk about the weather,
50   how the wind we're walking in means rain,
how the flood pushed cattle fifteen miles downriver.

These kids know mines like they know hound dogs
and how the sirens blow when something's wrong.
They know the blast, and the stories, how
55   the grown-ups drop whatever they are doing
to get out there. Story is shaped
by sound, and it structures what we know.
They told me this, and three of them
swore it was true, so I'll tell you
60   even though I know you do not know
this place, or how tight and dark the hills
pull in around the river and the railroad.

I'll say it as the children spoke it,
in the flat voice of my people:
65   down in Boone County, they sealed up
forty miners in a fire. The men who had come
to help tried and tried to get down to them,
but it was a big fire and there was danger,
so they had to turn around
70   and shovel them back in. All night long
they stood outside with useless picks and axes
in their hands, just staring at the drift mouth.
Here's the thing: what the sound must have been,
all those fire trucks and ambulances, the sirens,
75   and the women crying and screaming out
the names of their buried ones, who must have
called back up to them from deep inside
the burning mountain, right up to the end.

Don West (1906–1992)

Don West was a poet, preacher, educator, farmer, labor organizer, and political activist. Ecumenical in his political beliefs, harassed by the FBI for his politics and poetry, burned out by the Klan, Don West was, for sixty years, an undaunted crusader for social justice.

West was born near Burnt Mountain in Gilmer County, Georgia, to a family of farmers who, cash-poor, eventually had to drift into sharecropping and mill work. Raised on stories of mountain culture told by his grandfather, Kim Mulkey, West wrote prose and poetry, "little pieces of life," that spoke straightforwardly to the dispossessed. He attended Lincoln Memorial University, where he met other aspiring southern writers and Mabel "Connie" Adams, an art student and soon to be his wife and lifetime companion. He studied religion at Vanderbilt University, learned a Social Gospel approach to Christian theology, and was ordained as a minister. He won a scholarship to visit Danish folk schools and was inspired by an educational model that incorporated cultural heritage and cooperative learning. In 1932, he founded, with Myles Horton, the Highlander Folk School in Tennessee.

Writing in the vernacular of mountain culture, West published his first collection of poems, *Crab-Grass* in 1931, which sold a hundred thousand copies. During the 1930s, he published in left-wing journals, as well as in regional publications. His 1934 poem "I Am a Communist," published in *The Daily Worker* with the lines, "No body/With calloused hands/Is foreign to us," was used by the FBI and others to harass and blacklist West in the politically repressive decades that followed. In the mid- and late 1930s, he worked as an underground labor organizer under various aliases in Kentucky mining camps and continued to write, publish, and perform on the radio and to large rallies in southern Appalachia. *Songs for Southern Workers*, a southern version of the *Little Red Songbook*, and another collection, *Toil and Hunger*, were published in 1940. West published *Clods of Southern Earth* in 1946, a collection that included many previously published poems but excluded references to communism. After teaching for several years in Baltimore in the 1960s, Don and Connie West returned to the Mountain South and founded the Appalachian South Folklife Center in 1965. He continued performing and writing poetry, as well as publishing a series of pamphlets in the Tom Paine tradition. *O Mountaineers!* (1974), a collection of poems written over forty years was followed by *In a Land of Plenty: A Don West Reader* (1982). Like Okie poet Wilma Elizabeth McDaniel, he chose to write in the idiom of his own people, and like labor activist Florence Reese, he was very clear about whose side he was on.

CLODS OF SOUTHERN EARTH: INTRODUCTION (1946)

Once upon a time, not too long ago, authors wrote mainly about kings and nobles—the aristocracy. Many stories and poems were filled with debauchery and intrigues. Writers occupied themselves in turning out tales about the purity of lovely ladies and the daring of gallant gentlemen who never did a useful day's work in their lives.

The fact that systems of kings and nobles, of aristocratic ladies and useless gentlemen, were always reared upon the misery of masses of peasants, slaves, or workers, was carefully omitted from most books. The idea that these same peasants, slaves, or workers might themselves be fit material for literature would have been heresy.

You may think this is a strange sort of way to begin an introduction to a group of poems. You may be one of those Americans who say you don't like poetry anyhow. No one can blame you for that. I've often felt that way, too. Maybe it's because too many poets write in the old tradition. Using an obscure and "subtle" private language, they write only for the little clique of the "highly literate" elite. But in spite of their high and mighty intellectual snobbery, one finds them, after all, concerned mostly with minor themes. Such literary gentlemen, writing only for the "elite" ten percent, spurn the "crude" and "vulgar" masses. They still have their eyes full of star dust. They see neither the dirt and misery nor the beauty and heroism of common folk life.

You say you want a poem with its roots in the earth; a poem that finds beauty in the lives of common people, and perhaps a poem that may sometimes show the reasons for the heartache and sorrow of the plain folks and sometimes point the way ahead. I don't blame you. I sort of feel that way, too.

Does this sound like a strange notion about poetry? Maybe it is. Some people say I have strange notions anyhow. I don't know. Lots of things I don't know. I've been a preacher, and I've preached the working-man, Jesus, who had some strange notions himself about the poor and rich and the slaves. I've been a coal miner in Kentucky's Cumberlands and a textile worker in Carolina. I've been a radio commentator in Georgia and a deck hand on a Mississippi River steamboat. I've been a sailor, a farm owner, and farmer. I am now a school Superintendent. And I've wondered why it always seems that the folks who work less get more and those who work more get less. That puzzles me some. I've a notion it shouldn't be that way, and some say I have strange notions.

Maybe it's because of family background. You know, some people go in for that family stuff. I do come from an old Southern family. You've heard that one before, yes? Well, I don't mean what you think. Mine is a real old Southern family. Oh, I'm no sprig off the decadent tree of some bourbon, aristocratic, blue-blood family of the notorious slave-master tradition.

That's what is usually meant. You know—the professional Southerners who claim to be kind to Negroes—the tuxedoed gentlemen, the silk underweared, lace-dressed ladies coyly peeping from behind scented fans. No, I don't mean that. I'm more Southern than that. That represents only the small minority. My folks were the men who wore jean pants and the women who wore linsey petticoats. They had nothing to do with the genteel tradition. Some were the first white settlers of Georgia, and some were already settled when the white ones came.

Yes, on one limb of my family tree hangs a bunch of ex-jailbirds. They were good, honest (I hope, but it doesn't make a lot of difference now) working people in the old country. They were thrown in jails there because they were unemployed and couldn't raise money to pay their debts.

How in the devil a man is expected to pay a debt while lying in prison is hard to see. Maybe it satisfied the creditors to take it out on their hides. Anyhow, there they were, hundreds of them, and a man named Oglethorpe, who had a big warm heart and a real feeling for folks, asked the old king to let him take a group of these prisoners to the new land.

The king didn't warm up to the idea much at first, but finally he was convinced. These outcasts would make a nice buffer protection for the more blue-blooded settlers of the other colonies, against the Indians and Spanish. The place later to be known as Georgia was just the spot. The colonies warmed right up to the idea, too. Nice to have a gang of tough jailbirds known as "arrow-fodder" between them and the Indians. So, you see, Georgia was started. The plan worked.

Some Southerners love to boast about their families. And I reckon I do too, a little. At least none of mine ever made his living by driving slaves. There's nary a slave owner up my family tree. The old story that we don't look too closely for fear of finding a "horse thief" is commonplace, of course. Indeed, wouldn't it be shameful to find one of our grand-paws doing such a petty theft? Who could be proud of a great-grand-daddy with ambition no higher than stealing a horse? B'gad, we Americans go in for big stuff! Steal a horse? No! But steal a continent, a nation; steal the lives and labor of thousands of black men and women in slavery; steal the wages of underpaid workers; steal a railroad, a bank, a million dollars—oh boy, now you're talking! That's the real class. Those are the ancestors America's blue-bloods worship. But steal a horse—aw, heck, the guy might have been hanged for that!

Guess I'd better tell you about that other limb on my family tree now. From what I can uncover, it had just two main branches with a few sprigs sprouting off. A forked sort of bush, you know. On that other fork hangs a white slave (indentured servant) in Carolina and a kind hearted old Indian of the Cherokees in north Georgia. To make a long story short—though I think it is a beautiful, if tragic one—this white slave girl and her lover ran away from their master in the Carolina tidewater country. The girl was pregnant, but the master had been forcing his attentions on her and that was more than her lover could stand. They set out toward the Indian country of north Georgia. Hearing the pursuers close behind, the man stopped, telling the girl to keep going and he'd overtake her if he got a lucky shot. He never overtook her. She went on and finally, weary and near death, reached the Indian settlement around Tallulah Falls in north Georgia. The Indians put her to bed and cared for her. The baby, a boy, was born. The child grew up as an Indian, married into the tribe, and had other children.

This, then, is the other limb of our family tree.

Do you think I'm telling about this tree just because it's mine? You're partly right. But the main reason is that, to a greater or lesser degree, it represents the great majority of Southern whites. And their real story has never yet been adequately told. Some day I intend to do it, to tell about these people with rough hands, big feet, and hard bodies; about the real men and women of the South.

That old Southern family stuff that you've heard so much about, always meaning the aristocratic, slave-owning tradition, is worn about as thin as the blood of those families today. Our people, the real Southern mass majority of whites, are the ones the Negroes were taught to call "pore white trash." And we, in turn, were taught the hateful word "nigger." Nice little trick, isn't it? Hitler used it, too. And it is still being used today, by the whites from the big houses, who engineer lynchings and make it seem that the responsibility is the white workers'.

Our people, and the Negroes, made up about 98 percent of the Southern population before the Civil War.

In addition to all this, I'm a "hill-billy." My folks were mountain people. We lived on Turkey Creek. And what a place that is!

Turkey Creek gushes in white little splashes around the foot of Burnt Mountain and down to the Cartecay. The Cartecay crawls and gurgles—sometimes lazily, sometimes stormily—down the valleys and hollows between the hills to Ellijay. Over the cataracts and through the fords these waters have gone on since nobody knows when—except that summer when the drought saw sands scorching dry, and the river bed looked like a pided moccasin turned on its back to die in the sun.

Mountain houses are scattered along the banks of Cartecay. Mountain people live there, plain people to whom it is natural to ask a stranger to stay all night. They have lived there for generations—since the first white man pushed through the Tallulah gorge, and others came up from the lowlands to escape the slave system. Indians have also lived on the Cartecay. It was once their hunting grounds. But most of them were rounded up and marched west toward the setting sun. Mountain men on Cartecay have gone west too, in search of opportunity, but some have stayed.

The men who first settled the mountains of the South were fearless and freedom loving. Many, in addition to the prisoners, came to escape persecution in the old country. They had been outspoken in opposition to oppression and denial of liberties. Some came later into the friendly mountains seeking a few rocky acres they could till and call their own. They fled from the ever-encroaching wave of slave-holding planters in the lowlands. The "poor whites" in slavery days found themselves burdened down with slave labor competition. Their lot in many instances was very little better than that of the slave. In the lowlands of the planters they were considered a blight upon the community. They were pushed off the desirable lands. Left to them were the submarginal, undesirable ridges or swamps. Many, therefore, fled to the great mountain ranges of north Georgia and other states, where freedom of a sort was to be had. Disease, starvation, and illiteracy were the lot of tens of thousands of these "poor whites" who were forced to live in the hard, infertile regions of the South prior to the Civil War.

Now you may have thought, as I once did, that the old South was divided simply into whites and blacks—slave and master—and that everybody supported slavery from the beginning. I was taught that in school, from the history books, about my own state. But I'm going to let you in on a little secret that I didn't learn from the school text books. Here it is: Oglethorpe and the first settlers of Georgia were bitterly opposed to the whole institution of slavery. They fought resolutely against slavery ever coming to Georgia.

I dug this up from some old dusty records. Here is what Oglethorpe himself wrote in a letter to Granville Sharpe, October 13, 1776: "My friends and I settled the Colony of Georgia. . . . We determined not to suffer slavery there. But the slave merchants and their adherents occasioned us not only much trouble, but at last got the then government to favor them; we would, not suffer slavery . . . to be authorized under our authority; we refused, as trustees, to make a law permitting such a horrid crime. . . ."

But this isn't all. How deeply this idea of freedom and justice was planted in these early Georgians is further shown by a resolution passed January 12, 1775, endorsing the proceedings of the first American Congress, by "the Representatives of the extensive District of Darien, in the Colony of Georgia." It said:

> 5. To show the world that we are not influenced by any contracted or interested motives, but a general philanthropy for all mankind, of whatever climate, language or complexion, we hereby declare our disapprobation and abhorrence of the unnatural practice of slavery in America . . . a practice founded in injustice and cruelty, and highly dangerous to our liberties (as well as lives), debasing part of our fellow-creatures below men, and corrupting the virtues and morals of the rest; and laying the basis of the liberty we contended for . . . upon a very wrong foundation. We, therefore, resolve, at all times, to use our utmost endeavors for the manumission of slaves in this Colony. . . .

There it is! These were men who indeed did not fit into a system of power and privilege for a few. But eventually their opposition was beaten down (though never destroyed). There went on a general infiltration of the bluebloods who wanted slaves to do their work. Finally there was a civilization, a "culture," an aristocracy reared upon the institution of slavery, built upon the bent backs of human beings bought and sold like cattle, and upon the misery of the overwhelming majority of non-slave-holding Southern whites.

This, then, is the so-called and much lamented "culture" of the "lost cause"! The basis of wealth and privilege was the ownership of slaves. This privilege was concentrated in a very few hands. The total population of the South prior to the Civil War was about nine million. There was about four and a half million slaves, over four million non-slave-owning whites, and, at the most, not more than three hundred thousand actual slave owners.

Culture, education, and wealth were limited to this narrow oligarchy of a few hundred families. Since the overwhelming majority of Southern whites owned no slaves whatsoever, they had little voice in government. The local and state governments were virtually executive committees for the slave masters. For lack of free schools, ignorance and illiteracy were the lot of the poor whites who were bowed down under the heavy burden of taxation of a slave-master government.

And so there grew up in these Southern mountains, communities of non-slave-holding farmers, scratching a bare livelihood from the stubborn new-ground hillside patches. They hated the slave system and the slave masters. Many of them refused to fight for the "lost cause" in the Civil War. They reasoned: Why fight for a system that oppresses us as well as the black slaves?

Yes, these were my people. I come from the Devil's Hollow region close by Turkey Creek at the foot of Burnt Mountain in north Georgia. Earliest memories are woven around the struggles of my Dad and Mother to dig a living from our little mountain farm. Life always seemed hard—like an iron fist mauling them in the face, knocking them down every time they tried to get up. But they wanted their kids to go to school, get educated. We went, the whole bunch of us. There were nine kids, three now dead. All of the survivors today are progressive thinkers, working for a better South.

Yes, I got something in schools—Vanderbilt, Chicago University, Columbia, Oglethorpe, University of Georgia, in European schools. But my best education has not been from classrooms and formal professors. My real education has been beaten into me by the everlasting toil and hunger I've seen, by the struggles in textile and coal mining centers, where our people were lured down from the hills with false promises of a better life; by the hunger I have seen in the faces of sharecropper kids; by my own sister, wife of a sharecropper, dying young from overwork and worry. It is this education of life—of prisons and jails for innocent men—that caused a determination never to seek to rise upon the shoulders of others; to rise only when the great mass of plain people can also have a richer life. And some day we will!

I love the South. Like hundreds of other Southerners, I dislike some things about its customs and ways. But our folks have lived and died there. Our roots are sunk deeply from generations back. My own Dad died young—toil and hunger, too much work, and too little of the right kind of food are the only honest reasons any doctor could have given.

We had big hopes when we left the mountains to become sharecroppers in the cotton lowlands. But those hopes were dead long before we buried Dad in Hickory Grove Church Yard.

So I pass these poems on to you who may care enough to read. They are little pieces of life—and death—picked up along the way. May they help to kindle little sparks that will grow into big flames!

MOUNTAIN BOY

> You are more than a dirty child
> In patched overalls.
> You mountain boy . . . !
> The hills are yours.
> 5　The fragrant forests,
> The silver rivers
> Are your heritage.
>
> Dreamers. Thinkers.
> Rise up, young hillmen.

10   Sing your ballads.
Dream your future.
Up and down your valleys,
Over the ridge-roads.
Climb your jagged mountains.
15   Gaze into blue space . . .
Turn your thoughts free.
Nourish your imagination.

What will you do for your hills,
You mountain boy?

20   Love the soil.
Your father's blood
Made it rich.
His sweat has caused fruit to grow.
Sift the coarse soil
25   Between your fingers.
Exult when it runs between your toes
Through brogan shoes
As you follow the plow.
Yours is the poet's life.
30   You rhyme the soil,
Dig and plant
And watch the corn grow.
You are the heart of a nation—
Even America.

35   O farmer boy,
Rise up!
Sing your songs,
Live your life
Even as you know how!

CLODHOPPER

I'm the Clodhopper—
Have you heard about me—
The lump that feeds the world.
A lowland Georgia Cracker,
5   Song singer from the mountains—
A cotton-picking Brown Skin—
I'm the Clod-hopper
That puts clothes on the world . . .

Who said:
10   "Clodhoppers of the world,
Unite!
You have nothing to lose
But your clods—
Unite!"

15   Was that Jesus or Marx?
       Or maybe it was me
       Said that
       And:
       "Down with the clodhopper joke?
20   Up with the dignity of the clod.
       To every clodhopper a clod
       To wiggle between his toes!"

       Isn't it written:
       "The laborer is worthy
25   Of his wage,
       And the Hopper
       Of his clod?"

       If it isn't,
       I'll write it now . . .

30   Oh, I'm the Clodhopper
       That makes the tall corn grow,
       The artist that smears dignity
       Through the speckled cotton patch.
       I'm the man that fills
35   The belly of the world,
       And slips a petticoat
       Over her nakedness . . .

THERE'S ANGER IN THE LAND

Note: In the summer of 1950 I picked up a Negro hitch-hiker in South Georgia and brought him across the Chattahoochee at Eufala, Alabama. As we crossed the river he began telling me the story of how his brother was lynched and his body cut down from the limb and flung across the door-step of his mother's shack—broken, bleeding and lifeless.

       Oh, there's grieving in the plum-grove
       And there's weeping in the weeds,
       There is sorrow in the shanty
       Where a broken body bleeds . . .

5   For there's been another lynching
       And another grain of sand
       Swells the mountain of resentment—
       Oh, there's anger in the land!

       And a woman broods in silence
10   Close beside an open door
       Flung across the flimsy door-step
       Lies a corpse upon the floor!

       You'll not ask me why I'm silent;
       Thus the woman spoke to me.
15   Her two eyes blazed forked anger
       And her throat throbbed agony.

Let the wind go crying yonder
In the tree-tops by the spring,
Let its voice be soft and feeling
20   Like it was a living thing.

Once my heart could cry in sorrow
Now it lies there on the floor
In the ashes by the hearth-stone—
They can't hurt it anymore!

25   Did you ever see a lynching,
Ever see a frenzied mob
Mill around a swaying body
When it's done the hellish job?

Yes, the night was full of terror
30   And the deeds were full of wrong
Where they hung him to a beech-wood
After beating with a thong.

Oh, there's grieving in the plum-grove
And there's sobbing on the sand,
35   There is sorrow in the shanties—
And there's anger in the land!

NO LONESOME ROAD

For Byron Reece

Once I too said that all men walk
A solitary road
And that each one must grope alone
And drag his little load.

5   I thought that I must walk forlorn
Upon that lonesome street
All hedged about the granite walls
Of pride and self-conceit.

But now I've learned that all can trudge
10   Upon a common way
Thru moonlight night and stumbling dark
Or in the flaming day.

And men cry out in word and name
As they are passing by
15   To those whose faith and fortitude
Have shoved them near the sky

Like Galileo at the stake,
Jesus nailed to a tree.
Cold bleeding feet at Valley Forge
20   Are on that road with me.
And I would not forget the men
Who dig and plow the soil

And those who fight that all shall live
With simple lives of toil.

25   It is no lonesome road we tread
Though so the cynics say.
The poet, farmer, working man
Must walk a common way.

"I Am a Woman Worker": A Scrapbook of Autobiographies from the Summer Schools for Women Workers (1936)

Between 1921 and 1938, the summer schools for women workers offered nearly 1,700 women a rare summer hiatus. They could reside on a beautiful campus, attend lectures, study science, economics, and the liberal arts, and speak and write about their own experiences as workers. In a 1977 interview, Margaret Darin described her experience: "I debated a long time whether to go or not, because work had just started to pick up and I was helping my mother and my brother and sister-in-law. They said, 'Oh, Margie you go!' So I did. I went to the school for six weeks. They were the most beautiful weeks of my life. Would you believe being in Brynmawr College?"

The schools began in a climate of progressive support for women's rights and worker education. The National Women's Trade Union League asked the leaders of women's colleges to do their part to improve the lives of women workers. Bryn Mawr President M. Carey Thomas and Dean Hilda "Jane" Worthington Smith responded by starting the first school. The women workers were recruited through unions, primarily the ILGW (International Ladies Garment Workers Union), and through community organizations, such as the YWCA. A few slots were opened for women workers from abroad as well. The pedagogy was innovative—linking experience to learning—and the administrative approach was democratic—encouraging student involvement regarding the curriculum.

The stories presented here were written by women workers in several summer schools and gathered in one of many "scrapbooks" published by the Affiliated Schools for Workers in New York (1936). Responding to the question, "What happened to me?" posed by economics and English teachers, these anonymous writers offer firsthand accounts of the tedium, speed, and physicality of the job. These writing assignments were also intended as a mutual pedagogical strategy to "wake each other up"—a practice as relevant for the teachers as for the students in this important cross-class educational alliance.

SOLDERING

I reported for work at 8:00 in the morning. While I was waiting for the foreman to place me, the conveyor started. The place began to get smoky. I heard shouts "Up! the belt!" "Down! the belt!" Radios were turned on, radios were turned off. On and off, off and on! It was driving me mad. Suddenly the boss called me.

"Can you solder?"

"No."

"All right, I'll teach you," he said, and he handed me a soldering iron.

I felt the weight of it; "I can't hold it," I thought.

Then he gave me a piece of solder. "Watch me," he said, as he soldered two sets, four lugs on each.

"Can you do it?" he asked.

I answered half-frightened, "I'll try." I soldered one set.

He looked at it and said, "Not so bad, try another."

After I had done another set, "Okay," he said. "Now try just two lugs instead of the whole operation."

I soldered for about an hour. Then I began to get dizzy. It was the moving of the conveyor, and the inhaling of acid fumes. The place was a cloud of smoke. My wrist got weak. It felt as though it was breaking from the weight of the iron. I could not hold the iron steady. It slipped and burnt my fingers. My solder got caught in the plug from my iron and blew out the fuse. This made a terrible noise. Hot sparks flew from it. I could control myself no longer. I began to scream.

"Oh, I can't stand this, I can't." I was in great pain. My wrist felt as though it was broken. My fingers I had burnt were still stinging, and I had a large blister on one. My neck was stiff from bending over the conveyor. I ached all over. I began to cry; but I finally did learn the job.

ONE DAY OF LABOR

Six-forty-five A.M. How quiet it is in this place where thousands of workers bend their backs in hard monotonous toil, for the monster that drives the machinery still sleeps. How footsteps and voices carry through the silent rooms with their thousands of stilled belts, pulleys and millions of spindles.

But soon the silence is broken; the monster stirs. Trembling and quaking, the building groans as if in protest against the tremendous power within its walls. With a bellow to be heard for miles, the voice of the factory commands the arms and legs of the machinery to start work. Workers reluctantly slide levers and press buttons. Pulleys turn slowly, then gain speed. Belts hiss through close, hot air. Bobbins on their spindles revolve faster than eyes can see. The monster is awake, demanding, driving, compelling. On! On! On!

Night time is near. Hours of labor have passed in a perpetual grind. Heat! Mist! Dust! Work! All in a mad, endless whirl. Clothes wet with perspiration and the clammy thick mist from the hissing humidifiers. Dust, clinging and irritating. Work, hard work, sapping strength from the strongest, leaving the weak gasping. Tired eyes lift from their minute tasks to send swift glances at the slow-moving clock, but hands and arms continue without pause. Weariness, the vanguard of swift death, has spared none.

At last, the lights flicker and die. The voice has again bellowed, but this time unheard because of the clank and hum of tireless machines. With a last burst of speed, their tenders slam levers back; belts and pulleys halt reluctantly. With feet that feel like lead, the workers carry aching bodies through the now silent rooms. Free at last to leave. Free to rest as much as trembling bodies permit. It is the end of one day.

BEAN PICKING

About the middle of June every year, Mother would take us four children out to some country place to work. We usually picked beans. This was a back-breaking job. We had to be up at 4:30 every morning, go in the fields at 5:30, and work until dusk. If the crops were good, we made on an average of $15 to $17 a day. Some of the large families made as much as $25 to $30 a day. We were paid a penny a pound.

The shacks in which we lived were shabby, run-down, one room affairs. We had no electric bills. The wood was supplied by the boss. We usually ate what we could take from the fields. Therefore, we had very little expense.

The beds were made of straw piled on the floor and covered with sheets. The whole family slept in one bed. Whenever it rained, we would have to have pots under the places where the roof leaked. We had to make our own stoves from bricks and mud paste. Sometimes the stove would fall apart when it rained and we would have to make another one.

At night we would gather around the fire, from where we could see the bossman's home. A big, beautiful white home on the hill, surrounded by shrubbery, trees and flowers. We were not allowed to walk on his property—he said we would ruin his flowers.

Sometimes while working in the fields, some of the young boys and girls would start singing. The boss man would come over and tell us to stop. He said it made him nervous and, besides, we should work and not sing.

His son came home from college about this time. He would talk to us and be friendly while his father was not around, but he never recognized any of us when we went to town and he was among his own class.

One day the boss came to our shacks and insisted on searching them. We did not know what it was all about, but we soon found out. Some of his chickens were missing and he accused us of stealing them. The people could stand being accused of almost anything but stealing. We called a strike and refused to go to work the next morning. The boss tried to force us, but he saw it was no use. The next day he hired a truck and sent us home.

The Piece-Work System

I suggest that those people who invented piece-work be given a chance to work on that basis, under the same conditions as we piece-workers do, and see how they would like it.

I think that piece-work is a very unjust method of paying workers. If we realized how piece-work harms us mentally and physically, we might take it a little bit more seriously. Piece-work is paid on a plan that is more like guess-work than anything else. The employer cannot resist the temptation to cut prices when he sees that we are making more than he thinks we ought to make.

Often the employer picks the fastest girl in the place and gives her a certain amount of work to turn out, with a time-study method of ascertaining the time required. When she turns out more than the average worker, and so earns more, the employer usually cuts the prices accordingly. He may cut the rate again and again. And we have to work faster and faster in order to get a living wage. Our work is seasonal, so we are forced to make as much as we can to save some money for the slack time. The result is, that we get tired, disagreeable, and sometimes sick, so that we have to stay at home for a few days in the full season. I know a great number of girls who have been working long years in industry under the speed-up system who have heart disease or some other serious sickness.

Must we always be needlessly sacrificed to the desire for profit of the employers? Can not we discover some sort of "scientific management" which has as its aim the protection of the health and happiness of the workers, instead of the piling up of profits for the employers?

THE PRESIDENT VISITS THE MILL

One day at work, word was received that the President of our tobacco company was coming to visit the plant the next day. The boss sent me around to tell all the workers to get busy and start cleaning their machines. We had a half day to get everything ready for the President.

The next day, when the President came through he had several other men with him, some wearing diamond stick pins and rings which cost thousands of dollars. The President did not look at the cigarettes; he merely looked over the floor. When one of these very important looking men stopped at one of the cigarette machines that was making fourteen hundred cigarettes a minute, he found just one bad cigarette before the girl that was catching could get to it. (It is nothing unusual for a cigarette machine to run a bad cigarette once in a short time.) This man showed the bad cigarette to the President. The President called the foreman and had the girl fired.

This girl had a mother and a little sister to take care of on $11 a week. The men went on their way to another floor, while the girl trudged home with the news that she had no job.

Boxcar Bertha (Ben Reitman) (1879–1942)

*B*oxcar Bertha: An Autobiography (1937) begins with a confident announcement of subjective experience and authorship, the assertion of a particular, knowing voice: "I am thirty years old as I write this, and have been a hobo for fifteen years, a sister of the road, one of that strange and motley sorority which has increased its membership so greatly during the depression." Like much working-class autobiography, the writing serves to represent a community—the transient "sisterhood" of women who, by choice or necessity, live outside the confines of home, job, and often the law—as much as it represents the life of a unique individual. The life Bertha Thompson narrates was remarkable in its independence and range of experience. At the book's close, she is able to look back with a sense of achievement: "I had wanted to know how it felt to be a hobo, a radical, a prostitute, a thief, a reformer, a social worker, and a revolutionist. Now I knew." She might have added: a mother, a member of a free-love commune, and the lover of one man who died under a train and another hanged for murder. It is not surprising that Martin Scorsese directed the 1972 movie version of *Boxcar Bertha*. The book's enduring appeal, as a feminist odyssey and an underworld exposé, comes both from the pleasure that Bertha takes in her knowledge and experience and from her matter-of-fact narration, free of judgment and analysis—as the excerpt that follows, based on her work in a Chicago brothel, demonstrates.

It has been a shock to some readers to learn, in the book's 2002 reprinting as *Sister of the Road: The Autobiography of Boxcar Bertha*, that it was in fact written by Dr. Ben Reitman and that "Boxcar Bertha" is a fictional character composed from the stories of several women Reitman had known. Famous in Chicago as the "hobo doctor," Reitman had been riding the rails since his teenage years. After gaining his medical qualification, he devoted himself to the education and care of the migrant population, founding the Chicago Hobo College in 1907. Working among transient women as a physician, an advocate, and an amateur sociologist, Reitman specialized in the treatment of venereal disease, conducted interviews, and gathered statistics on prostitution. He was Emma Goldman's companion for many years and served as an informal manager for her tours on the anarchist lecture circuit. In 1919, he was jailed for six months on a charge of distributing literature that advocated birth control. *Boxcar Bertha* was his second book; the first was *The Second Oldest Profession* (1931), a study of pimping.

"ARE YOU BILL'S BROAD?" FROM *SISTER OF THE ROAD*: *THE AUTOBIOGRAPHY* OF *BOXCAR BERTHA*

The cab stopped in front of the Globe, an old three-story brick building on Erie Street near Clark. It had once been run as a man's lodging house. I walked up the steps and was met by the clerk at the desk.

"Are you Bill's broad?"

I nodded affirmation and he pressed a button back of the desk and a door opened. The inside man, Rudy, a pock-marked individual with over-hanging brows and an unhealthy odor about his feet, appeared.

"Right this way. Take your clothes off in this room. Did you bring a teddy with you? Take your drugs out of your pocket-book, and your make-up. Put your clothes in a bundle. Don't keep any money on you."

I took the things out of my purse Bill had provided for me the night before—a small tube of vaseline, a bar of germicidal soap, a small bottle of antiseptic, and my lipstick, rouge, powder and comb. Rudy took my bundle and put it in a small room called the get-away room, a secret escape leading to the outside. One of the wainscoting panels was on hinges, and led to a small opening between the floors which gave a passage to the roof. The girls could walk along this roof to a ladder that led up to another roof, on top of which was a cupola where they could hide until the police had gone.

After Rudy had explained the get-away he took me back and introduced Margaret, the colored maid, a high-yellow in her early thirties. She asked me my name, and I told her "Bertha."

"Now, honey, we's already got a Bertha, so we'll call you Dottie," she told me. "We work in turns 'til every girl 'breaks luck,' and then it's choice. You'll take the next man that comes in, unless he's someone's friend. Sit down."

We were in a large room, the parlor, a room full of mirrors, with a linoleum floor. It was well lighted. There were no chairs, but it had benches on three sides. There were six girls waiting. The other three were busy, and I met them later.

"This is Edna, and she is going to show you how we does business here."

Edna, or French Edna, as the girls called her, broke in most of the new girls. She was a bleached blonde, weighing about two hundred and fifteen pounds. I was glad to see someone larger than myself.

Edna did more business than any of the others, but she did not make the most money, for she was strictly a two-dollar woman. The next girl was Lorraine, the broad of Pollack, the manager. She was tall, nicely formed, red-haired. She always "topped the house," that is, made the most money.

Next to her sat Jackie, a little girl with a hooked nose that made her look like a guinea pig. She was a "nigger lover." Her pimp was a colored man. She was a mediocre hustler, and was known as a "three-way broad." She had the best street clothes of any girl there.

Irene was a thin, dark little woman of about thirty. She didn't have so many tricks but was a hard worker and made pretty good money. Chickie, a bleached blonde, didn't look very young, and had a mousey face. She was the mother of two kids, and her man was a gambler. In the corner sat Dolly and June, who looked, both of them, like statues, with hair combed back and expressionless faces. "They're French, and lady lovers," Edna whispered. "They both live with Earl Walker, a 'jigaboo' pimp from the south side."

Katherine was a mature, thoughtful-looking girl of about thirty, always reading a book when she wasn't busy. Her pimp, Scotty, was a guard at the county jail.

"And so," she greeted me, "you want to be a two-dollar whore, huh? I congratulate you. If you stay here more than sixty days, you belong here. Anybody can get into one of these joints accidentally, but the girl who remains here was born for the job."

Peggy, a peppy, bleached blonde, was like a young panther. She had a great line of bull and would say to most any man who looked like he had money, "Daddy, you're wonderful! Oh, you're such a fine lover. Won't you please take me out of here? If you'll let me have twenty dollars, I'll pay my debts to this gang and I'll meet you on the outside." Sol Rubenstein was her pimp, and he came for her every evening in a big Lincoln.

The last girl I met the first day was Alabama, a thin brunette who looked as though she might be tubercular. She was a comedienne, singing and telling stories and playing jokes, half-drunk most of the time, although it was against the rules of the house for the girls to drink much. She was a good money-maker. All the customers liked her. She had two pimps, one a married man, a cab driver with two kids, that she was supporting, and the other a bartender named Kelly, in a Loop hotel. Katherine said, "She told Kelly that the cab driver was her husband. He knows she's a liar, but he's satisfied as long as she slips him most of the money."

The turn-over in girls was very large, Margaret told me. All of the girls had pimps. I found out that the Globe was a syndicate joint, bossed by a mysterious personage that I never saw. They called him "the old man." He never came to the joint, but the girls said they met him occasionally at his cabaret.

The manager of the house was Pollack, a big-nosed, syphilitic, squint-eyed, bald-headed man known affectionately as "the slaver-driver." Besides being paid for his job, he was kept by four women, one in our place, Lorraine, and one in each of the other three syndicate joints. Next in authority was Rudy, the inside man. And then came Pork Chops, an Italian with a lowering countenance and a greasy vest, who stood on the corner and watched for the cops. When they were coming he gave us the "Air-loft," or warning to get away. The "roper," who stood in front and solicited business was Bad Eye, a tall, goofy kid of about twenty who had lost his eye from a gonococci infection picked up on a towel carelessly tossed in his mother's bathroom. Bad eye was the only man working there who did not have a girl of his own, but was constantly, "on the make." The last man was Chew-Tobacco Rocky, a big Italian with a cud constantly in his mouth. He ran errands for the girls and carried messages from one joint to another. He was Irene's man, and the girls called him a "coffee and" pimp, because Irene just gave him a dollar a day.

The person we girls had the most to do with was Margaret, the maid. When a "John," or customer, came in he was ushered into the parlor where half a dozen girls sat around. He would take his choice and they would go to a room. The girl asked him for the money as soon as they were alone. Although this house was known as a two-dollar joint, when a stranger came in the girls would hustle him for more money and get all they could. We were taught to say to strangers, "We'll give you a good time for five dollars." If they hesitated, we were to say, "Give me three dollars, and I'll take off all my clothes."

When a cab load came the maid would always say, before the men came into the parlor, "Portier," which meant to get as much as you could, because the cab driver would have to be paid a commission, four dollars out of ten, two out of five, and one dollar out of three. We weren't supposed to take less than five dollars from each man in the cab load. There were exceptions. If a "good man," one who had plenty of money to spend, came in, the maid would say "Friday." If he was a five-dollar trick, she said, "Holiday," and if he was a ten-dollar trick, "Double Holiday." In this way strange girls would never cheapen the good trade. It was Margaret's duty to remember every customer, and what he spent.

Just as soon as we got the money from the customer we went out and bought aluminum checks from Margaret, similar to the old-time brass beer checks. A two-dollar check was marked "Five Cents in Trade," and a three-dollar check was a little larger and said, "Ten Cents in Trade." If there was a ten-dollar trick, she'd give us two threes and two deuces.

As soon as Margaret had a bank of a hundred dollars she passed it on to Pollack, who later gave it to the collector, Solly, who came twice a day with a little handbag and two heavily armed guards; Boyle, an ex-police sergeant and another called "The Indian." They took the money from there to the Newland Hotel belonging to The Old Man. He had charge of about thirty joints, houses of prostitution and gambling joints, and was then Chief of the North Side Syndicate. None of the joints was owned by him or his partners.

It was easy to start a joint, I learned. An old hotel was taken on commission and the former owner of the hotel might be kept right on to run the place. All the old man did was to conduct his business for him, furnish him the girls, a staff and police protection. The original owner or manager of the hotel got anywhere from twenty-five to fifty per cent of the old man's share of the day's receipts. The girls were told that police protection cost ten percent. But Pollack, who had been in the game for twenty years, said that the police got very little. The old man had an "in" at the City Hall. He contributed heavily to every campaign fund, Democratic or Republican. He donated to all the politicians, was good to the poor and divided about two hundred dollars a week for each joint to the police. The captain, harness bulls and squad men got the most of it.

The day and night crew of the Globe consisted of twenty girls. Each girl made on an average of thirty dollars a day for the house. When we were "going good," it wasn't unusual for the house to clear as their end four thousand or five thousand dollars a week.

I had thought a house of prostitution would be very exciting. I was surprised to learn how quiet it was. Edna showed me how to put the footpad on the bed. No man ever took off his shoes, and a piece of blanket was laid on to protect the spread. Then she showed me how to examine a man, and told me not to take him if he showed any signs of disease.

Before Edna was through breaking me in, I had a definite feeling of having to make good on my job, just as I have felt when I started a new typing job anywhere. I felt she and the other girls knew more than I did and that they expected me to keep up with them.

My first trick was a bit of a shock to me, however, a big Hunky, a man of about fifty with a handle-bar moustache. He was clumsy and rough. He put his hands under my teddy and pinched me. I didn't mind the roughness, but his fingernails were filthy and he had a vile garlic breath.

The next dozen men were fairly easy. Then an old smooth-faced man of about seventy came in. All his manhood had left him, but he wanted me to pet him and kiss him, and do things. I tried but failed completely. I found myself sorry for him and wishing that I could help him, but it was impossible.

Toward evening a big roughneck came in. The minute I looked at him I knew he would be trouble. I made my first mistake by asking him to spend five dollars, and my second by insisting that he spend an extra dollar to see me take off my teddy. He wasn't going to wait for anything. He wouldn't let me examine him. He handed me two dollars, and picked me up and threw me on the bed. I protested, but he fought with me and wouldn't let me up. I called for Margaret, and he began abusing her. Margaret pushed the buzzer for Rudy, the bouncer.

He came in with Pollack right behind him, and while Rudy pulled the fellow off, Pollack said, "Let him have it!" Rudy hit him over the head with a "sap," a soft blackjack with shot in the end of it. While he was unconscious they dragged him down the back steps and put him into a car, took him a few blocks away and dumped him into an alley under the "L" tracks.

Some of the men were embarrassed. They chose a girl quickly without hardly looking at her. Or they pretended to be tough and tried rough jokes. One well-dressed man with a long thoughtful face picked me out by coming over and putting a hand on my shoulder. Then, and when we were alone, he never said a single word. I let him rest a few minutes in my arms when he was through, and when he went out he gave me a look like you've seen on the face of a hungry dog after you've fed it. Another one, just a youngster really, a little drunk, cried after he was satisfied and said he'd never been in a place like that before. But most of them seemed old customers and used to the joint.

During the course of the day at least half of my customers asked me if I were French. I said "No." Some of them coaxed, some of them threatened to get someone else, but no one made any serious trouble, until a young stub-nosed Italian came in, and when I flatly refused, he went out to Margaret and said, "I want a French broad. I don't have to come here for the regular. I can get that at home."

Margaret said something to Rudy, and he came in and sat beside me, gave me a cigarette and lit one.

"Kid, a notch house is a place of business and the customer must be satisfied. Nowadays few men want it straight. They want it half and half. Don't blame me. I didn't invent human nature. We're in the business, and if you're going to hustle in any kind of a joint you've got to learn to be French, and maybe Greek. Now don't be a damned fool. You get on to the tricks, and it will be easier that way than any other."

I learned quickly. The rest of the girls thought nothing of it. Enda said, "The big money is in the 'queer' guys. And what freaks some of 'em are! But that's the way nature made them and what are you going to do about it?"

At the end of the day I had forty tricks, forty sex-hungry men that I had satisfied.

In common with all the girls, I kept track of all my tricks in a little notebook. Here is an account of my first day's work as a prostitute:

10 men at $2.00 each		$40.00
10 men at	3.00	30.00
5 men at	5.00	25.00
2 men at	4.00	8.00
3 men at	10.00	30.00
Total		$133.00

At half-past six Margaret sent me into the office to cash in. I had a hundred and thirty-three checks and naturally thought I was to get half that much, or $66.50. Instead Pollack and Rudy counted my checks and handed me $40.

"Why only $40?" I asked. "I gave you $133. Where I went to school in North Dakota half of $133 is $66.50."

"Don't you know how we do business here?" Pollack answered me. And he took a pencil and showed me.

Tricks	$133.00
50% for the house	66.50
	66.50
10% for protection	6.50
	$60.00

"You see, kid, if there's a pinch we take care of you. You don't have to worry about a thing. We get you bondsmen and everything."

'Well, that still leaves twenty dollars unaccounted for," I protested.

"What the hell difference does it make, as long as you don't have anything to worry about? And we took three dollars off for the maid. She's supposed to get fifty cents on every sixteen checks, but we only took three dollars from you to-night because you're new and you haven't many friends. We gave Bad Eye two bucks for bringing in the business. How would you make any money if it wasn't for the roper? You've got to give Chew-Tobacco a buck for getting your cigarettes, your java, and your eats. We took off two bucks for towels. You used about four dozen, and it costs two bits a dozen to get 'em laundered. If you'd like to bring your own towels from home, you can. Then we bought you a teddy, and four pairs of stockings . . . that cost twelve dollars. So there you are."

Protection	$6.50
Teddy and stockings	12.00
Maid	3.00
Roper	2.00
The Runner	1.00
Towels	2.00
	$26.50

"Now, do you understand? How long have you been hustling? You'll get along better if you don't ask so many questions."

My spirits somewhat dampened, I accepted the forty dollars without further question, and went wearily back to my hotel. I didn't feel that anything had changed in me because I had become a prostitute. I just felt completely worn-out, as though I'd finished an unusually hard day's work.

Bill came into my room that night just long enough to order up my supper and say, "Good girl," and "How's tricks?" and to take my money. He took all but two dollars. I was too tired to protest. All I wanted was to bathe and sleep. I remember thinking as I dozed off how easily I had fallen into Bill's system. Only one day, and I was a full-fledged prostitute. That's the way it happened to women. The routine of every day after that would carry them on, just like it does in an office or factory. When their day was over they would be too tired to think.

Bill didn't offer to sleep with me. I couldn't have let him touch me, then. He knew enough to know that. I tried to remember, lying there, how he had felt to me when he took me in his arms, but I couldn't. Instead, I kept seeing the faces of the men who had come in to me that day. And I knew I would go back again and again until I had learned what I wanted to know about them and about the girls who received them.

Richard Wright (1908–1960)

Born on a plantation near Natchez, Mississippi, and largely self-educated, Richard Nathaniel Wright produced a body of work that transformed African American writing. His fiction and autobiographies brought unprecedented psychological depth and emotional power to the investigation of race and class in America. He also contributed several well-known poems of protest (see "I Have Seen Black Hands" in this section) to the revolutionary literary journals of the 1930s.

Wright spent most of his childhood in Memphis, raised by his mother and grandmother after his father, an illiterate sharecropper, left the family when Richard was six years old. To support his family (Wright's mother, a former schoolteacher, was often too ill to work), Wright began working early, clerking in an insurance agency and an optical company. He read avidly from the local library, using the library card of a white coworker for whom he would claim to be borrowing books. In 1927, he joined the migration of blacks from the Jim Crow South, moving to Chicago and a series of menial jobs before landing a position with the post office. Wright began writing sketches of black life, as he experienced and observed it around him, and in 1932 joined the local John Reed Club, a group of artists and writers supported by the Communist Party. His employment by the Federal Writers Project (the New Deal program to support unemployed writers during the Great Depression) gave Wright the time to complete his first book of stories, *Uncle Tom's Children* (1938) from which the story that follows is drawn.

A Guggenheim Fellowship in 1939 allowed Wright to complete the novel *Native Son* (1940), a Book-of-the-Month Club selection and an instant best-seller. Wright moved to New York in 1937, where he became the Harlem correspondent to the Communist Party's *Daily Worker*. He left the Party in 1944, disillusioned with its doctrinaire prescriptions for revolutionary literature. In 1947, he "chose exile" in Paris, rather than endure continued harassment from former comrades and persecution from anticommunists. During the McCarthy years, Wright could not find a publisher for two of his most radical books: his first novel *Lawd Today*, which treats his work in the post office (published posthumously in 1963), and *American Hunger* (1977), the second part of his autobiography detailing his dealings with the Communist Party, which had been omitted from *Black Boy* (1945). At his death, his papers included four thousand haiku, published in 1998 as *This Other World*.

I HAVE SEEN BLACK HANDS

I

I am black and I have seen black hands, millions and millions of them—
Out of millions of bundles of wool and flannel tiny black fingers have
    reached restlessly and hungrily for life.
Reached out for the black nipples at the black breasts of black mothers,
5   And they've held red, green, blue, yellow, orange, white, and purple toys
    in the childish grips of possession,
And chocolate drops, peppermint sticks, lollypops, wineballs, ice cream
    cones, and sugared cookies in fingers sticky and gummy,
And they've held balls and bats and gloves and marbles and jack-knives
10   and sling-shots and spinning tops in the thrill of sport and play,
And pennies and nickels and dimes and quarters and sometimes on New
    Year's, Easter, Lincoln's Birthday, May Day, a brand new green
    dollar bill,
They've held pens and rulers and maps and tablets and books in palms
15   spotted and smeared with ink,
And they've held dice and cards and half-pint flasks and cue sticks and
    cigars and cigarettes in the pride of new maturity . . .

II

I am black and I have seen black hands, millions and millions of them—
They were tired and awkward and calloused and grimy and covered with
20   hangnails,
And they were caught in the fast-moving belts of machines and snagged
    and smashed and crushed,
And they jerked up and down at the throbbing machines massing taller
    and taller the heaps of gold in the banks of bosses,

25 And they piled higher and higher the steel, iron, the lumber, wheat, rye,
    the oats, corn, the cotton, the wool, the oil, the coal, the meat, the
    fruit, the glass, and the stone until there was too much to be used,
   And they grabbed guns and slung them on their shoulders and marched
    and groped in trenches and fought and killed and conquered nations
30 who were customers for the goods black hands had made.
   And again black hands stacked goods higher and higher until there was
    too much to be used,
   And then black hands trembling at the factory gates the dreaded lay-off
    slip,
35 And the black hands hung idle and swung empty and grew soft and got
    weak and bony from unemployment and starvation,
   And they grew nervous and sweaty, and opened and shut in anguish and
    doubt and hesitation and irresolution . . .

III

   I am black and I have seen black hands, millions and millions of them—
40 Reaching hesitantly out of days of slow death for the goods they had
    made, but the bosses warned that the goods were private and did not
    belong to them,
   And the black hands struck desperately out in defense of life and there
    was blood, but the enraged bosses decreed that this too was wrong,
45 And the black hands felt the cold steel bars of the prison they had made,
    in despair tested their strength and found that they could neither
    bend nor break them,
   And the black hands fought and scratched and held back but a thousand
    white hands took them and tied them,
50 And the black hands lifted palms in mute and futile supplication to the
    sodden faces of mobs wild in the revelries of sadism,
   And the black hands strained and clawed and struggled in vain at the
    noose that tightened about the black throat,
   And the black hands waved and beat fearfully at the tall flames that
55 cooked and charred the black flesh . . .

IV

   I am black and I have seen black hands
   Raised in fists of revolt, side by side with the white fists of white workers,
   And some day—and it is only this which sustains me—
   Some day there shall be millions and millions of them,
60 On some red day in a burst of fists on a new horizon!

FIRE AND CLOUD

I

"A naughts a naught . . ."
As he walked his eyes looked vacantly on the dusty road, and the words rolled without movement from his lips, each syllable floating softly up out of the depths of his body.

"N five a figger . . ."

He pulled out his pocket handkerchief and mopped his brow without lessening his pace.

"All fer the white man . . ."

He reached the top of the slope and paused, head down.

"N none fer the nigger. . . ."

His shoulders shook in half-laugh and half-shudder. He finished mopping his brow and spat, as though to rid himself of some bitter thing. He thought. Thas the way its awways been! Wistfully he turned and looked back at the dim buildings of the town lying sprawled mistily on the crest of a far hill. Seems like the white folks jus erbout owns this whole worl! Looks like they done conquered *everything*. We black folks is jus los in one big white fog. . . . With his eyes still on the hazy buildings, he flexed his lips slowly and spoke under his breath:

"They could do something! They could do *something*, awright! Mabbe ef fiv er six thousan of us marched downtown we could *scare* em inter doin something! Lawd, mabbe them Reds *is* right!"

He walked again and tucked his handkerchief back into his pocket. He could feel the heat of the evening over all his body, not strongly, but closely and persistently, as though he were holding his face over a tub of steaming suds. Far below him at the bottom of the valley lay a cluster of bleak huts with window panes red-lit from dying sunlight. Those huts were as familiar to his eyes as a nest is to the eyes of a bird, for he had lived among them all his life. He knew by sight or sound every black man, woman and child living within those huddled walls. For a moment an array of soft black faces hovered before his eyes. N whut kin Ah tell em? Whut kin Ah say t em? He stopped, looked at the ground and sighed. And then he saw himself as he had stood but a few moments ago, facing the white woman who sat behind the brown, gleaming desk: her arms had been round, slender, snow-white, like cold marble; her hair had been the color of flowing gold and had glinted in the sunlight; her eyes had been wide and grey behind icily white spectacles. It seemed he could hear her saying in her dry, metallic voice: I'm sorry, Taylor. You'll just have to do the best you can. Explain it to them, make them understand that we cant do anything. Everybodys hongry, and after all, it's no harder on your people than it is on ours. Tell them they'll just have to wait. . . .

He wagged his head and his lips broke in a slow, sick smile. Whut she know erbout being hongry? Whut she know erbout it? He walked again, thinking, Here Ah is a man called by Gawd t preach n whut kin Ah do? Hongry folks looking t me fer hep n whut kin Ah do? Ah done tried everything n cant do *nuthin*! Shucks, mabbe Hadley n Greens right? They *might* be right. Gawd knows, they *might* be right.

He lifted his head and saw the wide fields plunging before him, down the hillside. The grass was dark and green. All this! he thought. All *this* n folks hongry! Good Gawd, whuts *wrong*! He saw the road running before him, winding, vanishing, the soft yellow dust filled with the ruts of wagon wheels and tiny threads of auto tires. He threw back his head and spoke out loud:

"The good Lawds gonna clean up this ol worl some day! Hes gonna make a new Heaven n a new Earth! N Hes gonna do it in a eye-twinkle change; Hes gotta do it! Things cant go on like this ferever! Gawd knows they cant!" He pulled off his coat and slung it under his left arm. "Waal, there ain nothing t do but go back n tell em. . . . Tell em the white folks wont let em eat. . . ."

The road curved, descending among the green fields that tumbled to a red sky. This was the land on which the Great God Almighty had first let him see the light of His blessed day. This was the land on which he had first taken unto himself a wife, leaving his mother and father to cleave to her. And it was on the green slopes of these struggling hills that his first-born son, Jimmy, had romped and played, growing to a strong, upright manhood. He wagged his head, musing: Lawd, them wuz the good ol days. . . . There had been plenty to eat; the blessings of God had been overflowing. He had toiled from sunup to sundown, and in the cool of the evenings his wife, May, had taught him to read and write. Then God had spoken to him, a quiet, deep voice coming out of the black night; God had called him to preach His word, to spread it to the four corners of the earth, to save His black people. And he had obeyed God and had built a church on a rock which the very gates of Hell could not prevail against. Yes, he had been like Moses, leading his people out of the wilderness into the Promised Land. He sighed, walking and taking his coat from his left arm and tucking it under his right. Yes, things had been clear-cut then. In those days there had stretched before his eyes a straight and narrow path and he had walked in it, with the help of a Gracious God. On Sundays he had preached God's Word, and on Mondays and Tuesdays and Wednesdays and Thursdays and Fridays and Saturdays he had taken old Bess, his mule, and his plow and had broke God's ground. For a moment while walking through the dust and remembering his hopes of those early years he seemed to feel again the plow handles trembling in his calloused hands and hear the earth cracking and breaking open, black, rich and damp; it seemed he could see old Bess straining forward with the plow, swishing her tail and tossing her head and snorting now and then. Yes, there had been something in those good old days when he had walked behind his plow, between the broad green earth and a blue sweep of sunlit sky; there had been in it all a surge of will, clean, full, joyful; the earth was his and he was the earth's; they were one; and it was that joy and will and oneness in him that God had spoken to when He had called him to preach His word, to save His black people, to lead them, to guide them, to be a shepherd to His flock. But now the whole thing was giving way, crumbling in his hands, right before his eyes. And every time he tried to think of some way out, of some way to stop it, he saw wide grey eyes behind icily white spectacles. He mopped his brow again. Mabbe Hadley n Greens right. . . . Lawd, Ah don know whut t do! Ef Ah fight fer things the white folk say Ahma bad nigger stirrin up trouble. N ef Ah don do nothin, we starve. . . . But somethings *gotta* be done! Mabbe ef we hada demonstration like Hadley n Green said, we could *scare* them white folks inter doin something. . . .

He looked at the fields again, half wistfully, half curiously. Lawd, we could make them ol fields bloom ergin. We could make em feed us. Thas whut Gawd put em there fer. Plows could break and hoes could chop and hands could pick and arms could carry. . . . On and on that could happen and people could eat and feel as he had felt with the plow handles trembling in his hands, following old Bess, hearing the earth cracking and breaking because he wanted it to crack and break; because he willed it, because the earth was his. And they could sing as he had sung when he and May were first married; sing about picking cotton, fishing, hunting, about sun and rain. They could. . . . But whuts the usa thinkin erbout stuff like this? Its all gone now. . . . And he had to go and tell his congregation, the folks the Great God Almighty had called him to lead to the Promised Land—he had to tell them that the relief would give them no food.

That morning he had sent a committee of ten men and women from his congregation to see the mayor. Wondah how they come out? The mayor tol em something, sho! So fer hes been pretty wid me even if he is a white man. As his feet sank softly into the dust he saw Mayor Bolton; he saw the red chin that always had a short, black stubble of beard; he saw the cigar glowing red in front of a pink, fat face. But he needs something t scare im now, he thought. Hes been running over us too long. . . .

He reached the bottom of the slope, turned into a cinder path, and approached the huts. N Lawd, when Ah do try t do somethin mah own folks wont stan by me, wont stick wid me. Theres old Deacon Smith a-schemin n a-plottin, just a-watchin me lika hawk, just a-waitin fer me t tak mah eyes off the groun sos he kin trip me up, sos he kin run t the white folks n tell em Ahm doin something wrong! A black snake in the grass! A black Judas! Thas all he is! Lawd, the Devils sho busy in this world. . . .

He was walking among the crowded huts now.

hello reveren

"How yuh tonight, sonny!" Let ol Deacon Smith tell it, no matter whut Ah *do*, Ahm wrong. . . .

good evenin reveren

"Good evenin, Sistah!" Hes been a-tryin t cheat me outta mah church ever since hes been erroun here. . . .

how yuh tonight reveren Taylor

"Jus fine. N how yuh tonight, Brother?" Hes awways a-whisperin berhin mah back, a-tryin t take mah congregation erway from me. . . . N when he ain doin that hes a-tryin his best t give me wrong advice, jus like the Devil a-tryin t tempt Jesus. But Ahm gonna march on wida hepa Gawd. . . . Yeah, Ah might preach a sermon erbout tha nex Sunday.

As he turned into the street leading to his home and church he saw a tall brown-skinned boy hurrying towards him. Here comes Jimmy! Ah bet hes lookin fer me. . . . Lawd, Ah hope ain nothin wrong. . . .

II

"Pa!" said Jimmy breathlessly when he was some twenty feet away.

Taylor stopped.

"Whuts the mattah, son?"

Jimmy came close.

"The mayors at home, waitin t see yuh," he whispered.

"The *mayor?*"

"Yeah, n two mo white men. One of em is the Chiefa Police."

"They there *now?*"

"Yeah; in the parlor."

"How long they been there?"

"Bout two-three minutes, Ah reckon. N lissen, Pa . . . Sam wuz by jus now. He say the white folks is ridin up n down the streets in their cars warning all the black folks t stay off the streets cause theres gonna be trouble. . . ."

"Sam say tha?"

"Thas whut he tol me. N lissen, Pa . . . Ahma git Sam n Pete n Bob n Jack n some mo boys together sos ef anything happens. . . ."

Taylor gripped Jimmy's shoulders.

"Naw, son! Yuh fixin t git us *all* inter trouble now! Yuh cant do nothing like tha! Yuh gotta be careful! If them white folks just *thought* we wuz doin somethin like that theyd crack down on us! Wed hava riot!"

"But we cant let em ride erroun n talk big n we do nothin!"

"Lissen here, son! Yuh do whut Ah tell yuh t do!" He shook Jimmy's shoulders and his voice was husky. "Yuh go tell them boys t do *nothin* till Ah see em, yuh hear me? Yuh young fools fixin t git us *all* murdered!"

"We jus as waal git killed fightin as t git killed doing nothin," said Jimmy sullenly.

"Yuh go n do whut Ah tol yuh, *hear* me? Ah gotta go n see tha mayor. . . ."

"Hes here t see yuh erbout tha demonstration," said Jimmy.

"How yuh know?"

"Cause thas whut everybodys sayin."

"Who yuh hear say tha?"

"Deacon Smiths spreadin the word."

Taylor winced as though struck by a blow and looked at the dust.

"Hes tellin alla deacons n the church membahs tha the mayors here t stop yuh," said Jimmy. "Hes tellin em yuhs mixed up wid the Reds."

"Deacon Smith there now, *too?*"

"Yeah; hes in the basement wida other deacons. Theys waitin t see yuh."

"How long they been there?"

"Bout hafa hour. N Hadley n Greens in the Bible Room, waitin t talk wid yuh, too. . . ."

Fear gripped Taylor and he stammered:

"Ddddid the mmmmayor ssssee em?"

"Naw, ain nobody seen em yit. Ah brought em in thu the back do and tol em t wait fer yuh. Ahm mighty scared wid them Reds waitin fer yuh in the Bible Room and that Chiefa Police waitin fer yuh in the parlor. Ef ol Deacon Smith knowed tha he sho would make a lotta trouble. . . ."

"Where you ma?"

"She upstairs, sewin"

"She know whuts happenin?"

"Naw, Pa."

Taylor stood still, barely breathing.

"Whut yuh gonna do, Pa?" asked Jimmy.

"Yuh go n tell them boys not t do nothin wrong, son. Go on n tell em now! Ah got too much on mah hands now widout yuh boys stirrin up mo trouble!"

"Yessuh."

"Yuh bettah go n do it *now!*"

"Yessuh."

He watched Jimmy hurry down the street. Lawd, Ah hope tha boy don go n git inter trouble. . . .

"Yuh do whut Ah tol yuh, Jimmy!" he yelled.

"Yessuh!" Jimmy hollered back.

He saw Jimmy turn a dusty corner, and go out of sight. Hadley n Greens there in the Bible Room n the Chiefa Police is waitin in the parlor! Ah cant let them white folks see them Reds! N ef Deacon Smith tells on me they'll lynch me. . . . Ah gotta git em out of tha church widout em seein each other. . . . Good Gawd, whut a mess!

III

No sooner had he opened the door of his church than he heard a crescendo of voices. They back awready! Tha committees back! Aw, Ah bet the mayor followed em here. . . . He walked down the hall, turned into the church's waiting room, and saw a roomful of black faces.

"Reveren Taylor! The mayor run us out!"

"He put the police on us!"

The black brothers and sisters ran to Taylor and surrounded him.

"The mayor tol us t git out n don come back no mo!"

A thin black woman swung onto Taylor's arm, crying:

"Whut Ahm gonna do? Ah ain gotta mouthful of bread at home!"

"Sistahs n Brothers, jusa minute," said Taylor. "Firs, tell me whut the mayor said. . . ."

"He say he cant do *nuthin!* N say fer us not t come back t his office no *mo!* N say ef we do hes gonna put us in jail!"

"In *jail?*" asked Taylor.

"Thas whut he said."

"N he tol us not t march, Reveren. He said ef we demonstrated hed put us *all* in jail."

"Who tol em yuh wuz gonna march?" asked Taylor.

"Ah bet it wuz tha ol Deacon Smith," said Sister Harris.

"The Bible says testify whut yuh see n speak whut yuh know," said Sister Davis to Sister Harris.

"Ah knows whut Ahm talkin erbout!" blazed Sister Harris.

"Sistahs n Brothers, les don start no fuss," said Taylor, sighing and dropping his shoulders.

"Whut they tell yuh at the relief station, Reveren Taylor?" asked Sister James.

"They say they cant do nothin," said Taylor.

The thin black woman came and knelt at Taylor's feet, her face in her hands.

"Reveren Taylor, it ain fer me Ahm astin! Its fer mah chillun! Theys hongry! It ain fer me, its fer them! Gawd, have mercy, theys hongry. . . ."

Taylor stepped back, ran his hand into his pocket and pulled out a palmful of loose coins.

"Here, Sistahs n Brothers, split this up between yuh all. Its ever cent Ah got in this worl, so hep me Gawd!"

He laid the coins on a small table. Brother Booker divided them as far as they would go. Then they swarmed around him again.

"Reveren, whut we gonna do?"

"Cant we make the white folks do something fer us?"

"Ahm tireda bein hongry!"

"Reveren, mah babys sick n Ah cant git her no milk!"

"Reveren, whut kin Ah tell mah wife?"

"Lawd knows, Ahm jus erbout sick of this!"

"Whut kin we do, Reveren?"

Taylor looked at them and was ashamed of his own helplessness and theirs.

"Sistahs n Brothers, les call on the great Gawd who made us n put us in this world. . . ."

He clasped his hands in front of him, closed his eyes, and bowed his head. The room grew still and silent.

"Lawd Gawd Awmighty, Yuh made the sun n the moon n the stars n the earth n the seas n mankind n the beasts of the fields!"

yes jesus

"Yuh made em all, Lawd, n Yuh tol em whut t do!"

yuh made em lawd

"Yuhs strong n powerful n Yo will rules this worl!"

yuh rules it lawd

"Yuh brought the chillun of Israel outta the lan of Egypt!"

yuh sho did

"Yuh made the dry bones rise up outta the valley of death n live!"

yuh made em live lawd

"Yuh saved the Hebrew chillun in the fiery furnace!"

yes jesus

"Yuh stopped the storm n Yuh made the sun stan still!"

yuh stopped it lawd

"Yuh knocked down the walls of Jericho n Yuh kept Jona in the belly of the whale!"

yuh kept im lawd

"Yuh let Yo son Jesus walk on watah n Yuh brought Im back from the dead!"

have mercy jesus

"Yuh made the lame walk!"

yuh did it lawd

"Yuh made the blin see!"

help us now lawd

"Yuh made the deaf hear!"

glory t the mos high

"Lawd, Yuhs a rock in the tima trouble n Yuhs a shelter in the tima storm!"

he is he is

"Lawd, Yuh said Yuhd strike down the wicked men who plagued Yo chillun!"

glory t gawd

"Yuh said Yuhd destroy this ol worl n create a new Heaven n a new Earth!"

wes waitin on yuh jesus

"Lawd, Yuh said call on Yo name n Yuhd answer!"

yuh said it lawd n now wes callin

"Yuh made us n put the breatha life in us!"

yuh did lawd

"Now look down on us, Lawd! Speak t our hearts n let us know what Yo will is! Speak t us like Yuh spoke t Jacob!"

speak lawd n our souls will be clay in yo hans

"Lawd, ack in us n well obey! Try us, Lawd, try us n watch us move t Yo will! Wes helpless at Yo feet, a-waitin fer Yo sign!"

send it lawd

"The white folks say we cant raise nothin on Yo earth! They done put the lans of the worl in their pockets! They done fenced em off n nailed em down! Theys a-trying t take Yo place, Lawd!"

speak t em lawd

"Yuh put us in this worl n said we could live in it! Yuh said this worl wuz Yo own! Now show us the sign like Yuh showed Saul! Show us the sign n well ack! We ast this in the name of Yo son Jesus who died tha we might live! Amen!"

amen amen

Taylor stopped and opened his eyes. The room was quiet; he could hear the clock ticking softly above his head, and from the rear came the sound of children playing back in the church. The sisters and brothers rose from their knees and began talking in subdued tones.

"But, Reveren, whut kin we *do*?"

"The issues wid Gawd now, Sistahs n Brothers."

"Is we gonna march?"

"Is yuh goin wid us t the mayor?"

"Have faith, Sistahs n Brothers. Gawd takes care of His own."

"But Ahm hongry, Reveren. . . ."

"Now, Sistahs n Brothers, Ah got t go. Ah got business t tend t. . . ."

He pushed ahead of the black hands that clung to his sleeve.

"Reveren Taylor. . . ."

The thin black woman wailed, kneeling:

"Please, Reveren, cant yuh do *somethin*. . . ."

He pushed through the door, closed it, and stood for a moment with his eyes shut and his fingers slowly loosening on the knob, his ears filled with the sound of wailing voices.

IV

How come all this gotta happen at *once*? Folks a-beggin fer bread n the mayor here t see me n them Reds a-waitin in the Bible Room. . . . Ef Deacon Smith knowed that hed ruin me sho! Ah cant let the mayor see them Reds. . . . Now, Gawd! He looked at a door at the far end of the room, then hurried to it and opened it softly.

"May!" he called in a hoarse whisper.

"Hunh?"

"C mere, quick!"

"Whutcha wan, Dan?"

"C mon in the *room*, May!"

She edged through the half-opened door and stood in front of him, wide-eyed.

"Whutcha wan, Dan?"

"Now, lissen. . . ."

"Ain nothin wrong, is it, Dan? Ain nothin happened, is it?"

He grabbed her arm.

"Naw, n don git scared!"

"Ah ain scared!"

"Yuh cant do whut Ah wan yuh t do ef yuhs scared!"

"Ah *ain* scared, Dan!"

"Lissen. . . ."

"Yeah?"

"The mayors here, in the parlor. N the Chiefa Police. . . ."

She stood stock still and seemed not to breathe.

"The *mayor*?"

"Yeah. . . ."

"*Ain* nothing wrong, is it, Dan?"

"There wont be ef yuh lissen n try to do right."

"Be careful, Dan!"

"Yeah," he said, his voice low and husky. "Go in and tell them white folks Ahm sick, hear?"

She stepped back from him and shook her head.

"Gawd *ain* wid yuh when yuh lie, Dan!"

"We *gotta* lie t white folks! Theys on our necks! They *make* us lie t them! Whut kin we do but lie?"

"*Dan!*"

"Lissen t whut Ahm telling yuh, May! Tell the mayor Ahm gittin outta bed t see him. Tell im Ahm dressin, see? Tell im t wait a few minutes."

"Yeah?"

"Then go t the basement n tell Deacon Smith Ahm wid the mayor. Tell im n the other deacons t wait."

"Now?"

"Yeah; but Ah ain thru yit. Yuh know Hadley n Green?"

"Them *Reds*?"

"Yeah. . . ."

"Dan!" said May, her lungs suspiring in one gasp of amazed helplessness.

"May, fer Chrissakes!"

She began to cry.

"Don do nothin wrong, Dan, please! Don't fergit Jimmy! Hes jus a young boy n hes gotta grow up in this town wid these white folks. Don go n do nothin n fix it so he wont have a chance. . . . Me n yuh don mattah, but thinka him."

Taylor swallowed and looked hard at her.

"Dan, please. . . ."

"May, yuh do whut Ah tell yuh t do! Ah know whut Ahm doin. Hadley n Green downstairs, in the Bible Room. Tell em so nobody kin hear yuh, hear?—tell em aftah yuh done tol the others—tell em t come in here. Let em in thru yo room. . . ."

"Naw!"

She tried to get through the door. He ran to her and caught her hand again.

"Yuh do whut Ah tell yuh, May!"

"Ah ain gonna have them Reds in *here* wid tha mayor n Chiefa Police out *there*! Ah *ain*!"

"Go on do whut Ah tell yuh, May!"

"Dan!"

"Go *ahead*, May!"

He pushed her. She went through the door, slowly, looking back at him. When the door was closed he rammed his hands deep into his pants' pockets, turned to the open window, and looked out into the street. It was profoundly quiet, save for the silvery sound of children's voices back of the church. The air was soft, warm, and full of the scent of magnolias and violets. Window panes across the street were blood-red from dying sunlight. A car sped past, lifting a great cloud of yellow-brown dust. He went to the center of the room and stood over a table littered with papers. He cocked his head, listening. He heard a door slam; footsteps echoed and ceased. A big eight-day clock above his head boomed six times; he looked and his eyes strayed up and rested on a gleaming, brass cross. Gawd, hep me now! Jus hep me t go thru wid this! Again he heard a door slam. Lawd, Ah hope May do right now. . . . N Ah hope Jimmy don go n ack a fool. . . . He crossed the floor on tiptoe, opened the door, and peeped into May's room. It was empty. A slender prism of dust-filled sunlight cut across the air. He closed the door, turned, pulled off his coat and threw it across the table. Then he loosened his collar and tie. He went to the window again and leaned with his back against the ledge, watching the door of May's room. He heard a hoarse voice rise and die. Footsteps again sounded and ceased. He frowned, listening. How come its takin May so long? He started when a timid knock came. He hurried to the door and cracked it.

V

"Hello, Reverend Taylor!" said Hadley, a white man.

"How yuh, Brother Hadley?"

"N how yuh, Reveren?" asked Green, a black man.

"Ahm fine, Brother Green. C mon in, yuh all."

Hadley and Green edged through the door.

"Say, whuts alla mystery?" asked Green.

"Sssh! Don't talk so loud," cautioned Taylor. "The mayor n the Chiefa Police is out there."

The Negro and the white man stood stone still.

"Do they know wes here?" asked Green.

"Naw, n don git scared. They done come t see me erbout tha demonstration. . . ."

Hadley and Green looked at each other.

"Pull down tha shade," whispered Green, pointing a shaking, black finger.

Quickly, Hadley moved to one side, out of range of the window. His cheeks flushed pink. Taylor lowered the shade and faced them in the semi-darkness. The eyes of the white man and the black man were upon him steadily.

"Waal?" said Green.

"Ah spose yuh know whuts up," said Taylor.

"Theyre here to scare you," said Hadley.

"Ahm trustin Gawd," sighed Taylor.

"Whut yuh gonna tell em?" asked Green.

"Thas whut Ah wanna see yuh all erbout," said Taylor.

"O.K. Whut kin we do?" asked Green.

Taylor looked around and motioned toward two chairs.

"Set down, Brothers."

"Naw, this is awright," said Green, still standing.

"Come on," said Hadley. "What's on your mind?"

Taylor folded his arms and half sat and half leaned on the edge of the table.

"Yuh all think wes gonna have many folks out in the mawnin fer the demonstration?"

"Whut yuh mean?" asked Green.

"When Ahm talkin wid the mayor and Chiefa Police Ah wanna know how many folks Ahm talkin fer. There ain no use in us havin a demonstration ef ain but a few of us is gonna be out there. The police will try t kill us then. . . ."

"How many folks we can get out tomorrow depends a great deal on you, Reverend," said Hadley.

"Hows that?" asked Taylor.

"If you had let us use your name on those handbills, we could say five thousand easily. . . ."

Taylor turned sharply to Hadley.

"Lissen, Brother, Ah done tol yuh Ah cant do tha! N there ain no use in us talkin erbout it no mo! Ah done told yuh Ah cant let them white folks know Ahm callin folks t demonstrate. Aftah all, Ahma preacher. . . ."

"Its yo duty, Reveren," said Green. "We owes it our black folks."

"Ahm doin mah duty as Gawd lets me see it," said Taylor.

"All right, Reverend," said Hadley. "Heres what happened: Weve covered the city with fifteen thousand leaflets. Weve contacted every organization we could think of, black and white. In other words, weve done all *we* could. The rest depends on the leaders of each group. If we had their active endorsement, none of us would have to worry about a crowd tomorrow. And if we had a crowd we would not have to worry about the police. If they see the whole town turning out, they'll not start any trouble. Now, youre known. White and black in this town respect you. If you let us send out another leaflet with your name on it calling for. . . ."

Taylor turned from them and drew his hand nervously across his face. Hadley and Green were silent, watching him. Taylor went to the window and pulled back the curtain slightly and peeped out. Without turning he said softly:

"Ah done tol yuh all Ah ain scareda lettin yuh use mah name."

"We don mean *that*," said Green hastily.

"Ef it wuz jus me who wuz takin the chance," said Taylor, "Ah wouldn't care none. But Gawd knows it ain right fer me to send them po folks out inter the streets in fronta police. Gawd knows, Ah cant do tha!"

"Honest, Reveren," said Green, touching Taylor's arm. "Ah don understan. Yuh done been thu harder things than this befo."

"N Ahll go thu wid em ergin," said Taylor proudly.

"All right!" said Hadley. "You can say the word that can make this thing a success. If you don't and we have no crowd, then youre to blame. . . ."

Taylor's eyes narrowed and when he spoke there was a note of anger in his voice.

"Gawd hep yuh ef yuhs a-tryin t say yuh gonna blame me ef things don go right!"

"Naw, Reveren!" said Green, coming hurriedly forward and spreading his black hands softly upon the air. "Don feel that way! Wes all jus in a jam. We got t do either two things: Call off this demonstration and let the folks stay hongry, er git as many as we kin together n go downtown in the mawnin. Ef we git five thousan down there the police wont bother us. Ef yuh let us send out yo name tellin the black folks. . . ."

"Naw, Brother!" said Taylor emphatically.

"Then the demonstrations going to be smashed," said Hadley. "*You* can stop it! You have the responsibility and the blame!"

Taylor sighed.

"Gawd knows Ah ain t blame. Ahm doin what mah heart tells me t do. . . ."

"Then whats keeping you from working with us?" asked Hadley. "Im a white man and Im here willing to fight for your peoples rights!"

"Ahm wid yuh, Brother!" said Taylor in a voice which carried a deep note of pleading. "Ahm wid yuh no mattah whut yuh *think*! But yuh *cant* use mah name! Ef them white folks knowed Ah wuz callin mah folks in the streets to demonstrate, they wouldn't never gimme a chance t git something fer mah folks ergin. . . ."

"Thats just it, Reverend," said Hadley. "Don't be afraid of their turning you down because youre fighting for your people. If they knew youd really fight, theyd dislike you; yes? But you can *make* them give something to *all* of your people, not just to *you*. Dont you see, Taylor, youre standing *between* your people and the white folks. You can make them give something to *all* of them. And the poor, hungry white folks will be with you."

"Ah cant lead mah folks t go ergin them white folks like tha," said Taylor. "Thas *war!*"

Hadley came close to Taylor.

"Reverend, cant you see thats just the way the white folks *want* you to feel? Are you leading your folks just because the white folks *say* you should, or are you leading them because you *want* to? Dont you believe in what youre doing? What kind of leaders are black people to have if the white folks pick them and tell them what to do?"

"Brothers, Ahma Christian, n whut yuhs asting fer is something tha makes blood!" thundered Taylor.

Hadley and Green looked at each other.

"Waal, whut yuh gonna tell the mayor?" asked Green.

Taylor stood in the center of the room with his hands in his pockets, looking down at his feet. His voice came low, as though he were talking to himself, trying to convince himself.

"Ahma tell em mah folks is hongry. Ahma tell em they wanna march. Ahma tell em if they march Ahma march wid em. Ahma tell em they wan bread. . . ."

"Reverend," asked Hadley, "why do you feel that this is so different from all the other times you've gone straight to the white folks and *demanded* things for your people?"

"It is different!" said Taylor.

"You didn't say that when you saved Scott from that *mob!*"

"Tha wuz different, Brother Hadley."

"I dont see it."

Taylor's voice came low.

"Ah feels differently erbout it, Brothers."

"You saved Scotts life. All right, youre saving the lives of your congregation now. Scott was one man, but there are five hundred starving people in your church."

"We ain facin no mob now, Brother Hadley."

"Then what in Gods name are we facin, Reverend? If those police wholl be out there in the morning with their guns and clubs arent a *legal* mob, then what. . . ."

"Its more than a mob, Brother Hadley."

Hadley and Green shook their heads.

"Ah don understand yuh, Reveren," said Green.

"When Ah saved Scott from tha mob, Ah wuz goin ergin *some* of the white folks. But this thing is going ergin em *all!* This is too much like war!"

"You mean youre going against the ones with *money* now!" said Hadley. "Over three thousand of the poor white folks will be with *us*. . . ."

"But, Brother Hadley, the white folks whos got moneys got *everything!* This is jus like civil war!"

"Reverend," said Hadley, "cant you see that if they were not afraid they wouldn't be here asking to *talk* with you? Go in and talk with them, speak to them in the name of five thousand hungry people. Tell the mayor and the Chief of Police that if they dont give the relief back we will demonstrate."

"Ah cant do tha, Brothers. Ah cant let these white folks think Ahm leadin mah folks tha way. Ah tol yuh Brothers when Ah ergreed t work wid yuh Ahd go as fer as Ah could. Waal, Ah done tha. Now, yuh here astin me t threaten this whole town n Ah ain gonna do tha!" said Taylor.

"Yuh astin fer bread, Reveren," said Green.

"Its threatenin, Brothers," said Taylor. "N tha ain Gawds way!"

"So youll let your folks starve before youll stand up and talk to those white folks?" asked Hadley.

"Ahm ackin as Gawd gives me the light to see," said Taylor.

There was silence. Then Hadley laughed, noiselessly.

"Well," he said. "I didn't know you felt this way, Reverend. I thought we could count on you. You know the Party will stand behind you no matter what happens."

"Ahm sorry, Brother Hadley," said Taylor.

"When kin we see yuh t fin out whut the mayor n Chiefa Police say?" asked Green.

Taylor looked at his watch.

"Its a little aftah six now. Make it half-pas six. Thall gimme time t see the Deacon Board."

Green sighed.

"O.K."

"O.K."

Taylor held the door for them. Then he stood in the center of the room and looked miles through the floor. Lawd, Ah hope Ahm doin right. N they think Ahm scared. . . . He flushed hot with shame and anger. He sat in a chair for a moment, then got right up. He drummed his fingers on the corner of the table. Shucks, Ah jus as waal see them white folks now n git it over wid. Ah knowed this wuz comin up! Ah knowed it! He went through May's room, walking slowly, softly, seeing in his mind the picture of the fat, pink face of Mayor Bolton and the lean, red face of Chief of Police Bruden. As he turned into the narrow hall that led to the parlor he heard children yelling in the playground. He went down a stairway, opened a door, and walked through his hushed, dim-lit church. Pale rose light fell slantwise through stained windows and glinted on mahogany pews. He lifted his eyes and saw the figure of Christ on a huge snow-white cross. Gawd, hep me now! Lemme do the right thing! He followed a red carpet to a door that opened into the parlor. He paused and passed his tongue over his dry lips. He could feel his heart beating. Ahll let them do all the talkin. Ahll just tell em mah folks is hongry. Thas all Ah kin do. Slowly, he turned the knob, his lips half parted in dread.

VI

"Why, hello, Dan!"

"Good evenin, Mistah Mayor."

"Howve you been, Dan?"

"Fairly well, wid de hepa Gawd, suh."

Taylor shook hands with a tall, fat white man in a blue serge suit.

"Its been a long time since Ive seen you, Dan."

"Yessuh. It sho has, yo Honah."

"Hows Jimmy?"

"Jus fine, suh."

"Thats a fine boy youve got, Dan."

"Ahm sho glad yuh think so, suh."

"If you raise that boy right he will be a leader of his people some day, Dan."

"Thas the one hope of mah life, suh," said Taylor with deep emotion.

"May was tellin me youre sick," said the mayor.

"Aw, it ain nothin, suh. Jusa summer col, suh."

"I didn't mean to bother you if youre sick, Dan."

"Thas awright, suh. Ahm feelin much bettah now, suh."

"Oh, youll pull through all right; itll take a lot more than a summer cold to kill old war-horses like you and me, eh, Dan?"

The mayor laughed and winked.

"Ahm hopin Gawd spares me a few mo years, suh," said Taylor.

"But at least you look all right now," said the mayor. "Say, Dan, I want you to meet Chief Bruden. This is Dan, Chief, the boy I was telling you about."

"How yuh, Mistah Chief?" asked Taylor.

A black cigar burned red in Bruden's mouth. He shifted his thin body and growled: "Hello, boy."

"And, Dan, this is Mr. Lowe, head of our fine Industrial Squad."

"How yuh, suh?" asked Taylor.

Lowe nodded with half-closed eyes.

"Sit down, Dan," said the mayor.

"Yessuh."

Taylor sat on the edge of a chair and rested his palms lightly on his knees.

"Maybe our little visit is a surprise, hunh?" asked the mayor.

"Yessuh. It is. But Ahm glad to be of any hep Ah kin, suh."

"Good; I knew youd talk that way. Now, Dan, we want you to help us. Youre a responsible man in this community; that's why we are here."

"Ah tries t do mah duty as Gawd shows it t me, suh."

"That's the spirit, Dan!" The mayor patted Taylor's knee. "Now, Im going to be perfectly frank with you, Dan." The mayor peeled a wrapper from a black cigar. "Here, have one."

"Thank yuh, suh." Taylor put the cigar into his vest pocket. "Ahll smoke it aftah dinner, suh."

There was a silence during which the three white men looked at Taylor.

"Dan," began the mayor, "its not every nigger Id come to and talk this way. Its not every nigger Id trust as Im about to trust you." The mayor looked straight at Taylor. "Im doing this because Ive faith in you. Ive known you for twenty-five years, Dan. During that time I think Ive played pretty fair with you, havent I?"

Taylor swallowed.

"Ahll have t say yuh have, yo Honah."

"Mister Lowe and the Chief here had another plan," said the mayor. "But I wouldn't hear of it. I told them Id work this thing *my* way. I thought *my* way would be much better. After all, Dan, you and I have worked together in the past and I dont see why we cant work together now. Ive backed you up in a lot of things, Dan. Ive backed you even when other white folks said you were wrong. But I believe in doing the right thing. After all, we are human beings, arent we?"

"Yessuh."

"What Ive done for you in the past Im willing to do again. You remember Scott, dont you?"

"Yessuh. Yuhs been a big hep t me n mah folks, suh."

"Well, Dan, my office is always open to you when you want to see me about any of your problems or the problems of your people," said the mayor.

"N Gawd knows Ah sho thanks yuh, suh."

The mayor bit off the tip of his cigar and spat it into a brass spittoon.

"I'm not going to beat about the bush, Dan."

The mayor paused again. There was silence. Taylor felt called upon to say something.

"Yessuh. Ah sho preciates tha, suh."

"You know these Goddam Reds are organizing a demonstration for tomorrow, dont you?" asked the mayor.

Taylor licked his lips before he answered.

"Yessuh. Ah done heard a lotta folks talkin erbout it, suh."

"That's too bad, Dan," said the mayor.

"Folks is talking erbout it everywhere. . . ." began Taylor.

"What *folks?*" interjected Bruden.

"Waal, mos everbody, suh."

Bruden leaned forward and shook his finger in Taylor's face.

"Listen, boy! I want you to get this straight! Reds aint *folks!* Theyre Goddam sonofabitching lousy bastard rats trying to wreck our country, see? Theyre stirring up race hate! Youre old enough to understand that!"

"Hes telling you straight, boy," said Lowe. "And furthermore. . . ."

"Say, whats all this?" demanded the mayor, turning to Lowe and Bruden. "Wait a minute! Whats the big idea of talking to Dan like that? Hes not mixed up in anything like that. Save that kind of talk for bad niggers. . . ."

"The quicker all you niggers get sense enough in your Goddam thick skulls to keep away from them Reds the better off you'll be!" said Bruden, ignoring the mayor.

"Aw, c mon," said the mayor. "Dans all right. Aint that right, Dan?"

Taylor looked down and saw at his feet a sharp jutting angle of sunshine falling obliquely through a window. His neck felt hot. This is the show-down, he thought. Theys tryin t trap me. . . . He cleared his throat and looked up slowly and saw the mayor gazing at him with cold grey eyes. He shifted his body slightly and saw the glint of Chief Bruden's police star; he saw Lowe's red lips twisted in half-smile and half-leer.

"Isnt that right, Dan?" the mayor asked again.

"Yessuh. Whut yuh white folks say is right. N Ah ergrees wid yuh. But Ah ain foolin wid nobody thas tryin t stir up race hate; naw, *suh!* Ah ain never done nothin like that n Ah never will, so hep me Gawd! Now, erbout this demonstration: Yessuh, Ah heard erbout it. Thas all everbodys been talking erbout erroun here fer a week, yo Honah. Waal, suh, Ahll tell yuh. Theys jus hongry. Theys marchin cause they don know whut else t do, n thas the truth from here t Heaven! Mistah Mayor, theys hongry! Jus plain *hongry!* Ah give mah las dime today t a woman wid eight chillun. . . ."

"We know all about that, Dan," said the mayor.

"Everybodys hungry," said Bruden.

"Boy, cant you see we are all in the *same* boat?" asked Lowe.

"Waal. . . ." drawled Taylor.

"Thingsll be straightened out soon, Dan," interjected the mayor soothingly. "We will see that nobody starves."

"Ah beg yo pardon, suh. A man died jus the other day from starvation. . . ."

Taylor's voice died in his throat and he looked at the floor. He knew that he had said too much.

"I reckon that makes you out a liar, don't it?" Bruden asked the mayor.

"Aw, naw, suh!" said Taylor eagerly. "Ah ain disputin nobodys word, suh. Ah jus thought yuh hadnt heard erbout it. . . ."

"We know all about it," said Bruden, turning his head away and looking out of the window, as though he was through with the conversation, as though his mind was made up.

"What do they think theyre going to get by marching?" asked Lowe.

"They think they kin git some bread," said Taylor.

"It wont get em a Goddam crumb!" said Lowe.

There was silence. Taylor looked again at the jutting angle of sunshine and heard the mayor's shoes shifting uneasily on the brown carpet. A match struck; he heard it drop with an angry hiss into the spittoon.

"I dont see why we cant get along, Dan," drawled the mayor.

"Ahm willin t git erlong, Mistah Mayor!" protested Taylor.

"Dan, here we all are, living in good old Dixie. There are twenty-five thousand people in this town. Ten thousand of those people are black, Dan. Theyre your people. Now, its our job to keep order among the whites, and we would like to think of you as being a responsible man to keep order among the blacks. Lets get together, Dan. You know these black people better than we do. We want to feel we can depend on you. Why dont you look at this thing the right way? You know Ill never turn you down if you do the right thing. . . ."

"Mistah Mayor, as Gawds mah judge, Ahm doin right when Ah tell yuh mah folks is hongry. . . ."

"Youre not doing right when you act like a Goddam Red!" said Lowe.

"These niggers around here trust you, Dan," said the mayor. "They'll do what you tell them to do."

"Speak to them," urged Lowe. "Tell them whats right."

"Mistah Mayor, Gawd in Heaven knows mah people is hongry," said Taylor humbly.

The mayor threw his body forward in the chair and rested his hands on his knees.

"Listen, Dan. I know just how you feel. We *all* feel that way. White people are hungry, too. But weve got to be prudent and do this thing right. Dan, youre a leader and youve got great influence over your congregation here." The mayor paused to let the weight of his words sink in. "Dan, I helped you to get that influence by doing your people a lot of favors through *you* when you came into my office a number of times." The mayor looked at Taylor solemnly. "I'm asking you now to use that influence and tell your people to stay *off* the streets tomorrow!"

When Taylor spoke he seemed to be outside of himself, listening to his own words, aghast and fearful.

"Ahm sho thankful as Gawd knows fer all yuh done done fer me n mah people, suh. But mah word don go so fer in times likes these, yo Honah. These folks is lookin t me fer bread n Ah cant give it t em. They hongry n Ah cant tell em where t eat. Theys gonna march no mattah whut Ah say. . . ."

"Youve got influence here, Dan, and you can use it!"

"They wouldnt be marchin ef they wuznt hongry, yo Honah!"

"Thats Red talk, nigger!" said Lowe, standing.

"Aw, thats all right, Lowe," said the mayor, placatingly.

"Im not going to sit here and let this Goddam nigger insult me to my face!" said Lowe. Taylor stood up.

"Ahm sorry, suh!"

"You *will* be sorry when you find a Goddam rope around your neck!" said Lowe.

"Now, now," said the mayor, laying his hand on Lowe's arm. He turned to Taylor. "You dont mean you wont speak to em, do you, Dan?"

"There ain nothin Ah kin say t em, Mistah Mayor. . . ."

"Youre doing the wrong thing, Dan!"

"Ahm lettin God be mah judge, suh!"

"If you dont do the right thing *we* will be your judges!" said Lowe.

"Ahm trustin Gawd, suh."

'Well, Goddammit, you better let Him guide you right!" said Bruden, jumping to his feet.

"But white folks!" pleaded Taylor. "Mah folks cant plant nothin! Its ergin the law! They cant git no work! Whut they gonna do? They don wan no trouble. . . ."

"Youre heading for a plenty right now!" said Bruden.

The mayor spoke and his voice was low and resigned.

"Ive done all I could, Dan. You wouldn't follow my advice, now the rest is up to Mister Lowe and Chief Bruden here."

Bruden's voice came with a shout:

"A niggers a nigger! I was against coming here talking to this nigger like he was a white man in the first place. He needs his teeth kicked down his throat!" Bruden poked the red tip of his cigar at Taylor's face. "Im the Chief of Police of this town, and Im here to see that orders kept! The Chamber of Commerce says therell be no demonstration tomorrow. Therell be three hundred police downtown in the morning to see that thats done. If you send them niggers down there, or if you let these Goddam Reds fool you into it, Ill not be responsible for whatll happen! Weve never had a riot in this town, but youre plotting one right now when you act like this! And you know wholl get the worst of it!"

"Cant yuh do something, Mistah Mayor? Cant yuh fix it sos we kin git some relief?"

The mayor did not answer; Lowe came close to him.

"We know youve been seeing Hadley and Green! We know whats going on! So watch yourself, nigger!"

"Suh?"

They went out. Taylor stood at the window and saw them get into their car and disappear in a cloud of dust around a corner. He sat down, feeling sweat over all his body. Gawd knows what t do. . . . He brought Lowe n Bruden here t threaten me. . . . N they know erbout Hadley and Green. . . . Somebody tol. . . . He looked up, hearing the soft boom of a clock. Hadley n Greens comin back here at six-thirty. . . . He went down the hall thinking, Lawd, ef Ah only knowed whut t do. . . .

VII

May met him in the hall.

"Whut they say, Dan?" she asked with suppressed hysteria.

"Don bother me now, May!"

"There wont be no trouble, will it, Dan?"

"Naw, May! Now, please! Yuh worrin me!"

"Yuhll spoil things fer Jimmy, Dan! Don do nothin wrong! Its fer Jimmy Ahm astin!"

"Itll be awright! Now, lemme go!"

He hurried down the hallway, leaving her crying. Good Gawd! How come she wont leave me erlone. Firs, its Jimmy; then its her. . . . Ef it ain one its the other. . . . He went to the end of the hall, down the steps, turned, and came to the door of the Deacon Room. He heard subdued voices. He knew that the deacons were waiting for him, waiting for some definite word. Shucks, Ahm willin t go thu wid tha march ef they is. Them white folks cant kill us *all*. . . . He pushed the door in. The voices ceased. He saw a dense cloud of tobacco smoke and a circle of black faces. He forced a wan smile.

"Good evenin, Brothers!" he said.

"How yuh, Reveren?" asked Deacon Bonds.

"Ahm sorry Ahm late," said Taylor.

"Wuz tha the mayor out there?" asked Deacon Williams.

Taylor paused and pulled out his handkerchief.

"Yeah, Brothers, it wuz the mayor. N the Chiefa Police n tha man Lowe from the Red Squad. . . ."

"RED SQUAD!" shouted Deacon Smith, jumping to his feet with an outraged look.

"Whut they say, Reveren?" asked Deacon Williams quietly, ignoring Deacon Smith.

Taylor sighed and looked at the floor. For a moment he loathed them because he knew they were expecting an answer to their questions. They were expecting him to speak now as he had always spoken, to the point, confidently, and finally. He had wanted them to do the talking, and now they were silent, waiting for him to speak. Lawd, Ah hope Ahm doin right. Ah don wanna lead these folks wrong. . . .

"They know all erbout tha demonstration," he said.

"But whut they *say?*" asked Deacon Bonds.

"Shucks, man! Yuh *know* whut they said!" said Deacon Smith. "Yuh *know* how them white folks feel erbout this thing!"

"They don wan us t march," said Taylor. "They said ef we march theyll put the police on us. . . ."

Deacon Smith leveled his forefinger at Taylor and intoned:

"AH TOL YUH SO!"

"They said therell be a riot," Taylor went on stubbornly.

"Yessuh! Brothers, wes gotta do *right!*" said Deacon Smith, banging his open palm down on the table. "Ah awways said wes gotta do *right*, Reveren!"

"Ahm prayin t Gawd t guide us right," said Taylor.

"Yuh sho don ack like it!" said Deacon Smith.

"Let the Reveren finish, will yuh?" asked Deacon Bonds.

"Wes gotta do right!" said Deacon Smith again, sitting down, folding his arms, crossing his legs and turning his face sternly away.

"Whut else they say, Reveren?" asked Deacon Bonds.

Taylor sighed.

"They say wes mixed up with the Reds. . . ."

"N by Gawd we 'is!" bawled Deacon Smith. "At least *yuh* is! Ah tol yuh t leave them Reds erlone! They don mean *nobody no* good! When men starts t deny Gawd, nothin good kin come from em!"

"Brother Smith, let the Reveren talk, will yuh?" asked Deacon Williams.

"He ain talkin *sense!*" said Deacon Smith.

"They say therell be three hundred police downtown in the mawnin," said Taylor, ignoring Smith. "They say only Washington kin do something erbout relief, n tha we must wait. . . ."

"N Gawd Awmighty knows thas all we kin do: wait!" said Deacon Smith.

"Fer Chrissakes, Brother Smith, let im talk!" said Deacon Williams. "We all know *yuhs* scared!"

"Ah ain scared! Ah got *sense!* Ah. . . ."

"Yuh sho don ack like it, the way yuh shoot off yo mouth!" said Deacon Williams.

Deacon Smith stood up.

"Yuh cant talk tha way t me!"

"Then keep yo big mouth shut!" said Deacon Williams.

"Whos gonna make me?"

"Brothers, please!" begged Taylor.

"A fool kin see tha the white folks is scared!" said Deacon Williams.

"N jus cause theys *scared*, theyll kill *any*body whuts fool ernuff t go downtown in the mawnin," said Deacon Smith.

"Shucks, Ahm willin t taka chance," said Deacon Hilton.

"Me too!"

"We ain got nothin t lose!"

"Any *fool* kin git his head busted!" said Deacon Smith.

"Brothers, fer the lova Gawd, quit fussin!" said Taylor.

They were silent. Taylor looked at them, letting his eyes rove from face to face.

"Brothers, this is the case," he said finally. "They threatenin us not t march, but they ain saying our folks kin git no relief. Now, Ah figgers ef we hada big crowd downtown in the mawnin they wont bother us . . ."

"Thas whut *yuh* think," sneered Deacon Smith.

"N ef we don hava big crowd, theyll smash us. Now, its up t us. . . ."

"Reveren, do the *po* white folks say they gonna be *wid* us?" asked Deacon Jones.

"Brother Hadley tol me theys gonna be wid us," said Taylor.

"Tha Hadley is a lie n the trutha Gawd ain in im!" shouted Deacon Smith. "Tha white man is jus tryin t trick yuh, Ahm telling yuh!"

"Waal, we kin never know less we try n see," said Deacon Bonds.

"Yeah, but they ain gonna let yuh try but *once*," said Deacon Smith.

"Waal, Ah ain got but *one* time t die!" said Deacon Bonds.

"Ah think the white folksll be there," said Taylor. "Theys hongry, too. . . ."

"Yuhll wake up *some* day!" said Deacon Smith.

"Whut yuh gonna do, Reveren?" asked Deacon Williams.

"Do the congregation wanna march?" asked Taylor.

"They say theys *gonna* march!"

"Waal, Ahll march wid em," said Taylor quietly. "They wont march erlone. . . ."

Deacon Smith waved his arms and screamed.

"Yeah, yuhll march! But yuhs scared t let em use yo name! Whut kinda leader *is* yuh? Ef yuhs gonna ack a fool n be a Red, then how come yuh wont come on out n say so sos we kin all hear it? Naw, you ain man ernuff t say whut yuh is! Yuh wanna stan in wid the white folks! Yuh wanna stan in wid the Reds! Yuh wanna stan in wid the congregation! Yuh wanna stan in wid the Deacon Board! Yuh wanna stan in wid *ever*body n yuh stan in wid *no*body!"

"Ahm ackin accordin t mah lights!" said Taylor.

"Waal, they ain lettin yuh see fer!" said Deacon Smith.

"Ef yuh gotta plan bettah than mine, Brother Smith, tell us erbout it!"

"AH SAY WE OUGHTNT MARCH!"

"Then, whut we gonna do?"

"Wait n see how things come out!"

"Ahm tireda waitin," said Taylor.

"How come yuh didnt send yo name out on them leaflets?" demanded Deacon Smith. Without waiting for Taylor to answer, he flared: "Ahll tell yuh why yuh didn't! Yuh *scared!* Yuh didnt wan them white folks t know yuhs mixed up in this demonstration. Yuh wanted em t think yuh wuz being pushed erlong by other folks n yuh couldn't help whut wuz happenin! But, Reveren, as sho as theres a Gawd in Heaven yuh ain foolin nobody!"

Taylor stood up.

"Brother Smith, Ah knows whut yuhs up t! Yuh tryin t run me outta mah church, but yuh cant! Gawd Awmighty Himself put me here n Ahm stayin till He says fer me t go! Yuh been schemin t git me out, but yuh cant do it this way! It ain right n Gawd knows it ain! Yeah; ef mah folks marches in the mawnin Ahm marchin wid em!"

"Thas the time, Reveren!"

"We kin show tha ol mayor something!"

"N therell be white folks wid us, too!"

"Ahll go wid the Reveren n the congregation!"

"Ahll go!"

"N me too!"

"Gawd ain wid yuh when yuh ain in the right!" said Deacon Smith.

"Gawd didnt mean fer folks t be hongry!" said Deacon Bonds.

"But He ain wid yuh when yuh stirrin up trouble, makin blood n riots!" said Deacon Smith. "N any man whut sets here n calls himself a leader called by Gawd t preach n leads his folks the wrong way is a fool n the spirita Gawd ain in im!"

"Now, wait a minute there, Brother Smith!" said Taylor. "Yuhs talkin *dangerous!*"

"Ah say any man whut leads his folks inter guns n police. . . ."

"Ain nobody leading us *nowhere!*" said Deacon Bonds.

"We gwine *ourselves!*" said Deacon Williams.

"Ah ain in this!" said Deacon Smith, jumping again to his feet. "Ah ain in this n Ahm gonna do whut Ah kin t hep mah people!"

The room grew quiet.

"Whut yuh mean, Brother Smith?" asked Taylor.

"Ah say Ahm gonna hep mah people!" said Deacon Smith again.

Taylor walked over to him.

"Is yuh gonna tell the white folks on us?"

Deacon Smith did not answer.

"Talk, Brother Smith!" said Taylor. "Tell us whut yuh mean!"

"Ah means whut Ah means!" said Deacon Smith; and he clamped his teeth tight, sat again, crossed his legs, folded his arms and stared at the blank wall.

Taylor swallowed and looked at the floor. Lawd, Ah don know whut to do! Ah wish this wuz over. . . . This niggers gonna tell on us! Hes gonna tell the white folks sos he kin stan in wid em. . . .

"Brother Smith. . . ." began Taylor.

The door opened and Jimmy stepped into the room.

"Say, Pa!"

"Whut yuh wan, son?"

"Somebodys out front t see yuh. Theys in a car. Theys white folks."

"Scuse me, Brothers," said Taylor. "Ahll be right back."

"Wes gonna set right here till yuh git back," said Deacon Smith.

When outside the door, Taylor turned to Jimmy.

"Who is they, Jimmy? How come they wouldnt come in?"

"Ah dunno, Pa. The car drove up just as Ah wuz comin thu the gate. They white men. They said fer yuh t come right out."

"Awright. N, son, yuh betta go see about yo ma."

"Whuts the mattah?"

"Shes jus upset erbout the demonstration."

"Is they gonna march, Pa?"

"Ah reckon so."

"Is many gonna be out?"

"Ah dunno, son. Ah hope so. Yuh bettah go see erbout yo ma now."

"Yessuh."

"Yuh tell them boys whut Ah tol yuh?"

"Yessuh."

Taylor paused at the front door and peeped out from behind a curtain. In front of his gate was a long black car. Who kin tha be? For a moment he thought the mayor had come back. But his cars grey. . . . He opened the door and walked slowly down the steps. Lawd, mabbe we oughtnt go thu wid this demonstration aftah all? We might all be sorry ef somebodys killed in the mawnin. . . . He walked along a flower-bordered path that smelt of violets and magnolias. Dust rested filmily on tree leaves. The sun was almost gone. As he came to the car a white face looked out.

"Yuh Taylor?"

"Yessuh," answered Taylor, smiling.

The rear door of the car opened and the white man stepped to the ground.

"So youre Taylor, hunh?"

"Yessuh," said Taylor again, still smiling, but puzzled. "Kin Ah be of service t yuh, suh?"

Taylor saw it coming, but could do nothing. He remembered afterward that he had wanted to ask, What yuh doin? The blow caught him flush on the point of the jaw, sending him flying backward. His head struck the edge of the runningboard; a flash of red shot before his eyes. He rolled, face downward, into a bed of thick violets. Dazed, he turned his head, trying to speak. He felt a hand grab the back of his collar and jerk him up.

"Get in the car, nigger!"

"Say, whut yuh. . . ."

"Shut up and get in the car, Goddam you!"

A blow came to his right eye. There were three white men now. They lifted him and rammed him down on the floor in the back of the car.

"Say, yuh cant do this!"

"Get your Goddam mouth shut, you bastard!"

A hard palm slapped him straight across his face. He struggled up, protesting.

"You. . . ."

The heel of a shoe came hard into his solar plexus. He doubled up, like a jackknife. His breath left, and he was rigid, half-paralyzed.

"You think you can run this whole Goddam town, don't you? You think a nigger can run over white folks and get away with it?"

He lay still, barely breathing, looking at blurred white faces in the semi-darkness of the roaring car.

VIII

The moment he tried to tell the direction in which the car was moving, he knew he had waited too long. He remembered dimly that they had turned corners at least three times. He lay with closed eyes and wondered what they were going to do with him. She gonna be worried t death, he thought, thinking of May. And then he thought of Jimmy and said to himself, Ah hope he don go n ack a fool now. . . . The numbness which had deadened most of his stomach and chest was leaving. He felt sweat on his back and forehead. The car slowed, turned; then it ran fast again. He knew by the way the rocks crunched beneath the humming rubber tires that they were speeding over gravel. Whut roads this? He could not tell. There were so many gravel roads leading out of town. He tried to recall how long he had lain there half-paralyzed from that kick in the solar plexus. He was confused; it might have been five minutes or it might have been an hour. The car slowed again, turning. He smelt the strong scent of a burning cigarette and heard the toll of a far off church bell. The car stopped; he heard the sound of other cars, gears shifting and motors throbbing. We mus be at some crossroads. But he could not guess which one. He had an impulse to call for help. But there would not be any use in his doing that now. Mabbe they white folks anyhow. He would be better off as he was; even six white men were better than a mob of white men. The car was speeding again, lurching. He smelt dust, clay dust. Then he heard a hard, rasping voice:

"How is he?"

"O.K."

"Keep im quiet!"

"O.K."

He said nothing. He began to wonder how many of them were in the car. Yes, he should have been watching for something like this. They been threatening me fer a long time. Now this is it. The car was gradually slowing with that long slow slowing preceding a final stop. He felt the rubber tires turning over rough ground; his head rocked from side to side, hitting against the lower back of the front seat. Then the car stopped; the motor stopped; for a moment there was complete silence. Then he heard wind sighing in trees. Wes out in the country somewhere. In the woods, he thought.

"O.K.?"

"O.K.!"

He heard a door open.

"C mon, nigger! Get up and watch yourself!"

He pulled up and caught a glimpse of starry sky. As his feet hit the ground his head began to ache. He had lain cramped so long the blood had left his limbs; he took a step, kicking out his legs to restore circulation. His arms were grabbed from behind and he felt the pressure of a kneecap in the center of his spine. He gasped and reeled backward.

"Where you think youre going?"

He rested on his knees, his body full of pain. He heard a car door slam.

"Awright, nigger! Lets go! Straight ahead!"

He got up and twisted his head about to see who had spoken. He saw four blurred white faces and then they were blotted out. He reeled backward again, his head striking the ground. A pain knotted in his temple.

"Get up, nigger! Keep your eyes in front, and walk, Goddammit!"

He pulled up and limped off, his head down. Mabbe they gonna shoot me? His feet and the feet behind him made a soft *cush-cush* in the dew-wet grass and leaves.

"Aw right, nigger!"

He stopped. Slowly he raised his eyes; he saw a tall white man holding a plaited leather whip in his hand, hitting it gently against his trousers' leg.

"You know what this is, nigger?"

He said nothing.

"Wont talk, hunh? Well, this is a nigger-lesson!"

The whip flashed in faint starlight. The blow numbed his lips. He tasted blood.

"You know what this is? Im asking you again, nigger!"

"Nawsuh," he whispered.

"This is a nigger-whip!"

The leather whacked across his shoulders.

"Mistah, Ah ain done nothin!"

"Aw, naw! You aint done nothing! You aint never done a Goddam thing, have you?" White men were standing close around him now. "All you ever do is play around with Reds, dont you? All you ever do is get crowds of niggers together to threaten white folks, dont you? When we get through with you to-night youll know how to stay in a niggers place! C mon! Get that Goddam vest off!"

He did not move. The whip wrapped itself around his neck, leaving a ring of fire.

"You want me to *beat* it off you?"

He pulled off the vest and held it in his hands.

"C mon! Get that shirt and undershirt off!"

He stripped to his waist and stood trembling. A night wind cooled his sweaty body; he was conscious of his back as he had never been before, conscious of every square inch of black skin there. One of the white men walked off a few paces and stopped.

"Bring im over here!"

"O.K.!"

They guided him with prods and kicks.

"On your knees, nigger!"

He did not move. Again his arms were caught from behind and a kneecap came into the center of his back. Breathless, he dropped, his hands and knees cooling in the wet grass.

He lifted his fingers to feel his swelling lips; he felt his wrists being grabbed and carried around the trunk of a tree. He held stiffly and struggled against a rope.

"Let go!"

His arms went limp. He rested his face against a cold tree-trunk. A rope cut into his wrists. They tied his feet together, drawing the rope tight about his ankles. He looked around; they stood watching.

"Well, nigger, what do you know?"

"Nothin, suh."

"Youre a preacher, aint you?"

"Yessuh."

"Well, lets hear you pray some!"

He said nothing. The whip lashed across his bare back, *whick!* He flinched and struggled against the rope that cut his wrists to the bone. The leather thong hummed again, *whick!* and his spine arched inward, like a taut bow.

"Goddam your black soul, pray!"

He twisted his face around, pleading:

"Please, Mistah! Don whip me! Ah ain done nothin. . . ."

Another lash came across his half-turned cheek, *whick!* He jerked around and sheltered his face against the treetrunk. The lash hit his back, *whick!*

"*Hit* that black bastard, Bob!"

"Let me have that whip!"

"Naw, wait a minute!"

He said nothing. He clenched his teeth, his whole body quivering and waiting. A split second after each blow his body would lurch, as though absorbing the shock.

"You going to pray? You want me to beat you till you *cant* pray?"

He said nothing. He was expecting each blow now; he could almost feel them before they came, stinging, burning. Each flick came straight on his back and left a streak of fire, a streak that merged with the last streak, making his whole back a sheet of living flame. He felt his strength ebbing; he could not clench his teeth any more. His mouth hung open.

"Let me have it, Bob?"

"Naw, its my turn!"

There was a pause. Then the blows came again; the pain burned its way into his body, wave upon wave. It seemed that when he held his muscles taut the blows hurt less; but he could not hold taut long. Each blow weakened him; each blow told him that soon he would give out. Warm blood seeped into his trousers, ran down his thighs. He felt he could not stand it any longer; he held his breath, his lungs swelling. Then he sagged, his back a leaping agony of fire; leaping as of itself, as though it were his but he could not control it any longer. The weight of his body rested on his arms; his head dropped to one side.

"Ahhlll ppppray," he sobbed.

"Pray, then! Goddam you, pray!"

He tried to get his breath, tried to form words, hearing trees sighing somewhere. The thong flicked again, *whick!*

"Ain't you going to pray!"

"Yyyyyessuh. . . ."

He struggled to draw enough air into his lungs to make his words sound.

"Ooour Fffather. . . ."

The whip cut hard, *whick!* pouring fire and fire again.

"Have mercy, Lawd!" he screamed.

"Pray, nigger! Pray like you *mean* it!"

". . . wwwhich aaaaart in hheaven . . . hhhallowed bbe Tttthy nname. . . ." The whip struck, *whick!* "Ahm prayin, Mmmmistah!"

"Goddam your black heart, *pray!*"

". . . Ttthine kkkindom ccome . . . Ttthy wwill bbe ddddone. . . ."

He sobbed, his breath leaving his lungs, going out from him, not wanting to stay to give sound to his words. The whip brought more fire and he could not stand it any longer; his heart seemed about to burst. He screamed, stretched his knees out and twisted his arms till he lay sideways, half on his stomach. The whip came into his stomach, *whick!* He turned over; it came on his back again, *whick!* He stopped struggling and hung limply, his weight suspended on arms he could not feel. Then fire flamed over all his body; he stiffened, glaring upward, wild-eyed.

"Whats the matter, nigger? You hurt?"

"Awright, kill me! Tie me n kill me! Yuh white trash cowards, kill me!"

"Youre tough, aint you? Just wait! Well kill you, you black sonofabitch!"

"Lemme have that whip!"

"C mon, now! Its my turn!"

"Give me that whip, Ellis!"

He was taut, but not feeling the effort to be taut.

"Well git yuh white trash some day! So hep me Gawd, we'll git yuh!"

The whip stopped.

"Say that again, Goddam you!"

The whip lashed, *whick!* but there was no streak of fire now; there was only one sheet of pain stretching all over his body, leaping, jumping, blazing in his flesh.

"Say it!"

He relaxed and closed his eyes. He stretched his legs out, slowly, not listening, not waiting for the whip to fall, *say it whick! say it whick! say it whick!* He groaned. Then he dropped his head and could not feel any more.

IX

Moonlight pained his eyeballs and the rustle of tree leaves thundered in his ears. He seemed to have only a head that hurt, a back that blazed, and eyes that ached. In him was a feeling that some power had sucked him deep down into the black earth, had drained all strength from him. He was waiting for that power to go away so he could come back to life, to light. His eyes were half-open, but his lids did not move. He was thirsty; he licked his lips, wanting water. Then the thunder in his ears died, rolling away. He moved his hand and touched his forehead; his arm fell limply in the wet grass and he lay waiting to feel that he wanted to move. As his blood began to flow swiftly again he felt sweat breaking out over his body. It seemed he could hear a tiny, faraway sound whispering over and over like a voice in an empty room: Ah got fever. . . . His back rested on a bed of fire, the imprint of leaves and grass searing him with a scalding persistence. He turned over on his stomach and groaned. Then he jerked up, half-sitting. He was fully conscious now, fighting for his strength, remembering the curses, the prayer and the whip. The voice whispered again, this time louder: Ah gotta git home. . . . With fumbling fingers he untied the rope from his ankles and wrists. They didnt kill me, he thought. He stood up and the dark earth swayed and the stars blurred. Lawd, have mercy! He found himself on his knees; he had not known when he had started falling; he just found himself on his knees. Lawd, Ahm weak! He stood up again, more slowly this time, holding onto a tree. He would have to get his shirt; he could not go through the streets with a naked and bleeding back. He put one foot in front of the other with conscious effort, holding his body stiffly. Each slight twist of his shoulders sent a wave of liquid metal over him. In the grass at his feet his shirt was smeared like a white blur. He touched it; it was wet. He held it, instinctively fearing to put it on. When it did touch, his whole back blazed with a pain so intense that it seemed to glow white hot. No, he could not put it on now. Stiffly, he went among the trees, holding the shirt in his hands, looking at the ground.

He stopped at the edge of a dirt road, conscious of the cool steady stars and the fire that smoldered in his back. What roads this? He could not tell. Then he heard a clock striking so faintly that it seemed to be tolling in his own mind. He counted, Wun, Tuh. . . . Its tuh erclock, he thought. He could not stay here all night; he had to go in one direction or another. He watched the brown dusty road winding away in the darkness, like a twisting ribbon. Then he ducked his head, being seared again with fire and feeling a slight rush of air brush across his face. A small bird wheeled past his eyes and fluttered dizzily in the starlight. He watched it veer and dip, then crash softly into a tree limb. It fell to the ground, flapping tiny wings blindly. Then the bird twittered in fright and sailed straight upward into the starlight, vanishing. He walked northward, not going anywhere in particular, but walked northward because the bird had darted in that direction.

The road curved, turned to gravel, crunching under his shoes. This mus be the way, he thought. There were fences along the sides of the road now. He went faster, holding his legs stiffly to avoid pulling the muscles in his back. A church steeple loomed in the starlight, slender and faint. Yeah, thas Houstons church. N Ah gotta go thu a white neighborhood, he thought with despair. He saw houses, white, serene and cool in the night. Spose Ah go to Houston? Naw, hes white. *White*. . . . Even tho he preaches the gospel Ah preaches, he might not take me in. . . . He passed a small graveyard surrounded by a high iron picket fence. A *white* graveyard, he thought and snickered bitterly. Lawd God in Heaven, even the dead cant be together! He stopped and held his shirt in his hands. He dreaded trying to put it on, but he had to. Ah cant go thu the streets like this. Gingerly, he draped the shirt over his shoulders; the whole mass of bruised and mangled flesh flamed, glowed white. With a convulsive movement he rammed his arms into the sleeves, thinking that the faster he did it the less pain there would be. The fire raged so he had a wild impulse to run, feeling that he would have no time then to suffer. But he could not run in a white neighborhood. To run would mean to be shot, for a burglar, or anything. Stiff-legged, he went down a road that turned from brown dust to black asphalt. Ahead street lamps glowed in round, rosy hazes.

Far down the shadow-dappled pavement he heard the sound of feet. He walked past a white man, then he listened to the white man's footsteps dying away behind him. He stopped at a corner and held onto a telephone pole. It would be better to keep in the residential district than to go through town. He would be stopped and questioned in town surely. And jailed maybe. Three blocks later on a white boy came up on him so softly and suddenly that he started in panic. After the boy had gone he turned to look; he saw the boy turning, looking at him. He walked on hurriedly. A block later a white woman appeared. When she was some fifty feet away she crossed to the other side of the street. Hate tightened his throat, then he emptied his lungs in a short, silent, bitter laugh. Ah ain gonna bother yuh, white lady. Ah only wan t git home. . . .

Like a pillar of fire he went through the white neighborhood. Some days theys gonna burn! Some days theys gonna burn in Gawd Awmightys fire! How come they make us suffer so? The worls got too mucha everything! Yit they bleed us! They fatten on us like leeches! There ain no groun yuh kin walk on that they don own! N Gawd knows tha ain right! He made the earth fer us all! He ain tol no lie when He put us in this worl n said be fruitful n multiply. . . . Fire fanned his hate; he stopped and looked at the burning stars. "Gawd, ef yuh gimme the strength Ahll tear this ol buildin down! Tear it down, Lawd! Tear it down like ol Samson tore the temple down!" He walked again, mumbling. "Lawd, tell me whut t do! Speak t me, Lawd!" He caught his breath; a dark figure came out of the shadows in front of him. He saw a glint of metal; it was a policeman. He held erect and walked rapidly. All stop, he thought. He wont have t ast me t stop. . . . He saw the white face drawing closer. He stopped and waited.

"Put your hands up, nigger!"

"Yessuh."

He lifted his arms. The policeman patted his hips, his sides. His back blazed, but he bit his lips and held still.

"Who you work for?"

"Ahma preacher, suh."

"A *preacher?*"

"Yessuh."

"What you doing out here this time of night?"

"Ah wuz visitin a sick man, a janitah, suh, whut comes t mah church. He works fer Miz Harvey. . . ."

"Who?"

"Miz Harvey, suh."

"Never heard of her, and I've been on this beat for ten years."

"She lives right back there, suh," he said, half turning and pointing.

"Well, you look all right. You can go on. But keep out of here at night."

"Yessuh."

He was near his own people now. Across a grassy square he could see the top of the round-house glinting dully in the moonlight. The black asphalt turned to cinders and the houses were low, close together, squatting on the ground as though hiding in fear. He saw his church and relaxed. He came to the steps. Caught hold of a banister and rested a moment.

When inside he went quietly down a hall, mounted the stairs, and came to the door of his room. He groped in the dark and felt the bed. He tried to pull off the shirt. It had stuck. He peeled it. Then he eased onto the bed and lay on his stomach. In the darkness his back seemed to take new fire. He went to the kitchen and wet a cloth with cold water. He lay down again with the cloth spread over him. That helped some. Then he began to shake. He was crying.

X

The door creaked.

"Tha yuh, Pa?"

"Son?"

"Good Gawd, wes been lookin all over fer yuh! Where yuh been? Mas worried t death!"

"C mon in, son, n close the do."

"Don yuh wanna light?"

"Naw; close the do."

There was a short silence.

"Whuts the mattah, Pa? Yuh sick?"

"Close the do n sit down, son!"

Taylor could hear Jimmy's breathing, then a chair scraping over the floor and the soft rustle of Jimmy's clothes as he sat.

"Whuts the mattah, Pa? Whut happened?"

Taylor stared in the darkness and slowly licked his swollen lips. He wanted to speak, but somehow could not. Then he stiffened, hearing Jimmy rise.

"Set *down*, son!"

"But, Pa. . . ."

Fire seethed not only in Taylor's back, but all over, inside and out. It was the fire of shame. The questions that fell from Jimmy's lips burned as much as the whip had. There rose in him a memory of all the times he had given advice, counsel, and guidance to Jimmy. And he wanted to talk to him now as he had in the past. But his impulses were deadlocked. Then suddenly he heard himself speaking, hoarsely, faintly. His voice was like a whisper rising from his whole body.

"They whipped me, son. . . ."

"Whipped yuh? Who?"

Jimmy ran to the bed and touched him.

"Son, set *down!*"

Taylor's voice was filled with a sort of tense despair. He felt Jimmy's fingers leaving him slowly. There was a silence in which he could hear only his own breath struggling in his throat.

"Yuh mean the *white folks?*"

Taylor buried his face in his pillow and tried to still the heaving in his chest.

"They beat me, son. . . ."

"Ahll git a doctah!"

"Naw!"

"But yuhs hurt!"

"Naw; lock the do! Don let May in here. . . ."

"Goddam them white bastards!"

"Set down, son!"

"Who wuz they, Pa?"

"Yuh cant do nothin, son. Yuhll have t wait. . . ."

"Wes been waitin too long! All we do is wait, *wait!*"

Jimmy's footsteps scuffed across the floor. Taylor sat up.

"Son?"

"Ahma git mah gun n git Pete n Bob n Joe n Sam! Theyll see they cant do this t us!"

Taylor groped in the darkness; he found Jimmy's shoulders.

"C mon son! Ahm awright. . . ."

"Thas the reason why they kill us! We take everything they put on us! We take everthing! *Everthing!*"

"Yuh cant do nothing *erlone,* Jimmy!"

Jimmy's voice was tense, almost hysterical.

"But we kin *make* em know they cant do this t us widout us doin something! Aw, hell, Pa! Is we gonna be dogs *all* the time?"

"But theyll kill yuh, son!"

"Somebody *has* t die!"

Taylor wanted to tell Jimmy something, but he could not find the words. What he wanted to say boiled in him, but it seemed too big to come out. He flinched from pain, pressing his fingers to his mouth, holding his breath.

"Pa?"

"Yeah, son?"

"Hadley n Green wuz here t see yuh three-fo times."

"Yeah?"

Jimmy said nothing. Taylor twisted around, trying to see his son's face in the darkness.

"Whut they say, son?"

"Aw, hell! It don mattah. . . ."

"Tell me whut they *said!*"

"Ttthey ssaid. . . . Aw, Paw, they didn't know!"

"Whut they *say?*"

"They said yuh had done run out on em. . . ."

"Run *out?*"

"Everbody wuz astin where yuh wuz," said Jimmy. "Nobody knowed. So they tol em yuh run out. N Brother Smith had the Deacon Board t vote yuh outta the church. . . ."

"Vote me *out?*"

"They said they didnt wan yuh fer pastah no mo. It was Smith who made em do it. He tol em yuh had planned a demonstration n lef em holdin the bag. He fussed n stormed at em. They thought they wuz doin right. . . ."

Taylor lay on his bed of fire in the darkness and cried. He felt Jimmy's fingers again on his face.

"Its awright, Pa. Well git erlong somehow. . . ."

"Seems like Gawds don lef me! Ahd die fer mah people ef Ah only knowed how. . . ."

"Pa. . . ."

"How come Ah cant never do nothin? All mah life Ah done tried n cant do nothin! *Nothin!*"

"Its awright, Pa!"

"Ah done lived all mah life on mah knees, a-beggin n a-pleadin wid the white folks. N all they gimme wuz crumbs! All they did wuz kick me! N then they come wida gun n ast me t give mah own soul! N ef Ah so much as talk lika man they try t kill me. . . ."

He buried his face in the pillow, trying to sink himself into something so deeply that he could never feel again. He heard Jimmy turning the key in the lock.

"Son!"

Again he ran to Jimmy and held him.

"*Don* do tha, son!"

"Thingsll awways be like this less we *fight!*"

"Set down, son! Yo po ol pas a-*beggin* yuh t set down!"

He pulled Jimmy back to the bed. But even then it did not seem he could speak as he wanted to. He felt what he wanted to say, but it was elusive and hard to formulate.

"Son. . . ."

"Ah ain gonna live this way, Pa!"

He groped for Jimmy's shoulders in the darkness and squeezed them till the joints of his fingers cracked. And when words came they seemed to be tearing themselves from him, as though they were being pushed upward like hot lava out of a mountain from deep down.

"Don be a fool, son! Don thow yo life erway! We cant do nothin erlone."

"But theys gonna treat us this way as long as we *let* em!"

He had to make Jimmy understand; for it seemed that in making him understand. in telling him, he, too, would understand.

"We gotta git wid the *people*, son. Too long we done tried t do this thing our way n when we failed we wanted t turn out n pay-off the white folks. Then they kill us up like flies. Its the *people*, son! Wes too much erlone this way! Wes los when wes erlone! Wes gonna be wid our folks. . . ."

"But theys killin us!"

"N theyll keep on killin us less we learn how t fight! Son, its the people we mus gid wid us! Wes empty n weak this way! The reason we cant do nothin is cause wes so much erlone. . . ."

"Them Reds wuz right," said Jimmy.

"Ah dunno," said Taylor. "But let nothin come tween yuh n *yo* people. Even the Reds cant do nothin ef yuh lose yo people. . . ." Fire burned him as he talked, and he talked as though trying to escape it. "Membah whut Ah tol yuh prayer wuz, son?"

There was silence, then Jimmy answered slowly:

"Yuh mean lettin Gawd be so real in yo life tha everthing yuh do is cause of Im?"

"Yeah, but its different now, son. Its the *people!* Theys the ones whut mus be real t us! Gawds wid the people! N the peoples gotta be real as Gawd t us! We cant hep ourselves er the people when wes erlone. Ah been wrong erbout a lotta things Ah tol yuh, son. Ah tol yuh them things cause Ah thought they wuz right. Ah told yuh t work hard n climb t the top. Ah told yuh folks would lissen t yuh then. But they wont, son! All the will, all the strength, all the power, all the numbahs is in the people! Yuh cant live by yoself! When they beat me tonight, they beat *me*. . . . There wuznt nothin Ah could do but lay there n hate n pray n cry. . . . Ah couldnt *feel* mah people, Ah couldnt *see* mah people, Ah couldnt *hear* mah people. . . . All Ah could feel wuz tha whip cuttin mah blood out. . . ."

In the darkness he imagined he could see Jimmy's face as he had seen it a thousand times, looking eagerly, his eyes staring before him, fashioning his words into images, into life. He hoped Jimmy was doing that now.

"Ahll awways hate them bastards! Ahll *awways* hate em!"

"Theres other ways, son."

"Yuhs sick, Pa. . . ."

'Wes all sick, son. Wes gotta think erbout the people, night n day, think erbout em so hard tha our po selves is fergotten. . . . Whut they suffer is whut Ah suffered las night when they whipped me. Wes gotta keep the people wid us."

Jimmy was silent. A soft knock came at the door.

XI

"Dan!"

"Thas Ma," said Jimmy.

Taylor heard Jimmy rise to his feet; he gripped Jimmy's hands.

"Please, Pa! Let her come in n hep yuh!"

"Naw."

"Dan!"

Jimmy broke from him; he heard the key turn in the lock. The door opened.

"Dan! Fer Gawds sake, whuts the mattah?"

Jimmy switched on the light. Taylor lay blinking at May's anxious face. He felt shame again, knowing that he should not feel it, but feeling it anyway. He turned over and buried his face in his hands.

"Dan!"

She ran and knelt at the side of the bed.

"They tried t kill im, Ma! They beat im!" said Jimmy.

"Ah knowed them white folks wuz gonna do something like this! Ah knowed it," sobbed May.

Taylor sat up.

"Yuh be still! Lay down!" said May.

She pushed him back onto the bed.

"Cant yuh do something fer im, Ma? Hes sufferin tha way."

Taylor heard May leave the room and come back.

"Hol still, Dan. This ain gonna hurt yuh. . . ."

He felt warm water laving him, then something cool that smelled of oil. He heard Jimmy moving to and fro, getting things for May. When his back was dressed he felt the bed had somehow changed. He wondered at the strange peace that seeped into his mind and body there in the room with May and Jimmy, with the white folks far off in the darkness.

"Feel bettah, Dan?"

"Ahm awright."

"Yuh hongry?"

"Naw."

He wanted to talk to Jimmy again, to tell him about the black people. But he could not think of words that would say what he wanted to say. He would tell it somehow later on. He began to toss, moving jerkily, more now from restlessness of mind than from the dying fire still lingering in his body.

XII

Suddenly the doorbell pealed. Taylor turned and saw May and Jimmy looking at each other.

"Somebody at the do," said Jimmy in a tense voice.

"Yuh reckon they white folks?" asked May.

"Yuh bettah go down, Jimmy," said Taylor.

"Ef its any white folks tell em Dans out," said May.

Jimmy's footsteps died away on the stairs. A door slammed. There were faint sounds of voices. Footsteps echoed, came on the stairs, grew loud. Taylor knew that more than one person was coming up. He lifted himself and sat on the edge of the bed.

"Dan, yuh cant git up! Yuhll make yoself sick!"

He ignored her. The door opened and Jimmy ran in.

"Its Brother Bonds, Pa!"

Bonds stood in the doorway with his head wrapped in blood-stained bandages. His face twitched and his eyes stared at something beyond the walls of the room, as though his attention had been riveted once and for always upon one fixed spot.

"Whut happened, Brother?" asked Taylor.

Bonds stared, dazed, with hunched and beaten shoulders. Then he sank to the floor, sobbing softly:

"They beat me! They beat mah chillun! They beat mah wife! They beat us all cause Ah tol em t git outta mah house! Lawd, how long Yuh gonna let em treat us this way? How long Yuh gonna let em make us suffer?"

May sobbed. Jimmy ran out of the room. Taylor caught him on the stairs.

"Don be a fool, boy! Yuh c mon back here, *now!*"

Jimmy flopped on the edge of a chair and mumbled to himself. The room was quiet save for the rustle of tree leaves that drifted in from the outside and the sound of Bonds sobbing on the floor. As Taylor stood his own suffering was drowned in a sense of widening horror. There was in his mind a vivid picture of all the little dingy huts where black men and women were crouched, afraid to stir out of doors. Bonds stopped crying and looked at Taylor; again that sense of shame spread over Taylor, inside and out. It stirred him to speech.

"Who else they beat, Brother?"

"Seem like everybody, Reveren! Them two Commoonists got beat something terrible n they put em in jail. N Ah heard they kilt one black man whut tried t fight back. They ketched everbody they kin on the streets n lettin em have it. They ridin up n down in cars. . . ."

Jimmy cursed. The doorbell pealed again.

"Git me a shirt, May!"

"Dan, yuh ain able t do nothin!"

The doorbell pealed again, then again. Taylor started toward the dresser; but May got there before he did and gave him a shirt.

"Dan, be careful!"

"C mon downstairs, Brother Bonds. N yuh, too, Jimmy," said Taylor.

XIII

The church's waiting room was full. Black men and women sat and stood, saying nothing, waiting. Arms were in slings; necks were wrapped in white cloth; legs were bound in bloodstained rags.

"LOOK AT WHUT YUH DONE DONE!" a voice bawled.

It was Deacon Smith. Taylor's eyes went from face to face; he knew them all. Every Sunday they sat in the pews of his church, praying, singing, and trusting the God he gave them. The mute eyes and silent lips pinned him to a fiery spot of loneliness. He wanted to protest that loneliness, wanted to break it down; but he did not know how. No parables sprang to his lips now to give form and meaning to his words; alone and naked, he stood ashamed. Jimmy came through the door and placed his hand on his shoulder.

"Its daylight, Pa. The folks is gatherin in the playground! Theys waiten fer yuh. . . ."

Taylor went into the yard with the crowd at his heels. It was broad daylight and the sun shone. The men in their overalls and the women with children stood about him on all sides, silent. A fat black woman elbowed her way in and faced him.

"Waal, Reveren, we done got beat up. Now, is we gonna march?"

"Yuh wanna march?" asked Taylor.

"It don make no difference wid me," she said. "Them white folks cant do no mo than theys already done."

The crowd chimed in.

"N Gawd knows they cant!"

"Ahll go ef the nex one goes!"

"Ah gotta die sometime, so Ah just as waal die now!"

"They cant kill us but once!"

"Ahm tired anyhow! Ah don care!"

"The white folks says theys gonna meet us at the park!"

Taylor turned to Jimmy.

"Son, git yo boys together n tell em t roun up everbody!"

"Yessuh!"

May was pulling at his sleeve.

"Dan, yuh *cant* do this. . . ."

Deacon Smith pushed his way in and faced him.

"Yuhll never set foot in a church ergin ef yuh lead them po black folks downtown t be killed!"

The crowd surged.

"Ain nobody leadin us nowhere!"

"We goin ourselves!"

"Is we gonna march, Reveren?"

"Yeah; soon as the crowd gits together," said Taylor.

"Ain nobody t blame but yuh ef yuh carry em t their *death!*" warned Deacon Smith.

"How come yuh don shut yo old big mouth n let the Reveren talk?" asked the fat woman.

"Sistah, Ah got as much right t speak as yuh!"

"Waal, don speak to me, yuh hear!"

"Somebody has t say something when ain *nobody* got no sense!"

"Man, don yuh tell me Ah ain got no sense!"

"Yuh sho don ack like it!"

"Ah got as much sense as yuh got!"

"How come yuh don use it?"

The fat sister slapped Deacon Smith straight across his face. Taylor ran between them and pried them apart. The crowd surged and screamed.

"Ef he touches Sistah Henry ergin Ahll kill im!"

"He ain got no bisness talkin tha way t a woman!"

Taylor dragged the fat woman toward the gate. The crowd followed, yelling. He stopped and faced them. They circled around, tightly, asking questions. May had hold of his sleeve. Jimmy came to him.

"Pa, theys comin!"

Taylor turned and walked across the yard with the crowd following. He took two planks and laid them upon the ends of two saw-horses and made a solid platform. He climbed up and stood in the quiet sunshine. He did not know exactly what it was he wanted to say, but whatever it was he would say it when they were quiet. He felt neither fear nor joy, just an humble confidence in himself, as though he were standing before his mirror in his room. Then he was conscious that they were quiet; he took one swift look over their heads, heads that stretched away to the street and beyond, a solid block of black, silent faces; then he looked down, not to the dust, but just a slight lowering of eyes, as though he were no longer looking at them, but at something within himself.

"Sistahs n Brothers, they tell me the Deacon Boards done voted me outta the church. Ef thas awright wid yuh, its awright wid me. The white folks says Ahma bad nigger n they don wanna have nothin else t do wid me. N thas awright, too. But theres one thing Ah wanna say. Ah knows how yuh feel erbout bein hongry. N how yuh feel is no different from how Ah feel. Yuh been waitin a week fer me t say whut yuh ought t do. Yuh been wonderin how come Ah didnt tell yuh whut yuh oughta do. Waal. . . ."

He paused and looked over the silent crowd; then again his eyes, his gaze, went inward.

"Sistahs n Brothers, the reason Ah didnt say nothin is cause Ah didnt know *whut* t say. N the only reason Ahm speakin now is cause Ah *do* know. Ah know whut t do. . . ."

He paused again, swallowing. The same feeling which had gripped him so hard last night when he had been talking to Jimmy seized him. He opened his mouth to continue; his lips moved several times before words came; and when they did come they fell with a light and hoarse whisper.

"Sistahs n Brothers, las night the white folks took me out t the woods. They took me out cause Ah tol em yuh wuz hongry. They ast me t tell yuh not t march, n Ah tol em Ah wouldnt. Then they beat me. They tied me t a tree n beat me till Ah couldnt feel no mo. They beat me cause Ah wouldnt tell yuh not t ast fer bread. They said yuhd blieve ever-thing Ah said. All the time they wuz hepin me, all the time they been givin me favors, they wuz doin it sos *they* could tell *me* to tell *yuh* how t ack! Sistahs n Brothers, as Gawds mah judge, Ah thought Ah wuz doin right when Ah did that. Ah thought Ah wuz doin right when Ah told yuh t do the things they said. N cause Ah wouldnt do it this time, they tied me t a tree n beat me till mah blood run. . . ."

Mist covered his eyes. He heard the crowd murmuring; but he did not care if they were murmuring for or against him; he wanted to finish, to say what he had been trying so hard to say for many long hours.

"Sistahs n Brothers, they whipped me n made me take the name of *Gawd* in vain! They made me say mah prayers n beat me n laughed! They beat me till Ah couldnt membah nothin! All last night Ah wuz lying stretched out on the ground wid mah back burnin. . . . All this mawning before day Ah wuz limpin thu white folks streets. Sistahs n Brothers, Ah *know* now! Ah done seen the *sign*! Wes gotta git together. Ah know whut yo life is! Ah done felt it! Its *fire*! Its like the fire that burned me las night! Its sufferin! Its hell! Ah cant bear this fire erlone! Ah know now whut t do! Wes gotta git close t one ernother! Gawds done spoke! Gawds done sent His sign. Now its fer us t ack. . . ."

The crowd started yelling:

"Well go ef yuh go!"

"Wes ready!"

"The white folks says theyll meet us at the park!"

The fat black woman started singing:

> So the sign of the fire by night
> N the sign of the cloud by day
> A-hoverin oer
> Jus befo
> As we journey on our way. . . .

Taylor got down. He moved with the crowd slowly toward the street. May went with him, looking, wondering, saying nothing. Jimmy was at his side. They sang as they marched. More joined along the way. When they reached the park that separated the white district from the black, the poor whites were waiting. Taylor trembled when he saw them join, swelling the mass that moved toward the town. He looked ahead and saw black and white marching; he looked behind and saw black and white marching. And still they sang:

"*So the sign of the fire by night. . . .*"

They turned into the street that led to town.

"*N the sign of the cloud by day. . . .*"

Taylor saw blue-coated policemen standing along the curb.

"*A -hoverin oer. . . .*"

Taylor felt himself moving between the silent lines of blue-coated white men, moving with a sea of placards and banners, moving under the sun like a pregnant cloud. He said to himself, They ain gonna bother us! They bettah *not* bother us. . . .

"*Jus befo. . . .*"

Across a valley, in front of him, he could see the buildings of the town sprawled on a hill.

"*As we journey on our way. . . .*"

They were tramping on pavement now. And the blue-coated men stood still and silent. Taylor saw Deacon Smith standing on the curb, and Smith's face merged with the faces of the others, meaningless, lost. Ahead was the City Hall, white and clean in the sunshine. The autos stopped at the street corners while the crowd passed; and as they entered the downtown section people massed quietly on the side-walks. Then the crowd began to slow, barely moving. Taylor looked ahead and wondered what was about to happen; he wondered without fear; as though whatever would or could happen could not hurt this many-limbed, many-legged, many-handed crowd that was he. He felt May clinging to his sleeve. Jimmy was peering ahead. A policeman came running up to him.

"You Taylor?"

"Yussuh," he said, quietly, his gaze straight and steady.

"The mayors down front; he wants to see you!"

"Tell im Ahm back here," said Taylor.

"But he wants to see the leader up front!"

"Tell im Ahm back here," said Taylor again.

The man hesitated, then left; they waited, quiet, still. Then the crowd parted. Taylor saw Mayor Bolton hurrying toward him, his face beet-red.

"Dan, tell your people not to make any trouble! We dont want any trouble, Dan. . . ."

"There ain gonna be no trouble, yo Honah!"

"Well, tell them they can get food if they go back home, peacefully. . . ."

"Yuh tell em, yo Honah!"

They looked at each other for a moment. Then the mayor turned and walked back. Taylor saw him mount the rear seat of an auto and lift his trembling hands high above the crowd, asking for silence, his face a pasty white.

A baptism of clean joy swept over Taylor. He kept his eyes on the sea of black and white faces. The song swelled louder and vibrated through him. This is the way! he thought. Gawd ain no lie! He ain no lie! His eyes grew wet with tears, blurring his vision: the sky trembled; the buildings wavered as if about to topple; and the earth shook. . . . He mumbled out loud, exultingly:

"Freedom belongs t the strong!"

Tillie Olsen (b. 1912 or 1913)

Born into a socialist family living in Omaha, Nebraska, Tillie Lerner was the second of six children. Her father was the state chair of the Socialist Party. She experienced cruelties when she crossed class lines to attend high school, where she wrote for the student paper under the byline "Tillie the Toiler." A year before graduation, she left school for paid employment and political activism. At sixteen, on one of her hauntings of secondhand bookshops, she bought an 1861 bound edition of the *Atlantic* and read *Life in the Iron Mills*, published anonymously. Even as a teenage reader, she knew the value of this story, and she kept it by her as a sign that working-class people could be the subject of great literature. By seventeen, she experienced jail for a period extended enough to cause her bodily harm and to convince her further of the need to resist illegitimate authority. She spent much of her lifetime in low-paid work and in political activism, in addition to mothering and housework. By the time she was in her mid-thirties, she had four daughters and a husband, Jack Olsen, whom she had met in the Young Communist League in the 1930s. We know from her accounts that she wrote daily in snatched time, even on buses or on lunch breaks, often on tiny bits of paper in a minuscule hand. Some short pieces, like "I Want You Women Up North to Know," were published in the 1930s, often to acclaim, but Olsen had no real time as a writer until the mid-1950s. Hence, her prize-winning collection of stories, *Tell Me a Riddle*, which included "I Stand Her Ironing" (presented in Part VI), appeared in 1961, when she was fifty.

Both the poem and the story charge the reader's courage to resist, the poem through the energy of the poet's fierce language, the story through the mother's confidence in the resilience of her daughter. Olsen's later work—the novella *Requa I* (1970), a lengthy biographical essay published with the novella *Life in the Iron Mills* by Rebecca Harding Davis, the novel *Yonnondio: From the Thirties* (1974), the essays *Silences* (1978), and the anthology *Mother to Daughter, Daughter to Mother* (1985)—all reflect Olsen's ability to capture the lives of working-class people in prose that needs no editor. She has also been, through more than forty years, a professor on many campuses, a mentor for hundreds of young writers, and an adviser to the Feminist Press and other presses about what needs publishing. She often said that she was educated in public libraries. Her extraordinary knowledge of literature, as a writer and a scholar, has helped to change the course of literary history.

Florence Howe

Tillie Olsen, I Want You Women Up North to Know[1]

The "Workers Correspondence" section of The Daily Worker *was a regular feature throughout the thirties. We who were reds then considered it a special (and thrilling) responsibility to elicit, to encourage the "voicing the unvoiced"; to help such letters into publication.*

I want you women up north to know
how those dainty children's dresses you buy
   at macy's, wannamakers, gimbels, marshall fields,
are dyed in blood, are stitched in wasting flesh,
5   down in San Antonio, "where sunshine spends the winter."
I want you women up north to see
the obsequious smile, the salesladies trill
   "exquisite work, madame, exquisite pleats"
vanish into a bloated face, ordering more dresses,
10   gouging the wages down,
dissolve into maria, ambrosa, catalina,
   stitching these dresses from dawn to night,
   In blood, in wasting flesh.

Catalina Rodriguez, 24,
15   body shrivelled to a child's at twelve,
catalina rodriguez, last stages of consumption,
   works for three dollars a week from dawn to midnight.
A fog of pain thickens over her skull, the parching heat
   breaks over her body,
20   and the bright red blood embroiders the floor of her room.
   White rain stitching the night, the bourgeois poet would say,
   white gulls of hands, darting, veering,
   white lightning, threading the clouds,
this is the exquisite dance of her hands over the cloth,
25   and her cough, gay, quick, staccato,
   like skeleton's bones clattering,
is appropriate accompaniment for the esthetic dance
   of her fingers,
and the tremolo, tremolo when the hands tremble with pain.
30   Three dollars a week,
two fifty-five,
seventy cents a week,
no wonder two thousand eight hundred ladies of joy
are spending the winter with the sun after he goes down—
35   for five cents (who said this was a rich man's world?) you can
   get all the lovin you want
"clap and syph aint much worse than sore fingers, blind eyes,
   and t.b."

Maria Vasquez, spinster,
40   for fifteen cents a dozen stitches garments for children she
   has never had,

---

[1] Based on a letter by Felipe Ibarro in *New Masses*, January 9, 1934. Originally published in *The Partisan* 1 (March 1934), when she was twenty-one, under her maiden name Tillie Lerner.

Catalina Torres, mother of four,
   to keep the starved body starving, embroiders from dawn
   to night.
45 Mother of four, what does she think of,
   as the needle pocked fingers shift over the silk—
   of the stubble-coarse rags that stretch on her own brood,
   and jut with the bony ridge that marks hunger's landscape
   of fat little prairie-roll bodies that will bulge in the
50   silk she needles?
(Be not envious, Catalina Torres, look!
   on your own children's clothing, embroidery,
   more intricate than any a thousand hands could fashion,
   there where the cloth is ravelled, or darned,
55   designs, multitudinous, complex and handmade by Poverty
   herself.)

Ambrosa Espinoza trusts in god,
   "Todos es de dios, everything is from god,"
   through the dwindling night, the waxing day, she bolsters
60   herself up with it—
but the pennies to keep god incarnate, from ambrosa,
and the pennies to keep the priest in wine, from ambrosa,
ambrosa clothes god and priest with hand-made children's dresses.

Her brother lies on an iron cot, all day and watches,
65 on a mattress of rags he lies.
For twenty-five years he worked for the railroad, then they laid him off.
   (racked days, searching for work; rebuffs; suspicious eyes of
   policemen.
   goodbye ambrosa, mebbe in dallas I find work; desperate
70   swing for a freight,
   surprised hands, clutching air, and the wheel goes over a
   leg,
   the railroad cuts it off, as it cut off twenty-five years of his life.)
She says that he prays and dreams of another world, as he lies
75   there, a heaven (which he does not know was brought to
   earth in 1917 in Russia, by workers like him).

Women up north, I want you to know
when you finger the exquisite hand-made dresses
what it means, this working from dawn to midnight,
80 on what strange feet the feverish dawn must come
   to maria, catalina, ambrosa,
how the malignant fingers twitching over the pallid faces jerk them
   to work,
and the sun and the fever mount with the day—
85   long plodding hours, the eyes burn like coals, heat jellies
   the flying fingers,
down comes the night like blindness.
   long hours more with the dim eye of the lamp, the breaking
   back,
90   weariness crawls in the flesh like worms, gigantic like earth's
   in winter.

And for Catalina Rodriguez comes the night sweat and the blood
    embroidering the darkness.
    for Catalina Torres the pinched faces of four huddled
95   children,
    the naked bodies of four bony children,
    the chant of their chorale of hunger.
And for twenty eight hundred ladies of joy the grotesque act gone
    over—the wink—the grimace—the "feeling like it baby?"
100 And for Maria Vasquez, spinster, emptiness, emptiness,
    flaming with dresses for children she can never fondle.
And for Ambrosa Espinoza—the skeleton body of her brother on
his mattress of rags, boring twin holes in the dark with his eyes
to the image of christ, remembering a leg, and twenty five years
105 cut off from his life by the railroad.

Women up north, I want you to know,
I tell you this can't last forever.

I swear it won't.

Filipe Ibarro's 1934 Letter in *New Masses*

Where the Sun Spends the Winter
San Antonio, Texas

Dear Editor:

I want the women of New York, Chicago and Boston who buy at Macy's, Wannamaker's, Gimbel's and Marshall Field to know that when they buy embroidered children's dresses labeled "hand made" they are getting dresses made in San Antonio, Texas, by women and girls with trembling fingers and broken backs.

These are bloody facts and I know, because I've spoken to the women who make them. Catalina Rodriguez is a 24-year-old Mexican girl but she looks like 12. She's in the last stages of consumption and works from six in the morning till midnight. She says she never makes more than three dollars a week. I don't wonder any more why in our city with a population of 250,000 the Board of Health has registered 8,000 professional "daughters of joy" and in addition, about 2,000 *Mujeres Alegres* (happy women), who are not registered and sell themselves for as little as five cents.

Catalina Torres has four children and her husband cracks pecans at thirty cents a hundred pounds. He makes about two dollars a week. She says that they pay her thirty cents a dozen for the embroidery and she can only make three dozen a week because of the children.

Maria Vasquez, a spinster, sews the children's dresses at home for fifteen cents a dozen. If she works from dawn to midnight she can make three dozen a day. For each new dress style you have to go to the office first and make a sample. I asked her if she passed the test every time. She ran inside and came out with an envelope in her hand. Read my diploma she says, and you won't ask any more foolish questions.

The "diploma" is a circular letter printed by the thousands on the company letterheads and is addressed to no one in particular. It says her work has been satisfactory and that they are proud of her, and any time she wants work they will be glad to give it to her. The company is the Juvenile Mfg. Corp. Their New York office is E. Edar, 1350 Broadway.

Several years ago our Chamber of Commerce launched a campaign in competition with Florida and California inviting tourists to come to San Antonio, "Where Sunshine Spends the Winter." I don't know whether the tourists came but Eastern manufacturers and Capital came and let out the children's dresses for home work. There are thousands of American-born Mexican girls and women and they work at any price.

Ambrosa Espinoza is thirty and she has worked the last seven years on these "hand made" dresses. I am enclosing her pay envelopes. One week three dollars, the next, two fifty-five and the third only seventy cents. With this she has to pay rent for her shack, pay insurance, support the Catholic Church and feed herself. When I try to talk to her she says: *Todos es de Dios, todos es de Dios*—everything is from God, everything is from God. She embroiders four dozen dresses a week at seventy-cents a dozen and works from morning till late at night. At night she uses a kerosene lamp. She says that times are getting harder and even American women will take the work. The boss knows this so he reduces the prices every week, and if you don't like it you can leave it. She also works for the Juvenile Mfg. Corp.

She tells me about her brother and how he lost his leg. For twenty-five years he worked for Southern Pacific Railway, and three years ago they laid him off. He looked high and low for work. Then he decided to look in North Texas and he tried to hop a freight. But he lost his balance and the train cut his leg the way the railroad cut the twenty-five years from his life.

As I got out of the shack I can't forget this brother who lies on his iron cot like a skeleton. He uses rags for mattress, and lies motionless, gazing on the Virgin of Guadalupe and the image of the young Jew of Galilee. He prays to them, dreaming of another world.

I want you women up North to know. I tell you this can't last forever. I swear it won't.

Felipe Ibarro

Source: Modern American Poetry, www.english.uiuc.edu/maps.

Meridel Le Sueur (1900–1996)

Born in 1900, Meridel Le Sueur had strong role models: her grandmother Antoinette McGovern Lucy, a leader of the Women's Christian Temperance Union, and her mother Marian Wharton, a founder of a socialist college in Kansas. When the family relocated to Minnesota in 1917, Le Sueur had already met the leading radicals of her day, including Eugene Debs, Big Bill Haywood, and Emma Goldman. She joined the IWW (Industrial Workers of the World) and the Communist Party and wrote for *The Masses* (later *The New Masses*) and *The Worker*. After the execution of Sacco and Vanzetti in 1927, she felt the need to "affirm life," as she later reflected, and gave birth to two daughters. She survived the 1930s by writing for both the radical press and commercial magazines. Her first story collection, *Salute to Spring*, appeared in 1941.

After World War II, Le Sueur was blacklisted and fell into obscurity. Interest in her work was revived by the feminist movement of the 1970s, resulting in publication of her stories by the Feminist Press (*Ripening*, 1982) and a novel by West End Press (*The Girl*, 1978). She published a novella, *The Dread Road*, in 1991 and left manuscripts of three other novels at her death in 1996. Even her most political writings were written from a first-person point of view. In her reportage, such as "I Was Marching" (1934), Le Sueur wrote as a strike participant as well as a journalist, earning the thanks of the union men, which she said "meant more to me than all the editors' comments I could have." In later vignettes, such as "Eroded Women" (1948), she exposed the dark side of exploitation, refusing to represent such a figure with the "official optimism" often demanded of communist writers. With unbending integrity reminiscent of her forebears, she tried to respect the personal truth of the working class.

John Crawford

I WAS MARCHING

I have never been in a strike before. It is like looking at something that is happening for the first time and there are no thoughts and no words yet accrued to it. If you come from the middle class, words are likely to mean more than an event. You are likely to think about a thing, and the happening will be the size of a pin point and the words around the happening very large, distorting it queerly. It's a case of "Remembrance of things past." When you are in the event, you are likely to have a distinctly individualistic attitude, to be only partly there, and to care more for the happening afterward than when it is happening. That is why it is hard for a person like myself and others to be in a strike.

Besides, in American life, you hear things happening in a far and muffled way. One thing is said and another happens. Our merchant society has been built upon a huge hypocrisy, a cut-throat competition which sets one man against another and at the same time an ideology mouthing such words as "Humanity," "Truth," the "Golden Rule," and such. Now in a crisis the word falls away and the skeleton of that action shows in terrific movement.

For two days I heard of the strike. I went by their headquarters. I walked by on the opposite side of the street and saw the dark old building that had been a garage and lean, dark young faces leaning from the upstairs windows. I had to go down there often. I looked in. I saw the huge black interior and live coals of living men moving restlessly and orderly, their eyes gleaming from their sweaty faces.

I saw cars leaving filled with grimy men, pickets going to the line, engines roaring out. I stayed close to the door, watching. I didn't go in. I was afraid they would put me out. After all, I could remain a spectator. A man wearing a polo hat kept going around with a large camera taking pictures.

I am putting down exactly how I felt, because I believe others of my class feel the same as I did. I believe it stands for an important psychic change that must take place in all. I saw many artists, writers, professionals, even business men and women standing across the street, too, and I saw in their faces the same longings, the same fears.

The truth is I was afraid. Not of the physical danger at all, but an awful fright of mixing, of losing myself, of being unknown and lost. I felt inferior. I felt no one would know me there, that all I had been trained to excel in would go unnoticed. I can't describe what I felt, but perhaps it will come near it to say that I felt I excelled in competing with others and I knew instantly that these people were NOT competing at all, that they were acting in a strange, powerful trance of movement *together*. And I was filled with longing to act with them and with fear that I could not. I felt I was born out of every kind of life, thrown up alone, looking at other lonely people, a condition I had been in the habit of defending with various attitudes of cynicism, preciosity, defiance, and hatred.

Looking at that dark and lively building, massed with men, I knew my feelings to be those belonging to disruption, chaos, and disintegration and I felt their direct and awful movement, mute and powerful, drawing them into a close and glowing cohesion like a powerful conflagration in the midst of the city. And it filled me with fear and awe and at the same time hope. I knew this action to be prophetic and indicative of future actions and I wanted to be part of it.

Our life seems to be marked with a curious and muffled violence over America, but this action has always been in the dark, men and women dying obscurely, poor and poverty marked lives, but now from city to city runs this violence, into the open, and colossal happenings stand bare before our eyes, the street churning suddenly upon the pivot of mad violence, whole men suddenly spouting blood and running like living sieves, another holding a dangling arm shot squarely off, a tall youngster, running, tripping over his intestines, and one block away, in the burning sun, gay women shopping and a window dresser trying to decide whether to put green or red voile on a mannikin.

In these terrible happenings you cannot be neutral now. No one can be neutral in the face of bullets.

The next day, with sweat breaking out on my body, I walked past the three guards at the door. They said, "Let the women in. We need women." And I knew it was no joke.

At first I could not see into the dark building. I felt many men coming and going, cars driving through. I had an awful impulse to go into the office which I passed, and offer to do some special work. I saw a sign which said "Get your button." I saw they all had buttons with the date and the number of the union local. I didn't get a button. I wanted to be anonymous.

There seemed to be a current, running down the wooden stairs, towards the front of the building, into the street, that was massed with people, and back again. I followed the current up the old stairs packed closely with hot men and women. As I was going up I could look down and see the lower floor, the cars drawing up to await picket call, the hospital roped off on one side.

Upstairs men sat bolt upright in chairs asleep, their bodies flung in attitudes of peculiar violence of fatigue. A woman nursed her baby. Two young girls slept together on a cot, dressed in overalls. The voice of the loudspeaker filled the room. The immense heat pressed down from the flat ceiling. I stood up against the wall for an hour. No one paid any attention to me. The commissary was in back and the women came out sometimes and sat down, fanning themselves with their aprons and listening to the news over the loudspeaker. A huge man seemed hung on a tiny folding chair. Occasionally some one tiptoed over and brushed the flies off his face. His great head fell over and the sweat poured regularly from his forehead like a spring. I wondered why they took such care of him. They all looked at him tenderly as he slept. I learned that he was a leader on the picket line and had the scalps of more cops to his name than any other.

Three windows flanked the front. I walked over to the windows. A red-headed woman with a button saying, "Unemployed Council," was looking out. I looked out with her. A thick crowd stood in the heat below listening to the strike bulletin. We could look right into the windows of the smart club across the street. We could see people peering out of the windows half hidden.

I kept feeling they would put me out. No one paid any attention. The woman said without looking at me, nodding to the palatial house, "It sure is good to see the enemy plain like that." "Yes," I said. I saw that the club was surrounded by a steel picket fence higher than a man. "They know what they put that there fence there for," she said. "Yes," I said. "Well," she said, "I've got to get back to the kitchen. Is it ever hot?" The thermometer said ninety-nine. The sweat ran off us, burning our skins. "The boys'll be coming in," she said, "for their noon feed." She had a scarred face. "Boy, will it be a mad house?" "Do you need any help?" I said eagerly. "Boy," she said, "some of us have been pouring coffee since two o'clock this morning, steady, without no let-up." She started to go. She didn't pay any special attention to me as an individual. She didn't seem to be thinking of me, she didn't seem to see me. I watched her go. I felt rebuffed, hurt. Then I saw instantly she didn't see me because she saw only what she was doing. I ran after her.

I found the kitchen organized like a factory. Nobody asks my name. I am given a large butcher's apron. I realize I have never before worked anonymously. At first I feel strange and then I feel good. The forewoman sets me to washing tin cups. There are not enough cups. We have to wash fast and rinse them and set them up quickly for buttermilk and coffee as the line thickens and the men wait. A little shortish man who is a professional dishwasher is supervising. I feel I won't be able to wash tin cups, but when no one pays any attention except to see that there are enough cups I feel better.

The line grows heavy. The men are coming in from the picket line. Each woman has one thing to do. There is no confusion. I soon learn I am not supposed to help pour the buttermilk. I am not supposed to serve sandwiches. I am supposed to wash tin cups. I suddenly look around and realize all these women are from factories. I know they have learned this organization and specialization in the factory. I look at the round shoulders of the woman cutting bread next to me and I feel I know her. The cups are brought back, washed and put on the counter again. The sweat pours down our faces, but you forget about it.

Then I am changed and put to pouring coffee. At first I look at the men's faces and then I don't look anymore. It seems I am pouring coffee for the same tense, dirty sweating face, the same body, the same blue shirt and overalls. Hours go by, the heat is terrific. I am not tired. I am not hot. I am pouring coffee. I am swung into the most intense and natural organization I have ever felt. I know everything that is going on. These things become of great matter to me.

Eyes looking, hands raising a thousand cups, throats burning, eyes bloodshot from lack of sleep, the body dilated to catch every sound over the whole city. Buttermilk? Coffee?

"Is your man here?" the woman cutting sandwiches asks me.

"No," I say, then I lie for some reason, peering around as if looking eagerly for someone, "I don't see him now."

But I was pouring coffee for living men.

For a long time, about one o'clock, it seemed like something was about to happen. Women seemed to be pouring into headquarters to be near their men. You could hear only lies over the radio. And lies in the paper. Nobody knew precisely what was happening, but everyone thought something would happen in a few hours. You could feel the men being poured out of the hall onto the picket line. Every few minutes cars left and more drew up and were filled. The voice at the loudspeaker was accelerated, calling for men, calling for picket cars.

I could hear the men talking about the arbitration board, the truce that was supposed to be maintained while the board sat with the Governor. They listened to every word over the loudspeaker. A terrible communal excitement ran through the hall like a fire through a forest. I could hardly breathe. I seemed to have no body at all except the body of this excitement. I felt that what had happened before had not been a real movement, these false words and actions had taken place on the periphery. The real action was about to show, the real intention.

We kept on pouring thousands of cups of coffee, feeding thousands of men.

The chef with a woman tattooed on his arm was just dishing the last of the stew. It was about two o'clock. The commissary was about empty. We went into the front hall. It was drained of men. "The men are massed at the market," he said. "Something is going to happen." I sat down beside a woman who was holding her hands tightly together, leaning forward listening, her eyes bright and dilated. I had never seen her before. She took my hands. She pulled me towards her. She was crying. "It's awful," she said. "Something awful is going to happen. They've taken both my children away from me and now something is going to happen to all those men." I held her hands. She had a green ribbon around her hair.

The action seemed reversed. The cars were coming back. The announcer cried, "This is murder." Cars were coming in. I don't know how we got to the stairs. Everyone seemed to be converging at a menaced point. I saw below the crowd stirring, uncoiling. I saw them taking men out of cars and putting them on the hospital cots, on the floor. At first I felt frightened, the close black area of the barn, the blood, the heavy movement, the sense of myself lost, gone. But I couldn't have turned away now. A woman clung to my hand. I was pressed against the body of another. If you are to understand anything you must understand it in the muscular event, in actions we have not been trained for. Something broke all my surfaces in something that was beyond horror and I was dabbing alcohol on the gaping wounds that buckshot makes, hanging open like crying mouths. Buckshot wounds splay in the body and then swell like a blow. Ness, who died, had thirty-eight slugs in his body, in the chest and in the back.

The picket cars keep coming in. Some men have walked back from the market, holding their own blood in. They move in a great explosion, and the newness of the movement makes it seem like something under ether, moving terrifically towards a culmination.

From all over the city workers are coming. They gather outside in two great half-circles, cut in two to let the ambulances in. A traffic cop is still directing traffic at the corner and the crowd cannot stand to see him. "We'll give you just two seconds to beat it," they tell him. He goes away quickly. A striker takes over the street.

Men, women, and children are massing outside, a living circle close packed for protection. From the tall office building business men are looking down on the black swarm thickening, coagulating into what action they cannot tell.

We have living blood on our skirts.

That night at eight o'clock a mass-meeting was called of all labor. It was to be in a parking lot two blocks from headquarters. All the women gather at the front of the building with collection cars, ready to march to the meeting. I have not been home. It never occurs to me to leave. The twilight is eerie and the men are saying that the chief of police is going to attack the meeting and raid headquarters. The smell of blood hangs in the hot, still air. Rumors strike at the taut nerves. The dusk looks ghastly with what might be in the next half hour.

"If you have any children," a woman said to me, "you better not go." I looked at the desperate women's faces, the broken feet, the torn and hanging pelvis, the worn and lovely bodies of women who persist under such desperate labors. I shivered, though it was 96 and the sun had been down a good hour.

The parking lot was already full of people when we got there and men swarmed the adjoining roofs. An elegant cafe stood across the street with water sprinkling from its roof and splendidly dressed men and women stood on the steps as if looking at a show.

The platform was the bullet riddled truck of the afternoon's fray. We had been told to stand close to this platform, so we did, making the center of a wide massed circle that stretched as far as we could see. We seemed buried like minerals in a mass, packed body to body. I felt again that peculiar heavy silence in which there is the real form of the happening. My eyes burn. I can hardly see. I seem to be standing like an animal in ambush. I have the brightest, most physical feeling with every sense sharpened peculiarly. The movements, the masses that I see and feel I have never known before. I only partly know what I am seeing, feeling, but I feel it is the real body and gesture of a future vitality. I see that there is a bright clot of women drawn close to a bullet riddled truck. I am one of them, yet I don't feel myself at all. It is curious, I feel most alive and yet for the first time in my life I do not feel myself as separate. I realize then that all my previous feelings have been based on feeling myself separate and distinct from others and now I sense sharply faces, bodies, closeness, and my own fear is not my own alone, nor my hope.

The strikers keep moving up cars. We keep moving back together to let cars pass and form between us and a brick building that flanks the parking lot. They are connecting the loudspeaker, testing it. Yes, they are moving up lots of cars, through the crowd and lining them closely side by side. There must be ten thousand people now, heat rising from them. They are standing silent, watching the platform, watching the cars being brought up. The silence seems terrific like a great form moving of itself. This is real movement issuing from the close reality of mass feeling. This is the first real rhythmic movement I have ever seen. My heart hammers terrifically. My hands are swollen and hot. No one is producing this movement. It is a movement upon which all are moving softly, rhythmically, terribly.

No matter how many times I looked at what was happening I hardly knew what I saw. I looked and I saw time and time again that there were men standing close to us, around us, and then suddenly I knew that there was a living chain of men standing shoulder to shoulder, forming a circle around the group of women. They stood shoulder to shoulder slightly moving like a thick vine from the pressure behind, but standing tightly woven like a living wall, moving gently.

I saw that the cars were now lined one close fitted to the other with strikers sitting on the roofs and closely packed on the running boards. They could see far over the crowd. "What are they doing that for?" I said. No one answered. The wide dilated eyes of the women were like my own. No one seemed to be answering questions now. They simply spoke, cried out, moved together now.

The last car drove in slowly, the crowd letting them through without command or instruction. "A little closer," someone said. "Be sure they are close." Men sprang up to direct whatever action was needed and then subsided again and no one had noticed who it was. They stepped forward to direct a needed action and then fell anonymously back again.

We all watched carefully the placing of the cars. Sometimes we looked at each other. I didn't understand that look. I felt uneasy. It was as if something escaped me. And then suddenly, on my very body, I knew what they were doing, as if it had been communicated to me from a thousand eyes, a thousand silent throats, as if it had been shouted in the loudest voice.

THEY WERE BUILDING A BARRICADE.

Two men died from that day's shooting. Men lined up to give one of them a blood transfusion, but he died. Black Friday men called the murderous day. Night and day workers held their children up to see the body of Ness who died. Tuesday, the day of the funeral, one thousand more militia were massed downtown.

It was still over ninety in the shade. I went to the funeral parlors and thousands of men and women were massed there waiting in the terrific sun. One block of women and children were standing two hours waiting. I went over and stood near them. I didn't know whether I could march. I didn't like marching in parades. Besides, I felt they might not want me.

I stood aside not knowing if I would march. I couldn't see how they would ever organize it anyway. No one seemed to be doing much.

At three-forty some command went down the ranks. I said foolishly at the last minute, "I don't belong to the auxiliary—could I march?" Three women drew me in. "We want all to march," they said gently. "Come with us."

The giant mass uncoiled like a serpent and straightened out ahead and to my amazement on a lift of road I could see six blocks of massed men, four abreast, with bare heads, moving straight on and as they moved, uncoiled the mass behind and pulled it after them. I felt myself walking, accelerating my speed with the others as the line stretched, pulled taut, then held its rhythm.

Not a cop was in sight. The cortege moved through the stop-and-go signs, it seemed to lift of its own dramatic rhythm, coming from the intention of every person there. We were moving spontaneously in a movement, natural, hardy, and miraculous.

We passed through six blocks of tenements, through a sea of grim faces, and there was not a sound. There was the curious shuffle of thousands of feet, without drum or bugle, in ominous silence, a march not heavy as the military, but very light, exactly with the heart beat.

I was marching with a million hands, movements, faces, and my own movement was repeating again and again, making a new movement from these many gestures, the walking, falling back, the open mouth crying, the nostrils stretched apart, the raised hand, the blow falling, and the outstretched hand drawing me in.

I felt my legs straighten. I felt my feet join in that strange shuffle of thousands of bodies moving with direction, of thousands of feet, and my own breath with the gigantic breath. As if an electric charge had passed through me, my hair stood on end. I was marching.

ERODED WOMAN

The sight of the shanty in the lead mine district brought back many strains of melancholy from my childhood in Oklahoma, and it was as if I had always remembered the bare-duned countryside and the tough, thin herb strains of men and women from the Indians of the Five Tribes to the lean migrants from Valley Forge. Standing before the shack, an old lean-to, pine bent and tense from the metal onslaught of sun, I was afraid to see the woman I knew would open the door.

The abandoned lead and zinc mines stand in a wasteland of ruined earth and human refuse. Ruin shows in the form of the shanty roof, in the shape of the awful knothole eye which admits chat-laden wind and light, in the loose swinging door. The insecurities of my childhood are awakened. The mine shaft openings glitter in the sunlight and the unreal day seems to shift and shatter and the old fear emanating from the land gnaws at me, fear of space, of moving, of the town, of what?

A union man in Joplin had told me to knock at this door. "The old lady is a fighter, her son is a fighter from way back! We had the blue card company union here first. They played all the tricks, control of relief, goons, they even had armed Indians against strikers, called everybody furriner and Communist, but we got railroaders blacklisted far back as the '94 strike, and old miners from Little Egypt who knew the score. We held out. Now we got a union. You go see the old lady."

She answered my knock. She was spare, clad in a kind of flour sack with a hole cut in the middle, showing the hulk of her bones and also the peculiar shyness, tenderness and dignity of a woman who has borne children, been much alone, and is still strong set against rebuff.

She was shy and I was shy. When I told her who sent me she let me into the rickety house which seemed only an extension of her gothic body. She wiped a chair with her skirt. "Set," she said. "It's the chat, overn everything."

"You lived here long?"

She looked at me. Her eyes seemed dusted with chat, their blueness dimmed and yet wide open and upon me, magnets of another human being. "A sight of time," she said, "too long. When we come we were always going back to the Ozarks to a farm." We both looked out of the crooked frame of the window. A chat pile rose up, there was not a tree, flower or bush. "Nothing will ever grow," she said, fixing her gnarled, knuckled hand in the flour sack of her lap. "Seems like you're getting sludge in yore blood."

We both looked out of the crooked window. More is said in silence than in words. It is in silence that she trusts me. "The Quapaws owned this land but the big oil scared them and they signed it over for ninety-nine years. I guess that's forever as us'n goes. I wouldn't sign over green land like that to some critters I never see.

"My son will be here. He will tell you. He's thinking all the time. Sometimes when he ain't working he makes me nervous setting thar but I know now he's thinking it out. Since the C.I.O. come here he's been thinking. Since they had that row and we was all out of work for so long and they broke up our meetings and they beat up my son. They beat him bad and my husband didn't say anything agin't. 'Ellie,' he said, 'he's fighting for his kin. He's fighting good.' And I tended him for two weeks bandaging his raw skin. His skin was peeled off'n him. Not an inch but what was pounded like a steak and I never said nothing to him. It looked like he was hurt for some reason that was not just hurt like in the mines, not just death. It makes you sore after awhile, no use seem to comin' of it. Like all the babies born so hard and dying so early."

A young man came up the walk. "It's my son that was in the strike," she said. "I been widowed twice. It's the chat hemorrhage both times. You drown in your own blood, you do. Hello, son," she said.

The boy was silent and shaggy, with the same blue eyes and a tense grievance in him. He sat on the edge of the bed, his cap in his hand. "Yes, we've got a union now, right of our blood we have. They done everything to us."

"They beat him," she said softly looking at him, and he looked fiercely and briefly at her.

"Yes, the Klan, the bosses, pickhandlers beat up every man with a CIO button. The merchants give dances and prizes if you belonged to the blue card."

"They tried to run him out, beat him up twice," she said.

"Don't lower your voice. The Klan don't rule here now, mamma," he said.

"I don't know. The Republicans are coming back. The Republicans sent the army. The army!" she said.

"Talk right up," he said.

"We would not give up fighting for the people and the land. I'm mighty proud of him not to lick the boots of the company. Now I'll be fixing the supper if you'll all excuse me."

When he got into it he was like a man in love. "Why," he said, "I'd kill a child of mine before he'd work in the mines. Children of lead, that's all we call them. I saw my father die, his lungs turned to stone, setting in that chair there till he held his breath and let his blood choke him and then he could lie down forever." Now the union was going to send him north to a school and he was going to learn. He didn't know anything. His mother would go with him and they would go north.

"Another migration," I said.

He looked at me. "You think we should stay? Stay put, eh?" He began to walk around the room, his hands in his pockets. The Mrs. came in. "Well," he said, "I got the seeds of unionism in me. My dad carried his union card in his heart for a long time, couldn't carry it nowheres else. He was always telling us a better life was coming through the union no matter how long we had to fight, he used to tell us. You can always do whatever you have to do to win."

The mother came to the door and said, "If you can eat what we eat, I guess like we used to say if we can stand it all year you can stand it for one meal."

We went into the lean-to kitchen. You could see the earth through the cracks but the boards were scrubbed clean as a butcher's table.

"I was a weaver back in Virginia," the mother said. "Why, if Mr. Baxter, the owner of the mill, was here this minute he could tell you, I could shore weave!"

The meal was a big plate of beans the color of dry locusts and some cornmeal bread. "If'n we had ketchup it would be tasty," he said. "Set!"

We bowed our heads. "Dear Lord, make us thankful fer what we are about to receive and fer all the blessing we receive at Thy hands. In Jesus' name we ask it, amen."

The son wanted to tell what he knew. He believed at first that the blue card union was the best because it "ain't furrin and it ain't Red" and you kept your job. Then the blue card had deliberately affiliated with the "furrin" union, the AF of L.

"A man don't know which way to turn. There was riot and killing in Galena. Lots of folks showed up here from all over. The Communists they help you and they ain't afeared. They call them furriners too."

"Henry," she laughed, "he says the whole darn district is getting furrin, he says he's gonna go on further west. Further west." They laughed.

She sang in a crooked voice. "*Ladies to the center, form a star, kill all furriners near and far.* We used to sing that. Don't never see how a union against the boss is always furrin. My man always was a union man and I don't always rightly understand but I am with him till the day I die and his thinking is my thinking and his way is mine. *Heigh ho, heigh ho, I joined the CIO, I give my dues to the goddamned Jews, heigh ho, heigh ho.* Not even a song like that got our boys to testify agin the CIO. They had to bring in a lot of wild boys and pay some drunk Indians to look like they was a big army agin the CIO. The pick-handle boys went around and the Klan come in."

"I got to be goin," the boy said.

"He's always off to a meeting," she said proudly.

He stopped at the door. "It's mighty fine, writing something. I hope you do it." He stood a moment. I held out my hand and he hesitated a moment in the dusky door, then in a rush he took it.

When he had gone it was dusk and the wood darkened. I said, "Don't light a lamp. It's nice to sit in the dusk."

"It's nice," she said sitting closer to me. "I should wash the dishes."

"I'll help you after a while. Let's just sit together." She was pleased.

I could feel the clearness of the woman, the edge, the honor, the gothic simplicity of the lean struggle and the clarity and honor with which she lived. She was close to the bone, her face honest as her house with the terrible nakedness of a tool, used as a tool is used, discarded as a tool, worked as a tool, uncared for as a human. And underneath there stirred the almost virginal delicate life of the woman, her modest delicate withdrawals, the bare and meager boundaries of her person kept intact, unviolated, with human tenderness emanating from her, like live energy. We sat close together.

"The long trek we been doin'. My children always thinkin' we are crossing a river or that the wind is on the wagon shaking and moving. We was movin' a lot. Why, we picked up everything when the mines open at Picher. Everyone was talking about a big lead and zinc vein over here, everybody was tearing out fer the new diggings jest across the line into Oklahoma, jest a hole in the road. It was a time I tell you when everybody was on the road. You see yore neighbor sticking his head outen his shack which was movin' comical right down the road and the living going on as usual, the kids hoppin' in and out shouting more'n usual. Farmers were a-coming from Arkansas and Alabama even and Tennessee scurrying like ants to a new corpse. Ozark hillbillies was comin' in on the freights, knocking on the door at night fer victuals, women even rode the blinds in with their children. Houses from Joplin carted, villages lifted right up and took on wheels, timber pulled by mules right onto the new diggins in Oklahoma.

"First we left the cotton hills, we come trying to git us'n a piece of land in Arkansas sharecropping, but we come on here in the night then when a friend comin' through in a covered wagon with his family said he is going to Galena for to work in the zinc thar. I didn't want my man to work ever again under the earth but he telling me then he says, No, Elly, you kin make a stake thar, we ain't aimin' to stay thar at all. We aimin' to make a little stake and then we goin' into that new territory of Oklahoma we stayin' thar, he says.

"We got us some of that land, that new good land and raisin' a crop of kids and whatever they are raisin' in them parts, but it's good land. That thar was years ago afore the twins died and layin' out thar in no proper earth I think sometimes I hear them playing in the woodshed. Now back in Kentucky, I recollect thar was good sweet earth with the sweet rot of leaves and it's just I think I hear them. I know I don't really hear them."

All of her teeth had gone, she said, by her fourth baby and her chin grew upward around as if to protect the sunken mouth and cheeks. "My man got as clever a turn as you want to see with everything. I got no education at all. We got one book, a hymn book. I know the words and I pointed them out to my son a long time afore he knew I couldn't read a scratch. I was ashamed. I never felt much like larnin' when I come from the mill. My pa was for larnin'. He said, you don't know, you air shut up. My ma couldn't read but she knew more'n any living woman I ever heard tell of. And when pa was kilt in the mill she worked as hard fer her family as cunning and strong you had to be. Born in Catawba County, her pa owned a farm there afore the rebel war. He never owned a slave and was bitter agin it saying the white man and the black man had to stand together, but all his sons was killed in it one way or another and it don't seem fair.

"Funny thing, the men always dyin' early. Hard life and dangerous, in my family the women is left with all the chilluns to raise and by that time you sure ain't in no shape to get another man.

"I remember we had beds of white maple pa made. Then he was one with his hands but hard times done us out of them, we sold them for quite a fancy price I remember. Pa worked in the field and raised a good part of what we et. We drawed ten cents a day in the mill. Ma drawed twenty-five. It were winter time when I begun to work. I recollect we went to work by lantern light and the kerosene lamps swinging away in the ceiling I thought they was some kinds of bugs swinging away there. Then my brother went to the mill, four of us drawing money. Hard times fer us, hard fer me. I got a fever I recollect, takes grit to get a body along. I just got over the typhoid and I went to the boss and I says I'm wuth more'n ten cents a day. I was a shy body, I just didn't think I had nothin' to lose, we couldn't eat with four of us working and he raised me to twenty cents and told me not to tell nobody.

"Do you think I'll meet them all in heaven? Do you believe they will be there now? I remember them all. Sadie, Goldie, Elijah, all of them and some of the dead ones more than the living. Oh, how it goes on and how you live through it! Claire, Kate and the dogs and cats and mules and cows and calves I have fed, always feeding something, day and midnight trying to get something to eat.

"I mourned and always mourn. Here was the pasture land and cows grazing and the green land I remember and crickets and in no time quicker than scat the green pasture was turned over like the palm of my hand and the mills was belching at the tailings and the gray chat begin to drift in all the cracks and the green land was agone forever agone and never coming back in our time."

She arose shyly. White in the gloom, the match struck sharp in her knuckled tree-bark weaver's hands. She held it, shaking a little, to the lamp wick. The light shook, distended like an eye, and the house sprang in the night in the ruined land. I saw the awkward, hunted, lost and wild endurance of her strong odored herb body which I could smell like night herb and I wanted to reach out and touch her but knew her flight. The door hung crooked outward and she went to close it. I saw the darkness, like an eye, through a knot-hole of the bleached skeletal sun-wracked pine—a thin boat in the night on a vacant sea. I saw the frail, sagging iron bed. The broken mirror held the light in a sharp rectangle. She was looking steadily at me, holding me in her silence. I saw a picture of a dead child. A picture of a bride and groom in a round frame, a garland of paper, faded roses about it.

I felt her deep exhaustion and her sorrow, wakened and warmed by unaccustomed talking, like soil stirred, the sorrow of its ruin reflected in her, the human and the land interlocked like doomed lovers.

I felt a kind of anguish as if we rode a Moby Dick of terror—as if a great beast rode under us not of earth but of a ruthless power that we could neither see nor call by name.

Her eyes in ambush look out at me for what I am thinking, gravely watchful. "My son will stay with a friend, if you would not mind to sleep with me."

I lay awake thinking of human waste, of injuries which reflect on the indifference and callousness of us all, of the unrecorded lives of dead children, the million-faceted darkness of their fear and sorrow like my own of being trapped far below ground in American life.

All over mid-America now lamplight reveals the old earth, reveals the story of water, and the sound of water in the darkness repeats the myth and legends of old struggles. The fields lie there, the plow handles wet, standing useless in the mud, the countless seeds, the little houses, the big houses, the vast spider network of us all in the womb of history, looking fearful, not knowing at this moment the strength, doubting the strength, often fearful of giant menace, fearful of peculiar strains and wild boar power and small eyes of the fox.

The lower continent underlying all speaks below us, the gulf, the black old land.

Muriel Rukeyser (1913–1980)

"In subjugated peoples, the poet emerges as prophet," Muriel Rukeyser writes in her essential *The Life of Poetry* (1949). Capacious, protean, radical, visionary, Rukeyser's life and work defy easy categorization. Above all, she was a writer of witness, but a witnessing that pushed beyond the event into the possibilities of human expansiveness achieved through struggle and solidarity. Born into a Jewish family in New York City, she attended Vassar and Columbia, as well as aviation school. Her first book of poems, *The Theory of Flight*, was published in the Yale Younger Poets Series in 1935. Enormously prolific, her books of poetry include *A Turning Wind* (1939), *Beast in View* (1944), *The Great Wave* (1948), *Elegies* (1949), *Body of Waking* (1958), *The Speed of Darkness* (1868), *Breaking Open* (1973), and *The Gates* (1976). Her poetry and life were foundational to a generation of women feminist poets writing in the 1970s and 1980s. Rukeyser also wrote plays and screenplays and translated the work of Octavio Paz. Rukeyser's work combines the artistic prowess of a great poet with a deep sense of political commitment. As a journalist, Rukeyser reported on the trial of the Scottsboro Boys and the 1936 People's Olympiad in Barcelona. She visited Hanoi as an opponent of the American War in Vietnam, fought for the human rights of writers around the world, and traveled with her friend photographer Nancy Naumberg to Gauley Bridge, West Virginia.

The poems that are sequentially excerpted here are selected from Rukeyser's *The Book of the Dead* (1938), part of a larger planned work, *U.S.1.* The story begins in 1929 when Union Carbide wanted to divert a river by excavating a tunnel from Gauley's Junction to Hawk's Nest in Fayette County, West Virginia, for a hydroelectric plant. In excavating the tunnel, the company seized the opportunity to mine pure silica. Instead of utilizing the standard safety techniques of the day, the company forced the workers (including a large number of African Americans) to dig *dry.* As a result, an estimated 476 to 2,000 miners were killed from silicosis, a painful and slow death. The corporate conglomerate set out to conceal the deaths through quick burials, bribed doctors and morticians, and blaming the victims' lifestyles instead of acknowledging the cause of their deaths. This story, first told through the Left press, became a much-publicized national scandal and resulted in congressional hearings. Rukeyser's twenty sequenced poems take the reader down into the actuality of the miners' experience through techniques of montage, collage, and intertextuality, including testimony, oral history, medical reports, portraits of workers, and descriptions of X rays. These poems of witness expose the reader to a site of technological virtuosity inseparable from the brutal disposability of workers' lives.

THE BOOK OF THE DEAD

THE ROAD

These are roads to take when you think of your country
and interested bring down the maps again,
phoning the statistician, asking the dear friend,

reading the papers with morning inquiry.
5   Or when you sit at the wheel and your small light
chooses gas gauge and clock; and the headlights

indicate future of road, your wish pursuing
past the junction, the fork, the suburban station,
well-travelled six-lane highway planned for safety.

10   Past your tall central city's influence,
outside its body: traffic, penumbral crowds,
are centers removed and strong, fighting for good reason.

These roads will take you into your own country.
Select the mountains, follow rivers back,
15   travel the passes. Touch West Virginia where

the Midland Trail leaves the Virginia furnace,
iron Clifton Forge, Covington iron, goes down
into the wealthy valley, resorts, the chalk hotel.

Pillars and fairway; spa; White Sulphur Springs.
20   Airport. Gay blank rich faces wishing to add
history to ballrooms, tradition to the first tee.

The simple mountains, sheer, dark-graded with pine
in the sudden weather, wet outbreak of spring,
crosscut by snow, wind at the hill's shoulder.

25 The land is fierce here, steep, braced against snow,
rivers and spring. KING COAL HOTEL, Lookout,
and swinging the vicious bend, New River Gorge.

Now the photographer unpacks camera and case,
surveying the deep country, follows discovery
30 viewing on groundglass an inverted image.

John Marshall named the rock (steep pines, a drop
he reckoned in 1812, called) Marshall's Pillar,
but later, Hawk's Nest. Here is your road, tying

you to its meanings: gorge, boulder, precipice.
35 Telescoped down, the hard and stone-green river
cutting fast and direct into the town.

GAULEY BRIDGE

Camera at the crossing sees the city
a street of wooden walls and empty windows,
the doors shut handless in the empty street,
and the deserted Negro standing on the corner.

5   The little boy runs with his dog
up the street to the bridge over the river where
nine men are mending road for the government.
He blurs the camera-glass fixed on the street.

Railway tracks here and many panes of glass
10 tin under light, the grey shine of towns and forests:
in the commercial hotel (Switzerland of America)
the owner is keeping his books behind the public glass.

Postoffice window, a hive of private boxes,
the hand of the man who withdraws, the woman who reaches her hand
15 and the tall coughing man stamping an envelope.

The bus station and the great pale buses stopping for food;
April-glass-tinted, the yellow-aproned waitress;
coast-to-coast schedule on the plateglass window.

The man on the street and the camera eye:
20 he leaves the doctor's office, slammed door, doom,
any town looks like this one-street town.

Glass, wood, and naked eye: the movie-house
closed for the afternoon frames posters streaked with rain,
advertise "Racing Luck" and "Hitch-Hike Lady."

25 Whistling, the train comes from a long way away,
slow, and the Negro watches it grow in the grey air,
the hotel man makes a note behind his potted palm.

Eyes of the tourist house, red-and-white filling station,
the eyes of the Negro, looking down the track,
30 hotel-man and hotel, cafeteria, camera.

And in the beerplace on the other sidewalk
always one's harsh night eyes over the beerglass
follow the waitress and the yellow apron.

The road flows over the bridge,
35   Gamoca pointer at the underpass,
opposite, Alloy, after a block of town.

What do you want—a cliff over a city?
A foreland, sloped to sea and overgrown with roses?
These people live here.

PRAISE OF THE COMMITTEE

These are the lines on which a committee is formed.
    Almost as soon as work was begun in the tunnel
    men began to die among dry drills. No masks.
    Most of them were not from this valley.
5   The freights brought many every day from States
    all up and down the Atlantic seaboard
    and as far inland as Kentucky, Ohio.
    After the work the camps were closed or burned.
    The ambulance was going day and night,
10   White's undertaking business thriving and
    his mother's cornfield put to a new use.
    "Many of the shareholders at this meeting
    "were nervous about the division of the profits;
    "How much has the Company spent on lawsuits?
15   "The man said $150,000. Special counsel:
    "I am familiar with the case. Not : one : cent.
    " 'Terms of the contract. Master liable.'
    "No reply. Great corporation disowning men who made. . . ."
    After the lawsuits had been instituted. . . .
20   *The Committee is a true reflection of the will of the people.*
    Every man is ill. The women are not affected,
    This is not a contagious disease. A medical commission,
    Dr. Hughes, Dr. Hayhurst examined the chest
    of Raymond Johnson, and Dr. Harless, a former
25   company doctor. But he saw too many die,
    he has written his letter to Washington.
    The Committee meets regularly, wherever it can.
    Here are Mrs. Jones, three lost sons, husband sick,
    Mrs. Leek, cook for the bus cafeteria,
30   the men: George Robinson, leader and voice,
    four other Negroes (three drills, one camp-boy)
    Blankenship, the thin friendly man, Peyton the engineer,
    Juanita absent, the one outsider member.
    Here in the noise, loud belts of the shoe-repair shop,
35   meeting around the stove beneath the one bulb hanging.
    They come late in the day. Many come with them
    who pack the hall, wait in the thorough dark.

This is a defense committee. Unfinished business:
Two rounds of lawsuits, 200 cases

40   Now as to the crooked lawyers
If the men had worn masks, their use would have involved
time every hour to wash the sponge at mouth.
Tunnel, 3^1/$_8$ miles long. Much larger than
the Holland Tunnel or Pittsburgh's Liberty Tubes.

45   Total cost, say, $16,000,000.
This is the procedure of such a committee:
To consider the bill before the Senate.
To discuss relief.
                Active members may be cut off relief,

50   16-mile walk to Fayetteville for cheque—
                WEST VIRGINIA RELIEF ADMINISTRATION, #22991,
                TO JOE HENIGAN, GAULEY BRIDGE, ONE AND 50/100,
                WINONA NATIONAL BANK. PAID FROM STATE FUNDS.
Unless the Defense Committee acts;

55   the *People's Press*, supporting this fight,
signed editorials, sent in funds.
Clothing for tunnel-workers.
                Rumored, that in the post-office
                parcels are intercepted.

60   Suspected: Conley. Sheriff, hotelman,
                head of the town ring—
                Company whispers. Spies,
                The Racket.
Resolved, resolved.

65   George Robinson holds all their strength together:
To fight the companies   to make somehow a future.
"At any rate, it is inadvisable to keep a community of dying
                persons intact."
"Senator Holt. Yes. This is the most barbarous example of

70   industrial construction that ever happened in the world."
Please proceed.
"In a very general way Hippocrates' *Epidemics* speaks
of the metal digger who breathes with difficulty,
having a pale and wan complexion.

75   Pliny, the elder. . . ."
"Present work of the Bureau of Mines. . . ."

The dam's pure crystal slants upon the river.
                A dark and noisy room, frozen two feet from stove.
                The cough of habit. The sound of men in the hall

80   waiting for word.

                These men breathe hard
                but the committee has a voice of steel.
                One climbs the hill on canes.
                They have broken the hills and cracked the riches wide.

85   In this man's face
                family leans out from two worlds of graves—

here is a room of eyes,
a single force looks out, reading out life.

Who stands over the river?
90   Whose feet go running in these rigid hills?
Who comes, warning the night,
shouting and young to waken our eyes?

Who runs through electric wires?
Who speaks down every road?
95   Their hands touched mastery; now they
demand an answer.

ABSALOM

I first discovered what was killing these men.
I had three sons who worked with their father in the tunnel:
Cecil, aged 23, Owen, aged 21, Shirley, aged 17.
They used to work in a coal mine, not steady work
5   for the mines were not going much of the time.
A power Co. foreman learned that we made home brew,
he formed a habit of dropping in evenings to drink,
persuading the boys and my husband—
give up their jobs and take this other work.
10   It would pay them better.
Shirley was my youngest son; the boy.
He went into the tunnel.

My heart   my mother   my heart   my mother
My heart   my coming into being.

15   My husband is not able to work.
He has it, according to the doctor.
We have been having a very hard time making a living since
    this trouble came to us.
I saw the dust in the bottom of the tub.
20   The boy worked there about eighteen months,
came home one evening with a shortness of breath.
He said, "Mother, I cannot get my breath."
Shirley was sick about three months.
I would carry him from his bed to the table,
25   from his bed to the porch, in my arms.

My heart is mine in the place of hearts,
They gave me back my heart, it lies in me.

When they took sick, right at the start, I saw a doctor.
I tried to get Dr. Harless to X-ray the boys.
30   He was the only man I had any confidence in,
the company doctor in the Kopper's mine,
but he would not see Shirley.
He did not know where his money was coming from.
I promised him half if he'd work to get compensation,
35   but even then he would not do anything.

I went on the road and begged the X-ray money,
the Charleston hospital made the lung pictures,
he took the case after the pictures were made.
And two or three doctors said the same thing.
40   The youngest boy did not get to go down there with me,
he lay and said, "Mother, when I die,
"I want you to have them open me up and
"see if that dust killed me.
"Try to get compensation,
45   "You will not have any way of making your living
"when we are gone,
"and the rest are going too."

     I have gained mastery over my heart
     I have gained mastery over my two hands
50   *I have gained mastery over the waters*
     I have gained mastery over the river.

The case of my son was the first of the line of lawsuits.
They sent the lawyers down and the doctors down;
they closed the electric sockets in the camps.
55   There was Shirley, and Cecil, Jeffrey and Oren,
Raymond Johnson, Clev and Oscar Anders,
Frank Lynch, Henry Palf, Mr. Pitch, a foreman;
a slim fellow who carried steel with my boys,
his name was Darnell, I believe. There were many others,
60   the towns of Glen Ferris, Alloy, where the white rock lies,
six miles away; Vanetta, Gauley Bridge,
Gamoca, Lockwood, the gullies,
the whole valley is witness.
I hitchhike eighteen miles, they make checks out.
65   They asked me how I keep the cow on $2.
I said one week, feed for the cow, one week, the children's flour.
The oldest son was twenty-three.
The next son was twenty-one.
The youngest son was eighteen.
70   They called it pneumonia at first.
They would pronounce it fever.
Shirley asked that we try to find out.
That's how they learned what the trouble was.

     I open out a way, they have covered my sky with crystal
75   *I come forth by day, I am born a second time,*
     I force a way through, and I know the gate
     I shall journey over the earth among the living.

He shall not be diminished, never;
I shall give a mouth to my son.

THE DISEASE

This is a lung disease. Silicate dust makes it.
The dust causing the growth of

This is the X-ray picture taken last April.
I would point out to you: these are the ribs;
5   this is the region of the breastbone;
this is the heart (a wide white shadow filled with blood).
In here of course is the swallowing tube, esophagus.
The windpipe. Spaces between the lungs.

Between the ribs?

10   Between the ribs. These are the collar bones.
Now, this lung's mottled, beginning, in these areas.
You'd say a snowstorm had struck the fellow's lungs.
About alike, that side and this side, top and bottom.
The first stage in this period in this case.

15   Let us have the second.

Come to the window again. Here is the heart.
More numerous nodules, thicker, see, in the upper lobes.
You will notice the increase : here, streaked fibrous tissue—

Indicating?

20   That indicates the progress in ten months' time.
And now, this year—short breathing, solid scars
even over the ribs, thick on both sides.
Blood vessels shut. Model conglomeration.

What stage?

25   Third stage. Each time I place my pencil point:
There and there and there, there, there.

"It is growing worse every day. At night
"I get up to catch my breath. If I remained
"flat on my back I believe I would die."
30   It gradually chokes off the air cells in the lungs?
I am trying to say it the best I can.
That is what happens, isn't it?
A choking-off in the air cells?

Yes.
35   There is difficulty in breathing.
Yes.
And a painful cough?
Yes.

Does silicosis cause death?

40   Yes, sir.

GEORGE ROBINSON: BLUES

Gauley Bridge is a good town for Negroes, they let us stand
    around, they let us stand
around on the sidewalks if we're black or brown.
Vanetta's over the trestle, and that's our town.

5 The hill makes breathing slow, slow breathing after you row the river,
   and the graveyard's on the hill, cold in the springtime blow,
   the graveyard's up on high, and the town is down below.

   Did you ever bury thirty-five men in a place in back of your house,
   thirty-five tunnel workers the doctors didn't attend,
10 died in the tunnel camps, under rocks, everywhere, world
     without end.

   When a man said I feel poorly, for any reason, any weakness or such,
   letting up when he couldn't keep going barely,
   the Cap and company come and run him off the job surely.

15 I've put them
   DOWN from the tunnel camps
   to the graveyard on the hill,
   tin-cans all about—it fixed them!—
   TUNNELITIS
20 hold themselves up
   at the side of a tree,
   I can go right now
   to that cemetery.

   When the blast went off the boss would call out, Come, let's go back,
25 when that heavy loaded blast went white, Come, let's go back,
   telling us hurry, hurry, into the falling rocks and muck.

   The water they would bring had dust in it, our drinking water;
   the camps and their groves were colored with the dust,
   we cleaned our clothes in the groves, but we always had the dust.
30 Looked like somebody sprinkled flour all over the parks and groves,
   it stayed and the rain couldn't wash it away and it twinkled
   that white dust really looked pretty down around our ankles.

   As dark as I am, when I came out at morning after the tunnel at night,
   with a white man, nobody could have told which man was white.
35 The dust had covered us both, and the dust was white.

THE BOOK OF THE DEAD

   These roads will take you into your own country.
   Seasons and maps coming where this road comes
   into a landscape mirrored in these men.

   Past all your influences, your home river,
5 constellations of cities, mottoes of childhood,
   parents and easy cures, war, all evasion's wishes.

   What one word must never be said?
   Dead, and these men fight off our dying,
   cough in the theatres of the war.

10 What two things shall never be seen?
   They : what we did. Enemy : what we mean.
   This is a nation's scene and halfway house.

What three things can never be done?
Forget.   Keep silent.   Stand alone.
15   The hills of glass, the fatal brilliant plain.

The facts of war forced into actual grace.
Seasons and modern glory.   Told in the histories,
    how first ships came

seeing on the Atlantic thirteen clouds
20   lining the west horizon with their white
    shining halations;

they conquered, throwing off impossible Europe—
could not be used to transform; created coast—
    breathed-in America.

25   See how they took the land, made after-life
fresh out of exile, planted the pioneer
    base and blockade,

pushed forests down in an implacable walk
west where new clouds lay at the desirable
30   body of sunset;

taking the seaboard. Replaced the isolation,
dropped cities where they stood, drew a tidewater
    frontier of Europe,

a moment, and another frontier held,
35   this land was planted home-land that we know.
    Ridge of discovery,

until we walk to windows, seeing America
lie in a photograph of power, widened
    before our forehead,

40   and still behind us falls another glory,
London unshaken, the long French road to Spain,
    the old Mediterranean

flashing new signals from the hero hills
near Barcelona, monuments and powers,
45   parent defenses.

Before our face the broad and concrete west,
green ripened field, frontier pushed back like river
    controlled and dammed;

the flashing wheatfields, cities, lunar plains
50   grey in Nevada, the sane fantastic country
    sharp in the south,

liveoak, the hanging moss, a world of desert,
the dead, the lava, and the extreme arisen
    fountains of life,

55   the flourished land, peopled with watercourses
to California and the colored sea;
     sums of frontiers

and unmade boundaries of acts and poems,
the brilliant scene between the seas, and standing,
60   this fact and this disease.

Half-memories absorb us, and our ritual world
carries its history in familiar eyes,
planted in flesh it signifies its music

in minds which turn to sleep and memory,
65   in music knowing all the shimmering names,
the spear, the castle, and the rose.

But planted in our flesh these valleys stand,
everywhere we begin to know the illness,
are forced up, and our times confirm us all.

70   In the museum life, centuries of ambition
yielded at last a fertilizing image:
the Carthaginian stone meaning a tall woman

carries in her two hands the book and cradled dove,
on her two thighs, wings folded from the waist
75   cross to her feet, a pointed human crown.

This valley is given to us like a glory.
To friends in the old world, and their lifting hands
that call for intercession. Blow falling full in face.

All those whose childhood made learn skill to meet,
80   and art to see after the change of heart;
all the belligerents who know the world.

You standing over gorges, surveyors and planners,
you workers and hope of countries, first among powers;
you who give peace and bodily repose,

85   opening landscapes by grace, giving the marvel lowlands
physical peace, flooding old battlefields
with general brilliance, who best love your lives;

and you young, you who finishing the poem
wish new perfection and begin to make;
90   you men of fact, measure our times again.

These are our strength, who strike against history.
These who corrupt cells owe their new styles of weakness
   to our diseases;

these carrying light for safety on their foreheads
95 descended deeper for richer faults of ore,
    drilling their death.

These touching radium and the luminous poison,
carried their death on their lips and with their warning
    glow in their graves.

100 These weave and their eyes water and rust away,
these stand at wheels until their brains corrode,
    these farm and starve,

all these men cry their doom across the world,
meeting avoidable death, fight against madness,
105   find every war.

Are known as strikers, soldiers, pioneers,
fight on all new frontiers, are set in solid
    lines of defense.

Defense is sight; widen the lens and see
110 standing over the land myths of identity,
    new signals, processes:

Alloys begin : certain dominant metals.
Deliberate combines add new qualities,
    sums of new uses.

115 Over the country, from islands of Maine fading,
Cape Sable fading south into the orange
    detail of sunset,

new processes, new signals, new possession.
A name for all the conquests, prediction of victory
120   deep in these powers.

Carry abroad the urgent need, the scene,
to photograph and to extend the voice,
    to speak this meaning.

Voices to speak to us directly. As we move.
125 As we enrich, growing in larger motion,
    this word, this power.

Down coasts of taken countries, mastery,
discovery at one hand, and at the other
    frontiers and forests,

130 fanatic cruel legend at our back and
speeding ahead the red and open west,
    and this our region,

desire, field, beginning. Name and road,
communication to these many men,
135 as epilogue, seeds of unending love.

Joseph Kalar (1906–1972)

Joseph Kalar (pronounced to rhyme with "tailor") was born April 4, 1906, in Merritt, Minnesota, the second son to poor Slovenian immigrants—his father an iron miner and his mother a barmaid in the local saloon. When Kalar was eight, his father moved the family to International Falls and took a job in the local paper mill. The remote location and months of being cooped up by the cold made young Joe into an avid reader at the local library. After graduating from the Bemidji Teachers College with honors, he went to work at a school in Wayland but disliked teaching. He returned to International Falls in 1926 and took a job in the paper mill. Soon Kalar's interest in labor activism and literature began to grow together. In little over a year, he was publishing in the most prominent communist literary magazines of the era: *New Masses, Anvil, International Literature, The Front,* and *The Morada.*

Despite this early success, Kalar never published a book of poems during his lifetime. His relative obscurity is not, however, the result of the quality of his work. Instead, it was an obscurity he *chose*; he chose to publish only in socialist and labor magazines; for reasons of self-doubt and overwork, he chose never to gather his poems into a collection; and, when he was not yet thirty years old, he became disenchanted by the meager effect of his poems and chose to quit writing permanently. Kalar died unknown in 1972. Ten years after his death, his poems, prose, and selected letters were gathered by his son in a privately printed edition, and in 2005, a selection of his best work was finally published by the University of Illinois Press as *Papermill: Poems 1927–1935,* edited by Ted Genoways. Kalar's unique perspective and unusual poetic skill have sparked this revival of interest in his work. Unlike many of his poet-activist contemporaries, Kalar wrote about social injustices that he witnessed firsthand as a worker in the isolated mills along Minnesota's border with Canada and, as such, his work has greater and more enduring value than he himself ever imagined.

Ted Genoways

NIGHT-SHIFT

Sleep aches in the eyes; taste of ashes
dryly sands the mouth, while lips are cracked
with mouthing gobs of stale brown plug;
hours have no periods, no precision, they
5   are merely hours, stretching into dawn
like a haze of fog greyly lifting over lumber
to warm compulsion of the sun; they are merely
the aching cry of the body for sleep, sleep,
sweet, sweet Jesus, sleep, sleep, the far cry
10 of drowsy tired blood: sleep, sleep, sleep.

Into the night, body a hunch against darkness,
jostling and bouncing on a wagon rigid
with stiffness, permitting no dreams of cotton,

creaking, groaning, a clot of shadow urgently
15　propelled down dark canyons of lumber, poking
fragrant load of pine between rows of piles
darkly reminiscent of western canyons of stone,
thoughts swarm drowsily behind the eyes of this man
who stares vacantly at the giant swell and roll
20　of horse buttocks dark and heaving before him,
thinking no more while muscles bulge terribly
like pistons moving smoothly under hide,
and the body is only a remembered cry for sleep.

In the morning when dawn has crept over the sky,
25　lips are a thin line not curving into the glow
of a smile, eyes are a lesson in brooding and vision,
and hands clutching at leather reins are ominous
with significance; though sleep is a phlegm of weariness
clothing his mind, hate is knowledge incandescent
30　bright illumination for a mind busy with planning,
and hands are rich with promise of a tomorrow
in which dreams will sprout beautifully into action,
and throats harsh with cursing will shout terribly
the words that will give meaning to hours,
35　precision to time, significance to bodies
now but a far painful cry in blood for sleep.

PROLETARIAN NIGHT

Now that work is done, the whistle blows,
its scream harsh as laughter out of steel,
piercing through the fat, pushing aside
the fur, the sleep, the dream,
5　finding each sad little cringing nerve
twitching in its cell of tired flesh,
while from the stack and the round mouths
of black dripping pipes, smoke puffs,
puffs, and sound dies, and giant wheels
10　cease their grinding, and pistons find rest
in the slimy clutch of oil and grease.
Now that work is done, the mill no longer
with a drone grinds gold out of flesh,
but with the night and its quiet dark
15　and sleep that presses on the eyes,
the tumult and the drive persist, and we find
remembrance in each nerve and bone and cell
of the grating sharp insistence of each wheel,
the slap of belts, tumultuous din of steel,
20　the insolent commands, the curses and the sneers
(with humility such a poor veil to hide
the hate that flames electric into the eyes);

> though the body cries for rest, writhing
> with aching flesh throughout the night,
> 25 and sleep descends with its blind crazy dreams,
> stuffing the mind with rags that dull,
> conviction, still inviolate, remains,
> that will not hail victory in,
> remove the steel thumbs of the mill
> 30 that gouge into the temples (here and here),
> return one beam of lost forgotten day,
> or drive one foe into the avenging street.

PAPERMILL

> Not to be believed, this blunt savage wind
> Blowing in chill empty rooms, this tornado
> Surging and bellying across the oily floor
> Pushing men out in streams before it;
> 5 Not to be believed, this dry fall
> Of unseen fog drying the oil
> And emptying the jiggling greasecups;
> Not to be believed, this unseen hand
> Weaving a filmy rust of spiderwebs
> 10 Over these turbines and grinding gears,
> These snarling chippers and pounding jordans;
> These fingers placed to lips saying shshsh:
> Keep silent, keep silent, keep silent;
> Not to be believed hardly, this clammy silence
> 15 Where once feet stamped over the oily floor,
> Dinnerpails clattered, voices rose and fell
> In laughter, curses, and songs. Now the guts
> Of this mill have ceased and red changes to black,
> Steam is cold water, silence is rust, and quiet
> 20 Spells hunger. Look at these men, now,
> Standing before the iron gates, mumbling,
> "Who could believe it? Who could believe it?"

WORKER UPROOTED

> The slow sleepy curl of cigarette smoke and butts
> glowing redly out of moving smiling mouths;
> now a whisper in the house, laughter muted,
> and warm words spoken no more to me.
> 5 Alien, I move forlorn among curses,
> laughing falsely, joking with tears
> aching at my eyes, now surely alien and lonely.
> Once I rubbed shoulders with sweating men,
> pulled when they pulled, strained, cursed,

10 comrade in their laughter,
 comrade in their pain,
 knowing fellowship of sudden smiles
 and the press of hands in silent speech.
 At noon hour, sprawled in the shade,
15 opening our lunches, chewing our sandwiches,
 laughing and spitting,
 we talked of the days and found joy
 in our anger, balm in our common contempt;
 thought of lumber falling with thump of lead
20 on piles geometrically exact; of horses
 sweating, puffing, bulging their muscles;
 of wagons creaking; of sawdust
 pouring from the guts of the mill.
 Now alien, I move forlorn, an uprooted tree,
25 feel the pain of hostile eyes
 lighting up no more for me;
 the forced silence, the awkward laugh,
 comrade no more in laughter and pain.

 And at dawn, irresolutely,
30 into the void . . .

Now that Snow Is Falling

 O the sky shall crack with laughter
 now that snow is falling,
 and all small timid things shall scent
 frozen petals of white and feel
5 knifeblades of cold sink into fur;
 yes, the bear shall suck his toes,
 and ants will sleep.
 If the sun, coming slowly after,
 warms flies and from frozen lethargy
10 to crawl again upon window panes,
 and you and I, hand in hand,
 shall make tracks in the snow,
 woolen gloves, and necks bound warmly
 against knifeblades of cold, and we
15 shall say: O most surely is the snow
 beautiful, and ask, what can we say
 now that snow is falling, and all
 the world is white, and clean, and beautiful,
 what can we say but that snow is beautiful
20 and snow tingles the sleepy blood
 into new surging awareness—what can
 we say if the sky is most suddenly rent
 with laughter, trees crack with mirth,
 and sparrows chatter in derision, as

25   a man walks by us clad thinly, shivering,
      hungry, vainly searching for bread,
      a job, and warm fires; what can we say,
      if such a man passes us bowed against
      the wind, and another, and yet more,
30   until he is as a multitude, a sad parade
      of hungry, cold, vague faces? What can we
      say, now that snow is falling?

Kenneth Patchen (1911–1972)

"I am the world-crier, and this is my dangerous career. . . . I am the one to call your bluff, and this is my climate," writes Kenneth Patchen. And few would doubt the maverick and engaged stance of his bold art in some thirty-six books of poetry and experimental fiction, as well as his recordings, picture-poems, and painted books experiments.

Born into the industrial Mahoning River Valley of Ohio, the son of a mill-worker, Patchen found a tradition of caring for the downtrodden in his father's unionist support and his mother's compassionate Catholicism. He witnessed firsthand the hardships of working-class families, the death of two sisters, and the quiet resignation of so many, and he gained the sense of outrage at the oppression of one class by another voiced in "The Orange Bears." The crash of the Great Depression sent him to work alongside his father and older brother in the steel mills. The Niles-Warren-Youngstown area had already born the violence and scars of betrayal from the Little Steel Strike of 1917, and Patchen's boyhood awareness now grew into a conscious identification with victims and a defiance at their plight. A year at the experimental college of Alexander Meikeljohn at the University of Wisconsin led to another at the Commonwealth Labor College in Arkansas, where he trained in labor history and organizing. This was followed by two years of "on the road" experience in which he embraced a lower-case socialism and began sending poems to small radical journals like Jack Conroy's *Rebel Poet*, which published his "Lenin" in 1932.

Settling for a time in New York's Greenwich Village, Patchen saw his tribute to a legendary figure of resistance, "Joe Hill Listens to the Praying" (1934), appear in Mike Gold's *New Masses*. By 1936, Random House published his *Before the Brave*, championing Patchen as their "American proletarian poet." This book was followed in 1939 by *First Will and Testament*, an early publication by James Laughlin's New Directions Publishing. Though Patchen would publish *Cloth of the Tempest* with Harper in 1943, the rest of his more than thirty-three books would all be published by independent presses, chiefly New Directions and Padell.

The 1950s found Patchen on the West Coast, where his art blossomed into the visual arts, poetry-jazz experiments, and a fuller thematic embracing of wonder in the world. During the 1960s and 1970s, his final bed-ridden years from a back injury, he continued to produce the daring and beautiful picture-poems that are seen in *What Shall We Do Without Us?* (1984). Patchen's work and life example remain a model of the engaged poet-artist in America.

Larry Smith

JOE HILL LISTENS TO THE PRAYING

Look at the steady rifles, Joe.
It's all over now—"Murder, first degree,"
The jury said. It's too late now
To go back. Listen Joe, the chaplain is reading:

5   *Lord Jesus Christ who didst*
So mercifully promise heaven
To the thief that humbly confessed
His injustice
                throw back your head

10   Joe; remember that song of yours
We used to sing in jails all over
These United States—tell it to him:
"I'll introduce to you
A man that is a credit to our Red, White
15   and Blue,
His head is made of lumber and solid as
a rock;
He is a Christian Father and his name is
Mr. Block."
20   Remember, Joe—
"You take the cake,
You make me ache,
Tie a rock on your block and jump
in the lake,
25   Kindly do that for Liberty's sake."

Behold me, I beseech Thee, with
The same eyes of mercy that
                        on the other
Hand we're driftin' into Jungles
30   From Kansas to the coast, wrapped
            round brake beams on a thousand
            freights; San Joaquin and Omaha
            brush under the wheels—"God made the summer
            for the hobo and the bummer"—we've been
35   everywhere, seen everything.
Winning the West for the good citizens;
Driving golden spikes into the U. P.;
Harvest hands, lumbermen drifting—
            now Iowa, now Oregon—
40   God, how clean the sky; the lovely wine
Of coffee in a can. This land
            is our lover. How greenly beautiful
Her hair; her great pure breasts
            that are
45   The Rockies on a day of mist and rain.

We love this land of corn and cotton,
            Virginia and Ohio, sleeping on
With our love, with our love—

O burst of Alabama loveliness, sleeping on
50 In the strength of our love; O Mississippi flowing
Through our nights, a giant mother.

Pardon, and in the end
                          How green is her hair,
              how pure are her breasts; the little farms
55   nuzzling into her flanks
              drawing forth life, big rich life
Under the deep chant of her skies
And rivers—but we, we're driftin'
Into trouble from Kansas to the coast, clapped
60   into the stink and rot of country jails
              and clubbed by dicks and cops
Because we didn't give a damn—
                                          remember Joe
How little we cared, how we sang
65   the nights away in their filthy jails;
              and how, when
We got wind of a guy called Marx
              we sang less, just talked
And talked. "Blanket-stiffs" we were
70 But we could talk, they couldn't jail us
For that—but they did—
        remember Joe

Of my life be strengthened
                          One Big Union:
75   our convention in Chi; the Red Cards,
              leaflets; sleeping in the parks,
              the Boul' Mich; "wobblies" now, cheering
              the guys that spoke our lingo, singing
              down the others. "Hear that train blow,
80 Boys, hear that train blow."

Now confessing my crimes, I may obtain
Millions of stars, Joe—millions of miles.
              Remember Vincent St. John
In the Goldfield strike; the timid little squirt
85   with the funny voice, getting onto the platform
              and slinging words at us that rolled
              down our chins and into our hearts,
              like boulders hell-bent down a mountain side.
And Orchard, angel of peace
90   —with a stick of dynamite in either hand.
              Pettibone and Moyer: "The strike
Is your weapon, to hell with politics."
              Big Bill—remember him—
At Boise—great red eye rolling like a lame bull
95   through the furniture and men
              of the courtroom—"This bastard,
His Honor."

Hobo Convention:
(Millions of stars, Joe—millions of miles.)
100   "Hallelujah, I'm a bum,
Hallelujah, I'm a bum." His Honor,
    the sonofabitch!
One Big Strike, Lawrence, Mass—
    23,000 strong, from every neck
105   of every woods in America, 23,000,
Joe, remember. "We don't need
    a leader. We'll fix things up
    among ourselves."
"Blackie" Ford and "Double-nose" Suhr in
110   Wheatland—"I. W. W.'s don't destroy
    property"—and they got life. "I've counted
The stars, boys, counted a million of these prison bars."

San Diego, soap boxes,
Hundreds of them! And always
115   their jail shutting out the sky,
    the clean rhythm of the wheels
    on a fast freight; disinfectant getting
    into the lung-pits, spitting blood
But singing—Christ, how we sang,
120   remember the singing
Joe, One Big Union,
       One Big

hope to be
With Thee
125 What do they matter, Joe, these rifles.
They can't reach the towns, the skies, the songs,
    that now are part of more
    than any of us—we were
The homeless, the drifters, but, our songs
130   had hair and blood on them.
There are no soap boxes in the sky.
We won't eat pie, now, or ever
    when we die,
        but Joe
135 We had something they didn't have:
    our love for these States
    was real and deep;
                 to be with Thee
In heaven. Amen.
140   (How steady are
the rifles.) We had slept
    naked on this earth on the coldest nights
    listening to the words of a guy named Marx.
Let them burn us, hang us, shoot us,
145   Joe Hill,
For at the last we had what it takes
    to make songs with.

THE ORANGE BEARS

The orange bears with soft friendly eyes
Who played with me when I was ten,
Christ, before I'd left home they'd had
Their paws smashed in the rolls, their backs
5   Seared by hot slag, their soft trusting
Bellies kicked in, their tongues ripped
Out, and I went down through the woods
To the smelly crick with Whitman
In the Haldeman-Julius edition,
10   And I just sat there worrying my thumbnail
Into the cover—What did he know about
Orange bears with their coats all stunk up with soft coal
And the National Guard coming over
From Wheeling to stand in front of the millgates
15   With drawn bayonets jeering at the strikers?

I remember you would put daisies
On the windowsill at night and in
The morning they'd be so covered with soot
You couldn't tell what they were anymore.

20   A hell of a fat chance my orange bears had!

Jack Conroy (1898–1990)

Jack Conroy was born and raised near Moberly, Missouri, in the "Monkey Nest" coal camp, which provided the setting for the first section of his autobiographical novel, *The Disinherited* (1933, excerpted here). His father, a formally educated Irishman, had immigrated to Canada in the 1880s. Failing to find work as a schoolteacher, he traveled to Missouri and a took job underground in the Eagle Mine, where he was killed in an accident when Jack was ten. The young Jack was an avid reader of everything from *Deadwood Dick* to Dickens to his father's union journals. Although his older brothers had to enter the mines, their mother arranged an apprenticeship for Jack at age thirteen in the Wabash Railroad shops, where he could learn a trade and continue his education in evening school. Conroy attended the University of Missouri–Columbia for one semester but was obliged to drop out because he refused to join the ROTC.

Increasingly radicalized during World War I and the Red Scare that followed, Conroy supported the nationwide railroad strike of 1922 and, as a result, lost his job in the Wabash shops. This began a period of traveling for work, to a steel mill in Des Moines, a rubber factory in Hannibal, and auto plants in Detroit and Toledo. Here he gathered much of the material—the workers' stories and their varied voices—for the writing he did during the short "proletarian nights" between the days of work. By 1929, Conroy joined the Rebel Poets, a group of writers connected to the Industrial Workers of the World, and was soon editing a journal of the same name. He also published several of his working-class sketches in the

American Mercury, where he had the support and encouragement of the far-from-radical editor, H. L. Mencken, who admired Conroy's direct first-person narratives: "What is the Depression really like? Read Jack Conroy's 'Hard Winter,' " Mencken advised his readers. "Hard Winter" was one of many sketches that Conroy wove into the text of *The Disinherited*, completed in 1932 but not issued until 1933, having been turned down by twelve publishers who feared that a realistic novel of the Great Depression, told in a worker's voice, would not sell. In a sense, they were correct: despite reviews that praised its authenticity and freedom from propaganda, the book sold only three thousand copies. It was not until its reprinting in the 1960s, and again in 1982, that Conroy's novel began to earn its place as an indispensable account of the early 1930s, a bold and original work of literature.

As editor of *The Anvil* (1933–1936), a midwestern radical alternative to New York's communist-affiliated *New Masses*, Conroy published and encouraged many fellow worker-writers, including Sanora Babb, Joseph Kalar, and Richard Wright. He was also the author of the novel, *A World to Win* (1935), and with Harlem Renaissance writer Arna Bontemps, of *They Seek a City* (1945). The collection *The Weed King and Other Stories* was published in 1985.

MONKEY NEST CAMP
FROM THE *DISINHERITED*

The Monkey Nest coal mine tipple stood twenty years; its dirt dump grew from a diminutive hillock among the scrub oaks to the height of a young mountain. Stubborn shrubs, wiry grasses, and persistent dewberries struggled for a roothold on it, but the leprous soapstone resists all vegetable growth, even in decay. Cold and white like the belly of some deep-sea monster incongruously cast out of the depths, the dump dominated Monkey Nest camp like an Old World cathedral towering over peasants' huts. To begin with, Mr. Stacpoole, the owner, had christened the mine the Eagle, but the miners had decided otherwise. Somebody had dubbed it the Monkey Nest, and so it remained—so it is yet in the memory of those who recall it or its history.

I first saw the Monkey Nest shaft when it was only head high to Old Man Vaughan. Father led me to the brink and I peered over fearsomely, clinging to his legs. Old Vaughan caught me under the armpits and swung me down; then he threatened to keep me there indefinitely, but I knew better. I was used to the miners' joshing. Three taciturn Italians were slicing the tough white clay with keen tile spades and throwing it clear of the edge, grunting "hah!" at each spadeful. Mike Riordan, the peg-leg sailor, was in the pit, and so was Lionel Stafford. Stafford was ruefully peeling blisters off his white hands. He said something to Mike about the iniquity of a world which forced a man with a bachelor's degree to toil at such arduous and menial labor. Mike couldn't spade with his peg, and if he bore down too hard on it, it sank into the earth. So he shoveled the crumbs from the Italians' and Stafford's spades. He pinched me playfully, and then gazed nonchalantly in another quarter.

"Looky here, Larry," said Vaughan. "A dad-blamed crawdad's hole and a crawpappy hisself at the bottom of it. I've follered that scoundrel from the grassroots and here's the bottom o' his hole finally. You know, when I've been diggin' a ditch or somethin', lots o' times I strike a crawdad's hole, and wonder just how far it runs in the ground. But I never *did* see the *bottom* o' one before, did you?"

The crawfish, a small lobster-like creature, angered and bewildered at this rude violation of his retreat, waved furious and menacing pincers. Vaughan was delighted, having realized a long-cherished ambition; and I was tickled, too, because I had often wondered just how far a crawfish burrowed into the soil. I have felt that thrill of accomplishment only a few times since.

The shaft bored past the clay, past the blue hardpan, blasted through the rock and into the coal. The Monkey Nest's tipple rose; its hoisting engine vibrated the heaps of slag and soapstone, oftentimes starting miniature avalanches down the dump. Cages shot up and down the shaft like office-building elevators. A mine tipple is like a gallows, especially if you chance to see its black timbers etched against a setting sun; and the cage dangles from the cathead like a hangman's rope. I have thought whimsically when a miner's head has appeared out of the shaft, apparently supported by the cable only, that his tongue should protrude and his legs kick spasmodically.

My brother Dan went to work in the mine when he was only twelve. There were nine children at home, and Father had more than he could do to feed us. It was against the law for a boy under sixteen to work in the pit unless he was with his father. But even with his father, the boy miner's cheeks blanch just the same; his shoulders stoop, apparently trying to fold in front of him like an angel's wings; and the hollow asthmatic cough begins before he is twenty—if he dodges rocks that long.

Father was despondent every time he was forced to take one of the boys to the mine. He wanted us all to get an education, but measles, whooping cough, scarlet fever and diphtheria assailed us. Most of the time we had no shoes, no pants with seats in them. When I was nine, I had been to school only a few weeks, but I could read rapidly and cipher passably.

On the morning of one of my periodic returns to school, I crept down the stairs. Mother bustled about filling dinner pails with water and food. Father and my brothers were putting on their dank, sweaty clothes. They stank from the foul, sulphurous air of the underground world. They lifted their shoes morosely, turned them upside down, and tapped on the soles. Pebbles rattled on the floor. Father rubbed his stiff sox. They had been muddy the night before. Now ascending motes rubbed from the sox were illuminated in a shaft of morning sunlight and they gleamed with iridescent hues. Father had talked about such things when he was younger, but he was a tired man now and getting to be an old man. He puffed when he bent over to lace the rawhide thongs in his shoes. You cannot use cloth shoe laces in a mine, for the acidulous slush and mud rot them away. My brothers' faces were sad, their limbs moved sluggishly. Mother had to shake and shake the boys to arouse them from their heavy sleep, and they yawned and knuckled their eyes even after they had eaten breakfast and set out for the tipple.

"Come here, son," Father said to me as I peered around the balustrade. "You're starting to school again. This time I want you to keep going. Don't mind if they laugh at your clothes. I want you to study hard; I don't want you to be a coal miner like me."

"I want to be like you," I answered, coming closer. "You went to school and got a good education, but you're a coal miner."

"It's different with me," he parried harshly. It always angered him to remind him that he was an educated man. "I'm in a deep ravine with no path to the heights again. I must follow my rut to the end. But your life is just beginning; so is Tim's. Maybe Dan and the other boys can rise from the mine again, but it's doubtful as that story about the fellow in Palestine arising from the tomb. The mine is a tomb and once the earth gets over you, it's hard to hump up and cast it off. It crushes them all in the end. So you want to study hard and maybe I can send you off to college. Maybe you can be a lawyer or a doctor."

Expert miners thump the roof inquiringly with a pick handle before they venture into their "rooms" of a morning. They learn the meaning of a whole octave of sounds indicating the solidity or lack of solidity in the ceiling, but pot rocks slip out as though they were well greased. They give no warning rattle. And bell rocks spring like panthers, leaving a smooth cup-like cavity. Always the rocks hang overhead like the fabled Damoclean sword, except that the sword was not too wide to allow some chance of jumping from beneath it.

When the cage delivered him up to the world of sun and daylight, Dan walked a quarter-mile bowed double before he could straighten his cramped spine. Evenings he lay on his back in the yard, staring at the stars. But he wasn't wondering where the Great Dipper or the Pleiades were located or whether there were people on Mars, as we used to do together. He never said a word, but only chewed the end of a timothy stalk. At nine o'clock, the very latest, he limped into the house to bed, and when I came in from playing, he snored loudly with his mouth hanging wide open. I never snored that way till ten years later, when I shoveled gravel all day long on the highway gang.

II

Our house wasn't a camp house. It had a neatly painted porch, and was a story and a half high. A barbed wire fence surrounded it and kept cows out of the yard. Below it the camp houses extended in a rough semicircle at the foot of the hill. At the extreme end of the semicircle perched Liam Ryan's Barroom, a favorite haunt of the miners.

The hillside was our commons, and on it we played wild horse, leap-frog, cowboy and Indian. Diamond Dick rode valorously to rescue his sweetheart Nell from scalping at the hands of the redskins just in the nick of time; while Handsome Harry, the old sarpint of Siiskiyou, proclaimed to the world that he was an extremely pisen rattler possessing sixteen rattles and a button; moreover, he was not a bit averse to biting viciously if he were provoked sufficiently.

The farmer boys were our natural enemies, and because of our communal life we easily triumphed in every combat. The isolated farm houses prevented any kind of defense organization, so we ambushed the rustics singly and collectively. Smarting under the implication—and, alas, the conviction—of social inferiority, we battled with extraordinary ferocity, fashioning spears out of horse weeds that grew rank in the creek bottoms, and charging the fleeing hinds with all the fervor of King Arthur in the lists at Camelot. We raided their school-house and even hunted the teacher far away through the brush, stuffing the chimney with rags and overturning the privy, which backed up to and squatted over a crick.

The older boys carried on the tradition, roaming the woods like satyrs, leaning against tree trunks and pumping doleful accordions, or sitting on fallen logs tootling merry flutes. They shot craps in the forest, and to the dour farmer youths they were mad and unholy. But the faunish farm girls giggled behind the buck bushes and squealed with mingled terror and delight when the miners chased them home. If one were imaginative enough one might fancy goat hooves and jaunty horns as the miners pursued their quarry through the second growth of oak saplings. Once a hired hand caught my brother Dick in a wild cherry tree where he had climbed after the fruit, and pelted him with Osage orange hedge-apples, as large as a small grapefruit and as hard as a cocoanut.

Ben Haskin was the most prosperous farmer thereabout, and he was the particular target of our wrath. Ben's cows gave down their milk in foaming abundance; his hens were never sluggards. His sprayed and pruned trees bore the most luscious fruits, and his fields were the envy of his neighbors. Ben's ruddy face wore a contemptuous look as he drove his sleek horses by the camp. We pelted him with mud balls and howled insults after him. He shook his store-bought buggy whip at us, the veins in his forehead bulging. Most of the farmers used hickory switches for whips, so Ben's buggy whip infuriated us. We considered it an effete gesture. He sure thinks he's smart, he'll get too big for his britches, we said bitterly.

I often lay like an Indian in ambush watching Ben and his family moving or working about the farm. Ben had wrested part of his farm from the woods and the woods wanted back the land. The oaks flung their acorns into the clearing and they rooted tenaciously there. The quickgrowing sumac and buck brush pushed into the field and kept Ben and his hired hand humping with mattock and axe. I watched from behind the boles of the larger trees and amused myself by throwing rocks at the men whenever they turned their backs.

Bonny Fern Haskin was Ben's only child. I despised her because she had everything that my sister Madge lacked. Bonny Fern's meticulously curled flaxen hair was bound with gaudy ribbons, her dresses were starched and immaculate. She wore shoes and stockings the year round. Madge had to stay inside in the bitterest weather to keep her feet from freezing. At other times she had to brave the frosts barefooted, and her soles were tough as whitleather.

Bonny Fern followed Ben and the hired man as they grubbed away at the tough sprouts. Whack! They struck at a young sapling; it was crushed to the ground, rebounding with only its bark bruised to slap them in the face. Ben swore fluently when Bonny Fern was not about, but now he merely exclaimed, "Wouldn't that cork you?" or something equally euphemistic.

"It's a good thing you ain't like them triflin' coal diggers," Bonny Fern piped sagely. "If you was, the saplin's 'd grow all over the place. All they do is lay around on the grass and let the jimson weeds and burdocks take the place. All they can raise is snotty-nosed younguns."

She had heard her mother saying this, and Ben laughed at the exact imitation of his wife's sour homily. But it infuriated me. I found a hefty sandstone and hurled it with true aim. It struck Bonny Fern in the temple and she sank down with a moan. Overwhelmed with terror and remorse I bounded away. I could hear Ben and the hired hand shouting angrily and beating the brush in search for me. I reached home out of breath and hid in the upstairs closet. I reflected over the advisability of pulling out for the Wild West and becoming an outlaw. I cocked my ears for the footsteps of the police, but they didn't come.

Within a day or so I was lurking around the clearing again. As I watched Bonny Fern I grew conscious of how pretty she was. Her cornsilk hair was so shiny; she kept so clean and never fingered her nose as my sister did. I hunted on shady hillsides till I found an exquisite ladyslipper. I carried it gingerly to avoid bruising the fragile blossom or snapping the slender stem. I watched Ben and the hired hand go to the farther end of the clearing and then approached the spot where Bonny Fern was playing alone.

"Who are you?" she challenged.

"I'm Larry Donovan. I brang you this flower. I thought maybe you'd like it. You don't see 'em every day. I hunted and hunted; they're hard as the devil to find."

"Oooh!" she squealed. "You swore! You're a dirty-mouthed little boy. Go wash your mouth out with soap!"

"I didn't aim to," I said contritely. "I didn't know that was a cuss-word. Everybody in the camp says that, even my pappy and Mr. Stafford, and they got college education."

"A camp kid," she shrieked, starting back as from a leper. "My daddy won't let me play with camp trash! You get off our farm, you camp trash!"

Ben had heard the racket, and he bounded across the field, not heeding the sprouts and buck brush lashing his legs.

"Haul out o' here, you young shitepoke," he bellowed. "And don't let me ketch any o' you camp kids hangin' 'round my land. Somebody like to 've murdered Bonny Fern day before yestiddy, and dollars to doughnuts it was one o' you hoodlums."

He fired clods at me as I retreated hastily into the woods. The clods were soft; they burst on tree trunks and showered me with dirt, but the hurt sank deep and intensified as I ran. Safe in the forest fastness, I sank down upon a rock to ease the stitch in my side.

Pietro Di Donato (1911–1992)

For many working-class and poor children in immigrant families, a childhood free from adult responsibilities is not possible. This was particularly true for Pietro di Donato. Born in West Hoboken, New Jersey, of Italian immigrant parents, di Donato went to work at age twelve as a bricklayer to support his mother and siblings after his father was killed in a preventable construction accident. This event—the unexpected loss of a father, husband, and the wages he earned—shaped di Donato's life. Di Donato retells it as literature in "Geremio," published as an autobiographical short story for *Esquire* in 1937 and named the "Best Short Story of 1938." Di Donato graphically describes that Good Friday in 1923 when his father Geremio and his Italian work crew of bricklayers were killed by "Job," work capitalized and personified as a devouring and demanding monster. Workers must support their families even if "[t]he scaffolds are not safe, for the rich must ever profit more." The critically acclaimed novel *Christ in Concrete* (1939) begins with "Geremio" and expands into episodic narratives about family, religion, laying bricks, Italian peasant culture, and, particularly, the interior life of Paul, the sensitive oldest child and his existential journey from religious faith to political consciousness. The power and complexity of *Christ in Concrete*—its operatic enthusiasm for life, its amalgamations of Italian and American idioms, and its questioning of the American ideology of upward mobility—make it an essential working-class text and a challenge for contemporary readers.

Di Donato, a conscientious objector during World War II, was stationed in Cooperstown, New York, where he met his wife, Helen Dean. He was the father of two sons and made his home on Long Island. His other works include a prequel to *Christ in Concrete*, *Three Circles of Light* (1960); an autobiographical novel, *This Woman* (1958); a biography, *Immigrant Saint: The Life of Mother Cabrini* (1960); *The Penitent* (1962), a collection of his writings; *Naked Author* (1970); and his unpublished opus, *The American Gospels*. In a 1985 interview, di Donato summed up his life's work: "I had never planned to be a writer. I'm a missionary, I'm a dreamer, I'm a visionary, a revolutionist, an idealist."

Geremio, From *Christ in Concrete*

March whistled stinging snow against the brick walls and up the gaunt girders. Geremio, the foreman, swung his arms about, and gaffed the men on.

Old Nick, the "Lean," stood up from over a dust-flying brick pile, tapped the side of his nose and sent an oyster directly to the ground. "Master Geremio, the Devil himself could not break his tail any harder than we here."

Burly Julio of the walrus mustache and known as the "Snoutnose" let fall the chute door of the concrete hopper and sang over in the Lean's direction: "Mari-Annina's belly and the burning night will make of me once more a milk-mouthed stripling lad . . ."

The Lean loaded his wheelbarrow and spat furiously. "Sons of two-legged dogs . . . despised of even the Devil himself! Work! Sure! For America beautiful will eat you and spit your bones into the earth's hole! Work!" And with that his wiry frame pitched the barrow violently over the rough floor.

Snoutnose waved his head to and fro and with mock pathos wailed, "Sing on, O guitar of mine . . ."

Short, cheery-faced Tomas, the scaffoldman, paused with hatchet in hand and tenpenny spike sticking out from small dicelike teeth to tell the Lean as he went by, in a voice that all could hear, "Ah, father of countless chicks, the old age is a carrion!"

Geremio chuckled and called to him. "Hey, little Tomas, who are you to talk? You and big-titted Cola can't even hatch an egg, whereas the Lean has just to turn the doorknob of his bedroom and old Philomena becomes a balloon!"

Coarse throats tickled and mouths opened wide in laughter.

The Lean pushed his barrow on, his face cruelly furrowed with time and struggle. Sirupy sweat seeped from beneath his cap, down his bony nose and turned icy at its end. He muttered to himself. "Saints up, down, sideways and inside out! How many more stones must I carry before I'm overstuffed with the light of day! I don't understand . . . blood of the Virgin, I don't understand!"

Mike the "Barrel-mouth" pretended he was talking to himself and yelled out in his best English . . . he was always speaking English while the rest carried on in their native Italian. "I don't know myself, but somebodys whose gotta bigga buncha keeds and he alla times talka from somebodys elsa!"

Geremio knew it was meant for him and he laughed. "On the tomb of Saint Pimple-legs, this little boy my wife is giving me next week shall be the last! Eight hungry little Christians to feed is enough for any man."

Tomas nodded to the rest. "Sure, Master Geremio had a telephone call from the next bambino. Yes, it told him it had a little bell between instead of a rose bush. . . . It even told him its name!"

"Laugh, laugh all of you," returned Geremio, "but I tell you that all my kids must be boys so that they someday will be big American builders. And then I'll help them to put the gold away in the basements!"

A great din of riveting shattered the talk among the fast-moving men. Geremio added a handful of Honest tobacco to his corncob, puffed strongly, and cupped his hands around the bowl for a bit of warmth. The chill day caused him to shiver, and he thought to himself: Yes, the day is cold, cold . . . but who am I to complain when the good Christ Himself was crucified?

Pushing the job is all right (when has it been otherwise in my life?), but this job frightens me. I feel the building wants to tell me something; just as one Christian to another. Or perhaps the Easter week is making of me a spirit-seeing pregnant woman. I don't like this. Mr. Murdin tells me, Push it up! That's all he knows. I keep telling him that the underpinning should be doubled and the old material removed from the floors, but he keeps the inspector drunk and . . . "Hey, Ashes-ass! Get away from under that pilaster? Don't pull the old work. Push it away from you or you'll have a nice present for Easter if the wall falls on you!" . . . Well, with the help of God I'll see this job through. It's not my first, nor the . . . "Hey, Patsy number two! Put more cement in that concrete; we're putting up a building, not an Easter cake!"

Patsy hurled his shovel to the floor and gesticulated madly. "The padrone Murdin-sa tells me, 'Too much, too much! Lil' bit is plenty!' And you tell me I'm stingy! The rotten building can fall after I leave!"

Six floors below, the contractor called. "Hey, Geremio! Is your gang of dagos dead?"

Geremio cautioned the men. "On your toes, boys. If he writes out slips, someone won't have big eels on the Easter table."

The Lean cursed that the padrone could take the job and all the Saints for that matter and shove it . . . !

Curly-headed Lazarene, the roguish, pigeon-toed scaffold-man, spat a cloud of tobacco juice and hummed to his own music . . . "Yes, certainly yes to your face, master padrone . . . and behind, This to you and all your kind!"

The day, like all days, came to an end. Calloused and bruised bodies sighed, and numb legs shuffled toward shabby railroad flats . . .

"Ah, bella casa mio. Where my little freshets of blood and my good woman await me. Home where my broken back will not ache so. Home where midst the monkey chatter of my piccolinos I will float off to blessed slumber with my feet on the chair and the head on the wife's soft full breast."

These great child-hearted ones leave one another without words or ceremony, and as they ride and walk home, a great pride swells the breast . . .

"Blessings to Thee, O Jesus. I have fought winds and cold. Hand to hand I have locked dumb stones in place and the great building rises. I have earned a bit of bread for me and mine."

The mad day's brutal conflict is forgiven, and strained limbs prostrate themselves so that swollen veins can send the yearning blood coursing and pulsating deliciously as though the body mountained leaping streams.

The job alone remained behind . . . and yet, they also, having left the bigger part of their lives with it. The cold ghastly beast, the Job, stood stark, the eerie March wind wrapping it in sharp shadows of falling dusk.

That night was a crowning point in the life of Geremio. He bought a house! Twenty years he had helped to mold the New World. And now he was to have a house of his own! What mattered that it was no more than a wooden shack? It was his own!

He had proudly signed his name and helped Annunziata to make her X on the wonderful contract that proved them owners. And she was happy to think that her next child, soon to come, would be born under their own rooftree. She heard the church chimes, and cried to the children, "Children, to bed! It is near midnight. And remember, shut-mouth to the paesanos! Or they will send the evil eye to our new home even before we put foot."

The children scampered off to the icy yellow bedroom where three slept in one bed and three in the other. Coltishly and friskily they kicked about under the covers; their black iron-cotton stockings not removed . . . what! and freeze the peanut-little toes?

Said Annunziata, "The children are so happy, Geremio; let them be, for even I would dance a Tarantella." And with that she turned blushing. He wanted to take her on her word. She patted his hands, kissed them, and whispered. "Our children will dance for us . . . in the American style someday."

Geremio cleared his throat and wanted to sing. "Yes, with joy I could sing in a richer feeling than the great Caruso." He babbled little old-country couplets and circled the room until the tenant below tapped the ceiling.

Annunziata whispered, "Geremio, to bed and rest. Tomorrow is a day for great things . . . and the day on which our Lord died for us."

The children were now hard asleep. Heads under the cover, over . . . snotty noses whistling, and little damp legs entwined.

In bed Geremio and Annunziata clung closely to each other. They mumbled figures and dates until fatigue stilled their thoughts. And with chubby Johnny clutching fast his bottle and warmed between them . . . life breathed heavily, and dreams entertained in far, far worlds, the nation-builder's brood.

But Geremio and Annunziata remained for a long while staring into the darkness . . . silently.

At last Annunziata spoke. "Geremio?"

"Yes?"

"This job you are now working . . ."

"So?"

"You used always to tell me about what happened on the jobs . . . who was jealous, and who praised . . ."

"You should know by now that all work is the same . . ."

"Geremio. The month you have been on this job, you have not spoken a word about the work . . . And I have felt that I am walking into a dream. Is the work dangerous? Why don't you answer . . . ?"

2

Job loomed up damp, shivery gray. Its giant members waiting.

Builders donned their coarse robes, and waited.

Geremio's whistle rolled back into his pocket and the symphony of struggle began.

Trowel rang through brick and slashed mortar rivets were machine-gunned fast with angry grind Patsy number one check Patsy number two check the Lean three check Julio four steel bellowed back at hammer donkey engines coughed purple Ashes-ass Pietro fifteen chisel point intoned stone thin steel whirred and wailed through wood liquid stone flowed with dull rasp through iron veins and hoist screamed through space Rosario the Fat twenty-four and Giacomo Sangini check . . . The multitudinous voices of a civilization rose from the surroundings and melted with the efforts of the Job.

The Lean as he fought his burden on looked forward to only one goal, the end. The barrow he pushed, he did not love. The stones that brutalized his palms, he did not love. The great God Job, he did not love. He felt a searing bitterness and a fathomless consternation at the queer consciousness that inflicted the ever mounting weight of structures that he *had to! had to!* raise above his shoulders! When, when and where would the last stone be? Never . . . did he bear his toil with the rhythm of song! Never . . . did his gasping heart knead the heavy mortar with lilting melody! A voice within him spoke in wordless language.

The language of worn oppression and the despair of realizing that his life had been left on brick piles. And always, there had been hunger and her bastard, the fear of hunger.

Murdin bore down upon Geremio from behind and shouted:

"Goddammit, Geremio, if you're givin' the men two hours off today with pay, why the hell are they draggin' their tails? And why don't you turn that skinny old Nick loose, and put a young wop in his place?"

"Now listen-a to me, Mister Murdin—"

"Don't give me that! And bear in mind that there are plenty of good barefoot men in the streets who'll jump for a day's pay!"

"Padrone—padrone, the underpinning gotta be make safe and . . ."

"Lissenyawopbastard! if you don't like it, you know what you can do!" And with that he swung swaggering away.

The men had heard, and those who hadn't knew instinctively.

The new home, the coming baby, and his whole background, kept the fire from Geremio's mouth and bowed his head. "Annunziata speaks of scouring the ashcans for the children's bread in case I didn't want to work on a job where. . . . But am I not a man, to feed my own with these hands? Ah, but day will end and no boss in the world can then rob me the joy of my home!"

Murdin paused for a moment before descending the ladder.

Geremio caught his meaning and jumped to, nervously directing the rush of work. . . . No longer Geremio, but a machinelike entity.

The men were transformed into single, silent beasts. Snoutnose steamed through ragged mustache whip-lashing sand into mixer Ashes-ass dragged under four-by-twelve beam Lean clawed wall knots jumping in jaws masonry crumbled dust billowed thundered choked . . .

At noon, dripping noses were blown, old coats thrown over shoulders, and foot-long sandwiches were toasted at the end of wire over the flames. Shadows were once again personalities. Laughter added warmth.

Geremio drank his wine from an old-fashioned magnesia bottle and munched a great pepper sandwich . . . no meat on Good Friday.

Said one, "Are some of us to be laid off? Easter is upon us and communion dresses are needed and . . ."

That, while Geremio was dreaming of the new house and the joys he could almost taste. Said he, "Worry not. You should know Geremio." It then all came out. He regaled them with his wonderful joy of the new house. He praised his wife and children one by one. They listened respectfully and returned him well wishes and blessings. He went on and on. . . . "Paul made a radio—all by himself, mind you! One can bear *Barney Google* and many American songs!"

"A radio!"

"An electric machine like magic—yes."

"With music and Christian voices?"

"That is nothing to what he shall someday accomplish!"

"Who knows," suggested Giacomo amazed, "but that Dio has deigned to gift you with a Marconi . . ."

"I tell you, son of Geremio shall never never lay bricks! Paulie mine will study from books—he will be the great builder! This very moment I can see him. . . . How proud he!"

Said they in turn: "Master Geremio, in my province it is told that for good luck in a new home, one is to sprinkle well with salt . . . especially the corners, and on moving day sweep with a new broom to the center and pick all up—but do not sweep it out over the threshold!"

"That may be, Pietro. But, Master Geremio, it would be better in my mind that holy water should bless. And also a holy picture of Saint Joseph guarding the door."

"The Americans use the shoe of a horse . . . there must be something in that. One may try . . ."

Snoutnose knew a better way. "You know, you know." He ogled his eyes and smacked his lips. Then, reaching out his hands over the hot embers . . . "To embrace a goosefat breast and bless the house with the fresh milk. And one that does not belong to the wife . . . that is the way!"

Acid-smelling di Nobilis were lit. Geremio preferred his corncob. And Lazarene "tobacco-eater" proudly chawed his quid . . . in the American style.

The ascent to labor was made, and as they trod the ladder, heads turned and eyes communed with the mute flames of the brazier whose warmth they were leaving, not with willing heart, and in that fleeting moment the breast wanted much to speak of hungers that never reached the tongue.

About an hour later, Geremio called over to Pietro, "Pietro see if Mister Murdin is in the shanty and tell him I must see him! I will convince him that the work must not go on like this . . . just for the sake of a little more profit!"

Pietro came up soon. "The padrone is not coming up. He was drinking from a large bottle of whisky and cursed in American words that if you did not carry out his orders—"

Geremio turned away disconcerted, stared dumbly at the structure and mechanically listed in his mind's eye the various violations of construction safety. An uneasy sensation hollowed him. The Lean brought down an old piece of wall and the structure palsied. Geremio's heart broke loose and out-thumped the floor's vibrations, a rapid wave of heat swept him and left a chill touch in its wake. He looked about to the men, a bit frightened. They seemed usual, life-size, and moved about with the methodical deftness that made the moment then appear no different than the task of toil had ever been.

Snoutnose's voice boomed into him. "Master Geremio, the concrete is re-ady!"

"Oh yes, yes, Julio." And he walked gingerly toward the chute, but not without leaving behind some part of his strength, sending out his soul to wrestle with the limbs of Job, who threatened in stiff silence. He talked and joked with Snoutnose. Nothing said anything, nor seemed wrong. Yet a vague uneasiness was to him as certain as the foggy murk that floated about Job's stone and steel.

"Shall I let the concrete down now, Master Geremio?"

"Well, let me see—no, hold it a minute. Hey, Lazarene! Tighten the chute cables!"

Snoutnose straightened, looked about, and instinctively rubbed the sore small of his spine. "Ah," sighed he, "all the men feel as I—yes, I can tell. They are tired but happy that today is Good Friday and we quit at three o'clock—"And he swelled in human ecstasy at the anticipation of food, drink and the hairy flesh-tingling warmth of wife, and then, extravagant rest.

Geremio gazed about and was conscious of seeming to understand many things. He marveled at the strange feeling which permitted him to sense the familiarity of life. And yet—all appeared unreal, a dream pungent and nostalgic.

Life, dream, reality, unreality, spiraling ever about each other. "Ha," he chuckled, "how and from where do these thoughts come?"

Snoutnose had his hand on the hopper latch and was awaiting the word from Geremio. "Did you say something, Master Geremio?"

"Why yes, Julio, I was thinking—funny! A—yes, what is the time—yes, that is what I was thinking."

"My American can of tomatoes says ten minutes from two o'clock. It won't be long now, Master Geremio."

Geremio smiled. "No, about an hour . . . and then, home."

"Oh, but first we stop at Mulberry Street, to buy their biggest eels, and the other finger-licking stuffs."

Geremio was looking far off, and for a moment happiness came to his heart without words, a warm hand stealing over. Snoutnose's words sang to him pleasantly, and he nodded.

"And Master Geremio, we ought really to buy the sea-fruits with the shells—you know, for the much needed steam they put into the—"

He flushed despite himself and continued, "It is true, I know it—especially the juicy clams . . . uhmn, my mouth waters like a pump."

Geremio drew on his unlit pipe and smiled acquiescence. The men around him were moving to their tasks silently, feeling of their fatigue, but absorbed in contemplations the very same as Snoutnose's. The noise of labor seemed not to be noise, and as Geremio looked about, life settled over him a gray concert—gray forms, atmosphere and gray notes. . . . Yet his off-tone world felt so near, and familiar.

"Five minutes from two," swished through Snoutnose's mustache.

Geremio automatically took out his watch, rewound and set it. Lazarene had done with the cables. The tone and movement of the scene seemed to Geremio strange, differently strange, and yet, a dream familiar from a timeless date. His hand went up in motion to Julio. The molten stone gurgled low, and then with heightening rasp. His eyes followed the stone-cementy pudding, and to his ears there was no other sound than its flow. From over the roofs somewhere, the tinny voice of *Barney Google* whined its way, hooked into his consciousness and kept itself a revolving record beneath his skullplate.

"Ah, yes, *Barney Google*, my son's wonderful radio machine . . . wonderful Paul." His train of thought quickly took in his family, home and hopes. And with hope came fear. Something within asked, "Is it not possible to breathe God's air without fear dominating with the pall of unemployment? And the terror of production for Boss, Boss and Job? To rebel is to lose all of the very little. To be obedient is to choke. O dear Lord, guide my path."

Just then, the floor lurched and swayed under his feet. The slipping of the under-pinning below rumbled up through the undetermined floors.

Was he faint or dizzy? Was it part of the dreamy afternoon? He put his hands in front of him and stepped back, and looked up wildly. "No! No!"

The men poised stricken. Their throats wanted to cry out and scream but didn't dare. For a moment they were a petrified and straining pageant. Then the bottom of their world gave way. The building shuddered violently, her supports burst with the crackling slap of wooden gunfire. The floor vomited upward. Geremio clutched at the air and shrieked agonizingly. "Brothers, what have we done? Ahhh-h, children of ours!" With the speed of light, balance went sickeningly awry and frozen men went flying explosively. Job tore down upon them madly. Walls, floors, beams became whirling, solid, splintering waves crashing with detonations that ground man and material in bonds of death.

The strongly shaped body that slept with Annunziata nights and was perfect in all the limitless physical quantities thudded as a worthless sack amongst the giant débris that crushed fragile flesh and bone with centrifugal intensity.

Darkness blotted out his terror and the resistless form twisted, catapulted insanely in its directionless flight, and shot down neatly and deliberately between the empty wooden forms of a foundation wall pilaster in upright position, his blue swollen face pressed against the form and his arms outstretched, caught securely through the meat by the thin round bars of reinforcing steel.

The huge concrete hopper that was sustained by an independent structure of thick timber wavered a breath or so, its heavy concrete rolling uneasily until a great sixteen-inch wall caught it squarely with all the terrific verdict of its dead weight and impelled it down-ward through joists, beams and masonry until it stopped short, arrested by two girders, an arm's length above Geremio's head; the gray concrete gushing from the hopper mouth, and sealing up the mute figure.

Giacomo had been thrown clear of the building and dropped six floors to the street gutter, where he lay writhing.

The Lean had evinced no emotion. When the walls descended, he did not move. He lowered his head. One minute later he was hanging in mid-air, his chin on his chest, his eyes tearing loose from their sockets, a green foam bubbling from his mouth and his body spasming, suspended by the shreds left of his mashed arms, pinned between a wall and a girder.

A two-by-four hooked little Tomas up under the back of his jumper and swung him around in a circle to meet a careening I-beam. In the flash that he lifted his frozen cherubic face, its shearing edge sliced through the top of his skull.

When Snoutnose cried beseechingly, "Saint Michael!" blackness enveloped him. He came to in a world of horror. A steady stream, warm, thick, and sickening as hot wine, bathed his face and clogged his nose, mouth, and eyes. The nauseous sirup that pumped over his face clotted his mustache red and drained into his mouth. He gulped for air, and swallowed blood. As he breathed, the pain shocked him to oppressive semiconsciousness. The air was wormingly alive with cries, screams, moans, and dust, and his crushed chest seared him with a thousand fires. He couldn't see, nor breathe enough to cry. His right hand moved to his face and wiped at the gelatinizing substance, but it kept coming on, and a heartbreaking moan wavered about him, not far. He wiped his eyes in subconscious despair. Where was he? What kind of a dream was he having? Perhaps he wouldn't wake up in time for work, and then what? But how queer; his stomach beating him, his chest on fire, he sees nothing but dull red, only one hand moving about, and a moaning in his face!

The sound and clamor of the rescue squads called to him from far off.

Ah, yes, he's dreaming in bed, and, far out in the streets, engines are going to a fire. Oh, poor devils! Suppose his house were on fire? With the children scattered about in the rooms he could not remember! He must do his utmost to break out of this dream! He's swimming under water, not able to raise his head and get to the air. He must get back to consciousness to save his children!

He swam frantically with his one right hand, and then felt a face beneath its touch. A face! It's Angelina alongside of him! Thank God, he's awake! He tapped her face. It moved. It felt cold, bristly, and wet. "It moves so. What is this?" His fingers slithered about grisly sharp bones and in a gluey, stringy, hollow mass, yielding as wet macaroni. Gray light brought sight, and hysteria punctured his heart. A girder lay across his chest, his right hand clutched a grotesque human mask, and suspended almost on top of him was the twitching, faceless body of Tomas. Julio fainted with an inarticulate sigh. His fingers loosed and the bodiless headless face dropped and fitted to the side of his face while the drippings above came slower and slower.

The rescue men cleaved grimly with pick and ax.

Geremio came to with a start . . . far from their efforts. His brain told him instantly what had happened and where he was. He shouted wildly. "Save me! Save me! I'm being buried alive!"

He paused exhausted. His genitals convulsed. The cold steel rod upon which they were impaled froze his spine. He shouted louder and louder. "Save me! I am hurt badly! I can be saved I can—save me before it's too late!" But the cries went no farther than his own ears. The icy wet concrete reached his chin. His heart appalled. "In a few seconds I will be entombed. If I can only breathe, they will reach me. Surely, they will!" His face was quickly covered, its flesh yielding to the solid sharp-cut stones. "Air! Air!" screamed his lungs as he was completely sealed. Savagely he bit into the wooden form pressed upon his mouth. An eighth of an inch of its surface splintered off. Oh, if he could only hold out long enough to bite even the smallest hole through to air! He must! There can be no other way! He must! There can be no other way! He is responsible for his family! He cannot leave them like this! He didn't want to die! This could not be the answer to life! He had bitten halfway through when his teeth snapped off to the gums in the uneven conflict. The pressure of the concrete was such, and its effectiveness so thorough, that the wooden splinters, stumps of teeth, and blood never left the choking mouth.

Why couldn't he go any farther?

Air! Quick! He dug his lower jaw into the little hollowed space and gnashed in choking agonized fury. Why doesn't it go through! Mother of Christ, why doesn't it give? Can there be a notch, or two-by-four stud behind it? Sweet Jesu! No! No! Make it give . . . Air! Air!

He pushed the bone-bare jaw maniacally; it splintered, cracked, and a jagged fleshless edge cut through the form, opening a small hole to air. With a desperate burst the lung-prisoned air blew an opening through the shredded mouth and whistled back greedily a gasp of fresh air. He tried to breathe, but it was impossible. The heavy concrete was settling immutably and its rich cement-laden grout ran into his pierced face. His lungs would not expand and were crushing in tighter and tighter under the settling concrete.

"Mother mine—mother of Jesu—Annunziata—children of mine—dear, dear, for, mercy, Jesu-Giuseppe e' Mari," his blue foamed tongue called. It then distorted in a shuddering coil and mad blood vomited forth. Chills and fire played through him and his tortured tongue stuttered, "Mercy, blessed Father—salvation, most kind Father—Saviour—Saviour of His children, help me—adored Saviour—I kiss your feet eternally—you are my Lord—there is but one God—you are my God of infinite mercy—Hail Mary divine Virgin—our Father who art in heaven hallowed be thy—name—our Father—my Father," and the agony excruciated with never-ending mount, "our Father—Jesu, Jesu, soon Jesu, hurry dear Jesu Jesu! Je-sssu . . . !" His mangled voice trebled hideously, and hung in jerky whimperings. Blood vessels burst like mashed flower stems. He screamed.

"Show yourself now, Jesu! Now is the time! Save me! Why don't you come! Are you there! I cannot stand it—ohhh, why do you let it happen—where are you? Hurry hurry hurry!"

His bones cracked mutely and his sanity went sailing distorted in the limbo of the sub-conscious. With the throbbing tones of an organ in the hollow background, the fighting brain disintegrated and the memories of a baffled lifetime sought outlet.

He moaned the simple songs of barefoot childhood, scenes flashed desperately on and off, and words and parts of words came pitifully high and low from his inaudible lips.

Paul's crystal-set earphones pressed the sides of his head tighter and tighter, the organ boomed the mad dance of the Tarentella, and the hysterical mind sang cringingly and breathlessly, "Jesu my Lord my God my all Jesu my Lord my God my all Jesu my Lord my God my all Jesu my Lord my God my all."

Tom Kromer (1906–1969)

Tom Kromer's *Waiting for Nothing* (1935) takes the reader deep inside the experience of being out of work and "on the bum" during the Great Depression. There is no romance of the open road for the hoboes and "stiffs" in Kromer's autobiographical novel. Instead, they endure a constant battle with hunger, joblessness, and humiliation, with little hope of change for the better. Kromer's achievement is partly a matter of literary form. The novel is constructed as a series of episodes, with no particular progression, each one dominated by the daily search for "three hots and a flop." These incidents are narrated in the first person and present tense, in a voice that blends the street language of the stiffs with an eerily simple syntax, allowing for some stark truth telling: "You ask for work and they laugh at you for asking for work. There is no work." The novel's power comes also from Kromer's firsthand knowledge of his subject. From 1929 to 1933, he was a homeless migrant, panhandling in the cities, riding the rails, and picking up occasional work as an agricultural laborer. He was imprisoned for vagrancy in Washington, DC, and at one point attempted suicide; the book is dedicated "to Jolene who turned off the gas." It was not until he enrolled in the California Conservation Corps in 1933, with regular food and work for the first time in years, that Kromer was able to begin shaping his experiences in writing.

Kromer was born in Huntington, West Virginia, the eldest of five children. In the preface to the British edition of *Waiting for Nothing*, he wrote:

> My people were working people. My father started to work in a coal-mine when he was eight years old. Later, he became a glass-blower, and unable to afford medical treatment, died of cancer at the age of forty-four. . . . My mother never wanted anything else than that the kids get an education so that they wouldn't have to worry about the factory closing down.

Kromer attended Marshall College for three years while working in a glass factory and as a newspaper proofreader. He taught in country schools for two years until the depression hit in 1929, the glass plant closed, and he headed west. After his novel drew favorable reviews in 1935, Kromer contributed articles and reviews to *New Masses* and other journals for a time and began a second novel, *Michael Kohler*, based on the life of his father. But he was already suffering from the pulmonary tuberculosis that incapacitated him, and deterred his writing, for the rest of his life.

"THREE HOTS AND A FLOP," FROM *WAITING FOR NOTHING*

It is night. I am walking along this dark street, when my foot hits a stick. I reach down and pick it up. I finger it. It is a good stick, a heavy stick. One sock from it would lay a man out. It wouldn't kill him, but it would lay him out. I plan. Hit him where the crease is in his hat, hard, I tell myself, but not too hard. I do not want his head to hit the concrete. It might kill him. I do not want to kill him. I will catch him as he falls. I can frisk him in a minute. I will pull him over in the shadows and walk off. I will not run. I will walk.

I turn down a side street. This is a better street. There are fewer houses along this street. There are large trees on both sides of it. I crouch behind one of these. It is dark here. The shadows hide me. I wait. Five, ten minutes, I wait. Then under an arc light a block away a man comes walking. He is a well-dressed man. I can tell even from that distance. I have good eyes. This guy will be in the dough. He walks with his head up and a jaunty step. A stiff does not walk like that. A stiff shuffles with tired feet, his head huddled in his coat collar, This guy is in the dough. I can tell that. I clutch my stick tighter. I notice that I am calm. I am not scared. I am calm. In the crease of his hat, I tell myself. Not too hard. Just hard enough. On he comes. I slink farther back in the shadows. I press closer against this tree. I hear his footsteps thud on the concrete walk. I raise my arm high. I must swing hard. I poise myself. He crosses in front of me. Now is my chance. Bring it down hard, I tell myself, but not too hard. He is under my arm. He is right under my arm, but my stick does not come down. Something has happened to me. I am sick in the stomach. I have lost my nerve. Christ, I have lost my nerve. I am shaking all over. Sweat stands out on my forehead. I can feel the clamminess of it in the cold, damp night. This will not do. This will not do. I've got to get me something to eat. I am starved.

I stagger from the shadows and follow behind this guy. He had a pretty good face. I could tell as he passed beneath my arm. This guy ought to be good for two bits. Maybe he will be good for four bits. I quicken my steps. I will wait until he is under an arc light before I give him my story. I do not have long to wait. He stops under an arc light and fumbles in his pocket for a cigarette. I catch up with him.

"Pardon me, mister, but could you help a hungry man get—"

"You goddam bums give me a pain in the neck. Get the hell away from me before I call a cop."

He jerks his hand into his overcoat pocket. He wants me to think he has a gun. He has not got a gun. He is bluffing.

I hurry down the street. The bastard. The dirty bastard. I could have laid him out cold with the stick. I could have laid him out cold with the stick, and he calls me a goddam bum. I had the stick over his head, and I could not bring it down. I am yellow. I can see that I am yellow. If I am not yellow, why am I shaking like a leaf? I am starved, too, and I ought to starve. A guy without enough guts to get himself a feed ought to starve.

I walk on up the street. I pass people, but I let them pass. I do not ding them. I have lost my nerve. I walk until I am on the main stem. Never have I been so hungry. I have got to get me something to eat. I pass a restaurant. In the window is a roast chicken. It is brown and fat. It squats in a silver platter. The platter is filled with gravy. The gravy is thick and brown. It drips over the side, slow. I stand there and watch it drip. Underneath it the sign says: "All you can eat for fifty cents." I lick my lips. My mouth waters. I sure would like to sit down with that before me. I look inside. It is a classy joint. I can see waitresses in blue and white uniforms. They hurry back and forth. They carry heavy trays. The dishes stick over the edge of the trays. There are good meals still left in these trays. They will throw them in the garbage cans. In the center of the floor a water fountain bubbles. It is made of pink marble. The chairs are red leather, bordered in black. The counter is full of men eating. They are eating, and I am hungry. There are long rows of tables. The cloths on them are whiter than white. The glassware sparkles like diamonds on its whiteness. The knives and forks on the table are silver. I can tell that they are pure silver from where I am standing on the street. They shine so bright. I cannot go in there. It is too classy, and besides there are too many people. They will laugh at my seedy clothes, and my shoes without soles.

I stare in at this couple that eat by the window. I pull my coat collar up around my neck. A man will look hungrier with his coat collar up around his neck. These people are in the dough. They are in evening clothes. This woman is sporting a satin dress. The blackness of it shimmers and glows in the light that comes from the chandelier that hangs from the dome. Her fingers are covered with diamonds. There are diamond bracelets on her wrists. She is beautiful. Never have I seen a more beautiful woman. Her lips are red. They are even redder against the whiteness of her teeth when she laughs. She laughs a lot.

I stare in at the window. Maybe they will know a hungry man when they see him. Maybe this guy will be willing to shell out a couple of nickels to a hungry stiff. It is chicken they are eating. A chicken like the one in the window. Brown and fat. They do not eat. They only nibble. They are nibbling at chicken, and they are not even hungry. I am starved. That chicken was meant for a hungry man. I watch them as they cut it into tiny bits. I watch their forks as they carry them to their mouths. The man is facing me. Twice he glances out of the window. I meet his eyes with mine. I wonder if he can tell the eyes of a hungry man. He has never been hungry himself. I can tell that. This one has always nibbled at chicken. I see him speak to the woman. She turns her head and looks at me through the window. I do not look at her. I look at the chicken on the plate. They can see that I am a hungry man. I will stand here until they come out. When they come out, they will maybe slip me a four-bit piece.

A hand slaps down on my shoulder. It is a heavy hand. It spins me around in my tracks.

"What the hell are you doin' here?" It is a cop.

"Me? Nothing," I say. "Nothing, only watching a guy eat chicken. Can't a guy watch another guy eat chicken?"

"Wise guy," he says. "Well, I know what to do with wise guys."

He slaps me across the face with his hand, hard. I fall back against the building. His hands are on the holster by his side. What can I do? Take it is all I can do. He will plug me if I do anything.

"Put up your hands," he says.

I put up my hands.

"Where's your gat?" he says.

"I have no gat," I say. "I never had a gat in my life."

"That's what they all say," he says.

He pats my pockets. He don't find anything. There is a crowd around here now. Everybody wants to see what is going on. They watch him go through my pockets. They think I am a stick-up guy. A hungry stiff stands and watches a guy eat chicken, and they think he is a stick-up guy. That is a hell of a note.

"All right," he says, "get down the street before I run you in. If I ever catch you stemming this beat, I will sap the living hell out of you. Beat it."

I hurry down the street. I know better than not to hurry. The lousy son of a bitch. I had a feed right in my lap, and he makes me beat it. That guy was all right in there. He was a good guy. That guy could see I was a hungry man. He would have fixed me up right when he came out.

I pass a small café. There are no customers in here. There is only a guy sitting by the cash register. This is my place. I go in and walk up to him. He is a fat guy with a double chin. I can see very well that he hasn't missed many meals in his life.

"Mister," I say, "have you got some kind of work like washing dishes I can do for something to eat? I am damn near starved. I'll do anything."

He looks hard at me. I can see right away that this guy is no good.

"Tell me," he says, "in God's name, why do you stiffs always come in here? You're the fourth guy in the last half-hour. I can't even pay my rent. There ain't been a customer in here for an hour. Go to some of the big joints where they do all the business."

"Could you maybe give me a cup of coffee?" I say. "That would hold me over. I've been turned down at about twenty places already."

"I can't give you nothing. Coffee costs money," he says. "Go to one of the chain stores and bum your coffee. When you've got any money, where do you go to spend it? You go to the chains. I can't do nothing for you."

I walk out. Wouldn't even give a hungry man a cup of coffee. Can you imagine a guy like that? The bastard. I'd like to catch him on a dark street. I'd give him a cup of coffee, and a sock on the snout he wouldn't soon forget. I walk. When I pass a place where there are no customers, I go in. They turn me down flat. No business, they say. Why don't I go to the big places? I am getting sick in the stomach. I feel like vomiting. I have to get me something to eat. What the hell? I will hit me one of these classy joints. Pride! What do I care about pride? Who cares about me? Nobody. The bastards don't care if I live or die.

I pass a joint. A ritzy place. It is all white inside. The tables are full. The counters are full. They are eating, and I am hungry. These guys pay good dough for a feed, and they are not even hungry. When they are through, they will maybe tip the waitress four bits. It is going to be cold tonight. Four bits will buy me a flop that will be warm, and not cold.

I go into this joint and walk up to the middle of the counter. I flop down in a seat. These cash customers gape at me. I am clean, but my front is seedy. They know I don't belong in here. I know I don't belong in here, too. But I am hungry. A hungry man belongs where there is food. Let them gape.

This waiter sticks the menu out to me. I do not take it. What do I want with a menu?

"Buddy," I say, "I am broke and hungry. Could you maybe give me something to eat?"

He shakes his head no, he cannot give me anything to eat.

"Busy. Manager's not in. Sorry."

I can feel my face getting red. They are all gaping at me. They crane their necks to gape at me. I get up out of this seat and walk towards the door. I can't get anything to eat anywhere. God damn them, if I could get my fingers on a gat.

"Say, buddy."

I turn around. A guy in a gray suit is motioning to me. He sits at the middle of the counter. I go back.

"You hungry?"

"I'm damn near starved. I have not eat in two days, and that is the God's truth."

"Down on your luck?" he says.

"Down so far I don't know how far," I say.

"Sit down. I've been down on my luck myself. I know how it is."

I sit down beside him.

"What'll it be?" he says.

"You order it," I say. "Anything you say."

"Order up anything you want. Fill up."

"A ham sandwich and a cup of coffee," I tell this waiter.

He is all smiles now, damn him. He sees where he can make a dime. I bet he owns this joint. He said the manager wasn't in, and I bet he's the manager himself.

"Give him a beef-steak dinner with everything that goes with it," says this guy in the gray suit.

"This man is hungry."

This is a good guy. He orders my steak dinner in a loud voice so everyone can see how big-hearted he is, but he is a good guy anyway. Any guy is a good guy when he is going to buy me a steak dinner. Let him show off a little bit. He deserves to show off a little bit. I sit here at this counter, and I feel like pinching myself. This is a funny world. Five minutes ago I was down in the dumps. Here I am now waiting on a steak dinner in a classy joint. Let them gape. What do I care? Didn't they ever see a hungry man before?

This waiter shoves my dinner in front of me. Christ, I've never seen anything look so good. This steak with all the trimmings is a picture for sore eyes. Big and thick and brown, it sits there. Around it, all around it, are tomatoes, sliced. I start in. I do not look up from my plate. They are all gaping at me. Fill up and get out of here, I tell myself.

The guy three seats down gets up and calls for his check. He is a little guy with horn-rimmed glasses. The check is thirty cents. I see it before the waiter turns it upside down. Why do they always have to turn a man's check upside down? Afraid the price will turn his stomach? This guy pulls a dollar out of his pocket and walks over to the cashier. I wonder how it feels to have a buck in your jeans. Four bits will set me on top of the world right now. A good warm flop tonight and breakfast in the morning. That's the way to live. Pay for what you get, and look every copper you pass on the street straight in the eye, and say: "You bastard, I don't owe you a cent."

The cashier hands this guy his change. He walks back and lays it down by my plate.

"Flop for tonight," he says.

He speaks low. He is not trying to show off like this guy in the gray suit. Not that I don't think that this guy in the gray suit is not all right. He is a good guy. He bought me a steak dinner when I was damn near starved. No, he is a good guy, but he likes to show off a little bit. I look up at this guy. He is walking out of the door. I do not thank him. He is too far away, and besides, what can I say? I can't believe it. Thirty cents, the check said. Thirty cents from a dollar. That makes seventy cents. I got seventy cents. A good warm flop tonight, breakfast in the morning, and enough left over for cigarettes. No fishing around in the gutters for snipes for me. I will have me a package of tailormade cigarettes. I pick up this change and stick it in my pocket. That guy is a mind-reader. I was sitting here wishing I had four bits, and before I know it, I got seventy cents. That guy is all right. I bet that guy has had troubles of his own some time. I bet he knows how it is to be hungry. I hurry up with my dinner. In here I am only a hungry stiff. Outside with seventy cents in my kick. I am as good as the next one. Say, I'd like to meet that guy, and I had a million dollars.

"Do you remember the time you give me seventy cents in a restaurant? You don't? Well, you give me seventy cents in a restaurant one time. I was damn near starved. I was just about ready to bump myself off, and you give me seventy cents."

I hand him a roll of bills. It is a big roll of bills. I walk off. That guy won't have to worry any more about dough. There was plenty in that roll to keep him in wheatcakes the rest of his life.

I finish my pie and get up.

"Thank you, Jack," I say to this guy in the gray suit. "I certainly appreciate what you done for me. I was damn near starved."

"That's all right, buddy," he says. "Glad to help a hungry man."

He speaks loud. They can hear him to the other end of the counter. He is a good guy, though. He bought me a steak dinner.

I walk outside. I put my hand in my pocket and jingle my money. It feels good to have money to jingle. I am not broke or hungry now. I cannot imagine I was broke and hungry an hour ago. No park for me tonight. No lousy mission flop.

I go down the street and walk through the park. I look at these benches with their iron legs and their wooden slats.

"To hell with you," I say. "I have nothing to do with you. I do not know you. You will leave no grooves in my back tonight. Tonight I will have me a good warm flop. I will have me a flop that will be warm, and not cold."

I look at these stiffs sprawled out on the benches. I like to walk to the time of the jingle in my pocket and think how miserable I was last night.

It is getting late, and I am tired. I head down the skid road and stop in front of my four-bit flop. There is no marquee in front to keep the guests from getting wet. There is no doorman dressed like a major in the Imperial Guards. They do not need these things, because all the suites are on the fourth floor. I am puffing when I get to the top of the rickety stairs. At the landing a guy squats on a stool in a wire cage.

"I want a four-bit flop," I say, "a four-bit flop with a clean bed."

This guy is hunched over a desk with his belly sticking out of a dirty green sweater. He rubs his hands together and shows his yellow teeth in a grin. He winks one of his puffy eyes.

"For a little extra, just a little extra," he says, "I can give you a nice room, a very nice room. But it is too big a room for one. You will be lonely. A little company will not go bad, eh? Especially if the company is very young and very pretty?" He licks his puffy lips. "We have a girl, a new girl. Only tonight she came. Because it is you, and she must learn, only a dollar extra, yes?"

I look at him, and I think of the fish-eyed, potbellied frogs I used to gig when I was a kid. I imagine myself sticking a sharp gig into his belly and watching him kick and croak.

"A four-bit flop is what I want," I say. "I do not wish to play nursemaid to your virgins. I am broke, and besides, I am sleepy."

"But you should see her," he says, "so tiny, so beautiful. I will get her. You will change your mind when you see her."

"I do not want to see her," I say.

"So high," he says. "Only so high she is, and so beautiful. I will get her. You will see how beautiful she is."

He climbs off his stool.

"Do I get me a flop or do I have to bury my foot in your dirty belly?" I say.

"Some other time, then," he says, "some other time when you have more money. You will see how very beautiful."

He waddles through the dirty hall. I follow him. His legs are swollen with dropsy. His ankles overflow his ragged house-slippers and hang down in folds over the sides. I can imagine I hear the water gurgling as he walks. He opens the door and holds out his hand for the money.

"How many beds in this room?" I say.

"Forty," he says, "but they are good, clean beds."

I walk into this room. It is a big room. It is filled with these beds. They do not look so hot to me. They are only cots. They look lousy. I bet they are lousy, but a stiff has got to sleep, lousy or not. Most of these beds are already full. I can hear the snores of the stiffs as they sleep. I pick me out a flop at the other end of the room. There is no mattress. Only two dirty blankets. They are smelly. Plenty of stiffs have slept under these blankets.

Four or five stiffs are gathered in a bunch over next to the wall. I watch them. I know very well what they are going to do. They are gas hounds, and they are going to get soused on derail.

"Give me that handkerchief," says this red-headed guy with the wens on his face. "I will squeeze more alky out of a can of heat than any stiff I know."

This little guy with the dirty winged collar examines this can of heat.

"The bastards," he says. "You know what? They're makin' the cans smaller and smaller. This can right here is smaller than they was yestiddy. The dirty crooks. They'd take the bread right out of your mouths, the bastards would."

He jumps up and down as he talks. His red eyes flash. The sweat stands in beads on his forehead. How can a guy get so mad about the size of a can of heat? Well, it does not take much to make you mad when you have been swigging heat for a year.

This red-headed guy takes this can of heat and empties it out in a handkerchief. The handkerchief is filthy, but that don't worry them none. What's a little filth to a gas hound? Pretty soon they will be high and nothing will worry them. Pretty soon they won't have any more troubles. This derail will see to that. They squeeze this stuff out of the handkerchief and let it drip into the glass. They pour water into the glass. The smell of this stuff will turn your stomach, but it don't turn their stomach. They are going to drink it. They take turns about taking a swig. They elbow each other out of the way to get at glass. When it is all gone, they squeeze out some more. They choke and gag when this stuff goes down, but they drink it. Pretty soon they have guzzled all the heat they have. In a little while they are singing. I do not blame these guys for getting soused on derail. A guy can't always be thinking. If a guy is thinking all the time, pretty soon he will go crazy. A man is bound to land up in the booby-hatch if he stays on the fritz. So these guys make derail and drink it.

This stiff in the bed next to mine turns up his nose at these guys who are soused up on derail.

"I got my opinion of a guy who will drink derail," he says. "A guy who will drink derail is lower down than a skunk."

He pulls a bottle out from under his pillow. It is marked: "Bay Rum." There are directions on the label. It says it will grow new hair. It says it will stop the old from falling out. But this guy does not need this stuff to keep his hair from falling out. This stiff has not had a haircut for a year.

"This is the stuff," he says. "I have been drinkin' this old stuff for a year, and I don't even get a headache afterwards."

He sticks this bottle up to his trap, and he does not take it down until he has emptied it.

"This is good stuff," he says. "It has got derail beat all to a frazzle."

I do not see how it can be such good stuff when he has to gag so much when he downs it. But, that is his business. If a guy has been drinking this stuff for a year, he ought to know if it is good stuff or not. Pretty soon this guy is dead to the world. He sprawls out on his bunk and sleeps. He sleeps with his eyes wide open. Christ, he gives me the willies with his eyes wide open like that. He looks like a dead man, but I never see a dead man with his face covered with sweat like his is. It is plenty chilly in this room, but his face is covered with sweat. That is the bay rum coming out of him. A guy that has been drinking this stuff for a year must have plenty inside him. I bet the inside of his gut is covered with hair. That would be a good way to find out if this bay rum is a fake or not. When this stiff croaks from swigging too much bay rum, just cut him open. If his gut is not covered with hair, then this bay rum is a fake.

I watch him. I cannot keep my eyes off him. His legs twitch. He quivers and jerks. He is having a spasm. He almost jumps off the bed. All time his eyes are wide open, and the sweat pours out of him. But he does not know what it is all about. He is dead to the world. If this is the good stuff, I will take the bad stuff. I will not even put this stuff on my hair. I would be afraid it would sink down into my gut and give me the spasms like this guy has got. The rest of these stiffs do not pay any attention to him. These bay horse fiends are old stuff to them. But they are not old stuff to me. It gets on my nerves. If this guy is going to act like this all night, I am going to walk the streets. It will be cold as hell walking the streets all night, but it will not be as bad as watching this guy jump up and down with his eyes wide open, and him dead to the world.

I cover up my head with this dirty blanket and try not to think about him.

Zora Neale Hurston (1891–1960)

The author of *Their Eyes Were Watching God* (1937), one of the most admired novels by an African American woman, kept her early years shrouded in a degree of uncertainty. Records indicate that she was born in 1891 in Notasulga, Alabama, rather than in Eatonsville, Florida, in 1901 or 1903, as she claimed. But her childhood was spent in Eatonsville, the small all-black township that provided the setting for her 1937 novel. Her father was a carpenter and Baptist preacher, and several times mayor of the town. Her schoolteacher mother died when Zora was thirteen, and she was passed around among relatives, eventually leaving town for jobs as a maid for white families. After more than a decade of traveling for work, Hurston was in Baltimore in 1917 and was given an opportunity to finish high school at Morgan Academy. The next year, still working as a maid and as a manicurist, she attended Howard University, where she was befriended by Alain Locke, a leading figure in the Harlem Renaissance.

In 1925, Hurston moved to New York with, as she put it, "$1.50, no job, no friends, and a lot of hope." She was admitted to Barnard College to study anthropology and there met the renowned Frank Boas, who became her mentor during the research and writing of *Mules and Men* (1935), the study of southern black folktales and voodoo practices that is excerpted here. Although she was a part of Harlem's artistic renaissance, collaborating with Langston Hughes on the play *Mule Bone: A Comedy of Negro Life* (1930), Hurston diverged from the movement's implicit politics. Neither a critic of white racism nor an advocate of civil rights, she preferred to use both her intimate firsthand knowledge and her "anthropologist's spyglass" to represent the richness and resilience of black imaginative and emotional life. The best of her fiction and her writings on folklore celebrate the cultural practices—especially the talk, songs, and stories, the "woofing" (trading comic insults) and "lying" (telling tall tales) on the porch or on the work gang—that form a distinct black community. Although more novels and an autobiography (*Dust Tracks on a Dirt Road*, 1942) would follow, Hurston and her work faded into relative obscurity through the 1940s. She spent the last decade of her life in Florida, living alone and working low-wage jobs until her death in January 1960 in the Saint Lucie County Welfare Home. The publication of Alice Walker's "In Search of Zora Neale Hurston" (*MS Magazine*, 1975) spurred the recovery of Hurston's remarkable body of work, including a reader of her short fiction and essays, *I Love Myself When I Am Laughing . . . And Then Again When I Am Looking Mean and Impressive*, edited in 1979 by Walker.

"POLK COUNTY BLUES," FROM *MULES AND MEN*

IV

Twelve miles below Kissimmee I passed under an arch that marked the Polk County line. I was in the famed Polk County.

> How often had I heard "Polk County Blues."
> "You don't know Polk County lak Ah do.
> Anybody been dere, tell you de same thing too."

The asphalt curved deeply and when it straightened out we saw a huge smoke-stack blowing smut against the sky. A big sign said, "Everglades Cypress Lumber Company, Loughman, Florida."

We had meant to keep on to Bartow or Lakeland and we debated the subject between us until we reached the opening, then I won. We went in. The little Chevrolet was all against it. The thirty odd miles that we had come, it argued, was nothing but an appetizer. Lakeland was still thirty miles away and no telling what the road held. But it sauntered on down the barkcovered road and into the quarters just as if it had really wanted to come.

We halted beside two women walking to the commissary and asked where we could get a place to stay, despite the signs all over that this was private property and that no one could enter without the consent of the company.

One of the women was named "Babe" Hill and she sent me to her mother's house to get a room. I learned later that Mrs. Allen ran the boarding-house under patronage of the company. So we put up at Mrs. Allen's.

That night the place was full of men—come to look over the new addition to the quarters. Very little was said directly to me and when I tried to be friendly there was a noticeable disposition to *fend* me off. This worried me because I saw at once that this group of several hundred Negroes from all over the South was a rich field for folk-lore, but here was I figuratively starving to death in the midst of plenty.

Babe had a son who lived at the house with his grandmother and we soon made friends. Later the sullen Babe and I got on cordial terms. I found out afterwards that during the Christmas holidays of 1926 she had shot her husband to death, had fled to Tampa where she had bobbed her hair and eluded capture for several months but had been traced thru letters to her mother and had been arrested and lodged in Bartow jail. After a few months she had been allowed to come home and the case was forgotten. Negro women *are* punished in these parts for killing men, but only if they exceed the quota. I don't remember what the quota is. Perhaps I did hear but I forgot. One woman had killed five when I left that turpentine still where she lived. The sheriff was thinking of calling on her and scolding her severely.

James Presley used to come every night and play his guitar. Mrs. Allen's temporary brother-in-law could play a good second but he didn't have a box so I used to lend him mine. They would play. The men would crowd in and buy soft drinks and woof at me, the stranger, but I knew I wasn't getting on. The ole feather-bed tactics.

Then one day after Cliffert Ulmer, Babe's son, and I had driven down to Lakeland together he felt close enough to tell me what was the trouble. They all thought I must be a revenue officer or a detective of some kind. They were accustomed to strange women dropping into the quarters, but not in shiny gray Chevrolets. They usually came plodding down the big road or counting railroad ties. The car made me look too prosperous. So they set me aside as different. And since most of them were fugitives from justice or had done plenty time, a detective was just the last thing they felt they needed on that "job."

I took occasion that night to impress the job with the fact that I was also a fugitive from justice, "bootlegging." They were hot behind me in Jacksonville and they wanted me in Miami. So I was hiding out. That sounded reasonable. Bootleggers always have cars. I was taken in.

The following Saturday was pay-day. They paid off twice a month and pay night is big doings. At least one dance at the section of the quarters known as the Pine Mill and two or three in the big Cypress Side. The company works with two kinds of lumber.

You can tell where the dances are to be held by the fires. Huge bonfires of faulty logs and slabs are lit outside the house in which the dances are held. The refreshments are parched[1] peanuts, fried rabbit, fish, chicken and chitterlings.

---

[1] Roasted.

The only music is guitar music and the only dance is the ole square dance. James Presley is especially invited to every party to play. His pay is plenty of coon dick, and he *plays*.

Joe Willard is in great demand to call figures. He rebels occasionally because he likes to dance too.

But all of the fun isn't inside the house. A group can always be found outside about the fire, standing around and woofing and occasionally telling stories.

The biggest dance on this particular pay-night was over to the Pine Mill. James Presley and Slim assured me that they would be over there, so Cliffert Ulmer took me there. Being the reigning curiosity of the "job" lots of folks came to see what I'd do. So it was a great dance.

The guitars cried out "Polk County," "Red River" and just instrumental hits with no name, that still are played by all good box pickers. The dancing was hilarious to put it mildly. Babe, Lucy, Big Sweet, East Coast Mary and many other of the well-known women were there. The men swung them lustily, but nobody asked me to dance. I was just crazy to get into the dance, too. I had heard my mother speak of it and praise square dancing to the skies, but it looked as if I was doomed to be a wallflower and that was a new role for me. Even Cliffert didn't ask me to dance. It was so jolly, too. At the end of every set Joe Willard would trick the men. Instead of calling the next figure as expected he'd bawl out, "Grab yo' partners and march up to de table and treat." Some of the men did, but some would bolt for the door and stand about the fire and woof until the next set was called.

I went outside to join the woofers, since I seemed to have no standing among the dancers. Not exactly a hush fell about the fire, but a lull came. I stood there awkwardly, knowing that the too-ready laughter and aimless talk was a window-dressing for my benefit. The brother in black puts a laugh in every vacant place in his mind. His laugh has a hundred meanings. It may mean amusement, anger, grief, bewilderment, chagrin, curiosity, simple pleasure or any other of the known or undefined emotions. Clardia Thornton of Magazine Point, Alabama, was telling me about another woman taking her husband away from her. When the show-down came and he told Clardia in the presence of the other woman that he didn't want her—could never use her again, she tole me "Den, Zora, Ah wuz so outdone, Ah just opened mah mouf and laffed."

The folks around the fire laughed and boisterously shoved each other about, but I knew they were not tickled. But I soon had the answer. A pencil-shaped fellow with a big Adam's apple gave me the key.

"Ma'am, whut might be yo' entrimmins?" he asked with what was supposed to be a killing bow.

"My whut?"

"Yo entrimmins? Yo entitlum?"

The "entitlum" gave me the cue, "Oh, my name is Zora Hurston. And whut may be yours?"

More people came closer quickly.

"Mah name is Pitts and Ah'm sho glad to meet yuh. Ah asted Cliffert tuh knock me down tuh yuh but he wouldn't make me 'quainted. So Ah'm makin' mahseff 'quainted."

"Ah'm glad you did, Mr. Pitts."

"Sho nuff?" archly.

"Yeah. Ah wouldn't be sayin' it if Ah didn't mean it."

He looked me over shrewdly. "Ah see dat las' crap you shot, Miss, and Ah fade yuh."

I laughed heartily. The whole fire laughed at his quick comeback and more people came out to listen.

"Miss, you know uh heap uh dese hard heads wants to woof at you but dey skeered."

"How come, Mr. Pitts? Do I look like a bear or panther?"

"Naw, but dey say youse rich and dey ain't got de nerve to open dey mouf."

I mentally cursed the $12.74 dress from Macy's that I had on among all the $1.98 mail-order dresses. I looked about and noted the number of bungalow aprons and even the rolled down paper bags on the heads of several women. I did look different and resolved to fix all that no later than the next morning.

"Oh, Ah ain't got doodley squat,"[2] I countered. "Mah man brought me dis dress de las' time he went to Jacksonville. We wuz sellin' plenty stuff den and makin' good money. Wisht Ah had dat money now."

Then Pitts began woofing at me and the others stood around to see how I took it.

"Say, Miss, you know nearly all dese niggers is after you. Dat's all dey talk about out in de swamp."

"You don't say. Tell 'em to make me know it.'

"Ah ain't tellin' nobody nothin'. Ah ain't puttin' out nothin' to no ole hard head but ole folks eyes and Ah ain't doin' dat till they dead. Ah talks for Number One. Second stanza: Some of 'em talkin' 'bout marryin' you and dey wouldn't know whut to do wid you if they had you. Now, dat's a fack."

"You reckon?"

"Ah know dey wouldn't. Dey'd 'spect you tuh git out de bed and fix dem some breakfus' and a bucket. Dat's 'cause dey don't know no better. Dey's thin-brainded. Now me, Ah wouldn't let you fix me no breakfus'. Ah git up and fix mah own and den, whut make it so cool, Ah'd fix *you* some and set it on de back of de cook-stove so you could git it when you wake up. Dese mens don't even know how to talk to nobody lak you. If you wuz tuh ast dese niggers somethin' dey'd answer you 'yeah' and 'naw.' Now, if you wuz some ole gator-black 'oman dey'd be tellin' you jus' right. But dat ain't de way tuh talk tuh nobody lak *you*. Now you ast *me* somethin' and see how Ah'll answer yuh."

"Mr. Pitts, are you havin' a good time?"

(In a prim falsetto) "Yes, Ma'am. See, dat's de way tuh talk tuh *you*."

I laughed and the crowd laughed and Pitts laughed. Very successful woofing. Pitts treated me and we got on. Soon a boy came to me from Cliffert Ulmer asking me to dance. I found out that that was the social custom. The fellow that wants to broach a young woman doesn't come himself to ask. He sends his friend. Somebody came to me for Joe Willard and soon I was swamped with bids to dance. They were afraid of me before. My laughing acceptance of Pitts' woofing had put everybody at his ease.

James Presley and Slim spied noble at the orchestra. I had the chance to learn more about "John Henry" maybe. So I strolled over to James Presley and asked him if he knew how to play it.

"Ah'll play it if you sing it," he countered. So he played and I started to sing the verses I knew. They put me on the table and everybody urged me to spread my jenk,[3] so I did the best I could. Joe Willard knew two verses and sang them. Eugene Oliver knew one; Big Sweet knew one. And how James Presley can make his box cry out the accompaniment!

By the time that the song was over, before Joe Willard lifted me down from the table I knew that I was in the inner circle. I had first to convince the "job" that I was not an enemy in the person of the law; and, second, I had to prove that I was their kind. "John Henry" got me over my second hurdle.

After that my car was everybody's car. James Presley, Slim and I teamed up and we had to do "John Henry" wherever we appeared. We soon had a reputation that way. We went to Mulberry, Pierce and Lakeland.

After that I got confidential and told them all what I wanted. At first they couldn't conceive of anybody wanting to put down "lies." But when I got the idea over we held a lying contest and posted the notices at the Post Office and the commissary. I gave four

---

[2] Nothing.
[3] Have a good time.

prizes and some tall lying was done. The men and women enjoyed themselves and the contest broke up in a square dance with Joe Willard calling figures.

The contest was a huge success in every way. I not only collected a great deal of material but it started individuals coming to me privately to tell me stories they had no chance to tell during the contest.

Cliffert Ulmer told me that I'd get a great deal more by going out with the swamp-gang. He said they lied a plenty while they worked. I spoke to the quarters boss and the swamp boss and both agreed that it was all right, so I strowed it all over the quarters that I was going out to the swamp with the boys next day. My own particular crowd, Cliffert, James, Joe Willard, Jim Allen and Eugene Oliver were to look out for me and see to it that I didn't get snake-bit nor 'gator-swallowed. The watchman, who sleeps out in the swamps and gets up steam in the skitter every morning before the men get to the cypress swamp, had been killed by a panther two weeks before, but they assured me that nothing like that could happen to me; not with the help I had.

Having watched some members of that swamp crew handle axes, I didn't doubt for a moment that they could do all that they said. Not only do they chop rhythmically, but they do a beautiful double twirl above their heads with the ascending axe before it begins that accurate and bird-like descent. They can hurl their axes great distances and behead moccasins or sink the blade into an alligator's skull. In fact, they seem to be able to do everything with their instrument that a blade can do. It is a magnificent sight to watch the marvelous co-ordination between the handsome black torsos and the twirling axes.

So next morning we were to be off to the woods.

It wasn't midnight dark and it wasn't day yet. When I awoke the saw-mill camp was a dawn gray. You could see the big saw-mill but you couldn't see the smoke from the chimney. You could see the congregation of shacks and the dim outlines of the scrub oaks among the houses, but you couldn't see the grey quilts of Spanish Moss that hung from the trees.

Dick Willie was the only man abroad. It was his business to be the first one out. He was the shack-rouser. Men are not supposed to over-sleep and Dick Willie gets paid to see to it that they don't. Listen to him singing as he goes down the line.

Wake up, bullies, and git on de rock. 'Tain't quite daylight but it's four o'clock.

Coming up the next line, he's got another song.

Wake up, Jacob, day's a breakin'. Git yo' hoe-cake a bakin' and yo' shirt tail shakin'.

What does he say when he gets to the jook and the long-house? I'm fixing to tell you right now what he says. He raps on the floor of the porch with a stick and says:

"Ah ha! What make de rooster crow every morning at sun-up?

"Dat's to let de pimps and rounders know de workin' man is on his way."

About that time you see a light in every shack. Every kitchen is scorching up fat-back and hoe-cake. Nearly every skillet is full of corn-bread. But some like biscuit-bread better. Break your hoe-cake half in two. Half on the plate, half in the dinner-bucket. Throw in your black-eyed peas and fat meat left from supper and your bucket is fixed. Pour meat grease in your plate with plenty of cane syrup. Mix it and sop it with your bread. A big bowl of coffee, a drink of water from the tin dipper in the pail. Grab your dinner-bucket and hit the grit. Don't keep the straw-boss[4] waiting.

This morning when we got to the meeting place, the foreman wasn't there. So the men squatted along the railroad track and waited.

---

[4] The low-paid poor white section boss on a railroad; similar to swamp boss who works the gang that gets the timber to the sawmill.

Joe Willard was sitting with me on the end of a cross-tie when he saw Jim Presley coming in a run with his bucket and jumper-jacket.

"Hey, Jim, where the swamp boss? He ain't got here yet."

"He's ill—sick in the bed Ah hope, but Ah bet he'll git here yet."

"Aw, he ain't sick. Ah bet you a fat man he ain't," Joe said.

"How come?" somebody asked him and Joe answered:

"Man, he's too ugly. If a spell of sickness ever tried to slip up on him, he'd skeer it into a three weeks' spasm."

Blue Baby stuck in his oar and said: "He ain't so ugly. Ye all jus' ain't seen no real ugly man. Ah seen a man so ugly till he could get behind a jimpson weed and hatch monkies."

Everybody laughed and moved closer together. Then Officer Richardson said: "Ah seen a man so ugly till they had to spread a sheet over his head at night so sleep could slip up on him."

They laughed some more, then Clifford Ulmer said:

"Ah'm goin' to talk with my mouth wide open. Those men y'all been talkin' 'bout wasn't ugly at all. Those was pretty men. Ah knowed one so ugly till you could throw him in the Mississippi river and skim ugly for six months."

"Give Cliff de little dog," Jim Allen said. "He done tole the biggest lie."

"He ain't lyin'," Joe Martin tole them. "Ah knowed dat same man. He didn't die—he jus' uglied away."

They laughed a great big old kah kah laugh and got closer together.

"Looka here, folkses," Jim Presley exclaimed. "Wese a half hour behind schedule and no swamp boss and no log train here yet. What yo' all reckon is the matter sho' 'nough?"

"Must be something terrible when white folks get slow about putting us to work."

"Yeah," says Good Black. "You know back in slavery Ole Massa was out in de field sort of lookin' things over, when a shower of rain come up. The field hands was glad, it rained so they could knock off for a while. So one slave named John says:

"More rain, more rest."

"Ole Massa says, 'What's dat you say?' "

"John says, 'More rain, more grass.' "

"There goes de big whistle. We ought to be out in the woods almost."

The big whistle at the saw-mill boomed and shrilled and pretty soon the log-train came racking along. No flats for logs behind the little engine. The foreman dropped off the tender as the train stopped.

"No loggin' today, boys. Got to send the train to the Everglades to fetch up the track gang and their tools."

"Lawd, Lawd, we got a day off," Joe Willard said, trying to make it sound like he was all put out about it. "Let's go back, boys. Sorry you won't git to de swamp, Zora."

"Aw, naw," the Foreman said. "Y'all had better g'wan over to the mill and see if they need you over there."

And he walked on off, chewing his tobacco and spitting his juice.

The men began to shoulder jumper-jackets and grab hold of buckets.

Allen asked: "Ain't dat a mean man? No work in the swamp and still he won't let us knock off."

"He's mean all right, but Ah done seen meaner men than him," said Handy Pitts.

"Where?"

"Oh, up in Middle Georgy. They had a straw boss and he was so mean dat when the boiler burst and blowed some of the men up in the air, he docked 'em for de time they was off de job."

Tush Hawg up and said: "Over on de East Coast Ah used to have a road boss and he was so mean and times was so hard till he laid off de hands of his watch."

Wiley said: "He's almost as bad as Joe Brown. Ah used to work in his mine and he was so mean till he wouldn't give God an honest prayer without snatching back 'Amen.'"

Ulmer says: "Joe Wiley, youse as big a liar as you is a man! Whoo-wee. Boy, you molds 'em. But lemme tell y'all a sho nuff tale 'bout Ole Massa."

"Go 'head and tell it, Cliff," shouted Eugene Oliver. "Ah love to hear tales about Ole Massa and John. John sho was one smart nigger."

So Cliff Ulmer went on.

You know befo' surrender Ole Massa had a nigger name John and John always prayed every night befo' he went to bed and his prayer was for God to come git him and take him to Heaven right away. He didn't even want to take time to die. He wanted de Lawd to come git him just like he was—boot, sock and all. He'd git down on his knees and say: "O Lawd, it's once more and again yo' humble servant is knee-bent and body-bowed—my heart beneath my knees and my knees in some lonesome valley, crying for mercy while mercy kin be found. O Lawd, Ah'm astin' you in de humblest way I know how to be *so* pleased as to come in yo' fiery chariot and take me to yo' Heben and its immortal glory. Come Lawd, you know Ah have such a hard time. Old Massa works me *so* hard, and don't gimme no time to rest. So come, Lawd, wid peace in one hand and pardon in de other and take me away from this sin-sorrowing world. Ah'm tired and Ah want to go home."

So one night Ole Massa passed by John's shack and heard him beggin' de Lawd to come git him in his fiery chariot and take him away; so he made up his mind to find out if John meant dat thing. So he goes on up to de big house and got hisself a bed sheet and come on back. He throwed de sheet over his head and knocked on de door.

John quit prayin' and ast: "Who dat?"

Ole Massa say: "It's me, John, de Lawd, done come wid my fiery chariot to take you away from this sin-sick world."

Right under de bed John had business. He told his wife: "Tell Him Ah ain't here, Liza."

At first Liza didn't say nothin' at all, but de Lawd kept right on callin' John: "Come on, John, and go to Heben wid me where you won't have to plough no mo' furrows and hoe no mo' corn. Come on, John."

Liza says: "John ain't here, Lawd, you hafta come back another time."

Lawd says: "Well, then Liza, you'll do."

Liza whispers and says: "John, come out from underneath dat bed and g'wan wid de Lawd. You been beggin' him to come git you. Now g'wan wid him."

John back under de bed not saying a mumblin' word. De Lawd out on de door step kept on callin'.

Liza says: "John, Ah thought you was so anxious to get to Heben. Come out and go on wid God!'

John says: "Don't you hear him say 'You'll do'? Why don't you go wid him?"

"Ah ain't a goin' nowhere. Youse de one been whoopin' and hollerin' for him to come git you and if you don't come out from under dat bed Ah'm gointer tell God youse here."

Ole Massa makin' out he's God, says: "Come on, Liza, you'll do."

Liza says: "O, Lawd, John is right here underneath de bed."

"Come on John, and go to Heben wid me and its immortal glory."

John crept out from under de bed and went to de door and cracked it and when he seen all dat white standin' on de doorsteps he jumped back. He says: "O, Lawd, Ah can't go to Heben wid you in yo' fiery chariot in dese ole dirty britches; gimme time to put on my Sunday pants."

"All right, John, put on yo' Sunday pants."

John fooled around just as long as he could, changing them pants, but when he went back to de door, de big white glory was still standin' there. So he says agin: "O, Lawd, de Good Book says in Heben no filth is found and I got on his dirty sweaty shirt. Ah can't go wid you in dis old nasty shirt. Gimme time to put on my Sunday shirt!"

"All right, John, go put on yo' Sunday shirt."

John took and fumbled around a long time changing his shirt, and den he went back to de door, but Ole Massa was still on de door step. John didn't had nothin' else to change so he opened de door a little piece and says:

"O, Lawd, Ah'm ready to go to Heben wid you in yo' fiery chariot, but de radiance of yo' countenance is *so* bright, Ah can't come out by you. Stand back jus' a li'l way please."

Ole Massa stepped back a li'l bit.

John looked out agin and says: "O, Lawd, you know dat po' humble me is less than de dust beneath yo' shoe soles. And de radiance of yo' countenance is so bright Ah can't come out by you. Please, please, Lawd, in yo' tender mercy, stand back a li'l bit further."

Ole Massa stepped back a li'l bit mo'.

John looked out agin and he says: "O, Lawd, Heben is so high and wese so low; youse so great and Ah'm so weak and yo' strength is too much for us poor sufferin' sinners. So once mo' and agin yo' humber servant is knee-bent and body-bowed askin' you one mo' favor befo' Ah step into yo' fiery chariot to go to Heben wid you and wash in yo' glory—be so pleased in yo' tender mercy as to stand back jus' a li'l bit further."

Ole Massa stepped back a step or two mo' and out dat door John come like a streak of lightning. All across de punkin patch, thru de cotton over de pasture—John wid Ole Massa right behind him. By de time dey hit de cornfield John was way ahead of Ole Massa.

Back in de shack one of de children was cryin' and she ast Liza: "Mama, you reckon God's gointer ketch papa and carry him to Heben wid him?"

"Shet yo' mouf, talkin' foolishness!" Liza clashed at de chile. "You know de Lawd can't outrun yo' pappy—specially when he's barefooted at dat."

Kah, Kah, Kah! Everybody laughing with their mouths wide open. If the foreman had come along right then he would have been good and mad because he could tell their minds were not on work.

Joe Willard says: "Wait a minute, fellows, wese walkin' too fast. At dis rate we'll be there befo' we have time to talk some mo' about Ole Massa and John. Tell another one, Cliffert."

"Aw, naw," Eugene Oliver hollered out.

Let *me* talk some chat. Dis is de real truth 'bout Ole Massa 'cause my grandma told it to my mama and she told it to me.

During slavery time, you know, Ole Massa had a nigger named John and he was a faithful nigger and Ole Massa lakted John a lot too.

One day Ole Massa sent for John and tole him, says: "John, somebody is stealin' my corn out de field. Every mornin' when I go out I see where they done carried off some mo' of my roastin' ears. I want you to set in de corn patch tonight and ketch whoever it is."

So John said all right and he went and hid in de field.

Pretty soon he heard somethin' breakin' corn. So John sneaked up behind him wid a short stick in his hand and hollered: "Now, break another ear of Ole Massa's corn and see what *Ah'll* do to you."

John thought it was a man all dis time, but it was a bear wid his arms full of roastin' ears. He throwed down de corn and grabbed John. And him and dat bear!

John, after while got loose and got de bear by the tail wid de bear tryin' to git to him all de time. So they run around in a circle all night long. John was so tired. But he couldn't let go of de bear's tail, do de bear would grab him in de back.

After a stretch they quit runnin' and walked. John swingin' on to de bear's tail and de bear's nose 'bout to touch him in de back.

Daybreak, Ole Massa come out to see 'bout John and he seen John and de bear walkin' 'round in de ring. So he run up and says: "Lemme take holt of 'im, John, whilst you run git help!"

John says: "All right, Massa. Now you run in quick and grab 'im just so."

Ole Massa run and grabbed holt of de bear's tail and said: "Now, John you make haste to git somebody to help us."

John staggered off and set down on de grass and went to fanning hisself wid his hat.

Ole Massa was havin' plenty trouble wid dat bear and he looked over and seen John settin' on de grass and he hollered:

"John, you better g'wan git help or else I'm gwinter turn dis bear aloose!"

John says: "Turn 'im loose, then. Dat's whut Ah tried to do all night long but Ah couldn't."

Jim Allen laughed just as loud as anybody else and then he said: "We better hurry on to work befo' de buckra[5] get in behind us."

"Don't never worry about work," says Jim Presley. "There's more work in de world than there is anything else. God made de world and de white folks made work."

"Yeah, dey made work but they didn't make us do it," Joe Willard put in. "We brought dat on ourselves."

"Oh, yes, de white folks did put us to work too," said Jim Allen.

Know how it happened? After God got thru makin' de world and de varmints and de folks, he made up a great big bundle and let it down in de middle of de road. It laid dere for thousands of years, then Ole Missus said to Ole Massa: "Go pick up dat box, Ah want to see whut's in it." Ole Massa look at de box and it look so heavy dat he says to de nigger, "Go fetch me dat big ole box out dere in de road." De nigger been stumblin' over de box a long time so he tell his wife:

"'Oman, go git dat box." So de nigger 'oman she runned to git de box. She says:

"Ah always lak to open up a big box 'cause there's nearly always something good in great big boxes." So she run and grabbed a-hold of de box and opened it up and it was full of hard work.

Dat's de reason de sister in black works harder than anybody else in de world. De white man tells de nigger to work and he takes and tells his wife.

"Aw, now, dat ain't de reason niggers is working so hard," Jim Presley objected.

Dis is de way *dat* was.

God let down two bundles 'bout five miles down de road. So de white man and de nigger raced to see who would git there first. Well, de nigger out-run de white man and grabbed de biggest bundle. He was so skeered de white man would git it away from him he fell on top of de bundle and hollered back: "Oh, Ah got here first and dis biggest bundle is mine." De white man says. "All right, Ah'll take yo' leavings," and picked up de li'l tee-ninchy bundle layin' in de road. When de nigger opened up his bundle he found a pick and shovel and a hoe and a plow and chop-axe and then de white man opened up his bundle and found a writin'-pen and ink. So ever since then de nigger been out in de hot sun, usin' his tools and de white man been sittin' up figgerin', ought's a ought, figger's a figger; all for de white man, none for de nigger.

"Oh lemme spread my mess. Dis is Will Richardson doin' dis lyin'."

You know Ole Massa took a nigger deer huntin' and posted him in his place and told him, says: "Now you wait right here and keep yo' gun reformed and ready. Ah'm goin' 'round de hill and skeer up de deer and head him dis way. When he come past, you shoot."

De nigger says: "Yessuh, Ah sho' will, Massa."

He set there and waited wid de gun all cocked and after a while de deer come tearin' past him. He didn't make a move to shoot de deer so he went on 'bout his business. After while de white man come on 'round de hill and ast de nigger: "Did you kill de deer?"

De nigger says: "Ah ain't seen no deer pass here yet."

Massa says: "Yes, you did. You couldn't help but see him. He come right dis way."

Nigger says: "Well Ah sho' ain't seen none. All Ah seen was a white man come along here wid a pack of chairs on his head and Ah tipped my hat to him and waited for de deer."

"Some colored folks ain't got no sense, and when Ah see 'em like dat," Ah say, "My race but not my taste."

---

5 West African word meaning white people.

John Steinbeck (1902–1968)

John Steinbeck was born and raised in Salinas, California, in the farming valley known at the time as the "Salad Bowl of the Nation." His most successful fiction, including the social protest novels of the 1930s—*Tortilla Flat* (1935), *In Dubious Battle* (1936), *Of Mice and Men* (1937), and *The Grapes of Wrath* (1939)—and his epic *East of Eden* (1952), are set in the towns and valleys surrounding his birthplace. His parents, John Steinbeck, Sr., a businessman and accountant, and Olive Hamilton, a former teacher, were prominent citizens of the town in which years later their son's Pulizer Prize-winning *The Grapes of Wrath* was banned at the Salinas Public Library. Although frequently vilified for its "crass" language and its critique of the farm labor system, Steinbeck's story of the Joads' migration from the Oklahoma dust bowl to California's fruit fields was the most widely read radical novel of the 1930s and came to symbolize the Depression-era dispossession of working-class Americans, in part because of its successful movie adaptation in 1940. Steinbeck prepared for the writing of the novel with several months of research, visiting the migrants' camps, advocating for them, and writing a series of articles, "The Harvest Gypsies," from which "Starvation Under the Orange Trees" is taken. The selected chapter from *The Grapes of Wrath* demonstrates his fictional reworking of this documentary material.

Primarily a novelist, Steinbeck also wrote short stories, Broadway plays (*Of Mice and Men* and *The Moon Is Down*), screenplays (*The Red Pony*, *The Pearl*, and *Viva Zapata!*), war reportage (*Bombs Away* and *Once There Was a War*), and travel narratives (*Sea of Cortez*, *A Russian Journey*, and *Travels with Charley*). When he was awarded the Nobel Prize in Literature in 1962, the honor was attacked in a *New York Times* editorial, "Does a Writer with a Moral Vision of the 1930s Deserve the Nobel Prize?" Although Steinbeck wrote to a friend, "This prize business is only different from the Lettuce Queen of Salinas in degree," he was stung, as he was throughout his career, by the criticism of his writing and its politics, and he wrote no more fiction. The last book to be published before his death, *America and Americans* (1966), registers his disenchantment with American greed and wastefulness, mistreatment of the environment, and continuing racial injustice. His final project, a modern rendering of Sir Thomas Mallory's *Morte d' Arthur*, which he had worked on through the 1950s and 1960s, was published posthumously in 1976.

STARVATION UNDER THE ORANGE TREES

The spring is rich and green in California this year. In the fields the wild grass is ten inches high, and in the orchards and vineyards the grass is deep and nearly ready to be plowed under to enrich the soil. Already the flowers are starting to bloom. Very shortly one of the oil companies will be broadcasting the locations of the wild-flower masses. It is a beautiful spring.

There has been no war in California, no plague, no bombing of open towns and roads, no shelling of cities. It is a beautiful year. And thousands of families are starving in California. In the county seats the coroners are filling in "malnutrition" in the spaces left for "causes of death." For some reason, a coroner shrinks from writing "starvation" when a thin child is dead in a tent.

For it's in the tents you see along the roads and in the shacks built from dump heap material that the hunger is, and it isn't malnutrition. It is starvation. Malnutrition means you go without certain food essentials and take a long time to die, but starvation means no food at all. The green grass spreads right into the tent doorways and the orange trees are loaded. In the cotton fields, a few wisps of the old crop cling to the black stems. But the people who picked the cotton, and cut the peaches and apricots, who crawled all day in the rows of lettuce and beans, are hungry. The men who harvested the crops of California, the women and girls who stood all day and half the night in the canneries, are starving.

It was so two years ago in Nipomo, it is so now, it will continue to be so until the rich produce of California can be grown and harvested on some other basis than that of stupidity and greed.

What is to be done about it? The Federal Government is trying to feed and give direct relief, but it is difficult to do quickly for there are forms to fill out, questions to ask, for fear someone who isn't actually starving may get something. The state relief organizations are trying to send those who haven't been in the state for a year back to the states they came from. The Associated Farmers, which presumes to speak for the farms of California and which is made up of such earth-stained toilers as chain banks, public utilities, railroad companies and those huge corporations called land companies, this financial organization in the face of the crisis is conducting Americanism meetings and bawling about reds and foreign agitators. It has been invariably true in the past that when such a close-knit financial group as the Associated Farmers becomes excited about our ancient liberties and foreign agitators, someone is about to lose something.

A wage cut has invariably followed such a campaign of pure Americanism. And of course any resentment of such a wage cut is set down as the work of foreign agitators. Anyway that is the Associated Farmers contribution to the hunger of the men and women who harvest their crops.

The small farmers, who do not belong to the Associated Farmers and cannot make use of the slop chest, are helpless to do anything about it. The little storekeepers at crossroads and in small towns have carried the accounts of the working people until they are near to bankruptcy.

And there are one thousand families in Tulare County, and two thousand families in Kings, fifteen hundred families in Kern, and so on. The families average three persons, by the way. With the exception of a little pea picking, there isn't going to be any work for nearly three months.

There is sickness in the tents, pneumonia and measles, tuberculosis. Measles in a tent, with no way to protect the eyes, means a child with weakened eyes for life. And there are varied diseases attributable to hunger, rickets and the beginning of pellagra.

The nurses in the county, and there aren't one-tenth enough of them, are working their heads off, doing a magnificent job, and they can only begin to do the work. The corps includes nurses assigned by the federal and state public health services, school nurses and county health nurses, and a few nurses furnished by the Council of Women for Home Missions, a national church organization. I've seen them, red-eyed, weary from far too many hours, and seeming to make no impression in the illness about them.

It may be of interest to reiterate the reasons why these people are in the state and the reason they must go hungry. They are here because we need them. Before the white American migrants were here, it was the custom in California to import great numbers of Mexicans, Filipinos, Japanese, to keep them segregated, to herd them about like animals, and, if there were any complaints, to deport or to imprison the leaders. This system of labor was a dream of heaven to such employers as those who now fear foreign agitators so much.

But then the dust and the tractors began displacing the sharecroppers of Oklahoma, Texas, Kansas and Arkansas. Families who had lived for many years on the little "cropper lands" were dispossessed because the land was in the hands of the banks and finance companies, and because these owners found that one man with a tractor could do the work of ten sharecropper families.

Faced with the question of starving or moving, these dispossessed families came west. To a certain extent they were actuated by advertisements and handbills distributed by labor contractors from California. It is to the advantage of the corporate farmer to have too much labor, for then wages can be cut. Then people who are hungry will fight each other for a job rather than the employer for a living wage.

It is possible to make money for food and gasoline for at least nine months of the year if you are quick on the getaway, if your wife and children work in the fields. But then the dead three months strikes, and what can you do then? The migrant cannot save anything. It takes everything he can make to feed his family and buy gasoline to go to the next job. If you don't believe this, go out in the cotton fields next year. Work all day and see if you have made thirty-five cents. A good picker makes more, of course, but you can't.

The method of concentrating labor for one of the great crops is this. Handbills are distributed, advertisements are printed. You've seen them. Cotton pickers wanted in Bakersfield or Fresno or Imperial Valley. Then all the available migrants rush to the scene. They arrive with no money and little food. The reserve has been spent getting there.

If wages happen to drop a little, they must take them anyway. The moment the crop is picked, the locals begin to try to get rid of the people who have harvested their crops. They want to run them out, move them on.

The county hospitals are closed to them. They are not eligible to relief. You must be eligible to eat. That particular locality is through with them until another crop comes in.

It will be remembered that two years ago some so-called agitators were tarred and feathered. The population of migrants left the locality just as the hops were ripe. Then the howling of the locals was terrible to hear. They even tried to get the army and the CCC ordered to pick their crops.

About the 15th of January the dead time sets in. There is no work. First the gasoline gives out. And without gasoline a man cannot go to a job even if he could get one. Then the food goes. And then in the rains, with insufficient food, the children develop colds because the ground in the tents is wet.

I talked to a man last week who lost two children in ten days with pneumonia. His face was hard and fierce and he didn't talk much.

I talked to a girl with a baby and offered her a cigarette. She took two puffs and vomited in the street. She was ashamed. She shouldn't have tried to smoke, she said, for she hadn't eaten for two days.

I heard a man whimpering that the baby was sucking but nothing came out of the breast. I heard a man explain very shyly that his little girl couldn't go to school because she was too weak to walk to school and besides the school lunches of the other children made her unhappy.

I heard a man tell in a monotone how he couldn't get a doctor while his oldest boy died of pneumonia but that a doctor came right away after it was dead. It is easy to get a doctor to look at a corpse, not so easy to get one for a live person. It is easy to get a body buried. A truck comes right out and takes it away. The state is much more interested in how you die than in how you live. The man who was telling about it had just found that out. He didn't want to believe it.

Next year the hunger will come again and the year after that and so on until we come out of this coma and realize that our agriculture for all its great produce is a failure.

If you buy a farm horse and only feed him when you work him, the horse will die. No one complains of the necessity of feeding the horse when he is not working. But we complain about feeding the men and women who work our lands. Is it possible that this state is so stupid, so vicious and so greedy that it cannot feed and clothe the men and women who help to make it the richest area in the world? Must the hunger become anger and the anger fury before anything will be done?

"THE SPRING IS BEAUTIFUL IN CALIFORNIA," FROM *THE GRAPES OF WRATH*

The spring is beautiful in California. Valleys in which the fruit blossoms are fragrant pink and white waters in a shallow sea. Then the first tendrils of the grapes, swelling from the old gnarled vines, cascade down to cover the trunks. The full green hills are round and soft as breasts. And on the level vegetable lands are the mile-long rows of pale green lettuce and the spindly little cauliflowers, the gray-green unearthly artichoke plants.

And then the leaves break out on the trees, and the petals drop from the fruit trees and carpet the earth with pink and white. The centers of the blossoms swell and grow and color: cherries and apples, peaches and pears, figs which close the flower in the fruit. All California quickens with produce, and the fruit grows heavy, and the limbs bend gradually under the fruit so that little crutches must be placed under them to support the weight.

Behind the fruitfulness are men of understanding and knowledge and skill, men who experiment with seed, endlessly developing the techniques for greater crops of plants whose roots will resist the million enemies of the earth: the molds, the insects, the rusts, the blights. These men work carefully and endlessly to perfect the seed, the roots. And there are the men of chemistry who spray the trees against pests, who sulphur the grapes, who cut out disease and rots, mildews and sicknesses. Doctors of preventive medicine, men at the borders who look for fruit flies, for Japanese beetle, men who quarantine the sick trees and root them out and burn them, men of knowledge. The men who graft the young trees, the little vines, are the cleverest of all, for theirs is a surgeon's job, as tender and delicate; and these men must have surgeons' hands and surgeons' hearts to slit the bark, to place the grafts, to bind the wounds and cover them from the air. These are great men.

Along the rows, the cultivators move, tearing the spring grass and turning it under to make a fertile earth, breaking the ground to hold the water up near the surface, ridging the ground in little pools for the irrigation, destroying the weed roots that may drink the water away from the trees.

And all the time the fruit swells and the flowers break out in long clusters on the vines. And in the growing year the warmth grows and the leaves turn dark green. The prunes lengthen like little green bird's eggs, and the limbs sag down against the crutches under the weight. And the hard little pears take shape, and the beginning of the fuzz comes out on the peaches. Grape blossoms shed their tiny petals and the hard little beads become green buttons, and the buttons grow heavy. The men who work in the fields, the owners of the little orchards, watch and calculate. The year is heavy with produce. And men are proud, for of their knowledge they can make the year heavy. They have transformed the world with their knowledge. The short, lean wheat has been made big and productive. Little sour apples have grown large and sweet, and that old grape that grew among the trees and fed the birds its tiny fruit has mothered a thousand varieties, red and black, green and pale pink, purple and yellow; and each variety with its own flavor. The men who work in the experimental farms have made new fruits: nectarines and forty kinds of plums, walnuts with paper shells. And always they work, selecting, grafting, changing, driving themselves, driving the earth to produce.

And first the cherries ripen. Cent and a half a pound. Hell, we can't pick 'em for that. Black cherries and red cherries, full and sweet, and the birds eat half of each cherry and the yellowjackets buzz into the holes the birds made. And on the ground the seeds drop and dry with black shreds hanging from them.

The purple prunes soften and sweeten. My God, we can't pick them and dry and sulphur them. We can't pay wages, no matter what wages. And the purple prunes carpet the ground. And first the skins wrinkle a little and swarms of flies come to feast, and the valley is filled with the odor of sweet decay. The meat turns dark and the crop shrivels on the ground.

And the pears grow yellow and soft. Five dollars a ton. Five dollars for forty fifty-pound boxes; trees pruned and sprayed, orchards cultivated—pick the fruit, put it in boxes, load the trucks, deliver the fruit to the cannery—forty boxes for five dollars. We can't do it. And the yellow fruit falls heavily to the ground and splashes on the ground. The yellowjackets dig into the soft meat, and there is a smell of ferment and rot.

Then the grapes—we can't make good wine. People can't buy good wine. Rip the grapes from the vines, good grapes, rotten grapes, wasp-stung grapes. Press stems, press dirt and rot.

But there's mildew and formic acid in the vats.

Add sulphur and tannic acid.

The smell from the ferment is not the rich odor of wine, but the smell of decay and chemicals.

Oh, well. It has alcohol in it, anyway. They can get drunk.

The little farmers watched debt creep up on them like the tide. They sprayed the trees and sold no crop, they pruned and grafted and could not pick the crop. And the men of knowledge have worked, have considered, and the fruit is rotting on the ground, and the decaying mash in the wine vats is poisoning the air. And taste the wine—no grape flavor at all, just sulphur and tannic acid and alcohol.

This little orchard will be a part of a great holding next year, for the debt will have choked the owner.

This vineyard will belong to the bank. Only the great owners can survive, for they own the canneries too. And four pears peeled and cut in half, cooked and canned, still cost fifteen cents. And the canned pears do not spoil. They will last for years.

The decay spreads over the State, and the sweet smell is a great sorrow on the land. Men who can graft the trees and make the seed fertile and big can find no way to let the hungry people eat their produce. Men who have created new fruits in the world cannot create a system whereby their fruits may be eaten. And the failure hangs over the State like a great sorrow.

The works of the roots of the vines, of the trees, must be destroyed to keep up the price, and this is the saddest, bitterest thing of all. Carloads of oranges dumped on the ground. The people came for miles to take the fruit, but this could not be. How would they buy oranges at twenty cents a dozen if they could drive out and pick them up? And men with hoses squirt kerosene on the oranges, and they are angry at the crime, angry at the people who have come to take the fruit. A million people hungry, needing the fruit—and kerosene sprayed over the golden mountains.

And the smell of rot fills the country.

Burn coffee for fuel in the ships. Burn corn to keep warm, it makes a hot fire. Dump potatoes in the rivers and place guards along the banks to keep the hungry people from fishing them out. Slaughter the pigs and bury them, and let the putrescence drip down into the earth.

There is a crime here that goes beyond denunciation. There is a sorrow here that weeping cannot symbolize. There is a failure here that topples all our success. The fertile earth, the straight tree rows, the sturdy trunks, and the ripe fruit. And children dying of pellagra must die because a profit cannot be taken from an orange. And coroners must fill in the certificates—died of malnutrition—because the food must rot, must be forced to rot.

The people come with nets to fish for potatoes in the river, and the guards hold them back; they come in rattling cars to get the dumped oranges, but the kerosene is sprayed. And they stand still and watch the potatoes float by, listen to the screaming pigs being killed in a ditch and covered with quicklime, watch the mountains of oranges slop down to a putrefying ooze; and in the eyes of the people there is the failure; and in the eyes of the hungry there is a growing wrath. In the souls of the people the grapes of wrath are filling and growing heavy, growing heavy for the vintage.

Sanora Babb (1907–2005)

The title of Sanora Babb's first novel, *Whose Names Are Unknown* (2004) is drawn from a legal eviction notice: "To John Doe and Mary Doe Whose True Names are Unknown." Set in the 1930s during the Great Plains dust bowl disaster that drove farmers off the land and into the migrant camps of California, Babb's documentary novel about the Dunne family gives a palpable identity to the "Does" of the world. It was a story that Babb knew firsthand. Born the year Oklahoma became a state—1907—Babb grew up in Cimarron County, the western end of the Oklahoma panhandle, in a poor family who moved frequently. After high school she supported herself by teaching in rural schools and with freelance writing until she moved to Los Angeles in 1929 to pursue a career as a journalist. She traveled with Tillie Olsen and novelist Harry Carlisle as representatives of the Los Angeles John Reed Clubs to New York to attend the 1935 Writers Congress.

Babb hitchhiked alone back to California, and in 1938 joined the Farm Security Administration as a volunteer and organizer in the migrant camps in the San Joaquin and Imperial Valleys. There she recorded her observations of the hardships faced by the displaced migrants as she corresponded with her own family still on the Plains. A letter from her mother describing the relentless dust storms in Kansas becomes the nearly verbatim "dust journal" of Julia Dunne (included here). Babb also shared her field notes with Tom Collins, a camp administrator who was sympathetic to the migrants. Collins, impressed with Babb's documentation, gave a copy of her notes to another California writer, John Steinbeck (who may or may not have read them). Babb began *Whose Names Are Unknown* while living in the camps and sent several chapters to Random House. Editor Bennett Cerf, recognizing the high quality of her novel, sent her an advance that allowed her to complete the manuscript in New York. As it happened, Steinbeck published his *The Grapes of Wrath* in 1939, and, consequently, Cerf and other editors decided that the market could not bear two books on the same topic and canceled the contract. More than sixty years later, this compelling novel of the struggles and dignity of ordinary people was finally published by the University of Oklahoma Press. Babb continued to publish essays, stories, and poems, as well as five other books: *The Lost Traveler* (1958, 1995), *An Owl on Every Post* (1970, 1994), *The Dark Earth* (1987), *Cry of the Tinamou* (1997), *Told in the Seed* (1998). Babb's husband was the cinematographer James Wong Howe, who won academy awards for *The Rose Tattoo* (1955) and *Hud* (1963).

Arthur Rothstein, "Dust Storm," Cimmaron County, Oklahoma, 1936. *Courtesy of Library of Congress, USF-Z62-11491-LC.*

"Dust," from *Whose Names Are Unknown*

"Dad boarded up the windows this morning as the dust was still blowing, looking like it would never stop." Julia brushed the dust from the rough school tablet paper and looked back at what she had written. She had decided to keep a record of the strange phenomenon of dust. The old man kept a record for years of the great storms, droughts, deep rains. He named the day and the year of natural disturbances the way another man names the events of his life.

She read her description of the first storm and felt frightened again, and pleased with herself. She closed the tablet and placed it on a shelf and went about her work.

April 4. A fierce dirty day. Just able to get here and there for things we have to do. It is awful to live in a dark house with the windows boarded up and no air coming in anywhere. Everything is covered and filled with dust.

April 5. Today is a terror.

April 6. Let up a little. We can see the fence but can't see any of the neighbors' houses yet. No trip to town today. Funny how you learn to get along even in this dust.

April 7. A beautiful morning. Everyone spoiling the happiness of a clear day by digging dust. Sunday afternoon we walked for miles to see other places. It was a sight. It looks like the desert you read about in books, desolation itself. The day began and ended as a real sunshiny western day.

April 8. Morning bright and skies clear. Ten o'clock. Dirt began to show up around the edges. By noon the sky and air full. We try to do our work as usual, thinking rain may fall and end our troubles for a while. We don't speak much of the wheat anymore. Going to bed. Dirt still blowing.

April 9. Sometime in the night about ten we think it started raining. We heard it and got up to put our heads out and get a fresh breath. Dad scared us. He heard it first and began to wake us up. He was excited and kept saying over and over. "It's raining! Hear it, it's raining!" We were so glad, we could hardly believe our ears. It rained on and off till morning. We all slept like dead.

This morning we all felt so happy over a smell of rain and the sight of it, but by nine o'clock dirt began to show up high in the heavens and got thicker and thicker. Mailman came by with another man along in case anything should happen. Had flit gun filled with water to shoot in car when dust got too thick. Also chain fastened to car and dragging, to ground electricity. He told us the town school buses go out with two drivers, mechanical air conditioners, water, everything needed for service in case they have to stay overnight. No school on worst days. The district school still closed. He told us he heard of some youngsters strayed off in wrong direction with dirt blinding them. Word was sent out over radio and men tied themselves together with rope to keep from getting lost in duster. The children were found out by the Cimarron River. At one town he said he heard on the radio it was blowing dirt and started raining and plastered the town with mud. Good to talk to somebody again.

April 10. Blowing all night again and all day today. Got up at 5:30, very dark and dirty. At nine o'clock a car stopped and people wanted a drink. Looked like bandits with noses and mouths tied up, faces and hair dirty, and clothes covered. They told us people in town were asked over radio to keep porch lights on overnight to aid someone who might have to get out. Said hospitals refuse to operate on anyone unless it's life or death. Some people getting dust pneumonia. 10 a.m. Just lighted lamp, fierce dark at times. Hope those people get where they are going safely.

Noon. Ate on a dirty dusty table. Took up 15 or 20 pounds of dust to make room for more. The dirt is in waves. Think someone's farm is in our house, maybe our own. Max brought over his little radio for us to use for a while. They have a big one. I washed my dishes and sat down in the dust to sew and listen to reports coming over radio. It took a big passenger bus from 7:30 a.m. till 3 p.m. to go 25 miles between towns. 3:30. Pitch dark, has been by spells all day, but the blackness is scarey and makes me feel creepy. Dad made a water spray for the house and one for barn. We needed something stronger than the fan. He stays in the barn most of the time spraying air for the cow and horses. The cow is sick with the dust. It's a wonder we all aren't. 4:30. Had to tend to the chickens. Some have died. It is terrible out. Monster gusts of dirt sweep across the yard like great clouds of black smoke from a fire. The kids hate to stay in the house so much. I wish it would clear up for even a day.

April 11. Everything covered from last night, and still blowing. But we have at least a peep of daylight through the dirt. 9:30. Still dirty. 10:00. Little lighter. 11:00. Still too dirty to start cleaning. We ate some potato soup standing up, too dirty to sit. Looks favorable to dust to keep up. 7:00. Cleaned up at last. We will sleep better tonight.

April 12. What a day! Sun out bright. No one could ever believe it was such a week. Must start in moving furniture and cleaning out. Milt shovels dirt up, takes it out in buckets. He's going to wash clothes while I clean. We can't lose a good day.

April 13. Dirty again and blowing. Sifting in all over my clean house. The last few years of dust are about more than people can stand but this year is just awful.

April 14. Dad found Bossy dying this morning. We all did everything we could think of but she was wheezing hard and choking and finally died. We had to tie the horses out till we got her out and skinned. The horses sniffed and rolled their eyes. They are frightened by death same as we are, poor things. Dad says he is going to sleep in the barn and spray the air at night. If we had a better barn it might help, but nothing would keep this dust out. The kids cried about Bossy, then we all did. The animals are like persons to us. I feel worried that the kids won't have milk now.

April 15. A real spring day. When it wants to be nice here it seems nicer than any place in the world. Looks desolate everywhere you look, but the sky is clear and you can see across the prairies to the end of nowhere. Cleaned again and put out a pretty wash. Myra and Lonnie played out all day. Milt and Dad walked all over the field, anxious to get to plowing for row crop, but we can't take chance on losing the seed if it doesn't rain enough and stop blowing. Maybe it will clear off now and be right. I feel like I could stand anything if the dust would stop. Mailman told me today that one of the little Long twins has a dust infection on her mouth, pretty bad. This blame dust has brought us all new worries. We sat in the yard tonight till bedtime.

April 16. Another spring day. If this keeps on we will try to get the ground in shape for planting. We need a good rain. School tomorrow. It's like coming back from another world.

April 17. Kids just left for school. It's so clear I can see the others walking from their homes. 9:30. Kinda hazy. 10:30. Teacher sent the kids home before it gets bad. They got here just in time but the dust is thin this time.

April 18. Blew all night but clear this morning. School today.

April 19. Rained a little last night and showered this morning. Myra came home from school saying the little Long girl died. Poor Mrs. Long.

April 20. Well, today is one of the worst we ever had. A black duster. Just when we thought it was better. I don't know where this dirt is coming from but not here. We listen to the radio and know we are not the only ones to suffer. It is just terrible for everyone. The drought years are bad enough but this is almost more than people can stand on top of being so poor from the depression and all.

April 21. Lovely morning. Cleaned and had everything fresh. We all took baths and changed our clothes and dressed up so nice and thought of driving over to Longs', and 1:30 came a fierce cloud sweeping on us, this time from the south. We hadn't finished our dinner and had to cover things as we ate. I was so discouraged I cried. If the land is ruined we can't just sit here and starve, and that's what we'll be doing if we can't grow our crops this year. This was about the last year most of us could stand the drought and keep from losing the farms. Seems queer that just at the time the world is hardest to make a living in, nature turns on us too. Well, as Mrs. Starwood is always saying, the meek shall inherit the *dearth.*

April 22. Cold but nice. I washed and ironed.

April 23. Dust. I am sick of writing about it.

April 24. A black one. Started at 7 a.m. and got worse and worse. We had to nail a cover over the door when we were inside. Everybody's house has canvas and boards on the windows and smells of this infernal dust. Blew all day. I notice Dad has a cough.

April 25. Blew all night and still blowing almost black. It is a terrible feeling to be in this blackness. You don't know what is going on outside and you imagine all kinds of things. It is so still, just blows and blows but as if there is no wind, just rolling clouds of dust. We haven't seen light for two days. I am worried about my chickens, some of them are acting droopy. Dad is sleeping in the barn again, worried about the horses.

April 26. A little lighter but still blowing. The sun looks sick and yellow above the dust. Mrs. Long stopped in on way home this morning. Had to stay in town all night. Yesterday the other twin was sick and she got scared and drove to town to doctor. She said she guessed she could stand the dust because she was so desperate, but the little girl began choking. She had to spit in her mouth. It was the only thing she could do to keep her from choking till she got to the doctor. He says she will be all right in a few days but kept her there out of the dust as nearly as possible. She said Gaylord's ceiling fell in with the weight of the dust in attic. Just heard on radio of 24 deaths this month so far. Might be worse if we had a flood but I'd like to see a little water. Some people get lost in the dust and choke. A lot of dust pneumonia. Suppose the effects of the dust will be showing up on a lot of people later.

April 27. Black as night nearly all day. This is one of the hardest weeks. Many nights we can hear the cattle bawling for water. They sound so pitiful and helpless, and there's nothing any of us can do. I hear them in my sleep. We need groceries today but don't dare venture out. With our wheat gone our credit won't be worth anything.

April 28. A beautiful morning, but everything is buried. Spent all morning cleaning house and getting ourselves cleaned up. Brownells came by in the afternoon and we drove all around. Nearly all the yuccas we saw had roots showing, even the thin ones that grow so long out around them. Maybe in a few years the country will be all right again but now it looks like a desert. It is sad every direction you look. No feed, water, cattle dying. People imprisoned in their own homes behind covered windows and doors. Myra and Lonnie wanted to visit Bossy, so we drove to the draw where her bones are. The wolves had dragged some of them away. I knew they would cry but they wanted to see her. Even Brownells have to mortgage something this year, but they can hold out several years maybe and the drought ought to be over by then. Max says the land may be ruined for years. Mrs. Brownell brought us some milk and butter. When it clears up, I'll make her a nice cake.

April 29. Dust came up in the night and still blowing. Something terrible happened. Poor Mr. Starwood got caught in it last night and when it got black he ran his truck into a ditch and couldn't get out. He turned the lights on and stayed in the truck afraid he'd get lost if he walked home. Nobody found him till this afternoon. He wrote his will on a paper sack, leaving what little he had to Mrs. Starwood. That wasn't much but the truck and luckily it's clear. He was revived but there isn't much chance for him. He is such a fine man, quiet and kind and hardworking. Hope the dust clears a little so I can go over and help Mrs. Starwood. Mailman told me that out where he used to live there was six square miles where not a soul lives and was thickly settled once. He says about every other place is vacant and he asked the papers to publish it and they said "No sir never."

April 30. Mr. Starwood died. Mailman just told me. We all feel bad. Mailman said he had carried life insurance for years and had to let it drop last few years when things got so bad. What a world! Dust is still blowing, sometimes light, sometimes dark. No use to keep on writing dust, dust, dust. Seems it will outlast us.

Wilma Elizabeth McDaniel (b. 1918)

In 1936, when she was seventeen, Wilma Elizabeth McDaniel and her family migrated out of the Oklahoma dust bowl into the promise and hope of California's San Joaquin Valley. She lived the experience Steinbeck reported and later fictionalized in *The Grapes of Wrath*. An indigenous American working-class poet, part Cherokee, McDaniel was born in 1918, the fourth of eight children, into a family of Oklahoma sharecroppers. With a characteristic eye for pithy details and with direct, vernacular diction, she describes her childhood and early adulthood as "forged in great rural poverty and hardship. It was a patchwork of rundown houses with privies. The daily struggle was for basic food, clothing, and shelter." Despite unremitting hardship, McDaniel responded as a young child with a poetic embrace of the world around her.

For over seventy years, most spent doing menial jobs, such as picking cotton or fruit, and despite ill health, she has sustained her calling as one tough poet with a great thirst for beauty. She says, she is "simply not a whiner." She does recognize her collective role as a poetic storyteller, witnessing for her people. A distinct, unequivocal voice, she has published more than fourteen small-press books, including *Sister Vayda's Song* (1982), *Martha and Mary* (1996), *We Live or Die in Pixley* (1999), *The Ketchup Bottle* (1996), *Getting Love Down Right* (2000), *Man with a Star Quilt* (1995) and *A Primer for Buford* (1990) from which come the selections presented here. An edited version of her collected writings (prose and poetry blur as genre distinctions) is expected from Heyday Books. Without grants, academic recognition, or supporting literary, labor, and political bases, she continues to express her own incisive poetic voice of radical humanism.

FROM *A PRIMER FOR BUFORD*

A PRIMER FOR BUFORD

Uncle Claudie Windham's life
has weathered to the color of
wisdom
only a few things bother him
5   now
mainly his grandson Buford Windham, Jr.

He laments
That boy ain't growing up right
in Berkeley where his mother teaches
10   I mean he don't know nothing
his daddy done
when he was a boy in Oklahoma

Why he don't even know our language
if you told him there was a roller
15   coming
he'd think you meant a steam roller

Uncle Claudie shakes his head
I reckon Buford needs a primer
like we had in the first grade
20   start from scratch
and learn where he come from

Pretty soon
there won't be anyone left that
can tell him

ORIGINS

By a still small voice

heard above the choking
winds

that had filled their mouths with
5   dust
instead of food

the Okies in California
always knew
where they had come from

FARM CHILDREN IN THE GRIP OF 1933

Coffee was grounds
flour was gone
cornmeal low
and fatback only a rind
5   February wind was ice
F.D.R. was a brand new voice

And we children played
a deadly game
each took a turn
10   at jumping off the top of the world
from a chicken house
calling
catch me
O-K-L-A-H-O-M-A
15   and didn't know why
we blamed our state

VIA DOLOROSA

Dustbowl women
cried special tears

on the Highway 66
Exodus to California

5   yellow
from snubs and fever
abusive stateline guards

purple
when tires went flat
10   and the waterhose broke

YOU CAN'T GO BACK

Willis Cates told Papa
out in the plum orchard

Things have changed Mister Mac
since our move in 'thirty-five

5   Nothing is the same for me and
mine

Coming West
you can't go back

to where you was
10   even if you could get there

OKIE BOY BOSS AT PUCCINELLO'S, 1936

The owner made him
shed boss at eighteen

tall
and thin
5   with Choctaw-color
eyes

he wore a planter's hat
and jeans
instead of overalls

10   Class
that's what he's got
I heard Beulah say
as Johnny Trueblood passed
with a box of peaches

15   It's a lot of things
that ring he wears
the way he walks
like he was gonna pounce
on someone any second

ABDICATION DAY

Uncle Bartis said to
us in the cold fog
of California 1936

If I was a king
5   you can bet
I wouldn't give up no throne
for a woman like
Mrs. Simpson

PICKING GRAPES, 1937

Magic seventeen
and new in California

working in bursting
sweet vineyards

5   hot sand on soul
one strap held by a
safety pin

a girl could be whatever
she desired

10   the first breath of
Eve in Paradise

the last gasp of Jean Harlow
in Hollywood

AMERICAN FOLK MUSIC, 1937

Fiddles fiddled
guitars strummed
pianos tinned
My Rose of San Antone
5   Bob Wills swing
O beat it out Leon

If Arlie Jones missed
a dance that summer
it broke his heart
10   until the next Saturday night

new shirt
ice cream pants
white shoes
and brilliantine on his hair

15   a waltz caught him up
and he danced with a girl
he'd never seen before

She smelled of rose talcum
and chewing gum
20   and they circled the floor
of sawdust dreams
to the refreshment stand

I'm crazy about Bob Wills'
music
25   the girl confided
with a coke bottle in her
hand
Makes you think you're
in another world

ROSTER

No alternative route
only one road leads from
yesterday

and every town
5   I pass through

is a place where someone
I have loved
died much too young

Merced
10   Fresno
and Malibu, California
Medford, Oregon
and El Paso, Texas

heaven forbid that
15   I should ever stop in
Boise, Idaho

Coda:
This is not a poem.
It is a cold fact.
20   Five of my brothers.
All young.

DAY OF RETURN, AUGUST 4, 1986

Bakersfield August
and its heat is modified hell
radio music has already begun to
stomp on me with fancy alligator
5   boots
everyone seems to have a cousin in
Kuzz
but it is good to be back in watermelon
country

10   a roadside stand reads Texas sweet
rattlesnake melons
plums 4 pounds for a dollar
cukes and stringbeans reasonable

entire new town
15   trying to hide its old roustabout
cotton picking past from me
high rise high price condominiums
occupants are not aware that I knew

their fathers and mothers
20   brothers and sisters
aunts and uncles at the end
of a long sharp hoe
shared many a tepid drink of
water from a wet burlap covered
25   jug

Woody Guthrie (1912–1967)

Woodrow Wilson Guthrie, named for the Democratic president elected in 1912, was born and raised in Okemah, Oklahoma, the third child of Charles and Nora Belle Guthrie. His mother, to whom Woody was deeply attached, suffered from an undiagnosed mental illness and was institutionalized in the state asylum when he was fifteen. His father was a real estate trader and small-town politician, whose land speculating eventually left the family in financial ruin. Charlie Guthrie played guitar and banjo, and both parents would sing, as Woody put it, "apart and together on hymns, spiritual songs, songs about how to save your lost and homeless soul and self." Woody's hometown also provided fertile ground for his budding musical imagination: "Okemah was one of the singingest, square dancingest, drinkingest, yellingest, preachingest, walkingest, talkingest, laughingest, cryingest, shootingest, fist fightingest, bleedingest, gamblingest, gun, club and razor carryingest of our ranch towns and farm towns, because it blossomed out into one of our first Oil Boom Towns." As *Bound for Glory* (1943), his autobiography of these early years demonstrates, the young Woody was both an enthusiastic observer and an occasional participant in the action.

The oil boom faded in 1931 as the Great Depression spread, and Guthrie left Okemah for Pampa, Texas, where he married his first (of three) wife, developed his guitar and harmonica playing, and formed a group called the Corn Cob Trio. When the dust storms hit in 1935, driving people from their farms, he joined tens of thousands of "dust bowl refugees" on the road to California in search of work and a new start. He began composing the songs that, along with Steinbeck's *The Grapes of Wrath* (which Woody later summarized in the twenty-verse ballad "Tom Joad"), made the experience of the migrants known to millions of Americans. In the years of "hard travelin" that followed —Los Angeles in 1937, New York in 1940, Washington State in 1941, the Merchant Marines in 1943, and back and forth between New York and California for several more years—Guthrie developed a deep appreciation of "his" people and their resourcefulness, as well as a love of the land he traveled through. These feelings inform his best-known song, "This Land Is Your Land" (permission to reprint this song was not granted). Written in response to Irving Berlin's "God Bless America," at the start of World War II, Woody's alternative national anthem originally concluded, "God blessed America for me." It was during his last recording session in 1952, at the height of the McCarthyite paranoia, that he changed the line to "This land is made for you and me," making clear that his optimism about America was based on an ethic of shared resources and expanded freedoms for all.

Although never a member, as he put it, of any "earthly organization," Guthrie sang in support of labor unions and contributed a weekly column to the Communist Party's newspaper, entitled "Woody Sez." Throughout the 1940s and into the early 1950s, he performed with Pete Seeger and other friends in the Almanac Singers and later the Weavers, groups that brought folk music and its tradition of protest into the mainstream of American popular music. In addition to *Dust Bowl Ballads* (1940) and numerous singles, Woody recorded the collections *Ballads of Sacco and Vanzetti* (1946) and *Songs to Grow on for Mother and Child* (released in 1956). In all, he contributed hundreds of songs to what Carl Sandburg called the "American Songbag," inspiring artists from Bob Dylan and Bruce Springsteen to Billy Bragg and Ani diFranco. The songs presented here—about Pretty

Boy Floyd, Sacco and Vanzetti, and the "massacre" in Calumet, Michigan—demonstrate Guthrie's strength as a writer and singer of stories about historical events in working-class life. In 1952, Woody Guthrie was diagnosed with Huntingdon's Chorea, the degenerative disease that, it was now clear, had also robbed his mother of her mental and physical faculties. He died in Brooklyn State Hospital on July 14, 1967.

PRETTY BOY FLOYD

If you'll gather 'round me, children,
A story I will tell
'Bout Pretty Boy Floyd, an outlaw,
Oklahoma knew him well.

5   It was in the town of Shawnee,
A Saturday afternoon,
His wife beside him in his wagon
As into town they rode.

There a deputy sheriff approached him
10   In a manner rather rude,
Using vulgar words of anger,
An' his wife she overheard.

Pretty Boy grabbed a log chain,
And the deputy grabbed his gun;
15   In the fight that followed
He laid that deputy down.

Then he took to the trees and timber
To live a life of shame;
Every crime in Oklahoma
20   Was added to his name.

But many a starving farmer
The same old story told
How the outlaw paid their mortgage
And saved their little homes.

25   Others tell you 'bout a stranger
That come to beg a meal,
Underneath his napkin
Left a thousand dollar bill.

It was in Oklahoma City,
30   It was on a Christmas Day,
There was a whole car load of groceries
Come with a note to say:

Well, you say that I'm an outlaw,
You say that I'm a thief.
35   Here's a Christmas dinner
For the families on relief.

Yes, as through this world I've wandered
I've seen lots of funny men;
Some will rob you with a six-gun,
40 And some with a fountain pen.

And as through your life you travel,
Yes, as through your life you roam,
You won't never see an outlaw
Drive a family from their home.

1913 MASSACRE

Take a trip with me in 1913,
To Calumet, Michigan, in the copper country.
I will take you to a place called Italian Hall,
Where the miners are having their big Christmas ball.

5   I will take you in a door and up a high stairs,
Singing and dancing is heard everywhere,
I will let you shake hands with the people you see,
And watch the kids dance around the big Christmas tree.

You ask about work and you ask about pay,
10   They'll tell you they make less than a dollar a day,
Working the copper claims, risking their lives,
So it's fun to spend Christmas with children and wives.

There's talking and laughing and songs in the air,
And the spirit of Christmas is there everywhere,
15   Before you know it you're friends with us all,
And you're dancing around and around in the hall.

Well a little girl sits down by the Christmas tree lights,
To play the piano so you gotta keep quiet,
To hear all this fun you would not realize,
20   That the copper boss' thug men are milling outside.

The copper boss' thugs stuck their heads in the door,
One of them yelled and he screamed, "there's a fire,"
A lady she hollered, "there's no such a thing.
Keep on with your party, there's no such thing."

25   A few people rushed and it was only a few,
"It's just the thugs and the scabs fooling you,"
A man grabbed his daughter and carried her down,
But the thugs held the door and he could not get out.

And then others followed, a hundred or more,
30   But most everybody remained on the floor,
The gun thugs they laughed at their murderous joke,
While the children were smothered on the stairs by the door.

Such a terrible sight I never did see,
We carried our children back up to their tree,
35   The scabs outside still laughed at their spree,
And the children that died there were seventy-three.

The piano played a slow funeral tune,
And the town was lit up by a cold Christmas moon,
The parents they cried and the miners they moaned,
40   "See what your greed for money has done."

Two Good Men

Say, there, did you hear the news?
Sacco worked at trimmin' shoes;
Vanzetti was a peddlin' man,
Pushed his fish cart with his hand.

5   Two good men a long time gone,
Two good men a long time gone,
Sacco an' Vanzetti are gone,
Left me here to sing this song.

Sacco's born across the sea,
10   Somewhere over in Italy;
Vanzetti born of parents fine,
Drank the best Italian wine.

Sacco sailed the sea one day,
Landed up in the Boston Bay.
15   Vanzetti sailed the ocean blue,
An' landed up in Boston, too.

Sacco's wife three children had;
Sacco was a family man.
Vanzetti was a dreamin' man,
20   His book was always in his hands.

Sacco earned his bread and butter
Bein' the factory's best shoe cutter.
Vanzetti spoke both day and night,
Told the workers how to fight.

25   I'll tell you if you ask me
'Bout this payroll robbery.
Two clerks was killed by the shoe fact'ry,
On the streets in South Braintree.

Judge Thayer told his friends around
30   That he had cut the radicals down.
"Anarchist bastard" was the name
Judge Thayer called these two good men.

I'll tell you the prosecutors' name,
Katzman, Adams, Williams, Kane.
35 The Judge and lawyers strutted down,
They done more tricks than circus clowns.

Vanzetti docked in nineteen eight;
Slept along the dirty street,
Told the workers "Organize,"
40 And on the 'lectric chair he dies.

All you people ought to be like me,
And work like Sacco and Vanzetti,
And every day find ways to fight
On the union side for the workers' rights.

45 Well, I ain't got time to tell this tale,
The dicks and bulls are on my trail.
But I'll remember these two good men
That died to show me how to live.

All you people in Suassos Lane,
50 Sing this song and sing it plain.
All you folks that's comin' along,
Jump in with me and sing this song.

CHRIST FOR PRESIDENT

Let's have Christ our President
Let us have him for our king
Cast your vote for the Carpenter
That you call the Nazarene

5 The only way we can ever beat
These crooked politician men
Is to run the money changers out of the temple
Put the Carpenter in

O It's Jesus Christ our President
10 God above our king
With a job and a pension for young and old
We will make hallelujah ring

Every year we waste enough
To feed the ones who starve
15 We build our civilization up
And we shoot it down with wars

But with the Carpenter on the seat
Way up in the Capital town
The USA would be on the way
20 Prosperity Bound!

"Listening to the Little Girls' Song Drift Out Across the Dark Wind," from *Bound for Glory*

For the next few months I took a spell of spending all of the money I could rake and scrape for brushes, hunks of canvas, and all kinds of oil paints. Whole days would go by and I wouldn't know where they'd went. I put my whole mind and every single thought to the business of painting pictures, mostly people.

I made copies of Whistler's "Mother," "The Song of the Lark," "The Angelus," and lots of babies and boys and dogs, snow and green trees, birds singing on all kinds of limbs, and pictures of the dust across the oil fields and wheat country. I made a couple of dozen heads of Christ, and the cops that killed Him.

Things was starting to stack up in my head and I just felt like I was going out of my wits if I didn't find some way of saying what I was thinking. The world didn't mean any more than a smear to me if I couldn't find ways of putting it down on something. I painted cheap signs and pictures on store windows, warehouses, barns and hotels, hock shops, funeral parlors and blacksmith shops, and I spent the money I made for more tubes of oil colors. "I'll make 'em good an' tough," I said to myself, "so's they'll last a thousand years."

But canvas is too high priced, and so is paint and costly oils, and brushes that you've got to chase a camel or a seal or a Russian red sable forty miles to get.

An uncle of mine taught me to play the guitar and I got to going out a couple of nights a week to the cow ranches around to play for the square dances. I made up new words to old tunes and sung them everywhere I'd go. I had to give my pictures away to get anybody to hang them on their wall, but for singing a song, or a few songs at a country dance, they paid me as high as three dollars a night. A picture—you buy it once, and it bothers you for forty years; but with a song, you sing it out, and it soaks in people's ears and they all jump up and down and sing it with you, and then when you quit singing it, it's gone, and you get a job singing it again. On top of that, you can sing out what you think. You can tell tales of all kinds to put your idea across to the other fellow.

And there on the Texas plains right in the dead center of the dust bowl, with the oil boom over and the wheat blowed out and the hard-working people just stumbling about, bothered with mortgages, debts, bills, sickness, worries of every blowing kind, I seen there was plenty to make up songs about.

Some people liked me, hated me, walked with me, walked over me, jeered me, cheered me, rooted me and hooted me, and before long I was invited in and booted out of every public place of entertainment in that country. But I decided that songs was a music and a language of all tongues.

I never did make up many songs about the cow trails or the moon skipping through the sky, but at first it was funny songs of what all's wrong, and how it turned out good or bad. Then I got a little braver and made up songs telling what I thought was wrong and how to make it right, songs that said what everybody in that country was thinking.

And this has held me ever since.

. . .

When night come down, everything got a little stiller, and you could walk around from one bunch of people to the other one and talk about the weather. Although the weather wasn't such an ace-high subject to talk about, because around Redding for nine months hand running the weather don't change (it's hot and dry, hot and dry, and tomorrow it's still going to be hot and dry), you can hear little bunches of folks getting acquainted with each other, saying, "Really hot, ain't it?" "Yeah, dry, too." "Mighty dry."

I run onto a few young people of twelve to twenty-five, mostly kids with their families, who picked the banjo or guitar, and sung songs. Two of these people drew quite a bunch every evening along toward sundown and it always took place just about the same way. An old bed was under a tree in their yard, and a baby boy romped around on it when the shade got cool, because in the early parts of the day the flies and bugs nearly packed him off. So this was his ripping and romping time, and it was the job of his two sisters, one around twelve and the other one around fourteen, to watch him and keep him from falling off onto the ground. Their dad parked his self back on an old car cushion. He throwed his eyes out over the rims of some two-bit specks just about every line or two on his reading matter, and run his Adam's apple up and down; and his wife nearby was singing what all the Lord had done for her, while the right young baby stood up for his first time, and jumped up and down, bouncing toward the edge of the mattress. The old man puckered up his face and sprayed a tree with tobacco juice, and said, "Girls. You girls. Go in the house and get your music box, and set there on the bed and play with the baby, so's he won't fall off."

One of the sisters tuned a string or two, then chorded a little. People walked from all over the camp and gathered, and the kid, mama, and dad, and all of the visitors, kept as still as daylight while the girls sang:

> Takes a worried man to sing a worried song
> Takes a worried man to sing a worried song
> Takes a worried man to sing a worried song
> I'm worried nowwww
> But I won't be worried long.

I heard these two girls from a-ways away where I was leaning back up against an old watering trough. I could hear their words just as plain as day, floating all around in the trees and down across the low places. I hung my guitar up on a stub of a limb, went down and stretched myself out on some dry grass, and listened to the girls for a long time. The baby kicked and bucked like a regular army mule whenever they'd quit their singing; but, as quick as they struck their first note or two on the next song, the kid would throw his wrist in his mouth, the slobbers would drip down onto his sister's lap, and the baby would kick both feet, but easy, keeping pretty good time to the guitar.

I don't know why I didn't tell them I had a guitar up yonder hanging on that tree. I just reared back and soaked in every note and every word of their singing. It was so clear and honest sounding, no Hollywood put-on, no fake wiggling. It was better to me than the loud squalling and bawling you've got to do to make yourself heard in the old mobbed saloons. And, instead of getting you all riled up mentally, morally and sexually—no, it done something a lot better, something that's harder to do, something you need ten times more. It cleared your head up, that's what it done, caused you to fall back and let your draggy bones rest and your muscles go limber like a cat's.

Two little girls were making two thousand working people feel like I felt, rest like I rested. And when I say two thousand, take a look down off across these three little hills. You'll see a hat or two bobbing up above the brush. Somebody is going, somebody is coming, somebody is kneeling down drinking from the spring of water trickling out of the west hill. Five men are shaving before the same crooked hunk of old looking-glass, using tin cans for their water. A woman right up close to you wrings out a tough work shirt, saves the water for four more. You skim your eye out around the south hill, and not less than a hundred women are doing the same thing, washing, wringing, hanging out shirts, taking them down dry to iron. Not a one of them is talking above a whisper, and the one that is whispering almost feels guilty because she knows that ninety-nine out of every hundred are tired, weary, have felt sad, joked and laughed to keep from crying. But these two little girls are telling about all of that trouble, and everybody knows it's helping. These songs say something about our hard traveling, something about our hard luck, our hard get-by, but the songs say we'll come through all of these in pretty good shape, and we'll be all right, we'll work, make ourself useful, if only the telegram to build the dam would come in from Washington.

I thought I could act a little bashful and shy, and not rush the people to get to knowing them, but something inside of me just sort of talked out and said, "Awful good singing. What's your name?"

The two little girls talked slow and quiet but it was not nervous, and it wasn't jittery, just plain. They told me their names.

I said, "I like the way you play that guitar with your fingers! Sounds soft, and you can hear it a long ways off. All of these three hills was just ringing out with your guitar, and all of these people was listening to you sing."

"I saw them listening," one sister said.

"I saw them too," the other sister said.

"I play with a flat celluloid pick. I've got to be loud, because I play in saloons and, well, I just make it my job to make more noise than they make, and they're sorry for me and give me nickels and pennies."

"I don't like old saloons," one little girl said.

"Me neither," the other little girl said.

I looked over at their daddy, and he sort of looked crossways out my side of his specks, pouched his lips up a little, winked at me, and said, "I'm against bars myself."

His wife talked up louder, "Yes, you're against bars! Right square up against them!"

Both of the sisters looked awful sober and serious at their dad. Everybody in the crowd laughed, and took on a new listening position, leaning back up against trees, squatting on smoky buckets turned upside down, stretched out in the grass, patting down places to lay in the short weeds.

I got up and strolled away and took my guitar down off of the sawed-off limb, and thought while I was walking back to where the crowd was, Boy howdy, old guitar, you been a lot of places, seen a lot of faces, but don't you go to actin' up too wild and reckless, 'cause these little girls and their mama don't like saloons.

I got back to where everybody was, and the two little sisters was singing "Columbus Stockade":

> Way down in Columbus stockade
> Where my gally went back on me;
> Way down in Columbus stockade,
> I'd ruther be back in Tennessee.

"Columbus Stockade" was always one of my first picks, so I let them run along for a little while, twisted my guitar up in tune with theirs, holding my ear down against the sounding box, and when I heard it was in tune with them I started picking out the tune, sort of note for note, letting their guitar play the bass chords and second parts. They both smiled when they heard me because two guitars being played this way is what's called the real article, and millions of little kids are raised on this kind of music. If you think of something new to say, if a cyclone comes, or a flood wrecks the country, or a bus load of school children freeze to death along the road, if a big ship goes down, and an airplane falls in your neighborhood, an outlaw shoots it out with the deputies, or the working people go out to win a war, yes, you'll find a train load of things you can set down and make up a song about. You'll hear people singing your words around over the country, and you'll sing their songs everywhere you travel or everywhere you live; and these are the only kind of songs my head or my memory or my guitar has got any room for.

So these two little girls and me sung together till the crowd had got bigger and it was dark under the trees where the moon couldn't hit us.

Takes a ten-dollar shoe to fit my feet
Takes a ten-dollar shoe to fit my feet
Takes a ten-dollar shoe to fit my feet, Lord God!
And I ain't a-gonna be treated this a-way!

When the night got late and the men in the saloons in town lost their few pennies playing framed-up poker, they drifted out to sleep the night in the jungle camp. We saw a bunch of twenty-five or thirty of them come running over the rim of the hill from town, yelling, cussing, kicking tin buckets and coffee pots thirty feet, and hollering like panthers.

And when the wild bunch run down the little trail to where we was singing—it was then that the whole drunk mess of them stood there reeling and listening in the dark, and then shushed each other to keep quiet and set down on the ground to listen. Everybody got so still that it almost crackled in the air. Men took seats and leaned their heads back against tree trunks and listened to the lightning bugs turn their lights on and off. And the lightning bugs must of been hushing each other, because the old jungle camp was getting a lot of good rest there listening to the little girls' song drift out across the dark wind.

Clifford Odets (1906–1963)

Imagine a January night in 1935 six years into the Great Depression. At the Civic Repertory Theater on 14th Street in New York City, a play about a 1934 taxi cab strike by an unknown playwright, Clifford Odets, ends with an audience of about fourteen hundred erupting and shouting, "Strike! Strike!" Imagine twenty-two curtain calls and a standing ovation of forty-five minutes, actors merging with audience into a chorus of hope in the face of economic despair, and you begin to see *Waiting for Lefty* in historical context. The son of Jewish immigrants, Clifford Odets was born in Philadelphia, but raised in New York City. When he was seventeen years old, he dropped out of school to become an actor. He joined the Group Theater, a politically left and avant-garde theater troupe in the 1930s and 1940s that was founded by Harold Clurman and method-acting master, Lee Strasberg.

Odets was part of a generation of artists and intellectuals from working-class and immigrant families who saw themselves, according to cultural historian Michael Denning, as "plebians." Educated through the public libraries and public schools, they were politically committed artists, writers, and musicians. Odets joined the American Communist Party in 1934. *Waiting for Lefty* is considered an example of "agit-prop" theater, a combination of "agitation" and "propaganda." Written in a familiar working-class idiom, these plays were intended as catalysts for collective social change, not as vehicles for individual celebrity. After *Waiting for Lefty*, Odets's plays *Awake and Sing!* (1935), *Till the Day I Die* (1935—one of the first anti-Nazi plays) *Paradise Lost* (1935), and *Golden Boy* (1937) were produced on Broadway in association with the Group Theater. With his success as a New York playwright, Odets got offers to write screenplays for Hollywood. In California, he married his first wife, actress Luise Rainer, and continued writing stage plays including *The Big Knife* (1949) and *The Country Girl* (1950), as well as a successful adaptation of the Ernest Lehman novella, *The Sweet Smell of Success* (1957). Odets also painted and collected art and was the prototype for the idealistic playwright in the 1991 Coen brothers' film, *Barton Fink*.

CHARACTERS

fatt	clayton
joe	agate keller
edna	henchman
miller	reilly
fayette	dr. barnes
irv	dr. benjamin
florrie	a man
sid	

WAITING FOR LEFTY

As the curtain goes up we see a bare stage. On it are sitting six or seven men in a semi-circle. Lolling against the proscenium down left is a young man chewing a toothpick: a gunman. A fat man of porcine appearance is talking directly to the audience. In other words he is the head of a union and the men ranged behind him are a committee of workers. They are now seated in interesting different attitudes and present a wide diversity of type, as we shall soon see. The fat man is hot and heavy under the collar, near the end of a long talk, but not too hot: he is well fed and confident. His name is HARRY FATT.

FATT: You're so wrong I ain't laughing. Any guy with eyes to read knows it. Look at the textile strike—out like lions and in like lambs. Take the San Francisco tie-up—starvation and broken heads. The steel boys wanted to walk out too, but they changed their minds. It's the trend of the times, that's what it is. All we workers got a good man behind us now. He's top man of the country—looking out for our interests—the man in the White House is the one I'm referrin' to. That's why the times ain't ripe for a strike. He's working day and night—

VOICE (*from the audience*): For who? (*The* GUNMAN *stirs himself.*)

FATT: For you! The records prove it. If this was the Hoover régime, would I say don't go out, boys? Not on your tintype! But things is different now. You read the papers as well as me. You know it. And that's why I'm against the strike Because we gotta stand behind the man who's standin' behind us! The whole country——

ANOTHER VOICE: Is on the blink! (*The* GUNMAN *looks grave.*)

FATT: Stand up and show yourself, you damn red! Be a man, let's see what you look like! (*Waits in vain.*) Yellow from the word go! Red and yellow makes a dirty color, boys. I got my eyes on four or five of them in the union here. What the hell'll they do for you? Pull you out and run away when trouble starts. Give those birds a chance and they'll have your sisters and wives in the whore houses, like they done in Russia. They'll tear Christ off his bleeding cross. They'll wreck your homes and throw your babies in the river. You think that's bunk? Read the papers! Now listen, we can't stay here all night. I gave you the facts in the case. You boys got hot suppers to go to and——

ANOTHER VOICE: Says you!

GUNMAN: Sit down, Punk!

ANOTHER VOICE: Where's Lefty? (*Now this question is taken up by the others in unison.* FATT *pounds with gavel.*)

FATT: That's what I wanna know. Where's your pal, Lefty? You elected him chairman —where the hell did he disappear?

VOICES: We want Lefty! Lefty! Lefty!

FATT (*pounding*): What the hell is this—a circus? You got the committee here. This bunch of cowboys you elected. (*Pointing to man on extreme right end.*)

MAN: Benjamin.

FATT: Yeah, Doc Benjamin. (*Pointing to other men in circle in seated order*): Benjamin, Miller, Stein, Mitchell, Phillips, Keller It ain't my fault Lefty took a run-out powder. If you guys—

A GOOD VOICE: What's the committee say?

OTHERS: The committee! Let's hear from the committee! (FATT *tries to quiet the crowd, but one of the seated men suddenly comes to the front. The* GUNMAN *moves over to center stage, but* FATT *says:*)

FATT: Sure, let him talk. Let's hear what the red boys gotta say! (*Various shouts are coming from the audience.* FATT *insolently goes back to his seat in the middle of the circle. He sits on his raised platform and relights his cigar. The* GUNMAN *goes back to his post.* JOE, *the new speaker, raises his hand for quiet. Gets it quickly. He is sore.*)

JOE: You boys know me. I ain't a red boy one bit! Here I'm carryin' a shrapnel that big I picked up in the war. And maybe I don't know it when it rains! Don't tell me red! You know what we are? The black and blue boys! We been kicked around so long we're black and blue from head to toes. But I guess anyone who says straight out he don't like it, he's a red boy to the leaders of the union. What's this crap about goin' home to hot suppers? I'm asking to your faces how many's got hot suppers to go home to? Anyone who's sure of his next meal, raise your hand! A certain gent sitting behind me can raise them both. But not in front here! And that's why we're talking strike—to get a living wage!

VOICE: Where's Lefty?

JOE: I honest to God don't know, but he didn't take no run-out powder. That Wop's got more guts than a slaughter house. Maybe a traffic jam got him, but he'll be here. But don't let this red stuff scare you. Unless fighting for a living scares you. We gotta make up our minds. My wife made up my mind last week, if you want the truth. It's plain as the nose on Sol Feinberg's face we need a strike. There's us comin' home every night—eight, ten hours on the cab. "God," the wife says, "eighty cents ain't money—don't buy beans almost. You're workin' for the company," she says to me, "Joe! you ain't workin' for me or the family no more!" She says to me, "If you don't start . . ."

I. JOE AND EDNA

The lights fade out and a white spot picks out the playing space within the space of seated men. The seated men are very dimly visible in the outer dark, but more prominent is FATT *smoking his cigar and often blowing the smoke in the lighted circle.*

A tired but attractive woman of thirty comes into the room, drying her hands on an apron. She stands there sullenly as JOE *comes in from the other side, home from work. For a moment they stand and look at each other in silence.*

JOE: Where's all the furniture, honey?

EDNA: They took it away. No installments paid.

JOE: When?

EDNA: Three o'clock.

JOE: They can't do that.

EDNA: Can't? They did it.

JOE: Why, the palookas, we paid three-quarters.

EDNA: The man said read the contract.

JOE: We must have signed a phoney. . . .

EDNA: It's a regular contract and you signed it.

JOE: Don't be so sour, Edna. . . . (*Tries to embrace her.*)

EDNA: Do it in the movies, Joe—they pay Clark Gable big money for it.

JOE: This is a helluva house to come home to. Take my word!

EDNA: Take MY word! Whose fault is it?

JOE: Must you start that stuff again?

EDNA: Maybe you'd like to talk about books?

JOE: I'd like to slap you in the mouth!

EDNA: No you won't.

JOE (*sheepishly*): Jeez, Edna, you get me sore some time. . . .

EDNA: But just look at me—I'm laughing all over!

JOE: Don't insult me. Can I help it if times are bad? What the hell do you want me to do, jump off a bridge or something?

EDNA: Don't yell. I just put the kids to bed so they won't know they missed a meal. If I don't have Emmy's shoes soled tomorrow, she can't go to school. In the meantime let her sleep.

JOE: Honey, I rode the wheels off the chariot today. I cruised around five hours without a call. It's conditions.

EDNA: Tell it to the A & P!

JOE: I booked two-twenty on the clock. A lady with a dog was lit . . . she gave me a quarter tip by mistake. If you'd only listen to me—we're rolling in wealth.

EDNA: Yeah? How much?

JOE: I had "coffee and—" in a beanery. (*Hands her silver coins.*) A buck four.

EDNA: The second month's rent is due tomorrow.

JOE: Don't look at me that way, Edna.

EDNA: I'm looking through you, not at you. . . . Everything was gonna be so ducky! A cottage by the waterfall, roses in Picardy. You're a four-star-bust! If you think I'm standing for it much longer, you're crazy as a bedbug.

JOE: I'd get another job if I could. There's no work—you know it.

EDNA: I only know we're at the bottom of the ocean.

JOE: What can I do?

EDNA: Who's the man in the family, you or me?

JOE: That's no answer. Get down to brass tacks. Christ, gimme a break, too! A coffee and java all day. I'm hungry, too, Babe. I'd work my fingers to the bone if—

EDNA: I'll open a can of salmon.

JOE: Not now. Tell me what to do!

EDNA: I'm not God!

JOE: Jeez, I wish I was a kid again and didn't have to think about the next minute.

EDNA: But you're not a kid and you do have to think about the next minute. You got two blondie kids sleeping in the next room. They need food and clothes. I'm not mentioning anything else—But we're stalled like a flivver in the snow. For five years I laid awake at night listening to my heart pound. For God's sake, do something, Joe, get wise. Maybe get your buddies together, maybe go on strike for better money. Poppa did it during the war and they won out. I'm turning into a sour old nag.

JOE (*defending himself*): Strikes don't work!

EDNA: Who told you?

JOE: Besides that means not a nickel a week while we're out. Then when it's over they don't take you back.

EDNA: Suppose they don't! What's to lose?

JOE: Well, we're averaging six-seven dollars a week now.

EDNA: That just pays for the rent.

JOE: That is something, Edna.

EDNA: It isn't. They'll push you down to three and four a week before you know it. Then you'll say, "That's somethin'," too!

JOE: There's too many cabs on the street, that's the whole damn trouble.

EDNA: Let the company worry about that, you big fool! If their cabs didn't make a profit, they'd take them off the streets. Or maybe you think they're in business just to pay Joe Mitchell's rent!

JOE: You don't know a-b-c, Edna.

EDNA: I know this—your boss is making suckers outa you boys every minute. Yes, and suckers out of all the wives and the poor innocent kids who'll grow up with crooked spines and sick bones. Sure, I see it in the papers, how good orange juice is for kids. But damnit our kids get colds one on top of the other. They look like little ghosts. Betty never saw a grapefruit. I took her to the store last week and she pointed to a stack of grapefruits. "What's that!" she said. My God, Joe—the world is supposed to be for all of us.

JOE: You'll wake them up.

EDNA: I don't care, as long as I can maybe wake you up.

JOE: Don't insult me. One man can't make a strike.

EDNA: Who says one? You got hundreds in your rotten union!

JOE: The union ain't rotten.

EDNA: No? Then what are they doing? Collecting dues and patting your back?

JOE: They're making plans.

EDNA: What kind?

JOE: They don't tell us.

EDNA: It's too damn bad about you. They don't tell little Joey what's happening in his bitsie witsie union. What do you think it is—a ping pong game?

JOE: You know they're racketeers. The guys at the top would shoot you for a nickel.

EDNA: Why do you stand for that stuff?

JOE: Don't you wanna see me alive?

EDNA (*after a deep pause*): No . . . I don't think I do, Joe. Not if you can lift a finger to do something about it, and don't. No, I don't care.

JOE: Honey, you don't understand what—

EDNA: And any other hackie that won't fight . . . let them all be ground to hamburger!

JOE: It's one thing to—

EDNA: Take your hand away! Only they don't grind me to little pieces! I got different plans. (*Starts to take off her apron.*)

JOE: Where are you going?

EDNA: None of your business.

JOE: What's up your sleeve?

EDNA: My arm'd be up my sleeve, darling, if I had a sleeve to wear. (*Puts neatly folded apron on back of chair.*)

JOE: Tell me!

EDNA: Tell you what?

JOE: Where are you going?

EDNA: Don't you remember my old boy friend?

JOE: Who?

EDNA: Bud Haas. He still has my picture in his watch. He earns a living.

JOE: What the hell are you talking about?

EDNA: I heard worse than I'm talking about.

JOE: Have you seen Bud since we got married?

EDNA: Maybe.

JOE: If I thought . . . (*He stands looking at her.*)

EDNA: See much? Listen, boy friend, if you think I won't do this it just means you can't see straight.

JOE: Stop talking bull!

EDNA: This isn't five years ago, Joe.

JOE: You mean you'd leave me and the kids?

EDNA: I'd leave *you* like a shot! ·

JOE: No. . . .

EDNA: Yes! (JOE *turns away, sitting in a chair with his back to her. Outside the lighted circle of the playing stage we hear the other seated members of the strike committee. "She will . . . she will . . . it happens that way," etc. This group should be used throughout for various comments, political, emotional and as general chorus. Whispering. . . . The fat boss now blows a heavy cloud of smoke into the scene.*)

JOE (*finally*): Well, I guess I ain't got a leg to stand on.

EDNA: No?

JOE (*suddenly mad*): No, you lousy tart, no! Get the hell out of here. Go pick up that bull-thrower on the corner and stop at some cushy hotel downtown. He's probably been coming here every morning and laying you while I hacked my guts out!

EDNA: You're crawling like a worm!

JOE: You'll be crawling in a minute.

EDNA: You don't scare me that much! (*Indicates a half inch on her finger.*)

JOE: This is what I slaved for!

EDNA: Tell it to your boss!

JOE: He don't give a damn for you or me!

EDNA: That's what I say.

JOE: Don't change the subject!

EDNA: This is the subject, the *exact subject!* Your boss makes this subject. I never saw him in my life, but he's putting ideas in my head a mile a minute. He's giving your kids that fancy disease called the rickets. He's making a jelly-fish outa you and putting wrinkles in my face. This is the subject every inch of the way! He's throwing me into Bud Haas' lap. When in hell will you get wise——

JOE: I'm not so dumb as you think! But you are talking like a red.

EDNA: I don't know what that means. But when a man knocks you down you get up and kiss his fist! You gutless piece of boloney.

JOE: One man can't——

EDNA (*with great joy*): I don't say one man! I say a hundred, a thousand, a whole million, I say. But start in your own union. Get those hack boys together! Sweep out those racketeers like a pile of dirt! Stand up like men and fight for the crying kids and wives. Goddamnit! I'm tired of slavery and sleepless nights.

JOE (*with her*): Sure, sure! . . .

EDNA: Yes. Get brass toes on your shoes and know where to kick!

JOE (*suddenly jumping up and kissing his wife full on the mouth*): Listen, Edna, I'm goin' down to 174th Street to look up Lefty Costello. Lefty was saying the other day . . . (*He suddenly stops.*) How about this Haas guy?

EDNA: Get out of here!

JOE: I'll be back! (*Runs out. For a moment* EDNA *stands triumphant. There is a blackout and when the regular lights come up,* JOE MITCHELL *is concluding what he has been saying*):

JOE: You guys know this stuff better than me. We gotta walk out!

(*Abruptly he turns and goes back to his seat.*)

Blackout

II. LAB ASSISTANT EPISODE

Discovered: MILLER, *a lab assistant, looking around; and* FAYETTE, *an industrialist.*

FAY: Like it?

MILLER: Very much. I've never seen an office like this outside the movies.

FAY: Yes, I often wonder if interior decorators and bathroom fixture people don't get all their ideas from Hollywood. Our country's extraordinary that way. Soap, cosmetics, electric refrigerators—just let Mrs. Consumer know they're used by the Crawfords and Garbos—more volume of sale than one plant can handle!

MILL: I'm afraid it isn't that easy, Mr. Fayette.

FAY: No, you're right—gross exaggeration on my part. Competition is cutthroat today. Market's up flush against a stone wall. The astronomers had better hurry—open Mars to trade expansion.

MILL: Or it will be just too bad!

FAY: Cigar?

MILL: Thank you, don't smoke.

FAY: Drink?

MILL: Ditto, Mr. Fayette

FAY: I like sobriety in my workers . . . the trained ones, I mean. The pollacks and niggers, they're better drunk—keeps them out of mischief. Wondering why I had you come over?

MILL: If you don't mind my saying—very much.

FAY (*patting him on the knee*): I like your work.

MILL: Thanks.

FAY: No reason why a talented young man like yourself shouldn't string along with us—a growing concern. Loyalty is well repaid in our organization. Did you see Siegfried this morning?

MILL: He hasn't been in the laboratory all day.

FAY: I told him yesterday to raise you twenty dollars a month. Starts this week.

MILL: You don't know how happy my wife'll be.

FAY: Oh, I can appreciate it. (*He laughs.*)

MILL: Was that all, Mr. Fayette?

FAY: Yes, except that we're switching you to laboratory A tomorrow. Siegfried knows about it. That's why I had you in. The new work is very important. Siegfried recommended you very highly as a man to trust. You'll work directly under Dr. Brenner. Make you happy?

MILL: Very. He's an important chemist!

FAY (*leaning over seriously*): We think so, Miller. We think so to the extent of asking you to stay within the building throughout the time you work with him.

MILL: You mean sleep and eat in?

FAY: Yes. . . .

MILL: It can be arranged.

FAY: Fine. You'll go far, Miller.

MILL: May I ask the nature of the new work?

FAY (*looking around first*): Poison gas. . . .

MILL: Poison!

FAY: Orders from above. I don't have to tell you from where. New type poison gas for modern warfare.

MILL: I see.

FAY: You didn't know a new war was that close, did you?

MILL: I guess I didn't.

FAY: I don't have to stress the importance of absolute secrecy.

MILL: I understand!

FAY: The world is an armed camp today. One match sets the whole world blazing in forty-eight hours. Uncle Sam won't be caught napping!

MILL (*addressing his pencil*): They say 12 million men were killed in that last one and 20 million more wounded or missing.

FAY: That's not our worry. If big business went sentimental over human life there wouldn't be big business of any sort!

MILL: My brother and two cousins went in the last one.

FAY: They died in a good cause.

MILL: My mother says "no!"

FAY: She won't worry about you this time. You're too valuable behind the front.

MILL: That's right.

FAY: All right, Miller. See Siegfried for further orders.

MILL: You should have seen my brother—he could ride a bike without hands. . . .

FAY: You'd better move some clothes and shaving tools in tomorrow. Remember what I said—you're with a growing organization.

MILL: He could run the hundred yards in 9:8 flat. . . .

FAY: Who?

MILL: My brother. He's in the Meuse-Argonne Cemetery. Mama went there in 1926. . . .

FAY: Yes, those things stick. How's your handwriting, Miller, fairly legible?

MILL: Fairly so.

FAY: Once a week I'd like a little report from you.

MILL: What sort of report?

FAY: Just a few hundred words once a week on Dr. Brenner's progress.

MILL: Don't you think it might be better coming from the Doctor?

FAY: I didn't ask you that.

MILL: Sorry.

FAY: I want to know what progress he's making, the reports to be purely confidential —between you and me.

MILL: You mean I'm to watch him?

FAY: Yes!

MILL: I guess I can't do that. . . .

FAY: Thirty a month raise . . .

MILL: You said twenty. . . .

FAY: Thirty!

MILL: Guess I'm not built that way.

FAY: Forty. . . .

MILL: Spying's not in my line, Mr. Fayette!

FAY: You use ugly words, Mr. Miller!

MILL: For ugly activity? Yes!

FAY: Think about it, Miller. Your chances are excellent. . . .

MILL: No.

FAY: you're doing something for your country. Assuring the United States that when those goddamn Japs start a ruckus we'll have offensive weapons to back us up! Don't you read your newspapers, Miller?

MILL: Nothing but Andy Gump.

FAY: If you were on the inside you'd know I'm talking cold sober truth! Now, I'm not asking you to make up your mind on the spot. Think about it over your lunch period.

MILL: No.

FAY: Made up your mind already?

MILL: Afraid so.

FAY: You understand the consequences?

MILL: I lose my raise——

                 MILL: And my job!

Simultaneously: FAY: And your job!

                 MILL: You misunderstand——

MILL: Rather dig ditches first!

FAY: That's a big job for foreigners.

MILL: But sneaking—and making poison gas—that's for Americans?

FAY: It's up to you.

MILL: My mind's made up.

FAY: No hard feelings?

MILL: Sure hard feelings! I'm not the civilized type, Mr. Fayette. Nothing suave or sophisticated about me. Plenty of hard feelings! Enough to want to bust you and all your kind square in the mouth! (*Does exactly that.*)

Blackout

III. THE YOUNG HACK AND HIS GIRL

Opens with girl and brother. FLORENCE *waiting for* SID *to take her to a dance.*

FLOR: I gotta right to have something out of life. I don't smoke, I don't drink. So if Sid wants to take me to a dance, I'll go. Maybe if you was in love you wouldn't talk so hard.

IRV: I'm saying it for your good.

FLOR: Don't be so good to me.

IRV: Mom's sick in bed and you'll be worryin' her to the grave. She don't want that boy hanging around the house and she don't want you meeting him in Crotona Park.

FLOR: I'll meet him anytime I like!

IRV: If you do, yours truly'll take care of it in his own way. With just one hand, too!

FLOR: Why are you all so set against him?

IRV: Mom told you ten times—it ain't him. It's that he ain't got nothing. Sure, we know he's serious, that he's stuck on you. But that don't cut no ice.

FLOR: Taxi drivers used to make good money.

IRV: Today they're makin' five and six dollars a week. Maybe you wanta raise a family on that. Then you'll be back here living with us again and I'll be supporting two families in one. Well . . . over my dead body.

FLOR: Irv, I don't care—I love him!

IRV: You're a little kid with half-baked ideas!

FLOR: I stand there behind the counter the whole day. I think about him—

IRV: If you thought more about Mom it would be better.

FLOR: Don't I take care of her every night when I come home? Don't I cook supper and iron your shirts and . . . you give me a pain in the neck, too. Don't try to shut me up!

I bring a few dollars in the house, too. Don't you see I want something else out of life. Sure, I want romance, love, babies. I want everything in life I can get.

IRV: You take care of Mom and watch your step!

FLOR: And if I don't?

IRV: Yours truly'll watch it for you!

FLOR: You can talk that way to a girl. . . .

IRV: I'll talk that way to your boy friend, too, and it won't be with words! Florrie, if you had a pair of eyes you'd see it's for your own good we're talking. This ain't no time to get married. Maybe later—

FLOR: "Maybe Later" never comes for me, though. Why don't we send Mom to a hospital? She can die in peace there instead of looking at the clock on the mantelpiece all day

IRV: That needs money. Which we don't have!

FLOR: Money, Money, Money!

IRV: Don't change the subject.

FLOR: This is the subject!

IRV: You gonna stop seeing him? (*She turns away.*) Jesus, kiddie, I remember when you were a baby with curls down your back. Now I gotta stand here yellin' at you like this.

FLOR: I'll talk to him, Irv.

IRV: When?

FLOR: I asked him to come here tonight. We'll talk it over.

IRV: Don't get soft with him. Nowadays is no time to be soft. You gotta be hard as a rock or go under.

FLOR: I found that out. There's the bell. Take the egg off the stove I boiled for Mom. Leave us alone Irv. (SID *comes in—the two men look at each other for a second.* IRV *exits.*)

SID (*enters*): Hello, Florrie.

FLOR: Hello, Honey. You're looking tired.

SID: Naw, I just need a shave.

FLOR: Well, draw your chair up to the fire and I'll ring for brandy and soda . . . like in the movies.

SID: If this was the movies I'd bring a big bunch of roses.

FLOR: How big?

SID: Fifty or sixty dozen—the kind with long, long stems—big as that. . . .

FLOR: You dope. . . .

SID: Your Paris gown is beautiful.

FLOR (*acting grandly*): Yes, Percy, velvet panels are coming back again. Madame La Farge told me today that Queen Marie herself designed it.

SID: Gee . . . !

FLOR: Every princess in the Balkans is wearing one like this (*Poses grandly.*)

SID: Hold it. (*Does a nose camera—thumbing nose and imitating grinding of camera with other hand. Suddenly she falls out of the posture and swiftly goes to him, to embrace him, to kiss him with love. Finally*):

SID: You look tired, Florrie.

FLOR: Naw, I just need a shave. (*She laughs tremulously.*)

SID: You worried about your mother?

FLOR: No.

SID: What's on your mind?

FLOR: The French and Indian War.

SID: What's on your mind?

FLOR: I got us on my mind, Sid. Night and day, Sid!

SID: I smacked a beer truck today. Did I get hell! I was driving along thinking of US, too. You don't have to say it—I know what's on your mind. I'm rat poison around here.

FLOR: Not to me. . . .

SID: I know to who . . . and I know why. I don't blame them. We're engaged now for three years. . . .

FLOR: That's a long time. . . .

SID: My brother Sam joined the navy this morning—get a break that way. They'll send him down to Cuba with the hootchy-kootchy girls. He don't know from nothing, that dumb basket ball player!

FLOR: Don't you do that.

SID: Don't you worry, I'm not the kind who runs away. But I'm so tired of being a dog, Baby, I could choke. I don't even have to ask what's going on in your mind. I know from the word go, 'cause I'm thinking the same things, too.

FLOR: It's yes or no—nothing in between.

SID: The answer is no—a big electric sign looking down on Broadway!

FLOR: We wanted to have kids. . . .

SID: But that sort of life ain't for the dogs which is us. Christ, Baby! I get like thunder in my chest when we're together. If we went off together I could maybe look the world straight in the face, spit in its eye like a man should do. Goddamnit, it's trying to be a man on the earth. Two in life together.

FLOR: But something wants us to be lonely like that—crawling alone in the dark. Or they want us trapped.

SID: Sure, the big shot money men want us like that.

FLOR: Highly insulting us——

SID: Keeping us in the dark about what is wrong with us in the money sense. They got the power and mean to be damn sure they keep it. They know if they give in just an inch, all the dogs like us will be down on them together—an ocean knocking them to hell and back and each singing cuckoo with stars coming from their nose and ears. I'm not raving, Florrie——

FLOR: I know you're not, I know.

SID: I don't have the words to tell you what I feel. I never finished school. . . .

FLOR: I know. . . .

SID: But it's relative, like the professors say. We worked like hell to send him to college—my kid brother Sam, I mean—and look what he done—joined the navy! The damn fool don't see the cards is stacked for all of us. The money man dealing himself a hot royal flush. Then giving you and me a phony hand like a pair of tens or something. Then keep on losing the pots 'cause the cards is stacked against you. Then he says, what's the matter you can't win—no stuff on the ball, he says to you. And kids like my brother believe it 'cause they don't know better. For all their education, they don't know from nothing. But wait a minute! Don't he come around and say to you—this millionaire with a jazz band—listen Sam or Sid or what's-your-name, you're no good, but here's a chance. The whole world'll know who you are. Yes sir, he says, get up on that ship and fight those bastards who's making the world a lousy place to live in. The Japs, the Turks, the Greeks. Take this gun—kill the slobs like a real hero, he says, a real American. Be a hero! And the guy you're poking at? A real louse, just like you, 'cause they don't let him catch more than a pair of tens, too. On that foreign soil he's a guy like me and Sam, a guy who wants his baby like you and hot sun on his face! They'll teach Sam to point the guns the wrong way, that dumb basket ball player!

FLOR: I got a lump in my throat, Honey.

SID: You and me—we never even had a room to sit in somewhere.

FLOR: The park was nice . . .

SID: In winter? The hallways . . . I'm glad we never got together. This way we don't know what we missed.

FLOR (in a burst): Sid, I'll go with you—we'll get a room somewhere.

SID: Naw . . . they're right. If we can't climb higher than this together—we better stay apart.

FLOR: I swear to God I wouldn't care.

SID: You would, you would—in a year, two years, you'd curse the day. I seen it happen.

FLOR: Oh, Sid. . . .

SID: Sure, I know. We got the blues, Babe—the 1935 blues. I'm talkin' this way 'cause I love you. If I didn't, I wouldn't care. . . .

FLOR: We'll work together, we'll—

SID: How about the backwash? Your family needs your nine bucks. My family——

FLOR: I don't care for them!

SID: You're making it up, Florrie. Little Florrie Canary in a cage.

FLOR: Don't make fun of me.

SID: I'm not, Baby.

FLOR: Yes, you're laughing at me.

SID: I'm not. (They stand looking at each other unable to speak. Finally, he turns to a small portable phonograph and plays a cheap, sad, dance tune. He makes a motion with his hand; she comes to him. They begin to dance slowly. They hold each other tightly, almost as though they would merge into each other. The music stops, but the scratching record continues to the end of the scene. They stop dancing. He finally looses her clutch and seats her on the couch, where she sits, tense and expectant.)

SID: Hello, Babe.

FLOR: Hello. (For a brief time they stand as though in a dream.)

SID (finally): Good-bye, Babe. (He waits for an answer, but she is silent. They look at each other.)

SID: Did you ever see my Pat Rooney imitation? (He whistles Rosy O'Grady and soft-shoes to it. Stops. He asks:)

SID: Don't you like it?

FLOR (finally): No. (Buries her face in her hands. Suddenly he falls on his knees and buries his face in her lap.)

Blackout

IV. LABOR SPY EPISODE

FATT: You don't know how we work for you. Shooting off your mouth won't help. Hell, don't you guys ever look at the records like me? Look in your own industry. See what happened when the hacks walked out in Philly three months ago! Where's Philly? A thousand miles away? An hour's ride on the train.

VOICE: Two hours!!

FATT: Two hours . . . what the hell's the difference. Let's hear from someone who's got the practical experience to back him up. Fellers, there's a man here who's seen the whole parade in Philly, walked out with his pals, got knocked down like the rest—and blacklisted after they went back. That's why he's here. He's got a mighty interestin' word to say. (*Announces*): *Tom Clayton!* (*As* CLAYTON *starts up from the audience,* FATT *gives him a hand which is sparsely followed in the audience.* CLAYTON *comes forward.*)

Fellers, this is a man with practical strike experience—Tom Clayton from little ole Philly.

CLAYTON *a thin, modest individual*: Fellers, I don't mind your booing. If I thought it would help us hacks get better living conditions, I'd let you walk all over me, cut me up to little pieces. I'm one of you myself. But what I wanna say is that Harry Fatt's right. I only been working here in the big town five weeks, but I know conditions just like the rest of you. You know how it is—don't take long to feel the sore spots, no matter where you park.

CLEAR VOICE (*from audience*): Sit down!

CLAYTON: But Fatt's right. Our officers is right. The time ain't ripe. Like a fruit don't fall off the tree until it's ripe.

CLEAR VOICE: Sit down, you fruit!

FATT (*on his feet*): Take care of him, boys.

VOICE (*in audience, struggling*): No one takes care of me. (*Struggle in house and finally the owner of the voice runs up on stage, says to speaker*):

SAME VOICE: Where the hell did you pick up that name! Clayton! This rat's name is Clancy, from the old Clancys, way back! Fruit! I almost wet myself listening to that one!

FATT (*gunman with him*): This ain't a barn! What the hell do you think you're doing here!

SAME VOICE: Exposing a rat!

FATT: You can't get away with this. Throw him the hell outa here.

VOICE (*preparing to stand his ground*): Try it yourself. . . .
When this bozo throws that slop around. You know who he is? That's a company spy.

FATT: Who the hell are you to make—

VOICE: I paid dues in this union for four years, that's who's me! I gotta right and this pussy-footed rat ain't coming in here with ideas like that. You know his record. Lemme say it out——

FATT: You'll prove all this or I'll bust you in every hack outfit in town!

VOICE: I gotta right. I gotta right. Looka *him*, he don't say boo!

CLAYTON: You're a liar and I never seen you before in my life!

VOICE: Boys, he spent two years in the coal fields breaking up any organization he touched. Fifty guys he put in jail. He's ranged up and down the east coast—shipping, textiles, steel—he's been in everything you can name. Right now——

CLAYTON: That's a lie!

VOICE: Right now he's working for that Bergman outfit on Columbus Circle who furnishes rats for any outfit in the country, before, during, and after strikes. (*The man who is the hero of the next episode goes down to his side with other committee men.*)

CLAYTON: He's trying to break up the meeting, fellers!

VOICE: We won't search you for credentials. . . .

CLAYTON: I got nothing to hide. Your own secretary knows I'm straight.

VOICE: Sure. Boys, you know who this sonovabitch is?

CLAYTON: I never seen you before in my life!!

VOICE: Boys, I slept with him in the same bed sixteen years.

HE'S MY OWN LOUSY BROTHER!!

FATT (*after pause*): Is this true? (*No answer from* CLAYTON.)

VOICE (*to* CLAYTON): Scram, before I break your neck! (CLAYTON *scrams down center aisle.* VOICE *says, watching him:* Remember his map—he can't change that—Clancy! (*Standing in his place says*): Too bad you didn't know about this, Fatt! (*After a pause.*) The Clancy family tree is bearing nuts! (*Standing isolated clear on the stage is the hero of the next episode.*)

Blackout

V. INTERNE EPISODE

Dr. Barnes, an elderly distinguished man, is speaking on the telephone. He wears a white coat.

DR. BARNES: No, I gave you my opinion twice. You outvoted me. You did this to Dr. Benjamin yourself. That is why you can tell him yourself. (*Hangs up phone, angrily. As he is about to pour himself a drink from a bottle on the table, a knock is heard.*)

BARNES: Who is it?

BENJAMIN (*without*): Can I see you a minute, please?

BARNES (*hiding the bottle*): Come in, Dr. Benjamin, come in.

BENJ: It's important—excuse me—they've got Leeds up there in my place—He's operating on Mrs. Lewis—the historectomy—it's my job. I washed up, prepared . . . they told me at the last minute. I don't mind being replaced, Doctor, but Leeds is a damn fool! He shouldn't be permitted——

BARNES (*dryily*): Leeds is the nephew of Senator Leeds.

BENJ: He's incompetent as hell.

BARNES (*obviously changing subject, picks up lab. jar*): They're doing splendid work in brain surgery these days. This is a very fine specimen. . . .

BENJ: I'm sorry, I thought you might be interested.

BARNES (*still examining jar*): Well, I am, young man, I am! Only remember it's a charity case!

BENJ: Of course. They wouldn't allow it for a second, otherwise.

BARNES: Her life is in danger?

BENJ: Of course! You know how serious the case is!

BARNES: Turn your gimlet eyes elsewhere, Doctor. Jigging around like a cricket on a hot grill won't help. Doctors don't run these hospitals. He's the Senator's nephew and there he stays.

BENJ: It's too bad.

BARNES: I'm not calling you down either. (*Plopping down jar suddenly.*) Goddamnit, do you think it's my fault?

BENJ (*about to leave*): I know . . . I'm sorry.

BARNES: Just a minute. Sit down.

BENJ: Sorry, I can't sit.

BARNES: Stand then!

BENJ (*sits*): Understand, Dr. Barnes, I don't mind being replaced at the last minute this way, but . . . well, this flagrant bit of class distinction—because she's poor——

BARNES: Be careful of words like that—"class distinction." Don't belong here. Lots of energy, you brilliant young men, but idiots. Discretion! Ever hear that word?

BENJ: Too radical?

BARNES: Precisely. And some day like in Germany, it might cost you your head.

BENJ: Not to mention my job.

BARNES: So they told you?

BENJ: Told me what?

BARNES: They're closing Ward C next month. I don't have to tell you the hospital isn't self-supporting. Until last year that board of trustees met deficits. . . . You can guess the rest. At a board meeting Tuesday, our fine feathered friends discovered they couldn't meet the last quarter's deficit—a neat little sum well over $100,000. If the hospital is to continue at all, its damn——

BENJ: Necessary to close another charity ward!

BARNES: So they say. . . . (*A wait.*)

BENJ: But that's not all?

BARNES (*ashamed*): Have to cut down on staff too. . . .

BENJ: That's too bad. Does it touch me?

BARNES: Afraid it does.

BENJ: But after all I'm top man here. I don't mean I'm better than others, but I've worked harder.

BARNES: And shown more promise. . . .

BENJ: I always supposed they'd cut from the bottom first.

BARNES: Usually.

BENJ: But in this case?

BARNES: Complications.

BENJ: For instance? (BARNES *hesitant.*)

BARNES: I like you, Benjamin. It's one ripping shame.

BENJ: I'm no sensitive plant—what's the answer?

BARNES: An old disease, malignant, tumescent. We need an anti toxin for it.

BENJ: I see.

BARNES: What?

BENJ: I met that disease before—at Harvard first.

BARNES: You have seniority here, Benjamin.

BENJ: But I'm a Jew! (BARNES *nods his head in agreement.* BENJ *stands there a moment and* *blows his nose.*)

BARNES (*blows his nose*): Microbes!

BENJ: Pressure from above?

BARNES: Don't think Kennedy and I didn't fight for you!

BENJ: Such discrimination, with all those wealthy brother Jews on the board?

BARNES: I've remarked before—doesn't seem to be much difference between wealthy Jews and rich Gentiles. Cut from the same piece!

BENJ: For myself I don't feel sorry. My parents gave up an awful lot to get me this far. They ran a little dry goods shop in the Bronx until their pitiful savings went in the crash last year. Poppa's peddling neckties. . . . Saul Ezra Benjamin—a man who's read Spinoza all his life.

BARNES: Doctors don't run medicine in this country. The men who know their jobs don't run anything here, except the motormen on trolley cars. I've seen medicine change—plenty—anesthesia, sterilization—but not because of rich men—in *spite* of them! In a rich man's country your true self's buried deep. Microbes! Less. . . . Vermin! See this ankle, this delicate sensitive hand? Four hundred years to breed that. Out of a revolutionary background! Spirit of '76! Ancestors froze at Valley Forge! What's it all mean! Slops! The honest workers were sold out then, in '76. The Constitution's for rich men then and now. Slops! (*The phone rings.*)

BARNES (*angrily*): Dr. Barnes. (*Listens a moment, looks at* BENJAMIN.) I see. (*Hangs up, turns slowly to the younger Doctor.*) They lost your patient. (BENJ *stands solid with the shock of this news but finally hurls his operation gloves to the floor.*)

BARNES: That's right . . . that's right. Young, hot, go and do it! I'm very ancient, fossil, but life's ahead of you, Dr. Benjamin, and when you fire the first shot say, "This one's for old Doc Barnes!" Too much dignity—bullets. Don't shoot vermin! Step on them! If I didn't have an invalid daughter——

(BARNES *goes back to his seat, blows his nose in silence*): I have said my piece, Benjamin.

BENJ: Lots of things I wasn't certain of. Many things these radicals say . . . you don't believe theories until they happen to you.

BARNES: You lost a lot today, but you won a great point.

BENJ: Yes, to know I'm right? To really begin believing in something? Not to say, "What a world!", but to say, "Change the world!" I wanted to go to Russia. Last week I was thinking about it—the wonderful opportunity to do good work in their socialized medicine——

BARNES: Beautiful, beautiful!

BENJ: To be able to work——

BARNES: Why don't you go? I might be able——

BENJ: Nothing's nearer what I'd like to do!

BARNES: Do it!

BENJ: No! Our work's here—America! I'm scared. . . . What future's ahead, I don't know. Get some job to keep alive—maybe drive a cab—and study and work and learn my place—

BARNES: And step down hard!

BENJ: Fight! Maybe get killed, but goddamn! We'll go ahead! (BENJAMIN *stands with clenched fist raised high.*)

Blackout

AGATE: *Ladies and Gentlemen*, and don't let anyone tell you we ain't got some ladies in this sea of upturned faces! Only they're wearin' pants. Well, maybe I don't know a thing; maybe I fell outa the cradle when I was a kid and ain't been right since—you can't tell!

VOICE: Sit down, cockeye!

AGATE: Who's paying you for those remarks, Buddy?—Moscow Gold? Maybe I got a *glass eye*, but it come from working in a factory at the age of eleven. They hooked it out because they didn't have a shield on the works. But I wear it like a medal 'cause it tells the world where I belong—deep down in the working class! We had delegates in the union there—all kinds of secretaries and treasurers . . . walkin' delegates, but not with blisters on their feet! Oh no! On their fat little ass from sitting on cushions and raking in mazuma. (SECRETARY *and* GUNMAN *remonstrate in words and actions here.*) Sit down, boys. I'm just sayin' that about unions in general. I know it ain't true here! Why no, our officers is all aces. Why, I seen our own secretary Fatt walk outa his way not to step on a cockroach. No boys, don't think——

FATT (*breaking in*): You're out of order!

AGATE (*to audience*): Am I outa order?

ALL: No, no. Speak. Go on, etc.

AGATE: Yes, our officers is all aces. But I'm a member here—and no experience in Philly either! Today I couldn't wear my union button. The damnest thing happened. When I take the old coat off the wall, I see she's smoking. I'm a sonovagun if the old union button isn't on fire! Yep, the old celluloid was makin' the most god-awful stink: the land-lady come up and give me hell! You know what happened? That old union button just blushed itself to death! Ashamed! Can you beat it?

FATT: Sit down, Keller! Nobody's interested!

AGATE: Yes they are!

GUNMAN: Sit down like he tells you!

AGATE (*continuing to audience*): And when I finish—— (*His speech is broken by* FATT *and* GUNMAN *who physically handle him. He breaks away and gets to other side of stage. The two are about to make for him when some of the committee men come forward and get in between the struggling parties.* AGATE's *shirt has been torn.*)

AGATE (*to audience*): What's the answer, boys? The answer is, if we're reds because we wanna strike, then we take over their salute too! Know how they do it? (*Makes Communist salute.*) What is it? An uppercut! The good old uppercut to the chin! Hell, some of us boys ain't even got a shirt to our backs. What's the boss class tryin' to do—make a nudist colony outa us? (*The audience laughs and suddenly* AGATE *comes to the middle of the stage so that the other cabmen back him up in a strong clump.*)

AGATE: Don't laugh! Nothing's funny! This is your life and mine! It's skull and bones every incha the road! Christ, we're dyin' by inches! For what? For the debutant-ees to have their sweet comin' out parties in the Ritz! Poppa's got a daughter she's gotta get her picture in the papers. Christ, they make 'em with our blood. Joe said it. Slow death or fight. It's war! (*Throughout this whole speech* AGATE *is backed up by the other six workers, so that from their activity it is plain that the whole group of them are saying these things. Several of them may take alternate lines out of this long last speech.*)

You Edna, God love your mouth! Sid and Florrie, the other boys, oid Doc Barnes—fight with us for right! It's war! Working class, unite and fight! Tear down the slaughter house of our old lives! Let freedom really ring.

These slick slobs stand here telling us about bogeymen. That's a new one for the kids—the reds is bogeymen! But the man who got me food in 1932, he called me Comrade! The one who picked me up where I bled—he called me Comrade too! What are we waiting for. . . . Don't wait for Lefty! He might never come. Every minute——— (*This is broken into by a man who has dashed up the center aisle from the back of the house. He runs up on stage, says*):

MAN: Boys, they just found Lefty!

OTHERS: What? What? What?

SOME: Shhh. . . . Shhh. . . .

MAN: They found Lefty. . . .

AGATE: Where?

MAN: Behind the car barns with a bullet in his head!

AGATE (*crying*): Hear it, boys, hear it? Hell, listen to me! Coast to coast! HELLO AMERICA! HELLO. WE'RE STORMBIRDS OF THE WORKING-CLASS. WORKERS OF THE WORLD. . . . OUR BONES AND BLOOD! And when we die they'll know what we did to make a new world! Christ, cut us up to little pieces. We'll die for what is right! put fruit trees where our ashes are!

(*To audience*): Well, what's the answer?

ALL: STRIKE!

AGATE: LOUDER!

ALL: STRIKE!

AGATE and OTHERS on Stage: AGAIN!

ALL: STRIKE, STRIKE, STRIKE!!!

Curtain

Thomas Bell (1903–1961)

Thomas Bell's short story with the unromantic title, "Zinc Works Craneman to Wed," is a finely focused glimpse into working-class expectations in the late 1930s in Pittsburgh's Monongahela Valley—then still the heart of the American steel industry. Published in 1939 in *Story* magazine, "Craneman" can be read as a rehearsal for Bell's masterpiece, the novel *Out of This Furnace* (1941). The story is likely a spin-off of trips back home to his steel-town roots to research details for his novel: visiting family, documenting (sometimes with a camera) the old towns and neighborhoods (Braddock and Donora, Pennsylvania), interviewing local officials of the CIO's Steelworkers Organizing Committee, which in 1937 had finally won recognition by Big Steel—undoubtedly the event that spurred Bell to write his major novel. Compared to the short story, *Out of This Furnace* is a large canvas, covering sixty years and two and a half generations in an immigrant Slovak family whose typical male task is steel labor. The book achieves an epic effect as it moves through the generations, picking up many subjects: women's work (hiring out as domestics, keeping boarders, rearing children), corrupt ward politics, company domination,

"Americanization," ethnic prejudice, shoddy housing, environmental degradation, work accidents, and lousy pay. In *Out of This Furnace*, Bell celebrates the triumph of the union in 1937 as the best hope for a democratic future—although he emphasizes that the problems are large.

Bell was born Adalbert Thomas Belejcak in Braddock, Pennsylvania, the son of an immigrant Slovak father and a first-generation Slovak American mother, and raised within a couple of blocks of U.S. Steel's Edgar Thomson Works. At fifteen, he started to work in the mills and later trained as an electrician. After the death of both parents, Bell moved in his late teens to the East Coast, settled in New York City, and was writing seriously by the mid-1920s. He wrote half a dozen novels in all, of which two others, *All Brides Are Beautiful* (1936) and *Till I Come Back to You* (1943), received good public notice when they first came out. Throughout his career, his best work always dealt with the detail of proletarian life.

David Demarest

Zinc Works Craneman to Wed

They left Braddock at ten. Mary coughed as they stood in the quiet street, waiting for Johnny to unlock the Chevvy. At this end of town there was no air that wasn't impregnated with smoke; it made space, the darkness, an almost palpable thing, harsh in the throat, blurring the street lamps. Dust from the blast furnaces grated underfoot.

The girls got into the back; Dave sat in front with Johnny. "Take 51," Ann said to her husband. "I hate that 48, it's all curves."

"Who's drivin' this car?" Johnny said.

"You heard me."

They went along Braddock Avenue, past the light at 13th, past the mill. The red neon sign on top of the machine shop, Carnegie-Illinois Steel Company, Edgar Thomson Works, floated in a haze of smoke and steam. Farther on a Bessemer Converter, vomiting flame, threw a light against the bleak, eroded hills that exposed every rock and gully.

Ann said, "Give me Donora any time. Zinc works and all."

"What's the matter with Braddock?" Johnny asked. "Braddock's a good town. I was born and raised in Braddock. So was Dave."

"Every time I come here it looks dirtier. I'll bet it's one of the dirtiest towns in the United States."

"You don't know what you're talking about. Plenty people wouldn't live any place but Braddock."

"They can have it."

They passed under the high concrete arch of the new bridge, crossed Turtle Creek and went up the hill, the Westinghouse sprawling up the valley to their left. Its thousand windows were greenish with "daylight" lamps.

"Westinghouse seems to be workin' good," Dave said.

"I hear they're puttin' in a new shop for mass production or something."

"Yeah. They call it little Ford."

"It's liable to do away with a lot of jobs."

"Show me something nowadays that don't."

After a while Johnny said, "So you don't like Braddock. I take notice you had to come to Braddock when you wanted to see a fashion show."

"Get any ideas?" Dave asked.

"They were showing mostly extreme things," Mary said. "I was surprised they showed so much. Hostess gowns, Sunday night dresses, cocktail dresses, stuff like that."

"Well," Johnny said, "they don't put on a fashion show to show you house dresses."

"I know, but they certainly can't expect to sell any in Braddock. A woman whose husband works in the mill isn't going to spend her money on hostess gowns."

"They don't expect to sell any," Johnny said. "They just wanted to put on a show to advertise the store."

"Listen to him," Ann said in Slovak, "how smart he's getting."

"Did they have a bride?" Dave asked.

"At the very end. I didn't care much for her dress. I want something simple."

"Don't be foolish," Ann said. "This is one time in your life you have a right to dress up. I'm half sorry I came," she went on. "Seeing all those clothes." She sighed gustily.

"It didn't bother me," Mary said.

"I used to be worse. I'd go to Pittsburgh and come home sick. Staying home you forget how many nice things there are until you go into one of those big stores."

"I like to look at them but it doesn't bother me."

"Wait till you've been married a while and find out you never can have them. You still have half a hope you'll get them some day."

Mary didn't reply.

They went down the hill into McKeesport, through McKeesport, through Glassport. There was a glow of floodlights on top of the hill on the other side of the river where a new plate mill was being built. Then they were out of town and rolling along the quiet river road. The air was clearer here. The river reflected the lights of the Clairton by-products plant. They passed a sternwheeler and barges that sat motionless on the water, waiting, pointing a still pencil of light up the valley.

"You thought of trying for a job in the new mill?"

"I've thought of it," Dave said. "I guess you have to know somebody, though."

"It don't hurt. They say it'll be the only mill in the country on top of a hill. It is a hell of a place to put a mill when you come to think of it."

"I guess they know what they're doing."

Mary said, "Just so you get out of the zinc works I don't care where you work."

"Oh. Startin' to boss him already. What's the matter with the zinc works?"

"I notice you quit the first chance you got."

"I didn't quit because my wife ordered me, did I sweetheart?"

"I'll sweetheart you."

"Why you want him out of the zinc works?" Johnny asked. "Runnin' that ore bridge is supposed to be a pretty good job."

"I ain't on the ore bridge any more," Dave said. "I only had that while Johnny Fisher was sick. I'm on that monorail that runs along the river."

"In all that smoke," Mary said.

"It has arsenic in it," Ann said.

"Arsenic, sulphur, God knows what," Mary said. "Look at the way it's killed everything on the hills, and they're on the other side of the river. Not even grass can grow."

"I wonder if that farmer ever got anything."

"I don't know. You hear he did and you hear he didn't."

"They sure ruined his farm."

"It's not doing Dave any good," Mary said. "He's lost ten pounds this year. Sometimes he'll come to see me and you'd think he couldn't keep his eyes open. It's all I can do to get a word out of him."

"It makes you sort of numb," Dave said.

"No wonder them Spaniards drink so much. Pretty soon nobody but Spaniards will be workin' there."

"They ain't Spaniards," Ann said. "They're Mexicans."

"All right, Mexicans. But they speak Spanish."

"It makes him shiver, too," Mary said. "He used to have to wear a sweater on the hottest day, couldn't get warm. When was it you came home that time and got under the blankets with a hot water bottle? I know it was summer. And when he finally sweated, his sweat made the sheet blue. Actually left a blue stain."

"I never heard of anything like that," Ann said.

"Do you think he'd tell me? Only way I found out was Mrs. Duran told me. She noticed the stains when she made his bed. Did I give it to him. I wanted him to quit then and there."

"There you go," Johnny said. "Boy, I never saw anything like it. Soon's they're sure of a man they start bossin' him. Why don't you let the poor guy alone? He's only got a month left of bein' his own boss. Why don't you let him enjoy it?"

"You shut up," Ann said. "Mind your own business."

They went down into Elizabeth, turned left and went up the short cut through the hills, away from the river, through the dark countryside.

"Oh, Mary's right," Dave said after a while. "Best thing I could do is get out of there altogether. It ain't only the smoke. What I do, see, is after they've taken all the metal out of the furnaces they shove what's left into buckets. It's like slag, you might say, only instead of being liquid it's dust. Red hot. Then I pick it up and dump it into railroad cars. The heat and the dust are bad enough but when it rains it's worse. The buckets stand in the yard and get water in them."

"But they're full of dust when you get them."

"Yeah. Damp on the bottom and red hot on top."

"I don't see how that could be."

"Come down some day after it's been raining and watch. When I drop the bottom of the bucket the damp stuff sticks to the sides, and when the red hot stuff slides past that you get some real interesting effects."

Dave lit a cigarette.

"Couple weeks ago I came in and I said to myself, this is going to be a second 4th of July. It'd rained all night. The first bucket I took over looked all right. I had one hand on my dump lever and one on the crane, the idea being to be dumping and moving away from it at the same time. But it went boom just the same and I got a shower of hot dust that damn near baked me standing up. You know how those monorails are, the cab's right over the bucket, practically."

"Well," Johnny said, "you're still livin'."

"Yeah. Then the millwright came and inspected all around and when he took a look at the cab supports he found the rivets almost sheared through. Only about a quarter-inch left."

"That was nice. Did they fix it?"

"When they got around to it. For while there every time the crane bumped over a joint in the rail I expected the damn cab to keep right on goin' down, and me with it. Wouldn't be the first time that's happened. Those monorails've made more cripples."

"Wasn't Andy what's-his-name in an accident like that?"

"You mean Andy Bielak. Yeah. He was on one of the monorails down the other end of the mill by the roasting furnaces. First they dry out the ore and then they roast it red hot to burn out the sulphur or something. Then Andy takes it to the sintering plant. You know where Scott Street goes down through the mill? Well, he was on his way to the sintering plant with a full bucket and just as he gets about the middle of the street his crane drops."

"I heard about that. The whole crane just dropped right off the rail."

"That's right. There was a girder below him, I don't know what it's there for, you have to carry your bucket high to pass it. Well, the crane was moving when it let go and the momentum I guess worked it so the bucket cable caught on this girder with the bucket on one side and the cab on the other. It just hung there for a second and then the bucket started to spill and then the cable let go and everything hit the street. Andy still don't know how he got out of the cab. He must've started climbing out of it while it was still falling."

"It must be a hell of a feeling."

"He says he saw that red hot ore coming at him but how he didn't get buried under it he still don't know. He just got his arms and back burned. He was in the hospital a while but he's back on the job now."

"Same job?"

"Yeah."

"He's got more guts than I'd have."

"It ain't guts especially. He used to be a chipper and he got the idea he'd like to run a crane, nothing to do but ride around all day. So they transferred him to the zinc works and how he's stuck with it. He thought he'd get a crane in the steel mill or the wire mill."

"Why don't you ask for a transfer?"

"I been down to the office a dozen times. Once they got you down as a zinc works man you stay zinc works. Only thing I can do is to get out of town altogether. I'm figuring on trying Pittsburgh Steel, either Monesson or Allenport."

"You'll need a car to get back and forth. Unless you move."

"There's guys from Donora workin' in Allenport that have cars. Ray Shedlock's runnin' a crane in the tube mill up there; I could ride with him for a quarter a day."

"That ore bridge looks like a pretty good job," Johnny said reflectively.

"Oh, if I could get that job steady I'd marry it. There's some smoke from the driers but nothing like up at this end. You fill your hoppers and you're through for a while. In winter the ore freezes and you have to wait for the labor gang to break it up for you, it's a picnic. Takes longer in the driers, too. Oh, I couldn't ask for a better job. But there ain't a chance."

"You get out of the zinc works altogether," Mary said. "That's all I ask."

"I'm tryin',"

"I mean it. I won't pack your lunch."

"You want to get married, don't you?" Johnny said. "You can't get married if he ain't got a job. And the zinc works is steady; they go right along workin' full time when the steel mills are down to three days a week. If you want to get married—"

"You shut your big mouth," Ann said.

They turned off 51 and went down Ella Hollow and came out on the river road again, turned left. Ahead of them, across the river, was the zinc works, and beyond it, behind the row of monumental stacks, taller than anything in a steel mill, the lights of the town. The furnaces were hot so there wasn't much smoke; freshly charged, they poured out acrid, bluish-gray smoke that filled the valley from hill to hill, sometimes made auto headlights necessary in the streets and set the river boat pilots to cursing God.

"I'll tell you what gets me," Dave said. "I can stand the dust and the smoke and the wet days, but what gets me is when something goes wrong and I have to walk that rail. The damn crane never breaks down near a ladder. So I have to get out and walk that rail. It ain't a foot wide and it's easy thirty feet above ground. I'm no iron worker and I'm telling you my knees are shakin' when I reach the ground."

"I'll have to come down and watch you sometime," Johnny said. "It ought to be good."

"Then I have to walk it again with the electrician or the millwright, and if he decides he needs something who goes for it? Me. I come back with my hands full, which just makes it that much better. If it's cold weather there's just enough frost on the rail to make the goin' good. And sometimes I think those goddam engineers wait on purpose till I'm on the rail to come along under me throwing up smoke and sparks."

Johnny laughed.

They were opposite the zinc works now, the tall cement stacks, the row of furnaces with their sides crawling with thousands of small, tongue-like flames, blue, green and yellow. It was prettier to look at than work with.

In the back seat Mary looked at the furnaces and listened to the men talking; and in the back of her head she was thinking, not really feeling but just thinking as a person thinks about something before he begins to feel it, begins getting hopeless or angry; she was thinking, Next month I'm going to marry him. I'm going to be his wife and see him go out in the morning. During the day I'll think of him in that crane, working; and late in the afternoon, with the house smelling of supper, I'll stand behind the curtains in the front room, watching the street, waiting for him to come around the corner.

William Attaway (1911–1986)

William Attaway's powerful novel *Blood on the Forge* is an important depiction of the doomed Great Steel Strike of 1919 in Pittsburgh's Monongahela Valley and of the experience of the African American men who were imported from the South in boxcars to work in the North as strikebreakers. Attaway's rendering of the Great Migration follows the careers of the three Moss brothers—Chinatown, Melody, and Big Mat—through the wrenching transition from a pre-cash feudal economy of their native Kentucky, with its organic sun-and-season time sense, to the industrial world of clock-time in the steel-ruined geography of the Mon Valley. The novel's spare poetic style, the depth of feeling with which the Moss brothers are understood and presented, and the epic quality of their migration make the novel very effective. In and out of print several times since its original publication in 1941, *Blood on the Forge* invites comparison with Thomas Bell's *Out of This Furnace*, also published in 1941. Both are retrospective novels, written toward the end of the 1930s proletarian renaissance, depicting major events in the history of steel labor from within different ethnic experiences: Eastern European immigrant and African American migrant.

Attaway was born in Greenville, Mississippi, but his parents, a doctor and a teacher, moved the family to Chicago when he was five because, according to Attaway, his father "had a notion that Negro kids brought up in the South unconsciously accept the white's estimate of them. They never get to know what it is to be a human among humans." After two years of college, Attaway dropped out and, like so many others during the Great Depression, hoboed out west, working and writing when he could. Back in Chicago in the mid-1930s, he completed college and became involved with the Illinois branch of the Federal Writers Project, which fostered a number of significant black writers, including Richard Wright, with whom Attaway became friends. Attaway's first novel, *Let Me Breathe Thunder*, was published in 1939, quickly followed by *Blood on the Forge* in 1941. Neither novel sold well, and after World War II, Attaway went into radio and television writing. He also became a prolific songwriter and arranger, especially of West Indian music; his best-known credit was Harry Belefonte's hit, "Day-O." His final publications were *The Calypso Songbook* (1957) and *Hear America Singing* (1967).

David Demarest

"THE MOSS BROTHERS ENTER THE MILL," FROM *BLOOD ON THE FORGE*

Squatted on the straw-spread floor of a boxcar, bunched up like hogs headed for market, riding in the dark for what might have been years, knowing time only as dippers of warm water gulped whenever they were awake, helpless and drooping because they were headed into the unknown and there was no sun, they forgot even that they had eyes in their heads and crawled around in the boxcar, as though it were a solid thing of blackness.

There were so many men in the car that for a long time Big Mat was lost from his brothers. Somebody had started to crawl around in the dark. Soon everyone was moving about. Big Mat had ended in a corner. He crouched there, body shaking with the car. Now and then his head struck against the wall with a noise that was lost in greater noises. His big muscles cried out for movement. Warm urine began to flow into the corner where he sat. He did not move. He was in misery, but his misery was a part of everything else. The air, fetid with man smell and nervous sweat, the pounding of the wheels shaking the car and its prisoners like a gourd full of peas, the piercing scream of the wheels fighting the rails on a curve, the uniform dark—those things were common to all. The misery that stemmed from them was a mass experience. Big Mat could not defend his identity against the pack.

The rattle and jar of the wheels kept Melody from singing, although he was feeling bad and had his box with him. The wheels seemed to be saying crazy things, laughing crazy laughs, trying to draw him into the present, trying to make him crazy like they were. Whatever came into his head was copied by the wheels.

Once he called out: "Big Mat, where you?"

The wheels swallowed up the cry and clicked it out, louder and louder, faster and faster. It made his head spin to try and keep up with the fast-talking wheels. He had to shift to another word in order to keep sane. Soon the wheels had him racing along with the new word. Melody was a sounding board for all rhythms. If it had not been for Chinatown and what he said, everything might have become mixed up with those crazy wheels.

Chinatown was sitting shoulder to shoulder with Melody. His grinning jaws ached with the effort of holding his teeth clamped tight. Every time he dozed off the jar of the car would begin to bang his teeth together. Painfully he dozed and started awake. After a while the fear of dozing began to work in his head. He was the first one in the car to crack up. Melody forgot himself, in trying to comfort his brother. The noise of the car was deafening, but they put their cheeks together, and each yelled in the other's ear.

"Ascared to sleep—ascared to sleep! Car shake so it liable to knock the gold tooth right outen my head. Can't lose that tooth—can't 'ford to lose that tooth. Now I go to sleep, and maybe it gits knocked out. . . . Ascared to sleep, and I tired. . . . I tired. . . ."

"Whoa now, whoa, boy!" Melody calmed him like he would an excited mule. "We be outen here 'fore long."

"I tired and can't sleep. All my life I think 'bout a gold tooth, then I gits one. Now maybe I go to sleep, and it gits knocked out. Somebody steal it sure if it gits knocked out."

"Sure, boy—whoa, boy!"

"It gittin' loose now. You kin feel it. Feel it."

Melody put a shaking hand on the tooth.

"It feel all right, China."

"You ain't foolin'?"

"Naw, boy."

"It ain't even loose?"

"Naw, boy."

"You a good kid, Melody," said Chinatown, greatly eased. "Reckon this damn rattlin' an' all drivin' me off my nut."

"That's it, boy—that's all to it."

"You know me, Melody, since I a little rhiney fella. Little Chinatown then. Now it's Big Chinatown. Never was nothin'—still ain't nothin'. But nobody treat a nigger like he got to git tired sometime."

Melody tried to quiet him again. "Sure, boy, I know how it is."

"Yeah, but you got your box to sit with. Everybody call me no-good nigger. Boss man walk by when he ain't got nothin' for to work. When there a job he kicks me if I slows and calls me a no-good nigger. All that make a man feel like he ain't nothin', and a man got to have somethin' he kin grin a little to hisself about."

"Sure is so, boy."

"When I jest Little Chinatown I seen the way things is an' I know I got to have somethin' to make me feel like I somebody. So all the time I dream 'bout a gold tooth, shinin' an' makin' everybody look when Chinatown smile."

"Sure do shine, China."

"Reckon it do. Work for that tooth when all I wants to do is laze in the sun. But that's all right—I gits the tooth. And I jest got to have that tooth. Without it I ain't nobody. Now everybody turn and see who it is when Chinatown smile."

"Sure do, China. Sure do, boy."

The train gave a lurch. They were pounded against the wall.

"Watch out for me, Melody. I do something for you sometime. Keep talkin', so's I won't go to sleep. Sure as I do I git to boundin' and knock out this here tooth. Somebody steal it then sure. Can't 'ford to lose this tooth. I ain't nothin' when I loses this tooth. I tired—tired. . . . But you and me keep talkin', Melody—keep talkin'. . . ."

Riding away from the hills they were born and raised on wasn't easy. Riding with the rattle of wheels in their ears when they were in the dark, not knowing where they were headed, wasn't easy. It was enough to make them all brittle. Melody knew that. He knew that later on Chinatown would not want to think about the crazy secret things he was saying then. . . . But the shiny tooth did not drop out, and Melody was glad. His brother's voice was the only sound, outside of the wheels, that was real.

When the car finally stopped for a long time and some men unsealed and slid back the big door they were blinded by the light of a cloudy day. In all their heads the train wheels still clicked. Their ears still heard the scream of steel on the curves. Their bodies were motionless, but inside they still jerked to the movement of a bouncing freight car.

A brakeman had to rouse them. "C'mon, stretch your legs on West Virginia ground, boys. Tomorrow you'll be in Allegheny County."

They hunched against one another, whispering and wondering, and big drops of rain, grayed with slag and soot, rolled on the long wooden bunkhouse. Passing the makings back and forth, they burned cigarettes until their tongues felt like flannel in their jaws. There was a crap game going on in the bunkhouse, but the newcomers didn't have any money to put on the wood. There was nothing for them to do that first day, except smoke and keep walking the rows of bunks. Windows stretched in the long wooden walls around them. And outside they could see the things that they would see for a long time to come.

A giant might have planted his foot on the heel of a great shovel and split the bare hills. Half buried in the earth where the great shovel had trenched were the mills. The mills were as big as creation when the new men had ridden by on the freight. From the bunkhouse they were just so much scrap iron, scattered carelessly, smoking lazily. In back of them ran a dirty-as-a-catfish-hole river with a beautiful name: the Monongahela. Its banks were lined with mountains of red ore, yellow limestone and black coke. None of this was good to the eyes of men accustomed to the pattern of fields.

Most of the crap shooters had been in the valley a long time. Some of them took time from the game to come back and talk with the green men.

"See them towers? That's where I works. The iron blast. Don't take the blast if you kin help it. It ain't the work—it's the head blower. Goddamn tough mick. Why, I seen the time when the keeper on my furnace mess up the blast, and the furnace freeze before you know it. That head blower don't stop to find who the fault go to. Naw, he run up and right quick lays out three men with a sow. One of the hunkies yanks a knife on him, but that hunky gits laid out too. I reckon somebody woulda got that mick 'fore this. Only a man ain't much fer a fight when he's makin' four hundred tons of fast iron from one sun to the other."

The men from the hills were not listening. They were not talking. Their attitude spoke. Like a refrain:

We have been tricked away from our poor, good-as-bad-ground-and-bad-white-men-will-let-'em-be hills. What men in their right minds would leave off tending green growing things to tend iron monsters?

"Lots of green guys git knocked out by the heat—'specially hunkies. They don't talk nothin' but gobbler talk. Don't understand nothin' else neither. Foreman tell one old feller who was workin' right next to me to put leather over his chest. Foreman might jest as well been whistlin', 'cause when the heat come down there that hunky lays with a chest like a scrambled egg."

Yes, them red-clay hills was what we call stripped ground, but there was growing things everywhere and crab-apple trees bunched—stunted but beautiful in the sun.

"Them old fellers hadn't oughta be put on a furnace. Course, a green man got to expect to git pitted up some. Lots o' young'uns got lead in their pants, and they gits tagged when the flame come jumpin' for their shovel. There always burns, too, when the furnace gits tapped and the slag spills over into the pit. But the quicker a man learn to move around on his feet the longer he stays livin'."

A man don't git to know what the place where he's born looks like until he goes someplace else. Then he begins to see with his mind things that his eyes had never been able to see. To us niggers who are seeing the red-clay hills with our minds this Allegheny County is an ugly, smoking hell out of a backwoods preacher's sermon.

"Mebbe they start you new boys out on the skull buster. That's a good way to git broke in. But jest keep minded that you got to be keerful o' that old devil, skull buster. Kill many a green man. How? Well, magnet lift the steel ball thirty feet up and drop her. Steel ball weigh nigh eight tons. That eight tons bust the hell out of old scrap metal. Got to be keerful not to git some of it in your skull. Yessir, many a green man long gone 'cause he couldn't keep old skull buster from aimin' at his head."

What's the good in strainin' our eyes out these windows? We can't see where nothin' grows around here but rusty iron towers and brick stacks, walled up like somebody's liable to try and steal them. Where are the trees? They so far away on the tops of the low mountains that they look like the fringe on a black wear-me-to-a-wake dress held upside down against the sky.

"Skull buster don't git as many as whores git. Roll mill help the gals out. Feller sees all that hot steel shooting along the runout tables, all them red-and-white tongues licking 'twixt them rollers. Feller go hog wild fer any gal what 'll take his money. She don't have to work him up none—he's hot from that bakin' steel."

The sun on the red hillsides baked a man, but it was only a short walk to the bottoms and the mud that oozed up between his toes like a cool drink to hot black feet, steppin' easy, mindful of the cotton-mouth.

"On the floor, under the Bessemers, you ain't got time to think what a gal's got 'tween her legs. . . ."

Melody and Chinatown went out into the wet. The door closed behind them. The rain had lessened to a drizzle. They could hear the clank of the mills over the steady swish of the rain. Melody led the way. He turned away from the river and walked toward the town.

"Boy, this here North don't seem like nothin' to me," complained Chinatown. "All this smoke and stuff in the air! How a man gonna breathe?"

The drizzle stopped. Thin clouds rolled. Melody looked up. "Sun liable to break through soon."

"Won't make no difference to us if the sun don't shine."

"How come?"

"There won't be no crop to make or take out."

"Sun make you feel better," said Melody.

"Couldn't shine through the smoke, nohow. Long time ago a fella told me a nigger need sun so's he kin keep black."

Melody kicked Chinatown with his knee. Chinatown kicked back. Soon they were kicking and dodging around the ash piles. They were laughing when they came to the weedy field at the edge of town. Both men stopped. The laughter died.

Quivering above the high weeds were the freckled white legs of a girl. She struggled with a small form—a little boy who wanted to be turned loose. Other children were peeping through the wet grass. They began to chant, "Shame, shame! Mary and her brother—shame!"

Chinatown and Melody wheeled and hurried away. They had no need to speak to each other. In both of them was the fear brought from Kentucky: that girl might scream. Back in the hills young Charley had been lynched because a girl screamed.

Breathing hard, they followed the path until it became a dirt street. In front of them was a long line of women waiting in front of a pump shed. A few boys crouched underneath one corner of the shelter, held by a game with a jackknife.

"Look—more hunkies!" breathed Chinatown.

"Keep shut," warned Melody.

The pump at the edge of town watered about fifty families. Every Saturday the women were here in line. This day they carried bathing water home. The rain had soaked into their shawl head coverings. They stood patiently.

Then one of the boys spied the three strangers. He was on his feet in a second. "Ya-a-a . . ."

A rock whizzed between Melody and Chinatown. The two men halted, confused. In the eyes of all the Slavs was a hatred and contempt different from anything they had ever experienced in Kentucky. Another rock went past. Chinatown started to back away.

"We ain't done nothin'," cried Melody. He took a step toward the pump shed. The women covered their faces with their shawls.

"We ain't done nothin'," he cried again.

His words were lost in the shrill child voices: "Ya-a-a . . . ya-a-a . . . ya-a-a . . ."

Melody backed after his half brother. A little distance away they turned and trotted riverward.

"So this how the North different from the South," panted Chinatown.

"Musta mistook us for somebody," said Melody.

"When white folks git mad all niggers look alike," said Chinatown.

"Musta mistook us," insisted Melody.

It should have been easy for them to find the bunkhouse. The river was a sure landmark. But, in turning in among a series of knolls, they lost direction and found themselves back at the town. Before them a dirt road ran between rows of frame shacks. A large pile of garbage blocked the far end of the road.

"Oughta be somebody we kin ask where the bunkhouse," said Chinatown.

"Well, I ain't knockin' on nobody's door to ask nothing."

"All we got to do is start back to the river."

"Which way the river?" puzzled Melody, craning his neck around.

The light rain had started again. A mist had arisen through the rain. The low mountains were no longer visible. The mills along the water were blotted out. Their sound seemed to come from all directions.

"Maybe if I climbs that garbage . . ."

Chinatown started at a run down the road. At the top of the garbage pile he got his bearings. To the west the gray was tinged with faint streaks of orange.

"Over yonder apiece," he yelled, pointing westward.

At the cry, white faces appeared in the doorway opposite him. Nothing was said. Little faces grimaced between the overalled legs of the bearded father. With a movement of her hands beneath an apron, the mother fanned the breadth of her hips at him. An old Slav bent like a burned weed out of the window. Great handle-bar mustaches dripped below his chin. With eyes a snow-washed blue, he looked contempt at Chinatown. Then he wrinkled his nose and spat.

Chinatown slid down the pile of wet garbage. Hardly daring to hurry, he walked the middle of the road to the place where Melody waited.

"These here folks ain't mistook nobody."

They made quick tracks in the mud to the west.

At the river they did not stop to rest or look around. They wanted the shelter of the bunkhouse. This new place was full of hatreds that they did not understand. Melody led the way down-river. They had been going ten minutes when he stopped. There was no sign of the bunkhouse. Nothing but the river looked familiar.

"You reckon we been goin' wrong?" asked Chinatown.

"Got to be one way or the other," said Melody. He turned and looked behind him.

A fat-cheeked black girl moved along the river-front road. Bright red lipstick had turned to purple on her lips. A man's hat was pulled down over her ears. She wore an old overall coat over a stained satin dress.

Melody stared at her. She drew the coat tight around her hips and began to swagger. He was drawn by her eyes. They were cold pieces of wet glass.

"Wish I knowed what the way to Kentucky," Chinatown was moaning. He turned and saw the woman. "Man! Man! Kentucky kin wait."

The girl passed them. Her swimming eyes invited. They caught a heavy scent of perfume. Under the perfume was a rot stink. The stink sickened them. They were unnerved.

"Howdy, boys. Green, huh?"

They whirled and faced a small, dark man. He shifted from one foot to the other. His movements were like a squirrel's.

"Howdy," said Chinatown.

"How come you know we green?" asked Melody.

"They give all green niggers the same clothes," said the man.

"Oh . . ." Melody's gaze followed the woman.

"Beside, only a green man stop to look at that there gal."

They questioned him with their eyes.

"Her left breast 'bout rotted off." The man laughed. "You kin smell it a mile away."

"What you know!" Chinatown laughed.

Melody was stunned. He could not get the wet eyes out of his mind. All he could think to say was, "We lost from the bunkhouse."

"You been goin' wrong," said the man. "Back the other way a piece."

"Obliged," said Melody.

"I got to pass by there. Point it out."

"Obliged."

They walked along together.

"You work around here?" Chinatown asked.

"Blast. Boss of stove gang," said the man.

"Oh," said Chinatown. He looked at the old overalls.

"Sparks," explained the little man. "They'll git you too."

"Oh."

A group of Slav workmen came out of a gate in front of one of the mills. They moved with a slow stiffness, hardly shaking their drooping mustaches. There was dignity in the way they walked.

"Uh-uh," groaned Chinatown.

The workmen paused at the gate. One of them turned and waved at the little black man.

"Hallo, Bo."

The little man waved back. That greeting was the easy familiarity of men who had known each other over a period of years.

Chinatown voiced what was in his mind: "That there's the first white guy we seen don't hate niggers."

Bo asked, "You been havin' trouble?"

"Everybody treat us like poison," said Chinatown.

"Everythin' be smooth in a coupla weeks," said Bo. "Always hate new niggers round here."

"How come?"

"Well, company bring them in when there strike talk. Keep the old men in line."

"Oh . . ." said Chinatown. They walked a little. "There strike talk now?"

Bo looked him in the eye. "Looka here, boy. I don't know nothin' but my job."

"Yessir," said Chinatown.

"Don't mean nothin' by talkin' short," said Bo, "only it ain't a good thing for a feller to go spoutin' off."

"That's like Kentucky," said Chinatown.

Within sight of the bunkhouse, Bo stopped in the open to let water.

"Good idea," he said. "The outhouse always full of flies. Smells because nobody sprinkle ashes like they supposed to." He laughed. "Sometime a lizard use your behind for a bridge when you on the hole."

The men from the hills had always let water in the open. It made a feller feel free—space around him and the warm water running in the weeds. Nothing overhead but what God first put there. This touch of the past relaxed them. Their recent experiences became the unreality. This was the reality. They felt for a minute like Bo was an old friend.

"Well, so long," said Bo. "Be keerful. They puts green men on the hot jobs afore they know enough to keep alive."

They stood and watched him cut across the weedy ground to the cinder path leading to the lunch car.

Back in the bunkhouse. Big Mat, Chinatown, Melody—the Moss boys—walking around in a place so strange that one of them might have been dreaming it for the other two. In the bare boards underneath one of the windows there was a knothole. It had a swirl like the top of an onion gone to seed. To the Moss boys that knothole was bigger than all the steel mills.

Later they were in their bunks but far from sleep. They could hear the noises of the dice game, still going strong. One of the men had told them that the game had been going on for years, the night shift taking over when the day shift was at work.

The Irish foreman broke the noises of the game, assigning the shifts. Most of the new men would work in the yards. A few would stoke the "mules," small engines that hauled steel along the river front.

That word "mule"—it sounded like home.

A shift was anywhere from ten to fourteen hours in the heat. Everybody averaged around twelve hours a day. Knowing that, they should have slept but they listened to the high, whining voice of a crippled Negro called Smothers. One of the men whispered that Smothers was off his nut. Yet they listened and heard a different sort of tale:

"It's wrong to tear up the ground and melt it up in the furnace. Ground don't like it. It's the hell-and-devil kind of work. Guy ain't satisfied with usin' the stuff that was put here for him to use—stuff of top of the earth. Now he got to git busy and melt up the ground itself. Ground don't like it, I tells you. Now they'll be folks laugh when I say the ground got feelin'. But I knows what it is I'm talkin' about. All the time I listen real hard and git scared when the iron blast holler to git loose, an' them big redhead blooms screamin' like the very heart o' the earth caught between them rollers. It jest ain't right.

"So what happen? There a ginny falls when they pourin'—and the preacher got to say service over a hundred tons o' steel. For no reason there's somethin' freeze in the blast furnace. Then it slip, and hot coke and metal rain down through the roof on the fellers round the bosh. Any time you foolin' round fast metal it liable to blow up. It always blow for no reason at all, 'ceptin' it want to. . . .

"Listen close now, an' I'm goin' to talk to you so you know something. Steel want to git you. Onliest thing—it ain't gittin' you fast enough. So there trouble in the mills. Guys wants to fight each other—callin' folks scabs and wants to knock somebody in the head. Don't nobody know why. I knows why. It's 'cause steel got to git more men than it been gittin'. . . .

"Can't blame the ground none. It give warnin'. Yessir, they was warnin' give a long time ago. Folks say one night there's somethin' fall right outen the sky, blazin' down, lightin' up this ol' river in the black o' night. Guys ain't stop meltin' long enough to see what it is but next morning they finds it. A solid hunk o' iron it be, big around as a house, fused together like it been worked by a puddler with a arm size of a hundred-foot crane. Where it come from? Where this furnace in the sky? You don't know. I don't know. But it were a warning to quit meltin' up the ground."

Smothers pulled himself to his feet by taking hold of the bunk above him. His eyes held all the green men until he got his crutches underneath his armpits. Then he shook his head in a last warning and hobbled out like a parched-up hopper-grass.

"It ain't quite daylight, but it's four o'clock,
So wake up, niggers, an' piss on the rock. . . ."

One of the boys woke the green men with that cry. He had done time on a Georgia chain gang. Outside, the light had not pierced the morning smoke cloud. Through the windows the men saw the red ball on the horizon. It was a strange waking to a muted sunrise. It was hard to realize the morning.

Some of the old hands kidded, "You ain't never goin' to work in daylight. Now it too early. Next week you work the night shift, and it too late."

The new men had heard how they changed to the night shift. One crew would have to work twenty-four hours in the heat. That did not mean anything to them now. Now they did not like the taste of the sooty air. They missed the sun.

"Got to blow the chimneys ever' night," they were told.

"When the air gits good guys is hungry," they were told.

Everything was too strange for the green men to comprehend. In a daze, they were herded to the mill gates and checked in. The night shift was getting off. They mingled for a few minutes at the mill gates. All of them were gray in the dirty river mists, but the men who had finished a turn were easy to pick out. Their shoulders sagged as though the weights of their coats were too much. The green men carried overall coats over their arms. They had been told to put something on after a turn, that even on a hot day a guy chills, coming away from the heat. They had on long underwear also. That would be good to take the sweat off when the heat really came down. The men from the hills hated the heavy shoes cramping toes used to gripping the dust.

The Moss boys waited in line with the rest. They were given numbers and keys to lockers. Their eyes were open, but they were not seeing the mills yet. They did not know how they arrived at the locker room. All around them men were changing into working clothes. The green men were given cold stares. Nobody spoke to them. They sat on a bench at one side.

An open-hearth worker had the locker next to the Moss boys. He was an Italian. Everybody called him Mike. Mike had a good heart. He showed them how to tie handkerchiefs around their necks. He made sure they had smoked glasses and heavy gloves. He warned them to wear two pairs of pants if they were put on a hot job—hot-job men always had a lot of holes burned in their clothes. Mike told them what had happened to him on the hearth.

"So there I, workin' Goddamn number eight. Pete throw switch, and furnace go over." He showed them how far the furnace had tilted, slanting his hands. "Goddamn slag run over at door. Some go in buggy car in pit. Some miss Goddamn slag hole. So sp-t-t-t-t-t—I think I Goddamn lucky not get burn bad. One, two, three hour later I standing up between Goddamn furnace catch little sleep. I wake up Goddamn cold. Fellas laugh like hell, 'cause spark burn right round pants top, an' Goddamn pants drop off my behind. Maybe I lucky not get burned, huh?"

The men laughed. Laughing, they broke up in little groups, headed for the places where strong metal was fighting to get loose. The shaping mills were far down the river, but he could hear the awful screams when the saws bit into the hot metal. The blast was a million bees in a drum. The open hearth was full of agony. The daylight was orange yellow with the droning flames of the Bessemers.

Melody whispered to Chinatown, "Wouldn't surprise me none if the Judgment turn out to be jest a steel mill. . . ." He was not joking.

"Sound like circus animals tryin' to git loose," whispered Chinatown.

To get to the pit they had to pass underneath the hearth furnaces. The foreman led the way under number four. All of the men but Chinatown and Melody got through without difficulty. When they ducked to follow the crew a curtain of fire appeared in front of them. Slag was dripping down through a hole to the floor of the pit, and there was no buggy in place to catch it. A couple of thin branches of liquid fire followed the slag. The branches grew large as a man's arm and flowed into one another. That liquid fire was "fast" steel. It hit on top of the slag and spattered. Chinatown yelled. His clothes began to smoke in a dozen places. They lost no time in getting out of there.

They came through under number five. O'Casey, the little pit boss, was there to give them hell.

"What in blue blazes you guys think this is?" he shouted. "You bastards ought to be docked half pay for takin' your own Goddamn time gettin' here."

"We couldn't git under——" began Melody.

O'Case left him in the middle of the words. The red face glowered up at the rest of the crew.

"What the blue blazes you guys waitin' for? Hop it! Clean up that mess front of number four!"

Half of the cleanup gang was made up of Slavs. They took their time getting to work. They knew that all pit bosses raised hell. It was the thing for a pit boss to do. Big Mat grabbed a pick and was at the slag before they could spit enough to slick their hands. They looked their disfavor. Big Mat would outwork everybody. He would spoil the rhythm of the crew. That would give the pit boss something else to raise hell about. Chinatown and Melody worked with a young Slovac. He wielded the pick; Chinatown shoveled, and Melody handled the wheelbarrow. The pile of stuff they were workin on was red hot; its core was still molten. Their feet heated and blistered.

Chinatown said, "When I think how we usta throw wiggle worms in hot ashes jest for fun I feels like crying."

Melody laughed.

"What you find to laugh for?" asked the Slovac. "This three-, four-hour work."

"Sonabitch let furnace go to hell," grumbled another of the men.

"You guys talk too much," yelled O'Casey from across the pit. "Get to diggin'."

"Stuff too hot for pick," yelled the Slovac. He dropped his pick. O'Casey came on the run.

"What the blue blazes!" he cried. "Git back on that stuff!"

"Too hot for a pick."

"You wasn't hired to work in no ice house," yelled the pit boss.

Some of the other men on the gang dropped their tools and backed away from the hot mass. O'Casey looked around desperately for a minute. Then he walked up to the biggest man on the floor of the pit—Big Mat. His head not as high as Big Mat's tobacco pocket, he had to lean backward to look the big man in the eye.

"You big dumb hulk of a bastard," cried the pit boss, "where's your brains?"

Big Mat dropped his shovel and glared down at the pit boss.

"Ain't you got brains enough to know what to do when the stuff is too hot?" cried the little man.

Big Mat opened his mouth to speak, but the words did not come out. His eyes glazed. He stood like a stupid child taking deserved punishment.

"Git the hell over there and find a hose!" commanded O'Casey.

Big Mat trotted away. O'Casey turned to the rest of the gang. His glance flashed over them with new confidence.

"Stand back and wait for that hose! Then hop to it! This furnace's due to pour in a half a hour."

The men stood back. O'Casey walked to the other side of the pit and expelled his breath in a long sigh.

A couple of the Slavs were too close when Big Mat turned the hose on the hot mass. There was a great hiss, and steam reached out and enveloped the two men. Cursing in their own tongues, they danced a crazy pattern. If Big Mat had not been so big he would have had a fight on his hands.

While the men were grumbling there came a long "Look o-o-o-out below!" Nobody had to tell the green men what to do. They scrambled under one of the furnaces. Maybe a crane had broken, and its ladle of hot metal would come pounding down to destroy the pit. But the danger was not overhead. It was only a spout flowing on number seven. The mud had burned out of the tap hole, and the fast steel was pitting the ground in a bright flood. They had to put on dark glasses to watch it. It was over in a few minutes. The furnace was tilted back so that the flow stopped.

The men who had been grumbling forgot all about Big Mat.

"This is an unlucky day," one of them sadly remarked.

"Don' no sonabitch know how fix spout round here?" screamed the young Slovac to everybody within listening distance.

"My feets is burnin' up," Chinatown said to Melody.

"Mine is hot too," Melody told him.

"Yeah, but if we got to clean up that there steel my feets goin' to git mad an' take me on out of here." He half grinned.

Melody grinned with him. The foreman was sending another crew to clean up the new mess.

They pried up the last of the slag with crowbars. And then there was time to take on a fresh jaw of cut plug. Big Mat went to watch the crew tap number two. Chinatown and Melody went to sit between the furnaces. It was cooler there. Melody took out his sack of tobacco and rolled a smoke. Chinatown got his chew soft and spat a long brown stream against a wheelbarrow. He stretched his arms over his head.

"Guy don't git no chance to sleep round here," he complained.

Later he would know the truth of his words through experience. It would always be time to start back to work before he was completely rested from the previous shift. Then if he went with the other fellows to raise a little hell before turning in he wouldn't get any rest at all.

"Think I knock off a few winks right now." Chinatown yawned.

"Sure, boy. I keep a lookout," promised Melody.

The thanks died on Chinatown's lips. His eyes closed, and he snored easily. Melody did not mind keeping watch. Chinatown was doing well to keep any kind of job. Melody thought about himself and Chinatown dozing in the sun back in Kentucky. The heat of the pit was like the sun at midday. Maybe they were in Kentucky. Maybe Maw was alive and in the back-door garden. Maybe Hattie would come in the doorway and say, "Wake up, you two lazy scapers. Vittles is done." He could not rouse himself, and Hattie was yanking at his shoulder.

It was Big Mat shaking him. Slowly he came to himself. He couldn't remember just when he had fallen asleep.

"Wazza matter?"

"'Nother cleanup job," said Big Mat. "Pit boss been raisin' hell."

Melody sprang to his feet.

"Pit boss jump on me 'cause you guys ain't around," said Big Mat.

"I think O'Casey got it in for you."

They got Chinatown on his feet. When they joined the rest of the gang O'Casey cursed Big Mat for taking so much time. Then they were hitting the hot slag again. The green men were not in the rhythm of the crew. Their pace was uneven. They grew very weary. There was nothing like working on hot slag for tiring a man, they thought. You worked a little while, and then the needles started all over your back, and you just had to lean on your shovel for a spell. They couldn't understand it. The slag was very light. Maybe it was the heat.

When the foreman told them to go to lunch most of the green men could hardly drag away to the mill yard. Big Mat was untouched by the toil, but Chinatown and Melody staggered as they walked. Chinatown did not want any food. He was too tired for eating. His muscles ached. Tears rolled down his face. Melody thought that all his life he would be seeing curtains of fire flowing down through slag holes. And when he thought about the long day ahead he got sick in his belly.

VI

Affluence, Cold War, and the Other America: 1940s–1970s

Whose neck shall I stand on, to make me feel superior?
And what will I get out of it? I don't want anything lower
than I am. I'm low enough already. I want to rise. And push
everything up with me as I go. . . .

—Esperanza, *Salt of the Earth*[1]

This thirty-year period of selected working-class literature calls for certain adjustments to one's angle of vision. The dust had settled, so to speak, after the trauma of economic depression, war, and atomic explosions. The clarity of a line drawn between capital and labor blurs into murkier relationships. The public face of labor is less *dramatically* visible. The world of workers has simultaneously expanded, spurred by new technologies, and, ironically, shrunk into more recessed and private spaces. The starting point (particularly for women writers) is inside, rather than outside—private and domestic spaces of the bedroom or kitchen—rather than the arena of the shop floor or the speaker's soapbox. Labor has not disappeared. This writing is no less communal in its sensibility than the labor songs or agitprop of previous decades, as shown in the quietly stirring words of Esperanza, a miner's wife from the film *Salt of the Earth* (1954). But Esperanza is not just fighting for safer working conditions and better pay for her husband and the other miners, she is also insisting on improved sanitation and indoor plumbing for herself and all the women— Mexican and Anglo. Esperanza's inclusive vision echoes an ethos of solidarity that fueled the proletarian writing of the 1930s. Her words also presage a more gender and racially inclusive shift in American literature, which is represented here and expanded more fully in Part VII. Beneath Esperanza's wish for a collective, rather than an individualistic, rising lie some of the fault lines in the promise of American democracy that mark this period of contractual unionism, anticommunism, wars in Korea and Vietnam, civil rights marches and legislation, antiwar demonstrations, women's liberation movements, and the slippage of citizenship into consumerism.[2] Did everyone rise with Esperanza Quintero? Did she?

From the victorious end of World War II in 1945 to the withdrawal of U.S. forces from Vietnam in 1975, the American working class—never of one voice, mind, or political vision—became more fractured, particularly as material circumstances improved for many (but not all) whites, but not for most black, immigrant, and migrant workers. The wartime Fair Employment Practices Commission, created in response to pressure by civil rights leaders to pry open the economic doors of defense work to black workers, was dismantled

Facing Page: "Bermuda Day" demonstration, 1954: As District Council 37, American Federation of State, County and Municipal Employees, AFL-CIO, pressed Mayor Wagner for collective bargaining rights, he took off for a vacation in Bermuda. Thousands marched at City Hall. Repeated demonstrations finally won an Executive Order providing for the right of city workers to organize, and directing all departments to establish grievance procedures. *District Council 37, American Federation of State, County and Municipal Employees, AFL-CIO. Courtesy of Bill Schleicher.*

after the war, ending a degree of equal protection and opportunity for minorities and women. White women factory workers—remembered as Rosie the Riveter—were expected to return to the home, and black male workers faced last hired, first fired seniority rules.[3] Black women workers continued to endure a restrictive, race- and gender-segregated work world, in which the worst jobs seemed to be saved for them.[4] Alice Childress's stories amusingly and bitingly present the black domestic worker's perspective on the white middle-class world she has no choice but to work in. Other stories, set in wartime, such as Ann Petry's "Like a Winding Sheet," show how societal racism can build to a point of explosion in the private life of a black couple.

These selections also offer a view from the immigrant margins. The concrete hardships and the abstracted hopes of immigrant workers are well represented in Filipino writer Carlos Bulosan's "The Story of a Letter" and his sweeping democratic poem "If You Want to Know What We Are." Hisaye Yamamoto's multilayered story "Seventeen Syllables" exposes some of the cultural clashes and intergenerational differences between Issei, first-generation Japanese immigrants, and Nisei, second-generation Japanese Americans, in the context of a larger historical backdrop in which thousands of West Coast Japanese were interned in wartime detention camps, including author Yamamoto and her family.

For the most part, though, the larger national narrative of homecoming and victory displaced such stories of immigrants and minorities. When the war ended in 1945, worker-soldiers returned home with a sense of affirmation that *they* were vital to winning it. And they were. With wage increases deferred and wartime shortages endured, returning veterans and their families wanted their fair share of corporate war profits. What ensued was a massive series of strikes between 1945 and 1946 led by autoworkers, followed by coal and rail workers. This pivotal moment in labor's strength—with union membership at an all-time high—was resisted by corporations and businesses through government lobbying and funding of pro-business legislators. The result was a major setback for organized labor: the Taft-Hartley (Labor Management Relations Act) of 1947. The Taft-Hartley Act curbed, if not overtly banned, labor's most powerful tool—the strike. Closed shops (workplaces in which only union members could be hired) were outlawed; strikes were curtailed by "cooling-off periods"; federal employees were not allowed to strike; and, among other provisions, union officers could not be members of the Communist Party.

Although workers, particularly male and white ones, achieved a measure of economic stability and prosperity in the two decades that followed, the seeds of unrest were sown as cities declined and suburbs developed and as industries built plants in previously rural areas, leaving workers who could not follow behind in urban ghettos. Big unions evolved into bureaucratic, increasingly conservative, hierarchies affiliating with and taking their political direction from government. Economic stability was traded for a deradicalized labor movement and the purging of left-wing and communist labor leaders. The Cold War with the Soviet Union advanced an extensive Red Scare, with a congressional witch hunt lead by Wisconsin Republican Senator Joseph McCarthy and hearings by the House Un-American Activities Committee (HUAC, 1953–1954). Carlos Bulosan, Edwin Rolfe, Tom McGrath, Tillie Olsen, and Studs Terkel were a few of the many writers, intellectuals, artists, and teachers on the Left who were harassed, questioned, and hounded by HUAC and the FBI during these years (a political censoring that some believe continues to this day). Rolfe sums up the critical question in his poem, "Are You Now or Have You Ever Been." The military budget jumped from $12 billion a year in 1950 to $40 billion in 1953 as the United States became involved in the often-forgotten Korean War or "Conflict" from 1950 to 1953. Homophobia accompanied the Red Scare, and homosexuals were barred from governmental service in 1953.[5]

Journalist David Halberstam describes the 1950s as "captured in black and white, most often by still photographers" and the decade that followed as "caught in living color on tape and film."[6] Images increasingly defined this period as *Life* magazine, ubiquitous advertisements, and television shaped Americans' view of themselves. Whose America was represented or reflected back?

The working-class writers of this period answer "whose America?" with many shades of black, white, and color. But whether in the regional portraits of James Wright's Ohio River Valley or Breece D'J. Pancake's Vietnam-era story of class and military service or Gwendolyn Brooks's peopled streetscapes, the writers tend to use smaller canvases to illuminate larger working-class realities. Brooks places her Chicago teenage gang, The Blackstone Rangers as inside and outside—"Their country is a Nation on no map." Harriette Arnow's dollmaker, Gertie Nevels, must leave her Kentucky home to follow her husband north to the industrial assembly-line jobs and consequently loses her grounding and identity as a powerfully skillful mountain woman—as well as her children. The mother in Tillie Olsen's iconic, "I Stand Her Ironing," moving back and forth with her iron, does not flatten the fabric of working-class lives, but embosses them, shows their complexity, and insists that such lives can never be so easily totaled up or dismissed. Judy Grahn's "Common Woman Poems" are seven extraordinary portraits of ordinary women, intended to present "everyday women without making us look either superhuman or pathetic."

Master oral historian Studs Terkel's classic collection *Working* is an indispensable panorama of working people and their views of their own jobs. Toni Bambara's much-anthologized "The Lesson," told from a child's perspective, reveals not just the measurable material differences between the rich and the poor, but is a lesson for everyone on the relationality of class—how class is hidden and exposed and known in this society. Toni Cade Bambara, in "Language and the Writer" (published posthumously in 1996), sums up the dilemma of engaged artists and cultural workers "in producing a desirable vision of the future" in a commercialized context in which "the tools of . . . trade are colonized. The creative imagination has been colonized. The global screen has been colonized. And the audience—readers and viewers—is in bondage to an industry."[7] Working-class literature of this period—and in all the parts of this anthology—attempts to resist that colonizing process.

Notes

1. Michael Wilson (screenplay), *Salt of the Earth*, 1953 (New York: Feminist Press, 1978), 82.

2. Lizabeth Cohen, *A Consumers' Republic: The Politics of Mass Consumption in Postwar America* (New York: Alfred A. Knopf, 2003).

3. Paul LeBlanc, *A Short History of the U.S. Working Class* (New York: Humanity Books, 1999), 95–96.

4. Jacqueline Jones, *A Short History of the Laboring Classes* (Malden, MA: Blackwell, 1999), 103, and the documentary, *The Life and Times of Rosie the Riveter*, Director, Connie Field, 1980.

5. Priscilla Murolo and A. B. Chitty, *From the Folks Who Brought You the Weekend* (New York: New Press, 2001), 235.

6. David Halberstam, *The Fifties* (New York: Villard Books, 1993), ix.

7. Toni Cade Bambara, *Deep Sightings and Rescue Missions* (New York: Pantheon, 1996), 139–140.

Ann Petry (1908–1997)

Born in Old Saybrook, Connecticut of four generations of African American New Englanders, Ann Lane Petry was the youngest of three daughters in a middle-class family. Her father, a pharmacist who owned his own drugstore, and her mother, a chiropodist and entrepreneur, provided an enclave of secure black family life in a predominately white community. Ann's mother was a storyteller and used stories to historicize racial prejudice. Although Ann enjoyed writing in high school, she trained to join the family business by earning a degree in pharmacy from Connecticut College in 1931. She moved to New York in 1938 after marrying George D. Petry, a mystery writer, and soon started writing for the *Amsterdam News* and *The People's Voice* and becoming involved in Harlem's vibrant wartime community life. Petry helped form Negro Women, Inc., a black women's consumer advocacy and community action group, and developed programs for children in a Harlem school. She studied painting, piano, and creative writing and performed in a production of the American Negro Theater. Her short story, "On Saturday the Siren Sounds at Noon," published in *Crisis*, caught the attention of editors at Houghton Mifflin and won her an advance and literary fellowship that led to the publication of her enormously successful first novel *The Street* (1946).

Petry had great powers of observation, combined with an equally large capacity to make an imaginative leap into the lives of individual figures, either historically, as in her books for young readers, *Harriet Tubman: Conductor on the Underground Railroad* (1955) and *Tituba of Salem Village* (1964), or contemporaneously in her characters' struggle to survive in *The Street*. She returned to Old Saybrook in 1948 with her husband and raised a daughter. She published, among other works, two more novels, *Country Place* (1947) and *The Narrows* (1953), and a collection of stories, *Miss Muriel and Other Stories* (1971). "Like a Winding Sheet" (1945) first appeared in *Crisis* and was collected in Martha Foley's *Best American Short Stories of 1946*.

Like a Winding Sheet

He had planned to get up before Mae did and surprise her by fixing breakfast. Instead he went back to sleep, and she got out of bed so quietly, he didn't know she wasn't there beside him until he woke up and heard the queer soft gurgle of water running out of the sink in the bathroom.

He knew he ought to get up, but instead he put his arms across his forehead to shut the afternoon sunlight out of his eyes, pulled his legs up close to his body, testing them to see if the ache was still in them.

Mae had finished in the bathroom. He could tell because she never closed the door when she was in there and now the sweet smell of talcum powder was drifting down the hall and into the bedroom. Then he heard her coming down the hall.

"Hi, babe," she said affectionately.

"Hum," he grunted, and moved his arms away from his head, opened one eye.

"It's a nice morning."

"Yeah." He rolled over, and the sheet twisted around him, outlining his thighs, his chest. "You mean afternoon, don't ya?"

Mae looked at the twisted sheet and giggled. "Looks like a winding sheet," she said. "A shroud—" Laughter tangled with her words, and she had to pause for a moment before she could continue. "You look like a huckleberry—in a winding sheet—"

"That's no way to talk. Early in the day like this," he protested.

He looked at his arms silhouetted against the white of the sheets. They were inky black by contrast, and he had to smile in spite of himself, and he lay there smiling and savoring the sweet sound of Mae's giggling.

"Early?" She pointed a finger at the alarm clock on the table near the bed and giggled again. "It's almost four o'clock. And if you don't spring up out of there, you're going to be late again."

"What do you mean 'again'?"

"Twice last week. Three times the week before. And once the week before, and—"

"I can't get used to sleeping in the daytime," he said fretfully. He pushed his legs out from under the covers experimentally. Some of the ache had gone out of them, but they weren't really rested yet. "It's too light for good sleeping. And all that standing beats the hell out of my legs."

"After two years you oughta be used to it," Mae said.

He watched her as she fixed her hair, powdered her face, slipped into a pair of blue denim overalls. She moved quickly, and yet she didn't seem to hurry.

"You look like you'd had plenty of sleep," he said lazily. He had to get up, but he kept putting the moment off, not wanting to move, yet he didn't dare let his legs go completely limp because if he did he'd go back to sleep. It was getting later and later, but the thought of putting his weight on his legs kept him lying there.

When he finally got up, he had to hurry, and he gulped his breakfast so fast that he wondered if his stomach could possibly use food thrown at it at such a rate of speed. He was still wondering about it as he and Mae were putting their coats on in the hall.

Mae paused to look at the calendar. "It's the thirteenth," she said. Then a faint excitement in her voice, "Why, it's Friday the thirteenth." She had one arm in her coat sleeve, and she held it there while she stared at the calendar. "I oughta stay home," she said. "I shouldn't go outa the house."

"Aw, don't be a fool," he said. "Today's payday. And payday is a good luck day everywhere, any way you look at it." And as she stood hesitating, he said, "Aw, come on."

And he was late for work again because they spent fifteen minutes arguing before he could convince her she ought to go to work just the same. He had to talk persuasively, urging her gently, and it took time. But he couldn't bring himself to talk to her roughly or threaten to strike her like a lot of men might have done. He wasn't made that way.

So when he reached the plant he was late, and he had to wait to punch the time clock because the day-shift workers were streaming out in long lines, in groups and bunches that impeded his progress.

Even now, just starting his workday, his legs ached. He had to force himself to struggle past the outgoing workers, punch the time clock, and get the little cart he pushed around all night, because he kept toying with the idea of going home and getting back in bed.

He pushed the cart out on the concrete floor, thinking that if this was his plant, he'd make a lot of changes in it. There were too many standing-up jobs, for one thing. He'd figure out some way most of 'em could be done sitting down, and he'd put a lot more benches around. And this job he had—this job that forced him to walk ten hours a night, pushing this little cart—well, he'd turn it into a sitting-down job. One of those little trucks they used around railroad stations would be good for a job like this. Guys sat on a seat, and the thing moved easily, taking up little room and turning in hardly any space at all, like on a dime.

He pushed the cart near the foreman. He never could remember to refer to her as the forelady even in his mind. It was funny to have a white woman for a boss in a plant like this one.

She was sore about something. He could tell by the way her face was red and her eyes were half-shut until they were slits. Probably been out late and didn't get enough sleep. He avoided looking at her and hurried a little, head down, as he passed her, though he couldn't resist stealing a glance at her out of the corner of his eyes. He saw the edge of the light-colored slacks she wore and the tip end of a big tan shoe.

"Hey, Johnson!" the woman said.

The machines had started full blast. The whirr and the grinding made the building shake, made it impossible to hear conversations. The men and women at the machines talked to each other, but looking at them from just a little distance away, they appeared to be simply moving their lips because you couldn't hear what they were saying. Yet the woman's voice cut across the machine sounds—harsh, angry.

He turned his head slowly. "Good evenin', Mrs. Scott," he said, and waited.

"You're late again."

"That's right. My legs were bothering me."

The woman's face grew redder, angrier looking. "Half this shift comes in late," she said. "And you're the worst one of all. You're always late. Whatsa matter with ya?"

"It's my legs," he said. "Somehow they don't ever get rested. I don't seem to get used to sleeping days. And I just can't get started."

"Excuses. You guys always got excuses." Her anger grew and spread. "Every guy comes in here late always has an excuse. His wife's sick or his grandmother died or some-body in the family had to go to the hospital." She paused, drew a deep breath. "And the niggers is the worst. I don't care what's wrong with your legs. You get in here on time. I'm sick of you niggers—"

"You got the right to get mad," he interrupted softly. "You got the right to cuss me four ways to Sunday, but I ain't letting nobody call me a nigger."

He stepped closer to her. His fists were doubled. His lips were drawn back in a thin narrow line. A vein in his forehead stood out swollen, thick.

And the woman backed away from him, not hurriedly but slowly—two, three steps back.

"Aw, forget it," she said. "I didn't mean nothing by it. It slipped out. It was an accident." The red of her face deepened until the small blood vessels in her cheeks were purple. "Go on and get to work," she urged. And she took three more slow back-ward steps.

He stood motionless for a moment and then turned away from the sight of the red lipstick on her mouth that made him remember that the foreman was a woman. And he couldn't bring himself to hit a woman. He felt a curious tingling in his fingers, and he looked down at his hands. They were clenched tight, hard, ready to smash some of those small purple veins in her face.

He pushed the cart ahead of him, walking slowly. When he turned his head, she was staring in his direction, mopping her forehead with a dark blue handkerchief. Their eyes met and then they both looked away.

He didn't glance in her direction again but moved past the long work benches, carefully collecting the finished parts, going slowly and steadily up and down, back and forth the length of the building, and as he walked he forced himself to swallow his anger, get rid of it.

And he succeeded so that he was able to think about what had happened without getting upset about it. An hour went by, but the tension stayed in his hands. They were clenched and knotted on the handles of the cart as though ready to aim a blow.

And he thought he should have hit her anyway, smacked her hard in the face, felt the soft flesh of her face give under the hardness of his hands. He tried to make his hands relax by offering them a description of what it would have been like to strike her because he had the queer feeling that his hands were not exactly a part of him anymore—they had developed a separate life of their own over which he had no control. So he dwelt on the pleasure his hands would have felt—both of them cracking at her, first one and then the other. If he had done that, his hands would have felt good now—relaxed, rested.

And he decided that even if he'd lost his job for it, he should have let her have it, and it would have been a long time, maybe the rest of her life, before she called anybody else a nigger.

The only trouble was, he couldn't hit a woman. A woman couldn't hit back the same way a man did. But it would have been a deeply satisfying thing to have cracked her narrow lips wide open with just one blow, beautifully timed and with all his weight in back of it. That way he would have gotten rid of all the energy and tension his anger had created in him. He kept remembering how his heart had started pumping blood so fast he had felt it tingle even in the tips of his fingers.

With the approach of night, fatigue nibbled at him. The corners of his mouth drooped, the frown between his eyes deepened, his shoulders sagged; but his hands stayed tight and tense. As the hours dragged by, he noticed that the women workers had started to snap and snarl at each other. He couldn't hear what they said because of the sound of machines, but he could see the quick lip movements that sent words tumbling from the sides of their mouths. They gestured irritably with their hands and scowled as their mouths moved.

Their violent jerky motions told him that it was getting close on to quitting time, but somehow he felt that the night still stretched ahead of him, composed of endless hours of steady walking on his aching legs. When the whistle finally blew, he went on pushing the cart, unable to believe that it had sounded. The whirring of the machines died away to a murmur, and he knew then that he'd really heard the whistle. He stood still for a moment, filled with a relief that made him sigh.

Then he moved briskly, putting the cart in the storeroom, hurrying to take his place in the line forming before the paymaster. That was another thing he'd change, he thought. He'd have the pay envelopes handed to the people right at their benches so there wouldn't be ten or fifteen minutes lost waiting for the pay. He always got home about fifteen minutes late on payday. They did it better in the plant where Mae worked, brought the money right to them at their benches.

He stuck his pay envelope in his pants pocket and followed the line of workers heading for the subway in a slow-moving stream. He glanced up at the sky. It was a nice night, the sky looked packed full to running over with stars. And he thought if he and Mae would go right to bed when they got home from work, they'd catch a few hours of darkness for sleeping. But they never did. They fooled around—cooking and eating and listening to the radio, and he always stayed in a big chair in the living room and went almost but not quite to sleep, and when they finally got to bed, it was five or six in the morning and daylight was already seeping around the edges of the sky.

He walked slowly, putting off the moment when he would have to plunge into the crowd hurrying toward the subway. It was a long ride to Harlem, and tonight the thought of it appalled him. He paused outside an all-night restaurant to kill time, so that some of the first rush of workers would be gone when he reached the subway.

The lights in the restaurant were brilliant, enticing. There was life and motion inside. And as he looked through the window, he thought that everything within range of his eyes gleamed—the long imitation marble counter, the tall stools, the white porcelain-topped tables, and especially the big metal coffee urn right near the window. Steam issued from its top, and a gas flame flickered under it—a lively, dancing, blue flame.

A lot of the workers from his shift—men and women—were lining up near the coffee urn. He watched them walk to the porcelain-topped tables carrying steaming cups of coffee, and he saw that just the smell of the coffee lessened the fatigue lines in their faces. After the first sip their faces softened, they smiled, they began to talk and laugh.

On a sudden impulse he shoved the door open and joined the line in front of the coffee urn. The line moved slowly. And as he stood there, the smell of the coffee, the sound of the laughter and of the voices, helped dull the sharp ache in his legs.

He didn't pay any attention to the white girl who was serving the coffee at the urn. He kept looking at the cups in the hands of the men who had been ahead of him. Each time a man stepped out of the line with one of the thick white cups, the fragrant steam got in his nostrils. He saw that they walked carefully so as not to spill a single drop. There was a froth of bubbles at the top of each cup, and he thought about how he would let the bubbles break against his lips before he actually took a big deep swallow.

Then it was his turn. "A cup of coffee," he said, just as he had heard the others say.

The white girl looked past him, put her hands up to her head, and gently lifted her hair away from the back of her neck, tossing her head back a little. "No more coffee for a while," she said.

He wasn't certain he'd heard her correctly, and he said, "What?" blankly.

"No more coffee for a while," she repeated.

There was silence behind him and then uneasy movement. He thought someone would say something, ask why or protest, but there was only silence and then a faint shuffling sound as though the men standing behind him had simultaneously shifted their weight from one foot to the other.

He looked at the girl without saying anything. He felt his hands begin to tingle, and the tingling went all the way down to his fingertips, so that he glanced down at them. They were clenched tight, hard, into fists. Then he looked at the girl again. What he wanted to do was hit her so hard that the scarlet lipstick on her mouth would smear and spread over her nose, her chin, out toward her cheeks, so hard that she would never toss her head again and refuse a man a cup of coffee because he was black.

He estimated the distance across the counter and reached forward, balancing his weight on the balls of his feet, ready to let the blow go. And then his hands fell back down to his sides because he forced himself to lower them, to unclench them and make them dangle loose. The effort took his breath away because his hands fought against him. But he couldn't hit her. He couldn't even now bring himself to hit a woman, not even this one, who had refused him a cup of coffee with a toss of her head. He kept seeing the gesture with which she had lifted the length of her blond hair from the back of her neck as expressive of her contempt for him.

When he went out the door, he didn't look back. If he had, he would have seen the flickering blue flame under the shiny coffee urn being extinguished. The line of men who had stood behind him lingered a moment to watch the people drinking coffee at the tables, and then they left just as he had without having had the coffee they wanted so badly. The girl behind the counter poured water in the urn and swabbed it out, and as she waited for the water to run out, she lifted her hair gently from the back of her neck and tossed her head before she began making a fresh lot of coffee.

But he had walked away without a backward look, his head down, his hands in his pockets, raging at himself and whatever it was inside of him that had forced him to stand quiet and still when he wanted to strike out.

The subway was crowded, and he had to stand. He tried grasping an overhead strap, and his hands were too tense to grip it. So he moved near the train door and stood there swaying back and forth with the rocking of the train. The roar of the train beat inside his head, making it ache and throb, and the pain in his legs clawed up into his groin so that he seemed to be bursting with pain, and he told himself that it was due to all that anger-born energy that had piled up in him and not been used, and so it had spread through him like a poison—from his feet and legs all the way up to his head.

Mae was in the house before he was. He knew she was home before he put the key in the door of the apartment. The radio was going. She had it tuned up loud, and she was singing along with it.

"Hello, babe," she called out, as soon as he opened the door.

He tried to say hello and it came out half grunt and half sigh.

"You sure sound cheerful," she said.

She was in the bedroom, and he went and leaned against the doorjamb. The denim overalls she wore to work were carefully draped over the back of a chair by the bed. She was standing in front of the dresser, tying the sash of a yellow housecoat around her waist and chewing gum vigorously as she admired her reflection in the mirror over the dresser.

"Whatsa matter?" she said. "You get bawled out by the boss or somep'n?"

"Just tired," he said slowly. "For God's sake, do you have to crack that gum like that?"

"You don't have to lissen to me," she said complacently. She patted a curl in place near the side of her head and then lifted her hair away from the back of her neck, ducking her head forward and then back.

He winced away from the gesture. "What you got to be always fooling with your hair for?" he protested.

"Say, what's the matter with you anyway?" She turned away from the mirror to face him, put her hands on her hips. "You ain't been in the house two minutes and you're picking on me."

He didn't answer her because her eyes were angry and he didn't want to quarrel with her. They'd been married too long and got along too well, and so he walked all the way into the room and sat down in the chair by the bed and stretched his legs out in front of him, putting his weight on the heels of his shoes, leaning way back in the chair, not saying anything.

"Lissen," she said sharply. "I've got to wear those overalls again tomorrow. You're going to get them all wrinkled up leaning against them like that."

He didn't move. He was too tired, and his legs were throbbing now that he had sat down. Besides the overalls were already wrinkled and dirty, he thought. They couldn't help but be, for she'd worn them all week. He leaned farther back in the chair.

"Come on, get up," she ordered.

"Oh, what the hell," he said wearily, and got up from the chair. "I'd just as soon live in a subway. There'd be just as much place to sit down."

He saw that her sense of humor was struggling with her anger. But her sense of humor won because she giggled.

"Aw, come on and eat," she said. There was a coaxing note in her voice. "You're nothing but an old hungry nigger trying to act tough, and"—she paused to giggle and then continued—"you—"

He had always found her giggling pleasant and deliberately said things that might amuse her and then waited, listening for the delicate sound to emerge from her throat. This time he didn't even hear the giggle. He didn't let her finish what she was saying. She was standing close to him, and that funny tingling started in his fingertips, went fast up his arms, and sent his fist shooting straight for her face.

There was the smacking sound of soft flesh being struck by a hard object, and it wasn't until she screamed that he realized he had hit her in the mouth—so hard that the dark red lipstick had blurred and spread over her full lips, reaching up toward the tip of her nose, down toward her chin, out toward her cheeks.

The knowledge that he had struck her seeped through him slowly, and he was appalled but he couldn't drag his hands away from her face. He kept striking her, and he thought with horror that something inside him was holding him, binding him to this act, wrapping and twisting about him so that he had to continue it. He had lost all control over his hands. And he groped for a phrase, a word, something to describe what this thing was like that was happening to him, and he thought it was like being enmeshed in a winding sheet—that was it—like a winding sheet. And even as the thought formed in his mind, his hands reached for her face again and yet again.

Carlos Bulosan (1911–1956)

Filipino writer Carlos Bulosan emigrated from the Pangasinan province in Luzon to the United States in 1930 at the age of sixteen. He worked his way from Seattle south, employed in canneries and the fields like the other Pinoys of his generation. Never forgetting the Philippines, he regarded America not only as his adopted land, but as the promise of democracy; this was the lesson he had learned in the colonial schools as a boy. As Bulosan's English improved, so did his determination to demand that America keep its promise to immigrants like himself. For a time, he worked as a union organizer. Hospitalized for tuberculosis and leg tumors in Los Angeles in 1936, befriended by American radicals, he read and wrote at a furious pace and began to publish his poems and stories. The advent of World War II deepened his sense of urgency. Alongside Filipino cohorts Ben Santos and Jose Garcia Villa, he worked in the War Office in Washington, DC. Failing in health, he published his masterpiece, the novel *America Is in the Heart* in 1946. Hounded in later years by McCarthyism, his health further compromised by alcoholism, he died at age forty-two in 1956, leaving several collections of short stories, a sheaf of poems, and several novellas. Bulosan's stature as a writer comes largely from his storytelling, in which he creates a persona sufficiently expansive to give an epic account of struggle, suffering, and hope. In "The Story of a Letter," his seemingly artless narrator reveals a family history of Filipinos striving to fulfill their destiny. The Whitmanesque poem "If You Want to Know What We Are" raises the political demands of a generation of immigrants whose vision is not restricted to that of the Filipinos.

John Crawford

IF YOU WANT TO KNOW WHAT WE ARE

I

If you want to know what we are who inhabit
forest, mountain, rivershore, who harness
beast, living steel, martial music (that classless
language of the heart), who celebrate labor,
5   wisdom of the mind, peace of the blood;

If you want to know what we are who become
animate at the rain's metallic ring, the stone's
accumulated strength, who tremble in the wind's
blossoming (that enervates earth's potentialities),
10   who stir just as flowers unfold to the sun;

If you want to know what we are who grow
powerful and deathless in countless counterparts,
each part pregnant with hope, each hope supreme,
each supremacy classless, each classlessness
15   nourished by unlimited splendor of comradeship;

Dorothea Lange, "Stoop Labor." *Courtesy of Library of Congress, Farm Security Administration.*

We are multitudes the world over, millions everywhere;
in violent factories, sordid tenements, crowded cities,
in skies and seas and rivers, in lands everywhere;
our numbers increase as the wide world revolves
20 and increases arrogance, hunger, disease and death.

We are the men and women reading books, searching
in the pages of history for the lost word, the key
to the mystery of living peace, imperishable joy;
we are factory hands field hands mill hands everywhere,
25 molding creating building structures, forging ahead,

Reaching for the future, nourished in the heart;
we are doctors scientists chemists discovering,
eliminating disease and hunger and antagonisms;
we are soldiers navy-men citizens guarding
30 the imperishable will of man to live in grandeur.

We are the living dream of dead men everywhere,
the unquenchable truth that class-memories create
to stagger the infamous world with prophecies
of unlimited happiness—a deathless humanity;
35 we are the living and the dead men everywhere . . .

II

If you want to know what we are, observe
the bloody club smashing heads, the bayonet
penetrating hollowed breasts, giving no mercy;
watch the bullet crashing upon armorless citizens;
40   look at the tear-gas choking the weakened lung.

If you want to know what we are, see the lynch
trees blossoming, the hysterical mob rioting;
remember the prisoner beaten by detectives to confess
a crime he did not commit because he was honest,
45   and who stood alone before a rabid jury of ten men.

And who was sentenced to hang by a judge
whose bourgeois arrogance betrayed the office
he claimed his own; name the marked man,
the violator of secrets; observe the banker,
50   the gangster, the mobster who kill and go free:

We are the sufferers who suffer for natural love
of man for man, who commemorate the humanities
of every man; we are the toilers who toil
to make the starved earth a place of abundance,
55   who transform abundance into deathless fragrance.

We are the desires of anonymous men everywhere,
who impregnate the wide earth's lustrous wealth
with a gleaming florescence; we are the new thoughts
and the new foundations, the new verdure of the mind;
60   we are the new hope new joy life everywhere.

We are the vision and the star, the quietus of pain;
we are the terminals of inquisition, the hiatuses
of a new crusade; we are the subterranean subways
of suffering; we are the will of dignities;
65   we are the living testament of a flowering race.

If you want to know what we are—
                    WE ARE REVOLUTION!

The Story of a Letter

When my brother Berto was thirteen he ran away from home and went to Manila. We did not hear from him until eight years later, and he was by that time working in a little town in California. He wrote a letter in English, but we could not read it. Father carried it in his pocket all summer hoping the priest in our village would read it.

The summer ended gloriously and our work on the farm was done. We gathered firewood and cut grass on the hillsides for our animals. The heavy rains came when we were patching the walls of our house. Father and I wore palm raincoats and worked in the mud, rubbing vinegar on our foreheads and throwing it around us to keep the lightning away. The rains ceased suddenly, but the muddy water came down the mountains and flooded the river.

We made a bamboo raft and floated slowly along on the water. Father sat in the center of the raft and took the letter from his pocket. He looked at it for a long time, as though he were commiting it to memory. When we reached the village church it was midnight, but there were many people in the yard. We tied our raft to the river bank and dried our clothes on the grass.

A woman came and told us that the priest had died of overeating at a wedding. Father took our clothes off the grass and we put them on. We untied our raft and rowed against the slow currents back to our house. Father was compelled to carry the letter for another year, waiting for the time when my brother Nicasio would come home from school. He was the only one in our family who could read and write.

When the students returned from the cities, Father and I went to town with a sack of fresh peanuts. We stood under the arbor tree in the station and watched every bus that stopped. We heated a pile of dry sand with burning stones and roasted peanuts. At night we sat in the coffee shop and talked to the loafers and gamblers. Then the last student arrived, but my brother Nicasio was not with them. We gave up waiting and went to the village.

When summer came again we plowed the land and planted corn. Then we were informed that my brother Nicasio had gone to America. Father was greatly disappointed. He took the letter from his pocket and locked it in a small box. We put our minds on our work and after two years the letter was forgotten.

Toward the end of my ninth year, a tubercular young man appeared in our village. He wanted to start a school for the children and the men were enthusiastic. The drummer went around the village and announced the good news. The farmers gathered in a vacant lot not far from the cemetery and started building a schoolhouse. They shouted at one another with joy and laughed aloud. The wind carried their laughter through the village.

I saw them at night lifting the grass roof on their shoulders. I ran across the fields and stood by the well, watching them place the rafters on the long bamboo posts. The men were stripped to the waist and their cotton trousers were boldly rolled up to their thighs. The women came with their earthen jars and hauled drinking water, pausing in the clear moonlight to watch the men with secret joy.

Then the schoolhouse was finished. I heard the bell ring joyfully in the village. I ran to the window and saw boys and girls going to school. I saw Father on our *carabao*, riding off toward our house. I took my straw hat off the wall and rushed to the gate.

Father bent down and reached for my hands. I sat behind him on the bare back of the animal and we drove crazily to the schoolhouse. We kicked the animal with our heels. The children shouted and slapped their bellies. When we reached the school yard the *carabao* stopped without warning. Father fell on the ground and rolled into the well, screaming aloud when he touched the water. I grabbed the animal's tail and hung on it till it rolled on its back in the dust.

I rushed to the well and lowered the wooden bucket. I tied the rope to the post and shouted for help. Father climbed slowly up the rope to the mouth of the well. The bigger boys came down and helped me pull Father out. He stood in the sun and shook the water off his body. He told me to go into the schoolhouse with the other children.

We waited for the teacher to come. Father followed me inside and sat on a bench at my back. When the teacher arrived we stood as one person and waited for him to be seated. Father came to my bench and sat quietly for a long time. The teacher started talking in our dialect, but he talked so fast we could hardly understand him.

When he had distributed some little Spanish books, Father got up and asked what language we would learn. The teacher told us that it was Spanish. Father asked him if he knew English. He said he knew only Spanish and our dialect. Father took my hand and we went out of the schoolhouse. We rode the *carabao* back to our house.

Father was disappointed. He had been carrying my brother's letter for almost three years now. It was still unread. The suspense was hurting him and me, too. He wanted me to learn English so that I would be able to read it to him. It was the only letter he had received in all the years that I had known him, except some letters that came from the government once a year asking him to pay his taxes.

When the rains ceased, a strong typhoon came from the north and swept away the schoolhouse. The teacher gave up teaching and married a village girl. Then he took up farming and after two years his wife gave birth to twins. The men in the village never built a schoolhouse again.

I grew up suddenly and the desire to go see other places grew. It moved me like a flood. It was impossible to walk a kilometer away from our house without wanting to run away to the city. I tried to run away a few times, but whenever I reached the town, the farm always called me back. I could not leave Father because he was getting old.

Then our farm was taken away from us. I decided to go to town for a while and live with Mother and my two little sisters. I left the farm immediately, but Father remained in the village. He came to town once with a stack of wild tomatoes and bananas, but the village called him back again.

I left our town and traveled to other places. I went to Baguio in the northern part of the Philippines and worked in the market-place posing in the nude for American tourists who seemed to enjoy the shameless nudity of the natives. An American woman, who claimed that she had come from Texas, took me to Manila.

She was a romantic painter. When we arrived in the capital she rented a nice large house where the sun was always shining. There were no children of my age. There were men and women who never smiled. They spoke through their noses. The painter from Texas asked me to undress every morning; she worked industriously. I had never dreamed of making my living by exposing my body to a stranger. That experience made me roar with laughter for many years.

One time, while I was still at the woman's house, I remembered the wide ditch near our house in the village where young girls used to take a bath in the nude. A cousin of mine stole the girls' clothes and then screamed behind some bushes. The girls ran at random with their hands between their legs. I thought of this incident when I felt shy, hiding my body with my hands from the woman painter. When I had saved a little money I took a boat for America.

I forgot my village for a while. When I went to a hospital and lay in bed for two years, I started to read books with great hunger. My reading was started by a nurse who thought I had come from China. I lied to her without thinking of it, but I made a good lie. I had had no opportunity to learn when I was outside in the world but the security and warmth of the hospital had given it to me. I languished in bed for two years with great pleasure. I was no longer afraid to live in a strange world and among strange peoples.

Then at the end of the first year, I remembered the letter of my brother Berto. I crept out of bed and went to the bathroom. I wrote a letter to Father asking him to send the letter to me for translation. I wanted to translate it, so that it would be easy for him to find a man in our village to read it to him.

The letter arrived in America six months later. I translated it into our dialect and sent it back with the original. I was now better. The doctors told me that I could go out of the hospital. I used to stand by the window for hours asking myself why I had forgotten to laugh in America. I was afraid to go out into the world. I had been confined too long. I had forgotten what it was like on the outside.

I had been brought to the convalescent ward when the Civil War in Spain started some three years before. Now, after the peasants' and workers' government was crushed,

I was physically ready to go out into the world and start a new life. There was some indignation against fascism in all the civilized lands. To most of us, however, it was the end of a great cause.

I stood at the gate of the hospital, hesitating. Finally, I closed my eyes and walked into the city. I wandered in Los Angeles for some time looking for my brothers. They had been separated from me since childhood. We had, separately and together, a bitter fight for existence. I had heard that my brother Nicasio was in Santa Barbara, where he was attending college. Berto, who never stayed in one place for more than three months at a time, was rumored to be in Bakersfield waiting for the grape season.

I packed my suitcase and took a bus to Santa Barbara. I did not find my brother there. I went to Bakersfield and wandered in the streets asking for my other brother. I went to Chinatown and stood in line for the free chop suey that was served in the gambling houses to the loafers and gamblers. I could not find my brother in either town. I went to the vineyards looking for him. I was convinced that he was not in that valley. I took a bus for Seattle.

The hiring halls were full of men waiting to be shipped to the canneries in Alaska. I went to the dance halls and poolrooms. But I could not find my brothers. I took the last boat to Alaska and worked there for three months. I wanted to save my money so that I could have something to spend when I returned to the mainland.

When I came back to the United States, I took a bus to Portland. Beyond Tacoma, near the district where Indians used to force the hop pickers into marriage, I looked out the window and saw my brother Berto in a beer tavern. I knew it was my brother although I had not seen him for many years. There was something in the way he had turned his head toward the bus that made me think I was right. I stopped at the next town and took another bus back to Tacoma. But he was already gone.

I took another bus and went to California. I stopped in Delano. The grape season was in full swing. There were many workers in town. I stood in the poolrooms and watched the players. I went to a beer place and sat in a booth. I ordered several bottles and pondered over my life in America.

Toward midnight a man in a big overcoat came in and sat beside me. I asked him to drink beer with me without looking at his face. We started drinking together and then, suddenly, I saw a familiar face in the dirty mirror on the wall. I almost screamed. He was my brother Nicasio—but he had grown old and emaciated. We went outside and walked to my hotel.

The landlady met me with a letter from the Philippines. In my room I found that my letter to Father, when I was in the hospital, and the translation of my brother Berto's letter to him had been returned to me. It was the strangest thing that ever happened to me. I had never lived in Delano before. I had never given my forwarding address to anybody. The letter was addressed to me at a hotel I had never seen before.

It was now ten years since my brother Berto had written the letter to Father. It was eighteen years since he had run away from home. I stood in the center of my room and opened it. The note attached to it said that Father had died some years before. It was signed by the postmaster of my town.

I bent down and read the letter—the letter that had driven me away from my village and had sent me half way around the world—read it the very day a letter came from the government telling me that my brother Berto was already serving in the Navy—and the same day that my brother Nicasio was waiting to be inducted into the Army. I held the letter in my hand and, suddenly, I started to laugh—choking with tears at the mystery and wonder of it all.

"Dear Father (my brother wrote): America is a great country. Tall buildings. Wide good land. The people walking. But I feel sad. I am writing you this hour of my sentimental. Your son.—Berto."

Harriette Arnow (1908–1986)

A descendent of a long line of Kentucky ancestors who lived along the big South Fork
of the Cumberland River and traced their roots back to the American Revolution,
Harriette Louisa Simpson Arnow inherited the gift of storytelling and wanted to be a
writer from an early age. Her parents were schoolteachers and her father supplemented his
modest teacher's salary with manual jobs to support a family of six children. Harriette was
educated in rural schools, at home, and in boarding school before she attended Berea
College, where she earned a teaching certificate, taught in a one-room schoolhouse in
Kentucky, and then earned a B.S. at the University of Louisville. Against her family's
wishes, she moved to Cincinnati in 1934 and, determined to be a writer, supported
herself primarily as a waitress. Through the 1930s, she wrote short fiction and a first novel
Mountain Path (1936), which was favorably reviewed.

In 1938, she met and later married newspaperman Harold Arnow while working for
the Works Progress Administration (WPA) in Cincinnati. For five years, they barely managed as subsistence farmers on land that they purchased in southern Kentucky. They moved
to Detroit after Harold became a reporter for the *Detroit Times*, lived in cramped public
wartime housing, and witnessed the dislocation of rural mountain people who were forced
by war and the need for cash to migrate to the industrial North. While raising two children
and giving birth to two others who did not survive, Arnow wrote *Hunter's Horn* (1949)
a best-seller, and after moving to Ann Arbor, Michigan, published her great novel, *The
Dollmaker* (1954). In the first chapter (excerpted here) she presents the confluence of
forces affecting the lives of Kentucky farming families—war, disease, poverty, class prejudice,
modernity—through the central character Gertie Nevels, whose working-class heroism
seems ordinary and natural. Honoring Gertie's mountain knowledge and thwarted artistic
expression, Arnow gives new meaning to literary conceptions of tragedy. She was the recipient of many honors and awards, and in addition to her novels, published social histories of
the Cumberland and a memoir. Arnow moved away from her Kentucky home but carried
with her the love of language, story, and the land that was her inheritance and became her
unsentimental gift to her readers.

"I'M GERTIE NEVELS FROM BALLEW, KENTUCKY," FROM *THE DOLLMAKER*

Dock's shoes on the rocks up the hill and his heavy breathing had shut out all sound so
that it seemed a long while she had heard nothing, and Amos lay too still, not clawing at
the blanket as when they had started. They reached the ridge top where the road ran
through scrub pine in sand, and while the mule's shoes were soft on the thick needles she
bent her head low over the long bundle across the saddle horn, listening. Almost at once
she straightened, and kicked the already sweat-soaked mule hard in the flanks until he
broke into an awkward gallop. "I know you're tired, but it ain't much furder," she said in
a low tight voice.

She rode on in silence, her big body hunched protectingly over the bundle. Now and
then she glanced worriedly up at the sky, graying into the thick twilight of a rainy afternoon in October; but mostly her eyes, large, like the rest of her, and the deep, unshining

gray of the rain-wet pine trunks, were fixed straight ahead of the mule's ears, as if by much looking she might help the weary animal pull the road past her with her eyes.

They reached the highway, stretching empty between the pines, silent, no sign of cars or people, as if it were not a road at all, but some lost island of asphalt coming from no place, going nowhere. The mule stopped, his ears flicking slowly back and forth as he considered the road. She kicked him again, explaining, "It's a road fer automobiles; we'll have to ride it to stop a car, then you can git back home."

The mule tried to turn away from the strange black stuff, flung his head about, danced stiff-leggedly back into the familiar sanctuary of soft ground and pine trees. "No," the woman said, gripping his thin flanks with her long thighs, "no, you've got to git out in th middle so's we can stop a car a goen toward th doctor's. You've got to." She kicked him again, turned him about. He tried one weary, half-hearted bucking jump; but the woman only settled herself in the saddle, gripped with her thighs, her drawn-up knees, her heels. Her voice was half pleading, half scolding: "Now, Dock, you know you cain't buck me off, not even if you was fresh—an you ain't. So git on."

The great raw-boned mule argued with his ears, shook the bridle rein, side-stepped against a pine tree, but accepted soon the fact that the woman was master still, even on a strange road. He galloped again, down the middle of the asphalt that followed a high and narrow ridge and seemed at times like a road in the sky, the nothingness of fog-filled valleys far below on either side.

A car passed. Dock trembled at the sound, and sidestepped toward the edge, but the woman spoke gently and held him still. "It won't hurt you none. It's a car like th coal truck; we ain't a stoppen it. It's a goen th wrong way."

The mule, in spite of all the woman's urging, was slow in getting through his fright from the passing of the car. He fought continually to stay on the edge of the road, which was beginning to curve sharply and down so that little of it could be seen in either direction. The woman's head was bent again, listening above the bundle, when the mule plunged wildly toward the pines. She jerked hard on the bridle, so swiftly, so fiercely, that he whirled about, reared, came down, then took a hard, stiff-legged jump that landed him for an instant crosswise in the road.

The roar of a car's coming grew louder. Terrified by the strange sound, the unfamiliar road, and the strangeness of the woman's ways, the mule fought back toward the pines. The woman gripped with her legs, pulled with her hand, so that they seemed to do some wild but well rehearsed dance, round and round in the road, the mule rearing, flinging his head about, fighting to get it down so that he could buck.

She eased her hold an instant, jerked hard with all her strength. He reared but stayed in the road. Yellow fog lights, pale in the gray mists, washed over them, shone on the red sandy clay on one of the woman's shoes, a man's shoe with cleats holding leather thongs, pressed hard against the mule's lifted body as if it pointed to a place in the bridle mended with a piece of rawhide. It seemed a long time she sat so, the mule on his hind legs, the car lights washing over her, the child unshaken in the crook of her left arm while she talked to the mule in the same low urgent voice she had used to get him onto the highway: "Don't be afeared, Dock. They'll stop. We'll make em stop. They dassn't take these downhill curves too fast. They'll have to stop. We'll all go over th bluff together."

There was a loud, insistent honking; brakes squealed and rubber squeaked while the fingers of light swept away from the woman and out into the fog above the valley. Then, as the car skidded, the lights crossed the woman again, went into the pines on the other side of the road, swept back, as the car, now only a few feet behind her but on the other side of the road, came out of its skid. The woman's voice was low, pressed down by some terrible urgency as she begged under the screaming of the horn, "Crosswise, crosswise; it'll git by us on t'other side."

She jerked, kicked the mule, until he, already crazed with fright, jumped almost directly in front of the car, forcing it to swerve again, this time so sharply that it went completely off the road. It plowed partway into a thicket of little pines, then stopped on the narrow sandy shoulder above the bluff edge. The woman looked once at the car, then away and past the trembling mule's ears; and though she looked down it was like searching the sky on a cloudy day. There was only fog, thickened in splotches, greenish above a pasture field, brownish over the corn far down in the valley below the tree tops by the bluff edge.

"You done good, real good," she whispered to the mule. Then all in one swift motion she swung one long leg over the mule's back, looped the bridle over the saddle horn, turned the dazed mule southward, slapping him on the shoulder. "Git," she said. She did not look after him as he leaped away, broken ribbons of foam flying down his chin, and blood oozing from a cut on his left hind leg where the car had grazed him.

She hurried the few steps along the bluff edge to the car as if afraid it would be off again; but her hand was reaching for the front door handle before the door opened slowly, cautiously, and a soldier, his head almost to her chin, got out. He stared up at her and did not answer when she begged all in a breath: "I've got tu have a lift. My little boy he's . . ."

The soldier was no longer looking at her. His eyes, blue, and with the unremembering look of a very old man's eyes, were fixed on the poplar tops rising above the bluff edge. He looked past them down into the valley, then slowly taking his glance away he reached for the handle of the back door, but dropped his hand when he saw that the window in the door was opening.

The woman turned to the down-dropping window and watched impatiently while first a hard and shiny soldier's cap rose above it, then a man's face, straight and neat and hard-appearing as the cap, but flushed now with surprise and anger. The mouth was hardly showing before it spoke, quickly, but with a flat, careful pronunciation of the words. "You realize you've run me off the road. If you can't manage a horse, don't ride one on the highway. Don't you know there's a war and this road carries . . ."

The woman had listened intently, watching the man's lips, her brows drawn somewhat together like one listening to a language only partly understood. "I know they's a war," she said, reaching for the door handle. "That's why th doctor closest home is gone. It was a mule," she went on. "I managed him. I had to make you stop. I've got to git my little boy to a doctor—quick." She had one foot inside the door, the child held now in her two hands as she prepared to lay him on the seat.

The man, plainly irritated because he had neglected to hold the door shut, continued to sit by it, his legs outspread, barring her way. His hand moved slowly, as if he wanted her to see it touch the pistol in a polished holster by his side, let the pistol speak to her more than his toneless, unruffled words when he said, "You must use other means of getting your child to the doctor." He reached swiftly, jerked the door so that she, bent as she was, and with the heavy bundle in her two hands, staggered. Her head flopped downward to his knees, but she righted herself and kept one foot in the door.

"If my business were not so urgent," he said, not taking his hand from the door, "I would have you arrested for sabotage. I travel from"—he hesitated—"an important place on urgent business." The voice still was not a man's voice, but the shiny cap, the bright leather, the pistol. It sharpened a little when he said, turning from her to the driver, "Get back into the car and drive on." He looked once at the bundle where one small sun-burned but blue-nailed hand waved aimlessly out of the blanket folds. Then, letting the door swing wide, he jerked it swiftly so that it struck hard against the woman's back, bent again as she searched for his eyes.

She straightened, put the hand under the blanket, but continued to stand between door and car. "I'm sorry you're th army; frum Oak Ridge, I reckon, but I'd a stopped you enyhow." Her voice was quiet as the voice below the cap. "You can shoot me now er give me an this youngen a lift to th closest doctor." And even in the man's work shoes, the long and shapeless coat, green-tinged with age, open, giving glimpses of a blue apron faded in strange squares as if it might have at one time been something else—a man's denim trousers or overall jumper—she held herself proudly, saying: "You want my name; I'm Gertie Nevels frum Ballew, Kentucky. Now, let me lay my little boy down. You cain't go . . ."

The officer had flung the door suddenly outward again. Still she did not fall when he banged it back against her, though in her attempts to keep from falling forward into the car and onto the child she dropped to her knees, her feet sliding through the gravel to the bluff edge. The officer gripped the pistol butt, and his voice shrilled a little as he said to the young soldier who had stood stiff and silent, staring at the woman: "Get in and drive on. She'll have to drop off then."

The other took his eyes from the blanket, still now. He saluted, said, "Yes, sir," but continued to stand, his body pressed against the car, his glance going again to the tree-tops below his feet.

"Back up on the road and drive on," the other repeated, his face reddening, his eyes determinedly fixed straight in front of him.

"Yes, sir?" the other said again, unmoving. There was in his questioning acceptance of the command some slight note of pleasure. He looked up at the tall woman as if he would share it with her. Their glances crossed, but the trouble, the urgency of her need would let nothing else come into her eyes.

She looked again at the other. "You want him to go over th bluff?" And her voice was weary to breaking, like an overwrought mother speaking to a stubborn child.

The older man for the first time looked past the woman and realized that what he had taken for a continuation of the brush and scrub pine was the tops of tall-growing trees below a bluff. He looked quickly away and began a rapid edging along the seat to the opposite door. It was only when he was out of the car and a few feet from the bluff edge that he was able to speak with the voice of polished leather and pistol handle, and command the other to back out.

The woman, as soon as the officer moved, had laid the child on the seat, then stood a moment by the door, watching the driver, shaking her head slowly, frowning as he raced the motor until the car shivered and the smoking rear wheels dug great holes in the sandy shoulder. "That'll do no good," she said, then more loudly, her voice lifted above the roaring motor, "Have you got a ax?"

He shook his head, smiling a little, then his eyes were blank, prim like his mouth when the other told him to turn off the motor. The woman picked up a large sandrock, dropped it behind one of the deeply sunken rear wheels. "Have you got a jack?" she asked the officer. "You could heist it up with a jack, git rocks under them wheels, an back up on th road."

"Take your child out of the car and get on," he said, his voice no longer smooth. "We may be stuck here until I can get a tow truck. You'll be arrested."

She glanced at him briefly, smoothed back her straight dark brown hair with a bended arm, then drawing the bottom of her apron into one hand to form a kind of sack, she began gathering rocks with the other hand, going in a quick squatting run, never straightening in her haste, never looking up.

The young soldier had by now got out of the car and stood by it, his back and shoulders very straight, his hands dropped by his sides so that a band of colored ribbon was bright on his dull uniform. The woman glanced curiously at it as she dumped a load of rocks by a wheel. The officer looked at him, and his voice was shrill, akin to an angry woman's. "Hatcher, you're not on the parade ground."

"Yes, sir," the other said, drawing himself up still more rigidly.

"Get out the jack," the officer said, after frowning a moment at the woman as if loath to repeat her suggestion.

"Yes, hurry, please," the woman begged, not pausing in her rock gathering, but looking toward the child on the back seat. It had struggled until the blanket had fallen away from its head, showing dark hair above a face that through the window shone yellowish white, contorted with some terrible effort to cry or vomit or speak. Like the woman as she ran squatting through the mud, the struggling child seemed animal-like and unhuman compared to the two neatly dressed men.

The woman hurried up again with another apronful of rocks, dumped them, then went at her darting, stooping run along the bluff edge searching for more. The young soldier in the awkward, fumbling way of a man, neither liking nor knowing his business, got out the jack and set it in the sandy mud under the rear bumper. "That's no good," the woman said, coming up with more rocks; and with one hand still holding the apron she picked up the jack, put a flat rock where it had been, reset it, gave it a quick, critical glance. "That'll hold now," she said. She dumped her rocks by the wheel, but continued to squat, studying now the pines caught under the front of the car.

The officer stood at the edge of the asphalt, silent. Sometimes he looked up and down the road, and often he glanced at his wrist watch, but mostly his frowning glance was fixed on the car. He watched the woman now. Her hands had been busied with rocks and apron when she bent by the wheel; now one hand was still holding her emptied apron as she straightened, but in the other was a long knife, bright, thin, sharply pointed. The man, watching, took a quick step backward while his hand went again to the pistol butt. The woman, without looking at either man, knelt by the front of the car and, reaching far under with the knife, slashed rapidly at the entangled pine saplings while with the other hand she jerked them free and flung them behind her.

Finished with the pines, she went quickly along the bluff edge by the car, her glance searching through the window toward the child, still now, with the hand of one down-hanging arm brushing the floor. She watched only an instant and did not bend to listen, for clearly in the silence came the child's short choking gasps. She hurried on around the back of the car, and bent above the soldier, only now getting the jack into working position. "Hurry," she begged in the same tight, urgent voice she had used on the mule. "Please, cain't you hurry—he's a choken so," and in her haste to get a wheel on solid rock she began clawing at the muddy earth with her hands, pushing rocks under the tire as it slowly lifted.

In a moment the officer called, "That's enough; try backing out now."

Some of the woman's need for haste seemed to have entered the soldier. He straightened, glanced quickly toward the child, struggling with its head dangling over the edge of the seat, its eyes rolled back but unseeing. He turned quickly and hurried into the driver's seat without taking time to salute or say, "Yes, sir." The woman ran to the back wheel that had dug such a rut in the mud, and watched anxiously while the driver started the motor, raced it as he backed an inch or so. The car stopped, the motor roaring, the wheels spinning, smoking, flinging mud, rocks, and pine brush into the woman's face bent close above them in her frantic efforts with hands and feet to keep the brush and rocks under the wheel.

"Try rocking out," the officer said. "Pull up, then shift, quick, into reverse."

The soldier was silent, looking at the emptiness in front of him. With the bent young pines cut away, the bumper seemed to hang above the valley. He moved at last, a few inches forward, but slowly, while the woman pushed rocks behind the rear wheels, jumping from first one to the other as she tried to force the rocks into the earth with her heavy shoes. The car stopped. The driver shifted again into reverse. The woman stood waiting between the side of the car and the bluff, her long arms a little lifted, the big jointed fingers of her great hands wide spread, her eyes on the back fender, her shoulders hunched like those of an animal gathering itself for a spring.

The motor roared again, the back wheels bit an inch or so into the rocks and mud, then spun. The woman plunged, flinging her two hard palms against the fender. Her body arched with the push like a too tightly strung bow; her eyes bulged; the muscles of her neck and face writhed under the thin brown skin; her big shoes dug holes in the mud in their efforts to keep still against the power of the pushing hands. The car hung, trembling, shivering, and one of the woman's feet began to slide toward the bluff edge.

Then her body seemed slowly to lengthen, for the car had moved. The woman's hands stayed with the fender until it pulled away from them. She fell sideways by the bluff edge so that the front wheel scraped her hip and the bumper touched strands of the dark hair tumbled from the thick knob worn high on her head. She stayed a moment in the mud, her knees doubled under her, her hands dropped flat on the earth, her drooping head between her arms, her whole body heaving with great gasping breaths.

She lifted her head, shook it as if to clear some dimness from her eyes, smoothed back her hair, then got slowly to her feet. Still gasping and staggering a little, she hurried to the car, stopped again but ready to start with its wheels on the hard-packed gravel by the road.

She jerked the door open and started in, but with the awkwardness of one unused to cars she bumped her head against the doorframe. She was just getting her wide shoulders through, her eyes on the child's face, when the officer, much smaller and more accustomed to cars than she, opened the door on his side, stepped partway in, and tried to pick up the child. It seemed heavier than he had thought, and instead of lifting it he jerked it quickly, a hand on either shoulder, across the seat and through the door, keeping it always at arm's length as if it had been some vile and dirty animal.

The woman snatched at the child but caught only the blanket. She tried to jump into the car, but her long loose coattail got under her feet and she squatted an instant, unable to rise, trapped by the coattail. Her long, mud-streaked hair had fallen over her face, and through it her eyes were big, unbelieving, as the man said, straightening from pulling the child into the road a few feet from the car, "You've helped undo a little of the damage you've done, but"—he drew a sharp quick breath—"I've no time for giving rides. I'm a part of the Army, traveling on important business. If you must go with me, you'll leave your child in the road. He isn't so sick," he went on, putting his foot through the door, even though the woman, still crouching, struggled through the other door. "He seemed quite active, kicking around," and then to the driver, quietly now, with no trace of shrillness, "Go on."

The woman gave the driver a swift measuring glance, saw his stiff shoulders, his face turned straight ahead as if he were a part of the car to be stopped or started at the will of the other. The car moved slowly; the officer was in now, one hand on the back of the front seat, the other closing the door. She gave an awkward squatting lunge across the car, her hands flung palm outward as when she had flung herself against the fender. One hand caught the small man's wrist above his pistol, the other caught his shoulder, high up, close to the neck, pushing, grasping more than striking, for she was still entangled in her coat.

He half sat, half fell in the road, one foot across the child. She did not look at him, but reached from the doorway of the car for the child, and her voice came, a low breathless crying: "Cain't you see my youngen's choken tu death? I've got to git him to a doctor."

One of the child's hands moved aimlessly, weakly knocking the blanket from its face. She gave a gasping cry, her voice shrilling, breaking, as if all the tightness and calmness that had carried her through the ride on the mule and the stopping and the starting of the car were worn away.

"Amos, Amos. It's Mommie. Amos, honey, Amos?" She was whispering now, a questioning whisper, while the child's head dangled over her arm. His unseeing eyes were rolled far back; the whites bulged out of his dark, purplish face, while mucus and saliva dribbled from his blue-lipped swollen mouth. She ran her finger down his throat, bringing up yellow-tinged mucus and ill smelling vomit. He gave a short whispering breath that seemed to go no deeper than his choked-up throat. She blew in his mouth, shook him, turned him over, repeating the questioning whisper, "Amos, oh Amos?"

The driver, who had leaped from his seat when she pushed the other through the car, was still, staring at the child, his hands under the older man's elbows, though the latter was already up and straightening his cap. For the first time he really looked at the child. "Shake him by the heels—slap him on the back," the young soldier said.

"Yes, take him by the heels," the other repeated. "Whatever is choking him might come loose." And now he seemed more man than soldier, at once troubled and repelled by the sick child.

The woman was looking about her, shaking the child cradled in her arms with quick jerky motions. "It's a disease," she said. "They's no shaken it out." She saw what she had apparently been hunting. A few feet up the road was a smooth wide shelf of sandstone, like a little porch hung above the valley. She ran there, laid the child on the stone, begging of the men, "Help me; help me," meanwhile unbuttoning the little boy's blue cotton jumper and under it his shirt, straightening him on the stone as one would straighten the dead. "Bring me a rock," she said over her shoulder, "flat like fer a piller."

The young soldier gaped at her, looked around him, and at last picked up a squarish piece of sandrock. She slipped it high up under the child's shoulders so that the swollen neck arched upward, stretched with the weight of the head, which had fallen backward.

"Help me," she repeated to the young soldier. "You'll have to hold his head, tight." She looked up at the other, who had stopped a few feet away, and now stared at her, wondering, but no longer afraid. "You hold his hands and keep his feet down." She looked down at the blue swollen face, smoothed back the dark brown hair from a forehead high and full like her own. "He cain't fight it much—I think—I guess he's past feelen anything," and there was a hopelessness in her voice that made the officer give her a sharp appraising glance as if he were thinking she could be crazy.

"Wouldn't it be better," he said, "to go quickly to the nearest doctor? He's not—he still has a pulse, hasn't he?"

She considered, nodding her head a little like one who understood such things. "I kept a tryen to feel it back there—I couldn't on th mule—but his heart right now—it's not good." She looked at him, and said in a low voice: "I've seen youngens die. He ain't hardly breathen," then looked down again at the child. "Hold his hands an keep his feet down; they's no use a talken a gitten to th doctor; th war got th closest; th next is better'n fifteen miles down th road—an mebbe out a his office."

"Oh," the officer said, and hesitantly drew closer and stooped above the child, but made no move to touch him.

"Hold him," the woman repeated, "his hands," her voice low again and tight, but with a shiver through it as if she were very cold. Her face looked cold, bluish like the child's, with all the color drained away, leaving the tanned, weather-beaten skin of her high cheekbones and jutting nose and chin like a brown freckled mask painted on a cold and frightened face with wide, frightened eyes. She looked again at the child, struggling feebly now with a sharp hoarse breath, all her eyes and her thoughts for him so that she seemed alone by the sloping sandrock with the mists below her in the valley and the little fogdarkened pines a wall between her and the road. She touched his forehead, whispering, "Amos, I cain't let th war git you too." Then her eyes were on his neck bowed up above the rock pillow, and they stayed there as she repeated, "Hold him tight now."

The older man, with the air of one humoring a forlorn and helpless creature, took the child's hands in one of his and put the other about its ankles. The young soldier, gripping the child's head, drew a sharp, surprised breath, but the other, staring down at patched overall knees, saw nothing until when he looked up there was the long bright knife drawing swiftly away from the swollen neck, leaving behind it a thin line that for an instant seemed no cut at all, hardly a mark, until the blood seeped out, thickening the line, distorting it.

The woman did not look away from the reddening line, but was still like a stone woman, not breathing, her face frozen, the lips bloodless, gripped together, the large drops of sweat on her forehead unmoving, hanging as she squatted head bent above the child. The officer cried: "You can't do that! You're—you're killing. You can't do that!"

He might have been wind stirring fog in the valley for all she heard. The fingers of her left hand moved quickly over the cut skin, feeling, pulling the skin apart, holding it, thumb on one side, finger on the other, shaping a red bowed mouth grinning up from the child's neck. "Please," the man was begging, his voice choked as if from nausea.

The knife moved again, and in the silence there came a little hissing. A red filmed bubble streaked with pus grew on the red dripping wound, rose higher, burst; the child struggled, gave a hoarse, inhuman whistling cry. The woman wiped the knife blade on her shoe top with one hand while with the other she lifted the child's neck higher, and then swiftly, using only the one hand, closed the knife, dropped it into her pocket, and drew out a clean folded handkerchief.

She gently but quickly wiped the blood and pus from the gaping hole, whispering to the child as it struggled, giving its little hoarse, inhuman cries. "Save yer breath, honey; thet little ole cut ain't nothen fer a big boy like you nigh four years old." She spoke in a low jerky voice like one who has run a long way or lifted a heavy weight and has no breath to speak. She lay down the handkerchief, hunted with her free hand an instant in her back hair, brought out a hairpin, wiped it on the handkerchief, inserted the bent end in the cut, and then slowly, watching the hole carefully, drew her hand from under the child's neck, all the while holding the hole open with the hairpin.

The young soldier, who had never loosened his grip on the child's head, drew a long shivering breath and looked with admiration at the woman, searching for her eyes; but finding them still on the child, he looked toward the officer, and at once gave an angry, whispering, "Jee-*sus*."

The woman looked around and saw the officer who had collapsed all in a heap, his head on Amos's feet, one hand still clutching the child's hands. "He's chicken-hearted," she said, turning back to the child, saying over her shoulder, "You'd better stretch him out. Loosen his collar—he's too tight in his clothes enyhow. Go on, I can manage."

The young soldier got up, smiling a secret, pleased sort of smile, and the woman, glancing quickly away from the child, gave him an uneasy glance. "Don't you be a letten him roll off the bluff edge."

"No?" the other said, smiling down at Amos, breathing hoarsely and quickly, but breathing, his face less darkly blue. The soldier looked past the officer crumpled on the stone down to the wide valley, then up and across to the rows of hills breaking at times through shreds and banks of the low-hanging fog, at other places hidden so that the low hills, seen through the fog, seemed vast and mysterious, like mountains rising into the clouds. He waved his hand toward the hills. "I'll bet hunting there is good."

The woman nodded without looking up. "Mighty good—now. They ain't hardly left us a man able to carry a gun er listen to a hound dog."

"Where is—" the soldier began, then stopped, for the officer's head was slowly lifting, and at once it was as if the other had never looked at the hills or spoken to her. He straightened his shoulders, pulled down his coat, watched an instant longer. As the head continued to lift, he stepped closer, and after a moment's hesitation, and with a swift glance at Gertie, put his hands under the other's arms, standing in front of him so that the officer was between him and the bluff.

The woman gave the two a quick, worried glance. "It's high there; watch out."

"I'm quite all right," the officer said, shaking the other's hands away. He lifted a greenish, watery-eyed face that seemed no soldier's face at all, only an old man's face. "How's the little one?" he asked, getting slowly to his feet.

"Breathen," the woman said.

"You've done a thing many doctors would be afraid to do without an operating room or anything," he said, all his need for haste somehow dropped away. The other had handed him his cap, but he stood holding it, looking at the woman as if there were something he would like to say but could not.

The woman dabbed at the blood and mucus and pus bubbling through the hole. "If that stuff runs down his windpipe an into his lungs, it'll be bad," she said, as if talking to herself more than to the men. "You can give a sheep pneumonie if when you're a drenchen it water gits down into its lungs."

She looked about her: at the little pine trees, at the tops of the black gum and poplar rising by the bluff, then away across the road as if searching for something. "Once I saved a cow that was choked—an in her windpipe I put a piece a cane."

"What is it?" he asked, careful not to look at the child. "It doesn't seem like plain choking."

"It's—" She rubbed her bent arm up her forehead, back across her stringing hair. "I disremember what they call it now; used to be they said membranous croup. I thought it was jist plain croup, bad hard croup like he's had afore, till Aunt Sue Annie come. She told me word come in th mail last night Mealie Sexton's baby was dead. We thought it had th croup when she come a visiten my mother when she come in frum Cincinnati—her baby an him, they was together." She looked toward the young soldier, who stood in respectful silence a few feet behind the other. "Could you hold this open and watch him; I'll have to git somethin to put in it. It'll take jist a minnit. They's a little poplar right acrost th road."

He glanced as if for permission at the officer, but the other had turned away, looking greenish and sick again; and after a moment's hesitation the young one came with a fresh clean handkerchief of his own and took the hairpin and the woman's place by the child. She hurried across the road to a little poplar, and with one swift stroke cut a bough about the thickness of her middle finger, cut again; the bough with its yellow leaves unflecked with red or brown dropped away. Then, working as she walked back across the road, she stripped the gray bark from the short length of limb, glancing between each knife stroke at the child. She had crossed the road, when she stopped, knife lifted, to look at a red card lettered in black, tacked to a fair-sized pine tree. Most of the print was small, but large enough for men in passing cars to read were the words: MEN, WOMEN, WILLOW RUN, UNCLE SAM, LIVING QUARTERS. Her knife lifted, came down in one long thrust against the card. It fell and she walked on, the knife working now with swift, twisting cuts, forming a hole in one end of the wood.

"You shouldn't have done that," the older man said nodding toward the card at the foot of the pine. "They need workers badly—as much as soldiers almost."

She nodded, glancing again toward the child. "But in our settlement they ain't nobody else they can git," she said.

"Is your husband in the armed forces?" he asked.

She shook her head. "His examinen date is still about three weeks off."

"Does he work in a factory?"

"He hauls coal in his own truck—when he can git gas—an th miners can git dynamite an caps an stuff to work in th coal."

"The big mines are more efficient," he said. "They need materials worse."

'Th only miners they left us is two cripples an one real old."

"But a good miner back here in these little mines—I've seen them by the road— would be a waste of man power, working without machinery," he said.

She studied the cut in the child's neck, listened, frowning to his short whistling breaths. She nodded to the man's words at last, but grudgingly, as if she had heard the words many times but could not or would not understand, and her face was expressionless, watching now the knife in the soft wood, now glancing at the child.

"It's like the farmers," the officer went on, his voice slightly apologetic as he glanced toward the child, struggling again so that the soldier must lay down the handkerchief and hold his hands while the strain of holding the hairpin steady in the windpipe was bringing sweat to his forehead. "They can't exempt every little one-horse farmer who has little to sell. A man has to produce a lot of what the country needs."

She did not nod, but her lips tightened so that, as when she had cut the child's neck, her mouth was a pale straight slit below the long straight upper lip and the jutting nose. "They warn't a farmer in all our settlement big enough," she said, and her voice was low and sullen.

"Have you any relatives in the armed forces?" he asked, his voice somehow critical.

"Jist cousins an in-laws an sich—now."

"Now?"

"Since yesterday mornen—I had a brother till then."

"Oh." His voice had changed, filled with a kind of proper sadness. "Let us hope he is only missing and that—"

"Jesse—that's my man's brother—he's th one that's missen. Fer my brother th telegram said, 'Kilt in action.'" The knife was still, and she sat a moment staring out across the hills, repeating slowly, tonelessly, "Kilt in action." Then, still in the toneless talking-to-herself voice: "These same leaves was green when they took him—an he'd planted his corn. Some of it he saw come up."

"He was a farmer?" the man asked.

The knife moved in the wood again as she said, "One a them little ones." The knife fought the wood with sharp swift jabs, forming a hole the length of the short piece of poplar. The man, watching stiffly, uncomfortably, trying not to look at the child or the woman's face, said, "You are very skillful with a knife."

"I've allus whittled."

"What?"

"Oh, handles."

"Handles?"

She looked down at the hand that held the poplar wood, the back brown and wrinkled, fingernails black and ragged, then at the palm, smooth with the look of yellowed leather. It was as if the hand were a page engraved with names while, she looking now at the poplar wood, repeated: "Hoe handles, saw handles, ax handles, cornknife handles, broom handles, plow handles, grubben-hoe handles, churn-dasher handles, hammer handles, all kinds a handles—it takes a heap a handles. Sometimes I make em fer th neighbors."

He was silent, his glance fixed on her hands. "Handles," he said at last. "There wouldn't be much fun in handles."

Her face for an instant softened, and as she looked up something that might have been hatred was gone from her eyes. "I've never had much time fer whittlen foolishness. Oh, a few dolls. Cassie—that's my least girl—she's crazy over th dolls I whittle, but when I git all settled I'm aimen to work up a piece a wild cherry wood I've got. It's big enough fer th head an shoulders uv a fair-sized man if"—her voice was low again, wandering as if she talked to herself—"if I can ever hit on th right face." She glanced at the soldier struggling to keep the child's hands from clawing at his neck. "Hold out a little minute longer. I've about got this hole through."

The older man stood so that if he looked straight in front of him he could see the woman but not the child. "What kind of face?" he asked.

She shook the shavings out of the rapidly deepening hole, began on the other end. "I don't know. I've, thought on Christ—but somehow his face ain't never clear er somehen. Maybe some other—old Amos, I liked, or Ecclesiastes or Judas."

"Judas?" And he gave her a sharp, suspicious-seeming glance.

She looked again at the child, then nodded, her eyes on the knife blade as she talked. "Not Judas with his mouth all drooly, his hand held out fer th silver, but Judas given th thirty pieces away. I figger," she went on after blowing the shavings out of the hole, "they's many a one does meanness fer money—like Judas." Her eyes were on the poplar as she spoke, "But they's not many like him gives th money away an feels sorry onct they've got it."

She looked toward the child and met the eyes of the young soldier—there was a head nod in his eyes—but he was silent, for the other was saying, "You seem to be quite a student of the Bible."

She shook her head. "Th Bible's about th only thing I've ever read—when I was a growen up my mother was sick a heap an my father hurt his leg in th log woods. I had to help him, an never got much schoolen but what he give me."

"And he had you study the Bible."

"He had me git things by heart th way they used to do in th old days—poetry an th Constitution an a heap a th Bible." She rose, and still whittling walked toward the child. She stood above him, working swiftly until the hole in the tiny wooden pipe was to her liking, and then with the same gentle skill with which she had whittled she put the tube into the child's neck. She then wrapped him swiftly in the blanket, and with no glance at either man walked quickly to the car.

The officer pushed himself into a corner as far from the woman and child as possible. He sat stiffly, trying not to show his distaste for the big woman cluttering his speckless car, just as he tried not to look at the child or show that the inhuman gurgling cries it gave or the whispering bubbles of its breath nauseated him like the sight of the wooden tube beaded at times with pus and bloody mucus.

The woman sensed this and sat, trying to make herself as small as possible, her muddy feet unmoving by the door, her great shoulders hunched over the child, and slightly sideways. The driver stared straight ahead at the road. The woman mostly watched the wooden pipe. The officer looked first at one side of the road, then the other, unable to keep his glance from the child.

The road left the high pine ridges and followed the twisting course of a creek down into the valley of the Cumberland. Above them on the shoulder of the ridge lay a steep little clearing; stumpy first-year new ground it looked to be, not half tended. Even in the rainy twilight Gertie could see the leafless sprouts encircling the white oak stumps and the smallness of the fodder shocks—a woman's fodder shocks. Held up against the hillside on long front legs like stilts was a little plank house with a tarpaper roof. Chickens were going to roost in a crooked dogwood tree near the door, and a white-headed child came around the house, stumbling under the sticks of stovewood hugged in its arms, while on the high porch steps two other children, one too small to walk, played with a spotted hound.

Though it lay on the woman's side of the road, both glanced at it—the first house after miles of Cumberland National Forest. Then both saw the service flag with one star—blue—in the one front window by the door.

"What crops do they raise in this country?" the officer asked, as if he didn't much care but wanted to make some sound above the child's breathing.

"A little uv everthing."

"But what is their main crop?" he insisted.

"Youngens," she said, holding the child's hands that were continually wandering toward the hole in his neck. "Youngens fer th wars an them factories."

He turned his head sharply away, as if he wished to hear no more, but almost at once his unwilling glance was flicking the child's face where the blueness was thinning, and the eyes, less bulging now, showed their dark coloring through the half open lids. "Your child needs a hospital," he said, looking past her through the window. "You'd better go with us until we reach one."

"Th closest that ud take him with a disease like this is mebbe Lexington—an that's nigh a hunnert miles away." She wiped a trickle of yellowish saliva from one corner of his mouth. "He needs some drugs, like they give fer this, right now—he oughtn't to wait."

"He needs oxygen," the man said. They were silent again, and once more the sounds of the child's battle for breath filled the quiet car. "Do you farm?" the officer asked in the same aimless, desperate, sound-making voice.

"A little."

"I guess every family back in these hills has a little patch of land and keeps a cow or so and a few sheep."

The woman turned and looked at him, her quiet gray eyes questioning. She gave a slow headshake. "Not everbody has got a little piece a land."

"I suppose you have."

She shook her head again with a slowness that might have been weariness. "We're renten," she said, "on Old John Ballew's place; he gits half—we git half." She hesitated, then added slowly, in a low voice, as if not quite certain of her words. "Now, that is; but— we're aimen—we're buyen us a place—all our own."

"How nice," he said, still making sound, giving a quick glance at the child. "A place for you and your children to live while your husband is in service."

"Yes," she said. A warm look came into her troubled eyes as when she had spoken of the block of wood. "Silas Tipton's went off to Muncie to work in a factory. He wanted his wife an youngens with him, so he sold his place. It's a good place—old, a log house—big an built good like they built in th old days. He sold it to Old John Ballew fer to git money to move on. Old John don't want th place. His boys is all gone."

He nodded. "So you'll buy it; farm it while your husband's gone."

"Yes," she said, speaking with more certainty than before, as if her words had made the land her own. "My biggest boy, Reuben, he's twelve," and her eyes were warm again. "He likes farm work an he's a good hand."

"You like to farm," he said, not asking, glancing at her wide shoulders and muscle-corded wrists showing beneath the too short coat sleeves.

She nodded. "I've allus farmed. My father had a big farm—I hepped him when I was growen up. My brother is—" she stopped, went on again, but the words were a thick mumble. "Way younger than me."

After a little space of level road, they were going down again, and the rainy autumn dark came swiftly down like a settling bird. There were sharp steep curves where the dripping limestone cliffs above gave back the sound of the car's horn, and below them lay a narrow black plain pricked with lights. A train blew high above them somewhere in the limestone walls. The child started at the strange sound, and the woman whispered, "Nothen's goen tu hurt you, honey."

On the low road in the village by the Cumberland, the lighted windows of homes were squares of brightness behind the shadows of the leafless, dripping trees. Then came sidewalks with store windows bright above them, and the driver went more slowly, looking first this way and that. The woman looked at the windows filled with many different things, and on them all were pasted white or red or blue or yellow sheets of paper that bore pictures of Uncle Sam, of soldiers, of sailors, of airmen, of pretty girl soldiers with neat hair; but all held big black words like the red sign on the pine tree: "GIVE, RED CROSS—JOIN THE WACS—GIVE BLOOD—WORK AT WILLOW RUN."

The car stopped in a wash of light from a broad window, while high above the road more lights made a brightness on the wet leaf-plastered sidewalks that lay on either side the street. The woman, as if unaccustomed to so much brightness, squinched her eyes and twisted her head about as she drew the blanket more closely about the child.

"Wait," the officer said. "Hatcher, make certain there is a doctor's office close by and that he is in."

The woman watched the soldier go across the street, then glanced at the officer, who was looking out his window as he rolled it down. A door had opened on the street, and through it came a burst of juke-box music. The woman looked toward the sound, a shadow of girlish interest in her troubled eyes, then her glance went swiftly back to the officer's head, and not taking her eyes from him, she lifted the child on one arm, and with a quick and furtive movement reached into her coat pocket, her hand going down into the lining, searching. The man turned a little, glancing at her in his quick, impatient way, and her hand at once became still, and did not search again until he had turned away.

The hand was still again when the young soldier opened the door, saying, "The doctor's in his office right across the street."

The woman hesitated, moving toward the opened door, but looking at the officer, her hand, folded into a fist, coming slowly out of the bottom of her coat. She flushed, opening the fist, showing a worn and limp bill. "I want tu pay you fer th ride," she said, "but I can't find th right change."

The officer looked at the outstretched five-dollar bill, surprise and disgust reddening his face. "I wouldn't think of charging," he said, staring at the bill, so worn, so wrinkled, the five was hardly legible.

"But I aimed tu pay," she said, touching his hand with the money.

He reached quickly for the money like one suddenly changing his mind. "I can change it," he said, and turning away from her drew out a wallet; but it was only after she was out of the car that he put bills, folded closely together, into her hand, saying, "A dollar's fair enough, I guess." And then, "Good luck. Help her across the street, Hatcher."

"I can manage," she said, dropping the money into her apron pocket.

The young soldier stooped quickly and picked up a small bright thing fallen from the folds of the child's blanket. He handed it to her as they walked across the highway. "Keep it for the baby," he said. "Stars like that are kind of scarce."

"Oh," she said, "th man's star—I didn't mean to tear it off. You'd better give it back to him; somebody'ull git him fer losen it. I've heared they're mighty hard on soldiers if their clothes don't look right."

"Not on the likes of him," the other said. They had gone a little distance down the sidewalk when the man pointed to a lighted doorway a few steps back from the street. "There's the doctor's," he said.

She glanced timidly toward the door. "I ain't never been to a doctor before. Clovis, my husband, he's allus took th youngens th few times it was somethen Sue Annie couldn't cure."

His flat, absent-minded eyes opened wide in astonishment. "Lady, you can't be afraid of nothing. Just walk in."

Alice Childress (1920–1994)

Born in Charleston, South Carolina, to a working-class black family, Alice Herndon Childress moved as a child to Harlem, where she was raised primarily by her maternal grandmother. A mother at age fifteen, Childress did not finish high school but developed a passion for writing and drama with her grandmother's encouragement. In 1940, she joined the American Negro Theater, formed initially during the Harlem Renaissance, performing as an actress and eventually composing her own plays. Her first critical success came with *Florence* (1949), which, like much of Childress's work, centers on a theme with which she had direct experience: the conflict over a black mother's refusal to support her daughter's desire to go on the stage. *Trouble in Mind* (1956) was the first play by a woman to be awarded an Obie, for its portrayal of black actors challenging the expectation that they will play only stereotyped characters. *Wedding Band: A Love/Hate Story in Black and White* (1966), dealing with interracial romance in South Carolina, was initially shunned, but by 1973 had been adapted for television.

Later in her career, Childress turned also to fiction and continued her practice of opening up controversial subjects along the fault-lines of race, class, and sex. The popular young adult novel, *A Hero Ain't Nothin' but a Sandwich* (1973) was banned in schools because of its frank portrayal of teenage sexual relationships and conflict with parents; it, too, became a film, in 1977. The stories that follow come from a series of fictional columns that Childress contributed to the *Baltimore African American* and the journal *Freedom* in the

Marion Post Wolcott, "Negro man entering movie theater by 'colored' entrance," Belzoni, Mississippi, October 1939. *Courtesy of Library of Congress, LC-USF34-17417.*

early 1950s, under the heading "Here's Mildred." Published in her 1956 book, *Like One of the Family: Conversations from a Domestic's Life*, these satiric vignettes are cast as a dialogue between Mildred and her friend and fellow domestic Marge. Drawing on Childress's experience working as a maid for white families during her early years in the theater, they give dramatic voice to Mildred's wry humor, her sharp analyses of her employers, and her capacity for self-assertion and cross-race solidarity.

LIKE ONE OF THE FAMILY

Hi Marge! I have had me one hectic day. . . . Well, I had to take out my crystal ball and give Mrs. C . . . a thorough reading. She's the woman that I took over from Naomi after Naomi got married. . . . Well, she's a pretty nice woman as they go, and I have never had too much trouble with her, but from time to time she really gripes me with her ways.

When she has company, for example, she'll holler out to me from the living room to the kitchen: "Mildred dear! Be sure and eat *both* of those lamb chops for your lunch!" Now you know she wasn't doing a thing but tryin' to prove to the company how "good" and "kind" she was to the servant, because she had told me *already* to eat those chops.

Today she had a girlfriend of hers over to lunch, and I was real busy afterward clearing the things away, and she called me over and introduced me to the woman. . . . Oh no, Marge! I didn't object to that at all. I greeted the lady and then went back to my work. . . . And then it started! I could hear her talkin' just as loud . . . and she says to her friend, "We *just* love her! She's *like* one of the family and she *just adores* our little Carol! We don't know *what* we'd do without her! We don't think of her as a servant!" And on and on she went . . . and every time I came in to move a plate off the table, both of them would grin at me like chessy cats.

After I couldn't stand it anymore, I went in and took the platter off the table and gave 'em both a look that would have frizzled a egg. . . . Well, you might have heard a pin drop, and then they started talkin' about something else.

When the guest leaves, I go in the living room and says, "Mrs. C . . . , I want to have a talk with you."

"By all means," she says.

I drew up a chair and read her thusly: "Mrs. C . . . , you are a pretty nice person to work for, but I wish you would please stop talkin' about me like I was a *cocker spaniel* or a *poll parrot* or a *kitten*. . . . Now you just sit there and hear me out.

"In the first place, you do not *love* me; you may be fond of me, but that is all. . . . In the second place, I am *not* just like one of the family at all! The family eats in the dining room, and I eat in the kitchen. Your mama borrows your lace tablecloth for her company, and your son entertains his friends in your parlor, your daughter takes her afternoon nap on the living room couch, and the puppy sleeps on your satin spread . . . and whenever your husband gets tired of something you are talkin' about, he says. 'Oh, for Pete's sake, forget it.' So you can see I am not *just* like one of the family.

"Now for another thing, I do not *just adore* your little Carol. I think she is a likable child, but she is also fresh and sassy. I know you call it 'uninhibited,' and that is the way you want your child to be, but *luckily* my mother taught me some inhibitions, or else I would smack little Carol once in a while when she's talkin' to you like you're a dog, but as it is, I just laugh it off the way you do because she is *your* child and I am *not* like one of the family.

"Now when you say, 'We don't know *what* we'd do without her,' this is a polite lie . . . because I know that if I dropped dead or had a stroke, you would get somebody to replace me.

"You think it is a compliment when you say, 'We don't think of her as a servant,' but after I have worked myself into a sweat cleaning the bathroom and the kitchen . . . making the beds . . . cooking the lunch . . . washing the dishes and ironing Carol's pinafores . . . I do not feel like no weekend house guest. I feel like a servant, and in the face of that I have been meaning to ask you for a slight raise, which will make me feel much better toward everyone here and make me know my work is appreciated.

"Now I hope you will stop talkin' about me in my presence and that we will get along like a good employer and employee should."

Marge! She was almost speechless, but she *apologized* and said she'd talk to her husband about the raise. . . . I knew things were progressing because this evening Carol came in the kitchen, and she did not say, "I want some bread and jam!" but she did say, "*Please*, Mildred, will you fix me a slice of bread and jam."

I'm going upstairs, Marge. Just look . . . you done messed up that buttonhole!

Sometimes I Feel So Sorry

You oughta hear Mrs. B . . . moanin' and groanin' about her troubles. I tell you, if you listen long enough, you just might break down and cry your heart out. That woman don't have nothin' but one problem on top of the other! If it ain't her, it's her husband or her brother or her friends or some everlastin' sorrow tryin' her soul. She's got sixty-'leven jars of face cream and lotions and stuff, but she's gettin' a big frown creased 'cross the front of her forehead just the same.

Girl, you oughta see all the stuff she's got! A handsome mink coat, a big old apartment overlookin' the river, me and a cook and a nurse for the children, a summer cottage in the country, and a little speedboat that she can chug up and down the river in any time she might take the notion. . . . Hello! And what did you say! . . . Yes, indeed, that just should be me!

Today she was almost out of her mind about her brother. Her brother's name is Carl, and he is a caution! Seems like he doesn't know whether to paint pictures or write books, and it just keeps his mind in torment and turmoil. Whenever the problem gets too much for him, he drinks up a case of whiskey and goes into the shakes.

Whenever this happens, they get him into a private home that costs about three hundred dollars a week. He will hang around there while the doctors study his mind for about seven or eight weeks, and then he'll come out again to go through the same merry-go-round all over again.

. . . You ain't heard nothin' yet! She also had a very close friend who was a awful successful actress, but she got to be a dope addict, and Mrs. B—— told me that she got that way 'cause she had so much work and personal appearances 'til it drove her to the drugs. I told her that she could turn down some of that work and do just enough to take it kinda easy-like, but all Mrs. B—— said about that was, "Oh, the poor thing, I feel so sorry for her."

Another time her mother's arm broke out in a little rash, and that thing developed into the biggest long drawn out to-do! The doctors had to analyze that woman's mind for almost a year and even then they couldn't tell whether she had a rash because of her dog's fur or on account of her husband's personality. No, I don't know if the thing is straightened out yet.

This mornin' Mrs. B—— was all tore up because Carl wants to get married. Marge, she is in a pacin'-up-and-down fit! She thinks the girl will aggravate Carl's condition because she can paint pretty pictures, and it will hurt Carl because he can't. Honey, she worries my soul-case out with all them troubles. I have listened to more tales of woe comin' out of that woman. . . . No, she won't want no advice 'cause she never listens to a word you say. I do believe it would break her heart half-in-two if anybody told her somethin' that would end all the misery 'cause she's so used to it by now she wouldn't know what to do without it!

That woman has a pure-artful knack of turnin' the simplest things into a burnin' hellfire *problem*! When she gives a dinner party, she worries herself to death about whether she's invited the *wrong* people and left out the *right* ones! If her daughter ain't laughin' and talkin' every single minute of every single day, she turns herself inside-out worryin' if somethin' is the matter with her. If her husband sneezes, she annoys him to death until he goes to the doctor for a complete check-up. She will eat too much lobster salad and then swear she's got a heart ailment when one of them gas pains hit her in the chest. . . .

Whenever things go kinda smooth-like, she takes time out to worry about the stock-market and who's gonna be our next president! That poor woman has harried herself into the shadow of a wreck!

Marge, sometimes I think that all she would need to cure her is one good-sized real trouble. You know, like lookin' in your icebox and seein' nothin' but your own reflection! I guess she'd know what trial and trouble really was if she had a child with a toothache, no money, and a dispossess all at the same time! . . . That's what happened to Gloria last spring! . . . Sure, I guess Gloria cried a little, but she took that child to the clinic, and then they moved with her brother for a while, and her brother only had four rooms for his wife and their four children!

. . . Sure, I remember the time you lost your uncle and he didn't have any insurance! And what about the time I had to send all my little savin's down home so that my niece could stay in college? You know everybody's so busy talkin' 'bout us gettin' into these schools 'til it never crosses their mind what a hard time we have stayin' there. It costs money!

I bet Mrs. B—— would think twice about what trouble is if she had one dollar in the house and had to fix dinner for a bunch of kids, like Mrs. Johnson who lives downstairs. She'd also think twice if *her* husband had lost his job 'cause the boss had to cut down and decided to let the colored go first.

. . . Marge, you may be right, perhaps their troubles are as real to them as ours are to us. I don't know about that though. I don't think I'd be goin' through the same miseries if I was in her shoes.

I've seen some trouble in my life, and I know that if I was to call up my aunt and tell her that I'd been too quiet all day or had a hang-over or didn't know whether to paint or write or something like that, she'd say, "Girl, are you out of your mind! Don't be botherin' me with no foolishness!"

Hisaye Yamamoto (b. 1921)

Born in Redondo Beach, California, Hisaye Yamamoto is a Nisei (second-generation Japanese American); her parents were Issei (Japanese immigrants) from Kumamoto, Japan. In 1942, Hisaye Yamamoto, her family, and other Americans of Japanese descent on the West Coast were forced to leave their homes, businesses, and farms and move to internment camps. Yamamoto and her family lived for three years in Arizona's Poston

Relocation Center. There, Yamamoto, who began writing as a teenager, published articles and stories in the camp newspaper, the *Poston Chronicle*. Yamamoto was briefly relocated to Springfield, Massachusetts, but returned to Poston upon hearing the news that her brother Johnny, age nineteen, was killed while fighting with the American army in Italy. When the war ended in 1945, Yamamoto moved to Los Angeles and found work as a reporter for the *Los Angeles Tribune*, a black weekly newspaper. "The High-Heeled Shoes," her first published story, appeared in *Partisan Review* in 1948, the same year that she adopted a son, Paul. As she began publishing stories in national journals, she gained recognition as a postwar Japanese American writer. Influenced by Dorothy Day and the Catholic Worker movement, she declined a Stanford Writing Fellowship to move to a Catholic Worker community farm in Staten Island in 1953. In 1955, she married Anthony DeSoto and returned to Los Angeles. She had four more children and continued to write and publish stories particularly about Japanese American experiences. "Yoneko's Earthquake" was chosen for Best American Short Stories of 1952. In 1986, Yamamoto received an American Book Award for Lifetime Achievement from the Before Columbus Foundation. Two of her stories, including "Seventeen Syllables," were adapted for an American Playhouse/PBS film, *Hot Summer Winds*.

SEVENTEEN SYLLABLES

The first Rosie knew that her mother had taken to writing poems was one evening when she finished one and read it aloud for her daughter's approval. It was about cats, and Rosie pretended to understand it thoroughly and appreciate it no end, partly because she hesitated to disillusion her mother about the quantity and quality of Japanese she had learned in all the years now that she had been going to Japanese school every Saturday (and Wednesday, too, in the summer). Even so, her mother must have been skeptical about the depth of Rosie's understanding, because she explained afterwards about the kind of poem she was trying to write.

See, Rosie, she said, it was a *haiku*, a poem in which she must pack all her meaning into seventeen syllables only, which were divided into three lines of five, seven, and five syllables. In the one she had just read, she had tried to capture the charm of a kitten, as well as comment on the superstition that owning a cat of three colors meant good luck.

"Yes, yes, I understand. How utterly lovely," Rosie said, and her mother, either satisfied or seeing through the deception and resigned, went back to composing.

The truth was that Rosie was lazy; English lay ready on the tongue but Japanese had to be searched for and examined, and even then put forth tentatively (probably to meet with laughter). It was so much easier to say yes, yes, even when one meant no, no. Besides, this was what was in her mind to say: I was looking through one of your magazines from Japan last night, Mother, and towards the back I found some *haiku* in English that delighted me. There was one that made me giggle off and on until I fell asleep—

> It is morning, and lo!
> I lie awake, comme il faut,
> sighing for some dough.

Now, how to reach her mother, how to communicate the melancholy song? Rosie knew formal Japanese by fits and starts, her mother had even less English, no French. It was much more possible to say yes, yes.

It developed that her mother was writing the *haiku* for a daily newspaper, the *Mainichi Shimbun*, that was published in San Francisco. Los Angeles, to be sure, was closer to the farming community in which the Hayashi family lived and several Japanese vernaculars were printed there, but Rosie's parents said they preferred the tone of the northern paper. Once a week, the *Mainichi* would have a section devoted to *haiku*, and her mother became an extravagant contributor, taking for herself the blossoming pen name, Ume Hanazono.

So Rosie and her father lived for awhile with two women, her mother and Ume Hanazono. Her mother (Tome Hayashi by name) kept house, cooked, washed, and, along with her husband and the Carrascos, the Mexican family hired for the harvest, did her ample share of picking tomatoes out in the sweltering fields and boxing them in tidy strata in the cool packing shed. Ume Hanazono, who came to life after the dinner dishes were done, was an earnest, muttering stranger who often neglected speaking when spoken to and stayed busy at the parlor table as late as midnight scribbling with pencil on scratch paper or carefully copying characters on good paper with her fat, pale green Parker.

The new interest had some repercussions on the household routine. Before, Rosie had been accustomed to her parents and herself taking their hot baths early and going to bed almost immediately afterwards, unless her parents challenged each other to a game of flower cards or unless company dropped in. Now if her father wanted to play cards, he had to resort to solitaire (at which he always cheated fearlessly), and if a group of friends came over, it was bound to contain someone who was also writing *haiku*, and the small assemblage would be split in two, her father entertaining the nonliterary members and her mother comparing ecstatic notes with the visiting poet.

If they went out, it was more of the same thing. But Ume Hanazono's life span, even for a poet's, was very brief—perhaps three months at most.

One night they went over to see the Hayano family in the neighboring town to the west, an adventure both painful and attractive to Rosie. It was attractive because there were four Hayano girls, all lovely and each one named after a season of the year (Haru, Natsu, Aki, Fuyu), painful because something had been wrong with Mrs. Hayano ever since the birth of her first child. Rosie would sometimes watch Mrs. Hayano, reputed to have been the belle of her native village, making her way about a room, stooped, slowly shuffling, violently trembling (*always* trembling), and she would be reminded that this woman, in this same condition, had carried and given issue to three babies. She would look wonderingly at Mr. Hayano, handsome, tall, and strong, and she would look at her four pretty friends. But it was not a matter she could come to any decision about.

On this visit, however, Mrs. Hayano sat all evening in the rocker, as motionless and unobtrusive as it was possible for her to be, and Rosie found the greater part of the evening practically anaesthetic. Too, Rosie spent most of it in the girls' room, because Haru, the garrulous one, said almost as soon as the bows and other greetings were over. "Oh, you must see my new coat!"

It was a pale plaid of grey, sand, and blue, with an enormous collar, and Rosie, seeing nothing special in it, said, "Gee, how nice."

"Nice?" said Haru, indignantly. "Is that all you can say about it? It's gorgeous! And so cheap, too. Only seventeen-ninety eight, because it was a sale. The saleslady said it was twenty-five dollars regular."

"Gee," said Rosie. Natsu, who never said much and when she said anything said it shyly, fingered the coat covetously and Haru pulled it away.

"Mine," she said, putting it on. She minced in the aisle between the two large beds and smiled happily. "Let's see how your mother likes it."

She broke into the front room and the adult conversation and went to stand in front of Rosie's mother, while the rest watched from the door. Rosie's mother was properly envious. "May I inherit it when you're through with it?"

Haru, pleased, giggled and said yes, she could, but Natsu reminded gravely from the door, "You promised me, Haru."

Everyone laughed but Natsu, who shamefacedly retreated into the bedroom. Haru came in laughing, taking off the coat. "We were only kidding, Natsu," she said. "Here, you try it on now."

After Natsu buttoned herself into the coat, inspected herself solemnly in the bureau mirror, and reluctantly shed it, Rosie, Aki, and Fuyu got their turns, and Fuyu, who was eight, drowned in it while her sisters and Rosie doubled up in amusement. They all went into the front room later, because Haru's mother quaveringly called to her to fix the tea and rice cakes and open a can of sliced peaches for everybody. Rosie noticed that her mother and Mr. Hayano were talking together at the little table—they were discussing a *haiku* that Mr. Hayano was planning to send to the *Mainichi*, while her father was sitting at one end of the sofa looking through a copy of *Life*, the new picture magazine. Occasionally, her father would comment on a photograph, holding it toward Mrs. Hayano and speaking to her as he always did—loudly, as though he thought someone such as she must surely be at least a trifle deaf also.

The five girls had their refreshments at the kitchen table, and it was while Rosie was showing the sisters her trick of swallowing peach slices without chewing (she chased each slippery crescent down with a swig of tea) that her father brought his empty teacup and untouched saucer to the sink and said, "Come on, Rosie, we're going home now."

"Already?" asked Rosie.

"Work tomorrow," he said.

He sounded irritated, and Rosie, puzzled, gulped one last yellow slice and stood up to go, while the sisters began protesting, as was their wont.

"We have to get up at five-thirty," he told them, going into the front room quickly, so that they did not have their usual chance to hang onto his hands and plead for an extension of time.

Rosie, following, saw that her mother and Mr. Hayano were sipping tea and still talking together, while Mrs. Hayano concentrated, quivering, on raising the handleless Japanese cup to her lips with both her hands and lowering it back to her lap. Her father, saying nothing, went out the door, onto the bright porch, and down the steps. Her mother looked up and asked, "Where is he going?"

"Where is he going?" Rosie said. "He said we were going home now."

"Going home?" Her mother looked with embarrassment at Mr. Hayano and his absorbed wife and then forced a smile. "He must be tired," she said.

Haru was not giving up yet. "May Rosie stay overnight?" she asked, and Natsu, Aki, and Fuyu came to reinforce their sister's plea by helping her make a circle around Rosie's mother. Rosie, for once having no desire to stay, was relieved when her mother, apologizing to the perturbed Mr. and Mrs. Hayano for her father's abruptness at the same time, managed to shake her head no at the quartet, kindly but adamant, so that they broke their circle and let her go.

Rosie's father looked ahead into the windshield as the two joined him. "I'm sorry," her mother said. "You must be tired." Her father, stepping on the starter, said nothing. "You know how I get when its *haiku*," she continued, "I forget what time it is." He only grunted.

As they rode homeward silently, Rosie, sitting between, felt a rush of hate for both—for her mother for begging, for her father for denying her mother. I wish this old Ford would crash, right now, she thought, then immediately, no, no, I wish my father would laugh, but it was too late: already the vision had passed through her mind of the green pick-up crumpled in the dark against one of the mighty eucalyptus trees they were just riding past, of the three contorted, bleeding bodies, one of them hers.

Rosie ran between two patches of tomatoes, her heart working more rambunctiously than she had ever known it. How lucky it was that Aunt Taka and Uncle Gimpachi had come tonight, though, how very lucky. Otherwise she might not have really kept her half-promise to meet Jesus Carrasco. Jesus was going to be a senior in September at the same school she went to, and his parents were the ones helping with the tomatoes this year. She and Jesus, who hardly remembered seeing each other at Cleveland High where there were so many other people and two whole grades between them, had become great friends this summer—he always had a joke for her when he periodically drove the loaded pick-up up from the fields to the shed where she was usually sorting while her mother and father did the packing, and they laughed a great deal together over infinitesimal repartee during the afternoon break for chilled watermelon or ice cream in the shade of the shed.

What she enjoyed most was racing him to see who could finish picking a double row first. He, who could work faster, would tease her by slowing down until she thought she would surely pass him this time, then speeding up furiously to leave her several sprawling vines behind. Once he had made her screech hideously by crossing over, while her back was turned, to place atop the tomatoes in her green-stained bucket a truly monstrous, pale green worm (it had looked more like an infant snake). And it was when they had finished a contest this morning, after she had pantingly pointed a green finger at the miniature tomatoes evident in the lugs at the end of his row and he had returned the accusation (with justice), that he had startlingly brought up the matter of their possibly meeting outside the range of both their parents' dubious eyes.

"What for?" she had asked.

"I've got a secret I want to tell you," he said.

"Tell me now," she demanded.

"It won't be ready till tonight," he said.

She laughed. "Tell me tomorrow then."

"It'll be gone tomorrow," he threatened.

"Well, for seven hakes, what is it?" she had asked, more than twice, and when he had suggested that the packing shed would be an appropriate place to find out, she had cautiously answered maybe. She had not been certain she was going to keep the appointment until the arrival of mother's sister and her husband. Their coming seemed a sort of signal of permission, of grace, and she had definitely made up her mind to lie and leave as she was bowing them welcome.

So as soon as everyone appeared settled back for the evening, she announced loudly that she was going to the privy outside, "I'm going to the *benjo!*" and slipped out the door. And now that she was actually on her way, her heart pumped in such an undisciplined way that she could hear it with her ears. It's because I'm running, she told herself, slowing to a walk. The shed was up ahead, one more patch away, in the middle of the fields. Its bulk, looming in the dimness, took on a sinisterness that was funny when Rosie reminded herself that it was only a wooden frame with a canvas roof and three canvas walls that made a slapping noise on breezy days.

Jesus was sitting on the narrow plank that was the sorting platform and she went around to the other side and jumped backwards to seat herself on the rim of a packing stand. "Well, tell me," she said without greeting, thinking her voice sounded reassuringly familiar.

"I saw you coming out the door," Jesus said. "I heard you running part of the way, too."

"Uh-huh," Rosie said. "Now tell me the secret."

"I was afraid you wouldn't come," he said.

Rosie delved around on the chicken-wire bottom of the stall for number two tomatoes, ripe, which she was sitting beside, and came up with a left-over that felt edible. She bit into it and began sucking out the pulp and seeds. "I'm here," she pointed out.

"Rosie, are you sorry you came?

"Sorry? What for?" she said. "You said you were going to tell me something."

"I will, I will," Jesus said, but his voice contained disappointment, and Rosie fleetingly felt the older of the two, realizing a brand-new power which vanished without category under her recognition.

"I have to go back in a minute," she said, "My aunt and uncle are here from Wintersburg. I told them I was going to the privy."

Jesus laughed. "You funny thing," he said. "You slay me!"

"Just because you have a bathroom *inside*," Rosie said. "Come on, tell me."

Chuckling, Jesus came around to lean on the stand facing her. They still could not see each other very clearly, but Rosie noticed that Jesus became very sober again as he took the hollow tomato from her hand and dropped it back into the stall. When he took hold of her empty hand, she could find no words to protest; her vocabulary had become distressingly constricted and she thought desperately that all that remained intact now was yes and no and oh, and even these few sounds would not easily out. Thus, kissed by Jesus, Rosie fell for the first time entirely victim to a helplessness delectable beyond speech. But the terrible, beautiful sensation lasted no more than a second, and the reality of Jesus' lips and tongue and teeth and hands made her pull away with such strength that she nearly tumbled.

Rosie stopped running as she approached the lights from the windows of home. How long since she had left? She could not guess, but gasping yet, she went to the privy in back and locked herself in. Her own breathing deafened her in the dark, close space, and she sat and waited until she could hear at last the nightly calling of the frogs and crickets. Even then, all she could think to say was oh, my, and the pressure of Jesus' face against her face would not leave.

No one had missed her in the parlor, however, and Rosie walked in and through quickly, announcing that she was next going to take a bath. "Your father's in the bathhouse," her mother said, and Rosie, in her room, recalled that she had not seen him when she entered. There had been only Aunt Taka and Uncle Gimpachi with her mother at the table, drinking tea. She got her robe and straw sandals and crossed the parlor again to go outside. Her mother was telling them about the *haiku* competition in the *Mainichi* and the poem she had entered.

Rosie met her father coming out of the bathhouse. "Are you through, Father?" she asked. "I was going to ask you to scrub my back."

"Scrub your own back," he said shortly, going toward the main house.

"What have I done now?" she yelled after him. She suddenly felt like doing a lot of yelling. But he did not answer, and she went into the bathhouse. Turning on the dangling light, she removed her denims and T-shirt and threw them in the big carton for dirty clothes standing next to the washing machine. Her other things she took with her into the bath compartment to wash after her bath. After she had scooped a basin of hot water from the square wooden tub, she sat on the grey cement of the floor and soaped herself at exaggerated leisure, singing "Red Sails in the Sunset" at the top of her voice and using da-da-da where she suspected her words. Then, standing up, still singing, for she was possessed by the notion that any attempt now to analyze would result in spoilage and she believed that the larger her volume the less she would be able to hear herself think, she obtained more hot water and poured it on until she was free of lather. Only then did she allow herself to step into the steaming vat, one leg first, then the remainder of her body inch by inch until the water no longer stung and she could move around at will.

She took a long time soaking, afterwards remembering to go around outside to stoke the embers of the tin-lined fireplace beneath the tub and to throw on a few more sticks so that the water might keep its heat for her mother, and when she finally returned to the parlor, she found her mother still talking *haiku* with her aunt and uncle, the three of them on another round of tea. Her father was nowhere in sight.

At Japanese school the next day (Wednesday, it was), Rosie was grave and giddy by turns. Preoccupied at her desk in the row for students on Book Eight, she made up for it at recess by performing wild mimicry for the benefit of her friend Chizuko. She held her nose and whined a witticism or two in what she considered was the manner of Fred Allen; she assumed intoxication and a British accent to go over the climax of the Rudy Vallee recording of the pub conversation about William Ewart Gladstone; she was the child Shirley Temple piping, "On the Good Ship Lollipop"; she was the gentleman soprano of the Four Inkspots trilling, "If I Didn't Care." And she felt reasonably satisfied when Chizuko wept and gasped, "Oh, Rosie, you ought to be in the movies!"

Her father came after her at noon, bringing her sandwiches of minced ham and two nectarines to eat while she rode, so that she could pitch right into the sorting when they got home. The lugs were piling up, he said, and the ripe tomatoes in them would probably have to be taken to the cannery tomorrow if they were not ready for the produce haulers tonight. "This heat's not doing them any good. And we've got no time for a break today."

It *was* hot, probably the hottest day of the year, and Rosie's blouse stuck damply to her back even under the protection of the canvas. But she worked as efficiently as a flawless machine and kept the stalls heaped, with one part of her mind listening in to the parental murmuring about the heat and the tomatoes and with another part planning the exact words she would say to Jesus when he drove up with the first load of the afternoon. But when at last she saw that the pick-up was coming, her hands went berserk and the tomatoes started falling in the wrong stalls, and her father said, "Hey, hey! Rosie, watch what you're doing!"

"Well, I have to go to the *benjo*," she said, hiding panic.

"Go in the weeds over there," he said, only halfjoking.

"Oh, Father!" she protested.

"Oh, go on home," her mother said. "We'll make out for awhile."

In the privy Rosie peered through a knothole toward the fields, watching as much as she could of Jesus. Happily she thought she saw him look in the direction of the house from time to time before he finished unloading and went back toward the patch where his mother and father worked. As she was heading for the shed, a very presentable black car purred up the dirt driveway to the house and its driver motioned to her. Was this the Hayashi home, he wanted to know. She nodded. Was she a Hayashi? Yes, she said, thinking that he was a good-looking man. He got out of the car with a huge, flat package and she saw that he warmly wore a business suit. "I have something here for your mother then," he said, in a more elegant Japanese than she was used to.

She told him where her mother was and he came along with her, patting his face with an immaculate white handkerchief and saying something about the coolness of San Francisco. To her surprised mother and father, he bowed and introduced himself as, among other things, the *haiku* editor of the *Mainichi Shimbun*, saying that since he had been coming as far as Los Angeles anyway, he had decided to bring her the first prize she had won in the recent contest.

"First prize?" her mother echoed, believing and not believing, pleased and overwhelmed. Handed the package with a bow, she bobbed her head up and down numerous times to express her utter gratitude.

"It is nothing much," he added, "but I hope it will serve as a token of our great appreciation for your contributions and our great admiration of your considerable talent."

"I am not worthy," she said, falling easily into his style. "It is I who should make some sign of my humble thanks for being permitted to contribute."

"No, no, to the contrary," he said, bowing again.

But Rosie's mother insisted, and then saying that she knew she was being unorthodox, she asked if she might open the package because her curiosity was so great. Certainly she might. In fact, he would like her reaction to it, for personally, it was one of his favorite *Hiroshiges*.

Rosie thought it was a pleasant picture, which looked to have been sketched with delicate quickness. There were pink clouds, containing some graceful calligraphy, and a sea that was a pale blue except at the edges, containing four sampans with indications of people in them. Pines edged the water and on the far-off beach there was a cluster of thatched huts towered over by pine-dotted mountains of grey and blue. The frame was scalloped and gilt.

After Rosie's mother pronounced it without peer and somewhat prodded her father into nodding agreement, she said Mr. Kuroda must at least have a cup of tea after coming all this way, and although Mr. Kuroda did not want to impose, he soon agreed that a cup of tea would be refreshing and went along with her to the house, carrying the picture for her.

"Ha, your mother's crazy!" Rosie's father said, and Rosie laughed uneasily as she resumed judgment on the tomatoes. She had emptied six lugs when he broke into an imaginary conversation with Jesus to tell her to go and remind her mother of the tomatoes, and she went slowly.

Mr. Kuroda was in his shirtsleeves expounding some *haiku* theory as he munched a rice cake, and her mother was rapt. Abashed in the great man's presence, Rosie stood next to her mother's chair until her mother looked up inquiringly, and then she started to whisper the message, but her mother pushed her gently away and reproached, "You are not being very polite to our guest."

"Father says the tomatoes . . ." Rosie said aloud, smiling foolishly.

"Tell him I shall only be a minute," her mother said, speaking the language of Mr. Kuroda.

When Rosie carried the reply to her father, he did not seem to hear and she said again, "Mother says she'll be back in a minute."

"All right, all right," he nodded, and they worked again in silence. But suddenly, her father uttered an incredible noise, exactly like the cork of a bottle popping, and the next Rosie knew, he was stalking angrily toward the house, almost running in fact, and she chased after him crying, "Father! Father! What are you going to do?"

He stopped long enough to order her back to the shed. "Never mind!" he shouted. "Get on with the sorting!"

And from the place in the fields where she stood, frightened and vacillating, Rosie saw her father enter the house. Soon Mr. Kuroda came out alone, putting on his coat. Mr. Kuroda got into his car and backed out down the driveway onto the highway. Next her father emerged, also alone, something in his arms (it was the picture, she realized), and, going over to the bathhouse woodpile, he threw the picture on the ground and picked up the axe. Smashing the picture, glass and all (she heard the explosion faintly), he reached over for the kerosene that was used to encourage the bath fire and poured it over the wreckage. I am dreaming, Rosie said to herself, I am dreaming, but her father, having made sure that his act of cremation was irrevocable, was even then returning to the fields.

Rosie ran past him and toward the house. What had become of her mother? She burst into the parlor and found her mother at the back window watching the dying fire. They watched together until there remained only a feeble smoke under the blazing sun. Her mother was very calm.

"Do you know why I married your father?" she said without turning.

"No," said Rosie. It was the most frightening question she had ever been called upon to answer. Don't tell me now, she wanted to say, tell me tomorrow, tell me next week, don't tell me today. But she knew she would be told now, that the telling would combine with the other violence of the hot afternoon to level her life, her world to the very ground.

It was like a story out of the magazines illustrated in sepia, which she had consumed so greedily for a period until the information had somehow reached her that those wretchedly unhappy autobiographies, offered to her as the testimonials of living men and women, were largely inventions: Her mother, at nineteen, had come to America and married her father as an alternative to suicide.

At eighteen she had been in love with the first son of one of the well-to-do families in her village. The two had met whenever and wherever they could, secretly, because it would not have done for his family to see him favor her—her father had no money; he was a drunkard and a gambler besides. She had learned she was with child; an excellent match had already been arranged for her lover. Despised by her family, she had given premature birth to a stillborn son, who would be seventeen now. Her family did not turn her out, but she could no longer project herself in any direction without refreshing in them the memory of her indiscretion. She wrote to Aunt Taka, her favorite sister in America, threatening to kill herself if Aunt Taka would not send for her. Aunt Taka hastily arranged a marriage with a young man of whom she knew, but lately arrived from Japan, a young man of simple mind, it was said, but of kindly heart. The young man was never told why his unseen betrothed was so eager to hasten the day of meeting.

The story was told perfectly, with neither groping for words nor untoward passion. It was as though her mother had memorized it by heart, reciting it to herself so many times over that its nagging vileness had long since gone.

"I had a brother then?" Rosie asked, for this was what seemed to matter now; she would think about the other later, she assured herself, pushing back the illumination which threatened all that darkness that had hitherto been merely mysterious or even glamorous. "A half-brother?"

"Yes."

"I would have liked a brother," she said.

Suddenly, her mother knelt on the floor and took her by the wrists. "Rosie," she said urgently, "Promise me you will never marry!" Shocked more by the request than the revelation, Rosie stared at her mother's face. Jesus, Jesus, she called silently, not certain whether she was invoking the help of the son of the Carrascos or of God, until there returned sweetly the memory of Jesus' hand, how it had touched her and where. Still her mother waited for an answer, holding her wrists so tightly that her hands were going numb. She tried to pull free. Promise, her mother whispered fiercely, promise. Yes, yes, I promise, Rosie said. But for an instant she turned away, and her mother, hearing the familiar glib agreement, released her. Oh, you, you, you, her eyes and twisted mouth said, you fool. Rosie, covering her face, began at last to cry, and the embrace and consoling hand came much later than she expected.

Edwin Rolfe (1909–1954)

Born Solomon Fishman, Edwin Rolfe grew up in New York's Coney Island, in a family of Russian Jewish immigrants. His father was a shoemaker and a socialist labor-union official; his mother was a women's rights activist who later joined the Communist Party.

Their son took the pen-name Edwin Rolfe in high school when he joined the Young Communist League and began contributing to the party's newspaper, the *Daily Worker*. His first published poem, "The Ballad of the Subway Worker," appeared there in 1927. After two years of college at the University of Wisconsin, Rolfe returned to New York and became a full-time writer at the *Daily Worker*, doing book reviews and news articles as the Great Depression worsened and the mass movements of the time gathered force.

Encouraged by Mike Gold and Langston Hughes, Rolfe became a contributor to the movement's cultural front, submitting poetry to *New Masses*, the *Anvil*, and *Partisan Review*. His first book, *To My Contemporaries*, was published by Dynamo Press in 1936. With the outbreak of the Spanish Civil War in 1937, Rolfe's internationalist sympathies were drawn to the struggle against Franco's fascism. Rolfe joined the Abraham Lincoln Brigade, serving first as editor of the brigade's Madrid-based paper, *Volunteer for Liberty*, and then as a fighter at the front. As Rolfe's friend, poet Thomas McGrath wrote in his foreword to the post-humous collection, *Permit Me Refuge* (1955): "[Rolfe] was not just a writer, he fought for his belief. . . . He believed that the word must become flesh, that saying and doing must become one."

On his return from Spain in 1939, Rolfe published a history of the brigade entitled *The Lincoln Battalion*, then worked for the Soviet news agency TASS for several years. His political commitments were tested again in the late 1940s, when, after a move to Los Angeles and some initial success in writing for the movies, he was named a communist before the House Un-American Activities Committee (HUAC) investigating the "red menace" in Hollywood. Rolfe was blacklisted and for the rest of his life engaged in opposition to the inquisition, writing a series of powerful anti-McCarthy poems that no publisher of the time dared print. He was still being summoned to testify before HUAC, and refusing, when he died of a heart attack in 1954. The poems that follow illuminate, with subtle dramatic irony, the currents of suspicion and persecution that lay beneath the apparently placid surface of the 1950s. "Are You Now or Have You Ever Been" a member of the Communist Party was, of course, HUAC's "sixty-four-dollar question." Rolfe's *Collected Poems* were published in 1993 by the University of Illinois Press.

ARE YOU NOW OR HAVE YOU EVER BEEN

I admit it: there was a moment of pity
a vulnerable second of sympathy
my defenses were down
and I signed the letter asking clemency
5   for the six Negroes the letter
hereinafter known as Exhibit A

I signed the letter yes
the signature is indubitably mine
and later this at another time
10   I wrote a small check yes small
since my income is small
perhaps ten dollars not more
for the fund these people were collecting
to keep the refugees alive
15   and then again in a moment of weakness
I promised and kept my promise
to join the demonstration at the city hall

protesting the raising of rents
no you needn't show me the photograph
20   I was there I admit I was there

but please believe me
everything I did was done through weakness if you will
but it's strange how weakness of this kind snowballs
multiplies
25   before they approached me with that innocent petition
I was may it please the court exactly
like you like every other man
I lived my own life solely suffered
only my own sorrows and enjoyed my own triumphs
30   small ones I grant you
asked nothing from
gave nothing to
any man
except myself my wife my children
35   so there you have it
it is all true
Exhibits A and B and C
and the witnesses don't lie
I wanted to help those six men stay alive
40   I thought them innocent
I honestly believed the rents were too high
(no, I own no tenements)
and the anguish of the refugees starving far from home
moved me I admit more than it should have
45   perhaps because I still retain
a fleeting childhood picture of my great grandfather's face
he too was a refugee

LITTLE BALLAD FOR AMERICANS, 1954

Brother, brother, best avoid your workmate—
Words planted in affection can spout a field of hate.

Housewife, housewife, never trust your neighbor—
A chance remark may boomerang to five years at hard labor.

5   Student, student, keep your mouth shut and brain spry—
Your best friend Dick Merriwell's employed by the F.B.I.

Lady, lady, make your phone calls frugal—
The chief of all Inquisitors has ruled the wire-tap legal.

Daughter, daughter, learn soon your heart to harden—
10   They've planted stoolies everywhere; why not in kindergarten?

Lovers, lovers, be careful when you're wed—
The wire-tap grows in living-room, in auto, and in bed.

Give full allegiance only to circuses and bread;
No person's really trustworthy until he's dead.

Thomas McGrath (1916–1990)

Thomas McGrath was born near Sheldon, North Dakota, the eldest of six children. His Irish Catholic parents were the second generation of farmers on land that the family would not own until after World War II. Both his grandfathers had been laborers building the western railroads. McGrath attended local schools, earned a BA from the University of North Dakota in 1939, and was awarded a Rhodes Scholarship to Oxford University. Unable to take up this scholarship until after the war, McGrath earned an MA in English from Louisiana State University and then spent a year teaching in Maine. He moved to New York City, where he earned a living as a welder in the shipyards, among the radical workers to whom he would later dedicate his first book of poems, *Longshot O'Leary's Garland of Practical Poesie* (1949). From 1942 to 1945, McGrath served in the U.S. Army Air Force; from 1947–1948 he studied at Oxford; and in 1951 he took a position teaching at Los Angeles State University. In 1954, he was called to testify before the House Un-American Activities Committee (HUAC). Citing Blake, Shelley, and Garcia Lorca, McGrath told HUAC: "Poets have been notorious non-cooperators where committees of this sort are concerned. . . . I do not wish to bring dishonor upon my tribe." Fired by Louisiana State University for his refusal to give the names of his socialist friends, McGrath was blacklisted for the rest of the 1950s. In 1962, he returned to the northern Great Plains to teach at the University of North Dakota, Fargo, and from 1969 until his retirement in 1983, he taught at Moorhead State University, Minnesota.

Greatly admired by other poets—Philip Levine calls him "the most significant teacher in my life as a poet"—McGrath has not been widely read in the mainstream English curriculum, which is averse to poetry of political commitment. What McGrath describes as his "unaffiliated far-left political feelings" have their roots in the prairie populism of his upbringing, as well as his years as an organizer among industrial workers, for whom many of his poems of protest and praise, his elegies and rhymed parodies, were written. His work combines a sense of outrage with an ironist's humor and the deep tenderness demonstrated in a poem like "On the Memory of a Working-Class Girl." McGrath published mainly in small journals—from Jack Conroy's *New Anvil* to the journal *Crazyhorse*, which he founded in 1960—and his seventeen books of poetry issued from small presses. His work is collected in *The Movie at the End of the World* (Swallow Press, 1973) and *Selected Poems, 1938–1988* (Copper Canyon Press, 1988). *Letter to an Imaginary Friend*, a book-length poem in four parts, was first published in its entirety in 1997.

A Long Way Outside Yellowstone

Across the tracks in Cheyenne, behind the biggest billboard,
Are a couple of human beings who aren't in for the Rodeo.
A week out of Sacramento, Jack, who was once a choir boy,
And Judy, a jail-bird's daughter, make love against the cold.
5   He gets the night freight for Denver. She hitches out for Billings.
But now under one blanket they go about their business.
Suppose you go about yours. Their business is being human.
And because they travel naked they are fifty jumps ahead of you
And running with all their lights on while half the world is blacked out.

10   Poverty of all but spirit turns up love like aces
     That weren't in the deck at all.
                              Meanwhile the cold
     Is scattered like petals of flowers down from the mountains of exile
     And makes comradeship essential, though perhaps you choose not to believe it.
15   That doesn't matter at all, for their hands touching deny you,
     Becoming, poor blinded beggars, pilgrims on the road to heaven.

     Back in the Park, at the best hotel, it is true
     The mountains are higher, and the food oftener, and love
     As phony as a nine-dollar bill. Though perhaps
20   When the millionaire kisses the Princess farewell (he's going nowhere)
     She weeps attractively in the expensive dark, moving—
     O delicately—among the broken hearts, perhaps haunted,
     Wondering if hers is among them. Or perhaps not.

                                                     Cheyenne, Wyoming, 1940

ARS POETICA: OR: WHO LIVES IN THE IVORY TOWER?

     Perhaps you'd like a marching song for the embattled prolet-
          ariat, or a realistic novel, the hopeful poet
     Said, or a slice of actual life with the hot red heart's blood running,
     The simple tale of a working stiff, but better than Jack London?

5   Nobody wants your roundelay, nobody wants your sestina,
     Said the housewife, we want Hedy Lamarr and Gable at the cinema,
     Get out of my technicolor dream with your tragic view and your verses;
     Down with iambic pentameter and hurray for Louella Parsons.

     Of course you're free to write as you please, the liberal editor answered,
10   But take the red flags out of your poem—we mustn't offend the censor—
     And change this stanza to mean the reverse, and you must tone down this passage;
     Thank God for the freedom of the press and a poem with a message!

     Life is lousy enough without you should put it into a sonnet,
     Said the man in the street, so keep it out of the novel, the poem, the drama;
15   Give us a paean of murder and rape, or the lay of a willing maiden,
     And to hell with the Bard of Avalon and to hell with Eliot Auden.

     Recite the damn things all day long, get drunk on smoke come Sunday,
     I respect your profession as much as my own, but it don't pay off when you're hungry;
     You'll have to carry the banner instead—said the hobo in the jungle—
20   If you want to eat; and don't forget: it's my bridge you're sleeping under.

     Oh it's down with art and down with life and give us another reefer—
     They all said—give us a South Sea isle, where light my love lies dreaming;
     And who is that poet come in off the streets with a look unleal and lour?
     Your feet are muddy, you son-of-a-bitch, get out of our ivory tower.

A LITTLE SONG ABOUT CHARITY

(Tune of Matty Grove)

The boss came around at Christmas—
Oh smiling like a lamb—
He made me a present of a pair of gloves
And then cut off my hands—
5   Oh and then cut off my hands.

The boss came around on my birthday
With some shoes of a rich man's brand.
He smiled like a priest and he cut off my feet
Then he said: "Go out and dance"—
10   Oh he said: "Go out and dance."

The boss came around on May Day.
He said: "You may parade."
Then his cops shot us down in the open street
And they clubbed us into jail—
15   Oh they clubbed us into jail.

The preacher says on Sunday:
"Turn ye the other cheek."
Don't turn it to the boss on Monday morn:
He may knock out all your teeth—
20   Oh he may knock out your teeth.

So listen to me workers:
When the boss seems kind and good
Remember that the stain on the cutting tool
Is nothing but your blood—
25   Oh it's nothing but your blood.

If you love your wife and daughters,
And if you love your sons,
And if you love the working class
Then keep your love at home.
30   Don't waste it on the cockroach boss
But keep your love at home.

ON THE MEMORY OF A WORKING-CLASS GIRL

You run in the ruined light, bare-headed, lovely.
A stain of evening sun grows golden on your hair.
Under those flashing feet the streets of winter
Catch color as you go. Behind your shoulder
5   The riding shadows, misery of the years,
Seem kindly graces lured by that calm beauty
Filling your face, which at the tenement stair,
Turns on its stalk toward the wishing star.

Only a painter could keep you as you are:
10   Lovely and real, in the too-real doorway:
Keep you and the light from changing—like the running streets
Which under your feet run into the dark and the years.
If you could stay picture-perfect like that forever
I could forget you now—or if you were rich:
15   To wear the world, command the streets, your life—
But because you are not, I must give my love.

Wishing will change you. It will not change you enough
And you will change against your wishes: leaving
The girl who ran in the ruined slum of evening
20   For something other. Time is bourgeois—his
Best wish is for those who have—and though he ruin
All lives, both rich and poor, he doubly thus
Ruins your unwished one. No one, my dear,
Nothing can hold you, not even love hold back
25   The unwished horses of these riding years.

O'LEARY'S LAST WISH: IN CASE THE REVOLUTION SHOULD FAIL

I want to be buried in Arlington Cemetery,
Somewhere at the patriotic center of the American Death,
With my bones full of the sleepy dynamite of the class struggle
And the time-bomb of the century under my private's shirt.

5   I want to lie there and tick like a pulse among the defunct
Heroes, the quiet deserters of their own body and blood—
The ones who stood on expensive roads in the total shell fire of money
Being cut off at the balls for their own and the public good.

I'll be there, the anti-bourgeois neutrino of the irreconcilable proletariat,
10   Among the tame terrene charges of those patriotic stiffs.
Contra-Destiny Factors ring midnight, but there's no gold in their veins;
Cock crow chimes thrice. Reveille. No one is stirring yet

But under the ghost-overgrown honortabs to the wars,
The real estate and spirit-money my fellow-death-workers have won,
15   Is the Word of the Four Last Things of the Working Class, the rumored
Revolution of the Dead which Heaven, and the Boss, want put down.

Nevertheless, I'm still here, Hell's partisan, with my anti-god bomb,
Agitating toward the day when these stony dead
Shall storm up out of the ground in their chalky battalions
20   To judge wars, Presidents, Fates, God and His Own Elect.

Tillie Olsen*

I Stand Here Ironing

I stand here ironing, and what you asked me moves tormented back and forth with the iron.

"I wish you would manage the time to come in and talk with me about your daughter. I'm sure you can help me understand her. She's a youngster who needs help and whom I'm deeply interested in helping."

"Who needs help." . . . Even if I came, what good would it do? You think because I am her mother I have a key, or that in some way you could use me as a key? She has lived for nineteen years. There is all that life that has happened outside of me, beyond me.

And when is there time to remember, to sift, to weigh, to estimate, to total? I will start and there will be an interruption and I will have to gather it all together again. Or I will become engulfed with all I did or did not do, with what should have been and what cannot be helped.

She was a beautiful baby. The first and only one of our five that was beautiful at birth. You do not guess how new and uneasy her tenancy in her now-loveliness. You did not know her all those years she was thought homely, or see her poring over her baby pictures, making me tell her over and over how beautiful she had been—and would be, I would tell her—and was now, to the seeing eye. But the seeing eyes were few or non-existent. Including mine.

I nursed her. They feel that's important nowadays. I nursed all the children, but with her, with all the fierce rigidity of first motherhood, I did like the books then said. Though her cries battered me to trembling and my breasts ached with swollenness, I waited till the clock decreed.

Why do I put that first? I do not even know if it matters, or if it explains anything.

She was a beautiful baby. She blew shining bubbles of sound. She loved motion, loved light, loved color and music and textures. She would lie on the floor in her blue overalls patting the surface so hard in ecstasy her hands and feet would blur. She was a miracle to me, but when she was eight months old I had to leave her daytimes with the woman downstairs to whom she was no miracle at all, for I worked or looked for work and for Emily's father, who "could no longer endure" (he wrote in his good-bye note) "sharing want with us."

I was nineteen. It was the pre-relief, pre-WPA world of the depression. I would start running as soon as I got off the streetcar, running up the stairs, the place smelling sour, and awake or asleep to startle awake, when she saw me she would break into a clogged weeping that could not be comforted, a weeping I can hear yet.

After a while I found a job hashing at night so I could be with her days, and it was better. But it came to where I had to bring her to his family and leave her.

It took a long time to raise the money for her fare back. Then she got chicken pox and I had to wait longer. When she finally came, I hardly knew her, walking quick and

---

* See note on Tillie Olsen, page 461.

nervous like her father, looking like her father, thin, and dressed in a shoddy red that yellowed her skin and glared at the pockmarks. All the baby loveliness gone.

She was two. Old enough for nursery school they said, and I did not know then what I know now—the fatigue of the long day, and the lacerations of group life in the kinds of nurseries that are only parking places for children.

Except that it would have made no difference if I had known. It was the only place there was. It was the only way we could be together, the only way I could hold a job.

And even without knowing, I knew. I knew the teacher that was evil because all these years it has curdled into my memory, the little boy hunched in the corner, her rasp, "why aren't you outside, because Alvin hits you? that's no reason, go out, scaredy." I knew Emily hated it even if she did not clutch and implore "don't go Mommy" like the other children, mornings.

She always had a reason why we should stay home. Momma, you look sick, Momma. I feel sick. Momma, the teachers aren't there today, they're sick. Momma, we can't go, there was a fire there last night. Momma, it's a holiday today, no school, they told me.

But never a direct protest, never rebellion. I think of our others in their three-, four-year-oldness—the explosions, the tempers, the denunciations, the demands—and I feel suddenly ill. I put the iron down. What in me demanded that goodness in her? And what was the cost, the cost to her of such goodness?

The old man living in the back once said in his gentle way: "You should smile at Emily more when you look at her." What *was* in my face when I looked at her? I loved her. There were all the acts of love.

It was only with the others I remembered what he said, and it was the face of joy, and not of care or tightness or worry I turned to them—too late for Emily. She does not smile easily, let alone almost always as her brothers and sisters do. Her face is closed and sombre, but when she wants, how fluid. You must have seen it in her pantomimes, you spoke of her rare gift for comedy on the stage that rouses a laughter out of the audience so dear they applaud and applaud and do not want to let her go.

Where does it come from, that comedy? There was none of it in her when she came back to me that second time, after I had had to send her away again. She had a new daddy now to learn to love, and I think perhaps it was a better time.

Except when we left her alone nights, telling ourselves she was old enough.

"Can't you go some other time, Mommy, like tomorrow?" she would ask. "Will it be just a little while you'll be gone? Do you promise?"

The time we came back, the front door open, the clock on the floor in the hall. She rigid awake. "It wasn't just a little while. I didn't cry. Three times I called you, just three times, and then I ran downstairs to open the door so you could come faster. The clock talked loud. I threw it away, it scared me what it talked."

She said the clock talked loud again that night I went to the hospital to have Susan. She was delirious with the fever that comes before red measles, but she was fully conscious all the week I was gone and the week after we were home when she could not come near the new baby or me.

She did not get well. She stayed skeleton thin, not wanting to eat, and night after night she had nightmares. She would call for me, and I would rouse from exhaustion to sleepily call back: "You're all right, darling, go to sleep, it's just a dream," and if she still called, in a sterner voice, "now go to sleep, Emily, there's nothing to hurt you." Twice, only twice, when I had to get up for Susan anyhow, I went in to sit with her.

Now when it is too late (as if she would let me hold and comfort her like I do the others) I get up and go to her at once at her moan or restless stirring. "Are you awake, Emily? Can I get you something?" And the answer is always the same: "No, I'm all right, go back to sleep, Mother."

They persuaded me at the clinic to send her away to a convalescent home in the country where "she can have the kind of food and care you can't manage for her, and you'll be free to concentrate on the new baby." They still send children to that place. I see pictures on the society page of sleek young women planning affairs to raise money for it, or dancing at the affairs, or decorating Easter eggs or filling Christmas stockings for the children.

They never have a picture of the children so I do not know if the girls still wear those gigantic red bows and the ravaged looks on the every other Sunday when parents can come to visit "unless otherwise notified"—as we were notified the first six weeks.

Oh it is a handsome place, green lawns and tall trees and fluted flower beds. High up on the balconies of each cottage the children stand, the girls in their red bows and white dresses, the boys in white suits and giant red ties. The parents stand below shrieking up to be heard, and the children shriek down to be heard, and between them the invisible wall "Not To Be Contaminated by Parental Germs or Physical Affection."

There was a tiny girl who always stood hand in hand with Emily. Her parents never came. One visit she was gone. "They moved her to Rose Cottage" Emily shouted in explanation. "They don't like you to love anybody here."

She wrote once a week, the labored writing of a seven-year-old. "I am fine. How is the baby. If I write my leter nicly I will have a star. Love." There never was a star. We wrote every other day, letters she could never hold or keep but only hear read—once. "We simply do not have room for children to keep any personal possessions," they patiently explained when we pieced one Sunday's shrieking together to plead how much it would mean to Emily, who loved so to keep things, to be allowed to keep her letters and cards.

Each visit she looked frailer. "She isn't eating," they told us.

(They had runny eggs for breakfast or mush with lumps, Emily said later, I'd hold it in my mouth and not swallow. Nothing ever tasted good, just when they had chicken.)

It took us eight months to get her released home, and only the fact that she gained back so little of her seven lost pounds convinced the social worker.

I used to try to hold and love her after she came back, but her body would stay stiff, and after a while she'd push away. She ate little. Food sickened her, and I think much of life too. Oh she had physical lightness and brightness, twinkling by on skates, bouncing like a ball up and down up and down over the jump rope, skimming over the hill; but these were momentary.

She fretted about her appearance, thin and dark and foreign-looking at a time when every little girl was supposed to look or thought she should look a chubby blonde replica of Shirley Temple. The doorbell sometimes rang for her, but no one seemed to come and play in the house or be a best friend. Maybe because we moved so much.

There was a boy she loved painfully through two school semesters. Months later she told me how she had taken pennies from my purse to buy him candy. "Licorice was his favorite and I brought him some every day, but he still liked Jennifer better'n me. Why, Mommy?" The kind of question for which there is no answer.

School was a worry to her. She was not glib or quick in a world where glibness and quickness were easily confused with ability to learn. To her overworked and exasperated teachers she was an overconscientious "slow learner" who kept trying to catch up and was absent entirely too often.

I let her be absent, though sometimes the illness was imaginary. How different from my now-strictness about attendance with the others. I wasn't working. We had a new baby, I was home anyhow. Sometimes, after Susan grew old enough, I would keep her home from school, too, to have them all together.

Mostly Emily had asthma, and her breathing, harsh and labored, would fill the house with a curiously tranquil sound. I would bring the two old dresser mirrors and her boxes of collections to her bed. She would select beads and single earrings, bottle tops and shells, dried flowers and pebbles, old postcards and scraps, all sorts of oddments; then she and Susan would play Kingdom, setting up landscapes and furniture, peopling them with action.

Those were the only times of peaceful companionship between her and Susan. I have edged away from it, that poisonous feeling between them, that terrible balancing of hurts and needs I had to do between the two, and did so badly, those earlier years.

Oh there are conflicts between the others too, each one human, needing, demanding, hurting, taking—but only between Emily and Susan, no, Emily toward Susan that corroding resentment. It seems so obvious on the surface, yet it is not obvious. Susan, the second child, Susan, golden- and curly-haired and chubby, quick and articulate and assured, everything in appearance and manner Emily was not; Susan, not able to resist Emily's precious things, losing or sometimes clumsily breaking them; Susan telling jokes and riddles to company for applause while Emily sat silent (to say to me later: that was *my* riddle, Mother, I told it to Susan); Susan, who for all the five years' difference in age was just a year behind Emily in developing physically.

I am glad for that slow physical development that widened the difference between her and her contemporaries, though she suffered over it. She was too vulnerable for that terrible world of youthful competition, of preening and parading, of constant measuring of yourself against every other, of envy, "If I had that copper hair," "If I had that skin. . . ." She tormented herself enough about not looking like the others, there was enough of the unsureness, the having to be conscious of words before you speak, the constant caring—what are they thinking of me? without having it all magnified by the merciless physical drives.

Ronnie is calling. He is wet and I change him. It is rare there is such a cry now. That time of motherhood is almost behind me when the ear is not one's own but must always be racked and listening for the child cry, the child call. We sit for a while and I hold him, looking out over the city spread in charcoal with its soft aisles of light. "*Shoogily*," he breathes and curls closer. I carry him back to bed, asleep. *Shoogily*. A funny word, a family word, inherited from Emily, invented by her to say: *comfort*.

In this and other ways she leaves her seal, I say aloud. And startle at my saying it. What do I mean? What did I start to gather together, to try and make coherent? I was at the terrible, growing years. War years. I do not remember them well. I was working, there were four smaller ones now, there was not time for her. She had to help be a mother, and housekeeper, and shopper. She had to set her seal. Mornings of crisis and near hysteria trying to get lunches packed, hair combed, coats and shoes found, everyone to school or Child Care on time, the baby ready for transportation. And always the paper scribbled on by a smaller one, the book looked at by Susan then mislaid, the homework not done. Running out to that huge school where she was one, she was lost, she was a drop; suffering over the unpreparedness, stammering and unsure in her classes.

There was so little time left at night after the kids were bedded down. She would struggle over books, always eating (it was in those years she developed her enormous appetite that is legendary in our family) and I would be ironing, or preparing food for the next day, or writing V-mail to Bill, or tending the baby. Sometimes, to make me laugh, or out of her despair, she would imitate happenings or types at school.

I think I said once: "Why don't you do something like this in the school amateur show?" One morning she phoned me at work, hardly understandable through the weeping: "Mother, I did it. I won, I won; they gave me first prize; they clapped and clapped and wouldn't let me go."

Now suddenly she was Somebody, and as imprisoned in her difference as she had been in anonymity.

She began to be asked to perform at other high schools, even in colleges, then at city and statewide affairs. The first one we went to, I only recognized her that first moment when thin, shy, she almost drowned herself into the curtains. Then: Was this Emily? The control, the command, the convulsing and deadly clowning, the spell, then the roaring, stamping audience, unwilling to let this rare and precious laughter out of their lives.

Afterwards: You ought to do something about her with a gift like that—but without money or knowing how, what does one do? We have left it all to her, and the gift has as often eddied inside, clogged and clotted, as been used and growing.

She is coming. She runs up the stairs two at a time with her light graceful step, and I know she is happy tonight. Whatever it was that occasioned your call did not happen today.

"Aren't you ever going to finish the ironing, Mother? Whistler painted his mother in a rocker. I'd have to paint mine standing over an ironing board." This is one of her communicative nights and she tells me everything and nothing as she fixes herself a plate of food out of the icebox.

She is so lovely. Why did you want me to come in at all? Why were you concerned? She will find her way.

She starts up the stairs to bed. "Don't get me up with the rest in the morning." "But I thought you were having midterms." "Oh, those," she comes back in, kisses me, and says quite lightly, "in a couple of years when we'll all be atom-dead they won't matter a bit."

She has said it before. She *believes* it. But because I have been dredging the past, and all that compounds a human being is so heavy and meaningful in me, I cannot endure it tonight.

I will never total it all. I will never come in to say: She was a child seldom smiled at. Her father left me before she was a year old. I had to work her first six years when there was work, or I sent her home and to his relatives. There were years she had care she hated. She was dark and thin and foreign-looking in a world where the prestige went to blonde-ness and curly hair and dimples, she was slow where glibness was prized. She was a child of anxious, not proud, love. We were poor and could not afford for her the soil of easy growth. I was a young mother, I was a distracted mother. There were the other children pushing up, demanding. Her younger sister seemed all that she was not. There were years she did not want me to touch her. She kept too much in herself, her life was such she had to keep too much in herself. My wisdom came too late. She has much to her and probably little will come of it. She is a child of her age, of depression, of war, of fear.

Let her be. So all that is in her will not bloom—but in how many does it? There is still enough left to live by. Only help her to know—help make it so there is cause for her to know—that she is more than this dress on the ironing board, helpless before the iron.

Gwendolyn Brooks (1917–2000)

Born in Topeka, Kansas, Gwendolyn Brooks grew up on the South Side of Chicago in the black community that would become "Bronzeville" in the remarkable poetry she went on to create. Her mother had been an elementary school teacher, and her father, the son of an escaped slave, worked as a janitor. Both parents were readers and storytellers—their home contained the work of Paul Lawrence Dunbar and *Anne of Green Gables*, as well as a prized set of the Harvard Classics—and their daughter's love of writing and literature developed early. At age thirteen, Brooks had a poem published in a children's magazine, and at age seventeen, she was writing a poetry column for the *Chicago Defender*, a leading African American newspaper. Church was an important center of family and community life, and it was at church that she first met Langston Hughes, who became a mentor and, in some ways, a model. After graduating from Wilson Junior College, Brooks tried for a job at the *Defender*, and failing that, spent miserable months working as a maid for a well-to-do North Shore family and then as a typist for the pastor of a storefront church. These experiences are combined with matter-of-fact observation of the lives around her in her first book *A Street in Bronzeville* (1945), which drew immediate attention, leading to a Guggenheim Fellowship. Brooks's second book, *Annie Allen*, which explores the growth into married womanhood of a Bronzeville girl who is marked by poverty and loss, won the Pulitzer Prize for poetry in 1950, the first awarded to an African American writer.

In the fifty years that followed, during which Brooks became perhaps the country's foremost black woman poet, she remained engaged with her urban community, drawing stories and characters from happenings in its streets and homes. As a teacher, workshop leader, and small-press publisher, she supported the development of fellow black writers and artists. She had a special commitment to young people: running a writing workshop for the Blackstone Rangers street gang in the 1960s; sponsoring poetry events and contests in Chicago public schools; and writing several books for children, including *Bronzeville Boys and Girls* (1956) and *Young Poets Primer* (1981). Her poetry draws on a range of traditions: European sonnets and ballads; American innovators, such as Walt Whitman and Emily Dickinson; the free verse movement; the rhythms of jazz; and the cadences of black preaching. Through successive changes in poetic form, she has crafted a voice that is recognizably "Gwendolynian," as she puts it, and that succeeds in being both accessible and challenging to its wide audiences. In addition to many books of poetry, Brooks was the author of the acclaimed experimental novel *Maud Martha* (1953) and two volumes of autobiography, *Report from Part One* (1972) and *Report from Part Two* (1997). In 1968, she became the poet laureate of Illinois, succeeding Carl Sandburg. By the time of her death in 2000, she had received more than seventy-five honorary doctorates.

BRONZEVILLE WOMAN IN A RED HAT

hires out to Mrs. Miles

I

They had never had one in the house before.
   The strangeness of it all. Like unleashing
A lion, really. Poised
To pounce. A puma. A panther. A black
5   Bear.
There it stood in the door,
Under a red hat that was rash, but refreshing—
In a tasteless way, of course—across the dull dare,
The semi-assault of that extraordinary blackness.
10   The slackness
Of that light pink mouth told little. The eyes told of heavy care. . . .
But that was neither here nor there,
And nothing to a wage-paying mistress as should
Be getting her due whether life had been good

15   For her slave, or bad.
     There it stood
     In the door. They had never had
     One in the house before.

     But the Irishwoman had left!
20   A message had come.
     Something about a murder at home.
     A daughter's husband—"berserk," that was the phrase:
     The dear man had "gone berserk"
     And short work—
25   With a hammer—had been made
     Of this daughter and her nights and days.
     The Irishwoman (underpaid,
     Mrs. Miles remembered with smiles),
     Who was a perfect jewel, a red-faced trump,
30   A good old sort, a baker
     Of rum cake, a maker
     Of mustard, would never return.
     Mrs. Miles had begged the bewitched woman
     To finish, at least, the biscuit blending,
35   To tarry till the curry was done,
     To show some concern
     For the burning soup, to attend to the tending
     Of the tossed salad. "Inhuman,"
     Patsy Houlihan had called Mrs. Miles.
40   "Inhuman." And "a fool."
     And "a cool
     One."

     The Alert Agency had leafed through its files—
     On short notice could offer
45   Only this dusky duffer
     That now made its way to her kitchen and sat on her kitchen stool.

II

     Her creamy child kissed by the black maid! square on the mouth!
     World yelled, world writhed, world turned to light and rolled
     Into her kitchen, nearly knocked her down.

50   Quotations, of course, from baby books were great
     Ready armor; (but her animal distress
     Wore, too and under, a subtler metal dress,
     Inheritance of approximately hate.)
     Say baby shrieked to see his finger bleed,
55   Wished human humoring—there was a kind
     Of unintimate love, a love more of the mind
     To order the nebulousness of that need.
     —This was the way to put it, this the relief.
     This sprayed a honey upon marvelous grime.
60   This told it possible to postpone the reef.

Fashioned a huggable darling out of crime.
Made monster personable in personal sight
By cracking mirrors down the personal night.

Disgust crawled through her as she chased the theme.
65   She, quite supposing purity despoiled,
Committed to sourness, disordered, soiled,
Went in to pry the ordure from the cream.
Cooing, "Come." (Come out of the cannibal wilderness,
Dirt, dark, into the sun and bloomful air.
70   Return to freshness of your right world, wear
Sweetness again. Be done with beast, duress.)

Child with continuing cling issued his No in final fire,
Kissed back the colored maid,
Not wise enough to freeze or be afraid.
75   Conscious of kindness, easy creature bond.
Love had been handy and rapid to respond.

Heat at the hairline, heat between the bowels,
Examining seeming coarse unnatural scene,
She saw all things except herself serene:
80   Child, big black woman, pretty kitchen towels.

THE BALLAD OF RUDOLPH REED

Rudolph Reed was oaken.
His wife was oaken too.
And his two good girls and his good little man
Oakened as they grew.

5   "I am not hungry for berries.
I am not hungry for bread.
But hungry hungry for a house
Where at night a man in bed

"May never hear the plaster
10   Stir as if in pain.
May never hear the roaches
Falling like fat rain.

"Where never wife and children need
Go blinking through the gloom.
15   Where every room of many rooms
Will be full of room.

"Oh my home may have its east or west
Or north or south behind it.
All I know is I shall know it,
20   And fight for it when I find it."

It was in a street of bitter white
That he made his application.
For Rudolph Reed was oakener
Than others in the nation.

25   The agent's steep and steady stare
Corroded to a grin.
Why, you black old, tough old hell of a man,
Move your family in!

Nary a grin grinned Rudolph Reed,
30   Nary a curse cursed he,
But moved in his House. With his dark little wife,
And his dark little children three.

A neighbor would *look*, with a yawning eye
That squeezed into a slit.
35   But the Rudolph Reeds and the children three
Were too joyous to notice it.

For were they not firm in a home of their own
With windows everywhere
And a beautiful banistered stair
40   And a front yard for flowers and a back yard for grass?

The first night, a rock, big as two fists.
The second, a rock big as three.
But nary a curse cursed Rudolph Reed.
(Though oaken as man could be.)

45   The third night, a silvery ring of glass.
Patience ached to endure.
But he looked, and lo! small Mabel's blood
Was staining her gaze so pure.

Then up did rise our Rudolph Reed
50   And pressed the hand of his wife,
And went to the door with a thirty-four
And a beastly butcher knife.

He ran like a mad thing into the night.
And the words in his mouth were stinking.
55   By the time he had hurt his first white man
He was no longer thinking.

By the time he had hurt his fourth white man
Rudolph Reed was dead.
His neighbors gathered and kicked his corpse.
60   "Nigger—" his neighbors said.

Small Mabel whimpered all night long,
For calling herself the cause.
Her oak-eyed mother did no thing
But change the bloody gauze.

The Blackstone Rangers

I

As Seen by Disciplines

There they are
Thirty at the corner.
Black, raw, ready.
Sores in the city
5　that do not want to heal.

II

The Leaders

Jeff. Gene. Geronimo. And Bop.
They cancel, cure and curry.
Hardly the dupes of the downtown thing
the cold bonbon,
10　the rhinestone thing. And hardly
in a hurry.
Hardly Belafonte, King,
Black Jesus, Stokely, Malcolm X or Rap.
Bungled trophies.
15　Their country is a Nation on no map.

Jeff, Gene, Geronimo and Bop
in the passionate noon,
in bewitching night
are the detailed men, the copious men.
20　They curry, cure,
they cancel, cancelled images whose Concerts
are not divine, vivacious; the different tins
are intense last entries; pagan argument;
translations of the night.

25　The Blackstone bitter bureaus
(bureaucracy is footloose) edit, fuse
unfashionable damnations and descent;
and exulting, monstrous hand on monstrous hand,
construct, strangely, a monstrous pearl or grace.

III

Gang Girls

A Rangerette

30　Gang Girls are sweet exotics.
Mary Ann
uses the nutrients of her orient,
but sometimes sighs for Cities of blue and jewel
beyond her Ranger rim of Cottage Grove.
35　(Bowery Boys, Disciples, Whip-Birds will
dissolve no margins, stop no savory sanctities.)

Mary is
a rose in a whiskey glass.

Mary's
40   Februaries shudder and are gone. Aprils
fret frankly, lilac hurries on.
Summer is a hard irregular ridge.
October looks away.
And that's the Year!
45   Save for her bugle-love.
Save for the bleat of not-obese devotion.
Save for Somebody Terribly Dying, under
the philanthropy of robins. Save for her Ranger
bringing
50   an amount of rainbow in a string-drawn bag.
"Where did you get the diamond?" Do not ask:
but swallow, straight, the spirals of his flask
and assist him at your zipper; pet his lips
and help him clutch you.

55   Love's another departure.
Will there be any arrivals, confirmations?
Will there be gleaning?

Mary, the Shakedancer's child
from the rooming-flat, pants carefully, peers at
60   her laboring lover. . . .
        Mary! Mary Ann!
Settle for sandwiches! settle for stocking caps!
for sudden blood, aborted carnival,
the props and niceties of non-loneliness—
the rhymes of Leaning.

———

James Wright (1927–1980)

"**W**hen you love a place, really and most hopelessly love it, I think you love it for its signs of disaster, just as you come to realize how you love the particular irregularities and even scars of some person's face," declares James Wright, of the working-class people and landscape of his native Ohio Valley. In fifteen volumes of poetry beginning with his 1957 Yale Younger Poets volume *The Green Wall*, Wright etched portraits of his steel people and places in Martins Ferry, Ohio.

The son of a factory worker, Wright grew to become a Pulitzer Prize winning poet for his *Collected Poems* of 1971. Although he would travel far, he would never cease writing of his Ohio Valley home. His empathy for the people and his ambivalence toward the industrialized land carry throughout his verse. Wright, who played semiprofessional football, says of "Autumn Begins in Martins Ferry, Ohio," his most requested poem, "I know from my own experience that perpetual violence and the representations of violence have threatened my own capacity to feel. Often, through poetry, I've tried to find a way to restore that capacity, to keep it alive."

In the 1950s, Wright attended Kenyon College on a Robert Frost Memorial Scholarship. His years at Kenyon were followed by graduate study at the University of Washington with poets Theodore Rhoethke and Stanley Kunitz. When he was not given a teaching position there, Wright moved on to the University of Minnesota, where he struggled with mental illness and befriended Robert and Carol Bly. His second volume, *Saint Judas*, in which he identifies with the downtrodden and outcast, appeared in 1958.

With the support of Bly and his Sixties Press, Wright began translating poets George Trakl, Cesar Vallejo, Pablo Neruda, Herman Hesse, and Theodore Storm. This helped him to open his verse form and to produce one of his most beautiful books, *The Branch Will Not Break* (1963). It was while he was teaching at New York's Hunter College that he produced his later books, including *Shall We Gather at the River* (1968), *Collected Poems* (1971), *Two Citizens* (1973), and *To a Blossoming Pear Tree* (1977).

Wright never forgot his native land or its working-class people. He died of mouth cancer on March 25, 1980, and several posthumus volumes appeared, including *This Journey* (1982) and *Above the River: The Complete Poems* (1990).

Larry Smith

Autumn Begins in Martins Ferry, Ohio

In the Shreve High football stadium,
I think of Polacks nursing long beers in Tiltonsville,
And gray faces of Negroes in the blast furnace at Benwood,
And the ruptured night watchman of Wheeling Steel,
5 Dreaming of heroes.

All the proud fathers are ashamed to go home.
Their women cluck like starved pullets,
Dying for love.

Therefore,
10 Their sons grow suicidally beautiful
At the beginning of October,
And gallop terribly against each other's bodies.

Honey

My father died at the age of eighty. One of the last things he did in his life was to call his fifty-eight-year-old son-in-law "honey." One afternoon in the early 1930's, when I bloodied my head by pitching over a wall at the bottom of a hill and believed that the mere sight of my own blood was the tragic meaning of life, I heard my father offer to murder his future son-in-law. His son-in-law is my brother-in-law, whose name is Paul. These two grown men rose above me and knew that a human life is murder. They weren't fighting about Paul's love for my sister. They were fighting with each other because one strong man, a factory worker, was laid off from his work, and the other strong man, the driver of a coal truck, was laid off from his work. They were both determined to live their lives, and so they glared at each other and said they were going to live, come hell or high water. High water is not trite in southern Ohio. Nothing is trite along a river. My father died a good death. To die a good death means to live one's life. I don't say a good life.

I say a life.

Judy Grahn (b. 1940)

Born in Chicago, Judy Grahn grew up in a small New Mexico town where she was known as a combination tomboy and poet. "I was a working-class girl—and girl was the word—we had no money, no hope, no future." Unable to afford higher education, she took night jobs, attended trade school, and joined the air force. In the air force, she worked in a military hospital as a nurse's aid and was discharged because of her lesbianism. In 1969, as a member of a women's consciousness-raising group, she wrote seven poems, "The Common Woman Poems." These widely circulated, read, chanted, put-to-music poems reclaimed and honored the word *common* and satisfied a hunger for portraits of ordinary women, who were distinct, yet connected. "Vera, from my childhood" ostensibly about Grahn's mother, spoke to the uncommon and unrecognized strength and beauty of common women and satisfied Grahn's belief that art should be useful to other people.

A pioneering figure, Grahn created, with Pat Parker, one of the first all-women's presses, The Women's Press Collective in California. She personifies the revolutionary spirit of the radical feminist-lesbian movement in the 1970s, of what she describes as "banding together with like-minded people." Winner of a Lambda Literary Award for Lesbian Non-Fiction, her published works include *She Who: A Graphic Book of Poems with 54 Images of Women* (graphics designed by Karen Sjoholm and Wendy Cadden, 1977); *Blood, Bread and Roses: How Menstruation Created the World* (1993); a novel, *Mundane's World* (1988); *Another Mother Tongue: Gay Words, Gay Worlds* (1984); and two edited volumes of *True to Life Adventure Stories* (1978, 1980). Her collected poems, including *Edward the Dyke* (1970), *A Woman Is Talking To Death* (1974), and the poems presented here are in *The Work of a Common Woman* (1964–1977), published with an introduction by Adrienne Rich.

THE COMMON WOMAN

The Common Woman Poems have more than fulfilled my idealistic expectations of art as a useful subject—of art as a doer, rather than a passive object to be admired. All by themselves they went around the country. Spurred by the enthusiasm of women hungry for realistic pictures, they were reprinted hundreds of thousands of times, were put to music, danced, used to name various women's projects, quoted and then misquoted in a watered-down fashion for use on posters and T-shirts.

Their origin was completely practical: I wanted, in 1969, to read something which described regular, everyday women without making us look either superhuman or pathetic. The closest I could come to finding such an image was a Leonard Cohen song about a whimsical woman named Suzanne, who takes you down to her place by the river. This was on an album of Nina Simone's, and I played that song numberless times during the night I wrote the seven portraits. Oddly, although the song is not a waltz, the poems are. (Try reading them while someone else hums a waltz.) I conceived of them as flexible, self-defining sonnets, seeing that each woman would let me know how many lines were needed to portray her in one long, informative thought.

I paid particular attention to ways of linking them together, and of connecting the facts of their lives with images which called up various natural powers, hoping that these combinations would help break current stereotypes about women and the work we do.

I wanted to accentuate the strengths of their persons without being false about the facts of their lives. To admire them for what they are, already. I still do.

I. HELEN, AT 9 AM, AT NOON, AT 5:15

Her ambition is to be more shiny
and metallic, black and purple as
a thief at midday; trying to make it
in a male form, she's become as
5   stiff as possible.
Wearing trim suits and spike heels,
she says "bust" instead of breast;
somewhere underneath she
misses love and trust, but she feels
10   that spite and malice are the
prices of success. She doesn't realize
yet, that she's missed success, also,
so her smile is sometimes still
genuine. After a while she'll be a real
15   killer, bitter and more wily, better at
pitting the men against each other
and getting the other women fired.
She constantly conspires.
Her grief expresses itself in fits of fury
20   over details, details take the place of meaning,
money takes the place of life.
She believes that people are lice
who eat her, so she bites first; her
thirst increases year by year and by the time
25   the sheen has disappeared from her black hair,
and tension makes her features unmistakably
ugly, she'll go mad. No one in particular
will care. As anyone who's had her for a boss
will know
30   the common woman is as common
as the common crow.

II. ELLA, IN A SQUARE APRON, ALONG HIGHWAY 80

She's a copperheaded waitress,
tired and sharp-worded, she hides
her bad brown tooth behind a wicked
smile, and flicks her ass
5   out of habit, to fend off the pass
that passes for affection.
She keeps her mind the way men
keep a knife—keen to strip the game
down to her size. She has a thin spine,
10   swallows her eggs cold, and tells lies.
She slaps a wet rag at the truck drivers
if they should complain. She understands

the necessity for pain, turns away
the smaller tips, out of pride, and
15   keeps a flask under the counter. Once,
she shot a lover who misused her child.
Before she got out of jail, the courts had pounced
and given the child away. Like some isolated lake,
her flat blue eyes take care of their own stark
20   bottoms. Her hands are nervous, curled, ready
to scrape.
The common woman is as common
as a rattlesnake.

III. NADINE, RESTING ON HER NEIGHBOR'S STOOP

She holds things together, collects bail,
makes the landlord patch the largest holes.
At the Sunday social she would spike
every drink, and offer you half of what she knows,
5   which is plenty. She pokes at the ruins of the city
like an armored tank; but she thinks
of herself as a ripsaw cutting through
knots in wood. Her sentences come out
like thick pine shanks
10   and her big hands fill the air like smoke.
She's a mud-chinked cabin in the slums,
sitting on the doorstep counting
rats and raising 15 children,
half of them her own. The neighborhood
15   would burn itself out without her;
one of these days she'll strike the spark herself.
She's made of grease
and metal, with a hard head
that makes the men around her seem frail.
20   The common woman is as common as
a nail.

IV. CAROL, IN THE PARK, CHEWING ON STRAWS

She has taken a woman lover
whatever shall we do
she has taken a woman lover
how lucky it wasnt you
5   And all the day through she smiles and lies
and grits her teeth and pretends to be shy,
or weak, or busy. Then she goes home
and pounds her own nails, makes her own
bets, and fixes her own car, with her friend.
10   She goes as far
as women can go without protection
from men.
On weekends, she dreams of becoming a tree;

a tree that dreams it is ground up
15　and sent to the paper factory, where it
lies helpless in sheets, until it dreams
of becoming a paper airplane, and rises
on its own current; where it turns into a
bird, a great coasting bird that dreams of becoming
20　more free, even, than that—a feather, finally, or
a piece of air with lightning in it.
　　　she has taken a woman lover
　　　whatever can we say
She walks around all day
25　quietly, but underneath it
she's electric;
angry energy inside a passive form.
The common woman is as common
as a thunderstorm.

V. DETROIT ANNIE, HITCHHIKING

Her words pour out as if her throat were a broken
artery and her mind were cut-glass, carelessly handled.
You imagine her in a huge velvet hat with great
dangling black feathers,
5　but she shaves her head instead
and goes for three-day midnight walks.
Sometimes she goes down to the dock and dances
off the end of it, simply to prove her belief
that people who cannot walk on water
10　are phonies, or dead.
When she is cruel, she is very, very
cool and when she is kind she is lavish.
Fishermen think perhaps she's a fish, but they're all
fools. She figured out that the only way
15　to keep from being frozen was to
stay in motion, and long ago converted
most of her flesh into liquid. Now when she
smells danger, she spills herself all over,
like gasoline, and lights it.
20　She leaves the taste of salt and iron
under your tongue, but you dont mind
The common woman is as common
as the reddest wine.

VI. MARGARET, SEEN THROUGH A PICTURE WINDOW

After she finished her first abortion
she stood for hours and watched it spinning in the
toilet, like a pale stool.
Some distortion of the rubber
5　doctors with their simple tubes and complicated prices,
still makes her feel guilty.
White and yeasty.

All her broken bubbles push her down
into a shifting tide, where her own face
10 floats above her like the whole globe.
She lets her life go off and on
in a slow strobe.
At her last job she was fired for making
strikes, and talking out of turn;
15 now she stays home, a little blue around the edges.
Counting calories and staring at the empty
magazine pages, she hates her shape
and calls herself overweight.
Her husband calls her a big baboon.
20 Lusting for changes, she laughs through her
teeth, and wanders from room to room.
The common woman is as solemn as a monkey
or a new moon.

VII. VERA, FROM MY CHILDHOOD

Solemnly swearing, to swear as an oath to you
who have somehow gotten to be a pale old woman;
swearing, as if an oath could be wrapped around
your shoulders
5 like a new coat:
For your 28 dollars a week and the bastard boss
you never let yourself hate;
and the work, all the work you did at home
where you never got paid;
10 For your mouth that got thinner and thinner
until it disappeared as if you had choked on it,
watching the hard liquor break your fine husband down
into a dead joke.
For the strange mole, like a third eye
15 right in the middle of your forehead;
for your religion which insisted that people
are beautiful golden birds and must be preserved;
for your persistent nerve
and plain white talk—
20 the common woman is as common
as good bread
as common as when you couldnt go on
but did.
For all the world we didnt know we held in common
25 all along
the common woman is as common as the best of bread
and will rise
and will become strong—I swear it to you
I swear it to you on my own head
30 I swear it to you on my common
woman's
head

——————

Breece D'J Pancake (1952–1979)

Breece Dexter Pancake grew up in the small town of Milton, West Virginia. His father "Bud" worked at the Union Carbide chemical plant in South Charleston, where he was a shipping clerk for the last twenty-five years of his life. Father and son hiked, hunted, and fished in the hilly country around their home, where Pancake gathered the intimate sense of the land and the people who worked it that informed the short stories he would go on to write. Pancake left home to attend Marshall University, graduating in 1974 with a degree in English and hopes of a career as either a teacher or a newspaper writer. He taught for the next two years at military academies in Virginia and in 1976 was admitted to the University of Virginia in Charlottesville with a full fellowship in the graduate writing program. At a school that had traditionally served the sons of the southern aristo- cracy, Pancake did not fit in and, in response, may have accentuated what he presented as his "hillbilly" roots. He was admired and supported, however, by notable writers on the faculty and had his first short stories accepted for publication in the prestigious *Atlantic Monthly*. In the proofs for "Trilobites," his name was set up as "D'J," and Pancake decided to adopt the typographical error as part of his pen-name. In April 1979, Pancake took his own life in Charlottesville, not long before his twenty-seventh birthday. His twelve completed stories were collected and published in 1983, evoking comparisons to such masters of the short story as Hemingway, Joyce, Faulkner, and Flannery O'Connor. In the book's Afterword, his teacher John Casey recalled that Pancake "had an authentic sense, even memory, of ways of being he couldn't have known firsthand. It seemed he'd taken in an older generation's experience along with (not in place of) his own." As "The Honored Dead" attests, Pancake had a remarkable gift for rendering the mingled violence and tenderness in the lives of the sons and daughters of his Appalachian home territory.

THE HONORED DEAD

Watching little Lundy go back to sleep, I wish I hadn't told her about the Mound Builders to stop her crying, but I didn't know she would see their eyes watching her in the dark. She was crying about a cat run down by a car—her cat, run down a year ago, only today poor Lundy figured it out. Lundy is turned too much like her momma. Ellen never worries because it takes her too long to catch the point of a thing, and Ellen doesn't have any problem sleeping. I think my folks were a little too keen, but Lundy is her momma's girl, not jumpy like my folks.

My grandfather always laid keenness on his Shawnee blood, his half-breed mother, but then he was hep on blood. He even had an oath to stop bleeding, but I don't remember the words. He was a fair to sharp woodsman, and we all tried to slip up on him at one time or another. It was Ray at the sugar-mill finally caught him, but he was an old man by then, and his mind wasn't exactly right. Ray just came creeping up behind and laid a hand on his shoulder, and the old bird didn't even turn around; he just wagged his head and said, "That's Ray's hand. He's the first fellow ever slipped up on me." Ray could've done without that, because the old man never played with a full deck again, and we couldn't keep clothes on him before he died.

I turn out the lamp, see no eyes in Lundy's room, then it comes to me why she was so scared. Yesterday I told her patches of stories about scalpings and murders, mixed up the Mound Builders with the Shawnee raids, and Lundy chained that with the burial mound in the back pasture. Tomorrow I'll set her straight. The only surefire thing I know about Mound Builders is they must have believed in a God and hereafter or they never would have made such big graves.

I put on my jacket, go into the foggy night, walk toward town. Another hour till dawn, and both lanes of the Pike are empty, so I walk the yellow line running through the valley to Rock Camp. I keep thinking back to the summer me and my buddy Eddie tore that burial mound apart for arrowheads and copper beads gone green with rot. We were getting down to the good stuff, coming up with skulls galore, when of a sudden Grandad showed out of thin air and yelled, "*Wah-pah-nah-te-he*." He was waving his arms around, and I could see Eddie was about to shit the nest. I knew it was all part of the old man's Injun act, so I stayed put, but Eddie sat down like he was ready to surrender.

Grandad kept on: "*Wah-pah-nah-te-he*. You evil. Make bad medicine here. Now put the goddamned bones back or I'll take a switch to your young asses." He watched us bury the bones, then scratched a picture of a man in the dust, a bow drawn, aimed at a crude sun. "Now go home." He walked across the pasture.

Eddie said, "You Red Eagle. Me Black Hawk." I knew he had bought the game for keeps. By then I couldn't tell Eddie that if Grandad had a shot at the sixty-four-dollar question, he would have sold them on those Injun words: *Wah-pah-nah-te-he*—the fat of my ass.

So I walk and try to be like Ellen and count the pass-at-your-own-risk marks on the road. Eastbound tramples Westbound: 26–17. At home is my own darling Ellen, fast asleep, never knowing who won. Sometimes I wonder if Ellen saw Eddie on his last leave. There are lightning bugs in the fog, and I count them until I figure I'm counting the same ones over. For sure, Lundy would call them Mound Builder eyes, and see them as signals without a message, make up her own message, get scared.

I turn off the Pike onto the oxbow of Front Street, walk past some dark store windows, watch myself moving by their gloss, rippling through one pane and another. I sit on the Old Bank steps, wait for the sun to come over the hills; wait like I waited for the bus to the draft physical, only I'm not holding a bar of soap. I sat and held a bar of soap, wondering if I should shove it under my arm to hike my blood pressure into the 4-F range. My blood pressure was already high, but the bar of soap would give me an edge. I look around at Front Street and picture people and places I haven't thought of in years; I wonder if it was that way for Eddie.

I put out my hand like the bar of soap was in it and see its whiteness reflect blue from the streetlights long ago. And I remember Eddie's hand flattened on green felt, arched knuckles cradling the cue for a tough eight-ball shot, or I remember the way his hand curled around his pencil to hide answers on math tests. I remember his hand holding an arrowhead or unscrewing a lug nut, but I can't remember his face.

It was years ago, on Decoration Day, and my father and several other men wore their Ike jackets, and I was in the band. We marched through town to the cemetery in the rain; then I watched the men move sure and stiff with each command, and the timing between volleys was on the nose; the echoes rang four times above the clatter of their bolt weapons. The rain smelled from the tang of their fire, the wet wool of our uniforms. There was a pause and the band director coughed. I stepped up to play, a little off tempo, and another kid across the hills answered my taps. I finished first, snapped my bugle back. When the last tone seeped through to mist, it beat at me, and I could swear I heard the stumps of Eddie's arms beating the coffin lid for us to stop.

I look down at my hand holding the bugle, the bar of soap. I look at my hand, empty, older, tell myself there is no bar of soap in that hand. I count all five fingers with the other hand, tell myself they are going to stay there a hell of a long time. I get out a cigarette and smoke. Out on the Pike, the first car races by in the darkness, knowing no cops are out yet. I think of Eddie pouring on the gas, heading with me down the Pike toward Tin Bridge.

That day was bright, but the blink of all the dome lights showed up far ahead of us. We couldn't keep still for the excitement, couldn't wait to see what happened.

I said, "Did you hear it, man? I thought they'd dropped the Bomb."

"Hear? I felt it. The damn ground shook."

"They won't forget that much noise for a long time."

"For sure."

Cars were stopped dead-center of the road, and a crowd had built up. Eddie pulled off to the side behind a patrol car, then made his way through the crowd, holding his wallet high to show his volunteer fireman's badge. I kept back, but in the break the cops made, I saw the fire was already out, and all that was left of Beck Fuller's Chevy was the grille, the rest of the metal peeled around it from behind. I knew it was Beck's from the '51 grille, and I knew what had happened. Beck fished with dynamite and primer cord, and he was a real sport to the end. Beck could never get into his head he had to keep the cord away from the TNT.

Then a trooper yelled: "All right, make way for the wrecker."

Eddie and the other firemen put pieces of Beck the Sport into bags, and I turned away to keep from barfing, but the smell of burning hair drifted out to me. I knew it was the stuffing in old car-seats, and not Beck, but I leaned against the patrol car, tossed my cookies just the same. I wanted to stop being sick because it was silly to be sick about something like that. Under the noise of my coughings I could hear the fire chief cussing Eddie into just getting the big pieces, just letting the rest go.

Eddie didn't sit here with any bar of soap in his hand. He never had much gray matter, but he made up for it with style, so he would never sit here with any bar of soap in his hand. Eddie would never think about blowing toes away or cutting off his trigger finger. It just was not his way to think. Eddie was the kind who bought into a game early, and when the deal soured, he'd rather hold the hand a hundred years than fold. It was just his way of doing.

At Eight Ball, I chalked up while Eddie broke. The pool balls cracked, but nothing went in, and I moved around the table to pick the choice shot. "It's crazy to join," I said.

"What the hell—I know how to weld. They'll put me in welding school and I'll sit it out in Norfolk."

"With your luck the ship'll fall on you."

"Come on, Eagle, go in buddies with me."

"Me and Ellen's got plans. I'll take a chance with the lottery." I shot, and three went in.

"That's slop," Eddie said.

I ran the other four down, banked the eight ball to a side pocket, and stood back, made myself grin at him. The eight went where I called it, but I never believed I made the shot right, and I didn't look at Eddie, I just grinned.

I toss my cigarette into the gutter, and it glows back orange under the blue streetlight. I think how that glow would be just another eye for Lundy, and think that after a while she will see so many eyes in the night they won't matter anymore. The eyes will go away and never come back, and even if I tell her when she is grown, she won't remember.

By then real eyes will scare her enough. She's Ellen's girl, and sometimes I want to ask Ellen if she saw Eddie on his last leave.

Time ago I stood with my father in the cool evening shadow of the barn to smoke; he stooped, picked up a handful of gravel, and flipped them away with his thumb. He studied on what I said about Canada, and each gravel falling was a little click in his thoughts; then he stood, dusted his palms. "I didn't mind it too much," he said. "Me and Howard kept pretty thick in foxhole religion—never thought of running off."

"But, Dad, when I seen Eddie in that plastic bag . . ."

He yelled: "Why the hell'd you look? If you can't take it, you oughtn't to look. You think I ain't seen that? That and worse, by god."

I rub my hand across my face, hang my arm tight against the back of my neck, think I ought to be home asleep with Ellen. I think, if I was asleep with Ellen, I wouldn't care who won. I wouldn't count or want to know what the signals mean, and I wouldn't be like some dog looking for something dead to drag in.

When Eddie was in boot camp, me and Ellen sat naked in the loft at midnight, scratching fleas and the itch of hay. She went snooping through a box of old books and papers, and pulled out a bundle of letters tied with sea-grass string. Her flashlight beamed over my eyes as she stepped back to me, and watching her walk in the color tracings the light left in my eyes, I knew she would be my wife. She tossed the package in my lap, and I saw the old V-mail envelopes of my father's war letters. Ellen lay flat on her back, rested her head on my thigh, and I took up the flashlight to read.

"*Dear folks. We are in*—the name's been cut out."

"Why?" She rolled to her stomach, looked up at me.

I shrugged. "I guess he didn't know he couldn't say that. *The way they do thes people is awful bad. I found a rusky prisoner starven in the street and took him to a german house for a feed.*" I felt Ellen's tongue on the inside of my thigh and shivered, tried to keep reading. "*They didn't do nothin for him till I leveled off with my gun and Howard he raised hell with me only I seen that rusky eat one damn fine meal.*" I turned off the flashlight, moved down beside Ellen. He had never told that story.

But it's not so simple now as then, not easy to be a part of Ellen without knowing or wanting to know the web our kisses make. It was easy to leave the house with a bar of soap in my pocket; only the hardest part was sitting here, looking at it, and remembering.

I went through the hall with the rest of the kids between classes, and there stood Eddie at the top of the stairs. He grinned at me, but it was not his face anymore. His face had changed; a face gone red because the other kids snickered at his uniform. He stood at parade rest, his seaman's cap hanging from his belt, his head tilting back to look down on me, then he dragged his hands around like Jackie Gleason taking an away-we-go pool shot. We moved on down the hall to ditch my books.

"You on leave?" I said.

"Heap bad medicine. Means I'm getting shipped."

"How long?" I fumbled with the combination of my locker.

"Ten days," he said, then squinted at the little upside-down flag on my open locker door. "You sucker."

I watched him until he went out of sight down the steps, then got my books, went on to class.

The butt of my palm is speckled with black spots deep under the skin: cinders from a relay-race fall. The skin has sealed them over, and it would cost plenty to get them out.

Sometimes Ellen wants to play nurse with a needle, wants to pry them out, but I won't let her. Sometimes I want to ask Ellen if she saw Eddie on his last leave.

Coach said I couldn't run track because anyone not behind his country was not fit for a team, so I sat under the covered bridge waiting for the time I could go home. Every car passing over sprinkled a little dust between the boards, sifted it into my hair.

I watched the narrow river roll by, its waters slow but muddy like pictures I had seen of rivers on the TV news. In history class, Coach said the Confederate troops attacked this bridge, took it, but were held by a handful of Sherman's troops on Company Hill. Johnny Reb drank from this river. The handful had a spring on Company Hill. Johnny croaked with the typhoid and the Yankees moved south. So I stood and brushed the dust off me. My hair grew long after Eddie went over, and I washed it every night.

I put my fist under my arm like the bar of soap and watch the veins on the back of my hand rise with pressure. There are scars where I've barked the hide hooking the disk or the drag to my tractor; they are like my father's scars.

We walked the fields, checked the young cane for blight or bugs, and the late sun gave my father's slick hair a sparkle. He chewed the stem of his pipe, then stood with one leg across a knee and banged tobacco out against his shoe.

I worked up the guts: "You reckon I could go to college, Dad?"

"What's wrong with farming?"

"Well, sir, nothing, if that's all you ever want."

He crossed the cane rows to get me, and my left went up to guard like Eddie taught me, right kept low and to the body.

"Cute," he said. "Real cute. When's your number up?"

I dropped my guard. "When I graduate—it's the only chance I got to stay out."

He loaded his pipe, turned around in his tracks like he was looking for something, then stopped, facing the hills. "It's your damn name is what it is. Dad said when you was born, 'Call him William Haywood, and if he ever goes in a mine, I hope he chokes to death.'"

I thought that was a shitty thing for Grandad to do, but I watched Dad, hoped he'd let me go.

He started up: "Everybody's going to school to be something better. Well, when everybody's going this way, it's time to turn around and go that way, you know?" He motioned with his hands in two directions. "I don't care if they end up shitting gold nuggets, somebody's got to dig in the damn ground. Somebody's got to."

And I said, "Yessir."

The sky is dark blue and the fog is cold smoke staying low to the ground. In this first hint of light my hand seems blue, but not cold; such gets cold sooner or later, but for now my hand is warm.

Many's the time my grandfather told of the last strike before he quit the mines, moved to the valley for some peace. He would quit his Injun act when he told it, like it was real again, all before him, and pretty soon I started thinking it was *me* the Baldwin bulls were after. *I* ran through the woods till my lungs bled. *I* could hear the Baldwins and their dogs in the dark woods, and *I* could remember machine guns cutting down pickets, and all *I* could think was how the One Big Union was down the rathole. Then I could taste it in my mouth, taste the blood coming up from my lungs, feel the bark of a tree root where I fell, where I slept. When I opened my eyes, I felt funny in the gut, felt watched. There were no twig snaps, just the feeling that something was too close. Knowing it was a man, one man, hunting me, I took up my revolver. I could hear him breathing, aimed into the sound, knowing the only sight would come with the flash. I knew all my life I had lived to kill this man, this goddamned Baldwin man, and I couldn't do it. I heard him move away down the ridge, hunting his lost game.

I fold my arms tight like I did the morning the bus pulled up. I was thinking of my grandfather, and there was a bar of soap under my arm. At the draft physical, my blood pressure was clear out of sight, and they kept me four days. The pressure never went down, and on the fourth day a letter came by forward. I read it on the bus home.

Eddie said he was with a bunch of Jarheads in the Crotch, and he repaired radio gear in the field. He said the USMC's hated him because he was regular Navy. He said the chow was rotten, the quarters lousy, and the left side of his chest was turning yellow from holding smokes inside his shirt at night. And he said he knew how the guy felt when David sent him into the battle to get dibs on the guy's wife. Eddie said he wanted dibs on Ellen, ha, ha. He said he would get married and give me his wife if I would get him out of there. He said the beer came in Schlitz cans, but he was sure it was something else. Eddie was sure the CO was a fag. He said he would like to get Ellen naked, but if he stayed with this outfit he would want to get me naked when he came back. He asked if I remembered him teaching me to burn off leeches with a cigarette. Eddie swore he learned that in a movie where the hero dies because he ran out of cigarettes. He said he had plenty of cigarettes. He said he could never go Oriental because they don't have any hair on their twats, and he bet me he knew what color Ellen's bush was. He said her hair might be brown, but her bush was red. He said to think about it and say Hi to Ellen for him until he came back. Sometimes I want to ask Ellen if she saw Eddie on his last leave.

When I came back, Ellen met me at the trailer door, hugged me, and started to cry. She showed pretty well with Lundy, and I told her Eddie's letter said to say Hi. She cried some more, and I knew Eddie was not coming back.

Daylight fires the ridges green, shifts the colors of the fog, touches the brick streets of Rock Camp with a reddish tone. The streetlights flicker out, and the traffic signal at the far end of Front Street's yoke snaps on; stopping nothing, warning nothing, rushing nothing on.

I stand and my joints crack from sitting too long, but the flesh of my face is warming in the early sun. I climb the steps of the Old Bank, draw a spook in the window soap. I tell myself that spook is Eddie's, and I wipe it off with my sleeve, then I see the bus coming down the Pike, tearing the morning, and I start down the street so he won't stop for me. I cannot go away, and I cannot make Eddie go away, so I go home. And walking down the street as the bus goes by, I bet myself a million that my Lundy is up and already watching cartoons, and I bet I know who won.

Studs Terkel (b. 1912)

Born in the Bronx, New York, the third son of Russian Jewish parents, Louis Terkel moved at age eleven to Chicago, where his father found work as a tailor. The family later opened a rooming house for immigrants and then a small hotel. Terkel credits his knowledge of the world to the tenants who gathered in the hotel lobby and in nearby

Bughouse Square, a meeting place for workers, labor organizers, the homeless, and religious fanatics of many persuasions. After graduating from high school in 1928, Terkel went to the University of Chicago, where he received a law degree in 1934. The following year he found work producing radio shows as part of the Federal Writers Project. Terkel, who now adopted the name Studs (after James Farrell's proletarian novel, *Studs Lonigan*), also became involved in the Chicago Repertory Theatre. At the outbreak of World War II, Terkel joined the Red Cross but was not allowed to serve overseas because of his left-wing political views.

In 1949, after years as a familiar voice on Chicago radio, he began a television show, *Studs' Place*, but after he was investigated by the House Un-American Activities Committee in 1953, his contract was canceled. Terkel refused to give evidence against other left-wing activists and was blacklisted and prevented from appearing on television. His radio show, "The Studs Terkel Program," was heard on Chicago's fine arts station from 1952 to 1997. In the 1960s, Terkel became interested in oral history. His first book on the subject was *Division Street: America* (1967), followed by *Hard Times* (1970), which featured interviews with Americans talking about their experiences of the Great Depression, and *Working* (1974), subtitled "People Talk About What They Do All Day and How They Feel About What They Do" (see the selections presented here). His other books include the Pulitzer Prize-winning *The Good War* (1985), *Race: How Blacks and Whites Think and Feel About the American Obsession* (1992), *Talking to Myself: A Memoir of My Times* (1995), *American Dreams: Lost and Found* (1999), and *Hope Dies Last: Keeping the Faith in Difficult Times* (2003). He is the recipient of the Presidential National Humanities Medal, among many other awards, and is a Distinguished Scholar in Residence at the Chicago Historical Society.

Terkel calls himself a "guerilla journalist with a tape recorder." He built a career on the belief that just about anyone may be worth talking to—the rich and famous, murderers and Ku Klux Klansmen—but, most of all, the unexamined mass of American life in between. His favorite interview was with C. P. Ellis, a former Klan leader who ended up fighting for the union rights of black janitors. "Anybody can be redeemed," Terkel says, "I've seen it." The interviews in his books constitute an alternative history of the American twentieth century and a testament to the indefatigable spirit in people that Terkel himself has always embodied.

Ken Boas

DOLORES DANTE, WAITRESS, FROM *WORKING*

She has been a waitress in the same restaurant for twenty-three years. Many of its patrons are credit card carriers on an expense account—conventioneers, politicians, labor leaders, agency people. Her hours are from 5:00 P.M. to 2:00 A.M. six days a week. She arrives earlier "to get things ready, the silverware, the butter. When people come in and ask for you, you would like to be in a position to handle them all, because that means more money for you.

"I became a waitress because I needed money fast and you don't get it in an office. My husband and I broke up and he left me with debts and three children. My baby was six months. The fast buck, your tips. The first ten-dollar bill that I got as a tip, a Viking guy gave to me. He was a very robust, terrific atheist. Made very good conversation for us,' cause I am too.

"Everyone says all waitresses have broken homes. What they don't realize is when people have broken homes they need to make money fast, and do this work. They don't have broken homes because they're waitresses."

I have to be a waitress. How else can I learn about people? How else does the world come to me? I can't go to everyone. So they have to come to me. Everyone wants to eat, everyone has hunger. And I serve them. If they've had a bad day, I nurse them, cajole them. Maybe with coffee I give them a little philosophy. They have cocktails, I give them political science.

I'll say things that bug me. If they manufacture soap, I say what I think about pollution. If it's automobiles, I say what I think about them. If I pour water I'll say, "Would you like your quota of mercury today?" If I serve cream, I say, "Here is your substitute. I think you're drinking plastic." I just can't keep quiet. I have an opinion on every single subject there is. In the beginning it was theology, and my bosses didn't like it. Now I am a political and my bosses don't like it. I speak *sotto voce*. But if I get heated, then I don't give a damn. I speak like an Italian speaks. I can't be servile. I give service. There is a difference.

I'm called by my first name. I like my name. I hate to be called Miss. Even when I serve a lady, a strange woman, I will not say madam. I hate ma'am. I always say milady. In the American language there is no word to address a woman, to indicate whether she's married or unmarried. So I say milady. And sometimes I playfully say to the man milord.

It would be very tiring if I had to say, "Would you like a cocktail?" and say that over and over. So I come out different for my own enjoyment. I would say, "What's exciting at the bar that I can offer?" I can't say, "Do you want coffee?" Maybe I'll say, "Are you in the mood for coffee?" Or, "The coffee sounds exciting." Just rephrase it enough to make it interesting for me. That would make them take an interest. It becomes theatrical and I feel like Mata Hari and it intoxicates me.

People imagine a waitress couldn't possibly think or have any kind of aspiration other than to serve food. When somebody says to me, "You're great, how come you're *just* a waitress?" *Just* a waitress. I'd say, "Why, don't you think you deserve to be served by me?" It's implying that he's not worthy, not that I'm not worthy. It makes me irate. I don't feel lowly at all. I myself feel sure. I don't want to change the job. I love it.

Tips? I feel like Carmen. It's like a gypsy holding out a tambourine and they throw the coin. (Laughs.) If you like people, you're not thinking of the tips. I never count my money at night. I always wait till morning. If I thought about my tips I'd be uptight. I never look at a tip. You pick it up fast. I would do my bookkeeping in the morning. It would be very dull for me to know I was making so much and no more. I do like challenge. And it isn't demeaning, not for me.

There might be occasions when the customers might intend to make it demeaning— the man about town, the conventioneer. When the time comes to pay the check, he would do little things, "How much should I give you?" He might make an issue about it. I did say to one, "Don't play God with me. Do what you want." Then it really didn't matter whether I got a tip or not. I would spit it out, my resentment—that he dares make me feel I'm operating only for a tip.

He'd ask for his check. Maybe he's going to sign it. He'd take a very long time and he'd make me stand there, "Let's see now, what do you think I ought to give you?" He would not let go of that moment. And you knew it. You know he meant to demean you. He's holding the change in his hand, or if he'd sign, he'd flourish the pen and wait. These are the times I really get angry. I'm not reticent. Something would come out. Then I really didn't care. "Goddamn, keep your money!"

There are conventioneers, who leave their lovely wives or their bad wives. They approach you and say, "Are there any hot spots?" "Where can I find girls?" It is, of course, first directed at you. I don't mean that as a compliment, 'cause all they're looking for is females. They're not looking for companionship or conversation. I am quite adept at understanding this. I think I'm interesting enough that someone may just want to talk to me. But I would philosophize that way. After all, what is left after you talk? The hours have gone by and I could be home resting or reading or studying guitar, which I do on occasion. I would say, "What are you going to offer me? Drinks?" And I'd point to the bar,

"I have it all here." He'd look blank and then I'd say, "A man? If I need a man, wouldn't you think I'd have one of my own? Must I wait for you?"

Life doesn't frighten me any more. There are only two things that relegate us—the bathroom and the grave. Either I'm gonna have to go to the bathroom now or I'm gonna die now. I go to the bathroom.

And I don't have a high opinion of bosses. The more popular you are, the more the boss holds it over your head. You're bringing them business, but he knows you're getting good tips and you won't leave. You have to worry not to overplay it, because the boss becomes resentful and he uses this as a club over your head.

If you become too good a waitress, there's jealousy. They don't come in and say, "Where's the boss?" They'll ask for Dolores. It doesn't make a hit. That makes it rough. Sometimes you say, Aw hell, why am I trying so hard? I did get an ulcer. Maybe the things I kept to myself were twisting me.

It's not the customers, never the customers. It's injustice. My dad came from Italy and I think of his broken English—*injoost*. He hated injustice. If you hate injustice for the world, you hate more than anything injustice toward you. Loyalty is never appreciated, particularly if you're the type who doesn't like small talk and are not the type who makes reports on your fellow worker. The boss wants to find out what is going on surreptitiously. In our society today you have informers everywhere. They've informed on cooks, on coworkers. "Oh, someone wasted this." They would say I'm talking to all the customers. "I saw her carry such-and-such out. See if she wrote that on her check." "The salad looked like it was a double salad." I don't give anything away. I just give myself. Informers will manufacture things in order to make their job worthwhile. They're not sure of themselves as workers. There's always someone who wants your station, who would be pretender to the crown. In life there is always someone who wants somebody's job.

I'd get intoxicated with giving service. People would ask for me and I didn't have enough tables. Some of the girls are standing and don't have customers. There is resentment. I feel self-conscious. I feel a sense of guilt. It cramps my style. I would like to say to the customer, "Go to so-and-so." But you can't do that, because you feel a sense of loyalty. So you would rush, get to your customers quickly. Some don't care to drink and still they wait for you. That's a compliment.

There is plenty of tension. If the cook isn't good, you fight to see that the customers get what you know they like. You have to use diplomacy with cooks, who are always dangerous. (Laughs.) They're madmen. (Laughs.) You have to be their friend. They better like you. And your bartender better like you too, because he may do something to the drink. If your bartender doesn't like you, your cook doesn't like you, your boss doesn't like you, the other girls don't like you, you're in trouble.

And there will be customers who are hypochondriacs, who feel they can't eat, and I coax them. Then I hope I can get it just the right way from the cook. I may mix the salad myself, just the way they want it.

Maybe there's a party of ten. Big shots, and they'd say, "Dolores, I have special clients, do your best tonight." You just hope you have the right cook behind the broiler. You really want to pleasure your guests. He's selling something, he wants things right, too. You're giving your all. How does the steak look? If you cut his steak, you look at it surreptitiously. How's it going?"

Carrying dishes is a problem. We do have accidents. I spilled a tray once with steaks for seven on it. It was a big, gigantic T-bone, all sliced. But when that tray fell, I went with it, and never made a sound, dish and all (softly) never made a sound. It took about an hour and a half to cook that steak. How would I explain this thing? That steak was salvaged. (Laughs.)

Some don't care. When the plate is down you can hear the sound. I try not to have that sound. I want my hands to be right when I serve. I pick up a glass, I want it to be just right. I get to be almost Oriental in the serving. I like it to look nice all the way. To be a waitress, it's an art. I feel like a ballerina, too. I have to go between those tables, between those chairs . . . Maybe that's the reason I always stayed slim. It is a certain way I can go through a chair no one else can do. I do it with an air. If I drop a fork, there is a certain way I pick it up. I know they can see how delicately I do it. I'm on stage.

I tell everyone I'm a waitress and I'm proud. If a nurse gives service, I say, "You're a professional." Whatever you do, be professional. I always compliment people.

I like to have my station looking nice. I like to see there's enough ash trays when they're having their coffee and cigarettes. I don't like ash trays so loaded that people are not enjoying the moment. It offends me. I don't do it because I think that's gonna make a better tip. It offends me as a person.

People say, "No one does good work any more." I don't believe it. You know who's saying that? The man at the top, who says the people beneath him are not doing a good job. He's the one who always said, "You're nothing." The housewife who has all the money, she believed housework was demeaning, 'cause she hired someone else to do it. If it weren't so demeaning, why didn't *she* do it? So anyone who did her housework was a person to be demeaned. The maid who did all the housework said, "Well, hell, if this is the way you feel about it, I won't do your housework. You tell me I'm no good, I'm nobody. Well, maybe I'll go out and be somebody." They're only mad because they can't find someone to do it now. The fault is not in the people who did the—quote—lowly work.

Just a waitress. At the end of the night I feel drained. I think a lot of waitresses become alcoholics because of that. In most cases, a waiter or a waitress doesn't eat. They handle food, they don't have time. You'll pick at something in the kitchen, maybe a piece of bread. You'll have a cracker, a little bit of soup. You go back and take a teaspoonful of something. Then maybe sit down afterwards and have a drink, maybe three, four, five. And bartenders, too, most of them are alcoholics. They'd go out in a group. There are after-hour places. You've got to go release your tension. So they go out before they go to bed. Some of them stay out all night.

It's tiring, it's nerve-racking. We don't ever sit down. We're on stage and the bosses are watching. If you get the wrong shoes and you get the wrong stitch in that shoe, that does bother you. Your feet hurt, your body aches. If you come out in anger at things that were done to you, it would only make you feel cheapened. Really I've been keeping it to myself. But of late, I'm beginning to spew it out. It's almost as though I sensed my body and soul had had quite enough.

It builds and builds and builds in your guts. Near crying. I can think about it . . . (She cries softly.) 'Cause you're tired. When the night is done, you're tired. You've had so much, there's so much going . . . You had to get it done. The dread that something wouldn't be right, because you want to please. You hope everyone is satisfied. The night's done, you've done your act. The curtains close.

The next morning is pleasant again. I take out my budget book, write down how much I made, what my bills are. I'm managing. I won't give up this job as long as I'm able to do it. I feel out of contact if I just sit at home. At work they all consider me a kook. (Laughs.) That's okay. No matter where I'd be, I would make a rough road for me. It's just me, and I can't keep still. It hurts, and what hurts has to come out.

POSTSCRIPT: *"After sixteen years—that was seven years ago—I took a trip to Hawaii and the Caribbean for two weeks. Went with a lover. The kids saw it—they're all married now. (Laughs.) One of my daughters said, "Act your age." I said, "Honey, if I were acting my age, I wouldn't be walking. My bones would ache. You don't want to hear about my arthritis. Aren't you glad I'm happy?"*

MIKE LEFEVRE, STEELWORKER, FROM *WORKING*

*It is a two-flat dwelling, somewhere in Cicero, on the outskirts of Chicago. He is thirty-seven.
He works in a steel mill. On occasion, his wife Carol works as a waitress in a neighborhood
restaurant; otherwise, she is at home, caring for their two small children, a girl and a boy.*

*At the time of my first visit, a sculpted statuette of Mother and Child was on the floor,
head severed from body. He laughed softly as he indicated his three-year-old daughter: "She
Doctor Spock'd it."*

I'm a dying breed. A laborer. Strictly muscle work . . . pick it up, put it down, pick it up,
put it down. We handle between forty and fifty thousand pounds of steel a day. (Laughs)
I know this is hard to believe—from four hundred pounds to three- and four-pound
pieces. It's dying.

You can't take pride any more. You remember when a guy could point to a house he
built, how many logs he stacked. He built it and he was proud of it. I don't really think
I could be proud if a contractor built a home for me. I would be tempted to get in
there and kick the carpenter in the ass (laughs), and take the saw away from him. 'Cause
I would have to be part of it, you know.

It's hard to take pride in a bridge you're never gonna cross, in a door you're never
gonna open. You're mass-producing things and you never see the end result of it. (Muses)
I worked for a trucker one time. And I got this tiny satisfaction when I loaded a truck. At
least I could see the truck depart loaded. In a steel mill, forget it. You don't see where
nothing goes.

I got chewed out by my foreman once. He said, "Mike, you're a good worker but you
have a bad attitude." My attitude is that I don't get excited about my job. I do my work
but I don't say whoopee-doo. The day I get excited about my job is the day I go to a head
shrinker. How are you gonna get excited about pullin' steel? How are you gonna get
excited when you're tired and want to sit down?

It's not just the work. Somebody built the pyramids. Somebody's going to build something. Pyramids, Empire State Building—these things just don't happen. There's hard work
behind it. I would like to see a building, say, the Empire State, I would like to see on one
side of it a foot-wide strip from top to bottom with the name of every bricklayer, the name
of every electrician, with all the names. So when a guy walked by, he could take his son
and say, "See, that's me over there on the forty-fifth floor. I put the steel beam in." Picasso
can point to a painting. What can I point to? A writer can point to a book. Everybody
should have something to point to.

It's the not-recognition by other people. To say a woman is *just* a housewife is degrading,
right? Okay. *Just* a housewife. It's also degrading to say *just* a laborer. The difference is that
a man goes out and maybe gets smashed.

When I was single, I could quit, just split. I wandered all over the country. You worked
just enough to get a poke, money in your pocket. Now I'm married and I got two kids . . .
(trails off). I worked on a truck dock one time and I was single. The foreman came over
and he grabbed my shoulder, kind of gave me a shove. I punched him and knocked him
off the dock. I said, "Leave me alone. I'm doing my work, just stay away from me, just
don't give me the with-the-hands business."

Hell, if you whip a damn mule he might kick you. Stay out of my way, that's all.
Working is bad enough, don't bug me. I would rather work my ass off for eight hours a
day with nobody watching me than five minutes with a guy watching me. Who you gonna
sock? You can't sock General Motors, you can't sock anybody in Washington, you can't
sock a system.

A mule, an old mule, that's the way I feel. Oh yeah. See. (Shows black and blue marks
on arms and legs, burns.) You know what I heard from more than one guy at work?

"If my kid wants to work in a factory, I am going to kick the hell out of him." I want my kid to be an effete snob. Yeah, mm-hmm. (Laughs.) I want him to be able to quote Walt Whitman, to be proud of it.

If you can't improve yourself, you improve your posterity. Otherwise life isn't worth nothing. You might as well go back to the cave and stay there. I'm sure the first caveman who went over the hill to see what was on the other side—I don't think he went there wholly out of curiosity. He went there because he wanted to get his son out of the cave. Just the same way I want to send my kid to college.

I work so damn hard and want to come home and sit down and lay around. *But I gotta get it out.* I want to be able to turn around to somebody and say, "Hey, fuck you." You know? (Laughs.) The guy sitting next to me on the bus too. 'Cause all day I wanted to tell my foreman to go fuck himself, but I can't.

So I find a guy in a tavern. To tell him that. And he tells me too. I've been in brawls. He's punching me and I'm punching him, because we actually want to punch somebody else. The most that'll happen is the bartender will bar us from the tavern. But at work, you lose your job.

This one foreman I've got, he's a kid. He's a college graduate. He thinks he's better than everybody else. He was chewing me out and I was saying, "Yeah, yeah, yeah." He said, "What do you mean, yeah, yeah, yeah. Yes, *sir*." I told him, "Who the hell are you, Hitler? What is this *"Yes, sir"* bullshit? I came here to work, I didn't come here to crawl. There's a fuckin' difference." One word led to another and I lost.

I got broke down to a lower grade and lost twenty-five cents an hour, which is a hell of a lot. It amounts to about ten dollars a week. He came over—after breaking me down. The guy comes over and smiles at me. I blew up. He didn't know it, but he was about two seconds and two feet away from a hospital. I said, "Stay the fuck away from me." He was just about to say something and was pointing his finger. I just reached my hand up and just grabbed his finger and I just put it back in his pocket. He walked away. I grabbed his finger because I'm married. If I'd a been single, I'd a grabbed his head. That's the difference.

You're doing this manual labor and you know that technology can do it. (Laughs.) Let's face it, a machine can do the work of a man; otherwise they wouldn't have space probes. Why can we send a rocket ship that's unmanned and yet send a man in a steel mill to do a mule's work?

Automation? Depends how it's applied. It frightens me if it puts me out on the street. It doesn't frighten me if it shortens my work week. You read that little thing: what are you going to do when this computer replaces you? Blow up computers. (Laughs.) Really. Blow up computers. I'll be goddamned if a computer is gonna eat before I do! I want milk for my kids and beer for me. Machines can either liberate man or enslave 'im, because they're pretty neutral. It's man who has the bias to put the thing one place or another.

If I had a twenty-hour workweek, I'd get to know my kids better, my wife better. Some kid invited me to go on a college campus. On a Saturday. It was summertime. Hell, if I have a choice of taking my wife and kids to a picnic or going to a college campus, it's gonna be the picnic. But if I worked a twenty-hour week, I could go do both. Don't you think with that extra twenty hours people could really expand? Who's to say? There are some people in factories just by force of circumstance. I'm just like the colored people. Potential Einsteins don't have to be white. They could be in cotton fields, they could be in factories.

The twenty-hour week is a possibility today. The intellectuals, they always say there are potential Lord Byrons, Walt Whitmans, Roosevelts, Picassos working in construction or steel mills or factories. But I don't think they believe it. I think what they're afraid of is the potential Hitlers and Stalins that are there too. The people in power fear the leisure man. Not just the United States. Russia's the same way.

What do you think would happen in this country if, for one year, they experimented and gave everybody a twenty-hour week? How do they know that the guy who digs Wallace today doesn't try to resurrect Hitler tomorrow? Or the guy who is mildly disturbed at pollution doesn't decide to go to General Motors and shit on the guy's desk? You can become a fanatic if you had the time. The whole thing is time. That is, I think, one reason rich kids tend to be fanatic about politics: they have time. Time, that's the important thing.

It isn't that the average working guy is dumb. He's tired, that's all. I picked up a book on chess one time. That thing laid in the drawer for two or three weeks, you're too tired. During the weekends you want to take your kids out. You don't want to sit there and the kid comes up: "Daddy, can I go to the park?" You got your nose in a book? Forget it.

I know a guy fifty-seven years old. Know what he tells me? "Mike, I'm old and tired *all* the time." The first thing happens at work: when the arms start moving, the brain stops. I punch in about ten minutes to seven in the morning. I say hello to a couple of guys I like, I kid around with them. One guy says good morning to you and you say good morning. To another guy you say fuck you. The guy you say fuck you to is your friend.

I put on my hard hat, change into my safety shoes, put on my safety glasses, go to the bonderizer. It's the thing I work on. They rake the metal, they wash it, they dip it in a paint solution, and we take it off. Put it on, take it off, put it on, take it off, put it on, take it off . . .

I say hello to everybody but my boss. At seven it starts. My arms get tired about the first half-hour. After that, they don't get tired any more until maybe the last half-hour at the end of the day. I work from seven to three thirty. My arms are tired at seven thirty and they're tired at three o'clock. I hope to God I never get broke in, because I always want my arms to be tired at seven thirty and three o'clock. (Laughs.) 'Cause that's when I know that there's a beginning and there's an end. That I'm not brainwashed. In between, I don't even try to think.

If I were to put you in front of a dock and I pulled up a skid in front of you with fifty hundred-pound sacks of potatoes and there are fifty more skids just like it, and this is what you're gonna do all day, what would you think about—potatoes? Unless a guy's a nut, he never thinks about work or talks about it. Maybe about baseball or about getting drunk the other night or he got laid or he didn't get laid. I'd say one out of a hundred will actually get excited about work.

Why is it that the communists always say they're for the workingman, and as soon as they set up a country, you got guys singing to tractors? They're singing about how they love the factory. That's where I couldn't buy communism. It's the intellectuals' utopia, not mine. I cannot picture myself singing to a tractor, I just can't. (Laughs.) Or singing to steel. (Singsongs.) Oh whoop-dee-doo, I'm at the bonderizer, oh how I love this heavy steel. No thanks. Never happen.

Oh yeah, I daydream. I fantasize about a sexy blonde in Miami who's got my union dues. (Laughs.) I think of the head of the union the way I think of the head of my company. Living it up. I think of February in Miami. Warm weather, a place to lay in. When I hear a college kid say, "I'm oppressed," I don't believe him. You know what I'd like to do for one year? Live like a college kid. Just for one year. I'd love to. Wow! (Whispers) Wow! Sports car! Marijuana! (Laughs.) Wild, sexy broads. I'd love that, hell yes, I would.

Somebody has to do this work. If my kid ever goes to college, I just want him to have a little respect, to realize that his dad is one of those somebodies. This is why even on— (muses) yeah, I guess, sure—on the black thing . . . (Sighs heavily.) I can't really hate the colored fella that's working with me all day. The black intellectual I got no respect for. The white intellectual I got no use for. I got no use for the black militant who's gonna scream three hundred years of slavery to me while I'm busting my ass. You know what I mean? (Laughs.) I have one answer for that guy: go see Rockefeller. See Harriman. Don't bother me. We're in the same cotton field. So just don't bug me. (Laughs.)

After work I usually stop off at a tavern. Cold beer. Cold beer right away. When I was single, I used to go into hillbilly bars, get in a lot of brawls. Just to explode. I got a thing on my arm here (indicates scar). I got slapped with a bicycle chain. Oh, wow! (Softly) Mmm. I'm getting older. (Laughs.) I don't explode as much. You might say I'm broken in.

(Quickly) No, I'll never be broken in. (Sighs.) When you get a little older, you exchange the words. When you're younger, you exchange the blows.

When I get home, I argue with my wife a little bit. Turn on TV, get mad at the news. (Laughs.) I don't even watch the news that much. I watch Jackie Gleason. I look for any alternative to the ten o'clock news. I don't want to go to bed angry. Don't hit a man with anything heavy at five o'clock. He just can't be bothered. This is his time to relax. The heaviest thing he wants is what his wife has to tell him.

When I come home, know what I do for the first twenty minutes? Fake it. I put on a smile. I got a kid three years old. Sometimes she says, "Daddy, where've you been?" I say, "Work." I could have told her I'd been in Disneyland. What's work to a three-year-old kid? If I feel bad, I can't take it out on the kids. Kids are born innocent of everything but birth. You can't take it out on your wife either. This is why you go to a tavern. You want to release it there rather than do it at home. What does an actor do when he's got a bad movie? I got a bad movie every day.

I don't even need the alarm clock to get up in the morning. I can go out drinking all night, fall asleep at four, and bam! I'm up at six—no matter what I do. (Laughs.) It's a pseudo-death, more or less. Your whole system is paralyzed and you give all the appearance of death. It's an ingrown clock. It's a thing you just get used to. The hours differ. It depends. Sometimes my wife wants to do something crazy like play five hundred rummy or put a puzzle together. It could be midnight, could be ten o'clock, could be nine thirty.

What do you do weekends?

Drink beer, read a book. See that one? *Violence in America*. It's one of them studies from Washington. One of them committees they're always appointing. A thing like that I read on a weekend. But during the weekdays, gee . . . I just thought about it. I don't do that much reading from Monday through Friday. Unless it's a horny book. I'll read it at work and go home and do my homework. (Laughs.) That's what the guys at the plant call it—homework. (Laughs.) Sometimes my wife works on Saturday and I drink beer at the tavern.

I went out drinking with one guy, oh, a long time ago. A college boy. He was working where I work now. Always preaching to me about how you need violence to change the system and all that garbage. We went into a hillbilly joint. Some guy there, I didn't know him from Adam, he said, "You think you're smart." I said, "What's your pleasure?" (Laughs.) He said, "My pleasure's to kick your ass." I told him I really can't be bothered. He said, "What're you, chicken?" I said, "No, I just don't want to be bothered." He came over and said something to me again. I said, "I don't beat women, drunks, or fools. Now leave me alone."

The guy called his brother over. This college boy that was with me, he came nudging my arm, "Mike, let's get out of here." I said, "What are you worried about?" (Laughs.) This isn't unusual. People will bug you. You fend it off as much as you can with your mouth and when you can't, you punch the guy out.

It was close to closing time and we stayed. We could have left, but when you go into a place to have a beer and a guy challenges you—if you expect to go in that place again, you don't leave. If you have to fight the guy, you fight.

I got just outside the door and one of these guys jumped on me and grabbed me around the neck. I grabbed his arm and flung him against the wall. I grabbed him here (indicates throat), and jiggled his head against the wall quite a few times. He kind of slid down a little bit. This guy who said he was his brother took a swing at me with a garrison belt. He just missed and hit the wall. I'm looking around for my junior Stalin (laughs), who loves violence and everything. He's gone. Split. (Laughs.) Next day I see him at work. I couldn't get mad at him, he's a baby.

He saw a book in my back pocket one time and he was amazed. He walked up to me and he said, "You read?" I said, "What do you mean, I read?" He said, "All these dummies read the sports pages around here. What are you doing with a book?" I got pissed off at the kid right away. I said, "What do you mean, all these dummies? Don't knock a man who's paying somebody else's way through college." He was a nineteen-year-old effete snob.

Yet you want your kid to be an effete snob?

Yes. I want my kid to look at me and say, "Dad, you're a nice guy, but you're a fuckin' dummy." Hell yes, I want my kid to tell me that he's not gonna be like me . . .

If I were hiring people to work, I'd try naturally to pay them a decent wage. I'd try to find out their first names, their last names, keep the company as small as possible, so I could personalize the whole thing. All I would ask a man is a handshake, see you in the morning. No applications, nothing. I wouldn't be interested in the guy's past. Nobody ever checks the pedigree on a mule, do they? But they do on a man. Can you picture walking up to a mule and saying, "I'd like to know who his granddaddy was?"

I'd like to run a combination bookstore and tavern. (Laughs.) I would like to have a place where college kids came and a steelworker could sit down and talk. Where a working-man could not be ashamed of Walt Whitman and where a college professor could not be ashamed that he painted his house over the weekend.

If a carpenter built a cabin for poets, I think the least the poets owe the carpenter is just three or four one-liners on the wall. A little plaque: Though we labor with our minds, this place we can relax in was built by someone who can work with his hands. And his work is as noble as ours. I think the poet owes something to the guy who builds the cabin for him.

I don't think of Monday. You know what I'm thinking about on Sunday night? Next Sunday. If you work real hard, you think of a perpetual vacation. Not perpetual sleep . . . What do I think of on a Sunday night? Lord, I wish the fuck I could do something else for a living.

I don't know who the guy is who said there is nothing sweeter than an unfinished symphony. Like an unfinished painting and an unfinished poem. If he creates this thing one day—let's say, Michelangelo's Sistine Chapel. It took him a long time to do this, this beautiful work of art. But what if he had to create this Sistine Chapel a thousand times a year? Don't you think that would even dull Michelangelo's mind? Or if da Vinci had to draw his anatomical charts thirty, forty, fifty, sixty, eighty, ninety, a hundred times a day? Don't you think that would even bore da Vinci?

Way back, you spoke of the guys who built the pyramids, not the pharaohs, the unknowns. You put yourself in their category?

Yes. I want my signature on 'em, too. Sometimes, out of pure meanness, when I make something, I put a little dent in it. I like to do something to make it really unique. Hit it with a hammer. I deliberately fuck it up to see if it'll get by, just so I can say I did it. It could be anything. Let me put it this way: I think God invented the dodo bird so when we get up there we could tell him, "Don't you ever make mistakes?" and He'd say, "Sure, look." (Laughs.) I'd like to make my imprint. My dodo bird. A mistake, *mine*. Let's say the whole building is nothing but red bricks. I'd like to have just the black one or the white one or the purple one. Deliberately fuck up.

This is gonna sound square, but my kid is my imprint. He's my freedom. There's a line in one of Hemingway's books. I think it's from *For Whom the Bell Tolls*. They're behind the enemy lines, somewhere in Spain, and she's pregnant. She wants to stay with him. He tells her no. He says, "if you die, I die," knowing he's gonna die. But if you go, I go. Know what I mean? The mystics call it the brass bowl. Continuum. You know what I mean? This is why I work. Every time I see a young guy walk by with a shirt and tie and dressed up real sharp, I'm lookin' at my kid, you know? That's it.

Toni Cade Bambara (1939–1995)

Fiction writer, filmmaker, and activist, Toni Cade Bambara was born in Harlem, named Miltona Mirkin Cade after her father's white employer, Milton Mirkin. She changed her name after finding the signature "Bambara" on a sketchbook in her great-grandmother's trunk. Coming of age during the civil rights movement and inspired by her mother's example, Bambara's creativity took shape with a keen consciousness of racism as well as appreciation for her black neighborhood with its talkers and musicians and community helpers. Her mother, she writes, "had a deep respect for the life of the mind." Bambara dedicated her novel *The Salt Eaters* (1980) to "Mama . . . who in 1948, having come upon me daydreaming in the middle of the kitchen floor, mopped around me." Bambara attended Queens College, graduating with a BA in Theater Arts and English, and later—after periods of work and study in Italy and France—completed an MA degree while working as a social worker in Brooklyn. In the late 1960s, she taught at New York's City College. Bambara's first book, *The Black Woman* (1970), was a groundbreaking collection of fiction, poetry, and essays by Audre Lorde, Alice Walker, and Nikki Giovanni, among others. It made a double political and artistic statement characteristic of Bambara's work: putting women writers at the center of the Black Arts movement and at the same time asserting the place of black women in feminism's second wave. A second anthology, *Tales and Stories for Black Folks* (1971), gathered narratives from what she called "Our Great Kitchen Tradition." *Gorilla My Love* followed in 1972, a collection of Bambara's own stories focused on the lives of women and girls in the same New York neighborhood. "The Lesson," reprinted here, is widely admired for its exploration of racial and class divisions through the perspective and language of a street-smart but curious and determined preteen girl. The stories in *The Sea Birds Are Alive* (1977) reflect Bambara's travels in the mid–1970s to Cuba, Vietnam, and Atlanta, Georgia. In the 1980s, Bambara turned increasingly to theater and filmmaking. Her film *The Bombing of Osage Avenue*, about the 1985 police attack on the MOVE headquarters in Philadelphia, won an Oscar for Best Documentary in 1986. *Deep Sightings and Rescue Missions: Fiction, Essays, and Conversations* was published in 1996, after Bambara's death from cancer, a year that also saw the release of her film biography of W. E. B. DuBois. *Those Bones Are Not My Child*, a novel about the Atlanta child murders in the early 1980s, appeared in 1999, edited by Bambara's friend Toni Morrison.

THE LESSON

Back in the days when everyone was old and stupid or young and foolish and me and Sugar were the only ones just right, this lady moved on our block with nappy hair and proper speech and no makeup. And quite naturally we laughed at her, laughed the way we did at the junk man who went about his business like he was some big-time president and his sorry-ass horse his secretary. And we kinda hated her too, hated the way we did the winos who cluttered up our parks and pissed on our handball walls and stank up our hallways and stairs so you couldn't halfway play hide-and-seek without a goddamn gas mask. Miss Moore was her name. The only woman on the block with no first name. And she was black as hell, cept for her feet, which were fish-white and spooky. And she was always planning these boring-ass things for us to do, us being my cousin, mostly, who lived on the block cause we all moved North the same time and to the same apartment then spread out gradual to breathe. And our parents would yank our heads into some kinda shape and crisp up our clothes so we'd be presentable for travel with Miss Moore, who always looked like she was going to church, though she never did. Which is just one of things the grown-ups talked about when they talked behind her back like a dog. But when she came calling with some sachet she'd sewed up or some gingerbread she'd made or some book, why then they'd all be too embarrassed to turn her down and we'd get handed over all spruced up. She'd been to college and said it was only right that she should take responsibility for the young ones' education, and she not even related by marriage or blood. So they'd go for it. Specially Aunt Gretchen. She was the main gofer in the family. You got some ole dumb shit foolishness you want somebody to go for, you send for Aunt Gretchen. She been screwed into the go-along for so long, it's a blood-deep natural thing with her. Which is how she got saddled with me and Sugar and Junior in the first place while our mothers were in a la-de-da apartment up the block having a good ole time.

So this one day Miss Moore rounds us all up at the mailbox and it's puredee hot and she's knockin herself out about arithmetic. And school suppose to let up in summer I heard, but she don't never let up. And the starch in my pinafore scratching the shit outta me and I'm really hating this nappy-head bitch and her goddamn college degree. I'd much rather go to the pool or to the show where it's cool. So me and Sugar leaning on the mailbox being surly, which is a Miss Moore word. And Flyboy checking out what everybody brought for lunch. And Fat Butt already wasting his peanut-butter-and-jelly sandwich like the pig he is. And Junebug punchin on Q. T.'s arm for potato chips. And Rosie Giraffe shifting from one hip to the other waiting for somebody to step on her foot or ask her if she from Georgia so she can kick ass, preferably Mercedes'. And Miss Moore asking us do we know what money is, like we a bunch of retards. I mean real money, she say, like it's only poker chips or monopoly papers we lay on the grocer. So right away I'm tired of this and say so. And would much rather snatch Sugar and go to the Sunset and terrorize the West Indian kids and take their hair ribbons and their money too. And Miss Moore files that remark away for next week's lesson on brotherhood, I can tell. And finally I say we oughta get to the subway cause it's cooler and besides we might meet some cute boys. Sugar done swiped her mama's lipstick, so we ready.

So we heading down the street and she's boring us silly about what things cost and what our parents make and how much goes for rent and how money ain't divided up right in this country. And then she gets to the part about we all poor and live in the slums, which I don't feature. And I'm ready to speak on that, but she steps out in the street and hails two cabs just like that. Then she hustles half the crew in with her and hands me a five-dollar bill and tells me to calculate 10 percent tip for the driver. And we're off. Me and Sugar and Junebug and Flyboy hangin out the window and hollering to everybody, putting lipstick on each other cause Flyboy a faggot anyway, and making farts with our sweaty armpits. But I'm mostly trying to figure how to spend this money. But they all fascinated with the meter ticking and Junebug starts laying bets as to how much it'll read when Flyboy can't hold his breath no more. Then Sugar lays bets as to how much it'll be when we get there. So I'm stuck. Don't nobody want to go for my plan, which is to jump out at the next light and run off to the first bar-b-que we can find. Then the driver tells us to get the hell out cause we there already. And the meter reads eighty-five cents. And I'm stalling to figure out the tip and Sugar say give him a dime. And I decide he don't need it bad as I do, so later for him. But then he tries to take off with Junebug foot still in the door so we talk about his mama something ferocious. Then we check out that we on Fifth Avenue and everybody dressed up in stockings. One lady in fur coat, hot as it is. White folks crazy.

"This is the place," Miss Moore say, presenting it to us in the voice she uses at the museum. "Let's look in the windows before we go in."

"Can we steal?" Sugar asks very serious like she's getting the ground rules squared away before she plays. "I beg your pardon," say Miss Moore, and we fall out. So she leads us around the windows of the toy store and me and Sugar screamin, "This is mine, that's mine, I gotta have that, that was made for me, I was born for that," till Big Butt drowns us out.

"Hey, I'm goin to buy that there."

"That there? You don't even know what it is, stupid."

"I do so," he say punchin on Rosie Giraffe. "It's a microscope."

"Whatcha gonna do with a microscope, fool?"

"Look at things."

"Like what, Ronald?" ask Miss Moore. And Big Butt ain't got the first notion. So here go Miss Moore gabbing about the thousands of bacteria in a drop of water and the some-thinorother in a speck of blood and the million and one living things in the air around us is invisible to the naked eye. And what she say that for? Junebug go to town on that "naked" and we rolling. Then Miss Moore ask what it cost. So we all jam into the window smudgin it up and the price tag say $300. So then she ask how long'd take for Big Butt and Junebug to save up their allowances. "Too long," I say. "Yeh," adds Sugar, "outgrown it by that time." And Miss Moore say no, you never outgrow learning instruments. "Why, even medical students and interns and," blah, blah, blah. And we ready to choke Big Butt for bringing it up in the first damn place.

"This here costs four hundred eighty dollars," say Rosie Giraffe. So we pile up all over her to see what she pointin out. My eyes tell me it's a chunk of glass cracked with some-thing heavy, and different-color inks dripped into the splits, then the whole thing put into a oven or something. But for $480 it don't make sense.

"That's a paperweight made of semi-precious stones fused together under tremendous pressure," she explains slowly, with her hands doing the mining and all the factory work.

"So what's a paperweight?" asks Rosie Giraffe.

"To weigh paper with, dumbbell," say Flyboy, the wise man from the East.

"Not exactly," say Miss Moore, which is what she say when you warm or way off too. "It's to weigh paper down so it won't scatter and make your desk untidy." So right away me and Sugar curtsy to each other and then to Mercedes who is more the tidy type.

"We don't keep paper on top of the desk in my class," say Junebug, figuring Miss Moore crazy or lyin one.

"At home, then," she say. "Don't you have a calendar and a pencil case and a blotter and a letter-opener on your desk at home where you do your homework?" And she know damn well what our homes look like cause she nosys around in them every chance she gets.

"I don't even have a desk," say Junebug. "Do we?"

"No. And I don't get no homework neither," say Big Butt.

"And I don't even have a home," say Flyboy like he do at school to keep the white folks off his back and sorry for him. Send this poor kid to camp posters, is his specialty.

"I do," says Mercedes. "I have a box of stationery on my desk and a picture of my cat. My godmother bought the stationery and the desk. There's a big rose on each sheet and the envelopes smell like roses."

"Who wants to know about your smelly-ass stationery," say Rosie Giraffe fore I can get my two cents in.

"It's important to have a work area all your own so that . . ."

"Will you look at this sailboat, please," say Flyboy, cuttin her off and pointin to the thing like it was his. So once again we tumble all over each other to gaze at this magnificent thing in the toy store which is just big enough to maybe sail two kittens across the pond if you strap them to the posts tight. We all start reciting the price tag like we in assembly. "Handcrafted sailboat of fiberglass at one thousand one hundred ninety-five dollars."

"Unbelievable," I hear myself say and am really stunned. I read it again for myself just in case the group recitation put me in a trance. Same thing. For some reason this pisses me off. We look at Miss Moore and she lookin at us, waiting for I dunno what.

"Who'd pay all that when you can buy a sailboat set for a quarter at Pop's, a tube of glue for a dime, and a ball of string for eight cents? It must have a motor and a whole lot else besides," I say. "My sailboat cost me about fifty cents."

"But will it take water?" say Mercedes with her smart ass.

"Took mine to Alley Pond Park once," say Flyboy. "String broke, Lost it. Pity."

"Sailed mine in Central Park and it keeled over and sank. Had to ask my father for another dollar."

"And you got the strap," laugh Big Butt. "The jerk didn't even have a string on it. My old man wailed on his behind."

Little Q. T. was staring hard at the sailboat and you could see he wanted it bad. But he too little and somebody'd just take it from him. So what the hell. "This boat for kids, Miss Moore?"

"Parents silly to buy something like that just to get all broke up," say Rosie Giraffe.

"That much money it should last forever," I figure.

"My father'd buy it for me if I wanted it."

"Your father, my ass," say Rosie Giraffe getting a chance to finally push Mercedes.

"Must be rich people shop here," say Q. T.

"You are a very bright boy," say Flyboy. "What was your first clue?" And he rap him on the head with the back of his knuckles, since Q. T. the only one he could get away with. Though Q. T. liable to come up behind you years later and get his licks in when you half expect it.

"What I want to know is," I says to Miss Moore though I never talk to her, I wouldn't give the bitch that satisfaction, "is how much a real boat costs? I figure a thousand'd get you a yacht any day."

"Why don't you check that out," she says, "and report back to the group?" Which really pains my ass. If you gonna mess up a perfectly good swim day least you could do is have some answers. "Let's go in," she say like she got something up her sleeve. Only she don't lead the way. So me and Sugar turn the corner to where the entrance is, but when we get there I kinda hang back. Not that I'm scared, what's there to be afraid of, just a toy store. But I feel funny, shame. But what I got to be shamed about? Got as much right to go in as anybody. But somehow I can't seem to get hold of the door, so I step away for Sugar to lead. But she hangs back too. And I look at her and she looks at me and this is ridiculous. I mean, damn, I have never ever been shy about doing nothing or going nowhere. But then Mercedes steps up and then Rosie Giraffe and Big Butt crowd in behind and shove, and next thing we all stuffed into the doorway with only Mercedes squeezing past us, smoothing out her jumper and walking right down the aisle. Then the rest of us tumble in like a glued-together jigsaw done all wrong. And people lookin at us. And it's like the time me and Sugar crashed into the Catholic church on a dare. But once we got in there and everything so hushed and holy and the candles and the bowin and the handkerchiefs on all the drooping heads, I just couldn't go through with the plan. Which was for me to run up to the altar and do a tap dance while Sugar played the nose flute and messed around in the holy water. And Sugar kept givin me the elbow. Then later teased me so bad I tied her up in the shower and turned it on and locked her in. And she'd be there till this day if Aunt Gretchen hadn't finally figured I was lyin about the boarder takin a shower.

Same thing in the store. We all walkin on tiptoe and hardly touchin the games and puzzles and things. And I watched Miss Moore who is steady watchin us like she waitin for a sign. Like Mama Drewery watches the sky and sniffs the air and takes note of just how much slant is in the bird formation. Then me and Sugar bump smack into each other, so busy gazing at the toys, specially the sailboat. But we don't laugh and go into our fat-lady bump-stomach routine. We just stare at that price tag. Then Sugar run a finger over the whole boat. And I'm jealous and want to hit her. Maybe not her, but I sure want to punch somebody in the mouth.

"Watcha bring us here for, Miss Moore?"

"You sound angry, Sylvia. Are you mad about something?" Givin me one of them grins like she tellin a grown-up joke that never turns out to be funny. And she's lookin very closely at me like maybe she plannin to do my portrait from memory. I'm mad, but I won't give her that satisfaction. So I slouch around the store bein very bored and say, "Let's go."

Me and Sugar at the back of the train watchin the tracks whizzin by large then small then gettin gobbled up in the dark. I'm thinkin about this tricky toy I saw in the store. A clown that somersaults on a bar then does chin-ups just cause you yank lightly at his leg. Cost $35. I could see me askin my mother for a $35 birthday clown. "You wanna who that costs what?" she'd say, cocking her head to the side to get a better view of the hole in my head. Thirty-five dollars could buy new bunk beds for Junior and Gretchen's boy. Thirty-five dollars and the whole household could go visit Granddaddy Nelson in the country. Thirty-five dollars would pay for the rent and the piano bill too. Who are these people that spend that much for performing clowns and $1,000 for toy sailboats? What kinda work they do and how they live and how come we ain't in on it? Where we are is who we are, Miss Moore always pointin out. But it don't necessarily have to be that way, she always adds then waits for somebody to say that poor people have to wake up and demand their share of the pie and don't none of us know what kind of pie she talkin about in the first damn place. But she ain't so smart cause I still got her four dollars from the taxi and she sure ain't gettin it. Messin up my day with this shit. Sugar nudges me in my pocket and winks.

Miss Moore lines us up in front of the mailbox where we started from, seem like years ago, and I got a headache for thinkin so hard. And we lean all over each other so we can hold up under the draggy-ass lecture she always finishes us off with at the end before we thank her for borin us to tears. But she just looks at us like she readin tea leaves. Finally she say, "Well, what did you think of F. A. O. Schwartz?"

Rosie Giraffe mumbles, "White folks crazy."

"I'd like to go there again when I get my birthday money," says Mercedes, and we shove her out the pack so she has to lean on the mailbox by herself.

"I'd like a shower. Tiring day," say Flyboy.

Then Sugar surprises me by sayin, "You know, Miss Moore, I don't think all of us here put together eat in a year what that sailboat costs." And Miss Moore lights up like somebody goosed her. "And?" she say, urging Sugar on. Only I'm standin on her foot so she don't continue.

"Imagine for a minute what kind of society it is in which some people can spend on a toy what it would cost to feed a family of six or seven. What do you think?"

"I think," say Sugar pushing me off her feet like she never done before, cause I whip her ass in a minute, "that this is not much of a democracy if you ask me. Equal chance to pursue happiness means an equal crack at the dough, don't it?" Miss Moore is besides herself and I am disgusted with Sugar's treachery. So I stand on her foot one more time to see if she'll shove me. She shuts up, and Miss Moore looks at me, sorrowfully I'm thinkin. And somethin weird is goin on, I can feel it in my chest.

"Anybody else learn anything today?" lookin dead at me.

I walk away and Sugar has to run to catch up and don't even seem to notice when I shrug her arm off my shoulder.

"Well, we got four dollars anyway," she says.

"Uh hunh."

"We could go to Hascombs and get half a chocolate layer and then go to the Sunset and still have plenty money for potato chips and ice-cream sodas."

"Uh hunh."

"Race you to Hascombs," she say.

We start down the block and she gets ahead which is O.K. by me cause I'm goin to the West End and then over to the Drive to think this day through. She can run if she want to and even run faster. But ain't nobody gonna beat me at nuthin.

VII

The New World Order and
Its Consequences: 1980s to 2005

We could circle our words around the world . . .
if the screens were really in the hands of experts: us
think of it—our ideas whipping through the air
everything stored in an eyeflash
our whole history, ready and waiting.
        —Karen Brodine, "Woman Sitting at the Machine, Thinking"

The rust was setting into the post–World War II engines of industry and affluence by the mid-1970s. Corporations invested their capital overseas, closing factories in the United States and reopening them in countries where workers labored for much lower pay. In many of the plants that remained across the Rust Belt, technological advances (the use of robots in automaking, for example) threatened skilled shop-floor workers with obsolescence. Widespread shutdowns, layoffs and "downsizing" meant that part-time work, unemployment, and homelessness were again on the rise. From 1973, real incomes (i.e., wages adjusted for inflation) entered a period of decline that continued, with a brief respite in the 1990s, into the twenty-first century. Conditions for working people worsened sharply in the 1980s, as the conservative "Reagan Revolution"—which included deregulating the workplace, breaking trade unions, and cutting welfare and tuition benefits—began dismantling the New Deal "social contract" that had made possible the relative prosperity of the postwar decades. At the start of the twenty-first century, the gap between rich and poor in the United States had returned to the level of the Gilded Age: The top 20 percent of the population had seventy-five times the per capita wealth of the bottom 20 percent (the gap had been thirtyfold in 1960).[1] At the same time, the United States spent a smaller proportion of its gross domestic product on fighting poverty than any of the other twenty most developed nations.[2]

At the start of the period from which the literature that follows is selected, the American working class was broadly divided between a shrinking unionized blue-collar sector and a much larger low-wage workforce in the booming service economy. From the midcentury, white-collar workers in offices, stores, hospitals, schools, and banks began to outnumber blue-collar workers.[3] Although they were encouraged to see themselves as middle class—going home with their clothes relatively clean—their work was often as manual and repetitive and as rigorously supervised as was factory labor (as Karen Brodine's "Woman Sitting at the Machine, Thinking," based on her work typesetting by computer, makes clear). The majority of service workers were women, who today make up 50 percent of the labor force. Especially in the lower-paid clerical, sales, food, and janitorial services, many were African American or Latino/Latina. They were joined from the 1970s on by

Facing Page: From Milton Rogovin's *Triptychs: Buffalo's Lower West Side Revisited* (NY: W. W. Norton, 1994), taken (from the top down) 1972, 1985, 1992, in the neighborhood of Buffalo's Lower West Side. *Photographs by Milton Rogovin, reprinted by permission, The Rogovin Collection, LLC.*

"Fourth Wave" immigrants from Asia and Central and South America, who were often fleeing poverty and political repression in their homelands (see the work of Helena Viramontes, Martín Espada, and Melida Rodas). Some illegal immigrants were absorbed into sweatshops in the garment industries of New York and Los Angeles, while others became migrant farmworkers, enduring long days of stoop labor exposed to dangerous chemicals, low pay, and harsh treatment from contractors (see Cherríe Moraga's play, *Heroes and Saints*).

The labor movement was slow to mount a challenge. Unions had been weakened both by the shrinking of their traditional industrial base and by the attack on labor rights initiated by Ronald Reagan's destruction of PATCO, the air traffic controllers' union, in 1981. Several major strikes were lost before the AFL-CIO began to follow the lead of Hospital Workers Local 1199 and Cesar Chavez's United Farm Workers in organizing the unorganized, especially women and workers of color. Janitors, hospital orderlies, hotel maids, and farmworkers became some of the most militant and successful unionized workers. The decline in membership continued, however, with only 12 percent of workers in unions in 2005, down from 35 percent in the late 1950s. Since it was largely the unions, backed by New Deal legislation, that ensured workers' rights—to a living wage, health and retirement benefits, vacations, and overtime pay—the erosion of labor's power allowed corporations to drive down wages, cut benefits, and undermine health and safety regulations. The majority of the new jobs that were created during the Clinton-era boom in the 1990s were low-wage, low-skill, and part time. The ranks of the "working poor" swelled: that is, people living below the poverty line, despite holding jobs with the world's largest and most profitable companies, such as Wal-Mart and McDonald's.[4]

Contemporary working-class literature bears the imprint of distress and dislocation brought on by the twin forces of deindustrialization and globalization, as well as by the longer-term systemic legacies of racial and class oppression. In one sense, the American workforce and its literature have always been "globalized." The plantation economy imported its slave labor from Africa and exported its cash crops to Britain, and the Industrial Revolution was built on the labor of workers who were drawn from across Europe. The service economy relies on Fourth Wave immigrants arriving in numbers that rival the great influx of the 1890s to 1910s.[5] The U.S. working class has therefore always been many-cultured, and it stands now as one of the most racially and ethnically diverse among developed nations.

The literature gathered here reflects this multiculturalism of the contemporary working class, including its diversity in gender and sexuality, and its regional differences. Part VII also reflects its broad range of occupations. We hear from a secretary (in Nellie Wong), a medical orderly (Ernie Brill), a handyman (Dagoberto Gilb), a data-entry processor (Karen Brodine), farmworkers (Tomas Rivera), domestics (Hattie Gossett and Kate Rushin), kitchen workers (Martín Espada and Melida Rodas) and waitresses (in works by Dorothy Allison, Jan Beatty, and John Gilgun). Showing that it is premature to designate the United States as "postindustrial"—20 percent of American workers still labor in factories—we also meet workers in an auto plant (in Jim Daniels and Philip Levine), a chicken factory (Carolyn Chute), a glass factory (Peter Oresick), a textile mill (Michael Casey), a nuclear power plant (Bill Witherup), a frozen-food factory (Leslie Feinberg), and a lumber mill (Yusef Komunyakaa). And we hear from two women worker-writers, pioneers in the male blue-collar worlds of a construction site and a railroad machine shop (Susan Eisenberg and Sue Doro).

Writers responded to the circumstances of working-class lives in the era of the "New World Order" in ways that were both like and unlike writers of the 1930s. Like members of the proletarian movement, many are—or were when these pieces were conceived— active worker-writers: Dagoberto Gilb was a carpenter, Sue Doro was a machinist, Jan Beatty was a waitress, and Jeanne Bryner is a nurse. As in the 1930s, they began publishing in the new small journals and presses that arose to give voice to working-class and multi-cultural experience: *Working Classics, Mill Hunk Herald, Blue Collar Review*, Arte Público Press, Bottom Dog Press, Kitchen Table Press, Papier Maché Press, West End Press, and the Feminist Press. Unlike the 1930s, many of the writers collected here are university-educated children of working-class parents, some working now as teachers of students from families like theirs. In much of their poetry, fiction, and memoir they reach back to assess or reclaim the inheritance of an earlier generation whose lives were shaped by manual labor. These fathers (in works by Jeanne Bryner, Lucille Clifton, Yusef Komunyakaa, Peter Oresick, Simon J. Ortiz, Melida Rodas, and Lois-Ann Yamanaka) and mothers (in Dorothy Allison, John Gilgun, Linda Hogan, Marge Piercy, Kate Rushin, Larry Smith, and Bill Witherup) are remembered, among a range of other personal qualities, for their hard work, resilience, and creativity in "making do" and in providing for their children. They are often remembered also for acts of caring or resistance, small or large, from which their children learned what it meant to be working class.

For Native American and other writers of color, raised in cultures with strong tra-ditions of oral storytelling, stories themselves can offer power to heal the wounds of labor, poverty and colonization. Like the fabrics pieced together to form Lovey's homemade patchwork hip-huggers (in Lois-Ann Yamanaka's narrative), these stories name pieces of the past, carrying them forward as resources for the present. The emergence of these new voices of multicultural working-class expression is another difference from the 1930s. Although the accents have changed, however, and the locus of struggle has shifted since the days of national mass movements—becoming at times more internal, more local, or more global—the new writing has its own political force. "Beneath that cool green sea of money," writes Jimmy Santiago Baca, "millions and millions of people fight to live, / search for pearls in the darkest depths / of their dreams."[6] For Joy Harjo, "The world begins at a kitchen table."[7] And Linda Hogan adds: "Inside the walls / world changes are planned, bosses overthrown."[8] If there is to be a better life, beyond the era of "liars, thieves, and killers," writes Simon Ortiz, it will come

> By working in this manner,
> For the sake of the land and people
> To be in vital relation
> With each other,
> We will have life
> And it will continue.[9]

Given their diversity—in ethnicity, in forms of labor, in geography, in education, in politics—what do the writers in this section, and the working people they represent, have in common? Some would argue that the working class is now fragmented into distinct factions, so that common class feeling and class activism are things of the past. Others suggest that extreme disparities of wealth and poverty, coupled with a growing awareness of the damage of corporate globalization, are forging a new consciousness and new possibilities for united action. An example may be seen in the 1999 Seattle actions against the World Trade Organization, which brought together trade unions and peace and environmental groups to "challenge a global order that places profits over people."[10] Such movements for economic justice are facilitated, ironically, by the prime technology of that new world order: computer communications.

The working-class literature of the new era of globalization, the Internet, and the "war on terror" is still being written. One of its directions may be indicated by Martín Espada's "Alabanza: In Praise of Local 100," a poem dedicated to "the 43 members of Hotel and Restaurant Employees Local 100, working at the Windows on the World restaurant, who lost their lives in the attack on the World Trade Center." Published on the first anniversary of September 11, 2001, "Alabanza" is a praise-song for the unnamed men and women from "Ecuador, México, Republica Dominicana, Haiti, Yemen, Ghana, Bangladesh" who worked and died at the pinnacle of American global capitalism. As the retaliatory war against Afghanistan begins, Espada imagines two columns of smoke rising from Manhattan and Kabul:

> . . . and one said with an Afghan tongue:
> *Teach me to dance. We have no music here.*
> And the other said with a Spanish tongue:
> *I will teach you. Music is all we have.*

Notes

1. Joshua Holland, "In Praise of Prosperity," AlterNet, April 25, 2005.
2. Ibid.
3. Joshua Freeman et al., *Who Built America: Working People and the Nation's Economy, Politics, Culture, and Society* (Boston, Bedford/St. Martin's, 2000), 587.
4. *Union Members Summary* (USDL 05-112), January 27, 2005, (Washington, DC: Bureau of Labor Statistics). See also David K. Shipler, *The Working Poor: Invisible in America* (New York: Vintage, 2005).
5. Shipler, *The Working Poor*, and Freeman et al., *Who Built America*, 715.
6. "So Mexicans Are Taking Jobs From Americans," p. 848 in this volume.
7. "Perhaps the World Ends Here," p. 796 in this volume.
8. "The New Apartment, Minneapolis," p. 746 in this volume.
9. "We Have Been Told Many Things," p. 709 in this volume.
10. Priscilla Murolo and A. B. Chitty, *From the Folks Who Brought You the Weekend* (New York: The New Press, 2001), 328; Roni Krouzman, "WTO: The Battle in Seattle," in Howard Zinn and Anthony Arnove, *Voices of a People's History of the United States* (New York: Seven Stories Press), 584.

Philip Levine (b. 1928)

When Philip Levine's working-class portraits first appeared in the 1960s, there was little contemporary poetry about the hard industrial labor he knew from his own and his family's experience. Born and raised in Detroit, the grandson of Russian Jewish immigrants, Levine started writing as a worker at Chevy Gear and Axle while taking night classes at Wayne State University. "I believed even then," he writes in *The Bread of Time: Toward an Autobiography* (1994), "that if I could transform my experience into poetry I would give it the value and dignity it did not begin to possess on its own." Many of the poems in his best-known book *What Work Is* (1991) and in his earliest volumes, *On the Edge* (1963) and *Not This Pig* (1968) explore the blue-collar inheritance that tied whole families to factory work, as well as their dignity and kindness in the face of its grinding monotony: "In those terrible places designed to rob us of our bodies and spirits, we sustained each other." In *They Feed, They Lion* (1972), Levine explored the Detroit race riots of the late 1960s. While he moved away from Detroit—he has lived most of his life in California and spent several periods in Spain—his writing maintained a loyalty to his roots and a political sympathy for those who are trapped by one form or another of dehumanizing power. In *The Names of the Lost* (1976) and *7 Years from Somewhere* (1979), he combines elegies for family members and for antifascist fighters in the Spanish Civil War. *What Work Is*, from which two of the poems that follow—the title poem and "Among Children"—are drawn, won a 1991 National Book Award and confirmed Levine's reputation as the preeminent contemporary poet of industrial work and life in America. Levine has translated the poems of Gloria Fuertes and Jaime Sabines and edited *The Essential Keats* (1994). He was, until his retirement, a professor of English at Fresno State University.

You Can Have It

My brother comes home from work
and climbs the stairs to our room.
I can hear the bed groan and his shoes drop
one by one. You can have it, he says.

5   The moonlight streams in the window
and his unshaven face is whitened
like the face of the moon. He will sleep
long after noon and waken to find me gone.

Thirty years will pass before I remember
10   that moment when suddenly I knew each man
has one brother who dies when he sleeps
and sleeps when he rises to face this life,

and that together they are only one man
sharing a heart that always labors, hands
15   yellowed and cracked, a mouth that gasps
for breath and asks, Am I gonna make it?

All night at the ice plant he had fed
the chute its silvery blocks, and then I
stacked cases of orange soda for the children
20   of Kentucky, one gray box-car at a time

with always two more waiting. We were twenty
for such a short time and always in
the wrong clothes, crusted with dirt
and sweat. I think now we were never twenty.

25   In 1948 in the city of Detroit, founded
by de la Mothe Cadillac for the distant purpose
of Henry Ford, no one wakened or died,
no one walked the streets or stoked a furnace,

for there was no such year, and now
30   that year has fallen off all the old newspapers,
calendars, doctors' appointments, bonds,
wedding certificates, driver's licenses.

The city slept. The snow turned to ice.
The ice to standing pools or rivers
35   racing in the gutters. Then bright grass rose
between the thousands of cracked squares,

and that grass died. I give you back 1948.
I give you all the years from then

to the coming one. Give me back the moon
40   with its frail light falling across a face.

Give me back my young brother, hard
and furious, with wide shoulders and a curse
for God and burning eyes that look upon
all creation and say, You can have it.

AMONG CHILDREN

I walk among the rows of bowed heads—
the children are sleeping through fourth grade
so as to be ready for what is ahead,
the monumental boredom of junior high
5   and the rush forward tearing their wings
loose and turning their eyes forever inward.
These are the children of Flint, their fathers
work at the spark plug factory or truck
bottled water in 5 gallon sea-blue jugs
10   to the widows of the suburbs. You can see
already how their backs have thickened,
how their small hands, soiled by pig iron,
leap and stutter even in dreams. I would like
to sit down among them and read slowly
15   from *The Book of Job* until the windows
pale and the teacher rises out of a milky sea
of industrial scum, her gowns streaming
with light, her foolish words transformed
into song, I would like to arm each one
20   with a quiver of arrows so that they might
rush like wind there where no battle rages
shouting among the trumpets, Ha! Ha!
How dear the gift of laughter in the face
of the 8 hour day, the cold winter mornings
25   without coffee and oranges, the long lines
of mothers in old coats waiting silently
where the gates have closed. Ten years ago
I went among these same children, just born,
in the bright ward of the Sacred Heart and leaned
30   down to hear their breaths delivered that day,
burning with joy. There was such wonder
in their sleep, such purpose in their eyes
closed against autumn, in their damp heads
blurred with the hair of ponds, and not one
35   turned against me or the light, not one
said, I am sick, I am tired, I will go home,
not one complained or drifted alone,
unloved, on the hardest day of their lives.
Eleven years from now they will become
40   the men and women of Flint or Paradise,

the majors of a minor town, and I
will be gone into smoke or memory,
so I bow to them here and whisper
all I know, all I will never know.

WHAT WORK IS

We stand in the rain in a long line
waiting at Ford Highland Park. For work.
You know what work is—if you're
old enough to read this you know what
5   work is, although you may not do it.
Forget you. This is about waiting,
shifting from one foot to another.
Feeling the light rain falling like mist
into your hair, blurring your vision
10   until you think you see your own brother
ahead of you, maybe ten places.
You rub your glasses with your fingers,
and of course it's someone else's brother,
narrower across the shoulders than
15   yours but with the same sad slouch, the grin
that does not hide the stubbornness,
the sad refusal to give in to
rain, to the hours wasted waiting,
to the knowledge that somewhere ahead
20   a man is waiting who will say, "No,
we're not hiring today," for any
reason he wants. You love your brother,
now suddenly you can hardly stand
the love flooding you for your brother,
25   who's not beside you or behind or
ahead because he's home trying to
sleep off a miserable night shift
at Cadillac so he can get up
before noon to study his German.
30   Works eight hours a night so he can sing
Wagner, the opera you hate most,
the worst music ever invented.
How long has it been since you told him
you loved him, held his wide shoulders,
35   opened your eyes wide and said those words,
and maybe kissed his cheek? You've never
done something so simple, so obvious,
not because you're too young or too dumb,
not because you're jealous or even mean
40   or incapable of crying in
the presence of another man, no,
just because you don't know what work is.

Nellie Wong (b. 1934)

For San Francisco-based poet Nellie Wong, much of her writing is rooted in her experience as a working-class Asian American woman and in her commitments as an activist for labor and human rights. "A lot of my poems come from the workplace," she writes, "that's where I've experienced a great deal of sexism and racism. . . . The more I see some people fighting back, the more I see everyone acquiring the strength to fight back." Raised in Oakland, California, the first American-born child of Chinese immigrants, Wong worked as a waitress in her parents' restaurant while in school. On graduation from Oakland High School, she went to work as a secretary, spending eighteen years with the Bethlehem Steel Corporation. She began writing in the early 1970s while attending night school at San Francisco State University and went on to found the feminist literary and performance group, Unbound Feet. In 1983, Wong joined Tillie Olsen, Alice Walker, and Paule Marshall as a member of the first U.S. Women Writers Tour of China. Wong is the author of three books of poems, *Dreams in Harrison Park* (1977), *The Death of Long Steam Lady* (1986), and *Stolen Moments* (1997); she is also coeditor of a collection of political essays, *Voices of Color* (1999) and of the 2003 publication, *Three Asian American Writers Speak Out on Feminism*. Until her recent retirement, Wong worked as an analyst in the Office of Affirmative Action and Equal Opportunity at the University of California, San Francisco. She is member of the University Professional and Technical Employees (UPTE/CWA 9119) union, a delegate to the San Francisco Labor Council, and an organizer for the Freedom Socialist Party. "Unemployment" was first published in David Joseph's journal of literature by worker-writers, *Working Classics* in 1983.

Unemployment

has no wings or legs. Yet its eyes are dark granite piercing
my heart. It is a monster, huge, rising, rising
from the decays of capitalism, not from the depths
of the ocean, not from the mountains, not
5 from the burning rays of the sun.

My former employer still sends me "The Bethlehem Review."
A woman speaks about her mining experience at a meeting
of men. She speaks for equality, of course, and the men nod
their heads. The government and corporations exploit
10 Indian lands for uranium and yet, unemployment with its dark granite
eyes stares over them too.

What is an unemployment line at the Employment Development Department?
An unemployment line is mostly men and women of color,
young, middle-aged, in overalls, khakis, worn leather jackets,
15 jeans, dresses, quilted jackets. They stare at the walls, smoke, kid
with each other, read the want ads. And I read the Business Peach
and am told I should start an IRA account.

"Hello," my interviewer greets me, "my name is Liz."
Is this a tea party, I ask myself silently, won over

20   to the woman's warmth. She talks about Pennsylvania, home
of Bethlehem Steel where they've laid off 10,000 workers, nationwide.
She gushes about the Saucon Valley Country Club, and I see
visions of emerald-green lawns, clear blue skies, where only
a selected few, executives in polo shirts, white pants, can forget
25   business for a few hours or can drum up more business for profits.
The Saucon Valley Country Club could be a home
for the homeless, the unemployed. The people could take over
the land, work it to fill their bellies.

Liz approves my application. After 31 years as a secretary
30   I am led to meet Helen who specializes in helping the unemployed
find jobs. Liz drops me off with "who wants a super secretary
with 18½ years at Bethlehem Steel?" A woman next to Helen's desk
tells me I should keep Helen awake who is shuffling 5′ × 8′ cards
into a metal file box. All the workers look up, smile at this woman
35   who is newly unemployed.

Helen shows me a job order for a secretary to a vice president
of an airline. Starting salary $800 per month, which is negotiable,
of course. Or, here, here's one at $650 per month as an office manager
to help the disabled. When I do not respond with a smile,
40   with enthusiasm, Helen's eyes search my face.

"The salary holding you back?" Her hands move, quick as a bird's peck,
and find more job orders. "You'll have to make some adjustments,"
she warns, and thrusts a form at me that will tell her everything
I can do.

45   Type, file, edit, write, organize, supervise, administrate,
handling phone calls while my mind buzzes its own filing system
of things to do, things to plan, taking shorthand, putting
messages through the Rapidfax, pulling off wires, packaging mail,
planning itineraries, coordinating conferences. The gamut of things
50   I can do: they do not sparkle but are translucent like good jade,
beads upon beads that circulate through my mind and my body,
these hands, these hands that rarely touch earth, but touch
upon everything that I am, can do, and want to change.

With my skills and experience I can be hired tomorrow.
55   Good secretaries are hard to find, good secretaries
are not appreciated, not paid well, not respected.
Good secretaries can always find jobs. Helen knows this,
impressed with my credentials. Friends for two minutes,
Helen and I now are apart, two women workers
60   In a system that must change. Yet Helen makes me feel
uncomfortable, that I should be jumping at each job
she pulls out from her gray metal box.

I hear names being called out: Guerrero, Gibson, Tong, Wilder.
They float through the smoke-fitted air. One man dozes,
65   another shuffles his feet. And a young Black woman
in a jacket of fake pony, rushes up to the window to see
if she has been forgotten.

THE DEATH OF LONG STEAM LADY

If Paisley Chan had her way, she would not go to Long Steam Lady's funeral. But of course she must. If she didn't go, she couldn't forgive herself. Besides, she loved Long Steam Lady and she missed seeing the old woman sitting in the sun in Portsmouth Square. Long Steam Lady with the plastic shopping bag filled with bock choy, carrots and sometimes a roll or two of pressed crab apples. Long Steam Lady with her painted eyebrows and fat red lips which even made them thicker, more sensuous than Paisley thought she should have colored them. But who was she, Paisley Chan, to say, to judge how Long Steam Lady dressed, how Long Steam Lady decorated herself? Even in an old flowered nylon dress and a tattered wool coat, Long Steam Lady looked elegant, with her eyes closed, letting the sun beat down on her unlined face, her unwrinkled hands.

Paisley dressed herself slowly and deliberately. What to wear to a Chinese funeral these days? Though Paisley was not a blood relative, she would wear sensible navy blue, or perhaps her coffee-brown pantsuit and her beige polyester blouse, the one she could tie into a puffy bow. Yes, she'd look tailored, dignified, and she would not wear lipstick. Yes, she'd walk into Gum Moon Funeral Parlor at the edge of Portsmouth Square, and no one would know her. Paisley Chan, thirty six years old. Paisley Chan, who worked as a telephone receptionist in the Financial District for nineteen years. Paisley Chan, who discovered Long Steam Lady looking grand in a frayed purple cloche in Portsmouth Square, who found herself having lunch with a talkative old woman for the past three months, who found it refreshing to leave her office every day at lunch, a reprieve from the enforced sterility of saying, "Good morning, J & C Enterprises," as if she were a machine.

Paisley ran a tortoise comb through her thick curly hair. Then she grabbed an Afro comb and separated several stubborn strands, letting them curl away from her scalp, then watched the hair form commas, curving into each other like a chorus line of dancers in a dream. Long Steam Lady had told Paisley that she had been a dancer, a dancer at Imperial City, which was now a disco. Whether that was true Paisley didn't know and she didn't care. She loved sitting in Portsmouth Square listening to Long Steam Lady spin her stories of how she slithered in sequined gowns, how she danced in top hats and tails, how she tap danced, how she tangoed with her lover-partner, Alexander Hing, and how she never rose from bed until one o'clock in the afternoon after an exhausting performance.

One day when Paisley was nibbling on hom foon and getting her fingers all sticky, she asked Long Steam Lady how she got her name. Long Steam, *cheong hay*, a talker, a blabbermouth. "Why are you called *Cheong Hay Poa*?" Paisley had asked, licking her fingers and relishing the grease from the filled rice noodles. Several pigeons clustered at Paisley's and Long Steam Lady's feet, pecking at seeds that Long Steam Lady spread lovingly on the ground as she pantomimed a folk dance of planting rice for the autumn harvest.

Paisley had watched the old woman with wonder, with awe. "Well, aren't you ever going to tell me your real name?" Paisley had asked impatiently. "I really want to know. Is it Estelle, Miranda, Sylvia?" The old woman closed her eyes for a moment, ignoring the beautiful names that her young companion had tossed at her like newly burst fireworks. "Ah, *Nu*, that doesn't matter. No names matter, don't you know that? I am Long Steam Lady. I am *Cheong Hay Poa* because I talk too much. I talk so much that no one ever listens to me, and no one listens to me because they can't make sense of what I say. Who has time?" She shrugged her shoulders. "I talk about everything, this and that about love, not just worrying where my body will be laid to rest, whether it will be pointed in the right direction of heaven's blessing. Ah, no, life is too short to worry about dying, when all one has to do is to love. No name, child, just Long Steam Lady, just *Cheong Hay Poa.* That is enough."

Long Steam Lady had refused to continue the discussion any longer. She had begun to spread more seeds on the ground, and more pigeons clustered around her feet, pecking around her worn shoes, not Dr. Scholl's that were high laced, not in somber black leather, but silver sandals that she had danced in when she was young. The heels were badly worn and in need of repair, but somehow Long Steam Lady's legs were still slender, a dancer's legs with strength and vitality. Long Steam Lady had told Paisley she never married. She had only loved Alexander Hing. Yes, Alexander Hing who danced circles around Fred Astaire. Yes, Alexander Hing. Long Steam Lady's eyes got misty, but Alexander Hing already had a wife.

Paisley slipped on her pantyhose and cursed as she had slipped them on backwards. She removed them and began again. She stared out her apartment window and watched the leaves of a pink camellia bush glisten in the sunlight. She watched the nylon panels move lightly in the breeze. Autumn was her favorite season, Halloween, Thanksgiving, homemade oxtail stew and chrysanthemums. Yes, she'd visit Long Steam Lady with her spider chrysanthemums though she wasn't sure whether Long Steam Lady would be cremated or buried at Ning Yeong Cemetery at Colma.

Paisley didn't know whether Long Steam Lady had any relatives. Long Steam Lady had mentioned once a sister who lived in New York City. Perhaps Paisley would meet that sister today at the funeral, but Paisley didn't even know her last name. Whom would she ask for? Would she yell out, "Yoo hoo, is Long Steam Lady's sister here from New York City? Long Steam Lady, *Cheong Hay Poa*, the dancer, the old woman who died all alone?" Why that would be downright embarrassing for someone whose name she didn't even know. And if she did find the sister, then what? How would she describe her friendship with the old woman? Lunch friends, companions? Philosophers, sisters? Grandmother, granddaughter?

Paisley sighed, again wishing she didn't have to go to the funeral. She didn't want to see Long Steam Lady lying in her coffin, lifeless, painted grotesquely by morticians who knew nothing about her, morticians who would over-rouge her cheeks, morticians who would redesign her with no creativity, no imagination. If Paisley had her way, she would dress Long Steam Lady in a black gown of airy silk crepe, satin spaghetti straps, with a huge sunburst of rhinestones pinned on one shoulder, with a red silk rose tucked into her bunned hair. But no, the morticians would probably dress her in a wool suit of salt-and-pepper tweed, or in a house-dress with droopy lavender flowers, or worse yet, in an old coat sweater with large pockets and military buttons. The mourners would never know Long Steam Lady, the dancer. The mourners would never know, would never see the silver sandals that Long Steam Lady wore daily to the park. They would shake their heads. Women would weep and sniff into their handkerchiefs, and Paisley would hear them say, "Long Steam Lady was a good woman, she never harmed anyone." And she would hear them say, "never married, never had any sons to look after her in her old age."

Paisley had never heard Long Steam Lady complain about not getting married, about not having sons. Sometimes Long Steam Lady wandered in her conversations. Sometimes she jumped from talking about dancing at Imperial City to looking for a letter written to her from her village in Toishan. But always, Paisley remembered, Long Steam Lady's eyes sparkled, her eyes grew large and luminous as she fell into lapses of memory, smiling as if she harbored the most delicious secret in the world.

And then Long Steam Lady was no more. For the past week Paisley had gone looking for her at the bench nearest the elevator in Portsmouth Square. Paisley took roast beef sandwiches and Bireley's orange drinks as if those items would seduce Long Steam Lady's appearance from the dark. Even the pigeons clustered closer to Paisley as she searched for the slender old woman among the crowds of men huddled in their games, among children laughing and running from their mothers, among the men who exercised Tai Chi Chuan, among the shoppers who spilled out into the park.

Paisley kicked herself for not knowing where Long Steam Lady lived. It had to be somewhere in Chinatown, perhaps at Ping Yuen, perhaps up Jackson or Washington Street, or Mason near the cable car barn. But Long Steam Lady, as talkative as she was, never revealed where she slept, never revealed whether she had any relatives looking in on her. But that was what attracted Paisley in the first place. Long Steam Lady's elegance, her dignity, her independence. Though Long Steam Lady must have been at least seventy five, she never walked dragging her feet. She never hunched. She had moved with the agility of a younger person, younger perhaps than Paisley herself. Funny how Long Steam Lady used to call her "Pessalee" instead of Paisley, speaking to her in a mixture of English and Sze Yip dialect, in a language familiar and warm and endurably American. "Hah, hah," Long Steam Lady had laughed, "you have to learn how to jom the cow meat the right way. See, like this, not like that," and she had begun to move her hands in quick vertical rhythms, showing Paisley how to jom cow meat. "See, it's all in the way how you jom. Jomming, it's the best secret."

Of course, Long Steam Lady had to have a name. How else could relatives have arranged the funeral at Gum Moon? How else could mourners order wreaths of carnations and marigolds streaming with white ribbons, with Long Steam Lady's name brushed in black ink? Although Mr. Erg, the florist, had told Paisley that Long Steam Lady's funeral was Saturday, he never said Long Steam Lady's name. He had said he read her obituary in the *Gold Mountain Times*. Paisley rose from her vanity and searched through a stack of *Chronicles* on her hall table. It had never occurred to her to look through the obituaries in the *Chronicle*, but if there were services for Long Steam Lady, it had to be in the *Chronicle* too. Paisley flipped through the last three days' papers. Nothing on Long Steam Lady, nothing on names such as Wong, SooHoo, Young, Lee, Fong, Chin. Nothing on former dancers at Imperial City, on old women who fed pigeons in Portsmouth Square. On old men who died alone in their rooms. Not that Chinese people didn't die, not that waiters, laundrymen, seamstresses, dishwashers didn't die. Paisley lingered over an article on the death of a philanthropist, a member of the Pacific Union Club, a world-wide traveler, a grandfather of twelve, a civil servant. And if an obituary had appeared in the *Chronicle* on Long Steam Lady, would they have identified her as a talkative crazy old lady who fed pigeons in the park? Would they have described her silver sandals?

Well, she'd go to the funeral, she owed Long Steam Lady that. It didn't matter to Paisley that she wouldn't know any of Long Steam Lady's relatives. Who knows? Perhaps Alexander Hing might be there, an old Alexander Hing in his tapdancing shoes, an old Alexander Hing whose hair might still be black and shiny as Long Steam Lady had described him, whose pencil-thin mustache tickled Long Steam Lady as they kissed? Paisley smiled and pushed her bangs out of her eyes. Long Steam Lady and she sitting together in Portsmouth Square, laughing and talking loudly. Long Steam Lady and she devouring custard tarts as if they were gold. Long Steam Lady and she scolding panhandlers away from their pink boxes of cha siu bow and hah gow and hom foon.

In the sunlight Paisley walked up Washington Street to Gum Moon Funeral Parlor. She cast her eyes across Portsmouth Square, at the bench where she and Long Steam Lady spent many lunch hours together. She saw pigeons pecking near the garbage can. She saw felt hats, grey suits, plaid shirts. She saw beer cans roll across the pathway. Paisley shifted her gaze and began to daydream about silver sandals. At thirty six perhaps it was not too late to sign up for dancing lessons.

Tomás Rivera (1935–1984)

Born in Crystal City, Texas, the son of Mexican American migrant farmworkers, Tomás Rivera was at the time of his death the chancellor of the University of California, Riverside. Although his family traveled through the upper Midwest during the picking season, the children always attended school, and Tomás, who became an avid reader, was writing poetry by the time he was twelve. As a young adult, he continued migrant work during the summer months and, during the school year, completed high school, junior college, and, by 1958, a degree in English at Southwest Texas State University. Over the next decade, he taught public school in San Antonio, Crystal City, and League City, Texas, while pursuing advanced degrees, culminating in 1969 with a Ph.D. in romance languages and literature from the University of Oklahoma.

Tomás Rivera's masterwork . . . *y no se lo tragó la tierra* was first published in 1971, having been awarded the inaugural Quinto Sol prize for Chicano literature. In this bilingual edition, Rivera's Spanish was accompanied by Herminio Rios's English translation. The novel gives literary form to the social world of the migrant worker through a sequence of vignettes, mostly narrated by young boy who observes and responds but does not fully understand the action around him. Rivera later told an interviewer: "During that period [1945–1955] I became very conscious, in my own life, about the suffering and the strength and beauty of these people." He wanted to document both the suffering and the beauty: "Not just this and this happened, but to give a spiritual dimension to the people of that time." The novel was reissued in 1987 by Arte Público Press, with a new translation by poet Evangelina Vigil-Piñón, entitled *And the Earth Did Not Devour Him*. (The excepts that follow are from this translation.) During his lifetime, Rivera also published a collection of poems, *The Searchers* (1973). *The Harvest: A Collection of Short Fiction* (1989) and *Tomás Rivera: The Complete Works* (1991) appeared posthumously.

As a writer, Rivera was a member of the "Quinto Sol generation" (with Rudolfo Anaya and Ronaldo Hinojosa) of the Chicano Renaissance and a strong supporter of Mexican American writing and publishing. As an educator, Rivera devoted his administrative energies to opening the doors of higher education to students like himself. The University of Texas at San Antonio, where he was a professor of Spanish and vice-president, named its Tomás Rivera Center for Student Success in his honor. Rivera was working on a second novel, to be titled *La casa grande*, when he died in 1984.

FROM . . . *Y NO SE LO TRAGÓ LA TIERRA* / *AND THE EARTH DID NOT DEVOUR HIM*

IT'S THAT IT HURTS

It hurts a lot. That's why I hit him. And now what do I do? Maybe they didn't expel me from school. Maybe it ain't so, after all. Maybe it's not. *Sure it is!* It is so, they did expel me. And now what do I do?

I think it all started when I got so embarrassed and angry at the same time. I dread getting home. What am I going to tell Mother? And then when Dad gets home from the fields? They'll whip me for sure. But it's embarrassing and angering. It's always the same in these schools in the north. Everybody just stares at you up and down. And then they make fun of you and the teacher with her popsicle stick, poking your head for lice. It's embarrassing. And then when they turn up their noses. It makes you angry. I think it's better staying out here on the ranch, here in the quiet of this knoll, with its chicken coops, or out in the fields where you at least feel more free, more at ease.

"Come on, son, we're almost there."

"You gonna take me to the principal?"

"Of course not. Don't tell me you don't know how to speak English yet. Look, that's the entrance over there. Just ask if you don't know where to go. Don't be shy, ask someone. Don't be afraid."

"Why can't you go in with me?"

"Don't tell me you're scared. Look, that's probably the entrance there. Here comes someone. Now, you behave, you hear me?"

"But why don't you help me?"

"No. You'll do just fine, don't be afraid."

It's always the same. They take you to the nurse and the first thing she does is check you for lice. And, too, those ladies are to blame. On Sundays they sit out in front of the chicken coops picking lice from each other's heads. And the gringos, passing by in their cars, looking and pointing at them. Dad is right when he says that they look like monkeys in the zoo. But it's not all that bad.

"Mother, you won't believe it. They took me out of the room. I had just walked in, and they put me in with a nurse all dressed in white. And they made me take off my clothes and they even examined my behind. But where they took the longest was on my head. I had washed it, right? Well, the nurse brought out a jar of, like vaseline, it smelled like worm-killer, do I still smell? And she smeared it all over my head. It itched. And then she started parting my hair with a pencil. After a while they let me go but I was so ashamed because I had to take off my pants, even my underwear, in front of the nurse."

But now what do I tell them? That they threw me out of school? But it wasn't all my fault. I didn't like that gringo, right off. This one didn't laugh at me. He'd just stare and when they put me in the corner apart from everyone he kept turning to look at me, and then he'd make a gesture with his finger. I was mad but mostly I felt embarrassed because I was sitting away from everyone where they could see me better. Then when it was my turn to read, I couldn't. I could hear myself. And I could hear that no words were coming out . . . This cemetery isn't scarey at all. That's what I like best about the walk to school and back. The greenness! And everything so even. The roads all paved. It even looks like where they play golf. Today I won't have time to run up the hills and slide down tumbling. Nor to lie down on the grass and try to hear all the sounds. Last time I counted to 26 . . . If I hurry maybe I can go to the dump with Doña Cuquita. She heads out about this time when the sun's not so hot.

"Careful, children. Just be careful and don't step where there's fire burning underneath. Wherever you see smoke coming out, there's coals underneath. I know what I'm telling you, I once got a bad burn and I still have the scar . . . Look, each of you get a long stick and just turn the trash over briskly. If the dump man comes to see what we're doing, tell him we came to throw away some stuff. He's a kind man, but he likes to keep those little books with nasty pictures that people sometimes throw away . . . watch out for the train as you cross that bridge. It ran over a man last year . . . caught him right in middle of the bridge and he wasn't able to make it to the other side . . . Did they give you permission to come with me? . . . Don't eat anything until after you've washed it."

But if I go with her without permission they'll whip me even more. What am I going to tell them? Maybe they didn't expel me. *Sure, they did!* Maybe not. *Yeah, they did!* What am I going to tell them? But it wasn't all my fault. I couldn't wait anymore. While I was standing there in the restroom he's the one that started picking on me.

"Hey, Mex . . . I don't like Mexicans because they steal. You hear me?"
"Yes."
"I don't like Mexicans. You hear, Mex?"
"Yes."
"I don't like Mexicans because they steal. You hear me?"
"Yes."

I remember the first fight I had at school, I got real scared because everything happened so slow. There wasn't any reason, it's just that some of the older boys who already had mustaches and who were still in the second grade started pushing us against each other. And they kept it up until we started fighting, I think, 'cause we were plain scared. It was about a block from school, I remember, when they started pushing me towards Ramiro. Then we began to scuffle and hit at each other. Some ladies came out and broke us up. Since then I got to feeling bigger. But all it was, up until I fought, was plain fear.

This time it was different. He didn't warn me. I just felt a real hard blow on my ear and I heard something like when you put a conch to your ear at the beach. I don't remember anymore how or when I hit him but I know I did because someone told the principal that we were fighting in the restroom. Maybe they didn't throw me out? *Sure they did!* And then, I wonder who called the principal? And the janitor all scared and with his broom up in the air, ready to swat me if I tried to leave.

"The Mexican kid got into a fight and beat up a couple of our boys . . . No, not bad . . . but what do I do?"
" . . ."
"No, I guess not, they could care less if I expel him . . . They need him in the fields."
" . . ."
"Well, I just hope our boys don't make too much out about it to their parents. I guess I'll just throw him out."
" . . ."
"Yeah, I guess you're right."
" . . ."
"I know you warned me, I know, I know . . . but . . . yeah, ok."

But how could I even think of leaving knowing that everyone at home wanted me to go to school. Anyways, the janitor stood with his broom up in the air, ready for anything . . . And then they just told me to leave.

I'm halfway home. This cemetery is real pretty. It doesn't look anything like the one in Texas. That one *is* scarey, I don't like it at all. What scares me the most is when we're leaving after a burial and I look up and I read the letters on the arch over the gate that say, *Don't forget me.* It's like I can hear all the dead people buried there saying these words and then the sound of these words stays in my mind and sometimes even if I don't look up when I pass through the gate, I still see them. But not this one, this one is real pretty. Just lots of soft grass and trees, I guess that's why here when people bury somebody they don't even cry. I like playing here. If only they would let us fish in the little creek that runs through here, there's lots of fish. But no, you even need a license to fish and then they don't even sell us one 'cause we're from out of state.

I won't be able to go to school anymore. What am I going to tell them? They've told me over and over that our teachers are like our second parents . . . and now? And when we get back to Texas everyone will find out too. Mother and Dad will be angry; I might get more than just a whipping. And then my Uncle will find out and Grandpa. Maybe they might even send me to a reform school like the ones I've heard them talk about. There they turn you into a good person if you're bad. They're real hard on you. They leave you soft as a glove. But maybe they didn't expel me, *sure they did*, maybe not, *sure they did*. I could make like I'm going to school and stay here in the cemetery. That would be better. But then what? I could tell them that I lost my report card. And then what if I stay in the same grade? What hurt me the most is that now I won't be able to be a telephone operator like Dad wants me to. You need to finish school for that.

> "Vieja, call m'ijo out here . . . look, compadre, ask your godson what he wants to be when he grows up and finishes school."
> "What will you be, godson?"
> "I don't know."
> "Tell him! Don't be embarrassed. He's your godfather."
> "What will you be, son?"
> "A telephone operator."
> "Is that so?"
> "Yes, compadre, he's very determined, you know that? Every time we ask him he says he wants to be an operator. I think they pay well. I told the boss the other day and he laughed. I don't think he believes that my son can do it, but that's 'cause he doesn't know him. He's smarter than anything. I just pray God helps him finish school so he can become an operator."

That movie was good. The operator was the most important one. Ever since then I suppose that's why Dad has wanted me to study for that after I finish school. But . . . maybe they didn't throw me out. What if it's not true? Maybe not. *Sure, it is.* What do I tell them? What do I do? Now they won't be able to ask me what I'm going to be when I grow up. Maybe not. *No, yeah.* What do I do? It's that it hurts and it's embarrassing at the same time. I better just stay here. No, but then Mother will get scared like she does when there's lightning and thunder. I've gotta tell them. And when my padrino comes to visit us I'll just hide. No need for him to find out. Nor for me to read to him like Dad has me do every time he comes to visit us. What I'll do when he comes is hide behind the chest or under the bed. That way Dad and Mother won't feel embarrassed. And what if I really wasn't expelled? Maybe I wasn't? *No, yeah.*

▬▬▬▬▬

> "Why do y'all go to school so much?"
> "My Dad says it's to prepare us. He says that if someday there's an opportunity, maybe they'll give it to us."
> "Sure! If I were you I wouldn't worry about that. The poor can't get poorer. We can't get worst off than we already are. That's why I don't worry. The ones who have to be on their toes are the ones who are higher up. They've got something to lose. They can end up where we're at. But for us what does it matter?"

AND THE EARTH DID NOT DEVOUR HIM

The first time he felt hate and anger was when he saw his mother crying for his uncle and his aunt. They both had caught tuberculosis and had been sent to different sanitariums. So, between the brothers and sisters, they had split up the children among themselves and had taken care of them as best they could. Then the aunt died, and soon thereafter they brought the uncle back from the sanitarium, but he was already spitting blood. That was when he saw his mother crying every little while. He became angry because he was unable to do anything against anyone. Today he felt the same. Only today it was for his father.

> "You all should've come home right away, m'ijo. Couldn't you see that your Daddy was sick? You should have known that he'd suffered a sunstroke. Why didn't you come home?"

"I don't know. Us being so soaked with sweat, we didn't feel so hot, but I guess that when you're sunstruck it's different. But I did tell him to sit down under the tree that's at the edge of the rows, but he didn't want to. And that was when he started throwing up. Then we saw he couldn't hoe anymore and we dragged him and put him under a tree. He didn't put up a fuss at that point. He just let us take him. He didn't even say a word."

"Poor viejo, my poor viejo. Last night he hardly slept. Didn't you hear him outside the house. He squirmed in bed all night with cramps. God willing, he'll get well. I've been giving him cool lemonade all day, but his eyes still look glassy. If I'd gone to the fields yesterday, I tell you, he wouldn't have gotten sick. My poor viejo, he's going to have cramps all over his body for three days and three nights at the least. Now, you all take care of yourselves. Don't over-work yourselves so much. Don't pay any mind to that boss if he tries to rush you. Just don't do it. He thinks its so easy since he's not the one who's out there stooped."

He became even angrier when he heard his father moan outside the chicken coop. He wouldn't stay inside because he said it made him feel very anxious. Outside where he could feel the fresh air was where he got some relief. And also when the cramps came he could roll over on the grass. Then he thought about whether his father might die from the sunstroke. At times he heard his father start to pray and ask for God's help. At first he had faith that he would get well soon but by the next day he felt the anger growing inside of him. And all the more when he heard his mother and his father clamoring for God's mercy. That night, well past midnight, he had been awakened by his father's groans. His mother got up and removed the scapularies from around his neck and washed them. Then she lit some candles. But nothing happened. It was like his aunt and uncle all over again.

"What's to be gained from doing all that, Mother? Don't tell me you think it helped my aunt and uncle any. How come we're like this, like we're buried alive? Either the germs eat us alive or the sun burns us up. Always some kind of sickness. And every day we work and work. For what? Poor Dad, always working so hard. I think he was born working. Like he says, barely five years old and already helping his father plant corn. All the time feeding the earth and the sun, only to one day, just like that, get struck down by the sun. And there you are, helpless. And them, begging for God's help . . . why, God doesn't care about us . . . I don't think there even is . . . No, better not say it, what if Dad gets worse. Poor Dad, I guess that at least gives him some hope."

His mother noticed how furious he was, and that morning she told him to calm down, that everything was in God's hands and that with God's help his father was going to get well.

"Oh, Mother, do you really believe that? I am certain that God has no concern for us. Now you tell me, is Dad evil or mean-hearted? You tell me if he has ever done any harm to anyone."

"Of course not."

"So there you have it. You see? And my aunt and uncle? You explain. And the poor kids, now orphans, never having known their parents. Why did God have to take them away? I tell you, God could care less about the poor. Tell me, why must we live here like this? What have we done to deserve this? You're so good and yet you have to suffer so much."

"Oh, please, m'ijo, don't talk that way. Don't speak against the will of God. Don't talk that way, please, m'ijo. You scare me. It's as if already the blood of Satan runs through your veins."

"Well, maybe. That way at least, I could get rid of this anger. I'm so tired of thinking about it. Why? Why you? Why Dad? Why my uncle? Why my aunt? Why their kids? Tell me, Mother, why? Why us, burrowed in the dirt like animals with no hope for anything? You know the only hope we have is coming out here every year. And like you yourself say, only death brings rest. I think that's the way my aunt and uncle felt and that's how Dad must feel too."

"That's how it is, m'ijo. Only death brings us rest."

"But why us?"

"Well, they say that . . ."

"Don't say it. I know what you're going to tell me—that the poor go to heaven."

That day started out cloudy and he could feel the morning coolness brushing his eyelashes as he and his brothers and sisters began the day's labor. Their mother had to stay home to care for her husband. Thus, he felt responsible for hurrying on his brothers and sisters. During the morning, at least for the first few hours, they endured the heat but by ten-thirty the sun had suddenly cleared the skies and pressed down against the world. They began working more slowly because of the weakness, dizziness and suffocation they felt when they worked too fast. Then they had to wipe the sweat from their eyes every little while because their vision would get blurred.

"If you start blacking out, stop working, you hear me? Or go a little slower. When we reach the edge we'll rest a bit to get our strength back. It's gonna he hot today. If only it'd stay just a bit cloudy like this morning, then nobody would complain. But no, once the sun bears down like this not even one little cloud dares to appear out of fear. And the worst of it is we'll finish up here by two and then we have to go over to that other field that's nothing but hills. It's okay at the top of the hill but down in the lower part of the slopes it gets to be real suffocating. There's no breeze there. Hardly any air goes through. Remember?"

"Yeah."

"That's where the hottest part of the day will catch us. Just drink plenty of water every little while. It don't matter if the boss gets mad. Just don't get sick. And if you can't go on, tell me right away, all right? We'll go home. Y'all saw what happened to Dad when he pushed himself too hard. The sun has no mercy, it can eat you alive."

Just as they had figured, they had moved on to the other field by early afternoon. By three o'clock they were all soaked with sweat. Not one part of their clothing was dry. Every little while they would stop. At times they could barely breathe, then they would black out and they would become fearful of getting sunstruck, but they kept on working.

"How do y'all feel?"

"Man, it's so hot! But we've got to keep on. 'Til six, at least. Except this water don't help our thirst any. Sure wish I had a bottle of cool water, real cool, fresh from the well, or a coke ice-cold."

"Are you crazy? That'd sure make you sunsick right now. Just don't work so fast. Let's see if we can make it until six. What do you think?"

At four o'clock the youngest became ill. He was only nine years old, but since he was paid the same as a grown up he tried to keep up with the rest. He began vomiting. He sat down, then he laid down. Terrified, the other children ran to where he lay and looked at him. It appeared that he had fainted and when they opened his eyelids they saw his eyes were rolled back. The next youngest child started crying but right away he told him to stop and help him carry his brother home. It seemed he was having cramps all over his little body. He lifted him and carried him by himself and, again, he began asking himself *why?*

"Why Dad and then my little brother? He's only nine years old. Why? He has to work like a mule buried in the earth. Dad, Mom, and my little brother here, what are they guilty of?"

Each step that he took towards the house resounded with the question, *why?* About halfway to the house he began to get furious. Then he started crying out of rage. His little brothers and sisters did not know what to do, and they, too, started crying, but out of fear. Then he started cursing. And without even realizing it, he said what he had been wanting to say for a long time. He cursed God. Upon doing this he felt that fear instilled in him by the years and by his parents. For a second he saw the earth opening up to devour him. Then he felt his footsteps against the earth, compact, more solid than ever. Then his anger swelled up again and he vented it by cursing God. He looked at his brother, he no longer looked sick. He didn't know whether his brothers and sisters had understood the graveness of his curse.

That night he did not fall asleep until very late. He felt at peace as never before. He felt as though he had become detached from everything. He no longer worried about his father nor his brother. All that he awaited was the new day, the freshness of the morning. By daybreak his father was doing better. He was on his way to recovery. And his little brother, too; the cramps had almost completely subsided. Frequently he felt a sense of surprise upon recalling what he had done the previous afternoon. He thought of telling his mother, but he decided to keep it secret. All he told her was that the earth did not devour anyone, nor did the sun.

He left for work and encountered a very cool morning. There were clouds in the sky and for the first time he felt capable of doing and undoing anything that he pleased. He looked down at the earth and kicked it hard and said.

"Not yet, you can't swallow me up yet. Someday, yes. But I'll never know it."

A stroke left the grandfather paralyzed from the neck down. One day one of his grandsons came by to visit with him. The grandfather asked him how old he was and what he most desired in life. The grandson replied that what he most wanted was for the next ten years to pass by immediately so that he would know what had happened in his life. The grandfather told him he was very stupid and cut off the conversation. The grandson did not understand why he had called him stupid until he turned thirty.

The teacher was surprised when, hearing that they needed a button on the poster to represent the button industry, the child tore one off his shirt and offered it to her. She was surprised because she knew that this was probably the only shirt the child had. She didn't know whether he did this to be helpful, to feel like he belonged or out of love for her. She did feel the intensity of the child's desire and this was what surprised her most of all.

THE PORTRAIT

As soon as the people returned from up north the portrait salesmen began arriving from San Antonio. They would come to rake in. They knew that the workers had money and that was why, as Dad used to say, they would flock in. They carried suitcases packed with samples and always wore white shirts and ties. That way they looked more important and the people believed everything they would tell them and invite them into their homes without giving it much thought. I think that down deep they even longed for their children to one day be like them. In any event, they would arrive and make their way down the dusty streets, going house to house carrying suitcases full of samples.

I remember once I was at the house of one of my father's friends when one of these salesmen arrived. I also remember that that particular one seemed a little frightened and timid. Don Mateo asked him to come in because he wanted to do business.

"Good afternoon, traveler. I would like to tell you about something new that we're offering this year."

"Well, let's see, let's see . . ."

"Well, sir, see, you give us a picture, any picture you may have, and we will not only enlarge it for you but we'll also set it in a wooden frame like this one and with inlays, like this— three dimensional, as they say."

"And what for?"

"So that it will look real. That way . . . look, let me show you . . . see? Doesn't he look real, like he's alive?"

"Man, he sure does. Look, vieja. This looks great. Well, you know, we wanted to send some pictures to be enlarged . . . but now, this must cost a lot, right?"

"No, I'll tell you, it costs about the same. Of course, it takes more time."

"Well, tell me, how much?"

"For as little as thirty dollars we'll deliver it to you done with inlays just like this, one this size."

"Boy, that's expensive! Didn't you say it didn't cost a lot more? Do you take installments?"

"Well, I'll tell you, we have a new manager and he wants everything in cash. It's very fine work. We'll make it look like real. Done like that, with inlays . . . take a look. What do you think? Some fine work, wouldn't you say? We can have it all finished for you in a month. You just tell us what color you want the clothes to be and we'll come by with it all finished one day when you least expect, framed and all. Yes, sir, a month at the longest. But like I say, this man who's the new manager, he wants the full payment in cash. He's very demanding, even with us."

"Yes, but it's much too expensive."

"Well, yes. But the thing is, this is very fine work. You can't say you've ever seen portraits done like this, with wood inlays."

"No, well, that's true. What do you think, vieja?"

"Well, I like it a lot. Why don't we order one? And if it turns out good . . . my Chuy . . . may he rest in peace. It's the only picture we have of him. We took it right before he left for Korea. Poor m'ijo, we never saw him again. See . . . this is his picture. Do you think you can make it like that, make it look like he's alive?"

"Sure, we can. You know, we've done a lot of them in soldier's uniforms and shaped it, like you see in this sample, with inlays. Why, it's more than just a portrait. Sure. You just tell me what size you want and whether you want a round or square frame. What do you say? How should I write it down?"

"What do you say, vieja, should we have it done like this one?"

"Well, I've already told you what I think. I would like to have m'ijo's picture fixed up like that and in color."

"All right, go ahead and write it down. But you take good care of that picture for us because it's the only one we have of our son grown up. He was going to send us one all dressed up in uniform with the American and Mexican flags crossed over his head, but he no sooner got there when a letter arrived telling us that be was lost in action. So you take good care of it."

"Don't you worry. We're responsible people. And we understand the sacrifices that you people make. Don't worry. And you just wait and see. When we bring it to you'll see how pretty it's gonna look. What do you say, should we make the uniform navy blue?"

"But he's not wearing a uniform in that picture."

"No, but that's just a matter of fixing it up with some wood fiber overlays. Look at these. This one, he didn't have a uniform on but we put one on him. So what do you say? Should we make it navy blue?"

"All right."

"Don't you worry about the picture."

And that was how they spent the entire day going house to house, street by street, their suitcases stuffed with pictures. As it turned out, a whole lot of people had ordered enlargements of that kind.

"They should be delivering those portraits soon, don't you think?"

"I think so, it's delicate work and takes more time. That's some fine work those people do. Did you see how real those pictures looked?"

"Yeah, sure. They do some fine work. You can't deny that. But it's already been over a month since they passed by here."

"Yes, but from here they went on through all the towns picking up pictures . . . all the way to San Antonio for sure. So it'll probably take a little longer."

"That's true, that's true."

And two more weeks had passed by the time they made the discovery. Some very heavy rains had come and some children who were playing in one of the tunnels leading to the dump found a sack full of pictures, all worm-eaten and soaking wet. The only reason they could tell that these were pictures was because there were a lot of them and most of them the same size and with faces that could just barely be made out. Everybody caught on right away. Don Mateo was so angry that he took off to San Antonio to find the so and so who had swindled them.

"Well, you know, I stayed at Esteban's house. And every day I went with him to the market to sell produce. I helped him with everything. I had faith that I would run into that son of a gun some day soon. Then, after I'd been there for a few days, I started going out to the different barrios and I found out a lot that way. It wasn't so much the money that upset me. It was my poor vieja, crying and all because we'd lost the only picture we had of Chuy. We found it in the sack with all the other pictures but it was already ruined, you know."

"I see, but tell me, how did you find him?"

"Well, you see, to make a long story short, he came by the stand at the market one day. He stood right in front of us and bought some vegetables. It was like he was trying to remember who I was. Of course, I recognized him right off. Because when you're angry enough, you don't forget a face. I just grabbed him right then and there. Poor guy couldn't even talk. He was all scared. And I told him that I wanted that portrait of my son and that I wanted it three dimensional and that he'd best get it for me or I'd let him have it.

And I went with him to where he lived. And I put him to work right then and there. The poor guy didn't know where to begin. He had to do it all from memory."

"And how did he do it?"

"I don't know. I suppose if you're scared enough, you're capable of doing anything. Three days later he brought me the portrait all finished, just like you see it there on that table by the Virgin Mary. Now tell me, how do you like the way my boy looks?"

"Well, to be honest, I don't remember too well how Chuy looked. But he was beginning to look more and more like you, isn't that so?"

"Yes, I would say so. That's what everybody tells me now. That Chuy's a chip off the old block and that he was already looking like me. There's the portrait. Like they say, one and the same."

⸻

"They let Figueroa out. He's been out a week."

"Yeah, but he's not well. There in the pen, if they don't like someone, they'll give them injections so they'll die."

"Damn right. Who do you think turned him in?"

"Probably some gringo who couldn't stand seeing him in town with that white girl he brought back with him from Wisconsin. And no one to defend him. They say the little gringa was seventeen and it's against the law."

"I'll bet you he won't last a year."

"Well, they say he has a very strange disease."

WHEN WE ARRIVE

At about four o'clock in the morning the truck broke down. All night they stood hypnotized by the high-pitched whir of the tires turning against the pavement. When the truck stopped they awakened. The silence alone told them something was wrong. All along the way the truck had been overheating and then when they stopped and checked the motor they saw that it had practically burned up. It just wouldn't go anymore. They would have to wait there until daybreak and then ask for a lift to the next town. Inside the trailer the people awakened and then struck up several conversations. Then in the darkness their eyes had gradually begun to close and all became so silent that all that could be heard was the chirping of the crickets. Some were sleeping, others were thinking.

"Good thing the truck stopped here. My stomach's been hurting a lot for some time but I would've had to wake up a lot of people to get to the window and ask them to stop. But you still can't hardly see anything. Well, I'm getting off, see if I can find a field or a ditch. Must've been that chile I ate, it was so hot but I hated to let it go to waste. I hope my vieja is doing all right in there, carrying the baby and all."

"This driver that we have this year is a good one. He keeps on going. He doesn't stop for anything. Just gases up and let's go. We've been on the road over twenty-four hours. We should be close to Des Moines. Sure wish I could sit down for just a little while at least. I'd get out and lie down on the side of the road but there's no telling if there's snakes or some other kind of animal. Just before I fell asleep on my feet it felt like my knees were going to buckle. But I guess your body gets used to it right away 'cause it doesn't seem so hard anymore. But the kids must feel real tired standing like this all the way and with nothing to hold on to. Us grownups can at least hold on to this center bar that supports the canvas. And to think we're not as crowded as other times. I think there must be forty of us at the most. I remember that one time I traveled with that bunch of wetbacks, there were more than sixty of us. We couldn't even smoke."

"What a stupid woman! How could she be so dumb as to throw that diaper out the front of the truck. It came sliding along the canvas and good thing I had glasses on or I would even have gotten the shit in my eyes! What a stupid woman! How could she do that? She should've known that crap would be blown towards all of us standing up back here. Why the hell couldn't she just wait until we got to a gas station and dump the shit there!"

"El Negrito just stood there in disbelief when I ordered the fifty-four hamburgers. At two in the morning. And since I walked into the restaurant alone and I'm sure he didn't see the truck pull up loaded with people. His eyes just popped wide open . . . 'at two o'clock in the morning, hamburgers? Fifty-four of them? Man, you must eat one hell of a lot.' It's that the people hadn't eaten and the driver asked for just one of us to get out and order for everyone. El Negrito was astounded. He couldn't believe what I ordered, that I wanted fifty-four hamburgers. At two o'clock in the morning you can eat that many hamburgers very easily, especially when you're starving."

"This is the last fuckin' year I come out here. As soon as we get to the farm I'm getting the hell out. I'll go look for a job in Minneapolis. I'll be damned if I go back to Texas. Out here you can at least make a living at a decent job. I'll look for my uncle, see if he can find me a job at the hotel where he works as a bellboy. Who knows, maybe they'll give me a break there or at some other hotel. And then the gringas, that's just a matter of finding them."

"If things go well this year, maybe we'll buy us a car so we won't have to travel this way, like cattle. The girls are pretty big now and I know they feel embarrassed. Sometimes they have some good buys at the gas stations out there. I'll talk to my compadre, he knows some of the car salesmen. I'll get one I like, even if it's old. I'm tired of coming out here in a truck like this. My compadre drove back a good little car last year. If we do well with the onion crop, I'll buy me one that's at least half-way decent. I'll teach my boy how to drive and he can take it all the way to Texas. As long as he doesn't get lost like my nephew. They didn't stop to ask for directions and ended up in New Mexico instead of Texas. Or I'll get Mundo to drive it and I won't charge him for gas. I'll see if he wants to."

"With the money Mr. Thompson loaned me we have enough to buy food for at least two months. By then we should have the money from the beet crop. Just hope we don't get too much in debt. He loaned me two-hundred dollars but by the time you pay for the trip practically half of it is gone, and now that they've started charging me half-fare for the children . . . And then when we return, I have to pay him back double. Four-hundred dollars. That's too much interest, but what can you do? When you need it, you need it. Some people have told me to report him because that's way too much interest but now he's even got the deed to the house. I'm just hoping that things go okay for us with the beet crop or else we'll be left to the wind, homeless. We have to save enough to pay him back the four-hundred. And then we'll see if we have something left. And these kids, they need to start going to school. I don't know. I hope it goes okay for us, if not I don't know how we're going to do it. I just pray to God that there's work."

"Fuckin' life, this goddamn fuckin' life! This fuckin' sonofabitchin' life for being pendejo! pendejo! pendejo! We're nothing but a bunch of stupid, goddamn asses! To hell with this goddamn motherfuckin' life! This is the last time I go through this, standing up all the way like a goddamn animal. As soon as we get there I'm headed for Minneapolis. Somehow I'll find me something to do where I don't have to work like a fuckin' mule. Fuckin' life! One of these days they'll fuckin' pay for this. Sonofabitch! I'll be goddamn for being such a fuckin' pendejo!"

"Poor viejo. He must be real tired now, standing up the whole trip. I saw him nodding off a little while ago. And with no way to help him, what with these two in my arms. How I wish we were there already so we could lie down, even if it's on the hard floor. These children are nothing but trouble. I hope I'll be able to help him out in the fields, but I'm afraid that this year, what with these kids, I won't be able to do anything. I have to breastfeed them every little while and then they're still so little. If only they were just a bit older. I'm still going to try my best to help him out. At least along his row so he won't feel so overworked. Even if it's just for short whiles. My poor viejo . . . the children are still so little and already he wishes they could start school. I just hope I'll be able to help him. God willing, I'll be able to help him."

"What a great view of the stars from here! It looks like they're coming down and touching the tarp of the truck. It's almost like there aren't any people inside. There's hardly any traffic at this hour. Every now and then a trailer passes by. The silence of the morning twilight makes everything look like it's made of satin. And now, what do I wipe myself with? Why couldn't it always be early dawn like this? We're going to be here till midday for sure. By the time they find help in the town and then by the time they fix the motor . . . If only it could stay like early dawn, then nobody would complain. I'm going to keep my eyes on the stars till the last one disappears. I wonder how many more people are watching the same star? And how many more might there be wondering how many are looking at the same star? It's so silent it looks like it's the stars the crickets are calling to."

"Goddamn truck. It's nothing but trouble. When we get there everybody will just have to look out for themselves. All I'm doing is dropping them off with the growers and I'm getting the hell out. Besides, we don't have a contract. They'll find themselves somebody to take them back to Texas. Somebody's bound to come by and pick them up. You can't make money off beets anymore. My best bet is to head back to Texas just as soon as I drop these people off and then see how things go hauling watermelons. The melon season's almost here. All I need now is for there not to be anyone in this goddamn town who can fix the truck. What the hell will I do then? So long as the cops don't come by and start hassling me about moving the truck from here. Boy, that town had to be the worst. We didn't even stop and still the cop caught up with us just to tell us that he didn't want us staying there. I guess he just wanted to show off in front of the town people. But we didn't even stop in their goddamn town. When we get there, as soon as I drop them off, I'll turn back. Each one to fend for himself."

"When we get there I'm gonna see about getting a good bed for my vieja. Her kidneys are really bothering her a lot nowadays. Just hope we don't end up in a chicken coop like last year, with that cement floor. Even though you cover it with straw, once the cold season sets in you just can't stand it. That was why my rheumatism got so bad, I'm sure of that."

"When we arrive, when we arrive, the real truth is that I'm tired of arriving. Arriving and leaving, it's the same thing because we no sooner arrive and . . . the real truth of the matter . . . I'm tired of arriving. I really should say when we don't arrive because that's the real truth. We never arrive."

"When we arrive, when we arrive . . ."

Little by little the crickets ceased their chirping. It seemed as though they were becoming tired and the dawn gradually affirmed the presence of objects, ever so carefully and very slowly, so that no one would take notice of what was happening. And the people were becoming people. They began getting out of the trailer and they huddled around and commenced to talk about what they would do when they arrived.

Bartolo passed through town every December when he knew that most of the people had returned from work up north. He always came by selling his poems. By the end of the first day, they were almost sold out because the names of the people of the town appeared in the poems. And when he read them aloud it was something emotional and serious. I recall that one time he told the people to read the poems out loud because the spoken word was the seed of love in the darkness.

John Gilgun (b. 1935)

Poet and fiction writer John Gilgun grew up in Malden, Massachusetts, a small blue-collar town a few miles from Boston. His father, who, according to Gilgun, never read a book, delivered milk from door to door, and his mother, like the mother in "Counting Tips," worked as a waitress in a country inn. And like the son in his poem, Gilgun commuted to college at Boston University, graduating in 1957 with a degree in English. His novel, *Music I Never Dreamed Of*, written in the early 1960s but not published until 1989, presents the story of Stevie Riley, growing up gay and poor in an Irish Catholic neighborhood during 1950s, and, in the words of one reviewer, "living, loving, laughing, thriving anyway." Gilgun himself left the Catholic Church at age sixteen, having been told by the priest in confession that he was not permitted to read James Joyce and the proletarian writer James T. Farrell. Many of Gilgun's poems and short stories are rooted in the settings of his working-class upbringing and in his lifelong engagement with American literature, especially the texts of those who not only wrote but worked with their hands and muscles (see "Whitman's Hands," in this section). They are published in *Everything That Has Been Shall Be Again* (1981), *The Dooley Poems* (1991), *From the Inside Out* (1991), *Your Buddy Misses You* (1994), and *In the Zone: The Moby Dick Poems of John Gilgun* (2001). Gilgun taught college-level English—literature, composition, and creative writing—from 1960 until his retirement in 1999, most of that time at Missouri Western College in St. Joseph, an "open-door" institution serving mainly working-class students.

COUNTING TIPS

for Janet Zandy

My mother came home from work,
sat down at the kitchen table
and counted her tips, nickel by nickel,
quarter by quarter, dime by dime.
5   I sat across from her reading Yeats.
No moonlight graced our window
and it wasn't Pre-Raphaelite pallor
that bleached my mother's cheeks.
I've never been able to forget

10   the moment she said—
interrupting *The Lake Isle of Innisfree*—
"I told him to go to hell."
A Back Bay businessman
had held back the tip, asking,
15   "How much do you think you're worth?"
And she'd said, "You can go to hell!"
All evening at the Winthrop Room she'd fed
stockbrokers, politicians, mafioso capos.
I was eighteen, a commuter student at BU,
20   riding the MTA to classes every day
and she was forty-one in her frilly cap,
pink uniform, and white waitress shoes.
"He just laughed but his wife was there
and she complained and the boss fired me."
25   Later, after a highball, she cried
and asked me not to tell my father
(at least not yet) and Ben Franklin
stared up from his quarter
looking as if he thought she deserved it,
30   and Roosevelt, from his dime, reminded her
she was twenty years shy of Social Security.
But the buffalo on the nickel, he—
he seemed to understand.

WHITMAN'S HANDS

Were rough and as he held them out toward me
I saw that they were stained with resin,
For he was a carpenter,
And with blood, for he was a wound dresser,
5   And with ink, for he was a printer.
And as he cupped them near my nose,
I smelled the earth,
For these hands delved into the earth,
And sweat, for these hands
10   Were intimate with bodies.
These hands knew sea stones and surf,
The trembling backs of stallions,
Rushes, birds' eggs, beer, beef,
And the sharp blue gravel of roadways.
15   When he raised his hands above his head
The veins grouped themselves into stars
Which merged into a luminous band
Across the night sky—
And it was as if all the young men
20   Who had ever been born or ever would be born
Were coming up over the horizon,
Their arms filled with white lilacs.

Bill Witherup (b. 1935)

Bill Witherup was born in Kansas City, Missouri. In 1944, his family moved to Richland, Washington, the community that housed the Hanford Engineering Works. Hanford processed the plutonium that was used in the Trinity bomb and its twin, Fat Man. Witherup's father worked in the chemical separation plants, known as the "Queen Marys," where some of the most toxic work was done. Witherup attended several colleges, but never completed a formal degree. He joined the US Air Force in 1957 and was trained as a Russian voice-processing specialist. After discharge, he taught creative writing and theater at the Institute of American Indian Arts in Santa Fe, New Mexico, and Soledad Correctional Training Facility in California. For most of his life, Witherup worked the trades: construction worker, garbage man, warehouseman, furniture mover, fish cannery worker, book store clerk, artists' model, dishwasher, and lumber mill worker. About his work history, he says, "all the physical work I did kept me physically strong—my body remembers the tiredness, but also the skill and the pride in strength." He adds, "I wrote mostly when I was getting unemployment, or between jobs, or from notes jotted down during work, or before going to work." Witherup is the author of nine books of poems and poetry in translation. His most recent book is *Down Wind, Down River: New and Selected Poems* (2000). He coedited, with Joseph Bruchac, *Words from the House of the Dead: Prison Writings from Soledad* (1971) and is a contributing editor to *Learn to Glow: A Nuclear Reader* (2000). "Mother Witherup's Top Secret Cherry Pie" was first published in *Men at Work* (1990).

MOTHER WITHERUP'S TOP SECRET CHERRY PIE

I

I have come back to the A-type, government-built, double-decker duplex where I grew up in the Fifties, to visit my ailing father, seventy-seven, who has terminal bone cancer. Merv, as his brothers and friends call him, retired from N-Reactor in 1972, after thirty years at the Hanford Atomic Engineering Works.

Father and I disagree on nuclear matters and foreign policy. And on the virtue of holding a steady job. But I pull my Oedipal punches, in deference to his cancer. It is not for the Prodigal Son to pass judgement—dad's labors in the mills of the National Security State fed, clothed and housed a family of six.

Merv is frail now, down to 135 lbs. But his opinions have kept their weight and vigor. He keeps trying to bait me into a nuclear discussion, much like the hired hand in the Robert Frost poem, who wants one more chance to teach the college boy how to build a load of hay.

When one of the Hospice's nurses stops in to take his blood pressure, pop gets in a dig.

"This is my oldest son, Bill. He grew up here, but he's been trying to shut the place down ever since."

Rictus-like grin, for my part. In the past, when he was healthy, we could never have it out anyway. Rose, my mother, would not allow arguments or heated discussions in her territory. She would shut us off with, "It's time for dinner," or "How about some pie and ice cream?"

Behind every good man there stands a baker of pies, her rolling pin raised like a gavel to rap the house to order.

Here lies the crust of a tale.

II

It is an October afternoon, 1987. A high pressure ridge vaults up all along the west coast, and it is unseasonably warm. Seattle, 200 miles northeast, is talking water rationing. Due west, Mt. St. Helens heats a fresh cauldron of Lava Soup. Some thirty miles northeast of Richland, N-Reactor is on hold and simmer—11,000 cooks, preps and dishwashers sweat a lay-off. The reactor has been temporarily closed by Public Health: cockroaches were found swimming in the Uranium Soup; rats burrowing in the Plutonium Soufflé.

We have just finished an early dinner. Since father's retirement the elders have supped at 4:30 p.m. so they can catch People's Court at 5:00 on the boob. Mother apologizes for serving left-overs, even though her left-overs would put the main course at a classy restaurant to shame.

Merv has gone back to the living room couch, where he holds court now, attired in black Playboy pajamas with red piping. Wasting and bird-boned, he reminds me of a redwing black-bird perched on a cattail.

Here my mother says a variation of her standard line.

"I don't know why I bother cooking—your father doesn't eat enough to keep a bird alive."

Papa Witherup grew up during the Great Depression, one of four children of a grocer in Kansas City, Missouri. After he married mother, he first went to work in a paint store. Following Pearl Harbor, he was hired by Remington Arms, a Dupont subsidiary, in the Quality Control section to check the annealing on cartridges.

When the Manhattan Project kicked into gear, Dupont contracted to build the world's first plutonium reactor at Hanford. Dad was recruited to come west. His first job was, again, in Quality Control. He helped record each graphite block that made up the core of *Ur-Reactor.*

Mama Witherup, nee Nita Rosemond Allen, was the youngest of six children. Her father was a drummer who sold drugstore supplies across Missouri, Kansas and Nebraska.

Rose is one hell of a cook. Her forte was always dessert—especially pie. Her crusts are so light that the wedges levitate on their own and float into your mouth.

Dessert was always the bait and the reward for eating your veggies. Dinner opened with a Blessing and ended with a blessing—provided we four cubs could see our teeth in the cleaned plates.

III

Mother always eats her dessert, with a cup of decafe, directly after the main course, whereas father's habit, after retirement, was to have his pie and ice cream later in the evening.

Though I'm bloated from overeating, I signal weakly that I will join mother over her dessert. My extended visit has given her the excuse to be liberal with the commissary. Food is Love. It is also part of my wages for helping to spit-shine and buff the decks of The Good Ship Witherup—a working class frigate that has patrolled the Columbia River against the assaults of dirt and Communism for almost half a century!

We have our pie at the dining room table while father kibitzes from the sofa. With each visit home I've prodded the old folks to tell me about their childhoods and about the parts of the Richland/Hanford Saga that I wasn't privy to as a youngster.

Neither of my parents are great conversationalists—they are laconic, matter-of-fact, hard-working, Show-Me-Missourians still. But as it is Saturday and there is no People's Court, mother allows herself a bit of free-associating. She tells me about the time, not too long after the move to Richland, when her cherry pie was classified TOP SECRET.

IV

Hanford was one of three highly secret death factories engineered by General Leslie Groves to produce atomic bombs. The other two plants were at Los Alamos, New Mexico (Brain Center) and Oak Ridge, Tennessee (Uranium Milling).

All the engineers and production workers on the assembly line were kept in the political and moral dark about the product of their labors. They only knew that they were performing essential war work.

The workers were not supposed to tell their wives what they were doing at Hanford, or if working women, to discuss it with boyfriends or husbands. Children had even less of an idea. During my nine years of boyhood in Richland, I never knew what it was my father did exactly, as he left each day or swing or grave on *The Grey Goose* on the way to the satanic mills.

Hanford workers and their families, however, were checked and rechecked for political spots or moral stains. Every six months the plain-clothes guys from Military Intelligence would knock on the neighbors' doors and inquire about the Witherups; would rap on our door and discuss the neighbors.

Before the unions were voted in at Hanford, it was hard to make-do for a family of six. My mother cooked up the idea to cater desserts for a little extra grocery money. Her masterwork, the Cadillac of pies, was her cherry pie, with freshly picked Yakima Valley cherries as the nuclear core. She decided to advertise her wares in the local paper, *The Villager*.

V

Shortly after the advertisement appeared, the man from MI sniffed the wind and came knocking on our door. He had seen the advertisement, he said, and had dropped by to sample the product. Rose invited him in—she had a pie cooling in the kitchen. She set out a piece with a cup of coffee; hoped perhaps he was a local businessman.

"My, my," he said. "This is some pie. Sakes alive!"

Then he flashed his Gum-Shoe-Glow-In-The-Dark Badge.

"I'm sorry, Mrs. Witherup, we can't let you advertise your pies. It violates security precautions. But you keep on making these," he said generously, dabbing his mouth with a government issue hanky.

"You can sell these to friends, or by word-of-mouth, but any advertising by Hanford workers or their families is CLASSIFIED. Security, you know—we wouldn't want the Axis to find out what we are up to here, would we?"

VI

It is 4 a.m. I'm asleep in my old room upstairs. I always wake up about this time when I'm visiting, gasping for air like a carp out of water: my folks have converted the original government model to an air-tight, filter-controlled residence. (A Defense System to protect mother's sinuses from dust and nefarious pollens.)

This particular morning I bolt upright, awakened by a pulsing, steady siren.

"Christ!" I think—"N-Reactor has gone critical!"

I throw on a robe and hurry downstairs, open the front door as quietly as I can and listen intently to the radioactive air. Relieved, I decide the siren is merely a car alarm that has triggered, only a few blocks away.

But as I stand there I notice bulky shadows lurking about the remodeled A, B, C, D, E, and F houses—and I know it is the KGB snuffling window sills for home-baked pies—

for there, deep in the sweet juices and sexual hearts of cherry, peach and apple pie lie the State-of-the-Art secrets of the U.S. nuclear weaponry!

———

Lucille Clifton (b. 1936)

Lucille Clifton was born in Depew, New York, the daughter of working-class parents who nurtured her appreciation of literature and of the works of African American writers in particular. From her first acclaimed collection of poems, *Good Times* (1969), Clifton has written candidly and inspiringly of the lives of ordinary African American men, women, and children and of the black family as a source of strength, vision, creativity, and abiding love. Many of Clifton's characters inhabit urban and working-class landscapes and embrace them as places of resilience and self-discovery in which *home* is imagined not only as a physical location, but as life lived in connection with each other through shared history, memory, and culture. In *Generations: A Memoir* (1976), Clifton honors the voices and stories of family members descended from her African ancestor, the indomitable Dahomey woman renamed Caroline Donald Sale, "born free in Afrika in 1822/died free in America in 1910," whose female wisdom and strength provide an enduring spiritual legacy for each of the storytellers.

Clifton's work is widely praised for its disarming and uncompromising approach to matters of social justice and to the personal and collective need to speak out against tyrannies of all kinds. As she explains, "You see, we can't ignore history. . . . The past isn't back there, the past is *here* too." Her poems challenge readers to see how communal responsibility toward past and future generations involves each of us, regardless of our positions in history. In "at the cemetery, walnut grove plantation, south carolina, 1989," Clifton returns us to the site of slavery in America and to the forgotten work of the slaves "nobody mentioned"—their presence unacknowledged by the tour guide, their women omitted from the plantation's inventory. A brilliant example of Clifton's signature form, the lines are powerfully brief and understated: "somebody did this work . . ." the poem reminds us; "some of these slaves/were women/some of them did this/honored work." Clifton's unsentimental yet deeply caring gaze on the matters before her make her poems remarkable acts of safekeeping and self-definition: poems in which the human desire to redeem loss and to inspire positive change is actualized and celebrated. Her collections include *Two-Headed Woman* (1980), *Good Woman: Poems and a Memoir 1969–1980* (1987), *Quilting: Poems 1987–1990* (1991), the National Book Award-winning *Blessing the Boats: New and Selected Poems, 1988–2000* (2000), and more than sixteen books for children. A former Poet Laureate of Maryland, Clifton has served as a chancellor of the Academy of American Poets since 1999 and is Distinguished Professor of Humanities at St. Mary's College of Maryland.

Lois Williams

FROM *GENERATIONS: A MEMOIR*

Well my Mama was from Georgia. My Mama was born in Rome Georgia in 1914. She used to tell us that she was from Rome, and when we were little we thought she was Italian. But she was a round brown lady from Georgia, and as Daddy said, "Everybody from Georgia glad to be *from* there." Her father has sent for her and her mother and sisters and brothers to come to Depew after he had been North awhile. He had come on the same train as my Daddy, in the strikebreaking. My Daddy and my grandfather were friends and my Mama was twelve years younger than my Daddy. My Daddy's first wife was a good friend of my Mama and so was my little sister's mother and so was his last girlfriend. All friends.

When the colored people came to Depew they came to be a family. Everybody began to be related in thin ways that last and last. The generations of white folks are just people but the generations of colored folks are families.

Depew is where I was born. Depew New York, in 1936. Roosevelt time. It was a small town, mostly Polish, all its life turned like a machine around the steel mill. We lived in a house on Muskingum Street, and my Mama's family lived on Laverack. My grandparents lived in this big frame house on Laverack Street with one toilet. And in that house were my Mama's family, the Moores, and a lot of other people, lines of people, old and young.

There was an old man who was a deacon, a pillar of the church. I remember once in prayer meeting, he was praying and the lights went out . . . a blackout, you know, in the second world war. And he was deep in the middle of his best praying. He was a very religious man, a deacon, and all of a sudden the lights went out and he looked up and shouted "Dammit, now, God!" then went on with his prayer. A good prayer too.

Our whole family lived there. In Depew. All the Moores, I mean. All around the steel mill. My grandfather and Daddy and uncles and all our men. Turning around the plant.

Depew. One of the earliest things I remember was the goat in the backyard. Our house was on top of a big hill and across the yard and down the hill in the back were the Moores. And Grandma kept a goat back there. Depew.

The closest big city was Buffalo, twelve miles away. One time Daddy walked there to buy a dining room set. He was the first colored man in Depew to have a dining room set. And he walked to Buffalo to get it. He got it on credit from Peoples', a store where they gave colored people credit back then. This is what it was like: you got this credit from Peoples' store and the Peoples' man would come around to your house every week and collect. It would just be fifty cents or a dollar, but that was some money in those times and you know it went on for so long. So long. My Daddy paid something to the Peoples' man for as long as I can remember. Me and my brother used to hate him because he would come over every Saturday and collect and Daddy called him Mr. Pitterman but he called Daddy Sam. And his name was Samuel too, Samuel Pitterman, and if Daddy could be called Sam so could he. But he never was. Every Saturday he would come over and even after we moved to Buffalo when I was five or six, he would collect and then he would sit with Daddy on the porch and they would talk over old days. And Daddy would look forward to it.

He used to carry merchandise in the trunk of his car, Sam Pitterman, and he would sell things out of it. One Christmas he gave me and Punkin matching white crepe skirts, pleated all around. We put them in the bottom drawer of our dresser where the mice had gnawed and left them there.

Anyway, my Daddy wanted to have this dining room set and he walked to Buffalo to get it and when he got to Peoples' the salesman there told him he didn't need a dining room set. And Daddy told the man that his great-grandmother was a Dahomey woman and he could have anything he wanted. And so he got it. And walked back home, and they delivered the set. First colored man to own a dining room set in Depew New York.

Roosevelt time. War time.

I remember when my uncle came home from the second world war, my Mama's baby brother. He belonged to the ninety-second division, which was the colored infantry,

I think, and they had been in Italy. Oh we were all so proud of him, and one afternoon my Grandma was sitting by the window looking out, and my aunt came into the kitchen from getting the mail and said "Mother, we got a letter from Buddy . . . and Here It Is!" And my uncle come grinning through the door with his soldier's suit on and oh my Grandma Moore laughed and cried and laughed again. I always remember how my Grandma Moore just sang out "Oh here's my Buddy Buddy Buddy Buddy!"

She was my grandmother that called me Genius. My Mama's mother. The Moores moved to Buffalo a while after we did, and they moved to downtown. She believed that I was twelve years old until the day she died, and I was married and pregnant. Always thought I was twelve, and she called me Genius because she knew I went to college.

When I went away to college, well, that was some time. People couldn't get it straight that I was going to Howard and not Harvard. Nobody in our family had graduated from high school at that time, and at that time no member of our church had ever gone to college. I had won this scholarship, you know, and they gave me this big party at the church. The Baptist church.

Now we didn't know a thing about going to college. I remember I took my Grandma's wedding trunk, all held together with rope. Me and Mama went over to Peoples' and bought me a black silk skirt and a red see-through blouse and we packed Grandma Moore's wedding trunk. When they delivered it at Howard, all those ritzy girls from Chicago and Texas, oh I was so embarrassed I went down at night to pick it up. This old trunk with thick rope around it and Georgia Moore written in ink. Anyway, I went away to college, and before I left I had to go and say goodby to everybody.

And we went to see Grandma and she was watching for us, and when we started down her block, she ran out on the porch hollering "Everybody, Everybody, Here come my Genius!" And all her neighbor people come running out on the porch. And here I come, here I come.

My Grandma Moore told me to behave myself away from home, and I promised that I would. I had never been away from home and my own people before and let me tell you I was scared but I didn't let on. Then she asked me "Where was Moses when the lights went out?" and I said "Grandma, I just don't know," and she said "Well, that's all right, just keep your dress tail down," and I said "Yes, ma'am," because I understood that part.

There was another old lady, older than Grandma, named Miss Washington, and she had been born in slavery. I went to see her and she gave me these doilies, all these doilies she had crocheted with her own hands. She told me about when she was a tiny girl and Mr. Lincoln had come by in a parade and her mother had picked her up and made her wave her hand. She told me about this proud thing and gave me these doilies to take to college, and I went off to school.

I was sixteen years old and went away to college and I had never slept a night away from my Mama and when me and my friend Retha and my friend Betty got to Washington they had this huge train station. I had never seen a place like that and I started to almost cry and I said to Retha that as soon as I ate I was going back home. Then a Howard man came up to us and looked at Betty all little and cute with her college clothes and her name tag on and said "You'll love it here, and we'll love you," and he turned to me and asked me if I was her mother. From that moment I knew I wouldn't last. And I didn't. Two years. That was all.

But what a two years it was! What a time! I was from New York, so that was a big deal, and I was a drama major, so that was a big deal too. At that time, at Howard, if you weren't light-skinned or had long hair you had to have something pretty strong going for you. Well, I was a drama major from New York. They didn't know that Buffalo is a long way from New York City, and for them that did know, I could lay claim to Canada, so it worked out well enough.

My Daddy wrote me a letter my first week there, and my Daddy could only write his name. But he got this letter together and it said "Dear Lucilleman, I miss you so much but you are there getting what we want you to have be a good girl signed your daddy." I cried and cried because it was the greatest letter I ever read or read about in my whole life. Mama wrote me too and her letter said, "Your daddy has written you a letter and he worked all day."

Being away from home, I didn't even know how to do it. I used to think I was going to starve to death. Nobody had any notion of what I needed or anything. One time Mama sent me a box full of tuna fish. I hid it under my bed and at night I would take it out and open can after can of tuna fish. And I was always afraid I'd make a mistake and Daddy would find out. I knew he'd know whatever I did. Whatever I did. But I was proud. The first Thanksgiving I went back home and now I had only been gone since September but when I stepped off the train Daddy and my sister Jo were there and Jo said "Oh, she don't look so different," but I started talking with a Washington accent and I even had to try to remember the way home. I was a mess. I thought everything seemed so little.

AT THE CEMETERY, WALNUT GROVE PLANTATION, SOUTH CAROLINA, 1989

> among the rocks
> at walnut grove
> your silence drumming
> in my bones,
> 5   tell me your names.
>
> nobody mentioned slaves
> and yet the curious tools
> shine with your fingerprints.
> nobody mentioned slaves
> 10   but somebody did this work
> who had no guide, no stone,
> who moulders under rock.
>
> tell me your names,
> tell me your bashful names
> 15   and i will testify.
>
> *the inventory lists ten slaves*
> *but only men were recognized.*
>
> among the rocks
> at walnut grove
> 20   some of these honored dead
> were dark

> some of these dark
> were slaves
> some of these slaves
> 25   were women
> some of them did this ·
> honored work.
> tell me your names
> foremothers, brothers,
>
> 30   tell me your dishonored names.
> here lies
> here lies
> here lies
> here lies
> 35   hear

Marge Piercy (b. 1936)

One of America's most widely read feminist writers, Marge Piercy grew up in a racially mixed working-class neighborhood of Detroit. She was raised Jewish by her mother and her grandmother, who was the daughter of a rabbi in a Lithuanian shetl. Both women were great storytellers. One key story that Piercy came to know was that of her maternal grandfather, Morris, a union activist who was killed while organizing bakery workers. Piercy attended Detroit public schools, but in grade school suffered an illness from which she almost died. The alteration in her health and appearance drove her inward as a child and into the imagined worlds of books. She started writing poetry at age fifteen when the family moved to a larger house, where "for the first time," she writes, "I had a room of my own with a door that closed." The first member of her family to attend college, Piercy won a scholarship to the University of Michigan, graduating in 1957, and a fellowship to Northwestern University, where she earned an MA in 1958. After two years working low-wage jobs in Chicago and another two years teaching college English—while writing novels for which she found no publishers—Piercy decided in 1963 to devote herself to a career as a professional writer. Equally productive as a novelist and a poet, Piercy is the author of more than forty books, beginning with *Breaking Camp* (1968, poetry) and *Going Down Fast* (1969, a novel).

As an activist as well as a political writer, Piercy was involved in the civil rights movement, the antiwar movement, Students for a Democratic Society, and the woman's movement. Several of her works have become classics of feminist literature, including poetry collections *To Be of Use* (1973) and *My Mother's Body* (1985) and the time-travel novel *Woman on the Edge of Time* (1976). She describes her role as a writer as that of a "useful artisan": "What I mean by useful is simply that readers will find poems that speak to and for them. . . . To find ourselves spoken for in art gives dignity to our pain, our anger, our lust, our losses." Her recent books include *The Art of Blessing the Day: Poems with a Jewish Theme* (2000), *The Third Child: A Novel* (2003), and *Sleeping with Cats: A Memoir* (2003). *Louder, We Can't Hear You: the Political Poems of Marge Piercy* was published in 2004.

TO BE OF USE

The people I love the best
jump into work head first
without dallying in the shallows
and swim off with sure strokes almost out of sight.
5   They seem to become natives of that element,
the black sleek heads of seals
bouncing like half submerged balls.

I love people who harness themselves, an ox to a heavy cart,
who pull like water buffalo, with massive patience,
10   who strain in the mud and the muck to move things forward,
who do what has to be done, again and again.

I want to be with people who submerge
in the task, who go into the fields to harvest
and work in a row and pass the bags along,
15   who stand in the line and haul in their places,
who are not parlor generals and field deserters
but move in a common rhythm
when the food must come in or the fire be put out.

The work of the world is common as mud.
20   Botched, it smears the hands, crumbles to dust.
But the thing worth doing well done
has a shape that satisfies, clean and evident.
Greek amphoras for wine or oil,
Hopi vases that held corn, are put in museums
25   but you know they were made to be used.
The pitcher cries for water to carry
and a person for work that is real.

HER GIFTS

It was in the soup, I think
soup made from the unlaid eggs
scooped from the belly of the still warm
chicken Lucy killed for us, eggs
5   in shells, unshelled eggs, red
and yellow glowy balls that reminded
me of the most beautiful marbles
my brother left in a drawer.

It was in the apple cake she baked,
10   the apples set in circles
dusted dark with cinnamon.
It was in the savory lamb stew,
in the pot roast rich with onions
and seared carrots chopped into logs,

15   in the pancakes shaped like cartoon
     cats with tails curled up.

     It was in stories she told washing
     my hair with tar soap, rinsing it
     in vinegar. It was in everything
20   like salt dissolved in water,
     the longing, the hollow cry
     out of the long bone's marrow
     oh give me something better—
     something sweet, give back to me.

Sue Doro (b. 1937)

The process of machining, whether a piece of steel scratched and marred in the railyards, or a poem worked on in the hours squeezed between work and family, or the rebuilding of a life hammered by outside forces, this labor of mind and body signifies the life of worker-writer, Sue Doro. Doro grew up in a family of factory workers in Milwaukee, Wisconsin. As a single parent of five children, she fought for the right to train as a machinist and succeeded, eventually becoming the first woman machinist in three factories. The poems from *Blue Collar Goodbyes* excerpted here speak not only to the particularities of Doro's and her coworkers' lives as they face the closing of their plant, but illuminate the circumstances of millions of workers whose jobs have ended through no fault of their own. These poems have found their way from factories, labor union halls, and adult literacy classes into anthologies and course curricula, a tribute to Doro, the writer, and her unique yet collective sensibility that voices the complex music of working-class lives. After the closing of Milwaukee Road Railway, Doro moved to Oakland, California, with her second husband Larry Robbins and became director of San Francisco's Tradeswomen, a not-for-profit organization for women in blue-collar jobs. She is also poetry editor of the organization's quarterly, *Tradeswomen*. Her work has appeared in many anthologies, and she has published two other books of poetry and short stories *Of Birds and Factories* and *Heart, Home and Hard Hats* (1986), with a preface by Meridel Le Sueur, who writes of Doro: "She uses the experiences of the working class as the root and flower of her perception. She is without hesitancy, inferiority, or timidity, rising clear, serene in the criminal world of power and destruction, asserting among the ruins the clear, human solidarity with others, in a world that must not be destroyed."

THE CULTURAL WORKER

The poem waited for her outside the wheel shop door in the Menomonee Valley train yard. Waited, as if it were one of the countless raw cast-iron train wheels propped upright against the factory wall in the moonlight. Train wheels in long, neat rows leaning like round rusty-brown, 500-pound dominoes. Train wheels waiting to be machined.

So too, the poem waited. It had been waiting for her to finish work since 3:30 that afternoon. Now it was midnight. Soon she would step out of second shift into the dark of the going home night.

Hours ago in the early evening, the summer sun hung low and rosy over sidetracked freight cars in the yard. The poem had gone to look in the window nearest the machine the woman was operating that night. The poem thought that the sunset would surely get her attention. But then it saw her leaning across the table of a boring-mill machine, measuring inside the hub of a freight car wheel with her micrometer. She was straining on tiptoes to reach across the machine's table to the wheel's freshly cut center, and the poem could see she was too busy to be thinking poem words, so it did what it knew how to do.

It waited.

Measuring minutes against the sun's shadows on the dirty cream-colored brick wall, it waited. When five o'clock break time arrived, it waited and watched through a different window as the woman ate half her sandwich sitting at the lunch table by the men's locker room. She was sharing a newspaper and conversation with some of her coworkers. She kept on talking as she reached under the table to feed a bit of cheese to a dusty yellow, scrawny factory cat that grabbed the scrap of food in its mouth and bolted away.

The woman was the only female in the shop, and there were nights when she was lonely for the company of other women. But tonight the poem saw she was having a good time, laughing and joking with her work "buddies."

It was an hour and a half later when the poem checked in again. The woman was standing at the same machine working on a different wheel, listening intently to a short leathery-faced man with a chin full of gray quarter-inch whiskers. He wore a work-scratched green hard hat low over his dark eyes. His hands hung at his sides, glistening with soiled brown train bearing grease. In one hand he held a red-handled putty knife used to scrape lard-like gobs of grease off old train bearings. In his other hand, by their cuffs, he grasped a pair of oily black rubber gloves. The ring finger was missing on that hand. A cigarette bobbed up and down in his lips as he spoke, its ashes dusting the man's brown shirt every so often. The poem moved in closer to hear the conversation above the roar and clatter of the machine. It could catch only a few of the man's mumbling phrases: "love her . . . the kids don't talk . . . need more time." The woman was concentrating on the man's hesitant sentences with one eye on the boring-mill's cutting tool, ready to slap the stop button and flip the lever that pulled the cutting bar out of the wheel's center.

The poem went back to wait at the door until dinner break.

In summer, it was still light at eight o'clock in the evening when the break whistle blew, and the poem knew that the woman would go outside to relax on the long bench against the building. Most of the other second shifters would travel up the hill to the tavern, so she was generally alone. Some evenings after eating the rest of her saved sandwich, she'd take a stroll along the railroad tracks heading under the nearby freeway.

The walk was quiet and calming except for the faint rumble of cars far overhead. And if she walked a little further, the traffic noise faded completely. There was a small stream at that end of the valley, and a hill where she'd sit and gaze at the water, listening to it ripple over rocks and chunks of cement. Wildflowers grew along the riverbanks. In springtime there were baby asparagus plants and tiny green onions hidden in the tall, waving grass. Once when she brought a spray of yellow daisies back to the shop, one of the guys found and washed a mayonnaise jar to use as a vase. The flowers lit up the tool bench by the window, and everyone that passed by that night stopped to smell the daisies or to comment on the display. She was pleasantly surprised and happy that not one man teased her about it.

Other evenings found the woman writing in her journal. But tonight there was neither a walk nor journal writing happening at dinner break, and she wasn't alone. When the poem came around the corner of the building, it saw her leaning forward on the bench, holding a small open book and flipping through its pages. She referred to certain passages by tapping the index finger of her right hand on the page while she and a group of seven or eight men seemed to be talking at the same time: "contract . . . bargaining . . . Chicago . . . layoffs in July . . . four guys fired . . . bankruptcy . . . they can't . . . it's illegal . . . they'll try." The poem decided it was fruitless to try to get into her head. Then the sound of a factory whistle pierced the air, and moments later a foreman appeared in the doorway motioning everyone back to work.

The sun was beginning to slide down behind the freeway overpass. The poem stayed outside.

At ten o'clock the poem looked in the window by the woman again. She was staring out into the deep blackness of the night without even noticing the poem. Her eyes were taking in moonlight silhouettes of axles, train wheels, and oil drums. She watched three crows gliding like slow motion, velvet shadows in front of a glowing pink yard light—one of the many fifty-foot-tall globes illuminating the train yard. A shop cat scampered over a discarded train bearing lying in the grass at the base of the pole. A warm west wind brushed the woman's cheek. She sniffed the air, smiling a little, and the poem thought for a moment that she was thinking poem thoughts. She wasn't. She was simply relieved that the night smelled of sweet Menomonee Valley city wilderness thanks to the west wind, instead of the stockyards to the east of the wheel shop.

"A few more wheels," she commented aloud to no one in particular, and then turned away from the window. Thoughts of home and her sleeping family filled her with a flash of emotion—God, how she missed them on night shift. She shrugged her shoulders, shivering at the same time, like a cat shaking off water. Then she attacked the unfinished wheel in the machine with the frenzy of someone who wished to believe her own speed could control the clock.

And finally it was minutes away from midnight. A full moon waited high over the factory roof like a white ball with a golden ring, outshining any stars. Pink lights cast shadows on the path next to the tracks. The entire train yard was a watercolored wash of pink and black. The poem waited with the moon, holding its breath.

The woman was usually the first ready to leave because her locker was in the bathroom of the foreman's office near the door. On other nights she waited to walk to the parking lot with the guys; however, tonight felt different to her as she stepped out ahead of the whistle.

She was short, but her shadow was ten feet tall. She carried a paper sack of dirty work clothes. The poem was with her like another shadow, walking quickly. The farther away she got from the building, the taller her shadow grew, from the yard lights and the moon on her shoulders. Little rocks and pebbles at her feet crunched under her shoes. Each pebble had its own rosy shadow, like pink moon rocks under her feet. She smiled to herself, relishing the moment.

A cat meowed from the path ahead, scurrying away from the woman's flying feet. Stopping abruptly, the cat turned its head to stare back at her, its yellow eyes frozen in black midair. Then it disappeared under a parked freight car.

Night birds called in the distance.

Now her shadow split in two, growing taller, taller, taller. Racing past more pink lights. Stepping nimbly across one, two, three sets of train tracks. Passing flatbed cars stacked with unmachined axles and rows of wheels. Past lines of mounted wheel and axle sets waiting to be shipped out.

A lone crow cawed at her from a telephone wire. Something stirred in her brain. Some disjointed words seemed to come together. She laughed aloud, and the crow cawed again, leaving its perch to soar over her head into the blackness beyond the realm of pink lights. For a fleeting second she saw its dark wings gleam with a blush of pink. Then suddenly the woman threw back her head and shouted up into the pink and black sky. "HEY . . . I'm a midnight rider. A cat's eye glider. I'm a second shift mother goin' home!"

She laughed again. Surprised and delighted, the poem jumped *inside her* like a fetus kicking in the ninth month. She hurried along, faster now, running the last few yards past the guard shanty.

Finally, she was at her car in the parking lot. She plopped her dirty work clothes on the car hood to pull her keys out of her pocket. She unlocked the door, opened it, and flung the sack into the backseat. Jumping in, she started the car, revved its engine, put the car in gear, and aimed the old '68 Ford out of the lot. She saw the other workers, just then crossing the tracks, waving at her, and she beeped her car horn a couple times in response.

Now she would have time for herself. A smile, glorious as a weekend, spread across her face. She felt the uneasy urgency she'd buried deep inside all night leave her in a great, earthmoving sigh as she drove through the open gate and turned up the road to the ramp leading from the valley.

And a poem was born, comfortable as a well-fitting work shoe, satisfying as the end of the work day. The poem. The woman. The mother. The machinist. All became one. And she sang to the hum of her car:

> *I'm a midnight rider*
> *A cat's eye glider*
> *A second shift mother goin' home.*
>
> *I'm a moon rock walker*
> *A pink bird stalker*
> *A short tall shadow headin' home.*
>
> *I'm a cool old river*
> *A seasoned survivor*
> *I'm a factory workin' poet goin' home.*

Hard Times in the Valley

> one day at a time they tell us
> well that's fine for a tv comedy show
> but no way to plan a life
>
> jobs hanging on
> 5   i don't knows/maybes
> and bathroom rumors of transfers
> to Chicago or Minneapolis
>
> we deserve more than five days' notice
> on the bulletin board before
> 10 they yank us out of our boots
> without unlacing them
>
> we are the guts
> the muscle of this railroad
> we know how to run machines
> 15 that have long since passed their prime
> how to create singing axles and wheels
> out of mute steel
>
> we gave 10/20/30 years to this place
> came in every day to keep the railroad going

20 obligated to quality
    safety
    commitment
    to babies mothers fathers
    grain and toothbrushes riding on our work

25 now all we know for sure
    is no damn paycheck pays enough
    for these hard times in the valley

BLUE COLLAR GOODBYES

blue collar goodbyes are a jumpstart
on a frozen battery midnight parking lot
peering out of second shift propped open coffee eyes
wide as inch-and-a-quarter sockets
5   from a toolbox back at the radial drill machine
in Allis Chalmers Tractor Shop
where the only African-American on the housing line
teams up with the only female in maintenance repair
to move those tractors out the door

10 now Bill Dunlap's powerful hands fasten jumper cables
to plus and minus inside car hoods exposed to winter in Wisconsin
my '71 Ford and Bill's bran' new step-up van's competent motor
vibrating powdered snow like sifted cake flour
off a gleaming waxed finish revealing
15 Bill's stencil painted signature design
DADDY HIGH POCKETS
and his wife Bernice's
LADY LOW POCKETS
in the cold moon glow blue brightness

20 as my engine finally turns over
warming up goodbyes satisfying
as Bill and Bernice's faces across their kitchen table
heavy with platters of deep Southern-fried catfish
and hot cornbread put out for company
25 my home partner Larry and I over for Saturday night
and Bill waits inside his van to be sure
I'm not stuck in ice ruts
then fifteen years and a plant closure later
Bill's gone
30 I'm gone
Allis Chalmers is gone

blue collar goodbyes become letters and phone calls
from back home Bill and Bernice
and Milwaukee Road buddies Earl, Don, and Verona
35 veterans of yet another plant closing down, another buyout
by a hungrier corporation

another selling out up the hill
with nothing but our lunch buckets
more forced layoffs, a few paid severances,
40 don't know how many transfers to Chicago or Minneapolis
where the Soo Line promised jobs then
four years later about to go belly up too,
it offers those same people a chance to buy
their own failing railroad
45 in a town they never wanted to live in
blue collar goodbyes report Wisconsin to California
on lined school notebook paper stark and strong
THERE'S BACK PAY COMING . . . YOU BETTER CALL
and phoning find the Soo Line
50 would've kept my blood-earned money
if I had not been told

if I had not known
the hearts of survivors
that corporate minds will never know
55 survivors of shutdowns and forty-below-zero wind chills
work friends like family separated
by job change and cross-country miles
people who hold dear and remember lunch buckets
Saturday catfish and goin' home car rides that never say never
60 'cause we'll see you sometime
goodbyes like sparks of electricity through jumper cables
in a midnight parking lot

Simon J. Ortiz (b. 1941)

Native American writer and teacher Simon Ortiz was born in Albuquerque, New Mexico, and grew up in McCartys, a village of the Acoma Pueblo of which he is a member. His mother was a traditional potter, and his father was a stonemason who labored much of his life for the Santa Fe railroad, often working at a distance from his home and family (see the poem "Final Solution: Jobs, Leaving" in this section). Ortiz spoke the Acoma language at home and first experienced the clash of cultures he would explore in his later writing when that language was disallowed in his government-run school. As he wrote in his 1991 collection *Woven Stone*, "This early language from birth to six years of age in the Acoma family and community was the basis and source of all I would later do in poetry, short fiction, essay, and other work."

Although he did well academically in high school, where he read widely and wrote regularly in a personal journal, Ortiz went to work in the uranium mines of the Grants Mineral Belt near his home. In 1962, he began a three-year stint in the U.S. Army, after which he attended the University of New Mexico and won a fellowship to the University of Iowa writing program, where he earned an MFA. His first publication, *Naked in the Wind*, appeared in 1971 and has been followed by more than twenty books, including *From*

Sand Creek (1981, reprinted in 2000), *Fightin': new and collected stories* (1983), *The People Shall Continue* (1988), *Man on the Moon* (1999) and *Out There Somewhere* (2002). He has also edited several collections of Native American writing, including *Earth Power Coming: Short Fiction in Native American Writing* (1983). In much of his poetry, fiction, and nonfiction, Ortiz confronts the damage and dislocation—human, cultural and environmental —caused by colonizing power, against which he maintains an ethic of justice and a faith in healing based on the integrity of "the land and the People." Ortiz has taught writing at many universities and arts institutes and is a professor of English at the University of Toronto.

MY FATHER'S SONG

Wanting to say things,
I miss my father tonight.
His voice, the slight catch,
the depth from his thin chest,
5   the tremble of emotion
in something he has just said
to his son, his song:

We planted corn one spring at Acu—
we planted several times
10   but this one particular time
I remember the soft damp sand
in my hand.

My father had stopped at one point
to show me an overturned furrow;
15   the plowshare had unearthed
the burrow nest of a mouse
in the soft moist sand.

Very gently, he scooped tiny pink animals
into the palm of his hand
20   and told me to touch them.
We took them to the edge
of the field and put them in the shade
of a sand moist clod.

I remember the very softness
25   of cool and warm sand and tiny alive mice
and my father saying things.

FINAL SOLUTION: JOBS, LEAVING

They would leave
on Sundays from the depot in Grants.
It seemed always, always, so final.
Goodbye. Goodbye Daddy. Daddy,

5 please come back. Please don't go.
Daddy. But they would leave.

Winslow.
          Flagstaff.
                    Seligman.
10 Barstow.

We had to buy groceries,
had to have clothes, homes, roofs,
windows. Surrounded by the United States,
we had come to need money.

15   The solution was to change,
to leave, to go to jobs.
                    Utah.

California.
          Idaho.
20   Oregon.

The children would cry.
The women would be so angry.
So angry.
Silent, we left.
25 We didn't want to leave, but
we left.

          "I don't want you and your brothers
to ever have to work for the railroad."
They kept the railroad repaired,
30 and the trains raced through
their land. Hearts. Blood. Bones
and skin. Wrenched muscles.
"You ever pick up a rail?
With your bare hands." Your sweat
35 burning in your eyes. Blood. Heart.
Skin. Bones. And they died too.
"I hope." How much they hated,
how much they hoped. How much.

          American Fork, Utah, February, 1959.
40 Dear Mama & Children,
I hope you are all well
as I am. Children, help your mother
and take care of each others
and around our home. Remember
45 that you must always love
your mothers. Think of the prayers
for the land. Mama, I wish
I was home with all of you.
I will be home in a few weeks.
50 I love you all. Make sure
you feed the horses. My love

and hugs to each of you and Mama,
            Daddy.

      Saw him in Seligman.
55 Or was it Valentine. Or Phoenix.
Or somewhere. "He step off the train.
That was the last time
I saw him. My friend." Tears.
Wine doesn't work. They died too.

60   One week, two weeks, three weeks,
months, we waited. Years.
Train. O Daddy, O Daddy. Train
would come thundering, thundering
thundering toward us. Hearts.
65 Blood. Bones and skin. Love
and hope. O Daddy. Please train.

      The children would laugh or cry
or be so silent.
The women were so angry.

Yes, we would wait again. Weeks, weeks, months, but not those years again. O Daddy,
never those years. Never again those years. Our own solution will be strength: hearts, blood,
bones, skin, hope and love. The woman anger and courage risen as the People's voice again.

We Have Been Told Many Things
but We Know This to Be True

The land. The people.
They are in relation to each other.
We are in a family with each other.
The land has worked with us.
5 And the people have worked with it.
This is true:
          Working for the land
and the people—it means life
and its continuity.
10 Working not just for the people,
but for the land too.
We are not alone in our life;
we cannot expect to be.
The land has given us our life,
15 and we must give life back to it.

The land has worked for us
to give us life—
breathe and drink and eat from it
gratefully—
20 and we must work for it
to give it life.

Within this relation of family,
it is possible to generate life.
This is the work involved.
25   Work is creative then.
It is what makes for reliance,
relying upon the relation of land and people.
The people and the land are reliant
upon each other.
30   This is the kind of self-reliance
that has been—
before the liars, thieves, and killers—
and this is what we must continue
to work for.
35   By working in this manner,
for the sake of the land and people
to be in vital relation
with each other,
we will have life,
40   and it will continue.

We have been told many things,
but we know this to be true:
the land and the people.

Gloria Anzaldúa (1942–2004)

Gloria Evangelina Anzaldúa's life and work transformed borders into spaces of expanded consciousness. "I am a border woman," she wrote in the Preface to *Borderlands/La Frontera: The New Mestiza*, "I have been straddling the *tejas*-Mexican border, and others, all my life." Anzaldúa pioneered a literary form and cultural theory of mestiza that encompasses contradiction, multiple identities, and code-switching languages—a mélange of insider and outsider tongues, a Chicano Spanglish. The oldest child of six generations of Mexicanos from the Rio Grande Valley of south Texas, Anzaldúa began working alongside her sharecropping parents at the age of eleven. Her family settled in the border town of Hargill, Texas, and Anzaldúa juggled work in the fields with her high school and college education. When Anzaldúa was fourteen, her father died at the age of thirty-eight, "having worked himself to death." She earned BA and MA degrees in English and education and at first taught in a variety of bilingual and special education programs and later in university women's studies and Chicano studies.

Anzaldúa coedited (with Cherríe Moraga) *This Bridge Called My Back: Writings by Radical Women of Color*, an anthology that in 1981 revolutionized women's studies by centering political struggle, lesbianism, and radical feminism. *Borderlands* (1987), from which these poems are selected, ensured her place as a widely influential cultural theorist and genre-breaking writer. Her other books include *Making Face, Making Soul/Haciendo Caras* (1990), two bilingual children's books, a collection of interviews, and *this bridge we call home: radical visions for transformation*, (2002, coedited with AnaLouise Keating).

A recipient of many awards, she described herself as Shiva, "a many armed and legged body with one foot on brown soil, one on white, one in straight society, one in the gay world, the man's world, the women's, one limb in the literary world, another in the working class, the socialist, and the occult worlds. A sort of spider woman hanging by one thin strand of web."

WE CALL THEM GREASERS

I found them here when I came.
They were growing corn in their small *ranchos*
raising cattle, horses
smelling of woodsmoke and sweat.
5 They knew their betters:
took off their hats
placed them over their hearts,
lowered their eyes in my presence.

Weren't interested in bettering themselves,
10 why they didn't even own the land but shared it.
Wasn't hard to drive them off,
cowards, they were, no backbone.
I showed 'em a piece of paper with some writing
tole 'em they owed taxes
15 had to pay right away or be gone by *mañana*.
By the time me and my men had waved
that same piece of paper to all the families
it was all frayed at the ends.

Some loaded their chickens children wives and pigs
20 into rickety wagons, pans and tools dangling
clanging from all sides.
Couldn't take their cattle—
during the night my boys had frightened them off.
Oh, there were a few troublemakers
25 who claimed we were the intruders.
Some even had land grants
and appealed to the courts.
It was a laughing stock
them not even knowing English.
30 Still some refused to budge,
even after we burned them out.
And the women—well I remember one in particular.

She lay under me whimpering.
I plowed into her hard
35 kept thrusting and thrusting
felt him watching from the mesquite tree
heard him keening like a wild animal
in that instant I felt such contempt for her
round face and beady black eyes like an Indian's.
40 Afterwards I sat on her face until

her arms stopped flailing,
didn't want to waste a bullet on her.
The boys wouldn't look me in the eyes.
I walked up to where I had tied her man to the tree
45   and spat in his face. Lynch him, I told the boys.

TO LIVE IN THE BORDERLANDS MEANS YOU

are neither *hispana india negra española*
ni gabacha, eres mestiza, mulata, half-breed
caught in the crossfire between camps
while carrying all five races on your back
5   not knowing which side to turn to, run from;

To live in the Borderlands means knowing
that the *india* in you, betrayed for 500 years,
is no longer speaking to you,
that *mexicanas* call you *rajetas,*
10   that denying the Anglo inside you
is as bad as having denied the Indian or Black;

Cuando vives en la frontera
people walk through you, the wind steals your voice,
you're a *burra, buey,* scapegoat,
15   forerunner of a new race,
half and half—both woman and man, neither—
a new gender;

To live in the Borderlands means to
put *chile* in the borschr (borscht),
20   eat whole wheat *tortillas,*
speak Tex-Mex with a Brooklyn accent;
be stopped by *la migra* at the border checkpoints;

Living in the Borderlands means you fight hard to
resist the gold elixer beckoning from the bottle,
25   the pull of the gun barrel,
the rope crushing the hollow of your throat;

In the Borderlands
you are the battleground
where enemies are kin to each other;
30   you are at home, a stranger,
the border disputes have been settled
the volley of shots have shattered the truce
you are wounded, lost in action
dead, fighting back;

---

gabacha—a Chicano term for a white woman
rajetas—literally, "split," that is, having betrayed your word
burra—donkey
buey—oxen

35   To live in the Borderlands means
          the mill with the razor white teeth wants to shred off
          your olive-red skin, crush out the kernel, your heart
          pound you pinch you roll you out
          smelling like white bread but dead;

40   To survive the Borderlands
          you must live *sin fronteras*
          be a crossroads.

Hattie Gossett (b. 1942)

Writer and performer Hattie Gossett gives her birthplace as "a central New Jersey factory town" and has lived much of her adult life in New York City, based at the "intersection where the republic of Harlem meets the Dominican Republic." Educated with an MFA degree from New York University, Gossett's long list of experiences as a "wage slave" includes office girl, florist's assistant, playground attendant, teacher's aide, and waitress. She has also worked as a jazz drummer, a magazine journalist, and a teacher of typing. A long-time practitioner of the "spoken word" style of music-inflected writing, Gossett performs her work both solo and with her Poetry Jazz Band. In addition to her poetry, Gosset writes essays and plays and collaborates with theater and dance companies. She was a contributing editor at *Essence* magazine and has published in the *Village Voice, Jazz Spotlite News, Black Scholar, Heresies*, and *Union-Wage*. She has taught writing and African American literature in schools, prisons, art centers, and at Oberlin College and Rutgers University. Gossett is the author of the prose and poetry collection *Presenting . . . Sister No Blues* (1988), from which the following piece is taken, one of a series of first-person work-vignettes entitled "Labor Relations." Like Alice Childress's "Conversations from a Domestic's Life" at mid-century, Gossett's contemporary cleaning woman claims her own voice and finds a creative way to "speak truth to power." This prose-poem should be read aloud.

THE CLEANING WOMAN/LABOR RELATIONS #4

the doctors knew.

the lab people knew.

the secretaries knew.

the volunteers knew.

5   the patients knew.

the clinic was moving to a new spot and would be closed for a while and
      everybody knew ahead of time.

---

sin fronteras—without borders

everybody except the cleaning woman.

she only found out on closing day.

10   i dont know why no one thought to tell you before this the woman doctor said to
      the cleaning woman over the phone annoyance all up in her voice at being asked
      by the cleaning woman why they hadnt given her an earlier notice.

      i dont know why no one thought to tell you. anyway i have patients now and have
      no time for you.

15   it was the cleaning womans dime so she went for broke. but i am dependent on the
      salary you pay me and now suddenly it wont be there she protested. wouldnt it
      be fair to give me some kind of severance pay?

      severance pay! shrieked the woman doctor. look she snapped you havent been with
      us that long. only a few weeks. besides i have help at home you know and i . . .

20   its like this the cleaning woman interrupted not wanting to hear about the doctors
      help at home (at least not what the doctor was going to say) when you work for
      a salary you need some kind of reasonable notice when its going to be
      discontinued so you can prepare yourself. how would you like it if you were in
      my place?

25   the woman doctor then tried to offer the cleaning woman a job in the new clinic
      plus a job in her own new private office but neither of these jobs would start for
      some weeks. she never did say how she would feel being in the cleaning womans
      place. the cleaning woman realized she was dealing with people who really didnt
      care about her. as far as they were concerned she could starve for those few
30   weeks. she wondered how long you would have to work for these people before
      it was long enough for them to tell you at least 2 weeks ahead of time that they
      were closing. how long is long enough?

      forget it the cleaning woman told the woman doctor. she was pissed. she didnt like
      knowing that she was being shafted and that there wasnt anything she could do.
35   when do you want me to bring back your keys? because she cleaned at night or
      very early in the morning she had keys to the clinic.

      as soon as the woman doctor said anytime in a somewhat startled voice the cleaning
      woman hung up. she didnt slam down the phone. she put it down gently. but she
      didnt say goodbye or have a nice day.

40   damn the cleaning woman said to herself after she had hung up. here these people
      are supposed to be progressive and look at how they act. here they are running
      an alternative clinic for lesbians and gays and straights and yet they treat their help
      just as bad as the american medical association fools treat theirs. are they really an
      alternative she asked herself.

45   sure they treat their help bad herself answered laughingly.

      the cleaning woman looked up a little surprised because she hadnt heard herself
      come in. now herself sat down and started eating some of the cleaning womans
      freshly sliced pineapple.

      what do you mean girlfriend the cleaning woman asked herself.

50   have you forgotten that every sister aint a sister and every brother aint a brother
      herself began. where did you get this pineapple? its really sweet and fresh.

come on now. dont play games. tell me what you mean the cleaning woman said.

look herself said. some of these sisters and brothers aint nothing but secondhand
reprints out of the bidness as usual catalogue in spite of all their tongue flapping
55   to the contrary. and these secondhand reprints can be worse than the originals.
like they have to prove that they know how to abuse people even more
coldheartedly than the originals do. its getting harder and harder to tell the real
alternatives from the rank rapscallions. of course everybody else on the staff knew
that the gig was moving but you. in their book you aint nothing no way.

60   what could the cleaning woman say?

herself was right once again and the cleaning woman tried to tell herself this but
that girl didnt hear anything cuz she had already tipped on out taking the last
piece of pineapple with her.

so the cleaning woman laughed for a minute. then she stopped brooding over those
65   fools at the clinic.

she got on the phone and started lining up some more work.

later she sat down and wrote this story which she put in the envelope with the
clinic keys. she wrote the woman doctors name on the front of the envelope cuz
she wanted to be sure the woman doctor would be able to share the story. at the
70   bottom of the story the cleaning woman put not to be copied or reproduced by
any means without written permission from the author.

cuz one monkey sho nuff dont stop no show.

Larry Smith (b.1943)

In his memoir, *Milldust and Roses* (2002), Larry Smith sums up his life: "I was born into a working-class family of the Ohio Valley, a war baby and child of the forties; I spent my growing-up years in the fifties, went from being a student to a husband and teacher in the sixties, became a pacifist and father in the seventies, and a writer and teacher in the eighties, nineties, and into this new millennium." He calls it a "common life," meaning, what is shared in common, and sees the telling of his own life story as a way to "confirm the lives of others." Smith practices a working-class cultural ethos that he shares with others of his generation who were born into working-class families, earned an education, but did not leave their working-class cultural roots. Smith worked as a summer steel mill laborer and high school teacher. His family were blue-collar Ohio workers—riggers, railroaders, and homemakers. During the Vietnam War years, he was a teaching fellow at Kent State University, and his wife was a nurse at a nearby hospital when during an antiwar protest four students were killed on May 4, 1970, by National Guard troops.

Smith is a professor emeritus of English and Humanities at Firelands College of Bowling Green State University in Huron, Ohio. He is the author of six books of poetry; literary biographies of Kenneth Patchen and Lawrence Felinghetti; a novella, *Beyond Rust*; several coedited collections; and a book of translations from the Chinese. He also wrote and codirected documentary films on James Wright and Kenneth Patchen. He is managing editor of *Heartlands: A Magazine of Midwest Life and Art* and publisher of Bottom Dog Press. He lives in Huron, Ohio, with his wife Ann, a professor of nursing, and is the father of three adult children. "The Company of Widows," from *Milldust and Roses*, describes a return to the industrial Ohio Valley, where "work is the fabric of life."

The Company of Widows

Every couple of months or so I return to the industrial Ohio Valley with its deep green Appalachian walls along that big winding river. And lately as I come into town bouncing over the gaping potholes of Steubenville streets, stopping at the traffic light beside that huge bridge to West Virginia, I stare at the new monument to the steel valley, a statue of a laborer in shiny asbestos suit frozen at that moment when he taps a sample from the blast furnace floor. He seems intent upon his job, only there is no blast furnace floor, just this laborer alone in time and space. I admire the statue's simple directness, its human scale and respect for reality. For me, this whole steel valley remains as real and fluid as the hot flowing iron of memory.

As I round the curve under the Market Street Bridge, my windows down to make a summer breeze, there is that aftertaste of something burnt in the air, and I swear you can taste it too in the water, as bittersweet as rust. Heavy barges of coal and ore move down river beside me as the gray air billows from smokestacks, rises and crests in a dark heavy cloud. I am enough of an outsider now to notice this; insiders never do, or if it gets too heavy and they are forced to cough each time they speak, they blame it on the milltown across the river—"Smells like Follansbee!" This place along the edge, so marked by extremes of beauty and waste, is my place, my hometown, my family—and I breathe and swallow it again.

"It ain't all bad," as they say, and I look over to see my wife awake now as we come into "Mingo Town." She smiles too at being home; my son looks up from his computer game at the blast furnaces that loom over the town, and we wake our twelve year old daughter, who asks, "Are we at Grandma's yet?"

I smile as the car winds up the steep hill, and pulls in before a yellow brick home. I unload our bags and leave everyone at Ann's mother's, then drive down St. Clair hill, staring into the steaming cauldrons of the mill. At Murdock Street I turn right, coast downhill, and pull in behind my mother's car. She has taken down the front maple, leafless for years, so that the whole place looks a little different and a whole lot the same; a three-story wooden frame house with worn green shingles along the edge of Ohio Route 7.

Mrs. Maul nods to me as I get out—neighbors still, her yard still cared for like her retarded son who is now 33 and staring out the window at me. I wave then note how Mom's porch needs the mill dirt squirted off. I take the broom by the door, and start dancing it across the green painted concrete till she hears me, comes to the front window laughing, "Get in here, you nut."

It is at least a five minute wait as she wrestles her door locks, three of them where once there were none. But I don't object, I want her safe, and with the recent break-ins and thefts from cars, I tell her I will install another if she wants. "Don't worry," she says hugging me home, "We old girls keep an eye out for each other."

In Mom's house one never gets further than the "television room" where the set is always on. I've found her sleeping here some nights in her reclining chair in the glow of a snowy screen. We sit and she gives me news of who has died or been arrested, and word of my lost siblings; she offers me candy and a glass of root beer. She is sixty-four this year, my father's fatal heart attack upstairs, now three years past. Though we often speak of him, of what he'd think, of how he used to work so hard, of his joking with the kids, we never address his death. We both know that he is gone—the whole house echoes his absence, but we won't recall for each other those weeks around his death when we went through his things, sorting out tools and clothes, taking papers from the mill to the social security office in Steubenville. It still breaks my heart remembering my mother sitting in that office, hearing her say to the stranger, "My husband's dead, now what do I do?"

Only this time as she brings in a plate of store-bought cookies, I am surprised to hear her say, "That day your dad died, he took a handful of these and a glass of milk. I remember, he said he was just going upstairs to lie down. He said he had to rest."

I cannot breathe for the weight of this, something caught in my own chest which somehow asks, "Mom, what happened that day Dad died? Who found him, did you?"

Our eyes just touch before she goes to sit, "Oh, yes, it was me that found him—here in our bed, asleep I thought at first, yet somehow I knew." She takes a breath as the scene begins, "He'd come home from golfing with his buddies saying that his arm was hurting. He started golfing several times a week since the mill retired him." Her eyes look distant as she talks, like she's watching all this on a television screen somewhere. "I called to him, touched his arm, and he felt cold lying there. God I was scared, so I called Darlene and she called the emergency squad. They got here quick. His friend Brownie was with them. He's the one came downstairs to tell me, 'Jeanny,' he said, 'there's nothing more we can do'—I remember him standing right here where you are, saying that. 'There's nothing more we can do,'" and she sighs. "Brownie's a good old boy, been your father's friend since they were school boys."

"Was there a doctor who came?" I have to ask.

"No, just the paramedics, but then they took him straight to the hospital where he was pronounced dead." Suddenly she looks at me as though she has awakened out of a trance and is waiting for me to explain.

Only I can't. All I can say is, "It must have been hard for you. I'm sorry I wasn't around." There is a silence between us so still that we notice the hoot and crash of the mill as the trains take a haul of slag down to the pits. The mill is always there in this town—in the sounds and smells, the color of the air and in the talk—"What they got you workin', midnight?" "We'd come up, but Michael's workin' four-to-twelve next month. . . ." Work is the fabric of life here.

Married at eighteen, my father worked as a brakeman on the railroad at Weirton Steel for forty years, till they forced him to retire. All this is *there* inside the room—his awareness of a life.

"How'd you get through it all, Mom?"

"Well, Darlene was here, and your sister Debbie had come down by then. I think Dr. Ruksha came by and gave me something. I can't remember now. Debbie would."

There's another long silence as we think about all that's just been said. This is further than we've ever gone into it, the gritty details of a death, and it's almost as though we've stirred up a part of ourselves we thought was dead. I smile at her, "How come we never talked about this, Mom?"

She looks back, "I don't know." And then she thinks to say, "I know he's gone—Lord how I miss that old boy—but he's still here inside this house. You know, I can feel him sometimes. I think I hear him calling up from the basement, 'Honey, where's my work clothes?' or some such thing. I almost answer him, then I stop." She smiles quietly, "I guess I'm losing touch. But you know, I always feel better when I think of him, like having him back in a dream."

I go over and hug her in her chair, and we can both sense the grief in each other. "What does it all mean?" she sighs, and I just hold her, so frail and quiet.

"You did all you could, Mom. All anyone can."

Now it is I who have to move about, so I walk out into the kitchen for a drink. The radio is playing the area talk show—'Will the schools be forced to consolidate if the mills don't pay back taxes?' It is a mix of local gossip and preparing for the worst. My wife's uncle talks of retiring at forty-five. "What do I care?" he asks, "I can't let the mills decide my life. What's going to happen anyway, when it all shuts down? Have you thought of that?" And he shakes his head sitting on his front porch, "Who owns these mills? Who decides what happens here?" I shake my own head. "We steelmakers are a forgotten race," he concludes and I have no more answer for him than for my mother in the other room.

I could tell her of my own dreams of my father—of how he appeared in our house, smiling and tried to tell me a joke I couldn't get—how he laughed as if to say he was okay now. I know I felt good for a week, but dreams fade quicker than memories. Back in this valley the struggle toughens you or it breaks your heart. And where do you draw the line?

I think of how my father didn't complain of his arm or chest on the day he died, and wonder if he might not be alive if he had. But, wasn't he trained here not to feel the pain, not to complain? Pouring my coffee, measuring my cream, I wonder how much we give up to survive? How much did my father?

I stir it together and I know these are futile questions, yet somewhere I've learned that ignoring a truth creates another sort of pain and a kind of blind numbness around the heart. I remember how Dad, scoutmaster of my youth, would stop our car on the street to breakup a kids' fight; he couldn't let a wrong go on. His working so hard, sending two boys through college, may have been his own way of rebelling against a silent lie. I take a drink of valley coffee and sit back down on the couch.

While my mother goes to take her medication I leaf through the local *Herald Star*. When she returns I ask, "Mom, what's this parade they're having uptown in Steubenville today—Festival Homecoming? Do you want to go?"

She smiles, "Sure, when is it?" Like a child now she welcomes small adventures and a chance for company. I know that kitchen radio is her best friend most days, that's why I bought it for her, and to quell my own guilt for moving away to my quiet home along the lake.

"They say at 2:00, but there's already a street fair on Fourth and Market if you want to take that in. Have you seen it?"

"Debbie and Michael took Robin the other night," as she sits. "They said she rode a pony in the street. I can't imagine that. A pony in the middle of Market Street that used to be so busy with traffic."

"Yeah," I say, and we both know the story of how the old downtown of Steubenville died four years ago after the layoffs, then again with the opening of the Fort Steuben Shopping Mall. And we both secretly wish we could be wrong about this, that the town will yet survive. Somehow our valley toughness doesn't exclude a capacity to dream.

At noon I show up again having retrieved my wife, son and daughter. My mother-in-law Sue has joined us in this summer thirst for a celebration. A widow like Mom, Sue carries her John with her all the time. Instead of wearing a widow's black, she refused to smile for a year and a half. She's a strong Italian woman whose fierce integrity and hard work make her a legend in her neighborhood. John too did his 40 years in the mills, as a millwright—humble and happy on his job till they took it from him claiming his eyes were too weak. They were weak but twice as strong as the benefits the mill paid for his "early out." And while I know these forced retirements didn't kill our dads, I curse the thoughtless pain they brought to good people. Sue works now in the school cafeteria—baking cookies and cakes, fish and french fries for a troop of teenagers. They give her a hard time but love her cooking. They always ask whether she cooked it before they buy . . . she is seventy.

My wife Ann and daughter Suzanne are like her in their strong will. In the Valley you learn early, if you learn at all, that work and self-belief are your strongest tools. My mother-in-law's favorite saying, besides "The rich get richer, and the poor get poorer" and "At least we eat good," is . . . "Well we have each other."

Ann offers the front seat to my mother, but she refuses, climbing into the back—"No, no, we belong back here. Don't we, Sue? The merry widows and Suzanne." We all laugh, as Ann and Brian squeeze together; they begin to talk as I cruise up river to the celebration, to the hope a parade brings.

As we enter town from the North I search for a parking place—up close and free. I must prove to all these women that they haven't a fool for a son, husband or father.

Finally, we pull onto the hot asphalt of the city lot, and I feed dimes to the meter. We cross the light down Adams to the street fair. The parade will follow these outside streets and march a square around the intersection of Fourth and Market. It's a good thing too, as those two streets are packed with noisy citizens barking back at the game keepers, standing in line for rides, or wolfing down Italian sausage and onions with a sudsy Budweiser in the afternoon. The whole street smells like a local bar, and there is hardly room to pass as we bump good naturedly into our neighbors. A flow in this human river, pushed on, I almost lose my wife who waves a hand above the heads. We laugh on the street corner, "So many people," I say, and she adds, "And we actually know some of them," an inside joke to small-town emigrants living in anonymous suburbs where the faces seem familiar yet you know none of them.

As a rock band blasts and rumbles from the flatbed of a truck, we feel at "home." And though we know this busy downtown street will become a deserted crime area again come Monday, for a while, our memory is washed by the flood of our senses.

Sue tells Ann to tell me that it's time to find a place to watch the parade, and so I look around then lead us back from Washington Street, only this time along the sidewalk, past the back of the Italian and Irish booths smelling of spaghetti and corned beef with nearly matching flags, past the abandoned J. C. Penney's building, the closed furniture and clothing stores—so empty full of darkness—past the Slovak church's pirogi and raffle booth, to the corner of Fourth and Adams.

The old Capital Theatre has been leveled to build a store to sell tires and auto parts. It's been gone for years, but each time it hits me with its large sense of absence. In fact I realize that I have been vibrating with this same sense of presence and absence since we arrived. Struck by the sense of what is here and what is not, I struggle to assimilate the change.

In the midst of parents pushing their children toward a noisy, street merry-go-round, I recall how my wife and I once sat close together in the cushioned seats of the Capital Theatre while Tony and Maria of *West Side Story* sang so desperately of their love struggle. It was the first time we kissed. Perhaps my whole little family really began in search of such close moments? Perhaps. What I do know is that things change even in this old town. Facing that, I know my real problem is understanding the direction of that change.

Waiting here on the curb along the corner, I've been noticing things. Not just the noise and vacant stores but the changed sense of the place. What has survived and how? The angry fumes of the One-Hour Dry Cleaners still spill out onto the street and I remember its sickening smell and sticky feel as I picked up a suit standing there forced to breathe it as I watched the weary movement of the women at their mangles, caught the hurried tone of the clerks. And of course the bars are still here, one for every third storefront, and the Sports & Cigar places not driven out by the legal lottery. One bakery is still open, reminding me of time spent waiting for the bus breathing the hearty bread and donut smells till I had to purchase "Just one, please," from the Downtown Bakery. All the Five and Dime stores have been converted to self-serve drugstores, the restaurants to offices or video rentals, the clothing stores empty as night.

I stand there making this mental documentary when my daughter insists, "Dad, I'm hungry." We adults suddenly look to each other and realize she is right, we have forgotten lunch. I look back to the booths, then back at my son who is pointing down Adams Street; we smile, one of the brightest moments of the day, for we are a half block away from one of the best pizza shops in Ohio, perhaps the world.

"I'll be back in a minute," I tell them, and take my daughter's hand and follow Brian down the street to DiCarlo's Italian Pizza. Inside, the mixed aromas of Parmesan cheese, warm dough, spicy pepperoni and sauce bring me back. It is a Roman pizza they make, sold by the square, and the crust is crisp yet chewy with juicy chunks of tomato melting into the mozzarella cheese and pepperoni which they throw on last like scattered seed. I point this out to my child, all the while remembering those years of standing at this same counter watching the rich ritual of the men tossing dough hard on counters, of their moving the pizza up the oven drawers as it rose steadily to a climax, cut and boxed, a rubber band snapped around the corners, the holes popped to keep it crisp. We buy two dozen and hurry back to our crowd, to that first bite into the steaming slab, chewing it well, a piece at a time. And it's good to taste how some things stay the same.

Standing as we eat, I notice the need for napkins, to catch the dripping but also to keep it clean from all the street dirt blowing along the curb. "It's a shame," Sue clucks, nodding to the way litter lies along the street—not just cigarette butts, though there are plenty of those, but whole bags from Burger King, empty pop and beer cans that the residents step over, like hard stones on the sidewalk. "The city levy didn't pass," I am told, and I nod as if I understand, but it is all wrong. Like watching your child pulled from a sports game, I am really torn that what seems so precious to me feels so easily abused. Yet I check my sense of righteous-ness knowing how much I've moved away from here, to my suburban life, a college teaching job, a safe haven along Lake Erie. I do not wish to accent my estrangement. I eat my pizza with my son on the curb.

People begin lining the curbs standing or seated in their lawn chairs. They stand and talk or occasionally watch up the street for the start of things. The police walk by us, a kid waits then darts across the street. Something is about to begin. Watching the faces of people standing near me I look for the familiar but find only the strange . . . a woman in a POISON T-shirt yanking her child up by the arm smacking her really hard on the butt, screaming "I told you to pee before we left!" this time with a smack to the face, "Didn't I?" No one says anything. "Well, didn't I?" The child only wails while the mother bellows, "Now, you run home, Missy, and change those pants. You'll miss the parade." The straw haired woman seems oblivious to all around her, as though the street is her home. This is something our parents and neighbors never did, no dirty laundry aired in the street. Her husband joins her now on stage and, yes, he is a hairy guy with those dark blue tattoos flaming up and down his arms. He brushes by her. "Hey, Babe, I'm goin' for a beer!" falls off his lips like spit, as he pushes his way through the crowd. "Oh, no you're not!" she shouts at him. "You're not leaving me again with these kids!" And it seems her whole life is a series of exclamations as she walks off leaving her children at our feet. They don't seem to notice, and most of the crowd looks back up the street trained now at ignoring these small unforgivable scenes of communal violence.

It is my mother-in-law who hisses, "*Sceevo*" and folds her pizza away in her napkin. It's an Italian expression, a succinct verb that means, "It makes me sick," and I know it is not the pizza but the mean ugliness that has repulsed her. It haunts the streets as I look hard at the faces in the crowd of locals who seem as strangely foreign to me as the news from Iraq. It's like watching the films made in this area—Michael Cimino's *The Deer Hunter*, or Peter Strauss' *Hearts of Steel*. The setting is right but the people are all wrong—not because they are actors but because they are portraying the valley and its people at their most desperate to preach Hollywood despair or false hope. That film *life* feels close yet alien to anyone who knows this place, a twin hurt that confuses me like these wounded faces around me. They are not the faces I grew up with here, those who lived well though poor and somehow shared the good that they had and were.

As I watch this woman turn back, I try to feel her life, guess her age, but it is impossible—the facial lines and cold eyes, the young children at our feet. She turns to us, motions to her kids, yells to my puzzled mother, "I'll be right back!" And so we find ourselves baby-sitting her girls on the street corner. The children take no notice until we offer them a pizza which they grab and gobble down, thanking us with their eyes. It's a sad scene, and this human gesture seems the only way to dispel the curse of this family's life. I need to understand.

"Mom," I turn to ask her, "Do you know these people?"

"Oh, no, I don't know her," she says, then realizes what I've asked. "There's a new crowd that lives downtown now."

"Where did they come from?" I hear myself ask.

She answers, "When everyone started moving out of downtown, they started moving in." She gestures broadly to the old buildings across the street, and I see above the storefronts, the backs of buildings, windows with ragged curtains, bags of trash out in the street beside junked cars. And my heart sags like the dirty clouds or this child's heavy diaper.

Sue adds, "Apartments are cheap now, cause nobody wants to live where so many muggings go on." She goes on to report the worst and most recent incidents while I wonder which came first—the crime or the abandonment. She can't help telling these stories, because it has happened to her friends; it's a part of her life now. She plays out her old storyteller's hand—hoping by telling to somehow understand.

And I think of another conversation last week with a city planner now working as a car salesman. "No jobs for city planners," he jokes. So when I tell him of my dismay at understanding the way cities change, he describes for me the 'myth of urban renewal.' "See, they throw up a few new office buildings that look good to the outsiders. Right?" I remember nodding. "Only what you don't see is also what you get. To the city poor it means something else—less and worse housing. Where do you think all the 'homeless' people come from?" he asks while downing a half cup of coffee. "I'll tell you. Urban renewal drives some of them into the street and it drives a lot of others away to smaller cities like your hometown where they have no support, sense of past and no hope of a future. And so there they live unconnected, and just using up the present."

I had nothing more to say to him or now to myself as this parade begins. I just stand here thinking: of the fathers who worked this valley farming labor into families along the river land, and of the widows now forced to watch the rich soil used up, spoiled by greed and unconcern. I know that my father had no answer for this either, and for once I am glad he doesn't have to be here to watch it all happen. I just stare across the street at an older man tending cars in the parking lot. He moves aimlessly from car to car, checking tags, and I recognize something in his face. My mother whispers his name, a classmate of mine, his face a shadow of my own.

Held there on the curb of the Steubenville street that feels so close yet strange, I become my own mute statue.

As the parade goes by, I watch how the faces light up at so little. The children are smiling at a clown squirting water from his motorcycle. A float of Junior Women toss candy at our feet. My mother waves to friends. I find myself nodding to everyone, yet inside myself I am thinking of the five words given to me by my ex-city planner: "Abandonment creates its own culture." It sums up my own confused pain now, and I say it over and over to myself, "Abandonment creates its own culture." In the summer heat, the parade passes, we smile into late afternoon sun, and then we take the widows home.

Ernie Brill (b. 1945)

Ernie Brill was born and raised in Brooklyn and credits "the lively global world of New York City" as a major influence on his stories and poems. At eighteen, he worked as an orderly on a terminal cancer ward as part of a college work-study experience that transformed his life and planted the seed for the hospital-based stories that are collected in *I Looked Over Jordan* (1980), from which "Crazy Hattie Enters the Ice Age" is taken. Of the book's title story, Meridel LeSueur wrote, "This is a wonderful story, beautifully told. We must have places for such stories. They must be read so there will be more." "Crazy Hattie" was adapted for television by Ruby Dee for PBS's "Ossie and Ruby Show."

After moving to San Francisco in the mid-1960s, Brill continued working in hospitals throughout undergraduate and graduate school, as a ward clerk and as an interviewer on workmen's compensation claims. His poems based on these experiences appeared in such journals as *Poetry for the People* and *Foolkiller* and in Tom Wayman's pioneering collection of work-poetry, *Going for Coffee: Poetry on the Job* (1981). Brill earned a BA and MA in English and American literature from San Francisco State University, where he participated in 1968 in one of the nation's longest student strikes against racism. He now teaches English and creative writing at a public high school in Northampton, Massachusetts, where his students regularly read the poems of John Beecher, Gwendolyn Brooks, and Martín Espada. Brill's most recent fiction project is a collection of stories about middle-school children in Chinatown, based on his experiences teaching in New York City in the 1990s.

CRAZIE HATTIE ENTERS THE ICE AGE

We could hear Lodge and Crazy Hattie going at it. The three of us were trying to eat our lunch and at the same time listen to the muffled angry voices in the closed conference room across the hall. I was sympathetic; Hattie'd been pretty nice to me when I became the floor's wardclerk. ("Main thing you wanna do is always be on top of things when the patients need somethin'. Next thing is helpin' the peoples what come visit, and keepin' 'em offa our behinds so we can take care of their kin properly. You'll understand more of that when you're here a spell. Remember, the paperwork you can do anytime. Paperwork don't puke.") Hector, the Filipino orderly, aggressively supported Hattie. Often at the end of the shift, Hattie would put her arm through Hector's, smiling, "This here's my main man. He gonna ditch his wife and kids, and we gonna elope to Manila and live offa coconuts and roast goat balls." Hector would smile and with a wink add, "And love." Hattie would howl. As for Janie, she disliked Hattie ever since Hattie dubbed her "Chicken Little", explaining, "She ain't a bad nurse, 'cept every little thing goes wrong, we got a disaster movie on our hands." All three of us—Janie, Hector, and me—strained to hear the arguing voices rise, then drop in loaded silence.

"They are INTO it," Hector grinned grimly.

I nodded. Janie smoothed her blond tight curls, then opened a yellow tupperware bowl, and began eating salad. She ate rapidly with decreasing daintiness as hunger overtook form.

Suddenly, Luann, the aide at the other end of the floor, walked in, her dark-brown face frowning, her large hands pushing back her sweat-wetted, bunned hair. She went over to the sink, splashed her face with water, and dried herself, turning.

"That Hattie screamin' in there?"

We nodded.

"Hm. Hope when I get her age I'll know when to get out while the gettin's good."

"Why you say that, Luann?" Hector asked, an almost hurt look on his face. I stared at Luann.

"Nothin'. Skip it."

"Hattie would retire if she could afford it," I put in.

"Well," Luann sighed, "that's a real problem now. Too tired to step it up, and too broke to step down."

Janie leaned back in her chair, squinting at Luann, who eyed her.

"You know," Janie began carefully, "If you're really going to be honest about all this, you'll admit Hattie can't do the work she used to do. And she's becoming a real problem."

"How's that?" Luann asked.

Janie sighed, "You tell me."

"I can tell you this," Luann snapped, "that Maggie McDermott what been here goin' on two hundred years now and goes around talkin' to bedscales, they kept her on and she's the laughingstock of this place and been that for three years now with her Memorandum Coordination Service jive they set up just for her, only she's administration AND white— so you don't see no one evaluatin' her now, do you?"

"We're not talking about Maggie, Luann," Janie maintained. "We're talking about Hattie."

Luann folded her arms and moved toward the door. "Hell, I'm not even supposed to be in here. I just came to wash up."

"You know," Hector said, turning toward Janie, "Hattie gets her work done. So she's a little slow. If you really cared, you'd help figure out how we can maybe lighten up the work for her, you know?"

"Hattie don't need no charity, Hector," Luann snapped.

"Hey, I'm not talkin' about charity. Shit." Hector shook his head, disgusted.

"Everyone gets their daily assignments," Janie persisted cooly. "And if that's too much to handle each day, then something's wrong, and that person should be man or woman or whatever enough to admit it to themselves."

"From all I can see, Hattie does her work," I threw in, "and other peoples' too."

"Like when?" Janie scowled.

"Like the time she hung that I.V. pole when you had your hands full and the I.V. nurse hadn't gotten here yet, that's when. And she got a whole lot of shit for that."

Janie scowled. "Well, Josh, I think there's also alot you don't know and don't see."

No one said anything.

"O.k.," Janie nodded, "so she does help when someone needs help. But it slows her own work up, and she's not fast enough to do that. And she's always taking forever— FOREVER—with her charting and her temperatures and all of her paperwork. She's slow and there's just no getting around it."

"Right. She's the slowest sixty-five year old here," Hector remarked bitterly.

"Look," Janie said. "What it really boils down to is: can she do the work, or can't she?"

No one spoke. Across the hall, something slammed. Hector nodded toward the closed door and the sound.

"She can do the work if people quit breathin' down her neck all the time."

Luann frowned, silently taking out a pack of cigarettes and going toward the door. Janie, smoothing her blond curls, shrugged.

"Well, maybe she could transfer. To a different shift other than days. Or something."
Luann lit up.

"You're quiet all of a sudden, lady," Hector remarked.

"Way I see it," puffed Luann, "it's Hattie's business. She don't need advice from any of us, leastways from me. Hattie knows what's best for Hattie. Let's leave it at that."

Luann suddenly left the room. The tension lessened. I wondered if Hattie would last, wondering too if there was any place in the hospital for someone who slowed down a step. The voices grew louder across the hall. The door opened. We heard first the voice of Judy Lodge, the sixth floor supervisor.

"I want to speak to you Hattie. I'm not finished."

Hattie very slowly walked out of the conference room, gripping her brown lunch bag in one hand and in the other hand her black rhinestoned purse—her fabled trademark ever since the 1968 strike when she wacked a Tactical Squad officer with it across the head so hard he fell off his motorcycle. Hattie wore green surgery "scrubs", green tops, and green pants—her favorite outfit from the days when she had been training as a surgical technician, though they had long since cancelled the program. She walked down the hall slowly, staring straight ahead, erect, muttering.

I concentrated hard to hear her mumblings. Her face seemed to pout permanently, a strong dark black face with large-lidded deep brown eyes, a small nose, and a full mouth with the bright red lipstick she sported, bragging, "Never know when some fine man gonna get tired of all these silly young things and ache for someone with experience." She'd wink with her large brown eyes, which were like a shot deer—full of red veins. When she wanted to "put a fix on folks," she spoke monotonously, her eyes focusing on a pen in a shirt, a ring on the finger, a nearby chart. She babbled, then silently stared straight into the eyes just as she reached her point. It distracted the nurses and aggravated the doctors, especially the ones who wanted her to kowtow. If a doctor, giving orders for a patient's treatment, added, "How does that sound to you?" mechanically consulting Hattie, he'd be abruptly jarred by the slow, firm answer, "Don't sound too good," followed by the famous, "Now, the way I see it—"

I watched her proudly trudging, with Judy Lodge right on her heels, the voice whiney, tight.

"Hattie, I want you to sign this."

Lodge sighed, persisting, too tightly encased in a yellow uniform. Pink flowers merrily spread down the wide shoulders and sides, below a thick neck and a strained white freckled face. Lodge was built broad and squat. On her five foot three inches, her two hundred pounds looked like a huge square.

"Hattie!"

"Stomachs don't know paper," Hattie muttered, staring at the floor. "Not a thing. Stomachs don't."

Luann watched from the far end of the corridor. Hector smiled slightly. Janie greeted Lodge with a wave of the hand that Lodge acknowledged while turning toward me.

"Josh, isn't your break at one o'clock?"

"Well, yes, but things seemed slow so I thought I'd—"

"Take your lunch when it's scheduled from now on," Lodge snapped. "If you want to change it, ask me."

She moved down the hall after Hattie, almost on the backs of her shoes. "Hattie. Hattie."

I slipped behind the desk to my chair and started looking busy. Hector was slowly moving toward the lunch carts, trying to stay close. Luann hadn't moved a muscle. Staring, Janie almost collided with one of the dietary aides bringing up the lunch carts.

"Hattie, I'm talking to you," Lodge persisted, waving the paper.

Hattie turned and blinked. She frowned, then walked over to one of the lunch carts and took a packet of salt and a packet of pepper. The phone rang. I grabbed it, trying to hear Hattie as she approached Lodge.

"Is there a Mr. Kitchener in room 669?"

I rapidly scanned the patient list, and muttered, "Went home yesterday."

"Hah?"

"Yesterday. He went home. Bye—" I whispered, hearing a faint, "Well, thank you anyway." Still, I missed hearing Hattie—only saw her, with a tired look on her face, hand Lodge the packets of salt and pepper.

Lodge's reddening face jutted out as if she didn't believe what she was seeing and hearing. Hector laughed out loud. Lodge glared at him. Luann choked on her cigarette and grabbed her side with her free hand. Even Janie tried to stifle a smile.

Hattie headed toward the break room, gripping her lunch bag and her black rhinestoned purse. Just before going in, she turned and said to no one in particular, "I'm on break. Anyone needs me, you know where to find me."

II

NURSING MEMORANDUM: *CONFIDENTIAL*

FROM: Judy Lodge, R.N. M.S. Assistant to the Director of Nursing, Six South Supervisor.

TO: John Booth, R.N. M.B.S. Director of Nursing Services.

SUBJECT: Perkins, H.

TITLE: Nursing Assistant.

LOCATION: Six South.

SPECIFICS: Employee performance evaluation and employee reaction.

The following are my summary notes of a discussion I had on June 14, 1976 with Ms. Hattie Perkins concerning a mutual talk we had about her most recent employee performance evaluation.

Ms. Perkins, as you know, has been at the Medical Center now for over thirty-five years. She has had a consistently good work performance, excellent attendance, and has gotten along reasonably well with her co-employees and our housestaff. She has been quite popular with many of our patients, and at times has epitomized our credo: "The patient comes first." Therefore, it is all the more regrettable that in recent months, it has come to my attention, as well as to other employees on the floor, that several factors are adversely affecting Ms. Perkins' work performance to the point where it has become seriously questionable as to whether or not she can continue to function in the manner and standards we expect of our employees in the deliverance of patient care.

Ms. Perkins' patient care is dangerously erratic. She has difficulties in performing the simplest tasks. Just this morning I found her nearly unable to complete the simple task of helping a patient back into bed. Of a graver nature is the recent incident concerning the near-drowning of a patient who was left unattended by Ms. Perkins. Fortunately, the patient himself talked his own family out of filing a malpractice suit. These bouts of "forgetfulness", as Ms. Perkins has called them to other employees (she won't admit this to me), have, as you can see, reached a frightening point.

Ms. Perkins has also become noticeably slower, nearly to the point of painful embarrassment. While this is to be expected of someone of her age, it is reaching the stage where she cannot keep up with her work, particularly the increasing amounts of written work given to the aides in an attempt to begin in-service training and upgrading, such as more charting in the patient notes to free the nurses for more leadership responsibilities throughout the hospital.

Ms. Perkins also tends to argue with her superiors regarding the quality of care. She has, on several occasions, illegally performed the work of registered nurses, and then asked to be monetarily reimbursed for working in the registered nurse category. This is not only impermissible, but unlawful. Ms. Perkins has been seen putting up intravenous poles for patients. Again, this could lead to a potential situation of considerable harm to the patient as well as the hospital (again, in terms of malpractice). Ms. Perkins claims it is "common practice" throughout the Medical Center, due to what she claims is "understaffing". I might add that she has received several previous warnings about hanging I.V. poles, and that this particular item is being grieved through the union grievance procedure by Ms. Perkins and several other aides and orderlies.

I mainly mention the above to illustrate Ms. Perkins' attitude. I feel Ms. Perkins assumes that her length of service with us entitles her to privileges and freedoms unavailable to other employees in her job category. This seems to be part of a growing truculent attitude on her part. More than several of the housestaff have complained about her attitude towards them—she contradicts their orders and often calls them "children". Indeed, while most of our house staff are much younger than Ms. Perkins, housestaff, residents, and interns are, in the majority, grown men with wives and families of their own, and certainly deserve to command respect among all of our employees.

Before sitting down with Ms. Perkins, I offered her our new procedure where she could write up her own evaluation of herself, explaining how this was to encourage employee input and feedback into the evaluation process. She refused. Again, today, after showing her her evaluation, I told her she could write her own reply in the designated space on the employee performance evaluation sheet. Again, she refused. This is the second time in less than a year that Ms. Perkins has refused to sign an employee performance evaluation. When I informed her of this, she simply agreed, and said, "So what?"

In short, I find that Ms. Perkins' work performance and attitude have grown increasingly unsatisfactory. I also feel that she is taking advantage of the fact that she has been with us for a long time, and is somewhat personally popular with many employees, particularly other minorities like herself.

This brings me to an important and delicate point. Ms. Perkins has openly accused me of being a "racialist". I replied that if I was a "racialist", would I have been given so many different positions of increasing responsibility in such a relatively short period of time? I think my record speaks for itself. When I first came here three years ago, I was a floor R.N., and within three months volunteered to be team leader. By the year's end, I took the responsibility for supervising the entire sixth floor. Six months ago, I assumed the position of Assistant to the Director of Nursing, while also maintaining most of my duties as sixth floor supervisor. I have also served as treasurer for the Christmas Club Committee, secretary of the Credit Union, and most recently, as Director of the March of Dimes Fund Drive. In all instances I have tried to be fair to all, regardless of race, creed, or religion. I think that most of my employees would say I was more than fair, and that Ms. Perkins' criticisms were unwarranted.

My main concern is to inform you of a very difficult situation. We are, at present, forced to keep on an employee whose performance and attitude I find basically unsatisfactory. I would appreciate a conference with yourself and several of the other supervisors concerning this problem, which I consider somewhat representative, in that the improper resolution could set a negative precedent, particularly in regards to the handling of our senior employees.

I might add that Ms. Perkins has threatened "to go to the union first thing in the morning." I told her that, according to our contract with the union, that was her privilege according to the second step of the grievance process, since the first step—meeting with the immediate supervisor, myself—will obviously prove unsatisfactory. I felt at a loss to say anything further for fear of jeopardizing our future case. I think it would be an excellent idea at some future date to have a workshop concerning this.

This brings me to another point. There occurred a small incident at the end of today's discussion about Ms. Perkins' employee performance evaluation that I consider to strongly border on insubordination. However, it was unclear to me when and under what circumstances—exactly—an employee can be charged with insubordination, other than the obvious instances of outright slander and physical assault. This area, too, could merit a workshop with yourself, the four assistants to the director, the head of personnel, and someone from labor relations. I would even be glad to make it a coffee and cake evening at my house, if that would be found suitable and agreeable.

Well, not wishing to take up any more of your valuable time, I remain,

Sincerely yours,
Judy Lodge

CC: Orville Larson, Administrator.
       Ike Howes, Personnel.
       Larry Shields, Labor Relations.
ATTENTION FILES: MATERIAL MARKED "CONFIDENTIAL" SHOULD NOT
BE PLACED IN EMPLOYEE FILE.

III

She kept wavin' that piece of paper like she thought she was God and that little piece of paper was the Ten Commandments. And I wanted to say hey we ain't up on Mt. Sinai bitch; and I coulda played crazy but she was lookin' so like she thought she was God, I had to set her straight and play the hand out and tell her what for.

I seen her kind come and go, and I think her kind oughta just as soon as they get here go right down to the Man, pull his pants down, and start right in. Why pussyfoot around with all that polite shit. I mean that's what they here for—to move up that ladder like there was a house of cheese at the top. All this noise about patient this and service that. I seen her from the get. That's why she hates ol' Hattie—'cause she knows I know what she's about. She knows I had her number before it was on the board. Only what she don't know is I got her number on MY board. I got one of her hairs. Just in case. Though I don't know that much about what to do with it—just the stories—but if it gets to that I can find out. I got that hair all right. I caught her actually doin' some work one day. She wiped her forehead and this hair got loose and twisted and she pulled at it and wiped her fat self with a towel and put it in the dirty linen and I headed straight for it and held my breath and got that towel and that hair, plucked it right off that nasty thing and into a paper towel. I washed my hands for twenty minutes afterwards.

She make me mad enough I might get some more hair. Might have to pull on that bitch's head until I see some brains. And that might be a long, long time. Maybe I pull her head open and there's nothin'—just a bunch of memos and maybe a purse fulla that Godawful lipstick like what French whores wear or like she thinks she's a eighteen year old heifer and not a fat way-over-forty cow the Army got tired of. And don't know she's not in the Army no more, that we don't salute here. We just do the work—the salutin' you can forget the minute you walk in here 'cause I ain't saluted for twenty some years and ain't about to start now, all my yessin' and maamin' is over with cause I waited and seen alot and seen the union, and when folks say the union's fat I tell 'em you kids try workin' without it, honey, and you'll find out just how skinny you can get—to the bone—and I don't want to hear nothin' else about it.

And the look on her face when I said, "Well, I guess I'm gonna have to go to the union again," and tomorrow first thing after I soak these bones and shower, I'm gonna get dressed up and see my business agent before he gets the sleepcrust outta his eyes—he gonna SEE me—and we'll see who's goin' to be signin' what, 'cause I'm a dues payin' member goin' on thirty-three years. Maybe I could try and get HER ass fired. Maybe I could make up an employee performance for that do-nothin' bitch what talks and walks around doin' nothin' 'cept spyin' on people and botherin' everybody with this evaluation and that memorandum b.s. Talkin' all this shit like she couldn't just come out and say, "Hattie, you're too old."

And I woulda said, "You think I enjoy this? Draggin' my bones here everyday, cleanin' cranky old people's assholes, seein' folks cry cause their kin dyin' or ain't never gonna be the same? Gimme a decent pension and I'll be outta here so fast, you can blink and I'll be home fixin' dinner."

Only everyone here knows that our retirement plan is the joke of the world, and when I was at Spencer's—Spencer he makes good money as a longshoreman, they have a pension you can live on instead of take one look and wanna lay down and die—Spencer he heard how much we got and leaned closer, frownin' like his eyebrows was gonna shake hands, "Did I hear you right, Hattie? You know, I pride myself on my hearing, Hattie, but I don't think I heard you right."

And I said, "You heard right. Eighty-five dollars a month."

And Spencer said, "Hattie, this is 1976."

And I said, "That's what the calendar say."

And Spencer was like he couldn't believe where he was for a minute. Poured himself a new drink. Yelled at his kid five minutes later. For nothing.

And I wish I could get outta here 'cause they don't appreciate a thing you do. Like you try to do someone nice, and all of a sudden they got you as a murderer, and don't want to hear a word from you about it.

I brought this man in for his bath and everything was fine. I washed him and he smiled and asked me could he stay in the tub longer, and I said, "It says twenty minute bath," and he said, "Come on, please Hattie, my roommate's a royal pain in the ass." "Didn't I know it," I said. "Tell me about it, honey, I been carin' for that sucker for two weeks and if he ain't one of the funkiest, crankiest sonsabitches I ever run across, my name ain't Hattie Perkins." And the man laughed, "Then you understand what I mean," and I say, "Sure, stay as long as you want." And he say, "Thanks alot Hattie, you're a lifesaver." And I say "Just dry yourself good when you get out so you don't catch cold."

And how was I to know his family'd come lookin' for him, and he be startin' to doze off and got a few bubbles of water up his nose, and his family screamin' and fussin' to wake the dead about how come he was all alone, was we tryin' to drown the man, what negligence, and who was it. They wrote it up. How could we leave him by hisself the senile old man, and I said, "Senile my ass, he just wanted to have himself some privacy." And the resident gettin' huffy as hell sayin', "I said short baths, Mrs. Perkins," and I said, "I was usin' my judgment. It was a matter of judgment or do you think judgment is reserved only for you." And he said, "That's not the point," and I said, "If that ain't the point, then I don't know what is."

And the next day he and Lodge had their heads together like they was playin' football and she kept slidin' her weasel eyes over towards me thinkin' she was so slick, only I forced her to keep them on me 'cause I stared at her straight out and said, "Yeah?" (pretendin' she didn't see me, who did she think she was foolin'?)

And now that all gets translated into I tell doctors what to do and hates 'em all, which at times ain't too far from the truth, but the truth too is the ones treat me decent we get along fine—like that Dr. Hartman, now me and him are great friends. Maybe I should have him see that pack of lies she wrote up, maybe he could straighten her out since she just goes ga ga over any doctor, practically gets down on her hands and knees and tries to get her name legally changed to Fido.

So when she was wavin' that paper I thought of all that and then some. And once I sat down and read what she had put down I was mad. I was so hot I wondered if I said anything would there be flames comin' out of my mouth I was so mad. I told her she must be craftier than even I thought she was if she thought I was goin' to sign that mess—all those lies, up and down, unsatisfactory this and doesn't meet requirements that. And I been workin' here 30 years goin' on 40. She said sign it and write whatever you want in this little itty bitty space over here. And I said I didn't hire on here as a writer, besides if I do start writin' what I think of what you wrote here, we gonna be here til after dark and I got granddaughters to see and grandchildren to visit and neighbors what need my advice on things. So I ain't signin', I ain't writin', and that's all there is to it.

And that bitch made me so upset sayin' things just weren't done like that, and in a way I was glad 'cause I could see I was messin' her up—she wanted it all wrapped up tight. So I just walked away 'cause I was gettin' tired of her jawin'. And I walked past all these folks—Hector, Josh, Janie, and saw Luann down the hall, and the other aides and folks from the kitchen with the food. And she was followin' me callin', "Hattie, Hattie," like she thought sooner or later I was gonna have to sign that paper. I just shook my head. I was tired of it. I had all to do to not just turn around and flatten that fat bitch, only my legs was hurtin' so bad I didn't know if my joints would make the turn. I reminded myself to take me home some rubbing alcohol and take a nice warm bath, a long hot soak.

And I thought of how earlier on in the day she seen me tryin' to help that poor old man Moore back into his bed where for a second I thought neither of us was gonna make it and we was gonna both land up on the floor. And she just stood there watchin' me so she could write down on that piece of paper that Hattie Perkins can no longer help move a six foot, 200 pound man back into bed all by herself. And she didn't move a muscle but stood there with her fat bitch self in the doorway, while I liked to kill myself twistin' and turnin' that old man Moore who had a bad back to begin with.

Yeah, well they'll be throwin' snowballs in hell before they get me to sign. They can come to my grave with a five dollar Papermate, and I'll just turn over.

And that's when I grabbed some of that salt and pepper offa the lunch wagon and turned to her as best as I could turn and said, "Here, Judy, maybe you actin' funky and peculiar 'cause you're hungry. Why don't you just pretend that piece of paper is a steak, and go on and chew it up. Just chew slow so you don't make yourself sick now." And folks started laughin', some was coverin' their mouths so she couldn't see 'em laugh, and I just kept on goin'.

And didn't look back neither, 'cause I don't need anyone or any piece of paper to tell me I'm not as fast as I usta be. Only who appreciates what a 65-year-old woman can do, 'cause I can do things in less time than it takes these girls what every time they give a bedpan almost or change a wound, they fussin' and raisin' up a storm. And if they did less fussin' and runnin' and fidgetin' and ohmyGodin', they'd get it done a whole lot faster. I try to tell 'em, but some folks you can't tell them a damn thing. And they call me Crazy, just 'cause I like to say a few things to remind myself about this and that. They say, "No Hattie, you crazy 'cause you talk to yourself." And I just say, "Hey, you find me someone who's more interesting than me, and I'll talk to them." That tickled them. They had a good laugh behind that. And what can you tell some kid who's got her figure and knows she's fine, and sees me as her grandma what should be in some old folks home anyway? What are they gonna listen to me for? Though there used to be a time when they did listen. But when they in a jam who you think they come to? When there's some mess, who you bet even these college nurses run to? 'Cause no one said much about what happens when someone collapses on the floor bleedin' and shittin' all over theyselves while they at the other end of the floor helpin' someone who can't breathe. And when they want me to help 'em lift, or clean someone shitted up themselves, well all of a sudden no one's callin' me crazy then. And once I pointed that out. And no one said nothin'—suddenly everyone got busy writin' and foldin' linen and lookin' real hard at their fingernails.

And it's like all these years, one after another, they be runnin' up, "Oh Hattie, Hattie you're the ONLY ONE can help me," which always seemed strange to me seein' how there's so many of us around, yet year after year I'm the ONLY ONE, yet now they don't seem to need the ONLY ONE. 'Cause maybe they gonna get someone else to be the ONLY ONE. And maybe that person don't know they been selected yet to become the next me, and instead of Ol' Hattie, it gonna be Ol' Luann, or Ol' Hector, or Ol' Johnnie.

And oh the look on her face that time last evaluation when I said in front of everybody when she said, "We only have your best interests at heart, Hattie," and I said, "So what you gonna do now? Take me to the Colonel, and buy me the Ten Dollar Bucket?" And Luann and Hector and Josh was gigglin' and I kept on, "See? I rate. They takin' me to The Colonel. Money's no object. Nothin's too good for ol' Hattie. And they gonna guarantee me no wings, and no backs. How about THAT?"

And I remember that 30 year anniversary party, and that was nice for real. Real nice. They got us all front row seats at the Venetian Room in the Hilton, and there was the twenty-year folks, and the twenty-five year folks, and three of us thirty-year folks—me, Irish Katy what works in the kitchen, and Capek the old engineer from Slovokia or one of them countries where it rains all the time. And they got me and Irish corsages. She got red roses, and I took the yellow roses 'cause I was wearin' my green silk evenin' gown, and it went with it. They gave us gold pins. I have it at home. And we talked into the micro-phone and I said, "I'm not Johnny Carsons or anything, but thanks alot." And later on J.J. who been there almost long as me said I did that so slick and to such perfection that he was gonna call up Johnny Carsons himself and tell him watch out for Hattie Perkins, Johnny, she's a real comer. And that's what I like about J.J. 'cause he's always sayin' stuff like that to me make me feel good even if it is a complete lie—only it's different, like a fib or stretchin' things a bit, or a tall tale, like a lotta things.

And not a real lie a complete lie a white lie, say a white lie weighin' about 220—if she ain't wearin' her wig today. If she's wearin' her wig now, that probably ups it to 230. Where she got it I'll never know, all I know is it fits bad and makes her look like she stole if offa some orangutang, the bitch, and I could even see her real colors her ugly roots in my ear, "Sign, sign, sign, Hattie, Hattie."

And I got to thinkin' how you always think and say, "Now that's *cold*," and me always tellin' these kids, "I seen it all" and "That ain't nothin'," and yet how I can never get used to it. Never.

Like Spence sayin' about the pension, "This is like the Stone Age. This is some cold shit." And me sayin', "It's the Ice Age is what it is." And Spencer saying, "Yeah, yeah. And the Ice Age was all white, wasn't it now." And Spencer's wife laughin', "Well, I don't recall seein' any black Eskimos. In fact, I don't recall seein' any Eskimos whatsoever." And I said, "That's 'cause everybody froze to death. Every living thing froze to death."

And for a second just a second when I come to work that mornin' in the rain last week and that wind was blowin' that rain, "Hattie," I said to myself, "what in the world are you doin' fightin' this rain and this wind to walk into THIS fool place?"

And that same day that fat cow started in with this, "Here's your pre-evaluation form, Hattie. I want you to look it over. You'll see that you can evaluate yourself and put in whatever comments you'd like. So, feel free." It was some new bullshit. I saw that right off—'cause she wanted me to write down about myself so she could take it and study on it, and I just said, "Do I have to do this? Is this in the union book?"

"Well no," she say, "but it's a new procedure and—"

And I didn't let her finish, told her straight-off, "If it ain't in the book, then forget it." And the blue in her eyes got so dark they looked like they was snowin' razorblades and she stomped off.

And later in the rain I was thinkin' of them animals what you see in the museum, old and funky and trapped in the ice, with them long teeth like what elephants got, and they say these was kin to the elephants—their great, great grandfolks goin' way back, and so big the elephants was like little bits next to these mothers.

And I couldn't get that outta my mind. I told my daughter and she said, "Ma, you got more to do than to worry about them old time animals," and I just said, real quiet, "Do I? And how else are they dealin' with me?" And she didn't say a word, but just hugged me. And I wanted to tell her how I dreamed I was on break and lookin' through the National Geographic and saw a picture of one of them mammadons in the ice. And the picture got bigger and bigger and the ice got big like a mirror, and I saw my face and my skin with these wrinkles and these bad teeth, and I felt like I was inside an icecube and woke up shiverin' chilled to the bone on a night you don't even need a blanket, and all around me it was white and cold, and Hector handed me a serape and said, "Take care Hattie, it's real cold out," and I was scared like when I was five years old and you wouldn't think I was 65, and then I woke up for real, and right there in the dead of night was cookin' at three o'clock in the morning, and hungry like I hadn't eaten a decent meal in weeks.

And I'd like nothin' better than to be able to get out of it. I wouldn't be one of these peoples you hear about what retires, then goes off and dies straight off 'cause they don't know what to do with themselves—like when the wardclerk and Hector they asked me, "What would you do Hattie?" And I said, "First thing, I'm gonna buy me a motorcycle, and come back here and ride 'round and round. Maybe run a few people over." They started laughin' and I went on.

"And if they give me enough money I'll travel. I'll go dancin' down in Rio—Rio de Janeiro where they got the biggest Mardi Gras in the world, bigger than the one in New Orleans even. Yeah, I'll hit all them festivals in Brazil and Mexico and Africa—I'd like to see Africa, they say they got some of the oldest civilizations in the world. Yeah, I'll travel my ass off, get to all them places, go to Europe and have 'em show me around all them famous museums and things, and go to Egypt and hit the Pyramids, and India with all them fancyassed temples—" and they was all laughin'.

And suddenly I got hot 'cause I figured here I was again runnin' my fool mouth and where the hell was I goin' anyway and whose business was it anyway, and I said, "Their business is to give me enough of a pension so I can do it, and maybe we should stick to that, because without that all this is so much BULLSHIT, I mean I'll probably be lucky if I get enough to eat three meals a day and make the rent," and just sayin' that made me feel like I was on the floor and out in the rain again and I felt hot and said, "Yeah, its all so much shit."

And all of a sudden no one was askin' about what I wanted to do or would do, and Josh was lookin' down at his papers, and Hector got that hurt look on his face like he gets sometimes, and Luann lit up though I been tellin' her them smokes gonna cut her heart out, so I figured the hell with it and smiled to myself and said, "Hey, and you know what else?" They were still solemn-like but they looked at me, and I said, "The main thing is, if I get what's comin to me (and they started to smile but half a smile like they weren't sure what was comin' next cause with me its true you never know), "I'm gonna party me up a storm. The last you'll hear about me I'll be drinkin' the finest rum in the world at midnight in the Caribbean Islands, the real stuff, the real homemade brew. That's the number one choice when you get down to it 'cause in the Caribbean—and I know 'cause I was there on my honeymoon if you can believe that—in the Caribbean they got water so blue and so clear you can see clean through it, yet that water is cool and at the same time warm as a bathtub 'cause they about as near the sun as you can get—they call it The Torrid Zone and that's where you can write me, Hattie Perkins, care of The Torrid Zone—"

They was all laughin' now and sayin', "Sounds great," and stuff like that, and I said, "You damn right it sounds great. 'Cause they got evenings there where the stars are dripping like they was split open melons, that's how they look—it's like the whole sky was like my purse only brand new and a whole lot bigger—and maybe I'll find me some magician stud, some magic man, who can turn these rhinestones into diamonds and who appreciates and respects a woman of my bearing."

And they was going back to work slow and shakin' their heads and smilin', "Crazy Hattie", and I said, "That's me."

Karen Brodine (1947–1987)

Karen Brodine grew up in rural Woodinville, Washington, in a family with a tradition of radical politics. Her grandmother, in whose memory Brodine would later write the poem "Her Stubborn Spirit," was a postal worker hounded by the FBI for her socialist activities and blacklisted for her refusal to testify before the House Un-American Activities Committee. Both parents were music teachers, and Brodine studied ballet and modern dance from a young age. She worked as a VISTA volunteer in the schools of New York's Harlem and later majored in dance at the University of California at Berkeley, graduating with a BA in 1972. She performed with dance troupes in the Bay Area and worked as a dance instructor until a congenital knee problem ended that career. She had also been writing poetry for many years, and in 1974 she earned an MA in creative writing from San Francisco State University, where she taught evening courses for the next six years. From 1975 until 1986, the year before her death from breast cancer, Brodine's main livelihood came from the typesetting trade, and this experience inspired the work that follows. "Woman Sitting at the Machine, Thinking," first published in 1984 by Radical Women Publications and subtitled "a series of work poems," insists that the worker, even in mechanical and repetitive jobs, is also a thinker, a critic, a dreamer. In language and images that emerge from the work of her hands on the keyboard, Brodine evokes the precise tasks, the time-discipline of the office, her coworkers, and her bosses, as well as the daydreams, thoughts of a lover, worries about a parent, and fantasies of ways to fight back, that fill her days.

Brodine was not only a writer, but a committed activist. She helped to found the Women Writers Union and became a leader in the Freedom Socialist Party. "As an activist, teacher, and poet," she writes, "I feel that art and politics are inextricable, and that both are essential. Without feminism, I would never have written a word." She was the author of four collections of poems: *Slow Juggling* (1975), *Workweek* (1978), *Illegal Assembly* (1980), and the posthumously published collection, *Woman Sitting at the Machine, Thinking* (1990).

Woman Sitting at the Machine, Thinking:
A series of work poems

she thinks about everything at once without making a mistake.
no one has figured out how to keep her from doing this thinking
while her hands and nerves also perform every delicate complex
function of the work. this is not automatic or deadening.
5   try it sometime. make your hands move quickly on the keys
fast as you can, while you are thinking about:

the layers, fossils. the idea that this machine she controls
is simply layers of human workhours frozen in steel, tangled
in tiny circuits, blinking out through lights like hot, red eyes.
10   the noise of the machine they all sometimes wig out to, giddy,
zinging through the shut-in space, blithering atoms;
everyone's hands paused mid-air above the keys
while Neil or Barbara solo, wrists telling every little thing,
feet blipping along, shoulders raggly.

15   she had always thought of money as solid, stopped.
but seeing it as moving labor, human hours, why that means
it comes back down to her hands on the keys, shoulder aching,
brain pushing words through fingers through keys, trooping
out crisp black ants on the galleys. work compressed into
20   instruments, slim computers, thin as mirrors, how could
numbers multiply or disappear, squeezed in sideways like that
but they could, they did, obedient and elegant, how amazing.
the woman whips out a compact, computes the cost,
her face shining back from the silver case
25   her fingers, sharp tacks, calling up the digits.

when she sits at the machine, rays from the cathode stream
directly into her chest. when she worked as a clerk, the rays
from the xerox angled upward, striking her under the chin.
when she waited tables the micro oven sat at stomach level.
30   when she typeset for Safeway, dipping her hands in processor
chemicals, her hands burned and peeled and her chest ached
from the fumes.

well we know who makes everything we use or can't use.
as the world piles itself up on the bones of the years,
35   so our labor gathers.

while we sell ourselves in fractions. they don't want us all
at once, but hour by hour, piece by piece. our hands mainly
and our backs. and chunks of our brains. and veiled expressions
on our faces, they buy. though they can't know what actual
40   thoughts stand behind our eyes.

then they toss the body out on the sidewalk at noon and at five.
then they spit the body out the door at sixty-five.

each morning:

fresh thermos of coffee at hand; for the slowing down, shift
gears, unscrew the lid of the orange thermos, pour out a whiff
of home, morning paper, early light. a tangible pleasure
5　　against the unlively words.

funny, though. this set of codes slips through my hands, a
loose grid of shadows with big gaps my own thoughts sneak
through . . .

Call format o five. Reports, Disc 2, quad left
10　　return. name of town, address, zip. quad left
return. rollalong and there you are.
done with this one. start the next.

call format o five. my day so silent yet taken up with words.
floating through the currents and cords of my wrists
15　　into the screen and drifting to land, beached pollywogs.
all this language handled yet the room is so silent.
everyone absorbed in feeding words through the machines.

enter file execute.

Call file Oceana. name of town, Pacifica. name of street, Arbor.
20　　thinking about lovemaking last night, how it's another land,
another set of sounds, the surface of the water, submerged,
then floating free, the delicate fabric of motion and touch
knit with listening and humming and soaring.
never a clear separation of power because it is both our power
25　　at once. hers to speak deep in her body and voice to her own
rhythms. mine to ride those rhythms out and my own,
and call them out even more. a speaking together from body
to mouth to voice.

replace file Oceana.
30　　call file Island.

Scroll up . . . . scroll down.
What is there to justify?

the words gliding on the screen like the seal at the aquarium,
funny whiskers, old man seal, zooming by upside down
35　　smirking at the crowd, mocking us
and his friends the dolphins, each sharp black and cream marking
streamlined as the water

huh. ugh, they want this over and over:
M A Y 1 M A Y 1 M A Y 1 M A Y 1 M A Y 1 enough?
40　　M A Y 1 M A Y 1

once I have typeset all the pages, I run the job out on tape
and clip it to the videosetter to be punched out.
then I swing out the door to get another job.

down the stairs into the cramped room where Mary and Rosie
5   and Agnes sit in the limp draft of one fan.
"must be 95 in here." "yeah, and freezing in the other room."
"got to keep the computers cool, you know."

back up the stairs past management barricaded
behind their big desks on the way to everything.
10   on the way to the candy machine.
on the way to the bathroom.
on the way to lunch.
I pretend they are invisible.
I pretend they have great big elephant ears.

15   and because they must think we are stupid in order
to push us around, *they* become stupid.
knowing "something's going on," peering like moles.
how can they know the quirk of an eyebrow behind their back?
they suspect we hate them because they know
20   what they are doing to us—but we are only
stupid Blacks or crazy Puerto Ricans, or dumb blonds.

we are their allergy, their bad dream.
they need us too much, with their talk of
"carrying us" on the payroll.
25   we carry them, loads of heavy, dull metal,
outmoded and dusty.
they try to control us, building partitions,
and taking the faces off the phones.
they talk to us slow and loud,
30   HOW ARE YOU TODAY? HERE'S A CHECK FOR YOU.
As if it were a gift.

we say—even if they stretched tape
across our mouths
we could still speak to one another
35   with our eyebrows.

————————

hours staring me in the face
miles of straight copy
singlespaced, shut in.

when I called my mother
5   her words were all
turned but not quite is that
every perfect thing isn't sense,
I can't, she says, can't talk about it.
when I call her, the floor drops inches
10   and I am trying to be cheer.
wh–whts the matter? she says.

mother wears a dress all of blue
fabric of tiny wires and messages

veins knotted together, snagging,
15   and the hem gaping down
where the stitching ripped out.

don't care if things are hard
just want a whole cloth
not all these unravelled scraps and me
20   a rough thread trying to gut them
together, in and out.

when I see the boss, I hold
my face clear and solemn, thinking
pig. pig. it's true, too.
25   not rhetorical.

"if we stick you in the little room
with the heat on, you'll be happy.
that's what you wanted."

"you're an electronic technician,
30   not a typesetter. you're lucky
to be shut out of the union."

I know that typesetters
grow more capillaries
in our fingertips
35   from all that use.

here's a test: cut my fingers
and see if I bleed more.

_____

knowledge this power owned, not shared
owned and hoarded
to white men, lock stock dollar
skill passed down from manager
5   to steal, wrench it back
knowledge is something we have
this is the bitters column
around the chair, toe stubbing the floor
and I am here, legs twisted
10   on our own time the words clarify
with all we are not taught
I will know it and use it burning
I sneak it home and copy it
the Puerto Rican janitor, the older
15   woman, the Black women, our heads
held over stolen not granted
in my stomach for all the access
I have to sneak
language is something
20   get my hands on the machine
he takes it all as his right

eating lunch for granted his whole life
get my hands on the book
he's being taught what I am not
25   angry words swallowing my throat

to take   to take it back

        and open   and ribbon out   and share

The Bitters Column.

---

2 hours till lunch.
1 hour till lunch.
43 minutes till lunch.
13 minutes till lunch.
5   LUNCH.

they write you up if you're three minutes late.
three write-ups and you're out.

I rush back from lunch, short-cut
through the hall to the door
10   locked like the face of a boss.

I tug at the door, definitely locked.
peer in through the glass, watery and dark,
see two supervisors standing 25 yards in,
talking, faces turned away.
15   oh good, I think, they'll let me in.
I knock on the glass, cold to my fist.
not too loud, just enough to let them know.
they glance at me, continue talking.
I knock again, louder.
20   one man looks right at me, turns his back.
I am furious, let me in!
and knock again, my fist white where it is
clenched. BAM BAM BAM pause
BAM BAM BAM BAM BAM
25   they don't even look up.
I knock harder and harder, the glass
shaking in its frame.
I imagine my hand smashing through the pane,
shaking their collars, bloody but triumphant.

Sleepy afternoon . . . halfway through typing a long page
about building specifications, lost, wandering
through strange buildings, wide deep fields at dusk,
trying to find the way home.
5   I reach a deserted building, a warehouse, fenced off.
people hurry to work, not stopping to talk.
a low-level murmur hovers below the surface, like the

slight draft that makes the hair on your arm lift.
birds clot on the aerials, the light out of whack.

10 we notice a tightness right below the hollow of the neck
gathering to a deep chestpain, slowmoving and thick.
we notice it like smog, waking up each morning
short-breathed and headachy. the officials say nothing's wrong,
any slippage is small, no measurable effects gather.

15 none of us talk outloud about this to anyone.

now though, crowds begin to pool, huddling together.
I hurry to a circle of women, where a girl dodges cops.
she is agile, darting back and forth, panting,
slippery as soap, her hair damp and glistening.
20 they lunge, she skips, twists, breaks from the circle
and runs. we race after her in a tumbling crowd,
she is at my ear, whispering, "money . . . burning . . . tell . . .
say . . . shout."

we are afraid, locked in a windowless building, guarded.
25 the pain is still here the way summer heat insists.
I repeat the words which are about the phony soap
the guards have handed us, sickly sweet,
"will it wash it will it wash it away" and another
woman joins me, "soap fake soap," and another
30 and now all of us are chanting and the ones guarding us
look uncertain, scared, as if they too wonder
and we are all chanting and shouting now,
"fake soap, will it wash it won't it wash it away."

━━━━━━━━━━

Line corrections
Interview with Leola S.
Typesetter: Karen B.

Born in Shreveport, Leola
5 independence is important, she
one of fourteen children, her
housecleaning in San Mateo
divorced now, she lives alone in
serving dinner from 4–5 pm every
10 starting pay 1.53 per
h o u r

she and some co-workers
today more than ever in U.S.
h i s t o r y

15 posed to discrimination by sex,
race, color, religious or national
o r i g i n

more women go to work in

    enter the labor
20   70 percent of the average wage
    Black women lowest paid of
    to organize the continuing fight
    determined to be heard
    plaints against unfair policies
25   something worth fighting for
    sector of the working class
    w o m e n

———

    Rivera's mural, the women, rows of them
    similar, yet each unique, their hands
    the focus of the art
    bodies solid, leaning forward, these women,
5   facing the voices, knowledge running through them

    language the most basic of industry
    to gather our food
    to record exchange
    to give warning and call for help
10   to praise courage
    it flows through our hands and into metal
    they think it doesn't touch us

    a typesetter changes man to person
    will they catch her?
15   She files one job under union,
    another under lagoon,
    another under cash

    what if you could send anything in and call it out again?
    I file jobs under words I like—red, buzz, fury
20   search for tiger, execute
    the words stream up the screen till tiger trips the halt
    search for seal search for strike
    search for the names of women

    we could circle our words around the world
25   like dolphins streaking through water their radar
    if the screens were really in the hands of experts: us.
    think of it—our ideas whipping through the air
    everything stored in an eyeflash
    our whole history, ready and waiting.

———

    at night switching off the machines one by one
    each degree of quiet a growing pleasure
    we swallow the silence after hours of steady noise
    the last machine harrumphs off and it is so visibly quiet
5   switch off the fluorescent lights and it is so quietly dark

I say, goodby, see you tomorrow, and relax down the stairs
into the cavernous shop where the paper is stored
near the presses, huge cardboard cylinders of newsprint
stacked up ceiling high.

10   I curve toward the door in the shadows
smells sweet like a big barn
calm snowbanks these spools, or tree trunks
in the light sifting through the glazed windows

walking tired through the resting plant
15   past huge breathing rolls of paper
waiting to be used

some buildings never sleep
round the clock
three eight hour shifts
seven days a week
5   centrifugal force irons us flat
to the blank walls, speeding,
whirling, intent as astronauts,
eyes toward the clock,
hands on the keys,
10   shoulders pressed against the chair.

some buildings never sleep
never shut down
roaring and roaring and we shout,
WHAT DID YOU SAY? HUH? WHAT?
15   WHERE IS THE? WHAT DID YOU SAY?

continuous paper streams from the room
words ratatat through our brains
trains and earthquakes shudder the walls
the long whistle of wind under the door
20   all we know of outside

remember that fish
that lives so deep
it has grown its own light
energy glaring out the bulbs
25   of its eyes
remember that fish formed flat
under fathoms of water
bones streamlined as ribs of steel
precise and efficient, formed in duress,
30   reaching, spinning the tough wire
of its own life, and long before Edison
volting out through its own demands.

Linda Hogan (b. 1947)

Native American poet, essayist, and fiction writer, Linda Hogan was born in Denver, Colorado, into a military family that moved often. A member of the Chickasaw nation, Hogan considers the Oklahoma country where her father's family lives, as her spiritual home. She began writing in her late twenties, and in her first book of poems, *Calling Myself Home* (1978), she demonstrates the concern for the relationships of native people, especially women, with their environment and their history that marks much of her work. Hogan pursued her interest in literature and writing with a bachelor's degree from University of Colorado at Colorado Springs and an MA from Colorado University at Boulder, where she later became a member of the English faculty. In 1979, Hogan adopted two daughters of Lakota heritage, Tanya Thunder Horse and Sandra Dawn Protector, whom she addressed in her second book of poems, *Daughters, I love You* (1981). A prolific writer, Hogan's books of poems include *That Horse* (1985, a collaboration with her father Charles Colbert Henderson); *Red Clay: Poems and Stories* (1991); and *Book of Medicines* (1993). The poem, "The New Apartment, Minneapolis," which is presented here, is from *Savings* (1988), a collection in which Hogan exposes and explores the effects of urban relocation on Native American people. She is also the author of the novels *Mean Spirit* (1990), which narrates the Oklahoma oil boom of the 1920s from the point of view of the displaced Osage people, *Solar Storms* (1995), and *Power* (1998); of collections of essays, *Dwellings: A Spiritual History of the Living World* (1995) and *The Sweet Breathing of Plants: Women and the Green World* (2000); and of *The Woman Who Watches Over the World: A Native Memoir* (2001). An active environmentalist and a volunteer in wildlife rehabilitation projects, Hogan has coauthored with Brenda Peterson *Sightings: The Gray Whales' Mysterious Journey* (2002). The story "Making Do" was published in *The New Native American Novel: Works in Progress* (1986).

MAKING DO

Roberta James became one of the silent people in Seeker County when her daughter, Harriet, died at six years of age.

Harriet died of what they used to call consumption.

After the funeral, Grandmother Addie went to stay with Roberta in her grief, as she had done over the years with her children and grandchildren. Addie, in fact, had stayed with Roberta during the time of her pregnancy with Harriet, back when the fifteen-year-old girl wore her boyfriend's black satin jacket that had a map of Korea on the back. And she'd visited further back than that, back to the days when Roberta wore white full skirts and white blouses and the sun came in the door, and she lay there in that hot sun like it was ironed flat against the floor, and she felt good with clean hair and skin and singing a little song to herself. There were oak trees outside. She was waiting. Roberta was waiting there for something that would take her away. But the farthest she got was just outside her skin, that black jacket against her with its map of Korea.

Addie never told Roberta a word of what she knew about divided countries and people who wear them on their backs, but later Roberta knew that her grandmother had seen way down the road what was coming, and warned her in little ways. When she brushed Roberta's dark hair, she told her, "You were born to a different life, Bobbie."

After the funeral, Roberta's mother offered comfort in her own way. "Life goes on," Neva said, but she herself had long belonged to that society of quiet Indian women in Seeker, although no one would have guessed this of the woman who wore Peach Promise lipstick, smiled generously, and kissed the bathroom mirror, leaving a message for Roberta that said, "See you in the a.m. Love."

Grandma Addie tended Angela, Roberta's younger daughter. She fed the baby Angela spoonsful of meal, honey, and milk and held her day and night while Roberta went about the routines of her life. The chores healed her a little; perking coffee and cleaning her mother's lipstick off the mirror. She swept away traces of Harriet with the splintered broom, picking up threads from the girl's dress, black hair from her head, wiping away her footprints.

Occasionally Neva stopped in, clasped her daughter's thin cold hands between her warm ones, and offered advice. "That's why you ought to get married," she said. She wrapped Roberta's shoulders in a large gray sweater. "Then you'd have some man to help when things are down and out. Like Ted here. Well, anyway, Honey," she said at eye level to Roberta, "you sure drew a good card when Harriet was born. Didn't she, Ted?"

"Sure sugar, an ace."

But when Roberta wasn't looking, Neva shook her head slowly and looked down at the floor, and thought their lives were all hopeless.

Roberta didn't get married like her mother suggested. She did take some comfort on those long nights by loving Tom Wilkins. Each night she put pieces of cedar inside his Red Wing boots, to keep him close, and neatly placed them beneath her bed. She knew how to care for herself with this man, keeping him close in almost the same space Harriet had abandoned. She wept slightly at night after he held her and he said, "There now. There now," and patted her on the back.

He brought her favorite Windmill cookies with him from town and he sang late at night so that the ghost of Harriet could move on more easily, like he eventually moved on when Roberta stopped placing cedar in his boots.

"Why didn't that Wilkins boy come back?" Grandma asked. "Choctaw, wasn't he?"

Roberta shrugged as if she hadn't left his boots empty of cedar. "He was prettier than me." She pushed her straggly hair back from her face to show Grandma what she meant.

A month later, Roberta was relieved when the company summoned Tom Wilkins to Louisiana to work on a new oil field and she didn't have to run into him at the store any longer.

Roberta's next child, a son she named Wilkins after the father, died at birth, strangled on his own cord. Roberta had already worn a dark shawl throughout this pregnancy. She looked at his small roughbox and said, "He died of life and I know how that can happen."

She held on to her grandmother's hand.

Grandma Addie and Neva talked about Roberta. "A woman can only hold so much hurt," Grandma said.

"And don't think I don't know it," said Neva.

Roberta surfaced from her withdrawal a half year later, in the spring of 1974, when Angela looked at her like a little grandmother and said, "Mother, I know it is hard, but it's time for me to leave you" and immediately became feverish. Roberta bathed her with alcohol and made blessing-root tea, which she dropped into little Angela's rose-petal mouth with an eye dropper. She prayed fervently to God or Jesus, she had never really understood which was which, and to all the stones and trees and gods of the sky and inner earth that she knew well, and to the animal spirits, and she carried her little Angel to the hospital in the middle of praying, to that house made of brick and window and cinders where dying bodies were kept alive, carried the girl with soft child skin in a small quilt decorated with girls in poke bonnets, and thought how funny it was to wrap a dying child in such sweetness as those red-cheeked girls in the calico bonnets. She blamed herself for ignoring Angela in her own time of grief. Four days later Angela died, wearing a little corn necklace Roberta made, a wristlet of glass beads, and covered with that quilt.

"She even told Roberta she was about to die," Neva told Ted. "Just like an old woman, huh, Bert?"

Roberta went on with her silence through this third death, telling herself over and over what had happened, for the truth was so bad she could not believe it. The inner voice of the throat spoke and repeated the words of loss and Roberta listened hard. "My Angel. My Harriet. All my life gone and broken while I am so young. I'm too young for all this loss."

She dreamed of her backbone and even that was broken in pieces. She dreamed of her house in four pieces. She was broken like the country of Korea or the land of the tribe.

They were all broken, Roberta's thin-skinned father broken by the war. He and Neva raised two boys whose parents had "gone off" as they say of those who come under the control of genie spirits from whiskey bottles, and those boys were certainly broken. And Neva herself had once been a keeper of the gates; she was broken.

In earlier days she read people by their faces and bodies. She was a keeper of gates, opening and closing ways for people to pass through life. "This one has been eating too much grain," she'd say, or "That one was born too rich for her own good and is spoiled. That one is broken in the will to live by this and that." She was a keeper of the family gates as well. She closed doors on those she disliked, if they were dishonest, say, or mean, or small. There was no room for smallness in her life, but she opened the doors wide for those who moved her slightly, in any way, with stirrings of love or pity. She had lusty respect for belligerence, political rebellion, and for vandalism against automobiles or businesses or bosses, and those vandals were among those permitted inside her walls.

And now she was broken, by her own losses and her loneliness.

Roberta cried against Addie's old warm shoulder and Grandma Addie stayed on, moving in all her things, cartons of canning jars, a blue-painted porcelain horse, her dark dresses and aprons, pictures of her grandchildren and great-grandchildren, rose-scented candles of the virgin of Guadalupe, even though she was never a Catholic, and the antlers of the deer.

Roberta ignored her cousins from the churches of the brethren of this and that when they came to comfort her in their ways, telling her that all things were meant to be and that the Lord gives and takes.

Uncle James was older and so he said nothing, and she sat with him, those silent ones together.

Roberta's mother left messages on the bathroom mirror. "There is a time for everything in heaven."

With Grandma there to watch over Neva and the house, Roberta decided one day to pack her dishes, blankets, and clothes into the old Chevy she had bought from Ted, and she drove away from the little square tombstones named Angela, Wilkins, and Harriet, though it nearly broke her heart to leave them. She drove away from all those trying to comfort her with what comforted them. The sorrow in her was like a well too deep for young ground; the sides caved in with anger, but Roberta planned still to return for Grandma Addie. She stopped once, in the flat, neutral land of Goodland, Kansas, and telephoned back.

"You sure you don't want to come with me? It's kind of pretty out this way, Grandma," she lied. She smelled truck exhaust from the phone booth and she watched the long, red-faced boys walking past, those young men who had eaten so much cattle they began to look like them.

"Just go and get settled. I'll be out to visit as soon as you get the first load of laundry hung on the line."

Roberta felt her grandma smile. She hung up the phone and headed back to the overloaded, dusty white car.

She headed for Denver, but wound up just west of there, in a mountain town called The Tropics. Its name was like a politician's vocabulary, a lie. In truth, The Tropics was arid. It was a mine town, uranium most recently. Dust devils whirled sand off the mountains. Even after the heaviest of rains, the water seeped back into the ground, between stones, and the earth was parched again. Still, *Tropics* conjured up visions of tall grasses in outlying savannas, dark rivers, mists, and deep green forests of ferns and trees and water-filled vines. Sometimes it seemed like they were there.

Roberta told herself it was God's acres, that it was fate she had missed the Denver turn-offs from the freeway, that here she could forgive and forget her losses and get on with living. She rented a cabin, got a part-time job working down at the Tropics Grocery where she sold single items to customers who didn't want to travel to town. She sold a bag of flour to one, a can of dog food to another, candy to schoolchildren in the afternoon. She sold boxed doughnuts and cigarettes to work crews in the mornings and 3.2 beer to the same crews after five. She dusted and stacked the buckling shelves, and she had time to whittle little birds, as her Uncle James had done. She whittled them and thought of them as toys for the spirits of her children and put them in the windows so the kids would be sure and see them. "This one's for Harriet," she'd tell no one in particular.

When she didn't work she spent her time in bed, completely still and staring straight at the ceiling. They used to say if a person is motionless, their soul will run away from the body, and Roberta counted on that. They say that once a soul decides to leave, it can't be recalled. Roberta lay in that room with its blue walls and blue-flowered blanket. She lay there with her hair pulled back from her round forehead. She held the sunbonnet quilt in her hands and didn't move.

To her disappointment, she remained alive. Every night she prayed to die and join her kids, but every morning she was still living, breathing. Some mornings she pulled at her flesh just to be certain, she was so amazed and despairing to be still alive.

Her soul refused to leave. It had a mind of its own. So Roberta got up and began a restless walking. There were nights in The Tropics that she haunted the dirt roads like a large-shouldered, thin-hipped ghost, like a tough girl with her shoulders held high to protect her broken heart. Roberta Diane James with her dark hair that had been worn thin from the hours she spent lying down trying to send her soul away. Roberta, with her eyes the color of dark river water after a storm when the gold stirs up in it. The left eye still held the trace of a wink in it, despite the thinness of skin stretched over her forehead, the smell of Ivory soap on her as she tried over and over to wash the grief from her flesh.

2

When I first heard how bad things were going for Roberta, I thought about going home, but I heard my other voices tell me it wasn't time. "There is a season for all things," Mom used to say, and I knew Mom would be telling Roberta just that, in her own words, and that Roberta would be fuming inside as I had done with Mom's fifty-cent sayings.

I knew this much: Roberta would need to hold on to her grief and her pain.

Us Chickasaws have lost so much we hold on to everything. Even our muscles hold on to their aches. We love our lovers long after they are gone, better than when they were present.

When we were girls, Roberta and I saved the tops of Coke bottlecaps and covered them with purple cloth like grapes. We made clusters of grapes sitting out there on the porch, or on tire swings in the heat, and we sewed the grapes together. We made do. We drank tea from pickle jars. We used potato water to starch our clothes. We even used our skinny dark legs as paper for tic-tac-toe. Now the girls turn bleach containers into hats, cutting them in fours and crocheting them together.

Our Aunt Bell is famous for holding on and making do. There's a nail in her kitchen for plastic six-pack rings, a box for old jars, a shelf or box for everything, including all the black and white shoes she's worn out as a grown woman. Don't think those boxes or nails mean she's neat, either. She's not. She has hundreds of dusty salt and pepper shakers people gave her, and stacks of old magazines and papers, years of yellowed history all contained in her crowded rooms, and I love her for it, for holding on that way. I have spent hours of my younger life looking at those shakers and reading those papers. Her own children tell her it is a miracle the viruses of science aren't growing to maturity in there.

We save ourselves from loss in whatever ways we can, collecting things, going out to Danceland, getting drunk, reading westerns or finding new loves, but the other side of all this salvation is that we deny the truth. When some man from town steals our land, we say, "Oh, he wouldn't do that. Jimmy Slade is a good old boy. I knew his folks. I used to work for the Slades during the Depression." Never mind that the Slades were not the hungry ones back then.

Some of us southern Indians used to have ranches and cattle. They were all lost piece by piece, or sold to pay for taxes on some land that was also lost. Now and then someone comes around and tells us we should develop our land like we once did. Or they tell us just to go out in the world. We nod and smile at them.

Now and then some of us young people make a tidal wave in the ocean of our history, an anxiety attack in the heart monitor of our race. We get angry and scream out. We get in the news. We strip ourselves bare in the colleges that recruited us as their minority quota and we run out into the snowstorm naked and we get talked about for years as the crazy Indian that did this or that, the one that drove to the gas station and went on straight to Canada, the girl who took out the garbage and never turned and went back. We made do.

I knew some people from up north. You could always tell they were from up north because my friend's daughter had a wall-eye with a hook tattooed on her forearm. Once we went to a pow-wow together and some of the women of the People wore jingle dresses, with what looked like bells. "What are those?" I asked my friend.

They were snuff can lids. Those women of the forests and woodlands, so much making do just like us, like when we use silver salt cans in our dances instead of turtle-shell rattles. We make music of those saltshakers, though now and then some outsider decides we have no culture because we use store-bought shakers and they are not traditional at all.

I defy them: Salt is the substance of our blood, sweat, our secretions, our semen. It is the ocean of ourselves.

Once I saw a railroad engineer's hat in a museum. It was fully beaded. I thought it was a new style like the beaded tennis shoes or the new beaded truckers' hats. But it was made in the late 1800s when the Lakota were forbidden to make traditional items. The mothers took to beading whatever was available, hats of the engineers of death. They covered colony cotton with their art.

We make art out of our loss.

That's why when I heard Roberta was in Colorado and was carving wooden birds, I figured it made sense. Besides, we come from a long line of whittlers and table carvers, people who work with wood, including the Mexican great-grandfather who made santos and a wooden mask that was banned by the priests. Its presence got him excommunicated.

Uncle James carves chains out of trees. We laugh and say it sounds like something *they* would do.

Roberta was carving wooden birds, crows, mourning doves, and even a scissortail or two. She sent some of the birds back home to have Aunt Bell put them on the graves of her little ones.

I think she was trying to carve the souls of her children into the birds. She was making do.

The New Apartment, Minneapolis

The floorboards creak.
The moon is on the wrong side of the building,

and burns remain
on the floor.

5   The house wants to fall down
the universe when earth turns.

It still holds the coughs of old men
and their canes tapping on the floor.

I think of Indian people here before me
10 and how last spring white merchants hung an elder
on a meat hook and beat him;
he was one of The People.

I remember this war
and all the wars

15 and relocation like putting the moon in prison
with no food and that moon was a crescent

but be warned, the moon grows full again
and the roofs of this town are all red

and we are looking through the walls of houses
20 at people suspended in air.

Some are baking, with flour on their hands,
or sleeping on floor three, or getting drunk.

I see the businessmen who hit their wives
and the men who are tender fathers.

25 There are women crying or making jokes.
Children are laughing under beds.

Girls in navy blue robes talk on the phone all night
and some Pawnee is singing 49s, drumming the table.

Inside the walls
30 world changes are planned, bosses overthrown.

If we had no coffee,
cigarettes or liquor,

says the woman in room 12,
they'd have a revolution on their hands.

35 Beyond walls are lakes and plains,
canyons and the universe;

the stars are the key
turning in the lock of night.

Turn the deadbolt and I am home.
40 I have walked to the dark earth,

opened a door to nights where there are no apartments,
just drumming and singing;

The Duck Song, The Snake Song,
The Drunk Song.

45　No one here remembers the city
or has ever lost the will to go on.

Hello aunt, hello brothers, hello trees
and deer walking quietly on the soft red earth.

BLESSING

Blessed
are the injured animals
for they live in his cages.
but who will heal my father,
5　tape his old legs for him?

Here's his bird with the two broken wings
and her feathers are white as an angel
and she says goddamn stirring grains
in the kitchen. When the birds fly out
10　he leaves the cages open
and she kisses his brow for such
good works.

Work he says
all your damned life
15　and at the end
you don't own even a piece of land.

Blessed are the rich
for they eat meat every night.
They have already inherited the earth.

20　For the rest of us, may we just live
long enough
and unwrinkle our brows,
may we keep our good looks
and some of our teeth
25　and our bowels regular.

Perhaps we can go live in places
a rich man can't inhabit,
in the sunfish and jackrabbits,
in the cinnamon colored soil,
30　the land of red grass
and red people
in the valley
of the shadow of Elk
who aren't there.

35   He says the old earth
        wobbles so hard, you'd best hang on
        to everything. Your neighbors
        steal what little you got.

        Blessed are the rich
40   for they don't have the same old
        Everyday to put up with
        like my father
        who's gotten old,
            Chickasaw
45   chikkih asachi, which means
        they left as a tribe not a very great while ago.
        They are always leaving, those people.

        Blessed
        are those who listen
50   when no one is left to speak.

Carolyn Chute (b. 1947)

She says her books are "involuntarily researched. I have lived poverty. I didn't CHOOSE it. No one would choose humiliation, pain, and rage." Born in Portland, Maine, Carolyn Chute married at sixteen, divorced, and supported her daughter with such low-wage jobs as harvesting potatoes, driving a school bus, plucking chickens, and working for the Holy Innocents Homemaker Service. She became a grandmother at age thirty-seven, about the same time that her first novel, *The Beans of Egypt, Maine* (1985), was published. With caustic wit and unflinching fidelity to her own rural Maine folk, Chute challenges readers to see the complex, diverse, unromantic humanity behind such bland categories as the "rural poor." Her subsequent novels, *Letourneau's Used Auto Parts* (1988), *Merry Men* (1993), and *Snow Man* (1999), narrate the complicated relationships, anger, resilience, and sardonic humor of people who have been left behind by so-called technological progress, yuppie tourism, and regional development. Her assessment of class oppression is fully voiced in her nonfiction and newspaper columns. The real divide, she says, isn't "Left vs. Right—It's Up vs. Down." Chute takes particular aim at the Supreme Court ruling giving corporations various citizenship rights, "Have you felt as though corporations have become people and you are just a concept?" She is a leader of the "Wicked Good Militia," speaking at local meetings out of a Tom Paine populist tradition, yet her originality, political acumen, and intellectuality defy simple categorization. "Faces in the Hands" first appeared in *"I Was Content and Not Content": The Story of Linda Lord and the Closing of Penobscot Poultry* by Cedric N. Chatterley, Alicia J. Rouverol, and Stephen A. Cole (2000). On the surface, an encounter at a party between a young engineer-aspiring-manager and Chute, it evolves into a perspicacious analysis of class/corporate relationships in contemporary America. Chute lives in North Parsonfield, Maine, with her husband Michael.

FACES IN THE HANDS

There was this party I was at recently. I was on one end of a couch . . . a teal-colored couch, I think it was. I was picking from a platter of cheeses and pickles and olives and little cupcakes. A young man in a pastel shirt and pastel pants sat beside me, and we began to chat. After only a few moments of chatting, he let it be known that he was an engineer with a company. I let my eyes give him a little quick once-over, and it was plain he didn't mean the smiling waving train engine kind. He tells me about some people employed by his company, that they have the gall to be asking for higher pay and some more benefits. They weren't like him, he assured me. They were machine operators. "Just a pair of hands," said he with a simper.

Hands body-less against space?

My eyes now did a little quickie once-over of my own hands, hands that had worked the factories. *Had* these hands been body-less, soulless against the background of the great American business? My right hand fetched a cute green-tinted cupcake and stuffed it into my mouth. What could I say to this professional who to the wide world glowed so pastel and perfect pink in his successfulness? I squinted at my hands again, dumbfounded.

My brother, a weight lifter, was Mr. Maine a while ago. During that year, a new magazine for business people hit the mails. One of its first issues featured an article on what they called "the Maine work ethic." Is the Maine work ethic really dead? Experts discussed whether or not Maine people enjoyed backbreaking, boring work as much as they used to. Even with all the "experts," the general feeling of the article was puzzlement—though an uplifting and sunshiny resolution was tacked on in the final paragraph. The magazine's glossy cover showed my brother's arm body-less against a black background. "Gosh," I marveled, reaching for a couple of olives. Is that arm truly the way the pastel–dress jacket–necktie people see the worker who makes their business possible? Is this why it's okay for so many to pay their workers wages that won't cover a month's rent? Would they pay less if they could? If it weren't for unions and the minimum wage (obscenely small as that is), would businesses pay anything at all? Is it easier to exploit people who are faceless? "Yep," I said aloud around my mouthful of olives. The engineer glanced with a startled expression at my mouth. I reached for a pickle.

Just a pair of hands. Yep. How about just a stomach? That's what I was once . . . just a stomach, body-less against space, working on the bridge of a potato harvester . . . lurching about on a windy field, a sort of gray and stormy sea . . . my stomach body-less against space on the verge of throwing up . . . hour after hour . . . day after day. And where the harvester got stuck in the mud, the potatoes were not potatoes coming your way, but a gluey, putrid, white stench. I quit. The Maine work ethic wasn't on my mind that day. Having no mind . . . just a stomach. You know, it's like that with any pain or punishment . . . impossible to get your elevated thoughts together with such distractions.

Then it was the chicken factory. Each morning it was like a knife to my heart to leave my cooking, sewing, sweeping, wash-hanging . . . my beloved home and my little daughter. At the factory the grease of the yellowy cooked meat streaked my face and gave my hair an unnatural thickness. Scaled over with grease and the roaring thrumming heat, the meat and I were one.

And so the days passed . . . identical. As the soggy golden matter chugged by on the conveyor belt and my hands flew, I would daydream of the coming weekend, which seemed a hundred years away. Or of early mornings standing at the bathroom sink brushing my daughter Joannah's hair into two ponytails, knotting green yarn bows on them to match her green dress . . . or red to match her sailor dress . . . or blue to go with jeans. Against my fingers was *not* the chicken meat but her yellow hair, an aureate braille. Hands, when they are placed on a child, are not hands in space but hands connected to your past, to your future, to eternity. It's a powerful incentive to have more babies. The less rewarding your job is, the more important children become. Children are your individual creations, singular and intricate. A child is the ultimate masterpiece.

Back at the party, the engineer on the teal-colored couch beside me is telling me more about his career. He's using one hand to gesture, and I take note that the palm and five fingers are pink and silky as lips.

Meanwhile, back at the chicken factory, I was pondering what I was going to do on payday. Times had changed, prices had swelled, but the paycheck stayed eensy. And there were more and more things our legislators, town hall authorities, school authorities, insurance companies, and neighbors said we had to have. It's the law that you and your kids and your yard and your vehicle LOOK nice, laws of one kind or another. Dress codes, building codes, mandatory liability insurance, mandatory this, mandatory that . . . lawmakers always being so quick to legislate you a new expense, so slow to raise the minimum wage . . . and neighbors with their eye on you . . . garage mechanic looking under your car . . . everybody pointing at you . . . rusty this and rusty that . . . two weeks' pay for an exhaust system, two weeks' pay for your overdue liability insurance . . . cops squinting at your car, code man squinting at your house, teachers squinting at your kids, neighbors squinting, peering, gloating, "Got a backed up septic system, huh? Better get it fixed quick!" It was hard enough being able to afford not to be an outlaw, let alone afford luxuries like house payments, health insurance, gasoline, dish detergent, propane to heat the water and cook with, doctor bills and dentist bills that insurance wouldn't cover even if you *had* insurance, lightbulbs, shoes for my girl, food, toilet paper. Maybe I could sneak a roll of toilet paper from the chicken factory ladies' room. But they got ahead of me on that. They know how to deal with outlaws and thieves. They had the tissue dispenser locked.

Now and then the bosses would stroll through the plant to check up on things. When they did this, I know they saw my face as no different from the vacant dead stare of the electrically stunned, upside-down chickens with their throats cut, dangling along toward their predestined forms: chicken spread, chicken dog food, chicken hotdogs. But behind my dead eyes my brain saw the way my kitchen looked at home, yellow cat curled in the sun on a chair, and the born and unborn children of all time flashing by, the voice that is the family trait, the nose of my father's side, the smile of my mother's side, the precise and yet ethereal possible cries of "Mumma!" and "Mumma!" and "Mumma!" while on and on my hands tore the hot chicken muscle from bones and bosses passed to the next operation, satisfied.

The Maine work ethic. What the hell is that anyway, as opposed to the Rhode Island work ethic? Consider this quote from John Poor of Andover, Massachusetts, a railroad visionary: "The capacity of the human frame for labor is found to be greater in Maine than Massachusetts or any other state, south or west of it."

Having some North Carolina blood coming in on my father's side must have been why I was getting weary of the chicken factory life. I just couldn't seem to feel that great noble surge, that "Hi-ho! Hi-ho! It's off to work we go!" frame of mind as I chugged along in my outlaw car from my outlaw home, running out of gasoline along the way, scouting for unattended-looking gas stations that might not have their toilet paper dispensers locked.

What by gorry is *any* kind of work ethic? Is it work for the sake of work? In the dictionary, the word *ethic* is described as "moral duty." Duty to whom? Wasn't it Thomas Jefferson who said an industrialized nation cannot be a true democracy?

What was it like here before industrialism? Before technology-ism, computerism, shopping-mall-ism, business-meeting-and-banquet-at-a-nice-hotel-ism?

When we were an agricultural people, the farm, the home, the family was the product. This was your masterpiece. You watched it grow or fail. A new season might bring renewed hope if you failed last year. Life was full of surprises. Suspense. Broken tools. Broken bones. Bad weather. Insects. Work. Work. Work. Passion. Ideas. Big ideas. Good ideas. Bad ideas. Traditions. Surprises, more surprises. Pride. The whole family . . . mother and father, teens and babies, an uncle and maybe a couple of burly aunts, everybody together battling away at the godly and ungodly forces that trickled out food, water, heat. Family with one goal in common . . . the finish line, the home plate . . . the harvest, the woodpile, the *home.*

Of course, not everybody liked farming. But in those days if you got caught out behind the barn with a book, you might get the strap. Reading a book was goofing off. Funny how fashion goes, isn't it? Who is it that decides these things?

Family units. Life in common. Work in common. Misery in common.

Families are not necessary to industry. But work for the sake of work is necessary to industry.

If we, Maine, we, America, are going to have a *true* free enterprise system in the future, we're going to have to think seriously of why the work ethic is dying and if there ever was one.

And "family." Are we going to see the extinction of *that* "system"?

Will we someday be little more than individual ants with one great corporate queen-ant biz dictating from the top?

Another cupcake . . . chocolate with white nonpareils. And the voice from the other side of the couch chatting away about his latest project. But what is there for me to reply to this person who will not really ever know me, he a person who cannot understand anything but the academic A plus? My thoughts must remain my own this evening.

So whose babies *are* the mills? *Somebody* must love them. The owners, of course. The owners love their mills, dream of them all night. They feel a thrill over mills. Passion. Joy. Consternation. Challenge. Surprises. Incentive. Pride. They have a *great* sense of the work ethic. They bounce out of bed each morning to work on that baby, to make it grow and to keenly dwell on that margin of profit and to ask, "What's the matter with the workers? How come they don't work harder? And harder and harder? What's all this complaining about wanting more pay? How come they don't love my mill, my masterpiece, my baby?"

I quit that chicken-picking job, too. I do not have enough Maine work ethic. I am not a good person. I am not a good American. I went on welfare, which is even worse. Welfare people are lazy no-counts living off the dole, they say.

Years later, on the teal-colored couch, checking out more pickles, sweet and dill, one of each, I am wondering, What about businesses that quit the people? Especially the ones that move somewhere else to find cheaper and cheaper, more desperate help. Leaving the state. Leaving the country. Where's *their* moral, duty? *Their* patriotism?

And what about these big businesses that get the dole?

Why does the obligation, the duty, always wind up in the lap of the individual, the worker, and never, NEVER the big guys? And how come comfy Joe and Jane America, the ones who are themselves workers but somewhat better paid workers, are always so quick to blame higher prices, higher taxes, job shortages, and what-all on the lower paid worker or the out-of-work worker and sometimes the better paid union worker . . . but never do they blame the boss, the owner, Mr. Biz?

"Joe and Jane are worried," I mutter around a dill pickle. "Yep, that's it. They are worried sick by the terrible power of the great punishing Dad . . . Dad who is America, God, and Wealth . . . especially Wealth, for if you don't pray to it enough and honor and obey it, it won't trickle down. If you question its holiness, things might get seriously worse for you."

"Excuse me?" wonders the man in pastel on the couch beside me, looking with narrowed, bewildered eyes at my mouth. Was I thinking aloud again? I reach for a little embossed napkin and wipe the pickle juice from my fingers.

Our neighbor Glen stops by for tea sometimes. Stepping out of his truck, he always has that same embarrassed look most Mainers have these days having to drive around with VACATIONLAND and red lobsters on both front and back bumpers. Glen is a carpenter and does some work in the woods, logs and pulp, firewood. He is building his own house, a farm, he tells us . . . the slow old-fashioned few-boards-at-a-time way, the no-bank-loan way, the you-don't-get-it-all-at-once way. He is independent, thoughtful. With a tea mug in one hand, he gives his mustache a few deep-thought pulls with the other. He says he's been thinking about why workers in some places, like those plants in the Midwest that make cars, are never happy with their paychecks and benefits, even when they have pretty good paychecks, at least by the standards we Maine workers know. He says he thinks the reason is because no matter how much they make, they have this unexpressed knowing that they are possessed, owned. Body and soul. They know what they'll be doing tomorrow. They know what they'll be doing next week. Next year. They can see their lives stretching out before them unvaried, flat, and uniform. They have already lived their future. They are the living dead. Carcasses, if not slaves. What price would you put on your life? The price is never good enough.

And yet what does the business owner vow to you? That plant can shut you out tomorrow, leave you fifty-five years old and jobless.

Something moves. Gives me a start. It's the young engineer on the couch beside me, reaching for a pink cupcake. He turns it in his long fingers and asks, "What do *you* do?"

"Blipe," I say around a big bite of very sunshiny yellow cupcake. And another olive. I chew thoughtfully, nodding, smiling, stalling. I'm wondering if the engineer has children. But of course. It's his privilege. It's the low-pay people who aren't supposed to have kids. You hear it time and time again: "And there they were in that dumpy place with all those kids. Argh!" or "After a person *that* poor has more kids than she can afford, you start taking the kids away."

How come nobody threatens to take away the kids of the employer who pays his people too little? Why don't *those* types stop having kids? Look at what their kind has made this world into? Look at their high-pay, high-profit waste. They are smashing the world.

I am remembering Reuben. Am I enraged by his death? Or content? I want to tell you about Reuben, but first I have to tell you about his people, my people.

One of the things I admire most about my husband, Michael, is his hands. I remem- ber when I met him in a darkish lakeside barroom, even while falling in love with his voice and eyes, his beard, his lanky, sinewy height, my eyes scrutinized those hands. I remember thinking, yes, those are the hands, the hands of my people.

My people. Memories filled with hands. My grandfather died when I was eighteen. I was terrified of the "viewing room," where you stand around the open casket. I stayed out in the anteroom with my cousin Jane. Jane's father was my grandfather's brother, Jim. Jim had died young. Jim dug bait worms for a living in Belfast. When we went to Belfast to visit, I remember my aunt's hands breaking open clams in the slate sink. Jim took us kids to the shed. I'll never forget him unbolting the shed door and there, living in wet hay, was the prize, the longest stinging bait worm he'd ever dug. It looked like a red snake with legs. I was impressed.

Jim was dying even then. Later he spent most of his time in a chair in the kitchen. His black, black hair was long because he was too sick to have it cut, our aunt told us apologetically on one of our last visits before he died. But I thought that hair was the most beautiful thing, back in those days when you never saw anybody's true hair, back in those days of buzzers and crew cuts. I remember holding my eyes on him, dazzled. He was part Indian, death in his eyes, his hands in his lap.

After my grandfather's funeral, on the ride home, my mother said, "You were right, Carolyn, not to want to see him. It didn't look like him at all." She sighed. "Except his hands . . . his beautiful hands." I could see clearly the short fingers, one with a "claw," and his wedding ring . . . how he always bragged he had never taken that ring off since it was put there. Not ever. By the time he died, the ring was as thin as a yellow hair.

My husband, Michael, wears green workshirts and green workpants. His eyes are brown, hair black, a little long. My mother says he looks like our uncle Jim. Michael is respectful of and dazzled by all life. He has magic in his hands. I've seen him carry a spider to safety. Another time a mouse. I have a photograph of Michael with a butterfly calmly settled on one of his thumbs. He has a volunteer job these days. He takes meals around to old folks. Some days he goes back and spends afternoons with them. He feeds their pets for them. The old guys and Michael shoot the breeze. They cover woods, weather, guns, and other country stuff. Michael can only write his first and last name, not his middle name. He can't read my name at all. His pay job these days is mowing graves. Makes $1,000 a year thereabouts.

Back in school Michael was called dumb by a lot of his teachers. Some called him a troublemaker. One of them put him out in the hall every day in third grade. Later he went to a fate worse than the hallway. SPECIAL ED, OR "RETARD ED," as some of the kids called it. Just because of dyslexia, because words scrambled on the page before his eyes, he was scolded, jeered, punished, stigmatized.

Back then, even then, Michael loved old people, had a way with them . . . aunt, uncle, grandmother, gramp were what life was about to Michael. But public school doesn't give you a grade in OLD PEOPLE. That's not ACADEMIC enough. It's not a thing you can do at your desk. And now in adulthood, Michael finds his greatest gift is still not valued. Helping old people is not a product. It's not a thing rich people can buy shares in. So his talents will never earn him a paycheck. In the eyes of America, Michael is still a failure.

We had mixed feelings back when we discovered I was pregnant with Reuben. The world was not exactly waiting for Reuben with open arms. But I studied the prenatal pamphlets showing fetuses at all stages of growth, trying to imagine Reuben's face, cell by cell, our masterpiece.

If I slammed the door of our old truck or dropped a kettle lid, Reuben would startle inside me, jerking back his hands and feet. Other times he would yearn up toward his father's spread hand.

It was in the days when President Ronald Reagan was riding his horse and talking softly into the microphone and many people were mesmerized. "He will cut those lazy types off without a dime!" good-pay Americans cheered. "And then those lazy bums will have to get themselves REAL jobs."

I overheard a neighbor snorting, "The president will clean up the garbage" and rolled his eyes toward my pregnant belly.

People who heard I was on welfare, people who had good-pay jobs, said, "Why doesn't Mike get a better job? Why doesn't he get two jobs? Three jobs? When I was young, I worked twelve hours a day, six days a week for fifteen dollars a week, and *I* didn't complain, *I* didn't ask for welfare." Sometimes they said, "Why doesn't Mike get his high school diploma? You can't amount to anything without that."

Once, when someone said this, Michael's hands tightened in rage. He went to the bureau drawer, found his high school diploma, gave it a toss into the wood-stove, and said gravely, "I've wanted to do that for a long time."

The unborn baby grew big. On both sides of the family, nice big babies were the usual.

Meanwhile, Michael was at the dairy farm or the orchard, pruning apple trees, harvesting potatoes, or splitting other people's firewood . . . moving from job to job . . . salvage yard, gardening, cold storage work, jobs that didn't require him to read and write . . . jobs that didn't depend on self-esteem. Jobs that paid minimum wage or less.

Meanwhile, President Reagan was riding his horse and tipping his hat, and the good-pay Americans were cheering as he cut money to the states and as the state of Maine took away my medical card, which was giving me and my baby medical care that Michael's check wouldn't cover.

Meanwhile, industries were leaving Maine, the great conveyor belts silenced, the truck bays and loading docks empty . . . chicken . . . shoes . . . textiles. Gone. Everybody scrambling to grab up what was left of the jobs.

The governor said not to worry. New jobs were on the way. Tourism was coming. You'll have lots of jobs soon. We tried to grin and bear the VACATIONLAND red lobster license plates. Some tried to grin and bear the new tourist-related jobs that were always part-time jobs and that offered low pay and no benefits. People even grinned through seeing the tourists who decided to STAY and live in Maine where *life is as it ought to be* . . . tourists whose willingness to pay *any* price skyrocketed the price of a home . . . a price low-pay working people could not afford and better-pay working people *thought* they *could* afford, going into debt neck-deep.

Everybody was grinning.

They told Michael, "Go get a job at McDonalds."

"Raise your aspirations," said others. Educators especially. They love that word. ASPIRATIONS. All over the state you can hear that long word rolling off their tongues. It's something the low-income people don't have enough of, they say.

Aspirations???

Where are the little farms? A person with learning disabilities who wasn't born to be a pastel-shirt person could get by with his own little farm . . . could be *inter*dependent . . . could practice Yankee ingenuity and good Yankee sense. The farm . . . the farm . . . just a fading whisper . . . gone.

And now the mills. Going.

The governor says what we need is more tourist-related jobs. We should bring in more tourists. But then sometimes the governor says tourist-related jobs are bad. What's the matter with you people? Can't you raise your aspirations? The governor tells the schools to give the kids more homework and longer school days to help them raise their aspirations and get them out of those dead-end tourist jobs.

Somebody tells Michael, "Raise your aspirations! Computers are the thing."

Everything's getting fast, faster. Keep up or keep out. "That's life," the politicians say. "If you can't keep up, you fall by the wayside. Fact of life."

Meanwhile, with no welfare medical card, I lost my private doctor. The prenatal clinic I went to was crammed with those fallen by the wayside of the president's and the governor's cuts. The hospital was crammed . . . so crammed that I was in labor with a breech birth baby for two weeks and a temperature of 104 degrees before the hospital would let me in.

His name was Reuben. Thick auburn hair. Narrow-shouldered. Dehydrated. Starved. He is buried here in these hills among his ancestors going back 150 years, the farmers of small farms and their great independence and pride. When I visit his grave, I am content. I tell him I'm glad he's dead. Safe. Spared. I say, "Dear, dear Reuben . . . dear gentle person. What if you were born?"

Well, there he goes again. The governor is on the radio talking higher aspirations for us all . . . more homework, more school hours, more, more, more! That'll cure the problem, he assures us. Doesn't he realize that the higher the white-shirt pastel-people raise their aspirations for us who are already failing *their* idea of success, the more we lose sight of our own true aspirations and the deeper into complete failure they leave us?

Reuben, dear gentle person, maybe you inherited the learning disabilities of your father and me. Maybe your talents would have been unmarketable. Maybe you would have had to take time and care with everything you would do. Schools and jobs have no patience. Maybe by the time you were a man, you couldn't feel like a man. You'd break one of their laws. And soon there are going to be A LOT MORE LAWS . . . school classrooms packed like cattle pens, prisons full of people standing shoulder-to-shoulder, more capital punishment, capital punishment for lesser crimes to make room, more drugs, lots more drugs, more disease, less help from doctors, people getting mad, people in mobs . . . everybody falling by the wayside . . . no place for the gentle, old-fashioned people . . . room only for the high-aspirations people. "Better people!" Better, smarter, cleaner, spotless, odorless, hair that doesn't seem like hair, skin that doesn't smell like skin, hands and fingernails that are silky as lips, humanity with no trace of mammalhood but uniformly glib with accent-free voices. Such creatures! Polymerized, preserved, freed of flaw, soaring up, up, up, and away . . . the ultimate win.

Something shifts on the couch beside me. I see the pastel-shirt pastel-pants fellow is still admiring his pink cupcake, but he doesn't eat it. He is telling me about something "incredible" he has just read in the *New York Times* this week.

Meanwhile, at the Blaine House (fancy mansion the governor lives in), the governor is probably helping himself to a snack before the maids bring supper. With his right hand he reaches for a cracker, applies soft cheese with a knife, leans back into his chair, and nibbles. His hands brush crumbs from his pastel dress pants. Governors everywhere reaching. And the president. Not the one on the horse; now it's the one with the big gas-guzzling boat. He is perhaps in his office this evening, leaning back in his big groaning chair with wheels, reaching, munching. President munching. Governors munching. Hands brushing crumbs to the rug.

You hear it these days . . . a lot of talk about choices . . . good choices, bad choices. You are shepherds of your own destiny, they say. There are how-to books on making the right choices. There are high-price counselors you can go sit with to help you pick the right life.

Doesn't luck play into this game somewhere? Like having the great big good luck of having what you are naturally good at be marketable, highly paid, highly respected.

But the idea of luck might take away the moral aspect of things, the idea that good people make the right choices, bad people make bad choices, and people get what they deserve.

Work hard, you win. Goof off, you lose. This is the belief.

The words of yesteryear's Maine were WORKING TOGETHER. The word today is COMPETITION. Like sports. Like school spirit. Whose baby is reading first? Whose school has the better team of better babies? Whose SAT scores are higher? Whose school puts out more professional types, fewer flunk-outs? Whose country does? Are we beating the Russians with more smart, more knowledgeable, more high-drive graduates? Beating the Japanese? Whose country has, if not more work ethic, bigger tanks, bombs, rockets, nuke subs, cruise missiles, and various other winged monstrosities . . . in case the smarter, better, faster babies of other countries get too smart or just too big and pushy, too crowded, too used up in resources, or too greedy, too "crazy"?

Our leaders and experts are always saying about the low-pay people, "They've got to break the cycle." As if the low-pay people are the ones totally in control of the situation here. What about the leaders' and experts' cycles of greed and waste? And ignorance? Especially ignorance. Gosh, how *little* they know!

"Low-income people have got to escape," they say. Escape what? Do they mean *leave home*? Leave town? Like they did? Do they mean escape that life we have here in Maine with our family ties and hometown ties and go to . . . to . . . to Harvard or Yale, like they did? Live in a faraway city? Be a yuppie? Is that the only acceptable choice? Why was it so easy for *them* to leave *their* homes, these leaders, these experts, these professionals? Were their homes dysfunctional in a way social workers aren't trained to recognize?

And besides, I thought Maine was *where life is as it should be.*

Maybe by "escape" they mean something along the lines of . . . get out of the way. Like a long time ago when they gave the Maine natives reservations to live on. What do they have in mind for us this time? Cement block public housing?

Back then, were they telling the Maine folks (the Passamaquoddies and Penobscots), "You have choices. You are the shepherds of your own destinies. The reservation or Harvard—take your pick."

Down at the pub for pizzas, Michael and I see some of the box shop guys who have been laid off . . . some woolen mill folks . . . and those who work in the woods . . . talking weather, sports, war, and the god-awful price of a can of Spam. The light from the table lamps on these men's hands is yellow and fuzzy and forgiving. Their hands, like their faces, are expressing glee or rage. One of them has a short finger. One of them has a couple of short fingers and a fingernail like a claw. I look across the table at my husband's hands and at his dark green workshirt buttoned in a formal way at his throat. His hands on the table are empty. But to me and to many, he is the axis of the earth.

Meanwhile, the governors unfold their cloth napkins and pick up pretty forks. The open newspaper tells of some of the doings of the low-pay people OUT THERE . . . the trials and tribulations they cause, their peculiarities, their discontent . . . distant . . . distant beings . . . as distant as if on a small blue planet in the black firmament. "What the hell is going on with these low-income types?" the president wonders. "What are we going to do about the mess they cause?" And the governors scratch their heads. In their respective mansions, they reach for the crusty bread.

I turn. The engineer is waiting for me to say something. Here's my chance. Should I explain, "Dear young fellow, in the hands of the working people, I've seen life, death, patience, enduring patience, surrender, miracles, and mistakes. Working people are as human as you are. They need to eat and sleep and stay warm and have a doctor when they need one, just like you do." Or should I say, "If the queen bee were alone, she'd die. All of us humans working together ate a perfect thing, a human network of needs and gifts. Boss and worker, each is a gift to the other."

No, the truth is that there are too many people today . . . indeed . . . too many. In each other's way. Grabbing. Clawing. Overlapping. War and disease are ready to do nature's task . . . to cut us down. And as in employment, so in war and disease, the working people and out-of-work people, not the A-plus people, will bear most of the blows. Survival of the fittest is still the great law of the land. *The Capitalist creed.*

The truth is, I'm not looking at the young engineer's face. "You seen one yuppie, you seen 'em all," some say. I want to close my eyes to the fear and hate that rises in me. There is nothing he and I have to say to each other. Diplomatic talks only take place between two powers. Not one power and one powerless. And maybe he's not all that powerful anyway, just one small-time yuppie . . . just a guy trying to get through another party, another day.

I narrow my eyes on his right hand. It's not the future I see in this man's hands. It's just a pink cupcake.

Yusef Komunyakaa (b. 1947)

Born and raised in Bogalusa, Lousiana, the eldest of five children, Komunyakaa learned about hard work from his carpenter father. As the poems that follow make clear, he also learned about the psychic and physical costs of working as a black man in white-dominated world. His rural roots and family ties, the blues and jazz music of nearby New Orleans, and the violence and racism he witnessed during military service as a young man are strong influences on his poetry. On graduation from high school, Komunyakaa enlisted in the U.S. Army and served in Vietnam, where in 1969–1970 he was a correspondent and managing editor of the military newspaper *The Southern Cross*, work for which he was awarded the Bronze Star. He began writing poetry soon after he left the army in the early 1970s, while earning BA and MFA degrees in Colorado and California, but it was not until a decade after Vietnam that he started to compose the searing poems that address that experience, collected in *Dien Cai Dau* (1988).

Komunyakaa's poetry books include *Lost in the Bonewheel Factory* (1979); *Copacetic* (1984); *I Apologize for the Eyes in My Head* (1986); *Magic City* (1992); and *Neon Vernacular: New and Selected Poems*, a 1994 Pulitzer prize winner. His prose is collected in *Blues Notes: Essays, Interviews, and Commentaries* (2000). In a 1990 interview, Komunyakaa describes "a sameness about American poetry that I don't think represents the whole people. . . . I believe poetry has always been political, long before poets had to deal with the page and white space." In his poems, however, political force and emotional impact are built through image, suggestion and language play: "Poetry is a kind of distilled insinuation. It's a way of expanding and talking around an idea or a question. Sometimes more actually gets said through such a technique than a full frontal assault."

WORK

I won't look at her.
My body's been one
Solid motion from sunrise,
Leaning into the lawnmower's
5   Roar through pine needles
& crabgrass. Tiger-colored
Bumblebees nudge pale blossoms
Till they sway like silent bells
Calling. But I won't look.
10   Her husband's outside Oxford,
Mississippi, bidding on miles
Of timber. I wonder if he's buying
Faulkner's ghost, if he might run
Into Colonel Sartoris
15   Along some dusty road.
Their teenage daughter & son sped off
An hour ago in a red Corvette
For the tennis courts,
& the cook, Roberta,
20   Only works a half day
Saturdays. This antebellum house
Looms behind oak & pine
Like a secret, as quail
Flash through branches.
25   I won't look at her. Nude
On a hammock among elephant ears
& ferns, a pitcher of lemonade
Sweating like our skin.
Afternoon burns on the pool
30   Till everything's blue,
Till I hear Johnny Mathis
Beside her like a whisper.
I work all the quick hooks
Of light, the same unbroken
35   Rhythm my father taught me
Years ago: *Always give
A man a good day's labor.*
I won't look. The engine
Pulls me like a dare.
40   Scent of honeysuckle
Sings black sap through mystery,
Taboo, law, creed, what kills
A fire that is its own heart
Burning open the mouth.
45   But I won't look
At the insinuation of buds
Tipped with cinnabar.
I'm here, as if I never left,
Stopped in this garden,

50   Drawn to some Lotus-eater. Pollen
     Explodes, but I only smell
     Gasoline & oil on my hands,
     & can't say why there's this bed
     Of crushed narcissus
55   As if gods wrestled here.

THE WHISTLE

1

     The seven o'clock whistle
     Made the morning air fulvous
     With a metallic syncopation,
     A key to a door in the sky—opening
5   & closing flesh. The melody
     Men & women built lives around,
     Sonorous as the queen bee's fat
     Hum drawing workers from flowers,
     Back to the colonized heart.
10   A titanous puff of steam rose
     From the dragon trapped below
     Iron, bricks, & wood.
     The whole black machine
     Shuddered: blue jays & redbirds
15   Wove light through leaves
     & something dead under the foundation
     Brought worms to life.
     Men capped their thermoses,
     Switched off Loretta Lynn,
20   & slid from trucks & cars.
     The rip saws throttled
     & swung out over logs
     On conveyer belts.
     Daddy lifted the tongs
25   To his right shoulder . . . a winch
     Uncoiled the steel cable
     From its oily scrotum;
     He waved to the winchman
     & iron teeth bit into the pine.
30   Yellow forklifts darted
     With lumber to boxcars
     Marked for distant cities.
     At noon, Daddy would walk
     Across the field of goldenrod
35   & mustard weeds, the pollen
     Bright & sullen on his overalls.
     He'd eat on our screened-in
     Back porch—red beans & rice

With hamhocks & cornbread.
40   Lemonade & peach Jello.

The one o'clock bleat
Burned sweat & salt into afternoon
& the wheels within wheels
Unlocked again, pulling rough boards
45   Into the plane's pneumatic grip.
Wild geese moved like a wedge
Between sky & sagebrush,
As Daddy pulled the cable
To the edge of the millpond
50   & sleepwalked cypress logs.
The day turned on its axle
& pyramids of russet sawdust
Formed under corrugated
Blowpipes fifty feet high.
55   The five o'clock whistle
Bellowed like a bull, controlling
Clocks on kitchen walls;
Women dabbed loud perfume
Behind their ears & set tables
60   Covered with flowered oilcloth.

2

When my father was kicked by the foreman,
He booted him back,
& his dreams slouched into an aftershock
Of dark women whispering
5   To each other. Like petals of a black rose
In one of Busby Berkeley's
Oscillating dances in a broken room. Shadows,
Runagates & Marys.
The steel-gray evening was a canvas
10   Zigzagged with questions
Curling up from smokestacks, as dusky birds
Brushed blues into a montage
Traced back to L'Amistad & the psychosis
Behind Birth of a Nation.
15   With eyes against glass & ears to diaphanous doors,
I heard a cornered prayer.
Car lights rubbed against our windows,
Ravenous as snow wolves.
A brick fell into the livingroom like a black body,
20   & a riot of drunk curses
Left the gladioli & zinnias
Maimed. Double dares
Took root in night soil.
The whistle boiled
25   Gutbucket underneath silence
& burned with wrath.

But by then Daddy was with Uncle James
Outside The Crossroad,
Their calloused fingers caressing the .38
30   On the seat of the pickup;
Maybe it was the pine-scented moonglow
That made him look so young
& faceless, wearing his mother's powder blue
Sunday dress & veiled hat.

Michael Casey (b. 1947)

Born in Lowell, Massachusetts, Michael Casey is a graduate of the Lowell Public Schools and the Lowell Technological Institute, where he earned a B.S. degree in physics. After college, he was drafted into the U.S. Army in 1968 and trained at Fort Gordon, Georgia. During the Vietnam War, he served as a military policeman both at a base in Missouri and in Quang Ngai and Quang Tin Provinces. His first book of poems, *Obscenities*, based on his Vietnam experience, was published in the Yale Younger Poet Series, judged by Stanley Kunitz in 1972, and reissued by Carnegie Mellon University Press in 2002. His second book, *Millrat* (1996), from which the poems presented here are excerpted, is set in the dye house of a textile mill in Lawrence, Massachusetts, where Casey worked as a kettleman while completing an M.A. degree. In these poems, Casey brings his remarkable ear for speech and keen sense of the absurd to a series of official company notices posted in the plant. Casey's two most recent poetry chapbooks are *The Million Dollar Hole* (2001), about Fort Leonard Wood, Missouri, and *Raiding a Whorehouse* (2004), about the military police in Vietnam.

THE COMPANY POOL

ya want ta be in our pool?
I was gonna axk ya sooner
but I didn't know
if ya wanted ta
5   I'll show ya how it works
ya pay a dollar an a quarter
ya givit ta me
but you'll haf ta start next week
the dollar goes inta the home run pool
10   and ya don't haf ta pay the quarter
unless if ya want ta
we use The Record
and we check out the runs column
on the sports page
15   not that this paper's always right
in fact it usually aint right

but this is the paper we use anyway
ya gotta use something ta go by
the team with the most runs
20   at the end a the week
the guy with that team wins the pool
the quarter is for the thirteen run pool
if ya team gets exactly thirteen runs
ya win that
25   that don't happen too often
Alfred over there
made thirty bucks last week winning that
so if ya want ta
ya can be in that one too
30   ya see we pick the team from this can
every week
so one guy don't get stuck
with the same shitty team
the tricky thing is
35   that the week for the pool
starts on Thursday and for the paper
it starts on Monday
so we just carry it over
y'understand this?

Positivity Poster

picture a grandmotherly lady on a rocker

what's outdated about the textile business
we are
not the new machinery we have
5   or up to the minute end products
but just our old fashioned ideas
avoiding waste
pride of craftsmen
work as a team
10   the worth of experience
all these
add to the unequaled quality
at wholesale value
that make our patrons love us
15   the new old fashion
textile business

everyone in the mill
the dye house anyway
reading this stuff would think
20   of only one word bullshit
you can guess
what wall these posters were on

and without any effort at all
you memorize them
25   and with some creativity and even art
you write crude phrases
and drawings on them
it was a lot like team effort
group improvement of a product

POSITIVITY POSTER #75

perplexed??
be sure then to see your supervisor
PDQ   pretty darn quick

   picture of
5   a man in a pickle
      in a rowboat with paddles
      floating away
      in a bowl of soup
      in a jar of jam
10   in circles walking
      in a dog house

   whether your trouble
   is on the job or off
don't face it alone
15   have someone with you
on your side
your supervisor certainly
in every possible way
will help you
20   at the end of this I add
     OUT THE FUCKIN DOOR
I didn't disguise
my handwriting or anything
I knew Walter would blame Roland for it
25   as it turned
Walter liked the remark
and gave Roland all the credit

URGENT NEED FOR BLOOD

There is an urgent need in Massachusetts
for blood donors. This seems to be an
excellent opportunity for the company
family to do something for the neighbors
5   in our community. It's easy, painless, and
really worthwhile.

Here's How:
    When: August 7th
    Time: 12:00 to 2 PM Monday
10   Where: American Red Cross
    391 Lacoshua St., Lowell, Mass.
    Blood types needed: ALL

The only prerequisite is that you must
not have given blood within the last six
15 weeks. Personnel wanting to donate blood
may donate blood without loss of pay or
attendance bonus provided you report
back to work within ten minutes of
consuming the five free cookies.
20   Transportation is free. Contact the
personnel office now. Don't wait until the
last minute! Due to an unfortunate
accident after the last blood drive, personnel
from the dye house are excluded
25 from this offer.

POSITIVITY POSTER #76

picture of angry rhinoceros facing
hunter: the hunter is reaching for his rifle
but the gun bearer who looks like Oliver
Hardy with rifle is running away from the
5 hunter and toward a giant time clock

WHEN YOU LEAVE EARLY
SOMEONE ELSE
SUFFERS FOR IT
SOMEONE ELSE
10 HAS TO WORK HARDER
LET US BE FAIR
FROM NOW ON

the end of every day now
Roland runs to the time clock
15 yellin RHINO RHINO RHINO

strength and survival

Leslie Marmon Silko (b. 1948)

Leslie Marmon Silko was born in Albuquerque, New Mexico, of Pueblo, Mexican, and white descent, and the perspective of her mixed ethnicity is a prominent feature in her work. Growing up on the Laguna Pueblo reservation, she attended an Indian school and

22

later went on to the University of New Mexico. Silko published her first work, "Tony's Story" in 1969 and her first book, *Laguna Women Poems* in 1974. In *Ceremony* (1977), her acclaimed first novel of alienation and healing, Thought-Woman creates a story while Silko becomes only the teller of that story. Her words, she says, become "a storyteller's most valiant attempt to imagine what a character in a story would be like, and what she would see, and how in the logic of that old belief system, then, things would come into creation." Silko's concern with the power of storytelling to enable the people to overcome oppression is infused throughout her work. *Storyteller* (1981), from which "Lullaby" is taken, uses the stories passed on in her Native American tradition to re-create, through poetry and prose, histories of her own family. She writes, "With these stories of ours/ we can escape almost anything/ with these stories we will survive." In her eight-hundred-page novel *Almanac of the Dead*, (1991) Silko brings America's indigenous peoples' struggles together in a complex, dark narrative about "time, and what's called history, and story, and who makes the story, and who remembers." *Delicacy and the Strength of Lace: Letters* (1986) is an edited version of her correspondence with poet James Wright. *Yellow Woman* (1993) and *Yellow Woman and a Beauty of the Spirit* (1996) are works on Laguna society before Christian missionaries arrived, as well as political statements against racist practices. Her most recent novel is *Gardens in the Dunes* (1999). Silko has received many awards for her work, including the "genius award" from the MacArthur Foundation and the Native Writers' Circle of the Americas Lifetime Achievement Award.

Ken Boas

strength and survival

LULLABY

The sun had gone down but the snow in the wind gave off its own light. It came in thick tufts like new wool—washed before the weaver spins it. Ayah reached out for it like her own babies had, and she smiled when she remembered how she had laughed at them. She was an old woman now, and her life had become memories. She sat down with her back against the wide cottonwood tree, feeling the rough bark on her back bones; she faced east and listened to the wind and snow sing a high-pitched Yeibechei song. Out of the wind she felt warmer, and she could watch the wide fluffy snow fill in her tracks, steadily, until the direction she had come from was gone. By the light of the snow she could see the dark outline of the big arroyo a few feet away. She was sitting on the edge of Cebolleta Creek, where in the springtime the thin cows would graze on grass already chewed flat to the ground. In the wide deep creek bed where only a trickle of water flowed in the summer, the skinny cows would wander, looking for new grass along winding paths splashed with manure.

Ayah pulled the old Army blanket over her head like a shawl. Jimmie's blanket—the one he had sent to her. That was a long time ago and the green wool was faded, and it was unraveling on the edges. She did not want to think about Jimmie. So she thought about the weaving and the way her mother had done it. On the tall wooden loom set into the *Ayah* sand under a tamarack tree for shade. She could see it clearly. She had been only a little girl when her grandma gave her the wooden combs to pull the twigs and burrs from the raw, freshly washed wool. And while she combed the wool, her grandma sat beside her, spinning a silvery strand of yarn around the smooth cedar spindle. Her mother worked at the loom with yarns dyed bright yellow and red and gold. She watched them dye the yarn in boiling black pots full of beeweed petals, juniper berries, and sage. The blankets her mother made were soft and woven so tight that rain rolled off them like birds' feathers. Ayah remembered sleeping warm on cold windy nights, wrapped in her mother's blankets on the hogan's sandy floor.

similar to tee pee

The snow drifted now, with the northwest wind hurling it in gusts. It drifted up around her black overshoes—old ones with little metal buckles. She smiled at the snow which was trying to cover her little by little. She could remember when they had no black rubber overshoes; only the high buckskin leggings that they wrapped over their elkhide moccasins. If the snow was dry or frozen, a person could walk all day and not get wet; and in the evenings the beams of the ceiling would hang with lengths of pale buckskin leggings, drying out slowly.

She felt peaceful remembering. She didn't feel cold any more. Jimmie's blanket seemed warmer than it had ever been. And she could remember the morning he was born. She could remember whispering to her mother, who was sleeping on the other side of the hogan, to tell her it was time now. She did not want to wake the others. The second time she called to her, her mother stood up and pulled on her shoes; she knew. They walked to the old stone hogan together, Ayah walking a step behind her mother. She waited alone, learning the rhythms of the pains while her mother went to call the old woman to help them. The morning was already warm even before dawn and Ayah smelled the bee flowers blooming and the young willow growing at the springs. She could remember that so clearly, but his birth merged into the births of the other children and to her it became all the same birth. They named him for the summer morning and in English they called him Jimmie.

It wasn't like Jimmie died. He just never came back, and one day a dark blue sedan with white writing on its doors pulled up in front of the boxcar shack where the rancher let the Indians live. A man in a khaki uniform trimmed in gold gave them a yellow piece of paper and told them that Jimmie was dead. He said the Army would try to get the body back and then it would be shipped to them; but it wasn't likely because the helicopter had burned after it crashed. All of this was told to Chato because he could understand English. She stood inside the doorway holding the baby while Chato listened. Chato spoke English like a white man and he spoke Spanish too. He was taller than the white man and he stood straighter too. Chato didn't explain why; he just told the military man they could keep the body if they found it. The white man looked bewildered; he nodded his head and he left. Then Chato looked at her and shook his head, and then he told her, "Jimmie isn't coming home anymore," and when he spoke, he used the words to speak of the dead. She didn't cry then, but she hurt inside with anger. And she mourned him as the years passed, when a horse fell with Chato and broke his leg, and the white rancher told them he wouldn't pay Chato until he could work again. She mourned Jimmie because he would have worked for his father then; he would have saddled the big bay horse and ridden the fence lines each day, with wire cutters and heavy gloves, fixing the breaks in the barbed wire and putting the stray cattle back inside again.

She mourned him after the white doctors came to take Danny and Ella away. She was at the shack alone that day they came. It was back in the days before they hired Navajo women to go with them as interpreters. She recognized one of the doctors. She had seen him at the children's clinic at Cañoncito about a month ago. They were wearing khaki uniforms and they waved papers at her and a black ball-point pen, trying to make her understand their English words. She was frightened by the way they looked at the children, like the lizard watches the fly. Danny was swinging on the tire swing on the elm tree behind the rancher's house, and Ella was toddling around the front door, dragging the broomstick horse Chato made for her. Ayah could see they wanted her to sign the papers, and Chato had taught her to sign her name. It was something she was proud of. She only wanted them to go, and to take their eyes away from her children.

She took the pen from the man without looking at his face and she signed the papers in three different places he pointed to. She stared at the ground by their feet and waited for them to leave. But they stood there and began to point and gesture at the children.

Danny stopped swinging. Ayah could see his fear. She moved suddenly and grabbed Ella into her arms; the child squirmed, trying to get back to her toys. Ayah ran with the baby toward Danny; she screamed for him to run and then she grabbed him around his chest and carried him too. She ran south into the foothills of juniper trees and black lava rock. Behind her she heard the doctors running, but they had been taken by surprise, and as the hills became steeper and the cholla cactus were thicker, they stopped. When she reached the top of the hill, she stopped to listen in case they were circling around her. But in a few minutes she heard a car engine start and they drove away. The children had been too surprised to cry while she ran with them. Danny was shaking and Ella's little fingers were gripping Ayah's blouse.

She stayed up in the hills for the rest of the day, sitting on a black lava boulder in the sunshine where she could see for miles all around her. The sky was light blue and cloudless, and it was warm for late April. The sun warmth relaxed her and took the fear and anger away. She lay back on the rock and watched the sky. It seemed to her that she could walk into the sky, stepping through clouds endlessly. Danny played with little pebbles and stones, pretending they were birds eggs and then little rabbits. Ella sat at her feet and dropped fistfuls of dirt into the breeze, watching the dust and particles of sand intently. Ayah watched a hawk soar high above them, dark wings gliding; hunting or only watching, she did not know. The hawk was patient and he circled all afternoon before he disappeared around the high volcanic peak the Mexicans called Guadalupe.

Late in the afternoon, Ayah looked down at the gray boxcar shack with the paint all peeled from the wood; the stove pipe on the roof was rusted and crooked. The fire she had built that morning in the oil drum stove had burned out. Ella was asleep in her lap now and Danny sat close to her, complaining that he was hungry; he asked when they would go to the house. "We will stay up here until your father comes," she told him, "because those white men were chasing us." The boy remembered then and he nodded at her silently.

If Jimmie had been there he could have read those papers and explained to her what they said. Ayah would have known then, never to sign them. The doctors came back the next day and they brought a BIA policeman with them. They told Chato they had her signature and that was all they needed. Except for the kids. She listened to Chato sullenly; she hated him when he told her it was the old woman who died in the winter, spitting blood; it was her old grandma who had given the children this disease. "They don't spit blood," she said coldly. "The whites lie." She held Ella and Danny close to her, ready to run to the hills again. "I want a medicine man first," she said to Chato, not looking at him. He shook his head. "It's too late now. The policeman is with them. You signed the paper." His voice was gentle.

It was worse than if they had died: to lose the children and to know that somewhere, in a place called Colorado, in a place full of sick and dying strangers, her children were without her. There had been babies that died soon after they were born, and one that died before he could walk. She had carried them herself, up to the boulders and great pieces of the cliff that long ago crashed down from Long Mesa; she laid them in the crevices of sandstone and buried them in fine brown sand with round quartz pebbles that washed down the hills in the rain. She had endured it because they had been with her. But she could not bear this pain. She did not sleep for a long time after they took her children. She stayed on the hill where they had fled the first time, and she slept rolled up in the blanket Jimmie had sent her. She carried the pain in her belly and it was fed by everything she saw: the blue sky of their last day together and the dust and pebbles they played with; the swing in the elm tree and broomstick horse choked life from her. The pain filled her stomach and there was no room for food or for her lungs to fill with air. The air and the food would have been theirs.

boulders: rounded or worn rock; large

She hated Chato, not because he let the policeman and doctors put the screaming children in the government car, but because he had taught her to sign her name. Because it was like the old ones always told her about learning their language or any of their ways: it endangered you. She slept alone on the hill until the middle of November when the first snows came. Then she made a bed for herself where the children had slept. She did not lie down beside Chato again until many years later, when he was sick and shivering and only her body could keep him warm. The illness came after the white rancher told Chato he was too old to work for him anymore, and Chato and his old woman should be out of the shack by the next afternoon because the rancher had hired new people to work there. That had satisfied her. To see how the white man repaid Chato's years of loyalty and work. All of Chato's fine-sounding English talk didn't change things.

It snowed steadily and the luminous light from the snow gradually diminished into the darkness. Somewhere in Cebolleta a dog barked and other village dogs joined with it. Ayah looked in the direction she had come, from the bar where Chato was buying the wine. Sometimes he told her to go on ahead and wait; and then he never came. And when she finally went back looking for him, she would find him passed out at the bottom of the wooden steps to Azzie's Bar. All the wine would be gone and most of the money too, from the pale blue check that came to them once a month in a government envelope. It was then that she would look at his face and his hands, scarred by ropes and the barbed wire of all those years, and she would think, this man is a stranger; for forty years she had smiled at him and cooked his food, but he remained a stranger. She stood up again, with the snow almost to her knees, and she walked back to find Chato.

It was hard to walk in the deep snow and she felt the air burn in her lungs. She stopped a short distance from the bar to rest and readjust the blanket. But this time he wasn't waiting for her on the bottom step with his old Stetson hat pulled down and his shoulders hunched up in his long wool overcoat.

She was careful not to slip on the wooden steps. When she pushed the door open, warm air and cigarette smoke hit her face. She looked around slowly and deliberately, in every corner, in every dark place that the old man might find to sleep. The bar owner didn't like Indians in there, especially Navajos, but he let Chato come in because he could talk Spanish like he was one of them. The men at the bar stared at her, and the bartender saw that she left the door open wide. Snowflakes were flying inside like moths and melting into a puddle on the oiled wood floor. He motioned to her to close the door, but she did not see him. She held herself straight and walked across the room slowly, searching the room with every step. The snow in her hair melted and she could feel it on her forehead. At the far corner of the room, she saw red flames at the mica window of the old stove door; she looked behind the stove just to make sure. The bar got quiet except for the Spanish polka music playing on the jukebox. She stood by the stove and shook the snow from her blanket and held it near the stove to dry. The wet wool smell reminded her of new-born goats in early March, brought inside to warm near the fire. She felt calm.

In past years they would have told her to get out. But her hair was white now and her face was wrinkled. They looked at her like she was a spider crawling slowly across the room. They were afraid; she could feel the fear. She looked at their faces steadily. They reminded her of the first time the white people brought her children back to her that winter. Danny had been shy and hid behind the thin white woman who brought them. And the baby had not known her until Ayah took her into her arms, and then Ella had nuzzled close to her as she had when she was nursing. The blonde woman was nervous and kept looking at a dainty gold watch on her wrist. She sat on the bench near the small window and watched the dark snow clouds gather around the mountains; she was worrying about the unpaved road. She was frightened by what she saw inside too: the strips of venison drying on a rope across the ceiling and the children jabbering excitedly in a language she did not know. So they stayed for only a few hours. Ayah watched the government car disappear down the road and she knew they were already being weaned from these lava hills and from this sky. The last time they came was in early June, and Ella stared at her the way the men in the bar were now staring. Ayah did not try to pick her up; she smiled at her instead and spoke cheerfully to Danny. When he tried to answer her, he could not seem to remember and he spoke English words with the Navajo. But he gave her a scrap of paper that he had found somewhere and carried in his pocket; it was folded in half, and he shyly looked up at her and said it was a bird. She asked Chato if they were home for good this time. He spoke to the white woman and she shook her head. "How much longer?" he asked, and she said she didn't know; but Chato saw how she stared at the boxcar shack. Ayah turned away then. She did not say good-bye.

She felt satisfied that the men in the bar feared her. Maybe it was her face and the way she held her mouth with teeth clenched tight, like there was nothing anyone could do to her now. She walked north down the road, searching for the old man. She did this because she had the blanket, and there would be no place for him except with her and the blanket in the old adobe barn near the arroyo. They always slept there when they came to Cebolleta. If the money and the wine were gone, she would be relieved because then they could go home again; back to the old hogan with a dirt roof and rock walls where she herself had been born. And the next day the old man could go back to the few sheep they still had, to follow along behind them, guiding them, into dry sandy arroyos where sparse grass grew. She knew he did not like walking behind old ewes when for so many years he rode big quarter horses and worked with cattle. But she wasn't sorry for him; he should have known all along what would happen.

There had not been enough rain for their garden in five years; and that was when Chato finally hitched a ride into the town and brought back brown boxes of rice and sugar and big tin cans of welfare peaches. After that, at the first of the month they went to Cebolleta to ask the postmaster for the check; and then Chato would go to the bar and cash it. They did this as they planted the garden every May, not because anything would survive the summer dust, but because it was time to do this. The journey passed the days that smelled silent and dry like the caves above the canyon with yellow painted buffaloes on their walls.

He was walking along the pavement when she found him. He did not stop or turn around when he heard her behind him. She walked beside him and she noticed how slowly he moved now. He smelled strong of woodsmoke and urine. Lately he had been forgetting. Sometimes he called her by his sister's name and she had been gone for a long time. Once she had found him wandering on the road to the white man's ranch, and she asked him why he was going that way; he laughed at her and said, "You know they can't run that ranch without me," and he walked on determined, limping on the leg that had been crushed many years before. Now he looked at her curiously, as if for the first time, but he kept shuffling along, moving slowly along the side of the highway. His gray hair had grown long and spread out on the shoulders of the long overcoat. He wore the old felt hat pulled down over his ears. His boots were worn out at the toes and he had stuffed pieces of an old red shirt in the holes. The rags made his feet look like little animals up to their ears in snow. She laughed at his feet; the snow muffled the sound of her laugh. He stopped and looked at her again. The wind had quit blowing and the snow was falling straight down; the southeast sky was beginning to clear and Ayah could see a star.

"Let's rest awhile," she said to him. They walked away from the road and up the slope to the giant boulders that had tumbled down from the red sandrock mesa throughout the centuries of rainstorms and earth tremors. In a place where the boulders shut out the wind, they sat down with their backs against the rock. She offered half of the blanket to him and they sat wrapped together.

The storm passed swiftly. The clouds moved east. They were massive and full, crowding together across the sky. She watched them with the feeling of horses—steely blue-gray horses startled across the sky. The powerful haunches pushed into the distances and the tail hairs streamed white mist behind them. The sky cleared. Ayah saw that there was nothing between her and the stars. The light was crystalline. There was no shimmer, no distortion through earth haze. She breathed the clarity of the night sky; she smelled the purity of the half moon and the stars. He was lying on his side with his knees pulled up near his belly for warmth. His eyes were closed now, and in the light from the stars and the moon, he looked young again.

She could see it descend out of the night sky: an icy stillness from the edge of the thin moon. She recognized the freezing. It came gradually, sinking snowflake by snowflake until the crust was heavy and deep. It had the strength of the stars in Orion, and its journey was endless. Ayah knew that with the wine he would sleep. He would not feel it. She tucked the blanket around him, remembering how it was when Ella had been with her; and she felt the rush so big inside her heart for the babies. And she sang the only song she knew to sing for babies. She could not remember if she had ever sung it to her children, but she knew that her grandmother had sung it and her mother had sung it:

> The earth is your mother,
>   she holds you.
> The sky is your father,
>   he protects you.
> Sleep,
> sleep.
> Rainbow is your sister,
>   she loves you.
> The winds are your brothers,
>   they sing to you.
> Sleep,
> sleep.
> We are together always
> We are together always
> There never was a time
> when this
> was not so.

Dorothy Allison (b. 1949)

Dorothy Allison is best known as a lesbian-feminist writer who has exposed the experience and consequences of childhood physical and sexual abuse in literature of great daring and artistry. Her award-winning *Bastard Out of Carolina* (1992) was a break-through novel and later became a television movie. Allison insists, though, that her life and writing have been marked as much by poverty as by incest and by her sexuality. In the essay "A Question of Class," she writes:

But what may be the central fact of my life is that I was born in 1949 in Greenville, South Carolina, the bastard daughter of a white woman from a desperately poor family, a girl who had left the seventh grade the year before, worked as a waitress, and was just a month past fifteen when she had me. That fact, the inescapable impact of being born in a condition of poverty that this society finds shameful, contemptible, and somehow deserved, has had dominion over me. (*Skin: Talking About Sex, Class and Literature*, 1994)

She adds, "I have loved my family so stubbornly that every impulse to hold them in contempt has sparked in me a countersurge of pride." In "Mama," taken from the 1988 collection of stories *Trash*, Allison characteristically blends fiction and autobiography in paying tribute to her mother's complex, even contradictory, legacy: on the one hand, the toughness of "the survivor, the endurer," linked to the power of storytelling and of strong defiant language; on the other hand, the message of shame—"Don't show it. Don't tell anyone what is really going on"—and the limitation of hope: "*Do not want what you cannot have*, she told me."

Allison was the first member of her family to finish high school. She credits her discovery of feminism while in college for planting the hope that she could build her own life and career. She holds a master's degree in anthropology from New York's New School of Social Research. She is also the author of *The Women Who Hate Me* (poems, 1983; expanded edition in 1991), *Two or Three Things I Know for Sure* (memoir, 1995), and a second novel *Cavedweller* (1998). In 1998, she founded the Independent Spirit Awards, through the Astraea Lesbian Writers Fund, designed to support publication of risk-taking works that may otherwise go unread. "Without the bookstores, magazines, and presses that have encouraged and sustained my imagination, I would not have known what to do with the stories I wanted to tell."

MAMA

Above her left ankle my mother has an odd star-shaped scar. It blossoms like a violet above the arch, a purple pucker riding the muscle. When she was a little girl in South Carolina they still bled people in sickness, and they bled her there. I thought she was just telling a story, when she first told me, teasing me or covering up some embarrassing accident she didn't want me to know about. But my aunt supported her.

"It's a miracle she's alive, girl. She was such a sickly child, still a child when she had you, and then there was the way you were born."

"How's that?"

"Assbackward," Aunt Alma was proud to be the first to tell me, and it showed in the excitement in her voice. "Your mama was unconscious for three days after you were born. She'd been fast asleep in the back of your Uncle Lucius's car when they hit that Pontiac right outside the airbase. Your mama went right through the windshield and bounced off the other car. When she woke up three days later, you were already out and named, and all she had was a little scar on her forehead to show what had happened. It was a miracle like they talk about in Bible school, and I know there's something your mama's meant to do because of it."

"Oh, yeah," Mama shrugged when I asked her about it. "An't no doubt I'm meant for greater things—bigger biscuits, thicker gravy. What else could God want for someone like me, huh?" She pulled her mouth so tight I could see her teeth pushing her upper lip, but then she looked into my face and let her air out slowly.

"Your aunt is always laying things to God's hand that he wouldn't have interest in doing anyway. What's true is that there was a car accident and you got named before I could say much about it. Ask your aunt why you're named after her, why don't you?"

On my stepfather's birthday I always think of my mother. She sits with her coffee and cigarettes, watches the sun come up before she must leave for work. My mama lives with my stepfather still, though she spent most of my childhood swearing that as soon as she had us up and grown, she'd leave him flat. Instead, we left, my sister and I, and on my stepfather's birthday we neither send presents nor visit. The thing we do—as my sister has told me and as I have told her—is think about Mama. At any moment of the day we know what she will be doing, where she will be, and what she will probably be talking about. We know, not only because her days are as set and predictable as the schedule by which she does the laundry, we know in our bodies. Our mother's body is with us in its details. She is recreated in each of us, strength of bone and the skin curling over the thick flesh the women of our family have always worn.

When I visit Mama, I always look first to her hands and feet to reassure myself. The skin of her hands is transparent—large-veined, wrinkled and bruised—while her feet are soft with the lotions I rubbed into them every other night of my childhood. That was a special thing between my mother and me, the way she'd give herself the care of my hands, lying across the daybed, telling me stories of what she'd served down at the truck-stop, who had complained and who tipped specially well, and most important, who had said what and what she'd said back. I would sit at her feet, laughing and nodding and stroking away the tightness in her muscles, watching the way her mouth would pull taut while under her pale eyelids the pulse of her eyes moved like kittens behind a blanket. Sometimes my love for her would choke me, and I would ache to have her open her eyes and see me there, to see how much I loved her. But mostly I kept my eyes on her skin, the fine traceries of the veins and the knotted cords of ligaments, seeing where she was not beautiful and hiding how scared it made me to see her close up, looking so fragile, and too often, so old.

When my mama was twenty-five she already had an old woman's hands, and I feared them. I did not know then what it was that scared me so. I've come to understand since that it was the thought of her growing old, of her dying and leaving me alone. I feared those brown spots, those wrinkles and cracks that lined her wrists, ankles, and the soft shadowed sides of her eyes. I was too young to imagine my own death with anything but an adolescent's high romantic enjoyment; I pretended often enough that I was dying of a wasting disease that would give lots of time for my aunts, uncles, and stepfather to mourn me. But the idea that anything could touch my mother, that anything would dare to hurt her was impossible to bear, and I woke up screaming the one night I dreamed of her death—a dream in which I tried bodily to climb to the throne of a Baptist god and demand her return to me. I thought of my mama like a mountain or a cave, a force of nature, a woman who had saved her own life and mine, and would surely save us both over and over again. The wrinkles in her hands made me think of earthquakes and the lines under her eyes hummed of tidal waves in the night. If she was fragile, if she was human, then so was I, and anything might happen. If she was not the backbone of creation itself, then fear would overtake me. I could not allow that, would not. My child's solution was to try to cure my mother of wrinkles in the hope of saving her from death itself.

Once, when I was about eight and there was no Jergens lotion to be had, I spooned some mayonnaise out to use instead. Mama leaned forward, sniffed, lay back and laughed into her hand.

"If that worked," she told me, still grinning, "I wouldn't have dried up to begin with—all the mayonnaise I've eaten in my life."

"All the mayonnaise you've spread—like the butter of your smile, out there for everybody," my stepfather grumbled. He wanted his evening glass of tea, wanted his feet put up, and maybe his neck rubbed. At a look from Mama, I'd run one errand after another until he was settled with nothing left to complain about. Then I'd go back to Mama. But by that time we'd have to start on dinner, and I wouldn't have any more quiet time with her till a day or two later when I'd rub her feet again.

I never hated my stepfather half as much for the beatings he gave me as for those stolen moments when I could have been holding Mama's feet in my hands. Pulled away from Mama's side to run get him a pillow or change the television channel and forced to stand and wait until he was sure there was nothing else he wanted me to do, I entertained myself with visions of his sudden death. Motorcycle outlaws would come to the door, mistaking him for a Drug Enforcement Officer, and blow his head off with a sawed-off shotgun just like the one my Uncle Bo kept under the front seat in his truck. The lawn mower would explode, cutting him into scattered separate pieces the emergency squad would have to collect in plastic bags. Standing and waiting for his orders while staring at the thin black hairs on his balding head, I would imagine his scalp seen through blood-stained plastic, and smile wide and happy while I thought out how I would tell that one to my sister in our dark room at night, when she would whisper back to me her own version of our private morality play.

When my stepfather beat me I did not think, did not imagine stories of either escape or revenge. When my stepfather beat me I pulled so deeply into myself I lived only in my eyes, my eyes that watched the shower sweat on the bathroom walls, the pipes under the sink, my blood on the porcelain toilet seat, and the buckle of his belt as it moved through the air. My ears were disconnected so I could understand nothing—neither his shouts, my own hoarse shameful strangled pleas, nor my mother's screams from the other side of the door he locked. I would not come back to myself until the beating was ended and the door was opened and I saw my mother's face, her hands shaking as she reached for me. Even then, I would not be able to understand what she was yelling at him, or he was yelling at both of us. Mama would take me into the bedroom and wash my face with a cold rag, wipe my legs and, using the same lotion I had rubbed into her feet, try to soothe my pain. Only when she had stopped crying would my hearing come back, and I would lie still and listen to her voice saying my name—soft and tender, like her hand on my back. There were no stories in my head then, no hatred, only an enormous gratitude to be lying still with her hand on me and, for once, the door locked against him.

Push it down. Don't show it. Don't tell anyone what is really going on. We are not safe, I learned from my mama. There are people in the world who are, but they are not us. Don't show your stuff to anyone. Tell no one that your stepfather beats you. The things that would happen are too terrible to name.

Mama quit working honkytonks to try the mill as soon as she could after her marriage. But a year in the mill was all she could take; the dust in the air got to her too fast. After that there was no choice but to find work in a diner. The tips made all the difference, though she could have made more money if she'd stayed with the honkytonks or managed a slot as a cocktail waitress. There was always more money serving people beer and wine, more still in hard liquor, but she'd have had to go outside Greenville County to do that. Neither she nor her new husband could imagine going that far.

The diner was a good choice anyway, one of the few respectable ones downtown, a place where men took their families on Sunday afternoon. The work left her tired, but not sick to death like the mill, and she liked the people she met there, the tips and the conversation.

"You got a way about you," the manager told her.

"Oh yeah, I'm known for my ways," she laughed, and no one would have known she didn't mean it. Truckers or judges, they all liked my mama. And when they weren't slipping quarters in her pocket, they were bringing her things, souvenirs or friendship cards, once or twice a ring. Mama smiled, joked, slapped ass, and firmly passed back anything that looked like a down payment on something she didn't want to sell. She started taking me to work with her when I was still too short to see over the counter, letting me sit up there to watch her some, and tucking me away in the car when I got cold or sleepy.

"That's my girl," she'd brag. "Four years old and reads the funny papers to me every Sunday morning. She's something, an't she?"

"Something," the men would nod, mostly not even looking at me, but agreeing with anything just to win Mama's smile. I'd watch them closely, the wallets they pulled out of their back pockets, the rough patches on their forearms and scratches on their chins. Poor men, they didn't have much more than we did, but they could buy my mama's time with a cup of coffee and a nickel slipped under the saucer. I hated them, each and every one.

My stepfather was a truck driver—a little man with a big rig and a bigger rage. He kept losing jobs when he lost his temper. Somebody would say something, some joke, some little thing, and my little stepfather would pick up something half again his weight and try to murder whoever had dared to say that thing. "Don't make him angry," people always said about him. "Don't make him angry," my mama was always saying to us.

I tried not to make him angry. I ran his errands. I listened to him talk, standing still on one leg and then the other, keeping my face empty, impartial. He always wanted me to wait on him. When we heard him yell, my sister's face would break like a pool of water struck with a handful of stones. Her glance would fly to mine. I would stare at her, hate her, hate myself. She would stare at me, hate me, hate herself. After a moment, I would sigh—five, six, seven, eight years old, sighing like an old lady—tell her to stay there, get up and go to him. Go to stand still for him, his hands, his big hands on his little body. I would imagine those hands cut off by marauders sweeping down on great black horses, swords like lightning bolts in the hands of armored women who wouldn't even know my name but would kill him anyway. Imagine boils and blisters and wasting diseases; sudden overturned cars and spreading gasoline. Imagine vengeance. Imagine justice. What is the difference anyway when both are only stories in your head? In the everyday reality you stand still. I stood still. Bent over. Laid down.

"Yes, Daddy."

"No, Daddy."

"I'm sorry, Daddy."

"Don't do that, Daddy."

"Please, Daddy."

Push it down. Don't show it. Don't tell anyone what is really going on. We are not safe. There are people in the world who are, but they are not us. Don't show your fear to anyone. The things that would happen are too terrible to name.

Sometimes I wake in the middle of the night to the call of my name shouted in my mama's voice, rising from silence like an echo caught in the folds of my brain. It is her hard voice I hear, not the soft one she used when she held me tight, the hard voice she used on bill collectors and process servers. Sometimes her laugh comes too, that sad laugh, thin and foreshadowing a cough, with her angry laugh following. I hate that laugh, hate the sound of it in the night following on my name like shame. When I hear myself laugh like that, I always start to curse, to echo what I know was the stronger force in my mama's life.

As I grew up my teachers warned me to clean up my language, and my lovers became impatient with the things I said. Sugar and honey, my teachers reminded me when I sprinkled my sentences with the vinegar of my mama's rage—as if I was supposed to want to draw flies. And, "Oh honey," my girlfriends would whisper, "do you have to talk that way?" I did, I did indeed. I smiled them my mama's smile and played for them my mama's words while they tightened up and pulled back, seeing me for someone they had not imagined before. They didn't shout, they hissed; and even when they got angry, their language never quite rose up out of them the way my mama's rage would fly.

"Must you? Must you?" they begged me. And then, "For God's sake!"

"Sweet Jesus!" I'd shout back but they didn't know enough to laugh.

"Must you? Must you?"

Hiss, hiss.

"For God's sake, do you have to end everything with *ass*? An anal obsession, that's what you've got, a goddamn anal obsession!"

"I do, I do," I told them, "and you don't even know how to say *goddamn*. A woman who says *goddamn* as soft as you do isn't worth the price of a meal of shit!"

Coarse, crude, rude words, and ruder gestures—Mama knew them all. *You assfucker, get out of my yard*, to the cop who came to take the furniture. *Shitsucking bastard!* to the man who put his hand under her skirt. *Jesus shit a brick*, every day of her life. Though she slapped me when I used them, my mama taught me the power of nasty words. Say *goddamn*. Say anything but begin it with *Jesus* and end it with *shit*. Add that laugh, the one that disguises your broken heart. Oh, never show your broken heart! Make them think you don't have one instead.

"If people are going to kick you, don't just lie there. Shout back at them."

"Yes, Mama."

Language then, and tone, and cadence. Make me mad, and I'll curse you to the seventh generation in my mama's voice. But you have to work to get me mad. I measure my anger against my mama's rages and her insistence that most people aren't even worth your time. "We are another people. Our like isn't seen on the earth that often," my mama told me, and I knew what she meant. I know the value of the hard asses of this world. And I am my mama's daughter—tougher than kudzu, meaner than all the ass-kicking, bad-assed, cold-assed, saggy-assed fuckers I have ever known. But it's true that sometimes I talk that way just to remember my mother, the survivor, the endurer, but the one who could not always keep quiet about it.

We are just like her, my sister and I. That March when my sister called, I thought for a moment it was my mama's voice. The accent was right, and the language—the slow drag of matter-of-fact words and thoughts, but the beaten-down quality wasn't Mama, couldn't have been. For a moment I felt as if my hands were gripping old and tender flesh, the skin gone thin from age and wear, my granny's hands, perhaps, on the day she had stared out at her grandsons and laughed lightly, insisting I take a good look at them. "See, see how the blood thins out." She spit to the side and clamped a hand down on my shoulder. I turned and looked at her hand, that hand as strong as heavy cord rolled back on itself, my bare shoulder under her hand and the muscles there rising like bubbles in cold milk. I had felt thick and strong beside her, thick and strong and sure of myself in a way I have not felt since. That March when my sister called I felt old; my hands felt wiry and worn, and my blood seemed hot and thin as it rushed through my veins.

My sister's voice sounded hollow; her words vibrated over the phone as if they had iron edges. My tongue locked to my teeth, and I tasted the fear I thought I had put far behind me.

"They're doing everything they can—surgery again this morning and chemotherapy and radiation. He's a doctor, so he knows, but Jesus . . ."

"Jesus shit."

"Yeah."

Mama woke up alone with her rage, her grief. "Just what I'd always expected," she told me later. "You think you know what's going on, what to expect. You relax a minute and that's when it happens. Life turns around and kicks you in the butt."

Lying there, she knew they had finally gotten her, the *they* that had been dogging her all her life, waiting for the chance to rob her of all her tomorrows. Now they had her, her body pinned down under bandages and tubes and sheets that felt like molten lead. She had not really believed it possible. She tried to pull her hands up to her neck, but she couldn't move her arms. "I was so mad I wanted to kick holes in the sheets, but there wasn't no use in that." When my stepfather came in to sit and whistle his sobs beside the bed, she took long breaths and held her face tight and still. She became all eyes, watching everything from a place far off inside herself.

"Never want what you cannot have," she'd always told me. It was her rule for survival, and she grabbed hold of it again. She turned her head away from what she could not change and started adjusting herself to her new status. She was going to have to figure out how to sew herself up one of those breast forms so she could wear a bra. "Damn things probably cost a fortune," she told me when I came to sit beside her. I nodded slowly. I didn't let her see how afraid I was, or how uncertain, or even how angry. I showed her my pride in her courage and my faith in her strength. But underneath I wanted her to be angry, too. "I'll make do," she whispered, showing me nothing, and I just nodded.

"Everything's going to be all right," I told her.

"Everything's going to be all right," she told me. The pretense was sometimes the only thing we had to give each other.

When it's your mama and it's an accomplished fact, you can't talk politics into her bleeding. You can't quote from last month's article about how a partial mastectomy is just as effective. You can't talk about patriarchy or class or confrontation strategies. I made jokes on the telephone, wrote letters full of healthy recipes and vitamin therapies. I pretended for her sake and my own that nothing was going to happen, that cancer is an everyday occurrence (and it is) and death is not part of the scenario.

Push it down. Don't show it. Don't tell anybody what is really going on. My mama makes do when the whole world cries out for things to stop, to fall apart, just once for all of us to let our anger show. My mama clamps her teeth, laughs her bitter laugh, and does whatever she thinks she has to do with no help, thank you, from people who only want to see her wanting something she can't have anyway.

Five, ten, twenty years—my mama has had cancer for twenty years. "That doctor, the one in Tampa in '71, the one told me I was gonna die, that sucker choked himself on a turkey bone. People that said what a sad thing it was—me having cancer, and surely meant to die—hell, those people been run over by pickups and dropped down dead with one thing and another, while me, I just go on. It's something, an't it?"

It's something. Piece by piece, my mother is being stolen from me. After the hysterectomy, the first mastectomy, another five years later, her teeth that were easier to give up than to keep, the little toes that calcified from too many years working waitress in bad shoes, hair and fingernails that drop off after every bout of chemotherapy, my mama is less and less the mountain, more and more the cave—the empty place from which things have been removed.

"With what they've taken off me, off Granny, and your Aunt Grace—shit, you could almost make another person."

A woman, a garbage creation, an assembly of parts. When I drink I see her rising like bats out of deep caverns, a gossamer woman—all black edges, with a chrome uterus and molded glass fingers, plastic wire rib cage and red unblinking eyes. My mama, my grandmother, my aunts, my sister and me—every part of us that can be taken has been.

"Flesh and blood needs flesh and blood," my mama sang for me once, and laughing added, "but we don't need as much of it as we used to, huh?"

When Mama talked, I listened. I believed it was the truth she was telling me. I watched her face as much as I listened to her words. She had a way of dropping her head and covering her bad teeth with her palm. I'd say, "Don't do that." And she'd laugh at how serious I was. When she laughed with me, that shadow, so grey under her eyes, lightened, and I felt for a moment—powerful, important, never so important as when I could make her laugh.

I wanted to grow up to do the poor-kid-done-good thing, the Elvis Presley/Ritchie Valens movie, to buy my mama her own house, put a key in her hand and say, "It's yours—from here to there and everything in between, these walls, that door, that gate, these locks. You don't ever have to let anyone in that you don't want. You can lay in the sun if you want or walk out naked in the moonlight if you take the mood. And if you want to go into town to mess around, we can go do it together."

I did not want to be my mother's lover; I wanted more than that. I wanted to rescue her the way we had both wanted her to rescue me. *Do not want what you cannot have*, she told me. But I was not as good as she was. I wanted that dream. I've never stopped wanting it.

The day I left home my stepfather disappeared. I scoured him out of my life, exorcising every movement or phrase in which I recognized his touch. All he left behind was a voice on a telephone line, a voice that sometimes answered when I called home. But Mama grew into my body like an extra layer of warm protective fat, closing me around. My muscles hug my bones in just the way hers do, and when I turn my face, I have that same bulldog angry glare I was always ashamed to see on her. But my legs are strong, and I do not stoop the way she does; I did not work waitress for thirty years, and my first lover taught me the importance of buying good shoes. I've got Mama's habit of dropping my head, her quick angers, and that same belly-gutted scar she was so careful to hide. But nothing marks me so much her daughter as my hands—the way they are aging, the veins coming up through skin already thin. I tell myself they are beautiful as they recreate my mama's flesh in mine.

My lovers laugh at me and say, "Every tenth word with you is *mama*. Mama said. Mama used to say. My mama didn't raise no fool."

I widen my mouth around my drawl and show my mama's lost teeth in my smile.

Watching my mama I learned some lessons too well. Never show that you care, Mama taught me, and never want something you cannot have. Never give anyone the satisfaction of denying you something you need, and for that, what you have to do is learn to need nothing. Starve the wanting part of you. In time I understood my mama to be a kind of Zen Baptist—rooting desire out of her own heart as ruthlessly as any mountaintop ascetic. The lessons Mama taught me, like the lessons of Buddha, were not a matter of degree but of despair. My mama's philosophy was bitter and thin. She didn't give a damn if she was ever born again, she just didn't want to be born again poor and wanting.

I am my mama's daughter, her shadow on the earth, the blood thinned down a little so that I am not as powerful as she, as immune to want and desire. I am not a mountain or a cave, a force of nature or a power of the earth, but I have her talent for not seeing what I cannot stand to face. I make sure that I do not want what I do not think I can have, and I keep clearly in mind what it is I cannot have. I roll in the night all the stories I never told her, cannot tell her still—her voice in my brain echoing love and despair and grief and rage. When, in the night, she hears me call her name, it is not really me she hears, it is the me I constructed for her—the one who does not need her too much, the one whose heart is not too tender, whose insides are iron and silver, whose dreams are cold ice and slate—who needs nothing, nothing. I keep in mind the image of a closed door, Mama weeping on the other side. She could not rescue me. I cannot rescue her. Sometimes I cannot even reach across the wall that separates us.

On my stepfather's birthday I make coffee and bake bread pudding with bourbon sauce. I invite friends over, tell outrageous stories, and use horrible words. I scratch my scars and hug my lover, thinking about Mama twelve states away. My accent comes back and my weight settles down lower, until the ache in my spine is steady and hot. I remember Mama sitting at the kitchen table in the early morning, tears in her eyes, lying to me and my sister, promising us that the time would come when she would leave him—that as soon as we were older, as soon as there was a little more money put by and things were a little easier—she would go.

I think about her sitting there now, waiting for him to wake up and want his coffee, for the day to start moving around her, things to get so busy she won't have to think. Sometimes, I hate my mama. Sometimes, I hate myself. I see myself in her, and her in me. I see us too clearly sometimes, all the little betrayals that cannot be forgotten or changed.

When Mama calls, I wait a little before speaking.

"Mama," I say, "I knew you would call."

———

Leslie Feinberg (b. 1949)

Internationally known for *hir** pioneering transgendered coming-of-age novel, *Stone Butch Blues*, Buffalo native Leslie Feinberg disrupts and challenges fixed categories and assumptions about gender and sexual identity. Jess Goldberg, the "stone butch" of the title, is a working-class, Jewish, he/she, butch lesbian who seems to fit nowhere. Seeking community in the gay drag bars of Buffalo, New York, Jess must confront the brutal police oppression against lesbians, gays, drag queens, transsexuals, and transgendered people, particularly in the pre-Stonewall (1969) days. The novel is also a gendered working-class story of factory work, union organizing, earned respect, hard physical labor, and worker-for-worker solidarity as well as worker-against-worker violence, as shown in the two excerpts presented here. An activist and writer/editor for *Workers World*, Feinberg applies Marxist analysis to show the interconnections of transgender oppression with class and racial oppressions in hir nonfiction books, *Transgender Warriors* (1996) and *Trans Liberation: Beyond Pink or Blue* (1998). In the Afterword to the ten-year anniversary issue of *Stone Butch Blues*

———

* Feinberg coins a pronoun, "hir," to indicate a transgendered identity.

(1993, 2003), Feinberg describes hir intentions in writing the novel: "I wrote it not as an expression of individual 'high' art but as a working-class organizer mimeographs a leaflet—a call to action." As a "saga of struggle," *Stone Butch Blues* also marks an important moment in working-class literary history.

"IT WAS TIME TO FIND A FACTORY JOB," FROM *STONE BUTCH BLUES*

It was time to find a factory job. The butches urged me to try to get into steel or auto. Of course I already knew that. I wasn't a damn fool. The strength of the unions in those heavy industries had won liveable wages and decent benefits.

But Edwin said there was more to it than that. The trade unions safeguarded job security. She told me that unlike a nonunion shop if she had a run-in with a jerk on the plant floor, it didn't signal her last day on the job. You couldn't be fired just because some foreman didn't like your face. With union protection, all the butches agreed, a he-she could carve out a niche, and begin earning valuable seniority.

In the meantime, while I was waiting for an opening, I had to work through the temporary labor agencies at minimum wage. In early autumn the agency sent me to a one-day job on the loading docks of a frozen food plant. My heart leaped when I saw Grant walking into the factory ahead of me. I caught up to her and shook her hand.

Unloading trucks on the docks was male turf. It meant a lot to have another butch watch your back. Grant dug her gloved hands deep inside the pockets of her blue Navy coat. "Brrr," she shivered. "I'm freezin' my ass off out here, let's get inside." Then she sauntered very slowly toward the loading docks. She never hurried. She was so cool.

One of the truckers shouted, "He-shes at high noon!" Several guys peered out from inside the plant and shook their heads in disgust. It was going to be a long shift. I was glad we walked slowly, like we owned the god damn parking lot.

We climbed up on the dock. The foreman came out to look us over. Grant took off her glove and extended her hand. At first the foreman looked like he wasn't going to shake her hand, but he did. What little respect Grant got, she earned.

The afternoon was waning. The sun dipped low in the winter sky. A brutal wind blew off the frozen lake. The huge semi we were unloading served to block the wind, but not the cold. I shivered. We were told we would unload two of these long, long trucks during the shift. We both nodded. Personally, I had my doubts.

We worked in silence with two guys. Neither of the men spoke a word to us. They hardly spoke to each other. When Grant and I had to get around the men, we all dropped our eyes. It was harder to bear than a storm of insults.

The cartons of frozen food weren't as heavy as I thought, not for the first three or four hours. After that, they felt like they were filled with cold steel. My muscles ached and burned. I felt elated as the truck load emptied. I worked faster. Grant slowed me down with a well-intentioned glare. I had forgotten another semi was coming until I saw it parked, waiting in the lot.

We had a ten-minute breather as one truck pulled away and the other backed in. Then we began unloading the endless rows of cartons in its trailer.

Sweat ran in rivulets between my breasts. But my head was frozen and my ears burned like fire. That's when I noticed with horror that both of the men we were working with were missing pieces of their ears. Frostbite.

In some plants the men were missing a finger down to the second joint, or a thumb. Out here on the docks, which butt up against the frozen lake, the men gave up little exposed pieces of their bodies. It frightened me. I wondered what I would be forced to sacrifice in order to survive.

I shuddered. Grant gave me a slight push that made me focus again on the task at hand. She looked me up and down to make sure I was alright. She wouldn't ask out loud. In order to be safe on men's terrain it was necessary to work with dignity, as though the job was effortless. I also didn't want Grant to see me cold and scared and tired. She seemed fine. She wasn't even breathing hard.

When the shift finally ended we got the night foreman to sign our timecards and high-tailed it out to the parking lot. We sat in Grant's car smoking cigarettes in silence. My arms trembled with exhaustion. It was the first real break we'd had in eight hours. Our smoky breath formed ice crystals on the windshield. Grant revved up the engine and turned the radio on low as we waited for the car to warm up.

"Wasn't too bad," I said casually, "huh?"

"Are you kidding?" she asked me incredulously. "Halfway through I thought I'd die."

I registered shock. "For real? You made it look so easy!"

She laughed, "You must be joking. The only thing that got me through was it looked like it wasn't bothering you much. I figured I had to show you an old butch like me could still keep up with a young punk like you!"

For a moment I felt uneasy. If she relied on me, she had no idea what a thin reed she leaned on. Then I flushed with gratitude as I realized how she was holding me up, even at this moment. "You pulled it off, kid," she punched my shoulder lightly. "Jesus," she added, as a look of fear crossed her face. "Did you see the ears on those guys?"

We finished our cigarettes in silence, lost in similar thoughts.

It was always hard the first day I started working at a new factory; it wasn't easy for anyone. It took a while for a new person to be accepted into the community of a plant. Before coworkers invested their caring in you they wanted to know if you were staying. Many workers never came back after the first day, or couldn't make quota. Others made it almost to the eve of the ninety days required to join the union, only to be laid off.

I planned to stay at this bindery, if I could. I easily made quota the first day, feeding machines and packing skids. By day two I slowed down. If quota was made too effortlessly, the foreman would raise it.

I was being watched and I knew it. The first day I wore sunglasses, defensively, all day long. I didn't take off my denim jacket and kept it buttoned up over my black T-shirt.

This was a small sweatshop with a company union and I was the only he-she in the plant. If this were a big plant, I would be one of many he-shes, so many we would have our own baseball or bowling teams within the factory complex. There I would probably have bound my breasts at work, worn a white T-shirt with no jacket, and found my place among our own smaller societal structure within the life of the plant.

But despite the fact that I hadn't yet been initiated into this society, kindnesses were not withheld. At lunch I bought a bottle of pop from the machine near the time clock and sat down on a skid to eat my baloney sandwich. Muriel, one of the older Native women who worked near me on the line, offered me half her apple. I stood and thanked her. I ate it appreciatively. Each morning for the next week Muriel offered me coffee from her thermos. Everyone watched us, weighing everything they could observe.

Those moments before the whistle blew in the morning were precious because they were ours. Only the *kerchunk* of the time clock stole the last one from us. We all dragged ourselves out of bed a little earlier in the mornings to be at the plant a quarter hour before we had to punch in. We drank coffee and ate rolls, talked and laughed.

We talked all day long too. The owners only rented our hands, not our brains. But even talking had to be negotiated when it was on the bosses' time. If we seemed to be having too much fun, laughing and enjoying ourselves too much, the foreman would come up behind us and hit the solid wooden worktables with a lead pipe while he growled, "Get to work." Then we'd all look at our hands as we worked and press our lips together in silent anger. I think the foreman sometimes got nervous after he'd done that, sensing the murderous glances he received moments after he turned his back. But he was assigned to keep us under control. That required keeping us divided.

We came from many different nationalities and backgrounds. About half the women on the line were from the Six Nations. Most were Mohawk or Seneca. What we shared in common was that we worked cooperatively, day in and day out. So we remembered to ask about each other's back or foot pains, family crises. We shared small bits of our culture, favorite foods, or revealed an embarrassing moment. It was just this potential for solidarity the foreman was always looking to sabotage. It was done in little ways, all the time: a whispered lie, a cruel suggestion, a vulgar joke. But it was hard to split us up. The conveyor belt held us together.

Within weeks I was welcomed into the circle, teased, pelted with questions. My differences were taken into account, my sameness sought out. We worked together, we talked, we listened.

And then there were songs. When the whistle first blew in the mornings there was a shared physical letdown among all the women and men who worked between its imperative commands. We lumbered to our feet, stood silently in line to punch in, and took our places on the assembly line—next to each other, facing each other. We worked the first few moments in heavy silence. Then the weight was lifted by the voice of one of the Native women. They were social songs, happy songs that made you feel real good to hear them, even if you had no idea what the words meant.

I listened to the songs, trying to hear the boundaries of each word, the patterns and repetitions. Sometimes one of the women would explain to us later what the song meant, or for which occasion or time of year it was sung.

There was one song I loved the best. I found myself humming it after I punched out in the afternoons. One day, without thinking, I sang along. The women pretended not to notice, but they smiled at each other with their eyes, and sang a little louder to allow me to raise my own voice a bit. After that I started looking forward to the songs in the morning. Some of the other non-Native women learned songs, too. It felt good to sing together.

One wintry Friday night, before we punched out, Muriel invited me to go to an indoor pow-wow on Sunday. I said yes, of course. I felt honored.

There were a few other Black and white workers at the social—friendships too valuable to explore solely on company time. I began to go regularly and got strung out on fry bread and corn soup.

Once or twice I was cajoled to get up and join a round dance. I must say that although the pounding of the drum resounded in my heart, it never got as far down as my feet. I felt awkward dancing and self-conscious about being so butch.

Of course, Muriel's daughter Yvonne being there made me self-conscious too. I had a fierce crush on Yvonne. She worked in the front office of the same factory. Everyone knew she was the girlfriend of a local organized crime boss. That didn't stop us from knowing where each other was in the room during those socials. I think all the women noticed right away.

I'd already decided I wasn't even going to think about approaching Yvonne, even though she seemed to like me. Some of the older butches had warned me that sometimes on a job the guys would pressure one of the women to sleep with a he-she, as a joke, and then come back and tell everyone about it. That was the last day on the job for the butch, who usually left in shame. But sooner or later the stigma also came back around and stuck on the woman who slept with one of us, and she had to leave too.

I was afraid of this at first with Yvonne, but she wasn't like that at all. One night when a group of us went out after work and got drunk, she told me her boyfriend had suggested he wanted to watch us make love and she had told him to fuck off. Once that had been said out loud, however, it was hard not to think about making love with Yvonne.

Just before Christmas the crew from work went to a bar near the plant for a few beers. There was a heavy snowstorm outside. Inside, we drank and laughed. By the time we left, the snow had nearly covered the cars. I heated the car door key to Muriel's old Dodge with my lighter to defrost it. When I finally got the car door open, Yvonne kissed me right on the mouth. She left me in that parking lot, stunned and excited.

The next night I went to the Malibou and wondered the whole time what it would be like to bring Yvonne there.

I was happy at the plant, flirting with Yvonne, listening to Muriel's stories, waiting for the next social. On Friday nights we drank at the bar where we cashed our checks. Saturday nights I spent at the gay bar. I was feeling just fine.

Then one day, when the plant whistle blew, silence hung heavy in the air. I looked from face to face. Something was up. Muriel spoke first. "Today you start the song," she suggested casually, "any song you want." I looked around in disbelief, but she was serious. I felt the blood rise in my face. I didn't want to call attention to myself. I didn't want to hear my voice rise alone, even for a minute, above the sounds of the machines and the other women. In fact, I realized I felt ashamed of my own voice. "I can't," I protested. I felt near tears. No one said a word. They just kept working in silence. By lunchtime I realized there would be no songs until I began one.

Why? I wondered. *Why are the women doing this to me? Are they making fun of me?* I knew it wasn't true. They noticed how quietly I mouthed the words to songs. They were inviting my voice to join theirs. They were honoring me again.

That night I lay awake in panic. The daily routine wouldn't resume until I sang alone. My throat clenched at the very idea. I thought about calling in sick, but it was too cowardly and it wouldn't change anything. No one was going to forget I was asked to start the first song. Besides, the next day was Christmas Eve. I would lose my holiday pay if I called in sick. And immediately after the holiday I was eligible to join the union.

In the morning I tried to act normal at work. I was welcomed as usual. When Yvonne came in, I wondered if she had heard. Her smile let me know she had. The whistle blew. Each of us punched in. We took our places on the line. The tension was thick. I cleared my throat several times. Muriel watched her hands while she worked; she smiled gently.

This was it. I would try to find my voice and be proud of it. After several false starts my voice began to rise, singing the song I loved most—the first song I'd learned. Almost immediately the other women lifted their voices up with mine to spare me any pain. We all smiled at each other and sang with tears in our eyes.

After lunch the foreman called me into his office and handed me a pink slip. "Sorry," he said. He escorted me to my locker to get my things. I wasn't allowed to say goodbye to anyone.

I actually felt embarrassed about being fired. I knew it was because I was so close to getting into the union. And I knew management had been watching the growing solidarity with great trepidation. But my shame rekindled as I realized the foremen probably heard my voice rising alone in song.

I walked home in the snow. The deep drifts muffled all the sounds of the city. I felt pretty low. Immediately after the holiday I'd have to begin job-hunting all over again. When I got home I hoped the phone would ring. It didn't. I had nothing to look forward to except watching the "Perry Como Christmas Special." That made me feel much worse. Drinking didn't help either, not that it ever did.

I was thinking about going out to the Malibou when I heard footsteps thumping up the stairs. I opened the door. There was Muriel, Yvonne, and some of the other Native women from the plant. They brought me food and a few wrapped presents. They were on their way to a social. I was invited. Muriel watched my face with mock solemnity as she said, "Now you learn to dance." . . .

———

Jim Boney didn't show up for work on Monday. I was glad. I wouldn't have admitted this to anyone, but I was still scared of him. So when he called in sick Monday morning I walked around the plant feeling a little smug.

Jack pulled me off the line and led me to a die cutter, which punched school flash-cards into the shape of decks. Normally one of the guys used a powerful air hose to blow away the trim before it jammed the machine. "The air hose is being fixed," Jack shouted over the roar of the machinery. "You assist Jan when she needs help loading her skids. Every once in a while, you brush the shit off the press, like this." He ran his hand across the face of the die cutter in the split second between punches. "Don't let it jam," he warned me, before he walked away.

Jan looked at the machine and back at me. "Be careful," she cautioned.

I watched the die cutter punch the decks, trying to learn its rhythm like a song. My hand darted out and quickly brushed some of the trim away. I got most of it. My hands were trembling. When you work around machines you grow to respect their mesmerizing power. I tried to stay in sync with the punch press. Just once my hand was slow. Just once was all it took.

It happened so fast. One moment my fingers were all connected to me. The next moment I could feel my ring finger lying against my palm. My blood spurted in an arc across the machine, the decks of cards stacked on skids, and the wall in front of me.

I tried not to look at my left hand, but I did. My stomach heaved before my mind could even understand what my eyes saw. I couldn't have been heard over the thunder of the machines, but it didn't matter. I couldn't make a sound. Everything took place in slow motion. Jan waved her arms and shouted. People came near but froze in horror.

It occurred to me I should go to a hospital. I knew I couldn't drive my motorcycle. As I walked to the door I wondered if I had enough bus fare. Walter and Duffy ran after me.

The next thing I remember was being in a car. Walter had his arm around me. Duffy was driving and he kept turning around to look for a sign from Walter. My whole hand was bound up in a red-soaked cloth. I felt so sorry for my finger that hot tears of grief ran down my face. I was thinking maybe I should bury it. I wondered who I should invite.

Walter lifted my injured hand up high with one of his large, gentle hands, and held me tightly against him with the other. I shook violently. "It's gonna be OK, honey," he crooned. "I seen a lot of these things happen. It's gonna be alright."

The next thing I knew I was lying on an operating table. I panicked. What if they took my clothes off? There was no one around. A fly buzzed around me and landed on my hand. My body lurched. The fly circled and landed again. This time as my injured hand jerked, my finger seemed to move in a different direction. I passed out.

It was Duffy's face I saw as I drifted back to consciousness. He was smiling, but he looked upset, too. "Duffy," I whispered, "where's my finger?"

He winced. "It's OK, Jess. They saved your finger."

I didn't think it was true. I'd seen lots of movies where they lie to injured people like that. I lifted my head slightly to look at my hand. It was covered in layers of gauze and there was some kind of metal device running from my forearm into the gauze and then emerging at the tip of where my finger would be. Duffy nodded. "Your finger's OK, Jess.

The bone wasn't completely severed." He turned away as he said it. I thought maybe he was going to throw up.

I was still dressed in my bloody work clothes. "Get me out of here, Duffy."

He stopped at the pharmacy to fill my prescriptions and drove me home. When I awoke he was gone. There was a note on the nightstand explaining when I should take the pills. He also left his phone number and said I should call when I woke up. I was relieved to find I was still in my work clothes.

I called him later that night and he raced over. "Jack set you up, Jess." Duffy paced around my kitchen. "Just before he put you on that machine one of the guys saw Kevin removing the safety device. Jack could claim he took it off because the hose was on the blink, but ordering someone to put their hand in it was an out-and-out contract violation."

I had trouble following what Duffy was saying. It wasn't just that my mind was hazy with painkillers, I didn't want to understand.

"But get this, Jess," Duffy bent over the kitchen table and pounded it. "After we took you to the hospital Jack reinstalled the safety device and swears it was on all the time. The bastard set you up, Jess."

I felt woozy with fear. It reminded me of when my parents had me committed, or the cops opened my cell door. So many people in the world had so much power to control and hurt me. I shrugged as though it wasn't important to me. "Look, Duffy, it's over. Besides, the contract's up in two months. We got other things to worry about."

Duffy looked at me like I was crazy, but when he spoke his voice was calm. "No, Jess. We're going to worry a lot about this. We're going to prove what Jack did to you and we're going to tell management either he's out or we all walk out." I marveled at the idea that straight people would stand up for me, or for any he-she.

"You know," Duffy added, "I don't think I really realized how hard it is for you. I know what jerks the guys at work can be sometimes." He leaned up against the sink and folded his arms. "But when I went to the hospital with you, I saw how they treated you, how they talked about you," he rubbed his face. When he looked back up at me, I saw tears in his eyes. "I felt so helpless, you know? I kept yelling at them that you were a human being, that you mattered, and it was like they weren't even listening to me. I couldn't do anything to help you and I couldn't make them take care of you the way I wanted, you know?"

I nodded. I did know. And now I knew that Duffy did too.

Susan Eisenberg (b. 1950)

Boston-based master electrician and poet, Susan Eisenberg has devoted a good part of her life to studying, supporting, and writing about women who work in the skilled construction trades. When federal law under President Jimmy Carter required that construction sites accept women workers, Eisenberg was one of the first to enter and complete the four-year apprenticeship program of the International Brotherhood of Electrical Workers. Her experiences with the difficulties and rewards of that work, as well as the hazards of being a gender pioneer, form the core of her first book of poems, *It's a Good Thing I'm Not Macho* (1984). Responses to the book included letters from women workers in other trades around the country, work-stories swapped at readings of her work, and an invitation in 1986 to the Split Shift Colloquium on the "New Work Writing," organized by the Vancouver Industrial Writers Union. "I realized how strong the commonality of experience among us was," she writes. "The ongoing dialogue I have had with the national community of tradeswomen over the years has been invaluable to me as a writer." After leaving the trade herself, she has continued to write poems rooted in these shared experiences, many of them published in the journal *Tradeswomen* and collected in her 1998 book *Pioneering: Poems from the Construction Site*. More recent poems address the dangers of this work, the hostility encountered by women on the job, and the valued mentorship of exceptional male coworkers. Since 1987, Eisenberg has been a member of the faculty of the College of Public and Community Service at the University of Massachusetts, Boston, where she teaches courses in creative writing, literature, and argument, with a special focus on labor and women's studies. She is the author of the nonfiction book *We'll Call You if We Need You: Experiences of Women Working Construction* (1998) based on interviews with women carpenters, electricians, ironworkers, painters, and plumbers. Her most recent publications are *Greatest Hits—1982–2003* (2003) and the essay, "Still Waiting After All These Years: Women in the U.S. Construction Industry."

HOMAGE

Electricity! at its core
   poetic: the earth herself
an enormous generator.

Electricity! at its core
5   political: the human animal
a current-carrying conductor.

HANGING IN, SOLO (SO WHAT'S IT LIKE TO BE THE ONLY FEMALE ON THE JOB?)

On the sunshine rainbow days
womanhood
clothes me in a fuchsia velour jumpsuit
and crowns me with a diamond hardhat.
5   I flare my peacock feathers
and fly through the day's work.

Trombones sizzle
as my drill glides through cement walls
   through steel beams.
10   Bundles of pipe rise through the air
at the tilt
     of my thumb.
Everything I do
      is perfect.

15   The female of the species
advances 10 spaces and
takes an extra turn.

On the mudcold-gray-no-
sun-in-a-week days womanhood
20 weighs me down in colorless arctic fatigues
hands me an empty survival kit
and binds my head in an iron hardhat
three sizes too small.
I burrow myself mole-like into my work, but
25 my tampax leaks
my diamond-tip bit burns out after one hole
my offsets are backwards
all of my measurements are wrong.

At each mistake, a shrill siren
30 alerts all tradesmen on the job
to come laugh at me.
Everything I do
        must be redone.

The female of the species
35 loses her next turn
and picks a penalty card.

On most days, those
partly sunny days that bridge
the rainbow sunshine days and the mudcold-
40 gray days
        womanhood outfits me
in a flannel shirt and jeans
and hands me a hardhat just like
everyone else's. I go about my work
45 like a giraffe foraging the high branches:
stretching myself comfortably.
As I hang lighting fixtures and make splices
I sing to myself and tell myself stories.
Everything I do
50   is competent enough.

The female of the species
advances 1 space
and awaits her next turn.

First Day on a New Jobsite

Never again a first day like the
First Day
        that Very First one,
when only the sternest vigilance
5 kept the right foot following the left

Erica Harding, Apprentice Electrician, International Brotherhood of Electrical Workers (IBEW), Local #43, "Erica's Armor." *Reprinted with permission from unseenamerica, Bread and Roses, Local 1199 (SEIU).*

following the right following the left,
each step a decision, a victory of
willpower over fear, future over past.
Margaret's out there/Keep going/
10 *She's been working a few*
weeks already/she's managing/
*Keep going/*The legs buck
LA/Seattle/Detroit/women passing
through construction site gates for the
15 *first time/Keep going/*Right following
Go home if you want!/But
tomorrow/What'll you do for work
*tomorrow?/*left following right up to
the gate
20   where a man hands me hardhat and
goggles and points me toward a trailer
where the conversation
                                      stops
                                      as I enter:
25 *Well, what'll we talk about now.*
Can't talk about girls.

And then Ronnie, the one with beady eyes
and a gimp leg, who knows for a fact—
one of the girl apprentices
30   is a stripper in the Zone—

says to my partner
                    Give me your apprentice
and I follow him, tripping over cinderblocks,
to a small room
35   where he points to the ceiling:
I need some hangers 11 inches off the ceiling/
Here's the Hilti/
The rod and strut are in the corner/
The ceiling's marked where I want
40 *holes drilled* and leaves
                         without
                         explaining
                         hanger
                         rod
45   strut
or seeing that the bit on the heavy drill
barely reaches
                    the x-marks on the ceiling
when I stand tiptoe on the ladder's
50 top step.

                    *   *   *

Knowing which words to use
    what jokes to banter
    how to glide the body through dangers
        without knocking anything
55   or anyone;
learning to speak first
    and define the territory
                    of conversation.
Passing.

                    *   *   *

60 Another
            first day: the job new
the workers all strangers, all men
myself the only "female"
    and yet
65 we find, almost easily, the language
that is common:
    —*Get me some 4-inch squares*
        with three-quarter k-o's——
    —*Need any couplings or connectors?*
70 —*No, but grab some clips and c-clamps*
        and some half-inch quarter-twenties.
Passwords.
    —*You know what you're doing in a panel?*
    —*Sure.*
75 Mechanic to mechanic.
Never again a first day like the
First Day.

WIRETALK

Working three floors apart
two mechanics
         at either end of a pipe
feed and pull in meter,
5   keeping time
through a morse code of yanks and tugs:
fingertips
         against the vocal chords of wire.

Dagoberto Gilb (b. 1950)

Fiction writer and essayist Dagoberto Gilb grew up in the South-Central section of Los Angeles, the son of a Chicana mother who had immigrated illegally from Mexico City and an ex-Marine father of German descent. He began writing in "personal notebooks" while a student at the University of California, where he obtained degrees in philosophy and religious studies. After college, Gilb made a living for sixteen years as a construction worker, twelve of those years as a journeyman carpenter with the United Brotherhood of Carpenters. He says of this period, "For me, a guy who likes to write, it was great. I could work six months and then take off for three and write some stories." Publication was a long time coming, however, since many literary journals considered his stories about the daily lives of working-class Mexican Americans to be "too colloquial." Recognition came with the publication of *The Magic of Blood*, the collection from which "Romero's Shirt" is taken, which won a PEN/Hemingway Award for first fiction in 1993. Ray Gonzales, writing in *The Nation*, praised Gilb's stories as "written in fresh, startling language that says, 'I don't care. This is how it is.'" Gilb is the author of two other collections of stories—*Winners on the Pass Line* (1985) and *Woodcuts of Women* (2001)—a novel, *The Last Known Residence of Mickey Acuna* (1994), set in a YMCA in El Paso, and a collection of essays, *Gritos* (2003). He teaches creative writing at Southwest Texas State University and is a frequent contributor to the *New York Times* and National Public Radio.

ROMERO'S SHIRT

Juan Romero, a man not unlike many in this country, has had jobs in factories, shops, and stores. He has painted houses, dug ditches, planted trees, hammered, sawed, bolted, snaked pipes, picked cotton and chile and pecans, each and all for wages. Along the way he has married and raised his children and several years ago he finally arranged it so that his money might pay for the house he and his family live in. He is still more than twenty years away from being the owner. It is a modest house even by El Paso standards. The building, in an adobe style, is made of stone which is painted white, though the paint is gradually chipping off or being absorbed by the rock. It has two bedrooms, a den which is used as another, a small dining area, a living room, a kitchen, one bathroom, and a garage which, someday, he plans to turn into another place to live. Although in a development facing a paved street and in a neighborhood, it has the appearance of being on almost half an acre. At the front is a garden of cactus—nopal, ocotillo, and agave—and there are weeds that grow tall with yellow flowers which seed into thorn-hard burrs. The rest is dirt and rocks of various sizes, some of which have been lined up to form a narrow path out of the graded dirt, a walkway to the front porch—where, under a tile and one-by tongue and groove overhang, are a wooden chair and a love seat, covered by an old bedspread, its legless frame on the red cement slab. Once the porch looked onto oak trees. Two of them are dried-out stumps; the remaining one has a limb or two which still can produce leaves, but with so many amputations, its future is irreversible. Romero seldom runs water through a garden hose, though in the back yard some patchy grass can almost seem suburban, at least to him, when he does. Near the corner of his land, in the front, next to the sidewalk, is a juniper shrub, his only bright green plant, and Romero does not want it to yellow and die, so he makes special efforts on its behalf, washing off dust, keeping its leaves neatly pruned and shaped.

These days Romero calls himself a handyman. He does odd jobs, which is exactly how he advertises—"no job too small"—in the throwaway paper. He hangs wallpaper and doors, he paints, lays carpet, does just about anything someone will call and ask him to do. It doesn't earn him much, and sometimes it's barely enough, but he's his own boss, and he's had so many bad jobs over those other years, ones no more dependable, he's learned that this suits him. At one time Romero did want more, and he'd believed that he could have it simply through work, but no matter what he did his children still had to be born at the county hospital. Even years later it was there that his oldest son went for serious medical treatment because Romero couldn't afford the private hospitals. He tried not to worry about how he earned his money. In Mexico, where his parents were born and he spent much of his youth, so many things weren't available, and any work which allowed for food, clothes, and housing was to be honored—by the standards there, Romero lived well. Except this wasn't Mexico, and even though there were those who did worse even here, there were many who did better and had more, and a young Romero too often felt ashamed by what he saw as his failure. But time passed, and he got older. As he saw it, he didn't live in poverty, and *here*, he finally came to realize, was where he was, where he and his family were going to stay. Life in El Paso was much like the land—hard, but one could make do with what was offered. Just as his parents had, Romero always thought it was a beautiful place for a home.

Yet people he knew left—to Houston, Dallas, Los Angeles, San Diego, Denver, Chicago—and came back for holidays with stories of high wages and acquisition. And more and more people crossed the river, in rags, taking work, his work, at any price. Romero constantly had to discipline himself by remembering the past, how his parents lived; he had to teach himself to appreciate what he did have. His car, for example, he'd kept up since his early twenties. He'd had it painted three times in that period and he worked on it so devotedly that even now it was in as good a condition as almost any car could be. For his children he tried to offer more—an assortment of clothes for his daughter, lots of toys for his sons. He denied his wife nothing, but she was a woman who asked for little. For himself, it was much less. He owned some work clothes and T-shirts necessary for his jobs as well as a set of good enough, he thought, shirts he'd had since before the car. He kept up a nice pair of custom boots, and in a closet hung a pair of slacks for a wedding or baptism or important mass. He owned two jackets, a leather one from Mexico and a warm nylon one for cold work days. And he owned a wool plaid Pendleton shirt, his favorite piece of clothing, which he'd bought right after the car and before his marriage because it really was good-looking besides being functional. He wore it anywhere and everywhere with confidence that its quality would always be both in style and appropriate.

The border was less than two miles below Romero's home, and he could see, down the dirt street which ran alongside his property, the desert and mountains of Mexico. The street was one of the few in the city which hadn't yet been paved. Romero liked it that way, despite the run-off problems when heavy rains passed by, as they had the day before this day. A night wind had blown hard behind the rains, and the air was so clean he could easily see buildings in Juárez. It was sunny, but a breeze told him to put on his favorite shirt before he pulled the car up alongside the house and dragged over the garden hose to wash it, which was something he still enjoyed doing as much as anything else. He was organized, had a special bucket, a special sponge, and he used warm water from the kitchen sink. When he started soaping the car he worried about getting his shirt sleeves wet, and once he was moving around he decided a T-shirt would keep him warm enough. So he took off the wool shirt and draped it, conspicuously, over the juniper near him, at the corner of his property. He thought that if he couldn't help but see it, he couldn't forget it, and forgetting something outside was losing it. He lived near a school, and teenagers passed by all the time, and also there was regular foot-traffic—many people walked the sidewalk in front of his house, many who had no work.

After the car was washed, Romero went inside and brought out the car wax. Waxing his car was another thing he still liked to do, especially on a weekday like this one when he was by himself, when no one in his family was home. He could work faster, but he took his time, spreading with a damp cloth, waiting, then wiping off the crust with a dry cloth. The exterior done, he went inside the car and waxed the dash, picked up some trash on the floorboard, cleaned out the glove compartment. Then he went for some pliers he kept in a toolbox in the garage, returned and began to wire up the rear license plate which had lost a nut and bolt and was hanging awkwardly. As he did this, he thought of other things he might do when he finished, like prune the juniper. Except his old shears had broken, and he hadn't found another used pair, because he wouldn't buy them new.

An old man walked up to him carrying a garden rake, a hoe, and some shears. He asked Romero if there was some yard work needing to be done. After spring, tall weeds grew in many yards, but it seemed a dumb question this time of year, particularly since there was obviously so little ever to be done in Romero's yard. But Romero listened to the old man. There were still a few weeds over there, and he could rake the dirt so it'd be even and level, he could clip that shrub, and probably there was something in the back if he were to look. Romero was usually brusque with requests such as these, but he found the old man unique and likeable and he listened and finally asked how much he would want for all those tasks. The old man thought as quickly as he spoke and threw out a number. Ten. Romero repeated the number, questioningly, and the old man backed up, saying well, eight, seven. Romero asked if that was for everything. Yes sir, the old man said, excited that he'd seemed to catch a customer. Romero asked if he would cut the juniper for three dollars. The old man kept his eyes on the evergreen, disappointed for a second, then thought better of it. Okay, okay, he said, but, I've been walking all day, you'll give me lunch? The old man rubbed his striped cotton shirt at his stomach.

Romero like the old man and agreed to it. He told him how he should follow the shape which was already there, to cut it evenly, to take a few inches off all of it just like a haircut. Then Romero went inside, scrambled enough eggs and chile and cheese for both of them and rolled it all in some tortillas. He brought out a beer.

The old man was clearly grateful, but since his gratitude was keeping the work from getting done—he might talk an hour about his little ranch in Mexico, about his little turkeys and his pig—Romero excused himself and went inside. The old man thanked Romero for the food, and, as soon as he was finished with the beer, went after the work sincerely. With dull shears—he sharpened them, so to speak, against a rock wall—the old man snipped garishly, hopping and jumping around the bush, around and around. It gave Romero such great pleasure to watch that this was all he did from his front window.

The work didn't take long, so, as the old man was raking up the clippings, Romero brought out a five-dollar bill. He felt that the old man's dancing around that bush, in those baggy old checkered pants, was more inspiring than religion, and a couple of extra dollars was a cheap price to see old eyes whiten like a boy's.

The old man was so pleased that he invited Romero to that little ranch of his in Mexico where he was sure they could share some aguardiente, or maybe Romero could buy a turkey from him—they were skinny but they could be fattened—but in any case they could enjoy a bottle of tequila together, with some sweet lemons. The happy old man swore he would come back no matter what, for he could do many things for Romero at his beautiful home. He swore he would return, maybe in a week or two, for surely there was work that needed to be done in the back yard.

Romero wasn't used to feeling so virtuous. He so often was disappointed, so often dwelled on the difficulties of life, that he had become hard, guarding against compassion and generosity. So much so that he'd even become spare with his words, even with his family. His wife whispered to the children that this was because he was tired, and, since it wasn't untrue, he accepted it as the explanation too. It spared him that worry, and from having to discuss why he liked working weekends and taking a day off during the week, like this one. But now an old man had made Romero wish his family were there with him so he could give as much, *more*, to them too, so he could watch their spin around dances—he'd missed so many—and Romero swore he would take them all into Juárez that night for dinner. He might even convince them to take a day, maybe two, for a drive to his uncle's house in Chihuahua instead, because he'd promised that so many years ago—so long ago they probably thought about somewhere else by now, like San Diego, or Los Angeles. Then he'd take them there! They'd go for a week, spend whatever it took. No expense could be so great, and if happiness was as easy as some tacos and a five-dollar bill, then how stupid it had been of him not to have offered it all this time.

Romero felt so good, felt such relief, he napped on the couch. When he woke up he immediately remembered his shirt, that it was already gone before the old man had even arrived—he remembered they'd walked around the juniper before it was cut. Nevertheless, the possibility that the old man took it wouldn't leave Romero's mind. Since he'd never believed in letting down, giving into someone like that old man, the whole experience became suspect. Maybe it was part of some ruse which ended with the old man taking his shirt, some food, money. This was how Romero thought. Though he held a hope that he'd left it somewhere else, that it was a lapse of memory on his part—he went outside, inside, looked everywhere twice, then one more time after that—his cynicism had flowered, colorful and bitter.

Understand that it was his favorite shirt, that he'd never thought of replacing it and that its loss was all Romero could keep his mind on, though he knew very well it wasn't a son, or a daughter, or a wife, or a mother or father, not a disaster of any kind. It was a simple shirt, in the true value of things not very much to lose. But understand also that Romero was a good man who tried to do what was right and who would harm no one willfully. Understand that Romero was a man who had taught himself to not care, to not want, to not desire for so long that he'd lost many words, avoided many people, kept to himself, alone, almost always, even when his wife gave him his meals. Understand that it was his favorite shirt and though no more than that, for him it was no less. Then understand how he felt like a fool paying that old man who, he considered, might even have taken it, like a fool for feeling so friendly and generous, happy, when the shirt was already gone, like a fool for having all those and these thoughts for the love of a wool shirt, like a fool for not being able to stop thinking them all, but especially the one reminding him that this was what he had always believed in, that loss was what he was most prepared for.

And so then you might understand why he began to stare out the window of his home, waiting for someone to walk by absently with it on, for the thief to pass by, careless. He kept a watch out the window as each of his children came in, then his wife. He told them only what had happened and, as always, they left him alone. He stared out that window onto the dirt street, past the ocotillos and nopales and agaves, the junipers and oaks and mulberries in front of other homes of brick or stone, painted or not, past them to the buildings in Juárez, and he watched the horizon darken and the sky light up with the moon and stars, and the land spread with shimmering lights, so bright in the dark blot of night. He heard dogs barking until another might bark farther away, and then another, back and forth like that, the small rectangles and squares of their fences plotted out distinctly in his mind's eye as his lids closed. Then he heard a gust of wind bend around his house, and then came the train, the metal rhythm getting closer until it was as close as it could be, the steel pounding the earth like a beating heart, until it diminished and then faded away and then left the air to silence, to its quiet and dark, so still it was like death, or rest, sleep, until he could hear a grackle, and then another gust of wind, and then finally a car.

He looked in on his daughter still so young, so beautiful, becoming a woman who would leave that bed for another, his sons still boys when they were asleep, who dreamed like men when they were awake, and his wife, still young in his eyes in the morning shadows of their bed.

Romero went outside. The juniper had been cut just as he'd wanted it. He got cold and came back in and went to the bed and blankets his wife kept so clean, so neatly arranged as she slept under them without him, and he lay down beside her.

Joy Harjo (b. 1951)

S outhwestern poet, screenwriter, and musician, Joy Harjo was born and raised in Tulsa, Oklahoma, as a full member of the Muskogee tribe. Her extended family includes a number of traditional wordsmiths and artists; one grandfather was a noted Creek Indian preacher, and a grandmother and great-aunt were skilled Muskogee painters. Harjo left home to attend high school at Santa Fe's Institute of Native American Arts, where she studied painting, theater, and dance. It was as a senior at the University of New Mexico that she switched from visual arts to writing, making a "decision to work with words, and the power of words." Asked in a 1993 interview, "What can you do in poetry that painting could not achieve?" Harjo replied, "Speak directly in a language that was meant to destroy us." Her talent and conviction took her, a single mother with two young children, to the University of Iowa's Writing Workshop, where she earned an MFA in 1978. Harjo is the author of seven books of poems, including *What Moon Drove Me to This* (1979), *She Had Some Horses* (1983), *In Mad Love and War* (1990), *A Map to the Next World* (2000), and *How We Became Human: New and Selected Poems, 1975–2001* (2004). She is also coeditor, with Gloria Bird, of *Reinventing the Enemy's Language* (1998), an anthology of Native American Women's literature. As a singer and saxophonist, Harjo performs many of her poems to music on such discs as *Letter From the End of the 20th Century* (1997), with her band Poetic Justice, and *Native Joy for Real* (2004), which includes "The Woman Hanging From the 13th Floor."

The poems that follow express two of Harjo's major themes: the particular struggles of urban Native peoples, especially women, and the resilience and hope for renewal embodied in the collectivity of tribe and family. Harjo has been honored with numerous awards, including a Lifetime achievement Award from the Native Writers Circle of the Americas.

THE WOMAN HANGING FROM THE THIRTEENTH FLOOR WINDOW

She is the woman hanging from the 13th floor
window. Her hands are pressed white against the
concrete molding of the tenement building. She
hangs from the 13th floor window in east Chicago,
5　with a swirl of birds over her head. They could
be a halo, or a storm of glass waiting to crush her.

She thinks she will be set free.

The woman hanging from the 13th floor window
on the east side of Chicago is not alone.
10　She is a woman of children, of the baby, Carlos,
and of Margaret, and of Jimmy who is the oldest.
She is her mother's daughter and her father's son.
She is several pieces between the two husbands
she has had. She is all the women of the apartment
15　building who stand watching her, watching themselves.

When she was young she ate wild rice on scraped down
plates in warm wood rooms. It was in the farther
north and she was the baby then. They rocked her.
She sees Lake Michigan lapping at the shores of
20　herself. It is a dizzy hole of water and the rich
live in tall glass houses at the edge of it. In some
places Lake Michigan speaks softly, here, it just sputters
and butts itself against the asphalt. She sees
other buildings just like hers. She sees other
25　women hanging from many-floored windows
counting their lives in the palms of their hands
and in the palms of their children's hands.

She is the woman hanging from the 13th floor window
on the Indian side of town. Her belly is soft from
30　her children's births, her worn levis swing down below
her waist, and then her feet, and then her heart.
She is dangling.

The woman hanging from the 13th floor hears voices.
They come to her in the night when the lights have gone
35　dim. Sometimes they are little cats mewing and scratching
at the door, sometimes they are her grandmother's voice,
and sometimes they are gigantic men of light whispering
to her to get up, to get up, to get up. That's when she wants
to have another child to hold onto in the night, to be able
40　to fall back into dreams.

And the woman hanging from the 13th floor window
hears other voices. Some of them scream out from below
for her to jump, they would push her over. Others cry softly
from the sidewalks, pull their children up like flowers and
45   gather
      them into their arms. They would help her, like themselves.

But she is the woman hanging from the 13th floor window,
and she knows she is hanging by her own fingers, her
own skin, her own thread of indecision.
50   She thinks of Carlos, of Margaret, of Jimmy.
      She thinks of her father, and of her mother.
      She thinks of all the women she has been, of all
      the men. She thinks of the color of her skin, and
      of Chicago streets, and of waterfalls and pines.
55   She thinks of moonlight nights, and of cool spring storms.
      Her mind chatters like neon and northside bars.
      She thinks of the 4 a.m. lonelinesses that have folded
      her up like death, discordant, without logical and
      beautiful conclusion. Her teeth break off at the edges.
60   She would speak.

The woman hangs from the 13th floor window crying for
the lost beauty of her own life. She sees the
sun falling west over the grey plane of Chicago.
She thinks she remembers listening to her own life
65   break loose, as she falls from the 13th floor
      window on the east side of Chicago, or as she
      climbs back up to claim herself again.

PERHAPS THE WORLD ENDS HERE

The world begins at a kitchen table. No matter what,
we must eat to live.

The gifts of earth are brought and prepared, set on the
table. So it has been since creation, and it will go on.
5   We chase chickens or dogs away from it. Babies teethe
     at the corners. They scrape their knees under it.

It is here that children are given instructions on what
it means to be human. We make men at it,
we make women.

10   At this table we gossip, recall enemies and the ghosts
     of lovers.

Our dreams drink coffee with us as they put their arms
around our children. They laugh with us at our poor
falling-down selves and as we put ourselves back
15   together once again at the table.

This table has been a house in the rain, an umbrella
in the sun.

Wars have begun and ended at this table. It is a place
to hide in the shadow of terror. A place to celebrate
20   the terrible victory.

We have given birth on this table, and have prepared
our parents for burial here.

At this table we sing with joy, with sorrow.
We pray of suffering and remorse.
25   We give thanks.

Perhaps the world will end at the kitchen table,
while we are laughing and crying,
eating of the last sweet bite.

Jeanne Bryner (b. 1951)

Jeanne Bryner's family was part of Appalachia's outward migration. She was born in Waynesburg, Pennsylvania, and lived in West Virginia until age four. Her father, who began his working life as a fourteen-year-old coal miner, moved the family to Ohio when he found work in a steel mill. "When I think of my sense of location, it's fragmented," Bryner says. One of five children, she grew up in a crowded apartment in the projects of an Ohio steel mill town. The first in her family to get a professional education and university degree, Bryner is a registered nurse with specializations in pediatric, intensive, and emergency care. She is also an award-winning writer, who teaches writing workshops in cancer support groups, nursing homes, and universities. Her fiction, memoir, and poetry have been adapted for performance. Her books include *Breathless* (1995), *Blind Horse* (1999), *Eclipse* (2003), and *Tenderly Lift Me: Nurses Honored, Celebrated, and Remembered* (2004). She has also edited two collections of writing, photographs, and drawings by women who are living with cancer. About her dual life as a writer and nurse she says, "I love to write and dance around the light of a new poem, but I don't see a time when I'll quit nursing. I've seen men and women and children used as rags, and there's nothing romantic about such harshness. I try to work through angst with my writing. Who doesn't?" The poetry selections that follow are from her collection, *Blind Horse*.

THE STORY OF MY VILLAGE

Here is the story I write
about the men in my village,
my love for watching water.
The river was here first
5   and miles of hard road.
It is a small thing to believe
in order, believe in reaching.

My people came from blue mountains,
always the tribe sends men ahead
10   to build the fire. To describe this,
I must name our fathers: Clark,
Jenkins, Furriatti, who rose
with dawn, settled this valley.

Other men study oceans, handle
15   great nets, learn music of tides.
Because our river was here,
the steel mill came.
It isn't necessary to describe
its arms. I will say it cradled
20   our men, a poison wet nurse.

We were fragile and strange,
our men lost their language.
To describe this, I should name
their sickness: whiskey, wheezing,
25   tumors. Coils deafened; men grew numb.
They could not remember
the light of clear day.

One morning, big bosses inspected
30   our mill like Utah's desert
after the bomb tests—it was unfit.
They locked gates. To describe this,
I count what remains: ricocheting names
coughing in graveyards,
35   the thing that came first, our river,
and miles and miles of hard road.

MILEAGE

A few years near the blast furnace and every guy looks alike.
Thomas Geoghegan

Father had an eighth-grade education,
he'd worked the coal mines, didn't loathe
boxy darkness of our small garage,
where after his shift and before supper
5   men brought their cars:
the milkman's sedan, Ramblers, Chevys,
dying Fords driven by his union brothers.

After a full day, lying down is hard,
a barn with no heat, a father,
10   his door always closed, a smithy
in carbon-monoxide apron
fitting brakes like shoes
to the rim of hooves. They paid
him a little at a time.

15 He never whistled or hummed,
    but studied the black congestion
    beneath each hood, an old midwife,
    he felt the gush of warm fluids
    settle like blood on his shirt, trousers,
20 and shoes. Behind vapors, his wrench
    pawed heater hoses, partial rot of fan belts.

    Here was the muddled space of living
    below the surface, cells bound with conflicting
    loyalties. It's clearer now why he kept
25 a bottle hidden in his shop rags,
    rain to wet the brown leaf's membrane,
    a needle to ease the pain of fixing
    another's trouble, something to dull
    the thought of wanting the jack to fall.

RELEASE OF THE SPIRIT

    Even if we say the lives of ordinary people
    may be the dandelions blooming, coming
    always back, year after year,
    who will believe us?

5   We are the children raised in a town
    at the bottom of the ocean, an ocean
    which was never named, and our mill
    was a Spanish galleon destined to go down.

    Wasps humming in the guard shanty
10 are the kind voices of workers on the job,
    they let the sun pass through trembling
    on its knees. Is it wrong to lift a lantern,

    to search what's left of the wreck?
    Things keep calling us: the parking lot's
15 gray face where wind fingers the grass
    like a widow counting her pension—

    thin, green bills—and rows of steel dies
    sit mute, old men in robes above a chess board.
    How can we write the story of such a journey
20 with anything but blue ink?

    We have signed a contract with a no-strike clause.
    Even if we claim there were no hard times
    or hunger or fear of tomorrow,
    who'd believe us?

25 We are the children whose fathers learned
    the world is flat
    after work there's nothing,
    but the heart's quiet roar.

Earl Dotter, Detroit, Michigan, 1980. *Reprinted with permission by Earl Dotter, Photojournalist, Digital Stock Photography Image Library.*

BLUE COLLAR

You must change your life.
Rilke

We know, we surely must know
there are moments before explosions,
before any body count, when breaking
windows and screaming might have helped.

5   Serious bargaining over the old contract:
human dignity and ruling by fear.
No simple answers exist,
but when they tell you, *They got greedy*;

see, now it's gone, it's all gone.
10   What they really mean is, *it's OK
to let some furnaces go cold,
some children go hungry.*

Did your teachers ever make you memorize
the names of coal strikes? steel leaders?
15   tell you the story of the Triangle Shirtwaist Company?
the chicken factory in Hamlet, NC?

Learn the Gettysburg Address,
the Pledge of Allegiance,
the Preamble to the Constitution;
20   *study hard, and you may move up,* they said.

But the rules are the rules,
justice doesn't wear a flannel shirt.
Without the working class,
what is America? What is America?

25   Where are the great studies on buried miners,
burned women, displaced steel workers,
the lost towns gutted like deer,
people left to choose between the river and the sky?

Kate Rushin (b. 1951)

Kate Rushin grew up in the tiny African American community of Lawnside, New Jersey, a town that came into being after the Civil War, its founders having moved north with the help of abolitionists in the Philadelphia area. Her sense of being a community artist, working to capture in her poems "the faces, voices, and stories of African American women, family and history," is rooted in the support she experienced in her hometown and her desire to extend that sense of connectedness by communicating among people across differences of race and class. Her approach to writing was formed within the Black Arts movement of the 1970s, with Gwendolyn Brooks, Alice Walker, and especially poet Audre Lorde as major influences. The poem that follows is the title piece from *The Black Back-Ups*, published in 1993 by the small feminist press, Firebrand Books. Rushin has spent many years as a poet-in-the-schools in Massachusetts and was the Connecticut Poetry Circuit Poet in 1997. She teaches at Wesleyan University, where she is a member of the Center for African American Studies.

THE BLACK BACK-UPS

This is dedicated to Merry Clayton, Fontella Bass, Vonetta
Washington, Carolyn Franklin, Yolanda McCullough,
Carolyn Willis, Gwen Guthrie, Helaine Harris, and Darlene
Love. This is for all of the Black women who sang back-up
5   for Elvis Presley, John Denver, James Taylor, Lou Reed.
Etc. Etc. Etc.

I said Hey Babe
Take a Walk on the Wild Side
I said Hey Babe
10   *Take a Walk on the Wild Side*

And the colored girls say
Do dodo do do dodododo
Do dodo do do dodododo
Do dodo do do dodododo ooooo

15   This is for my Great-Grandmother Esther, my Grandmother
     Addie, my grandmother called Sister, my Great-Aunt
     Rachel, my Aunt Hilda, my Aunt Tine, my Aunt Breda,
     my Aunt Gladys, my Aunt Helen, my Aunt Ellie,
     my Cousin Barbara, my Cousin Dottie and my Great-Great-
20   Aunt Vene.

     This is dedicated to all of the Black women riding on buses
     and subways back and forth to the Main Line, Haddonfield,
     Cherry Hill and Chevy Chase. This is for the women who
     spend their summers in Rockport, Newport, Cape Cod and
25   Camden, Maine. This is for the women who open those
     bundles of dirty laundry sent home from those ivy-covered
     campuses.

     My Great-Aunt Rachel worked for the Carters
     Ever since I can remember
30   There was *The Boy*
     Whose name I never knew
     And there was *The Girl*
     Whose name was Jane

     Great-Aunt Rachel brought Jane's dresses for me to wear
35   Perfectly Good Clothes
     And I should've been glad to get them
     Perfectly Good Clothes
     No matter they didn't fit quite right
     Perfectly Good Clothes
40   Brought home in a brown paper bag
     With an air of accomplishment and excitement
     Perfectly Good Clothes
     Which I hated

     At school
45   In Ohio
     I swear to Gawd
     There was always somebody
     Telling me that the only person
     In their whole house
50   Who listened and understood them
     Despite the money and the lessons
     Was the housekeeper
     And I knew it was true
     But what was I supposed to say

55   I know it's true
     I watch her getting off the train
     Moving slowly toward the Country Squire
     With their uniform in her shopping bag
     And the closer she gets to the car

60   The more the two little kids jump and laugh
     And even the dog is about to
     Turn inside out
     Because they just can't wait until she gets there
     Edna Edna Wonderful Edna

65   But Aunt Edna to me, or Gram, or Miz Johnson, or
     Sister Johnson on Sundays
     And the colored girls say
     Do dodo do do dodododo
     Do dodo do do dodododo
70   *Do dodo do do dodododo ooooo*

     This is for Hattie McDaniel, Butterfly McQueen
     Ethel Waters
     Sapphire
     Saphronia
75   Ruby Begonia
     Aunt Jemima
     Aunt Jemima on the Pancake Box
     Aunt Jemima on the Pancake Box?
     AuntJemimaonthepancakebox?
80   Ainchamamaonthepancakebox?
     Ain't chure Mama on the pancake box?

     Mama Mama
     Get off that box
     And come home to me
85   And my Mama leaps off that box
     She swoops down in her nurse's cape
     Which she wears on Sunday
     And for Wednesday night prayer meeting
     And she wipes my forehead
90   And she fans my face
     And she makes me a cup of tea
     And it don't do a thing for my real pain
     Except she is my mama

     Mama Mommy Mammy
95   *Mam-mee Mam-mee*
     I'd Walk a Mill-yon Miles
     For one of your smiles

     This is for the Black Back-Ups
     This is for my mama and your mama
100 My grandma and your grandma

     This is for the thousand thousand Black Back-Ups
     And the colored girls say
     Do   dodo   do do   dodododo
     do   dodo
105 *dodo*
             do
               do

Cherríe Moraga (b. 1952)

Playwright, poet, essayist, editor, teacher, and activist, Cherríe Moraga is among those who pioneered a "Third-World feminism" that, in theory and practice, "walk[s] a freedom road that is both material and metaphysical. Sexual and spiritual. Third-World feminism is about feeding people in all their hungers." Born in Whittier, California, and raised in San Gabriel, Moraga experienced, in her words, "a huge disparity between what I was born into and what I grew to become." The daughter of a Chicana mother and an Anglo father, Moraga describes herself as "La Guera," fair-skinned. As she claimed her identity as a lesbian, Moraga transformed her twoness, her outward identity (white skin/Anglo education) and her interior subjectivity (Chicana mother/women's knowledge) into an integrated, "welded," vision.

She was one of the founders of Kitchen Table: Women of Color Press, which published *This Bridge Called My Back* (1981) (coedited with Gloria Anzaldúa), winner of the Before Columbus Foundation American Book Award in 1986. Her autobiographical *Loving in the War Years: Lo que nunca paso por sus labios* (1983) fuses the poetical and political, the acts of loving and resisting. As a playwright, Moraga moved from the personal voice of the essay to the multiple voices and perspectives of the stage. "Theater," she says, "allows for contradiction to reside among the characters. They show themselves and in the showing the political issues . . . are exposed through the 'living bodies' of the actors." Moraga is a recipient of an NEA Theater Playwriting Fellowship Award and is a significant artist in the Chicano/a Theater movement. Her many plays include *Watsonville: Some Place Not Here* (1996), *Heroes and Saints* (1992), *Shadow of a Man* (1990), and *Giving Up the Ghost* (1989). She has edited or coedited several collections including, *Cuentos/Short Stories by Latinas* (1983). More recently, she wrote about her life as a mother of a son in *Waiting in the Wings: Portrait of Queer Motherhood* (1997). She is an artist in residence at Stanford University.

HEROES AND SAINTS

AUTHOR'S NOTES

Although *Heroes and Saints* is fiction, it came in response to the numerous events that took place in 1988 which brought growing visibility to the United Farm Workers' grape boycott in protest against pesticide poisoning. The greatest public attention came as a result of the 36-day fast by the president of the union, Cesar Chávez, which ended on August 21, 1988. Less than a month later, the vice-president of the union, Dolores Huerta, was brutally beaten by a San Francisco policeman while holding a press conference protesting George Bush's refusal to honor the boycott.

Behind the scenes of these events are the people whose personal tragedy inspired a national political response. In the town of McFarland in the San Joaquin Valley of California, a so-called cancer cluster was discovered. Within a ten-year period from 1978 to 1988, a highly disproportionate number of children were diagnosed with cancer and were born with birth defects. After viewing the UFW's documentary video *The Wrath of Grapes*, which describes the McFarland situation, an image remained in my mind—a child with no arms or legs, born of a farm worker mother. The mother had been picking in pesticide-sprayed fields while her baby was still in the womb. This child became Cerezita, a character who came to me when I wondered of the child's future as we turn into the next century.

I want to thank Luis Valdez for his play *The Shrunken Head of Pancho Villa*, whose head character became, for me, a point of departure. I also wish to thank El Teatro Campesino for allowing me access to their archives on the McFarland situation. I am indebted to Marta Salinas, a mother and one of the chief organizers in McFarland, who opened her home and the homes of other McFarland families to me. The character of Doña Amparo is my tribute to her, as it is to Dolores Huerta, a woman whose courage and relentless commitment to Chicano/a freedom has served as a source of inspiration to two generations of Chicanas.

Finally, I dedicate this play to the memory and legacy of Cesar Chávez.

CHARACTERS

CEREZITA VALLE, *the head*

AMPARO, *the comadre and activista*

ANA PEREZ, *the news reporter*

DOLORES, *the mother*

BONNIE, *a neighbor's child "adopted" by* AMPARO *and* DON GILBERTO

YOLANDA, *the hairdresser sister*

MARIO, *the sometimes-student brother*

FATHER JUAN, *the "half-breed" leftist priest*

DON GILBERTO, *the compadre,* AMPARO's *husband*

POLICEMAN

EL PUEBLO, *the children and mothers of McLaughlin;* THE PEOPLE/PROTESTORS/ AUDIENCE *participating in the struggle (ideally,* EL PUEBLO *should be made up of an ensemble of people from the local Latino community)*

Notes on CEREZITA

CEREZITA *is a head of human dimension, but one who possesses such dignity of bearing and classical Indian beauty she can, at times, assume nearly religious proportions. (The huge head figures of the pre-Columbian Olmecas are an apt comparison.) This image, however, should be contrasted with the very real "humanness" she exhibits on a daily functioning level. Her mobility and its limits are critical aspects of her character. For most of the play,* CEREZITA *is positioned on a rolling, tablelike platform, which will be referred to as her "raite" (ride). It is automated by a button she operates with her chin. The low hum of its motor always anticipates her entrance. The raite can be disengaged at any time by flipping the hold on each wheel and pushing the chin piece out of her reach. At such times,* CEREZITA *has no control and can only be moved by someone manually.*

SETTING

The play takes place in McLaughlin, California, a fictional town in the San Joaquin Valley. The year is 1988.

McLaughlin is a one-exit town off Highway 99. On the east side of the highway sits the old part of town, consisting primarily of a main street of three blocks of small businesses—the auto supply store, a small supermarket, the post office, a laundromat, an old central bank with a recently added automatic teller machine, a storefront Iglesia de Dios and, of course, a video movie rental shop. Crossing the two-lane bridge over Highway 99, a new McLaughlin has emerged. From the highest point of the overpass, a large island of single-family stucco houses and apartments can be seen. The tracts

*were built in the late '70s and reflect a manicured uniformity in appearance, each house with its obli-
gatory crew-cut lawn and one-step front porch. Surrounding the island is an endless sea of agricultural
fields which, like the houses, have been perfectly arranged into neatly juxtaposed rectangles.*

*The hundreds of miles of soil that surround the lives of Valley dwellers should not be confused
with land. What was once land has become dirt, overworked dirt, overirrigated dirt, injected with
deadly doses of chemicals and violated by every manner of ground- and back-breaking machinery. The
people that worked the dirt do not call what was once the land their enemy. They remember what land
used to be and await its second coming.*

*To that end, the grape vineyards, pecan tree orchards and the endless expanse of the Valley's
agricultural life should be constant presences in the play and visibly press upon the intimate life of the
Valle family home. The relentless fog and sudden dramatic sunbreaks in the Valley sky physically alter
the mood of each scene. The Valle family home is modest in furnishing but always neat, and looks
onto EL PUEBLO through a downstage window. Scenes outside the family home can be represented
by simple, movable set pieces, e.g., a park bench for the street scenes, a wheelchair for the hospital, a
set of steps for the church, etc.*

ACT I

Scene One

*At rise in the distance, a group of children wearing calavera masks enters the grape vineyard. They carry
a small, child-size cross which they erect quickly and exit, leaving its stark silhouetted image against
the dawn's light. The barely distinguishable figure of a small child hangs from it. The child's hair and
thin clothing flap in the wind. Moments pass. The wind subsides. The sound of squeaking wheels and
a low, mechanical hum interrupt the silence. CEREZITA enters in shadow. She is transfixed by the
image of the crucifixion. The sun suddenly explodes out of the horizon, bathing both the child and
CEREZITA. CEREZITA is awesome and striking in the light. The crucified child glows, Christlike.
The sound of a low-flying helicopter invades the silence. Its shadow passes over the field. Black out.*

Scene Two

*Mexican rancheras can be heard coming from a small radio in the Valle home. ANA PEREZ is
on the street in front of the house. She holds a microphone and is expertly made up. AMPARO, a
stocky woman in her fifties, is digging holes in the yard next door. She wears heavy-duty rubber gloves.*

ANA PEREZ (*to the "cameraman"*): Bob, is my hair okay? What? . . . I have lipstick?
Where? Here? (*She wets her finger with her tongue, rubs the corner of her lip.*) Okay? . . . Good.
(*Addressing the "camera."*) Hello, I'm Ana Pérez and this is another edition of our Channel
Five news special: "Hispanic California." Today I am speaking to you from the town of
McLaughlin in the San Joaquin Valley. McLaughlin is commonly believed to be a cancer
cluster area, where a disproportionate number of children have been diagnosed with
cancer in the last few years. The town has seen the sudden death of numerous children, as
well as a high incidence of birth defects. One of the most alarming recent events which
has brought sudden public attention to the McLaughlin situation has been a series of . . .
crucifixions, performed in what seems to be a kind of ritualized protest against the dying
of McLaughlin children. (DOLORES, *a slender woman nearing fifty, enters. She carries
groceries.*) The last three children to die were each found with his corpse hanging from a
cross in the middle of a grape vineyard. The Union of Campesinos, an outspoken advocate
for pesticide control, is presently under investigation for the crime. (*Spying* DOLORES.)
We now are approaching the house of Dolores Valle. Her daughter Cerezita is one of
McLaughlin's most tragic cases.

*Upon sight of ANA PEREZ coming toward her with her microphone, DOLORES hurries
into the house. AMPARO intervenes.*

AMPARO: You should maybe leave her alone; she don' like the telebision cameras too much no more.

ANA PEREZ (*to the "camera"*): Possibly this neighbor can provide us with some sense of the emotional climate prevalent in this small, largely Hispanic farm worker town.

AMPARO: She says es como un circo—

ANA PEREZ (*to the camera*): A circus.

AMPARO: Que la gente . . . the peepo like tha' kina t'ing, to look at somebody else's life like that t'ing coont never happen to them. But Cerezita's big now. She got a lot to say if they give her the chance. It's important for the peepo to reelize what los rancheros—

ANA PEREZ (*overlapping*): The growers.

AMPARO: Are doing to us.

ANA PEREZ: Cerezita. That's an unusual name. Es una fruta ¿qué no?

AMPARO: That's what they call her because she look like tha' . . . a red little round cherry face. I think maybe all the blood tha' was apose to go to the resta her body got squeezed up into her head. I think tha's why she's so smart, too. Mario, her brother, el doctor-to-be, says the blood gots oxygen. Tha's gottu help with the brains. So pink pink pink she turn out.

ANA PEREZ: And how old is Cerezita now?

AMPARO: A big teenager already. Cerezita come out like this before anybody think too much about it. Now there's lotza nuevas because lotza kids are turning out all chuecos and with ugly things growing inside them. So our pueblito, pues it's on the map now. The gabachos, s'cuze me, los americanos are always coming through McLaughlin nowdays. Pero, not too much change. We still can' prove it's those chemcals they put on the plantas. But we know Cere turn out this way because Dolores pick en los files cuando tenía panza.

ANA PEREZ: Uh . . . pregnant, I think.

AMPARO: Dolores tells me que no le importa a la gente and maybe she's right. She says all the publeesty gives peepo somet'ing to do. Peepo que got a lotta free time. It gives them a purpose, she says—like God.

ANA PEREZ: Señora, what about the boy?

AMPARO: ¿Qué boy?

ANA PEREZ: The boy on the cross . . . in the field.

AMPARO: Memo?

ANA PEREZ: Yes. Memo Delgado.

AMPARO: He died a little santito, son angelitos todos.

ANA PEREZ: That's the third one.

AMPARO: Yes.

ANA PEREZ: Why would someone be so cruel, to hang a child up like that? To steal him from his deathbed?

AMPARO: No, he was dead already. Already dead from the poison.

ANA PEREZ: But ma'am . . .

AMPARO: They always dead first. If you put the children in the ground, the world forgets about them. Who's gointu see them, buried in the dirt?

ANA PEREZ: A publicity stunt? But who's—

AMPARO: Señorita, I don' know who. But I know they not my enemy. (*Beat.*) Con su permiso. (AMPARO *walks away.*)

ANA PEREZ (*with false bravado*): That concludes our Hispanic hour for the week, but watch for next week's show where we will take a five-hour drive north to the heart of San Francisco's Latino Mission District, for an insider's observation of the Day of the Dead, the Mexican Halloween. (*She holds a television smile for three full seconds. To the "cameraman":*) Cut! We'll edit her out later.

BONNIE *and a group of small* CHILDREN *enter wearing calavera masks. They startle her.*

THE CHILDREN: Trick or treat!

ANA PEREZ: No. I mean . . . I don't . . . have anything to give you. *She exits nervously.*

Scene Three

Crossfade to the Valle kitchen. It is late afternoon. YOLANDA *is breastfeeding her baby.* CEREZITA *observes.*

CEREZITA: I remember the first time I tasted fear, I smelled it in her sweat. It ran like a tiny river down her breast and mixed with her milk. I tasted it on my tongue. It was very bitter. Very bitter.

YOLANDA: That's why I try to keep calm. Lina knows when I'm upset.

CEREZITA: I stopped drinking. I refused to nurse from her again, bit at her breasts when she tried to force me.

YOLANDA: Formula is expensive. Breastfeeding is free. Healthier, too. I'll do it until Lina doesn't want it no more. (YOLANDA *buttons her blouse, puts the infant into her crib, sings to her softly.*) 'Duerme, duerme, negrito'. . . (*Continues singing.*)

CEREZITA: But imagine my sadness, my longing for the once-sweetness of her nipple.

YOLANDA *positions* CEREZITA *for her weekly beauty treatment. She takes out various beauty supplies from a bag.* MARIO *enters, towel wrapped around his hips. He is well built, endearingly macho in his manner. He is drying himself briskly.*

MARIO: ¡Hijo! It's freezing! These cold showers suck, man! We should all just get the fuck outta here. I'm gonna move us all the fuck outta here!

CEREZITA: Where to, Mario?

YOLANDA: Go 'head, chulo. You keep taking those showers purty boy and your skin's gonna fall off in sheets. Then who's gonna want you?

MARIO: The water was cold, man. Ice cold.

YOLANDA: I turned the water heater off.

MARIO: Great. My skin's gonna freeze off from the cold sooner than any chemicals. How can you stand it?

CEREZITA: Where you gonna move us to, Mario?

MARIO (*looking out the window*): What?

CEREZITA: Where we going?

MARIO: I dunno. Just away.

YOLANDA (*has filled up a glass of water from the faucet*): Here.

MARIO: Chale. The shit stinks.

YOLANDA: C'mon, chulo. Tómalo. Why don't you just throw it down your throat better? It's the same thing. You suck enough of it up through your skin taking those hot baths three times a day.

MARIO: Two.

YOLANDA *starts to spread the beauty mask onto* CEREZITA*'s face.*
DOLORES *can be seen coming up the porch steps after her day's work.*

YOLANDA: You wanna see Lina's nalguitas? They're fried, man. The hot water opens your pores and just sucks up the stuff. She cried all night last night. This shit's getting outta hand! Doña Amparo told me—

DOLORES (*entering*): Es una metiche, Amparo.

YOLANDA: They shot through her windows the last night.

CEREZITA: Who?

YOLANDA: Who knows? The guys in the helicopters . . . God.

DOLORES: Por eso, te digo she better learn to keep her damn mouth shut. Ella siempre gottu be putting la cuchara en la olla. I saw her talking to the TV peepo last week right in front of the house. It scare me.

YOLANDA: What are you scared of?

DOLORES: They come to talk to Amparo on the job yesterday.

MARIO: Who?

DOLORES: The patrones.

MARIO: The owners?

DOLORES: Not the owners, pero their peepo. They give her a warning que they don' like her talking about the rancheros.

YOLANDA: Cabrones.

DOLORES: She gointu lose her job.

MARIO: Got to hand it to Nina Amparo. She's got huevos, man.

DOLORES: She got a husband, not huevos. Who's gointu support Cere if I stop working?

The room falls silent. CERE*'s face is now covered in a facial mask.*

MARIO: Well, I better get ready. (*He starts to exit upstage,* DOLORES *stops him.*)

DOLORES: I better see you back el lunes temprano ¿m'oyes? I got the plaster falling down from the front of the house.

MARIO: Okay.

CEREZITA: Where you going, Mario?

DOLORES *goes to the stove, puts a pot of beans to boil.*

YOLANDA: Don't talk, Cere. You're gonna crack your face.

MARIO: ¡San Pancho, 'manita!

YOLANDA (*running a slab of facial down his cheek, softly*): Better stay away from the jotos, you don't wanna catch nothing.

MARIO (*"slabbing" it back, teasing*): I got it covered, hermana.

DOLORES: What are you two whispering about?

MARIO: Nothing, 'amá.

DOLORES: You know, secrets kill sometimes.

YOLANDA, It was nothing, 'amá.

DOLORES: You don' believe it, pero tha' place, it's crazy. They got all those crazy peepo que sleep on the street nowdays. You never know one could come up and shoot you right in the head.

YOLANDA: They're shooting us here anyway.

DOLORES: ¿Crees que soy una exagerada? We'll see.

MARIO (*mimicking*): "We'll see." ¡Hijo! I hate when she says that like she knows something we don't.

YOLANDA: I know.

DOLORES: Pues, maybe I do.

MARIO (*coming up behind DOLORES and wrapping his arms around her*): I'm fine, 'amá.

DOLORES (*softening*): "I'm fine, 'amá." ¿Qué sabes tú about "fine"?

AMPARO *can be seen coming up onto the porch. JUAN trails behind her carrying a five-gallon tank of spring water. He wears jeans and a flannel shirt.*

AMPARO: ¡Halo! Anybody home? I got a sorprise for you!

DOLORES: Abra la puerta, hijo.

AMPARO (*calling out behind her*): Right here! This is the house!

MARIO (*going to the door*): What's up, Nina?

AMPARO: ¡Ay! Te vez bien sexy.

DOLORES (*spying JUAN at the porch*): ¡Ay, Dios! (*She quickly pushes CEREZITA out of sight, drawing a curtain around her.*)

YOLANDA (*whispering*): Why do you do that to her?

DOLORES: Cállete tú.

MARIO (*to JUAN, with interest*): Hello.

JUAN: Hello.

AMPARO: This is my godson, Mario. (MARIO *takes the bottle from JUAN.*)

JUAN: Thanks.

MARIO: No problem.

AMPARO: That's Yolanda y su baby, Evalina.

YOLANDA: Hi.

AMPARO: And this is my comadre, Dolores Valle.

DOLORES: Halo.

JUAN: Mucho gusto.

DOLORES: ¿Habla español?

JUAN: Soy mexicano.

DOLORES: ¿Verdad?

AMPARO (*aside*): Half y half.

MARIO (*suggestively*): Like the cream?

AMPARO: And a priest. Father Juan Cunningham.

DOLORES: Mario, why you standing around sin ropa? Go put some clothes on.

MARIO: All right. I was just helping the man. I mean, the priest.

He puts the water onto the dispenser, then exits. JUAN's *eyes follow him.*

DOLORES: Siéntese, Father.

YOLANDA: So, where'd you get the water, Doña Amparo?

AMPARO: The Arrowhead donated it.

JUAN: Thanks to Doña Amparo. Last week's newscast stirred up everyone!

AMPARO: It wasn' me. It was la crucifixión. That's what brought the newspeepo here.

DOLORES: ¡Es una barbaridad!

AMPARO: The newspeepo, they wanted to talk to Cereza, comadre.

DOLORES: Y ¿por qué?

YOLANDA: Cere knows, 'amá.

DOLORES: Cerezita don' know nothing.

YOLANDA: She sees.

DOLORES: She sees nothing. (*To* JUAN:) She looks out the window all day, nomás. What can she see?

The lights crossfade to CEREZITA *at the window.* BONNIE *sits near her, playing with a doll. She prepares bandages for it, tearing a flour-sack cloth into strips and wrapping it around the doll's head.*

CEREZITA: The sheep drink the same water we do from troughs outside my window. Today it is an orange-yellow color. The mothers dip their heads into the long rusty buckets and drink and drink while their babies deform inside them. Innocent, they sleep inside the same poison water and are born broken like me, their lamb limbs curling under them.

BONNIE (*takes out a thermometer and puts it into her doll's mouth*): ¿Estás malita, mija? (*Checking the temperature.*) Yes. I think you got "it." (*She rubs the top of its head, chanting.*)

'Sana sana colita de rana, si no sanas hoy sanarás mañana.
Sana sana colita de rana, si no sanas hoy sanarás mañana.
Sana sana colita de rana, si no sanas hoy sanarás mañana.'
She puts the doll into a small box and covers it tenderly with the remains of the cloth.

CEREZITA: I watch them from my window and weep.

Fade out.

Scene Four

DOLORES *and* JUAN *are at the kitchen table. He is eating a taco of chorizo. She embroiders a dishcloth.*

DOLORES: And then I started working in the packing houses and the same thing was happening. The poison they put on the almonds, it would make you sick. The women would run out of the place coz they had to throw up. Sure, I dint wannu go back in there, pero after awhile you start to accept it because you gottu have a job.

JUAN: Where do you work now?

DOLORES: Otro packing house. (*Pause.*) ¿Le gusta la comida, Father?

JUAN: Sí, está muy sabrosa.

DOLORES: Pues, I'm glad you came. Most a the priests, they not like you, they don' come to the house no more unless you got money. It's not right, Padre.

JUAN: No, no es justo, Señora Valle.

DOLORES: But the priests should be worried because a lot a peepo they leaving la iglesia. ¿Sabe qué? A buncha my vecinos already turn into the "Holy Rollie."

JUAN: Holy Rollie?

DOLORES: Tha's what my Yolie calls them. They turn from the Catholic god. They "Chrishins" now.

JUAN: Oh, you mean Pentecostals.

DOLORES: One time I was feeling so tire, so lonely, just dragging myself home from work and I hear a tamborín coming out of the panadería. Now it's a church, but it usetu be la panadería de la familia Hernández. It still smell like pandulce un poco when you go by. An' it was like the tamborín me 'staba llamando, telling me to come inside, if only para quitarme el cansancio a little. So I go in and sit in the back. And they were all jumping up and down and shaking their hands in the air. Pura raza, singing songs like children. It scare me, Father. Their faces look kina dopey-like, kina like their eyes had turned to hard glass por las lágrimas que tienen all lock up inside them. Se llama "Iglesia de Dios," but there wasn' no God there. And too much noise. How can your soul even find God con tanto ruído?

JUAN: I guess they feel they find him with one another.

DOLORES: No es posible. God es una cosa privada, un secreto que guardas and nobody can touch that part of you. Even the priest has to forget every secret you tell him. (*She observes* JUAN *as he finishes the dripping taco. He licks his fingers.*) ¡Ay, qué pena! (*She brings him a clean dishtowel.*) You been a father a long time, Father?

JUAN: About ten years.

DOLORES: You still have the eyes of a man.

JUAN: ¿Perdón?

DOLORES: No importa. It's good you experience the world a little. Some of these priests, you confess to them your sins y que consejo te pueben ofrecer? A little life doesn' hurt nobody. (*Pause.*) Come see my Cerezita. She'll like you. It's been years since a priest come to see her.

JUAN: Would you like me to hear her confession?

DOLORES: What sins could a girl like her have, Padre? She was born this way. Es una santa. We should pray to her, I think.

They both rise.

Scene Five

Crossfade to CEREZITA *speaking into a tape recorder.*

CEREZITA: It is so, he came to meet her seeking the purity of nature he'd lost. He sought baptism in the fire of her original desire.

JUAN (*entering timidly*): Hello . . . (CEREZITA *turns the tape recorder off with her chin.*) Am I . . . interrupting? (*She doesn't respond.*) Your mother asked me to come by. I hope it's . . . all right with you?

CEREZITA: She must like you. Few people get past her inspection.

JUAN: Can you turn around? I'd like to talk to you face to face.

CEREZITA: You're wasting your time, Padre. I have no use for God.

JUAN: You don't believe?

CEREZITA: I don't care.

JUAN: I see (*Pause.*) Can I read you something? Your mother says you are quite a reader.

CEREZITA (*reluctantly*): What is it?

JUAN: Just something I'm reading. It struck me.

CEREZITA: I got ears.

JUAN (*reading from a small paperback*): "Then, they named rich the man of God, and poor the man of flesh. And they determined that the rich would care for and protect the poor in as much that through them, the rich had received such benefits."

CEREZITA: "Entonces llamaron rico al hombre de oro y pobre al hombre de carne. Y dispusieron que el rico cuidara y amparara al pobre por cuanto que de él había recibido beneficios.". . .

JUAN (*impressed*): "And they ordered that the poor would respond on behalf of the rich before the face of truth."

CEREZITA: "Y ordenaron que el pobre respondería por el rico ante la cara de la verdad.". . .

JUAN: "For this—"

CEREZITA (*slowly turning to him*): "For this reason our law states that no rich person can enter heaven without the poor taking him by the hand."

Seeing her fully for the first time, JUAN's face registers both awe and tenderness.

JUAN: Balun Canan. Rosario Castellanos.

CEREZITA: First, the Maya. (*Pause.*) Am I your pobre, Father?

Fade out.

Scene Six

Early morning. AMPARO and DOLORES come out of the house, wearing work clothes. DOLORES carries a small bucket of plaster and a trowel. AMPARO carries a shovel and heavy gloves.

DOLORES: This house is falling apart. ¡Ayúdanos, Dios!

AMPARO: You think God is gointu take care of it? Working is what changes things, not oraciones.

DOLORES: Ya te dije, I'm not going to your protesta.

AMPARO *puts on the gloves, begins digging into the yard. DOLORES goes over to the side of the house and starts applying plaster to it.*

AMPARO: ¿Sabes qué? I don' even go to church no more, ni recibir comunión . . . coz I'm tire of swallowing what they want to shove down my throat. Body of Christ . . . pedo.

DOLORES: I hate when you talk like this. It makes me sick to my stomach.

AMPARO (*digging more vigorously*): Pues, the truth aint so purty sometimes.

DOLORES: I'm not going. (*To herself.*) You'd think I could get the only son I got to do this for me, pero no. He's always gallivanting around con sus secretos.

AMPARO (*hitting upon something on the ground*): Mira. Hay algo aquí. Ayúdame.

DOLORES: Wha' chu find?

AMPARO: No sé. Help me.

They both get down on their hands and knees and dig. They pull out an old, thick rubber hose.

DOLORES: No es nada.

AMPARO: You don' believe me, but they bury all their poison under our houses. Wha' chu think that crack comes from? An earthquake? The house is sinking, te digo como quicksand.

DOLORES: It's the only house I got.

AMPARO: They lied to us, Lola. They thought we was too stupid to know the diference. They throw some dirt over a dump, put some casas de cartón on top of it y dicen que it's the "American Dream." Pues, this dream has turned to pesadilla.

DOLORES: Where we apose to go? Every three houses got a For Sale sign. Nobody's gointu buy from us now.

AMPARO: The gov'ment owes us the money.

DOLORES: Oh sí, and they're gointu drop it de los cielos. (*She sits on the porch step.*)

AMPARO: No, pero not'ing gointu change if you don' do not'ing. How can you jus' sit with your hands folded? You see Yolie's baby, ya 'stá malita.

DOLORES: She got a little rash, nomás. Anyway, I do somet'ing before and what good did it do me? Somos mas pobres que antes. A'least before I open my big mouth, Cerezita had a father.

AMPARO: What kina father? A father who wouldn' let his own child feel the sun on her face, who kept her hidden como algo cochino. And now you do the same thing to her. It's not right, Lola. You think hiding her is gointu bring Arturo back?

DOLORES: No. (*Pause.*) It wasn' fair what I did to him. I humiliate him.

AMPARO: Tha's an old tune, comadre. He never humiliate you?

DOLORES: The men are weaker. They can't take what a woman takes.

AMPARO: Adió. You did it to educate the peepo.

DOLORES: I did it to make him ashame. I tole him, "¿Ves? Half a father make half a baby." (*Pause.*) He believe it.

AMPARO: That was a long time ago. Wha' chu got to stop you now?

DOLORES (*returning to plastering*): Vete. Go to your marcha. No tiene nada que ver eso conmigo.

DOLORES *slaps some more plaster onto the wall.* AMPARO *tosses the hose into the junk heap and exits. The sound of a low-flying crop duster fills the stage.* DOLORES *stares up at it as its shadow passes over her. Fade out.*

Scene Seven

The wheels to CERE's raite can be heard in the darkness. At rise, MARIO *is on his back, tightening a bolt under the wheelchair.* CEREZITA *is reading a medical book, periodically turning the pages with her mouth. The infant sleeps in her crib.*

CEREZITA: So, what kind of cancer did Memo have?

MARIO: He had a neuroblastoma. Hand me that screwdriver, will you, Cere? (*She picks it up with her mouth, drops it down to him.*) Watch it. You almost hit me.

CEREZITA: I can't see you from up here.

MARIO: Pues, wátchale. (*He rolls the raite back and forth, it squeaks loudly.*) How's that feel?

CEREZITA: Fine, but can you do something about the squeak?

MARIO: Where's the oil?

CEREZITA: Check under the sink. (*He does.*) What's a neuroblastoma?

MARIO (*coming back with the oil*): A tumor. They usually arise in the adrenal gland or any place in the sympathetic chain. (*Pointing out a reference in the book.*) See.

CEREZITA: Like in the chest.

MARIO: Well, they can appear there. Memo's started in the abdomen.

CEREZITA: It says that the prognosis is worse than most leukemia.

MARIO (*applying the oil*): Usually even surgery can't cure it. (*He puts her chin piece back in place.* CEREZITA *gives the raite a little test drive.*) There, a smooth ride. Memo didn't have a chance, Cere. Kids' bodies are so vulnerable. They pick up stuff way before adults. They got no buffer zone. "The canary in the mine shaft" . . . that's exactly what they are. (*He puts the tools away, washes his hands, then runs a comb through his hair.*)

CEREZITA: You going out, Mario?

MARIO: Yeah.

CEREZITA: Tell me the story about the Mayan god before you go.

MARIO: Ah, Cere, my ride's coming.

CEREZITA: Please, don't go just yet.

MARIO: Okay, but the short version. (*Sitting down next to her.*) Cousin Freddie—

CEREZITA: Hadn't been in the states too long, maybe a few months and he liked everything American . . .

MARIO (*amused*): I guess even me. God, Freddie was beautiful. Dark. He had cheekbones to die for, like they were sculpted outta some holy Mayan rock. And he had this little twitch in the side of his jaw that would pulse whenever he got excited or upset or something. The party was still going on and I was supposed to be sleeping in the next room. But Nino Gilberto started singing and letting out those famous gritos of his. . . . (*Imitates "los gritos."*) So, no way, man, was I gonna get any sleep. I could hear Freddie laughing in the patio and I started following his voice around. I'd think about his smile, I'd imagine him waving his hands in people's faces while he talked, getting a little pálido from all the pisto. The next thing I know he's standing—

CEREZITA: No, you forgot the boleros.

MARIO: Right. When the boleros came on, I could hear him singing along with them and I'd think about those veined hands around Yolie's back while they danced, wishing I was there inside those hands. The next thing I know, my young god is standing at the foot of my bed. His shirt's open to his waist . . . more Mayan rock. It's kinda sticking to him from the sweat he's worked up on the dance floor. My little heart is pounding as he tells me how he just came in to check on me. "Mijo," he calls me.

CEREZITA: Mijo.

MARIO: That little twitch pulsing. (*A car horn sounds from the street. He gives* CEREZITA *a peck on the cheek.*) That's it.

CEREZITA: Ah, Mario.

MARIO (*spotting* YOLANDA *through the window*): Look-it, Yolie's coming home. Have her take you out back. It's nice out right now. Ay te watcho. (*He grabs a leather jacket, goes out the door.*)

YOLANDA: Your "friend" is waiting for you, ése. (MARIO *gives her a kiss and exits;* YOLANDA *comes indoors.*) That was one sleazy-looking gringo in that car.

CEREZITA: Mario doesn't like him.

YOLANDA: Well, for not liking him, he sure sees him a lot.

CEREZITA: He gives him things.

YOLANDA: That I believe.

CEREZITA: Take me outside, Yolie.

YOLANDA (*checking the baby in its crib*): Did Lina wake up?

CEREZITA: No. Take me outside, Yolie. Mom's gonna be home soon.

YOLANDA: Okay, let's go. Your hair's lookin' raggedy. I'm gonna give you a good conditioning later. (*Pushing the raite.*) Hey! What happened to the squeak?

CEREZITA (*with pride*): Mario fixed it.

Fade out.

Scene Eight

That evening. CEREZITA *is reading a book.* YOLANDA *passes by with a diaper over her shoulder and a small stack of them in her hands.*

CEREZITA: It recommends making a tea from flor de muerto. It's good for indigestion.

YOLANDA: I'm not giving my baby anything called "flower of the dead."

CEREZITA: It worked for the Aztecs. Zempasuchitl, the yellow marigold.

YOLANDA: Forget it.

YOLANDA *exits.* CEREZITA *shuts the book just as she spots* JUAN *coming up the front steps.*

CEREZITA: Come in.

JUAN (*entering*): Hello. You alone?

CEREZITA: No, Yolie's in back with the baby. Lina's been throwing up her milk.

JUAN: Oh.

CEREZITA: If you came to see my mom, she's next door.

JUAN: No. I came to see you.

CEREZITA: She's trying to get Don Gilberto to stop Amparo from leading the protest at the school tomorrow. Can you hear them?

JUAN: No.

CEREZITA: Sure, my mom's going, "What kina man are you, you can't control your own wife?" And Don Gilberto answers, "I don't gotta control her, I love her."

JUAN: I can't hear them.

CEREZITA: Yeah, but that's what they're saying. Are you going to the demonstration, Father?

JUAN: Yes. I was hoping your mother would bring you.

CEREZITA: No, I don't go out.

JUAN: Never?

CEREZITA: Never. (*She observes* JUAN *for a moment.*)

JUAN: I . . .

CEREZITA: Touch my hair, Father.

JUAN: What?

CEREZITA: Touch my hair. (*He hesitates.*) Go 'head. It's not gonna hurt you. I'm normal from the neck up. (*He touches a strand very gingerly.*)

CEREZITA: Well?

JUAN: It's very . . . smooth.

CEREZITA: Like silk, huh?

JUAN: Yes.

CEREZITA: Oughtabe. Yolie just gave it the works. She studies all these beauty magazines and tries out every new item that hits the market. She's into "natural" these days, which I'm very grateful for. Over the last five years, Yolie experimented in every fashion from beehives to buzzcuts. It was fun for a while, until my hair started falling out. And if my hair doesn't look decent, I don't have much going for me now, do I, Father?

JUAN (*pause*): No, I guess . . . not.

CEREZITA: So now my hair tends to smell more like an overripe tropical garden than anything else. You know, coconut and mango juice shampoo, avocado conditioners, et cetera.

JUAN: I wouldn't know.

CEREZITA: Now it just grows long and thick like a beautiful dark curtain. Nice huh?

JUAN (*touching it again*): Yes.

CEREZITA: I like it, too . . . sometimes just spin my head around and around so I can feel it brush past my cheeks. I imagine it's what those Arab women with the veils must feel like . . . all those soft cloths secretly caressing their bodies.

JUAN: You think about that?

CEREZITA: What, the Arab women? Give me a break, Padre. All I've got is this imagination.

JUAN: Yes . . .

CEREZITA: And a tongue.

JUAN: A tongue?

CEREZITA: Yeah, and mine's got the best definition I bet in the world, unless there's some other vegetable heads like me who survived this valley. Think about it, Padre. Imagine if your tongue and teeth and chin had to do the job of your hands . . . you know, (*She demonstrates.*) turning pages, picking up stuff, scratching an itch, pointing. I mean your tongue alone would have to have some very serious definition. For me . . . well, it's my most faithful organ. Look it up. (*She sticks out her tongue, "pointing" to the dictionary on the shelf.*)

JUAN: What?

CEREZITA: Get the dictionary. (*Pointing.*) Look up the word *tongue*.

JUAN: But why?

CEREZITA: You'll see. Check it out. (JUAN *gets the dictionary.*)

JUAN (*reading*): "Ton. Tonality. Tone. Tongue. Latin: Lingua."

CEREZITA: Spanish: Lengua.

JUAN: "1 a: a fleshy movable process of the floor of the mouths of most vertebrates that bears sensory end organs and functions especially in taking and swallowing food."

CEREZITA (*reciting from memory*): "2: The power of communication through speech." Your turn, Padre. (*He hesitates.*) Go on.

JUAN: "3: The flesh of the tongue used as food."

CEREZITA (*with JUAN*): "4 a: Language, especially a spoken language."

JUAN: "b: ecstatic usually unintelligible utterance accompanying religious excitement. c: the charismatic gift—"

CEREZITA (*overlapping*): "Of ecstatic speech."

JUAN: The gift of tongues!

CEREZITA: "d: the cry of a hound in sight of game—used especially in the phrase," italicized . . . (*Suggestively.*) "to give tongue." (*She pants like the hound.*)

JUAN: C'mon, now.

CEREZITA: Be a sport, Padre.

JUAN: "Verb. 1 *archaic*: scold."

CEREZITA: "2: to touch or lick with; to project in a tongue."

JUAN: "3: to articulate," parenthetically, "notes by". . . (*He hesitates.*)

CEREZITA: Yes?. . .

JUAN: "By tonguing."

CEREZITA: My brother Mario brought me a trumpet once, the old medieval kind. No fingering needed . . . just a good, strong tongue. "Tongue in cheek."

JUAN: "Characterized by insincerity, irony, or whimsical exaggeration."

CEREZITA (*provocatively*): "Tongue-lash."

JUAN: "To chide or—"

CEREZITA: Regañar.

JUAN: "Tongueless."

CEREZITA: "Lacking the power of speech."

JUAN: "Mute. Tongue-tied—disinclined or". . . (*He looks up at her.*)

CEREZITA: "Unable to speak freely."

Fade out.

Scene Nine

The school grounds. McLaughlin Elementary. BONNIE enters carrying a lunch box. DON GILBERTO is pushing a broom. He wears a janitor's uniform which reads McLaughlin School District on back. BONNIE sits, opens her lunch box and takes out an apple. She watches him sweep for a moment.

BONNIE: Don Gilberto, I dreamed Memo before he died.

DON GILBERTO: You did?

BONNIE: Yeah. I dreamed Memo alive playing on the merry-go-round like we used to before he got sick. He's in the middle of it, holding on real tight and I'm pushing the merry-go-round faster and faster. And then I see his face starts to get scared, so I try to stop the merry-go-round but I can't. I can't grab the bars. They just keep hitting my hands harder and harder and he's spinning around so fast that finally his face just turns into a blur. And then he disappears.

DON GILBERTO: Just like that?

BONNIE: Well, then I woke up. (*Pause.*) Now when I go to sleep, I make a prayer so I don't dream about nobody.

DON GILBERTO: What kind of prayer?

BONNIE: Just one that asks God that . . . when I'm sleeping, that he'll keep all the kids outta me. Maybe you make your dreams come true. Maybe you kill people that way.

DON GILBERTO (*taking out a handkerchief from his back pocket and polishing the apple*): Sometimes when you're worried or scared about something, hija, your dreams draw pictures in your sleep to show you what the feelings look like.

BONNIE: Like Memo blurring?

DON GILBERTO: Sí. (*He hands her back the polished apple.*)

BONNIE: I have to think about that, Don Gilberto.

DON GILBERTO: That's all right. You think about it. (*He kisses the top of her head, goes back to sweeping.*)

BONNIE: Look, Don Gilberto! It's the news lady!

ANA PEREZ *appears in front of the "cameras."* AMPARO *and a group of* PROTESTORS *are approaching, including* MARIO, JUAN, *and* YOLANDA. *They are carrying placards reading,* The School Board Lies! Save Our Children! Sin Agua No Tenemos Vida, *etc.* ANA PEREZ *straightens her jacket, lightly brushes back her hair. She addresses the "camera."*

ANA PEREZ: A crowd is beginning to form out here in front of the town of McLaughlin's elementary school. Mostly mothers and other neighbors have shown up this morning. There is no sign of school officials as of yet. Local residents are outraged by the school board's decision to refuse Arrowhead's offer of free drinking water for the schoolchildren. They believe local tap water, contaminated by pesticides, to be the chief cause of the high incidence of cancer among children in the area. They claim that the extensive spraying, especially aerial spraying, causes the toxic chemicals to seep into the public water system. The majority of residents are from a nearby housing tract of federally subsidized housing. It has been alleged that the housing was built on what was once a dump site for pesticides with the full knowledge of contractors. What we have here, Jack, appears to be a kind of 1980s Hispanic Love Canal.

The PROTESTORS *have arrived at the school grounds, led by* DOÑA AMPARO.

DON GILBERTO (*with affection*): She's gonna get me fired, mi vieja.

AMPARO (*under her breath, to* DON GILBERTO): I think I got the cold feet, Berto.

DON GILBERTO: Pues, warm 'em up quick. You got all this gente here esperán-dote. (*She hesitates.*) ¡Adelante, mujer!

ANA PEREZ: It looks like a local resident will be addressing the crowd.

DON GILBERTO *helps* AMPARO *up onto a bench. The crowd goes quiet. As the speech progresses, the* PROTESTORS *become more and more receptive, calling out in response.*

AMPARO (*tentatively*): Our homes are no longer our homes. They have become prisons. When the water that pours from the sink gots to be boiled three times before it can pass your children's lips, what good is the faucet, the indoor plumbing, the toilet that flushes pink with disease? (*Gaining confidence.*) We were better off when our padres hang some blankets from a tree and we slept under the pertection de las estrellas, because our roofs don' pertect us. A'least then, even if you had to dig a hole in the ground to do your biznis and wipe yourself with newspaper, you could still look up hasta los cielos and see God. But where is God now, amigos? ¿Y el diablo? El diablo hides between the pages of the papeles we sign that makes us afraid. The papeles they have no weight. ¡Ay! They could fly away en la brisa, they could burn hasta una ceniza with a simple household mecha. But our children are flesh and bone. They weigh mucho. You put them all together and they make hunerds and hunerds a pounds of Razita. (*Pause.*) Yesterday, the school board refuse the gift of clean water for our chil'ren's already poisoned throats. The board says, No, there's not'ing wrong with our water. We don' know for sure, it hasn' been prove. How much prove you need? How many babies' bodies pile all up on top of each other in the grave? (*Pause, coming downstage.*) Comadres, compadres. ¿Qué significa que the three things in life—el aire, el agua, y la tierra—que we always had enough of, even in our pueblitos en México, ya no tenemos? Sí, parece que tenemos all that we need. In the morning the air is cool y fresco, the ground stretches for miles, and all that the ranchero puts into it grows big and bright and the water pours from our faucets sin término. Pero, todo es mentira. Look into your children's faces. They tell you the truth. They are our future. Pero no tendremos ningún futuro si seguimos siendo víctimas.

> The PROTESTORS *come down into the audience, passing out pamphlets of information about the pesticide problem.* CEREZITA *has been looking out the window at the demonstration.* DOLORES *is sweeping, trying to ignore the sounds of the protest invading her house.*

CEREZITA: Mira, 'amá. They're all going house to house, giving out pamphlets. Father Juanito's there and Don Gilberto. They even got the news cameras.

DOLORES: Get your face out of the window.

CEREZITA: Nobody's looking over here.

DOLORES: Quítate de allí, te digo.

> DOLORES *disengages* CEREZITA's *raite and moves her away from the window.*

CEREZITA: Ah, 'amá!

DOLORES: Pues, you don't know who could be out there. All this protesta is bringing the guns down from the sky.

CEREZITA: I just wanted to see.

DOLORES: You don't need to see. (*She gets down on her hands and knees and begins picking up various books and newspapers that* CEREZITA *has left around the floor.*) Mira todos los libros que tienes. One a these days your brain's gointu explode por tantas palabras.

CEREZITA: Wha' else am I supposed to do?

DOLORES: You're suppose to do nothing. I'm suppose to do everything.

CEREZITA: Martyrs don't survive, 'amá.

DOLORES: Your brother teaches you tha' kina talk. Don' get smart with me.

CEREZITA: I am smart.

DOLORES: Maybe you read a lot, but tha' doesn' mean you know about life. You think you find life in a book?

CEREZITA: No, I don't think I find life in a book. (CERE *tosses her hair around, trying to feel it against her cheeks.*)

DOLORES: It's a pig's pen around here, you leave all your junk laying around . . . candy wrappers, the little crumbs from the erasers. (*On her hands and knees, picking at the rug.*) What do you do with them? Chew them?

CEREZITA: Erase.

DOLORES: Mentirosa. I seen you chew them.

CEREZITA: Well, sometimes . . . when I'm thinking.

DOLORES: Well, stop it. It makes a big mess. I can' get those tiny pieces out of l'alfombra. (CEREZITA *lays her face down on the raite, rubs it back and forth, trying to feel her hair against her face.* DOLORES *finds an open book on the floor.*) ¿Qué's esto? Cere?

CEREZITA: Huh? . . . Nothing. It's just one of Mario's old anatomy books.

DOLORES: Es cochino. Tha's what it is? I thought he give you the books to study about the sick peepo. This is not the sick peepo.

CEREZITA: God, Mom, it's just the body.

DOLORES: So, what biznis you got with the body? This jus' puts thoughts in your head. (*She flips through the book.*) ¿Qué tiene que ver una señorita con this kind of pictures? (*Slams it shut.*) I should call in the father.

CEREZITA: Father Juan?

DOLORES: Jus' cuz you don' got a body doesn' mean you can't sin. The biggest sins are in the mind.

CEREZITA: Oh God.

DOLORES: Tu eres una inocente. That's how God wanted it. There's a reason he made you like this. You're old enough now . . .

CEREZITA: I'm old enough now to go out!

DOLORES: Pues vete. (*She engages* CEREZITA's *wheels, puts the chin piece in place.*) You think you're so tough, go on. But we'll see how you feel the first time some stranger looks at you with cruel eyes.

DOLORES *goes to the table. After a pause,* CEREZITA *crosses to her.*

CEREZITA: Give me a chance, 'amá. If nobody ever sees me, how will I know how I look? How will I know if I scare them or make them mad or . . . move them? If people could see me, 'amá, things would change.

DOLORES: No, hija. Dios es mi testigo. I'll never let nobody look at my baby that way.

DOLORES *caresses her.* CERE's *face is rigid as the lights crossfade to* MARIO *and* JUAN *sitting on a park bench.*

JUAN: Why didn't you bring Cerezita out to this?

MARIO: My mom. She protects her.

JUAN: From what?

MARIO: Ridicule. The world.

JUAN: She wanted to be here.

MARIO: You bring her out, then. Maybe Lola would let you. You're God on earth, after all. You're all the protection she'd ever need.

JUAN: She needs you.

MARIO: Oh, Padre, they all need me, but I got other plans.

JUAN: Like what?

MARIO: Getting out. Finishing school. Having a life. One life, not two.

JUAN: Two?

MARIO: You don't know what it's like growing up in this valley.

JUAN: I was born in Sanger, Mario.

MARIO: Yeah? Don't show.

JUAN: My family left when I was about twelve.

MARIO: To LA, right?

JUAN: Right.

MARIO: At least you got out. (*Pause.*) When I was in high school, I used to sit out there in those fields, smoking, watching the cars go by on 99. I'd think about the driver, having somewhere to go. His foot pressed to the floorboard, cruisin'. He was always a gringo. And he'd have one arm draped over the steering wheel and the other around the back of the seat and it'd never occur to him that anybody lived there between those big checkerboard plots of tomatoes, strawberries, artichokes, brussels sprouts, and . . .

JUAN: Grapes.

MARIO: Hundreds of miles of grapes. He'd be headed home to his woman and TV set and sleeping kids tucked into clean sheets and he'd have a wad of bills in his pocket and he'd think he'd live forever. But I'm twenty-five and stuck here in this valley and I know I won't.

JUAN: But twenty-five's so young, Mario.

MARIO: I get high, Padre. I smoke and snort and suck up anything and anyone that will have me. Those are the facts. (*A car horn sounds from the street. MARIO jumps to his feet. He motions to the driver.*) Why did you come back, Father? All you'd need is a nice Buick, a full tank of gas and you'd be indistinguishable on that highway. Just don't stop to pick me up. Your type can destroy me.

MARIO *runs off.* JUAN *watches the car drive away. The lights fade to black.*

Scene Ten

JUAN *fills up a glass of water from the dispenser.*

JUAN: Some of the union people were at the rally. They were trying to enlist people to join in the fast with them. I agreed.

CEREZITA: That's good. People like to see priests and celebrities sacrificing. I'd do it, too, if anyone would notice me. The trick is to be noticed.

JUAN: Six months ago, that's the very thing that brought me here . . . to the Valley.

CEREZITA: What?

JUAN: The union's fast. I saw this newspaper photo of Cesar Chávez. He had just finished a thirty-three-day fast. He looked like a damn saint, a veritable Ghandi. Even the number was holy. Thirty-three.

CEREZITA: The age of Christ's death.

JUAN: So I came home. I came home to the valley that gave birth to me. Maybe as a priest it's vanity to believe you can have a home. The whole church is supposed to be your family, your community, but I can't pretend I don't get lonely.

CEREZITA: Why did you become a priest, Father Juan?

JUAN: Too many years as an altar boy. (*He takes a drink of water.*) And because of the fabric.

CEREZITA: The fabric?

JUAN: Yes. Literally, the cloth itself drew me to be a "man of the cloth." The vestments, the priest's body asleep underneath that cloth, the heavy weight of it tranquilizing him.

CEREZITA: Will you always be a priest, Father Juan?

JUAN: Yes. There's no choice in the matter. Once ordained, you've given up volition in that sense. The priesthood is an indelible mark. You are bruised by it, not violently, but its presence is always felt. A slow dull ache, a slight discoloration in the skin . . .

CEREZITA: A purple-red spot between the eyes, the size of a small stone.

JUAN: I wish I had a third eye, Cere.

CEREZITA: But that's your job, isn't it, Father, to make people see? The "theology of liberation." It's a beautiful term. The spiritual practice of freedom. On earth. Do you practice what you preach, Father?

JUAN: It's the people that are to be liberated, not the priests. We're still caught in the Middle Ages somewhere, battling our internal doubts Spanish Inquisition-style. (*Pause.*) I always wanted that kind of sixteenth-century martyr's death. To die nobly and misunderstood, to be exonerated centuries later by a world that was finally ready for me.

CEREZITA (*smiling*): You've been reading too much Lorca.

JUAN: He's my hero.

Fade out.

Scene Eleven

AMPARO *and* DOLORES *return home from work, wearing white uniforms. They are a little tipsy, having stopped off at the local bar for a few beers first. They are singing a ranchera. They come into the house and pull out a few chairs onto the porch.* BONNIE *rides up on a bicycle. Nueva canción music can be heard coming from the radio indoors.*

AMPARO: I dunno how much longer I could aguantar working in tha' place anyway. I dunno wha's worser, the bending to pick en los files or standing on your feet all day in the same damn spot. Me 'stoy poniendo vieja. (*They sit down in front of the house, take off their shoes.*) Mira los bunions. (BONNIE *joins them,* AMPARO *shows her her feet.*) You see how the toes all bunch up there on top of each other? . . . Mi viejo usetu tell me I had beautiful feet. Beautiful. Like a movie star. Ya no.

BONNIE: You want me to rub 'em, Doña Amparo?

AMPARO: ¿Qué, mija?

BONNIE: Your feet. You want me to rub 'em for you?

AMPARO: Pues, okay!

DOLORES: ¡Ay! The royal treatment. (BONNIE *massages* AMPARO's *feet.*)

AMPARO: Your feet get crooked when you gottu squeeze 'em into zapatos que take all the blood from you. They don' tell you cuando eras una chamaca tha' you suffer the rest a your life for the chooz you wear at sixteen. ¿Qué no?

DOLORES: Tha's for darn chure.

AMPARO: Tha's nice, hija. La verdad es que siempre he sido pura ranchera. If I had my way, I'd go barefoot. Ahora these patas don' fit into not'ing but the tenny shoes.

DOLORES (*rolling down her stockings*): What I got is the varicose venas. It's from the cement floors. They squeeze you from the soles up and then el cansancio press you from the neck down. In between, your venas jus' pop out.

BONNIE: Ouch!

AMPARO: Pinche jale. Who needs it?

YOLANDA *comes out onto the porch. She wears rubber gloves, stained with black hair dye.*

YOLANDA: I thought I heard you out here.

DOLORES: You got a custmer, mija?

YOLANDA: Señora Reyes. She's under the dryer.

AMPARO: What color she want this time?

YOLANDA: Midnight blue.

AMPARO: Ya no quiere ser güera.

YOLANDA: I think she's given up . . . tired of fighting the roots.

DOLORES: Bonnie, go get us a coupla beers from the refrigerador, eh?

BONNIE: Okay, Doña Lola. (*She goes to get the beer.*)

DOLORES: ¿Quieres una, mija?

YOLANDA: No. Looks like you two have already had a few.

DOLORES: Una, nomás.

AMPARO: 'Stamos celebrando.

YOLANDA: What?

DOLORES: The varicose venas y los bunions.

AMPARO: They kicked me from the job, hija.

DOLORES *getures to* YOLANDA *not to ask.*

YOLANDA: But . . . why?

AMPARO: They heard about the protesta. It affect "the workers' morale," me dijeron, que I set a bad example.

YOLANDA: They fired you for speaking at a rally?

AMPARO: Pues, también I was giving out los panfletos from the union.

DOLORES: I tole her not to.

YOLANDA: I can't believe they fired you.

AMPARO: Good thing I got the green card or right now I be on the bus back to Coahuila.

BONNIE *comes out with the beers, passes them to* DOLORES *and* AMPARO.

DOLORES: Gracias, mija.

BONNIE: Here you go, Doña Amparo.

AMPARO: Thank you, chula.

The radio music is suddenly interrupted by a news break.

RADIO VOICE: This is KKCF in Fresno. News brief. San Salvador. UPI reports that at 6 A.M. this morning six Jesuit priests, along with their housekeeper and her daughter, were found brutally murdered. The priests, from the Central American University, were outspoken opponents to the ruling rightist ARENA party.

DOLORES: Cere! ¡Baja la radio! (*To the women:*) We got enough bad news today without hearing about the rest a the world también. (*The volume lowers, then fades out.*) If she can't be in the world, she brings it into the house and we all gottu know about it. First, it's her brother and now it's the priest. He got her all metida en cosas she got no biznis knowing about.

AMPARO: How long you think you can shelter her from the suffering of the world, Lola? (DOLORES *doesn't respond, puts her shoes back on.*)

DOLORES (*to* YOLANDA): Did your brother come home?

YOLANDA: No. What're you gonna do now without a job, Doña Amparo?

AMPARO: Pues, first thing I put that husband of mine on a diet. (DOLORES *gets up, looks down the street.*) He still got a job, mija. We'll make it all right. But if they wannu shut me up, they thinking of a purty good way to do it.

DOLORES (*to* YOLANDA): Did he call?

YOLANDA: Who?

DOLORES: Tu hermano.

YOLANDA: Yeah, he said he's leaving on Saturday. He's already packed, 'amá.

DOLORES: Fine. I'm tired of worrying for him. This way, if you don' know nothing, you got nothing to worry about.

YOLANDA: He said if you wanted he'd come by Friday night.

DOLORES: Díle que no thank you. I don' wan' no good-byes. I had enough good-byes already in my life.

AMPARO: Pues, you tell mi querido ahijado he better not move nowhere without saying good-bye to his padrinos. It would break his Nino's heart.

YOLANDA: I'll tell him, Doña Amparo.

YOLANDA *goes back inside to check on Señora Reyes. Crossfade to* JUAN, *who is walking to the Valle home, books stuffed under one arm. He reads from a newspaper article.*

JUAN: They blasted their brains out in their sleep! Just like that!

DON GILBERTO *enters carrying a lunch pail, returning home from work.*

DON GILBERTO: ¿Qué le pasa, Padre? It looks like you saw one of those holy ghosts of yours.

JUAN: 'Scuze me?

DON GILBERTO: Read some bad news, Father?

JUAN: Yes. (*He shows* DON GILBERTO *the article.*)

DON GILBERTO: Did you know the guys?

JUAN: No, but they were Jesuits, my order.

DON GILBERTO: You'd think a priest in a Catholic country couldn't get shot up in his pajamas.

JUAN: But they were intellectuals.

DON GILBERTO: That didn't seem to matter too much to the bullets, Padre.

DON GILBERTO *pats* JUAN *on the shoulder, continues on home.* YOLANDA *comes out onto the porch.*

DOLORES: ¿Y la Señora Reyes?

YOLANDA: She fell asleep under the dryer.

AMPARO: I hope she like el cabello frito.

BONNIE: Fried hair?

AMPARO: Un estilo nuevo, mija.

The laughter of the women calls JUAN's *attention. He crosses to them.*

DOLORES: Oh, hello, Father.

JUAN: Buenas tardes.

YOLANDA: Visiting the sick again, Padre?

JUAN: No. Yes . . . I mean I have some books for Cerezita. (*To* DOLORES:) If that's all right with you, señora?

DOLORES: Go 'head. What else she gottu do, la pobre. (*He starts to go inside.*) Oh, Father . . . (*He stops at the door.*) Can you come over to the house Friday night? Mi hijo is moving to San Francisco and we gointu have a little get-together, nothing fancy, just some enchiladas rojas. Son Mario's fav'rit.

JUAN: Of course, I'd love to. . . . ¿Con su permiso?

DOLORES: Pásale. Pásale. (*He goes inside. To* AMPARO:) And bring tu viejo. This way he gets some food in his estómago antes que you start to starve him to death.

YOLANDA: ¡Orale! ¡Una pachanga!

DOLORES: I dint say nothing about una pachanga.

YOLANDA: You know what happens when Don Gilberto comes—it's party time!

DOLORES: Pues, it'll be nice to have some men in the house for a change.

AMPARO: And tha' priest, he's plenty a man.

YOLANDA: Yeah, I don't trust him.

DOLORES: He means well, hija.

AMPARO: Pero you know wha' they say, Lola. A man is a man first, no matter wha' he is. If he's a priest or an uncle or a brother, no importa.

THE WOMEN (*to* BONNIE): ¡Un hombre es un hombre!

They laugh. The lights fade out.

Scene Twelve

Música Norteña. At rise, a pachanga in full swing. The records are spinning, the beer and tequila are flowing. JUAN *sits at the kitchen table watching* MARIO *and* AMPARO *dance.* CEREZITA *is just finishing a game of Lotería with* BONNIE. DON GILBERTO *is playing la guitarra, while* DOLORES *sits on the couch, embroidering a dishcloth.* YOLANDA *sits next to her, holding the baby. After a few minutes,* DON GILBERTO, *who's pretty well plastered, puts his guitar down and pours himself another beer.*

DON GILBERTO: ¿Sabe qué, Padre? I love that muchacho. He's lo máximo. You wanna know the truth, Padre? That boy's not just my godson, he's my real son. That's right, mi propio hijo cuz I love him that much. Right, hijo?

MARIO: That's right, Nino.

DON GILBERTO: An' he's getting outta this pinche valle.

DOLORES: Compadre!

DON GILBERTO: I can talk like that with you. ¿No, Padre? You're off duty right now.

JUAN: Sure you can.

DON GILBERTO: That's right. God's back there in the church. The only men we got at this table are hombres de carne y hueso. Vieja!

AMPARO: ¿Qué?

DOLORES (*intervening*): Wha' chu handsome men wan' here?

DON GILBERTO: Tenemos sed, comadre.

DOLORES: Coming right up.

AMPARO *helps* DOLORES *with the drinks, preparing the tequila, salt and lemon. They take a few shots themselves.* MARIO *joins the men at the table.*

DON GILBERTO: She's got a heart of gold, that woman. And she loves her kids ¿sabe? There aint nothin' she wouldn't do for her kids. Look-it Cerezita over there. (CEREZITA *is radiant.*) 'Sta contenta because she knows she got a family, a mother, that loves her. It's hard, Padre. . . . You listenin' to me, Padre?

JUAN (*pulling his gaze from* CEREZITA): . . . Yes.

DON GILBERTO: You can imagine how hard it's been for Dolores, but she did it, and alone. My compadre . . . bueno, it's hard to even call him that now after leaving his family like he did. When a man leaves his wife alone to raise his kids, well to me that no longer qualifies him to be a man. A big macho, maybe. Maybe he can fool las viejas, act like que tiene huevos. But that's the easy part, jumping in and out of the sack. A real man tiene brazos. Nos llaman braceros because we work and love with our arms. Because we aint afraid to lift a sack of potatoes, to defend our children, to put our arms around la waifa at night. This family, they've suffered a lot, Padre. When a father leaves, it's like cutting off the arms of the family. (*Hugging* MARIO.) Even this guy. He had a lot on his shoulders. ¡Chihuahua! I usetu remember this little mocoso coming home from school all the time with his nose all bloody. He wasn' a fighter. But after so many times, finally, Dolores tells me, "Compadre, tienes que hacer algo." (*He brings* MARIO *to his feet, starts to box with him.*) So, I put the gloves on him and showed him my famous "apricot." (DON GILBERTO *winds up, lets out a wild "uppercut" in the air and ends up on his butt. They all rush to him.*) And they never messed with him again. Right, hijo?

MARIO: Right.

DON GILBERTO: ¡Eso!

JUAN: So, all your kids are grown, Don Gilberto?

DON GILBERTO: Well, I guess that's why la vieja and me, we kina adopt these guys. We couldn't have no children. Amparo's a good woman, she wanted kids bad! But it was me. She never tells nobody cuz she thinks I get ashamed. But it's biology, right, Padre? Mi madre, she had two of us, see. And my cuate, well it seems he just hogged up all the jugo, if you know what I mean. He got a pile of kids, nietos too. (*He takes another shot.*) ¿Y tú, Padre? What's your excuse?

JUAN: . . . I'm a priest.

DON GILBERTO: That's no excuse! (*Busting up.*) When los conquistadores come to América with their priests, half the Mexican population got fathers for fathers! (*Busting up again.*)

JUAN (*embarrassed*): I don't know. You just make choices, . . . I guess.

DON GILBERTO: Pues, sometimes you don't get to choose. But that just teaches you que you gotta make familia any way you can.

AMPARO: Ya, viejo. You gointu put the father to sleep con tanta plática. Mira, the father's glass is almost empty.

DON GILBERTO: Pues, fill it up then.

DOLORES: Aquí lo tengo ya. (*She carries a tray with drinks.*)

DON GILBERTO: ¡Tequila! ¡Sí! ¡Celebremos! You watch, mi ahijado's gointu go to the big university. He's gointu be a doctor someday and cure all the sickness que tiene nuestra raza. Right, mijo?

MARIO: That's right, Nino.

DON GILBERTO: Pues, lez drink to that. (*Toasting*.) ¡Salud! (*They all raise their glasses*.)

JUAN: Amor, dinero.

MARIO: Y tiempo para gozarlos.

DON GILBERTO: ¡Eso! (DON GILBERTO *picks up the guitar again and the family joins in singing "Volver."*)

'Y volver, volver, volver
a tus brazos otra vez.
Llegaré hasta donde 'stés.
Yo sé perder, yo sé perder.
Quiero volver, volver, volver.'

MARIO *rises, lights a cigarette, and steps out onto the porch*. DOLORES's *eyes follow him*.

JUAN (*to* DOLORES): May I have this dance?

DOLORES: You don' dance to "Volver," Padre. You cry.

JUAN: May I have this cry?

DOLORES: Bueno, I think this one, pues . . . it's all mine.

Crossfade to MARIO *smoking on the porch. He watches the sky as the fog begins to roll in. Sound of crop duster overhead. He waves back at it sarcastically.* DOLORES *comes out onto the porch.*

DOLORES: Why they spraying at night now?

MARIO: Nobody sees them that way. Nobody that matters anyway.

DOLORES: I'm tired of it. I wish we were all going away.

MARIO: I'm sorry.

DOLORES: Really.

MARIO: Yes.

DOLORES: But it doesn't stop you from leaving us.

MARIO: I want a future, 'amá.

DOLORES: The school is not why you're going. It's something else.

MARIO: What?

DOLORES: You're leaving with a secret.

MARIO: It's no secret, 'amá. You're the only one that doesn't want to see it.

DOLORES: I'm not talking about that. I know already for a long time. You think I dint know since the time you was little? How you want to do everything like Yolie. Play with her dolls, put on her dresses. "Jus' pertend," you say, "jus' pertend, mami." Pertend, nada. Me chocó the first time I seen your hands digging into Yolie's purse like they belong there. (*Grabbing his hands*.) Look at your hands, hijo. Son las manos de tu padre, las manos de un obrero. Why you wannu make yourself como una mujer? Why you wannu do this to the peepo who love you?

MARIO (*pulling his hands away*): Who loves me, 'amá?

DOLORES: Tienes familia.

MARIO: Family you don't take to bed.

DOLORES: You think those men who put their arms around you in the night are gointu be there to take care of you in the morning?

MARIO: No.

DOLORES: Necesitas familia, hijo. What you do fuera del matrimonio is your own biznis. You could have familia. Eres hombre. You don' gottu be alone, not like Yolie. Who's gointu want her con una niña already?

MARIO: I can't do that, 'amá. I can't put my body one place and my heart another. I'm not my father.

DOLORES: He loved us, hijo.

MARIO: He loved his women, too.

DOLORES: Can't you forget that? You hold that in your heart, it's gointu poison you.

MARIO: Can you? We've always been lonely, 'amá. You and me waiting for some-one to come along and just talk to us with a little bit of kindness, to tell us how fine and pretty we are, to lie to our face.

DOLORES: Me das asco.

MARIO: Why? Because I remind you of you. What love did you ever get from my dad? He had a sweet mouth, that's all. A syrupy tongue that every time he dragged himself home, could always talk you back into loving him. That's not the kind of man I want to be.

DOLORES: You'd rather suffer like a woman instead?

MARIO: No.

DOLORES: God made you a man and you throw it away. You lower yourself into half a man.

MARIO: I don't want to fight, 'amá. I'm leaving in the morning. Give me your blessing. Send me on my way with the sign of the cross and a mother's love.

DOLORES: No puedo.

MARIO: You don't have to approve of it, 'amá.

DOLORES: No puedo. Peepo like you are dying. They got tha' sickness. How can I give mi bendición para una vida que te va a matar. God makes this sickness to show peepo it's wrong what they do. Díme que te vas a cambiar y te doy mi bendición. Tu eres el único macho. I want you to live.

MARIO: I want to live, too. I can't make you see that. Your god's doing all the seeing for you.

MARIO *takes off down the street.*

Scene Thirteen

The party is over. CEREZITA *is looking out the window.* DON GILBERTO *is asleep in the chair.* AMPARO *and* JUAN *are just finishing the dishes.* YOLANDA *has retired with the baby.* BONNIE *is asleep on the couch.*

CEREZITA: Mario won't return to us. He will grow ill like his brother and we will ignore this brother, this son, this child of ours who failed in his manly destiny.

JUAN *puts the last of the dishes away.*

AMPARO: Gracias, Father. But don't tell Dolores I let you help me. She kill me. ¡Imagínese! A priest doing the dishes!

JUAN: I enjoyed it.

AMPARO: That's coz you don't haftu do it every day. (*She goes over to* BONNIE, *awakens her.*) C'mon, mija. Ya nos vamos.

BONNIE: Okay.

AMPARO: Bueno, I guess I better try to get this old man out of here.

JUAN: You need help?

AMPARO: No, I'm usetu it. (*She goes to* DON GILBERTO *and nudges him awake.*)

DON GILBERTO (*startled*): Soñé contigo, vieja. You had un montón de chamacos mamando tu pecho.

AMPARO (*helping him to his feet*): The only baby I got is right here.

DON GILBERTO: I was so proud!

AMPARO: You tell Dolores I talk to her in the morning.

JUAN: Sure.

AMPARO (*to* CEREZITA): Good night, mija.

CEREZITA: Good night, Doña Amparo . . . Don Gilberto. (DON GILBERTO *throws her a kiss.*)

BONNIE: 'Night, Cere.

CEREZITA: 'Night, mija.

They exit. JUAN *comes up behind* CEREZITA. *He stares out the window.*

JUAN: There's nothing to see. The fog's barely a foot from the window.

CEREZITA: Sometimes I wish it would swallow the whole house up. I don't blame Mario for leaving. I'd leave if I could.

JUAN: You're gonna miss him, aren't you?

CEREZITA: There's nothing for him here. No Mayan gods. Nothing.

JUAN (*awkwardly*): Well, I guess I better go, too. Do you . . . need something before I leave?

CEREZITA: Yeah, just put a towel over my cage like the canaries. Martyrs don't survive.

JUAN: Cere, I . . .

CEREZITA: I want out, Father! Out into that street! And I will not have time for anybody who can't help me.

She turns her face away. JUAN *hesitates for a moment, then leaves.*

JUAN (*passing* DOLORES *coming back into the yard*): Buenas noches, señora. Gracias.

DOLORES: Buenas noches, Padre.

JUAN *starts to say more, but she has already started toward the house. He exits. Moments later, the sound of the crop duster passes overhead again.* DOLORES *follows the sound.*

DOLORES: Why don't you just drop a bomb, cabrones! It'd be faster that way!

The lights fade to black.

ACT II

Scene One

Several months later, DOLORES *is sneaking around the outside of the front of the house. Crouching down behind a bush, she peaks into the windows, trying not to be seen.* JUAN *is passing by. He is saying prayers from his breviary, his lips moving silently.*

JUAN (*nearly bumping into her*): Señora Valle.

DOLORES: ¡Ay, Padre! Me asustó.

JUAN: ¿Qué hace, señora?

DOLORES (*conspiratorially*): I'm looking through the windows.

JUAN: But . . . why?

DOLORES: To know, Father.

JUAN: To know what?

DOLORES: To know what you can see inside the house at night. The peepo going by can see through the windows. ¿Qué vió, Padre, when you were coming up the street?

JUAN: No sé. I wasn't paying attention.

DOLORES: Next time, Father, you pay attention, eh? So you can tell me from how far away you can see wha's going on inside the house.

JUAN: Certainly, I . . .

DOLORES: Cere don' wan' the shades down. She wants to look at the street lamps, she say.

JUAN: Es todo lo que tiene, Señora Valle.

DOLORES: Sí, pero anybody que pasa por aquí can see we don' got no men in the house. Mire, Father. (*Indicates the window.* JUAN *crouches down next to her.*) Can you tell Cere is sick from here?

JUAN: What do you mean?

DOLORES: ¡Que no tiene cuerpo!

JUAN: No, no se ve.

DOLORES: It looks like she could just be sentada, no?

JUAN: Sí, sentada or stooping behind something.

DOLORES: Bueno, tha's all I needed to know. Gracias, Padre.

JUAN: Buenas noches.

DOLORES: Buenas noches.

JUAN *continues on with his prayers,* DOLORES *goes inside.* YOLANDA *sits near the baby's crib.* CEREZITA *is reading.*

YOLANDA: I can't get her to feed. She keeps pulling her face away.

DOLORES: Pues, no tiene hambre.

YOLANDA: Yesterday was the same. Look. She just sleeps. I have to wake her up to feed her.

DOLORES: ¿Tiene calentura?

YOLANDA: A little. I took her temperature about an hour ago.

DOLORES: ¿Y que te dijeron en la clínica?

YOLANDA: Nothing much. They say maybe there's something wrong with my milk. They gave me formula. She doesn't want that either.

DOLORES: A ver . . . (*Goes over to the baby, checks for a temperature.*) Todavía tiene un poco de calentura. Get some cold toallitas y pónselas en la frente. Tal vez that'll bring her fiebre down.

YOLANDA: I'm scared she's really sick, 'amá.

DOLORES: No pienses así. Traele la toallita. (YOLANDA *goes to get the wet cloth, applies it to the baby's forehead.* DOLORES *serves up sopa from the stove for* CERE, *puts a napkin under her chin, begins spooning the food into her mouth.*) Así me rechazabas when you was a baby. All of a sudden, you dint wan' the chichi no more.

CEREZITA: That was a long time ago, 'amá.

DOLORES: But a mother never forgets those things . . . cuando su bebé turns her face away like that.

She continues feeding CEREZITA, *periodically wiping her mouth.* AMPARO *enters carrying a large, rolled-up chart.*

AMPARO: I'm jus' in time for dinner, eh?

DOLORES: Sí, comadre. Ya 'stá caliente la cena.

AMPARO: No, no. I'm just kidding. Ya comí. (*Going to the baby.*) Ahora ¿cómo esta?

YOLANDA: Igual.

AMPARO: I'm sorry, hija. (*Beat.*) Vente. Quiero enseñarles algo.

YOLANDA: ¿Qué?

AMPARO: Hice un mapa. (*She unrolls the chart onto the table.*) A chart of all the houses en la vecindad que tiene gente con the health problems.

YOLANDA: Let me see.

AMPARO: Miren, the red dots mean those houses got someone with cancer. Estos puntos azules donde tienen tumores. Los green ones son para birth defects y los amarillos, the miscarriages.

YOLANDA: What are all these orange dots?

AMPARO: Bueno, smaller problems como problemas del estómago, las ronchas, cosas así.

YOLANDA: Cheezus, it's the whole damn neighborhood.

CEREZITA: Where's our house?

AMPARO: Aquí donde están the orange dot and the green dot.

CEREZITA: That's me, the green dot.

YOLANDA (*lightly*): You put us on the map, Cere.

CEREZITA: That's right. (*They laugh.*)

DOLORES: Go 'head, make the jokes. (*To* AMPARO:) ¿Por qué traes estas cosas a mi casa?

AMPARO: Bueno, I—

DOLORES: I got one baby que eighteen years later I still got to feed and clean and wipe, que no tiene ni la capacidad to put a spoon a food in her mouth. I got a grandchild si no 'stá llorando por las ronchas, she sleeps all day sin ganas de comer, and I got a son que might as well be dead coz almost a year go by and I don' know nothing about him. So, I don' need a chart to tell me que tengo problemas.

AMPARO: I'm not trying to tell you about your problems, comadre. I'm trying to tell you que no 'stás sola.

DOLORES: I am alone and I'm not gointu hold out my hand como una mendiga a nadie.

AMPARO: No one's going begging. It's not begging to make the government pay for what we got coming to us.

YOLANDA: We need help, 'amá.

DOLORES: Vete. Take tu comunismo someplace else.

AMPARO: Ay, Lola, me das vergüenza. Soy tu comadre. Don' make me into a stranger.

DOLORES: Pues ya no te reconozco. You change since they put your picture in the papers and on the TV. I think you like it.

YOLANDA: That's not fair, 'amá.

AMPARO: No, tiene razón tu madre. It does give me somet'ing. It makes me feel good to watch peepo que no tiene ni educación ni sus papeles, show the guts to fight para sus niños.

DOLORES: ¿Qué sabes tú? No tienes niños.

YOLANDA: 'Amá. (*The baby cries.* YOLANDA *starts toward it, but* DOLORES *intercepts.*)

DOLORES: This is my work. (*Patting the infant. The cries subside.*) When you got a baby, when you feel that baby come out entre las piernas, nothing is the same after that. You are chain to that baby. It doesn' matter how old they get or how far away they go, son tus hijos and they always take a piece of you with them. So you walk around full of holes from all the places they take from you. All the times you worry for them—where they are, who they with, what they doing. All the times you see them suffer on their faces and your hands are tied down from helping them. Como se puede sentir una mujer whole and strong como quieres tú with so many empty places in her body? El Dios es el único que nos llena. Not you and not your gov'ment. (*She goes to* AMPARO, *grabs the chart from her.*) This is the las' time I'm gointu say it, I don' wan' this biznis in my house.

DOLORES *throws the chart out the door and goes back to feeding* CEREZITA, *shoving the food into her mouth.* AMPARO *leaves in silence. Fade out.*

Scene Two

Lights rise on front room. CEREZITA *is watching* BONNIE *play. She is constructing a coffin out of a small shoe box.* DOLORES *sits on the sofa, softly murmuring the rosary.*

BONNIE: We knew she wouldn't make it. The cancer got her.

CEREZITA: How did you know?

BONNIE: She bled through all her openings: her mouth, her ears, her nose . . . even through her pee hole, she bled. It was outta control.

CEREZITA: What are you doing now?

BONNIE: I gotta bury her. I'm making her coffin.

CEREZITA: The shoe box is her coffin?

BONNIE: Yeah, but I'm making it real purty inside. I got some valentine cards in there and some of Yolie's ribbon for her hair. See, look. (*She shows* CEREZITA *the box.*)

CEREZITA: Yeah, Rosie will be nice and cozy in there.

YOLANDA *enters with an overnight bag. She stops at the door, riveted by* BONNIE's *words.*

BONNIE: Lina's gonna die, too, just like this. When they send the children to the hospital, they never come back. They keep 'em in the hospital bed until they put 'em in a box. Then they'll put dirt over her face. When she wakes up, she won't be able to breathe cuz the dirt will be in her nose and her mouth. (BONNIE *shows the box to* YOLANDA *as a kind of offering.*) Look, Yolie.

Horrified, YOLANDA *goes into the kitchen, pours herself a shot of tequila and sits at the table.* DOLORES *goes to her.*

DOLORES: I know what you're feeling. I know what it feels like to have a sick baby. When Cerezita come out of me, I dint even wannu look at her, I tole the doctors to put a blanket over her head to suffocate her, but she scream and scream so loud, the doctors couldn' do it. They tole me un grito así means the baby wants to live with all its heart and soul.

YOLANDA: Evalina's dying, 'amá. My baby's dying.

DOLORES: No hables así. You don' know tha'!

YOLANDA: I know it's a tumor. I know it's malignant. I know what that means.

DOLORES: It means you gottu pray to God. Fíjate. Cerezita es un milagro. Every day that she lives, it's prove que el Dios does not forget us.

YOLANDA: He's forgotten you and me and everybody else in this goddamn valley. (*Sound of low-flying helicopter suddenly fills the air. Searchlights flood the kitchen windows.* YOLANDA *rushes to the front door, swings it open, runs outside.*) Take me! You mutherfuckers!

DOLORES (*going after her*): Yolie! No, they'll see you! Mija! (YOLANDA *is ablaze with light. Chopper sounds grow nearer.*)

YOLANDA (*shouting into the sky*): C'mon, you sonavabitches! Take me! C'mon! Here I am! Look-it! Shoot me you mutherfuckers! Kill me!

DOLORES (*grabbing her*): No, mija! Come back in. (DOLORES *and* YOLANDA *fall to the ground together weeping as the chopper retreats.*)

YOLANDA: Don't you see, 'amá? I gotta find her killer. Put a face to him, a name, track him down and make him suffer the way we suffer. I want to kill him, 'amá. I want to kill some . . . goddamn body!

DOLORES (*stroking her*): Sí, mija. Sí. Ya lo sé, hija. I know.

DOLORES *helps her daughter to her feet and brings her back into the house. The lights fade to black.*

Scene Three

Lights rise to reveal a political demonstration. ANA PEREZ, *in an overcoat and scarf, stands before the "cameras" with a microphone. In the distance, the* PROTESTORS *are approaching, the* MOTHERS *wearing white bandanas. Their expressions are heavy with the faces of the dying and the memory of the already dead. The* PROTESTORS *carry signs reading, Boycott Grapes, No Compre Uvas, etc. One child holds up a sign saying, Quiero Vivir! and another, I Want to Live! The red-and-black Union of Campesino flags can be seen above their heads.* DON GILBERTO *and* JUAN *are among the protestors, as are* BONNIE *and the* CHILDREN. *A drum beats slowly.*

ANA PEREZ: It's a frostbitten morning here in Sacramento, Jack, but that hasn't discouraged the Mothers and Friends of McLaughlin from making the long trek up here from their home at the southernmost end of the San Joaquin Valley.

PROTESTORS (*chanting*): '¡El pueblo unido jamás será vencido!' (*They continue to the beat of the drum.*)

ANA PEREZ: The mothers' demands are quite concrete. They believe that the federal government should pay for their families' relocation to an environmentally safe community, since federal moneys subsidized the building of their housing tract. They further demand that the well which provides tap water for the area be shut down and never again be used for drinking water. And finally they urge the governor to see to the establishment of a free health clinic for affected families and to monitor the growing incidence of cancer in the region. (*The* PROTESTORS *begin to move downstage. They stand shoulder to shoulder.*) Amparo Manríquez, the founder of Mothers for McLaughlin, has approached the capitol steps. I understand they have prepared some kind of statement.

As AMPARO *steps forward, she holds up a picture of a dead child. Each of the* MOTHERS *follows in the same manner.*

AMPARO: Sandy Pérez. Died August 15, 1982. Ailment: acute leukemia. Age 9.

MOTHER: Frankie Gonzales. Died March 16, 1986. Ailment: bone cancer. Age 10.

MOTHER: Johnny Rodríguez. Died July 10, 1987. Ailment: adrenal gland tumor. Age 5.

MOTHER: Rosalinda Lorta. Died June 5, 1980. Ailment: chest muscle tumor. Age 5.

MOTHER: Maira Sánchez. Died August 30, 1987. Ailment pituitary tumor. Age 6.

MOTHER: Mario Bravo. Died November 26, 1987. Ailment: cancer of the liver. Age 14.

MOTHER: Memo Delgado. Died October 24, 1988. Ailment: adrenal gland tumor. Age 6.

YOLANDA: Evalina Valle. Died November 2, 1989. Ailment . . . ailment . . . era mi hija . . . era . . . ¡mi hija!

She collapses in AMPARO's *arms. The* PROTESTORS *advance, forming a line of resistance. A* POLICEMAN *in riot gear holds back the crowd. They continue to press forward.*

PROTESTORS: ¡Asesinos! ¡Asesinos! ¡Asesinos! . . .

BONNIE *slips.* AMPARO *steps out of the line to retrieve her. The* POLICEMAN *knocks* AMPARO *down with his nightstick.*

ANA PEREZ: She's been struck! Amparo Manríquez . . . oh my god! The policeman! . . . (*He continues to beat her in slow, methodical blows.*) Stop him! Jesus! Somebody stop him! No! No! Stop him!

DON GILBERTO *breaks through the line and throws his body over* AMPARO *to shield her. The* PROTESTORS *scatter. Black out.*

Scene Four

JUAN *has brought* CEREZITA *outdoors. The sun is setting. Black silhouettes of pecan trees on the horizon, grape vineyards in the foreground.* CEREZITA *is transfixed by the view.* JUAN *paces back and forth nervously.* BONNIE *is on the porch, softly singing a lullaby. She ties two twigs together in the shape of a cross, then hangs her doll onto it, wrapping string around its wrists and ankles.*

BONNIE:

> 'Duerme, duerme, negrito,
> que tu mama está en el campo, negrito.
> Te va a traer rica fruta para tí.
> Te va a traer muchas cosas para tí . . .'

JUAN: I got scared. I don't know why. I . . . I could have done something. They beat her so bad, Cere.

CEREZITA: Heroes and saints.

JUAN: What?

CEREZITA: That's all we can really have for now. That's all people want.

JUAN: They want blood?

CERE *glances at him, presses her mouth to the raite button, and comes downstage.* JUAN *looks over to* BONNIE. *She waves back with the crucified doll.*

CEREZITA: Look, Juan, it looks like a thousand mini-crucifixions out there.

JUAN: What?

CEREZITA: The vineyards. See all the crosses? It's a regular cemetery.

(JUAN *comes up behind her; his eyes scan the horizon.*) The trunk of each of the plants is a little gnarled body of Christ writhing in agony. Don't you see it?

JUAN: Sort of.

CEREZITA: See how the branches look like arms with the bulging veins of suffering. Each arm intertwined with the other little crucified Christs next to it. Thousands of them in neat orderly rows of despair. Syphilitic sacks of grapes hanging from their loins.

JUAN: How do you see these things, Cere?

CEREZITA: I see it all. A chain gang of Mexican Christs. Their grey wintered skin, their feet taking root into the trenches the machines have made.

JUAN: They *are* lifelike, aren't they?

CEREZITA: They're dead. (*Suddenly the sun bursts through a cloud. It bathes*
　　CEREZITA'*s face. She basks in it for a moment.*)

> The living dead of winter.
> Dead to the warmth of sun on my face
> melting into the horizon.
> Pecan trees like rigid skeletons
> black against the sky.
> Dead to the deep red and maroon
> the grapevines bleed.
> Dead to the smell of earth,
> split moist and open
> to embrace the seed.

BONNIE *approaches. She carries two small two-by-fours.*

BONNIE: I got the wood, Cere.

CEREZITA: Bring it here, mija.

JUAN (*stopping her*): No! Give it to me.

BONNIE *hesitates, looks to* CEREZITA.

CEREZITA: Dásela.

BONNIE (*handing the wood over to him*): Are you gonna make the cross, Father Juan?

He raises up the two pieces of wood, forming them into the shape of a small, child-sized cross. His eyes are fixed on CERE'*s.*

JUAN: Yes.

Sudden flute and tambor. Fade out.

Scene Five

The hospital. DON GILBERTO *brings* AMPARO *out in a wheelchair. She has a black eye and wears a hospital gown and carries a small purse on her lap.* JUAN *is with them.* DON GILBERTO *sits, takes out a racing form.*

AMPARO: They cut out my spleen, Father. It was completely smash.

DON GILBERTO: El Doctor Fong . . . es un Chino ¿sabes? He says que the spleen is the part of the body que 'stá conectado con el coraje.

JUAN: It's the place of emotion, of human passions.

AMPARO: Pues, that policia got another thing coming if he think he could take away mi pasión. ¿No, viejo?

DON GILBERTO: Yeah, she already been trying to pull me on top of her in the wheelchair. She gonna bust her stitches I tell her.

AMPARO: No seas exagerado. (*To* JUAN:) The doctor dice que me parezco a su madre, que I'm tough like his mother con el dolor.

DON GILBERTO (*teasing*): Mi Chinita.

AMPARO: Cállete el hocico tú. El padre came to visit me. I'm the sick one. (DON CILBERTO *smiles, starts reading the racing form. As the conversation ensues, he begins to nod off, then finally falls asleep. The newspaper lies draped across his chest.*) Y Dolores . . . ¿cómo 'stá?

JUAN: Yolanda seems to be handling the baby's death better than Señora Valle. I had to pull her out of the bushes last night.

AMPARO: ¿Otra vez?

JUAN: This was worse. It was already past midnight, and she wouldn't budge. She said she had seen Mario's ghost . . .

AMPARO: ¿Cómo?

JUAN: That Mario's ghost was trying to get back into the house.

AMPARO: ¡Qué raro!

JUAN: She was shaking . . . and as white as a ghost herself.

AMPARO: Pero ¿por qué dijo eso?

JUAN: I don't know. Nobody can reach Mario.

AMPARO: My comadre is a very scared woman, Father. (*Pause.*) Mira.

AMPARO *takes a news clipping out of her purse, unfolds it, hands it to* JUAN.

JUAN: It's Cerezita.

AMPARO: Barely two years old and in *The New York Times*. Fifteen years ago, Cere's face was in all the newspapers, then Dolores just shut up.

JUAN: Why?

AMPARO: She lost her husband on account of it.

JUAN: On account of what?

AMPARO: Advertising his sins. She believe Cere was a sign from God to make her husband change his ways. But he dint change, he left.

JUAN: But it was pesticides.

AMPARO: In her heart, Dolores feels difernt. Nobody wants to be a víctima, Father. Better to believe that it's the will of God than have to face up to the real sinners. They're purty powerful, those sinners. You start to take them on, pues you could lose. This way, por lo menos, you always get to win in heaven. Isn' that what the Church teaches, Father?

JUAN: Well, the Church counsels that—

AMPARO: You gointu do the rosary tonight, Father?

JUAN: Yes. At seven, then the vigil will go on all night.

AMPARO: And Cerezita will be there?

JUAN: Yes, it's at the house.

AMPARO (*looking over to make sure* DON GILBERTO *is asleep*): Cuídala, Father. Don' let her go out tonight.

JUAN: But Cere . . . never goes out.

AMPARO: The men in the helicopters, they're hired by the growers. Anybody out en los files tonight, they'll shoot them. They don' wan' no more publeesty about the crucifixions.

JUAN: Then you think Cere—

AMPARO: I don' think not'ing. I'm jus' asking you not to let your eyes leave her tonight. Hazme el favor.

JUAN: Of . . . course.

AMPARO: Bueno. Now give me one of those priest's prayers of yours. A ver si me ayuda.

JUAN: You want me to pray for you?

AMPARO: Insurance, Padre.

He smiles. AMPARO *closes her eyes as* JUAN *blesses her. The lights fade to black.*

Scene Six

Later that night. CEREZITA *is sleeping.* DOLORES *is standing by the small coffin. It is surrounded by candles and flowers. Trancelike, she takes one of the candles and places it on* CEREZITA's *raite. She kneels before her.*

DOLORES: I can't pray no more to a God no tiene oídos. Where is my Dios, mija? I turn to you coz I got nobody left now. Give me a sign mi querida virgencita. Enséñame como aliviarnos del dolor que nos persigue en este valle de lágrimas.

CEREZITA *slowly opens her eyes, sees her mother praying to her.*

CEREZITA: Go to sleep now, 'amá. I'll watch over Evalina.

DOLORES: Gracias, virgencita. (*She rises, carrying the candle, goes to the window.*) Mario carried death with him. I saw it in his cansancio, in the way his head fell down, tan pesada entre los hombros. In the way he put one foot onto the porch and then the other . . . and then he change his mind. (DOLORES *blows out the candle, as she does the others by the coffin. With each one, she names her progeny.*) I miss my babies, mi Evalina, mi Mario, mi Cerezita . . .

CEREZITA: I'm still here, 'amá.

DOLORES (*staring at her daughter, momentarily confused*): Arturo, do you remember when I was big with Cere and the whole house was full of babies?

She exits, quietly muttering to herself. CEREZITA *presses her mouth to the raite button and goes over to the small open coffin.*

CEREZITA: Before the grown ones come to put you in the ground, they'll untie the ropes around your wrists and ankles. By then you are no longer in your body. The child's flesh hanging from that wood makes no difference to you. It is . . . you are a symbol. Nada más.

JUAN *appears at the window, taps it lightly.*

CEREZITA (*whispering*): Juan?

JUAN: Yes, it's me.

CEREZITA: Come in.

JUAN (*entering with a duffel bag*): Is everyone asleep?

CEREZITA: Yes.

Trying to contain his excitement, JUAN *gets down on his knees and starts pulling things out of the bag.*

CEREZITA: You hardly look like a gravedigger.

JUAN: Shovel. Flashlight. Rope. Did I forget anything?

CEREZITA: Do you know how beautiful you are?

JUAN: What?

CEREZITA: I've never seen you like this. You're almost glowing.

JUAN: I am?

CEREZITA: Glowing.

JUAN: Are the children waiting? (*He repacks the duffel bag.*)

CEREZITA: They'll meet us in front of the church. There's time yet.

JUAN: I saw Amparo today. She knows, Cere.

CEREZITA: She wouldn't stop us.

JUAN: No, but . . .

CEREZITA: What?

JUAN: She says it's dangerous. She says they'll shoot anything that moves out there in the field tonight.

CEREZITA: Then we'll have to leave the kids behind. I don't need them now. I have you. You're not afraid are you, Juan?

JUAN: No. Yes, I'm scared, but it's exciting.

CEREZITA: Things are gonna change now, Juan. You'll see.

JUAN (*walks over to the coffin, blesses it*): She looks peaceful.

CEREZITA: She is. What we do to her body won't disturb her peace.

JUAN: Yes, I'm supposed to know that.

CEREZITA: Nobody's dying should be invisible, Juan. Nobody's.

There is a pause. JUAN *prays by the coffin.* CEREZITA *observes.*

CEREZITA: Juan? . . .

JUAN: Hmm? . . .

CEREZITA: You know when they killed those priests in El Salvador?

JUAN: The Jesuits.

CEREZITA: Did you know they killed the housekeeper and her daughter, too?

JUAN: Yes.

CEREZITA: If the Jesuits died as priests, does that make them saints?

JUAN: I don't know. They're martyrs, heroes. They spoke out against the government.

CEREZITA: Did the housekeeper and her daughter?

JUAN: What?

CEREZITA: Speak out against the government?

JUAN: I don't think so.

CEREZITA: I don't either. It wasn't their job. I imagine they just changed the priests' beds, kept a pot of beans going, hung out the sábanas to dry. At least, the housekeeper did and the girl, she helped her mother. She did the tasks that young girls do . . . girls still living under the roof of their mother. And maybe sometimes one of the priests read to the girl, maybe . . . he taught her to read and she . . . fell in love with him, the teacher. (*Pause.*) Touch my hair, Juan.

Coming up from behind her, he touches her hair very tenderly, brings a strand to his face. He smells it, puts his hand to her cheek, caresses her. She moves her cheek deeper into the palm of his hand, moans softly. She lifts her face to his. He hesitates, then kisses her at first awkwardly, trying to find her mouth at the right angle. CEREZITA moans. Suddenly, JUAN's face takes on a distanced look. He grabs CERE's cheeks between his hands.

CEREZITA: I want to taste you, Juan.

He hesitates, then kisses her again. CEREZITA's moaning increases, intensifies. He comes around behind her, presses his pelvis up against the backside of the raite. He brings her head against him, his fingers tangled in her hair.

CEREZITA: I want the ocean in my mouth.

She pulls at his shirt with her teeth, trying to bring him back around.

CEREZITA: Juan, help me. I need your hands.

JUAN *closes his eyes.*

CEREZITA: Juan, look at me.

He digs his pelvis into the raite, pulling her head deeper into him.

CEREZITA: Juan, where are you?

He pushes against her harder, deeper.

CEREZITA: Open your eyes. Juan.

He comes to orgasm.

CEREZITA: Juan.

He grabs the duffel bag and runs out.

CEREZITA: Juan!

After a few moments, the sound of an approaching helicopter, then gunshots are heard. Black out.

Scene Seven

Dawn. MARIO *is lying on a park bench, wearing a jacket, the collar turned up, a knapsack at his feet. He has a constant cough.* JUAN *walks by. Still in his priest's clothes, he appears somewhat disheveled.*

MARIO: Got a cigarette?

JUAN: Mario.

MARIO: Hello, Father.

JUAN: We'd almost given you up for lost.

MARIO: You're out pretty early.

JUAN: I . . . couldn't sleep.

MARIO: I've forgotten what sleep is.

JUAN: Why didn't you answer my messages?

MARIO: Wasn't even sure I was coming until I found myself hitching out on the interstate.

JUAN: You been to the house?

MARIO: Yes. Well . . . almost.

JUAN (*indicating the bench*): May I?

MARIO: For a cigarette.

JUAN: Oh, right.

MARIO *gets up.* JUAN *sits beside him, lights up a cigarette for each of them.*

JUAN: You shouldn't be smoking, Mario . . . with that cough.

MARIO: Lung cancer's the least of my worries, Padre. (*They sit in silence for a few moments. Sounds of the highway can be heard in the distance.*) This place is strange. Just one hundred yards off that highway, and you're already right smack back into the heart of the Valley. In minutes, it feels like you never left, like it won't ever let you leave again, . . . like a Chicano Bunuel movie. (JUAN *smiles.*)

JUAN: Except it's too real.

MARIO: The city's no different. Raza's dying everywhere. Doesn't matter if it's crack or . . . pesticides, AIDS, it's all the same shit.

JUAN: Do you regret going, Mario?

MARIO: No. (*Pause.*) I've always loved sex, Father, always felt that whatever I had crippled or bent up inside me that somehow sex could cure it, that sex could straighten twisted limbs, like . . . the laying on of hands.

JUAN: Like tongues of fire.

MARIO: Yeah. Even holy like that . . . with the right person. (*Pause.*) And when you love your own sex, and they got your own hungry dark eyes staring back at you, well you're convinced that you could even cure death. And so you jus' keep kissing that same purple mouth, deeper and harder, and you keep whispering, "I'm gonna wipe all that sickness outta you, cousin." And then weeks and months and maybe even a year or two go by, and suddenly you realize you didn't cure nothing and that your family's dissolving right there inside of your hands.

JUAN (*pause*): And your blood family, Mario? . . .

MARIO: I've had to choose, Father. I can't come home. I'm not strong enough, I'm not a woman. I'm not suited for despair. I'm not suited to carry a burden greater than the weight of my own balls. (*He picks up his knapsack.*)

JUAN: You're leaving?

MARIO: I'm sick, Father. Tell my family in whatever way you can. (*He starts to exit.*)

JUAN: Mario.

He hands him the pack of cigarettes. MARIO *smiles and walks off. Fade out.*

Scene Eight

A few hours later. YOLANDA *wears a black slip and is ironing a black blouse.* CEREZITA *watches her.*

YOLANDA: My mom hasn't said one word to me about Lina. She just keeps asking what time mi 'apá's coming. What are we gonna do? We barely got a family left. (*She puts on the blouse, starts to button it.*)

CEREZITA: You gotta leave this place.

YOLANDA (*grabbing her breasts*): ¡Carajo! I can't stop them. I can't stop them from running.

CEREZITA: What?

YOLANDA: My breasts. They're so heavy, Cere. They're killing me. Nothing takes the pain away. They want a mouth and there's no mouth to relieve them. They feel like they're gonna burst open. I wish they would, I wish they would spill onto everything, turn everything to milk. Sweet milk. My baby's sweet mouth, I miss my baby. (*Her breasts run.*) Look at me. I'm a mess. They're dripping all over me. (*She grabs a bunch of tissues, continues stuffing them into her bra, taking them out and stuffing more in.*) Every time I think of her, they run. Nobody told my body my baby is dead. I still hear her crying and my breasts bleed fucking milk. I remember the smell of her skin and they bleed again. My body got used to being a mother, Cere. And then it's cut off . . . like that! A child's not supposed to die before her mother. It's not natural. It's not right. That's why you hear about women throwing themselves in front of speeding cars, blocking bullets to save their kid. I get it now. It's not about sacrifice. It's instinct. (*She pulls at her breasts.*) I want to rip them off of me. They feel like tombstones on my chest!

CEREZITA (*presses the button to her raite, crosses to* YOLANDA): Sister! I wish I had arms to hold you.

YOLANDA: Cere . . .

CEREZITA: It's almost over now, 'mana. You gotta get outta here, start a new family.

YOLANDA: I'm afraid, Cere. I think my womb is poisoned.

CEREZITA: No. Let me take the pain away. Your breasts, they're so heavy.

YOLANDA *goes to her, opens her blouse and brings* CERE's *face to her breast. The lights fade to black.*

Scene Nine

BONNIE *holds her doll in one hand and a large pair of scissors in the other.*
CEREZITA *watches her as she begins to cut the doll's hair.*

BONNIE: This isn't going to hurt you, hija. It's for your own good.

CEREZITA: Bonnie, vente.

BONNIE *goes to her. They huddle together, speaking in whispers.*

CEREZITA (*aloud*): After this there will be no more sacrificial lambs. Not here in this valley. No more.

BONNIE *nods and exits as* JUAN *enters.* CEREZITA *will not look at him.*

JUAN: I came to see if you were all right. (*Pause.*) Cere, turn around. Please. . . . I heard there were gunshots. The children—

CEREZITA: The children were waiting for you. They were waiting for you with their little flashlights, their children's shovels, their children's hearts.

JUAN: I lost heart.

CEREZITA: Yes, you lost heart.

JUAN (*pause*): After I left here, I just started driving north. I didn't know where I was going, I was going nowhere. The fog was so thick. I could barely see the front end of the car. (*Pause.*) And it suddenly hit me, how this had happened once before, that I had done this before, somewhere else with some other—

CEREZITA: Pobre?

JUAN: Yes. (*Pause.*) I turned the car around.

CEREZITA: Why?

JUAN: I had to come back. See you.

CEREZITA: We had a plan, Juan, a plan of action. But your small fear stopped you.

JUAN: I couldn't after that. I—

CEREZITA: After what?

JUAN: It shouldn't have happened.

CEREZITA: Stop, Juan.

JUAN: I'm a priest, Cere. I'm not free. My body's not my own.

CEREZITA: It wasn't your body I wanted. It was mine. All I wanted was for you to make me feel like I had a body because, the fact is, I don't. I was denied one. But for a few minutes, a few minutes before you started *thinking*, I felt myself full of fine flesh filled to the bones in my toes. . . . I miss myself. Is that so hard to understand?

JUAN: No.

CEREZITA: And I'm sick of all this goddamn dying. If I had your arms and legs, if I had your dick for chrissake, you know what I'd do? I'd burn this motherless town down and all the poisoned fields around it. I'd give healthy babies to each and every childless woman who wanted one and I'd even stick around to watch those babies grow up! . . . You're a waste of a body.

JUAN: Cere . . .

BONNIE *reenters, carrying the small cross. The* CHILDREN *stand behind her.*

CEREZITA: I'm not gonna let you stop me, Juan. Nobody's going to stop me.

The lights fade to black.

Scene Ten

JUAN *has exited. In the half-darkness, the* CHILDREN *surround* CEREZITA *and begin to transform her as* BONNIE *cuts away at* CERE's *hair. Moments later, they scatter. The lights rise to reveal* DOLORES *standing in the doorway. A brilliant beam of light has entered the room and washes over* CEREZITA. *She is draped in the blue-starred veil of La Virgen de Guadalupe. Her head is tilted slightly toward the right, her eyes downcast in the Virgin's classic expression.* DOLORES *is riveted by the sight. The raite is covered in a white altar cross with the roses of Tepeyac imprinted upon it. The cross rests at the base of the raite. The light, brighter now, completely illuminates* CERE's *saintlike expression and the small cross.* DOLORES *drops to her knees.*

DOLORES: Mi virgen.

Black out.

Scene Eleven

The baby's coffin has been brought out, draped in a funeral cloth of white. DOLORES *stands by it, praying softly, then crosses to la virgen. She lifts up the veil slightly and touches* CEREZITA's *face.* DOLORES *exhibits a calm not previously witnessed in the play.*

DOLORES: And you usetu have such beautiful beautiful hair. But it was you, mi virgencita, that made this sacrificio para nosotros. (*Crossing herself with the rosary, she kneels before the image of la virgen.*) "El quinto misterio doloroso, la crucifixión." Querida virgen santísima, watch over nuestra baby Evalina.

She begins to pray the rosary. YOLANDA *enters, wearing a black chapel veil.*

YOLANDA: ¿Está lista, 'amá? . . . Cheezus! What's wrong with her?

Why are you praying to her?

DOLORES: It was a sign from God.

YOLANDA: What sign? Cere-girl. Answer me!

DOLORES: Ya no 'stá.

YOLANDA: Whadayou mean, she's not there? Cere?

DOLORES: She went already to another place.

YOLANDA: What place?

DOLORES: A place inside herself. She said she was going on a long jornada. She tole me with her eyes.

YOLANDA: No, 'amá.

DOLORES: She gave me a sign, a sign of the cross. Esta mañana I found it, just like this. (*She takes the cross, holds it up to her.*) The sun was coming in por la ventana y la cruz estaba iluminada en luz. We've had no pertection, hija. La virgencita will protect us now.

YOLANDA: Cere. Talk to me.

DOLORES: ¡Imagínate! Un milagro un nuestra propia casa.

YOLANDA: 'Amá, what did you do to her?

DOLORES (*pause*): I pray, hija.

In the distance the sound of singing and the slow beat of a tambor.

EL PUEBLO (*singing*):

> "Oh María, madre mía! Oh consuelo, del mortal!
> Amparadme y guiadme a la patria celestial!"

BONNIE *comes into the house and approaches* DOLORES.

DOLORES: ¿Qué quieres?

BONNIE: La cruz, Doña Lola. It's the funeral.

DOLORES (*as if realizing for the first time*): The funeral.

DOLORES *reluctantly hands the cross over to her.* YOLANDA *goes to the coffin, hesitates for a brief moment, then tenderly lifts it up and carries it out to meet the procession, following* BONNIE. *Hearing the voices approaching,* DOLORES *pulls the curtain around* CEREZITA. *Outside,* ANA PEREZ *addresses the "camera."*

ANA PEREZ: This is Ana Pérez coming to you live from McLaughlin, California. Today is the funeral of Evalina Valle, the tenth child to die of cancer in this small Valley town.

JUAN, *dressed in full vestments, accompanied by altar boys and* EL PUEBLO, *passes before the Valle house. They crane their necks to get a glimpse of* CEREZITA, *but* DOLORES *stands resolute before the window, shielding her from view.* YOLANDA *gives the altar boys the coffin. They all continue in procession,* BONNIE *leading with the cross.*

ANA PEREZ: Although funerals are becoming commonplace here in McLaughlin, rumors of a miracle occurrence in the family of the deceased have spread rapidly and have already attracted a huge following. Just before nine this morning, it was reported that Dolores Valle, the mother of Cerezita Valle, found a wooden cross in the disabled girl's sleeping chamber. The cross was illuminated in a wondrous glow and from that moment the young virgin has ceased to speak and has assumed an appearance and affect strikingly similar to the Virgin of Guadalupe . . . (*She spies* YOLANDA *as the procession passes.*) This . . . virgin, this saint is your sister?

YOLANDA: I don't want to talk to you.

ANA PEREZ: The priest asked me to be here.

YCLANDA: Father Juan?

ANA PEREZ: He said there was to be a crucifixion.

YOLANDA: My god! ¡Mi hija! (*She rushes off to catch up with the procession.*)

EL PUEBLO *have arrived at the church steps.* JUAN *prays over the coffin, blessing it with holy water.* YOLANDA *hovers near the coffin.* DON GILBERTO *arrives with* AMPARO *in the wheelchair.* ANA PEREZ *stands on the sidelines, observing. The church bells toll.*

JUAN: Señor, hazme un instrumento de tu paz. Donde hay odio . . .

EL PUEBLO: Que siembre yo amor;

JUAN: Donde hay injuria . . .

EL PUEBLO: Perdón;

JUAN: Donde hay duda . . .

EL PUEBLO: Fe;

JUAN: Donde hay deseperación . . .

EL PUEBLO: Esperanza;

They continue praying. In the Valle home, DOLORES *has covered her head with a black rebozo. She starts to exit.*

CEREZITA: Let me go, 'amá.

DOLORES: Hija?

CEREZITA: I know about death. I know how to stop death.

DOLORES: ¿Has visto la cara de Dios?

CEREZITA: Sí, 'amá. I've seen the face of God. But I'm not free.

DOLORES: No entiendo.

CEREZITA: You tie my tongue, 'amá. How can I heal without my tongue? Do I have arms or legs?

DOLORES: I cut them from you.

CEREZITA: No 'amá. You gave birth to me. Eres mi madre.

DOLORES: Sí . . .

CEREZITA: Now, let . . . me . . . go.

Church bells resonate throughout the town. They call her to action. She turns back the curtain. DOLORES *is stunned by the resolve in* CEREZITA's *eyes. There is no need for more words.* DOLORES *pushes the raite with la virgen out the door.*

JUAN: Pues es dando . . .

EL PUEBLO: Que recibimos;

JUAN: Es perdonando . . .

EL PUEBLO: Que somos perdonados;

JUAN: Y es muriendo . . .

EL PUEBLO: Que nacemos a la vida eter—

Upon the sight of la virgen, the prayer is interrupted. A hush falls over the crowd.

JUAN (*to himself*): My God, Cere, what have they done to you?

They arrive at the church steps. DOLORES *calls out to* ANA PEREZ.

DOLORES: Come, señorita. Come see how my baby se vuelve a santita. Come show the peepo.

ANA PEREZ *is noticeably shaken by the image of* CEREZITA. *She signals to the "cameraman" to begin filming. In procession,* EL PUEBLO *bring forth pictures of their dead and deformed children in offering to la virgen.*

EL PUEBLO (*singing*):

> "Oh María, madre mía! Oh consuelo, del mortal!
> Amparadme y guiadme a la patria celestial!"

The singing continues as they pin milagros to the white cloth of her raite. DOLORES *raises her hand to quiet the crowd.* CEREZITA's *eyes scan the faces of the people. There is a pause.*

CEREZITA: Put your hand inside my wound. Inside the valley of my wound, there is a people. A miracle people. In this pueblito where the valley people live, the river runs red with blood; but they are not afraid because they are used to the color red. It is the same color as the river that runs through their veins, the same color as the sun setting into the sierras, the same color of the pool of liquid they were born into. They remember this in order to understand why their fields, like the rags of the wounded, have soaked up the color and still bear no fruit. No lovely red fruit that el pueblo could point to and say yes, for this we bleed, for this our eyes go red with rage and sadness. They tell themselves red is as necessary as bread. They tell themselves this in a land where bread is a tortilla without maize, where the frijol cannot be cultivated. (*Pause.*) But we, we live in a land of plenty. The fruits that pass through your fingers are too many to count—luscious red in their strawberry wonder, the deep purple of the grape inviting, the tomatoes perfectly shaped and translucent. And yet, you suffer at the same hands. (*Pause.*) You are Guatemala, El Salvador. You are the Kuna y Tarahumara. You are the miracle people too, for like them the same blood runs through your veins. The same memory of a time when your deaths were cause for reverence and celebration, not shock and mourning. You are the miracle people because today, this day, that red memory will spill out from inside you and flood this valley con coraje. And you will be free. Free to name this land *Madre*. Madre Tierra. Madre Sagrada. Madre . . . Libertad. The radiant red mother . . . rising.

JUAN *moves to the center of the crowd to give a final bendición.* MARIO *appears upstage. He goes to* DOLORES. *They embrace.* EL PUEBLO *kneel as* JUAN *blesses them and all those witnessing the play.* BONNIE *approaches* JUAN *with the cross.*

BONNIE: Now is it time, Father?

JUAN *nods, then takes the cross from her. Another child brings* JUAN *some rope. He goes to* CEREZITA, *touches her cheek, and releases the locks on the raite. Her eyes do not leave him. He puts her mouthpiece attachment in place. They both turn to* YOLANDA. YOLANDA *now understands that she is to offer up her dead infant. She goes to the coffin, takes it from the altar boys, kisses it, then hands it over to* JUAN. CEREZITA *presses her mouth to the button of her raite and slowly turns toward the vineyard. The tambor begins to beat slowly, while* EL PUEBLO *watch in silence.* JUAN *and* CEREZITA *head out to the vineyard.* CEREZITA *pauses briefly as she passes her mother.*

CEREZITA: Mamá.

DOLORES *blesses her.* CEREZITA *and* JUAN *proceed offstage into the vineyards. Moments later, the shadow and sound of a helicopter pass overhead.* EL PUEBLO *watch the sky. Then there is the sudden sound of machine gun fire.* EL PUEBLO *let out a scream and drop to the ground, covering their heads in terror.* MARIO *suddenly rises, raises his fist into the air.*

MARIO: Burn the fields!

EL PUEBLO (*rising with him*): ¡Enciendan los files! (*They all, including* ANA PEREZ, *rush out to the vineyards, shouting as they exit.*) ¡Asesinos! ¡Asesinos! ¡Asesinos!

Moments later, there is the crackling of fire as a sharp red-orange glow spreads over the vineyard and the Valle home. The lights slowly fade to black.

Jimmy Santiago Baca (b. 1952)

Jimmy Santiago Baca was born in Santa Fe, New Mexico, of Chicano and Apache descent. Raised by grandparents, at age seven he was sent to an orphanage when his grandfather died. A teenage runaway who hated books, Baca lived by his wits on the streets, sometimes holding down a job but often drifting. Fighting and run-ins with police led to stints in jail and, at age twenty-one, to a five-year sentence in a maximum security prison on drug charges. Baca taught himself to read and write while incarcerated, using his literacy as a defense against the assault on body and sanity exacted upon him by prison life. Through poetry, Baca re-formed himself, nurturing a life-saving sense of freedom, identity, and power that could not be undone by his encounters with brutality and racism. As he explains in *A Place To Stand* (2001), "language . . . opened the way toward a future that was based not on fear or bitterness or apathy but on compassionate involvement and a belief that I belonged."

Baca's poems speak with passion and beautiful directness about the hard work of living: of keeping it together, of dealing with the damning isolation of being poor or brown or undesired in an America that values affluence and whiteness above all. His poems celebrate the life force of creativity, showing how one's language, ancestry, and circumstances can forge a wakeful and authentic life. Baca portrays characters toughened and made soulful by an urgency to survive and thrive. In "Perfecto Flores," a Mexican bricklayer banters proudly that we could "sharpen a file on these hands"—the same hands whose craft and ingenuity have built from scraps a literally solid life: three houses for his family. In "The New Warden," Baca playfully imagines a prison transformed: a place without bars and death chairs—a place of true workmanship made over from the ground up in a spirit of reconciliation. His vision suggests that real work—work of the will and imagination, not of the enforcer—generates genuine purpose and change.

Baca's work as a poet, novelist, and scriptwriter is widely acclaimed. His poetry collections include *Immigrants in Our Own Land* (1979), National Book Award-winning *Martin and Meditations on the South Valley* (1987), *Black Mesa Poems* (1989), *Healing Earthquakes* (2001), and *Winter Poems Along the Rio Grande* (2004). In 2001, Baca coedited, with James Stacy, *The Heat: Steelworker Lives and Legends*, a collection of stories written by workers in Gary, Indiana, and Baltimore steel mills.

                                                                                Lois Williams

THE NEW WARDEN

He sat in the cool morning.
He had a handful of seeds in his palm.
He sat there contemplating
Where he would plant them.
5   A month later he tore the kitchen down
and planted apple seeds there.
Some of the convicts asked him why:
"Apples," he said, "is one of America's
great traditional prides. Remember
10   the famous ballad Johnny Apple Seed?"
Nobody had heard of it, so he set up
A poetry workshop where the death house had been.
The chair was burned in a great ceremony.
Some of the Indian convicts performed
15   Ancient rituals for the souls of those executed in the past.
He sold most of the bricks and built
Little ovens in the earth with the rest.
The hospital was destroyed except for one new wing
To keep the especially infirm aged ones.
20   And funny thing, no one was ever sick.
The warden said something about freedom being the greatest cure
For any and all ailments. He was right.
The cellblocks were razed to the ground.
Some of the steel was kept and a blacksmith shop went up.
25   With the extra bricks the warden purchased
Tents, farming implements and bought a big yellow bus.
The adjoining fields flowed rich with tomatoes, pumpkins,
Potatoes, corn, chili, alfalfa, cucumbers.
From the nearby town of Florence, and as far away as Las Cruces,
30   People came to buy up loads and loads of vegetables.
In one section of the compound the artists painted
Easter and Christmas and other holiday cards, on paper
previously used for disciplinary reports.
The government even commissioned some of the convicts
35   To design patriotic emblems.
A little group of engineers, plumbers, electricians
Began building solar heating systems and sold them
To elementary schools way under cost. Then,
Some citizens grew interested. Some high school kids
40   Were invited to learn about it, and soon,
Solar systems were being installed in the community.
An agricultural program opened up.
Unruly convicts were shipped out to another prison.
After the first year, the new warden installed ballot boxes.
45   A radio and TV shop opened. Some of the convicts' sons
And daughters came into prison to learn from their fathers'
trades and talking with them about life.
This led to several groups opening up sessions dealing with
Language, logic, and delving into past myths and customs.

50   Blacks, Mejicanos, Whites, all had so much to offer.
      They were invited to speak at the nearby university
      Discussing what they found to be untouched by past historians.
      Each day six groups of convicts went into the community,
      Working for the aged and infirmed.
55   One old convict ended up marrying the governor's mother.

So Mexicans Are Taking Jobs from Americans

      0 Yes? Do they come on horses
      with rifles, and say,
                          Ese gringo, gimmee your job?
      And do you, gringo, take off your ring,
5   drop your wallet into a blanket
      spread over the ground, and walk away?

      I hear Mexicans are taking your jobs away.
      Do they sneak into town at night,
      and as you're walking home with a whore,
10   do they mug you, a knife at your throat,
      saying, I want your job?
      Even on TV, an asthmatic leader
      crawls turtle heavy, leaning on an assistant,
      and from a nest of wrinkles on his face,
15   a tongue paddles through flashing waves
      of lightbulbs, of cameramen, rasping
      "They're taking our jobs away."

      Well, I've gone about trying to find them,
      asking just where the hell are these fighters.
20   The rifles I hear sound in the night
      are white farmers shooting blacks and browns
      whose ribs I see jutting out
      and starving children,
      I see the poor marching for a little work,
25   I see small white farmers selling out
      to clean-suited farmers living in New York,
      who've never been on a farm,
      don't know the look of a hoof or the smell
      of a woman's body bending all day long in fields.

30   I see this, and I hear only a few people
      got all the money in this world, the rest
      count their pennies to buy bread and butter.

      Below that cool green sea of money,
      millions and millions of people fight to live,
35   search for pearls in the darkest depths
      of their dreams, hold their breath for years
      trying to cross poverty to just having something.

The children are dead already. We are killing them,
that is what America should be saying;
40   on TV, in the streets, in offices, should be saying,
"We aren't giving the children a chance to live."

Mexicans are taking our jobs, they say instead.
What they really say is, let them die,
and the children too.

PERFECTO FLORES

We banter
back and forth
the price
for laying brick.
5   "You people only pay
the rich, those who
already have money.
I have a whole yard of bricks
collected over thirty years
10   working as a mason.
I offer you a good price,
load them on the truck,
bring sand and gravel,
do the work almost for nothing,
15   and you won't pay me
half what Hunter charges."
He was right, I relented,
paid him seventy cents a block.
The next day
20   he brought them,
towing cement mixer
behind his old truck.
He rounded the weeping willow
trunk with blocks
25   left over from apartments
he worked on
six years ago,
then poured cement
and troweled it smooth.
30   After he was done, he asked,
"Can I have that roll of wire back there?"
He lives by scraps, built three houses
for his daughters with construction site
scraps.
35   In English
his name is Perfect Flower.
Brawny man with bull shoulders,
who forty years ago came from Mexico,

tired of the mines, the somnolent
40   spirit of Mexicans. ". . . I was the first one
to say I wouldn't ride the old bus.
It was falling apart. I refused, and
the rest followed, and soon a new bus
was brought up the mountain."
45   I gave him our old Falcon
for pouring cement floor
in the guest cottage,
jar of blessed black-purple
Acoma corn kernels
50   for helping me uproot a tree,
gave him seven rabbits
and a box of chickens
for helping me cut adobe arches.
We curse and laugh as we work.
55   He proudly hefts a wheelbarrow
brimmed with cement. "Ah! Sixty-two, *cabrón*!
And you, naa! You would break your back!"
He ribs me, proud of his strength.
He has nothing that glows his face
60   so much as stories of his working years,
feats of courage in the mines
when he was called upon to defuse dynamite
that didn't explode. Short, stocky
gray-haired man, always in his yard
65   scattering chicken seed, nailing, sawing,
always in jean overalls.
Chews a ground weed,
carries a stub pencil and grimy wad of paper
for figuring, and
70   always turns to me when I drive
or walk into his yard
with a roguish grin,
his love of telling stories
competing with mine.
75   He growls with laughter
at the blisters on my hands,
takes his gloves off,
spreads his palms up—
a gallery owner who strips black cloth
80   off his prized Van Gogh painting,
"Look! You could sharpen a file
on these hands," he grins proudly.

Jan Beatty (b. 1952)

Poet, teacher, and radio host, Jan Beatty was born in the Roselia Foundling Home in Pittsburgh's Hill District. Adopted at birth, she was raised in a steel-working family in nearby Whitehall Borough and educated in parochial schools. "Being an adoptee is like being a permanent stranger," she says, "I began writing poetry as a small child. I think it gave me a place to live in." Beatty graduated from West Virginia University with a degree in social work and held jobs as a welfare caseworker and a counselor in a rape crisis center, an abortion clinic, and a maximum-security prison. The work to which she regularly returned between other jobs was waiting tables—in burger joints, jazz clubs, and diners. The poems that follow explore that work world and the voices and desires of the people who animate it: coworkers, dishwashers, customers, and college kids passing through. After fifteen years of waitressing, Beatty returned to college to earn an MFA in poetry at the University of Pittsburgh. Her two major books, *Mad River* (1995, winner of the Agnes Lynch Starrett Prize), and *Boneshaker* (2002), were published by the University of Pittsburgh Press. Of *Boneshaker*, Gerald Stern writes: "There is a school of poetry where the poems have content, where they communicate, where beauty is not forgotten. It is about work, family, and the lost towns. Grief. Jan is a central figure in this school." Beatty now teaches poetry at several colleges in Pittsburgh and in community workshops. She is the host of "Prosody," a weekly public radio show of interviews and readings with local and national writers. "People need to have access to poetry all the time," she says. "There needs to be more of it around—in the schools, in hotels, on the buses. Poetry should be for everybody."

AWAKE IN A STRANGE LANDSCAPE

Deep in my gut,
large stones scrape each other
to dust at night, rising into coughs
until my mouth is white chalk in the morning.

5 Something has become intolerable.

I work as a waitress.
Every day, rich customers,
their fingers beckoning me like feathers.

The dishwasher empties trash in the back.

10 I work with people too young to remember
Vietnam, or even Watergate.
They speak in airy voices of becoming
accountants, going into advertising.
They say it must have been neat
15 to live in the sixties.

The black cooks rap to L. L. Cool J in the kitchen.

The fat woman wants to order half of a grilled sandwich.
I tell her we will have to throw the other half away.
She says that's okay, waving her diamond hands,
20   her Talbot's bag at her side.

    I am heaping trash on the dishwasher.
    He is still singing under piles of remains,
    wet cigarettes soaked with coffee,
    everything that is used.
25   With strong black arms, he scrapes the blood-
    colored lipstick from wine glasses
    for three dollars an hour.

The waitresses are talking about how fat they are,
about working out, about spring break,
30   about the real job they will get.

    I don't know how to tell them what I'm thinking.
    I'm thinking of the taste of chalk in the morning,
    I'm thinking that we are Americans,
    lost steer crashing into landscape,
35   herds rumbling to some black sea.

LOUISE

Table 5,
single woman at a four-top,
smoking relentlessly.

    Hi, how ya doin? I say.

5   *Honey, let me tell you*
exactly what I want—
Give me a cheeseburger with no cheese,
I want that medium-well, no blood, honey.

    She grabs my arm, her smoke hits my face.

10   *If there's blood on the plate,*
I can't eat it, I'm sick to my stomach,
I just talked to my daughter,
do you have kids, honey?

    No.

15   *Don't ever do it—they'll break your heart.*
And if there's blood on the bun,
I won't be able to eat, okay honey?
What kind of buns do you serve here?

    I guess they're kaiser rolls.

20   *Well, it doesn't matter, I know*
what you have, I've eaten here before,
but honey, tell the chef to toast the bun,
not too dark—

      She stares at me through thick glasses,
25   her eyes dark, magnified. She's maybe
      fifty-five, her mouse-brown hair frizzed,
      intractable. I don't know her losses;
      I know her faded rose blouse and lumpy
      wool skirt say: working class: apart.

30   *And if you put lettuce and tomato on it,*
      don't put it on top of the bread.

      I try to go back over this:
      You said a cheeseburger with no cheese?

      Yes, that's right, honey, no cheese.

35   *So—you want a hamburger?*

      No, I want a cheeseburger with no cheese.

      Okay. Toasted bun, not burnt,
      lettuce and tomato on the side—

      You can put it on the same plate, honey,
40   *just watch the bun.*

      I deliberately loiter for a minute,
      thinking people must often run from her.
      She looks up at me like I'm wasting her time.

      That's all, she says.

45   Now the fat man's being seated in my section—
      the one who never wants anything green:
      no pickles, no lettuce, and don't just separate
      the lettuce and tomato—he wants nothing
      that has ever *touched* green. At the door, the rich
50   saboteur who plants hair in his fries
      to get a free lunch; the homeless young
      mother who sips at her coffee
      for hours.

      Is what they need so little, so large?
55   I've walked into these strange lives
      only to go back to the kitchen wondering
      how to explain Louise to the cooks,
      how I'll be able to get her
      what she wants.

THE ROLLING ROCK MAN

      It's not me shouting at no one
      in Cadillac Square: it's God
      roaring inside me, afraid
      to be alone.

               —*Lawrence Joseph*

Never talks, never tips,
drinks two Rolling Rock draughts,
maybe three as he sits for hours
in the restaurant, wears too many clothes
5   for the weather, his combat jacket,
his navy blue cap, oblivious
to the people eating lunch around him.
Can I get you something to drink? I say,
afraid to say, *How about a Rolling Rock*,
10   afraid to be familiar with a man like this.
Somebody already waited on me, he said.
Okay, good, I said.
You lost some weight.
Yeah, I said, *a little*,
15   amazed that he is speaking, that
he has noticed a change in me.
I look straight at him, one of his eyes
is blood, a red blotch from a punch—
he said, *You look like you have AIDS,*
20   *you better go to the hospital,*
you're gonna die soon.
I felt the evil wash over me
as I walked to my next table, stunned
by this backwash of words, this bold
25   sickness, this butcher world that's in
and around us, *Someone please, pray for us.*
Minutes later, he started shouting at no one,
Body bags, he yelled, *Body bags.*
I heard the words as I watched a five-year-old girl
30   stare at him, afraid for her. *Vietnam*, he shouted,
as customers looked up from their chicken salads,
women three feet away sucked Bloody Marys
and fingered their circle pins—he heard a song
and he spoke the words—I don't know
35   what he saw or heard.

A Waitress' Instructions on Tipping or Get the Cash Up and Don't Waste My Time

Twenty percent minimum as long as the waitress doesn't inflict bodily harm.
If you're two people at a four top, tip extra.
If you sit a long time, pay rent.
Double tips for special orders.
5   Always tip extra when using coupons.
Better yet, don't use coupons.
Never leave change instead of bills, no pennies.
Never hide a tip for fun.
Overtip, then tip some more.
10   Remember, I am somebody's mother or daughter.

No separate piles of change for large parties.
If people in your party don't show up, tip *for* them.
Don't wait around for gratitude.
Take a risk. Don't adjust your tip so your credit card total is even.
15   Don't ever, ever pull out a tipping guide in public.
If you leave 10% or less, eat at home.
If I call a taxi for you, tip me.
If I hang up your coat for you, tip me.
If I get cigarettes for you, tip me.
20   Better yet, do it yourself.
Don't fold a bill and hand it to me like you're a big shot.
Don't say, *There's a big tip in it for you if* . . .
Don't say, *I want to make sure you get this*, like a busboy would steal it.
Don't say, *Here, honey, this is for you*—ever.
25   If you buy a $50 bottle of wine, pull out a ten.
If I serve you one cocktail, don't hand me 35¢.
If you're just having coffee, leave a five.

THE WAITRESS ANGELS SPEAK TO ME IN A VISION

Another tough Friday night, only fifty bucks
to show, I throw my stash of dirty bills on
the table, leave the change in the apron
that smells like two weeks of roadkill & smoke.
5   The mayonnaise stains gleam, otherworldly
in the beam of kitchen light. I'm tired
of waiting on drunks, coming home to myself
and these 4:00 AM flashbacks of men
trying to put their hands on me, regulars
10   who think they own me, I'm sitting here staring
at the cobwebs in the ceiling corner and that's
when they came to me: You've heard of
dust to dust, well this was dust to angels,
but these were real women with hard faces,
15   lifers in white, these were tough broads,
broads with cigarettes, pockets full of
guest checks and loose change—sassy babes
with big hair, gravelly laughs and downtown talk,
smackin each other on the back, saying,
20   "Honey, you're full o' shit," the whole time
my chest bursting with pride and relief
at the end of virginal blue, pressed palms,
and bowed heads. Death to Silent Acceptance!
No More Vale of Tears! Their hands on their
25   hips said: *Hey, we're brash, we're trashy,*
we're happenin—you got a problem with that?
These were no walking-behind-Jesus-babes,
no eyes-to-the-floor-floaters, these dolls
were sportin jewelry and mascara, they were

30   serious as a heart attack—and there I was,
      ready to flee the corporeal glut of my life
      for this hip heaven, when I asked to join them
      and they shut me down: "Look, sweetie
      this ain't no picnic here—we're on break right now—
35   flyin out to shake down some bad tippers—besides,
      this celestial trip is overrated. Check it out,
      your life ain't so bad."

Helena María Viramontes (b. 1954)

Combining her artistry as a writer, her knowledge of the physicality of labor, and her commitment to social change and the education of children, Viramontes infuses a political consciousness into her carefully wrought novels, short stories, and screenplays. Born in East Los Angeles, one of nine children, she witnessed the gendered work of her parents—her father as a construction worker and her mother as a housewife—as well as their support for Mexican migrants who crossed the border into California looking for work. Her writing and life demonstrate a sense of camaraderie and respect for those who do stoop labor in the fields and sustaining labor in the family, with particular attention to the hopes and latent power of young Latinas. Winner of numerous awards, her books include a collection of short stories, *The Moths and Other Stories* (1985) (in which the cinematic "Cariboo Cafe" appears), a second collection of stories and screenplay, *Paris Rats in E.L.A.* (1993), and novels *Under the Feet of Jesus* (1995) and *Their Dogs Came with Them* (1996). She has also coedited, with Maria Herrera Sobek, two nonfiction collections, *Chicana Creativity and Criticism* (1987) and *Chicana Writers—On Word and Film* (1994). In "Why I Write" (1993), Viramontes speaks to the linkages that are inherent in her work and working-class literature: "I believe that language is a powerful tool for social change. Through writing I have learned to protect the 'souls' of my feet from the broken glass. Writing is the only way I know how to pray."

THE CARIBOO CAFE

I

They arrived in the secrecy of night, as displaced people often do, stopping over for a week, a month, eventually staying a lifetime. The plan was simple. Mother would work, too, until they saved enough to move into a finer future where the toilet was one's own and the children needn't be frightened. In the meantime, they played in the back alleys, among the broken glass, wise to the ways of the streets. Rule one: never talk to strangers, not even the neighbor who paced up and down the hallways talking to himself. Rule two: the police, or "polie" as Sonya's popi pronounced the word, was La Migra in disguise and thus should always be avoided. Rule three: keep your key with you at all times—the four walls of the apartment were the only protection against the streets until Popi returned home.

Sonya considered her key a guardian saint and she wore it around her neck as such until this afternoon. Gone was the string with the big knot. Gone was the key. She hadn't noticed its disappearance until she picked up Macky from Mrs. Avila's house and walked home. She remembered playing with it as Amá walked her to school. But lunch break came, and Lalo wrestled her down so that he could see her underwear, and it probably fell somewhere between the iron rings and sandbox. Sitting on the front steps of the apartment building, she considered how to explain the missing key without having to reveal what Lalo had seen, for she wasn't quite sure which offense carried the worse penalty.

She watched people piling in and spilling out of the buses, watched an old man asleep on the bus bench across the street. He resembled a crumbled ball of paper, huddled up in the security of a tattered coat. She became aware of their mutual loneliness and she rested her head against her knees, blackened by the soot of the playground asphalt.

The old man eventually awoke, yawned like a lion's roar, unfolded his limbs and staggered to the alley where he urinated between two trash bins. (She wanted to peek, but it was Macky who turned to look.) He zipped up, drank from a paper bag, and she watched him until he disappeared around the corner. As time passed, buses came less frequently, and every other person seemed to resemble Popi. Macky became bored. He picked through the trash barrel; later, and to Sonya's fright, he ran into the street after a pigeon. She understood his restlessness, for waiting was as relentless as long lines to the bathroom. When a small boy walked by, licking away at a scoop of vanilla ice cream, Macky ran after him. In his haste to outrun Sonya's grasp, he fell and tore the knee of his denim jeans. He began to cry, wiping snot against his sweater sleeve.

"See?" she asked, dragging him back to the porch steps by his wrist. "See? God punished you!" It was a thing she always said because it seemed to work. Terrified by the scrawny tortured man on the cross, Macky wanted to avoid His wrath as much as possible. She sat him on the steps in one gruff jerk. Seeing his torn jeans and her own scraped knees, she wanted to join in his sorrow and cry. Instead, she snuggled so close to him she could hear his stomach growling.

"Coke," he said. Mrs. Avila gave him an afternoon snack which usually held him over until dinner. But sometimes Macky got lost in the midst of her own six children and . . .

Mrs. Avila! It took Sonya a few moments to realize the depth of her idea. They could wait there, at Mrs. Avila's. And she'd probably have a stack of flour tortillas, fresh off the comal, ready to eat with butter and salt. She grabbed his hand. "Mrs. Avila has Coke."

"Coke!" He jumped up to follow his sister. "Coke," he cooed.

At the major intersection, Sonya quietly calculated their next move while the scores of adults hurried to their own destinations. She scratched one knee as she tried retracing her journey home in the labyrinth of her memory. Things never looked the same when backwards and she searched for familiar scenes. She looked for the newspaperman who sat in a little house with a little T.V. on and sold magazines with naked girls holding beach balls. But he was gone. What remained was a little closet-like shed with chains and locks, and she wondered what happened to him, for she thought he lived there with the naked ladies.

They finally crossed the street at a cautious pace, the colors of the street lights brighter as darkness descended, a stereo store blaring music from two huge, blasting speakers. She thought it was the disco store she passed, but she didn't remember if the sign was green or red. And she didn't remember it flashing like it was now. Studying the neon light, she bumped into a tall, lanky dark man. Maybe it was Raoul's Popi. Raoul was a dark boy in her class that she felt sorry for because everyone called him spongehead. Maybe she could ask Raoul's Popi where Mrs. Avila lived, but before she could think it all out, red sirens flashed in their faces and she shielded her eyes to see the polie.

The polie are men in black who get kids and send them to Tijuana, says Popi. Whenever you see them, run, because they hate you, says Popi. She grabs Macky by his sleeve and they crawl under a table of bargain cassettes. Macky's nose is running, and when he sniffles, she puts her finger to her lips. She peeks from behind the poster of Vincente Fernandez to see Raoul's father putting keys and stuff from his pockets onto the hood of the polie car. And it's true, they're putting him in the car and taking him to Tijuana. Popi, she murmured to herself. Mamá.

"Coke." Macky whispered, as if she had failed to remember.

"Ssssh. Mi'jo, when I say run, you run, okay?" She waited for the tires to turn out, and as the black and white drove off, she whispered "Now," and they scurried out from under the table and ran across the street, oblivious to the horns.

They entered a maze of alleys and dead ends, the long, abandoned warehouses shadowing any light. Macky stumbled and she continued to drag him until his crying, his untied sneakers, and his raspy breathing finally forced her to stop. She scanned the boarded-up boxcars, the rows of rusted rails to make sure the polie wasn't following them. Tired, her heart bursting, she leaned him against a tall chain-link fence. Except for the rambling of some railcars, silence prevailed, and she could hear Macky sniffling in the darkness. Her mouth was parched and she swallowed to rid herself of the metallic taste of fear. The shadows stalked them, hovering like nightmares. Across the tracks, in the distance, was a room with a yellow glow, like a beacon light at the end of a dark sea. She pinched Macky's nose with the corner of her dress, took hold of his sleeve. At least the shadows will be gone, she concluded, at the zero-zero place.

II

Don't look at me. I didn't give it the name. It was passed on. Didn't even know what it meant until I looked it up in some library dictionary. But I kinda liked the name. It's, well, romantic, almost like the name of a song, you know, so I kept it. That was before JoJo turned fourteen even. But now if you take a look at the sign, the paint's peeled off 'cept for the two O's. The double zero cafe. Story of my life. But who cares, right? As long as everyone 'round the factories knows I run an honest business.

The place is clean. That's more than I can say for some people who walk through that door. And I offer the best prices on double-burger deluxes this side of Main Street. Okay, so it's not pure beef. Big deal, most meat markets do the same. But I make no bones 'bout it. I tell them up front, "yeah, it ain't dogmeat, but it ain't sirloin either." 'Cause that's the sort of guy I am. Honest.

That's the trouble. It never pays to be honest. I tried scrubbing the stains off the floor, so that my customers won't be reminded of what happened. But they keep walking as if my cafe ain't fit for lepers. And that's the thanks I get for being a fair guy.

Not once did I hang up all those stupid signs. You know, like "We reserve the right to refuse service to anyone," or "No shirt, no shoes, no service." To tell you the truth— which is what I always do though it don't pay—I wouldn't have nobody walking through that door. The streets are full of scum, but scum gotta eat too is the way I see it. Now, listen. I ain't talkin 'bout out-of-luckers, weirdos, whores, you know. I'm talking 'bout five-to-lifers out of some tech. I'm talking Paulie.

I swear Paulie is thirty-five, or six. JoJo's age if he were still alive, but he don't look a day over ninety. Maybe why I let him hang out is 'cause he's JoJo's age. Shit, he's okay as long as he don't bring his wigged-out friends whose voices sound like a record at low speed. Paulie's got too many stories and they all get jammed up in his mouth so I can't make out what he's saying. He scares the other customers, too, acting like he is shadow boxing, or like a monkey hopping on a frying pan. You know, nervous, jumpy, his jaw all falling and his eyes bulgy and dirt-yellow. I give him the last booth, coffee, and yesterday's donut holes to keep him quiet. After a few minutes, out he goes, before lunch. I'm too old, you know, too busy making ends meet to be nursing the kid. And so is Delia.

That Delia's got these unique titties. One is bigger than the other. Like an orange and grapefruit. I kid you not. They're like that on account of when she was real young she had some babies, and they all sucked only one favorite tittie. So one is bigger than the other, and when she used to walk in with Paulie, huggy-huggy and wearing those tight leotard blouses that show the nipple dots, you could see the difference. You could tell right off that Paulie was proud of them, the way he'd hang his arm over her shoulder and squeeze the grapefruit. They kill me, her knockers. She'd come in real queen-like, smacking gum and chewing the fat with the illegals who work in that garment warehouse. They come in real queen-like, too, sitting in the best booth near the window, and order cokes. That's all. Cokes. Hey, but I'm a nice guy. So what if they mess up my table, bring their own lunches and only order small cokes, leaving a dime as tip? So sometimes the place ain't crawling with people, you comprende, buddy? A dime's a dime as long as its in my pocket.

Like I gotta pay my bills, too. I gotta eat. So like I serve anybody whose got the greens, including that crazy lady and the two kids that started all the trouble. If only I had closed early. But I had to wash the dinner dishes on account of I can't afford a dishwasher. I was scraping off some birdshit glue stuck to this plate, see, when I hear the bells jingle against the door. I hate those fucking bells. That was Nell's idea. Nell's my wife; my ex-wife. So people won't sneak up on you, says my ex. Anyway, I'm standing behind the counter staring at this short woman. Already I know that she's bad news because she looks street to me. Round face, burnt-toast color, black hair that hangs like straight ropes. Weirdo, I've had enough to last me a lifetime. She's wearing a shawl and a dirty slip is hanging out. Shit if I have to dish out a free meal. Funny thing, but I didn't see the two kids 'til I got to the booth. All of a sudden I see these big eyes looking over the table's edge at me. It shook me up, the way they kinda appeared. Aw, maybe they were there all the time.

The boy's a sweetheart. Short Order don't look nothing like his mom. He's got dried snot all over his dirty cheeks and his hair ain't seen a comb for years. She can't take care of herself, much less him or the doggie of a sister. But he's a tough one, and I pinch his nose 'cause he's a real sweetheart like JoJo. You know, my boy.

It's his sister I don't like. She's got these poking eyes that follow you 'round 'cause she don't trust no one. Like when I reach for Short Order, she flinches like I'm 'bout to tear his nose off, gives me a nasty, squinty look. She's maybe five, maybe six, I don't know, and she acts like she owns him. Even when I bring the burgers, she doesn't let go of his hand. Finally, the fellow bites it and I wink at him. A real sweetheart.

In the next booth, I'm twisting the black crud off the top of the ketchup bottle when I hear the lady saying something in Spanish. Right off I know she's illegal, which explains why she looks like a weirdo. Anyway, she says something nice to them 'cause it's in the same tone that Nell used when I'd rest my head on her lap. I'm surprised the illegal's got a fiver to pay, but she and her tail leave no tip. I see Short Order's small bites on the bun.

You know, a cafe's the kinda business that moves. You get some regulars, but most of them are on the move, so I don't pay much attention to them. But this lady's face sticks like egg yolk on a plate. It ain't 'til I open a beer and sit in front of the B & W to check out the wrestling matches that I see this news bulletin 'bout two missing kids. I recognize the mugs right away. Short Order and his doggie sister. And all of a sudden her face is out of my mind. Aw, fuck, I say, and put my beer down so hard that the foam spills onto last month's Hustler. Aw, fuck.

See, if Nell was here, she'd know what to do: call the cops. But I don't know. Cops ain't exactly my friends, and all I need is for bacon to be crawling all over my place. And seeing how her face is vague now, I decide to wait 'til the late news. Short Order don't look right neither. I'll have another beer and wait for the late news. The alarm rings at four and I have this headache, see, from the sixpak, and I gotta get up. I was supposed to do something, but I got all suck-faced and forgot. Turn off the T.V., take a shower, but that don't help my memory any.

Hear sirens near the railroad tracks. Cops. I'm supposed to call the cops. I'll do it after I make the coffee, put away the eggs, get the donuts out. But Paulie strolls in looking partied out. We actually talk 'bout last night's wrestling match between BoBo Brazil and the Crusher. I slept through it, you see. Paulie orders an O.J. on account of he's catching a cold. I open up my big mouth and ask about De. Drinks the rest of his O.J., says real calm-like, that he caught her eaglespread with the vegetable fatso down the block. Then, very politelike, Paulie excuses himself. That's one thing I gotta say about Paulie. He may be one big Fuck-Up, but he's got manners. Juice gave him shit cramps, he says.

Well, leave it to Paulie. Good ole Mr. Fuck-Up himself to help me with the cops. The prick O.D.'s in my crapper; vomits and shits are all over—I mean all over the fuckin' walls. That's the thanks I get for being Mr. Nice Guy. I had the cops looking up my ass for the stash. Says one, the one wearing a mortician's suit, We'll be back, we'll be back when you ain't looking. If I was pushing, would I be burning my goddamn balls off with spitting grease? So fuck 'em, I think. I ain't gonna tell you nothing 'bout the lady. Fuck you, I say to them as they drive away. Fuck your mother.

That's why Nell was good to have 'round. She could be a pain in the ass, you know, like making me hang those stupid bells, but mostly she knew what to do. See, I go bananas. Like my mind fries with the potatoes and by the end of the day, I'm deader than dogshit. Let me tell you what I mean. A few hours later, after I swore I wouldn't give the fuckin' pigs the time of day, the green vans roll up across the street. While I'm stirring the chili con carne, I see all these illegals running out of the factory to hide, like roaches when the lightswitch goes on. I taste the chile, but I really can't taste nothing on account of I've lost my appetite after cleaning out the crapper, when three of them run into the Cariboo. They look at me as if I'm gonna stop them, but when I go on stirring the chile, they run to the bathroom. Now look, I'm a nice guy, but I don't like to be used, you know? Just 'cause they're regulars don't mean jackshit. I run an honest business. And that's what I told them agents. See, by that time, my stomach being all dizzy, and the cops all over the place, and the three illegals running in here, I was all confused, you know. That's how it was, and well, I haven't seen Nell for years, and I guess that's why I pointed to the bathroom.

I don't know. I didn't expect handcuffs and them agents putting their hands up and down their thighs. When they walked passed me, they didn't look at me. That is, the two young ones. The older one, the one that looked silly in the handcuffs on account of she's old enough to be my grandma's grandma, looks straight at my face with the same eyes Short Order's sister gave me yesterday. What a day. Then, to top off the potatoes with the gravy, the bells jingle against the door and in enters the lady again with the two kids.

III

He's got lice. Probably from living in the detainers. Those are the rooms where they round up the children and make them work for their food. I saw them from the window. Their eyes are cut glass, and no one looks for sympathy. They take turns, sorting out the arms from the legs, heads from the torsos. Is that one your mother? one guard asks, holding a mummified head with eyes shut tighter than coffins. But the children no longer cry. They just continue sorting as if they were salvaging cans from a heap of trash. They do this until time is up and they drift into a tunnel, back to the womb of sleep, while a new group comes in. It is all very organized. I bite my fist to keep from retching. Please, God, please don't let Geraldo be there.

For you see, they took Geraldo. By mistake, of course. It was my fault. I shouldn't have sent him out to fetch me a mango. But it was just to the corner. I didn't even bother to put his sweater on. I hear his sandals flapping against the gravel. I follow him with my eyes, see him scratching his buttocks when the wind picks up swiftly, as it often does at such unstable times, and I have to close the door.

The darkness becomes a serpent's tongue, swallowing us whole. It is the night of La Llorona. The women come up from the depths of sorrow to search for their children. I join them, frantic, desperate, and our eyes become scrutinizers, our bodies opiated with the scent of their smiles. Descending from door to door, the wind whips our faces. I hear the wailing of the women and know it to be my own. Geraldo is nowhere to be found.

Dawn is not welcomed. It is a drunkard wavering between consciousness and sleep. My life is fleeing, moving south towards the sea. My tears are now hushed and faint.

The boy, barely a few years older than Geraldo, lights a cigarette, rests it on the edge of his desk, next to all the other cigarette burns. The blinds are down to keep the room cool. Above him hangs a single bulb that shades and shadows his face in such a way as to mask his expressions. He is not to be trusted. He fills in the information, for I cannot write. Statements delivered, we discuss motives.

"Spies," says he, flicking a long burning ash from the cigarette onto the floor, then wolfing the smoke in as if his lungs had an unquenchable thirst for nicotine. "We arrest spies. Criminals." He says this with cigarette smoke spurting out from his nostrils like a nosebleed. "Spies? Criminal?" My shawl falls to the ground. "He is only five and a half years old." I plead for logic with my hands. "What kind of crimes could a five-year old commit?"

"Anyone who so willfully supports the Contras in any form must be arrested and punished without delay." He knows the line by heart. I think about moths and their stupidity. Always attracted by light, they fly into fires, or singe their wings with the heat of the single bulb and fall on his desk, writhing in pain. I don't understand why nature has been so cruel as to prevent them from feeling warmth. He dismisses them with a sweep of a hand. "This," he continues, "is what we plan to do with the Contras and those who aid them." He inhales again.

"But, Señor, he's just a baby."

"Contras are tricksters. They exploit the ignorance of people like you. Perhaps they convinced your son to circulate pamphlets. You should be talking to them, not us." The cigarette is down to his yellow finger tips, to where he can no longer continue to hold it without burning himself. He throws the stub on the floor, crushes it under his boot. "This," he says, screwing his boot into the ground, "is what the Contras do to people like you."

"Señor. I am a washerwoman. You yourself see I cannot read or write. There is my X. Do you think my son can read?" How can I explain to this man that we are poor, that we live as best we can? "If such a thing has happened, perhaps he wanted to make a few centavos for his mamá. He's just a baby."

"So you are admitting his guilt?"

"So you are admitting he is here?" I promise, once I see him, hold him in my arms again, I will never, never scold him for wanting more than I can give. "You see, he needs his sweater . . ." The sweater lies limp on my lap.

"Your assumption is incorrect."

"May I check the detainers for myself?"

"In time."

"And what about my Geraldo?"

"In time." He dismisses me, placing the forms in a big envelope crinkled by the day's humidity.

"When?" I am wringing the sweater with my hands.

"Don't be foolish, woman. Now off with your nonsense. We will try to locate your Pedro."

"Geraldo."

Maria came by today with a bowl of hot soup. She reports, in her usual excited way, that the soldiers are now eating the brains of their victims. It is unlike her to be so scandalous. So insane. Geraldo must be cold without his sweater.

"Why?" I ask as the soup gets cold. I will write Tavo tonight.

At the plaza, a group of people are whispering. They are quiet when I pass, turn to one another and put their finger to their lips to cage their voices. They continue as I reach the church steps. To be associated with me is condemnation.

Today I felt like killing myself, Lord. But I am too much of a coward. I am a washerwoman, Lord. My mother was one, and hers, too. We have lived as best we can, washing other people's laundry, rinsing off other people's dirt until our hands crust and chap. When my son wanted to hold my hand, I held soap instead. When he wanted to play, my feet were in pools of water. It takes such little courage, being a washerwoman. Give me strength, Lord.

What have I done to deserve this, Lord? Raising a child is like building a kite. You must bend the twigs enough, but not too much, for you might break them. You must find paper that is delicate and light enough to wave on the breath of the wind, yet must withstand the ravages of a storm. You must tie the strings gently but firmly so that it may not fall apart. You must let the string go, eventually, so that the kite will stretch its ambition. It is such delicate work, Lord, being a mother. This I understand, Lord because I am. But you have snapped the cord, Lord. It was only a matter of minutes and my life is lost somewhere in the clouds. I don't know, I don't know what games you play, Lord.

These four walls are no longer my house; the earth beneath it, no longer my home. Weeds have replaced all good crops. The irrigation ditches are clodded with bodies. No matter where we turn, there are rumors facing us, and we try to live as best we can under the rule of men who rape women then rip their fetuses form their bellies. Is this our home? Is this our country? I ask Maria. Don't these men have mothers, lovers, babies, sisters? Don't they see what they are doing? Later, Maria says, these men are babes farted out from the Devil's ass. We check to make sure no one has heard her say this.

Without Geraldo, this is not my home; the earth beneath it, not my country. This is why I have to leave. Maria begins to cry. Not because I am going, but because she is staying.

Tavo. Sweet Tavo. He has sold his car to send me the money. He has just married and he sold his car for me. Thank you, Tavo. Not just for the money. But also for making me believe in the goodness of people again . . . The money is enough to buy off the border soldiers. The rest will come from the can. I have saved for Geraldo's schooling and it is enough for a bus ticket to Juarez. I am to wait for Tavo there.

I spit. I do not turn back.

Perhaps I am wrong in coming. I worry that Geraldo will not have a home to return to, no mother to cradle his nightmares away, soothe the scars, stop the hemorrhaging of his heart. Tavo is happy I am here, but it is crowded with the three of us, and I hear them arguing behind their closed door. There is only so much a nephew can provide. I must find work. I have two hands willing to work. But the heart. The heart wills only to watch the children playing in the street.

The machines, their speed and dust, make me ill. But I can clean. I clean toilets, dump trash cans, sweep. Disinfect the sinks. I will gladly do whatever is necessary to repay Tavo. The baby is due any time and money is tight. I volunteer for odd hours, weekends, since I really have very little to do. When the baby comes, I know Tavo's wife will not let me hold it, for she thinks I am a bad omen. I know it.

Why would God play such a cruel joke, if he isn't my son? I jumped the curb, dashed out into the street, but the street is becoming wider and wider. I've lost him once and can't lose him again and to hell with the screeching tires and the horns and the headlights barely touching my hips. I can't take my eyes off him because, you see, they are swift and cunning and can take your life with a snap of a finger. But God is a just man and His mistakes can be undone.

My heart pounds in my head like a sledgehammer against the asphalt. What if it isn't Geraldo? What if he is still in the detainer waiting for me? A million questions, one answer: Yes. Geraldo, yes. I want to touch his hand first, have it disappear in my own because it is so small. His eyes look at me in total bewilderment. I grab him because the earth is crumbling beneath us and I must save him. We both fall to the ground.

A hot meal is in store. A festival. The cook, a man with shrunken cheeks and the hands of a car mechanic, takes a liking to Geraldo. Its like birthing you again, mi'jo. My baby.

I bathe him. He flutters in excitement, the water gray around him. I scrub his head with lye to kill off the lice, comb his hair out with a fine-tooth comb. I wash his rubbery penis, wrap him in a towel, and he stands in front of the window, shriveling and sucking milk from a carton, his hair shiny from the dampness.

He finally sleeps. So easily, she thinks. On her bed next to the open window he coos in the night. Below, the sounds of the city become as monotonous as the ocean waves. She rubs his back with warm oil, each stroke making up for the days of his absence. She hums to him softly so that her breath brushes against his face, tunes that are rusted and crack in her throat. The hotel neon shines on his back and she covers him.

All the while the young girl watches her brother sleeping. She removes her sneakers, climbs into the bed, snuggles up to her brother, and soon her breathing is raspy, her arms under her stomach.

The couch is her bed tonight. Before switching the light off, she checks once more to make sure this is not a joke. Tomorrow she will make arrangements to go home. Maria will be the same, the mango stand on the corner next to the church plaza will be the same. It will all be the way it was before. But enough excitement. For the first time in years, her mind is quiet of all noise and she has the desire to sleep.

The bells jingle when the screen door slaps shut behind them. The cook wrings his hands in his apron, looking at them. Geraldo is in the middle, and they sit in the booth farthest away from the window, near the hall where the toilets are, and right away the small boy, his hair now neatly combed and split to the side like an adult, wrinkles his nose at the peculiar smell. The cook wipes perspiration off his forehead with the corner of his apron, finally comes over to the table.

She looks so different, so young. Her hair is combed slick back into one thick braid and her earrings hang like baskets of golden pears on her finely sculptured ears. He can't believe how different she looks. Almost beautiful. She points to what she wants on the menu with a white, clean fingernail. Although confused, the cook is sure of one thing— it's Short Order all right, pointing to him with a commanding finger, saying his only English word: coke.

His hands tremble as he slaps the meat on the grill; the patties hiss instantly. He feels like vomiting. The chile overboils and singes the fires, deep red trail of chile crawling to the floor and puddling there. He grabs the handles, burns himself, drops the pot on the wooden racks of the floor. He sucks his fingers, the patties blackening and sputtering grease. He flips them, and the burgers hiss anew. In some strange way he hopes they have disappeared, and he takes a quick look only to see Short Order's sister, still in the same dress, still holding her brother's hand. She is craning her neck to peek at what is going on in the kitchen.

Aw, fuck, he says, in a fog of smoke, his eyes burning tears. He can't believe it, but he's crying. For the first time since JoJo's death, he's crying. He becomes angry at the lady for returning. At JoJo. At Nell for leaving him. He wishes Nell here, but doesn't know where she's at or what part of Vietnam JoJo is all crumbled up in. Children gotta be with their parents, family gotta be together, he thinks. It's only right. The emergency line is ringing.

Two black and whites roll up and skid the front tires against the curb. The flashing lights carousel inside the cafe. She sees them opening the screen door, their guns taught and cold like steel erections. Something is wrong, and she looks to the cowering cook. She has been betrayed, and her heart is pounding like footsteps running, faster, louder, faster, and she can't hear what they are saying to her. She jumps up from the table, grabs Geraldo by the wrist, his sister dragged along because, like her, she refuses to release his hand. Their lips are mouthing words she can't hear, can't comprehend. Run, Run is all she can think of to do, Run through the hallway, out to the alley, Run because they will never take him away again.

But her legs are heavy and she crushes Geraldo against her, so tight, as if she wants to conceal him in her body again, return him to her belly so that they will not castrate him and hang his small blue penis on her door, not crush his face so that he is unrecognizable, not bury him among the heaps of bones, and ears, and teeth, and jaws, because no one but she cared to know that he cried. For years he cried and she could hear him day and night. Screaming, howling, sobbing, shriveling and crying because he is only five years old, and all she wanted was a mango.

But the crying begins all over again. In the distance, she hears crying.

She refuses to let go. For they will have to cut her arms off to take him, rip her mouth off to keep her from screaming for help. Without thinking, she reaches over to where two pots of coffee are brewing and throws the steaming coffee into their faces. Outside, people begin to gather, pressing their faces against the window glass to get a good view. The cook huddles behind the counter, frightened, trembling. Their faces become distorted and she doesn't see the huge hand that takes hold of Geraldo and she begins screaming all over again, screaming so that the walls shake, screaming enough for all the women of murdered children, screaming, pleading for help from the people outside, and she pushes an open hand against an officer's nose, because no one will stop them and he pushes the gun barrel to her face.

And I laugh at his ignorance. How stupid of him to think that I will let them take my Geraldo away just because he waves that gun like a flag. Well, to hell with you, you pieces of shit, do you hear me? Stupid, cruel pigs. To hell with you all, because you can no longer frighten me. I will fight you for my son until I have no hands left to hold a knife. I will fight you all because you're all farted out of the Devil's ass, and you'll not take us with you. I am laughing, howling at their stupidity because they should know by now that I will never let my son go. And then I hear something crunching like broken glass against my forehead and I am blinded by the liquid darkness. But I hold onto his hand. That I can feel, you see, I'll never let go. Because we are going home. My son and I.

Peter Oresick (b. 1955)

Peter Oresick was born and grew up in the small mill town of Ford City, on the Allegheny River in western Pennsylvania. His grandparents were Ukranian and Ruthyn immigrants. They and his father worked in the town's glass-manufacturing plant, where Oresick also worked summers, packing automobile windshields. Oresick's first book of poems *The Story of Glass* (1977) portrays that work and the lives of family and coworkers outside of work—in bars, at a company picnic, during periods of layoff—with an insider's knowledge and a young man's questions about the meaning of this work legacy at a time of "deindustrialization." Oresick earned a BA in education from the University of Pittsburgh and taught high school English for a number of years while working on an MFA degree in writing. While teaching high school, he began collecting contemporary poems that he felt would be interesting and relevant to his largely working-class students. This expanding collection formed the basis of the anthology *Working Classics: Poems on Industrial Life* (1990), coedited with Nicholas Coles. A second anthology, *For a Living: The Poetry of Work* (1995), gathered poems from a range of nonindustrial service and professional occupations. Oresick also coedited, with Ed Ochester, *The Pittsburgh Book of Contemporary American Poetry*, featuring work from the Poetry Series of the University of Pittsburgh Press, where Oresick was for many years a senior staff member. His other books of poetry are *Other Lives* (1985), *An American Peace* (1985), and *Definitions* (1990), which includes the early poems from *The Story of Glass*, reprinted here.

MY FATHER

My father was four years in the war,
and afterward, according to my mother,
had nothing to say. She says he trembled
in his sleep the next four years.
5   My father was twice the father of sons
miscarried, and afterward, said nothing.
My mother keeps this silence also.
Four times my father was on strike,
and according to my mother, had nothing
10   to say. She says the company didn't understand,
nor can her son, the meaning
of an extra 15 cents an hour in 1956
to a man tending a glass furnace in August.

I have always remembered him a tired man.
15   I have respected him like a guest
and expected nothing.
It is April now.
My life lies before me
enticing as the woman at my side.
20   Now, in April, I want him to speak.
I want to stand against the worn body
of his pain. I want to try it on
like a coat that does not fit.

THE STORY OF GLASS

From the holes of the earth, from
truck, from silo, from cullet,
from scale, batch, tank, heat-wind; from

heat, from ribbon, from flow, roll
5   roll, from lehr, they feed the line.

They crosscut, snap, they flour lites,
plates, plates, plates on belts, coveys,
glass, glass you grab, you pull, you

lift, you pack, you kick, you count,
10   and you turn, they feed the line.

You reach, you grab, you pack, you
tap, into skid, into crane,
into pack, uncut and cut-

down, they stock, they bay, they stack
15   skid, skid on skid, box, and they

feed the line. They multi-cut,
they Race 1, they feed you glass
and it comes, it waits, you pack,

it moves, stops, and you pack, it
20   comes, it comes, it comes without

pause, it comes without thought, it
comes without Jesus or Marx,
it comes, it comes, you pack, they

feed the line. You band, you crimp,
25   you ship to Kuwait, Detroit,

to Crestline, Ohio, they
profit, it comes, they feed the
line. You eat, you sleep, you bail

glass from your dreams, you drown, you
30   faint, you rest, you rage, you love,

feed, they feed
the line, glass, industry you,
from earth.

AFTER THE DEINDUSTRIALIZATION OF AMERICA, MY FATHER ENTERS TELEVISION REPAIR

My hands hold, my father's solder the wires—
picture rolls once, then steadies . . . an English castle!
The voice-over drones about Edward I,
who, to subdue the Welsh, built castles.
5   Some sixty years, dozens of engineers, the masses
conscripted from the villages.

My father moves on to a Zenith
with a bad tuner. TVs interest him, not the English
with their damp, historical programming.

10   Here there were Indians, mound builders.
     Here, an English fort, a few farmers.
     And here the industrialist settled his ass,
     John Ford on the river dredging sand
     for making glass. Plate glass.
15   (Why should America buy from Europe?)
     Some half dozen years, German engineers, and hundreds
         of Slavic peasants.

     Grandfather sat on his samovar
     warming himself and making excuses,
20   but finally, he set off.
     Got a room, became a shoveler.
     Got a wife, a company house.
     Ford City: a valley filling with properties.

     No one got along—
25   not Labor and Capital, not Germans and Slavs,
     not husbands and wives, for that matter.

▪▪▪▪▪▪▪▪▪▪

     Edward's castles were ruins
     by the 15th century. Not from Welsh armies,
     but the rise of the middle class.
30   The towns around a castle thrived:
     tailors, smithies, cobblers, coopers.
     Drawing in the Welsh peasants.
     And what with intermarriage and the rise of capitalism . . .
     a castle grew obsolescent.

35   I turn off the set. My father hunts
     cigarettes at the Kwik-Mart on the corner.
     Overhead, my mother's footsteps,
     the tonk of bottles,
     the scraping of plates.

▪▪▪▪▪▪▪▪▪▪

40   During Eisenhower's reign
     my grandfather retired and mowed his lawn
     until I took over. He primed the filter,
     set the choke, then we took turns pulling
     till the sputtering engine caught.
45   ("Somanabitch," he'd spit.)
     And watch me as I mowed
     back and forth for two dollars.

     Once in the garage he showed me a scythe.
     He mowed hay in the old country, and the women
50   would follow, raking it in windrows.

▪▪▪▪▪▪▪▪▪▪

The factories today are mostly closed down,
or full of robots or far off in Asia.
Ford City lives through the mail:
compensation, a thin pension,
55   and, of course, Social Security.

I always drive along the factory, windows rolled down;
I want my kids in the back seat to see.
Seven or eight, probably pensioners, congregate
on the corner, each man dressed quite alike:
60   Sears jacket, cigarette, salt-and-pepper hair.

"Honk the horn," my oldest begs.
He waves and waves zealously
until a man turns—a man
with my face, but full of sweetness now,
65   silence and clarity.

Toward the Heaven of Full Employment

Out of love for the dead Kennedys,
    out of fear of her laid-off spouse,
Aunt Sophie lit candles and prayed an extra rosary
    so God would make the payment on the house.

5   Even then factories like carriers at sea
        steamed off toward the Far East.
Even then the men, paging magazines,
        smoked more, grew bored and obese.

Mock on, mock on, Mr. Marx & Mr. Engels,
10   this America of the idle and decadent.
Haul us up, slow God, speed us like angels
        toward the heaven of full employment.

Now

Now the silence. Now the peace.
Now the empty hands uplifted. And my father, now
the pensioner, recites a psalm before
the ikon, addresses praise to the cloudy
5   forehead of God.
      Now the morning, all crammed with
heaven, and the mystery of cigarettes and coffee.
Behind the cup and smoke, behind the radio's low mutter
he empties his head, turning more inward hourly.
10   I want said what needs said: his story wide and long now,
a public account, out of the furnace of the private life.
I want to trust it, to own it, to sit between boredom
and wonder watching it rise beneath the dome of stars, over

the tender years, over the wars, over the mill's crooked
15   gloom, the long arcs rising, rising toward the triumphant,
toward the end of historical time. I want his silence
broken now and what is mine.

No, he says, *I have no story.*
The story tells me. Even now.

Jim Daniels (b. 1956)

Jim Daniels grew up in Detroit in a family of autoworkers. His father, grandfather, brothers, and most of his friends worked in the factories, and Daniels worked summers on the assembly line at Ford's axle plant, earning money for college. Blue-collar work and family life have been dominant themes in his poetry from his earliest chapbooks, *Factory Poems* (1979) and *On The Line* (1981). The poems in *Places/Everyone* (1985) explore the "places" to which workers are assigned by the regime of the job, as well as the dramas taking place in the homes and neighborhoods to which they return at night. *Punching Out* (1990) dramatizes in detail the world of a single auto plant—its harsh music, its camaraderie, its cast of diverse characters and the many ways they have of surviving or resisting its boredom and control—through the experience of a new hire named Digger, a persona that Daniels says he developed "to explore in depth the effects of that work on an individual." In *Digger's Territory* (1989) and *Digger's Blues* (2002), we see Daniels's "autoworker's everyman" maturing but still stuck as he faces layoffs, counts the years to retirement, takes a vacation, takes a break in the bar, and so forth. Daniels's gaze on the world that formed him and the language in which he expresses that gaze are direct, unsentimental, and often comic or surprisingly tender. Robert Creeley calls Daniels "a poet of unique commitment and ability. He makes poetry an act of deep caring and recognition." In addition to thirteen books of poems, he is the author of two collections of short stories, *No Pets* (1999) and *Detroit Tales* (2003), and the editor of *Letters to America: Contemporary American Poetry of Race* (1995). Daniels teaches at Carnegie-Mellon University in Pittsburgh.

DIGGER THINKS ABOUT NUMBERS

You look at the number
above the freeway to see
how many cars have been made
in America this year.
5   The car drifts
and you swerve back
into your lane.
Each time you have to look.

Every day you're supposed to make
10   800 axle housing tubes.
If you make 800
you sit down for the rest of the day.
Some days you try to make it
and do. Some days you try
15   but the machine breaks down.
Some days you break down.

And every day you start back at zero
like you never made those parts
the day before.

20   You want them to put a sign over the freeway:
"Digger made 160,000 parts so far this year."
You want your neighbor to come over
and congratulate you. But
he ties brake cables—he'd want a sign too.

25   Your wife hits your arm:
"What are you trying to do, get us killed?"
You think of the sign at the police station:
auto injuries ———
fatalities ———.
30   You grab the wheel and hunch over,
guarding the only life
you're ever going to have.

Digger Goes on Vacation

The maps from AAA, the tourbooks,
you are well-prepared:
Florida here we come.
For the first time
5   your son will not go with you.
He has a legitimate excuse:
a job at the corner store.
It is only you and the girls.
You think of your wife
10   as a girl.
You think
that you have given her nothing.
At the first Stuckey's on the road
you buy her a box of peanut brittle
15   and smile weakly
as she kisses your cheek.
Then you think of the plant
she is kissing you good-bye
in the morning.

20   You feel a chill
maybe wind on your neck.
You have two weeks.
Your body shakes
as you pull back on the road:
25   you have fifteen more years.

First night
you stop at a motel
off of I-75 in Kentucky.
At a diner
30   you eat a late dinner
the girls nodding off to sleep
in their hamburgers.
You look at your wife.
If somehow she could lose some weight.
35   Then you look at your belly
hanging over your belt:
but mine's hard, you tell yourself,
muscle.

You punch your gut:
40   *if we could just lose*
all this weight.

"Digger?"
"Oh . . . yeah."
You pay the bill
45   and walk across the street
to the motel
squeezing your wife's hand
like a snowball
you want to melt.

---

50   You lie in the sand
the sun crisp on your back.
You will get burned.
You always do.
You try to read a book
55   in the bright glare—
the same book you brought
on vacation last year:
The Godfather.
At a cabin in Northern Michigan
60   you read 150 pages
and killed mosquitoes.
She packed it to keep me busy,
keep my eyes off the women.

You look over at your wife
65   wearing a floppy sun hat and bulging out
from her bathing suit.
You throw sand on her belly:
"hey Loretta, gimme a beer."
She hands you one
70   from the cooler by her side.

She really does
care about me,
you think, and suddenly
you are happy and smile.
75   You put the cold beer
against her neck
and she jumps up screaming.
"Hey baby, I love you."
"What?"
80   She takes off her sunglasses
and smiles, hugging you.
"You haven't said that since . . .
last year's vacation!"

You stare out at the sea of skin
85   and wonder when
you'll say it again.

━━━━

At the beach
your foot in the sand
outlines the part
90   you weld onto axles.
"What's that, Daddy?"
You kick sand
over the drawing,
"Nothin'."
95   But no matter how many times
you kick the sand
it still looks like
something.

━━━━

In a motel in Tennessee
100   you peel off your skin
to gross your daughters out.
"Oh Daddy, that's sick!"
You laugh
and rub your vacation beard:
105   "when all this skin is gone
I'll be a new person."
"Who will you be then, Daddy?"
"I'll be an astronaut.

So I could get lost in space."
110 "You're already lost in space,"
your wife shouts from the bathroom.

That night after dinner
you drink alone
at a local bar.
115 Your hands hold up your head
like obedient stilts.
This is how you always
become a new person.
You talk to the bartender:
120 "I used to be an astronaut."
And he believes you.

DIGGER LAID OFF

Eight years since
the last time. Never thought
it would happen again.

You thought your seniority
5 was a hole you were digging—
the deeper you dug, the safer
you felt.

At the unemployment office
you shuffle in line with the rest,
10 shifting from foot to foot,
wobbling like a bowling pin.
Angry, but you don't know
at who or what.

When you were a kid, you waited
15 in line for football physicals.
Naked, nowhere to hide.
You can't pick your eyes up
off the floor. If they ask you,
you will cough.

DIGGER, THE BIRTHDAY BOY

40 years old. 20 at the plant.
When you started, you said
two years tops. Enough money
to get ahead a little
5 *till I figure out what I*
really want to do.
When someone calls you a lifer now
you do not object.

Your buddy Frank took an early
10   retirement buyout, moved down south
near his parents. He sent a picture—
it's on the bulletin board—he's holding
his belly like a watermelon:
I'm going crazy
15   *down here. Heard any good jokes?*
30 years. And out.

He got an aerial view of the plant
that everyone signed—the company gift.
Roof and parking lot. He squinted,
20   shook his head, forced a laugh,
like it was a bachelor party, everybody
trying hard to be funny, drinking fast.

And him a lifetime bachelor.
You don't see any of the guys after work
25   anymore. No quick showers
to head out to the bars, hair wet
and shiny, the night fresh with possibility.
No card games, ball games, no picnics.
Just talk at breaks about cars, sports, tv.

30   Family. All you have. You sit in the car
after work today, wondering what you'll get
when you get home—a card from the kids,
your favorite meal, steak on the grill,
cake and ice cream. You back your car out
35   and smile, swerving onto Mound Road toward home,
toward the off-key voices,
the new shirt, socks, shovel. The love.

DIGGER'S TERRITORY

Some would say
there's not much to
a life lived on your street.
They might say you're dumb
5   that you watch too much tv
that you drink too much
fart and belch and laugh too loud
dress funny and eat too many hamburgers.

But tonight after work
10   after you wash your hands
eat a good meal
wrestle with the dog a little
after you grab a beer
and sit with your family
15   on your porch sharing a laugh
with a couple of neighbors

while the sun sets behind
the bowling alley, after a man parks
his car carefully behind
20 your Impala up on blocks
and walks stiff up your driveway
in his suit and briefcase and perfect hair
and holds out a soft hand,
you all smile at each other
25 because no matter what he knows
you're going to teach him a few things.

Martín Espada (b. 1957)

Martín Espada was born and raised in Brooklyn, New York, with a Puerto Rican heritage that instilled a strong sense of commitment to social justice. His father, Frank Espada, was a civil rights activist and a photographer who documented life in his Puerto Rican community. Espada's first book of poems, *The Immigrant Iceboy's Bolero* (1982), features his father's photographs. Espada started writing poetry in his late teens and in his early work was influenced by writers in the Nyorican tradition (that is, Puerto Ricans raised in New York City), Pedro Pietri, Piri Thomas, and Miguel Piñero in particular. He names as later influences Carl Sandburg, Pablo Neruda, Langston Hughes, and Walt Whitman. Espada obtained a BA degree in history from the University of Wisconsin and a JD in law from Northeastern University. It was in Boston that he worked as a tenants-rights lawyer for low-income, Spanish-speaking residents of Chelsea, people and experiences that he writes about in *City of Coughing and Dead Radiators* (1993), which includes two of the poems that follow. Of this period of his life and work, Espada says, "Both as a poet and a lawyer, I was engaged in the business of advocacy, speaking on behalf of those without an opportunity to be heard." He is also the author of *Imagine the Angels of Bread* (1996), a collection of essays *Zapata's Disciple* (1998), and *Alabanza: New and Selected Poems (1982–2002)*, the title poem of which was first published in *The Nation* on the anniversary of the September 11, 2001, attacks on the World Trade Center. He is the editor of *Poetry Like Bread: An Anthology of Political Poets* (1994) and *El Coro: A Chorus of Latino and Latina Poets* (1998). In a 2002 interview, Espada spoke about the political aesthetic of his work: "The crossroads of poetry and politics is a place where craft encounters commitment, where the spirit of dissent encounters the imagination, where we labor to create a culture of conscience. There the dynamic of oppression and resistance distills itself through the image, the senses. . . . We must work to give history a human face, eyes, nose, mouth."

WHO BURNS FOR THE PERFECTION OF PAPER

At sixteen, I worked after high school hours
at a printing plant
that manufactured legal pads:
Yellow paper

5 stacked seven feet high
and leaning
as I slipped cardboard
between the pages,
then brushed red glue
10 up and down the stack.
No gloves: fingertips required
for the perfection of paper,
smoothing the exact rectangle.
Sluggish by 9 PM, the hands
15 would slide along suddenly sharp paper,
and gather slits thinner than the crevices
of the skin, hidden.
Then the glue would sting,
hands oozing
20 till both palms burned
at the punchclock.

Ten years later, in law school,
I knew that every legal pad
was glued with the sting of hidden cuts,
25 that every open lawbook
was a pair of hands
upturned and burning.

THE TOOLMAKER UNEMPLOYED

—Connecticut River Valley, 1992

The toolmaker
is sixty years old,
unemployed
since the letter
5 from his boss
at the machine shop.

He carries
a cooler of soda
everywhere,
10 so as not to carry
a flask of whiskey.

During the hours
of his shift,
he is building a barn
15 with borrowed lumber
or hacking at trees
in the yard.

The family watches
and listens to talk

20   of a bullet
      in the forehead,
      maybe for himself,
      maybe for the man
      holding the second mortgage.

25   Sometimes
      he stares down
      into his wallet.

ALABANZA: IN PRAISE OF LOCAL 100

For the 43 members of Hotel Employees and Restaurant Employees Local 100, working at the
Windows on the World restaurant, who lost their lives in the attack on the World Trade Center

      Alabanza. Praise the cook with a shaven head
      and a tattoo on his shoulder that said *Oye,*
      a blue-eyed Puerto Rican with people from Fajardo,
      the harbor of pirates centuries ago.
5   Praise the lighthouse in Fajardo, candle
      glimmering white to worship the dark saint of the sea.
      Alabanza. Praise the cook's yellow Pirates cap
      worn in the name of Roberto Clemente, his plane
      that flamed into the ocean loaded with cans for Nicaragua,
10   for all the mouths chewing the ash of earthquakes.
      Alabanza. Praise the kitchen radio, dial clicked
      even before the dial on the oven, so that music and Spanish
      rose before bread. Praise the bread. *Alabanza.*

      Praise Manhattan from a hundred and seven flights up,
15   like Atlantis glimpsed through the windows of an ancient aquarium.
      Praise the great windows where immigrants from the kitchen
      could squint and almost see their world, hear the chant of nations:
      Ecuador, México, Republica Dominicana,
      Haiti, Yemen, Ghana, Bangladesh.
20   *Alabanza.* Praise the kitchen in the morning,
      where the gas burned blue on every stove
      and exhaust fans fired their diminutive propellers,
      hands cracked eggs with quick thumbs
      or sliced open cartons to build an altar of cans.
25   *Alabanza.* Praise the busboy's music, the *chime-chime*
      of his dishes and silverware in the tub.
      Alabanza. Praise the dish-dog, the dishwasher
      who worked that morning because another dishwasher
      could not stop coughing, or because he needed overtime
30   to pile the sacks of rice and beans for a family
      floating away on some Caribbean island plagued by frogs.
      Alabanza. Praise the waitress who heard the radio in the kitchen
      and sang to herself about a man gone. *Alabanza.*

After the thunder wilder than thunder,
35   after the shudder deep in the glass of the great windows,
after the radio stopped singing like a tree full of terrified frogs,
after night burst the dam of day and flooded the kitchen,
for a time the stoves glowed in darkness like the lighthouse in Fajardo,
like a cook's soul. Soul I say, even if the dead cannot tell us
40   about the bristles of God's beard because God has no face,
soul I say, to name the smoke-beings flung in constellations
across the night sky of this city and cities to come.
Alabanza I say, even if God has no face.

Alabanza. When the war began, from Manhattan and Kabul
45   two constellations of smoke rose and drifted to each other,
mingling in icy air, and one said with an Afghan tongue:
Teach me to dance. We have no music here.
And the other said with a Spanish tongue:
I will teach you. Music is all we have.

Lois-Ann Yamanaka (b. 1961)

Lois-Ann Yamanaka was born in Hoolchua, on the island of Molokai, Hawaii, the eldest of four daughters and a fourth-generation descendant of Japanese immigrant laborers in Hawaii's fruit and sugar plantations. The family later moved to Hawaii Island, where her father worked as a taxidermist and her mother as a primary school teacher. Yamanaka earned a B.Ed. degree from the University of Hawaii at Manoa in 1983 and began work in the Hawaii public schools. Teaching a group of "at-risk" students in a tough Honolulu neighborhood, she became convinced of the power of writing to address issues of class shame and ethnic prejudice. While working on a master's degree, she was encouraged by poet Faye Kicknosway to use pidgin (officially Hawaiian Creole English) in her writing, the dialect spoken by most working-class Hawaiians and the language of her home and of the plantation communities. Pidgin, however, was discouraged in the public schools, and Kamanaka's first book *Saturday Night at the Pahala Theatre* (1993), a series of verse novellas narrated by working-class teenagers, was banned from several schools as much for its use of pidgin as for its realistic treatment of issues of drug use, sexuality, and abusive relationships. Her first novel *Wild Meat and the Bully Burgers* (1996) explores adolescence from the point of view of twelve-year-old Lovey Nariyoshi, who is treated as an outsider at school by both whites and middle-class Japanese because of her second-hand clothes, her pidgin English, and her status as a "slow learner." Out of her shame at her family's make-do existence and her desire to show up her classmates, Lovey literally pieces together, in the story that follows, a fabric that expresses both her individual sense of style and her knowledge of her family's past. Yamanaka is also the author of the novels *Blu's Hanging* (1997), *Heads by Harry* (1999), *Name Me Nobody* (a young adult novel, 1999), and *Father of the Four Passages* (2001). She says of her writing: "My work involves bringing to the page the utter complexity, ferocious beauty and sometimes absurdity of our ethnic relationships here in the islands. The way we language about each other and with each other in our 'talk story' communities resonates in me with every word I write."

LOVEY'S HOMEMADE SINGER SEWING CLASS
PATCHWORK DENIM HIPHUGGERS

Grandma makes quilts. All grandmas do. Calhoon and me can spread our quilts out over the living-room floor and tell you whose dress or shirt is there right under us.

Aunty Bing's last year's May Day muumuu. Mother's shortie muumuu for Uncle Steven's New Year's mochi-pounding party. Grandma's favorite lavender aloha print church dress. Calhoon's and my matching County Fair clothes from three years ago with matching bikini bottoms.

And whenever we get a new grandma-made quilt, we lay it down on the floor to see who's there. The more we know, the more we fight for the blanket.

There is an old blanket on the floor of the garage. Paper boxes ripped apart and blood dripping from the carcass of an axis deer hanging by its antlers from a hook on the ceiling of the garage.

Before the gully, there is a field of grass, rolling hills, and ohia-log wire fences far off in the distance. I imagine "The Sound of Music" playing, Julie Andrews spinning in her peasant dress and apron, and what Austria might look like. When I hear the shots from the gully, I spread the blanket on the bed of the truck and get ready to go home.

"Cal grab one antler, Lovey grab the odda one, and heave, ho. Pull um up, hurry up befo' the blood drip on you guys' slippas." Under the lychee tree, everybody poses with the buck, purple tongue hanging out, eyes purple clear, the flies swarming fat and black.

"Careful how you skin the hide, Ed," says Father. "We gonna sew us hunting vests with all the scrap hide I get in the freeza. For the *real* huntas for wear under the army jacket. Betta than down vest, I tell you, and I going sew um myself."

Mother says Cal and me should go to sewing lessons down in the cool basement of the Singer store. Concrete floors and the whirwhirwhir of the machine wheels. Bobbins all over the floor of the sewing class, strips of pattern tissue. Tracing paper in all colors spread out over the cutting table and tracing wheels with red-and-green handles hanging on little nails.

"I making a skirt first," I tell Calhoon. "McCall's 1064 or Simplicity 2761."

Mother says, "No Vogue patterns—too expensive and Butterick don't fit the Japanee bodies right. Even Grandma says so 'cause the Japanee get long body and short daikon legs, thass why. The waist of the Butterick pattern is right under your chi-chi."

Teruko Nakamura, the sewing teacher, wears a green tape measure around her neck. Every girl except for Cal and me, who share a sewing kit, has all of the following:

A satin pastel pincushion.

Sewing pins with colorful heads.

A huge plastic, see-through sewing chest.

And a shiny, silver, official Singer's scissors from the locked showcase.

We got this:

Grandma's old wicker chest. The string that holds the cover to the basket ripped off on one side, so the cover hangs when you open the basket. Rusty hinges and a lock that doesn't pop open. We gotta pry the chest open.

A cheapo tomato pincushion.

Needles that don't have heads. The kind the kindergarten teacher used to pin notes to your dress at the end of the day.

And the greatest shame, the poultry shears for sewing scissors.

Cut the body open from jaw to belly. Slice the hide off the head. Gelatin eyes, skeleton teeth—black-and-green smiling teeth hidden behind all that skin.

The fat bubbles where my father slices and the sound of Saran Wrap stretched and cut as he separates the hide from the body, careful not to leave meat on the hide. So much salt for one body, throw the rock salt over the carcass as he works. The flies buzz around the pieces of meat sliced from the hide and flicked off the hand, stuck on the floor of the garage.

From Hilo town as we leave in the morning, I see the *purplemountainmajesty*—Mauna Kea. I know exactly what the song means every time I see the mountain in the middle of my island. There on the slopes of Mauna Kea, we find a place to hide. Stay low.

Hide. Daddy filming us stalking the mouflons nibbling the shoots off the mamane tree. Huge-horned rams, blonds and browns. Mixedbreed mouflons and native sheep with one and a half curls on the horns. Ewes and babies.

Lava fields and brush all around and no sign of purple this close to the summit. The wind and the whirwhirwhir of the 8-millimeter camera filming this huge flock of sheep as evidence when we tell Uncle Ed about the hunt he missed for golf. So close and so many to shoot, upwind, perfect—Daddy, Cal, and me.

Cal takes off her fluorescent-orange hunting hat, wipes her head, and all of a sudden, the flock scatters, heads straight for us, gunshots, duck your head, scramble for cover, hoofs on rock, and sheep crying in all directions. Gunshots and Daddy screaming, "Who the hell's firing?!"

The black ewe that's hit scrambles to her feet, pulling her hindquarters. Father straightens his glasses—twisted sideways on his face—shoves the camera to me, and shoots her in the head. Thick gelatin blood spurts and sticks to our faces and black blood pools on the lava as Father kicks her to make sure she's dead.

"No can even mount this sunnafabitch. Look too old for meat. Gunfunnit, you, Cal. Why you wen' wave your hat like that fo'? Sheezus Christmas. And who the hell fired their gun? Dammit, Lovey. You coulda kill somebody. Freak accidents happen when somebody shoot stupid, *Stupid*. Here, you skin this sheep." Father snaps the buck knife to the ground and its blade cuts into the dirt. "Take the hide and leave the rest. I ain't carrying back this heavy shit-for-nothing sheep. Pick the best part of the hide for the vest I going sew. And pick good."

Teruko helps me pick my brown skirt material. It's gauzy but stiff and she charges the material and pellon for the waistband to my mother's account.

I cut the pattern carefully right outside the black lines. I lay the pattern down and measure the nap. Cut with the poultry shears slowly so that I hear the scissors' crunch, crunch, crunch on the Formica tabletop. I read the instructions two times over before I even pin the fabric together. Sew stitch by stitch a perfect five-eighths and zigzag, not pink, the seams. Steam-press every seam.

So how come Teruko doesn't tell me to iron the hem when I'm done is unclear to me. Why my mother expected Teruko, who is from Japan, to tell me to iron the damn hem before I wear the damn skirt to school is also unclear to me.

So that when Gina Oshiro says, "Oh wow, Lovey. Homemade skirt? Can tell. You neva iron the hem, that's why." It doesn't make sense to me. And I swear, I pull and tug the hem all day and nothing does it like Mother's iron when I get home.

Why didn't they tell me?

I make a beige gauze hippy blouse with gathers in the front. I iron the hem and wear it with my hiphuggers. A huge leather belt with painted engraved butterflies and flowers and a tarnished bronze buckle. Gina says in Period One, real loud, "The hiphuggas from J. C. Penney's and the shirt from Lovey's Singer sewing class." She's right and I gotta wear the damn clothes for another five periods.

I hate sewing. I want to quit.

I try to see who else in school wears Singer sewing class clothes. I cannot tell. Maybe Lori Shigemura and Laura Murayama, but their clothes look like they could pass for store-made.

From then on, I make throw pillows in sewing class with pink and red corduroy. For my bed. For the living room. For Mother's bed. And throw pillows for Grandma out of printed terry cloth.

Calhoon in the meanwhile makes the nicest jacket with fake patchwork denim with waistband ribbing and a real jacket zipper from the expensive zipper section in Singer's. It looks so real and so good until I borrow it for school one day and everybody says, "Rip-off patchwork denim. Phony-ass, fake stuff. Looks Wigwam or worse yet. Homemade."

Goddammit, I quit sewing for good.

"And no quit. Only losers give up the ship," my father says. "One day you be the best hunter, no worry. But, eh, maybe you ain't made fo' be *just* one hunter. I mean, maybe you be the vest seamstress. You help Daddy and Uncle Ed make their vest, and with the scraps, I make *you* one, okay? Only the top game hunters wear the kine vest we going make."

My father starts tanning the hides for the two vests for him and Uncle Ed. He throws the defrosted hides one by one over the sawhorse and slices the meat off the hides. "Gotta make sure no mo' nothing on the hide bumbye the bugga rotten right on your body," he says and flings the meat at me but misses and it sticks to the side of the Land Rover. Father removes the fat gelatin skin layer from each of the hides.

"Salt and air dry this bugga. Go put um out for dry under the lychee tree. Gotta be in the shade, let the breeze dry um out."

My father pickle-bathes the hides in lots of rock salt and water in the totan by the bathhouse, then puts them in the tanning solution.

In a few days, me and him running each piece of hide through the breaker, rubbing it back and forth on the cane knife until the hides are soft, softer than suede.

And Daddy says, "For my vest, my spirit is the axis deer and the mouflon we wen' catch up Mauna Loa, so half my vest going be deer and the odda half sheep. Ed one is the odda half of the axis deer and the pig he wen' catch up by Moniz them pastureland up Uka side. And nobody, nobody but you, me, and Ed can name um, the place where these hides all from, and how we wen' catch um, you hear? And for mo' power, I tanning the deer balls for my pocket on the inside of my vest and the pig balls for Ed 'cause the bugga almost snatch his leg befo' he blass um in the head. And the minute you tell, all this fo' nothing."

And then I know what I have to do. Daddy makes me thread the long hooked needle with black nylon thread. I stab it into the top of his worktable. We trace the tissue paper from the Simplicity 8132 from Singer onto oaktag from the stationery store and cut out the hides with the X-acto knife.

Put right sides together like Teruko says and stitch. "Take your time and make um good. Like each stitch is for make this vest strong." Poke the hooked needle, the sound of leather being punctured, slow. We take all afternoon and that night in front of the TV.

"See, Hubert, lucky thing I sent Lovey sewing lessons, eh?" my mother says. "And there you was, grumble, grumble, grumble about the money. So you need help, let me know, even if those hides smell like ten dead goats in a barrel of oil."

When I'm done, no hems to press, raw edges without zigzag, balls for pockets, Daddy says, "We going catch one big one next time we go hunting, I tell you." And Daddy wears his vest to sleep.

I choose for my vest:

Bully hide for the cow we couldn't eat who cried like a man.

Goat hide though it's not my Nanny, I wear it to scare away billies and for goat smell on my skin.

Ewe hide for the black one from Mauna Kea who dragged herself with a bullet in the side—a bullet behind her eye in a pool of dark blood.

Rabbit hides for Clyde, Lani, and Hokulani on my shoulders, killed by dogs, but close to my face. To dominate.

And no one—no one can name them but me.

"Rip-off patchwork denim. Phony-ass, fake stuff. Looks Wigwam or worse yet. Homemade."

And then I know what I have to do.

Calhoon says she'll help me make the real patchwork denim hiphugger bell-bottoms from Simplicity 1013. I go back for another lesson. Only losers give up the ship.

Calhoon hunts for her old kindergarten sleeping bag. Grandma digs in her three giant trash bags full of quilt scraps for my pieces of denim and sends it air mail to me from Moloka'i. We whirwhirwhir the fabric together.

Father brings his old chambray work shirts from the Salvation Army boxes outside in the aluminum shed. Cal and me sew all the denim pieces together but it's not quite enough. When Mother donates her old Baptist camp Levi's, all faded but rugged and washed out, we can finish the fabric.

Calhoon and me lay the pattern down and pin the nap carefully. We cut with the poultry shears that work extra well with the thick patchwork denim. To make it look really store-bought, my mother tells us to sew the bell-bottom hiphuggers on Aunt Helen's Bernina so the topstitch looks like store-bought.

When I put it on with my unbleached-muslin wildflower-embroidered halter top, suck in my stomach and show a little bit of belly button, the fabric rubs me right—the patchwork jeans with Dutch clogs and a leather-fringe shoulder bag.

Gina Oshiro in Period One can't say anything about home-sewn clothes that look so expensive and store-bought that she resorts to say, "Eh, Lovey, pull up your hiphuggas. Can see your ass cleavage."

I say, "Hey, man, I planned it that way."

Grandma, Mother, Calhoon, Father, and me at that moment in the patchwork denim bell-bottom hiphuggers whose scraps nobody in the room could name but me.

Melida Rodas (b. 1972)

$\mathbf{M}$elida Rodas was born in Guatemala, and as a child was surrounded by Mayan art and folklore, Spanish architecture, and religious icons. In 1979, when she was seven years old, she and her family set out for *Los Estados* to join Rodas's father who led the way six months earlier. The family migrated from their native country in a Greyhound bus to search for a better life and to escape economic and political oppression in Guatemala. "*El Olor de Cansancio*" is inspired by her father's life: "In America my papa stares at me glassy eyed holding my hands across the kitchen table. I am old enough now to hear his stories, stories of the forest of his youth, the Guatemalan army, and La Migra. . . . The man who once wore suits and ties to work would provide for his three daughters and his wife by enduring the excessive hours of labor in the scolding kitchens of restaurants and delis." Rodas's mother found work in an unventilated rug factory, but, crippled by rheumatoid arthritis and osteoporosis, she was no longer able to do factory work.

Inheriting her family's oral tradition of storytelling, Rodas braided her memories of Guatemala with her experiences in America and began telling her own stories through art and poetry. She expressed herself visually from an early age, and her sculptures, photographs, and paintings have been exhibited in public spaces and galleries throughout New Jersey. Her passion for words was supported by her family, friends, and, particularly, her college teacher Edvige Giunta who introduced her to memoir writing. She is a wife, mother, legal assistant, and part of *Chilltown*, an underground poetry movement in downtown Jersey City. She is at work on a memoir, *Me Llamo Guadalupe*. "My work," she says, is "like a Mayan tapestry, a work of color embroidered by memories, and threaded by Mayan art, urban life, religious tradition, and spiritualism."

EL OLOR DE CANSANSIO (THE SMELL OF FATIGUE)

My father hangs up the phone. He puts away our colorful new kite. He puts away his smile and his Tuesday clothes as he prepares for a new battle. I watch him put on the white shirt. The checkered pants. The boots. He folds a crisp white apron and places it in the pocket of his jacket. I admire the fresh white shirt, the crisp crease that runs down his black-and-white pants. Smelling like soap and shaving cream, he returns to the restaurant where he has been slaving ever since we moved to New Jersey from Guatemala in 1979.

I see him walk slowly, tired. Another cook has left. Another dishonorable discharge, I suppose. My father is brought in to hold down the fort on his day off. The way he always does, like a respectable soldier.

Each day I see my father's hair get grayer. It won't be long before it's silver, like the buttons on a new cadet's jacket, silver like water in the sun. His hands are small. Always callused. Always pink. He holds my face like a moon before he says good-bye. "Next week," he promises, as he points to the drawer that keeps our kite. I wish that he would stay. I try to keep my eyes from telling him as he holds my face. His hands feel so strong. Strong from carrying pots of heavy soup. Strong from fighting the ambush of dinner specials, lunch specials, breakfast specials with eggs, home fries, bacon, silver dollar pancakes, California cheeseburgers, Caesar salads, BLTs, mashed potatoes, French fries with gravy, toast with marmalade, jelly, butter, cream cheese.

Noune Manjares, Filipino Workers Center, "Mom Looking Out the Window." *Reprinted with permission from unseenamerica, Bread and Roses, Local 1199 (SEIU).*

My father has always worked hard. Ever since the age of seven when he sold peanuts, which he carried in small bags on a cardboard box. Ever since he shared the streets with the other children who sold Chicklets and shined shoes. With the blind man who sold tickets *de lotteria* and the *viejita* who begged for money outside El Palacio National. He's worked hard ever since his toes were small and wrinkled in the rain because the leather from his shoes had finally surrendered.

Life has always been as hard as the soles of my father's feet. Like the callused hand my face melts into. He holds it like the cantaloupe before a fruit salad. Like life before America. Before it's sliced, devoured, consumed. Guatemala feels like a memory, just a memory. A humble memory that moves slowly and peacefully. It is a place not so gray with buildings. It is a landscape with green mountains, blue skies, and sweet air. It is a place where you don't fear the *Migra*. The force. The clan that comes to take you away. They search in kitchens and factories for their victims. They send them back with suitcases full of postcards of the Statue of Liberty that never got sent, subway tokens, wrinkled letters with Spanish writing decorated with exotic pressed flowers, stamped with colorful postage, smelling like perfume and crayon. Everyone who is here on borrowed time, with expired visas and false documentation, fears the *Migra*. Because it doesn't matter that you have spent all your *centavos* to buy a piece of the American pie. So what if you risked your life crossing the desert with a *coyote*, the man who guides you through the desert and river to the American border? Once you reach the line, once you dodge the bullets that the border patrol has fired at you, once you say *El Salve Maria*, you crawl to American soil. *Mojado. Indocumentado.* No visa. Your wet clothes stick to your tired back. Pictures of your children, of your family, stick to your almost empty wallet.

We come to America by bus. It takes us five days to reach *Los Estados*. We leave our colorful beautiful Guatemala for gray buildings and a promise that here we will have a better life. Here my father doesn't wear a suit and tie to work. Here there is no garden, no fruit trees, no space. Here we live in an apartment. People don't smile. People don't say hello, except for the Puerto Rican lady my mother calls Donna Ortega. She's the only one who is friendly with us when we first arrive. Americans don't want to know us. Not even the children. Patrick, who lives next door, calls me a spic. One day he spits on my face on the way home from school.

Today my father leaves our apartment for the restaurant. The awful place that fatigues him. His shoulders are small and round. His feet are heavy. The image is familiar. I realize that I've seen it before. It is the picture of a wounded soldier who returns to the battle. I feel a large *jocote* in my throat as I try to imagine the number of potatoes my father has peeled. Oh, the difficulty of surviving an infantry of dishes, a Sunday morning rush! And the heat of August days. The sweat on his brow, the napkin he wraps around his forehead to prevent it from blinding him. How do you endure the battles, such battles, Father, with pans and pots as your only allies? Vegetables, meats, oil as your weapons? When is it time to surrender the ladle, the whisk, the spoon?

My father's boots. They alone tell the story of the war. With their greasy suede and vegetable pulp trapped underneath them. When he enters our home, he sheds the boots on the floor, as if never wanting to see them again. A reminder of the American Dream gone sour. Of times that don't get better, just get harder. Every day I've seen life take the years from my father. Years taken with unsympathetic conviction. As I walk past restaurant alleys, I remember the smell of my father's clothes when he comes home.

Sometimes the hours are so hard and so long that he asks me to take off his heavy boots. Proudly, I reach for his feet and try to give him a sense of home and gratitude. I untie the hardened laces. I dispose of the fragments of lettuce and tomato caught between them. I remove his boots like a heavy cast. His feet give off the heat of labor and *cansansio*. His socks I peel off with the delicate care of an archeologist revealing precious Mayan fossils. His pale feet wait to be freed from their torture. I squeeze fatigue away from his toes. I rejuvenate his ankles. I make his beautiful rough heels feel like they can carry him to the front line again tomorrow.

My father leaves our small apartment when the sky is still purple. He leaves when the newspapers outside the candy store are still wrapped with string and the bakery rolls are still warm in large paper bags. He leaves when the chill of Aurora glues me to a poncho my *abuelo* has sent. My father leaves when the house doesn't yet smell like tea, syrup, and eggs. When the only one who hears his footsteps is my mother, as she tries to keep the warmth he has left in their bed.

My father returns when the sky is purple again. When the first stars are saying hello. He comes home when homework is done. When you've brushed your teeth. When dishes have been used, washed, dried, and put away. My father comes home when others have taken off their ties or panty hose, have eaten dinner, paid their bills, and read their favorite book. When the day has simmered and night begins. When the enemy has ceased fire. My father comes home when you grow tired of waiting. When you surrender to the weight of your eyelids and you wish you could have told him that you made honor roll again today.

Contents by Genre

Journals, Memoir, Autobiography, Oral History

Petitions, Speeches, Addresses, Lectures

Essays

Plays

Letters

Short Stories

Novel Excerpts

Select Bibliography

The bibliography that follows is intended to extend the range of working-class literature beyond the necessary limits of an anthology that is designed primarily for classroom use. Many texts are named here that the editors would have included if space allowed—texts we have taught in our own classes and that we recommend reading alongside those included here. As resources for further study, we also list commentaries and historical writings that have shaped our understanding of this literature and of the field of working-class studies more broadly. The bibliography is divided into four distinct lists: (1) books by individual authors (a note on genre follows each entry where this is not indicated in the title), (2) collections and anthologies, (3) literary and cultural commentary, and (4) labor and working-class history.

In selecting titles to be included here, we accepted two limitations that readers should be aware of. First, we list only published full-length books—no articles or journal and magazine publications, no chapbooks, and no unpublished manuscripts. As this book's contents indicate, however, the cultural production of the American working class is much more extensive and diverse than can be represented by books alone. Second, we have listed in the first section primarily books that are currently in print and therefore available for classroom use by teachers and students. For further, and in some cases more focused lists, readers can consult Laura Hapke, *Labor's Text: The Worker in American Fiction* (see Section 3); Paul Lauter "Working-Class Women's Literature: An Introduction to Study" (in *Women in Print I*, Joan E. Hartman and Ellen Messer-Davidow, eds, New York: Modern Language Association, 1982); Cheryl Cline, "Autobiographies by American Working-Class Women: A Bibliography" (in Janet Zandy, ed. *What We Hold in Common*—see Section 3); and the lists of fiction, poetry, and film maintained by the Center for Working-Class Studies on its web site <www.as.ysu.edu/~cwcs/workingclasslit>. For labor and working-class film, see Tom Zaniello, *Working Stiffs, Union Maids, Reds, and Riffraff: An Organized Guide to Films about Labor* (see Section 3).

1. Books by Individual Authors

Agee, James, and Walker Evans. *Let Us Now Praise Famous Men: Three Tenant Families*. Boston: Houghton Mifflin, 1941. Photography-journalism

Alcott, Louisa May. *Work: A Story of Experience*. New York: Penguin Classics; Reprint ed., 1994. Novel

Alexie, Sherman. *Reservation Blues*. New York: Warner, 1996. Novel

Algren, Nelson. *Somebody in Boots: A Novel*. 1935; New York: Thunder's Mouth Press, 1987.

——. *Neon Wilderness*. 1947; New York: Seven Stories Press, 2002. Novel

Allen, Paula Gunn. *Life is a Fatal Disease: Selected Poems, 1962–1995*. Albuquerque, NM: West End Press, 1996.

Allison, Dorothy. *Bastard Out of Carolina*. New York: Dutton, 1992. Novel

——. *Trash*. Ithaca, NY: Firebrand, 1988. Short stories

Anderson, Edward. *Hungry Men*. 1935; Norman: University of Oklahoma Press, 1993. Novel

Anzaldúa, Gloria. *Borderlands/La Frontera: The New Mestiza*. San Francisco: Aunt Lute, 1987. Multigenre

Arnow, Harriette. *The Dollmaker*. 1954; New York: Avon, 1999. Novel

Attaway, William. *Blood on the Forge*. 1941; New York: New York Review Books, 2005. Novel

Babb, Sonora. *Whose Names Are Unknown*. Norman: University of Oklahoma Press, 2004. Novel

Baca, Jimmy Santiago. *Immigrants in Our Own Land*. New York: New Directions, 1990. Poems

———. *Working in the Dark: Reflections of a Poet of the Barrio*. Santa Fe, NM: Red Crane, 1992. Memoir

Bambara, Toni Cade. *The Salt Eaters*. New York: Vintage, 1980. Novel

———. *Gorilla, My Love*. New York: Vintage, 1992. Short stories

Barrio, Raymond. *The Plum Plum Pickers*. 1981; Tempe, AZ: Bilingual Review Press, 1984. Novel

Bell, Thomas. *Out of This Furnace*. 1940; Pittsburgh: University of Pittsburgh Press, 1976. Novel

Bencastro, Mario. *Odyssey to the North*. Houston: Arte Publico Press, 1998. Novel

Berlin, Lucia. *Homesick: New and Selected Stories*. Santa Rosa, CA: Black Sparrow Press, 1990.

Blair, Peter. *Last Heat*. Washington, DC: Word Works, 2000. Poems

Bonosky, Phillip. *Burning Valley*. 1953; Urbana: University of Illinois Press, 1998. Novel

Bontemps, Arna Wendell, and Jack Conroy. *Anyplace but Here*. 1966; Columbia: University of Missouri Press, 1997. History/Oral history

Brady, Maureen. *Folly*. 1982; New York: Feminist Press, 1994. Novel

Brant, Beth. *Mohawk Trail*. Ithaca, NY: Firebrand Books, 1985. Multigenre

Brill, Ernie. *I Looked Over Jordan and Other Stories*. Boston: South End Press, 1980. Short fiction

Brooks, Gwendolyn. *Selected Poems*. New York: Harper and Row, 1963.

Brown, Claude. *Manchild in the Promised Land*. 1965; New York: Simon and Schuster, 1999. Autobiography

Brown, Rita Mae. *Rubyfruit Jungle*. 1973; New York: Bantam; reissue ed., 1983. Novel

Brown, Sterling A. [Michael Harper, ed.] *The Collected Poems of Sterling A. Brown*. Evanston, IL: Triquarterly Books, 1996.

Bryant, Dorothy. *Miss Giardino*. 1978; New York: Feminist Press, 1997. Novel

Bukowski, Charles. *Post Office*. Santa Rosa, CA: Black Sparrow Press, 1971. Novel

Bulosan, Carlos. *America Is in the Heart*. 1946; Seattle: University of Washington Press, 1973. Autobiography

Burke, Fielding. *Call Home the Heart*. 1932; New York: Feminist Press, 1983. Novel

Burke, James Lee. *To the Bright and Shining Sun*. New York: Hyperion, 1989. Novel

Cahan, Abraham. *The Rise of David Levinsky*. 1917; New York: Penguin, 1993. Novel

Caldwell, Erskine. *Tobacco Road*. 1932; Athens: University of Georgia Press, 1995. Novel

Cervantes, Lorna Dee. *Emplumada*. Pittsburgh: University of Pittsburgh Press, 1981. Poems

———. *From the Cables of Genocide: Poems of Love and Hunger*. Houston: Arte Publico Press, 1991.

Chute, Carolyn. *The Beans of Egypt, Maine*. New York: Warner, 1987. Novel

———. *Letourneau's Used Auto Parts*. New York: Harper and Row, 1988. Novel

Cisneros, Sandra. *The House on Mango Street*. New York: Vintage, 1984. Short stories

———. *Woman Hollering Creek and Other Stories*. New York: Vintage, 1991. Short stories

Coleman, Wanda. *African Sleeping Sickness*. 1979; Santa Rosa, CA: Black Sparrow Press, 1990. Stories and poems

Crane, Stephen. *Maggie: A Girl of the Streets, and Other Bowery Tales*. 1893; New York: Random House, 2001. Novella

Conroy, Jack. *The Disinherited*. 1933; Columbia: University of Missouri Press, 1991. Novel

Curran, Mary Doyle. *The Parish and the Hill*. 1948; New York: Feminist Press, 1986. Novel

Dahlberg, Edward. *Bottom Dogs*. New York: G. P. Putnam's Sons, 1929. Novel

Daniels, Jim. *Punching Out*. Detroit: Wayne State University Press, 1989. Poems

———. *No Pets*. Huron, OH: Bottom Dog Press, 1999. Short stories

Davis, Rebecca Harding. *Life in the Iron Mills*. 1861; New York, Feminist Press, 1972. Novella

Debs, Eugene. *Debs: His Life, Writings and Speeches*. Honolulu: University Press of the Pacific, 2002.

Denby, Charles. *Indignant Heart: A Black Worker's Journal*. Detroit: Wayne State University Press, 1989. Autobiography

DeRosa, Tina. *Paper Fish*. 1980; New York: Feminist Press, 1996. Novel

Diaz, Junot. *Drown and Other Stories*. New York: Riverhead, 1996. Short stories

DiDonato, Pietro. *Christ in Concrete*. 1939; New York: Signet, 1993. Novel

Dobler, Patricia. *Talking to Strangers*. Madison: University of Wisconsin Press, 1986. Poems

Doro, Sue. *Blue Collar Goodbyes*. 1992; Huron, OH: Bottom Dog Press, 2000. Poems

———. *Heart, Home, and Hardhats*. Minneapolis: Midwest Villages and Voices, 1986. Stories and poems

Dorris, Michael. *Working Men*. New York: Warner, 1994. Short stories

Dos Passos, John. *USA: The 42nd Parallel/1919/The Big Money*. New York: Library of America, 1996. Trilogy of novels

Doubiago, Sharon. *Hard Country*. 1982; Tucson: University of New Mexico Press, 1999.

Douglass, Frederick. *Narrative of the Life of Frederick Douglass, An American Slave: Written by Himself*. 1845; New Haven, CT: Yale University Press, 2001.

Dreiser, Theodore. *Sister Carrie*. 1900; New York: Signet, 2000. Novel

Eisenberg, Susan. *Pioneering: Poems from the Construction Site*. Ithaca, NY: ILR Press, 1998. Poems

———. *We'll Call You if We Need You: Experiences of Women Working Construction*. Ithaca, NY: ILR Press, 1999. Oral history, memoir

Ellison, Ralph. *Invisible Man*. 1952; New York: Vintage, 1995. Novel

Espada, Martin. *City of Coughing and Dead Radiators*. New York: Norton, 1994. Poems

———. *Alabanza: New and Selected Poems, 1982–2002*. New York: Norton, 2003.

Farrell, Thomas. *Studs Lonigan: A Trilogy Comprising Young Lonigan, the Young Manhood of Studs Lonigan, and Judgement Day*. 1933–35; Urbana: University of Illinois Press, 1993. Trilogy of novels

Fast, Howard. *Freedom Road*. 1944; Armonk, NY: M. E. Sharpe, 1995. Novel

———. *The Passion of Sacco and Vanzetti: A New England Legend*. New York: Bodley Head, 1954. Nonfiction

Feinberg, Leslie. *Stone Butch Blues*. 1993; Los Angeles: Alyson, 2004. Novel

Fell, Mary. *The Persistence of Memory*. New York: Random House, 1984. Poems

Flynn, Elizabeth Gurley. *The Rebel Girl: An Autobiography, My First Life (1906–1926)*. New York, International Publishers 1973.

Fuchs, Daniel. *The Williamsburg Trilogy*. 1934–1937; Berkeley, CA: Carroll and Graf, 1983. Trilogy of novels

Gardner, Leonard. *Fat City*. 1969; Berkeley: University of California Press, 1996. Novel

Garson, Barbara. *All the Livelong Day: The Meaning and Demeaning of Routine Work*. 1975; New York: Penguin, 1994. Reportage, oral history

Giardina, Denise. *Storming Heaven*. New York: Ballantine, 1988. Novel

———. *The Unquiet Earth*. New York: Norton, 1992. Novel

Gilb, Dagoberto. *The Magic of Blood*. New York: Grove Press, 1993. Short stories

———. *Woodcuts of Women*. New York: Grover, 2001. Short stories

Gold, Michael. *Jews Without Money*. 1930; Berkeley, CA: Carroll and Graf, 1996. Novel

Goldman, Emma. *Living My Life*. Vols. 1 and 2. New York: Dover, 1930. Autobiography

———. *Red Emma Speaks: An Emma Goldman Reader*. Amherst, NY: Prometheus Books, 1996.

Grahn, Judy. *The Work of a Common Woman*. New York: St. Martin's Press, 1978. Poems

Guthrie, Woody. *Bound for Glory*. 1917; New York: Plume Books, 1995. Autobiography

Gwaltney, John Langston, ed. *Drylongso: A Self-Portrait of Black America*. 1980; New York: New Press, 1993. Oral history

Hamper, Ben. *Rivethead: Tales from the Assembly Line* 1986; New York: Warner, 1992. Work narrative

Hayward, William. *The Autobiography Big Bill Haywood*. New York: International Publishers, 1966.

Hesse, Karen. *Out of the Dust*. New York: Scholastic, 1997. [Young adult] verse novel

Herbst, Josephine. *Pity Is Not Enough*. Urbana: University of Illinois Press, 1998. Novel

Himes, Chester. *If He Hollers Let Him Go*. 1945; New York: Thunder's Mouth Press, 1995. Novel

Hughes, Langston. Faith Berry, ed. *Good Morning Revolution: Uncollected Writings of Social Protest.* Secaucus, NJ: Citadel Press, 1992.

——, Susan Duffy, ed. *The Political Plays of Langston Hughes.* Carbondale: Southern Illinois University Press, 2001.

Hurston, Zora Neale. Alice Walker, ed. *I Love Myself When I'm Laughing . . . and Then Again When I Am Looking Mean and Impressive: A Zora Neale Hurston Reader.* New York: Feminist Press, 1989. Stories, articles

——, *Their Eyes Were Watching God.* 1937; New York: Harper, 1998. Novel

Jacobs, Harriet. *Incidents in the Life of a Slave Girl.* 1861; New York: Dover, 2001. Autobiography, slave narrative

Jones, Mary Harris. *The Autobiography of Mother Jones.* 1925; Chicago: C. H. Kerr, 1990.

Karr, Mary. *The Liars' Club: A Memoir.* New York: Penguin, 1995.

Kelley, Edith Summers. *Weeds.* 1923; New York: Feminist Press, 1982. Novel

Kingsolver, Barbara. *The Bean Trees.* New York: Harper and Row, 1988. Novel

——, *Holding the Line: Women in the Great Arizona Mine Strike of 1983.* Ithaca, NY: ILR Press, 1997 History, oral history

Kingston, Maxine Hong. *China Men.* New York: Vintage, 1989. Multigenre

Kromer, Tom. *Waiting for Nothing.* 1935; Athens: University of Georgia Press, 1986. Novel

Larcom, Lucy. *A New England Girlhood, Outlined from Memory.* 1889; Boston: Northeastern University Press, 1986. Memoir

LeSueur, Meridel. *The Girl.* 1938; Albuquerque: University of New Mexico Press, 2000. Novel

——, *Ripening: Selected Work, 1927–1980.* 1982; New York: Feminist Press, 1990. Stories, articles

Levine, Philip. *What Work Is.* New York: Knopf, 1992. Poems

Llewellyn, Chris. *Steam Dummy and Fragments from the Fire: The Triangle Shirtwaist Company Fire of March 25, 1911.* 1987; Huron, OH: Bottom Dog Press, 1993. Poems

London, Jack. *Martin Eden.* 1884; New York: Penguin, 1993. Novel

——. *People of the Abyss.* 1903; New York: Lawrence Hill Books, 2004. Reportage

Lorde, Audre. *Zami: A New Spelling of My Name.* Freedom, CA: Crossing Press, 1983. Autobiography

Lumpkin, Grace. *To Make My Bread.* 1932; Urbana: University of Illinois Press, 1995. Novel

Lynn, Loretta, with George Vecsey. *Coal Miner's Daughter.* 1976; New York: Da Capro Press, 1996. Autobiography

Malkiel, Theresa S. *The Diary of a Shirtwaist Worker.* 1910; Ithaca, NY: Cornell University Press, 1990. Novel

Mangione, Jerre. *An Ethnic at Large: Memoirs of America in the Thirties and Forties.* 1978; Syracuse University Press, 2002.

Marshall, Paule. *Brown Girl, Brownstones.* 1959; New York, Feminist Press, 1981. Novel

Mason, Bobbie Ann. *In Country.* New York: HarperCollins, 1993. Novel

McCarriston, Linda. *Eva-Mary.* Evanston, IL: Triquarterly Books, 1994. Poems

McDaniel, Wilma Elizabeth. *The Last Dust Storm.* Brooklyn, NY: Hanging Loose Press, 1995. Poems

McKenney, Ruth. *Industrial Valley.* 1939; Ithaca, NY: Cornell University Press, 1992. Novel

McGrath, Thomas. *Movie at the End of the World: Collected Poems.* Athens, OH: Swallow Press, 1972.

Meriwether, Louise. *Daddy Was a Numbers Runner.* New York: Feminist Press, 1986. Novel

Miner, Valerie. *Winter's Edge.* New York: Feminist Press, 1997. Short Stories

Moraga, Cherrie. *Heroes and Saints and Other Plays.* Albuquerque, NM: West End Press, 1994.

Mori, Toshio. *Unfinished Message: Selected Works of Toshio Mori.* Berkeley, CA: Heyday Books, 2000. Short fiction, letters, interviews

Naylor, Gloria. *The Women of Brewster Place: A Novel in Seven Stories.* New York: Penguin, 1983.

Ng, Fae Myenne. *Bone.* New York: Harper Perennial, 1994. Novel

Nowack, Mark. *Shut Up Shut Down.* Minneapolis: Coffee House Press, 2004. Poems, photography

Noyes, Henry. *Hand Over Fist.* Boston: South End Press, 1980. Novel

Odets, Clifford. *Waiting for Lefty/Collected Plays.* 1935; New York: Grove Press, 1993. Plays

Olsen, Tillie. *Yonnondio: From the Thirties*. 1974; New York: Delacorte Press, 1979. Unfinished novel
——, *Tell Me a Riddle*. 1961; New Brunswick, NJ: Rutgers University Press, 1995. Short fiction
Ortiz, Simon. *Fightin': New and Collected Stories*. 1984; New York: Thunder's Mouth Press, 1988.
Page, Myra. *Daughter of the Hills*. 1950; New York: Feminist Press, 1983. Novel
Pancake, Breece. *The Stories of Breece D'J Pancake*. 1983; New York: Henry Holt, 1988. Short Stories
Petry, Ann Lane. *The Street*. 1946; Boston: Houghton Mifflin, 1988. Novel
Phelps, Elizabeth Stuart. *The Silent Partner*. 1871; New York: Feminist Press, 1983. Novel
Pinzer, Maimie. *The Maimie Papers: Letters from an Ex-Prostitute*. New York: Feminist Press, 1997.
Porter, Connie. *All Bright Court*. New York: Harper, 1991. Novel
Potrebenko, Helen. *Hey Waitress and Other Stories*. Vancouver, BC: Lazara Press, 1990.
——, *Taxi!* Vancouver, BC: New Star Press, 1989. Short Stories
Rechy, John. *City of Night*. 1963; New York: Grove Press, 1988. Novel
Reed, John. *John Reed for the Masses*. Jefferson, NC: Mcfarland, 1987. Reportage
Register, Cheri. *Packinghouse Daughter: A Memoir*. New York: Perennial, 2001.
Reitman, Ben. *Sister of the Road: The Autobiography of Boxcar Bertha*. 1937; Oakland, CA: AK Press, 2002. Fictional autobiography
Reznikoff, Charles. *Poems, 1918–1975: The Complete Poems of Charles Reznikoff*. Santa Rosa, CA: Black Sparrow Press, 1989. Poems
Richardson, Dorothy. *The Long Day: The Story of a New York Working Girl*. 1904; Charlottesville: University Press of Virginia, 1990. Novel
Riis, Jacob. *How the Other Half Lives*. 1890; New York: Penguin Classics, 1997. Photography/journalism
Rivera, Tomás. *. . . y no se lo trago la tierra / . . . And the Earth Did Not Devour Him*. Houston: Arte Publico Press, 1987. Bilingual novel
Rodriguez, Luis. *Always Running: La Vida Loca: Gang Days in LA*. New York: Touchstone, 1994. Memoir
Rolfe, Edwin. *Collected Poems*. Urbana: University of Illinois Press, 1997.
Rolvaag, Ole. *Giants in the Earth: A Saga of the Prairie*. 1927; New York: HarperCollins, 1999. Novel
Rose, Wendy. *The Halfbreed Chronicles and Other Poems*. Albuquerque: University of New Mexico Press, 1986.
Rossi, Agnes. *The Quick: A Novella and Other Stories*. New York: Norton, 1992.
Roth, Henry. *Call It Sleep*. 1934; New York: Noonday Press, 1992. Novel
Rukeyser, Muriel. *The Collected Poems of Muriel Rukeyser*. University of Pittsburgh Press, 2005. Includes *The Book of the Dead* (1938) Poems
Sanchez, Sonia. *Homegirls and Handgrenades*. 1984; New York: Thunder's Mouth Press, 1997. Poems and vignettes
Sandburg, Carl. *The Complete Poems of Carl Sandburg*. New York: Harcourt, 2003. Includes *The People, Yes* (1934)
Sapphire (Ramona Lofton). *PUSH: A Novel*. New York: Vintage Contemporaries, 1997.
Saxton, Alexander. *The Great Midland*. 1948; Urbana: University of Illinois, 1997. Novel
Selby, Hubert. *Last Exit to Brooklyn*. 1957; New York: Grove Press, 1988. Novel
Silko, Leslie Marmon. *Ceremony*. New York: Penguin, 1989. Novel
——, *Storyteller*. Champaign, IL: Arcade, 1989. Multigenre
Sinclair, Jo. *The Seasons: Death and Transfiguration*. New York: Feminist Press, 1993. Memoir.
Sinclair, Upton. *The Jungle*. 1906; New York: Bantam Classics, 1981. Novel
Smedley, Agnes. *Daughter of Earth*. 1929; New York: Feminist Press, 1987. Novel
Sorrentino, Gilbert. *Steelwork*. 1970; Normal, IL: Dalkey Archive Press, 1992. Novel
Spewack, Bella. *Streets: A Memoir of the Lower East Side*. New York: Feminist Press, 1995.
Stein, Julia. *Under the Ladder to Heaven*. Albuquerque, NM: West End Press, 1984. Poems
Steinbeck, John. *In Dubious Battle*. 1936; New York: Penguin, 1992. Novel
——. *The Grapes of Wrath*. 1939; New York: Penguin, 2002. Novel
Swados, Harvey. *On the Line: Stories About a Life on the Assembly Line*. 1957; Urbana: University of Illinois, 1990. Short stories

Thomas, Piri. *Down These Mean Streets*. 1967; New York: Vintage, 1997. Autobiography

Traven, B. *The Death Ship*. 1934; New York: Lawrence Hill Books, 1991. Novel

Viramontes, Helen. *The Moths and Other Stories*. Houston, TX: Arte Publico Press, 1995.

——. *Under the Feet of Jesus*. New York: Plume, 1996. Novel

Vorse, Mary Heaton. Dee Garrison, ed. *Rebel Pen: The Writings of Mary Heaton Vorse*. New York: Monthly Review Press, 1986. Journalism

——, *Strike!* 1930; Urbana: University of Illinois Press, 1991. Novel

Walker, Alice. *The Color Purple*. 1982; New York: Washington Square Press, 1996. Novel

Wayman, Tom. *Introducing Tom Wayman: Selected Poems, 1973–1980*. Seattle, WA: Left Bank Books, 1980.

——. *I'll Be Right Back: New and Selected Poems, 1980–1996*. New York: Ontario Review Press, 1997.

West, Don. *In a Land of Plenty: A Don West Reader*. Washington, DC: West End Press, 1982. Poems

Wideman, John Edgar. *Brothers and Keepers*. New York: Vintage, 1995. Memoir

Wilson, August. *Fences*. 1986; New York: New American Library, 1995. Play

Wilson, Harriet. Henry Louis Gates Jr., ed. *Our Nig: Or, Sketches from the Life of a Free Black*. 1859; New York: Random House, 1983. Novel

Wilson, Michael. *Salt of the Earth*. 1954; New York: Feminist Press, 1977. Screenplay

Wong, Nellie. *The Death of Long Steam Lady*. Los Angeles: West End Press, 1986. Poems and stories

Wright, Richard. *Black Boy (American Hunger)*. 1944; New York: HarperCollins, 1998. Autobiography

——. *Native Son*. 1940; New York: HarperCollins, 1989. Novel

——. *Uncle Tom's Children: Four Novellas*. 1938; New York: HarperCollins, 1993.

Yamauchi, Wakako. *Songs My Mother Taught Me*. New York: Feminist Press, 1994. Songs, Plays, Memoir

Yezierska, Anzia. *Bread Givers*. 1925; New York: Persea Press, 1995. Novel

——. Alice Kessler-Harris, ed. *The Open Cage: An Anzia Yezierska Collection*. New York: Persea, 1979. Short stories

2. Collections and Anthologies

Baca, Jimmy Santiago, ed. *The Heat: Steelworker Lives and Legends*. Mena, AZ: Cedar Hill, 2001.

Banks, Ann, ed. *First Person America*. 1981; New York: Norton, 1991. Oral history from the Federal Writers Project

Berkinow, Louise, ed. *The World Split Open: Four Centuries of Women Poets in England and America, 1552–1950*. New York: Vintage, 1974.

Byerly, Victoria. *Hard Times Cotton Mill Girls: Personal Histories of Womanhood and Poverty in the South*. Ithaca, NY: ILR Press, 1987.

Carlsson, Chris and Mark Leger, eds. *Bad Attitude: The Processed World Anthology*. New York: Verso, 1990.

Carson, Robert, ed. *The Waterfront Writers: The Literature of Work*. San Francisco: Harper and Row, 1979. Poems, Stories, Play, Work narratives

Coles, Nicholas, and Peter Oresick, eds. *For a Living: The Poetry of Work*. Urbana: University of Illinois Press, 1995.

Daniels, Jim, ed. *Letters to America: Contemporary American Poetry on Race*. Detroit: Wayne State University Press, 1995.

Delacoste, Frederique, and Pricilla Alexander, eds. *Sex Work: Writings by Women in the Sex Industry*. 1987; Pittsburgh: Cleis Press, 1998.

Dublin, Thomas, ed. *Farm to Factory, Women's Letters, 1830–1860*. New York: Columbia University Press, 1981

Eisler, Benita, ed. *The Lowell Offering: Writings by New England Mill Women, 1840–1845*. 1980; New York: Norton, 1997.

Espada, Martín, ed. *Poetry Like Bread: Poets of the Political Imagination*. Willimantic, CT: Curbstone Press, 2000.

Foner, Philip, and Ronald L. Lewis, eds. *American Labor Songs of the Nineteenth Century*. Urbana: University of Illinois Press, 1975.

Fowke, Edith, and Joe Glazer, eds. *Songs of Work and Protest*. 1960; New York: Dover, 1973.

Franklin, Bruce, ed. *Prison Literature in America: The Victim as Criminal and Artist*. New York: Oxford University Press, 1989.

Grahn, Judy, ed. *True to Life Adventure Stories*. Santa Cruz, CA: Crossing Press, 1983.

Hoffman, Nancy, and Florence Howe, eds. *Women Working: An Anthology of Stories and Poems*. New York: Feminist Press, 1979.

Hongo, Garrett, ed. *The Open Boat: Poems from Asian America*. New York: Anchor Press, 1993.

Hourwich, Andria Taylor, and Gladys L. Palmer, eds. *I Am a Woman Worker: A Scrapbook of Autobiographies*. 1936; Manchester, NH: Ayer, 1980.

Howe, Forence, ed. *No More Masks: An Anthology of Twentieth-Century American Women Poets*. New York: HarperCollins, 1993.

Lauter, Paul, and Ann Fitzgerald, eds. *Literature, Class, and Culture: An Anthology*. New York: Longman, 2001.

Lerner, Gerda, ed. *Black Women in White America: A Documentary History*. 1973; New York: Vintage, 1992.

Lomax, Alan, Woody Guthrie and Pete Seeger, eds. *Hard Hitting Songs for Hard Hit People*. 1967; Lincoln: University of Nebraska Press, 1999.

Lynd, Staughton, and Alice, eds. *Rank and File: Personal Histories by Working-Class Organizers* 1981; Ithaca, NY: ILR Press, 1999.

Martz, Sandra, ed. *If I Had a Hammer: Women's Work in Poetry, Fiction, and Photographs*. Watsonville, CA: Papiev Mache Press, 1990.

Moraga, Cherrie, and Gloria Anzaldua, eds. *This Bridge Called My Back: Writings by Radical Women of Color*. 1981; Latham, NY: Kitchen Table Press, 1984.

Mullen, Bill, ed. *Revolutionary Tales: African American Women's Short Stories*. New York: Laurel, 1995.

Nekola, Charlotte, and Paula Rabinowitz, eds. *Writing Red: An Anthology of American Women Writers, 1930–1940*. New York: Feminist Press, 1987.

North, Joseph, ed. *New Masses: An Anthology of Rebel Thirties*. New York: International Publishers, 1969.

Oresick, Peter, and Nicholas Coles, eds. *Working Classics: Poems on Industrial Life*. Urbana: University of Illinois Press, 1990.

Overtime: Punchin' Out with the Mill Hunk Herald Magazine (1979–1989). Tucson: University of New Mexico Press, 1990.

Raffo, Susan, ed. *Queerly Classed: Gay Men and Lesbians Write About Class*. Boston: South End Press, 1997.

Roediger, David, ed. *The Haymarket Scrapbook*. Chicago: Charles H. Kerr, 1986.

Salzman, Jack. ed. *Years of Protest: A Collection of American Writings of the 1930s*. New York: Pegasus, 1967.

Seeger, Pete, and Bob Reiser. *Carry It On: A History in Song and Pictures of America's Working Men and Women*. New York: Simon and Shuster, 1985.

Shevin, David, and Larry Smith, eds. *Getting By: Stories of Working Lives*. Huron, OH: Bottom Dog Press, 1996.

Sinclair, Upton, Edward Sagarin, Albert Teichner, eds. *The Cry for Justice: An Anthology of the Literature of Social Protest*. 1915; Fort Lee, NJ: Barricade Books, 1996.

Smith, Barbara. *Homegirls: Black Feminist Anthology*. 1983; New Brunswick, NJ: Rutgers University Press, 2000.

Smith, Larry, ed. *Our Working Lives: Short Stories oe People and Work*. Huron, OH: Bottom Dog Press, 2000.

Solomon, Barbara, ed. *The Haves and the Have-Nots: 30 Stories About Money and Class in America*. New York: Signet, 1999.

Terkel, Studs. *Working: People Talk About What They Do All Day and How They Feel About What They Do*. 1972; New York: New Press, 1997.

Washington, Mary Helen, ed. *Invented Lives: Narratives of Black Women, 1860–1960*. New York: Anchor, 1987.

——. *Memory of Kin: Stories About Families by Black Writers*. New York: Anchor Press, 1991.

Wayman, Tom, ed. *Going for Coffee: Poetry on the Job*. Seattle, WA: Left Bank Books, 1981.

——, *Paperwork*. Madiera Park, BC: Harbour Press, 1991.

Wolf, Robert, ed. *An American Mosaic: Prose and Poetry by Everyday Folk*. New York: Oxford University Press, 1999.

Wray, Matt, and Annalee Newitz, eds. *White Trash: Race and Class in America*. New York: Routledge, 1997. Essays

Zandy, Janet, ed. *Calling Home: Working-Class Women's Writings, An Anthology*. New Brunswick, NJ: Rutgers University Press, 1990.

——, *Liberating Memory: Our Work and Our Working-Class Consciousness*. New Brunswick, NJ: Rutgers University Press, 1994.

Zinn, Howard and Anthony Arnove, eds. *Voices of a People's History of the United States*. New York: Seven Stories Press, 2004.

3. Literary and Cultural Commentary

Aaron, Daniel. *Writers on the Left: Episodes in American Literary Communism*. 1961; New York: Columbia University Press, 1992.

Allison, Dorothy. *Skin: Talking About Sex, Class, and Literature*. Ithaca, NY: Firebrand, 1994.

Berke, Nancy. *Women Poets on the Left: Lola Ridge, Genevieve Taggard, Margaret Walker*. Gainesville: University Press of Florida, 2001.

Bromell, Nicholas Knowles. *By the Sweat of the Brow: Literature and Labor in Ante-Bellum America*. Chicago: Chicago University Press, 1993.

Coiner, Constance. *Better Red: The Writing and Resistance of Tillie Olsen and Meridel LeSueur*. New York: Oxford University Press, 1995.

Denning, Michael. *Cultural Front: The Laboring of American Culture in the Twentieth Century*. New York: Verso, 1998.

——. *Mechanic Accents: Dime Novels and Working-Class Culture in America*. New York: Verso, 1998.

Ellis, Jacqueline. *Silent Witnesses: Representations of Working-Class Women in the United States*. Bowling Green OH: Bowling Green State University Press, 1998.

Foley, Barbara. *Radical Representations: Politics and Form in U.S. Proletarian Fiction, 1929–1941*. Durham, NC: Duke University Press, 1993.

Halker, Clark D. *For Democracy, Workers, and God: Labor Song-Poems and Labor Protest*. Urbana: University of Illinois Press, 1991.

Hapke, Laura. *Daughters of the Great Depression: Women, Work, and Fiction in the American 1930s*. Athens: University of Georgia Press, 1995.

——. *Labor's Text: The Worker in American Fiction*. New Brunswick, NJ: Rutgers University Press, 2001.

——. *Tales of the Working Girl: Wage-Earning Women in American Literature, 1890–1925*. New York: Twayne, 1992.

Hollis, Karen. *Resisting Voices: Writing at the Bryn Mawr Summer School for Women Workers, 1921–1938*. Englewood Cliffs, NJ: Prentice Hall, 1996.

Hooks, Bell. *Where We Stand: Class Matters*. New York: Routledge, 2000.

Klaus, Gustav, ed. *The Literature of Labor: Two Hundred Years of Working-Class Writing*. New York: St. Martin's Press, 1985.

Lauter, Paul. *Canons and Contexts*. New York: Oxford University Press, 1991.

Lenhart, Gary. *The Stamp of Class: Reflections on Poetry and Social Class*. Ann Arbor: University of Michigan Press, 2006.

Levine, Lawrence. *Black Culture and Black Consciousness: Afro-American Folk Thought from Slavery to Freedom*. New York: Oxford University Press, 1978.

Linkon, Sherry Lee, ed. *Teaching Working Class*. Amherst: University of Massachusetts Press, 1999.

Mirabella, M. Bella, and Lennard Davis, eds. *Left Politics and the Literary Profession*. New York: Columbia University Press, 1991.

Murphy, James. *The Proletarian Moment: The Controversy over Leftism in Literature*. Urbana: University of Illinois Press, 1991.

Nelson, Cary. *Repression and Recovery: Modern American Poetry and the Politics of Cultural Memory*. Madison: University of Wisconsin Press, 1989.

——. *Revolutionary Memory: Recovering the Poetry of the American Left*. New York: Routledge, 2003.

Olsen, Tillie. *Silences*. 1978; New York: Feminist Press, 2003.

Prestridge, Victoria. *The Worker in American Fiction: An Annotated Bibliography*. Champaign: University of Illinois Press, 1954.

Rabinowitz, Paula. *Labor and Desire: Women's Revolutionary Fiction in Depression America*. Chapel Hill: University of North Carolina Press, 1991.

Rideout, Walter. *The Radical Novel in the United States, 1900–1954: Some Interrelations of Literature and Society*. New York: Columbia University Press, 1992.

Robinson, Lillian. *Sex, Class, and Culture*. Bloomington: Indiana University Press, 1978.

Scully, James. *Line Break: Poetry as Social Practice*. Seattle, WA: Bay Press, 1988.

Shevin, David, Janet Zandy, Larry Smith, eds. *Writing Work: Writers on Working-Class Writing*. Huron, OH: Bottom Dog Press, 1999.

Shepard, Alan, John McMillan, and Gary Tate, eds. *Coming to Class: Pedagogy and the Social Class of Teachers*. Portsmouth, NH: Boynton/Cook, 1998.

Smith, Barbara. *The Truth That Never Hurts: Writings on Race, Gender, and Freedom*. New Brunswick, NJ: Rutgers University Press, 2000.

Walker, Alice. *In Search of Our Mothers' Gardens*. New York: Harcourt, 1983.

Wayman, Tom. *Inside Job: Essays on the New Work Writing*. 1983; Toronto: University of Toronto Press, 1986.

Wixson, Douglas C. *Worker-Writer in America: Jack Conroy and the Tradition of Midwestern Literary Radicalism, 1898–1990*. Urbana: Illinois University Press, 1994.

Zandy, Janet, ed. *What We Hold in Common: An Introduction to Working-Class Studies*. New York: Feminist Press, 2001.

——. *Hands: Physical Labor, Class, and Cultural Work*. New Brunswick, NJ: Rutgers University Press, 2004.

Zaniello, Tom. *Working Stiffs, Union Maids, Reds, and Riffraff: An Organized Guide to Films about Labor*. Ithaca, NY: Cornell University Press, 1996.

4. Labor and Working-Class History

Buhle, Paul and Nicole Shulman. *Wobblies! A Graphic History of the Industrial Workers of the World*. New York: Verso, 2005.

Clark, Christopher, Nancy A, Hewitt et al. *Who Built America? Working People and the Nation's Economy, Politics, Culture, and Society (Volume 1, to 1877)*. American Social History Project. New York: Worth, 2000.

Davis, Mike. *Prisoners of the American Dream: Politics and Economy in the History of the U.S. Working Class*. New York: Verso, 1986.

Demarest, David, ed. *"The River Ran Red": Homestead 1892*. Pittsburgh: University of Pittsburgh Press, 1992.

Ehrenreich, Barbara. *Nickel and Dimed: On (Not) Getting By in America*. New York: Metropolitan, 2001.

Foner, Philip. *First Facts of American Labor*. New York: Holmes and Meier, 1983.

Gutman, Herbert. *Work, Culture and Society in Industrializing America*. New York: Vintage, 1977.

Jones, Jacqueline. *Labor of Love, Labor of Sorrow: Black Woman, Work, and the Family from Slavery to the Present*. New York: Basic Books, 1985.

——. *A Social History of the Laboring Classes: From Colonial Times to the Present*. Oxford, England: Blackwell, 1999.

Kessler-Harris, Alice. *Out to Work: A History of Wage-Earning Women in the United States*. New York: Oxford University Press, 1982, 2003.

Le Blanc, Paul. *A Short History of the U.S. Working Class: From Colonial Times to the Twenty-first Century*. Amherst, NY: Humanity Books, 1999.

Lichtenstein, Nelson, Joshua Freeman et al. *Who Built America? Working People and the Nation's Economy, Politics, Culture, and Society (Volume 2, 1877 to the Present)*. American Social History Project. Boston: Bedford/St. Martin's Press, 2000.

Linebaugh, Peter, and Marcus Rediker. *The Many-Headed Hydra: Sailors, Slaves, Commoners, and the Hidden History of the Revolutionary Atlantic*. Boston: Beacon Press, 2000.

Murolo, Priscilla and A. B. Chitty. *From the Folks Who Brought You the Weekend: A Short Illustrated History of Labor in the United States*. New York: New Press, 2001.

Roediger, David. *The Wages of Whiteness: Race and the Making of the American Working Class*. London: Verso, 1991, 1999.

Saxton, Alexander. *The Rise and Fall of the White Republic: Class, Politics, and Mass Culture in Nineteenth-Century America*. New York: Verso, 1990.

Shipler, David. *The Working Poor: Invisible in America*. New York: Vintage, 2004.

Takaki, Ronald. *A Different Mirror: A History of Multicultural America*. Boston: Little, Brown, 1993.

Zieger, Robert H. and Gilbert J. Gall. *American Workers, American Unions*. Baltimore: Johns Hopkins University Press, 1986, 2002.

Zinn, Howard. *A People's History of The United States*. New York: Harper, 1980.

Zweig, Michael. *The Working Class Majority: America's Best Kept Secret*. Ithaca, NY: ILR/Cornell University Press, 2000.

——, ed. *What's Class Got to Do With It? American Society in the Twenty-First Century*. Ithaca, NY: ILR/Cornell University Press, 2004.

A Timeline of American Working-Class History

I. EARLY AMERICAN LABOR: HARD, BOUND, AND FREE

Colonial Period / American Revolution

1619	Imported child workers and Africans first sold into servitude in Virginia
1676	Bacon's Rebellion of indentured servants, slaves, and poor farmers
1712	Slave rebellion in New York City
1734	New York City Maidservants protest sexual harassment from mistresses' husbands
1739	Stono rebellion, uprising of South Carolina slaves
1765	Sons of Liberty organize in opposition to British rule
1770	Boston Massacre: Crispus Attucks and other workers killed by British soldiers
1773	Boston Tea Party: protest by Sons of Liberty against British tea tax
1775	Philadelphia Quakers adopt abolitionism
1775–1783	Revolutionary War of Independence
1776	Declaration of Independence from Britain
1786	Shays Rebellion in Massachusetts; printers' strike in Philadelphia
1787	U.S. Constitution adopted
1791	Bill of Rights added to the Constitution; Philadelphia carpenters strike for a ten-hour day
1792	First trade union formed: Journeyman Cordwainers (shoemakers) of Philadelphia
1793	Eli Whitney invents the cotton gin; first U.S. textile factory opens in Pawtucket Falls, Rhode Island
1798	Alien and Sedition Act curtails rights to free political expression
1803	Louisiana Purchase: The United States doubles its land area, expanding between the Mississippi River and the Rocky Mountains
1807	Trial of Philadelphia shoe workers—unions judged to be criminal conspiracies
1808	Importation of slaves abolished in the United States
1812–1815	War with the British

II. NEW KINDS OF WORK, OLD PRACTICES: 1820s–1850s

Antebellum Period / First Industrial Revolution

1817–1825	Construction of Erie Canal links Great Lakes to Hudson River
1819–1822	Economic depression
1825	Campaign for a ten-hour day initiated in Boston and Philadelphia
1825	United Tailoresses of New York formed

1827	*Mechanics Free Press* begins publication in Philadelphia
1828	Working Men's Party, first labor political party, founded in Philadelphia; construction begins on Baltimore and Ohio Railroad
1830	Indian Removal Act; tribes pressured to sign away lands
1831	Nat Turner's slave rebellion in Virginia
1834	National Trades Union founded; Antiblack riots in New York City; first "turn out" of mill girls in Lowell, Massachusetts, to protest wage cuts
1835	General Strike for a ten-hour day, Philadelphia
1836	Poets John Greenleaf Whittier and William Cullen Bryant defend New York Journeymen Tailors; Massachusetts passes first state law restricting children's labor
1837	"Panic of 1837" (economic depression); "Flour riots" in New York City against high rents and food prices
1838	"Trail of Tears": Cherokees forcibly relocated to Oklahoma on foot
1840	*Lowell Offering* begins publishing writing by women textile workers; ten-hour work day instituted for federal employees
1842	Lowell, Massachusetts, textile workers petition legislature for a ten-hour day; children's labor limited to ten hours in Massachusetts and Connecticut
1846–1848	Mexican War results in the geographic expansion of slavery; entry of Mexican American workers to low-wage labor force
1848	First Chinese immigrants arrive in San Francisco; first American convention for women's rights held in Seneca Falls, New York, organized by Elizabeth Cady Stanton, Lucretia Mott, and others
1849	Harriet Tubman escapes slavery; begins her work on the Underground Railroad
1850	Fugitive Slave Act; American League of Colored Laborers formed in New York City with Frederick Douglass, president
1857	In Dred Scott decision, Supreme Court affirms that slaves are "property" of their owners
1859	John Brown's raid on federal arsenal in Harper's Ferry, Virginia
1860	Pemberton Mill in Lawrence, Massachusetts, collapses killing 90—first major industrial accident; Great Shoemakers Strike by 20,000 in Lynn, Massachusetts

III. BENEATH THE GILDED SURFACE: 1860–1890s

Civil War / Reconstruction / Gilded Age

1860–1900	About 14 million people immigrate, mostly from the British Isles, Germany, and Scandinavia
1861–1865	Civil War, America's second revolutionary war
1862	Homestead Act opens the West to settlement
1863	Conscription Act; Draft Riots in New York City claim 105 lives
1863	Emancipation Proclamation; Lincoln's Gettysburg Address
1864	Sand Creek massacre of Cheyennes and Arapaho in Colorado Territory; 150 killed
1865	13th Amendment to the Constitution abolishes slavery in the United States
1866	National Labor Union formed; Colored Caulkers' Trade Union Society of Baltimore, first black union founded; Ku Klux Klan founded in Tennessee
1867	Daughters of St. Crispin (shoemakers) founded, first national women's labor organization; Reconstruction Act affirms African American political rights in former slave states

1868	14th Amendment to the Constitution defines US citizenship and requires equal protection under the law for all persons
1869	Knights of Labor founded, for men and women of "every craft, creed, and color"; railroad link between Atlantic and Pacific coasts completed
1870	15th Amendment to the Constitution confirms the right to vote regardless of race, color, or previous servitude
1873	Severe depression and widespread unemployment
1877	"Compromise of 1877" ends Reconstruction, federal troops leave Southern states; "Great Uprising," first nationwide strike begins with railroad workers and is crushed by federal troops, with over 100 killed; 10 coalminers, members of the "Molly Maguires," hanged in Pennsylvania
1880	By this date, the United States is the world's largest industrial producer
1881	Atlanta laundresses form a trade organization, the Washing Society, and strike over wages
1882	First Labor Day parade held in New York City; Chinese Exclusion Act prohibits entry of Chinese workers for ten years
1884	Federation of Organized Trades and Labor Unions initiates two-year campaign for an eight-hour day
1886	Movement for an eight-hour day culminates in massive strikes on May 1; Haymarket Massacre in Chicago; Knights of Labor collapses; American Federation of Labor formed; 1 million workers are union members
1887	Eight "anarchists" charged with a bombing in Chicago's Haymarket Square are sentenced to death—four are hanged
1889	Time-clock patented, widely adopted in factories over the next few years
1890	Wounded Knee massacre: federal troops kill 146 Sioux in South Dakota; United Mine Workers of America founded; Farmers' Alliance captures four state governorships
1892	"Battle of Homestead": iron and steel workers win battle against Pinkertons, lose in lockout by Carnegie Steel in Homesetad, Pennsylvania; People's ("Populist") Party founded
1894	Pullman Strike supported by American Railway Union led by Eugene V. Debs
1893–1896	Major economic depression
1894	"Coxey's Army" of unemployed marches on Washington, DC
1895	*Appeal to Reason*, mass circulation socialist paper, begins publication in Kansas
1896	In *Plessy v. Ferguson*, the U.S. Supreme Court affirms racial segregation and southern states' "Jim Crow" laws
1898	Frederick Taylor introduces "scientific management" at Midvale Steel Works, Pennsylvania

IV. REVOLT, REPRESSION, AND CULTURAL FORMATIONS: 1990s–1929s

Progressive Era / Roaring Twenties

1900–1930	About 18 million immigrate, the majority from Central and Southern Europe
1901	U.S. Steel Corporation formed in Pittsburgh, the world's first billion-dollar corporation, Socialist Party of America founded
1902	United Mine Workers strike for an eight-hour day in the anthracite coal region

1903	Mother Jones leads "March of the Mill Children" from Philadelphia to Oyster Bay, New York; Mexican and Japanese workers form the first agricultural union, the Sugar Beet and Farm Laborers' Union of Oxnard, California; Women's Trade Union League formed at AFL convention
1905	Industrial Workers of the World (IWW) formed with William D. ("Big Bill") Haywood as chairman
1907	Financial panic and depression; mine explosion in Monogagh, West Virginia, kills 361
1909	National Association for the Advancement of Colored People created
1909–1910	"Uprising of the 20,000": general strike of women garment workers, led by Clara Lemlich; IWW "Free Speech" actions in Western cities
1910–1920	Great Migration: hundreds of thousands of African Americans leave the South, most settling in northern cities
1911	Triangle Shirtwaist Factory Fire in New York City takes 146 lives, mostly Italian and Jewish immigrant women and girls; 128 Alabama convict miners killed in explosion
1912	Lawrence "Bread and Roses" Textile Strike led by IWW; Massachusetts passes first minimum wage law; Eugene V. Debs's Socialist Party wins 6 percent of the presidential vote
1913	Pageant of Paterson Strike performed by striking silk workers at Madison Square Garden, New York: IWW's *Little Red Songbook* distributed
1914	Ludlow Massacre: Colorado militia attack tent colony of striking miners' families; Henry Ford pioneers assembly-line production for Model-T
1914–1918	World War I
1915	Joe Hill, IWW organizer and songwriter, executed in Utah; Commission on Industrial Relations links labor unrest to concentration of wealth
1916	Boll weevils attack cotton crops across the South
1917	Bolshevik Revolution in Russia; United States enters World War I, reinstitutes conscription; antiblack riots in East St. Louis leave 49 dead; the Espionage Act curtails the expression of dissent
1918	100 IWW members found guilty of violating the Espionage Act
1919	Nationwide Great Steel Strike ends in defeat; race riots in Washington, DC, and Chicago
1920	19th Amendment to the Constitution affirms women's voting rights; 6,000 radical workers arrested in Palmer Raids; IWW suppressed; Sacco and Vanzetti charged with murder; Eugene V. Debs gets 1 million votes for president while in jail for an antiwar speech
1921–1923	Wave of strikes by miners wins union recognition and an eight-hour day
1925	A. Philip Randolph helps found the Brotherhood of Sleeping Car Porters
1927	Italian-born radical workers Sacco and Vanzetti executed despite worldwide protest
1929	U.S. stock market crashes on "Black Thursday," October 24

V. ECONOMIC DEPRESSION AND CULTURAL RESURGENCE: 1930s

Great Depression / New Deal / Proletarian Movement

1929	Gastonia textile strike, singer-organizer Ella May Wiggins murdered
1929–1934	*New Masses* edited by Michael Gold

1931	First National Hunger March in Washington, DC; Davis-Bacon Act requires the payment of "prevailing wages" on publicly funded construction projects
1932	Bonus Army marches on Washington, "Hooverville" attacked; Roosevelt elected president; national convention of John Reed Clubs
1933	Strike by International Ladies Garment Workers Union wins wage increases; Unemployed Councils organized by Communist and Socialist Parties, merge to form Workers Alliance of America in 1935
1933–1935	Dust storms across the Great Plains force exodus from farm lands
1934	General strikes in Minneapolis, San Francisco, and Toledo; Southern Tenant Farmers Union formed in Arkansas; *Anvil: Stories for Workers* begins publication in Missouri
1935	"New Deal" includes pro-labor Wagner Act, Social Security Act, Works Progress Administration, Federal Writers Project; Committee for Industrial Organization (CIO, later the Congress of Industrial Organizations) formed; CP adopts "Popular Front" against fascism
1936	National Negro Congress formed; Flint Sitdown Strike against General Motors in Michigan; U.S. Steel signs contract with Steel Workers Organizing Committee
1937	Nationwide strike wave; "Memorial Day Massacre," police kill ten workers in Chicago; Pullman signs first contract with Brotherhood of Sleeping Car Porters
1938	Fair Labor Standards Act prohibits child labor, sets minimum wage and forty-hour workweek
1939	Cotton sharecroppers organize roadside sitdown strikes in Missouri
1939–1945	World War II
1941	Pearl Harbor attacked, United States enters World War II; Fair Employment Practices Committee established; 33 percent of American workers are union members

VI. AFFLUENCE, COLD WAR, AND THE OTHER AMERICA, 1940s–1970s

Postwar Boom / Social Contract / Civil Rights Era

1942	National War Labor Relations Board established to protect collective bargaining during unions' wartime no-strike pledge
1943	Smith-Connally Act makes it a crime to advocate work stoppages; United Mine Workers defy no-strike pledge with "wildcat" strikes
1945–1946	Nationwide strike wave involves 5 million workers
1947	Taft-Hartley (Labor Management Relations Act) curbs right to strike; United Mine Workers win first health and pension package
1947–1960s	House Un-American Activities Committee spearheads purge of radical dissenters
1949	CIO expels nine left-wing trade unions
1950–1953	Korean War
1953	Film *Salt of the Earth*, about New Mexico zinc workers' strike, is made by blacklisted Hollywood professionals and Mexican American workers
1954	Senate votes to censure Joseph McCarthy, Wisconsin Republican, who led anticommunist crusade; in *Brown v. Board of Education* U.S. Supreme Court rules that racial segregation of schools is unconstitutional
1955	American Federation of Labor and Congress of Industrial Organizations merge (AFL-CIO); Rosa Parks's protest initiates bus boycott in Montgomery, Alabama

1959	Local 1199, New York City hospital workers' strike, extending union movement (along with SEIU and AFSCME) to the service industry; National Steel Strike ends in victory after 119 days, affirming safety standards
1960	Negro American Labor Council forms to pursue organizing black workers and to address racism in unions
1962	National Farm Workers Association convenes with Cesar Chavez as president
1963	Martin Luther King delivers "I Have a Dream" speech at March for Jobs and Freedom in Washington, DC; Equal Pay Act bans wage discrimination based on gender
1964–1973	Vietnam War
1964	Civil Rights Act outlaws discrimination based on race, creed, sex, or national origin
1965	Voting Rights Act removes most barriers to African American voting in southern states
1965	United Farm Workers (UFW) organizes boycott of California grape growers
1966	National Organization for Women (NOW) formed
1968	Martin Luther King and Robert Kennedy assassinated
1969	Miners form Black Lung Association, march on Charleston, West Virginia; Stonewall Inn Riot sparks gay rights movement
1970	UFW signs the first union agreement with California vineyards; Occupational Safety and Health Act (OSHA) signed into law; Congress creates Environmental Protection Agency
1972	Equal Rights Amendment (ERA) to the Constitution fails to win ratification by states
1973	In *Roe v. Wade*, Supreme Court upholds women's right to abortion; Karen Silkwood, chemical worker and union activist, killed en route to revealing safety violations at nuclear plant in Oklahoma
1974	Coalition of Labor Union Women formed in Chicago; 50 percent of mothers with school-age children work outside the home
1975–1976	In Boston, whites violently oppose busing for racial desegregation
1979	Three Mile Island nuclear accident in Pennsylvania

VII. THE NEW WORLD ORDER AND ITS CONSEQUENCES: 1980s TO 2005s

Technological revolution / Globalization / End of the Social Contract

1980	Ronald Reagan's election as president initiates "conservative revolution" of military buildup, tax cuts, soaring deficits, and antiunion crusade
1981	Professional Air Traffic Controllers Organization (PATCO) strikes over working conditions—President Reagan fires 13,000 strikers, decertifies union; Microsoft introduces DOS operating system on IBM computers
1985	United Food and Commercial Workers wages unsuccessful strike of Hormel meat-packing company in Austin, Minnesota; Service Employees International Union initiates "Justice for Janitors" campaign in Los Angeles
1989	United Mine Workers eleven-month strike of Pittston Coal Company, Virginia
1991	First Gulf War; televised beating of black motorist Rodney King by Los Angeles police—their acquittal triggers riots in South Central Los Augeles
1992	National debt reaches $3 trillion, having quadrupled since 1980; world's largest shopping mall, Mall of America, opens in Bloomington, Minnesota

1993	North American Free Trade Agreement (NAFTA) leads to loss of hundreds of thousands of Americans' jobs, mostly to Mexico
1994	"Proposition 187" becomes law in California, denying education and medical services to undocumented aliens—later overturned by federal courts
1996	Welfare Reform Act eliminates Aid to Families with Dependent Children, safety net program dating from the New Deal of 1935
1997	Teamsters challenge United Parcel Service over involuntary part-time labor and benefit cuts—victorious strike by 185,000 "brown-collar" workers wins broad public support
1999	"Battle of Seattle": tens of thousands disrupt meeting of World Trade Organization, protesting neglect of labor rights and environmental protection in its oversight of capitalist globalization
2000	Predicted "Y2K" worldwide computer disaster fails to occur; Democrat Al Gore loses to George W. Bush, despite winning popular vote for president, after Supreme Court halts Florida recount
2001	Terrorist suicide missions attack Pentagon and destroy the World Trade Center in New York City—three thousand die in coordinated attacks on September 11; Bush launches "War on Terror," signs USA PATRIOT Act into law
2002	WalMart Stores becomes the world's largest company
2003	Second Gulf War begins—United States and Britain invade Iraq
2005	Hurricane Katrina causes flooding of New Orleans—kills 1,300 and displaces more than 1 million from Gulf states; the Teamsters, SEIU, UNITE, UFW and other unions leave AFL-CIO and form Change to Win Coalition

Sources: Christopher Clark, Nancy A, Hewitt et al., *Who Built America? Working People and the Nation's Economy, Politics, Culture, and Society, Volume 1, to 1877* (New York: Worth, 2000); Philip Foner, *First Facts of American Labor* (New York: Holmes and Meier, 1983); Paul Le Blanc, *A Short History of the U.S. Working Class: From Colonial Times to the Twenty-first Century* (Amherst, NY: Humanity Books, 1999); Nelson Lichtenstein, Joshua Freeman et al. *Who Built America? Working People and the Nation's Economy, Politics, Culture, and Society, Volume 2, 1877 to the Present* (Boston: Bedford/St. Martin's, 2000); Robert H. Zieger and Gilbert J. Gall. *American Workers, American Unions* (Baltimore: Johns Hopkins University Press, 1986, 2002); AFL/CIO website <www.aflcio.org/aboutus/history/history/timeline.cfm>.

Credits

Index by Author

Index by Title

About the Editors

Nicholas Coles is Associate Professor of English at the University of Pittsburgh, where he teaches and writes about literacy and pedagogy, working-class literature, contemporary poetry, and teacher-research. He is the coeditor, with Peter Oresick, of two collections of poetry, *Working Classics: Poems on Industrial Life* (1990) and *For a Living: The Poetry of Work* (1995), both from the University of Illinois Press. Coles is Director of Composition at Pitt and serves as Field Director for the National Writing Project, based at the University of California, Berkeley.

Janet Zandy is Professor of English at the Rochester Institute of Technology. She is the author of *Hands: Physical Labor, Class, and Cultural Work* (Rutgers University Press, 2004), and the editor of *Calling Home: Working-Class Women's Writings* (Rutgers, 1990); *Liberating Memory: Our Work and Our Working-Class Consciousness* (Rutgers, 1994); and *What We Hold in Common: An Introduction to Working-Class Studies* (The Feminist Press, 2001). She was general editor of *Women's Studies Quarterly* from 1997–2001. Recognized as a pioneer in working-class studies, she lectures and publishes widely on working-class culture. She is the interim chair of the Department of English.